Gross Domestic Product, 1959–2002 (continued)
(billions of dollars, except as noted)

Year	Net Exports of Goods and Services			Government Consumption Expenditures and Gross Investment					Final Sales of Domestic Product	Gross Domestic Purchases[1]	Addendum: Gross National Product[2]	Percent Change from Preceding Period	
					Federal								
	Net Exports	Exports	Imports	Total	Total	National Defense	Nondefense	State and Local				Gross Domestic Product	Gross Domestic Purchases[1]
1959	−1.7	20.6	22.3	112.5	67.4	56.0	11.4	45.1	503.5	509.1	510.3		
1960	2.4	25.3	22.8	113.8	65.9	55.2	10.7	47.9	524.1	525.0	530.6	3.9	3.1
1961	3.4	26.0	22.7	121.5	69.5	58.1	11.3	52.0	542.7	542.3	549.3	3.5	3.3
1962	2.4	27.4	25.0	132.2	76.9	62.8	14.1	55.3	580.4	584.1	590.7	7.5	7.7
1963	3.3	29.4	26.1	138.5	78.5	62.7	15.8	59.9	613.1	615.4	623.2	5.5	5.4
1964	5.5	33.6	28.1	145.1	79.8	61.8	18.0	65.3	659.6	658.9	669.4	7.4	7.1
1965	3.9	35.4	31.5	153.7	82.1	62.4	19.7	71.6	710.9	716.2	725.5	8.4	8.7
1966	1.9	38.9	37.1	174.3	94.4	73.8	20.7	79.9	775.7	787.4	794.5	9.6	9.9
1967	1.4	41.4	39.9	195.3	106.8	85.8	21.0	88.6	824.2	832.6	839.5	5.7	5.7
1968	−1.3	45.3	46.6	212.8	114.0	92.2	21.8	98.8	902.4	912.7	917.6	9.3	9.6
1969	−1.2	49.3	50.5	224.6	116.1	92.6	23.5	108.5	976.2	986.5	991.5	8.1	8.1
1970	1.2	57.0	55.8	237.1	116.4	90.9	25.5	120.7	1,037.7	1,038.5	1,046.1	5.5	5.3
1971	−3.0	59.3	62.3	251.0	117.6	89.0	28.6	133.5	1,120.3	1,131.6	1,136.2	8.6	9.0
1972	−8.0	66.2	74.2	270.1	125.6	93.5	32.2	144.4	1,231.3	1,248.4	1,249.1	9.9	10.3
1973	.6	91.8	91.2	287.9	127.8	93.9	33.9	160.1	1,369.7	1,384.9	1,398.2	11.7	10.9
1974	−3.1	124.3	127.5	322.4	138.2	99.7	38.5	184.2	1,487.0	1,504.2	1,516.7	8.3	8.6
1975	13.6	136.3	122.7	361.1	152.1	107.9	44.2	209.0	1,641.4	1,621.6	1,648.4	8.9	7.8
1976	−2.3	148.9	151.1	384.5	160.6	113.2	47.4	223.9	1,806.8	1,826.2	1,841.0	11.5	12.6
1977	−23.7	158.8	182.4	415.3	176.0	122.6	53.5	239.3	2,009.1	2,055.1	2,052.1	11.4	12.5
1978	−26.1	186.1	212.3	455.6	191.9	132.0	59.8	263.8	2,270.1	2,322.0	2,318.0	13.0	13.0
1979	−24.0	228.7	252.7	503.5	211.6	146.7	65.0	291.8	2,548.4	2,590.4	2,599.3	11.8	11.6
1980	−14.9	278.9	293.8	569.7	245.3	169.6	75.6	324.4	2,801.9	2,810.5	2,830.8	8.9	8.5
1981	−15.0	302.8	317.8	631.4	281.8	197.8	84.0	349.6	3,101.5	3,146.3	3,166.1	12.0	12.0
1982	−20.5	282.6	303.2	684.4	312.8	228.3	84.5	371.6	3,274.1	3,279.8	3,295.7	4.1	4.2
1983	−51.7	277.0	328.6	735.9	344.4	252.5	92.0	391.5	3,540.7	3,586.6	3,571.8	8.5	9.4
1984	−102.0	303.1	405.1	800.8	376.4	283.5	92.8	424.4	3,867.3	4,034.7	3,968.1	11.3	12.5
1985	−114.2	303.0	417.2	878.3	413.4	312.4	101.0	464.9	4,191.2	4,327.2	4,238.4	7.1	7.2
1986	−131.9	320.3	452.2	942.3	438.7	332.2	106.5	503.6	4,446.3	4,584.7	4,468.3	5.7	6.0
1987	−142.3	365.6	507.9	997.9	460.4	351.2	109.3	537.5	4,715.3	4,884.7	4,756.2	6.5	6.5
1988	−106.3	446.9	553.2	1,036.9	462.6	355.9	106.8	574.3	5,089.8	5,214.6	5,126.8	7.7	6.8
1989	−80.7	509.0	589.7	1,100.2	482.6	363.2	119.3	617.7	5,461.4	5,569.8	5,509.4	7.5	6.8
1990	−71.4	557.2	628.6	1,181.4	508.4	374.9	133.6	673.0	5,788.7	5,874.7	5,832.2	5.7	5.5
1991	−20.7	601.6	622.3	1,235.5	527.4	384.5	142.9	708.1	5,986.4	6,006.9	6,010.9	3.2	2.3
1992	−27.9	636.8	664.6	1,270.5	534.5	378.5	156.0	736.0	6,303.9	6,346.8	6,342.3	5.6	5.7
1993	−60.5	658.0	718.5	1,293.0	527.3	364.9	162.4	765.7	6,621.2	6,702.8	6,666.7	5.1	5.6
1994	−87.1	725.1	812.1	1,327.9	521.1	355.1	165.9	806.8	6,991.8	7,141.4	7,071.1	6.2	6.5
1995	−84.3	818.6	902.8	1,372.0	521.5	350.6	170.9	850.5	7,367.5	7,484.8	7,420.9	4.9	4.8
1996	−89.0	874.2	963.1	1,421.9	531.6	357.0	174.6	890.4	7,783.2	7,902.1	7,831.2	5.6	5.6
1997	−89.4	966.4	1,055.8	1,487.9	538.2	352.6	185.6	949.7	8,318.4	8,407.7	8,325.4	6.5	6.7
1998	−151.7	964.9	1,116.6	1,538.5	539.2	349.1	190.1	999.3	8,781.5	8,933.3	8,778.1	5.6	6.3
1999	−249.9	989.3	1,239.2	1,641.0	565.0	364.3	200.7	1,076.0	9,274.3	9,524.2	9,297.1	5.6	6.3
2000	−365.5	1,101.1	1,466.6	1,751.0	589.2	374.9	214.3	1,161.8	9,824.6	10,190.1	9,848.0	5.9	7.0
2001	−348.9	1,034.1	1,383.0	1,858.0	628.1	399.9	228.2	1,229.9	10,082.2	10,431.0	10,104.1	2.6	2.4
2002	−418.1	1,017.6	1,435.7	1,973.1	693.5	447.5	246.0	1,279.0	10,442.1			3.6	4.1

ECONOMICS

ECONOMICS

Fifth Edition

DAVID C. COLANDER

Middlebury College

McGraw Hill Irwin

Boston Burr Ridge, IL Dubuque, IA Madison, WI New York San Francisco St. Louis
Bangkok Bogotá Caracas Kuala Lumpur Lisbon London Madrid Mexico City
Milan Montreal New Delhi Santiago Seoul Singapore Sydney Taipei Toronto

The McGraw-Hill Companies

McGraw-Hill Irwin

ECONOMICS
Published by McGraw-Hill/Irwin, a business unit of The McGraw-Hill Companies, Inc., 1221 Avenue of the Americas, New York, NY, 10020.
Some ancillaries, including electronic and print components, may not be available to customers outside the United States.

This book is printed on acid-free paper.

domestic 3 4 5 6 7 8 9 0 DOW/DOW 0 9 8 7 6 5 4
international 2 3 4 5 6 7 8 9 0 DOW/DOW 0 9 8 7 6 5 4 3

ISBN 0-07-254902-5

Publisher: *Gary Burke*
Executive sponsoring editor: *Lucille Sutton*
Developmental editor: *Katie Crouch*
Marketing manager: *Martin D. Quinn*
Senior producer, Media technology: *Melissa Kansa*
Project manager: *Destiny Rynne*
Senior production supervisor: *Rose Hepburn*
Lead designer: *Pam Verros*
Photo research coordinator: *Jeremy Cheshareck*
Photo researcher: *Teri Stratford*
Lead supplement producer: *Becky Szura*
Senior digital content specialist: *Brian Nacik*
Cover design: *JoAnne Schopler*
Cover image: © *Freeman Patterson/Masterfile*
Typeface: *10.3/12 Goudy*
Compositor: *GAC/Indianapolis*
Printer: *RRD/Willard*

Library of Congress Cataloging-in-Publication Data

Colander, David C.
Economics / David C. Colander.—5th ed.
p. cm.
Includes index.
ISBN 0-07-254902-5 (alk. paper) — ISBN 0-07-121447-X (international : alk. paper)
1. Economics. I. Title.
HB171.5.C788 2004
330—dc21

2003044959

INTERNATIONAL EDITION ISBN 0-07-121447-X

www.mhhe.com

Dedicated to the memory of Frank Knight and
Thorstein Veblen, both of whose economics have significantly
influenced the contents of this book.

About the Author

David Colander is the Christian A. Johnson Distinguished Professor of Economics at Middlebury College. He has authored, coauthored, or edited 35 books and over 100 articles on a wide range of economic topics.

He earned his B.A. at Columbia College and his M.Phil and Ph.D. at Columbia University. He also studied at the University of Birmingham in England and at Wilhelmsburg Gymnasium in Germany. Professor Colander has taught at Columbia College, Vassar College, and the University of Miami, as well as having been a consultant to Time-Life Films, a consultant to Congress, a Brookings Policy Fellow, and Visiting Scholar at Nuffield College, Oxford. In 2001–2002, he was the Kelley Professor of Distinguished Teaching at Princeton University.

He belongs to a variety of professional associations and has served on the board of directors and as vice president and president of both the History of Economic Thought Society and the Eastern Economics Association. He has also served on the editorial boards of the *Journal of Economic Perspectives*, *The Journal of Economic Education*, *The Journal of Economic Methodology*, *The Journal of the History of Economic Thought*, *The Journal of Socio-Economics*, and *The Eastern Economic Journal*.

He is married to a pediatrician, Patrice, who has a private practice in Middlebury, Vermont. In their spare time, the Colanders designed and built their oak post-and-beam house on a ridge overlooking the Green Mountains to the east and the Adirondacks to the west. The house is located on the site of a former drive-in movie theater. (They replaced the speaker poles with fruit trees and used the I-beams from the screen as support for the second story of the carriage house and the garage. Dave's office and library are in the former projection room.)

Preface

"Imagine . . . a textbook that students enjoy!" That comment, from Glen Waddell, who teaches at Purdue, was e-mailed to me as I was struggling to write the preface to the fourth edition. That comment still captures what I believe to be the most distinctive feature of my book. I've always felt that the books students read in their courses should speak to them and be as enjoyable as possible to read. Those beliefs continue to be the guiding principle for my writing.

▲ For Those Who Are New to the Book

For those of you who haven't used earlier editions, let me briefly describe where I see this book fitting in the panoply of top-selling books. Principles books are often categorized as old-style or new-style. Old-style books have macro first. Within macro, short-run stabilization comes before growth; generally the flavor is Keynesian activist macro policy. New-style books have micro first and later, within macro, do growth before stabilization, often with little coverage of stabilization issues, such as multiplier analysis; they generally have a Classical laissez-faire, macro-policy flavor.

This book is new-style in organization—it puts micro and the long run first—but it is not new-style in terms of coverage; it presents stabilization as an important issue, and it doesn't have that laissez-faire flavor of some new-style books. I like to think of the flavor of this book as neither old- nor new-style, but instead cutting-edge style. Much of the conceptual foundations for the theory underlying it are derived from the new work in behavioral economics, nonlinear dynamics, complexity, and strategic game theory.

Within this new-style work, everything is less certain than in either the new- or the old-style theory. Cutting-edge theory recognizes that Keynes and Keynesians had some important policy insights that need to be part of what we teach. However, it also recognizes that much of Keynesian policy was oversold, and that it underestimated government failure. So while theory may not tell us that laissez-faire is a desirable policy, a study of history and politics and the complexity of the system warns us about activist policy, even when our hearts tell us that government action is needed. Both these views show through in the presentations.

Similarly with micro policy. The cutting-edge style sees economic theory taking us only so far in answering policy questions about whether or not the government should intervene in the economy. At the cutting edge of modern theory, no side is totally right or totally wrong in the ongoing policy debates. It's that ongoing debate about policy that makes economics so interesting to me.

Another way in which principles books are classified is on the easy–medium–difficult spectrum. This book is definitely in the medium range. Based on writing style alone, it would probably be placed in the easy range, but since it tackles difficult conceptual topics that will challenge even the brightest students, it should be considered a medium-range text. Why do I choose that combination? Because I believe that most students have the ability to understand economic concepts even though on exams it often appears as if they have serious problems. In my opinion many of those problems are not conceptual; rather, they are problems in motivation, reading, and math. The economics found in principles courses is not students' highest priority; it certainly wasn't mine when I was 18. I'm continually amazed at how many supposedly not-so-good students are conceptually bright. The reality is that most principles books bore this MTV generation. To teach them effectively, we've got to get their attention and hold it.

One way I try to get students' attention is to use a colloquial style. The book is written in a style that talks to students and makes them feel that in the textbook they have a second teacher who is urging them on to study harder, and trying to explain the material to them. That colloquial style helps with one of the biggest problems in the course—getting students to read the book. Some professors don't always like the style, but even some of those have written me that they use the book anyway because their students will read it. And if the students have read the book, teaching is more rewarding.

Another way the book relates to students is through its focus on policy. This book is not written for future economics majors, because most students aren't going to go on in economics. It is written for students who will probably take only one or two economics courses in their lifetime. These students are interested in policy, and what I try to present to them is the basics of economic reasoning as it relates to policy questions. So, throughout the book, I turn the discussion to policy. This discussion presents policy as students see it in the news: policy questions are seldom clear-cut; a book that presents policy any other way is unfair to students.

A final way in which this book differs from some of the others is that it emphasizes the importance of institutions and history. Modern work in game theory and strategic decision making is making it clear that the implications of economic reasoning depend on the institutional setting. To understand economics requires an understanding of existing institutions and the historical development of those institutions. In a principles course, while we don't have time to present much about history and institutions, we can at least let students know that we know that these issues are important. And that's what I try to do.

▲ For Those Who Have Used the Book Before

Those of you who have who have used earlier editions will find that this fifth edition has the same basic structure and tone as the fourth edition, and that it has fewer changes than in previous revisions. The reason for the fewer changes is that reviewers said that in the last edition I'd reached a nice equilibrium—I'd made the book consistent with the standard presentations, but I also had kept enough of the historical and institutional approaches and informal, student-friendly writing style to make the book distinctive. I guess the process of reviewing and rewriting does finally lead to something like a steady-state equilibrium. But even in the steady state, changes are still necessary to ensure that (1) the views provided express the latest standard views of economists, and (2) that the exposition relates as closely as possible to recent economic events. Let me briefly take you through the changes.

Changes in the Introductory Section (Chapters 1–5)

The introductory section had the largest revisions. I significantly reorganized and reworked Chapters 2 and 3 to make the book easier to use and to allow more choice in presentation of this material. Specifically, Chapter 2 is now titled "Trade, Trade-Offs, and Government Policy"; it focuses on the production possibility curve, comparative advantage, and trade. To keep the focus on policy so that students are not presented with a tool out of context, I moved the discussion of the roles of government previously found in Chapter 5 to this chapter. Chapter 3 is now titled "The Evolving U.S. Economy in Perspective." It covers economic systems, institutions, the U.S. economy, and the problems of regulating trade both domestically and internationally. It concludes with a discussion of how globalization has affected the U.S. economy.

The following should give you a sense of the chapter-by-chapter changes that were made in the introductory section:

- Chapter 1 (Economics and Economic Reasoning): I added a discussion of economics as an observational science.
- Chapter 2: (Trade, Trade-Offs, and Government Policy): The chapter now centers on a discussion of comparative advantage, the production possibility curves, and government policy toward trade. Finally, since this is the first chapter in which graphs are used in an analytic manner, I conclude the chapter with a graphing appendix.
- Chapter 3 (The Evolving U.S. Economy in Perspective): This chapter now discusses both economic systems and economic institutions, concluding with a policy discussion of globalization.
- Chapter 4 (Supply and Demand): This chapter presents the basic issues that students need to know about supply and demand for the macro course, including the effect of shifting demand and supply curves and the limitations of supply/demand analysis. Thus, professors who want to move right into macro issues can skip Chapter 5, Using Supply and Demand, without any loss of continuity.
- Chapter 5 (Using Supply and Demand): This chapter gives many real-world examples and deepens students' understanding of the supply/demand model. It begins with two real-world examples of supply and demand, and no longer includes discussions of the roles of government (now covered in Chapter 2). Third-party-payer markets are an addition to this chapter.

Changes in the Micro Section (Chapters 6–21)

The biggest change in the micro section involved reorganizing the chapters to make them better fit the way most people teach the course. I moved up the antitrust chapter to the section covering market structure; I also moved up the factor market section to earlier in the book. This allowed me to collapse the two policy sections into one. The goals of these changes were to match the structure to the way most people teach the course and to make it easier for professors to pick and choose among the policy chapters. The majority of the other changes in the micro section involved improving the exposition and updating examples. The following list should give you a brief idea of the type of changes I made. (A more extensive list can be found on the book's website.)

Section I: Microeconomics: The Basics

- Chapter 6 (Describing Supply and Demand: Elasticities): I eliminated the term *arc elasticity* to simplify the presentation, updated the estimates of elasticities, and added new examples.
- Chapter 7 (Taxation and Government Intervention): Consumer surplus and producer surplus are now introduced in this chapter (moved from Chapter 4).

Section II: Foundations of Supply and Demand

- Chapter 8 (The Logic of Individual Choice): I expanded some examples and clarified the importance of the budget constraint.
- Chapter 9 (Production and Cost Analysis I): I added a short discussion of corporations and issues of accounting, and clarified that all fixed costs are assumed to be sunk costs.
- Chapter 10 (Production and Cost Analysis II): I added additional problems and exercises relating to technical and economic efficiency.

Section III: Market Structure and Policy

- Chapter 11 (Perfect Competition): I updated the shutdown decision example to refer to Kmart.
- Chapter 12 (Monopoly): I added a discussion of monopolists that failed so that students see that monopolies may make a loss.
- Chapter 13 (Monopolistic Competition, Oligopoly, and Strategic Pricing): I added examples about Microsoft and Amazon, and added a box on John Nash.
- Chapter 14 (Real-World Competition and Technology): I reworked this chapter significantly by moving the discussion of globalization to Chapter 3, and concentrating the discussion on technology and the process of competition.
- Chapter 15 (Antitrust Policy and Regulation): I updated the discussion of the Microsoft case and added newer examples throughout.

Section IV: Factor Markets

- Chapter 16 (Work and the Labor Market): I moved the appendix on nonwage income and property rights into a box within the chapter and added a discussion of the living-wage movement.
- Chapter 17 (Who Gets What? The Distribution of Income): I added a box about Armartya Sen's views of the goals of society and a box assessing the 1996 welfare-to-work law.

Section V: Applying Economic Reasoning to Policy

- Chapter 18 (Government Policy and Market Failures): I shortened the discussion of licensing and health care.
- Chapter 19 (Politics and Economics: The Case of Agricultural Markets): I updated the discussion of farm laws to include the 2002 agricultural support bill.
- Chapter 20 (Microeconomic Policy, Economic Reasoning, and Beyond): I updated the value-of-human-life statistics.
- Chapter 21 (International Trade Policy): I added a discussion of empirical measures of trade, updated examples, and added a new box on the forces of antiglobalization.

Changes in the Macro Section (Chapters 22–34)

Changes in the macro section involved two changes in content and two changes in organization. The most substantial change in content involved the switch from a horizontal to an upward-sloping *AS* curve. I made this change in content because reviewers told me that an upward-sloping *AS* curve is easier to teach. The other change in content is the use of the term *marginal propensity to expend (mpe)* rather than *marginal propensity to consume (mpc)* to avoid the algebraic manipulation necessary to add endogenous imports and taxes to the model. This allowed me to make the policy discussions richer right from the beginning.

The major reorganization involved adding fiscal policy discussions to the two theory chapters. This change allowed me to integrate the material that had been in the concluding chapter into a summary chapter on demand management policy. Another substantial change was the addition of a development chapter back from an earlier edition. A number of instructors said they missed it. In addition, the order of some chapters was changed to better fit the way most professors teach the course. Finally, I removed the coverage of international trade in the international chapter to concentrate on international financial issues. Those professors who want to teach trade can assign that material from the micro part of the book. Thus, the new structure of the macro section is: introduction, theory, money and inflation, policy issues in depth, and international policy issues. As has always been the case, the chapters are written for flexibility.

Examples of the types of changes made in the macro chapters are the following:

Section I: Macroeconomic Problems

- Chapter 22 (Economic Growth, Business Cycles, Unemployment, and Inflation): Data have been updated. I've added a discussion of accounting scandals, the recession of 2001, and the stock market crash.

- Chapter 23 (National Income Accounting): I added a table that shows the relationship between GDP and national income, and I clarified the circular flow diagram to show that upper arrows reflected the income approach and lower arrows reflected the expenditures approach.

Section II: The Macroeconomic Framework

- Chapter 24 (Growth, Productivity, and the Wealth of Nations): I added a box on aggregate demand's role as a possible determinant of growth, and added examples of entrepreneurs.
- Chapter 25 (Aggregate Demand, Aggregate Supply, and Modern Macroeconomics): I made the AS curve upward-sloping rather than horizontal and added a discussion of fiscal policy to the chapter. Also, what had been called the potential output curve is now called the long-run aggregate supply curve to conform to standard terminology.
- Chapter 26 (The Multiplier Model): I switched the discussion of the multiplier to focus on the broader *mpe*, and showed how that becomes the *mpc* under certain conditions. This change makes the chapter less technical and allows room for a discussion of fiscal policy. With fewer and fewer books devoting significant space to the multiplier, this cleaner exposition, which gets right to the bottom line for policy rather than spending a lot of time developing the components of expenditures, makes the exposition shorter and more policy-focused. Those who want to include the components of the *mpe* can do so with the appendix.

Section III: Money, Inflation, and Monetary Policy

- Chapter 27 (Money, Banking, and the Financial Sector): I updated the data and added a section on valuing stocks and bonds to the appendix.
- Chapter 28 (Monetary Policy and the Debate about Macro Policy): I added a discussion of a typical Federal Open Market Committee meeting and a diagram about Fed tools. I discussed the Fed response to the September 11, 2001, terrorist attacks.
- Chapter 29 (Inflation and Its Relationship to Unemployment and Growth): I added a discussion of deflation and moved the discussion about demand-pull and cost-push inflation into the text.

Section IV: Macro Policy in Perspective

- Chapter 30 (Aggregate Demand Policy in Perspective): Since the discussion of fiscal policy is now contained in the theory chapters, it was removed from this chapter. I added a discussion of credibility and policy regimes, which have become much more important in policy discussions.
- Chapter 31 (Politics, Deficits, and Debt): Since the U.S. government's surpluses of the late 1990s have disappeared, the focus of this chapter was reoriented toward deficits.
- Chapter 32 (Macro Policies in Developing Countries): This chapter was in the third but not the fourth edition; a number of users asked that it be included in the fifth edition, so we revised it and put it back in.

Section V: International Policy Issues

- Chapter 33 (International Financial Policy): I removed the discussion of trade policy to avoid overlap with the international trade chapter and added a section on foreign exchange rates and the euro.
- Chapter 34 (Monetary and Fiscal Policy in a Global Setting): I revised the discussions of monetary and fiscal policy to concentrate on simpler relationships, and updated the chapter to include a discussion of the euro.

▲ A Final Comment

A number of my friends keep asking me why I spend so much thought and time about what goes into the book. The answer is that I care about teaching economic ideas, which I think is the most important job that society has assigned to academic economists. Research is nice, but good teaching is priceless, and if the writing and the ideas in this book contribute to good teaching, then I'm happy. As I get older, I find that I'm happier with less grandiose goals, and to have turned a few students on to economics seems like a worthwhile legacy.

▲ Ancillaries

All reviewers agreed that the fourth edition's ancillaries were top rate. We have continued to work hard to maintain that level of excellence.

Study Guide

This guide—written by myself, Douglas Copeland of Johnson County Community College, and Jenifer Gamber—reviews the main concepts from each chapter and applies those concepts in a variety of ways: short-answer questions, matching terms with definitions, problems and applications, a brainteaser, multiple-choice questions, and potential essay questions. Since students learn best not by just knowing the right answer but by understanding how to get there, each answer comes with an explanation. Timed cumulative pretests help students prepare for exams.

Instructor's Manual

In the fifth edition, Tom Adams of Sacramento City College continues to maintain the high standard set in previous editions. Class preparation is easier than ever. "Chapter Overview" and "What's New" provide a quick review of each chapter. "What's New" will be invaluable when modifying lecture notes to fit the new edition. The manual provides you with comprehensive lecture outlines, but it also offers help for inevitable classroom trouble spots. "Discussion Starters" will help engage students and keep them thinking. "Tips for Teaching Large Sections," written by Gail Hoyt of the University of Kentucky for micro and Dave Colander for macro, offers innovative ideas for teaching very large classes. "Student Stumbling Blocks" provides additional explanations or examples that help clarify difficult concepts. "Ties to the Tools" helps bring those text boxes into the classroom; a comprehensive list of relevant URLs brings the Internet in too. Every chapter's 10-question "Pop Quiz" will help students prepare for exams. The "Case Studies" provide contemporary, real-world economic examples. The entire instructor's manual is available in print, on the Instructor's CD-ROM, and on the Colander website.

Test Banks

James DeVaut of Lafayette College and Susan Dadres of Southern Methodist University revised Test Banks A and B (the 10,500-question multiple-choice test banks). Each question is categorized by chapter learning objective; level of difficulty (easy, medium, hard); skill being tested (recall, comprehension, application); and type of question (word problem, calculation, graph). In addition, James Chasey has tagged all the questions that are best suited for a high school AP course. Approximately 30 percent of the questions are new or revised. Each question was reviewed by Jenifer or myself for accuracy, clarity, and consistency with the textbook. They are available in print form and in the Diploma electronic test generating system on the Instructor's CD-ROM.

Test Bank C, revised by Rashid Al-Hmoud of Texas Tech University, now consists of approximately 600 short-answer questions, essay questions, and graphical and mathematical problems. Questions vary in level of difficulty and type of skill being tested. They are available in print and on the Instructor's CD-ROM.

DiscoverEcon

The DiscoverEcon software, developed by Gerald Nelson of the University of Illinois at Urbana-Champaign, is the best-selling academic economics software. It functions like an interactive text; software chapters parallel text chapters, and software pages include specific page references to the text. Each chapter of the software includes a multiple-choice quiz, essay questions with online links, two Web questions, and match-the-terms exercises. Interactive graphs, animated charts, and live tables allow students to manipulate variables and study the outcomes. E-submission is a new feature of DiscoverEcon to accompany the fifth edition. Using the Web-based version, instructors can now set up their courses for e-submission so that all exercise results for each student can be viewed and downloaded to other Windows applications. For those instructors using a course management system, specific "pages" in DiscoverEcon can now be linked to specific parts of the course website. This makes student navigation and therefore self-assessment easier than ever for both student and instructor.

The software is available online with a password code card; it is also available on a single CD that can be installed and run over a network. Link to DiscoverEcon online through the Colander book website: www.mhhe.com/economics/colander5.

PowerPoint Presentation

Anthony Zambelli of Cuyameca College has once again prepared an extensive slide program that includes all text exhibits and key concepts. He has reduced the number of slides in each chapter to give the presentations more focus. They are available on CD-ROM and on our website.

Overhead Transparencies

We offer all key text exhibits in full-color acetate form for use with overhead projectors.

Economics Web Newsletter

This electronic newsletter contains 10 questions related to current economic events that can be used as an in-class quiz and reprints one recent *Wall Street Journal* article along with 5 in-depth questions (and answers) that are tied to specific text chapters. Seven new exercises will be added each semester.

Classic Readings in Economics

This collection includes selections from the writings of economists, such as Smith, Marx, Hayek, or Veblen, who have raised questions that changed the direction of economic thinking. This material is especially useful for courses that stress the importance of economic ideas.

Economics: An Honors Companion

The *Honors Companion* presents mathematical techniques that underlie numerous basic economic concepts. It presupposes a solid student background in algebra and geometry and some familiarity with basic calculus, thereby giving *Economics, Fifth Edition*, flexibility for use in more rigorous classes.

▲ www.mhhe.com/economics/colander5

The Online Learning Center with PowerWeb to accompany Colander's fifth edition is a website full of exciting new content that follows the text chapter by chapter. Students and instructors alike will find a wealth of new online resources.

For the Student Center, Douglas Copeland of Johnson County Community College has prepared chapter-level study aids, including Chapter Introductions, Tutorials (3–5 problems per chapter using interactive graphing applets), and Practice Exercises (3–5 problems per chapter, with answers). Students can also choose from four levels of multiple-choice quizzes: easy, medium, hard, and an assortment, plus Learning Objectives, end-of-chapter Web Questions, Web Newsletters, a section called Writing about Economics, a Glossary, a Colloquial Glossary, and answers to even-numbered end-of-chapter questions.

Kit Taylor of Bellevue Community College has developed a Current Events section, updated quarterly, with "mini-readers" that use *New York Times* and *Business Week* articles to explore economics in the news today. Each new section will include suggested Web resources for further research, brief background notes, suggested paper topics—and will tie it all to the appropriate book chapters. Kit has also updated the WebNotes from the book; this feature extends the text discussion onto the Web. WebNotes are signified in the book by a globe icon in the margin and shown here on the left. In addition, a *New York Times* Web feed presents students with economics-related news headlines. Thanks to embedded PowerWeb content, students can get quick access to real-world news and essays that pertain to economics.

Instructors will find downloadable PowerPoints, the Instructor's Manual, Sample Syllabi, a link to Dave Colander's own website, and Help for AP Courses. We also provide a link to "Best Practices for Teaching Principles of Economics," a compilation of brief exercises provided by professors across the country that is edited by Kim Marie McGoldrick and Peter Schuhmann.

The entire website content can be delivered multiple ways—through the textbook website, through PageOut, or within a course management system (i.e., WebCT or Blackboard).

I'm very proud of the ancillary package. I think you will find that its high quality, enormous diversity, and exceptional utility make the book a complete learning system.

▲ People to Thank

A book this size is not the work of a single person, despite the fact that only one is listed as author. So many people have contributed so much to this book that it is hard to know where to begin thanking them. But I must begin somewhere, so let me begin by thanking the fifth edition reviewers, whose insightful comments kept me on track.

Rashid Al-Hmoud
Texas Tech University

Frank Albritton
Seminole Community College

Steven Balkin
Roosevelt College

Mohsen Bahmani-Oskoee
University of Wisconsin–Milwaukee

Taradas Bandyopadhyay
University of California–Riverside

David J. Berri
California State University–Bakersfield

Gerald Bialka
University of North Florida

Jeanne Boeh
Augsburg College

Rhead S. Bowman
Southern Utah University

Edward Castronova
California State University–Fullerton

Don Cole
Drew University

Fred Curtis
Drew University

Gregory DeFreitas
Hofstra University

Matthew J. Easton
Pueblo Community College

Robert R. Ebert
Baldwin-Wallace College

Rich Einhorn
Coe College

Richard England
University of New Hampshire

Rudy Fichtenbaum
Wright State University

Garry Fleming
Roanoke College

Edward N. Gamber
Lafayette College

Robert Gilette
University of Kentucky–Lexington

Larry Gullickson
Kilian Community College

Randal Gunden
Goshen College

Simon Hakim
Temple University

Hadley S. Hartman
Santa Fe Community College

Tom Head
George Fox University

Jannett Highfill
Bradley University

Matthew Hyle
Winona State University

Rodney E. Kingery
Hawkeye Community College

Morris Knapp
Miami Dade Community College

K. T. Magnusson
Salt Lake Community College

Farooq Malik
Pennsylvania State University

Mary Ellen Mallia
Siena College

Richard McIntyre
University of Rhode Island

Mark A. McLeod
Virginia Tech

Philip J. McLewin
Ramapo College

Gary Mongiovi
St. John's University

Barbara A. Moore
University of Central Florida

James T. Moyer
Albright College

Keith Neergaard
Pacific Union College

Neil Niman
University of New Hampshire

A. Papathanasis
Central Connecticut State University

Jay Patyk
Foothill College

Brian Peterson
Manchester College

Reza Ramazani
Saint Michael's College

Brian Rungeling
University of Central Florida

William Shambora
Ohio University

Timothy J. Stanton
Mount Saint Mary's College

Della L. Sue
Marist College

W. Scott Trees
Siena College

David Tufte
Southern Utah University

Ken Woodward
Saddleback College

Chiou-nan Yeh
Alabama State University

I'd also like to thank the reviewers of the previous four editions. This new book builds on their insights.

Jack Adams
University of Arkansas

Tom Adams
Sacramento City College

Peter Alexander
Hartwick College

Rashid Al-Hmoud
Texas Tech University

Fatma Antar
Manchester Community College

Stan Antoniotti
Bridgewater State College

Lenard Anyanwu
New Jersey Institute of Technology

Laura Argys
University of Colorado–Denver

Mahmoud P. Arya
Edison Community College

John Atkins
Pensacola Junior College

James Q. Aylsworth
Lakeland Community College

Bruce Barnett
Grossmont College

Peter S. Barth
University of Connecticut

Diann Benesh
University of Wisconsin–Eau Claire

David Berrian
Shoreline Community College

Michael Best
Berea College

David Black
University of Toledo

Geoffrey Black
Marist College

John Blair
Wright State University

George Bohler
University of North Florida

William W. Boorman
Palm Beach Community College

Bijit K. Bora
Carleton College

Ginny Brannon
Arapahoe Community College

Michael D. Brasselero
Forest Range Community College

Gerald E. Breger
Grand Rapids Junior College

H. L. Brockman
Central Piedmont Community College

Kathleen K. Bromley
Monroe Community College

Byron Brown
Michigan State University

Marie Bussing-Burks
University of Southern Indiana

Mario Cantu
Northern Virginia Community College

Kathleen Carroll
University of Maryland, Baltimore Campus

Sidney L. Carroll
University of Tennessee–Knoxville

Tom Carroll
Central Oregon Community College

Thomas Cate
Northern Kentucky University

Marc C. Chopin
Louisiana Tech University

Carol A. M. Clark
Guilford College

Chris Clark
BCIT

Curtis Clarke
Mountain View College

Roy Cohn
Illinois State University

Don Cole
Drew University

Roger Conover
Azusa Pacifica University

Douglas Copeland
Johnson County Community College

John Costley
Iowa Wesleyan College

Eleanor D. Craig
University of Delaware

James Craven
Clark College

Jerry L. Crawford
Arkansas State University

Antoinette Criss
Foothill Junior College

Al Culver
California State University, Chico

Norman V. Cure
Macomb Community College

Susan Dadres
Southern Methodist University

Bridget Daldy
University of Waikato

Lisa C. DeFelice
University of New Hampshire

Ed Dennis
Franklin Pierce College

Romesh Diwan
Rensselaer Polytechnical Institute

Thomas Drennen
Hobart & William Smith Colleges

Phillip Droke
Highline Community College

Tran Huu Dung
Wright State University

James W. Eden
Portland Community College

Ishita Edwards
Oxnard College

Rex Edwards
Moorpark College

James P. Egan
University of Wisconsin–Eau Claire

Fred Englander
Fairleigh Dickinson University

Valerie Englander
St. John's University

Sharon Erenberg
Eastern Michigan University

John P. Farrell
Oregon State University

David N. Feglio
University of Oregon

David W. Findlay
Colby College

Charles Fisk, Jr.
Saint Leo's College

Fred Folvary
John F. Kennedy University

Peter Fortura
Algonquin College

Ann J. Fraedrich
Marquette University

Rhona C. Free
Eastern Connecticut State University

Landreth Freeman
Randolph-Macon Woman's College

Mary Gade
Oklahoma State University

Julie Galloway
Southwest Missouri State University

Roger Garrison
Auburn University

Joseph Garwood
Valencia Community College

Bernard Gauci
Hollins College

Robert Gentennar
Hope College

Jack B. Goddard
Northeastern State University

Deniek Gondwee
Gettysburg College

John W. Graham
Rutgers University

Joe Green
Dixie College

Louis Green
San Diego State University

Mark E. Haggerty
Clarion University of Pennsylvania

David R. Hakes
University of Northern Iowa

John B. Hall
Portland State University

William Hall
University of North Carolina–Wilmington

Jay Paul Hamilton
California State University–San Bernadino

Richard Hansen
Southeast Missouri State University

Bassim Harik
Western Michigan University

Raymond N. Harvey
Niagara County Community College

Tom Head
George Fox University

Paul Heise
Lebanon Valley College

Marc Herold
University of New Hampshire

Jannett Highfill
Bradley University

George E. Hoffer
Virginia Commonwealth University

Vern Hoglund
Hutchinson Community College

Alexander Holmes
University of Oklahoma

Ric Holt
Southern Oregon University

Andy Howard
Rio Hondo College

Gail Hoyt
University of Kentucky

Kathryn Hulett
Arizona Western College

Scott Hunt
Columbus State Community College

Matthew Hyle
Winona State University

Joseph A. Ilacqua
Bryant College

Robert Jantzen
Iona College

Robert Jerome
James Madison University

Roger Johnson
Messiah College

Walter Johnson
University of Missouri

Susan Kamp
University of Alberta

Nicholas Karatjas
Indiana University of Pennsylvania

Stan Keil
Ball State University

R. E. Kingery
Hawkeye Community College

Robert Kirk
Indiana University/Purdue University Indianapolis

Philip A. Klein
The Pennsylvania State University

Morris Knapp
Miami-Dade Community College

Andrew Kohen
James Madison University

Diana E. Kraas
Augustana College

Penny Kugler
Central Missouri State University

Randy LaHote
Washtenaw Community College

Leonard Lardaro
University of Rhode Island

Mehrene Larudee
University of Kansas

Jodey Lingg
City University of Renton

Randall Lutter
State University of New York–Buffalo

Raymond Mack
Community College of Allegheny County, Boyce Campus

Drew Mattson
Anoka-Ramsey Community College

Evanthis Mavrokordatos
Tarrant County Junior College N.E.

Ann Marie May
University of Nebraska

Diana L. McCoy
Truckee Meadows Community College

Bruce McCrea
Lansing Community College

Richard McIntyre
University of Rhode Island

H. Neal McKenzie
Dalton College

Robert T. McLean
Harrisburg Area Community College

Shah M. Mehrabi
Montgomery College

Debbie A. Meyer
Brookdale Community College

Dennis D. Miller
Baldwin Wallace College

Jon R. Miller
University of Idaho

Craig Milnor
Clarke College

Eric Mitchell
Randolph-Macon Woman's College

Barbara Moore
University of Central Florida

Maria Mora
New Mexico State University

William Morgan
University of Wyoming

Mark Morlock
California State University–Chico

H. Richard Moss
Ricks College

James Murphy
Western Carolina University

Theodore Muzio
St. Vincent College

James E. Needham
Cuyahoga Community College

Reynold Nesiba
Augustana College

Hillar Neumann, Jr.
Northern State University

Maureen O'Brien
University of Minnesota–Duluth

Bill O'Connor
Saddleback College

Patrick O'Neill
University of North Dakota

Norman P. Obst
Michigan State University

Albert Okunade
University of Memphis

Adenike Osoba
Texas Tech University

Amar Pari
State University of New York–Fredonia

Tim Payne
Shoreline Community College

Steve Pecsok
Middlebury College

Don Peppard
Connecticut College

Michael Perelman
California State University–Chico

E. Dale Peterson
Late of Mankato State University

Bill Phillips
University of Southern Maine

Harmanna Poen
Houston Community College

Irene Powell
Grinnell College

Daniel Powroznik
Chesapeake College

Leila J. Pratt
University of Tennessee–Chattanooga

Renee Prim
Gonzaga University

James J. Rakowski
University of Notre Dame

Jaishankar Raman
Valparaiso University

Edward R. Raupp
Augsburg College

Donald Reddick
Kwantlen College

Mitchell Redlo
Monroe Community College

Angela Ritzert
University of New Hampshire

Steve Robinson
University of North Carolina–Wilmington

Denise Robson
University of Wisconsin, Oshkosh

Richard Rosenberg
University of Wisconsin

Brian Rungeling
University of Central Florida

Balbir S. Sahni
Concordia University

George D. Santopietro
Radford University

Linda Schaeffer
California State University–Fresno

Ted Scheinman
Mt. Hood Community College

Timothy Schibik
University of Southern Indiana

Dennis Shannon
Belleville Area College

Dorothy Siden
Salem State College

R. J. Sidwell
Eastern Illinois University

Amrick Singh Dua
Mt. San Antonio College

Garvin Smith
Daytona Beach Community College

John D. Snead
Bluefield State College

Susan Snyder
Virginia Polytechnic Institute

John Somers
Portland Community College

Jacob Sonny
Dowling College

Ugur Soytas
Texas Tech University

Annie Spears
University of Prince Edward Island

G. Anthony Spira
University of Tennessee

Timothy Stanton
Mount Saint Mary's College

Delores W. Steinhauser
Brookdale Community College

Mitch Stengel
University of Michigan–Dearborn

Robert Stonebreaker
Indiana University of Pennsylvania

John Stoudenmire
Methodist College

Martha Stuffler
Irvine Valley Community College

Osman Suliman
Millersville University

Frank Taylor
McLennan Community College

Kit Taylor
Bellevue Community College

Neil Terry
West Texas A&M

Wade Thomas
State University of New York College–Oneonta

Deborah L. Thorsen
Palm Beach Community College

Joe Turek
Illinois Benedictine College

Kay Unger
University of Montana

Alejandro Velez
St. Mary's University

Marion Walsh
Lansing Community College

James Watson
Jefferson College

David Weinberg
Xavier University

Robert Wofford
University of the Ozarks

David Wong
California State University–Fullerton

Edgar W. Wood
University of Mississippi

Kenneth Woodward
Saddleback College

In addition to the input of the formal reviewers listed above, I have received helpful comments, suggestions, encouragement, and assistance from innumerable individuals. Their help made the book better than it otherwise would have been. They include Betty Britt, Deb Quenichet, David Horlacher, Carl Hooker, Tom Adams, Martina Downey, Evan Dixon, Natasha M. Yust, Juan Camilo Gonzalez, Josiah Blackwell, George Harrington Butts, Peter Davis, Sarah Cooper, Wade Pfau, Jonathan Bydlak, Natalie Ram, Nicole Walton Golden, Gregory Czar, Patricia Chamberlain, Skip Moedinger, Kai Chan, Tommy Klym, Dave Anthony, Alison Jonas, Joseph Batin, Don Uy-Barretta, Jim Barbour, Scott Davis, James Chasey, Steve Pecsok, George A. Jouganatos, Steve Payson, John Zembron, Olexandra Astafyeva, Justas Staisiunas, Fred Folvary, Gail Hoyt, Glen Waddell, James Craven, James DeVault, Jim Swaney, Paul Wonnacott, Perry Mehrling, Peter M. Lichtenstein, Phil Shannon, Rashid Al-Hmoud and Ric Holt. I would also like to thank the many other economists who helped me along the way with a suggestion at a conference or via e-mail.

Special thanks to our supplements authors. Jenifer Gamber guided the ancillary team of Tom Adams, Sacramento City College; Douglas Copeland, Johnson County Community College; Kit Taylor, Bellevue Community College; Gail Hoyt, University of Kentucky; James DeVault, Lafayette College; Susan Dadres, Southern Methodist University; Rashid Al-Hmoud, Texas Tech University; Gerald Nelson, University of Illinois; Anthony Zambelli, Cuyameca College; Harry Landreth, Centre College; Sunder Ramaswamy, Middlebury College; and Kailash Khandke, Furman University. They did a great job.

There is another group of people who helped at various stages. Helen Reiff proofread, prepared the glossary, and provided valuable research assistance. A special thank-you goes to Jenifer Gamber, whose role in the book cannot be overestimated. She helped me clarify its vision by providing research, critiquing expositions and often improving them, guiding the ancillaries, and being a good friend. She has an amazing set of skills and I thank her for using them to improve the book.

Next there is the entire McGraw-Hill team: Lucille Sutton, the executive editor; Gary Burke, the publisher; Katie Crouch, the developmental editor; Destiny Rynne, the project manager; Rose Hepburn, the senior production supervisor; book designer Pam Verros; Becky Szura, the supplements coordinator; Janet Renard, the copy editor; Marty Quinn, the marketing manager; David Littlehale, the national sales manager; and the sales representatives who have been so supportive and helpful. They did a great job and I thank them all.

Finally, I want to thank Pat, my wife, and my sons, Kasey and Zach, for helping me keep my work in perspective, and for providing a loving environment in which to work.

Cutting-Edge Approach

Macro

The text considers the limitations of applying the macro model. Models cannot be applied in a mechanistic way; instead they are a guide for reasoning.

Shifts in Expenditures Might Reflect Desired Shifts in Supply and Demand

There is an implicit assumption in the multiplier model that shifts in demand are not reflections of shifts in desired production or supply. Reality is much more complicated. Shifts can occur for many reasons, and many shifts can reflect desired shifts in aggregate production, which are accompanied by shifts in aggregate expenditures. An example of such a change occurred in Japan in the 1990s as Japan's industries lost their competitive edge to Korean, Chinese, and Taiwanese industries. The Japanese economy faltered, but the problem was not simply a fall in aggregate demand, and therefore the solution to it was not simply to increase aggregate demand. There was a simultaneous shift in aggregate supply that had to be dealt with.

Suppliers operate in the future—shifting supply, not to existing demand, but to expected demand, making the relationship between aggregate production and current demand far more complicated than it seems in the multiplier model. Expansion of this line of thought has led some economists (in an earlier chapter called *real-business-cycle economists*) to develop the **real-business-cycle theory** of the economy: *the theory that fluctuations in the economy reflect real phenomena—simultaneous shifts in supply and demand, not simply supply responses to demand shifts*. Let's consider an example—the expansion of the U.S. economy in the late 1990s. The *AS/AD* model would attribute that to a shift of the *AD* curve to the right, combined with a relatively fixed *SAS* curve that did not shift up as output expanded. The real-business-cycle theory would attribute that shift in income to businesses' decision to increase supply due to technological developments, and a subsequent increase in demand via Say's law.

Micro

Colander explores the latest information in the field of behavioral economics. He looks at the application of psychology to economics in the following Beyond the Tools box:

Psychology and Economics

Beyond the Tools

More and more psychology is being integrated into economics and economic reasoning. Instead of just assuming that individuals act rationally, modern economists are conducting experiments to determine how individuals act. In 2002 the Nobel Prize Committee recognized this change when it awarded the Nobel Prize in Economics to a professor of psychology, Danny Kahneman, and to an economist, Vernon Smith.

Smith was given the award for being a leader in experimental economics. He has played a central role in getting economists to test their theories with laboratory experiments, in which one can observe, rather than assume, how people behave. In these experiments economists have found that individuals have a sense of fairness along with economic rationality that guides their decisions.

Kahneman, together with Amos Tversky (who died in 1996), developed the theory of behavioral economics and argued that people aren't as calculating as economists often assume and that they repeatedly make errors in judgment that can be predicted and categorized. For example, a principle of economic rationality is that a sunk cost is a sunk cost, and should not be taken into account in decisions. But consistently individuals take sunk costs into account. He found that people are far less likely to sell a share of stock that they bought for $90 for $70 than they are to sell a share of stock for $70 that they bought for $50, even though economic rationality says that a rational person will not take into account the purchase price of a stock when deciding whether to sell it; they will only take into account future stock prices. Such insights are changing the face of modern economics, but they should be seen as complements to, rather than substitutes for, standard economic reasoning.

Upward Sloping AS Curve

The text now uses the standard upward sloping short-run aggregate supply curve along with standard explanations of how the economy moves from a short-run to a long-run equilibrium.

Figure 25-7 (a, b, and c) Short- and Long-Run Frameworks

The economy is in both short-run and long-run equilibrium when all three curves intersect in the same location. When the economy is in short-run equilibrium but not long-run equilibrium, the position of the *SAS* curve is determined by the relationship between output and potential output. If output is below potential, the *SAS* curve is pulled down by falling input prices, as shown in (**b**). If output is above potential, the *SAS* curve is pulled up by rising input prices, as shown in (**c**).

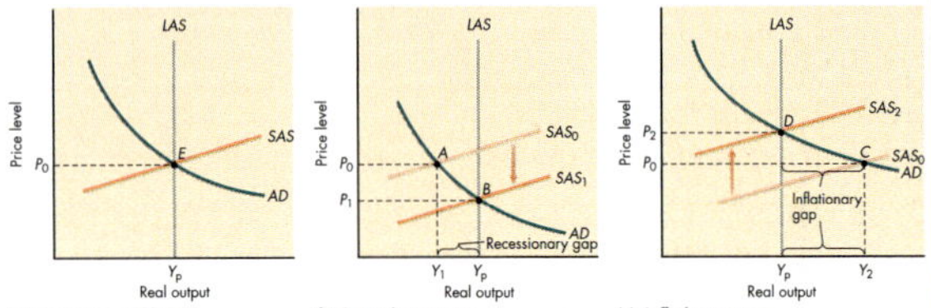

(a) Long-run equilibrium **(b) Recessionary gap** **(c) Inflationary gap**

Colloquial Style

Colander's writing style reaches students on an individual level and makes them feel that in the textbook they have a second teacher. The author doesn't hide behind his words; he's a constant presence throughout the text, coaching students through the difficult spots and adding humor along the way.

[1]This book is written by a person, not a machine. That means that I have my quirks, my odd sense of humor, and my biases. All textbook writers do. Most textbooks have the quirks and eccentricities edited out so that all the books read and sound alike—professional but dull. I choose to sound like me—sometimes professional, sometimes playful, and sometimes stubborn. In my view, that makes the book more human and less dull. So forgive me my quirks—don't always take me too seriously—and I'll try to keep you awake when you're reading this book at 3 A.M. the day of the exam. If you think it's a killer to read a book this long, you ought to try writing one.

WebNotes

Web Note 2.1
Wine and Cloth

Throughout the book, web icons appear in the margin with a label (such as "2.1 Wine and Cloth"). When students go to the book website, they will find a discussion of the topic that extends out to the web by linking to relevant websites.

Focus on Policy

For many students, the principles of economics course will be the only economics course they ever take. These students are most interested in the basics of economic reasoning as it relates to policy questions. Colander relates the economic principles to policy issues, taking into account all the messiness of the real world.

Micro

The Antiglobalization Forces

Applying the Tools

Often when there is a meeting of the World Trade Organization or of a similar type organization promoting free trade, protests (sometimes violent ones) are held by a loosely organized collection of groups opposing globalization. The goals of these groups are varied. Some argue that trade hurts developed countries such as the United States; others argue that it hurts developing countries by exploiting poor workers so that Westerners can get luxuries cheaply. Still others argue against a more subtle Western economic imperialism in which globalization spreads Western cultural values and undermines developing countries' social structures.

Paul Conklin/Photoedit

Each of these arguments has some appeal, although making the first two simultaneously is difficult because it says that voluntary trade hurts both parties to the trade. But the arguments have had little impact on the views of most policymakers and economists.

Supporting free trade does not mean that globalization does not have costs. It does, but many of the costs associated with free trade are really the result of technological changes. The reality is that technological developments, such as those in telecommunications and transportation, are pushing countries closer together and will involve difficult social and cultural changes, regardless of whether trade is free or not. Restricting trade might temporarily slow these changes but is unlikely to stop them.

Most empirical studies have found that, with regard to material goods, the workers in developing countries involved in trade are generally better off than those not involved in trade. That's why most developing countries work hard to encourage companies to move production facilities into their countries. From a worker's perspective, earning $4 a day can look quite good when the alternative is earning $3 a day. Would the worker rather earn $10 a day? Of course, but the higher the wages in a given country, the less likely it is that firms are going to locate production there.

Many economists are sympathetic to various antiglobalization arguments, but they often become frustrated at the lack of clarity of the antiglobalization groups' views. To oppose something is not enough; to effect positive change, one must not only understand how the thing one opposes works but also have a realistic plan for a better alternative.

Macro

State Government Finance and Procyclical Fiscal Policy

Automatic stabilizers are sometimes offset by other institutional structures that work as a type of automatic *destabilizer*. Examples of such destabilizers are states' constitutional provisions to maintain balanced budgets. These provisions mean that whenever a recession hits, states are faced with declining tax revenue. To maintain balanced budgets, the states must cut spending, increase tax rates, or both. For example, during the 2001–2002 recession, state governments struggled to balance their budgets by cutting expenditures on education, transportation, health care, and a variety of other programs while raising income and sales taxes. These actions deepened the recession. Similarly, during the previous 10-year expansion, state revenue rose; and states increased spending and decreased tax rates. The expansionary effect of these changes further increased total income. The result is what economists call **procyclical fiscal policy**—*changes in government spending and taxes that increase the cyclical fluctuations in the economy instead of reducing them*.

Coverage of Institutions and History

Economic Institutions

To know whether you can apply economic theory to reality, you must know about economic institutions—laws, common practices, and organizations in a society that affect the economy. Corporations, governments, and cultural norms are all examples of economic institutions. Many economic institutions have social, political, and religious dimensions. For example, your job often influences your social standing. In addition, many social institutions, such as the family, have economic functions. If any institution significantly affects economic decisions, I include it as an economic institution because you must understand that institution if you are to understand how the economy functions.

Economic institutions differ significantly among countries. For example, in Germany banks are allowed to own companies; in the United States they cannot. This

Recent research suggests that the implications of economic reasoning depend on the institutional setting. Colander is well-known for his inclusion of detailed material on existing institutions and the historical development of those institutions. This historical perspective allows students to examine how institutions impact economic decisions.

Tools Boxes

"Applying the Tools," "Knowing the Tools," and "Beyond the Tools" are included in most chapters to reinforce the economic tools presented in the text and help students learn the basics.

Laissez-Faire is Not Anarchy

Beyond the Tools

Most reasons for government intervention discussed in this chapter are debatable.

There is, however, one governmental role that even the strongest laissez-faire advocates generally accept. That role is for government to set up an appropriate institutional and legal structure within which markets can operate.

The reason there's little debate about this role is that all economists recognize that markets do not operate when there is anarchy. They require institutional structures that determine the rules of ownership, what types of trade are allowable, how contracts will be enforced, and what productive institutions are most desirable.

Before anyone conducts business, he or she needs to know the rules of the game and must have a reasonable expectation that those rules will not be changed. The operation of the modern economy requires that contractual arrangements be made among individuals. These contractual arrangements must be enforced if the economy is to operate effectively.

Economists differ significantly on what the rules for such a system should be and whether any rules that already exist should be modified. Even if the rules are currently perceived as unfair, it can be argued that they should be kept in place. Individuals have already made decisions based on those rules, and it's unfair to them to change the rules in the middle of the game.

Stability of rules is a benefit to society. When the rules are perceived as unfair, and changing them is also perceived as unfair, the government must find a balance between the two degrees of unfairness. Government often finds itself in that difficult position. Thus, while there's little debate about government's role in providing some institutional framework, there's heated debate about which framework is most appropriate.

www.mhhe.com/economics/colander5

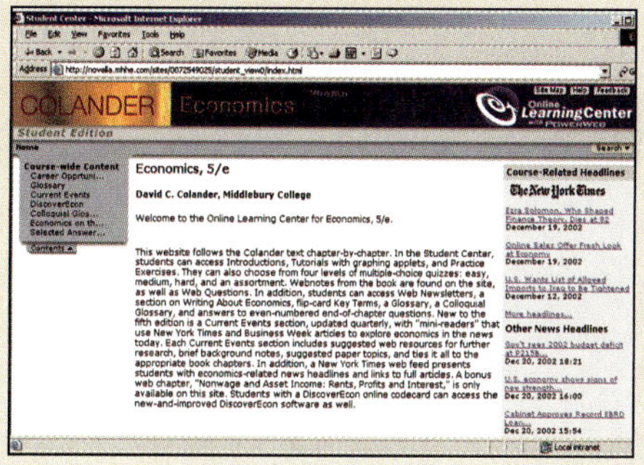

The Online Learning Center with PowerWeb to accompany Colander's fifth edition is full of exciting new content. In the Student Center, you'll find multiple-choice quizzes at three levels of difficulty, interactive graphs, a current events section with web resources and paper topics, WebNotes from the text, a New York Times headline feed, and chapter-level PowerWeb content, and more. The Instructor Center includes helpful instructional aids such as a compilation of instructors' favorite classroom exercises ("Best Practices") and "Help for AP Courses," in addition to the Instructor's Manual, PowerPoints, and Sample Syllabi.

DiscoverEcon

The DiscoverEcon software is the bestselling academic economics software.

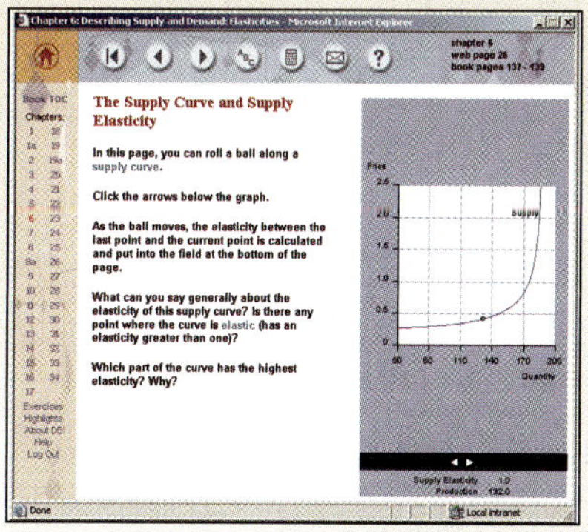

The chapter-level content features multiple-choice quizzes, essay questions, web questions, interactive graphs, live tables, and more. The version of DiscoverEcon to accompany the fifth edition of Colander will allow students to electronically submit their quiz and essay results directly to their professors. DiscoverEcon is more helpful and accessible than ever.

BRIEF CONTENTS

I

INTRODUCTION: THINKING LIKE AN ECONOMIST

II

MICROECONOMICS

III

MACROECONOMICS

CONTENTS

I

INTRODUCTION: THINKING LIKE AN ECONOMIST

Section II
Foundations of Supply and Demand

8 The Logic of Individual Choice: The Foundation of Supply and Demand 178

9 Production and Cost Analysis I 203

10 Production and Cost Analysis II 220

Section III
Market Structure and Policy

15 Antitrust Policy and Regulation 328

Section IV
Factor Markets

16 Work and the Labor Market 354

17 Who Gets What? The Distribution of Incomc 384

20 Microeconomic Policy, Economic Reasoning, and Beyond 442

21 International Trade Policy 460

III

MACROECONOMICS

Section I
Macroeconomics Problems

Section II
The Macroeconomic Framework

PART I

INTRODUCTION: THINKING LIKE AN ECONOMIST

Part I is an introduction, and an introduction to an introduction seems a little funny. But other sections have introductions, so it seemed a little funny not to have an introduction to Part I; and besides, as you will see, I'm a little funny myself (which, in turn, has two interpretations; I'm sure you will decide which of the two is appropriate). It will, however, be a very brief introduction, consisting of questions you probably have and some answers to those questions.

SOME QUESTIONS AND ANSWERS

Why study economics?
Because it's neat and interesting and helps provide insight into events that are constantly going on around you.

Why is this book so big?
Because there's a lot of important information in it and because the book is designed so your teacher can pick and choose. You'll likely not be required to read all of it, especially if you're on the quarter system. But once you start it, you'll probably read it all anyhow. (Would you believe?)

Why does this book cost so much?
To answer this question you'll have to read the book.

Will this book make me rich?
No.

Will this book make me happy?
It depends.

This book doesn't seem to be written in a normal textbook style. Is this book really written by a professor?
Yes, but he is different. He misspent his youth working on cars; he married his high school sweetheart after they met again at their 20th high school reunion. Twenty-five years after graduating from high school, his wife went back to medical school and got her MD because she was tired of being treated poorly by doctors. Their five kids make sure he doesn't get carried away in the professorial cloud.

Will the entire book be like this?
No, the introduction is just trying to rope you in. Much of the book will be hard going. Learning happens to be a difficult process: no pain, no gain. But the author isn't a sadist; he tries to make learning as pleasantly painful as possible.

What do the author's students think of him?
Weird, definitely weird—and hard. But fair, interesting, and sincerely interested in getting us to learn. (Answer written by his students.)

So there you have it. Answers to the questions that you might never have thought of if they hadn't been put in front of you. I hope they give you a sense of me and the approach I'll use in the book. There are some neat ideas in it. Let's now briefly consider what's in the first five chapters.

A SURVEY OF THE FIRST FIVE CHAPTERS

This first section is really an introduction to the rest of the book. It gives you the background necessary so that the later chapters make sense. Chapter 1 gives you an overview of the entire field of economics as well as an introduction to my style. Chapter 2 focuses on the production possibility curve, comparative advantage, and trade. It explains how trade increases production possibilities but also why, in the real world, free trade and no government regulation may not be the best policy. Chapter 3 gives you some history of economic systems and introduces you to the institutions of the U.S. economy. It also discusses the challenges that globalization presents for the U.S. economy. Chapters 4 and 5 introduce you to supply and demand, and show you not only the power of those two concepts but also the limitations.

Now let's get on with the show.

1 Economics and Economic Reasoning

After reading this chapter, you should be able to:

- Define economics and list three coordination problems that an economy must solve.
- Explain how to make decisions by comparing marginal costs and marginal benefits.
- Define opportunity cost and explain its relationship to economic reasoning.
- Explain real-world events in terms of economic forces, social forces, and political forces.
- Differentiate between microeconomics and macroeconomics.
- Distinguish among positive economics, normative economics, and the art of economics.

In my vacations, I visited the poorest quarters of several cities and walked through one street after another, looking at the faces of the poorest people. Next I resolved to make as thorough a study as I could of Political Economy.

—*Alfred Marshall*

When an artist looks at the world, he sees color. When a musician looks at the world, she hears music. When an economist looks at the world, she sees a symphony of costs and benefits. The economist's world might not be as colorful or as melodic as the others' worlds, but it's more practical. If you want to understand what's going on in the world that's really out there, you need to know economics.

I hardly have to convince you of this fact if you keep up with the news. Unemployment is down; the price of gas is up; interest rates are down; businesses are going bankrupt. . . . The list is endless. So let's say you grant me that economics is important. That still doesn't mean that it's worth studying. The real question then is: How much will you learn? Most of what you learn depends on you, but part depends on the teacher and another part depends on the textbook. On both these counts, you're in luck; since your teacher chose this book for your course, you must have a super teacher.[1]

What Economics Is

Economics is *the study of how human beings coordinate their wants and desires, given the decision-making mechanisms, social customs, and political realities of the society.* One of the key words in the definition of the term "economics" is *coordination*. Coordination can mean many things. In the study of economics, coordination refers to how the three central problems facing any economy are solved. These central problems are:

[1]This book is written by a person, not a machine. That means that I have my quirks, my odd sense of humor, and my biases. All textbook writers do. Most textbooks have the quirks and eccentricities edited out so that all the books read and sound alike—professional but dull. I choose to sound like me—sometimes professional, sometimes playful, and sometimes stubborn. In my view, that makes the book more human and less dull. So forgive me my quirks—don't always take me too seriously—and I'll try to keep you awake when you're reading this book at 3 A.M. the day of the exam. If you think it's a killer to read a book this long, you ought to try writing one.

1. What, and how much, to produce.
2. How to produce it.
3. For whom to produce it.

Three central coordination problems any economy must solve are what to produce, how to produce it, and for whom to produce it.

How hard is it to make the three decisions? Imagine for a moment the problem of living in a family: the fights, arguments, and questions that come up. "Do I have to do the dishes?" "Why can't I have piano lessons?" "Bobby got a new sweater. How come I didn't?" "Mom likes you best." Now multiply the size of the family by millions. The same fights, the same arguments, the same questions—only for society the questions are millions of time more complicated. In answering these questions, economies generally find that individuals want more than is available, given how much they're willing to work. That means that in our economy there is a problem of **scarcity**—*the goods available are too few to satisfy individuals' desires*.

The coordination questions faced by society are complicated.

Scarcity has two elements—our wants and our means of fulfilling those wants. These can be interrelated since wants are changeable and partially determined by society. The way we fulfill wants can affect those wants. For example, if you work on Wall Street you will probably want upscale and trendy clothes. Up here in Vermont, I am quite happy wearing Levi's and flannel.

The degree of scarcity is constantly changing. The quantity of goods, services, and usable resources depends on technology and human action, which underlie production. Individuals' imagination, innovativeness, and willingness to do what needs to be done can greatly increase available goods and resources. Who knows what technologies are in our future—nannites or micromachines that change atoms into whatever we want could conceivably eliminate scarcity of goods we currently consume. But they would not eliminate scarcity entirely since new wants are constantly developing.

The quantity of goods, services, and usable resources depends on technology and human action.

In all known economies, coordination has involved some type of coercion—limiting people's wants and increasing the amount of work individuals are willing to do to fulfill those wants. The reality is that many people would rather play than help solve society's problems. So the basic economic problem involves inspiring people to do things that other people want them to do, and not to do things that other people don't want them to do. Thus, an alternative definition of economics is that it is the study of how to get people to do things they're not wild about doing (such as studying) and not to do things they are wild about doing (such as eating all the lobster they like), so that the things some people want to do are consistent with the things other people want to do.

To understand an economy you need to learn:

1. *Economic reasoning*.
2. *Economic terminology*.
3. *Economic insights* economists have about issues, and theories that lead to those insights.
4. Information about *economic institutions*.
5. Information about the *economic policy options* facing society today.

Let's consider each in turn.

To understand an economy you need to learn:

1. Economic reasoning.
2. Economic terminology.
3. Economic insights.
4. Economic institutions.
5. Economic policy options.

A Guide to Economic Reasoning

People trained in economics think in a certain way. They analyze everything critically; they compare the costs and the benefits of every issue and make decisions based on those costs and benefits. For example, say you're trying to decide whether a policy to eliminate terrorist attacks on airlines is a good idea. Economists are trained to put their emotions aside and ask: What are the costs of the policy, and what are the benefits?

Thus, they are open to the argument that security measures, such as conducting body searches of every passenger or scanning all baggage with bomb-detecting machinery, might not be the appropriate policy because the costs might exceed the benefits. To think like an economist is to address almost all issues using a cost/benefit approach. Economic reasoning—how to think like an economist, making decisions on the basis of costs and benefits—is the most important lesson you'll learn from this book.

Economic reasoning is making decisions on the basis of costs and benefits.

Economic reasoning, once learned, is infectious. If you're susceptible, being exposed to it will change your life. It will influence your analysis of everything, including issues normally considered outside the scope of economics. For example, you will likely use economic reasoning to decide the possibility of getting a date for Saturday night, and who will pay for dinner. You will likely use it to decide whether to read this book, whether to attend class, whom to marry, and what kind of work to go into after you graduate. This is not to say that economic reasoning will provide all the answers. As you will see throughout this book, real-world questions are inevitably complicated, and economic reasoning simply provides a framework within which to approach a question. In the economic way of thinking, every choice has costs and benefits, and decisions are made by comparing them.

Marginal Costs and Marginal Benefits

The relevant costs and relevant benefits to economic reasoning are the expected *incremental,* or additional, costs incurred and the expected *incremental* benefits that result from a decision. Economists use the term *marginal* when referring to additional or incremental. Marginal costs and marginal benefits are key concepts.

Web Note 1.1
Costs and Benefits

A **marginal cost** is *the additional cost to you over and above the costs you have already incurred*. That means not counting **sunk costs**—*costs that have already been incurred and cannot be recovered*—in the relevant costs when making a decision. Consider, for example, attending class. You've already paid your tuition; it is a sunk cost. So the marginal (or additional) cost of going to class does not include tuition.

Similarly with marginal benefit. A **marginal benefit** is *the additional benefit above what you've already derived*. The marginal benefit of reading this chapter is the *additional* knowledge you get from reading it. If you already knew everything in this chapter before you picked up the book, the marginal benefit of reading it now is zero. The marginal benefit is not zero if by reading the chapter you learn that you are prepared for class; before, you might only have suspected you were prepared.

Comparing marginal (additional) costs with marginal (additional) benefits will often tell you how you should adjust your activities to be as well off as possible. Just follow the **economic decision rule:**

If the marginal benefits of doing something exceed the marginal costs, do it. If the marginal costs of doing something exceed the marginal benefits, don't do it.

> *If the marginal benefits of doing something exceed the marginal costs, do it.*
>
> *If the marginal costs of doing something exceed the marginal benefits, don't do it.*

As an example, let's consider a discussion I might have with a student who tells me that she is too busy to attend my classes. I respond, "Think about the tuition you've spent for this class—it works out to about $30 a lecture." She answers that the book she reads for class is a book that I wrote, and that I wrote it so clearly she fully understands everything. She goes on:

Q.1 Say you bought a share of Sun Microsystems for $100 and a share of Cisco for $10. The price of each is currently $15. Assuming taxes are not an issue, which would you sell if you need $15?

> I've already paid the tuition and whether I go to class or not, I can't get any of the tuition back, so the tuition is a sunk cost and doesn't enter into my decision. The marginal cost to me is what I could be doing with the hour instead of spending it in class. I value my time at $75 an hour [people who understand everything value their time highly], and even though I've heard that your lectures are super, I estimate that

Economic Knowledge in One Sentence: TANSTAAFL

Knowing the Tools

Once upon a time, Tanstaafl was made king of all the lands. His first act was to call his economic advisers and tell them to write up all the economic knowledge the society possessed. After years of work, they presented their monumental effort: 25 volumes, each about 400 pages long. But in the interim, King Tanstaafl had become a very busy man, what with running a kingdom of all the lands and all. Looking at the lengthy volumes, he told his advisers to summarize their findings in one volume.

Despondently, the economists returned to their desks, wondering how they could summarize what they'd been so careful to spell out. After many more years of rewriting, they were finally satisfied with their one-volume effort, and tried to make an appointment to see the king. Unfortunately, affairs of state had become even more pressing than before, and the king couldn't take the time to see them. Instead he sent word to them that he couldn't be bothered with a whole volume, and ordered them, under threat of death (for he had become a tyrant), to reduce the work to one sentence.

The economists returned to their desks, shivering in their sandals and pondering their impossible task. Thinking about their fate if they were not successful, they decided to send out for one last meal. Unfortunately, when they were collecting money to pay for the meal, they discovered they were broke. The disgusted delivery man took the last meal back to the restaurant, and the economists started down the path to the beheading station. On the way, the delivery man's parting words echoed in their ears. They looked at each other and suddenly they realized the truth. "We're saved!" they screamed. "That's it! That's economic knowledge in one sentence!" They wrote the sentence down and presented it to the king, who thereafter fully understood all economic problems. (He also gave them a good meal.) The sentence?

There **A**in't **N**o **S**uch **T**hing **A**s **A** **F**ree **L**unch—
TANSTAAFL

the marginal benefit of your class is only $50. The marginal cost, $75, exceeds the marginal benefit, $50, so I don't attend class.

I congratulate her on her diplomacy and her economic reasoning, but tell her that I give a quiz every week, that students who miss a quiz fail the quiz, that those who fail all the quizzes fail the course, and that those who fail the course do not graduate. In short, she is underestimating the marginal benefits of attending my course. Correctly estimated, the marginal benefits of attending my class exceed the marginal costs. So she should attend my class.

Economics and Passion

Recognizing that everything has a cost is reasonable, but it's a reasonableness that many people don't like. It takes some of the passion out of life. It leads you to consider possibilities like these:

- Saving some people's lives with liver transplants might not be worth the additional cost. The money might be better spent on nutritional programs that would save 20 lives for every 2 lives you might save with transplants.
- Maybe we shouldn't try to eliminate all pollution, because the additional cost of doing so may be too high. To eliminate all pollution might be to forgo too much of some other worthwhile activity.
- Providing a guaranteed job for every person who wants one might not be a worthwhile policy goal if it means that doing so will reduce the ability of an economy to adapt to new technologies.

Economic reasoning is based on the premise that everything has a cost.

- It might make sense for the automobile industry to save $12 per car by not installing a safety device, even though without the safety device some people will be killed.

You get the idea. This kind of reasonableness is often criticized for being cold-hearted. But, not surprisingly, economists disagree; they argue that their reasoning leads to a better society for the majority of people.

Q-2 Can you think of a reason why a cost/benefit approach to a problem might be inappropriate? Can you give an example?

Economists' reasonableness isn't universally appreciated. Businesses love the result; others aren't so sure, as I discovered some years back when my then-girlfriend told me she was leaving me. "Why?" I asked. "Because," she responded, "you're so, so . . . reasonable." It took me many years after she left to learn what she already knew: There are many types of reasonableness, and not everyone thinks an economist's reasonableness is a virtue. I'll discuss such issues later; for now, let me simply warn you that, for better or worse, studying economics will lead you to view questions in a cost/benefit framework.

Opportunity Cost

Opportunity cost is the basis of cost/benefit economic reasoning; it is the benefit forgone, or the cost, of the next-best alternative to the activity you've chosen. In economic reasoning, that cost is less than the benefit of what you've chosen.

Putting economists' cost/benefit rules into practice isn't easy. To do so, you have to be able to choose and measure the costs and benefits correctly. Economists have devised the concept of opportunity cost to help you do that. The **opportunity cost** of undertaking an activity is *the benefit forgone by undertaking that activity*. The benefit forgone is the benefit that you might have gained from choosing the next-best alternative. To obtain the benefit of something, you must give up (forgo) something else—namely, the next-best alternative. All activities that have a next-best alternative have an opportunity cost.

Let's consider some examples. The opportunity cost of going out once with Natalie (or Nathaniel), the most beautiful woman (attractive man) in the world, might well be losing your solid steady, Margo (Mike). The opportunity cost of cleaning up the environment might be a reduction in the money available to assist low-income individuals. The opportunity cost of having a child might be two boats, three cars, and a two-week vacation each year for five years.

Examples are endless, but let's consider two that are particularly relevant to you: your choice of courses and your decision about how much to study. Let's say you're a full-time student and at the beginning of the term you had to choose four or five courses to take. Taking one precluded taking some other, and the opportunity cost of taking an economics course may well have been not taking a course on theater. Similarly with studying: You have a limited amount of time to spend studying economics, studying some other subject, sleeping, or partying. The more time you spend on one activity, the less time you have for another. That's opportunity cost.

Opportunity costs have always made choice difficult, as we see in the early-19th-century engraving, "One or the Other."
Bleichroeder Print Collection, Baker Library, Harvard Business School.

Notice how neatly the opportunity cost concept takes into account costs and benefits of all other options, and converts these alternative benefits into costs of the decision you're now making.

The relevance of opportunity cost isn't limited to your individual decisions. Opportunity costs are also relevant to government's decisions, which affect everyone in society. A common example is the guns-versus-butter debate. The resources that a society has are limited; therefore, its decision to use those resources to have more guns (more weapons) means that it must have less butter (fewer consumer goods).

Thus, when society decides to spend $50 billion more on an improved health care system, the opportunity cost of that decision is $50 billion not spent on helping the homeless, paying off some of the national debt, or providing for national defense.

The opportunity cost concept has endless implications. It can even be turned upon itself. For instance, it takes time to think about alternatives; that means that there's a cost to being reasonable, so it's only reasonable to be somewhat unreasonable. If you followed that argument, you've caught the economic bug. If you didn't, don't worry. Just remember the opportunity cost concept for now; I'll infect you with economic thinking in the rest of the book.

Q.3 John, your study partner, has just said that the opportunity cost of studying this chapter is about 1/35 the price you paid for this book, since the chapter is about 1/35 of the book. Is he right? Why or why not?

Economic and Market Forces

The opportunity cost concept applies to all aspects of life and is fundamental to understanding how society reacts to scarcity. When goods are scarce, those goods must be rationed. That is, a mechanism must be chosen to determine who gets what. Society must deal with the scarcity, thinking about and deciding how to allocate the scarce good.

Q.4 Ali, your study partner, states that rationing health care is immoral—that health care should be freely available to all individuals in society. How would you respond?

Let's consider some specific real-world rationing mechanisms. Dormitory rooms are often rationed by lottery, and permission to register in popular classes is often rationed by a first-come, first-registered rule. Food in the United States, however, is generally rationed by price. If price did not ration food, there wouldn't be enough food to go around. All scarce goods or rights must be rationed in some fashion. These rationing mechanisms are examples of **economic forces,** *the necessary reactions to scarcity*.

One of the important choices that a society must make is whether to allow these economic forces to operate freely and openly or to try to rein them in. A **market force** is *an economic force that is given relatively free rein by society to work through the market*. Market forces ration by changing prices. When there's a shortage, the price goes up. When there's a surplus, the price goes down. Much of this book will be devoted to analyzing how the market works like an invisible hand, guiding economic forces to coordinate individual actions and allocate scarce resources. The **invisible hand** is *the price mechanism, the rise and fall of prices that guides our actions in a market*.

When an economic force operates through the market, it becomes a market force.

Economic reality is controlled by three forces:

1. Economic forces (the invisible hand),
2. Social and cultural forces, and
3. Political and legal forces.

Societies can't choose whether or not to allow economic forces to operate—economic forces are always operating. However, societies can choose whether to allow market forces to predominate. Social, cultural, and political forces play a major role in deciding whether to let market forces operate. Economic reality is determined by a contest among these various forces.

Let's consider an example in which social forces prevent an economic force from becoming a market force: the problem of getting a date for Saturday night. If a school (or a society) has significantly more people of one gender than the other (let's say more men than women), some men may well find themselves without a date—that is, men will be in excess supply—and will have to find something else to do, say study or go to a movie by themselves. An "excess supply" person could solve the problem by paying someone to go out with him or her, but that would probably change the nature of the date in unacceptable ways. It would be revolting to the person who offered payment and to the person who was offered payment. That unacceptability is an example of the complex social and cultural norms that guides and limits our activities. People don't try to buy dates because social forces prevent them from doing so.

Social and cultural forces can play a significant role in the economy.

Now let's consider another example in which political and legal influences stop economic forces from becoming market forces. Say you decide that you can make some money delivering mail in your neighborhood. You try to establish a small business, but suddenly you are confronted with the law. The U.S. Postal Service has a legal exclusive right to deliver regular mail, so you'll be prohibited from delivering regular mail

Q.5 Your study partner, Joan, states that market forces are always operative. Is she right? Why or why not?

Economics in Perspective

Beyond the Tools

All too often, students study economics out of context. They're presented with sterile analysis and boring facts to memorize, and are never shown how economics fits into the larger scheme of things. That's bad; it makes economics seem boring—but economics is not boring. Every so often throughout this book, sometimes in the appendixes and sometimes in boxes, I'll step back and put the analysis in perspective, giving you an idea from whence the analysis sprang and its historical context. In educational jargon, this is called *enrichment.*

I begin here with economics itself.

First, its history: In the 1500s there were few universities. Those that existed taught religion, Latin, Greek, philosophy, history, and mathematics. No economics. Then came the *Enlightenment* (about 1700), in which reasoning replaced God as the explanation of why things were the way they were. Pre-Enlightenment thinkers would answer the question "Why am I poor?" with "Because God wills it." Enlightenment scholars looked for a different explanation. "Because of the nature of land ownership" is one answer they found.

Such reasoned explanations required more knowledge of the way things were, and the amount of information expanded so rapidly that it had to be divided or categorized for an individual to have hope of knowing a subject. Soon philosophy was subdivided into science and philosophy. In the 1700s, the sciences were split into natural sciences and social sciences. The amount of knowledge kept increasing, and in the late 1800s and early 1900s social science itself split into subdivisions: economics, political science, history, geography, sociology, anthropology, and psychology. Many of the insights about how the economic system worked were codified in Adam Smith's *The Wealth of Nations,* written in 1776. Notice that this is before economics as a subdiscipline developed, and Adam Smith could also be classified as an anthropologist, a sociologist, a political scientist, and a social philosopher.

Throughout the 18th and 19th centuries, economists such as Adam Smith, Thomas Malthus, John Stuart Mill, David Ricardo, and Karl Marx were more than economists; they were social philosophers who covered all aspects of social science. These writers were subsequently called *classical economists.* Alfred Marshall continued in that classical tradition, and his book, *Principles of Economics,* published in the late 1800s, was written with the other social sciences much in evidence. But Marshall also changed the questions economists ask; he focused on those questions that could be asked in a graphical supply/demand framework.

This book falls solidly in the Marshallian tradition. It sees economics as a way of thinking—as an engine of analysis used to understand real-world phenomena.

Marshallian economics is primarily about policy, not theory. It sees institutions as well as political and social dimensions of reality as important, and it shows you how economics ties in to those dimensions.

---

in competition with the post office. Economic forces—the desire to make money—led you to want to enter the business, but in this case political forces squash the invisible hand.

Economic forces are always operative; society may allow market forces to operate.

Often political and social forces work together against the invisible hand. For example, in the United States there aren't enough babies to satisfy all the couples who desire them. Babies born to particular sets of parents are rationed—by luck. Consider a group of parents, all of whom want babies. Those who can, have a baby; those who can't have one, but want one, try to adopt. Adoption agencies ration the available babies. Who gets a baby depends on whom people know at the adoption agency and on the desires of the birth mother, who can often specify the socioeconomic background (and many other characteristics) of the family in which she wants her baby to grow up. That's the economic force in action; it gives more power to the supplier of something that's in short supply.

Web Note 1.2
Society and Markets

If our society allowed individuals to buy and sell babies, that economic force would be translated into a market force. The invisible hand would see to it that the quantity of babies supplied would equal the quantity of babies demanded at some price. The market, not the adoption agencies, would do the rationing.[2]

Most people, including me, find the idea of selling babies repugnant. But why? It's the strength of social forces reinforced by political forces.

What is and isn't allowable differs from one society to another. For example, in Cuba and North Korea, many private businesses are against the law, so not many people start their own businesses. In the United States, until the 1970s, it was against the law to hold gold except in jewelry and for certain limited uses such as dental supplies, so most people refrained from holding gold. Ultimately a country's laws and social norms determine whether the invisible hand will be allowed to work.

Social and political forces are active in all parts of your life. Political forces influence many of your everyday actions. You don't practice medicine without a license; you don't sell body parts or certain addictive drugs. These actions are against the law. But many people do sell alcohol; that's not against the law if you have a permit. Social forces also influence us. You don't make profitable loans to your friends (you don't charge your friends interest); you don't charge your children for their food (parents are supposed to feed their children); many sports and media stars don't sell their autographs (some do, but many consider the practice tacky); you don't lower the wage you'll accept in order to get a job away from someone else (you're no scab). The list is long. You cannot understand economics without understanding the limitations that political and social forces place on economic actions.

In summary, what happens in a society can be seen as the reaction to, and interaction of, these three forces: economic forces, political and legal forces, and social and historical forces. Economics has a role to play in sociology, history, and politics, just as sociology, history, and politics have roles to play in economics.

Economics is about the real world. Throughout this book I'll use the forces just described to talk about real-world events and the interrelationships of economics, history, sociology, and politics.

What happens in society can be seen as a reaction to, and interaction of, economic forces, political forces, social forces, and historical forces.
Rachel Epstein/Photoedit

Economic Terminology

Economic terminology needs little discussion. It simply needs learning. As terms come up, you'll begin to recognize them. Soon you'll begin to understand them, and finally you'll begin to feel comfortable using them. In this book I'm trying to describe how economics works in the real world, so I introduce you to many of the terms that occur in business and in discussions of the economy. Whenever possible I'll integrate the introduction of new terms into the discussion so that learning them will seem painless. In fact I've already introduced you to a number of economic terms: *opportunity cost, the invisible hand, market forces, economic forces,* just to name a few. By the end of the book I'll have introduced you to hundreds more.

Economic Insights

Economists have thought about the economy for a long time, so it's not surprising that they've developed some insights into the way it works.

---

[2]Even though it's against the law, some babies are nonetheless "sold" on a semilegal market, also called a gray market. At the turn of the century, the "market price" for a healthy baby was about $30,000. If it were legal to sell babies (and if people didn't find it morally repugnant to have babies in order to sell them), the price would be much lower, because there would be a larger supply of babies. (It was not against the law to sell human eggs in the early 2000s, and one human egg was sold for $50,000. The average price was much lower; it varied with donor characteristics such as SAT scores and athletic accomplishments.)

These insights are often based on generalizations, called theories, about the workings of an abstract economy. Theories tie together economists' terminology and knowledge about economic institutions. Theories are inevitably too abstract to apply in specific cases, and thus a theory is often embodied in an **economic model**—*a framework that places the generalized insights of the theory in a more specific contextual setting*—or in an **economic principle**—*a commonly held economic insight stated as a law or general assumption*. Then these theories, models, and principles are empirically tested (as best one can) to ensure that they correspond to reality. Because economics is an observational, not a laboratory, science, economists cannot test their models with controlled experiments. Instead, economists must carefully observe the economy and try to figure out what is affecting what. To do so they look for natural experiments, where something has changed in one place (say the minimum wage in New Jersey) but has not changed somewhere else (say the minimum wage in Pennsylvania) and compare the results in the two cases. But even in cases where there is a natural experiment, it is impossible to hold "other things constant," as is done in laboratory experiments, and thus the empirical results in economics are often subject to dispute.

Theories, models, and principles must be combined with a knowledge of real-world economic institutions to arrive at specific policy recommendations.

While economic models and principles are less general than theories, they are still usually too general to apply in specific cases. Theories, models, and principles must be combined with a knowledge of real-world economic institutions to arrive at specific policy recommendations.

To see the importance of principles, think back to when you learned to add. You didn't memorize the sum of 147 and 138; instead you learned a principle of addition. The principle says that when adding 147 and 138, you first add 7 + 8, which you memorized was 15. You write down the 5 and carry the 1, which you add to 4 + 3 to get 8. Then add 1 + 1 = 2. So the answer is 285. When you know just one principle, you know how to add millions of combinations of numbers.

The Invisible Hand Theory

In the same way, knowing a theory gives you insight into a wide variety of economic phenomena, even though you don't know the particulars of each phenomenon. For example, much of economic theory deals with the *pricing mechanism* and how the market operates to coordinate *individuals' decisions*. Economists have come to the following insights:

Q-6 There has been a superb growing season and the quantity of tomatoes supplied exceeds the quantity demanded. What is likely to happen to the price of tomatoes?

> When the quantity supplied is greater than the quantity demanded, price has a tendency to fall.
>
> When the quantity demanded is greater than the quantity supplied, price has a tendency to rise.

Using these generalized insights, economists have developed a theory of markets that leads to the further insight that, under certain conditions, markets are efficient. That is, the market will coordinate individuals' decisions, allocating scarce resources to their best possible use. **Efficiency** means *achieving a goal as cheaply as possible*. Economists call this insight the **invisible hand theory**—*a market economy, through the price mechanism, will tend to allocate resources efficiently*.

Theories, and the models used to represent them, are enormously efficient methods of conveying information, but they're also necessarily abstract. They rely on simplifying assumptions, and *if you don't know the assumptions, you don't know the theory*. The result of forgetting assumptions could be similar to what happens if you forget that you're supposed to add numbers in columns. Forgetting that, yet remembering all the steps, can lead to a wildly incorrect answer. For example,

Winston Churchill and Lady Astor

Applying the Tools

There are many stories about Nancy Astor, the first woman elected to Britain's Parliament. A vivacious, fearless American woman, she married into the English aristocracy and, during the 1930s and 1940s, became a bright light on the English social and political scenes, which were already quite bright.

One story told about Lady Astor is that she and Winston Churchill, the unorthodox genius who had a long and distinguished political career and who was Britain's prime minister during World War II, were sitting in a pub having a theoretical discussion about morality. Churchill suggested that as a thought experiment Lady Astor ponder the following question: If a man were to promise her a huge amount of money—say a million pounds—for the privilege, would she sleep with him? Lady Astor did ponder the question for a while and finally answered, yes, she would, if the money were guaranteed. Churchill then asked her if she would sleep with him for five pounds. Her response was sharp: "Of course not. What do you think I am—a prostitute?" This time Churchill won the battle of wits by answering, "We have already established that fact; we are now simply negotiating about price."

One moral that economists might draw from this story is that economic incentives, if high enough, can have a powerful influence on behavior. An equally important moral of the story is that noneconomic incentives can also be very strong. Why do most people feel it's wrong to sell sex for money, even if they would be willing to do so if the price were high enough? Keeping this second moral in mind will significantly increase your economic understanding of real-world events.

$$\begin{array}{r} 147 \\ +\ 138 \\ \hline \end{array}$$

1,608 is wrong.

Knowing the assumptions of theories and models allows you to progress beyond gut reaction and better understand the strengths and weaknesses of various economic systems. Let's consider a central economic assumption: the assumption that individuals behave rationally—that what they choose reflects what makes them happiest, given the constraints. If that assumption doesn't hold, the invisible hand theory doesn't hold.

Presenting the invisible hand theory in its full beauty is an important part of any economics course. Presenting the assumptions on which it is based and the limitations of the invisible hand is likewise an important part of the course. I'll do both throughout the book.

Economic Theory and Stories

Theory is a shorthand way of telling a story.

Economic theory, and the models in which that theory is presented, often developed as a shorthand way of telling a story. These stories are important; they make the theory come alive and convey the insights that give economic theory its power. In this book I present plenty of theories and models, but they're accompanied by stories that provide the context that makes them relevant.

At times, because there are many new terms, discussing models and theories takes up much of the presentation time and becomes a bit oppressive. That's the nature of the beast. As Albert Einstein said, "Theories should be as simple as possible, but not more so." When a theory or a model becomes oppressive, pause and think about the underlying story that the theory is meant to convey. That story should make sense and be concrete. If you can't translate the theory into a story, you don't understand the theory.

Microeconomics and Macroeconomics

Economic theory is divided into two parts: microeconomic theory and macroeconomic theory. Microeconomic theory considers economic reasoning from the viewpoint of individuals and firms and builds up from there to an analysis of the whole economy. I define **microeconomics** as *the study of individual choice, and how that choice is influenced by economic forces*. Microeconomics studies such things as the pricing policies of firms, households' decisions on what to buy, and how markets allocate resources among alternative ends. Our discussion of opportunity cost was based on microeconomic theory. The invisible hand theory comes from microeconomics.

Microeconomics is the study of how individual choice is influenced by economic forces.

As one builds up from microeconomic analysis to an analysis of the entire economy, everything gets rather complicated. Many economists try to uncomplicate matters by taking a different approach—a macroeconomic approach—first looking at the aggregate, or whole, and then breaking it down into components. I define **macroeconomics** as *the study of the economy as a whole*. It considers the problems of inflation, unemployment, business cycles, and growth. Macroeconomics focuses on aggregate relationships such as how household consumption is related to income and how government policies can affect growth. A micro approach would analyze a person by looking first at each individual cell and then building up. A macro approach would start with the person and then go on to his or her components—arms, legs, fingernails, feelings, and so on. Put simply, microeconomics analyzes from the parts to the whole; macroeconomics analyzes from the whole to the parts.

Macroeconomics is the study of the economy as a whole. It considers the problems of inflation, unemployment, business cycles, and growth.

Microeconomics and macroeconomics are very much interrelated. Clearly, what happens in the economy as a whole is based on individual decisions, but individual decisions are made within an economy and can be understood only within that context. For example, whether a firm decides to expand production capacity will depend on what the owners expect will happen to the demand for their products. Those expectations are determined by macroeconomic conditions. Likewise, decisions by the federal government to change the welfare program in the mid-1990s had to be made based on how those changes would affect the decisions of millions of individuals. Because microeconomics focuses on the individual and macroeconomics focuses on the whole economy, traditionally microeconomics and macroeconomics are taught separately, even though they are interrelated.

Q-7 Classify the following topics as macroeconomic or microeconomic:

1. The impact of a tax increase on aggregate output.
2. The relationship between two competing firms' pricing behavior.
3. A farmer's decision to plant soy or wheat.
4. The effect of trade on economic growth.

Economic Institutions

To know whether you can apply economic theory to reality, you must know about economic institutions—laws, common practices, and organizations in a society that affect the economy. Corporations, governments, and cultural norms are all examples of economic institutions. Many economic institutions have social, political, and religious dimensions. For example, your job often influences your social standing. In addition, many social institutions, such as the family, have economic functions. If any institution significantly affects economic decisions, I include it as an economic institution because you must understand that institution if you are to understand how the economy functions.

To apply economic theory to reality, you've got to have a sense of economic institutions.

Economic institutions differ significantly among countries. For example, in Germany banks are allowed to own companies; in the United States they cannot. This contributes to a difference in the flow of resources into investment in Germany as compared to the flow in the United States. Alternatively, in the Netherlands workers are highly unionized, while in the United States they are not. Unions in the Netherlands

Economists and Market Solutions

Applying the Tools

Economic reasoning is playing an increasing role in government policy. Consider the regulation of pollution. Pollution became a policy concern in the 1960s as books such as Rachel Carson's *Silent Spring* were published. In 1970, in response to concerns about the environment, the Clean Air Act was passed. It capped the amount of pollutants (such as sulfur dioxide, carbon monoxide, nitrogen dioxides, lead, and hydrocarbons) that firms could emit. This was a "command-and-control" approach to regulation, which brought about a reduction in pollution, but also brought about lots of complaints by firms that either found the limits costly to meet or couldn't afford to meet them and were forced to close.

Enter economists. They proposed an alternative approach, called cap-and-trade, that achieved the same overall reduction in pollution, but at a lower overall cost. In the plan they proposed, government still set a pollution cap that firms had to meet, but it gave individual firms some flexibility. Firms that reduced emissions by less than the required limit could buy pollution permits from other firms that reduced their emissions by more than their limit. The price of the permits would be determined in an "emissions permit market." Thus, firms that had a low cost of reducing pollution would have a strong incentive to reduce pollution by more than their limit in order to sell these permits, or rights to pollute, to firms that had a high cost of reducing pollution and therefore reduced their pollution by less than what was required. The net reduction was the same, but the reduction was achieved at a lower cost.

In 1990 Congress adopted economists' proposal and the Clean Air Act was amended to include tradable emissions permits. An active market in emissions permits developed and it is estimated that the tradable permit program has lowered the cost of reducing sulfur dioxide emissions by $1 billion a year. Economists today are using this same argument to promote an incentive-based solution to world pollution in an agreement among some countries to reduce world pollution known as the Kyoto Protocol.

therefore have the power to agree to restrain wage demands in exchange for job creation. This means that inflation control policy is different in these two countries; recently, the Netherlands has been able to keep the unemployment rate at about 2 percent, compared to 6 percent in the United States.

Economic institutions sometimes seem to operate in ways quite different than economic theory predicts. For example, economic theory says that prices are determined by supply and demand. However, businesses say that prices are set by rules of thumb—often by what are called cost-plus-markup rules. That is, you determine what your costs are, multiply by 1.4 or 1.5, and the result is the price you set. Economic theory says that supply and demand determine who's hired; experience suggests that hiring is often done on the basis of whom you know, not by economic forces.

These apparent contradictions have two complementary explanations. First, economic theory abstracts from many issues. These issues may account for the differences. Second, there's no contradiction; economic principles often affect decisions from behind the scenes. For instance, supply and demand pressures determine what the price markup over cost will be. In all cases, however, to apply economic theory to reality—to gain the full value of economic insights—you've got to have a sense of economic institutions.

Economic Policy Options

Economic policies are *actions (or inaction) taken by government to influence economic actions*. The final goal of the course is to present the economic policy options facing our society today. For example, should the government restrict mergers between firms?

Should it run a budget deficit? Should it do something about the international trade deficit? Should it decrease taxes?

I saved this discussion for last because there's no sense talking about policy options unless you know some economic terminology, some economic theory, and something about economic institutions. Once you know something about them, you're in a position to consider the policy options available for dealing with the economic problems our society faces.

To carry out economic policy effectively one must understand how institutions might change as a result of the economic policy.

Policies operate within institutions, but policies can also influence the institutions within which they operate. Let's consider an example: welfare policy and the institution of the two-parent family. In the 1960s, the United States developed a variety of policy initiatives designed to eliminate poverty. These initiatives directed income to single parents with children, and assumed that family structure would be unchanged by these policies. But family structure did not remain unchanged; it changed substantially, and, very likely, these policies to eliminate poverty played a role in increasing the number of single-parent families. The result was a failure of the programs to eliminate poverty. Now this is not to say that we should not have programs to eliminate poverty, or that two-parent families are always preferable to one-parent families; it is only to say that we must build into our policies their effect on institutions.

Q-8 True or false? Economists should focus their policy analysis on institutional changes because such policies offer the largest gains.

Some policies are designed to change institutions directly. While these policies are much more difficult to implement than policies that don't, they also offer the largest potential for gain. Let's consider an example. In the 1990s, a number of Eastern and Central European countries decided to replace central planning with market economies. The result: Output in those countries fell enormously as the old institutions fell apart. While most Central European countries have rebounded from their initial losses, some countries of former Soviet Union have yet to do so. The hardships these countries continue to experience show the enormous difficulty of implementing policies involving major institutional changes.

OBJECTIVE POLICY ANALYSIS

Q-9 John, your study partner, is a free market advocate. He argues that the invisible hand theory tells us that the government should not interfere with the economy. Do you agree? Why or why not?

Web Note 1.3
The Art of Economics

Good economic policy analysis is objective; that is, it keeps the analyst's value judgments separate from the analysis. Objective analysis does not say, "This is the way things should be," reflecting a goal established by the analyst. That would be subjective analysis because it would reflect the analyst's view of how things should be. Instead, objective analysis says, "This is the way the economy works, and if society (or the individual or firm for whom you're doing the analysis) wants to achieve a particular goal, this is how it might go about doing so." Objective analysis keeps, or at least tries to keep, subjective views—value judgments—separate.

Positive economics is the study of what is, and how the economy works.

Normative economics is the study of what the goals of the economy should be.

To make clear the distinction between objective and subjective analysis, economists have divided economics into three categories: *positive economics*, *normative economics*, and the *art of economics*. **Positive economics** is *the study of what is, and how the economy works*. It asks such questions as: How does the market for hog bellies work? How do price restrictions affect market forces? These questions fall under the heading of economic theory. **Normative economics** is *the study of what the goals of the economy should be*. Normative economics asks such questions as: What should the distribution of income be? What should tax policy be designed to achieve? In discussing such questions, economists must carefully delineate whose goals they are discussing. One cannot simply assume that one's own goals for society are society's goals.

The *art of economics* is the application of the knowledge learned in positive economics to the achievement of the goals determined in normative economics.

The **art of economics** is *the application of the knowledge learned in positive economics to the achievement of the goals one has determined in normative economics*. It looks at such questions as: To achieve a certain distribution of income, how would you go about it, given the way the economy works?[3] Most policy discussions fall under the art of economics.

In each of these three branches of economics, economists separate their own value judgments from their objective analysis as much as possible. The qualifier "as much as possible" is important, since some value judgments inevitably sneak in. We are products of our environment, and the questions we ask, the framework we use, and the way we interpret empirical evidence all embody value judgments and reflect our backgrounds.

Maintaining objectivity is easiest in positive economics, where one is working with abstract models to understand how the economy works. Maintaining objectivity is harder in normative economics. You must always be objective about whose normative values you are using. It's easy to assume that all of society shares your values, but that assumption is often wrong.

It's hardest to maintain objectivity in the art of economics because it embodies the problems of both positive and normative economics. Because noneconomic forces affect policy, to practice the art of economics we must make judgments about how these noneconomic forces work. These judgments are likely to embody our own value judgments. So we must be exceedingly careful to be as objective as possible in practicing the art of economics.

Q-10 Tell whether the following five statements belong in positive economics, normative economics, or the art of economics.

1. We should support the market because it is efficient.
2. Given certain conditions, the market achieves efficient results.
3. Based on past experience and our understanding of markets, if one wants a reasonably efficient result, markets should probably be relied on.
4. The distribution of income should be left to markets.
5. Markets allocate income according to contributions of factors of production.

Policy and Social and Political Forces

When you think about the policy options facing society, you'll quickly discover that the choice of policy options depends on much more than economic theory. Politicians, not economists, determine economic policy. To understand what policies are chosen, you must take into account historical precedent plus social, cultural, and political forces. In an economics course, I don't have time to analyze these forces in as much depth as I'd like. That's one reason there are separate history, political science, sociology, and anthropology courses.

While it is true that these other forces play significant roles in policy decisions, specialization is necessary. In economics, we focus the analysis on the invisible hand, and much of economic theory is devoted to considering how the economy would operate if the invisible hand were the only force operating. But as soon as we apply theory to reality and policy, we must take into account political and social forces as well.

An example will make my point more concrete. Most economists agree that holding down or eliminating tariffs (taxes on imports) and quotas (numerical limitations on imports) makes good economic sense. They strongly advise governments to follow a policy of free trade. Do governments follow free trade policies? Almost invariably they do not. Politics leads society in a different direction. If you're advising a policy maker, you need to point out that these other forces must be taken into account, and how other forces should (if they should) and can (if they can) be integrated with your recommendations.

Conclusion

There's tons more that could be said by way of introducing you to economics, but an introduction must remain an introduction. As it is, this chapter should have:

[3]This three-part distinction was made back in 1896 by a famous economist, John Neville Keynes, father of John Maynard Keynes, the economist who developed macroeconomics. This distinction was instilled into modern economics by Milton Friedman and Richard Lipsey in the 1950s. They, however, downplayed the art of economics, which J. N. Keynes had seen as central to understanding the economist's role in policy.

1. Introduced you to economic reasoning.
2. Surveyed what we're going to cover in this book.
3. Given you an idea of my writing style and approach.

We'll be spending long hours together over the coming term, and before entering into such a commitment it's best to know your partner. While I won't know you, by the end of this book you'll know me. Maybe you won't love me as my mother does, but you'll know me.

This introduction was my opening line. I hope it also conveyed the importance and relevance that belong to economics. If it did, it has served its intended purpose. Economics is tough, but tough can be fun.

Summary

- The three coordination problems any economy must solve are what to produce, how to produce it, and for whom to produce it. In solving these problems economies have found that there is a problem of scarcity.
- Economic reasoning structures all questions in a cost/benefit frame: If the marginal benefits of doing something exceed the marginal costs, do it. If the marginal costs exceed the marginal benefits, don't do it.
- Sunk costs are not relevant to the economic decision rule.
- The opportunity cost of undertaking an activity is the benefit you might have gained from choosing the next-best alternative.
- "There ain't no such thing as a free lunch" (TANSTAAFL) embodies the opportunity cost concept.
- Economic forces, the forces of scarcity, are always working. Market forces, which ration by changing prices, are not always allowed to work.
- Economic reality is controlled and directed by three types of forces: economic forces, political forces, and social forces.
- Under certain conditions the market, through its price mechanism, will allocate scarce resources efficiently.
- Economics can be divided into microeconomics and macroeconomics. Microeconomics is the study of individual choice and how that choice is influenced by economic forces. Macroeconomics is the study of the economy as a whole. It considers problems such as inflation, unemployment, business cycles, and growth.
- Economics can be subdivided into positive economics, normative economics, and the art of economics. Positive economics is the study of what is, normative economics is the study of what should be, and the art of economics relates positive to normative economics.

Key Terms

art of economics *(16)*
economic decision rule *(6)*
economic force *(9)*
economic model *(12)*
economic policy *(15)*
economic principle *(12)*
economics *(4)*
efficiency *(12)*
invisible hand *(9)*
invisible hand theory *(12)*
macroeconomics *(14)*
marginal benefit *(6)*
marginal cost *(6)*
market force *(9)*
microeconomics *(14)*
normative economics *(16)*
opportunity cost *(8)*
positive economics *(16)*
scarcity *(5)*
sunk cost *(6)*

Questions for Thought and Review

1. What is the textbook author's reasoning for focusing the definition of economics on coordination rather than on scarcity?
2. List two recent choices you made and explain why you made those choices in terms of marginal benefits and marginal costs.
3. At times we all regret decisions. Does this necessarily mean we did not use the economic decision rule when making the decision?
4. What is the opportunity cost of buying a $20,000 car?
5. Suppose you currently earn $30,000 a year. You are considering a job that will increase your lifetime earnings by $300,000 but that requires an MBA. The job will mean also attending business school for two years at an annual cost of $25,000. You already have a bachelor's degree, for which you spent $80,000 in tuition and books. Which of the above information is relevant to your decision whether to take the job? What other information would be relevant?
6. Suppose your college has been given $5 million. You have been asked to decide how to spend it to improve your college. Explain how you would use the economic decision rule and the concept of opportunity costs to decide how to spend it.
7. Name three ways a limited number of dormitory rooms could be rationed. How would economic forces determine individual behavior in each? How would social or legal forces determine whether those economic forces become market forces?
8. Give two examples of social forces and explain how they keep economic forces from becoming market forces.
9. Give two examples of political or legal forces and explain how they might interact with the invisible hand.
10. What is an economic model? What besides a model do economists need to make policy recommendations?
11. Does economic theory prove that the free market system is best? Why?
12. List two microeconomic and two macroeconomic problems.
13. Name an economic institution and explain how it either embodies economic principles or affects economic decision making.
14. Is a good economist always objective? Why?

Problems and Exercises

1. You rent a car for $29.95. The first 150 miles are free, but each mile thereafter costs 15 cents. You drive it 200 miles. What is the marginal cost of driving the car?
2. Calculate, using the best estimates you can:
   a. Your opportunity cost of attending college.
   b. Your opportunity cost of taking this course.
   c. Your opportunity cost of attending yesterday's lecture in this course.
3. Individuals have two kidneys but most of us need only one. People who have lost both kidneys through accident or disease must be hooked up to a dialysis machine, which cleanses waste from their bodies. Say a person who has two good kidneys offers to sell one of them to someone whose kidney function has been totally destroyed. The seller asks $30,000 for the kidney, and the person who has lost both kidneys accepts the offer. Who benefits from the deal? Who is hurt? Should a society allow such market transactions? Why?
4. For some years, China has had a one-child-per-family policy. For cultural reasons, there are now many more male than female children born in China. How is this likely to affect who pays the cost of dates in China in 15 or 20 years? Explain your response.
5. State whether the following are microeconomic or macroeconomic policy issues:
   a. Should the U.S. government use a policy of free trade with China to encourage China to advance human rights?
   b. Will the fact that more and more doctors are selling their practices to managed care networks increase the efficiency of medical providers?
   c. Should the current federal income tax structure be eliminated in favor of a flat tax?
   d. Should the federal minimum wage be raised?
   e. Should AT&T and Verizon both be allowed to build local phone networks?
   f. Should commercial banks be required to provide loans in all areas of the territory from which they accept deposits?
6. Go to two stores: a supermarket and a convenience store.
   a. Write down the cost of a gallon of milk in each.
   b. The prices are most likely different. Using the terminology used in this chapter, explain why that is the case and why anyone would buy milk in the store with the higher price.
   c. Do the same exercise with shirts or dresses in Wal-Mart (or its equivalent) and Saks (or its equivalent).
7. State whether the following statements belong in positive economics, normative economics, or the art of economics.

a. In a market, when quantity supplied exceeds quantity demanded, price tends to fall.
b. When determining tax rates, the government should take into account the income needs of individuals.
c. What society feels is fair is determined largely by cultural norms.
d. When deciding which rationing mechanism is best (lottery, price, first-come/first-served), one must take into account the goals of society.
e. California currently rations water to farmers at subsidized prices. Once California allows the trading of water rights, it will allow economic forces to be a market force.

8. Adam Smith, who wrote *The Wealth of Nations* and is seen as the father of modern economics, also wrote *The Theory of Moral Sentiments*, in which he argued that society would be better off if people weren't so selfish and were more considerate of others. How does this view fit with the discussion of economic reasoning presented in the chapter?

Web Questions

1. Find an employment Web page (an example is www.monster.com) and search for available jobs using "economist" as a keyword. List five jobs that economists have and write a one-sentence description of each.
2. Use an online periodical (an example is www.movingideas.org) to find two examples of political or legal forces at work. Do those forces keep economic forces from becoming market forces?
3. Using an Internet mapping page (an example is www.mapquest.com), create a map of your neighborhood and answer the following questions:
   a. How is the map like a model?
   b. What are the limitations of the map?
   c. Could you use this map to determine change in elevation in your neighborhood? Distance from one place to another? Traffic speed? What do your answers suggest about what to consider when using a map or a model?

Answers to Margin Questions

The numbers in parentheses refer to the page number of each margin question.

1. Since the price of both stocks is now $15, it doesn't matter which one you sell (assuming no differential capital gains taxation). The price you bought them for doesn't matter; it's a sunk cost. Marginal analysis refers to the future gain, so what you expect to happen to future prices of the stocks—not past prices—should determine which stock you decide to sell. *(6)*
2. A cost/benefit analysis requires that you put a value on a good, and placing a value on a good can be seen as demeaning it. Consider love. Try telling an acquaintance that you'd like to buy his or her spiritual love, and see what response you get. *(8)*
3. John is wrong. The opportunity cost of reading the chapter is primarily the time you spend reading it. Reading the book prevents you from doing other things. Assuming that you already paid for the book, the original price is no longer part of the opportunity cost; it is a sunk cost. Bygones are bygones. *(9)*
4. Whenever there is scarcity, the scarce good must be rationed by some means. Free health care has an opportunity cost in other resources. So if health care is not rationed, to get the resources to supply that care, other goods would have to be more tightly rationed than they currently are. It is likely that the opportunity cost of supplying free health care would be larger than most societies would be willing to pay. *(9)*
5. Joan is wrong. Economic forces are always operative; market forces are not. *(9)*
6. According to the invisible hand theory, the price of tomatoes will likely fall. *(12)*
7. (1) Macroeconomics; (2) Microeconomics; (3) Microeconomics; (4) Macroeconomics. *(14)*
8. False. While such changes have the largest gain, they may also have the largest cost. The policies economists should focus on are those that offer the largest net gain—benefits minus costs—to society. *(16)*
9. He is wrong. The invisible hand theory is a positive theory and does not tell us anything about policy. To do so would be to violate Hume's dictum that a "should" cannot be derived from an "is." This is not to say that government should or should not interfere; whether government should interfere is a very difficult question. *(16)*
10. (1) Normative; (2) Positive; (3) Art; (4) Normative; (5) Positive. *(17)*

Trade, Trade-Offs, and Government Policy

2

Economics is a science of thinking in terms of models, joined to the art of choosing models which are relevant to the contemporary world.

—*J. M. Keynes*

After reading this chapter, you should be able to:

- Demonstrate opportunity cost with a production possibility curve.
- Relate the concept of comparative advantage to the production possibility curve.
- State the principle of increasing marginal opportunity cost.
- State how through comparative advantage and trade, production possibilities increase.
- State six roles of government.
- Compare the regulation of international markets to the regulation of domestic markets.

Every economy must solve three main coordination problems:

1. What, and how much, to produce.
2. How to produce it.
3. For whom to produce it.

In Chapter 1, I suggested that you can boil down all economic knowledge into the single phrase "There ain't no such thing as a free lunch." There's obviously more to economics than that, but it's not a bad summary of the core of economic reasoning—it's relevant for an individual, for nonprofit organizations, for governments, and for nations. Oh, it's true that once in a while you can snitch a sandwich, but what economics tells you is that if you're offered something that approaches free-lunch status, you should also be on the lookout for some hidden cost.

A key element in getting people to recognize that lunches aren't free is the concept of opportunity cost—every decision has a cost in forgone opportunities—which I introduced you to in Chapter 1. Economists have a model, the production possibility model, that conveys the concept of opportunity costs both numerically and graphically. This model is important for understanding not only opportunity cost but also why people specialize in what they do and trade for the goods they need. Through specialization and trade, individuals, firms, and countries can achieve greater levels of production than they could otherwise achieve.

The Production Possibilities Model

The production possibilities model shows trade-offs and can be presented both in a table and in a graph. I'll start with the table and then move from that to the graph. Opportunity cost can be seen numerically with a **production possibility table**—*a table that lists a choice's opportunity costs by summarizing what alternative outputs you can achieve with your inputs*. An **output** is simply *a result of an activity,*

Figure 2-1 (a and b) A Production Possibility Table and Curve for Grades in Economics and History
The production possibility table (**a**) shows the highest combination of grades you can get with only 20 hours available for studying economics and history. The information in the production possibility table in (**a**) can be plotted on a graph, as is done in (**b**). The grade received in economics is on the vertical axis, and the grade received in history is on the horizontal axis.

Hours of Study in History	Grade in History	Hours of Study in Economics	Grade in Economics
20	98	0	40
19	96	1	43
18	94	2	46
17	92	3	49
16	90	4	52
15	88	5	55
14	86	6	58
13	84	7	61
12	82	8	64
11	80	9	67
10	78	10	70
9	76	11	73
8	74	12	76
7	72	13	79
6	70	14	82
5	68	15	85
4	66	16	88
3	64	17	91
2	62	18	94
1	60	19	97
0	58	20	100

(a) Production possibility table

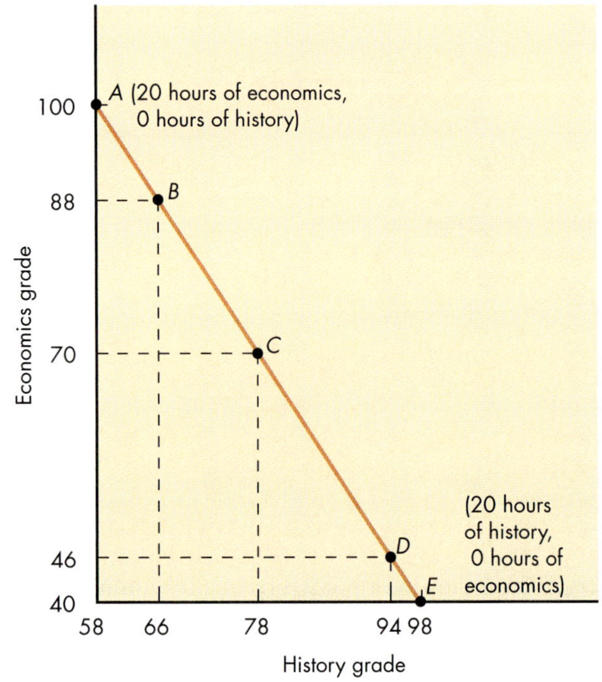

(b) Production possibility curve

and an **input** is *what you put into a production process to achieve an output.* For example, your grade in a course is an output and your study time is an input.

A Production Possibility Curve for an Individual

Q-1 What is the opportunity cost of producing an extra unit of good *X* in terms of good *Y*?

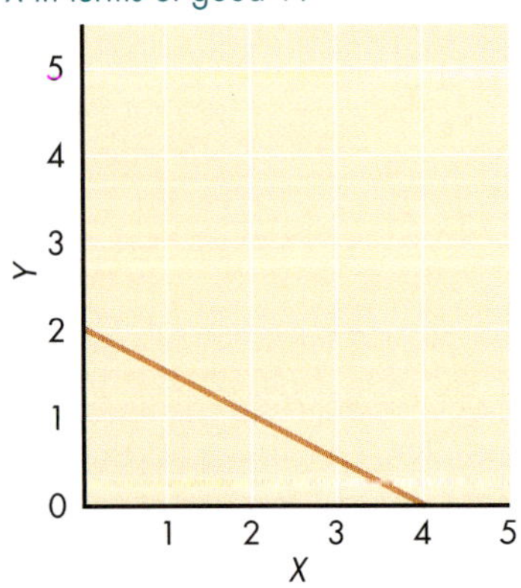

Let's consider the study-time/grades example. Say you have exactly 20 hours a week to devote to two courses: economics and history. (So maybe I'm a bit optimistic.) Grades are given numerically and you know that the following relationships exist: If you study 20 hours in economics, you'll get a grade of 100; 18 hours, 94; and so forth.[1]

Let's say that the best you can do in history is a 98 with 20 hours of study a week; 19 hours of study guarantees a 96, and so on. The production possibility table in Figure 2-1(a) shows the highest combination of grades you can get with various allocations of the 20 hours available for studying the two subjects. One possibility is getting 70 in economics and 78 in history.

Notice that the opportunity cost of studying one subject rather than the other is embodied in the production possibility table. The information in the table comes from

[1]Throughout the book I'll be presenting numerical examples to help you understand the concepts. The numbers I choose are often arbitrary. After all, you have to choose something. As an exercise, you might choose different numbers than I did, numbers that apply to your own life, and work out the argument using those numbers.

Dealing with Math Anxiety

Knowing the Tools

Knowing my own students, I can see the red flags rising, the legs tensing up, the fear flooding over many of you. Here it comes—the math and the graphs.

I wish I could change things by saying to you, "Don't worry—the mathematics and graphical analysis are easy." But I can't. That doesn't mean math and graphical analysis aren't wonderful tools that convey ideas neatly and efficiently. They are. But I've had enough teaching experience to know that somewhere back in elementary school some teacher blew it and put about 40 percent of you off mathematics for life. A tool that scares you to death is not useful; it can be a hindrance, not a help, to learning. Nothing your current teacher or I now can say, write, or do is going to completely reassure you, but I'll do my best to relieve your anxiety.

Try to follow the numerical and graphical examples carefully, because they not only cement the knowledge into your minds; they also present in a rigorous manner the ideas I'm discussing. The ideas conveyed in the numerical and graphical examples will be explained in words—and the graphical analysis (the type of mathematical explanation most used in introductory economics) generally will simply be a more precise presentation of the accompanying discussion in words. In most economics courses the exams pose the questions in graphical terms, so there's no getting around the need to understand the ideas graphically. And it is easier than you think. (Appendix A at the end of this chapter discusses the basics of graphical analysis.)

experience: We are assuming that you've discovered that if you transfer an hour of study from economics to history, you'll lose 3 points on your grade in economics and gain 2 points in history. Thus, the opportunity cost of a 2-point rise in your history grade is a 3-point decrease in your economics grade.

The information in the production possibility table can also be presented graphically in a diagram called a production possibility curve. A **production possibility curve** is *a curve measuring the maximum combination of outputs that can be obtained from a given number of inputs*. It is a graphical presentation of the opportunity cost concept.

The production possibility curve is a curve measuring the maximum combination of outputs that can be obtained from a given number of inputs.

A production possibility curve is created from a production possibility table by mapping the table in a two-dimensional graph. I've taken the information from the table in Figure 2-1(a) and mapped it into Figure 2-1(b). The history grade is mapped, or plotted, on the horizontal axis; the economics grade is on the vertical axis.

As you can see from the bottom row of Figure 2-1(a), if you study economics for all 20 hours and study history for 0 hours, you'll get grades of 100 in economics and 58 in history. Point A in Figure 2-1(b) represents that choice. If you study history for all 20 hours and study economics for 0 hours, you'll get a 98 in history and a 40 in economics. Point E represents that choice. Points B, C, and D represent three possible choices between these two extremes.

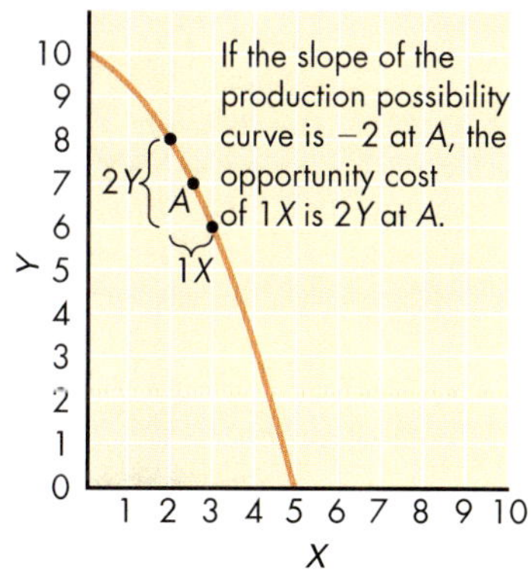

The slope of the production possibility curve tells you the opportunity cost of good X in terms of good Y. You have to give up 2Y to get 1X when you're around point A.

Notice that the production possibility curve slopes downward from left to right. That means that there is an inverse relationship (a trade-off) between grades in economics and grades in history. The better the grade in economics, the worse the grade in history, and vice versa. That downward slope represents the opportunity cost concept—you get more of one benefit only if you get less of another benefit.

The production possibility curve not only represents the opportunity cost concept but also measures the opportunity cost. For example, in Figure 2-1(b), say you want to raise your grade in history from a 94 to a 98 (move from point D to point E). The opportunity cost of that 4-point increase would be a 6-point decrease in your economics grade, from 46 to 40.

To summarize, the production possibility curve demonstrates that:

Figure 2-2 (a and b) A Production Possibility Table and Curve

The table in (a) contains information on the trade-off between the production of guns and butter. This information has been plotted on the graph in (b). Notice in (b) that as we move along the production possibility curve from *A* to *F*, trading butter for guns, we get fewer and fewer guns for each pound of butter given up. That is, the opportunity cost of choosing guns over butter increases as we increase the production of guns. This concept is called the principle of increasing marginal opportunity cost. The phenomenon occurs because some resources are better suited for the production of butter than for the production of guns, and we use the better ones first.

% of Resources Devoted to Production of Guns	Number of Guns	% of Resources Devoted to Production of Butter	Pounds of Butter	Row
0	0	100	15	*A*
20	4	80	14	*B*
40	7	60	12	*C*
60	9	40	9	*D*
80	11	20	5	*E*
100	12	0	0	*F*

(a) Production possibility table

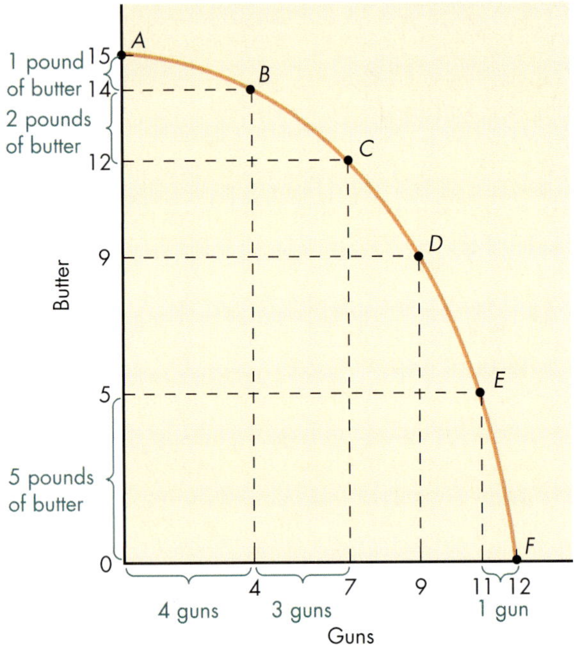

(b) Production possibility curve

1. There is a limit to what you can achieve, given the existing institutions, resources, and technology.
2. Every choice you make has an opportunity cost. You can get more of something only by giving up something else.

A Production Possibility Curve for a Society

The grade example shows a production possibility curve representing the choices facing an individual. The production possibility curve can also be used to model how societies must consider opportunity costs in their decisions, so let's now move on to an example of such a societal production possibility curve. In this example I also discuss how opportunity costs typically change over a range of decisions and how that change in opportunity cost influences the shape of the curve.

I chose an unchanging trade-off in the study-time/grade example because it made the initial presentation of the production possibility curve easier. Since, by assumption, you could always trade two points on your history grade for three points on your economics grade, the production possibility curve was a straight line. But is that the way we'd expect reality to be? Probably not. So let's use a more realistic, outward-bowed production possibility curve, as in Figure 2-2(b).

Why are production possibility curves typically bowed outward? Because some resources are better suited for the production of certain kinds of goods than they are for the production of other kinds of goods. To make the answer more concrete, let's talk specifically about society's choice between defense spending (guns) and spending on

Production Possibility Curves

Knowing the Tools

Definition	Shape	Shifts	Points In, Out, and On
The production possibility curve is a curve that measures the maximum combination of outputs that can be obtained with a given number of inputs.	Most are outward bowed because of increasing marginal opportunity cost; if opportunity cost doesn't change, the production possibility curve is a straight line.	Increases in inputs or increases in the productivity of inputs shift the production possibility curve out; decreases have the opposite effect; the production possibility curve shifts along the axis whose input is changing.	Points inside the production possibility curve are points of inefficiency; points on the production possibility curve are points of efficiency; points outside the production possibility curve are not obtainable.

domestic needs (butter). The graph in Figure 2-2(b) is derived from the table in Figure 2-2(a).

Let's see what the shape of the curve means in terms of numbers. Let's start with society producing only butter (point *A*). Giving up a little butter (1 pound) initially gain us a lot of guns (4), moving us to point *B*. The next 2 pounds of butter we give up gain us slightly fewer guns (point *C*). If we continue to trade butter for guns, we find that at point *D* we gain very few guns from giving up a pound of butter. The opportunity cost of choosing guns over butter increases as we increase the production of guns.

The reason the opportunity cost of guns increases as we produce more guns is that some resources are relatively better suited to producing guns, while others are relatively better suited to producing butter. Put in economists' terminology, some resources have a **comparative advantage** over other resources—*the ability to be better suited to the production of one good than to the production of another good*. In this example, some resources have a comparative advantage over other resources in the production of butter, while other resources have a comparative advantage in the production of guns.

Q-2 If no resource had a comparative advantage in the production of any good, what would the shape of the production possibility curve be? Why?

When making small amounts of guns and large amounts of butter, in the production of those guns we use the resources whose comparative advantage is in the production of guns. All other resources are devoted to producing butter. Because the resources used in producing guns aren't good at producing butter, we're not giving up much butter to get those guns. As we produce more and more of a good, we must use resources whose comparative advantage is in the production of the other good—in this case, more suitable for producing butter than for producing guns. As we remove resources from the production of butter to get the same additional amount of guns, we must give up increasing amounts of butter. An alternative way of saying this is that the opportunity cost of producing guns becomes greater as the production of guns increases. As we continue to increase the production of guns, the opportunity cost of more guns becomes very high because we're using resources to produce guns that have a strong comparative advantage for producing butter.

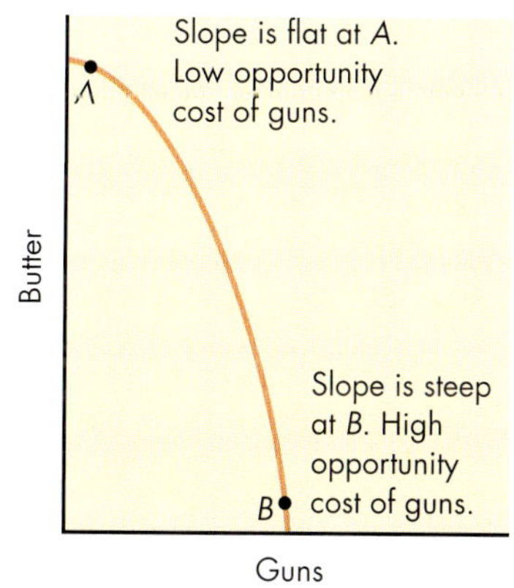

Let's consider two more examples. Say the United States suddenly decides it needs more wheat. To get additional wheat, we must devote additional land to growing it. This land is less fertile than the land we're already using, so our additional output of wheat per acre of land devoted to wheat will be less. Alternatively, consider the use of relief pitchers in a baseball game. If only one relief pitcher is needed, the manager sends in the best; if he must send in a second one, then a third, and even a fourth, the likelihood of winning the game decreases.

Choices in Context

Beyond the Tools

The production possibility curve presents choices in a timeless fashion and therefore makes opportunity costs clear-cut; there are two choices, one with a higher cost and one with a lower cost. The reality is that most choices are dependent on other choices; they are made sequentially. With sequential choices you cannot simply reverse your decision. Once you have started on a path, to take another path you have to return to the beginning. Thus, following one path often lowers the costs of options along that path, but it raises the costs of options along another path.

Such sequential decisions can best be seen within the framework of a decision tree—a visual description of sequential choices. A decision tree is shown in the accompanying figure.

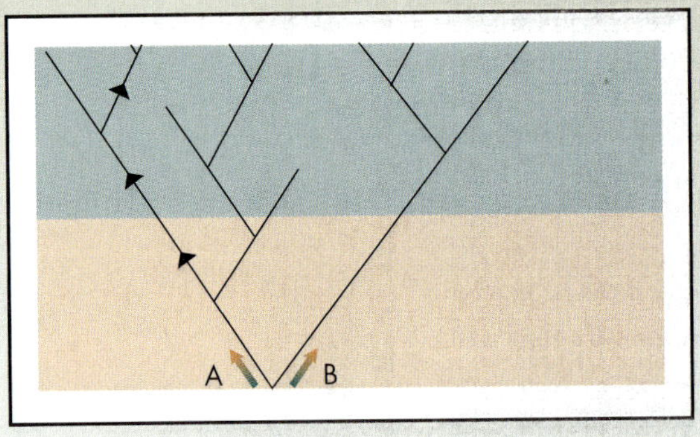

Once you make the initial decision to go on path A, the costs of path B options become higher; they include the costs of reversing your path and starting over. The decision trees of life have thousands of branches; each decision you make rules out other paths, or at least increases your costs highly. (Remember that day you decided to blow off your homework? That decision may have changed your future life.)

Another way of putting this same point is that *all decisions are made in context:* What makes sense in one context may not make sense in another. For example, say you're answering the question "Would society be better off if students were taught literature or if they were taught agriculture?" The answer depends on the institutional context. In a developing country whose goal is large increases in material output, teaching agriculture may make sense. In a developed country, where growth in material output is less important, teaching literature may make sense.

Recognizing the contextual nature of decisions is important when interpreting the production possibility curve. Because decisions are contextual, what the production possibility curve for a particular decision looks like depends on the existing institutions, and the analysis can be applied only in institutional and historical context. The production possibility curve is not a purely technical phenomenon. The curve is an engine of analysis to make contextual choices, not a definitive tool to decide what one should do in all cases.

Increasing Marginal Opportunity Cost

The principle of increasing marginal opportunity cost states that opportunity costs increase the more you concentrate on the activity. In order to get more of something, one must give up ever-increasing quantities of something else.

For many of the choices society must make, opportunity costs tend to increase as we choose more and more of an item. The reason is that the resources we devote to its production will be less and less good at producing it. (Remember, we use those resources with the greatest comparative advantage first.). Such a phenomenon about choice is so common, in fact, that it has acquired a name: the **principle of increasing marginal opportunity cost.** That principle states:

> *In order to get more of something, one must give up ever-increasing quantities of something else.*

In other words, initially the opportunity costs of an activity are low, but they increase the more we concentrate on that activity. Sometimes this law is called the flowerpot law because, if it didn't hold, all the world's food could be grown in a flowerpot. But it can't be. As we add more seeds to a fixed amount of soil, there won't be enough nutrients or room for the roots, so output per seed decreases.

Figure 2-3 (a, b, and c) Efficiency, Inefficiency, and Technological Change
The production possibility curve helps us see what is meant by efficiency. At point A, in (**a**), all inputs are used to make 4 pounds of butter and 6 guns. This is inefficient since there is a way to obtain more of one without giving up any of the other, that is, to obtain 6 pounds of butter and 6 guns (point C) or 8 guns and 4 pounds of butter (point *B*). All points inside the production possibility curve are inefficient. With fixed inputs and given technology, we cannot go beyond the production possibility curve. For example, point *D* is unattainable.

A technological change that improves production techniques will shift the production possibility curve outward, as shown in both (**b**) and (**c**). How the curve shifts outward depends on how technology improves. For example, if we become more efficient in the production of both guns and butter, the curve will shift out as in (**b**). If we become more efficient in producing butter, but not in producing guns, then the curve will shift as in (**c**).

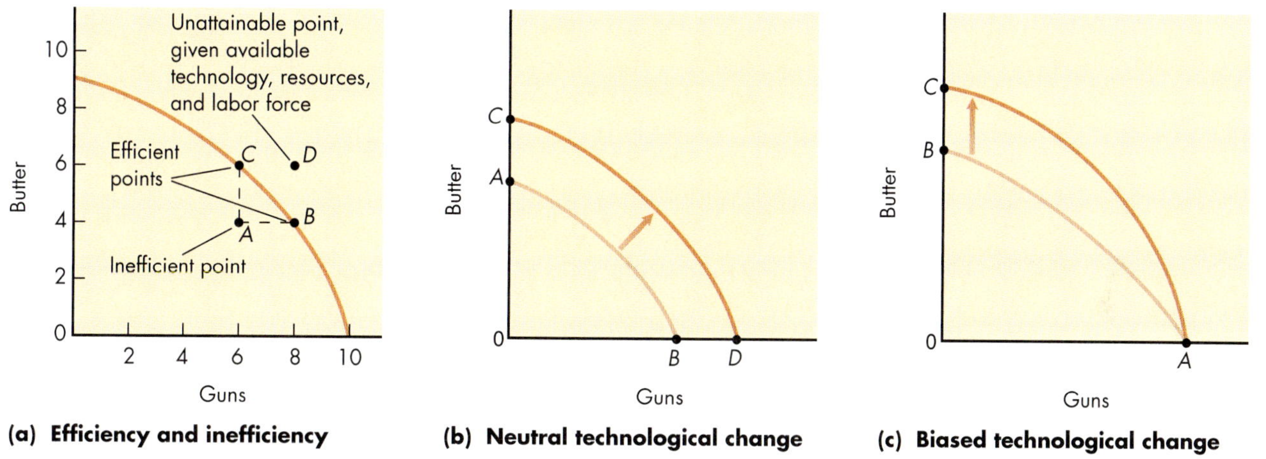

EFFICIENCY

We would like, if possible, to get as much output as possible from a given amount of inputs or resources. That's **productive efficiency**—*achieving as much output as possible from a given amount of inputs or resources*. We would like to be efficient. The production possibility curve helps us see what is meant by productive efficiency. Consider point A in Figure 2-3(a), which is inside the production possibility curve. If we are producing at point A, we are using all our resources to produce 6 guns and 4 pounds of butter. Point A represents **inefficiency**—*getting less output from inputs which, if devoted to some other activity, would produce more output*. That's because with the same inputs we could be getting either 8 guns and 4 pounds of butter (point *B*) or 6 pounds of butter and 6 guns (point C). As long as we prefer more to less, both points B and C represent **efficiency**—*achieving a goal using as few inputs as possible*. We always want to move our production out to a point on the production possibility curve.

Why not move out farther, to point *D*? If we could, we would, but by definition the production possibility curve represents the most output we can get from a certain combination of inputs. So point *D* is unattainable, given our resources and technology.

When technology improves, when more resources are discovered, or when the economic institutions get better at fulfilling our wants, we can get more output with the same inputs. What this means is that when technology or an economic institution improves, the entire production possibility curve shifts outward from *AB* to *CD* in Figure 2-3(b). How the production possibility curve shifts outward depends on how the technology improves. For example, say we become more efficient in producing butter, but not more efficient in producing guns. Then the production possibility curve shifts outward to *AC* in Figure 2-3(c).

Q-3 Identify the point(s) of inefficiency and efficiency. What point(s) are unattainable?

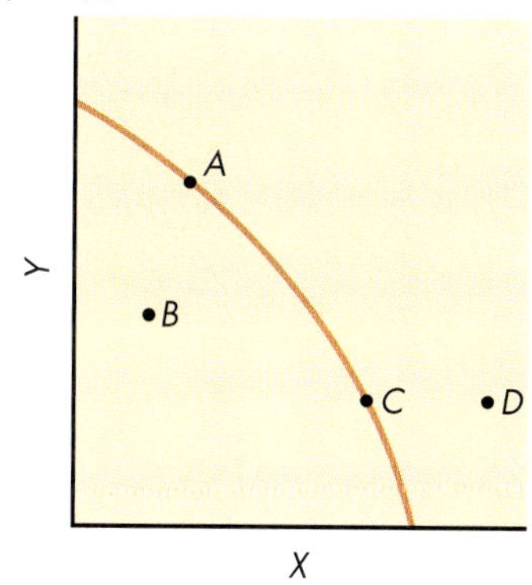

Efficiency involves achieving a goal as cheaply as possible. Efficiency has meaning only in relation to a specified goal.

Figure 2-4 Examples of Shifts in Production Possibility Curves
Each of these curves reflects a different type of shift. Your assignment is to match these shifts with the situations given in the text.

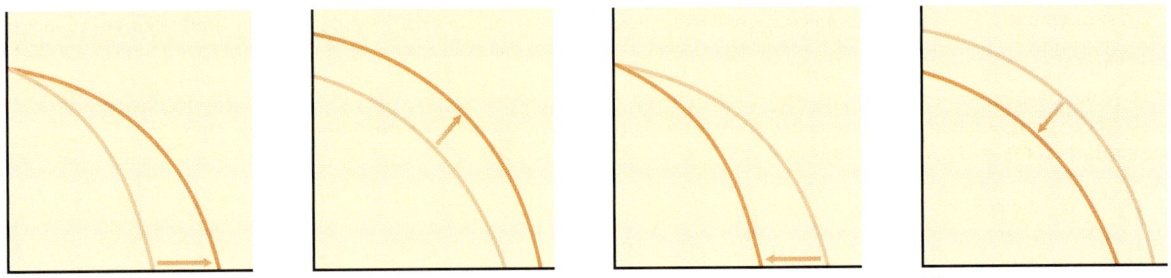

(a) **(b)** **(c)** **(d)**

Q-4 Your firm is establishing a trucking business in Saudi Arabia. The managers have noticed that women are generally paid much less than men in Saudi Arabia, and they suggest that hiring women would be more efficient than hiring men. What should you respond?

Innovations such as the automation of production shown here shifts the production possibility curve out. Photodisc

Distribution and Productive Efficiency

In discussing the production possibility curve for a society, I avoided questions of distribution: Who gets what? But such questions cannot be ignored in real-world situations. Specifically, if the method of production is tied to a particular income distribution and choosing one method will help some people but hurt others, we can't say that one method of production is efficient and the other inefficient, even if one method produces more total output than the other. As I stated above, the term *efficiency* involves achieving a goal as cheaply as possible. The term has meaning only in regard to a specified goal. Say, for example, that we have a society of ascetics who believe that consumption above some minimum is immoral. For such a society, producing more for less (productive efficiency) would not be efficient since consumption is not its goal. Or say that we have a society that cares that what is produced is fairly distributed. An increase in output that goes to only one person and not to anyone else would not necessarily be efficient.

In our society, however, most people prefer more to less, and many policies have relatively small distributional consequences. On the basis of the assumption that more is better than less, economists use their own kind of shorthand for such policies and talk about efficiency as identical to productive efficiency—increasing total output. But it's important to remember the assumption under which that shorthand is used: that the distributional effects that accompany the policy aren't undesirable and that we, as a society, prefer more output.

Examples of Shifts in the Production Possibility Curve

To see whether you understand the production possibility curve, let us now consider some situations that can be shown with it. In Figure 2-4 I demonstrate four situations with production possibility curves. Below, I list four situations. To test your understanding of the curve, match each situation to one of the curves in Figure 2-4.

1. A meteor hits the world and destroys half the earth's natural resources.
2. Nanotechnology is perfected that lowers the cost of manufactured goods.
3. A new technology is discovered that doubles the speed at which all goods can be produced.
4. Global warming increases the cost of producing agricultural goods.

Q-5 When a natural disaster hits the midwestern United States, where most of the U.S. butter is produced, what happens to the U.S. production possibility curve for guns and butter?

The correct answers are: 1–d; 2–a; 3–b; 4–c.

If you got them all right, you are well on your way to understanding the production possibility curve.

TRADE AND COMPARATIVE ADVANTAGE

Figure 2-5 Comparative Advantage and the Production Possibility Curve

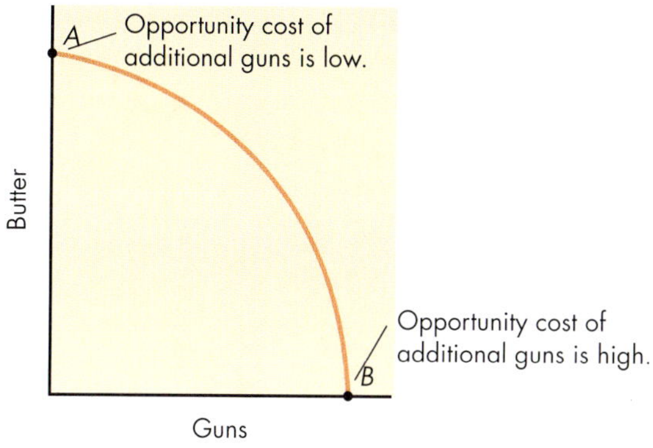

Now that we have gone through the basics of the production possibility curve, let's dig a little deeper. From the above discussion, you know that production possibility curves are generally bowed outward and that the reason for this is comparative advantage. To remind you of the argument, consider Figure 2-5, which is the guns and butter production possibility example I presented earlier.

At point *A*, all resources are being used to produce butter. As more guns are produced, we take resources away from producing butter that had a comparative advantage in producing guns, so we gain a lot of guns for little butter (the opportunity cost of additional guns is low). As we continue down the curve, the comparative advantage of the resources we use changes, and as we approach *B*, we use almost all resources to produce guns, so we are using resources that aren't very good at producing guns. Thus, around point *B* we gain few guns for a lot of butter (the opportunity cost of additional guns is high).

A society wants to be on the frontier of its production possibility curve. This requires that individuals produce those goods for which they have a comparative advantage. The question for society, then, is how to direct individuals toward those activities. For a firm, the answer is easy. A manager can allocate the firm's resources to their best use. For example, he or she can assign an employee with good people skills to the human resources department and another with good research skills to research and development. But our economy has millions of individuals, and no manager directing everyone what to do. How do we know that these individuals will be directed to do those things for which they have a comparative advantage? It was this question that was central to a British moral philosopher named Adam Smith when he wrote his most famous book, *The Wealth of Nations* (1776). In it he argued that it was humankind's proclivity to trade that leads to individuals using their comparative advantage. He writes:

> This division of labour, from which so many advantages are derived, is not originally the effect of any human wisdom, which foresees and intends that general opulence to which it gives occasion. It is the necessary, though very slow and gradual consequence of a certain propensity in human nature which has in view no such extensive utility; the propensity to truck, barter, and exchange one thing for another. . . . [This propensity] is common to all men, and to be found in no other race of animals, which seem to know neither this nor any other species of contracts. . . . Nobody ever saw a dog make a fair and deliberate exchange of one bone for another with another dog. Nobody ever saw one animal by its gestures and natural cries signify to another, this is mine, that yours; I am willing to give this for that.

As long as people trade, Smith argues, the market will guide people, like an invisible hand, to gravitate toward those activities for which they have a comparative advantage. By specializing in the production of goods in which they have a comparative advantage, they will produce the most goods they can. They can then trade with other people who specialize in the production of other goods. For Smith, what was especially neat about this process was that it could take place without enormous amounts of government intervention. Smith writes:

Adam Smith argued that it was humankind's proclivity to trade that leads to individuals using their comparative advantage.

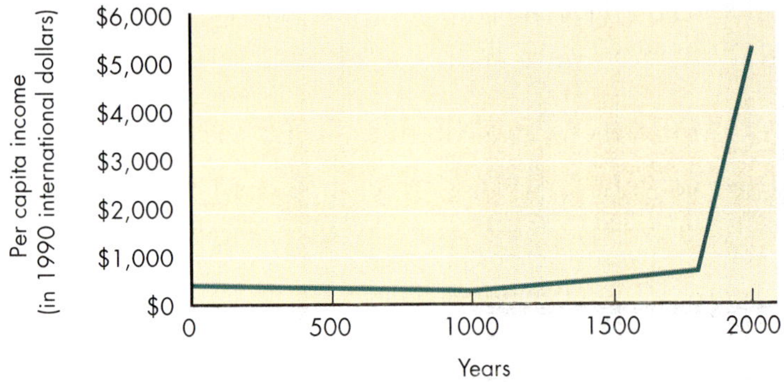

Figure 2-6 Growth in the Past Two Millennia
For 1,700 years the world economy grew very slowly. Then at the end of the 18th century with the introduction of markets and the spread of democracy, the world economy has grown at increasing rates.

Source: Angus Maddison, *Monitoring the World Economy*, OECD, 1995; Angus Maddison, "Poor Until 1820," *The Wall Street Journal*, January 11, 1999.

Man has almost constant occasion for the help of his brethren, and it is in vain for him to expect it from their benevolence only. He will be more likely to prevail, if he can interest their self-love in his favour, and show them that it is for their own advantage to do for him what he requires of them. Whoever offers to another a bargain of any kind proposes to do this. Give me that which I want, and you shall have that which you want, is the meaning of every such offer; and it is in this manner that we obtain from one another the far greater part of those good offices which we stand in need of. It is not from the benevolence of the butcher, the brewer, or the baker, that we expect our dinner, but from their regard to their own interest. We address ourselves, not to their humanity but to their self-love, and never talk to them of our own necessities but of their advantages.

Markets, Specialization, and Growth

Markets can be very simple or very complicated.
Jon Riley/Stone/Getty Images

We can see the effect of trade on our well-being empirically by considering the growth of economies. As you can see from Figure 2-6, for 1,700 years the world economy grew very slowly. Then, at the end of the 18th century, the world economy started to grow, and it has grown at an increasing rate since then.

What changed? The introduction of markets that facilitate trade and the spread of democracy. There's something about markets that leads to economic growth. Markets allow specialization and encourage trade. The bowing out of the production possibilities from trade is part of the story, but a minor part. As individuals compete and specialize they learn by doing, becoming even better at what they do. Markets also foster competition, which pushes individuals to find better ways of doing things. They devise new technologies that further the growth process.

The new millennium is offering new ways for individuals to specialize and compete. More and more businesses are trading on the Internet. For example, colleges, such as the University of Phoenix, are providing online competition for traditional colleges. Similarly, online bookstores and drugstores are proliferating. As Internet technology becomes built into our economy, we can expect more specialization, more division of labor, and the economic growth that follows.

The Benefits of Trade

The reasons why markets can direct people to use their comparative advantages follows from a very simple argument: When people freely enter into a trade, both parties can be expected to benefit from the trade; otherwise, why would they have traded in the first place? So when the butcher sells you meat, he's better off with the money you give him, and you're better off with the meat he gives you.

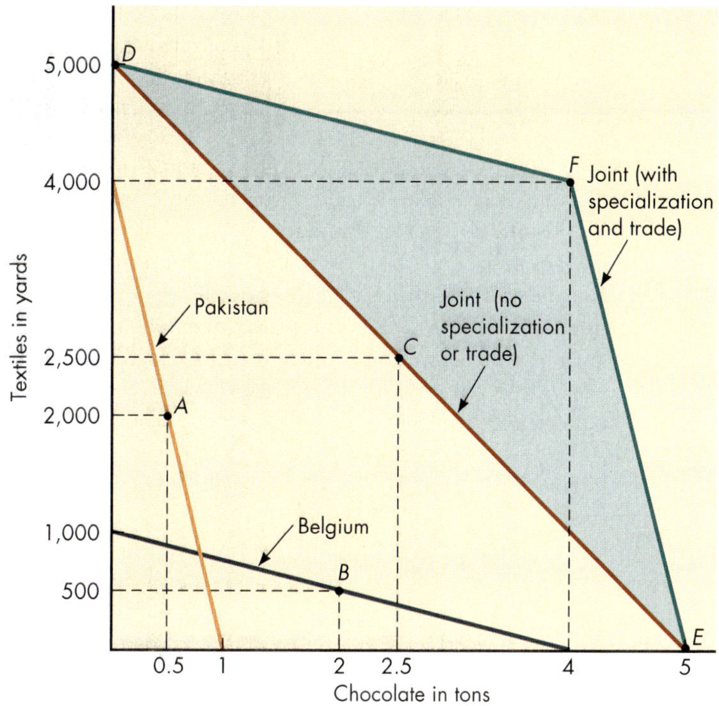

Figure 2-7 The Gains from Trade
Trade makes those involved in the trade better off. When the countries produce goods in equal proportions and don't specialize or trade, their combined production possibilities curve is shown by the red line. If each country specializes and takes advantage of its comparative advantage, the combined production possibilities curve becomes bowed outward. The blue shaded region represents the gains from specialization and trade.

When there is competition in trading, such that individuals are able to pick the best trades available to them, each individual drives the best bargain he or she can. The end result is that both individuals in the trade benefit as much as they possibly can, given what others are willing to trade. This argument for the benefits from trade underlies the general policy of **laissez-faire**—*an economic policy of leaving coordination of individuals' actions to the market.* (*Laissez-faire,* a French term, means "Let events take their course; leave things alone.")

Web Note 2.1
Wine and Cloth

Laissez-faire is an economic policy of leaving coordination of individuals' actions to the market.

Let's consider a numerical example of the gains that accrue to two countries when they trade, and show how that trade increases the production possibilities, creating the bowed shape of the production possibility curve. I use an international trade example so that you can see that the argument holds for international trade as well as domestic trade.

Q.6 What argument underlies the general laissez-faire policy argument?

Let's say that the two countries are Pakistan and Belgium, and that Pakistan has a comparative advantage in producing textiles, while Belgium has a comparative advantage in producing chocolate. Specifically, Pakistan can produce 4,000 yards of textiles a day, or 1 ton of chocolate a day, or any proportional combination in between. (Pakistan's opportunity cost of 1 ton of chocolate is 4,000 yards of textiles.) Pakistan's production possibility curve is shown by the orange line in Figure 2-7. In a given day Belgium can produce either 1,000 yards of textiles, 4 tons of chocolate, or any proportion in between. (Belgium's opportunity cost of 1 ton of chocolate is 250 yards of textiles.) Its production possibility curve is shown by the purple line in Figure 2-7.

The most each country can produce is some combination along its production possibility curve. Say Pakistan has chosen to produce 2,000 yards of textiles and 0.5 tons of chocolate (point *A*), while Belgium has chosen to produce 500 yards of textiles and 2 tons of chocolate (point *B*). Together the countries produce 2.5 tons of chocolate and 2,500 thousand yards of textiles, as shown in the following table:

Pakistan	2,000 yards textiles	0.5 ton chocolate
Belgium	500 yards textiles	2 tons chocolate
Total	2,500 yards textiles	2.5 tons chocolate

This combination is also shown as point C in Figure 2.7. Point C is just one possible combination. The two countries could select other production combinations. Let's assume each country has the same consumption pattern and devotes the same proportion of resources to the consumption of each good. Two extreme combinations are both countries producing only chocolate and both producing only textiles. These cases are 5,000 yards of textiles and no chocolate (point *D*) and 5 tons of chocolate and no textiles (point *E*). Generally, however, countries want to consume a mix of goods such as combination C. The red line connecting points *D* and *E* represents all possible combinations (including C) of chocolate and textiles where the countries produce goods in the same proportions.

What if each specialized, doing what it does best, and then traded with the other for the goods it wants? This separates the production and consumption decisions. It makes sense for Pakistan to specialize in textiles, producing 4,000 yards. Similarly, it makes sense for Belgium to specialize in chocolate, producing 4 tons. By specializing, the countries together produce 4 tons of chocolate and 4,000 yards of textiles—point *F* in Figure 2-7. By specializing and trading, they can each have the same amount of chocolate and textiles as before (point C), *plus an additional 1,500 yards of textiles and 1.5 tons of chocolate to split up between them*. The following table summarizes these gains:

Specialization and trade create gains that make all better off.

	Combined Production Possibilities		
	(I) No Specialization or Trade	(II) Specialization and Trade	(III) Gains to Trade
Fabric	2,500 yards	4,000 yards	1,500 yards
Chocolate	2.5 tons	4 tons	1.5 tons

Column I shows the combination with no specialization or trade. Column II represents the amount the countries can produce if each specializes in what it does best and then trades. Column III is the difference between Column II and Column I. How these gains are distributed is up to negotiation, but the total combination of goods has risen. It is these gains from trade that lead to economists' support of free trade and their opposition to barriers to trade.

Q-7 Steve can bake either 4 loaves of bread or 8 dozen cookies a day. Sarah can bake either 4 loaves of bread or 4 dozen cookies a day. Show, using production possibility curves, that Steve and Sarah would be better off specializing in their baking activities and then trading, rather than baking only for themselves.

The numbers in the table represent one possibility of the gains from specialization and trade. Other combinations are possible. Connecting points *D*, *E*, and *F* in Figure 2-7 tells us all potential combinations of output with trade. The extremes (points *D* and *E*) are where both countries are using all their resources in the production of one or the other goods. Point *F* represents the combined total output when each specializes in the good for which it has a comparative advantage. Connecting points *D*, *E*, and *F* (the blue line) gives us the combined production possibility curve with specialization and trade. The shaded area graphically represents the gains from specialization and trade.

Q-8 True or false? Two countries can achieve the greatest gains from trade by each producing the goods for which the opportunity costs are greatest and then trading those goods.

Notice that the combined production possibility curve has the same slope as Belgium's from *D* to *F*, and the same slope as Pakistan's from *F* to *E*. That is because, when trade is allowed, the slope of the combined production possibility curve is determined by the country with the lowest opportunity cost. It is by producing where costs are lowest that countries can achieve gains from trade. This principle—*lowest cost rules*—gives us a sense of what happens when we expand the production possibility curve analysis to include many countries rather than just two: The production possibility curve becomes smoother as each country's comparative advantage governs a smaller portion of the shape. Eventually, as the number of countries that trade gets large, it becomes the smooth bowed curve we drew above for guns and butter.

U.S. Textile Production and Trade

When each country follows its comparative advantage, production becomes more efficient and the production possibilities curve increases the amount of goods that can be produced. Because of these benefits, most economists support free markets and free trade. The market system gives individual firms an incentive to search for comparative advantages, and to produce with lowest-cost methods at lowest-cost locations. This pressures other producers to lower their costs or get out of the business.

The pressure to find comparative advantages is never ending, in part because comparative advantage can change. Two hundred years ago the United States had a comparative advantage in producing textiles. It was rich in natural resources and labor, and it had a low-cost source of power (water). As the cost of U.S. labor went up, and as trade opportunities widened, that comparative advantage disappeared. As it did, the United States moved out of the textile industry. Countries with cheaper labor, such as Bangladesh, today have the comparative advantage in textiles. As firms have relocated textile production to Bangladesh, total costs have fallen. The gains from trade show up as higher pay for Bangladeshi workers and lower-priced cloth for U.S. consumers. Of course, trade is a two-way street. In return for Bangladesh's textiles, the United States sends computer software and airplanes, products that would be highly expensive, indeed almost impossible, for Bangladesh to produce on its own. So Bangladeshi consumers, on average, are also made better off by the trade.

The pressure to find comparative advantages is never ending.

Web Note 2.2
Wage Comparison

Regulating Trade: Institutions, Government, and Trade

We've spent a lot of time going through the production possibility curve model, and the underlying comparative advantage argument. Now let's turn to the implications of the model for policy. Clearly, one of the lessons of the model and its analysis is that *trade is good*—if that conclusion didn't hit you over the head, you probably were daydreaming as you read the preceding sections. But does the model mean that we should fully support free trade and a laissez-faire policy? What policy should society have regarding trade? The answers to these questions are more subtle than the general conclusion. To find the answers, you have to know not only what the model is telling us about policy but also what assumptions—both implicit and explicit—are included in the model, because it is those assumptions that lead us to that conclusion. (Here is an example of the proposition I presented in Chapter 1: To truly know a model you have to know both the model and its assumptions.)

To apply the model one must know its assumptions; thus, while the model tells us that trade is generally good, it may not be good in particular instances.

Let's start with the easy part: What is the model, given its assumptions, telling us about policy? Trade expands the production possibilities one faces and, by encouraging individuals to take advantage of their comparative advantage, it allows individuals to achieve gains they couldn't otherwise achieve. This argument is quite robust and can be applied in many different instances. Now let's turn to the harder part—the assumptions of the model upon which that argument is based. The important assumption of the model that we're going to concentrate on here is that trade is costless, or, put another way, that there are no transactions costs to trade. This assumption is not true in the real world. Trade can be extraordinarily costly. For markets to develop, trading partners need to cooperate, which requires a complex institutional environment. Rules and methods of trading need to become codified. To have ongoing trade you have to have enforceable contracts, a commercial code (laws about what is allowable in trade and what isn't), rules about what happens when someone does not fulfill an obligation they incur in trade, methods to make trade easier, and a whole lot more. Somebody has to supply all that, and in the United States (and, more generally, in domestic economies) that somebody is the government of the country. In countries where an effective government does not exist, as in Somalia, you don't have these institutions and you don't have effective markets.

Q-9 True or false? If a country doesn't have an effective government, then the market will be more efficient because the government will have to follow a laissez-faire policy.

One way domestic governments make trading easier is to limit private restrictions on trade. U.S. states, for example, are not allowed to place taxes on goods as they cross their borders. (In countries where there is not an effective government, such as Afghanistan, that is not the case; warlords charge for any goods passing through their territory, making trade difficult and costly.) Another way is to provide a common currency for traders to use. In the United States you can spend a dollar in any state. Cross the border into Canada or Mexico, and you have to switch currencies. Common currencies provided by government make trades much easier, which is why the European Union, for example, has organized to establish a common currency—the euro. I could go on, but the examples given so far should make my point: Domestic governments are part and parcel of modern functioning markets. An important reason why international trade is much more difficult than domestic trade is that no world government exists to assist in that trade. Instead, voluntary organizations, such as the World Bank, the World Court, the International Monetary Fund, and the World Trade Organization fill some of the roles internationally that a national government fills domestically.

When you think about policy, don't think about government and markets as totally separate.

I raise these issues here to point out to you that while we rely on government to regulate markets, government is also part of the institutional structure of markets (because it provides the institutional environment in which markets exist). So when you think about policy, don't think of government and markets as totally separate. Think of them as intertwined entities, both of whose continued existence depends on the existence of the other. (We'll talk more about such issues in later chapters.)

You must use the insight that institutions and government are central to trade when interpreting the implications of the production possibilities model for policy. It tells us that while markets work like an invisible hand—guiding individuals to make choices that work for the good of society, even as those individuals pursue their own welfare—we can't think of markets as operating alone. Instead we must think of them as operating in conjunction with social and political forces. The invisible hand works as well as it does only because it is part of a broader institutional structure. Society appropriately regulates markets, preventing trades that are harmful to its members and encouraging trades that are helpful. Who decides what hurts and what helps? Within the United States, the government decides. Government stands as the arbiter of whether the trade is actually helping society or not.

Roles of government in a market economy are:

1. providing a stable set of institutions and rules,
2. promoting effective and workable competition,
3. correcting for externalities,
4. ensuring economic stability and growth,
5. providing public goods, and
6. adjusting for undesired market results.

Roles of Government in a Market

Economists have thought a lot about why government should not allow some trades and should limit or highly regulate others. This thinking goes back to Adam Smith, who in *The Wealth of Nations* explored a number of roles for government in a market economy. Later economists have expanded thinking about those roles. So let us now take a look at the roles of government in restricting trade. These roles include (1) providing a stable set of institutions and rules, (2) promoting effective and workable competition, (3) correcting for externalities, (4) ensuring economic stability and growth, (5) providing public goods, and (6) adjusting for undesired market results.

Laissez-Faire is Not Anarchy

Beyond the Tools

Most reasons for government intervention discussed in this chapter are debatable.

There is, however, one governmental role that even the strongest laissez-faire advocates generally accept. That role is for government to set up an appropriate institutional and legal structure within which markets can operate.

The reason there's little debate about this role is that all economists recognize that markets do not operate when there is anarchy. They require institutional structures that determine the rules of ownership, what types of trade are allowable, how contracts will be enforced, and what productive institutions are most desirable.

Before anyone conducts business, he or she needs to know the rules of the game and must have a reasonable expectation that those rules will not be changed. The operation of the modern economy requires that contractual arrangements be made among individuals. These contractual arrangements must be enforced if the economy is to operate effectively.

Economists differ significantly on what the rules for such a system should be and whether any rules that already exist should be modified. Even if the rules are currently perceived as unfair, it can be argued that they should be kept in place. Individuals have already made decisions based on those rules, and it's unfair to them to change the rules in the middle of the game.

Stability of rules is a benefit to society. When the rules are perceived as unfair, and changing them is also perceived as unfair, the government must find a balance between the two degrees of unfairness. Government often finds itself in that difficult position. Thus, while there's little debate about government's role in providing some institutional framework, there's heated debate about which framework is most appropriate.

Provide a Stable Set of Institutions and Rules A basic role of government is to provide a stable institutional framework that includes the set of laws specifying what can and cannot be done as well as a mechanism to enforce those laws. For example, if someone doesn't pay you, you can't go take what you are owed; you have to go through the government court system. The government restricts individuals from enforcing contracts; it retains that role for itself. Before people conduct business, they need to know the rules of the game and have a reasonable belief about what those rules will be in the future. These rules can initially develop spontaneously, but as society becomes more complex, the rules must be codified; enforcement mechanisms must be established. The modern market economy requires enforceable complex contractual arrangements among individuals. Where governments don't provide a stable institutional framework, as often happens in developing and transitional countries, economic activity is difficult; usually such economies are stagnant. Zimbabwe in the early 2000s is an example. As various groups fought for political control, the Zimbabwe economy stagnated.

Promote Effective and Workable Competition In a market economy the forces of monopoly—the control of a market by one firm—and competition are always in conflict, and the government must decide what role it is to play in protecting or promoting competition. Thus, when Microsoft gained a monopolistic control of the computer operating system market with Windows, the U.S. government took the company to court and challenged that monopoly.

Historically, U.S. sentiment runs against **monopoly power**—*the ability of individuals or firms currently in business to prevent other individuals or firms from entering the same kind of business*. Monopoly power gives existing firms and individuals the ability to raise their prices. Similarly, individuals' or firms' ability to enter freely into business activities is generally seen as good. Government's job is to promote competition and prevent excess monopoly power from limiting competition.

What makes this a difficult function for government is that most individuals and firms believe that competition is far better for the other guy than it is for themselves, that their own monopolies are necessary monopolies, and that competition facing them is unfair competition. For example, most farmers support competition, but these same farmers also support government farm subsidies (payments by government to producers based on production levels) and import restrictions. Likewise, most firms support competition, but these same firms also support tariffs, which protect them from foreign competition. Most professionals, such as architects and engineers, support competition, but they also support professional licensing, which limits the number of competitors who can enter their field. Now, as you will see in reading the newspapers, there are always arguments for limiting entry into fields. The job of the government is to determine whether these arguments are strong enough to overcome the negative effects those limitations have on competition.

When there are externalities, there is a potential role for government.
Charles O'Rear/Corbis

Correct for Externalities When two people freely enter into a trade or agreement, they both believe that they will benefit from the trade. But unless they're required to do so, traders are unlikely to take into account any effect that an action may have on a third party. Economists call *the effect of a decision on a third party not taken into account by the decision maker* an **externality.** An externality can be positive (in which case society as a whole benefits from the trade between the two parties) or negative (in which case society as a whole is harmed by the trade between the two parties).

An example of a positive externality is education. When someone educates herself or himself, all society benefits, since better-educated people usually make better citizens and are better equipped to figure out new approaches to solving problems—approaches that benefit society as a whole. An example of a negative externality is pollution. Air conditioners emit a small amount of chlorofluorocarbons into the earth's atmosphere and contribute to the destruction of the ozone layer. Since the ozone layer protects all living things by filtering some of the sun's harmful ultraviolet light rays, a thinner layer of ozone can contribute to cancer and other harmful or fatal conditions. Neither the firms that produce the air conditioners nor the consumers who buy them take those effects into account. This means that the destruction of the ozone layer is an externality—the result of an effect that is not taken into account by market participants.

When there are externalities, there is a potential role for government to adjust the market result. If one's goal is to benefit society as much as possible, actions with positive externalities should be encouraged and actions with negative externalities should be restricted. Governments can step in and change the rules so that the actors must take into account the effect of their actions on society as a whole. I emphasize that the role is a potential one for two reasons. The first is that government often has difficulty dealing with externalities in such a way that society gains. For example, even if the U.S. government totally banned products that emit chlorofluorocarbons, other countries might not do the same and the ozone layer would continue to be destroyed. The second reason is that government is an institution that reflects, and is often guided by, politics and vested interests. It's not clear that, given the political realities, government intervention to correct externalities would improve the situation. In later chapters I'll have a lot more to say about government's role in correcting for externalities.

Ensure Economic Stability and Growth In addition to providing general stability, government has the potential role of providing economic stability. If it's possible, most people would agree that government should prevent large fluctuations in the level of economic activity, maintain a relatively constant price level, and provide an economic environment conducive to economic growth. These aims, which became the goals of the U.S. government in 1946 when the Employment Act was passed, are generally considered macroeconomic goals. They're justified as appropriate aims for government to pursue because they involve **macroeconomic externalities** (*externalities that affect the levels of unemployment, inflation, or growth in the economy as a whole*).

A macroeconomic externality is the effect of an individual decision that affects the levels of unemployment, inflation, or growth in an economy as a whole but is not taken into account by the individual decision maker.

Here's how a macro externality could occur. When individuals decide how much to spend, they don't take into account the effects of their decision on others; thus, there may be too much or too little spending. Too little spending often leads to unemployment. But in making their spending decision, people don't take into account the fact that spending less might create unemployment. So their spending decisions can involve a macro externality. Similarly, when people raise their price and don't consider the effect on inflation, they too might be creating a macro externality.

Provide for Public Goods Another role for government is to supply public goods. A **public good** is *a good that if supplied to one person must be supplied to all and whose consumption by one individual does not prevent its consumption by another individual.* In contrast, a **private good** is *a good that, when consumed by one individual, cannot be consumed by another individual.* An example of a private good is an apple; once I eat that apple, no one else can consume it. An example of a public good is national defense. In order to supply defense, governments must force people to pay for it with taxes, rather than leaving it to the market to supply it.

There are very few pure public goods, but many goods have public good aspects to them, and in general economists use the term *public good* to describe goods that are most efficiently provided collectively rather than privately. Parks, playgrounds, roads, and (as noted above) national defense are examples. Let's consider national defense more closely. For technological reasons national defense must protect all individuals in an area; a missile system cannot protect some houses in an area without protecting others nearby.

Everyone agrees that national defense is needed, but not everyone takes part in it. If someone else defends the country, you're defended for free; you can be a **free rider**—*a person who participates in something for free because others have paid for it.* Because self-interested people would like to enjoy the benefits of national defense while letting someone else pay for it, everyone has an incentive to be a free rider. But if everyone tries to be a free rider, there won't be any national defense. In such cases government can step in and require that everyone pay part of the cost of national defense, reducing the free rider problem.

Adjust for Undesired Market Results A controversial role for government is to adjust the results of the market when those market results are seen as socially undesirable. Government redistributes income, taking it away from some individuals and giving it to others whom it sees as more deserving or more in need. In doing so, it attempts to see that the outcomes of trades are fair. Determining what's fair is a difficult philosophical question. Let's consider two of the many manifestations of the fairness problem. Should the government use a **progressive tax** (*a tax whose rates increase as a person's income increases*) to redistribute money from the rich to the poor? (A progressive income tax schedule might tax individuals at a rate of 15 percent for income up to $20,000; at 25 percent for income between $20,000 and $40,000; and at 35 percent for every dollar earned over $40,000.) Or should government impose a **regressive tax** (*a tax whose rates decrease as income rises*) to redistribute money from the poor to the rich? Or should government impose a flat or **proportional tax** (*a tax whose rates are constant at all income levels, no matter what a taxpayer's total annual income is*)? Such a tax might be, say, 25 percent of every dollar of income. The United States has chosen a somewhat progressive income tax, while the Social Security tax is a proportional tax up to a specified earned income. Economists can tell government the effects of various types of taxes and

Web Note 2.3
Minimum Wage

forms of taxation, but we can't tell government what's fair. That is for the people, through the government, to decide.

Another example of this role involves having government decide what's best for people, independently of their desires. The market allows individuals to decide. But what if people don't know what's best for themselves? Or what if they do know but don't act on that knowledge? For example, people might know that addictive drugs are bad for them, but because of peer pressure, or because they just don't care, they may take drugs anyway. Government action prohibiting such activities through laws or high taxes may then be warranted. *Goods or activities that government believes are bad for people even though they choose to use the goods or engage in the activities* are called **demerit goods or activities.** Illegal drugs are a demerit good and using addictive drugs is a demerit activity.

With merit and demerit goods, individuals are assumed not to be doing what is in their self-interest.

Alternatively, there are some activities that government believes are good for people, even if people may not choose to engage in them. For example, government may believe that going to the opera or contributing to charity is a good activity. But in the United States only a small percentage of people go to the opera, and not everyone in the United States contributes to charity. Similarly, government may believe that whole-wheat bread is more nutritious than white bread. But many consumers prefer white bread. Goods like whole-wheat bread and activities like contributing to charity are known as **merit goods or activities**—*goods and activities that government believes are good for you even though you may not choose to engage in the activities or consume the goods*. Government sometimes provides support for them through subsidies or tax benefits.

Market Failures and Government Failures

Q-10 If there is an externality, does that mean that the government should intervene in the market to adjust for that externality?

The reasons for government intervention are often summed up in the phrase *market failure*. **Market failures** are *situations in which the market does not lead to a desired result*. In the real world, market failures are pervasive—the market is always failing in one way or another. But the fact that there are market failures does not mean that government intervention will improve the situation. There are also **government failures**—*situations in which the government intervenes and makes things worse*. Government failures are pervasive in the government—the government is always failing in one way or another. So real-world policymakers usually end up choosing which failure—market failure or government failure—will be least problematic.

Regulating Markets Internationally

When thinking about the various roles of government, it is useful to contrast what happens domestically with what happens internationally, where there is no central world government. As I stated above, internationally, some of the roles of a government are not performed and others are performed by voluntary organizations or statelike institutions. For example, some countries have entered into free trade agreements and trade organizations that limit their ability to restrict trade. Similarly, other countries have entered into agreements to have a common currency. So these roles of government seem to carry over to situations where there is no government, and voluntary institutions are created to provide those roles.

While governments enter into voluntary agreements to fulfill some of the roles of government in the international market, for other roles we see far fewer agreements. For example, we see far less attempted redistribution of income at the international level than at the domestic level (foreign aid accounts for about 0.1 percent of U.S. income) and far less provision of public goods. Because there is no way to force countries to

The Emergence of Free Trade Associations

Applying the Tools

There are strong pressures to secure and institutionalize the benefits of free international trade, and numerous international institutions have developed, or are developing, to achieve that end. Let's consider some of them.

EU

In 1957, several governments of Europe formed the European Economic Community (EEC). This organization has undergone many changes since its founding, changes that have strengthened the economic and political ties among the countries. The EEC eventually came to be called the European Union (EU) as it evolved into both an economic free trade area and a loose political organization. In the EU, as in any economic union, members allow free trade among themselves to help their economies by providing a larger marketplace and more competition for their own companies. Economic union also increases the market power of the combined countries. In 2002 the EU currently had 15 members, 12 of which shared a common currency, the euro. Thirteen other countries from southern and eastern Europe plan to join the EU in the next few years. (For more information, you can go to www.europa.eu.int.)

NAFTA

Partly in response to the growing strength of the EU, in 1994 the United States entered into a free trade agreement with Canada and Mexico called the North American Free Trade Agreement (NAFTA). Under NAFTA, trade barriers between the United States, Canada, and Mexico will be eliminated over a 15-year period. U.S. firms will be able to produce in Mexico and Canada—and vice versa—subject to Mexican or Canadian regulations and at each country's wage rates, and ship directly to the United States without international legal hurdles or barriers to trade. (To read the agreement go to www.nafta-sec-alena.org.)

MERCOSUR

In 1991, a group of four South American countries (Argentina, Paraguay, Uruguay, Brazil) launched Mercosur (Mercado Comun del Sur, meaning "common market of the south") to develop a common market without trade barriers and coordinated economic policies. Since 1991, Bolivia and Chile have joined. (Go to www.mercosur.org to find out more.) In 1994 an effort began to develop an even larger free trade area that encompasses both NAFTA and Mercosur, called the Free Trade Area of the Americas (FTAA). While negotiations regarding the structure of the trade agreement among 34 proposed members are due to be completed in 2005, it is unclear whether such an agreement will ever be accepted. (Go to www.ftaa-alca.org to check the progress.)

AFTA

Asia does not have a free trade association, but it is working toward one, and the Association of Southeast Asian Nations (ASEAN) has been discussing the creation of what would be called the Asian Free Trade Association (AFTA). Even though its work toward a free trade association is not complete, ASEAN includes many agreements to limit tariffs and to facilitate trade among its member countries. (Go to www.aseansec.org.)

WTO

Economists are of two minds about the regional free trade associations described above. While such associations promote trade among themselves, they often also establish strong barriers with outside countries and thereby limit free trade. Thus, many economists argue that the policy focus should be on the World Trade Organization (WTO), whose purpose is to promote free trade among all member countries.

comply with international agreements, governments have been unable to come up with an effective means of dealing with various environmental issues, such as global warming, and disputes among countries can lead to war and terrorism rather than being solved by a system of world courts. The point I am making is that, internationally, we don't have world government failure because we don't have a world government. But we also don't get the benefits that a world government would provide.

International policymaking differs from domestic policymaking because there is no international government.

The push for globalization that has characterized the last decades of international relations is also a push for stronger international organizations that can make trading easier. Whether establishing those stronger organizations makes sense is an open question, but its existence shows the interconnection between markets and governments.

The Production Possibilities Model and Government Policy

As you can see, there are many roles for government that are consistent with the production possibilities model, once we modify the model to fit the real world. The model says that trade is good and that it therefore makes sense for us to rely on the market to solve our problems. The model applied to the real world (which means we take its assumptions into account) says that trade can be good, although at times it can cause problems and government regulation may be needed to adjust for those problems. This latter lesson is far less precise than the former, but it is more accurate. Debate often exists among economists about whether government should intervene.

Models are important because they structure the discourse of debate about regulating the market.

If the real-world policy implications of the model are ambiguous, why learn the model in the first place? The answer is: because the model structures the discourse of debate about regulating the market. Economists will say, "Oh, that's an externality problem," "That's a public good problem," or "That's a government failure problem"—and policymakers will know what they mean. Then the policymakers go back and study similar events in history to determine how those events worked out in the real world, and to see if this instance is any different. They then come up with a policy position in relation to the model, to history, and to politics. That's what we mean by the art of economics.

Conclusion

While the production possibility curve model does not give unambiguous answers as to what government's role should be in regulating trade, it does serve a very important purpose. It is a geometric tool that summarizes a number of ideas in economics—opportunity cost, comparative advantage, efficiency, and how trade leads to efficiency. These ideas are all essential to economists' conversations. They provide the framework within which those conversations take place. Thinking of the production possibility curve (and picturing the economy as being on it) directs you to think of the trade-offs involved in every decision.

The production possibility curve represents the tough choices society must make.

Look at questions such as: Should we save the spotted owl or should we allow logging in the western forests? Should we expand the government health care system or should we strengthen our national defense system? Should we emphasize policies that allow more consumption now or should we emphasize policies that allow more consumption in the future? Such choices involve difficult trade-offs that can be pictured by the production possibility curve.

Not everyone recognizes these trade-offs. For example, politicians often talk as if the production possibility curve were nonexistent. They promise voters the world, telling them, "If you elect me, you can have more of everything." When they say that, they obscure the hard choices and increase their probability of getting elected.

Economists continually point out that seemingly free lunches often involve significant hidden costs.

Economists do the opposite. They promise little except that life is tough, and they continually point out that seemingly free lunches often involve significant hidden costs. Alas, political candidates who exhibit such reasonableness seldom get elected. Economists' reasonableness has earned economics the nickname *the dismal science*.

Summary

- The production possibility curve measures the maximum combination of outputs that can be obtained from a given number of inputs. It embodies the opportunity cost concept.
- In general, in order to get more and more of something, we must give up ever-increasing quantities of something else. This is the principle of increasing marginal opportunity cost.
- Trade allows people to use their comparative advantage and shift out society's production possibility curve.
- The rise of markets coincided with significant increases in output. Specialization, trade, and competition have all contributed to the increase.
- Points inside the production possibility curve are inefficient, points along the production possibility curve are efficient, and points outside are unattainable.
- By specializing in producing those goods for which one has a comparative advantage (lowest opportunity cost), one can produce the greatest amount of goods with which to trade. Doing so shifts the production possibility curve out.
- The typical outward bow of the production possibility curve is the result of comparative advantage and trade.
- There is no central world government. Governments enter voluntary agreements that perform the role of regulating international markets.
- Six roles of government are (1) to provide a stable set of institutions and rules, (2) to promote effective and workable competition, (3) to correct for externalities, (4) to ensure economic stability and growth, (5) to provide public goods, and (6) to adjust for undesired market results.

Key Terms

comparative advantage *(25)*
demerit good or activity *(38)*
efficiency *(27)*
externality *(36)*
free rider *(37)*
government failure *(38)*
inefficiency *(27)*
input *(22)*
laissez-faire *(31)*
macroeconomic externality *(37)*
market failure *(38)*
merit good or activity *(38)*
monopoly power *(35)*
output *(21)*
principle of increasing marginal opportunity cost *(26)*
private good *(37)*
production possibility curve *(23)*
production possibility table *(21)*
productive efficiency *(27)*
progressive tax *(37)*
proportional tax *(37)*
public good *(37)*
regressive tax *(37)*

Questions for Thought and Review

1. Design a grade production possibility table and curve that embody the principle of increasing marginal opportunity cost.
2. What would the production possibility curve look like if there were decreasing marginal opportunity costs? Explain. What is an example of decreasing marginal opportunity costs?
3. Show how a production possibility curve would shift if a society became more productive in its output of widgets but less productive in its output of wadgets.
4. Show how a production possibility curve would shift if a society became more productive in the output of both widgets and wadgets.
5. How does the theory of comparative advantage relate to production possibility curves?
6. When all people use economic reasoning, inefficiency is impossible, because if the benefit of reducing that inefficiency were greater than the cost, the inefficiency would be eliminated. Thus, if people use economic reasoning, it's impossible to be on the interior of a production possibility curve. Is this statement true or false? Why?
7. How does the democratic political system lead politicians to emphasize points outside the production possibility curve?
8. If neither of two countries has a comparative advantage in either of two goods, what will their combined production possibility curve look like?
9. If neither of two countries has a comparative advantage in either of two goods, what are the gains from trade?

10. If income distribution is tied to a particular production technique, how might that change one's view of alternative production techniques?
11. Does the fact that the production possibilities model tells us that trade is good mean that in the real world free trade is necessarily the best policy? Explain.
12. What are the six roles of government listed in the text? Which do you believe is the most controversial? Why?
13. You've set up the rules for a game and started the game, but now realize that the rules are unfair. Should you change the rule?
14. Say the government establishes rights to pollute so that without a pollution permit you aren't allowed to emit pollutants into the air, water, or soil. Firms are allowed to buy and sell these rights. In what way will this correct for an externality?

Problems and Exercises

1. A country has the following production possibility table:

Resources Devoted to Clothing	Output of Clothing	Resources Devoted to Food	Output of Food
100%	20	0%	0
80	16	20	5
60	12	40	9
40	8	60	12
20	4	80	14
0	0	100	15

   a. Draw the country's production possibility curve.
   b. What's happening to marginal opportunity costs as output of food increases?
   c. Say the country gets better at the production of food. What will happen to the production possibility curve?
   d. Say the country gets equally better at producing both food and clothing. What will happen to the production possibility curve?

2. Suppose the United States and Japan have the following production possibility tables:

Japan		United States	
Bolts of Cloth	Tons of Wheat	Bolts of Cloth	Tons of Wheat
1,000	0	500	0
800	100	400	200
600	200	300	400
400	300	200	600
200	400	100	800
0	500	0	1,000

   a. Draw each country's production possibility curve.
   b. In what good does the United States have a comparative advantage? Japan?
   c. Draw the joint possibility curve if the United States and Japan devote the same proportion of resources to the production of both goods and do not trade.
   d. Draw their joint production possibility curve if the countries take advantage of their comparative advantages and trade.

3. Assume the United States can produce Toyotas at the cost of $8,000 per car and Chevrolets at $6,000 per car. In Japan, Toyotas can be produced at 1,000,000 yen and Chevrolets at 500,000 yen.
   a. In terms of Chevrolets, what is the opportunity cost of producing Toyotas in each country?
   b. Who has the comparative advantage in producing Chevrolets?
   c. Assume Americans purchase 500,000 Chevrolets and 300,000 Toyotas each year. The Japanese purchase far fewer of each. Using productive efficiency as the guide, which country should most likely produce Chevrolets and which should produce Toyotas, assuming Chevrolets are going to be produced in one country and Toyotas in the other?
4. Lawns produce no crops but occupy more land (25 million acres) in the United States than any single crop, such as corn. This means that the United States is operating inefficiently and hence is at a point inside the production possibility curve. Right? If not, what does it mean?
5. Groucho Marx is reported to have said, "The secret of success is honesty and fair dealing. If you can fake those, you've got it made." What would likely happen to society's production possibility curve if everyone could fake honesty? Why? (Hint: Remember that society's production possibility curve reflects more than just technical relationships.)
6. Go to a store in your community.
   a. Ask what limitations the owners faced in starting their business.
   b. Were these limitations necessary?
   c. Should there have been more or fewer limitations?
   d. Under what heading of reasons for government intervention would you put each of the limitations?
   e. Ask what kinds of taxes the business pays and what benefits it believes it gets for those taxes.
   f. Is it satisfied with the existing situation? Why? What would it change?

7. Give an example of a merit good, a demerit good, a public good, and a good that involves an externality.
   a. How might individuals disagree about the government's role in intervening in the market for each of the goods you listed?
   b. Discuss the concepts of market failure and government failure in relation to the goods you listed.

WEB QUESTIONS

1. Select a foreign country and, using the CIA World Factbook (www.cia.gov/cia/publications/factbook), answer the following questions:
   a. What goods does the country produce? Purchase from another country?
   b. In what goods does it have a comparative advantage? Explain your answer.
   c. Name one of its trading partners. Why do you think that country is a trading partner?
2. Go to www.libertarian.org to read about libertarians and to answer the following questions:
   a. Click "Intro." What is a libertarian's defining belief?
   b. Click "Policy." Take the world's smallest quiz and report your score. Do you agree with the result?
   c. Continue with "Policy." What are libertarians' main objections to government regulation?

ANSWERS TO MARGIN QUESTIONS

1. You must give up 2 units of good *Y* to produce 4 units of good *X*, so the opportunity cost of *X* is ½ *Y*. *(22)*
2. If no resource had a comparative advantage, the production possibility curve would be a straight line connecting the points of maximum production of each product as in the graph below.

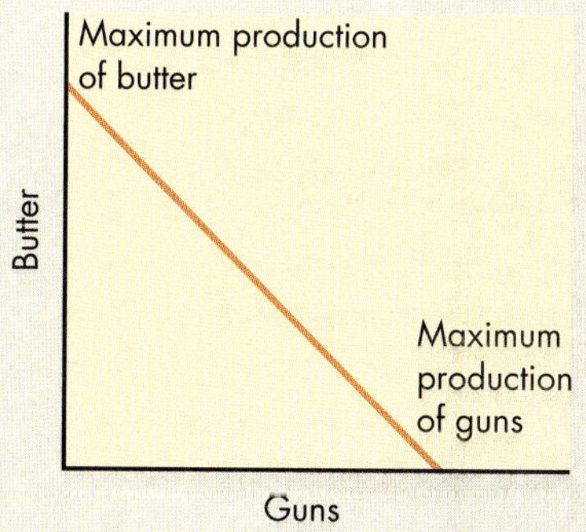

At all points along this curve, the opportunity cost of producing guns and butter is equal. *(25)*

3. Points *A* and *C* are along the production possibility curve, so they are points of efficiency. Point *B* is inside the production possibility curve, so it is a point of inefficiency. Point *D* is to the right of the production possibility curve, so it is unattainable. *(27)*
4. I remind them of the importance of cultural forces. In Saudi Arabia women are not allowed to drive. *(28)*
5. The production possibility curve shifts in along the butter axis as in the graph below. *(28)*

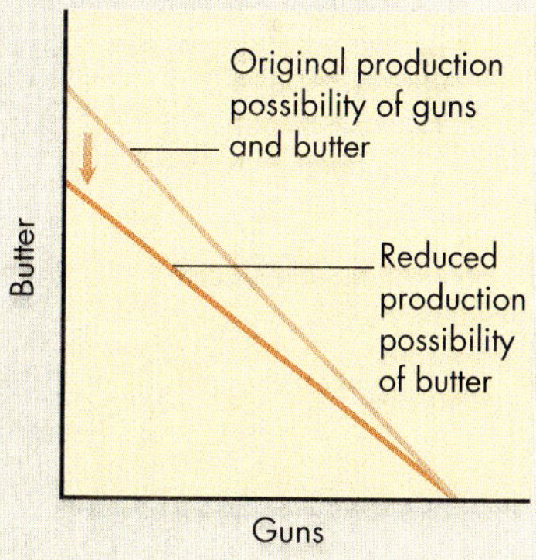

6. The argument that underlies the general laissez-faire policy argument is that when there is competition in trade, individuals are able to pick the best trades available to them and the end result is that both parties to the trade benefit as much as they possibly can. *(31)*
7. If Steve and Sarah devote the same resources to baking each good and do not trade, the combined production possibility is the orange line in the graph on the following page. Their combined production possibility curve is shown in blue. The production possibility curve with specialization and trade is farther to the right than the one without trade. Steve and Sarah can each end up with more bread and cookies if they take advantage of their

comparative advantages and trade than if they work on their own. (32)

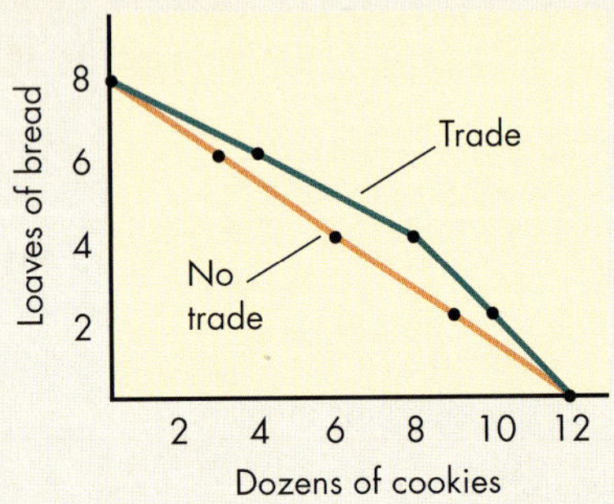

8. False. By producing the good for which it has a comparative advantage (lowest opportunity cost) a country will have the greatest amount of goods with which to trade and will reap the greatest gains from trade. (32)
9. False. Governments are needed for effective markets to function. At a minimum, they must provide the rules and the institutional structure within which the market operates. (34)
10. Not necessarily. The existence of an externality creates the possibility that government intervention might help. But there are also government failures in which the government intervenes and makes things worse. (38)

APPENDIX A

Graphish: The Language of Graphs

A picture is worth 1,000 words. Economists, being efficient, like to present ideas in **graphs,** *pictures of points in a coordinate system in which points denote relationships between numbers*. But a graph is worth 1,000 words only if the person looking at the graph knows the graphical language: *Graphish*, we'll call it. (It's a bit like English.) Graphish is usually written on graph paper. If the person doesn't know Graphish, the picture isn't worth any words and Graphish can be babble.

I have enormous sympathy for students who don't understand Graphish. A number of my students get thrown for a loop by graphs. They understand the idea, but Graphish confuses them. This appendix is for them, and for those of you like them. It's a primer in Graphish.

TWO WAYS TO USE GRAPHS

In this book I use graphs in two ways:

1. To present an economic model or theory visually, to show how two variables interrelate.
2. To present real-world data visually. To do this, I use primarily bar charts, line charts, and pie charts.

Actually, these two ways of using graphs are related. They are both ways of presenting visually the *relationship* between two things.

Graphs are built around a number line, or axis, like the one in Figure A2-1(a). The numbers are generally placed in order, equal distances from one another. That number line allows us to represent a number at an appropriate point on the line. For example, point *A* represents the number 4.

The number line in Figure A2-1(a) is drawn horizontally, but it doesn't have to be; it can also be drawn vertically, as in Figure A2-1(b).

How we divide our axes, or number lines, into intervals is up to us. In Figure A2-1(a), I called each interval 1; in Figure A2-1(b), I called each interval 10. Point A appears after 4 intervals of 1 (starting at 0 and reading from left to right), so it represents 4. In Figure A2-1(b), where each interval represents 10, to represent 5, I place point *B* halfway in the interval between 0 and 10.

So far, so good. Graphish developed when a vertical and a horizontal number line were combined, as in Figure A2-1(c). When the horizontal and vertical number lines are put together, they're called *axes*. (Each line is an axis. *Axes* is the plural of *axis*.) I now have a **coordinate system**—*a two-dimensional space in which one point represents two numbers*. For example, point A in Figure A2-1(c) represents the numbers (4, 5)—4 on the horizontal number line and 5 on the vertical number line. Point *B* represents the numbers (1, 20). (By convention, the horizontal numbers are written first.)

Being able to represent two numbers with one point is neat because it allows the relationships between two numbers to be presented visually instead of having to be expressed verbally, which is often cumbersome. For example, say the cost of producing 6 units of something is \$4 per unit and the cost of producing 10 units is \$3 per unit. By

Figure A2-1 (a, b, and c) Horizontal and Vertical Number Lines and a Coordinate System

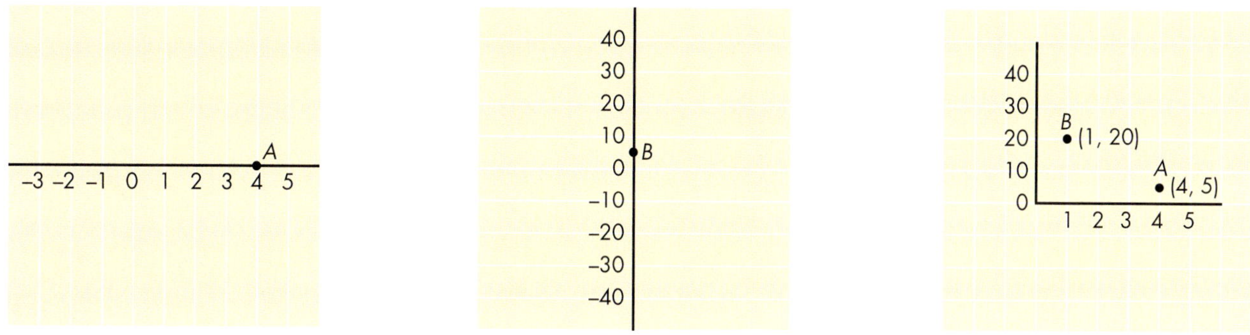

(a) Horizontal number line **(b) Vertical number line** **(c) Coordinate system**

putting both these points on a graph, we can visually see that producing 10 costs less per unit than does producing 6.

Another way to use graphs to present real-world data visually is to use the horizontal line to represent time. Say that we let each horizontal interval equal a year, and each vertical interval equal $100 in income. By graphing your income each year, you can obtain a visual representation of how your income has changed over time.

Using Graphs in Economic Modeling

I use graphs throughout the book as I present economic models, or simplifications of reality. A few terms are often used in describing these graphs, and we'll now go over them. Consider Figure A2-2(a), which lists the number of pens bought per day (column 2) at various prices (column 1).

We can present the table's information in a graph by combining the pairs of numbers in the two columns of the table and representing, or plotting, them on two axes. I do that in Figure A2-2(b).

By convention, when graphing a relationship between price and quantity, economists place price on the vertical axis and quantity on the horizontal axis.

I can now connect the points, producing a line like the one in Figure A2-2(c). With this line, I interpolate the numbers between the points (which makes for a nice visual presentation). That is, I make the **interpolation assumption**—*the assumption that the relationship between variables is the same between points as it is at the points*. The interpolation assumption allows us to think of a line as a collection of points and therefore to connect the points into a line.

Even though the line in Figure A2-2(c) is straight, economists call any such line drawn on a graph a *curve*. Because it's straight the curve in A2-2(c) is called a **linear curve**—*a curve that is drawn as a straight line*. Notice that this curve starts high on the left-hand side and goes down to the right. Economists say that any curve that looks like that is *downward-sloping*. They also say that a downward-sloping curve represents an **inverse relationship**—*a relationship between two variables in which when one goes up, the other goes down*. In this example, the line demonstrates an inverse relationship between price and quantity—that is, when the price of pens goes up, the quantity bought goes down.

Figure A2-2(d) presents a **nonlinear curve**—*a curve that is drawn as a curved line*. This curve, which really is curved, starts low on the left-hand side and goes up to the right. Economists say any curve that goes up to the right is *upward-sloping*. An upward-sloping curve represents a **direct relationship**—*a relationship in which when one variable goes up, the other goes up too*. The direct relationship I'm talking about here is the one between the two variables (what's measured on the horizontal and vertical lines). *Downward-sloping* and *upward-sloping* are terms you need to memorize if you want to read, write, and speak Graphish, keeping graphically in your mind the image of the relationships they represent.

Slope

One can, of course, be far more explicit about how much the curve is sloping upward or downward by defining it in terms of **slope**—*the change in the value on the vertical axis divided by the change in the value on the horizontal axis*. Sometimes the slope is presented as "rise over run":

$$\text{Slope} = \frac{\text{Rise}}{\text{Run}} = \frac{\text{Change in value on vertical axis}}{\text{Change in value on horizontal axis}}$$

Figure A2-2 (a, b, c, and d) A Table and Graphs Showing the Relationships between Price and Quantity

	Price per Pen	Quantity of Pens Bought per Day
A	$3.00	4
B	2.50	5
C	2.00	6
D	1.50	7
E	1.00	8

(a) Price quantity table

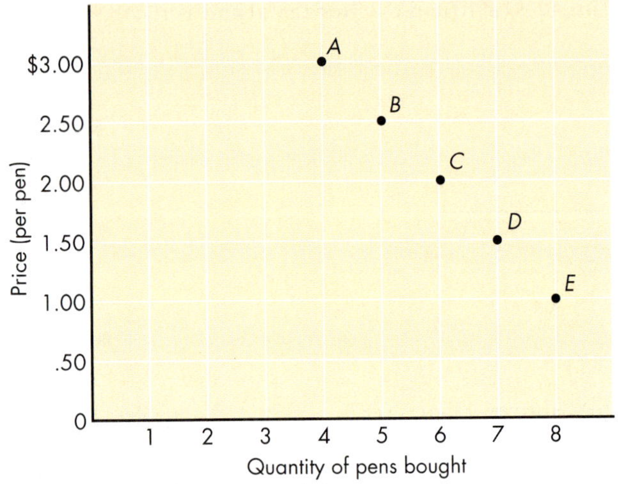

(b) From a table to a graph (1)

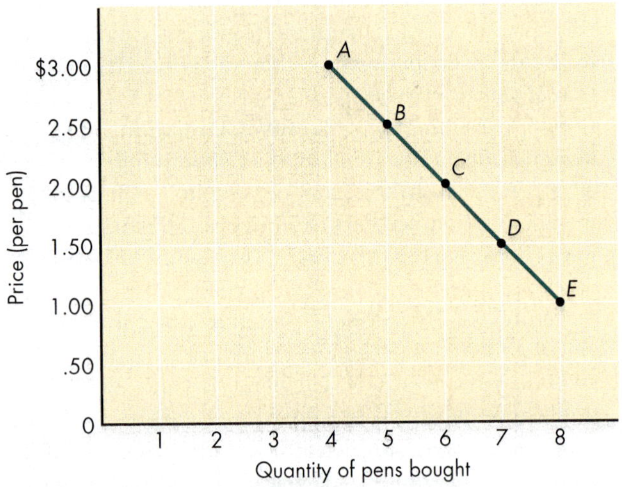

(c) From a table to a graph (2)

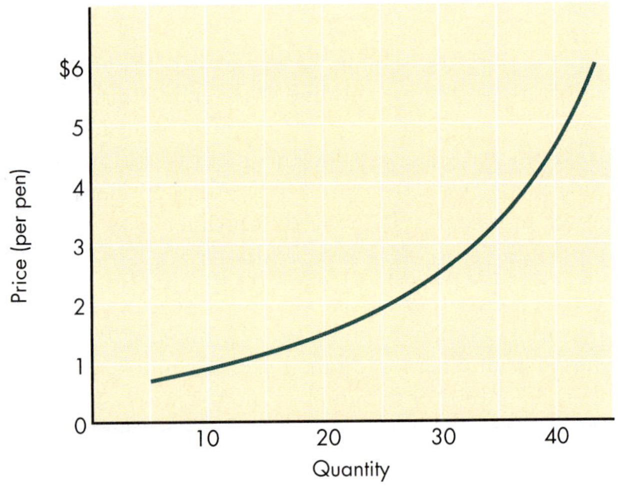

(d) Nonlinear curve

Slopes of Linear Curves

In Figure A2-3, I present five linear curves and measure their slope. Let's go through an example to show how we can measure slope. To do so, we must pick two points. Let's use points A (6, 8) and B (7, 4) on curve *a*. Looking at these points, we see that as we move from 6 to 7 on the horizontal axis, we move from 8 to 4 on the vertical axis. So when the number on the vertical axis falls by 4, the number on the horizontal axis increases by 1. That means the slope is −4 divided by 1, or −4.

Notice that the inverse relationships represented by the two downward-sloping curves, *a* and *b*, have negative slopes, and that the direct relationships represented by the two upward-sloping curves, *c* and *d*, have positive slopes. Notice also that the flatter the curve, the smaller the numerical value of the slope; and the more vertical, or steeper, the curve, the larger the numerical value of the slope. There are two extreme cases:

1. When the curve is horizontal (flat), the slope is zero.
2. When the curve is vertical (straight up and down), the slope is infinite (larger than large).

Knowing the term *slope* and how it's measured lets us describe verbally the pictures we see visually. For example, if I say a curve has a slope of zero, you should picture in your mind a flat line; if I say "a curve with a slope of minus one," you should picture a falling line that makes a 45° angle with the horizontal and vertical axes. (It's the hypotenuse of an isosceles right triangle with the axes as the other two sides.)

Figure A2-3 Slopes of Curves
The slope of a curve is determined by rise over run. The slope of curve *a* is shown in the graph. The rest are shown below:

	Rise	÷	Run	=	Slope
b	−1		+2		−.5
c	1		1		1
d	4		1		4
e	1		1		1

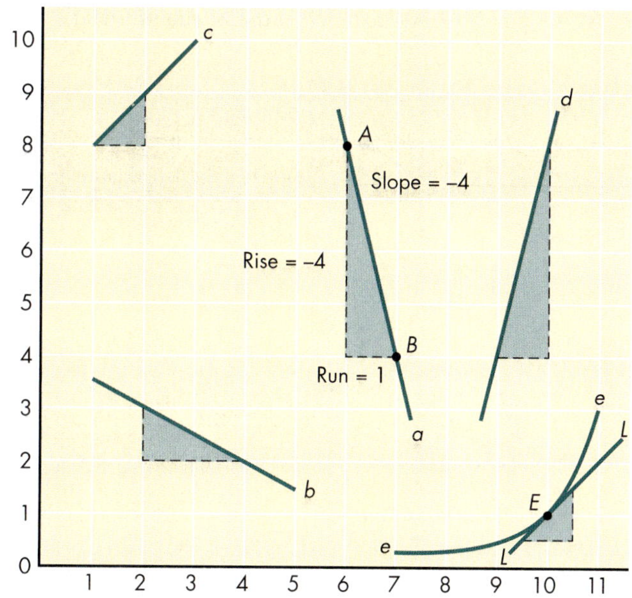

Inverse and Direct Relationships

Knowing the Tools

Inverse relationship:
When *X* goes up, *Y* goes down.
When *X* goes down, *Y* goes up.

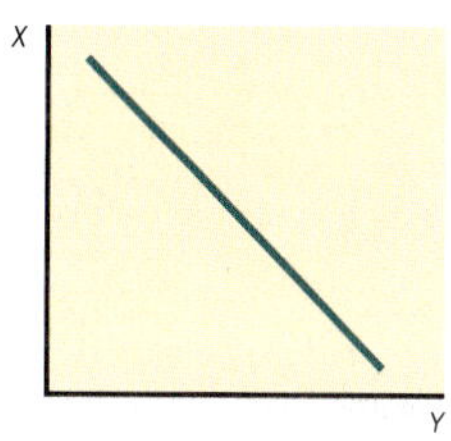

Direct relationship:
When *X* goes up, *Y* goes up.
When *X* goes down, *Y* goes down.

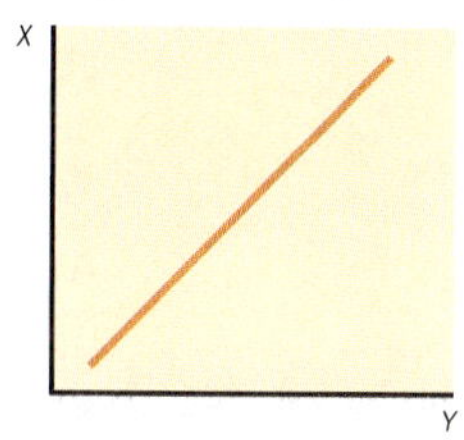

Slopes of Nonlinear Curves

The preceding examples were of *linear (straight) curves*. With *nonlinear curves*—the ones that really do curve—the slope of the curve is constantly changing. As a result, we must talk about the slope of the curve at a particular point, rather than the slope of the whole curve. How can a point have a slope? Well, it can't really, but it can almost, and if that's good enough for mathematicians, it's good enough for us.

Defining the slope of a nonlinear curve is a bit more difficult. The slope at a given point on a nonlinear curve is determined by the slope of a linear (or straight) line that's tangent to that curve. (A line that's tangent to a curve is a line that just touches the curve, and touches it only at one point in the immediate vicinity of the given point.) In Figure A2-3, the line *LL* is tangent to the curve *ee* at point *E*. The slope of that line, and hence the slope of the curve at the one point where the line touches the curve, is +1.

Maximum and Minimum Points

Two points on a nonlinear curve deserve special mention. These points are the ones for which the slope of the curve is zero. I demonstrate those in Figure A2-4(a) and (b). At point A we're at the top of the curve, so it's at a maximum point; at point B we're at the bottom of the curve, so it's at a minimum point. These maximum and minimum points are often referred to by economists, and it's important to realize that the value of the slope of the curve at each of these points is zero.

There are, of course, many other types of curves, and much more can be said about the curves I've talked about. I won't do so because, for purposes of this course, we won't need to get into those refinements. I've presented as much Graphish as you need to know for this book.

Figure A2-4 (a and b) A Maximum and a Minimum Point

(a) Maximum point **(b) Minimum point**

Figure A2-5 A Shifting Curve versus a Movement along a Curve

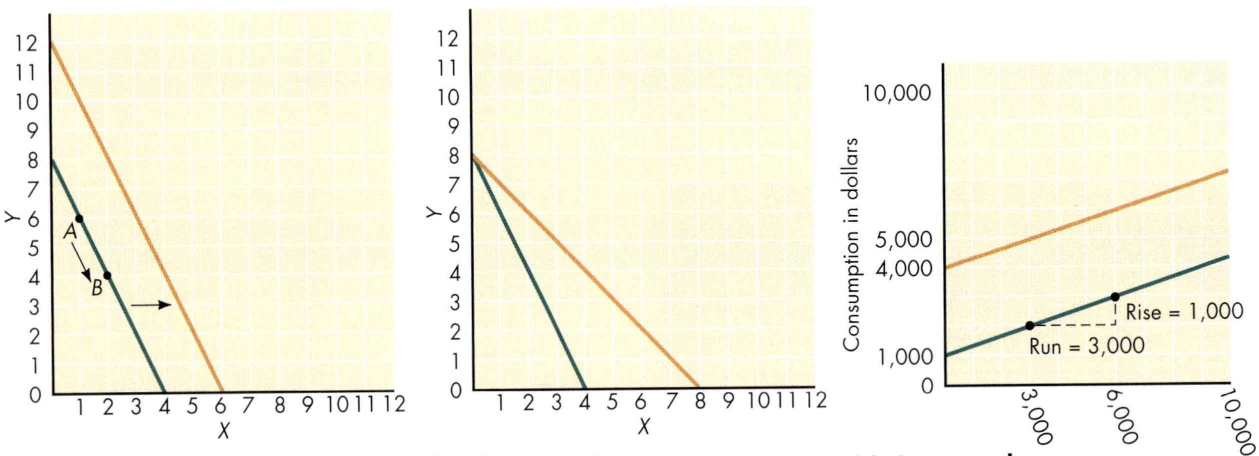

(a) Shifting curve **(b) Changing slope** **(c) An example**

Equations and Graphs

Sometimes economists depict the relationships shown in graphs using equations. Since I present material algebraically in the appendixes to a few chapters, let me briefly discuss how to translate a linear curve into an equation. Linear curves are relatively easy to translate because all linear curves follow a particular mathematical form: $y = mx + b$, where y is the variable on the vertical axis, x is the variable on the horizontal axis, m is the slope of the line, and b is the vertical-axis intercept. To write the equation of a curve, look at that curve, plug in the values for the slope and vertical-axis intercept, and you've got the equation.

For example, consider the blue curve in Figure A2-5(a). The slope (rise over run) is -2 and the number where the curve intercepts the vertical axis is 8, so the equation that depicts this curve is $y = -2x + 8$. It's best to choose variables that correspond to what you're measuring on each axis, so if price is on the vertical axis and quantity is on the horizontal axis, the equation would be $p = -2q + 8$. This equation is true for any point along this line. Take point A (1, 6), for example. Substituting 1 for x and 6 for y into the equation, you see that $6 = -2(1) + 8$, or $6 = 6$. At point B, the equation is still true: $4 = -2(2) + 8$. A move from point A to point B is called a *movement along a curve*. A movement along a curve does not change the relationship of the variables; rather, it shows how a change in one variable affects the other.

Sometimes the relationship between variables will change. The curve will either shift, change slope, or both shift and change slope. These changes are reflected in changes to the m and b variables in the equation. Suppose the vertical-axis intercept rises from 8 to 12, while the

Figure A2-6 (a, b, and c) Presenting Information Visually

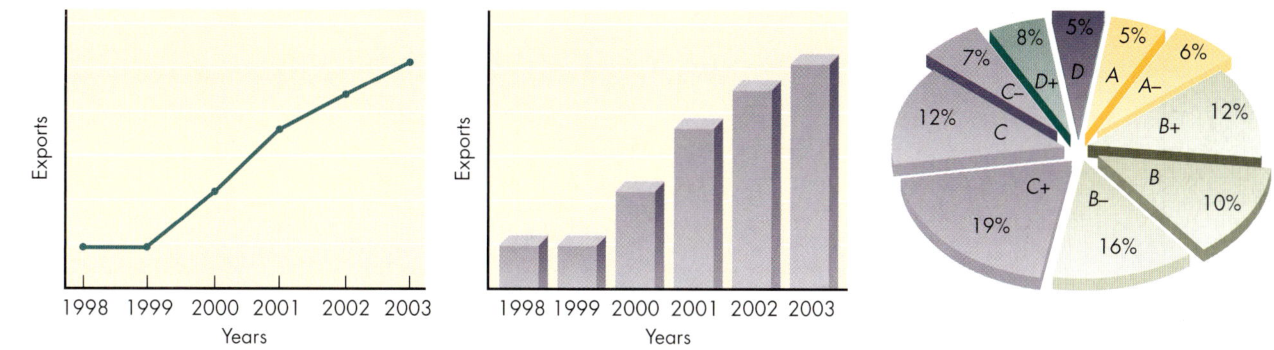

(a) Line graph **(b) Bar graph** **(c) Pie chart**

slope remains the same. The equation becomes $y = -2x + 12$; for every value of y, x has increased by 4. Plotting the new equation, we can see that the curve has *shifted* to the right, as shown by the orange line in Figure A2-5(a). If instead the slope changes from -2 to -1, while the vertical-axis intercept remains at 8, the equation becomes $y = -x + 8$. Figure A2-5(b) shows this change graphically. The original blue line stays anchored at 8 and rotates out along the horizontal axis to the new orange line.

Here's an example for you to try. The lines in Figure A2-5(c) show two relationships between consumption and income. Write the equation for the blue line.

The answer is $C = \frac{1}{3}Y + \$1{,}000$. Remember to write the equation you need to know two things: the vertical-axis intercept ($1,000) and the slope ($\frac{1}{3}$). If the intercept changes to $4,000, the curve will shift up to the orange line as shown.

Presenting Real-World Data in Graphs

The previous discussion treated the Graphish terms that economists use in presenting models which focus on hypothetical relationships. Economists also use graphs in presenting actual economic data. Say, for example, that you want to show how exports have changed over time. Then you would place years on the horizontal axis (by convention) and exports on the vertical axis, as in Figure A2-6(a) and (b). Having done so, you have a couple of choices: you can draw a **line graph**—*a graph where the data are connected by a continuous line;* or you can make a **bar graph**—*a graph where the area under each point is filled in to look like a bar.* Figure A2-6(a) shows a line graph and Figure A2-6(b) shows a bar graph.

Another type of graph is a **pie chart**—*a circle divided into "pie pieces," where the undivided pie represents the total amount and the pie pieces reflect the percentage of the whole pie that the various components make up*. This type of graph is useful in visually presenting how a total amount is divided. Figure A2-6(c) shows a pie chart, which happens to represent the division of grades on a test I gave. Notice that 5 percent of the students got As.

There are other types of graphs, but they're all variations on line and bar graphs and pie charts. Once you understand these three basic types of graphs, you shouldn't have any trouble understanding the other types.

Interpreting Graphs about the Real World

Understanding Graphish is important because, if you don't, you can easily misinterpret the meaning of graphs. For example, consider the two graphs in Figure A2-7(a) and (b). Which graph demonstrates the larger rise in income? If you said (a), you're wrong. The intervals in the vertical axes differ, and if you look carefully you'll see that the curves in both graphs represent the same combination of points. So when considering graphs, always make sure you understand the markings on the axes. Only then can you interpret the graph.

Quantitative Literacy: Avoiding Stupid Math Mistakes

The data of economics are often presented in graphs and tables. Numerical data are compared by the use of percentages, visual comparisons, and simple relationships based on quantitative differences. Economists who have

Figure A2-7 (a and b) The Importance of Scales

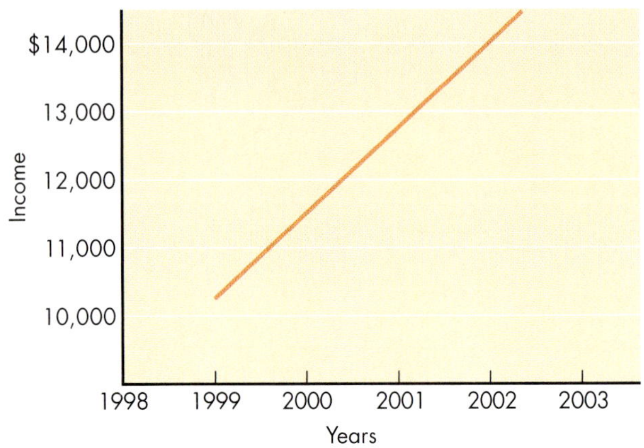

(a) Income over time (1)

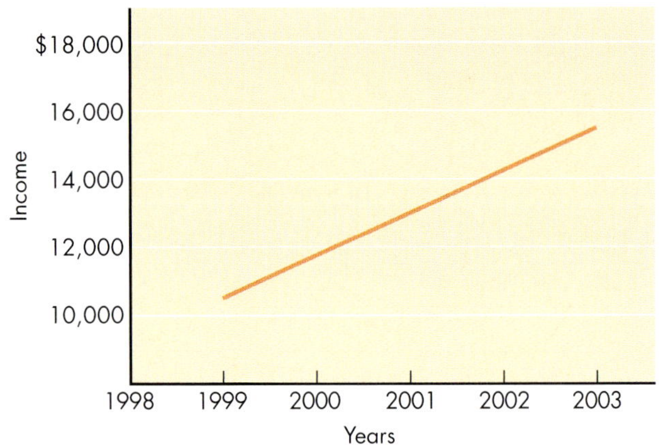

(b) Income over time (2)

studied the learning process of their students have found that some very bright students have some trouble with these presentations. Students sometimes mix up percentage changes with level changes, draw incorrect implications from visual comparisons, and calculate quantitative differences incorrectly. This is not necessarily a math problem—at least in the sense that most economists think of math. The mistakes are in relatively simple stuff—the kind of stuff learned in fifth, sixth, and seventh grades. Specifically, as reported in "Student Quantitative Literacy: Is the Glass Half-full or Half-empty?" (Robert Burns, Kim Marie McGoldrick, Jerry L. Petr, and Peter Schuhmann, 2002 University of North Carolina at Wilmington Working Paper) when the professors gave a test to students at a variety of schools, they found that a majority of students missed the following questions.

1. What is 25 percent of 400?
   a. 25 b. 50 c. 100
   d. 400 e. none of the above
2. Consider Figure A2-8 where U.S oil consumption and U.S. oil imports are plotted for 1990–2000. Fill in the blanks to construct a true statement: U.S. domestic oil consumption has been steady while imports have been ________; therefore U.S. domestic oil production has been ________.
   a. rising; rising b. falling; falling
   c. rising; falling d. falling; rising
3. Refer to the following table to select the true statement.

Figure A2-8

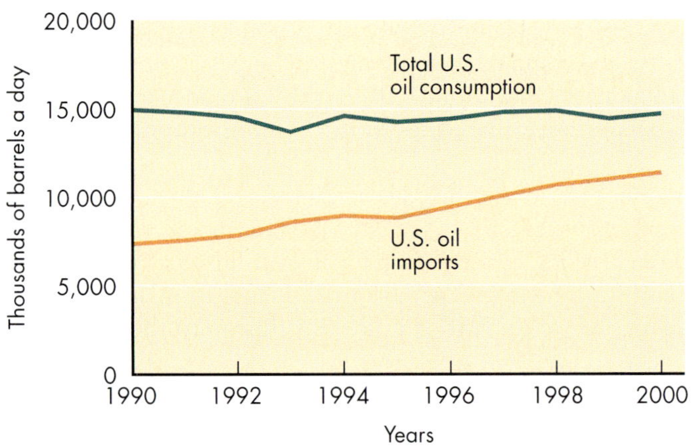

Economic Growth in Poland

Percent Increase in GDP, 1990–1994				
1990	1991	1992	1993	1994
−11.7	−7.8	−1.5	4.0	3.5

a. GDP in Poland was larger in 1992 than in 1991.
b. GDP in Poland was larger in 1994 than in 1993.
c. GDP in Poland was larger in 1991 than in 1992.
d. GDP in Poland was larger in 1993 than in 1994.
e. Both b and c are true.

4. If U.S. production of corn was 60 million bushels in 2002 and 100 million bushels in 2003, what was the percentage change in corn production from 2002 to 2003?
   a. 40 b. 60 c. 66.67
   d. 100 e. 200

The reason students got these questions wrong is unknown. Many of them had had higher-level math courses, including calculus, so it is not that they weren't trained in math. I suspect that many students missed the questions because of carelessness: the students didn't think about the question carefully before they wrote down the answer.

Throughout this book we will be discussing issues assuming a quantitative literacy sufficient to answer these questions. Moreover, questions using similar reasoning will be on exams. So it is useful for you to see whether or not you fall in the majority. So please answer the four questions given above now if you haven't done so already.

Now that you've answered them, I give you the correct answers upside-down in the footnote at the bottom of the page.[1]

If you got all four questions right, great! You can stop reading this appendix now. If you missed one or more, read the explanations of the correct answers carefully.

1. The correct answer is c. To calculate a percentage, you multiply the percentage times the number. Thus 25 percent of 400 is 100.
2. The correct answer is c. To answer it you had to recognize that U.S. consumption of oil comes from U.S. imports and U.S. production. Thus, the distance between the two lines represents U.S. production, which is clearly getting smaller from 1990 to 2000.
3. The correct answer is e. The numbers given to you are percentage changes, and the question is about levels. If the percentage change is positive, as it is in 1993 and 1994, the level is increasing. If the percentage change is negative, as it is in 1992, the level is falling. Thus 1994 is greater (by 3.5 percent) than 1993, even though the percentage change is smaller than in 1993. Because income fell in 1992, the level of income in 1991 is greater than the level of income in 1992.
4. The correct answer is c. To calculate percentage change, you first need to calculate the change, which in this case is 100− 60 or 40. So corn production started at a base of 60 and rose by 40. To calculate the percentage change that this represents you divide the amount of the rise, 40, by the base, 60. Doing so gives us $40/60 = 2/3 = .6667$, which is 66.67 percent.

Now that I've given you the answers I suspect that most of you will recognize that they are the right answers. If, after reading the explanations, you still don't follow the reasoning, you should look into getting some extra help in the course either from your teacher, your TA, or from some program the college has. If, after reading the explanations, you follow them and believe that if you had really thought about them you would have gotten them right, then the next time you see a chart or a table of numbers being compared *really think about them*. Be a bit slower in drawing inferences since they are the building blocks of economics discussions. If you want to do well on exams it probably makes sense to practice some similar questions to make sure that you have concepts down.

A Review

Let's now review what we've covered.

- A graph is a picture of points on a coordinate system in which the points denote relationships between numbers.
- A downward-sloping line represents an inverse relationship or a negative slope.
- An upward-sloping line represents a direct relationship or a positive slope.
- Slope is measured by rise over run, or a change of y (the number measured on the vertical axis) over a change in x (the number measured on the horizontal axis).
- The slope of a point on a nonlinear curve is measured by the rise over run of a line tangent to that point.
- At the maximum and minimum points of a nonlinear curve, the value of the slope is zero.
- A linear curve has the form $y = mx + b$.
- A shift in a linear curve is reflected by a change in the b variable in the equation $y = mx + b$.
- A change in the slope of a linear curve is reflected by a change in the m variable in the equation $y = mx + b$.
- In reading graphs, one must be careful to understand what's being measured on the vertical and horizontal axes.

[1] 1-c; 2-c; 3-e; 4-c.

KEY TERMS

bar graph (49)
coordinate system (44)
direct relationship (45)
graphs (44)
interpolation assumption (45)
inverse relationship (45)
line graph (49)
linear curve (45)
nonlinear curve (45)
pie chart (49)
slope (45)

QUESTIONS FOR THOUGHT AND REVIEW

1. Create a coordinate space on graph paper and label the following points:
   a. (0, 5)
   b. (−5, −5)
   c. (2, −3)
   d. (−1, 1)
2. Graph the following costs per unit, and answer the questions that follow.

Horizontal Axis: Output	Vertical Axis: Cost per Unit
1	$30
2	20
3	12
4	6
5	2
6	6
7	12
8	20
9	30

   a. Is the relationship between cost per unit and output linear or nonlinear? Why?
   b. In what range in output is the relationship inverse? In what range in output is the relationship direct?
   c. In what range in output is the slope negative? In what range in output is the slope positive?
   d. What is the slope between 1 and 2 units?
3. Within a coordinate space, draw a line with:
   a. Zero slope.
   b. Infinite slope.
   c. Positive slope.
   d. Negative slope.
4. Calculate the slope of lines *a* to *e* in the following coordinate system.

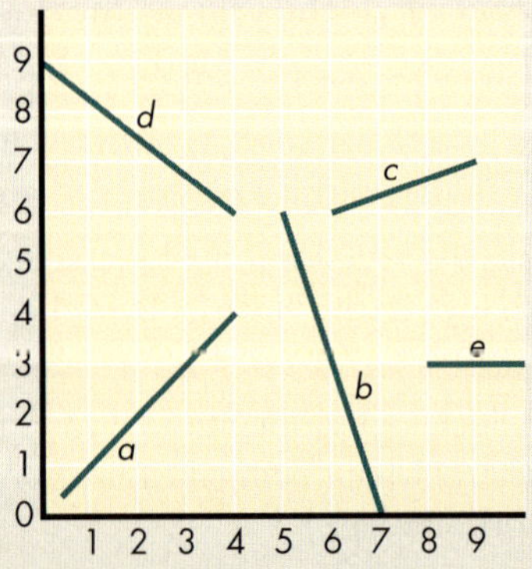

5. Given the following nonlinear curve, answer the following questions:

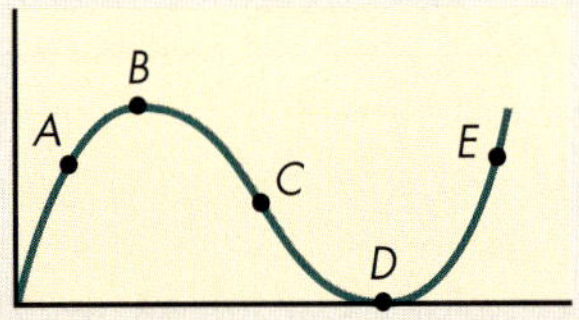

   a. At what point(s) is the slope negative?
   b. At what point(s) is the slope positive?
   c. At what point(s) is the slope zero?
   d. What point is the maximum? What point is the minimum?
6. Draw the graphs that correspond to the following equations:
   a. $y = 3x - 8$
   b. $y = 12 - x$
   c. $y = 4x + 2$
7. Using the equation $y = 3x + 1{,}000$, demonstrate the following:
   a. The slope of the curve changes to 5.
   b. The curve shifts up by 500.
8. State what type of graph or chart you might use to show the following real-world data:
   a. Interest rates from 1929 to 2003.
   b. Median income levels of various ethnic groups in the United States.
   c. Total federal expenditures by selected categories.
   d. Total costs of producing between 100 and 800 shoes.

THE EVOLVING U.S. ECONOMY IN PERSPECTIVE

3

Nobody can be a great economist who is only an economist—and I am even tempted to add that the economist who is only an economist is likely to become a nuisance if not a positive danger.

—*F. Hayek*

After reading this chapter, you should be able to:

- Define *market economy.*
- Compare and contrast socialism with capitalism.
- Describe how businesses, households, and government interact in a market economy.
- Summarize briefly the advantages and disadvantages of various types of businesses.
- Explain why, even though households have the ultimate power, much of the economic decision making is done by business and government.
- Distinguish the government's role as an actor from its role as a referee.
- Explain how globalization has changed competition.

The powerful U.S. economic machine generates enormous economic activity and provides a high standard of living (compared to most other countries) for almost all its inhabitants. It also provides economic security for a large majority of its citizens. Starvation is far from most people's minds. Ultimately, what underlies the U.S. economy's strength is its people and its other resources. The United States has vast central plains that are extraordinarily fertile, as are areas in its West and South. It is the world's second-largest producer, and largest exporter, of grains. It has excellent ports and almost 8 million kilometers (5 million miles) of roads.

The positive attributes of the U.S. economy don't mean that the United States has no problems. Critics point out that economic resources such as oil and minerals are declining, the environment is deteriorating, the distribution of income is skewed toward the rich, companies mislead investors and channel profits to managers and directors, and enormous economic effort goes into economic gamesmanship (real estate deals, stock market deals, deals about deals) that seems simply to reshuffle existing wealth, not to create new wealth. But even with all its problems, the U.S. economy is the awe of many people around the world.

In much of this book I present economic reasoning. But to apply that reasoning you need a sense of the economy you are reasoning about. So in this chapter I introduce you to the U.S. economy and an important problem facing it in the early 2000s—how to deal with the increasing economic globalization. I begin by looking at the U.S. economic system in historical perspective, considering how it evolved and how it relates to other historical economic systems. Then I consider some of the central institutions of the modern U.S. economy, and how they influence the way in which the economy works. Finally, I look at the challenges that globalization presents for the U.S. economy.

THE U.S. ECONOMY IN HISTORICAL PERSPECTIVE

A market economy is an economic system based on private property and the market. It gives private property rights to individuals, and relies on market forces to coordinate economic activity.

The first thing to note about the U.S. economy is that it is a market economy. A **market economy** is *an economic system based on private property and the market in which, in principle, individuals decide how, what, and for whom to produce*. In a market economy, individuals are encouraged to follow their own self-interest, while market forces of supply and demand are relied on to coordinate those individual pursuits. Businesses, guided by prices in the market, produce goods and services that they believe people want and that will earn a profit for the business. Prices in the market guide businesses in deciding what to produce. Distribution of goods is to each individual according to his or her ability, effort, and inherited property.

Q-1 John, your study partner, is telling you that the best way to allocate property rights is through the market. How do you respond?

Reliance on market forces doesn't mean that political, social, and historical forces play no role in coordinating economic decisions. These other forces do influence how the market works. For example, for a market to exist, government must allocate and defend **private property rights**—*the control a private individual or firm has over an asset or a right*. The concept of private ownership must exist and must be accepted by individuals in society. When you say, "This car is mine," it means that it is unlawful for someone else to take it without your permission. If someone takes it without your permission, he or she is subject to punishment through the legal system.

HOW MARKETS WORK

Markets work through a system of rewards and payments. If you do something, you get paid for doing that something; if you take something, you pay for that something. How much you get is determined by how much you give. This relationship seems fair to most people. But there are instances when it doesn't seem fair. Say someone is unable to work. Should that person get nothing? How about Joe down the street, who was given $10 million by his parents? Is it fair that he gets lots of toys, like Corvettes and skiing trips to Aspen, and doesn't have to work, while the rest of us have to work 40 hours a week and maybe go to school at night?

I'll put those questions about fairness off at this point—they are very difficult questions. For now, all I want to present is the underlying concept of fairness that a market economy embodies: "Them that works, gets; them that don't, starve."[1] In a market economy, individuals are encouraged to follow their own self-interest.

In market economies, individuals are free to do whatever they want as long as it's legal. The market is relied on to see that what people want to get, and want to do, is consistent with what's available. Price is the mechanism through which people's desires are coordinated and goods are rationed. If there's not enough of something to go around, its price goes up; if more of something needs to get done, the price given to individuals willing to do it goes up. If something isn't wanted or doesn't need to be done, its price goes down. In a market economy, fluctuations in prices play a central role in coordinating individuals' wants.

Fluctuations in prices play a central role in coordinating individuals' wants in a market economy.

[1]How come the professor gets to use rotten grammar but screams when he sees rotten grammar in your papers? Well, that's fairness for you. Actually, I should say a bit more about writing style. All writers are expected to know correct grammar; if they don't, they don't deserve to be called writers. Once you know grammar, you can individualize your writing style, breaking the rules of grammar where the meter and flow of the writing require it. In college you're still proving that you know grammar, so in papers handed in to your teacher, you shouldn't break the rules of grammar until you've proved to the teacher that you know them. Me, I've done lots of books, so my editors give me a bit more leeway than your teachers will give you.

What's Good about the Market?

Web Note 3.1
What Are Markets?

Is the market a good way to coordinate individuals' activities? Much of this book will be devoted to answering that question. The answer that I, and most U.S. economists, come to is: Yes, it is a reasonable way. True, it has problems; the market can be unfair, mean, and arbitrary, and sometimes it is downright awful. Why then do economists support it? For the same reason that Oliver Wendell Holmes supported democracy—it is a lousy system, but, based on experience with alternatives, it is better than all the others we've thought of.

The primary debate among economists is not about using markets; it is about how markets should be structured, and whether they should be modified and adjusted by government regulation. Those are much harder questions, and on these questions, opinions differ enormously.

The primary debate among economists is not about using markets but about how markets are structured.

Capitalism and Socialism

The view that markets are a reasonable way to organize society has not always been shared by all economists. Throughout history strong arguments have been made against markets. These arguments are both philosophical and practical. The philosophical argument against the market is that it brings out the worst in people—it glorifies greed. It encourages people to beat out others rather than to be cooperative. As an alternative some economists have supported socialism. In theory **socialism** is *an economic system based on individuals' goodwill toward others, not on their own self-interest, and in which, in principle, society decides what, how, and for whom to produce*. The concept of socialism developed as a description of a hypothetical economic system to be contrasted with the predominant market-based economic system of the time, which was called capitalism. **Capitalism** is defined as *an economic system based on the market in which the ownership of the means of production resided with a small group of individuals called capitalists*.

Q-2 Which would be more likely to attempt to foster individualism: socialism or capitalism?

You can best understand the idea behind theoretical socialism by thinking about how decisions are made in a family. In most families, benevolent parents decide who gets what, based on the needs of each member of the family. When Sabin gets a new coat and his sister Sally doesn't, it's because Sabin needs a coat while Sally already has two coats that fit her and are in good condition. Victor may be slow as molasses, but from his family he still gets as much as his superefficient brother Jerry gets. In fact, Victor may get more than Jerry because he needs extra help.

Q-3 Are there any activities in a family that you believe should be allocated by a market? What characteristics do those activities have?

Markets have little role in most families. In my family, when food is placed on the table we don't bid on what we want, with the highest bidder getting the food. In my family, every person can eat all he or she wants, although if one child eats more than a fair share, that child gets a lecture from me on the importance of sharing. "Be thoughtful; be considerate. Think of others first" are lessons that many families try to teach.

In theory, socialism was an economic system that tried to organize society in the same way as most families are organized, trying to see that individuals get what they need. Socialism tried to take other people's needs into account and adjust people's own wants in accordance with what's available. In socialist economies, individuals were urged to look out for the other person; if individuals' inherent goodness does not make them consider the general good, government would make them. In contrast, a capitalist economy expected people to be selfish; it relied on markets and competition to direct that selfishness to the general good.[2]

Socialism is, in theory, an economic system that tries to organize society in the same way as most families are organized—all people contribute what they can, and get what they need.

[2]As you probably surmised, the above distinction is too sharp. Even capitalist societies wanted people to be selfless, but not too selfless. Children in capitalist societies were generally taught to be selfless at least in dealing with friends and family. The difficulty parents and societies face is finding a midpoint between the two positions: selfless but not too selfless; selfish but not too selfish.

As I stated above, the term *socialism* originally developed as a description of a hypothetical, not an actual, economic system. Actual socialist economies came into being only in the early 1900s, and when they developed they differed enormously from the hypothetical socialist economies that writers had described earlier.

In practice socialist governments had to take a strong role in guiding the economy. Socialism became known as an economic system based on government ownership of the means of production, with economic activity governed by central planning. Such economies were often called **Soviet-style socialist economies**—*economies that used administrative control or central planning to solve the coordination problems: what, how, and for whom*—because it was the system used by the former Soviet Union. In that Soviet-style socialist economic system, government planning boards set society's goals and then directed individuals and firms as to how to achieve those goals.

Soviet-style socialist economies used administrative control or central planning to solve the coordination problems: what, how, and for whom.

Q-4 What is the difference between socialism in theory and socialism in practice?

For example, if government planning boards decided that whole-wheat bread was good for people, they directed firms to produce large quantities and priced it exceptionally low. Planners, not prices, coordinated people's actions. The results were often not quite what the planners desired. Bread prices were so low that pig farmers fed bread to their pigs even though pig feed would have been better for the pigs and bread was more costly to produce. At the low price the quantity of bread demanded was so high that there were bread shortages; consumers had to stand in long lines to buy bread for their families.

As is often the case, over time the meaning of the word *socialism* expanded and evolved further. It was used to describe the market economies of Western Europe, which by the 1960s had evolved into economies that had major welfare support systems and governments that were very much involved in their market economies. For example, Sweden, even though it relied on markets as its central coordinating institution, was called a socialist economy because its taxes were high and it provided a cradle-to-grave welfare system.

When the Union of Soviet Socialist Republics (USSR) broke apart, Russia and the countries that evolved out of the USSR adopted a market economy as their organizing framework. China, which is ruled by the Communist Party, also adopted many market institutions. As they did, the terms *capitalism* and *socialism* fell out of favor. Since the 1990s, people have talked little about the differences in economic systems such as capitalism and socialism; instead they have talked about the differences in the institutions of the various economies. Most economies today are differentiated primarily by the degree to which their economies rely on markets, not whether they are a market, capitalist, or socialist economy.[3]

Since the 1990s people have talked little about differences in economic systems; instead they have talked about differences in institutions.

Even countries that call themselves socialist economies are, to many observers, hardly differentiable from market economies. For example, even as China began to adopt market institutions such as stock markets and private ownership of businesses, the Communist Party maintained its control of government, arguing that in doing so it was maintaining a socialist economy. The result was a tension between the political and economic sectors. The Communist Party was defined as a party of workers, and "capitalists" (owners of private businesses, and individuals who received much of their income from stock) were prevented from joining. Communist leaders feared that the rising capitalist power base with no political representation would lead to political instability. In 2002, the Chinese Communist Party resolved the tension by taking the unprecedented step of allowing capitalists to be members. In many people's eyes that

[3]Cuba and North Korea are the two countries that still saw themselves as Soviet-style socialist economies in the early 2000s.

Tradition and Today's Economy

Applying the Tools

In a tradition-based society, the social and cultural forces create an inertia (a tendency to resist change) that predominates over economic and political forces.

"Why did you do it that way?"

"Because that's the way we've always done it."

Tradition-based societies had markets, but they were peripheral, not central, to economic life. In feudal times what was produced, how it was produced, and for whom it was produced were primarily decided by tradition.

In today's U.S. economy, the market plays the central role in economic decisions. But that doesn't mean that tradition is dead. As I said in Chapter 1, tradition still plays a significant role in today's society, and, in many aspects of society, tradition still overwhelms the invisible hand. Consider the following:

1. The persistent view that women should be homemakers rather than factory workers, consumers rather than producers.
2. The raised eyebrows when a man is introduced as a nurse, secretary, homemaker, or member of any other profession conventionally identified as women's work.
3. Society's unwillingness to permit the sale of individuals or body organs.
4. Parents' willingness to care for their children without financial compensation.

Each of these tendencies reflects tradition's influence in Western society. Some are so deeply rooted that we see them as self-evident. Some of tradition's effects we like; others we don't—but we often take them for granted. Economic forces may work against these traditions, but the fact that they're still around indicates the continued strength of tradition in our market economy.

change meant the end of what was known as communism and the transformation of the party into a ruling autocracy with little connection to communism.

Evolving Economic Systems[4]

An important lesson of the above discussion is that economic systems and the institutions that make them up are constantly evolving, and will likely continue to evolve. Let's consider that evolution briefly. What became known as capitalism came into widespread existence in the mid-1700s; socialism came into existence in the early 1900s. Before capitalism and socialism, other forms of economic systems existed, including **feudalism**—*an economic system in which traditions rule*. In feudalism if your parents were serfs (small farmers who lived on a manor), you would be a serf. Feudalism dominated the Western world from about the 8th century to the 15th century.

Feudalism is an economic system in which traditions rule.

Throughout the feudalistic period merchants and artisans (small manufacturers who produced goods by hand) grew in importance and wealth, and eventually their increased importance led to a change in the economic system from feudalism to **mercantilism**—*an economic system in which government determines the what, how, and for whom decisions by doling out the rights to undertake certain economic activities*.

Mercantilism is an economic system in which government doles out the rights to undertake economic activities.

Mercantilism remained the dominant economic system until the 1700s, when the **Industrial Revolution**—*a time when technology and machines rapidly modernized industrial production and mass-produced goods replaced handmade goods*—led to a decrease in power

[4]The appendix to this chapter traces the development of economic systems from feudalism to mercantilism to capitalism to socialism to modern-day forms of market economies in a bit more detail.

The Rise of Markets in Perspective

Beyond the Tools

Back in the Middle Ages, markets developed spontaneously. "You have something I want; I have something you want. Let's trade" is a basic human attitude we see in all aspects of life. Even children quickly get into trading: chocolate ice cream for vanilla, a candy bar for a ride on a motor scooter. Markets institutionalize such trading by providing a place where people know they can go to trade. New markets are continually being formed. Today there are markets for baseball cards, pork bellies (which become bacon and pork chops), rare coins, and so on. The Internet, with sites like eBay, is expanding markets enormously, allowing ordinary people to trade with people thousands of miles away.

Throughout history, societies have tried to prevent some markets from operating because they feel those markets are ethically wrong or have undesirable side effects. Societies have the power to prevent markets, to make some kinds of markets illegal. In parts of the United States, the addictive drug market, the baby market, and the sex market, to name a few, are illegal. In Soviet-style socialist countries, markets in a much wider range of goods (such as clothes, cars, and soft drinks) and activities (such as private business for individual profit) have been illegal.

But, even if a society prevents the market from operating, society cannot escape the invisible hand. If there's excess supply, there will be downward pressure on prices; if there's excess demand, there will be upward pressure on prices. To maintain an equilibrium in which the quantity supplied does not equal the quantity demanded, a society needs a strong force to prevent the invisible hand from working. In the Middle Ages, that strong force was religion. The Church told people that if they got too far into the market mentality—if they followed their self-interest—they'd go to Hell.

Until recently, in socialist society the state provided the preventive force. The educational system in socialist countries emphasized a more communal set of values. They taught students that a member of socialist society does not try to take advantage of other human beings but, rather, lives by the philosophy "From each according to his ability; to each according to his need."

For whatever reason—whether it be that true socialism wasn't really tried, or that people's self-interest is too strong—the "from each according to his ability; to each according to his need" approach didn't work in socialist countries. They have switched (some say succumbed) to greater reliance on the market.

---

of small producers, an increase in power of capitalists, and eventually to a revolution instituting capitalism as the dominant economic system.

I mention feudalism and mercantilism because aspects of both continue in economies today. For example, governments in Japan and Germany play significant roles in directing their economies. Their economic systems are sometimes referred to as *neomercantilist economies*.

Revolutionary shifts that give rise to new economic systems are not the only way economic systems change. Systems also evolve internally, as I discussed above. For example, the U.S. economy, is and has always been a market economy, but it has changed over the years, evolving with changes in social customs, political forces, and the strength of markets. In the 1930s, during the Great Depression, the U.S. economy integrated a number of what might be called socialist institutions into its existing institutions. Distribution of goods was no longer, even in theory, only according to ability; need also played a role. Governments began to play a larger role in the economy, taking control over some of the *how*, *what*, and *for whom* decisions. In the 1990s, the process was reversed. The United States became even more market oriented and the government tried to pull back its involvement in the market in favor of private enterprise. Whether that movement will continue remains to be seen, but we can expect institutions to continue to change.

Figure 3-1 Diagrammatic Representation of a Market Economy
This circular flow diagram of the economy is a good way to organize your thinking about the aggregate economy. As you can see, the three sectors—households, government, and business—interact in a variety of ways.

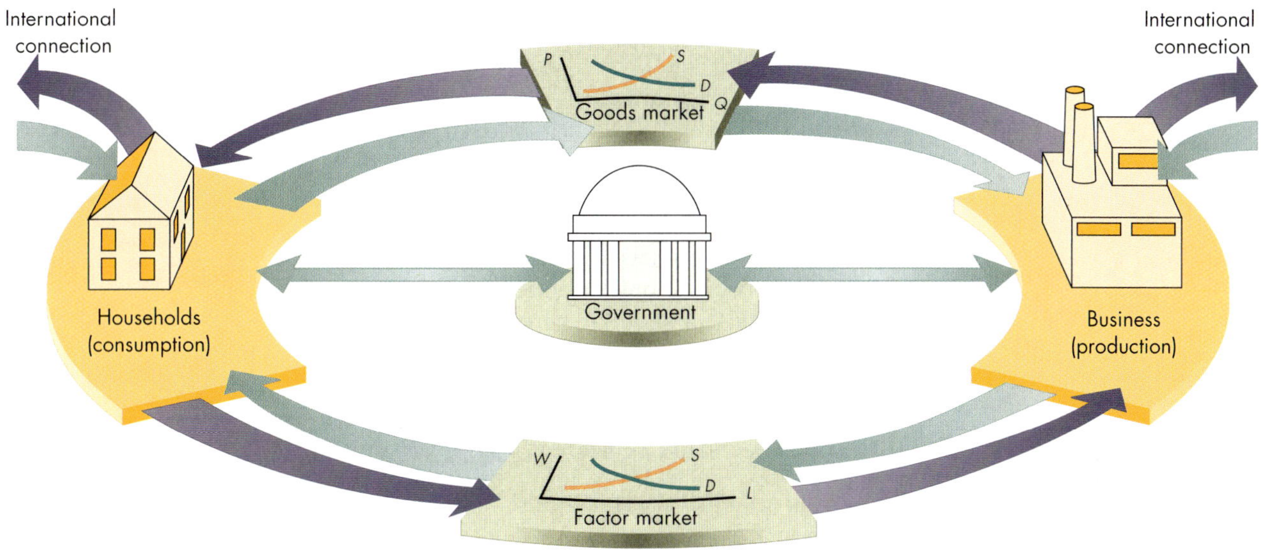

THE U.S. ECONOMY

Q-5 Into what three groups are market economies generally broken up?

Now that we have put the U.S. economic system in historical perspective, let's consider some of its main institutions. The U.S. economy can be divided up into three groups: businesses, households, and government, as Figure 3-1 shows. Households supply labor and other factors of production to businesses and are paid by businesses for doing so. The market where this interaction takes place is called a *factor market*. Businesses produce goods and services and sell them to households and government. The market where this interaction takes place is called the *goods market*.

Each of the three groups is interconnected; moreover, the entire U.S. economy is interconnected with the world economy. Notice also the arrows going out to and coming in from both business and households. Those arrows represent the connection of an economy to the world economy. It consists of interrelated flows of goods (exports and imports) and money (capital flows). Finally, consider the arrows connecting government with households and business. Government taxes business and households. It buys goods and services from business and buys labor services from households. Then, with some of its tax revenue, it provides services (e.g., roads, education) to both business and households and gives some of its tax revenue directly back to individuals. In doing so, it redistributes income. But government also serves a second function. It oversees the interaction of business and households in the goods and factor markets. Government, of course, is not independent. The United States, for instance, is a democracy, so households vote to determine who shall govern. Similarly, governments are limited not only by what voters want but also by their relationships with other countries. They are part of an international community of countries, and they must keep up relations with other countries in the world. For example, the United States is a member of many international organizations and has signed international treaties in which it has agreed to limit its domestic actions, such as its ability to tax imports.

Now let's look briefly at the individual components.

Business

Web Note 3.2
Starting a Business

President Calvin Coolidge once said, "The business of America is business." That's a bit of an overstatement, but business is responsible for over 80 percent of U.S. production. (Government is responsible for the other 20 percent.) In fact, anytime a household decides to produce something, it becomes a business. **Business** is simply the name given to *private producing units in our society*.

Businesses in the United States decide *what* to produce, *how* much to produce, and *for whom* to produce it.

Businesses in the United States decide *what* to produce, *how* much to produce, and *for whom* to produce it. They make these central economic decisions on the basis of their own feelings, which are influenced by market incentives. Anyone who wants to can start a business, provided he or she can come up with the required cash and meet the necessary regulatory requirements. Each year, about 600,000 businesses are started.

Don't think of business as something other than people. Businesses are ultimately made up of a group of people organized together to accomplish some end. Although corporations account for about 90 percent of all sales, in terms of numbers of businesses, most are one or two person operations. Home-based businesses are easy to start. All you have to do is say you're in business, and you are. However, some businesses require licenses, permits, and approvals from various government agencies. That's one reason why **entrepreneurship** (*the ability to organize and get something done*) is an important part of business.

What Do U.S. Firms Produce?

Producing physical goods is only one of a society's economic tasks. Another task is to provide services (activities done for others). Services do not involve producing a physical good. When you get your hair cut, you buy a service, not a good. Much of the cost of the physical goods we buy actually is not a cost of producing the good, but is a cost of one of the most important services: distribution (getting the good to where the consumer is). After a good is produced, it has to get to the individuals who are going to consume it at the time they need it. If the distribution system gets botched up, it's as if the good had never been produced.

Let's consider an example. Take hot dogs at a baseball game. How many of us have been irked that a hot dog that costs 25¢ to fix at home costs $4 at a baseball game? But a hot dog at home isn't the same as a hot dog at a game. Distribution of the good is as important as production; you're paying the extra $3.75 for distribution, which is a central component of a service economy.

The importance of the service economy can be seen in modern technology companies. They provide information and methods of handling information, not physical goods. Operating systems, such as Linux and Windows, can be supplied over the Internet; no physical production is necessary. As the U.S. economy has evolved, the relative importance of services has increased. Today, services make up 51 percent of the U.S. economy, compared to 20 percent in 1947 and services are likely to continue to rise in importance in the future.

Consumer Sovereignty and Business

Although businesses decide what to produce, they are guided by consumer sovereignty.

To say that businesses decide what to produce isn't to say that **consumer sovereignty** (*the consumer's wishes determine what's produced*) doesn't reign in the United States. Businesses decide what to produce based on what they believe will sell. A key question a person in the United States should ask about starting a business is: Can I make a profit from it? **Profit** is *what's left over from total revenues after all the appropriate costs have been subtracted*. Businesses that guess correctly what the consumer wants generally make a profit. Businesses that guess wrong generally operate at a loss.

People are free to start businesses for whatever purposes they want. No one asks them: "What's the social value of your term paper assistance business, your Twinkies business, your pornography business, or your textbook publishing business?" Yet the U.S. economic system is designed to channel individuals' desire to make a profit into the general good of society. That's the invisible hand at work. As long as the business violates no law and conforms to regulations, people in the United States are free to start whatever business they want, if they can get the money to finance it.

Q-6 In the United States the invisible hand ensures that only socially valuable businesses are started. True or false? Why?

Forms of Business The three primary forms of business are sole proprietorships, partnerships, and corporations. Of the 25 million businesses in the United States, approximately 72 percent are sole proprietorships, 8 percent are partnerships, and 20 percent are corporations, as we see in Figure 3-2(a). In terms of total receipts, however, we get a quite different picture, with corporations far surpassing all other business forms, as Figure 3-2(b) shows. In fact, the largest 500 corporations account for about 80 percent of the total receipts of all U.S. businesses.

Q-7 Are most businesses in the United States corporations? If not, what are most businesses?

Sole proprietorships—*businesses that have only one owner*—are the easiest to start and have the fewest bureaucratic hassles. **Partnerships**—*businesses with two or more owners*—create possibilities for sharing the burden, but they also create unlimited liability for each of the partners. **Corporations**—*businesses that are treated as a person, and are legally owned by their stockholders who are not liable for the actions of the corporate "person"*—are the largest form of business when measured in terms of receipts. In corporations, ownership is separated from control of the firm. When a corporation is formed, it issues **stock** (*certificates of ownership in a company*), which is sold or given to individuals. Proceeds from the sale of that stock make up what is called the *equity capital* of a company.

Corporations were developed as institutions to make it easier for company owners (i.e., stockholders) to be separated from company management. A corporation provides the owners with **limited liability**—*the stockholder's liability is limited to the amount that stockholder has invested in the company*. With the other two forms of business, owners can lose everything they possess even if they have only a small amount invested in the company, but in a corporation the owners can lose only what they have invested in that corporation. If you've invested $100, you can lose only $100. In the other kinds of business, even if you've invested only $100, you could lose everything; the business's losses must be covered by the individual owners. Corporations' limited liability makes it easier for

Figure 3-2 (a and b) Forms of Business
The charts divide firms by the type of ownership. Approximately 72 percent of businesses in the United States are sole proprietorships (a). In terms of annual receipts, however, corporations surpass all other forms (b).

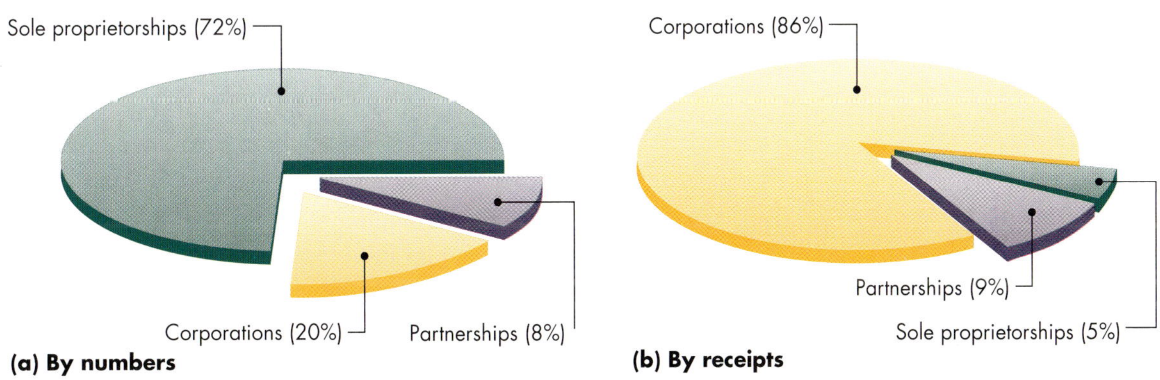

Source: *Statistics of Income*, IRS, Summer 2002 (www.irs.ustreas.gov).

them to attract investment capital. Corporations pay taxes, but they also offer their individual owners ways of legally avoiding taxes.[5]

The advantages and disadvantages of each are summarized in the following table:

Advantages and Disadvantages of Various Forms of For-Profit Businesses

	Sole Proprietor	Partnership	Corporation
Advantages	1. Minimum bureaucratic hassle 2. Direct control by owner	1. Ability to share work and risks 2. Relatively easy to form	1. No personal liability 2. Increasing ability to get funds 3. Ability to shed personal income and gain added expenses
Disadvantages	1. Limited ability to get funds 2. Unlimited personal liability	1. Unlimited personal liability (even for partner's blunder) 2. Limited ability to get funds	1. Legal hassle to organize 2. Possible double taxation of income 3. Monitoring problems

Finance and Business Much of what you hear in the news about business concerns financial assets—assets that acquire value from an obligation of someone else to pay. Stocks are one example of a financial asset; bonds are another. Financial assets are traded in markets such as the New York Stock Exchange. Trading in financial markets can make people rich (or poor) quickly. Stocks and bonds can also provide a means through which corporations can finance expansions and new investments.

An important tool investors use to decide where to invest is the accounting statements firms provide. From these, individuals judge how profitable firms are, and how profitable they are likely to be in the future. In the early 2000s, investors' trust in firms was shattered by a series of accounting frauds, which kept many people from investing in stocks and decreased the efficiency of the financial system.

E-Commerce and the Digital Economy Stocks were particularly important in the late 1990s to the development and expansion of new ".com" (read: dot-com) companies based on **e-commerce** (*buying and selling over the Internet*). E-commerce comes in a variety of forms, depending on who is buying and selling from whom. The following table provides the standard classifications. (The *B* refers to businesses and the C consumers.)

B2B	B2C
C2B	C2C

Notice that e-commerce includes business selling to business (B2B), business selling to consumers (B2C), consumers selling to business (C2B), and consumers selling to consumers (C2C). Most of you will see the influence of e-commerce in the B2C and C2C

[5]As laws have evolved, the sharp distinctions among forms of businesses have blurred. Today there are many types of corporations and types of partnerships that have varying degrees of limited liabilities.

Knowing the Tools

Stocks are usually traded on a *stock exchange*—a formal market in which stocks are bought and sold. The figure below shows a typical stock exchange listing. Each stock sold on this stock exchange—the New York Stock Exchange—has only one price listed. That's because the exchange has a "specialist" market-maker system, in which a particular broker markets a particular group of stocks. This specialist always stands ready to buy or sell shares of a stock at some price. The specialist sets a price and then varies it according to whether he or she is receiving more buy orders or more sell orders.

In order to buy or sell a stock, you contact a stockbroker (or simply contact the company through the Web—it's cheaper that way) and say you want to buy or sell whatever stock you've decided on—say Ford Motor Company. The commission you're charged for having the broker sell you the stock (or sell it for you) varies. It usually starts at some minimum between $10 and $30, and then is so much per share.

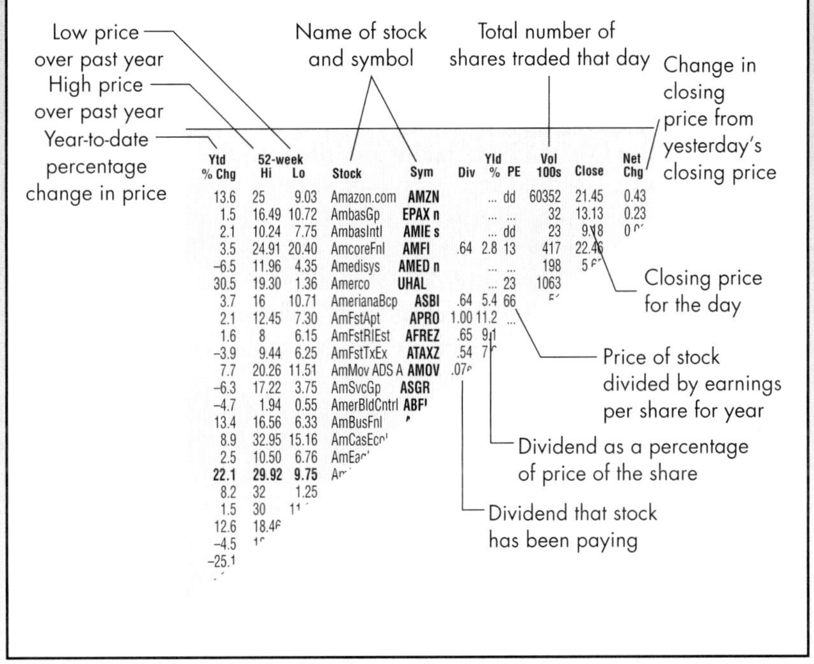

Source: *The Wall Street Journal*, Jan. 10, 2003. Reprinted by permission of *The Wall Street Journal* © 2003 Dow Jones & Company, Inc. All rights reserved worldwide.

There are a number of stock exchanges. The two most familiar in the United States are the New York Stock Exchange and the National Association of Securities Dealers Automated Quotations (Nasdaq). Somewhere around 90 million individuals own stock they bought on the New York Stock Exchange.

To judge how stocks as a whole are doing, a number of indexes have been developed. These include Standard and Poor's (S&P 500), the Wilshire Index, the Russell 2000, and the Dow Jones Industrial Average. The Dow Jones is the one you're most likely to hear about in the news.

When a share of a corporation's existing stock is sold on the stock exchange, corporations get no money from that sale. The sale is simply a transfer of ownership from one individual (or organization) to another. The only time a corporation gets money from the sale of stock is when it first issues the shares.

areas. Amazon.com and eBay are examples. But even more significant gains are now being made in the B2B area. With increasing frequency, companies are advertising specifications for needed parts and are accepting bids from a variety of new companies all over the world. The result is increased competition for existing suppliers, lower prices, and increased productivity—the output that comes out of a given amount of inputs.

E-commerce is growing in importance in the other areas too. More and more individuals are buying cars, books, and prescription drugs on the Internet. Even when they don't buy on the Internet, they will often compare prices on the Internet before making a purchase. Traditional "brick-and-mortar" firms that don't adapt to this new reality will not stay competitive and will be forced out of business. Car dealers, for example, now face consumers who have shopped dealer prices and dealer costs on the Internet. Similarly, local bookstores must compete with Amazon.com, which they do by both reducing their prices and providing services that can be provided only on-site, such as book groups and cafés to make the shopping experience more enjoyable. Other brick-and-mortar companies are starting their own Internet divisions, and will combine with Internet providers. For example, Lands' End was recently bought by Sears, and the combined company will offer goods in Sears stores, over the Internet, and by catalog.

E-commerce brings people together at a low cost in a virtual marketplace where geographic location doesn't matter.

E-commerce brings people together at a low cost in a virtual marketplace where geographic location doesn't matter. By reducing the importance of location, e-commerce broadens the potential marketplace. No longer is Main Street, USA, or The Mall, the market; the market is much broader, and can be as wide as the world. This gives companies for which location is not important a comparative advantage by reducing the need for buildings, shelving, or a large retail staff. E-commerce also changes the nature of the office. Firms can have employees all over the world, hiring those people who are the best in their field and creating virtual office space with chat rooms and group e-mails. By reducing overhead, the Internet and e-commerce reduce the costs of production and product prices.

As people touted the new Internet companies as the wave of the future, investors entered the market, bidding up the prices of Internet stock. Stocks of dot-com companies sold for enormous values, making many dot-com millionaires. Most economists advised people that the technology stock market had a financial bubble, which would likely burst. In fact, the previous edition of this textbook (and most other economics textbooks) warned readers of that likely fate. In 2000, the bubble burst; prices of the dot-coms' stocks fell enormously, and many dot-com companies went out of business. What had been called the new economy was shown to simply be the evolving old economy.

Whereas in the late 1990s most economists were saying that dot-com companies were overvalued and that the stock market overestimated the immediate impact of the Internet on the economy, economists today are much more open to arguments about the importance of the Internet in the economy. The difference is that today the discussion is about evolution, not revolution. Most economists agree that, over time, the Internet and new technology will substantially change the way business is done, and the way the economy operates.

E-commerce adds competition, increases information, and reduces the importance of geography.

Why is e-commerce an important new development? Because it adds significant competition to the economy, increases the amount of information available to consumers, and reduces the importance of geography and location for firms. These changes will place pressure on existing firms to lower prices and to redefine their business models. E-commerce's long-run effect on the U.S. economy is uncertain but what is not uncertain is that it will have an impact. To understand our economy is to understand that it has always been evolving and will continue to evolve in the future.

Households

The second classification we'll consider in this overview of U.S. economic institutions is households. **Households** (*groups of individuals living together and making joint decisions*) are the most powerful economic institution. They ultimately control government and business, the other two economic institutions. Households' votes in the political arena determine government policy; their decisions about supplying labor and capital determine what businesses will have available to work with; and their spending decisions or expenditures (the "votes" they cast with their dollars) determine what business will be able to sell.

In the economy, households vote with their dollars.

The Power of Households While the ultimate power does in principle reside with the people and households, we, the people, have assigned much of that power to representatives. As I discussed above, corporations are only partially responsive to owners of their stocks, and much of that ownership is once-removed from individuals. Ownership of 1,000 shares in a company with a total of 2 million shares isn't going to get you any influence over the corporation's activities. As a stockholder, you simply accept what the corporation does.

A major decision that corporations make independently of their stockholders concerns what to produce. True, ultimately we, the people, decide whether we will buy what business produces, but business spends a lot of money telling us what services we want, what products make us "with it," what books we want to read, and the like. Most economists believe that consumer sovereignty reigns—that we are not fooled or controlled by advertising. Still, it is an open question in some economists' minds whether we, the people, control business or the business representatives control people.

Consumer sovereignty reigns, but it works indirectly by influencing businesses.

Because of this assignment of power to other institutions, in many spheres of the economy households are not active producers of output but merely passive recipients of income, primarily in their role as suppliers of labor.

Suppliers of Labor The largest source of household income is wages and salaries (the income households get from labor). Households supply the labor with which businesses produce and government governs. The total U.S. labor force is about 140 million people, about 4.3 percent (5.9 million) of whom were unemployed in 1999. The average U.S. workweek is 42.4 hours for males and 36.2 hours for females. The average pay in the United States was $618 per week for males and $473 for females, which translates to $15.45 per hour for males and $11.83 for females. Of course, that average represents enormous variability and depends on the occupation and region of the country where one is employed. For example, lawyers often earn $100,000 per year; physicians earn about $150,000 per year; and CEOs of large corporations often make $2 million per year or more. A beginning McDonald's employee generally makes about $12,000 per year.

The table below shows predicted growth rates of certain jobs. Notice that many of the fastest-growing jobs are in service industries; many of the fastest declining are in manufacturing and agriculture. This is not surprising, since the United States has become largely a service economy.

Fastest-Growing Jobs*	Fastest-Declining Jobs*
Computer engineers (100%)	Railroad switch operators (−61%)
Computer support specialists (97%)	Telephone operators (−35%)
Computer software engineers (90%)	Loan interviewers and clerks (−28%)
Network administrators (82%)	Farmers and ranchers (−25%)

*Projection for 2000–2010, based on moderate growth assumptions.

Source: *Employment and Earnings,* Bureau of Labor Statistics, and Occupational Outlook Handbook, 2002–2003 (http://stats.bls.gov).

Government

The third major U.S. economic institution I'll consider is government, which I introduced you to in Chapter 2. Government plays two general roles in the economy. It's both a referee (setting the rules that determine relations between business and households) and an actor (collecting money in taxes and spending that money on its own projects, such as defense and education). Let's first consider government's role as an actor.

Figure 3-3 (a and b) Income and Expenditures of State and Local Governments
The charts give you a sense of the importance of state and local governments—where they get (**a**) and where they spend (**b**) their revenues.

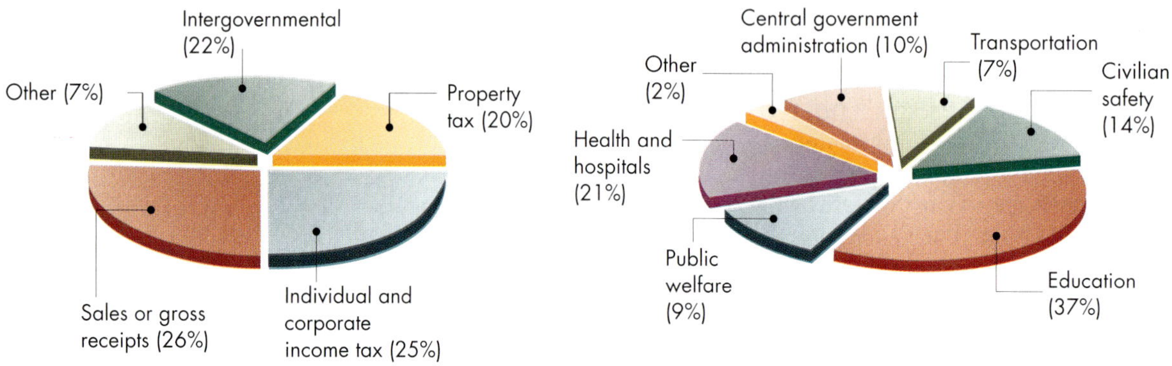

(a) Income **(b) Expenditures**

Source: *Survey of Current Business*, 2002, Bureau of Economic Analysis (www.bea.doc.gov), and *State and Local Government Finance Estimates*, Bureau of the Census (www.census.gov/govs/www/estimate.html).

Web Note 3.3
Government Websites

Government as an Actor The United States has a federal government system, which means we have various levels of government (federal, state, and local), each with its own powers. Together they consume about 20 percent of the country's total output and employ over 21 million individuals. The various levels of government also have a number of programs that redistribute income through taxation or through an array of social welfare and assistance programs designed to help specific groups.

State and local governments employ over 18 million people and spend over $1 trillion a year. As you can see in Figure 3-3(a), state and local governments get much of their income from taxes: property taxes, sales taxes, and state and local income taxes. They spend their tax revenues on public welfare, administration, education (education through high school is available free in U.S. public schools), and roads, as Figure 3-3(b) shows.

Q-8 The largest percentage of federal expenditures is in what general category?

Probably the best way to get an initial feel for the federal government and its size is to look at the various categories of its tax revenues and expenditures in Figure 3-4(a). Notice income taxes make up about 50 percent of the federal government's revenue, while Social Security taxes make up about 36 percent. That's more than 80 percent of the federal government's revenues, most of which shows up as a deduction from your paycheck. In Figure 3-4(b), notice that the federal government's two largest categories of spending are income security and national defense, with expenditures on interest payments close behind.

Government as a Referee Even if government spending made up only a small proportion of total expenditures, government would still be central to the study of economics. The reason is that, in a market economy, government sets the rules of interaction between households and businesses, and acts as a referee, changing the rules when it sees fit. Government decides whether economic forces will be allowed to operate freely.

Some examples of U.S. laws regulating the interaction between households and businesses today are:

Figure 3-4 (a and b) Income and Expenditures of the Federal Government
The pie charts show the sources and uses of federal government revenue. It is important to note that, when the government runs a deficit, expenditures exceed income and the difference is made up by borrowing, so the size of the income and expenditure pies may not be equal.

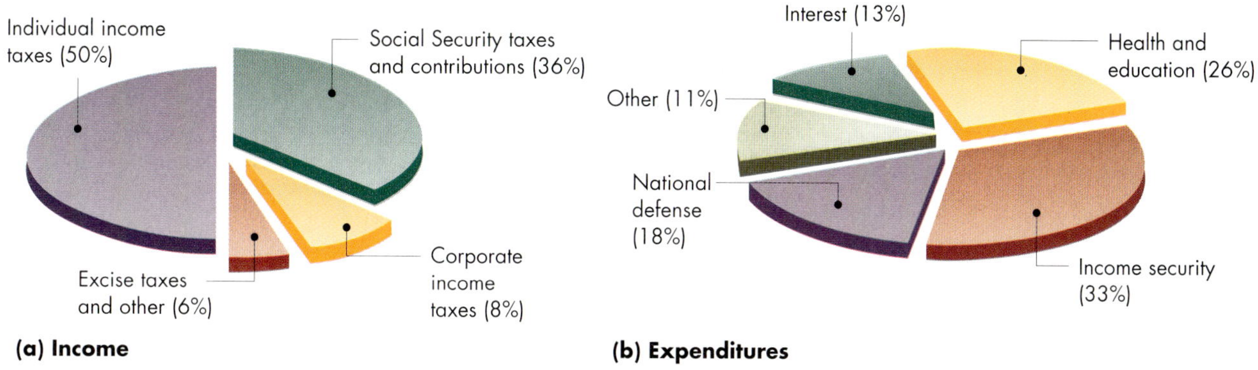

Source: *Survey of Current Business*, 2002, Bureau of Economic Analysis (www.bea.doc.gov).

1. Businesses are not free to hire and fire whomever they want. They must comply with equal opportunity and labor laws. Even closing a plant requires 60 days' notice for many kinds of firms.
2. Many working conditions are subject to government regulation: safety rules, wage rules, overtime rules, hours of work rules, and the like.
3. Businesses cannot meet with other businesses to agree on prices they will charge.
4. In some businesses workers must join a union to work at certain jobs.

Most of these laws evolved over time. Up until the 1930s, household members, in their roles as workers and consumers, had few rights. Businesses were free to hire and fire at will and, if they chose, to deceive and take advantage of consumers.

Over time, new laws to curb business abuses have been passed, and government agencies have been formed to enforce these laws. Many people think the pendulum has swung too far the other way. They believe businesses are saddled with too many regulatory burdens.

One big question that I'll address throughout this book is: What referee role should the government play in an economy? For example, should government use its taxing powers to redistribute income from the rich to the poor? Should it allow mergers between companies? Should it regulate air traffic? Should it regulate prices? Should it attempt to stabilize fluctuations of aggregate income?

THE U.S. ECONOMY AND GLOBALIZATION

What we've done so far in this chapter is to put the U.S. economy in historical and institutional perspective. In this last section we put it into perspective relative to the world economy. By doing so, we gain a number of insights into the U.S. economy. First, it is successful; the U.S. economy makes up 25 percent of world output and consumption, a percentage that is much larger than its relative size by geographic area (6 percent of world's land mass) or by population (less than 5 percent of world population). Second, it is becoming more integrated; it is impossible to talk about U.S. economic institutions without considering how those institutions integrate with the world economy.

Our International Competitors

Knowing the Tools

The world economy is often divided into three main areas or trading blocs: the Americas, Europe and Africa, and East Asia. These trading blocs are shown in the map below.

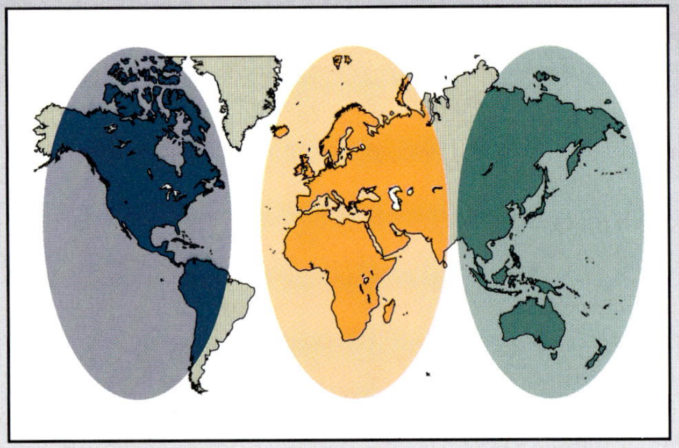

The three dominant economies in these trading blocs are the United States, Germany, and Japan. Each area has a major currency. In the Americas, it is the dollar; in Europe it is the euro, a currency recently created by the European Union; and in East Asia it is the Japanese yen.

The table below gives you a sense of the similarities and differences in the economies of the United States, Japan, and Europe.

	United States	Japan	European Union
Area (square miles)	3,536,341	145,814	915,330
Population	290 million	127 million	378 million
GDP, 2001	$10.6 trillion	$3.45 trillion	$8.5 trillion
Percentage of world output	22%	7%	18%
GDP per capita	$36,800	$27,000	$22,500
Natural resources	Coal, copper, lead, and others	Very few mineral resources, fish	Coal, iron ore, natural gas, fish, and others
Exports as a percentage of GDP	10%	9%	11%
Imports as a percentage of GDP	14%	8%	12%
Currency value (as of January, 2002)	Dollar ($1 = $1)	Yen (¥133 = $1)	Euro (€0.90 = $1)

Source: *Eurostat Yearbook 2002* (europa.eu.int/comm/eurostat), *CIA World Factbook 2002* (www.cia.gov)

Global Corporations

Global corporations are corporations with substantial operations on both the production and sales sides in more than one country.

Consider corporations. Most large corporations today are not U.S., German, or Japanese corporations; they are **global corporations** (*corporations with substantial operations on both the production and sales sides in more than one country*). Just because a car has a Japanese or German name doesn't mean that it was produced abroad. Many Japanese and German companies now have manufacturing plants in the United States, and many U.S. firms have manufacturing plants abroad. Others, such as Chrysler and Daimler Benz (they make Mercedes) have merged. When goods are produced by global corporations, corporate names don't always tell much about where a good is produced. As global corporations' importance has grown, most manufacturing decisions are made in reference to the international market, not the U.S. domestic market. This means that the consumer sovereignty that guides decisions of firms is becoming less and less U.S. consumer sovereignty, and more and more global consumer sovereignty.

Global corporations offer enormous benefits for countries. They create jobs; they bring new ideas and new technologies to a country, and they provide competition for domestic companies, keeping them on their toes. But global corporations also pose a

A World Economic Geography Quiz

Applying the Tools

Economic geography isn't much covered in most economics courses because it requires learning enormous numbers of facts, and college courses aren't a good place to learn facts. College is designed to teach you how to interpret and relate facts. Unfortunately, if you don't know facts, much of what you learn in college isn't going to do you much good. You'll be relating and interpreting air. The following quiz presents some facts about the world economy. Below I list characteristics of 20 countries or regions in random order. Beneath the characteristics, in alphabetical order, I list 20 countries or regions. Associate the characteristics with the country or region.

If you answer 15 or more correctly, you have a reasonably good sense of economic geography. If you don't, I strongly suggest learning more facts. The study guide for this text has other projects, information, and examples. An encyclopedia has even more, and your library has a wealth of information. You could spend the entire semester following the economic news carefully, paying attention to where various commodities are produced and picturing in your mind a map whenever you hear about an economic event.

____ 1. Former British colony, now small independent island country famous for producing rum.

____ 2. Large sandy country contains world's largest known oil reserves.

____ 3. Very large country with few people; produces 25 percent of the world's wool.

____ 4. Temperate country ideal for producing wheat, soybeans, fruits, vegetables, wine, and meat.

____ 5. Small tropical country produces abundant coffee and bananas.

____ 6. Has world's largest population and world's largest hydropower potential.

____ 7. Second-largest country in Europe; famous for wine and romance.

____ 8. Former Belgian colony with vast copper mines.

____ 9. European country; exports luxury clothing, footwear, and automobiles.

____ 10. Country that has depleted many of its natural resources but that has the highest level of GDP of any country in the world.

____ 11. Long, narrow country of four main islands; most thickly populated country in the world; second most technologically powerful economy in the world.

____ 12. The European Union's most populous and richest country; one important product is steel.

____ 13. Second-largest country in the world; a good neighbor to the United States; leading paper exporter.

____ 14. European country for centuries politically repressed; now becoming industrialized; chemicals are one of its leading exports.

____ 15. 96 percent of its people live on 4 percent of the land; much of the world's finest cotton comes from here.

____ 16. Politically and radically troubled African nation has world's largest concentration of gold.

____ 17. Huge, heavily populated country eats most of what it raises but is a major tea exporter.

____ 18. Country that is a top producer of oil and gold; has recently undergone major political and economic changes.

____ 19. Has only about 50 people per square mile but lots of trees; timber and fish exporter.

____ 20. Sliver of a country on Europe's Atlantic coast; by far the world's largest exporter of cork.

A. Argentina
B. Australia
C. Barbados
D. Canada
E. China
F. Costa Rica
G. Egypt
H. France
I. Germany
J. India
K. Italy
L. Japan
M. Portugal
N. Russia
O. Saudi Arabia
P. South Africa
Q. Spain
R. Sweden
S. United States
T. Democratic Republic of the Congo

Answers: 1–C, 2–O, 3–B, 4–A, 5–F, 6–E, 7–H, 8–T, 9–K, 10–S, 11–L, 12–I, 13–D, 14–Q, 15–G, 16–P, 17–J, 18–N, 19–R, 20–M.

number of problems for governments. One is their implication for domestic and international policy. A domestic corporation exists within a country and can be dealt with using policy measures within that country. A global corporation exists within many countries and there is no global government to regulate or control it. If it doesn't like the policies in one country—say taxes are too high or regulations too tight—it can shift its operations to other countries.

Global Markets

The rise of global corporations is a reflection of how integrated the world economy has become. Over the past 20 years markets have become more global in a number of other ways as well. Through the General Agreement on Tariffs and Trade, which became the **World Trade Organization (WTO)**—*an organization committed to getting countries to agree not to impose new tariffs or other trade restrictions except under certain limited conditions*—tariffs and other barriers to trade have been lowered significantly. Political tensions among world superpowers have eased, leading firms to be more confident that they can diversify their production and their sources of inputs. Communication costs have fallen dramatically, which has lowered the cost of searching for the lowest-cost source of inputs and location for production. The global economy gives firms a lot more places to search, and the Internet reduces the costs of that search significantly.

Because of globalization U.S. companies' strategic decision makers must take into account more than just domestic competitors. They face competition from foreign firms and see their potential market as the world, not just the United States.

Globalization has two effects on firms. The first is positive; it increases the size of the gain to the winner. Because the world economy is so much larger than the domestic economy, the rewards for winning globally are much larger than the rewards for winning domestically. The second effect is negative; globalization makes it much harder to win, or even to stay in business. A company may be the low-cost producer in a particular country yet may face foreign competitors that can undersell it. The global economy increases the number of competitors for the firm. Consider the automobile industry. Two companies are headquartered in the United States, but more than 20 automobile companies operate worldwide. U.S. automakers face stiff competition from foreign automakers; unless they meet that competition, they will not survive.

The global economy increases the number of competitors for the firm.

These two effects are, of course, related. When you compete in a larger market, you have to be better to survive, but if you do survive the rewards are greater.

Globalization increases competition by allowing greater specialization and division of labor, which, as Adam Smith first observed in *The Wealth of Nations*, increases growth and improves the standard of living for everyone. Thus, in many ways globalization is simply another name for increased specialization. Globalization allows (indeed, forces) companies to move operations to countries with a comparative advantage. As they do so, they lower costs of production. Globalization leads to companies specializing in smaller portions of the production process because the potential market is not just one country but the world. Such specialization can lead to increased productivity as firms learn from doing.

Globalization leads to specialization, which leads to increased productivity.

Web Note 3.4
Surviving in a Global Economy

Surviving in a Global Economy

In order to survive in the global economy, companies must be continually looking for ways to organize production that will improve efficiency and lower costs. One important way they are doing this is by breaking down the production process into its component parts and considering new ways of organizing not only production but also the firm.

Specialization in the modern economy involves dividing production (which includes manufacturing, distribution, sales, research, management, and advertising) into component parts, and searching for the cheapest method of producing each component. Firms may keep production within the company but parcel out portions of it to divisions located in different parts of the world. Or they may simply outsource (buy from another firm) the part of production that can be done more cheaply by other domestic or foreign firms. Globalization lets companies take advantage of cost differentials across countries for different aspects of production. An example of a cost differential is the cost of labor. Labor is a significant input to production whose costs differ widely among countries.

Q-9 How does globalization reduce the cost of production?

Table 3-1 lists hourly compensation for workers in various countries. For example, average hourly wages in manufacturing are $20.32 in the United States but only $5.70 in Taiwan.

Table 3-1 Hourly Compensation for Production Workers

Country	Cost in U.S. Dollars
United States	$20.32
Canada	15.64
Mexico	2.34
Japan	19.59
Korea	8.09
Taiwan	5.70
Germany	22.86
Hong Kong	5.96

Source: International Comparisons of Manufacturing Hourly Compensation Costs, 2002. Bureau of Labor Statistics (http://stats.bls.gov).

Labor-intensive parts of production might be relocated to Taiwan. Keep in mind that labor costs are only one part of the decision to relocate production. Firms also take into account differences in the quality of labor, the infrastructure, and regulations within countries. The fact remains, however, that barriers among countries have been lowered, allowing companies to consider moving parts of their operations across the world. Firms are using comparative advantage not just in producing an entire product but in producing portions of the product. Firms are reevaluating the entire production process, asking where the production process for each component should occur.

Consider automobiles again. GM, Ford, and DaimlerChrysler all have production facilities throughout the world. When you buy a GM car, its components will likely have come from 50 different companies, and a Toyota car may have more U.S.-made components than a GM car. Components of the U.S. Air Force's F-16 fighter aircraft are produced in 11 countries, and the aircraft is assembled in 4 countries.

Production within companies is often divided among many countries.

This specialization and division of labor due to globalization means that competition takes place not just in the market for finished products but in numerous layers of the production process. Global competition helps hold down prices and wages firms pay to the factors of production. Those layers that do not face significant global competition may still be able to use lower-cost inputs to production, while maintaining their own high product prices. For example, U.S. legal work, as yet, gets very little international competition because (1) services are difficult to transport cheaply, (2) countries regulate the practice of law within their borders, and (3) laws tend to be country-specific. Hence, the prices U.S. lawyers get for their services remain high. The manufacturing layer of production, however, is quite susceptible to foreign competition. This

Made in China?

Applying the Tools

Barbie and her companion Ken are as American as apple pie, and considering their origins gives us some insight into the modern U.S. economy and its interconnection with other countries. Barbie and Ken are not produced in the United States; they never were. When Barbie first came out in 1959 she was produced in Japan. Today, it is unclear where Barbie and Ken are produced. If you look at the box they come in, it says "Made in China," but looking deeper we find that Barbie and Ken are actually made in five different countries, each focusing on an aspect of production that reflects its comparative advantage. Japan produces the nylon hair. China provides much of what is normally considered manufacturing—factory spaces, labor, and energy for assembly—but it imports many of the components. The oil for the plastic comes from Saudi Arabia, which is refined into plastic pellets in Taiwan. The United States even provides some of the raw materials that go into the manufacturing process—it provides the cardboard, packing, paint pigments, and mold.

Michael Newman/Photoedit

The diversification of parts that go into the manufacturing of Barbie and Ken is typical of many goods today. As the world economy has become more integrated, the process of supplying components of manufacturing has become more and more spread out, as firms have divided up the manufacturing process in search of the least-cost location for each component.

But the global diversity in manufacturing and supply of components is only half the story of modern production. The other half is the shrinking of the relative importance of that manufacturing, and it is this other half that explains how the United States maintains its position in the world when so much of the manufacturing takes place elsewhere. It does so by maintaining its control over the distribution and marketing of the goods. In fact, of the $15 retail value of a Barbie or Ken, $12 can be accounted for by activities not associated with manufacturing—design, transportation, merchandising, and advertising. And, luckily for the United States, many of these activities are still done in the United States, allowing the country to maintain its high living standard even as manufacturing spreads around the globe.

competition has placed downward pressure on U.S. manufacturing prices. Faced with increasing foreign competition, manufacturing workers are forced to accept lower pay. If the workers don't accept lower pay, the company will outsource the manufacturing to a foreign country in which costs are lower.

Consider the letters for the game Scrabble. Until recently these wooden tiles were made in a small Vermont town. In 1998, a Hong Kong company offered to produce the tiles at a lower price, and now Vermont lumber is shipped to Hong Kong, where the Scrabble tiles are made and shipped back to the United States. Hasbro, which makes Scrabble, is still a U.S. company; its marketing and distribution is run from the United States, but the production of its tiles is outsourced to a foreign firm. This is only one of many possible examples.

Does Globalization Eliminate Jobs?

It is sometimes argued that global competition eliminates jobs in the United States. To some degree this is absolutely true, but it is important to see global trade as something that increases total production and simultaneously creates jobs. Lowering costs of production can lead to lower product prices, which benefits consumers. Lower prices boost sales and, as sales rise, demand for the inputs to production rises, which can raise the prices of inputs and/or profits. This potentially benefits laborers and others who supply the various inputs to production. Consumers, producers, and suppliers of the factors of production all can potentially benefit.

The reality is that over the past decade the U.S. economy has added 23 million jobs even though U.S. markets have faced increased global competition. How has that happened? U.S. firms, even small ones, more and more see themselves as global companies and are structuring themselves to compete on the global market. As they do so, their costs of production fall or the design of their products improves, putting them in a better position to sell their products. This increases the demand for those aspects of production—generally advertising, marketing, financial services, management, and distribution—which are still U.S.-based. This has helped keep the demand high for U.S. goods and, hence, increased the demand for U.S. labor.

Globalization eliminates jobs, but it also creates jobs.

Until recently, European firms have led a far more sheltered life. European governments' movement toward the **European Union (EU)** (*an economic and political union of a number of European countries*) and the euro, the common European currency, are both attempts to add broader competition within European markets and to better prepare European firms to compete in the global economy. Trade restrictions between EU members have been eliminated, and when the euro became the common currency of many member nations in 2002, comparison shopping became much easier.

Dealing with Globalization

To deal with the problems that globalization presents, institutions are changing. Some argue that to oversee global businesses, one needs a global government, with power to regulate businesses wherever they are. But, as we discussed in Chapter 2, no such government exists. The closest institution there is to a world government is the United Nations (UN), which according to critics is simply a debating society. It has no ability to tax and no ability to impose its will separate from the political and military power of its members. When the United States opposes a UN mandate, it can, and often does, ignore it. Hence, international problems must be dealt with through negotiation, consensus, bullying, and concessions.

Governments have, however, developed a variety of international institutions to promote negotiations and coordinate economic relations among countries. Besides the United Nations, these include the World Bank, the World Court, and the International Monetary Fund (IMF). These organizations have a variety of goals. For example, the World Bank is a multinational, international financial institution that works with developing countries to secure low-interest loans, channeling such loans to them to foster economic growth. The International Monetary Fund (IMF) is a multinational, international financial institution concerned primarily with monetary issues. It deals with international financial arrangements. When developing countries encountered financial problems in the 1980s and had large international debts that they could not pay, the IMF helped work on repayment plans.

In addition to these formal institutions, there are informal meetings of various countries. These include the Group of Five, which meets to promote negotiations and coordinate economic relations among countries. The Five are Japan, Germany, Britain, France, and the United States. The Group of Eight also meets to promote negotiations and coordinate economic relations among countries. The Eight are the five countries just named plus Canada, Italy, and Russia.

Since governmental membership in international organizations is voluntary, their power is limited. When the United States doesn't like a World Court ruling, it simply states that it isn't going to follow the ruling. When the United States is unhappy with

Since governmental membership in international organizations is voluntary, their power is limited.

Q-10 If the United States chooses not to follow a World Court decision, what are the consequences?

what the United Nations is doing, it withholds some of its dues. Other countries do the same from time to time. Other member countries complain but can do little to force compliance. It doesn't work that way domestically. If you decide you don't like U.S. policy and refuse to pay your taxes, you'll wind up in jail.

What keeps nations somewhat in line when it comes to international rules is a moral tradition: Countries want to (or at least want to look as if they want to) do what's "right." Countries will sometimes follow international rules to keep international opinion favorable to them. But perceived national self-interest often overrides international scruples.

Conclusion

This has been a whirlwind introduction to the U.S. economy and the challenges that globalization presents. The U.S. economy in the 21st century is a global economy with links through both its trade sector and its financial sector. To understand it, you must understand its components—business, households, and government—and their interrelationship.

The economy is undergoing significant changes because of technological change. E-commerce is growing exponentially and is making markets more global. On the Internet the location of a trade doesn't matter. Countries, however, pose barriers to trade, and there will likely be much conflict as the push for free trade comes up against national boundaries.

Summary

- A market economy is an economic system based on private property and the market. It gives private property rights to individuals and relies on market forces to solve the *what*, *how*, and *for whom* problems.
- In a market economy price is the mechanism through which people's desires are coordinated and goods are rationed. The U.S. economy today is a market economy.
- In principle, under socialism society solves the *what*, *how*, and *for whom* problems in the best interest of the individuals in society. It is based on individual's goodwill toward one another.
- In practice socialism became known as Soviet-style socialism, an economic system based on government ownership of the means of production, with economic activity governed by central planning.
- The predominant market-based system during the early 1900s was capitalism, an economic system based on the market in which the ownership of production resided with a small group of individuals called capitalists.
- In feudalism, tradition rules, in mercantilism, the government rules; in capitalism, the market rules.
- Economic systems are in a constant state of evolution.
- A diagram of the U.S. market economy shows the connections among businesses, households, and government. It also shows the U.S. economic connection to other countries.
- In the United States, businesses make the *what*, *how much*, and *for whom* decisions.

- Although businesses decide what to produce, they succeed or fail depending on their ability to meet consumers' desires. That's consumer sovereignty.
- The three main forms of business are corporations, sole proprietorships, and partnerships. Each has its advantages and disadvantages.
- Although households are the most powerful economic institution, they have assigned much of their power to government and business. Economics focuses on households' role as the supplier of labor.
- Government plays two general roles in the economy: (1) as a referee, and (2) as an actor.
- To understand the U.S. economy, one must understand its role in the world economy.
- Global corporations are corporations with significant operations in more than one country. They are increasing in importance.
- Globalization increases competition by providing more competitors to domestic firms at all levels of production and by allowing firms to specialize. Globalization also increases the gain to the industry leader by reducing costs of production and by increasing the size of the market.

KEY TERMS

business *(60)*
capitalism *(55)*
consumer sovereignty *(60)*
corporation *(61)*
e-commerce *(62)*
entrepreneurship *(60)*
European Union *(73)*
feudalism *(57)*
global corporation *(68)*
households *(64)*
Industrial Revolution *(57)*
limited liability *(61)*
market economy *(54)*
mercantilism *(57)*
partnership *(61)*
private property right *(54)*
profit *(60)*
socialism *(55)*
Soviet-style socialist economy *(56)*
sole proprietorship *(61)*
stock *(61)*
World Trade Organization (WTO) *(70)*

QUESTIONS FOR THOUGHT AND REVIEW

1. In a market economy, what is the central coordinating mechanism?
2. In Soviet-style socialism, what is the central coordinating mechanism?
3. How does a market economy solve the what, how, and for whom to produce problems?
4. How does Soviet-style socialism solve the what, how and for whom to produce problems?
5. Is capitalism or socialism the better economic system? Why?
6. What arguments can you give for supporting a socialist organization of a family and a market-based organization of the economy?
7. True or false? As economic systems have evolved, there has been less need for planning.
8. Why does an economy's strength ultimately reside in its people?
9. A market system is often said to be based on consumer sovereignty—the consumer determines what's to be produced. Yet business decides what's to be produced. Can these two views be reconciled? How? If not, why?
10. Why is entrepreneurship a central part of any business?
11. You're starting a software company in which you plan to sell software to your fellow students. What form of business organization would you choose? Why?
12. What are the two largest categories of federal government expenditures?
13. A good measure of a country's importance to the world economy is its area and population. True or false? Why?
14. What are the qualities of the Internet that has put competitive pressures on businesses?
15. What effect has globalization had on the ability of firms to specialize? How has this affected the competitive process?

Problems and Exercises

1. Tom Rollins heads a company called Teaching Co. He has taped lectures at the top universities, packaged the lectures on audio and videocassettes, and sells them for $90 and $150 per eight hour series.
   a. Discuss whether such an idea could be expanded to include college courses that one could take at home.
   b. What are the technical, social, and economic issues involved?
   c. If it is technically possible and cost effective, will the new venture be a success?
2. Economists Edward Lazear and Robert Michael have calculated that the average family spends two and a half times as much on each adult as they do each child.
   a. Does this mean that children are deprived and that the distribution is unfair?
   b. Do you think these percentages change with family income? If so, how?
   c. Do you think that the allocation would be different in a family in a Soviet-style socialist country than in a capitalist country? Why?
3. Poland, Bulgaria, and Hungary (all former socialist countries) were in the process of changing to a market economy in the early 1990s.
   a. Go to the library and find the latest information about their transitions.
   b. Explain what has happened in the markets, political structures, and social customs of those countries.
4. One of the specific problems Soviet-style socialist economies had was keeping up with capitalist countries technologically.
   a. Can you think of any reason inherent in a centrally planned economy that would make innovation difficult?
   b. Can you think of any reason inherent in a capitalist country that would foster innovation?
   c. Joseph Schumpeter, a famous Harvard economist of the 1930s, predicted that as firms in capitalist societies grew in size they would innovate less. Can you suggest what his argument might have been?
   d. Schumpeter's prediction did not come true. Modern capitalist economies have had enormous innovations. Can you provide explanations as to why?
5. In 2002 the hourly cost to employers per German industrial worker was $22.86. The hourly cost to employers per U.S. industrial worker was $20.32, while the average cost per Taiwanese industrial worker was $5.70.
   a. Give three reasons why firms produce in Germany rather than in a lower-wage country.
   b. Germany has just entered into an agreement with other EU countries that allows people in any EU country, including Greece and Italy, which have lower wage rates, to travel and work in any EU country, including high-wage countries. Would you expect a significant movement of workers from Greece and Italy to Germany right away? Why or why not?
   c. Workers in Thailand are paid significantly less than workers in Taiwan. If you were a company CEO, what other information would you want before you decided where to establish a new production facility?

Web Questions

1. Go to Levi Strauss's home page (www.levistrauss.com) and answer the following questions:
   a. Is Levi Strauss a sole proprietorship, partnership, or corporation? What reasons do you suspect it has chosen that form of business?
   b. Is Levi Strauss a global corporation? Explain your answer.
   c. Are the shares of Levi Strauss publicly traded?
2. The Social Security system is a program that is significant to the evolution of capitalism in the United States. Go to the Social Security Administration's home page (www.ssa.gov) and describe how changes in the Social Security system have moved the U.S. economy away from a market economy. What proposals are being discussed that will change the nature of Social Security? What does this say about the evolution of the U.S. economy?

Answers to Margin Questions

1. He is wrong. Property rights are required for a market to operate. Once property rights are allocated, the market will allocate goods, but the market cannot distribute the property rights that are required for the market to operate. *(54)*
2. Capitalism places much more emphasis on fostering individualism. Socialism tries to develop a system in which the individual's needs are placed second to society's needs. *(55)*

3. Most families allocate basic needs through control and command. The parents do (or try to do) the controlling and commanding. Generally they are well-intentioned, trying to meet their perception of their children's needs. However, some family activities that are not basic needs might be allocated through the market. For example, if one child wants a go-cart and is willing to do extra work at home in order to get it, go-carts might be allocated through the market, with the child earning chits that can be used for such nonessentials. *(55)*
4. In theory, socialism is an economic system based upon individuals' goodwill. In practice, socialism followed the Soviet model and involved central planning and government ownership of the primary means of production. *(56)*
5. Market economies are generally broken up into businesses, households, and government. *(59)*
6. False. In the United States individuals are free to start any type of business they want, provided it doesn't violate the law. The invisible hand sees to it that only those businesses that customers want earn a profit. The others lose money and eventually go out of business, so in that sense only businesses that customers want stay in business. *(61)*
7. As can be seen in Figure 3-2, most businesses in the United States are sole proprietorships, not corporations. Corporations, however, generate the most revenue. *(61)*
8. The largest percentage of federal expenditures is for income security. *(66)*
9. Globalization reduces the cost of production in two ways. First, it allows companies to specialize in smaller portions of the production process, which increases competition and lowers cost at all levels of the production process. Second, it allows companies to locate parts of the production process in those countries with comparative advantage in that portion of the production process. *(71)*
10. The World Court has no enforcement mechanism. Thus, when a country refuses to follow the court's decisions, the country cannot be directly punished except through indirect international pressures. *(74)*

Appendix A

The History of Economic Systems

In the text I made the distinction between market and economic forces: Economic forces have always existed—they operate in all aspects of our lives; but market forces have not always existed. Markets are social creations societies use to coordinate individuals' actions. Markets developed, sometimes spontaneously, sometimes by design, because they offered a better life for at least some—and usually a large majority of—individuals in a society.

To understand why markets developed, it is helpful to look briefly at the history of the economic systems from which our own system descended.

Feudal Society: Rule of Tradition

Let's go back in time to the year 1000 when Europe had no nation-states as we now know them. (Ideally, we would have gone back further and explained other economic systems, but, given the limited space, I had to draw the line somewhere—an example of a trade-off.) The predominant economic system at that time was feudalism. There was no coordinated central government, no unified system of law, no national patriotism, no national defense, although a strong religious institution simply called the Church fulfilled some of these roles. There were few towns; most individuals lived in walled manors, or "estates." These manors "belonged to" the "lord of the manor." (Occasionally the "lord" was a lady, but not often.) I say "belonged to" rather than "were owned by" because most of the empires or federations at that time were not formal nation-states that could organize, administer, and regulate ownership. No documents or deeds gave ownership of the land to an individual. Instead, tradition ruled, and in normal times nobody questioned the lord's right to the land. The land "belonged to" the lord because the land "belonged to" him—that's the way it was.

Without a central nation-state, the manor served many functions a nation-state would have served had it existed. The lord provided protection, often within a walled area surrounding the manor house or, if the manor was large enough, a castle. He provided administration and decided disputes. He also decided *what* would be done, *how* it would be done, and *who* would get what, but these decisions were limited. In the same way that the land belonged to the lord because that's the way it always had been, what people did and how they did it were determined by what they always had done. Tradition ruled the manor more than the lord did.

Problems of a Tradition-Based Society

Feudalism developed about the 8th and 9th centuries and lasted until about the 15th century, though in isolated countries such as Russia it continued well into the 19th century, and in all European countries its influence lingered for hundreds of years (as late as about 140 years ago in some parts of Germany). Such a long-lived system must have done some things right, and feudalism did: It solved the *what, how,* and *for whom* problems in an acceptable way.

But a tradition-based society has problems. In a traditional society, because someone's father was a baker, the son must also be a baker, and because a woman was a homemaker, she wouldn't be allowed to be anything but a homemaker. But what if Joe Blacksmith, Jr., the son of Joe Blacksmith, Sr., is a lousy blacksmith and longs to knead dough, while Joe Baker, Jr., would be a superb blacksmith but hates making pastry? Tough. Tradition dictated who did what. In fact, tradition probably arranged things so that we will never know whether Joe Blacksmith, Jr., would have made a superb baker.

As long as a society doesn't change too much, tradition operates reasonably well, although not especially efficiently, in holding the society together. However, when a society must undergo change, tradition does not work. Change means that the things that were done before no longer need to be done, while new things do need to get done. But if no one has traditionally done these new things, then they don't get done. If the change is important but a society can't figure out some way for the new things to get done, the society falls apart. That's what happened to feudal society. It didn't change when change was required.

The life of individuals living on the land, called *serfs*, was difficult, and feudalism was designed to benefit the lord. Some individuals in feudal society just couldn't take life on the manor, and they set off on their own. Because there was no organized police force, they were unlikely to be caught and forced to return to the manor. Going hungry, being killed, or both, however, were frequent fates of an escaped serf. One place to which serfs could safely escape, though, was a town or city—the remains of what in Roman times had been thriving and active cities. These cities, which had been decimated by plagues, plundering bands, and starvation in the preceding centuries, nevertheless remained an escape hatch for runaway serfs because they relied far less on tradition than did manors. City dwellers had to live by their wits; many became merchants who lived predominantly by trading. They were middlemen; they would buy from one group and sell to another.

Trading in towns was an alternative to the traditional feudal order because trading allowed people to have an income independent of the traditional social structure. Markets broke down tradition. Initially merchants traded using barter (exchange of one kind of good for another): silk and spices from the Orient for wheat, flour, and artisan products in Europe. But soon a generalized purchasing power (money) developed as a medium of exchange. Money greatly expanded the possibilities of trading because its use meant that goods no longer needed to be bartered. They could be sold for money, which could then be spent to buy other goods.

In the beginning, land was not traded, but soon the feudal lord who just had to have a silk robe but had no money was saying, "Why not? I'll sell you a small piece of land so I can buy a shipment of silk." Once land became tradable, the traditional base of the feudal society was undermined. Tradition that can be bought and sold is no longer tradition—it's just another commodity.

From Feudalism to Mercantilism

Toward the end of the Middle Ages (mid-15th century), markets went from being a sideshow, a fair that spiced up people's lives, to being the main event. Over time, some traders and merchants started to amass fortunes that dwarfed those of the feudal lords. Rich traders settled down; existing towns and cities expanded and new towns were formed. As towns grew and as fortunes shifted from feudal lords to merchants, power in society shifted to the towns. And with that shift came a change in society's political and economic structure.

As these traders became stronger politically and economically, they threw their support behind a king (the strongest lord) in the hope that the king would expand their ability to trade. In doing so, they made the king even stronger. Eventually, the king became so powerful that his will prevailed over the will of the other lords and even over the will of the Church. As the king consolidated his power, nation-states as we know them today evolved. *The government became an active influence on economic decision making.*

As markets grew, feudalism evolved into mercantilism. The evolution of feudal systems into mercantilism occurred in the following way: As cities and their markets grew in size and power relative to the feudal manors and the traditional economy, a whole new variety of possible economic activities developed. It was only natural that individuals began to look to a king to establish a new tradition that would determine who would do what. Individuals in particular occupations organized into groups called *guilds*, which were similar to strong labor unions today. These guilds, many of which had financed and supported the king, now expected the king and his government to protect their interests.

As new economic activities, such as trading companies, developed, individuals involved in these activities similarly depended on the king for the right to trade and for help in financing and organizing their activities. For example, in 1492, when Christopher Columbus had the wild idea that by sailing west he could get to the East Indies and trade for their riches, he went to Spain's Queen Isabella and King Ferdinand for financial support.

Since many traders had played and continued to play important roles in financing, establishing, and supporting the king, the king was usually happy to protect their interests. The government doled out the rights to undertake a variety of economic activities. By the late 1400s, Western Europe had evolved from a feudal to a mercantilist economy.

The mercantilist period was marked by the increased role of government, which could be classified in two ways: by the way it encouraged growth, and by the way it limited growth. Government legitimized and financed a variety of activities, thus encouraging growth. But government also limited economic activity in order to protect the monopolies of those it favored, thus limiting growth. So mercantilism allowed the market to operate, but it kept the market under its control. The market was not allowed to respond freely to the laws of supply and demand.

From Mercantilism to Capitalism

Mercantilism provided the source for major growth in Western Europe, but mercantilism also unleashed new tensions within society. Like feudalism, mercantilism limited entry into economic activities. It used a different form of limitation—politics rather than social and cultural tradition—but individuals who were excluded still felt unfairly treated.

The most significant source of tension was the different roles played by craft guilds and owners of new businesses, who were called industrialists or capitalists (businesspeople who have acquired large amounts of money and use it to invest in businesses). Craft guild members were artists in their own crafts: pottery, shoemaking, and the like. New business owners destroyed the art of production by devising machines to replace hand production. Machines produced goods cheaper and faster than craftsmen.[1] The result was an increase in supply and a downward pressure on the price, which was set by the government. Craftsmen didn't want to be replaced by machines. They argued that machine-manufactured goods didn't have the same quality as hand-crafted goods, and that the new machines would disrupt the economic and social life of the community.

Industrialists were the outsiders with a vested interest in changing the existing system. They wanted the freedom to conduct business as they saw fit. Because of the enormous cost advantage of manufactured goods over crafted goods, a few industrialists overcame government opposition and succeeded within the mercantilist system. They earned their fortunes and became an independent political power.

Once again the economic power base shifted, and two groups competed with each other for power—this time, the guilds and the industrialists. The government had to decide whether to support the industrialists (who wanted government to loosen its power over the country's economic affairs) or the craftsmen and guilds (who argued for strong government limitations and for maintaining traditional values of workmanship). This struggle raged in the 1700s and 1800s. But during this time, governments themselves were changing. This was the Age of Revolutions, and the kings' powers were being limited by democratic reform movements—revolutions supported and financed in large part by the industrialists.

The Need for Coordination in an Economy

Craftsmen argued that coordination of the economy was necessary, and the government had to be involved. If government wasn't going to coordinate economic activity, who would? To answer that question, a British moral philosopher named Adam Smith developed the concept of the invisible hand, in his famous book *The Wealth of Nations* (1776), and used it to explain how markets could coordinate the economy without the active involvement of government.

As stated in the Chapter 2, Smith argued that the market's invisible hand would guide suppliers' actions toward

[1]Throughout this section I use *men* to emphasize that these societies were strongly male-dominated. There were almost no business women. In fact, a woman had to turn over her property to a man upon her marriage, and the marriage contract was written as if she were owned by her husband!

the general good. No government coordination was necessary.

With the help of economists such as Adam Smith, the industrialists' view won out. Government pulled back from its role in guiding the economy and adopted a laissez-faire policy.

The Industrial Revolution

The invisible hand worked; capitalism thrived. Beginning about 1750 and continuing through the late 1800s, machine production increased enormously, almost totally replacing hand production. This phenomenon has been given a name, the Industrial Revolution. The economy grew faster than ever before. Society was forever transformed. New inventions changed all aspects of life. James Watt's steam engine (1769) made manufacturing and travel easier. Eli Whitney's cotton gin (1793) changed the way cotton was processed. James Kay's flying shuttle (1733),[2] James Hargreaves' spinning jenny (1765), and Richard Arkwright's power loom (1769), combined with the steam engine, changed the way cloth was processed and the clothes people wore.

The need to mine vast amounts of coal to provide power to run the machines changed the economic and physical landscapes. The repeating rifle changed the nature of warfare. Modern economic institutions replaced guilds. Stock markets, insurance companies, and corporations all became important. Trading was no longer financed by government; it was privately financed (although government policies, such as colonial policies giving certain companies monopoly trading rights with a country's colonies, helped in that trading). The Industrial Revolution, democracy, and capitalism all arose in the middle and late 1700s. By the 1800s, they were part of the institutional landscape of Western society. Capitalism had arrived.

From Capitalism to ~~Socialism~~ *Welfare Capitalism*

Capitalism was marked by significant economic growth in the Western world. But it was also marked by human abuses—18-hour workdays, low wages, children as young as five years old slaving long hours in dirty, dangerous factories and mines—to produce enormous wealth for an elite few. Such conditions and inequalities led to criticism of the capitalist or market economic system.

Marx's Analysis

The best-known critic of this system was Karl Marx, a German philosopher, economist, and sociologist who wrote in the 1800s and who developed an analysis of the dynamics of change in economic systems. Marx argued that economic systems are in a constant state of change, and that capitalism would not last. Workers would revolt, and capitalism would be replaced by a socialist economic system.

Marx saw an economy marked by tensions among economic classes. He saw capitalism as an economic system controlled by the capitalist class (businessmen). His class analysis was that capitalist society is divided into capitalist and worker classes. He said constant tension between these economic classes causes changes in the system. The capitalist class made large profits by exploiting the proletariat class—the working class—and extracting what he called surplus value from workers who, according to Marx's labor theory of value, produced all the value inherent in goods. Surplus value was the additional profit, rent, or interest that, according to Marx's normative views, capitalists added to the price of goods. What standard economic analysis sees as recognizing a need that society has and fulfilling it, Marx saw as exploitation.

Marx argued that this exploitation would increase as production facilities became larger and larger and as competition among capitalists decreased. At some point, he believed, exploitation would lead to a revolt by the proletariat, who would overthrow their capitalist exploiters.

By the late 1800s, some of what Marx predicted had occurred, although not in the way that he thought it would. Production moved from small to large factories. Corporations developed, and classes became more distinct from one another. Workers were significantly differentiated from owners. Small firms merged and were organized into monopolies and trusts (large combinations of firms). The trusts developed ways to prevent competition among themselves and ways to limit entry of new competitors into the market. Marx was right in his predictions about these developments, but he was wrong in his prediction about society's response to them.

The Revolution That Did Not Occur

Western society's response to the problems of capitalism was not a revolt by the workers. Instead, governments

[2]The invention of the flying shuttle frustrated the textile industry because it enabled workers to weave so much cloth that the spinners of thread from which the cloth was woven couldn't keep up. This challenge to the textile industry was met by offering a prize to anyone who could invent something to increase the thread spinners' productivity. The prize was won when the spinning jenny was invented.

stepped in to stop the worst abuses of capitalism. The hard edges of capitalism were softened.

Evolution, not revolution, was capitalism's destiny. The democratic state did not act, as Marx argued it would, as a mere representative of the capitalist class. Competing pressure groups developed; workers gained political power that offset the economic power of businesses.

In the late 1930s and the 1940s, workers dominated the political agenda. During this time, capitalist economies developed an economic safety net that included government-funded programs, such as public welfare and unemployment insurance, and established an extensive set of regulations affecting all aspects of the economy. Today, depressions are met with direct government policy. Antitrust laws, regulatory agencies, and social programs of government softened the hard edges of capitalism. Laws were passed prohibiting child labor, mandating a certain minimum wage, and limiting the hours of work. Capitalism became what is sometimes called welfare capitalism.

Due to these developments, government spending now accounts for about a fifth of all spending in the United States, and for more than half in some European countries. Were an economist from the late 1800s to return from the grave, he'd probably say socialism, not capitalism, exists in Western societies. Most modern-day economists wouldn't go that far, but they would agree that our economy today is better described as a welfare capitalist economy than as a capitalist, or even a market, economy. Because of these changes, the U.S. and Western European economies are a far cry from the competitive "capitalist" economy that Karl Marx criticized. Markets operate, but they are constrained by the government.

The concept *capitalism* developed to denote a market system controlled by one group in society, the capitalists. Looking at Western societies today, we see that domination by one group no longer characterizes Western economies. Although in theory capitalists control corporations through their ownership of shares of stock, in practice corporations are controlled in large part by managers. There remains an elite group who control business, but *capitalist* is not a good term to describe them. Managers, not capitalists, exercise primary control over business, and even their control is limited by laws or the fear of laws being passed by governments.

Governments in turn are controlled by a variety of pressure groups. Sometimes one group is in control; at other times, another. Government policies similarly fluctuate. Sometimes they are proworker, sometimes proindustrialist, sometimes progovernment, and sometimes prosociety.

From Feudalism to Socialism

You probably noticed that I crossed out *Socialism* in the previous section's heading and replaced it with *Welfare Capitalism*. That's because capitalism did not evolve to socialism as Karl Marx predicted it would. Instead, Marx's socialist ideas took root in feudalist Russia, a society that the Industrial Revolution had in large part bypassed. Arriving at a different place and a different time than Marx predicted it would, you shouldn't be surprised to read that socialism arrived in a different way than Marx predicted. The proletariat did not revolt to establish socialism. Instead, World War I, which the Russians were losing, crippled Russia's feudal economy and government. A small group of socialists overthrew the czar (Russia's king) and took over the government in 1917. They quickly pulled Russia out of the war, and then set out to organize a socialist society and economy.

Russian socialists tried to adhere to Marx's ideas, but they found that Marx had concentrated on how capitalist economies operate, not on how a socialist economy should be run. Thus, Russian socialists faced a huge task with little guidance. Their most immediate problem was how to increase production so that the economy could emerge from feudalism into the modern industrial world. In Marx's analysis, capitalism was a necessary stage in the evolution toward the ideal state for a very practical reason. The capitalists exploit the workers, but in doing so capitalists extract the necessary surplus—an amount of production in excess of what is consumed. That surplus had to be extracted in order to provide the factories and machinery upon which a socialist economic system would be built. But since capitalism did not exist in Russia, a true socialist state could not be established immediately. Instead, the socialists created *state socialism*—an economic system in which government sees to it that people work for the common good until they can be relied upon to do that on their own.

Socialists saw state socialism as a transition stage to pure socialism. This transition stage still exploited the workers; when Joseph Stalin took power in Russia in the late 1920s, he took the peasants' and small farmers' land and turned it into collective farms. The government then paid farmers low prices for their produce. When farmers balked at the low prices, millions of them were killed.

Simultaneously, Stalin created central planning agencies that directed individuals what to produce and how to produce it, and determined for whom things would be produced. During this period, *socialism* became synonymous with *central economic planning*, and Soviet-style socialism became the model of socialism in practice.

Also during this time, Russia took control of a number of neighboring states and established the Union of Soviet Socialist Republics (USSR), the formal name of the Soviet Union. The Soviet Union also installed Soviet-dominated governments in a number of Eastern European countries. In 1949 most of China, under the rule of Mao Zedong, adopted Soviet-style socialist principles.

Since the late 1980s, the Soviet socialist economic and political structure has fallen apart. The Soviet Union as a political state broke up, and its former republics became autonomous. Eastern European countries were released from Soviet control. Now they faced a new problem: transition from socialism to a market economy. Why did the Soviet socialist economy fall apart? Because workers lacked incentives to work; production was inefficient; consumer goods were either unavailable or of poor quality; and high Soviet officials were exploiting their positions, keeping the best jobs for themselves and moving themselves up in the waiting lists for consumer goods. In short, the parents of the socialist family (the Communist party) were no longer acting benevolently; they were taking many of the benefits for themselves.

Recent political and economic upheavals in Eastern Europe and the former Soviet Union suggest the kind of socialism these societies tried did not work. However, that failure does not mean that socialist goals are bad; nor does it mean that no type of socialism can ever work. To overthrow socialist-dominated governments it is not necessary to accept capitalism, and many citizens of these countries are looking for an alternative to both systems. Most, however, want to establish market economies. These changes have led some socialists to modify their view that state socialism is the path from capitalism to true socialism, and instead to joke: "Socialism is the longest path from capitalism to capitalism."

SUPPLY AND DEMAND

4

> Teach a parrot the terms *supply* and *demand* and you've got an economist.
>
> —*Thomas Carlyle*

After reading this chapter, you should be able to:

- State the law of demand and draw a demand curve from a demand table.
- Explain the importance of substitution to the laws of supply and demand.
- Distinguish a shift in demand from a movement along the demand curve.
- State the law of supply and draw a supply curve from a supply table.
- Distinguish a shift in supply from a movement along the supply curve.
- Explain how the law of demand and the law of supply interact to bring about equilibrium.
- Show the effect of a shift in demand and supply on equilibrium price and quantity.
- State the limitations of demand and supply analysis.

Supply and demand. Supply and demand. Roll the phrase around in your mouth, savor it like a good wine. *Supply* and *demand* are the most-used words in economics. And for good reason. They provide a good off-the-cuff answer for any economic question. Try it.

Why are bacon and oranges so expensive this winter? *Supply and demand.*

Why are interest rates falling? *Supply and demand.*

Why can't I find decent wool socks anymore? *Supply and demand.*

The importance of the interplay of supply and demand makes it only natural that, early in any economics course, you must learn about supply and demand. Let's start with demand.

DEMAND

People want lots of things; they "demand" much less than they want because demand means a willingness and ability to pay. Unless you are willing and able to pay for it you may *want* it, but you don't *demand* it. For example, I want to own a Maserati. But, I must admit, I'm not willing to do what's necessary to own one. If I really wanted one, I'd mortgage everything I own, increase my income by doubling the number of hours I work, not buy anything else, and get that car. But I don't do any of those things, so at the going price, $240,000, I do not demand a Maserati. Sure, I'd buy one if it cost $10,000, but from my actions it's clear that, at $240,000, I don't demand it. This points to an important aspect of demand: The quantity you demand at a low price differs from the quantity you demand at a high price. Specifically, the quantity you demand varies inversely—in the opposite direction—with price.

Prices are the tool by which the market coordinates individuals' desires and limits how much people are willing to buy—how much they demand. When goods become scarce, the market reduces the quantity of those scarce goods people demand; as their prices go up, people buy fewer goods. As goods become abundant, their prices go down, and people want more of them. The invisible hand—the price mechanism—sees to it that what people demand (do what's necessary to get) matches what's available. In doing so, the invisible hand coordinates individuals' demands.

The Law of Demand

The law of demand states that the quantity of a good demanded is inversely related to the good's price.

The ideas expressed above are the foundation of the **law of demand:**

Quantity demanded rises as price falls, other things constant.

Or alternatively:

Quantity demanded falls as price rises, other things constant.

When price goes up, quantity demanded goes down. When price goes down, quantity demanded goes up.

This law is fundamental to the invisible hand's ability to coordinate individuals' desires: as prices change, people change how much of a particular good they're willing to buy.

What accounts for the law of demand? Individuals' tendency to substitute other goods for goods whose relative price has gone up. If the price of music downloads from the Internet rises but the price of CDs stays the same, you're more likely to buy that new Sheryl Crow recording on CD than to download it from the Internet.

To see that the law of demand makes intuitive sense, just think of something you'd really like but can't afford. If the price is cut in half, you—and other consumers—become more likely to buy it. Quantity demanded goes up as price goes down.

Web Note 4.1
Markets without Money

Just to be sure you've got it, let's consider a real-world example: demand for vanity—specifically, vanity license plates. When the North Carolina state legislature increased the vanity plates' price from $30 to $40, the quantity demanded fell from 60,334 at $30 a year to 31,122 at $40 a year. Assuming other things remained constant, that is the law of demand in action.

The Demand Curve

A **demand curve** is *the graphic representation of the relationship between price and quantity demanded.* Figure 4-1 shows a demand curve.

Q-1 Why does the demand curve slope downward?

As you can see, in graphical terms, the law of demand states that as the price goes up, the quantity demanded goes down, other things constant. An alternative way of saying the same thing is that price and quantity demanded are inversely related, so the demand curve slopes downward to the right.

"Other things constant" places a limitation on the application of the law of demand.

Notice that in stating the law of demand, I put in the qualification "other things constant." That's three extra words, and unless they were important I wouldn't have put them in. But what does "other things constant" mean? Say that over a period of two years, both the price of cars and the number of cars purchased rise. That seems to

Figure 4-1 A Sample Demand Curve
The law of demand states that the quantity demanded of a good is inversely related to the price of that good, other things constant. As the price of a good goes up, the quantity demanded goes down, so the demand curve is downward-sloping.

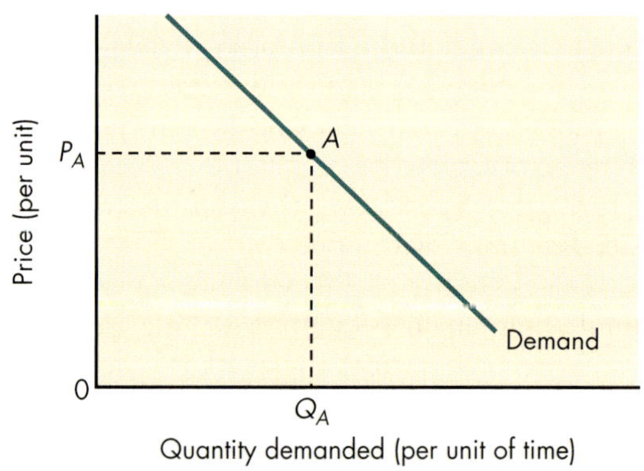

violate the law of demand, since the number of cars purchased should have fallen in response to the rise in price. Looking at the data more closely, however, we see that a third factor has also changed: Individuals' income has increased. As income increases, people buy more cars, increasing the demand for cars.

The increase in price works as the law of demand states—it decreases the number of cars bought. But in this case, income doesn't remain constant; it increases. That rise in income increases the demand for cars. That increase in demand outweighs the decrease in quantity demanded that results from a rise in price, so ultimately more cars are sold. If you want to study the effect of price alone—which is what the law of demand refers to—you must make adjustments to hold income constant. That's why the qualifying phrase "other things constant" is an important part of the law of demand.

The other things that are held constant include individuals' tastes, prices of other goods, and even the weather. Those other factors must remain constant if you're to make a valid study of the effect of an increase in the price of a good on the quantity demanded. In practice, it's impossible to keep all other things constant, so you have to be careful when you say that when price goes up, quantity demanded goes down. It's likely to go down, but it's always possible that something besides price has changed.

Shifts in Demand versus Movements along a Demand Curve

To distinguish between the effects of price and the effects of other factors on how much of a good is demanded, economists have developed the following precise terminology—terminology that inevitably shows up on exams. The first distinction to make is between demand and quantity demanded.

- **Demand** refers to *a schedule of quantities of a good that will be bought per unit of time at various prices, other things constant.*
- **Quantity demanded** refers to *a specific amount that will be demanded per unit of time at a specific price, other things constant.*

In graphical terms, the term *demand* refers to the entire demand curve. Demand tells how much of a good will be bought *at various prices*. *Quantity demanded* tells how much of a good will be bought at a specific price; it refers to a point on a demand curve, such as point A in Figure 4-1. This terminology allows us to distinguish between *changes in quantity demanded* and *shifts in demand*. A change in the quantity demanded refers to the effect of a price change on the quantity demanded. It refers to a **movement along a demand curve**—*the graphical representation of the effect of a change in price on the quantity demanded.* A **shift in demand** refers to *the effect of anything other than price on demand.*

Q-2 The uncertainty caused by the terrorist attacks of September 11, 2001, made consumers reluctant to spend on luxury items. This reduced ________. Should the missing words be *demand for luxury goods* or *quantity of luxury goods demanded?*

Shift Factors of Demand

Shift factors of demand are factors that cause shifts in the demand curve. A change in anything that affects demand besides price causes a shift of the entire demand curve.

Important shift factors of demand include:

1. Society's income.
2. The prices of other goods.
3. Tastes.
4. Expectations.
5. Taxes on and subsidies to consumers.

Income From our example above of "the other things constant" qualification, we saw that a rise in income increases the demand for goods. For most goods this is true. As individuals' income rises, they can afford more of the goods they want, such as steaks, computers, or clothing. These are normal goods. For other goods, called inferior goods, an increase in income reduces demand. An example is urban mass transit. A person whose income has risen tends to stop riding the bus to work because she can afford to buy a car and rent a parking space.

Price of Other Goods Because people make their buying decisions based on the price of related goods, demand will be affected by the prices of other goods. Suppose the price of jeans rose from $25 to $35, but the price of khakis remained at $25. Next time you need pants, you're apt to try khakis instead of jeans. They are substitutes. When the price of a substitute declines, demand for the good whose price has remained the same will fall. Or consider another example. Suppose the price of movie tickets falls. What will happen to the demand for popcorn? You're likely to increase the number of times you go to the movies, so you'll also likely increase the amount of popcorn you purchase. The lower cost of a movie ticket increases the demand for popcorn because popcorn and movies are complements. When the price of a good declines, the demand for its complement rises.

Q-3 Explain the effect of each of the following on the demand for new computers:

1. The price of computers falls by 30 percent.
2. Total income in the economy rises.

Tastes An old saying goes: "There's no accounting for taste." Of course, many advertisers believe otherwise. Changes in taste can affect the demand for a good without a change in price. As you become older, you may find that your taste for rock concerts has changed to a taste for an evening at the opera or local philharmonic.

Expectations Finally, expectations will also affect demand. Expectations can cover a lot. If you expect your income to rise in the future, you're bound to start spending some of it today. If you expect the price of computers to fall soon, you may put off buying one until later.

Taxes and Subsidies Taxes levied on consumers increase the cost of goods to consumers and therefore reduce demand for those goods. Subsidies to consumers have the opposite effect. When states host tax-free weeks during August's back-to-school shopping season, consumers load up on products to avoid sales taxes. Demand for retail goods rises during the tax holiday.

These aren't the only shift factors. In fact anything—except the price of the good itself—that affects demand (and many things do) is a shift factor. While economists agree these shift factors are important, they believe that no shift factor influences how much is demanded as consistently as does price of the specific item. That's what makes economists focus first on price as they try to understand the world. That's why economists make the law of demand central to their analysis.

Change in price causes a movement along a demand curve; a change in a shift factor causes a shift in demand.

To make sure you understand the difference between a movement along a demand curve and a shift in demand, let's consider an example. Singapore has one of the world's highest number of cars per mile of road. This means that congestion is considerable. Singapore adopted two policies to reduce road use: It increased the fee charged to use roads, and it provided an expanded public transportation system. Both policies reduced congestion. Figure 4-2(a) shows that increasing the toll charged to use roads from $1 to $2 per 50 miles of road reduces quantity demanded from 200 to 100 cars per mile every hour (a movement along the demand curve). Figure 4-2(b) shows that providing alternative methods of transportation such as buses and subways shifts the demand curve for roads. Demand for road use shifts in to the left so that at every price, demand drops by 100 cars per mile every hour (the demand curve shifts to the left).

Figure 4-2 Shift in Demand versus a Change in Quantity Demanded
A rise in a good's price results in a reduction in quantity demanded and is shown by a movement up along a demand curve from point *A* to point *B* in (**a**). A change in any other factor besides price that affects demand leads to a shift in the entire demand curve, as shown in (**b**).

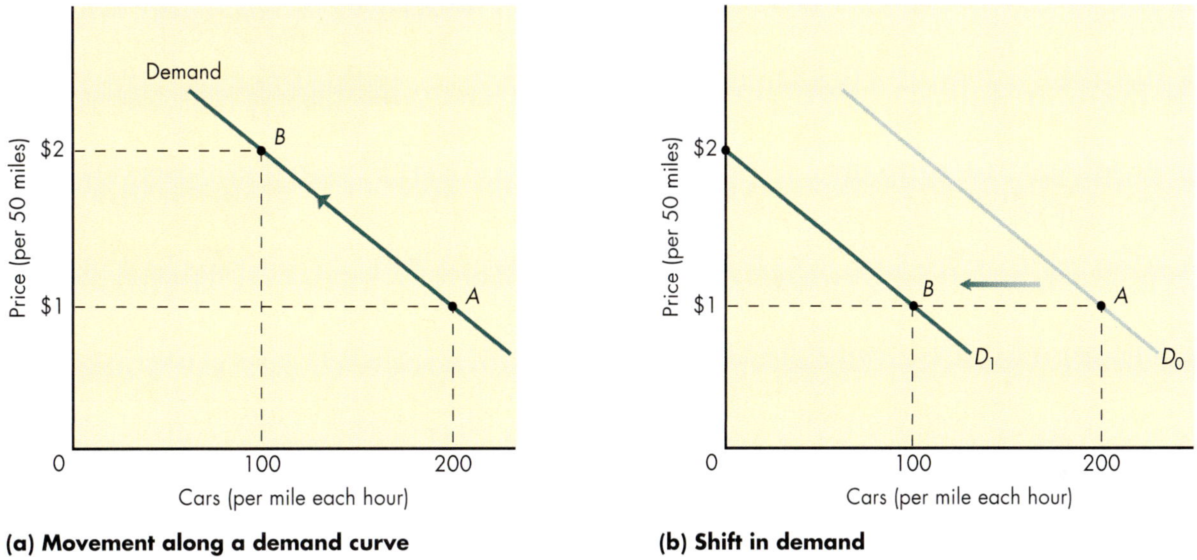

A Review

Let's test your understanding by having you specify what happens to your demand curve for videocassettes in the following examples: First, let's say you buy a DVD player. Next, let's say that the price of videocassettes falls; and finally, say that you won $1 million in a lottery. What happens to the demand for videocassettes in each case? If you answered: It shifts in to the left; it remains unchanged; and it shifts out to the right—you've got it.

The Demand Table

As I emphasized in Chapter 2, introductory economics depends heavily on graphs and graphical analysis—translating ideas into graphs and back into words. So let's graph the demand curve.

Figure 4-3(a), a demand table, describes Alice's demand for renting DVDs. For example, at a price of $2 Alice will rent (buy the use of) 6 DVDs per week, and at a price of 50 cents she will rent 9.

There are four points about the relationship between the number of DVDs Alice rents and the price of renting them that are worth mentioning. First, the relationship follows the law of demand: As the rental price rises, quantity demanded decreases. Second, quantity demanded has a specific *time dimension* to it. In this example demand refers to the number of DVD rentals per week. Without the time dimension, the table wouldn't provide us with any useful information. Nine DVD rentals per year is quite a different concept from 9 DVD rentals per week. Third, Alice's DVD rentals are interchangeable—the 9th DVD rental doesn't significantly differ from the 1st, 3rd, or any other DVD rental. The fourth point is already familiar to you: The schedule assumes that everything else is held constant.

Figure 4-3 (a and b) From a Demand Table to a Demand Curve
The demand table in (a) is translated into a demand curve in (b). Each combination of price and quantity in the table corresponds to a point on the curve. For example, point A on the graph represents row A in the table: Alice demands 9 DVD rentals at a price of 50 cents. A demand curve is constructed by plotting all points from the demand table and connecting the points by a line.

	Price per DVD	DVD rentals demanded per week
A	$0.50	9
B	1.00	8
C	2.00	6
D	3.00	4
E	4.00	2

(a) A demand table

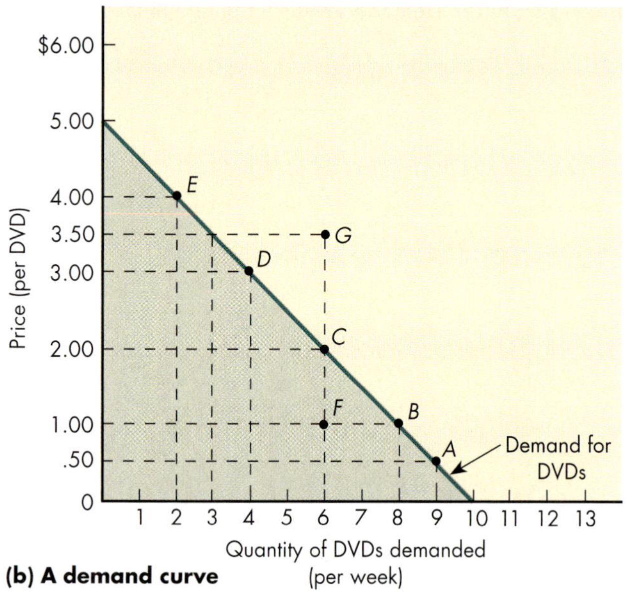

(b) A demand curve

FROM A DEMAND TABLE TO A DEMAND CURVE

Figure 4-3(b) translates the demand table in Figure 4-3(a) into a graph. Point A (quantity = 9, price = $.50) is graphed first at the (9, $.50) coordinates. Next we plot points *B*, *C*, *D*, and *E* in the same manner and connect the resulting dots with a solid line. The result is the demand curve, which graphically conveys the same information that's in the demand table. Notice that the demand curve is downward sloping (from left to right), indicating that the law of demand holds in the example.

The demand curve represents the maximum price that an individual will pay.

The demand curve represents the *maximum price* that an individual will pay for various quantities of a good; the individual will happily pay less. For example, say someone offers Alice 6 DVD rentals at a price of $1 each (point *F* of Figure 4-3(b)). Will she accept? Sure; she'll pay any price within the shaded area to the left of the demand curve. But if someone offers her 6 rentals at $3.50 each (point G), she won't accept. At a rental price of $3.50 apiece, she's willing to rent only 3 DVDs.

Q-4 Derive a market demand curve from the following two individual demand curves:

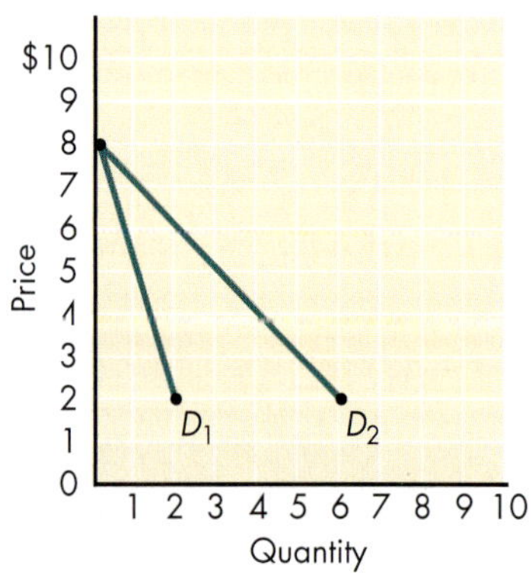

INDIVIDUAL AND MARKET DEMAND CURVES

Normally, economists talk about market demand curves rather than individual demand curves. A **market demand curve** is *the horizontal sum of all individual demand curves*. Market demand curves are what most firms are interested in. Firms don't care whether individual A or individual B buys their goods; they only care that *someone* buys their goods.

It's a good graphical exercise to add individual demand curves together to create a market demand curve. I do that in Figure 4-4. In it I assume that the market consists of three buyers, Alice, Bruce, and Carmen, whose demand tables are given in Figure 4-4(a). Alice and Bruce have demand tables similar to the demand tables discussed previously. At a price of $3 each, Alice rents 4 DVDs; at a price of $2, she rents 6. Carmen is an all or nothing individual. She rents 1 DVD as long as the price is equal to or below $1; otherwise she rents nothing. If you plot Carmen's demand curve, it's a vertical line. However, the law of demand still holds: As price increases, quantity demanded decreases.

Figure 4-4 (a and b) From Individual Demands to a Market Demand Curve

The table (**a**) shows the demand schedules for Alice, Bruce, and Carmen. Together they make up the market for DVD rentals. Their total quantity demanded (market demand) for DVD rentals at each price is given in column 5. As you can see in (**b**), Alice's, Bruce's, and Carmen's demand curves can be added together to get the total market demand curve. For example, at a price of \$2, Carmen demands 0, Bruce demands 3, and Alice demands 6, for a market demand of 9 (point *D*).

	(1) Price (per DVD)	(2) Alice's demand	(3) Bruce's demand	(4) Carmen's demand	(5) Market demand
A	\$0.50	9	6	1	16
B	1.00	8	5	1	14
C	1.50	7	4	0	11
D	2.00	6	3	0	9
E	2.50	5	2	0	7
F	3.00	4	1	0	5
G	3.50	3	0	0	3
H	4.00	2	0	0	2

(a) A demand table

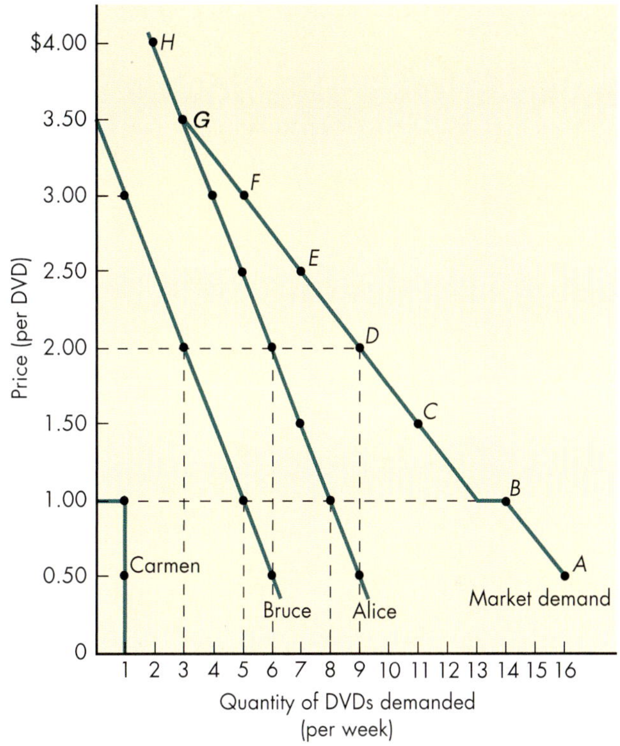

(b) Adding demand curves

The quantity demanded by each consumer is listed in columns 2, 3, and 4 of Figure 4-4(a). Column 5 shows total market demand; each entry is the horizontal sum of the entries in columns 2, 3, and 4. For example, at a price of \$3 apiece (row *F*), Alice demands 4 DVD rentals, Bruce demands 1, and Carmen demands 0, for a total market demand of 5 DVD rentals.

Figure 4-4(b) shows three demand curves: one each for Alice, Bruce, and Carmen. The market, or total, demand curve is the horizontal sum of the individual demand curves. To see that this is the case, notice that if we take the quantity demanded at \$1 by Alice (8), Bruce (5), and Carmen (1), they sum to 14, which is point *B* (14, \$1) on the market demand curve. We can do that for each price. Alternatively, we can simply add the individual quantities demanded, given in the demand tables, prior to graphing (which we do in column 5 of Figure 4-4(a)), and graph that total in relation to price. Not surprisingly, we get the same total market demand curve.

In practice, of course, firms don't measure individual demand curves, so they don't sum them up in this fashion. Instead, they estimate total demand. Still, summing up individual demand curves is a useful exercise because it shows you how the market demand curve is the sum (the horizontal sum, graphically speaking) of the individual demand curves, and it gives you a good sense of where market demand curves come from. It also shows you that, even if individuals don't respond to small changes in price, the market demand curve can still be smooth and downward sloping. That's because, for the market, the law of demand is based on two phenomena:

1. At lower prices, existing demanders buy more.
2. At lower prices, new demanders (some all or nothing demanders like Carmen) enter the market.

For the market, the law of demand is based on two phenomena:

1. At lower prices, existing demanders buy more.
2. At lower prices, new demanders enter the market.

Six Things to Remember about a Demand Curve

Knowing the Tools

- A demand curve follows the law of demand: When price rises, quantity demanded falls; and vice versa.
- The horizontal axis—quantity—has a time dimension.
- The quality of each unit is the same.
- The vertical axis—price—assumes all other prices remain the same.
- The curve assumes everything else is held constant.
- Effects of price changes are shown by movements along the demand curve. Effects of anything else on demand (shift factors) are shown by shifts of the entire demand curve.

Supply

In one sense, supply is the mirror image of demand. Individuals control the factors of production—inputs, or resources, necessary to produce goods. Individuals' supply of these factors to the market mirrors other individuals' demand for those factors. For example, say you decide you want to rest rather than weed your garden. You hire someone to do the weeding; you demand labor. Someone else decides she would prefer more income instead of more rest; she supplies labor to you. You trade money for labor; she trades labor for money. Her supply is the mirror image of your demand.

For a large number of goods and services, however, the supply process is more complicated than demand. For many goods there's an intermediate step in supply: individuals supply factors of production to firms.

Let's consider a simple example. Say you're a taco technician. You supply your labor to the factor market. The taco company demands your labor (hires you). The taco company combines your labor with other inputs like meat, cheese, beans, and tables, and produces tacos (production), which it supplies to customers in the goods market. For produced goods, supply depends not only on individuals' decisions to supply factors of production but also on firms' ability to produce—to transform those factors of production into usable goods.

Supply of produced goods involves a much more complicated process than demand and is divided into analysis of factors of production and the transformation of those factors into goods.

The supply process of produced goods is generally complicated. Often there are many layers of firms—production firms, wholesale firms, distribution firms, and retailing firms—each of which passes on in-process goods to the next layer of firms. Real-world production and supply of produced goods is a multistage process.

The supply of nonproduced goods is more direct. Individuals supply their labor in the form of services directly to the goods market. For example, an independent contractor may repair your washing machine. That contractor supplies his labor directly to you.

Thus, the analysis of the supply of produced goods has two parts: an analysis of the supply of factors of production to households and to firms, and an analysis of the process by which firms transform those factors of production into usable goods and services.

The Law of Supply

There's a law of supply that corresponds to the law of demand. The **law of supply** states:

Quantity supplied rises as price rises, other things constant.

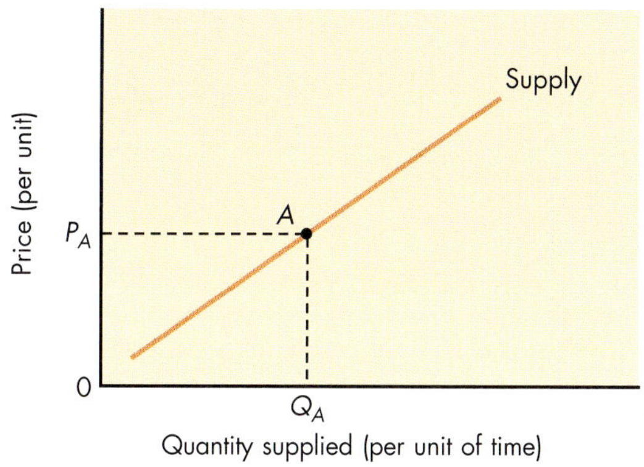

Figure 4-5 A Sample Supply Curve
The supply curve demonstrates graphically the law of supply, which states that the quantity supplied of a good is directly related to that good's price, other things constant. As the price of a good goes up, the quantity supplied also goes up, so the supply curve is upward sloping.

Or alternatively:

Quantity supplied falls as price falls, other things constant.

Price regulates quantity supplied just as it regulates quantity demanded. Like the law of demand, the law of supply is fundamental to the invisible hand's (the market's) ability to coordinate individuals' actions.

What accounts for the law of supply? When the price of a good rises, individuals and firms can rearrange their activities in order to supply more of that good to the market. They want to supply more because the opportunity cost of *not* producing the goods rises as its price rises. Thus, the law of supply is based on a firm's ability to substitute production of one good for another, or vice versa. If the price of corn rises and the price of wheat has not changed, farmers will grow less wheat and more corn, other things constant.

The law of supply is based on substitution and the expectation of profits.

With firms, there's a second explanation of the law of supply. Assuming firms' costs are constant, a higher price means higher profits (the difference between a firm's revenues and its costs). The expectation of those higher profits leads it to increase output as price rises, which is what the law of supply states.

The Supply Curve

A **supply curve** is *the graphical representation of the relationship between price and quantity supplied.* A supply curve is shown graphically in Figure 4-5.

Notice how the supply curve slopes upward to the right. That upward slope captures the law of supply. It tells us that the quantity supplied varies *directly*—in the same direction—with the price.

As with the law of demand, the law of supply assumes other things are held constant. Thus, if the price of wheat rises and quantity supplied falls, you'll look for something else that changed—for example, a drought might have caused a drop in supply. Your explanation would go as follows: Had there been no drought, the quantity supplied would have increased in response to the rise in price, but because there was a drought, the supply decreased, which caused prices to rise.

As with the law of demand, the law of supply represents economists' off-the-cuff response to the question "What happens to quantity supplied if price rises?" If the law seems to be violated, economists search for some other variable that has changed. As was the case with demand, these other variables that might change are called shift factors.

Shifts in Supply versus Movements along a Supply Curve

The same distinctions in terms made for demand apply to supply.

Supply refers to *a schedule of quantities a seller is willing to sell per unit of time at various prices, other things constant.*

Quantity supplied refers to *a specific amount that will be supplied at a specific price.*

Q-5 In the 1980s and 1990s, as animal activists caused a decrease in the demand for fur coats, the prices of furs fell. This made __________ decline. Should the missing words be *the supply* or *the quantity supplied?*

In graphical terms, supply refers to the entire supply curve because a supply curve tells us how much will be offered for sale at various prices. "Quantity supplied" refers to a point on a supply curve, such as point A in Figure 4-5.

The second distinction that is important to make is between the effects of a change in price and the effects of shift factors on how much of a good is supplied. Changes in price cause changes in quantity supplied; such changes are represented by a **movement along a supply curve**—*the graphic representation of the effect of a change in price on the quantity supplied.* If the amount supplied is affected by anything other than price, that is, by a shift factor of supply, there will be a **shift in supply**—*the graphic representation of the effect of a change in a factor other than price on supply.*

Shift Factors of Supply

Other factors besides price that affect how much will be supplied include the price of inputs used in production, technology, expectations, and taxes and subsidies. Let's see how.

Price of Inputs Firms produce to earn a profit. Since their profit is tied to costs, it's no surprise that costs will affect how much a firm is willing to supply. If costs rise, profits will decline, and a firm has less incentive to supply. Supply falls when the price of inputs rises. If costs rise substantially, a firm might even shut down.

Q-6 Explain the effect of each of the following on the supply of romance novels:

1. The price of paper rises by 20 percent.
2. Government increases the sales tax on producers on all books by 5 percentage points.

Technology Advances in technology change the production process, reducing the number of inputs needed to produce a given supply of goods. Thus, a technological advance that reduces the number of workers will reduce costs of production. A reduction in the costs of production increases profits and leads suppliers to increase production. Advances in technology increase supply.

Expectations Supplier expectations are an important factor in the production decision. If a supplier expects the price of her good to rise at some time in the future, she may store some of today's supply in order to sell it later and reap higher profits, decreasing supply now and increasing it later.

Taxes and Subsidies Taxes on suppliers increase the cost of production by requiring a firm to pay the government a portion of the income from products or services sold. Because taxes increase the cost of production, profit declines and suppliers will reduce supply. The opposite is true for subsidies. Subsidies to suppliers are payments by the government to produce goods; thus, they reduce the cost of production. Subsidies increase supply. Taxes on suppliers reduce supply.

These aren't the only shift factors. As was the case with demand, a shift factor of supply is anything that affects supply, other than its price.

A Shift in Supply versus a Movement along a Supply Curve

The same "movement along" and "shift of" distinction that we developed for demand exists for supply. To make that distinction clear, let's consider an example: the supply of

Figure 4-6 Shift in Supply versus Change in Quantity Supplied
A change in quantity supplied results from a change in price and is shown by a movement along a supply curve like the movement from point *A* to point *B* in (**a**). A shift in supply—a shift in the entire supply curve—brought about by a change in a nonprice factor is shown in (**b**).

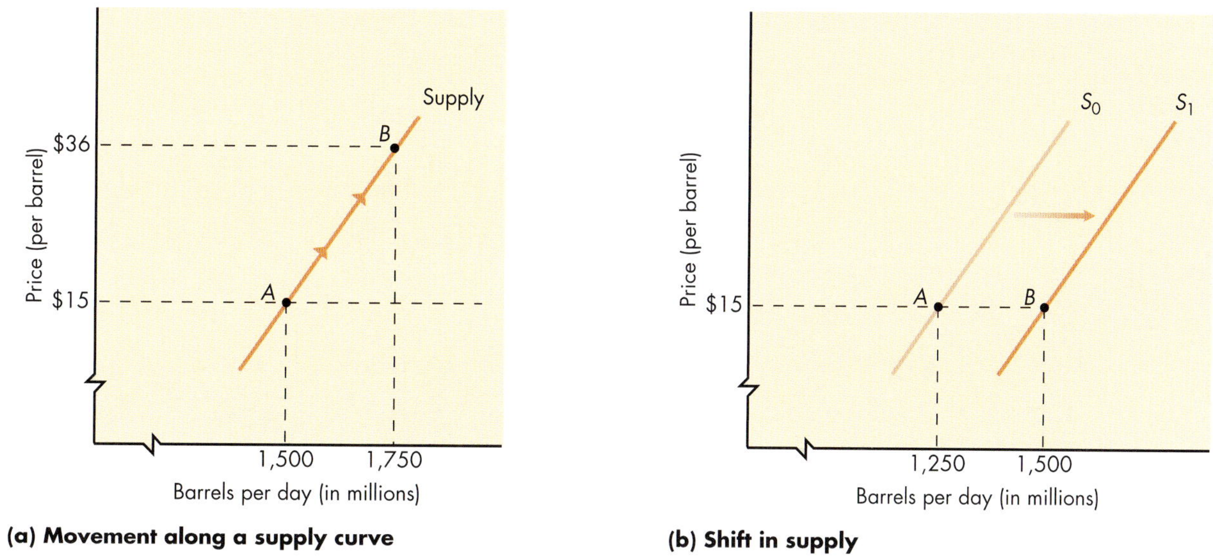

oil. In 1990 and 1991, world oil prices rose from $15 to $36 a barrel when oil production in the Persian Gulf was disrupted by the Iraqi invasion of Kuwait. U.S. oil producers, seeing that they could sell their oil at a higher price, increased oil production. As the price of oil rose, domestic producers increased the quantity of oil supplied. The change in domestic quantity supplied in response to the rise in world oil prices is illustrated in Figure 4-6(a) as a movement up along the U.S. supply curve from point *A* to point *B*. At $15 a barrel, producers supplied 1,500 million barrels of oil a day, and at $36 a barrel they supplied 1,750 million barrels per day.

Photodisc

Earlier, in the 1980s, technological advances in horizontal drilling more than doubled the amount of oil that could be extracted from some oil fields. Technological innovations such as this reduced the cost of supplying oil and shifted the supply of oil to the right, as shown in Figure 4-6(b). Before the innovation, suppliers were willing to provide 1,250 million barrels of oil per day at $15 a barrel. After the innovation, suppliers were willing to supply 1,500 million barrels of oil per day at $15 a barrel.

A Review

To be sure you understand shifts in supply, explain what is likely to happen to your supply curve for labor in the following cases: (1) You suddenly decide that you absolutely need a new car. (2) You win a million dollars in the lottery. And finally, (3) the wage you earn doubles. If you came up with the answers: shift out to the right, shift in to the left, and no change—you've got it down. If not, it's time for a review.

Do we see such shifts in the supply curve often? Yes. A good example is computers. For the past 30 years, technological changes have continually shifted the supply curve for computers out to the right.

Figure 4-7 (a and b) From Individual Supplies to a Market Supply

As with market demand, market supply is determined by adding all quantities supplied at a given price. Three suppliers—Ann, Barry, and Charlie—make up the market of DVD suppliers. The total market supply is the sum of their individual supplies at each price, shown in column 5 of (**a**).

Each of the individual supply curves and the market supply curve have been plotted in (**b**). Notice how the market supply curve is the horizontal sum of the individual supply curves.

	(1)	(2)	(3)	(4)	(5)
Quantities supplied	Price (per DVD)	Ann's supply	Barry's supply	Charlie's supply	Market supply
A	$0.00	0	0	0	0
B	0.50	1	0	0	1
C	1.00	2	1	0	3
D	1.50	3	2	0	5
E	2.00	4	3	0	7
F	2.50	5	4	0	9
G	3.00	6	5	0	11
H	3.50	7	5	2	14
I	4.00	8	5	2	15

(a) A supply table

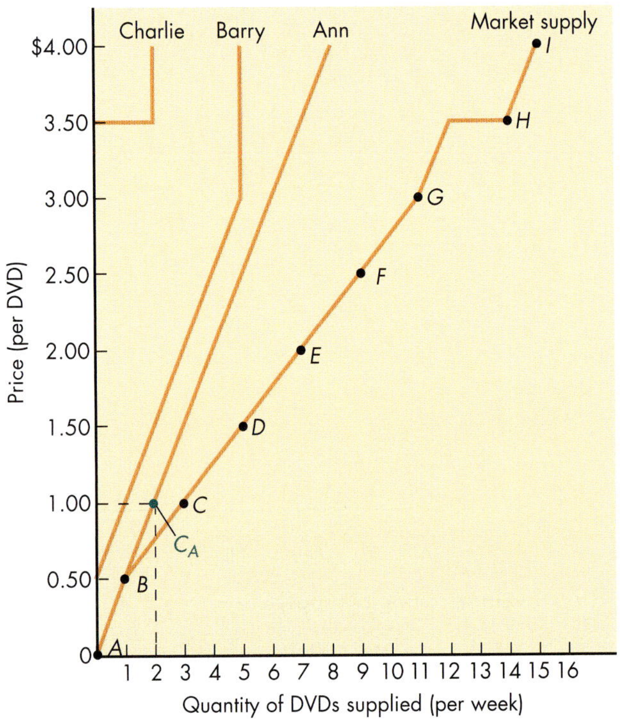

(b) Adding supply curves

The Supply Table

Remember Figure 4-4(a)'s demand table for DVD rentals? In Figure 4-7(a), columns 2 (Ann), 3 (Barry), and 4 (Charlie), we follow the same reasoning to construct a supply table for three hypothetical DVD suppliers. Each supplier follows the law of supply: When price rises, each supplies more, or at least as much as each did at a lower price.

From a Supply Table to a Supply Curve

Figure 4-7(b) takes the information in Figure 4-7(a)'s supply table and translates it into a graph of each supplier's supply curve. For instance, point C_A on Ann's supply curve corresponds to the information in columns 1 and 2, row C. Point C_A is at a price of $1 per DVD and a quantity of 2 DVDs per week. Notice that Ann's supply curve is upward sloping, meaning that price is positively related to quantity. Charlie's and Barry's supply curves are similarly derived.

The supply curve represents the set of *minimum* prices an individual seller will accept for various quantities of a good. The market's invisible hand stops suppliers from charging more than the market price. If suppliers could escape the market's invisible hand and charge a higher price, they would gladly do so. Unfortunately for them, and fortunately for consumers, a higher price encourages other suppliers to begin selling DVDs. Competing suppliers' entry into the market sets a limit on the price any supplier can charge.

Six Things to Remember about a Supply Curve

Knowing the Tools

- A supply curve follows the law of supply. When price rises, quantity supplied increases, and vice versa.
- The horizontal axis—quantity—has a time dimension.
- The quality of each unit is the same.
- The vertical axis—price—assumes all other prices remain constant.
- The curve assumes everything else is constant.
- Effects of price changes are shown by movements along the supply curve. Effects of nonprice determinants of supply are shown by shifts of the entire supply curve.

Individual and Market Supply Curves

The market supply curve is derived from individual supply curves in precisely the same way that the market demand curve was. To emphasize the symmetry, I've made the three suppliers quite similar to the three demanders. Ann (column 2) will supply 2 at $1; if price goes up to $2, she increases her supply to 4. Barry (column 3) begins supplying at $1, and at $3 supplies 5, the most he'll supply regardless of how high price rises. Charlie (column 4) has only two units to supply. At a price of $3.50 he'll supply that quantity, but higher prices won't get him to supply any more.

The **market supply curve** is *the horizontal sum of all individual supply curves*. In Figure 4-7(a) (column 5), we add together Ann's, Barry's, and Charlie's supplies to arrive at the market supply curve, which is graphed in Figure 4-7(b). Notice that each point on it corresponds to the information in columns 1 and 5 for each row. For example, point *H* corresponds to a price of $3.50 and a quantity of 14.

The market supply curve's upward slope is determined by two different sources: by existing suppliers supplying more and by new suppliers entering the market. Sometimes existing suppliers may not be willing to increase their quantity supplied in response to an increase in prices, but a rise in price often brings brand-new suppliers into the market. For example, a rise in teachers' salaries will have little effect on the amount of teaching current teachers do, but it will increase the number of people choosing to be teachers.

The law of supply is based on two phenomena:

1. At higher prices, existing suppliers supply more.
2. At higher prices, new suppliers enter the market.

The Interaction of Supply and Demand

Thomas Carlyle, the English historian who dubbed economics "the dismal science," also wrote this chapter's introductory tidbit. "Teach a parrot the terms *supply* and *demand* and you've got an economist." In earlier chapters, I tried to convince you that economics is *not* dismal. In the rest of this chapter, I hope to convince you that, while supply and demand are important to economics, parrots don't make good economists. If students think that when they've learned the terms *supply* and *demand* they've learned economics, they're mistaken. Those terms are just labels for the ideas behind supply and demand, and it's the ideas that are important. What matters about supply and demand isn't the labels but how the concepts interact. For instance, what happens if a freeze kills the blossoms on the orange trees? The quantity of oranges supplied isn't expected to equal the quantity demanded. It's in understanding the interaction of supply and demand that economics becomes interesting and relevant.

EQUILIBRIUM

Web Note 4.2
Online Markets

When you have a market in which neither suppliers nor consumers collude and in which prices are free to adjust, the forces of supply and demand interact to arrive at an equilibrium. The concept of equilibrium comes from physics—classical mechanics. **Equilibrium** is *a concept in which opposing dynamic forces cancel each other out*. For example, a hot-air balloon is in equilibrium when the upward force exerted by the hot air in the balloon equals the downward pressure exerted on the balloon by gravity. In supply/demand analysis, equilibrium means that the upward pressure on price is exactly offset by the downward pressure on price. **Equilibrium price** is *the price toward which the invisible hand drives the market*. At the equilibrium price, quantity demanded equals quantity supplied. **Equilibrium quantity** is *the amount bought and sold at the equilibrium price*.

So much for what equilibrium is. Now let's consider what it isn't.

WHAT EQUILIBRIUM ISN'T

First, equilibrium isn't a state of the world. It's a characteristic of the model—the framework you use to look at the world. The same situation could be seen as an equilibrium in one framework and as a disequilibrium in another. Say you're describing a car that's speeding along at 100 miles an hour. That car is changing position relative to objects on the ground. Its movement could be, and generally is, described as if it were in disequilibrium. However, if you consider this car relative to another car going 100 miles an hour, the cars could be modeled as being in equilibrium because their positions relative to each other aren't changing.

Equilibrium is not inherently good or bad.

Second, equilibrium isn't inherently good or bad. It's simply a state in which dynamic pressures offset each other. Some equilibria are awful. Say two countries are engaged in a nuclear war against each other and both sides are blown away. An equilibrium will have been reached, but there's nothing good about it.

What happens if the market is not in equilibrium—if quantity supplied doesn't equal quantity demanded? You get either excess supply or excess demand, and a tendency for prices to change.

EXCESS SUPPLY

Bargain hunters can get a deal when there is excess supply.
Elena Rooraid/Photoedit

If there is **excess supply** (a surplus), *quantity supplied is greater than quantity demanded*, and some suppliers won't be able to sell all their goods. Each supplier will think: "Gee, if I offer to sell it for a bit less, I'll be the lucky one who sells my goods; someone else will be stuck with not selling their goods." But because all suppliers with excess goods will be thinking the same thing, the price in the market will fall. As that happens, consumers will increase their quantity demanded. So the movement toward equilibrium caused by excess supply is on both the supply and demand sides.

EXCESS DEMAND

The reverse is also true. Say that instead of excess supply, there's **excess demand** (a shortage)—*quantity demanded is greater than quantity supplied*. There are more consumers who want the good than there are suppliers selling the good. Let's consider what's likely to go through demanders' minds. They'll likely call long-lost friends who just happen to be sellers of that good and tell them it's good to talk to them and, by the way, don't they want to sell that . . . ? Suppliers will be rather pleased that so many of their old friends have remembered them, but they'll also likely see the connection between excess demand and their friends' thoughtfulness. To stop their phones from ringing all the time, they'll likely raise their price. The reverse is true for excess supply. It's amazing how friendly suppliers become to potential consumers when there's excess supply.

PRICE ADJUSTS

This tendency for prices to rise when the quantity demanded exceeds the quantity supplied and for prices to fall when the quantity supplied exceeds the quantity demanded is a central element to understanding supply and demand. So remember:

When quantity demanded is greater than quantity supplied, prices tend to rise.
When quantity supplied is greater than quantity demanded, prices tend to fall.

Prices tend to rise when there is excess demand and fall when there is excess supply.

Two other things to note about supply and demand are (1) the greater the difference between quantity supplied and quantity demanded, the more pressure there is for prices to rise or fall, and (2) when quantity demanded equals quantity supplied, the market is in equilibrium.

People's tendencies to change prices exist as long as there's some difference between quantity supplied and quantity demanded. But the change in price brings the laws of supply and demand into play. As price falls, quantity supplied decreases as some suppliers leave the business (the law of supply). And as some people who originally weren't really interested in buying the good think, "Well, at this low price, maybe I do want to buy," quantity demanded increases (the law of demand). Similarly, when price rises, quantity supplied will increase (the law of supply) and quantity demanded will decrease (the law of demand).

Whenever quantity supplied and quantity demanded are unequal, price tends to change. If, however, quantity supplied and quantity demanded are equal, price will stay the same because no one will have an incentive to change.

THE GRAPHICAL INTERACTION OF SUPPLY AND DEMAND

Figure 4-8 shows supply and demand curves for DVD rentals and demonstrates the force of the invisible hand. Let's consider what will happen to the price of DVD in three cases:

1. When the price is \$3.50 each;
2. When the price is \$1.50 each; and
3. When the price is \$2.50 each.

1. When price is \$3.50, quantity supplied is 7 and quantity demanded is only 3. Excess supply is 4. Individual consumers can get all they want, but most suppliers can't sell all they wish; they'll be stuck with DVDs that they'd like to rent. Suppliers will tend to offer their goods at a lower price and demanders, who see plenty of suppliers out there, will bargain harder for an even lower price. Both these forces will push the price as indicated by the *A* arrows in Figure 4-8.

Now let's start from the other side.

2. Say price is \$1.50. The situation is now reversed. Quantity supplied is 3 and quantity demanded is 7. Excess demand is 4. Now it's consumers who can't get what they want and suppliers who are in the strong bargaining position. The pressures will be on price to rise in the direction of the *B* arrows in Figure 4-8.
3. At \$2.50, price is at its equilibrium: quantity supplied equals quantity demanded. Suppliers offer to sell 5 and consumers want to buy 5, so there's no pressure on price to rise or fall. Price will tend to remain where it is (point *E* in Figure 4-8). Notice that the equilibrium price is where the supply and demand curves intersect.

Figure 4-8 The Interaction of Supply and Demand
Combining Ann's supply from Figure 4-7 and Alice's demand from Figure 4-4, let's see the force of the invisible hand. When there is excess demand there is upward pressure on price. When there is excess supply there is downward pressure on price. Understanding these pressures is essential to understanding how to apply economics to reality.

Price (per DVD)	Quantity supplied	Quantity demanded	Surplus (+)/ shortage (−)
$3.50	7	3	+4
$2.50	5	5	0
$1.50	3	7	−4

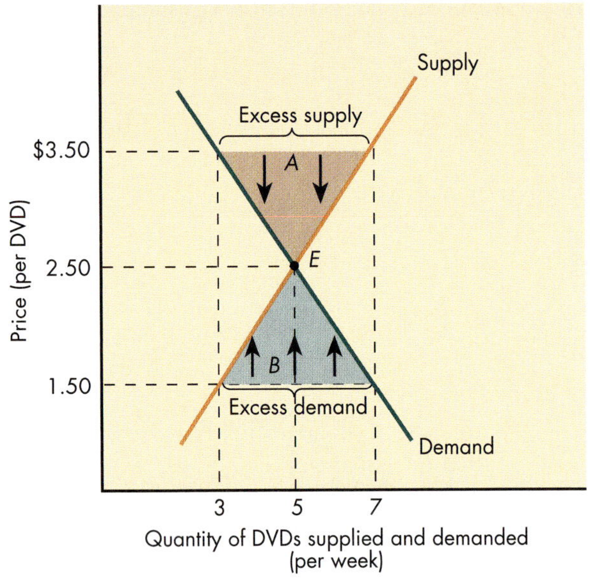

Political and Social Forces and Equilibrium

When I discussed equilibrium, I emphasized that equilibrium is a characteristic of the framework of analysis, not of the real world. Understanding that idea is important in applying economic models to reality. For example, in the preceding description I said equilibrium occurs where quantity supplied equals quantity demanded. In a model where the invisible hand is the only force operating, that's true. In the real world, however, other forces—political and social forces—are operating. These will likely push price away from that supply/demand equilibrium. Were we to consider a model that included all these forces—political, social, and economic—equilibrium would be likely to exist where quantity supplied isn't equal to quantity demanded. For example:

- Farmers use political pressure to obtain prices that are higher than supply/demand equilibrium prices.
- Social pressures often offset economic pressures and prevent unemployed individuals from accepting work at lower wages than currently employed workers receive.
- Existing firms conspire to limit new competition by lobbying Congress to pass restrictive regulations and by devising pricing strategies to scare off new entrants.
- Renters often organize to pressure local government to set caps on the rental price of apartments.

If social and political forces were included in the analysis, they'd provide a counterpressure to the dynamic forces of supply and demand. The result would be an equilibrium with continual excess supply or excess demand if the market were considered only in reference to economic forces. The invisible hand pushing toward a supply/demand equilibrium would be thwarted by social and political forces pushing in the other direction.

Figure 4-9 (a and b) Shifts in Supply and Demand
When there is an increase in demand (the demand curve shifts outward), there is upward pressure on the price, as shown in (**a**). If demand increases from D_0 to D_1, the quantity of DVD rentals that was demanded at a price of \$2.25, 8, increases to 10, but the quantity supplied remains at 8. This excess demand tends to cause prices to rise. Eventually, a new equilibrium is reached at the price of \$2.50, where the quantity supplied and the quantity demanded is 9 (point *B*).

If supply of DVD rentals decreases, then the entire supply curve shifts inward to the left, as shown in (**b**), from S_0 to S_1. At the price of \$2.25, the quantity supplied has now decreased to 6 DVDs, but the quantity demanded has remained at 8 DVDs. The excess demand tends to force the price upward. Eventually, an equilibrium is reached at the price of \$2.50 and quantity 7 (point C).

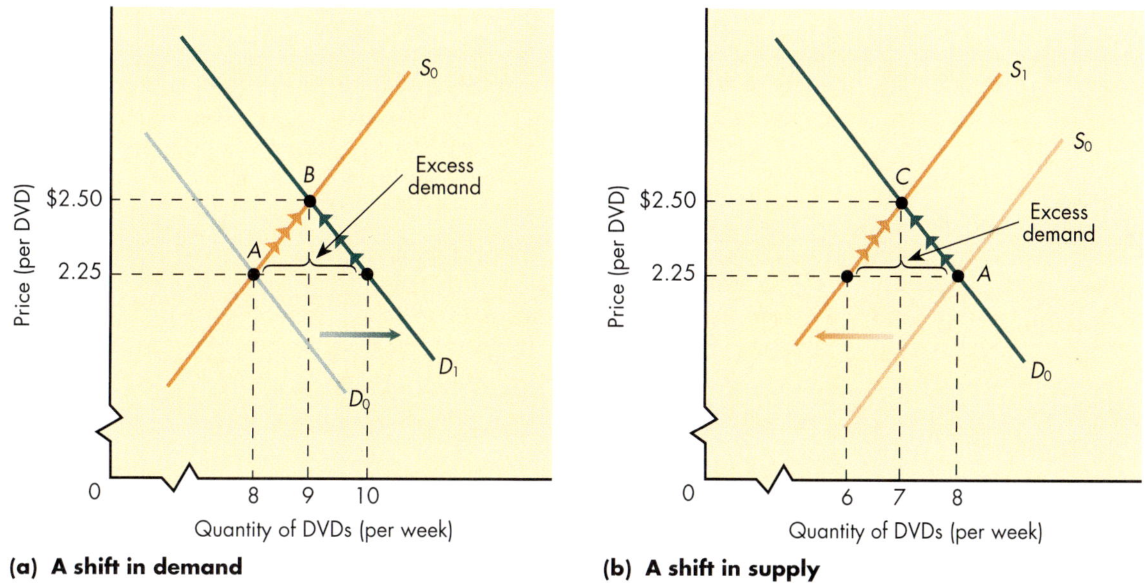

Shifts in Supply and Demand

Supply and demand are most useful when trying to figure out what will happen to equilibrium price and quantity if either supply or demand shifts. Figure 4-9(a) deals with an increase in demand. Figure 4-9(b) deals with a decrease in supply.

Let's consider again the supply and demand for DVD rentals. In Figure 4-9(a), the supply is S_0 and initial demand is D_0. They meet at an equilibrium price of \$2.25 per DVD and an equilibrium quantity of 8 DVDs per week (point *A*). Now say that the demand for DVD rentals increases from D_0 to D_1. At a price of \$2.25, the quantity of DVD rentals supplied will be 8 and the quantity demanded will be 10; excess demand of 2 exists.

Q-7 Demonstrate graphically the effect of a heavy frost in Florida on the equilibrium quantity and price of oranges.

The excess demand pushes prices upward in the direction of the small arrows, decreasing the quantity demanded and increasing the quantity supplied. As it does so, movement takes place along both the supply curve and the demand curve.

The upward push on price decreases the gap between the quantity supplied and the quantity demanded. As the gap decreases, the upward pressure decreases, but as long as that gap exists at all, price will be pushed upward until the new equilibrium price (\$2.50) and new quantity (9) are reached (point *B*). At point *B*, quantity supplied equals quantity demanded. So the market is in equilibrium. Notice that the adjustment is twofold: The higher price brings about equilibrium by both increasing the quantity supplied (from 8 to 9) and decreasing the quantity demanded (from 10 to 9).

Figure 4-9(b) begins with the same situation that we started with in Figure 4-9(a); the initial equilibrium quantity and price are 8 DVDs per week and \$2.25 per DVD

THE SUPPLY AND DEMAND FOR CHILDREN

Beyond the Tools

In Chapter 1, I distinguished between an economic force and a market force. Economic forces are operative in all aspects of our lives; market forces are economic forces that are allowed to be expressed through a market. My examples in this chapter are of market forces—of goods sold in a market—but supply and demand can also be used to analyze situations in which economic, but not market, forces operate. An economist who is adept at this is Gary Becker of the University of Chicago. He has applied supply and demand analysis to a wide range of issues, even the supply and demand for children.

Becker doesn't argue that children should be bought and sold. But he does argue that economic considerations play a large role in people's decisions on how many children to have. In farming communities, children can be productive early in life; by age six or seven, they can work on a farm. In an advanced industrial community, children provide pleasure but generally don't contribute productively to family income. Even getting them to help around the house can be difficult.

Becker argues that since the price of having children is lower for a farming society than for an industrial society, farming societies will have more children per family. Quantity of children demanded will be larger. And that's what we find. Developing countries that rely primarily on farming often have three, four, or more children per family. Industrial societies average fewer than two children per family.

(point A). In this example, however, instead of demand increasing, let's assume supply decreases—say because some suppliers change what they like to do, and decide they will no longer supply DVDs. That means that the entire supply curve shifts inward to the left (from S_0 to S_1). At the initial equilibrium price of $2.25, the quantity demanded is greater than the quantity supplied. Two more DVDs are demanded than are supplied. (Excess demand = 2.)

Q-8 Demonstrate graphically the likely effect of an increase in the price of gas on the equilibrium quantity and price of compact cars.

This excess demand exerts upward pressure on price. Price is pushed in the direction of the small arrows. As the price rises, the upward pressure on price is reduced but will still exist until the new equilibrium price, $2.50, and new quantity, 7, are reached. At $2.50, the quantity supplied equals the quantity demanded. The adjustment has involved a movement along the demand curve and the new supply curve. As price rises, quantity supplied is adjusted upward and quantity demanded is adjusted downward until quantity supplied equals quantity demanded where the new supply curve intersects the demand curve at point C, an equilibrium of 7 and $2.50.

Here is an exercise for you to try. Demonstrate graphically how the price of computers could have fallen dramatically in the past 10 years, even as demand increased. (Hint: Supply has shifted even more, so even at lower prices, far more computers have been supplied than were being supplied 10 years ago.)

THE LIMITATIONS OF SUPPLY/DEMAND ANALYSIS

Supply and demand are tools, and, like most tools, they help us enormously when used appropriately. Used inappropriately, however, they can be misleading. Throughout the book I'll introduce you to the limitations of the tools, but let me discuss an important one here.

In supply/demand analysis other things are assumed constant. If other things change, then one cannot directly apply supply/demand analysis. Sometimes supply and demand are interconnected, making it impossible to hold other things constant. Let's take an example. Say we are considering the effect of a fall in the wage rate. In supply/demand analysis, you would look at the effect that fall would have on workers' decisions to supply labor, and on business's decision to hire workers. But there are also other effects. All actions have a multitude of ripple and possible feedback effects—they create waves, like those that spread out from a stone thrown into a pool. For instance, the fall in the wage lowers people's income and thereby reduces demand. That reduction may feed back to firms and reduce the demand for their goods and that reduction might reduce the firms' demand for workers. If these effects do occur, and are important enough to affect the result, those effects have to be added to the analysis in order for you to have a complete analysis.

Q-9 When determining the effect of a shift factor on price and quantity, in which of the following markets could you likely assume that other things will remain constant?

1. Market for eggs.
2. Labor market.
3. World oil market.
4. Market for luxury boats.

There is no single answer to the question of which ripples must be included, and much debate among economists involves which ripple effects to include. But there are some general rules. Supply/demand analysis, used without adjustment, is most appropriate for questions where the goods are a small percentage of the entire economy. That is when the other-things-constant assumption will most likely hold. As soon as one starts analyzing goods that are a large percentage of the entire economy, the other-things-constant assumption is likely not to hold true. The reason is found in the **fallacy of composition**—*the false assumption that what is true for a part will also be true for the whole*.

The fallacy of composition is the false assumption that what is true for a part will also be true for the whole.

Consider the example of one supplier lowering the price of his or her good. People will substitute that good for other goods, and the quantity of the good demanded will increase. But what if all suppliers lower their prices? Since all prices have gone down, why should consumers switch? The substitution story can't be used in the aggregate. There are many such examples.

An understanding of the fallacy of composition is of central relevance to macroeconomics. In the aggregate, whenever firms produce (whenever they supply), they create income (demand for their goods). So in macro, when supply changes, demand changes. This interdependence is one of the primary reasons we have a separate macroeconomics. In macroeconomics, the other-things-constant assumption central to microeconomic supply/demand analysis cannot hold.

Q-10 Why is the fallacy of composition relevant for macroeconomic issues?

It is to account for these interdependencies that we separate macro analysis from micro analysis. In macro we use curves whose underlying foundations are much more complicated than the supply and demand curves we use in micro.

It is to account for interdependency between aggregate supply decisions and aggregate demand decisions that we have a separate micro analysis and a separate macro analysis.

One final comment: The fact that there may be an interdependence between supply and demand does not mean that you can't use supply/demand analysis; it simply means that you must modify its results with the interdependency that, if you've done the analysis correctly, you've kept in the back of your head. Thus, using supply and demand analysis is generally a step in any good economic analysis, but you must remember that it may be only a step.

Conclusion

Throughout the book I'll be presenting examples of supply and demand. So I'll end this chapter here because its intended purposes have been served. What were those intended purposes? First, I exposed you to enough economic terminology and economic thinking to allow you to proceed to my more complicated examples. Second, I have set your mind to work putting the events around you into a supply/demand framework. Doing that will give you new insights into the events that shape all our lives. Once you incorporate the supply/demand framework into your way of looking at the world, you will have made an important step toward thinking like an economist.

Summary

- The law of demand states that quantity demanded rises as price falls, other things constant.
- The law of supply states that quantity supplied rises as price rises, other things constant.
- Factors that affect supply and demand other than price are called shift factors. Shift factors of demand include income, prices of other goods, tastes, expectations, and taxes on and subsidies to consumers. Shift factors of supply include the price of inputs, technology, expectations, and taxes on and subsidies to producers.
- A change in quantity demanded (supplied) is a movement along the demand (supply) curve. A change in demand (supply) is a shift of the entire demand (supply) curve.
- The laws of supply and demand hold true because individuals can substitute.
- A market demand (supply) curve is the horizontal sum of all individual demand (supply) curves.
- When quantity supplied equals quantity demanded, prices have no tendency to change. This is equilibrium.
- When quantity demanded is greater than quantity supplied, prices tend to rise. When quantity supplied is greater than quantity demanded, prices tend to fall.
- When the demand curve shifts to the right (left), equilibrium price rises (declines) and equilibrium quantity rises (falls).
- When the supply curve shifts to the right (left), equilibrium price declines (rises) and equilibrium quantity rises (falls).
- In the real world, one must add political and social forces to the supply/demand model. When you do, equilibrium is likely not going to be where quantity demanded equals quantity supplied.
- In macro, small side effects that can be assumed away in micro are multiplied enormously. Thus, they can significantly change the results and cannot be ignored. To ignore them is to fall into the fallacy of composition.

Key Terms

demand *(85)*
demand curve *(84)*
equilibrium *(96)*
equilibrium price *(96)*
equilibrium quantity *(96)*
excess demand *(96)*
excess supply *(96)*
fallacy of composition *(101)*
law of demand *(84)*
law of supply *(90)*
market demand curve *(88)*
market supply curve *(95)*
movement along a demand curve *(85)*
movement along a supply curve *(92)*
quantity demanded *(85)*
quantity supplied *(92)*
shift in demand *(85)*
shift in supply *(92)*
supply *(92)*
supply curve *(91)*

Questions for Thought and Review

1. State the law of demand. Why is price inversely related to quantity demanded?
2. State the law of supply. Why is price directly related to quantity supplied?
3. List four shift factors of demand and explain how each affects demand.
4. Distinguish the effect of a shift factor of demand on the demand curve from the effect of a change in price on the demand curve.
5. Mary has just stated that normally, as price rises, supply will increase. Her teacher grimaces. Why?
6. List four shift factors of supply and explain how each affects supply.

7. Derive the market supply curve from the following two individual supply curves.

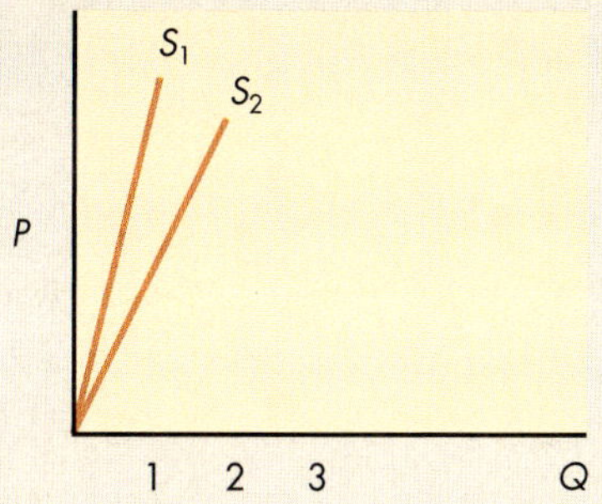

8. It has just been reported that eating red meat is bad for your health. Using supply and demand curves, demonstrate the report's likely effect on the equilibrium price and quantity of steak sold in the market.
9. Why does the price of airline tickets rise during the summer months? Demonstrate your answer graphically.
10. Why does sales volume rise during weeks when states suspend taxes on sales by retailers? Demonstrate your answer graphically.
11. What is the expected impact of increased security measures imposed by the federal government on airlines on fares and volume of travel? Demonstrate your answer graphically.
12. Explain what a sudden popularity of "Economics Professor" brand casual wear would likely do to prices of that brand.
13. In a flood, usable water supplies ironically tend to decline because the pumps and water lines are damaged. What will a flood likely do to prices of bottled water?
14. Oftentimes, to be considered for a job, you have to know someone in the firm. What does this observation tell you about the wage paid for that job?
15. In most developing countries, there are long lines of taxis at airports, and these taxis often wait two or three hours. What does this tell you about the price in that market? Demonstrate with supply and demand analysis.
16. Define the fallacy of composition. How does it affect the supply/demand model?
17. Why is a supply/demand analysis that includes only economic forces likely to be incomplete?
18. In which of the following three markets is there likely to be the greatest feedback effects: market for housing, market for wheat, market for manufactured goods?

Problems and Exercises

1. You're given the following individual demand tables for comic books.

Price	John	Liz	Alex
$ 2	4	36	24
4	4	32	20
6	0	28	16
8	0	24	12
10	0	20	8
12	0	16	4
14	0	12	0
16	0	8	0

a. Determine the market demand table.
b. Graph the individual and market demand curves.
c. If the current market price is $4, what's total market demand? What happens to total market demand if price rises to $8?
d. Say that an advertising campaign increases demand by 50 percent. Illustrate graphically what will happen to the individual and market demand curves.

2. You're given the following demand and supply tables:

	Demand		
P	D_1	D_2	D_3
$37	20	4	8
47	15	2	7
57	10	0	6
67	5	0	5

	Supply		
P	S_1	S_2	S_3
$37	0	4	14
47	0	8	16
57	10	12	18
67	10	16	20

a. Draw the market demand and market supply curves.
b. What is excess supply/demand at price $37? Price $67?
c. Label equilibrium price and quantity.

3. Draw hypothetical supply and demand curves for tea. Show how the equilibrium price and quantity will be affected by each of the following occurrences:
   a. Bad weather wreaks havoc with the tea crop.
   b. A medical report implying tea is bad for your health is published.
   c. A technological innovation lowers the cost of producing tea.
   d. Consumers' income falls. (Assume tea is a normal good.)
4. You're a commodity trader and you've just heard a report that the winter wheat harvest will be 2.09 billion bushels, a 44 percent jump, rather than an expected 35 percent jump to 1.96 billion bushels.
   a. What would you expect would happen to wheat prices?
   b. Demonstrate graphically the effect you suggested in *a*.
5. In the United States, gasoline costs consumers about \$1.50 per gallon. In Italy it costs consumers about \$5 per gallon. What effect does this price differential likely have on:
   a. The size of cars in the United States and in Italy?
   b. The use of public transportation in the United States and in Italy?
   c. The fuel efficiency of cars in the United States and in Italy? What would be the effect of raising the price of gasoline in the United States to \$4 per gallon?
6. State whether supply/demand analysis used without significant modification is suitable to assess the following:
   a. The impact of an increase in the demand for pencils on the price of pencils.
   b. The impact of an increase in the supply of labor on the quantity of labor demanded.
   c. The impact of an increase in aggregate savings on aggregate expenditures.
   d. The impact of a new method of producing CDs on the price of CDs.

WEB QUESTIONS

1. Go to the U.S. Census Bureau's home page (www.census.gov) and navigate to the population pyramids for 2000, for 2025, and for 2050. What is projected to happen to the age distribution in the United States? Other things constant, what do you expect will happen in the next 50 years to the relative demand and supply for each of the following, being careful to distinguish between shifts of and a movement along a curve:
   a. Nursing homes.
   b. Prescription medication.
   c. Baby high chairs.
   d. College education.
2. Go to the Energy Information Administration's home page (www.eia.doe.gov) and look up its most recent "Short-Term Energy Outlook" and answer the following questions:
   a. List the factors that are expected to affect demand and supply for energy in the near term. How will each affect demand? Supply?
   b. What is the EIA's forecast for world oil prices? Show graphically how the factors listed in your answer to *a* are consistent with the EIA's forecast. Label all shifts in demand and supply.
   c. Describe and explain EIA's forecast for the price of gasoline, heating oil, and natural gas. Be sure to mention the factors that are affecting the forecast.
3. Go to the Tax Administration home page (www.taxadmin.org) and look up sales tax rates for the 50 U.S. states.
   a. Which states have no sales tax? Which state has the highest sales tax?
   b. Show graphically the effect of sales tax on supply, demand, equilibrium quantity, and equilibrium price.
   c. Name two neighboring states that have significantly different sales tax rates. How does that affect the supply or demand for goods in those states?

ANSWERS TO MARGIN QUESTIONS

1. The demand curve slopes downward because price and quantity demanded are inversely related. As the price of a good rises, people switch to purchasing other goods whose prices have not risen by as much. *(84)*
2. *Demand for luxury goods*. The other possibility, *quantity of luxury goods demanded*, is used to refer to movements along (not shifts of) the demand curve. *(85)*
3. (1) The decline in price will increase the quantity of computers demanded (movement down along the demand curve); (2) With more income, demand for computers will rise (shift of the demand curve out to the right). *(86)*
4. When adding two demand curves, you sum them horizontally, as in the accompanying diagram. *(88)*

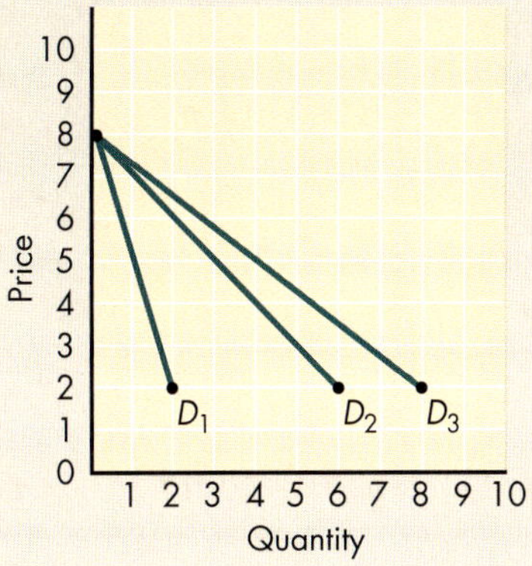

5. *The quantity supplied* declined because there was a movement along the supply curve. The supply curve itself remained unchanged. *(92)*
6. (1) The supply of romance novels declines since paper is an input to production (supply shifts in to the left); (2) the supply of romance novels declines since the tax increases the cost to the producer (supply shifts in to the left). *(92)*
7. A heavy frost in Florida will decrease the supply of oranges, increasing the price and decreasing the quantity demanded, as in the accompanying graph. *(99)*

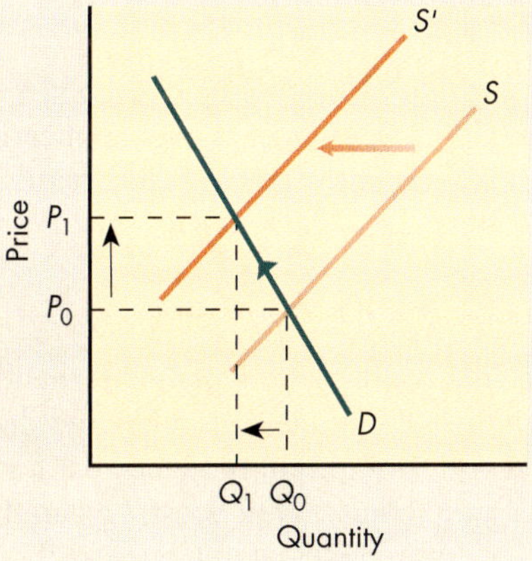

8. An increase in the price of gas will likely increase the demand for compact cars, increasing their price and increasing the quantity supplied, as in the accompanying graph. *(100)*

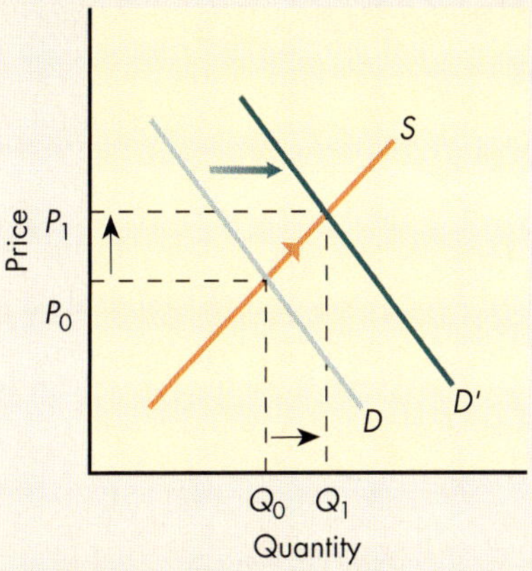

9. Other things are most likely to remain constant in the egg and luxury boat markets because each is a small percentage of the whole economy. Factors that affect the world oil market and the labor market will have ripple effects that must be taken into account in any analysis. *(101)*
10. The fallacy of composition is relevant for macroeconomic issues because it reminds us that, in the aggregate, small effects that are immaterial for micro issues can add up and be material. *(101)*

5 Using Supply and Demand

After reading this chapter, you should be able to:

- Explain real-world events using supply and demand.
- Discuss how exchange rates are determined using supply and demand.
- Demonstrate the effect of a price ceiling and a price floor on a market.
- Explain the effect of excise taxes and tariffs on equilibrium price and quantity.
- Explain the effect of a third-party-payer system on equilibrium price and quantity.

It is by invisible hands that we are bent and tortured worst.

—*Nietzsche*

Supply and demand give you a lens through which to view the economy. That lens brings into focus issues that would otherwise seem like a muddle. In this chapter we use the supply/demand lens to consider real-world events.

Real-World Supply and Demand Applications

I begin this section by presenting various applications of supply/demand analysis to show you how the supply/demand model works. These applications show you the power of supply and demand and also how the invisible hand interacts with social and political forces.

The Market for Advertising

From the supply/demand analysis in Chapter 4, you might get the idea that prices are constantly fluctuating in response to changes in supply and demand. This is true for commodities such as gold and agricultural products, but for 90 percent of final goods sold, prices are often slow to adjust. That doesn't mean that supply and demand forces aren't working and that prices won't eventually adjust. It just means that the process of adjustment takes time, often because other forces are influencing events. In our example, we consider a market in which supply and demand are operating but are affecting actions in a way that does not show up directly in reported prices.

Companies spend a lot of resources to influence your buying habits, so the market for television advertising is a big market. Companies in the United States spend in excess of $100 billion each year on advertising. Advertising creates brand-name recognition and that "gotta-have" feeling among consumers. The supply in this market is relatively constant—there are only so many minutes on shows that they can fill up with advertising (although the amount has been creeping up so that now the typical half-hour show is really only 19 minutes; the remainder is advertising).

The advertising market is highly competitive, and the ads are expensive. A 30-second advertising slot on a typical prime-time television show costs over $60,000. During the Super Bowl, that price goes up to $2 million.

Companies know that people don't like advertising and often try to avoid it. A remote in the hands of a man (somehow men seem to like the control much more than women) means that three programs can be watched at once (although stations often run the commercials simultaneously to stop this), but firms recognize that much of their advertising is "clicked" away.

Because advertising budgets are often directly related to sales, the demand for advertising fluctuates significantly. Thus, when the economy slows down, the demand for advertising also slows down. In 2001, that's precisely what happened. The U.S. economy began to slow, and companies cut advertising budgets significantly. The advertising market fell into its worst decline since World War II, with advertisers cutting their demand by 10 percent.

The decline in the demand for advertising is represented by a shift of the demand curve to the left, as Figure 5-1 shows. From supply/demand analysis, you'd expect the price of advertisements to fall from P_0 to P_1 and the quantity of advertisements to decline from Q_0 to Q_1. But price didn't decline, at least not initially. Instead of reducing their prices, television companies offered extras to advertisers. Although such extras didn't show up in reported prices, they were equivalent to a decline in price, because the product the advertisers were getting was qualitatively better. One of the ways in which media companies provided advertisers extra value was to weave advertisements into the media's content. In magazines this meant that products were mentioned in articles, and in TV it meant that products were mentioned positively in the show or became part of the story line. This got the message to more people, including the "remote-clickers."

Prices are often slow to adjust to changes in supply and demand.

There are many examples of this phenomenon, but one will suffice. The example is advertising for the fast-food company Wendy's on the *Rosie O'Donnell Show*. Wendy's was a standard advertiser between show segments. When the advertising market slumped, Wendy's required more for the standard fee. It asked that Rosie eat a Wendy's salad as part of the show's segment on dieting. And Rosie did precisely that, having

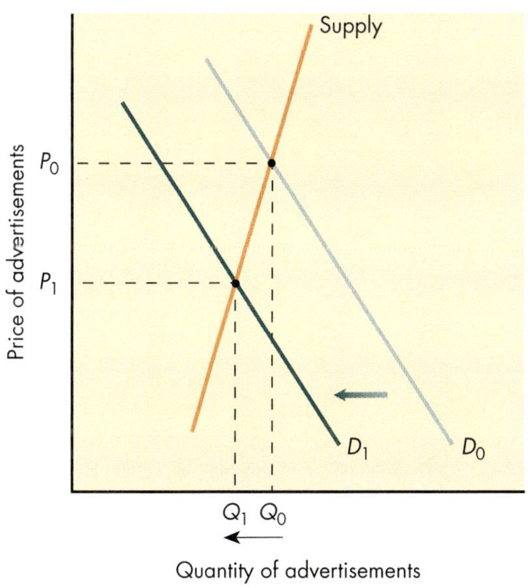

Figure 5-1 Decline in the Demand for Advertising
In 2001, the demand for advertising declined. As this figure shows, one would expect the effect would be to reduce the equilibrium price and quantity. This didn't happen, at least not initially. Instead the media offered higher-quality advertising at the same price. Although the price didn't fall, the value received for the price rose.

received an urgent instruction to do so from offstage. Upon eating the salad, she declared, "Mmmm, that's good." Wendy's was happy. So, in this case, even though the price Wendy's paid for advertising didn't fall, the value that Wendy's received for the price rose. With some modification—adjusting price for the value received—the supply/demand framework can explain why companies were able to get so much more advertising value during a slump in the market.

The Price of a Foreign Currency

The next market we consider is the market for foreign currencies, which is called the foreign exchange (forex) market. It is this market that determines the **exchange rates**—*the price of one currency in terms of another currency*—that are reported daily in newspapers in tables such as the following:

Q-1 You are going to Chile and plan to exchange $100. According to the foreign exchange rate table in the text, how many Chilean pesos will you receive?

Wednesday, January 8, 2003

EXCHANGE RATES

The foreign exchange mid-range rates below apply to trading among banks in amounts of $1 million and more, as quoted at 4 p.m. Eastern time by Reuters and other sources. Retail transactions provide fewer units of foreign currency per dollar.

	U.S. $ EQUIVALENT		CURRENCY PER U.S. $	
Country	**Wed**	**Tue**	**Wed**	**Tue**
Argentina (Peso)-y	.3035	.3044	3.2949	3.2852
Australia (Dollar)	.5766	.5739	1.7343	1.7425
Bahrain (Dinar)	2.6523	2.6522	.3770	.3770
Brazil (Real)	.2991	.3046	3.3434	3.2830
Canada (Dollar)	.6403	.6399	1.5618	1.5627
Chile (Peso)	.001406	.001405	711.24	711.74
China (Renminbi)	.1208	.1208	8.2781	8.2781
Colombia (Peso)	.0003457	.003439	2892.68	2907.82
Czech. Rep (Koruna)				
Commercial rate	.03335	.03327	29.985	30.057
Denmark (Krone)	.1413	.1403	7.0771	7.1276
Ecuador (Sucre)	1.0000	1.0000	1.0000	1.0000
Hong Kong (Dollar)	.1282	.1282	7.8003	7.8003
Hungary (Forint)	.004459	.004429	224.27	225.78
India (Rupee)	.02086	.02086	47.939	47.939
Indonesia (Rupiah)	.0001120	.0001120	8929	8929
Israel (Shekel)	.2069	.2078	4.8333	4.8123
Japan (Yen)	.008395	.008303	119.12	120.44
Jordan (Dinar)	1.4092	1.4092	.7096	.7096
Kuwait (Dinar)	3.3417	3.3343	.2992	.2999
Lebanon (Pound)	.0006634	.0006634	1507.39	1507.39
Malaysia (Ringgit)-b	.2632	.2632	3.7994	3.7994
Malta (Lira)	2.5086	2.4933	.3986	.4011

	U.S. $ EQUIVALENT		CURRENCY PER U.S. $	
Country	**Tue**	**Mon**	**Tue**	**Mon**
Mexico (Peso)				
Floating rate	.0957	.0966	10.4450	10.3541
New Zealand (Dollar)	.5328	.5300	1.8769	1.8868
Norway (Krone)	.1451	.1442	6.8918	6.9348
Pakistan (Rupee)	.01719	.01720	58.173	58.140
Peru (new Sol)	.2865	.2861	3.4904	3.4953
Philippines (Peso)	.01868	.01870	53.533	53.476
Poland (Zloty)	.2614	.2606	3.8256	3.8373
Russia (Ruble)-a	.03136	.03137	31.888	31.878
Saudi Arabia (Riyal)	.2667	.2666	3.7495	3.7509
Singapore (Dollar)	.5760	.5729	1.7367	1.7455
Slovak Rep. (Koruna)	.02537	.02528	39.417	39.557
South Africa (Rand)	.1169	.1155	8.5543	8.6580
South Korea (Won)	.0008446	.0008453	1183.99	1183.01
Sweden (Krona)	.1154	.1149	8.6655	8.7032
Switzerland (Franc)	.7202	.7146	1.3885	1.3994
Taiwan (Dollar)	.02895	.02899	34.542	34.495
Thailand (Baht)	.02342	.02332	42.699	42.882
Turkey (Lira)	.00000060	.00000059	1666667	1694915
U.K. (Pound)	1.6123	1.6046	.6202	.6232
United Arab (Dirham)	.2723	.2723	3.6724	3.6724
Uruguay (Peso)				
Financial	.03600	.03600	27.778	27.778
Venezuela (Bolivar)	.000642	.000695	1602.56	1438.85
SDR	1.3532	1.3593	.7390	.7357
Euro	1.0493	1.0518	.9530	.9599

Special Drawing Rights (SDR) are based on exchange rates for the U.S., British, and Japanese currencies. Source: International Monetary Fund.

a-Russian Central Bank rate. b-Government rate. y-Floating rate.

This table shows the cost of various currencies in terms of dollars and dollars in terms of other currencies. From it you can see that on January 8, 2003, one riyal cost about 27 cents and one rand cost 12 cents. (If you are wondering what riyal and rand are, look at the table.)

People demand currencies of other countries to buy those countries' goods and assets.

Unless you collect currencies, the reason you want the currency of another country is that you want to buy something that country produces or an existing asset of that country. Say you want to buy a Hyundai car that costs 13.476 million South Korean won. Looking at the table, you see that 1 won costs $0.000845. This means that 13.476 million won will cost you $11,387.22. So before you can buy the Hyundai, somebody must go to a forex market with $11,387.22 and exchange those dollars for 13.476 million won. Only then can the car be bought in the United States. Most final buyers don't do this; the importer does it for them. But whenever a foreign good is bought, someone must trade currencies.

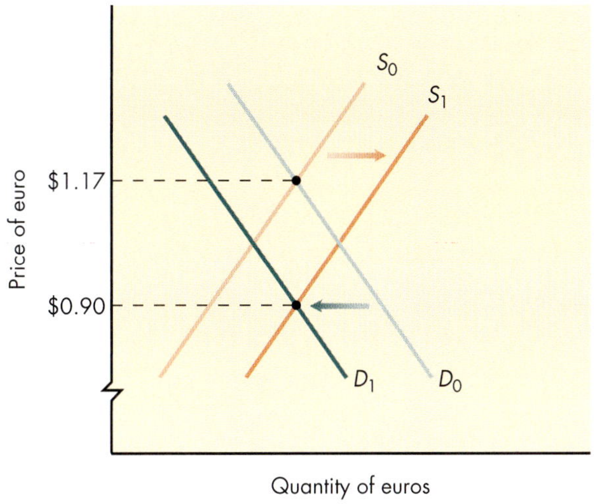

Figure 5-2 The Market for Euros
The price of the euro declined for a few years after it was introduced because the U.S. stock market was rising and was expected to continue to rise. European investors increased their supply of euros to buy dollars and invest in the U.S. stock market, while American investors sold European stocks to buy American stocks, which required reducing their demand for euros. The combined effect was a drop in the dollar price of euros.

To see what determines exchange rates let's consider the price of the **euro**—*the currency used by 12 of the members of the European Union*. When the euro was first introduced in 1999, one euro sold for $1.17. Over the next two years, the price of the euro fell to about $0.90. What caused its price to fall? Supply and demand. Once you recognize that a currency is just another good, what may appear to be a hard subject (the determination of exchange rates) becomes an easy subject (what determines a good's price). All you have to do is to replace the good I used in Chapter 4 (DVDs) with euros, and apply the same reasoning process we've used so far to determine the equilibrium price of the euro.

The determination of exchange rates is the same as the determination of price. A currency is just another good.

Figure 5-2 shows supply and demand curves for the euro. As with any good, the supply of euros represents those people who are selling euros and the demand for the euro represents those people who are buying euros. Sellers of euros are Europeans who want to buy U.S. goods and assets. Buyers of euros are U.S. citizens who want to buy European goods and assets. (For simplicity, we assume that the only countries that exist are the United States and European countries that use the euro as their currency.)

The fall in the value of the euro after it was introduced occurred for a number of reasons. The one we will focus on here is the phenomenal rise in U.S. stock prices in the late 1990s and into early 2000. The initial demand, D_0, and supply, S_0, for euros resulted in an equilibrium price of $1.17 in 1999. Because U.S. stock prices were rising, and were expected to continue to rise, Europeans wanted to buy U.S. stocks. To buy U.S. stocks, they needed to pay in U.S. dollars. They had to sell their euros for dollars, increasing the supply of euros from S_0 to S_1. Americans, for their part, decided to buy more U.S. stocks and therefore fewer European stocks. Americans reduced their demand for euros from D_0 to D_1. Both forces contributed to a decline in the price of the euro, and the equilibrium price of the euro fell to $0.90 in 2000.

There is more to the determination of exchange rates than this, but as is often the case, supply/demand analysis gives you a good first entry into what is otherwise a potentially confusing issue.

Three Real-World Examples

Now that we've been through two examples of applying supply and demand analysis, let's see how *you* do in using supply/demand analysis. Below are three events. After reading each, try your hand at explaining what happened, using supply and demand curves.

Q-2 True or false? If supply rises, price will rise.

Figure 5-3 (a, b, and c)
In this exhibit, three shifts of supply and demand are shown. Your task is to match them with the events listed in the chapter.

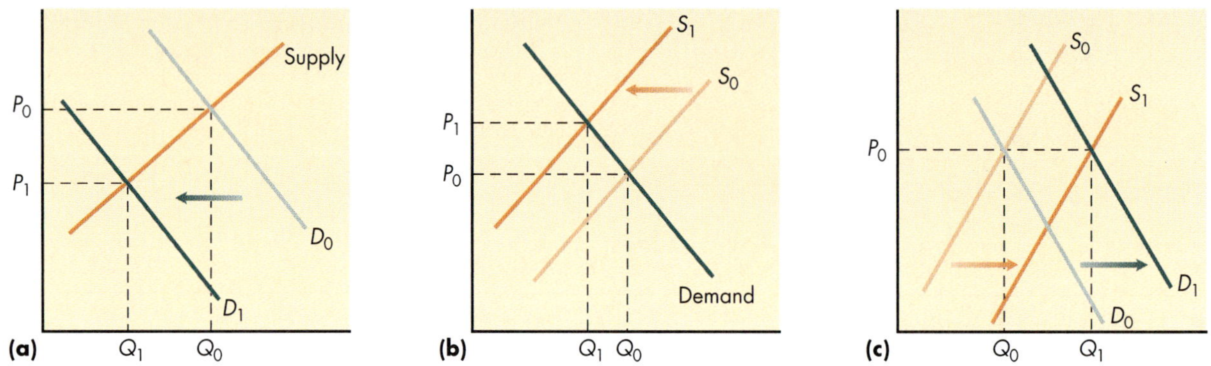

Answers: 1:b; 2:a; 3:c.

To help you in the process Figure 5-3 provides some diagrams. *Before* reading my explanation, try to match the shifts to the examples. In each, be careful to explain which curve, or curves, shifted and how those shifts affected equilibrium price and quantity.

A freeze can ruin a crop causing supply to shift in to the left and price to rise.
Tony Ranze/AFP/Corbis

Web Note 5.1
Fad Markets

1. A 1997 freeze caused more than \$300 million in damage to Florida crops. Prices of some vegetables rose by 25 percent just one week after the freeze. Squash, for example, which had cost \$1.16 per pound on January 17, cost \$1.40 per pound on January 24. Market: Vegetables.
2. In 2001, when the Taliban was ousted from Afghanistan, a five-year law requiring women to completely cover their bodies in public with a wrap-around garment called a burkha was eliminated. Many women stopped wearing burkhas and sellers found they had more burkhas than they could sell. Within days, the price of burkhas fell 20 percent.
3. Due to the entry of new coffee-growers (such as Vietnam) in the market, improved growing techniques, and favorable growing weather, the price of raw coffee beans fell from about \$2.00 a pound in 1997 to less than \$0.50 a pound in 2002. Some growers have proposed a marketing campaign to boost demand to match the increase in supply. While it's unlikely to be successful, for this analysis, let's assume it is. Market: raw coffee beans.

Now that you've matched them, let's see if your analysis matches mine.

Florida Freeze The weather is invariably uncooperative. Nearly every other year, Florida or some other state is hit with a crop damaging freeze. This is a shift factor of supply because it raises the cost of supplying the remaining vegetables. The 1997 freeze shifted the supply curve for Florida vegetables in to the left, as shown in Figure 5-3(b). At the original price, \$1.16 per pound (shown by P_0), quantity demanded exceeded quantity supplied and the invisible hand of the market pressured the price to rise until quantity demanded equaled quantity supplied at \$1.40 per pound (shown by P_1).

Burkhas in Afghanistan Before the Taliban rule began in 1996, many working Afghan women wore Western business clothes. The Taliban outlawed that practice, and

Supply and Demand in Action

Knowing the Tools

Sorting out the effects of the shifts of supply or demand or both can be confusing. Here are some helpful hints to keep things straight:

- Draw the initial demand and supply curves and label them. The equilibrium price and quantity is where these curves intersect. Label them.
- If only price has changed, no curves will shift and a shortage or surplus will result.
- If a nonprice factor affects demand, determine the direction demand has shifted and add the new demand curve. Do the same for supply.
- Equilibrium price and quantity is where the new demand and supply curves intersect. Label them.
- Compare the initial equilibrium price and quantity to the new equilibrium price and quantity.

See if you can describe what happened in the three graphs below.

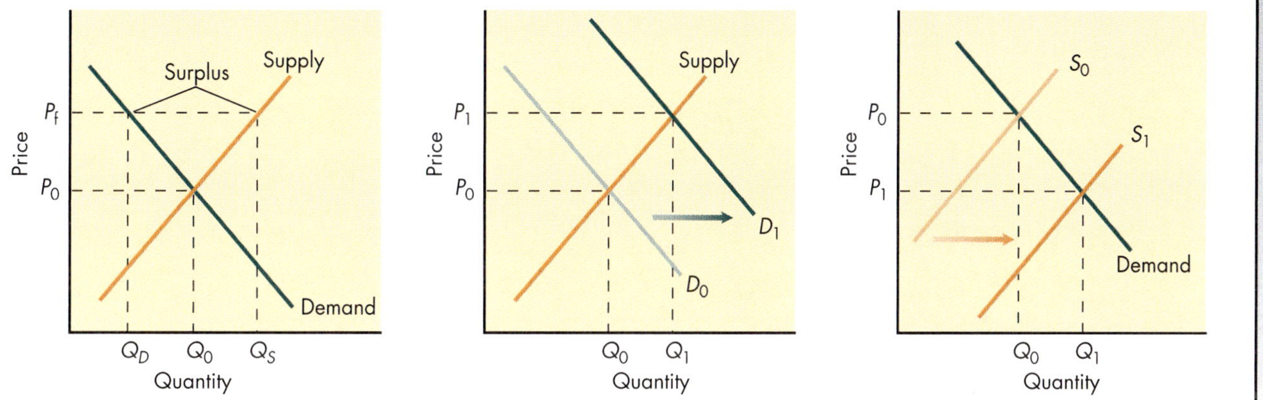

A change in price **A shift in demand** **A shift in supply**

required all women to wear burkhas. That was a boon to the burkha business. But when the Taliban were ousted in 2001, the demand for burkhas fell, shifting demand to the left as shown in Figure 5-3(a). At the original price (shown by P_0) shopkeepers found they had more burkhas than they could sell and began to offer heavy discounts. Afghani women could purchase burkhas at a much lower price (shown by P_1).

Coffee Beans Increased rainfall in Brazil, as well as more efficient farm machinery, has increased the coffee bean yield per acre. The entry of Vietnam into the coffee market has added more coffee beans on the market. This increase in supply is represented by a shift of the supply curve out to the right, as Figure 5-3(c) shows. Equilibrium price declined from \$2.00 to \$0.50 per pound in just two years and equilibrium quantity rose (where D_0 and S_1 intersect). Let's now consider the Coffee Growers' Federation recommended marketing coffee so that increases in demand matched increases in consumption. If successful, this would shift the demand curve out to the right sufficiently to raise the price of coffee back to \$2.00 a pound and raising equilibrium quantity even further. So in this case both supply and demand shift out.

A Review

Anything other than price that affects demand or supply will shift the curves.

As you can see, in using supply/demand analysis, it is important that you separate shifts in demand and supply from movements along the supply and demand curves. Remember: Anything that affects demand and supply other than price of the good will shift the curves. Changes in the price of the good result in movements along the curves. Another thing to recognize is that when both curves are shifting you can get a change in price but little change in quantity, or a change in quantity but little change in price.

Q-3 Say a hormone has been discovered that increases cows' milk production by 20 percent. Demonstrate graphically what effect this discovery would have on the price and quantity of milk sold in a market.

To test your understanding, I'll now give you six generic results from the interaction of supply and demand. Your job is to decide what shifts produced those results. This exercise is a variation of the first. It goes over the same issues, but this time without the graphs. On the left-hand side of the table below, I list combinations of movements of observed prices and quantities, labeling them 1–6. On the right I give six shifts in supply and demand, labeling them *a–f*.

If you don't confuse your "shifts of" with your "movements along," supply and demand provide good off-the-cuff answers for any economic questions.

Price and Quantity Changes			Shifts in Supply and Demand
1.	P↑	Q↑	*a.* Supply shifts in. No change in demand.
2.	P↑	Q↓	*b.* Demand shifts out. Supply shifts in.
3.	P↑	Q?	*c.* Demand shifts in. No change in supply.
4.	P↓	Q?	*d.* Demand shifts out. Supply shifts out.
5.	P?	Q↑	*e.* Demand shifts out. No change in supply.
6.	P↓	Q↓	*f.* Demand shifts in. Supply shifts out.

You are to match the shifts with the price and quantity movements that best fit each described shift, using each shift and movement only once. My recommendation to you is to draw the graphs that are described in *a–f*, decide what happens to price and quantity, and then find the match in 1–6.

Q-4 If both demand and supply shift in to the left, what happens to price and quantity?

Now that you've worked them, let me give you the answers I came up with. They are: 1:*e;* 2:*a;* 3:*b;* 4:*f;* 5:*d;* 6:*c*. How did I come up with the answers? I did what I suggested you do—took each of the scenarios on the right and predicted what happens to price and quantity. For case *a*, supply shifts in to the left and there is a movement up along the demand curve. Since the demand curve is downward-sloping, the price rises and quantity declines. This matches number *2* on the left. For case *b*, demand shifts out to the right. Along the original supply curve, price and quantity would rise. But supply shifts in to the left, leading to even higher prices but lower quantity. What happens to quantity is unclear, so the match must be number 3. For case *c*, demand shifts in to the left. There is movement down along the supply curve with lower price and lower quantity. This matches number 6. For case *d*, demand shifts out and supply shifts out. As demand shifts out, we move along the supply curve to the right and price and quantity rise. But supply shifts out too, and we move out along the new demand curve. Price declines, erasing the previous rise, and the quantity rises even more. This matches number 5.

I'll leave it up to you to confirm my answers to *e* and *f*. Notice that when supply and demand both shift, the change in either price or quantity is uncertain—it depends on the relative size of the shifts. As a summary, I present a diagrammatic of the combinations in Table 5-1.

Table 5-1 Diagram of Effects of Shifts of Demand and Supply on Price and Quantity
This table provides a summary of the effects of shifts in supply and demand on equilibrium price and equilibrium quantity. Notice that when both curves shift, the effect on either price or quantity depends on the relative size of the shifts.

	No change in supply.	Supply shifts out.	Supply shifts in.
No change in demand.	No change.	P↓ Q↑ Price declines and quantity rises.	P↑ Q↓ Price rises. Quantity declines.
Demand shifts out.	P↑ Q↑ Price rises. Quantity rises.	P? Q↑ Quantity rises. Price could be higher or lower depending upon relative size of shifts.	P↑ Q? Price rises. Quantity could rise or fall depending upon relative size of shifts.
Demand shifts in.	P↓ Q↓ Price declines. Quantity declines.	P↓ Q? Price declines. Quantity could rise or fall depending upon relative size of shifts.	P? Q↓ Quantity declines. Price rises or falls depending upon relative size of shifts.

Q-5 If price and quantity both fell, what would you say was the most likely cause?

Government Intervention in the Market

People don't always like the market-determined price. If the invisible hand were the only determinant of prices, that would be tough for them; they would have to accept it. But it isn't; social and political forces are also important determinants of price. For example, when prices fall, sellers look to government for ways to hold prices up; when prices rise, buyers look to government for ways to hold prices down. Let's now consider the effect of such actions. Let's start with an example of the price being held down.

Price Ceilings

When government wants to hold prices down, it imposes a **price ceiling**—*a government-imposed limit on how high a price can be charged.* That limit is generally below equilibrium price. (A price ceiling that is above the equilibrium price will not have any effect at all.) From Chapter 4, you already know the effect of a price that is below equilibrium price—quantity demanded will exceed quantity supplied and there will be excess demand. Let's now look at an example of **rent control**—*a price ceiling on rents, set by government*—and see how that excess demand shows up in the real world.

Web Note 5.2 Rent Control

Rent controls exist today in a number of American cities as well as other cities throughout the world. Many of the laws governing rent were first instituted during the two world wars in the first half of the 20th century. Consider Paris, for example. During World War I, the Paris government froze rent to ease the financial burden of those families whose wage earners were sent to fight in the war. When the soldiers returned at the

Figure 5-4 Rent Control in Paris
A price ceiling imposed on housing rent in Paris during World War I created a shortage of housing when World War I ended and veterans returned home. The shortage would have been eliminated if rents had been allowed to rise to $17 per month.

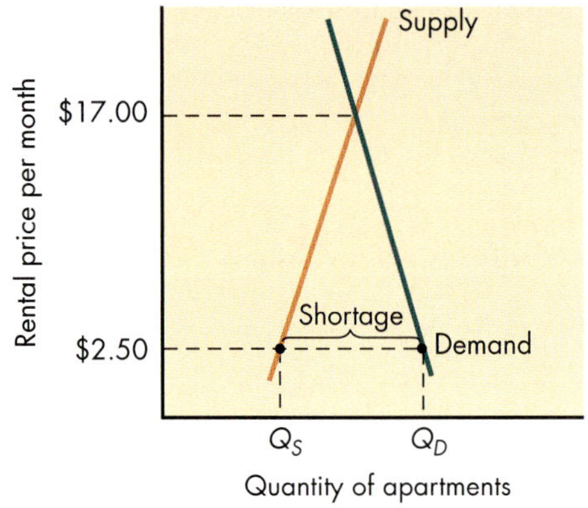

end of the war, the rent control was continued; removing it would have resulted in a tripling of rents, and that was felt to be an unfair burden for veterans. During World War II, the rent control laws were reaffirmed and additional housing was placed under government control. At the end of World War II, maximum rent was set at $2.50 a month. Without rent control, an apartment would have cost $17 a month.

Figure 5-4 shows this situation. The below-market rent set by government created an enormous shortage of apartments. Initially this shortage didn't bother those renting apartments, since they got low-cost apartments. But it created enormous hardships for those who didn't have apartments. Many families moved in with friends or extended families. Others couldn't find housing at all and lived on the streets. However, eventually the rent controls started to cause problems even for those who did have apartments. The reason why is that owners of buildings cut back on maintenance. More than 80 percent of Parisians had no private bathrooms and 20 percent had no running water. Since rental properties weren't profitable, no new buildings were being constructed and existing buildings weren't kept in repair. It was even harder for those who didn't have apartments.

Since market price was not allowed to ration apartments, alternative methods of rationing developed. People paid bribes up to $1,500 per room or watched the obituaries and then simply moved in their furniture before anyone else did. Eventually the situation got so bad that rent controls were lifted.

The system of rent controls is not only of historical interest. Below I list some phenomena that existed in New York City recently.

Q-6 What is the effect of the price ceiling, P_c, shown in the graph below on price and quantity?

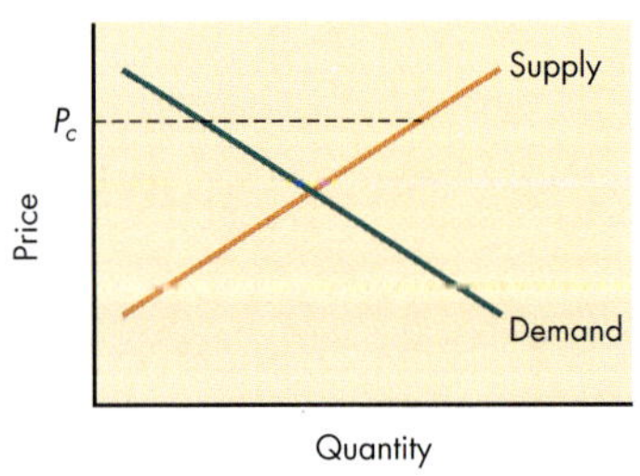

1. A couple paid $350 a month for a two-bedroom Park Avenue apartment with a solarium and two terraces, while another individual paid $1,200 a month for a studio apartment shared with two roommates.
2. The vacancy rate for apartments in New York City was 3.5 percent. Anything under 5 percent is considered a housing emergency.
3. The actress Mia Farrow paid $2,900 a month (a fraction of the market-clearing rent) for 10 rooms on Central Park West. It was an apartment her mother first leased 50 years ago.
4. Would-be tenants made payments, called key money, to current tenants or landlords to get apartments.

Your assignment is to explain how these phenomena might have come about, and to demonstrate, with supply and demand, the situation that likely caused them. (Hint: New York City does have rent control.)

Now that you have done your assignment (you have, haven't you?), let me give you my answers so that you can check them with your answers.

The situation is identical with that presented above in Figure 5-4. Take the first item. The couple lived in a rent-controlled apartment while the individual with roommates did not. If rent control were eliminated, rent on the Park Avenue apartment would rise and rent on the studio would most likely decline. Item 2: The housing emergency was a result of rent control. Below-market rent resulted in excess demand and little vacancy. Item 3: That Mia Farrow rents a rent-controlled apartment was the result of nonprice rationing. Instead of being rationed by price, other methods of rationing arose. These other methods of rationing scarce resources are called nonprice rationing. In New York City, strict rules determined the handing down of rent-controlled apartments from family member to family member. Item 4: New residents searched for a long time to find apartments to rent, and many discovered that illegal payments to landlords were the only way to obtain a rent-controlled apartment. Key money is a black market payment for a rent-controlled apartment. Because of the limited supply of apartments, individuals were willing to pay far more than the controlled price. Landlords used other methods of rationing the limited supply of apartments—instituting first-come, first-served policies, and, in practice, selecting tenants based on gender, race, or other personal characteristics, even though such discriminatory selection was illegal.

With price ceilings, existing goods are no longer rationed entirely by price. Other methods of rationing existing goods arise called nonprice rationing.

If rent controls had only the bad effects described above, no community would institute them. They are, however, implemented with good intentions—to cope with a sudden increases in demand for housing that would otherwise cause rents to explode and force many poor people out of their apartments. The negative effects occur over time as buildings begin to deteriorate and the number of people looking to rent and unable to find apartments increases. As this happens, people focus less on the original renters and more on new renters excluded from the market and on the inefficiencies of price ceilings. Since politicians tend to focus on the short run, we can expect rent control to continue to be used when there are sudden increases in demand.

PRICE FLOORS

Sometimes political forces favor suppliers, sometimes consumers. So let us now go briefly through a case when the government is trying to favor suppliers by attempting to prevent the price from falling below a certain level. **Price floors**—*government-imposed limits on how low a price can be charged*—do just this. The price floor is generally above the existing price. (A price floor below equilibrium price would be ineffective.) When there is an effective price floor, quantity supplied exceeds quantity demanded and the result in excess supply.

Q.7 What is the effect of the price floor, P_f, shown in the graph below on price and quantity?

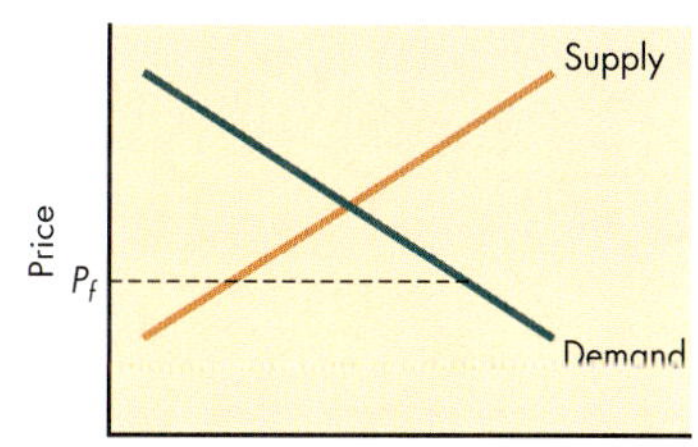

An example of a price floor is the minimum wage. Both individual states and the federal government impose **minimum wage laws**—*laws specifying the lowest wage a firm can legally pay an employee*. The U.S. federal government first instituted a minimum wage of 25 cents per hour in 1938 as part of the Fair Labor and Standards Act. It has been raised many times since, and in the early 2000s there was a push to raise it to over $6.00 an hour. (With inflation, that's a much smaller increase than it looks.) In 2001 about 1.6 million hourly wage earners received the minimum wage, or about 1.6 percent of workers, most of whom are unskilled. The market-determined equilibrium wage for skilled workers is generally above the minimum wage.

The effect of a minimum wage on the unskilled labor market is shown in Figure 5-5. The government-set minimum wage is above equilibrium, as shown by W_{min}. At the market-determined equilibrium wage W_e, the quantity of labor supplied and demanded equals Q_e. At the higher minimum wage, the quantity of labor supplied rises to Q_1 and

Figure 5-5 A Minimum Wage
A minimum wage, W_{min}, above equilibrium wage, W_e, helps those who are able to find work, shown by Q_2, but hurts those who would have been employed at the equilibrium wage but can no longer find employment, shown by $Q_e - Q_2$. A minimum wage also hurts producers who have higher costs of production and consumers who may face higher product prices.

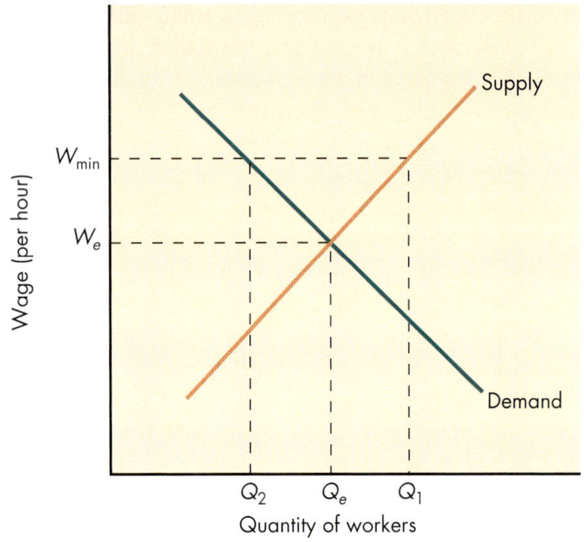

the quantity of labor demanded declines to Q_2. There is an excess supply of workers (a shortage of jobs) represented by the difference $Q_2 - Q_1$. This represents people who are looking for work but cannot find it.

The minimum wage helps some people and hurts others.

Who wins and who loses from a minimum wage? The minimum wage improves the wages of the Q_2 workers who are able to find work. Without the minimum wage, they would have earned W_e per hour. The minimum wage hurts those, however, who cannot find work at the minimum wage but who are willing to work, and would have been hired, at the market-determined wage. These workers are represented by the distance $Q_e - Q_2$ in Figure 5-5. The minimum wage also hurts firms that now must pay their workers more, increasing the cost of production. The minimum wage also hurts consumers to the extent that firms are able to pass that increase in production cost on in the form of higher product prices.

All economists agree that the above analysis is logical and correct. But they disagree about whether governments should have minimum wage laws. One reason is that the empirical effects of minimum wage laws are relatively small; in fact, some studies have found them to be negligible. (There is, however, much debate about these estimates, since "other things" never remain constant.) A second reason is that some real-world labor markets are not sufficiently competitive to fit the supply/demand model. The third reason is that the minimum wage affects the economy in ways that some economists see as desirable and others see as undesirable. I point this out to remind you that the supply/demand framework is a tool to be used to analyze issues. It does not provide final answers about policy. (In microeconomics, economists explore the policy issues of interferences in markets much more carefully.)

Because the federal minimum wage is low, and not binding for most workers, a movement called the living-wage movement has begun. The living-wage movement focuses on local governments, calling on them to establish a minimum wage at a *living wage*—a wage necessary to support a family at or above the federally determined poverty line. In 2002, 51 local governments had passed living-wage laws, with minimum wages ranging between \$6.25 an hour in Milwaukee and \$10.75 in San Jose. The analysis of these living-wage laws is the same as that for minimum wages.

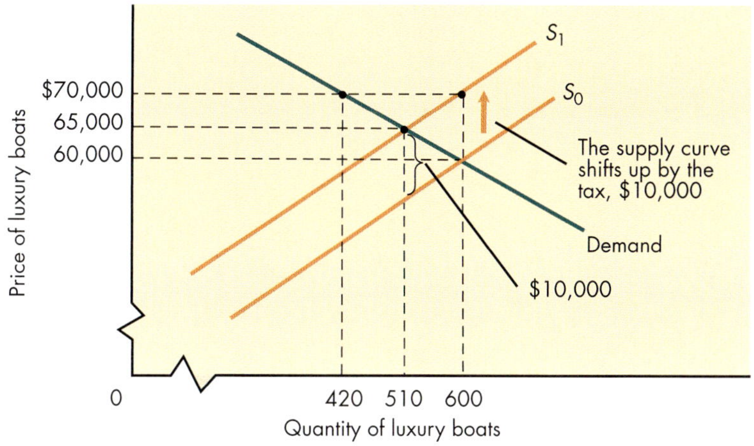

Figure 5-6 The Effect of an Excise Tax
An excise tax on suppliers shifts the entire supply curve up by the amount of the tax. Since at a price equal to the original price plus the tax there is excess supply, the price of the good rises by less than the tax.

Excise Taxes

Let's now consider an example of the government entering into a market and modifying the results of supply/demand analysis in the form of a tax. An **excise tax** is *a tax that is levied on a specific good.* The luxury tax on expensive cars that the United States imposed in 1991 is an example. A **tariff** is *an excise tax on an imported good.* What effect will excise taxes and tariffs have on the price and quantity in a market?

A tax on suppliers shifts the supply curve up by the amount of the tax.

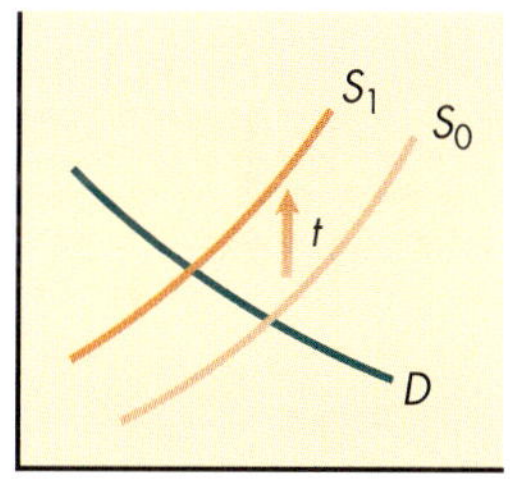

To lend some sense of reality, let's take the example from the early 1990s, when the United States put a tax on the suppliers of some luxury goods, in this case expensive boats. Say the price of a boat before the luxury tax was $60,000, and 600 boats were sold at that price. Now the government places a tax of $10,000 on the sale of such boats. What will the new price of the boat be, and how many will be sold?

If you were about to answer "The new price will be $70,000," be careful. Ask yourself whether I would have given you that question if the answer were that easy. By looking at supply and demand curves in Figure 5-6, you can see why $70,000 is the wrong answer.

To supply 600 boats, suppliers must be fully compensated for the tax. So the tax of $10,000 on the supplier shifts the supply curve up from S_0 to S_1. However, at $70,000, consumers are not willing to purchase 600 boats. They are willing to purchase only 420 boats. Quantity supplied exceeds quantity demanded at $70,000. Suppliers lower their prices until quantity supplied equals quantity demanded at $65,000, the new equilibrium price. Consumers increase the quantity of boats they are willing to purchase to 510, still less than the original 600 at $60,000. Why? At the higher price of $65,000 some people choose not to buy boats and others find substitute vehicles or purchase their boats outside the United States.

Q-8 Your study partner, Umar, has just stated that a tax on demanders of $2 per unit will raise the equilibrium price from $4 to $6. How do you respond?

Notice that at the new equilibrium the new price is $65,000, not $70,000. The reason is that at the higher price, the quantity of boats people demand is less. This is a movement up along a demand curve to the left. Excise taxes reduce the quantity of goods demanded. That's why boat manufacturers were up in arms after the tax was imposed and why the revenue generated from the tax was less than expected. Instead of collecting $10,000 × 600 ($6 million), revenue collected was only $10,000 × 510 ($5.1 million). The tax was repealed in 1993.

A tariff has the same effect on the equilibrium price and quantity as an excise tax. The difference is that only foreign producers sending goods into the United States pay the tax. An example is the 30 percent tariff imposed on steel imported into the United

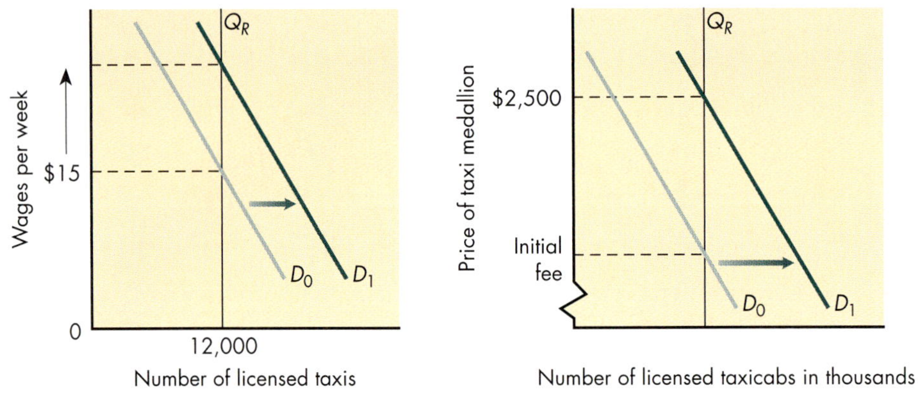

Figure 5-7 (a and b) Quantity Restrictions in the Market for Taxi Licenses
In 1937, New York City limited the number of taxi licenses to 12,000 as a way to increase the wages of taxi drivers. It had the intended effect, as **(a)** shows. A secondary effect, however, was the development of a taxi medallion market. Because taxi medallions were limited in supply, as demand for taxi services rose, so did the demand for medallions. Their price rose from the minimal license fee to $2,500 in 1947, as **(b)** shows. They sell for $250,000 today.

States in 2002. The Bush administration instituted the tariffs because U.S. steelmakers were having difficulty competing with lower-cost foreign steel. The tariff increased the price of imported steel, making U.S. steel more competitive to domestic buyers. As expected, the price of imported steel rose by over 15 percent, to about $230 a ton, and the quantity imported declined. Tariffs don't hurt just the foreign producer. Tariffs increase the cost of imported products to domestic consumers. In the case of steel, manufacturing companies such as automakers faced higher production costs. The increase in the cost of steel will likely lower production in those industries and increase the cost of a variety of goods to U.S. consumers.

Quantity Restrictions

Q-9 What is the effect of the quantity restrictions, Q_R, shown in the graph below on equilibrium price and quantity?

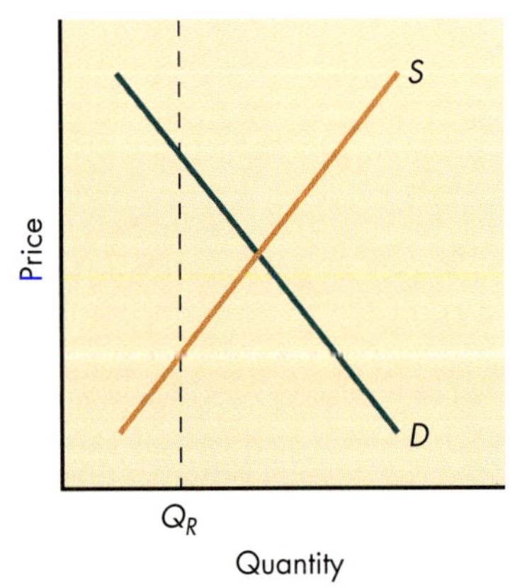

Another way in which governments often interfere with, or regulate, markets is with licenses, which limit entry into a market. For example, to be a doctor you need a license; to be a vet you need a license; and in some places to be an electrician, a financial planner, a cosmetologist, or to fish, you need a license. There are many reasons for licenses, and we will not consider them here. Instead, we will simply consider what effect licenses have on the price and quantity of the activity being licensed. Specifically, we'll look at a case where the government issues a specific number of licenses and holds that number constant. The example we'll take is licenses to drive a taxi. In New York City these are called taxi medallions because the license is an aluminum plate attached to the hood of a taxi. Taxi medallions were established in 1937 as a way to increase the wages of licensed taxi drivers. Wages of taxi drivers had fallen from $26 a week in 1929 to $15 a week in 1933. As wages fell, the number of taxi drivers fell from 19,000 to about 12,000. The remaining 12,000 taxi drivers successfully lobbied New York City to grant drivers with current licenses who met certain requirements permanent rights to drive taxis—medallions. Thereafter it held the number of medallions constant. The restriction had the desired effect. As the economy grew, demand for taxis grew (the demand for taxis shifted out) and because the supply of taxis remained at 12,000, the wages of the taxi drivers owning medallions increased, as is shown in Figure 5-7(a).

Issuing taxi medallions had a secondary effect. Because New York City also granted medallion owners the right to sell their medallions, a market in medallions developed. Those fortunate enough to have been granted a medallion by the city found that they had a valuable asset. A person wanting to drive a taxi, and earn those high wages, had to buy a medallion from an existing driver. This meant that while new taxi drivers

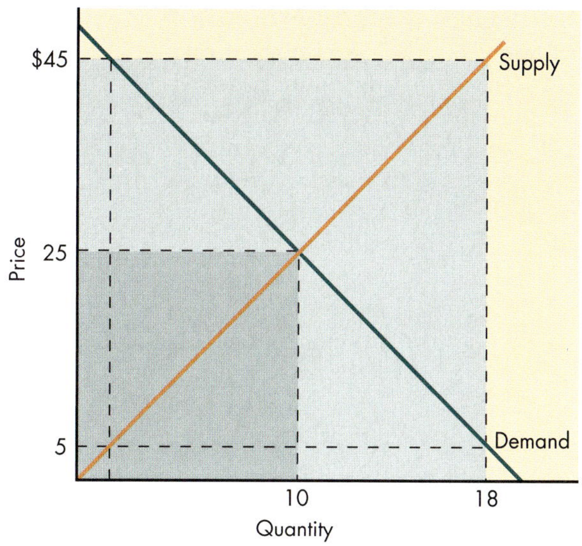

Figure 5-8 Third-Party-Payer Markets
In a third-party-payer system, the person who chooses the product doesn't pay the entire cost. In this example, with a co-payment of $5, consumers demand 18 units. Sellers require $45 per unit for that quantity. Total expenditures with such a system, shown by the entire shaded region, are much greater compared to when the consumer pays the entire cost, shown by just the dark shaded region.

would earn a higher wage once they had bought a license, their wage after taking into account the cost of the license would be much lower.

Quantity restrictions tend to increase price.

Because the number of medallions was limited, the medallions became more and more valuable as the demand for taxis rose. The effect on the price of medallions is shown in Figure 5-7(b). The quantity restriction, Q_R, means that any increases in demand lead only to price increases. Although the initial license fee was minimal, increases in demand for taxis quickly led to higher and higher medallion prices. In 1947, for example, a medallion cost $2,500.

The demand for taxi medallions continues to increase each year as the New York City population grows, but no additional taxi medallions have been issued. The result is that the price of a taxi medallion continues to rise. Today taxi medallions cost about $250,000, giving anyone who has bought that license a strong reason to oppose an expansion in the number of licenses being issued.[1]

THIRD-PARTY-PAYER MARKETS

As a final example for this chapter, let's consider third-party-payer markets. In **third-party-payer markets,** *the person who receives the good differs from the person paying for the good.* Figure 5-8 shows what happens in the supply/demand model when there is a third-party-payer market and a small co-payment. In the normal case, when the individual demander pays for the good, equilibrium quantity is where quantity demanded equals quantity supplied—in this case at an equilibrium price of $25 and an equilibrium quantity of 10.

Under a third-party-payer system, the person who chooses how much to purchase doesn't pay the entire cost. Because the co-payment faced by the consumer is much lower, quantity demanded is much greater. In this example with a co-payment of $5, the consumer demands 18. Given an upward-sloping supply curve, the seller requires a higher price, in this case $45 for each unit supplied to provide that quantity. Assuming

[1]As is usually the case, the analysis is more complicated in real life. In New York there are both individual and corporate licenses. But the general reasoning carries through: Effective quantity restrictions increase the value of a license.

In third-party-payer markets, equilibrium quantity and total spending is much higher.

the co-payment is for each unit, the consumers pay $5 of that price for total out-of-pocket cost of $90 ($5 times 18). The third-party payer pays the remainder, $40, for a cost of $720 ($40 times 18). Total spending is $810. This compares to total spending of only $250 (25 times 10) if the consumer had to pay the entire price. Notice that with a third-party-payer system, total spending, represented by the large shaded rectangle, is much higher than total spending if the consumer paid, represented by the small darker rectangle.

The third-party-payer system describes much of the health care system in the United States today. Typically, a person with health insurance makes a fixed co-payment of $5 to $10 for an office visit, regardless of procedures and tests provided. Given this payment system, the insured patient has little incentive to limit the procedures offered by the doctor. The doctor charges the insurance company, and the insurance company pays. The rise in health care costs over the past decades can be attributed in part to the third-party-payer system.

Q-10 If the cost of textbooks were included in tuition, what would likely happen to their prices? Why?

A classic example of how third-party-payer systems can affect choices is a case where a 70-year-old man spent weeks in a hospital recovering from surgery to address abdominal bleeding. The bill, to be paid by Medicare, was nearing $275,000 and the patient wasn't recovering as quickly as expected. The doctor finally figured out that the patient's condition wasn't improving because ill-fitting dentures didn't allow him to eat properly. The doctor ordered the hospital dentist to fix the dentures but the patient refused the treatment. Why? The patient explained as follows: "Seventy-five dollars is a lot of money." The $75 procedure wasn't covered by Medicare.

Third-party-payer systems are not limited to health care. (Are your parents or the government paying for part of your college? If you were paying the full amount, would you be demanding as much college as you currently are?) Anytime a third-party-payer system exists, the quantity demanded will be higher than it otherwise would be. Market forces will not hold down costs as much as they would otherwise because the person using the service doesn't have an incentive to hold down costs. Of course, that doesn't mean that there are no pressures. The third-party payers—parents, employers, and government—will respond to this by trying to limit both the quantity of the good individuals consume, and the amount they pay for it. For example, parents will put pressure on their kids to get through school quickly rather than lingering for five or six years, and government will place limitations on what procedures Medicare and Medicaid patients can use. The goods will be rationed through social and political means. Such effects are not unexpected; they are just another example of supply and demand in action.

Conclusion

I began this chapter by pointing out that supply and demand are the lens through which economists look at reality. It takes practice to use that lens, and this chapter gave you some practice. Focusing the lens on a number of issues highlighted certain aspects of those issues. The analysis was simple but powerful and should, if you followed it, provide you with a good foundation for understanding the economist's way of thinking about policy issues.

SUMMARY

- Firms respond to demand and supply pressures in other ways than changing observed prices. If observed equilibrium prices and quantities don't match your supply/demand analysis, look at other dimensions of the market or for other forces that may affect price and quantity.
- The determination of prices of currencies—the determination of foreign exchange rates—can be determined by supply and demand analysis, in the same way supply and demand analysis applies to any other good.
- By minding your *P*s and *Q*s—the shifts of and movements along curves—you can describe almost all events in terms of supply and demand.
- A price ceiling is a government-imposed limit on how high a price can be charged. Price ceilings below market price create shortages.
- A price floor is a government-imposed limit on how low a price can be charged. Price floors above market price create surpluses.
- Taxes and tariffs paid by suppliers shift the supply curve up by the amount of the tax or tariff. They raise the equilibrium price (inclusive of tax) and decrease the equilibrium quantity.
- Quantity restrictions increase equilibrium price and reduce equilibrium quantity.
- In a third-party-payer market, the consumer and the one who pays the cost differ. Quantity demanded, price, and total spending are greater when a third party pays than when the consumer pays.

KEY TERMS

exchange rate *(108)*
excise tax *(117)*
euro *(109)*
minimum wage law *(115)*
price ceiling *(113)*
price floor *(115)*
rent control *(113)*
tariff *(117)*
third-party-payer market *(119)*

QUESTIONS FOR THOUGHT AND REVIEW

1. Say that the equilibrium price and quantity both rose. What would you say was the most likely cause?
2. Say that equilibrium price fell and quantity remained constant. What would you say was the most likely cause?
3. Demonstrate graphically the effect of a price ceiling.
4. Demonstrate graphically why rent controls might increase the total payment that new renters pay for an apartment.
5. Demonstrate graphically the effect of a price floor.
6. Graphically show the effects of a minimum wage on the number of unemployed.
7. Demonstrate graphically the effect of a tax of $4 per unit on equilibrium price and quantity.
8. The dollar price of the South African rand fell from 29 cents to 22 cents in 1996, the same year the country was rocked by political turmoil. Using supply/demand analysis, explain why the turmoil led to a decline in the price of the rand.
9. Quotas, like medallions, are quantity restrictions on imported goods. Demonstrate the effect of a quota on the price of imported goods.
10. Supply/demand analysis states that equilibrium occurs where quantity supplied equals quantity demanded, but in U.S. agricultural markets quantity supplied almost always exceeds quantity demanded. How can this be?
11. In what ways is the market for public post-secondary education an example of a third-party payer market? What's the impact of this on total educational expenditures?
12. What reasons might governments have to support third-party-payer markets?

Problems and Exercises

1. Since 1981, the U.S. government has supported the price of sugar produced by U.S. sugar producers by limiting import of sugar into the United States. Restricting imports is effective because the United States consumes more sugar than it produces.
   a. Using supply/demand analysis, demonstrate how import restrictions increases the price of domestic sugar.
   b. What other import policy could the government implement to have the same effect as the import restriction?
   c. Under the Uruguay Round of the General Agreement on Tariffs and Trade in 1997, the United States agreed to permit at least 1.25 million tons of sugar to be imported into the United States. How does this affect the U.S. sugar price support program?
2. In some states and localities "scalping" is against the law, although enforcement of these laws is spotty (difficult).
   a. Using supply/demand analysis and words, demonstrate what a weakly enforced antiscalping law would likely do to the price of tickets.
   b. Using supply/demand analysis and words, demonstrate what a strongly enforced antiscalping law would likely do to the price of tickets.
3. Apartments in New York City are often hard to find. One of the major reasons is that there is rent control.
   a. Demonstrate graphically how rent controls could make apartments hard to find.
   b. Often one can get an apartment if one makes a side payment to the current tenant. Can you explain why?
   c. What would be the likely effect of eliminating rent controls?
   d. What is the political appeal of rent controls?
4. Until recently, angora goat wool (mohair) has been designated as a strategic commodity (it used to be utilized in some military clothing). Because of that, in 1992 for every dollar's worth of mohair sold to manufacturers, ranchers received $3.60.
   a. Demonstrate graphically the effect of the elimination of this designation and subsidy.
   b. Explain why the program was likely kept in existence for so long.
   c. Say that a politician has suggested that the government should pass a law that requires all consumers to pay a price for angora goat wool high enough so that the sellers of that wool would receive $3.60 more than the market price. Demonstrate the effect of the law graphically. Would consumers support it? How about suppliers?
5. The technology is now developing so that road use can be priced by computer. A computer in the surface of the road picks up a signal from your car and automatically charges you for the use of the road.
   a. How could this technological change contribute to ending bottlenecks and rush hour congestion?
   b. What are some of the problems that might develop with such a system?
   c. How would your transportation habits likely change if you had to pay to use roads?
6. In 1938 Congress created a Board of Cosmetology in Washington, D.C., to license beauticians. In 1992 this law was used by the board to close down a hair braiding salon specializing in cornrows and braids operated by Mr. Uqdah, even though little was then taught in cosmetology schools about braiding and cornrows.
   a. What possible reason can you give for why this board exists?
   b. What options might you propose to change the system?
   c. What will be the political difficulties of implementing those options?
7. In the Oregon health care plan for rationing Medicaid expenditures, therapy to slow the progression of AIDS, and treatment for brain cancer were covered, while liver transplants and treatment for infectious mononucleosis were not covered.
   a. What criteria do you think were used to determine what was covered and what was not covered?
   b. Should an economist oppose the Oregon plan because it involves rationing?
   c. How does the rationing that occurs in the market differ from the rationing that occurs in the Oregon plan?
8. Airlines and hotels have many frequent flyer and frequent visitor programs in which individuals who fly the airline or stay at the hotel receive bonuses that are the equivalent to discounts.
   a. Give two reasons why these companies have such programs rather than simply offering lower prices.
   b. Can you give other examples of such programs?
   c. What is the likely reasons why firms don't monitor these programs?
9. You're given the following supply and demand tables:

Demand		Supply	
P	Q	*P*	Q
$ 0	1,200	$ 0	0
2	900	2	0
4	600	4	150
6	300	6	300
8	0	8	600
10	0	10	600
12	0	12	750
14	0	14	900

a. What is equilibrium price and quantity in a market system with no interferences?
b. If this were a third-party-payer market where the consumer pays $2, what is the quantity demanded? What is the price charged by the seller?
c. What is total spending in the two situations described in *a* and *b*?

Web Questions

1. Go to the Cato Institute's home page (www.cato.org) and search for the article "How Rent Control Drives Out Affordable Housing" by William Tucker. After reading the article, answer the following questions:
   a. What is a shadow market, and why does one develop when there is rent control?
   b. Why is housing a particularly easy good to hoard? How does this affect newcomers to a city?
   c. How do vacancy rates compare among cities with and without rent control? Does this make sense within the supply/demand framework?
2. Go to the Economic Policy Institute's home page (www.epinet.org) and search the publications catalog for the article "Time to Repair the Wage Floor" by Jared Bernstein and Jeff Chapman (Brief 180). Using that article, answer the following questions:
   a. What has happened to the minimum wage adjusted for inflation since the 1970s? Within the standard supply/demand framework, how does this affect unemployment resulting from the minimum wage?
   b. Who is affected by the minimum wage?
   c. How do the authors think it will impact the U.S. economic recovery in 2002? What evidence do they cite?

Answers to Margin Questions

1. You will receive 65,616.80 pesos. 1 Chilean peso = $.001406, so dividing $100 by $.001406 gives you, with rounding, 71,123.76 pesos. *(108)*
2. False. When supply rises supply shifts out to the right. Price falls because demand slopes downward. *(109)*
3. A discovery of a hormone that will increase cows' milk production by 20 percent will increase the supply of milk, pushing the price down and increasing the quantity demanded, as in the accompanying graph. *(112)*

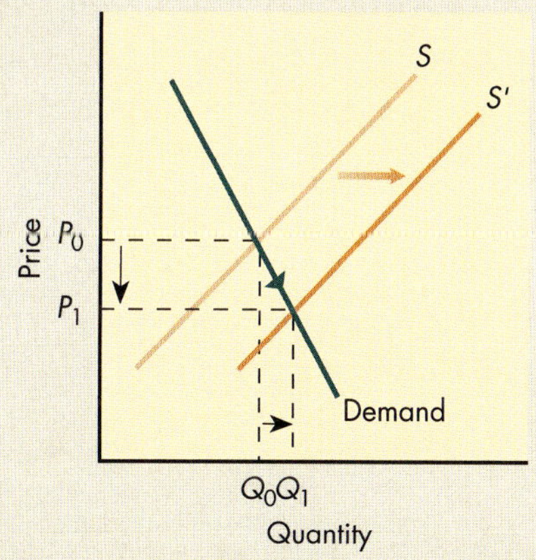

4. Quantity decreases but it is unclear what happens to price. *(112)*
5. It is likely demand shifted in and supply remained constant. *(113)*
6. Since the price ceiling is above the equilibrium price, it will have no effect on the market-determined equilibrium price and quantity. *(114)*
7. Since the price floor is below the equilibrium price, it will have no effect on the market-determined equilibrium price and quantity. *(115)*
8. I state that the tax will most likely raise the price by less than $2 since the tax will cause the quantity demanded to decrease. This will decrease quantity supplied, and hence decrease the price the suppliers receive. In the diagram below, Q falls from Q_0 to Q_1 and the price the supplier receives falls from $4 to $3, making the final price $5, not $6. *(117)*

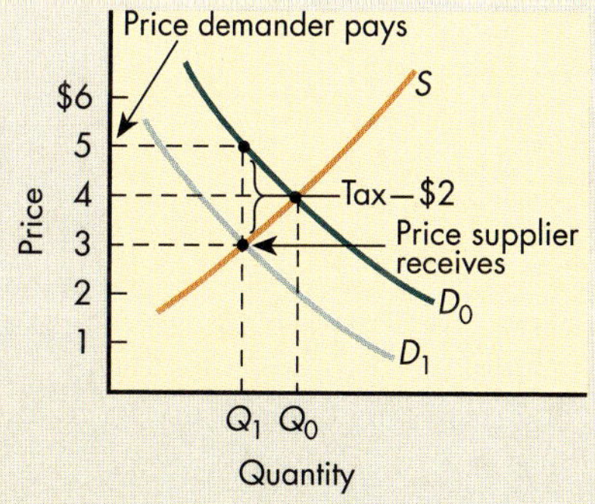

9. Given the quantity restriction equilibrium quantity will be Q_R and equilibrium price will be P_0, which is higher than the market equilibrium price of P_e. *(118)*

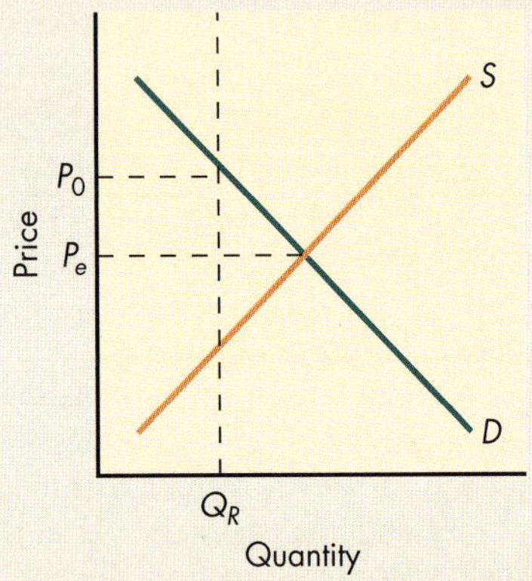

10. Universities would probably charge the high tuition they do now, but they would likely negotiate with publishers for lower textbook prices, because they are both demanding and paying for the textbook. *(120)*

Appendix A

Algebraic Representation of Supply, Demand, and Equilibrium

In this chapter and Chapter 4, I discussed demand, supply, and the determination of equilibrium price and quantity in words and graphs. These concepts can also be presented in equations. In this appendix I do so, using straight line supply and demand curves.

The Laws of Supply and Demand in Equations

Since the law of supply states that quantity supplied is positively related to price, the slope of an equation specifying a supply curve is positive. (The quantity intercept term is generally less than zero since suppliers are generally unwilling to supply a good at a price less than zero.) An example of a supply equation is:

$$Q_S = -5 + 2P$$

where Q_S is units supplied and P is the price of each unit in dollars per unit. The law of demand states that as price rises, quantity demanded declines. Price and quantity are negatively related, so a demand curve has a negative slope. An example of a demand equation is:

$$Q_D = 10 - P$$

where Q_D is units demanded and P is the price of each unit in dollars per unit.

Determination of Equilibrium

The equilibrium price and quantity can be determined in three steps using these two equations. To find the equilibrium price and quantity for these particular demand and supply curves, you must find the quantity and price that solve both equations simultaneously.

Step 1: Set the quantity demanded equal to quantity supplied:

$$Q_S = Q_D \rightarrow -5 + 2P = 10 - P$$

Step 2: Solve for the price by rearranging terms. Doing so gives:

$$3P = 15$$
$$P = \$5$$

Thus, equilibrium price is \$5.

Step 3: To find equilibrium quantity, you can substitute \$5 for P in either the demand or supply equation. Let's do it for supply: $Q_S = -5 + (2 \times 5) = 5$ units. I'll leave it to you to confirm that the quantity you obtain by substituting $P = \$5$ in the demand equation is also 5 units.

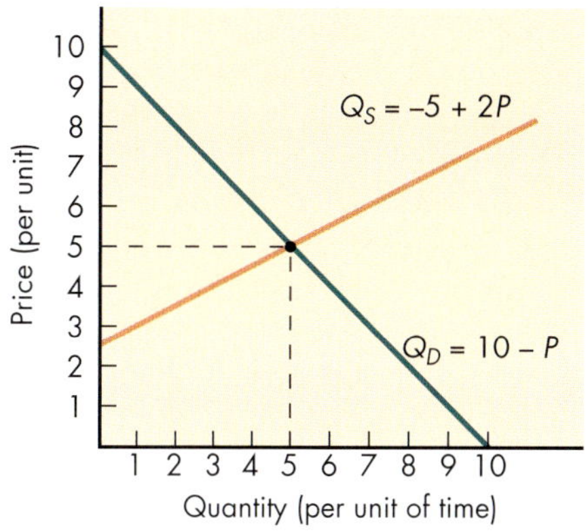

Figure A5-1 Supply and Demand Equilibrium
The algebra in this appendix leads to the same results as the geometry in the chapter. Equilibrium occurs where quantity supplied equals quantity demanded.

The answer could also be found graphically. The supply and demand curves specified by these equations are depicted in Figure A5-1. As you can see, demand and supply intersect; quantity demanded equals quantity supplied at a quantity of 5 units and a price of $5.

Movements along a Demand and Supply Curve

The demand and supply curves above represent schedules of quantities demanded and supplied at various prices. Movements along each can be represented by selecting various prices and solving for quantity demanded and supplied. Let's create a supply and demand table using the above equations—supply: $Q_S = -5 + 2P$; demand: $Q_D = 10 - P$.

P	$Q_S = -5 + 2P$	$Q_D = 10 - P$
$ 0	−5	10
1	−3	9
2	−1	8
3	1	7
4	3	6
5	5	5
6	7	4
7	9	3
8	11	2
9	13	1
10	15	0

As you move down the rows, you are moving up along the supply schedule, as shown by increasing quantity supplied, and moving down along the demand schedule, as shown by decreasing quantity demanded. Just to confirm your equilibrium quantity and price calculations, notice that at a price of $5, quantity demanded equals quantity supplied.

Shifts of a Demand and Supply Schedule

What would happen if suppliers' changed their expectations so that they would be willing to sell more goods at every price? This shift factor of supply would shift the entire supply curve out to the right. Let's say that at every price, quantity supplied increases by 3. Mathematically the new equation would be $Q_S = -2 + 2P$. The quantity intercept increases by 3. What would you expect to happen to equilibrium price and quantity? Let's solve the equations mathematically first.

Step 1: To determine equilibrium price, set the new quantity supplied equal to quantity demanded:

$$10 - P = -2 + 2P$$

Step 2: Solve for the equilibrium price:

$$12 = 3P$$
$$P = \$4$$

Step 3: To determine equilibrium quantity, substitute P in either the demand or supply equation:

$$Q_D = 10 - (1 \times 4) = 6 \text{ units}$$
$$Q_S = -2 + (2 \times 4) = 6 \text{ units}$$

Equilibrium price declined to $4 and equilibrium quantity rose to 6, just as you would expect with a rightward shift in a supply curve.

Now let's suppose that demand shifts out to the right. Here we would expect both equilibrium price and equilibrium quantity to rise. We begin with our original supply and demand curves—supply: $Q_S = -5 + 2P$; demand: $Q_D = 10 - P$. Let's say at every price, the quantity demanded rises by 3. The new equation for demand would be $Q_D = 13 - P$. You may want to solve this equation for various prices to confirm that at every price, quantity demanded rises by 3. Let's solve the equations for equilibrium price and quantity.

Step 1: Set the quantities equal to one another:

$$13 - P = -5 + 2P$$

Step 2: Solve for equilibrium price:

$$18 = 3P$$
$$P = \$6$$

Step 3: Substitute P in either the demand or supply equation:

$$Q_D = 13 - (1 \times 6) = 7 \text{ units}$$
$$Q_S = -5 + (2 \times 6) = 7 \text{ units}$$

Equilibrium price rose to $6 and equilibrium quantity rose to 7 units, just as you would expect with a rightward shift in a demand curve.

Just to make sure you've got it, I will do two more examples. First, suppose the demand and supply equations for wheat per year in the United States can be specified as follows (notice that the slope is negative for the demand curve and positive for the supply curve):

$$Q_D = 500 - 2P$$
$$Q_S = -100 + 4P$$

P is the price in dollars per thousand bushels and Q is the quantity of wheat in thousands of bushels. Remember that the units must always be stated. What is the equilibrium price and quantity?

Step 1: Set the quantities equal to one another:

$$500 - 2P = -100 + 4P$$

Step 2: Solve for equilibrium price:

$$600 = 6P$$
$$P = \$100$$

Step 3: Substitute P in either the demand or supply equation:

$$Q_D = 500 - (2 \times 100) = 300$$
$$Q_S = -100 + (4 \times 100) = 300$$

Equilibrium quantity is 300 thousand bushels.

As my final example, take a look at Alice's demand curve depicted in Figure 4-4(b) in Chapter 4. Can you write an equation that represents the demand curve in that figure? It is $Q_D = 10 - 2P$. At a price of zero, the quantity of DVD rentals Alice demands is 10, and for every increase in price of $1, the quantity she demands falls by 2. Now look at Ann's supply curve shown in Figure 4-7(b) in Chapter 4. Ann's supply curve mathematically is $Q_S = 2P$. At a zero price, the quantity Ann supplies is zero, and for every $1 increase in price, the quantity she supplies rises by 2. What is the equilibrium price and quantity?

Step 1: Set the quantities equal to one another:

$$10 - 2P = 2P$$

Step 2: Solve for equilibrium price:

$$4P = 10$$
$$P = \$2.5$$

Step 3: Substitute P in either the demand or supply equation:

$$Q_D = 10 - (2 \times 2.5) = 5, \text{ or}$$
$$Q_S = 2 \times 2.5 = 5 \text{ DVDs per week}$$

Ann is willing to supply 5 DVDs per week at $2.50 per rental and Alice demands 5 DVDs at $2.50 per DVD rental. Remember that in Figure 4-8 in Chapter 4, I showed you graphically the equilibrium quantity and price of Alice's demand curve and Ann's supply curve. I'll leave it up to you to check that the graphic solution in Figure 4-8 is the same as the mathematical solution we came up with here.

Price Ceilings and Price Floors

Let's now consider a price ceiling and price floor. We start with the supply and demand curves:

$$Q_S = -5 + 2P$$
$$Q_D = 10 - P$$

This gave us the solution:

$$P = 5$$
$$Q = 5$$

Now, say that a price ceiling of $4 is imposed. Would you expect a shortage or a surplus? If you said "shortage," you're doing well. If not, review the chapter before continuing with this appendix. To find out how much the shortage is we must find out how much will be supplied and how much will be demanded at the price ceiling. Substituting $4 for price in both lets us see that $Q_S = 3$ units and $Q_D = 6$ units. There will be a shortage of 3 units. Next, let's consider a price floor of $6. To determine the surplus we follow the same exercise. Substituting $6 into the two equations gives a quantity supplied of 7 units and a quantity demanded of 4 units, so there is a surplus of 3 units.

TAXES AND SUBSIDIES

Next, let's consider the effect of a tax of $1 placed on the supplier. That tax would decrease the price received by suppliers by $1. In other words:

$$Q_S = -5 + 2(P - 1)$$

Multiplying the terms in parentheses by 2 and collecting terms results in

$$Q_S = -7 + 2P$$

This supply equation has the same slope as in the previous case, but a new intercept term—just what you'd expect. To determine the new equilibrium price and quantity, follow steps 1 to 3 discussed earlier. Setting this new equation equal to demand and solving for price gives

$$P = 5\tfrac{2}{3}$$

Substituting this price into the demand and supply equations tells us equilibrium quantity:

$$Q_S = Q_D = 4\tfrac{1}{3} \text{ units}$$

Of that price, the supplier must pay $1 in tax, so the price the supplier receives net of tax is $4⅔.

Next, let's say that the tax were put on the demander rather than on the supplier. In that case, the tax increases the price for demanders by $1 and the demand equation becomes

$$Q_D = 10 - (P + 1), \text{ or}$$
$$Q_D = 9 - P$$

Again solving for equilibrium price and quantity requires setting the demand and supply equations equal to one another and solving for price. I leave the steps to you. The result is:

$$P = 4\tfrac{2}{3}$$

This is the price the supplier receives. The price demanders pay is $5⅔. The equilibrium quantity will be 4⅓ units.

These are the same results we got in the previous cases showing that, given the assumptions, it doesn't matter who actually pays the tax: The effect on equilibrium price and quantity is identical no matter who pays it.

QUOTAS

Finally, let's consider the effect of a quota of 4⅓ placed on the market. Since a quota limits the quantity supplied, as long as the quota is less than the market equilibrium quantity the supply equation becomes:

$$Q_S = 4\tfrac{1}{3}$$

where Q_S is the actual amount supplied. The price that the market will arrive at for this quantity is determined by the demand curve. To find that price substitute the quantity 4⅓ into the demand equation ($Q_D = 10 - P$):

$$4\tfrac{1}{3} = 10 - P$$

and solve for P:

$$P = 5\tfrac{2}{3}$$

Since consumers are willing to pay $5⅔, this is what suppliers will receive. The price that suppliers would have been willing to accept for a quantity of 4⅓ is $4⅔. This can be found by substituting the amount of the quota in the supply equation:

$$4\tfrac{1}{3} = -5 + 2P$$

and solving for P:

$$2P = 9\tfrac{1}{3}$$
$$P = 4\tfrac{2}{3}$$

Notice that this result is very similar to the tax. For demanders it is identical; they pay $5⅔ and receive 4⅓ units. For suppliers, however, the situation is much preferable; instead of receiving a price of $4⅔, the amount they received with the tax, they receive $5⅔. With a quota, suppliers receive the "implicit tax revenue" that results from the higher price.

QUESTIONS FOR THOUGHT AND REVIEW

1. Suppose the demand and supply for milk are described by the following equations: $Q_D = 600 - 100P$; $Q_S = -150 + 150P$, where P is price in dollars, Q_D is quantity demanded in millions of gallons per year, and Q_S is quantity supplied in millions of gallons per year.
   a. Create demand and supply tables corresponding to these equations.
   b. Graph supply and demand and determine equilibrium price and quantity.

c. Confirm your answer to *b* by solving the equations mathematically.

2. Beginning with the equations in question 1, suppose a growth hormone is introduced that allows dairy farmers to offer 125 million more gallons of milk per year at each price.
   a. Construct new demand and supply curves reflecting this change. Describe with words what happened to the supply curve and to the demand curve.
   b. Graph the new curves and determine equilibrium price and quantity.
   c. Determine equilibrium price and quantity by solving the equations mathematically.
   d. Suppose the government set the price of milk at $3 a gallon. Demonstrate the effect of this regulation on the market for milk. What is quantity demanded? What is quantity supplied?
3. Write demand and supply equations that represent demand, D_0, and supply, S_0, in Figure A5-1 in this appendix.
   a. Solve for equilibrium price and quantity mathematically. Show your work.
   b. Rewrite the demand equation to reflect an increase in demand of 3 units. What happens to equilibrium price and quantity?
   c. Rewrite the supply equation to reflect a decrease in supply of 3 units at every price level. What happens to equilibrium price and quantity using the demand curve from *b*?
4. a. How is a shift in demand reflected in a demand equation?
   b. How is a shift in supply reflected in a supply equation?
   c. How is a movement along a demand (supply) curve reflected in a demand (supply) equation?
5. Suppose the demand and supply for wheat is described by the following equations: $Q_D = 10 - P$; $Q_S = 2 + P$, where P is the price in dollars; Q_D is quantity demanded in millions of bushels per year; and Q_S is quantity supplied in millions of bushels per year.
   a. Solve for equilibrium price and quantity of wheat.
   b. Would a government-set price of $5 create a surplus or a shortage of wheat? How much? Is $5 a price ceiling or a price floor?
6. Suppose the U.S. government imposes a $1 per gallon of milk tax on dairy farmers. Using the demand and supply equations from question 1:
   a. What is the effect of the tax on the supply equation? The demand equation?
   b. What is the new equilibrium price and quantity?
   c. How much do dairy farmers receive per gallon of milk after the tax? How much do demanders pay?
7. Repeat question 6 assuming the tax is placed on the buyers of milk. Does it matter who pays the tax?
8. Repeat question 6 assuming the government pays a subsidy of $1 per gallon of milk to farmers.
9. Suppose the demand for DVDs is represented by $Q_D = 15 - 4P$, and the supply of DVDs is represented by $Q_S = 4P - 1$. Determine if each of the following is a price floor, price ceiling, or neither. In each case, determine the shortage or surplus.
   a. $P = \$3$
   b. $P = \$1.50$
   c. $P = \$2.25$
   d. $P = \$2.50$

PART II

MICROECONOMICS

> In my vacations, I visited the poorest quarters of several cities and walked through one street after another, looking at the faces of the poorest people. Next I resolved to make as thorough a study as I could of Political Economy.

You may remember having already seen this quotation from Alfred Marshall. It began the first chapter. I chose this beginning for two reasons. First, it gives what I believe to be the best reason to study economics. Second, the quotation is from a hero of mine, one of the economic giants of all times. His *Principles of Economics* was the economists' bible in the late 1800s and early 1900s. How important was Marshall? It was Marshall who first used the supply and demand curves as an engine of analysis.

I repeat this quotation here in the introduction to the microeconomics section because for Marshall economics was microeconomics, and it is his vision of economics that underlies this book's approach to microeconomics. For Marshall, economics was an art that was meant to be applied—used to explain why things were the way they were, and what we could do about them. He had little use for esoteric theory that didn't lead to a direct application to a real-world problem. Reflecting on the state of economics in 1906, Marshall wrote to a friend:

> I had a growing feeling in the later years of my work at the subject that a good mathematical theorem dealing with economic hypotheses was very unlikely to be good economics: and I went more and more on the rules—(1) Use mathematics as a shorthand language, rather than as an engine of inquiry. (2) Keep to them until you have done. (3) Translate into English. (4) Then illustrate by examples that are important in real life. (5) Burn the mathematics. (6) If you can't succeed in (4), burn (3). This last I did often. (From a letter from Marshall to A. L. Bowley, reprinted in A. C. Pigou, *Memorials of Alfred Marshall*, p. 427.)

Marshall didn't feel this way about mathematical economics because he couldn't do mathematics. He was trained as a formal mathematician, and he was a good one. But, for him, mathematics wasn't economics, and the real world was too messy to have applied to it much of the fancy mathematical economic work that some of his fellow economists were doing. Marshall recognized the influence of market, political, and social forces and believed that all three had to be taken into account in applying economic reasoning to reality.

Since 1906, when Marshall wrote this letter, the economics profession has moved away from its Marshallian roots. The profession has found other heroes who have created a mathematical foundation for economics that's both impressive and stultifying. Mathematical economics that has only the slightest connection to the real world has overwhelmed much of the real-world economics that Marshall followed. That's sad.

Not to worry. You won't see such highfalutin mathematical economics in these microeconomic chapters. The chapters follow the Marshallian methodology and present the minimum of formal theory necessary to apply the concepts of economics to the real world, and then they do just that: start talking about real-world issues.

Section I, Microeconomics: The Basics (Chapters 6 and 7), and Section II, Foundations of Supply and Demand (Chapters 8–10), present the background theory necessary to understand the economic way of thinking. These sections introduce you to the foundations of economic reasoning and to some central terms and ideas of microeconomics. But even in these theoretical chapters the focus is on intuition, policy, and on putting the economic approach to problems into perspective, rather than on presenting technique for the sake of technique.

Section III, Market Structure and Policy (Chapters 11–15), introduces you to various market structures, providing you with a way of approaching real-world markets. Chapter 15 provides an overview of government's policy on market structure—antitrust policy.

Section IV, Factor Markets (Chapters 16–17), looks at a particular set of markets—factor markets. These markets play a central role in determining the distribution of income. These chapters won't tell you how to get rich (you'll have to wait for the sequel for that), but they will give you new insights into how labor markets work.

Section V, Applying Economic Reasoning to Policy (Chapters 18–21), provides an overview of the implications of microeconomics for policy. It includes both general overviews and analyses of specific issues.

6 Describing Supply and Demand: Elasticities

After reading this chapter, you should be able to:

- Use the terms *price elasticity of supply* and *price elasticity of demand* to describe the responsiveness of quantity supplied and quantity demanded to changes in price.
- Calculate elasticity graphically and numerically.
- Distinguish five elasticity terms that are used to differentiate varying degrees of responsiveness.
- Explain the importance of substitution in determining elasticity of supply and demand.
- Relate price elasticity of demand to total revenue.
- State how other elasticity concepts are useful in describing the effect of shift factors on demand.
- Explain how the concept of *elasticity* makes supply and demand analysis more useful.

The master economist must understand symbols and speak in words. He must contemplate the particular in terms of the general, and touch abstract and concrete in the same flight of thought.

—*J. M. Keynes*

Chapters 4 and 5 gave you a good sense of supply and demand. In this chapter I introduce you to the concept of elasticity, a term economists use to describe supply and demand. Elasticity refers to responsiveness; for example, elasticity can be used to describe the responsiveness of quantity supplied or quantity demanded to price.

In economics the term elasticity comes up continually. For example, policymakers use it to describe by how much quantity demanded will fall in response to an increase in taxes. Firms use elasticity to describe the responsiveness of consumers to an increase in price. In general, the greater the elasticity, the more responsive quantity is to a change in price.

Information about elasticity is extremely important to firms in making their pricing decisions, and to economists in their study of the economy. Consider the decision by America West Airlines to cut airfares for business travelers by 50 percent. That decision was based on the prediction that lowering price would entice a large number of business travelers to switch carriers and book travel with America West. That is, the airline was hoping that quantity demanded was very responsive to a change in price, or, in other words, that demand for business travel was elastic. Alternatively, consider some school boards' decisions to raise teachers' salaries by 10 percent because of a shortage of teachers in their districts. The boards were hoping that the number of individuals choosing jobs as teachers would increase significantly with a rise in salaries; that is, they were hoping that the supply of teachers was highly elastic.

Price Elasticity

The most commonly used elasticity concept is price elasticity of demand and supply. **Price elasticity of demand** is *the percentage change in quantity demanded divided by the percentage change in price:*

$$E_D = \frac{\text{Percentage change in quantity demanded}}{\text{Percentage change in price}}$$

Price elasticity of supply is *the percentage change in quantity supplied divided by the percentage change in price:*

Price elasticity is the percentage change in quantity divided by the percentage change in price.

$$E_S = \frac{\text{Percentage change in quantity supplied}}{\text{Percentage change in price}}$$

Let's consider some numerical examples. Say the price of a good rises by 10 percent and, in response, quantity demanded falls by 20 percent. The price elasticity of demand is 2 (−20 percent/10 percent). Notice that I said 2, not −2. Because quantity demanded is inversely related to price, the calculation for the price elasticity of demand comes out negative. Despite this fact, economists talk about price elasticity of demand as a positive number. (Those of you who remember some math can think of elasticity as an *absolute value* of a number, rather than a simple number.) Using this convention makes it easier to remember that a *larger* number for price elasticity of demand means quantity demanded is *more responsive* to price.

Q-1 If when price rises by 4 percent, quantity supplied rises by 8 percent, what is the price elasticity of supply?

To make sure you have the idea down, let's consider two more examples. Say that when price falls by 5 percent, quantity supplied falls by 2 percent. In this case, the price elasticity of supply is 0.4 (2 percent/5 percent). And, finally, say the price goes up by 10 percent and in response the quantity demanded falls by 15 percent. Price elasticity of demand is 1.5 (15 percent/10 percent).

What Information Price Elasticity Provides

Price elasticity of demand and supply gives us information about the exact quantity response to a change in price. A price elasticity of demand of 0.3 tells us that a 10 percent rise in price will lead to a 3 percent decline in quantity demanded. If the elasticity of demand were a larger number, say 5, the same 10 percent rise in price will lead to a 50 percent decline in quantity demanded. As elasticity increases, responsiveness of quantity to price increases.

Classifying Demand and Supply as Elastic or Inelastic

It is helpful to classify elasticities by relative responsiveness. Economists usually describe supply and demand by the terms *elastic* and *inelastic*. Formally, demand or supply is **elastic** if *the percentage change in quantity is greater than the percentage change in price* ($E > 1$). Conversely, demand or supply is **inelastic** if *the percentage change in quantity is less than the percentage change in price* ($E < 1$). In the last two examples, an elasticity of supply of 0.3 means supply is inelastic ($E_S < 1$), and an elasticity of supply of 5 means supply is elastic ($E_S > 1$).

Elastic: $E > 1$
Inelastic: $E < 1$

The commonsense interpretation of these terms is the following: An *inelastic* supply means that the quantity supplied doesn't change much with a change in price. For example, say the price of land rises. The amount of land supplied won't change much, so the supply of land is inelastic. An *elastic* supply means that quantity supplied changes by a larger percentage than the percentage change in price. For example, say the price of pencils doubles. What do you think will happen to the quantity of pencils supplied? I suspect it will more than double, which means that the supply of pencils is elastic.

The same terminology holds with demand. Consider a good such as a brand A ballpoint pen that has a close substitute, a brand B ballpoint pen. If brand A's price rises, the quantity demanded will fall a lot as people shift to the substitute (a brand B ballpoint pen). So the demand for brand A ballpoint pens would be highly elastic. Alternatively, consider table salt, which has no close substitute at current prices. Demand for table salt

Q-2 If price elasticity of demand is greater than 1, what would we call demand: elastic or inelastic?

is highly inelastic. That is, a rise in the price of table salt does not result in a large decline in quantity demanded.

Elasticity Is Independent of Units

Percentages allow us to have a measure of responsiveness that is independent of units, making comparisons of responsiveness among different goods easier.

Before continuing, notice that elasticity measures the percentage, not the absolute, change in variables. Using percentages allows us to have a measure of responsiveness that is independent of units, making comparisons of responsiveness among different goods easier. Say a $1 increase in the price of a $2,000 computer decreases the quantity demanded by 1, from 10 to 9. Say also that a $1 increase in the price of a pen, from $1 to $2, decreases quantity demanded by 1—from 10,000 to 9,999. Using absolute numbers, the $1 price increase reduced the quantities demanded for both pens and computers by 1. But such a comparison of absolute numbers is not very helpful. To see that, ask yourself if you were planning on raising your price, which good you'd rather be selling.

The computer price increased by 1/2,000 of its original price, a relatively small percentage increase, and quantity demanded declined by 1/10 of original sales, a large percentage decline. The percentage decline in quantity demanded exceeded the percentage rise in price, so your total revenue (Price × Quantity) would decrease. The percentage increase in price of pens was relatively large—100 percent—and the percentage decline in quantity demanded was relatively small—1/10 of 1 percent. So if you raise the price of pens, total revenue increases. Clearly, if you're raising your price in these examples, you'd rather be selling pens than computers.

By using percentages, this is made clear: With computers, a 0.05 percent increase in price decreases quantity demanded by 10 percent, so the elasticity is 200. With pens, a 100 percent increase in price decreases quantity demanded by 0.01 percent—an elasticity of 0.0001.

Calculating Elasticities

To see that you've got the analysis down, calculate price elasticity of demand or supply in the following three real-world examples:

> *Case 1:* In 2000, the Metropolitan Atlanta Rapid Transit Authority (MARTA) proposed raising one-way bus fare by 12.5 percent and estimated that ridership would decline by 5 percent.
>
> *Case 2:* In the 1980s, when gasoline prices rose by 9 percent in Washington, D.C., the quantity of gasoline demanded there fell by 40 percent.
>
> *Case 3:* In the mid-1990s, when the minimum wage in Vermont rose by 10 percent, the quantity of labor supplied for relevant jobs increased by about 1.8 percent.

In the first case price elasticity of demand is 0.4. The quantity of rides demanded in the MARTA system was not expected to respond much to the increase in price. Elasticity was less than 1, so demand was inelastic. In the second case, price elasticity of demand is 4.4. The quantity of gas demanded in Washington, D.C., responded by a lot to a relatively small change in gas prices. Elasticity was greater than 1, so demand was elastic. The price elasticity of supply in the third case is 0.18. The quantity of labor supplied did not respond much to the change in wage. Elasticity was less than 1, so supply was inelastic.

Let's now calculate some elasticities graphically. Let's begin by determining the price elasticity of demand between points *A* and *B* in Figure 6-1(a).

The demand curve in the figure is a hypothetical demand for WolfPack Simulation Software. You can see that as the price of the software rises from $20 to $26, the quantity demanded falls from 14,000 to 10,000 units a year. To determine the price elasticity

Figure 6-1 (a, b, and c) Graphs of Elasticities
In (**a**) we are calculating the elasticity of the demand curve between A and B. We essentially calculate the midpoint and use that midpoint to calculate percentage changes. This gives us a percentage change in price of 26 percent and a percentage change in quantity of 33 percent, for an elasticity of 1.27. In (**b**) the percentage change in price is 10.53 percent and the percentage change in quantity is 1.87 percent, giving an elasticity of 0.18. In (**c**), the calculations are left for you to do.

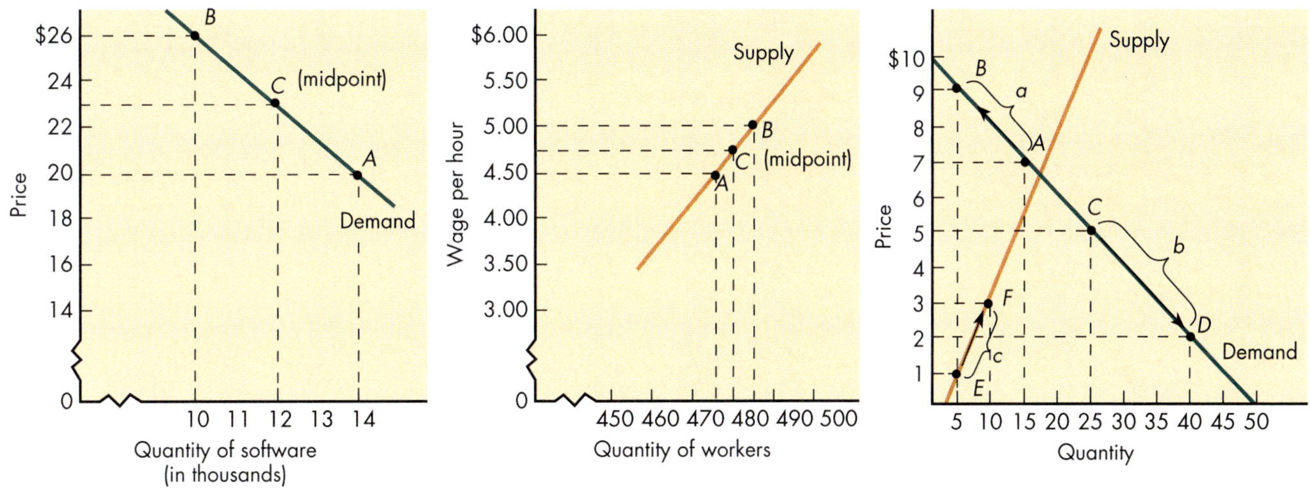

(a) Elasticity of demand **(b) Elasticity of supply** **(c) Some examples**

Answers to (c): $a = 4$; $b = 0.54$; $c = 0.67$

of demand, we need to determine the percentage change in quantity and the percentage change in price. In doing so, there is a small problem that is sometimes called the *end-point problem:* The percentage change differs depending on whether you view the change as a rise or a decline. For example, say you calculate the rise in price from \$20 to \$26, starting from \$20. That gives you a percentage increase in price of [(20 − 26)/20] × 100 = 30 percent. If, however, you calculate that same change in price, \$6, as a fall in price from \$26 to \$20, the percentage decrease in price is [(26 − 20)/26] × 100 = 23 percent. The easiest way to solve this problem is to use the average of the two end values to calculate percentage change. In our example, instead of using 20 or 26 as a starting point, you use (20 + 26)/2, or 23. So the percentage change in price is

Economists use the average of the two end values to get around the end-point problem.

$$\frac{P_2 - P_1}{\frac{1}{2}(P_1 + P_2)} = \frac{(26 - 20)}{23} \times 100 = 26 \text{ percent}$$

Similarly the percentage change in quantity is

$$\frac{Q_2 - Q_1}{\frac{1}{2}(Q_1 + Q_2)} = \frac{(10 - 14)}{12} \times 100 = -33 \text{ percent}$$

Having done this, we can calculate elasticity as usual by dividing the percentage change in quantity by the percentage change in price:

$$\text{Elasticity} = \frac{\text{Percentage change in quantity}}{\text{Percentage change in price}} = \frac{-33}{26} = 1.27^{1}$$

[1]I dropped the negative sign because, as discussed earlier, economists talk about price elasticity of demand as a positive number.

Calculating Elasticity at a Point

Knowing the Tools

The text explained how to calculate elasticity of a range along a demand and supply curve. But what if you're asked to calculate elasticity at a specific point and you don't know the percentage change in price and quantity? In that case, you can use the following procedure.

Say you want to determine the elasticity at point *A* in Figure (a). First create a line segment, with the point as the segment's midpoint. The segment can be of any length. In Figure (a) I have selected a segment that begins 4 units on the quantity axis before the quantity at *A* and extends 4 units beyond the quantity at *A*. Thus, the quantity extends from 20 to 28. Next, determine the price relevant for the quantities chosen. In the example, the price corresponding to the quantity 28 is $3, and the price corresponding to the quantity 20 is $5.

I've now got my line segment, so I am ready to calculate the relevant percent changes. Percentage change in quantity = [(28 − 20)/24] × 100 = 33 percent. Percentage change in price = [(5 − 3)/4] × 100 = 50 percent. Elasticity at point *A* is 33/50 = 0.66.

To see that you've got the calculation down, in Figure (b) I present four points—two on the demand curve and two on a supply curve. Your assignment is to determine the elasticity of the four points on your own.

Now that you've done the calculations—you have, right?—you can look at the bottom of Figure (b), where I give you the correct answers. If you got all four right, you're in good shape. If not, it's time for a review. (And if you're taking the easy road and not calculating them on your own, it's time to get yourself in gear and start studying—remember, this stuff doesn't get into your head through osmosis.)

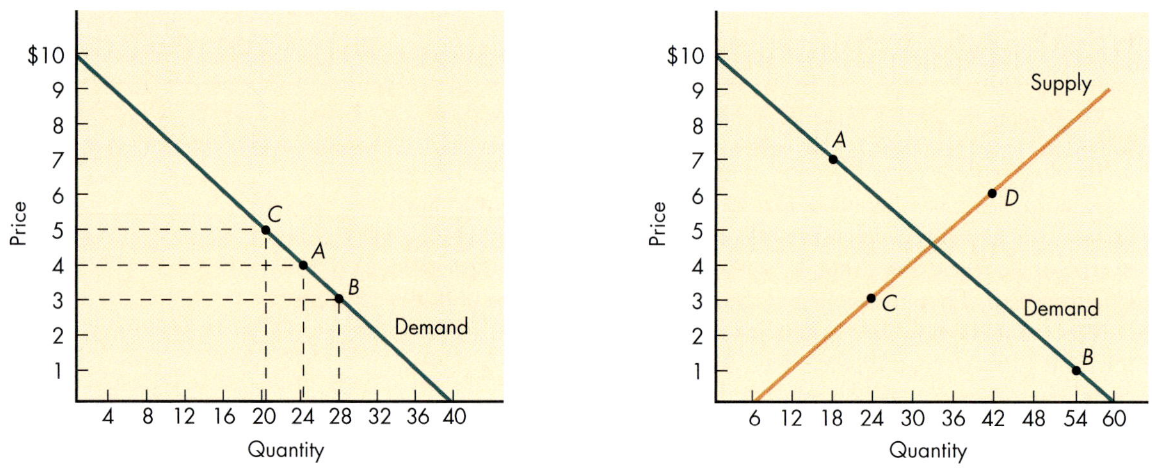

(a) Elasticity of demand **(b) Some examples**

Answers to **(b)**: *A* = 2.33; *B* = 0.11; *C* = 0.75; *D* = 0.86.

The elasticity of demand between points A and *B* is approximately 1.3. This means that a 10 percent increase in price will cause a 13 percent fall in quantity demanded. Thus, demand between *A* and *B* is elastic.

Other Examples

In Figure 6-1(b) I go through another example, this time using the supply elasticity from case 3 on p. 134. Initially, the Vermont minimum wage was $4.50 an hour; it was then raised to $5 an hour. The average of the two end points is $4.75 and so the percentage change in price is (0.50/4.75) × 100 = 10.53 percent. The initial quantity of labor supplied I estimated for my area in Vermont was 476; the rise in the minimum wage increased that number to 485, which gives us a percentage change in quantity of (9/480.5) × 100 = 1.87 percent. To calculate the elasticity of supply, divide the percentage change in quantity by the percentage change in price to get 1.87/10.53 = 0.18. A 10 percent rise in the minimum wage will bring about a 1.8 percent increase in quantity of labor supplied. The minimum-wage labor supply in Vermont is inelastic.

Learning the mechanics of calculating elasticities takes some practice, so in Figure 6-1(c) I give you three additional examples, leaving the calculations for you.

a. Move from *A* to *B* on the demand curve.

b. Move from *C* to *D* on the demand curve.

c. Move from *E* to *F* on the supply curve.

Now that you've calculated them (you have, haven't you?), I'll let you know that the answers can be found upside down at the bottom of the figure.

Q-3 What is the approximate elasticity between points *A* and *B* on the graph below?

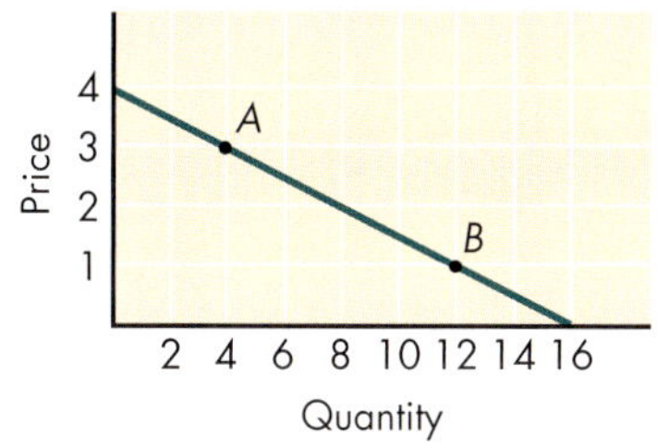

ELASTICITY AND SUPPLY AND DEMAND CURVES

There are two important points to remember about elasticity and supply and demand curves. The first is that elasticity is related to (but is not the same as) slope, and the second is that elasticity changes along straight-line demand and supply curves.

ELASTICITY IS NOT THE SAME AS SLOPE

Let's begin with the first point. The relationship between elasticity and slope is the following: The steeper the curve becomes at a given point, the less elastic is supply or demand. The limiting examples of this are a vertical curve (most steep), shown in Figure 6-2(a), and a horizontal (least steep) curve, shown in Figure 6-2(b).

The vertical demand curve shown in Figure 6-2(a) demonstrates how a change in price leads to no change in quantity demanded. Economists describe this curve as **perfectly inelastic**—*quantity does not respond at all to changes in price* ($E = 0$). Curves that are vertical are perfectly inelastic. The demand curve shown in Figure 6-2(b), in contrast, is horizontal. A change in price from above or below P_0 results in an infinitely large increase in quantity demanded. This curve is **perfectly elastic**, reflecting the fact that *quantity responds enormously to changes in price* ($E = \infty$). Horizontal curves are perfectly elastic. From these extreme cases, you can see that steeper (more vertical) curves at a given point are more *in*elastic and less steep (more horizontal) curves at a given point are more elastic. Elasticity, however, is not the same as slope. The second point illustrates this well.

ELASTICITY CHANGES ALONG STRAIGHT-LINE CURVES

Q-4 Your study partner, Nicole, has just stated that a straight-line demand curve is inelastic. How do you respond?

On straight-line supply and demand curves, slope does not change, but elasticity does. Figure 6-2(c and d) shows how elasticity changes along demand and supply curves. At the price intercept of the demand curve in Figure 6-2(c), demand is perfectly elastic ($E_D = \infty$); elasticity becomes smaller as price declines until it becomes perfectly inelastic ($E_D = 0$) at the quantity intercept. At one point along the demand curve, between an elasticity of infinity and zero, demand is **unit elastic**—*the percentage change in quantity equals the percentage change in price* ($E = 1$). In Figure 6-2(c) demand is unit elastic at a price of \$5. To confirm this, calculate elasticity of demand between \$4 and \$6. The percentage change in price is (2/5) × 100 = 40 percent, and the percentage change in quantity is (2/5) × 100 = 40 percent. The point at which demand is unit elastic divides

Figure 6-2 (a–d) Elasticities and Supply and Demand Curves
In (**a**) and (**b**), two special elasticity cases are shown. A perfectly inelastic curve is vertical; a perfectly elastic curve is horizontal. In (**c**) and (**d**), I show how elasticity generally varies along both supply and demand curves. Along demand curves it always goes from infinity at the vertical axis intercept to zero at the horizontal axis intercept. How elasticity of supply varies depends on which axis the supply curve intersects. If it intersects the vertical axis, elasticity starts at infinity and declines, and eventually approaches 1. If it intersects the horizontal axis, it starts at zero and increases, and eventually approaches 1. The one exception is when the supply curve intersects the origin. A good exercise is to determine what happens to elasticity in that case. (Hint: See Knowing the Tools box on page 139.)

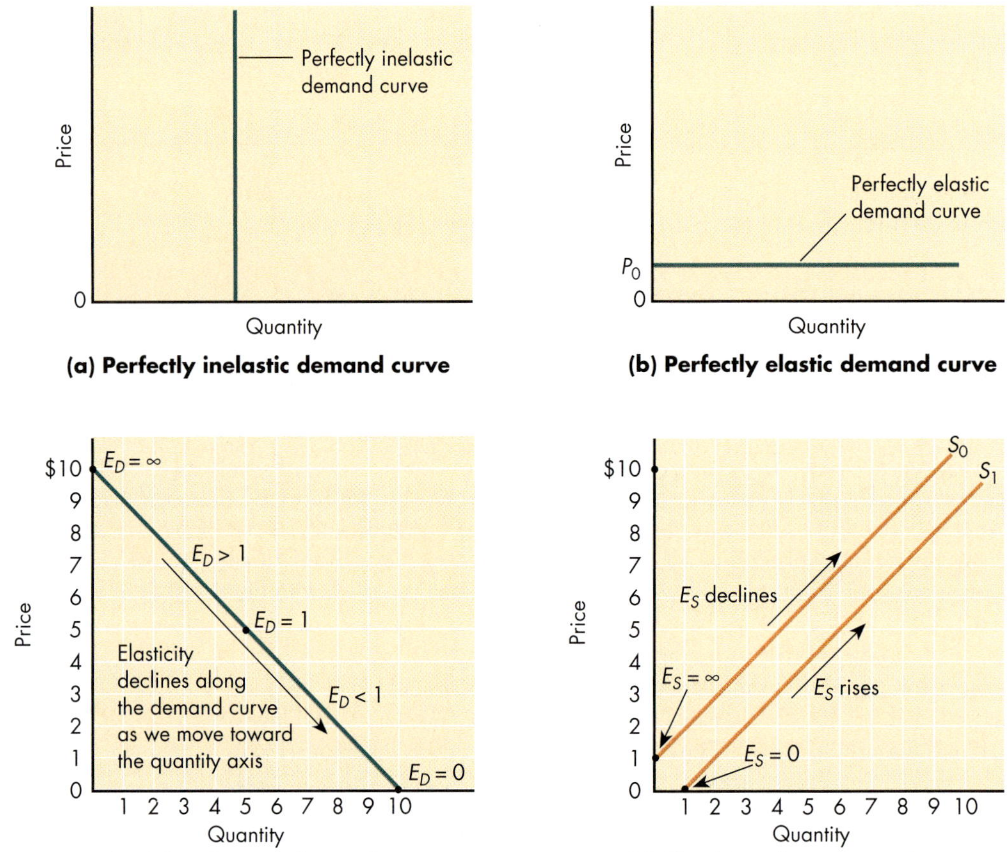

(a) Perfectly inelastic demand curve **(b) Perfectly elastic demand curve**

(c) Elasticity along a demand curve **(d) Elasticity along a supply curve**

the demand curve into two sections—an elastic portion ($E_D > 1$) above the point at which demand is unit elastic and an inelastic portion ($E_D < 1$) below the point at which demand is unit elastic.

The change in elasticity along a supply curve is less dramatic. At the point on a straight-line supply curve that intercepts the price axis, supply is perfectly elastic ($E_S = \infty$). Points become less elastic as you move out along the supply curve. At the point on a straight-line supply curve that intercepts the quantity axis, supply is perfectly inelastic ($E_S = 0$); it becomes more elastic as you move out along the supply curve. These changes are labeled in Figure 6-2(d). I leave it to you to determine what happens to the elasticity of the supply curve if the supply curve intercepts the origin. (Hint: See the Knowing the Tools box "Geometric Tricks for Estimating Price Elasticity.")

As a review, the five terms to describe elasticity along a curve are listed here from most to least elastic:

GEOMETRIC TRICKS FOR ESTIMATING PRICE ELASTICITY

Knowing the Tools

There are a couple of tricks that are useful in determining whether a point on a straight-line supply or demand curve is elastic or inelastic. The trick with demand is the following: (1) Determine where the demand curve intersects the price and quantity axes. (2) At a point midway between the origin and the quantity line intersection, draw a vertical line back up to the demand curve. The point where it intersects the demand curve will have an elasticity of 1; it will be unit elastic; all points to the left of that line will be elastic, and all points to the right of that will be inelastic.

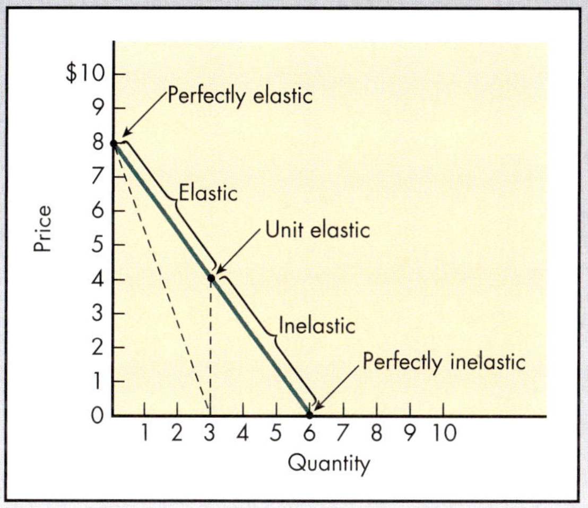

To determine whether a straight-line supply curve is elastic or inelastic you simply extend it to one of the axes, as in the following graph. The point at which this extension intersects the axes indicates the elasticity of the supply curve:

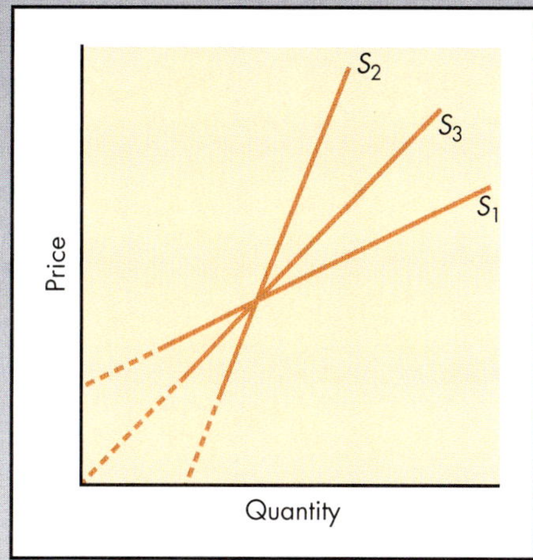

- If the extension intersects the vertical (price) axis, as does S_1, all points on the supply curve have an elasticity greater than 1; the supply curve is elastic.
- If the extension intersects the horizontal (quantity) axis, as does S_2, all points on the supply curve have an elasticity less than 1; the supply curve is inelastic.
- If the extension intersects the two axes at the origin, the supply curve has an elasticity of 1; the supply curve has unit elasticity.

If you combine these tricks with a knowledge that a perfectly elastic supply or demand curve is horizontal and crosses the price axis, and a perfectly inelastic supply or demand curve is vertical and crosses the quantity axis, you can even remember which is which. If a straight-line supply curve crosses the quantity axis, all points on it are inelastic; if it crosses the price axis, all points on it are elastic. Similarly, the top half of the demand curve (the part that crosses the price axis) is elastic; the bottom half (the part that crosses the quantity axis) is inelastic.

1. *Perfectly elastic:* Quantity responds enormously to changes in price ($E = \infty$).
2. *Elastic:* The percentage change in quantity exceeds the percentage change in price ($E > 1$).
3. *Unit elastic:* The percentage change in quantity is the same as the percentage change in price ($E = 1$).
4. *Inelastic:* The percentage change in quantity is less than the percentage change in price ($E < 1$).
5. *Perfectly inelastic:* Quantity does not respond at all to changes in price ($E = 0$).

Five elastic terms are: perfectly elastic ($E = \infty$); elastic ($E > 1$); unit elastic ($E = 1$); inelastic ($E < 1$); and perfectly inelastic ($E = 0$).

Now that you have seen that elasticity changes along straight-line supply and demand curves, the first point—that elasticity is related to but not the same as slope—should be clear. Whereas elasticity changes along a straight-line curve, slope does not.

Substitution and Elasticity

Now that you know how to measure elasticity, let's consider some of the factors that are likely to make supply and demand more or less elastic.

The most important determinant of price elasticity of demand is the number of substitutes for the good.

How responsive quantity demanded and quantity supplied will be to changes in price can be summed up in one word: substitution. As a general rule, the more substitutes a good has, the more elastic is its supply or demand.

The reasoning is as follows: If a good has substitutes, a rise in the price of that good will cause the consumer to shift consumption to those substitute goods. Put another way, when a satisfactory substitute is available, a rise in that good's price will have a large effect on the quantity demanded. For example, I think a Whopper is a satisfactory substitute for a Big Mac. If most people agree with me, the demand for Big Macs would be very elastic.

Factors that affect a good's substitutability of demand differ from factors that affect a good's substitutability of supply. So I will consider each separately. I begin with demand.

Substitution and Demand

The number of substitutes a good has is affected by several factors. Four of the most important are:

1. The time period being considered.
2. The degree to which a good is a luxury.
3. The market definition.
4. The importance of the good in one's budget.

These four reasons are derivatives of the substitution factor. Let's consider each to see why.

The more substitutes, the more elastic the demand and the more elastic the supply.

1. *The period being considered.* The larger the time interval considered, or the longer the run, the more elastic is the good's demand curve. There are more substitutes in the long run than in the short run. That's because the long run provides more alternatives. For example, let's consider the World War II period, when the price of rubber went up considerably. In the short run, there were few substitutes; the demand for rubber was inelastic. In the long run, however, the rise in the price of rubber stimulated research for alternatives. Many alternatives were found. Today automobile tires, which were all made of rubber at the time World War II broke out, are almost entirely made from synthetic materials. In the long run, the demand curve was very elastic.

2. *The degree to which a good is a luxury.* The less a good is a necessity, the more elastic is its demand curve. Because by definition one cannot do without necessities, they tend to have fewer substitutes than do luxuries. Insulin for a diabetic is a necessity; the demand is highly inelastic. Chocolate Ecstasy cake, however, is a luxury. A variety of other luxuries can be substituted for it (for example, cheesecake or a ball game).

Q.5 What are four important factors affecting the number of substitutes a good has?

3. *The market definition.* As the definition of a good becomes more specific, demand becomes more elastic. If the good we're talking about is broadly defined (say, transportation), there aren't many substitutes and demand will be inelastic. If you want to get from A to B, you need transportation. If the definition of the good is narrowed—say, to "transportation by bus"—there are more substitutes. Instead of taking a bus you

can walk, ride your bicycle, or drive your car. In that case the demand curve is more elastic.

4. *The importance of the good in one's budget.* Demand for goods that represent a large proportion of one's budget are more elastic than demand for goods that represent a small proportion of one's budget. Goods that cost very little relative to your total expenditures aren't worth spending a lot of time figuring out whether there's a good substitute. An example is pencils. Their low price means most people would buy just as many even if their price doubled. Their demand is inelastic. It is, however, worth spending lots of time looking for substitutes for goods that take a large portion of one's income. The demand for such goods tends to be more elastic. Many colleges have discovered this as they tried to raise tuition when other colleges did not. The demand curve they faced was elastic.

Substitution and Supply

The same general issues involving substitution are relevant when considering determinants of the elasticity of supply. But when it comes to supply, economists focus on time rather than on other factors because time plays such a central role in determining supply elasticity. The general rule is: The longer the time period considered, the more elastic is the supply curve. The reasoning is the same as with demand; in the long run there are more alternatives, so it is easier (less costly) for suppliers to change and produce other goods.

The longer the time period considered, the more elastic the supply.

To emphasize the importance of time, economists distinguish three time periods relevant to supply:

1. In the instantaneous period, quantity supplied is fixed, so supply is perfectly inelastic. This supply is sometimes called the momentary supply.
2. In the short run, some substitution is possible, so the short-run supply curve is somewhat elastic.
3. In the long run, significant substitution is possible; the supply curve becomes very elastic.

Q-6 Is supply generally more elastic in the short run or in the long run?

In determining the elasticity of supply, one must, however, remember an additional factor: Many supplied goods are produced, so we must take into account how easy it is to increase production of those same goods. For example, if the cost per unit of producing a good is constant, its supply is likely highly elastic. Before we can discuss such issues in detail, we need to talk about the production process in detail. And that will take two entire chapters, so I will put off the discussion for now.

How Substitution Factors Affect Specific Decisions

Let's consider how some of the substitution factors affect a specific decision. Let's say you've been hired by two governments (the city of Washington, D.C., and the U.S. government) to advise them about the effect that raising the gas tax by 10 percent will have on tax revenues. You look at the three factors that affect elasticity of demand.

In your report to the two governments, you would point out that in the short run the demand curve is less elastic than in the long run, since people aren't going to trade in their gas-guzzling cars for fuel-efficient cars immediately in response to a 10 percent rise in gas taxes—partly because they can't afford to, partly because they don't want to, and partly because not that many fuel-efficient cars are available to buy at the moment. When the time comes, however, that they would ordinarily purchase a new car, they're likely to switch to cars that are more fuel-efficient than their old cars, and to switch as much as they can to forms of transportation that are more fuel-efficient than cars. In the long run the demand will be far more elastic.

In the long run, demand generally becomes more elastic.

The second point you'd note is that gasoline is generally considered a necessity, although not all driving is necessary. However, since gasoline is only a small part of what it costs to drive a car, demand will probably tend to be inelastic.

As for the third factor (how specifically the good is defined) you have to be careful. It makes your recommendations for the government of the city of Washington, D.C., and the U.S. government quite different from each other. For the U.S. government, which is interested in the demand for gasoline in the entire United States, gasoline has a relatively inelastic demand. The general rule of thumb is that a 1-cent rise in tax will raise tax revenues by $1 billion. That inelasticity can't be carried over to the demand for gasoline in a city such as Washington, D.C. Because of the city's size and location, people in Washington have a choice. A large proportion of the people who buy gas in Washington could as easily buy gas in the adjacent states of Maryland or Virginia. Gasoline in Washington is a narrowly defined good and therefore has a quite elastic demand. A rise in price will mean a large fall in the quantity of gas demanded.

I mention this point because someone forgot about it when the city of Washington, D.C., raised the tax on a gallon of gasoline by 8 cents, a rise at that time of about 9 percent (this was case 2 in our discussion of calculating elasticities on p. 134). In response, monthly gasoline sales in Washington fell from 16 million gallons to less than 11 million gallons, a 40 percent decrease! The demand for gas in Washington was not inelastic, as it was for the United States as a whole; it was very elastic (E_D = 4.4). Washingtonians went elsewhere to buy gas.

The fact that smaller geographic areas have more elastic demands limits how highly state and local governments can tax goods relative to their neighboring localities or states. Where there are tax differences, new stores open all along the border and existing stores expand to entice people to come over that border and save on taxes. For example, the liquor tax is higher in Vermont than in New Hampshire, so it isn't surprising that right across the border from Vermont, New Hampshire has a large number of liquor stores. Here's one final example: If you look at license plates in Janzen Beach, Oregon (right across the Washington state border), you'll see a whole lot of Washington license plates. Why? If you answered that it likely has something to do with differential sales taxes in Washington and Oregon, you've got the idea.

Empirical Estimates of Elasticities of Demand and Supply

Table 6-1 presents empirical estimates of elasticity of demand. Notice that, as expected, different estimates are provided for the short- and long-run elasticities of each good. Also notice that the estimates are for the entire United States; estimates for a specific region in the United States could be expected to show more elasticity.

Taking an example from Table 6-1, notice that the long-run demand for movies is elastic. If movie theaters raise their prices, it's relatively easy for individuals simply to stay home and watch television. Movies have close substitutes, so we would expect the demand to be relatively elastic.

As a second example, in the short run the demand for electricity is highly inelastic. Either people have electrical appliances or they don't. In the long run, however, it becomes elastic since people can shift to gas for cooking and oil for heating, and can buy more energy-efficient appliances. As an exercise, you might see if you can explain why each of the other goods listed in the table has the elasticity of demand reported.

There are many fewer empirical measurements of supply than there are of demand. The reason concerns the structure of markets of produced goods, and the complicated nature of production. Most retail markets have seller-set or posted prices—you go to the

Table 6-1 Short-Run and Long-Run Elasticities of Demand

Product	Price Elasticity Short-Run	Long-Run
Tobacco products	0.46	1.89
Electricity (for household consumption)	0.13	1.89
Health services	0.20	0.92
Toys (nondurable)	0.30	1.02
Movies/motion pictures	0.87	3.67
Foreign travel by U.S. residents	0.14	1.77
Beer	.56	1.39
Wine	.68	.84
University tuition	.52	—
Rail transit	.62	1.59

Sources: Hendrik S. Houthakker and Lester D. Taylor, *Consumer Demand in the United States: Analyses and Projections,* 2nd ed. (Cambridge, Mass.: Harvard University Press, 1970); W. S. Comanor and T. A. Wilson, *Advertising and Market Power* (Cambridge, Mass.: Harvard University Press, 1974); Shermon Folland, Allen C. Goodman, and Miron Stano, *The Economics of Health Care* (New York: Macmillan, 1993); Yu Hsing and Hui S. Chang, "Testing Increasing Sensitivity of Enrollment at Private Institutions to Tuition and Other Costs," *The American Economist* 41, no. 1 (Spring 1996); Richard Voith, "The Long-Run Elasticity of Demand for Commuter Rail Transportation," *Journal of Urban Economics* 30 (1991).

store and pay the listed price of toothpaste. You can buy as much as you want at that price, so in a sense the supply of toothpaste (and most retail goods) is perfectly elastic until the store runs out, whereupon the supply becomes perfectly inelastic. But in another sense there is no supply curve since the selling price is determined by the seller's pricing strategy, not by the market. I will hold off discussion of such issues until after we discuss costs, production, and various market structures.

We do find empirical measurements of supply in factor markets, such as the market for labor services. For example, economist David Blau has estimated that the supply of child care labor is elastic—it may be as high as 1.9—which means that a 10 percent rise in the wages paid to child care workers will lead to a 19 percent increase in the quantity of child care workers. More generally, economists have estimated that the labor supply elasticity of heads of households is about 0.1, and for secondary workers is about 1.1. A good test of whether you intuitively understand elasticities is whether you can explain why the latter is more elastic.

Other areas in which elasticities of supply are estimated are agricultural and raw materials markets. Estimating supply elasticities here is possible because these goods are often sold in auction markets where price is directly determined by supply and demand, rather than in posted-price markets. In these markets, economists have generally found that the short-run supplies are highly inelastic and that the long-run supplies are highly elastic.

Elasticity, Total Revenue, and Demand

For sellers, knowing elasticity of demand is useful because from it they can tell whether the total revenue will go up or down when they raise or lower their prices. The total revenue a supplier receives is the price he or she charges times the quantity he or she sells. (Total revenue equals total quantity sold multiplied by the price of the good.) Elasticity tells sellers what will happen to total revenue if their price changes. Specifically:

- If demand is elastic ($E_D > 1$), a rise in price lowers total revenue. (Price and total revenue move in opposite directions.)

Figure 6-3 (a, b, and c) Elasticity and Total Revenue
Total revenue is measured by the rectangle produced by extending lines from the demand curve to the price and quantity axes. The change in total revenue resulting from a change in price can be estimated by comparing the sizes of the before and after rectangles. If price is being raised, total revenue increases by rectangle C and decreases by rectangle B. As you can see, the effect of a price rise on total revenue differs significantly at different points on a demand curve; **(a)** shows an almost unitary elastic range, **(b)** shows an inelastic range, and **(c)** shows an elastic range.

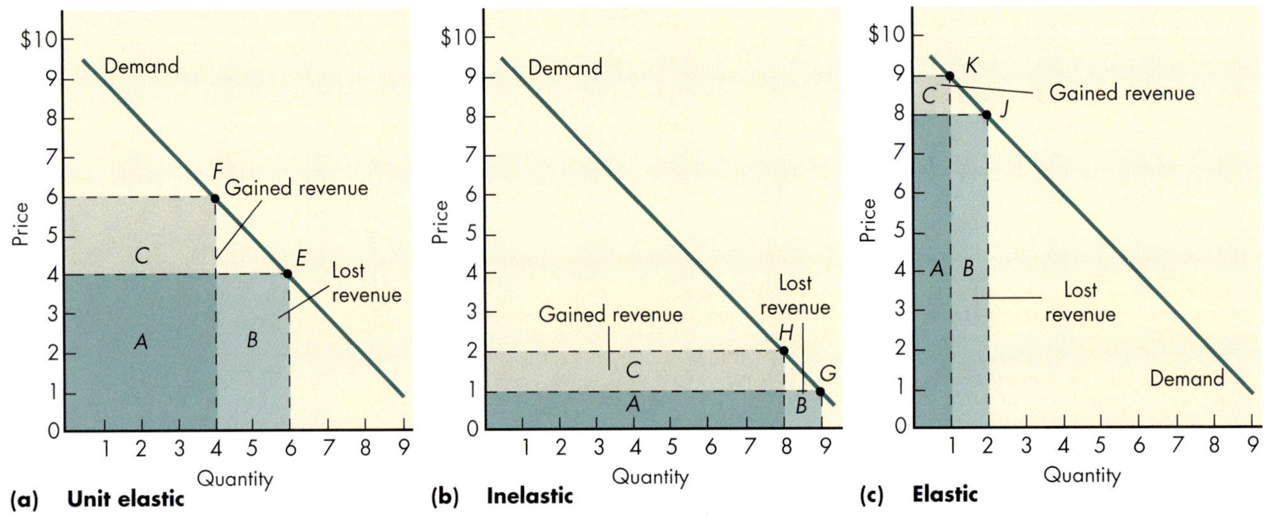

Q-7 If demand is inelastic and a firm raises price, what happens to total revenue?

- If demand is unit elastic ($E_D = 1$), a rise in price leaves total revenue unchanged.
- If demand is inelastic ($E_D < 1$), a rise in price increases total revenue. (Price and total revenue move in the same direction.)

The relationship between elasticity and total revenue is no mystery. There's a very logical reason why they are related, which can be seen most neatly by recognizing that total revenue ($P \times Q$) is represented by the area under the demand curve at that price and quantity. For example, at point *E* on the demand curve in Figure 6-3(a), the total revenue at price $4 and quantity 6 is the area designated by the *A* and *B* rectangles, $24.

If we increase price to $6, quantity demanded decreases to 4, so total revenue is still $24. Total revenue has remained constant, so the demand curve from point *E* to point *F* is unit elastic. The new total revenue is represented by the A and C rectangles. The difference between the old total revenue (A and B) and the new total revenue (A and C) is the difference between the rectangles B and C. Comparing these rectangles provides us with a visual method of estimating elasticities.

Figure 6-3(b) shows an inelastic range; Figure 6-3(c) shows a highly elastic range. While in Figure 6-3(b) the slope of the demand curve is the same as in Figure 6-3(a), we begin at a different point on the demand curve (point G). If we raise our price from $1 to $2, quantity demanded falls from 9 to 8. The gained area (rectangle C) is much greater than the lost area (rectangle B). In other words, total revenue increases significantly, so the demand curve between points *H* and G is highly inelastic.

In Figure 6-3(c) the demand curve is again the same, but we begin at still another point, *J*. If we raise our price from $8 to $9, quantity demanded falls from 2 to 1. The gained area (rectangle C) is much smaller than the lost area (rectangle *B*). In other words, total revenue decreases significantly, so the demand curve from points *J* to *K* is highly elastic.

Figure 6-4 (a and b) How Total Revenue Changes
Total revenue is at a maximum when elasticity equals 1, as you can see in (a) and (b). When demand is elastic, total revenue decreases with an increase in price. When demand is inelastic, total revenue increases with an increase in price.

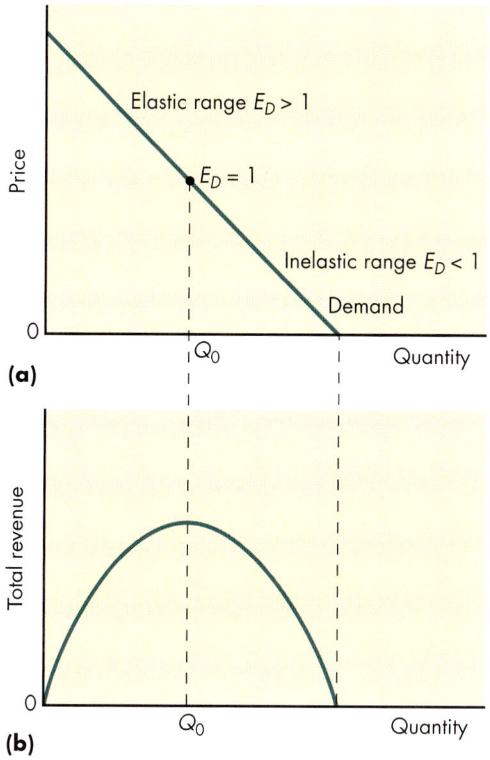

Relationship between Elasticity (*E*) and Total Revenue (*TR*)

	Price Rise	Price Decline
Elastic ($E_D > 1$)	*TR* ↓	*TR* ↑
Unit Elastic ($E_D = 1$)	*TR* constant	*TR* constant
Inelastic ($E_D < 1$)	*TR* ↑	*TR* ↓

Total Revenue along a Demand Curve

The way in which elasticity changes along a demand curve and its relationship to total revenue can be seen in Figure 6-4. When output is zero, total revenue is zero; similarly, when price is zero, total revenue is zero. That accounts for the two end points of the total revenue curve in Figure 6-4(b). Let's say we start at a price of zero, where demand is perfectly inelastic. As we increase price (decrease quantity demanded), total revenue increases significantly. As we continue to do so, the increases in total revenue become smaller until finally, after output of Q_0, total revenue actually starts decreasing. It continues decreasing at a faster and faster rate until finally, at zero output, total revenue is zero.

With elastic demands, a rise in price decreases total revenue. With inelastic demands, a rise in price increases total revenue.

As an example of where such calculations might come in handy, recall the vanity license plates that we used to illustrate the law of demand in Chapter 4. A rise in the price of vanity plates of about 29 percent, from \$30 to \$40, decreased the quantity demanded about 64 percent, from 60,334 to 31,122, so the price elasticity of demand was about 0.64/0.29 = 2.2. Since demand was elastic, total revenue fell. Specifically, total revenue fell from \$1,810,020 (\$30 × 60,334) to \$1,244,880 (\$40 × 31,122).

Web Note 6.1
Elasticity and Cartels

Elasticity of Individual and Market Demand

In thinking about elasticity of demand, keep in mind the point made in Chapter 4: The market demand curve is the horizontal summation of individual demand curves; some individuals have highly inelastic demands and others have highly elastic demands. A slight rise in the price of a good will cause some people to stop buying the good; the slight increase won't affect other people's quantity demanded for the good at all. Market demand elasticity is influenced both by how many people drop out totally and by how much an existing consumer marginally changes his or her quantity demanded.

Firms have a strong incentive to separate out people with less elastic demand and charge them a higher price.

If a firm can somehow separate the people with less elastic demand from those with more elastic demand, it can charge more to the individuals with inelastic demands and less to individuals with elastic demands. Economists call this *price discrimination*. We see firms throughout the economy trying to use price discrimination. Let's consider three examples:

1. Airlines' Saturday stay-over specials. If you stay over a Saturday night, usually you can get a much lower airline fare than if you don't. The reason is that businesspeople have inelastic demands and don't like to stay over Saturday nights, while pleasure travelers have more elastic demands. By requiring individuals to stay over Saturday night, airlines can separate out businesspeople and charge them more.
2. The phenomenon of selling new cars. Most new cars don't sell at the listed price. They sell at a discount. Salespeople are trained to separate out comparison shoppers (who have more elastic demands) from impulse buyers (who have inelastic demands). By not listing the selling price of cars so that the discount can be worked out in individual negotiations, salespeople can charge more to customers who have inelastic demands.
3. The almost-continual-sale phenomenon. Some items, such as washing machines, go on sale rather often. Why don't suppliers sell them at a low price all the time? Because some buyers whose washing machines break down have inelastic demand. They can't wait, so they'll pay the "unreduced" price. Others have elastic demands; they can wait for the sale. By running sales (even though they're frequent sales), sellers can separate consumers with inelastic demand curves from consumers with elastic demand curves.

Other Elasticity Concepts

There are many other elasticity concepts besides the price elasticity of demand and the price elasticity of supply. Since these other elasticities can be useful in specifying the effects of shift factors on the demand for a good, I will introduce you to two of them: income elasticity of demand and cross-price elasticity of demand.

Income elasticity of demand shows the responsiveness of demand to changes in income.

The definition of these concepts is straightforward. **Income elasticity of demand** is defined as *the percentage change in demand divided by the percentage change in income*. Put another way,

$$\text{Income elasticity of demand} = \frac{\text{Percentage change in demand}}{\text{Percentage change in income}}$$

It tells us the responsiveness of demand to changes in income. (Notice I used *demand*, not *quantity demanded*, to emphasize that in response to a change in anything but the price of that good, the entire demand curve shifts; there's no movement along the demand curve.) **Cross-price elasticity of demand** is defined as *the percentage change in demand divided by the percentage change in the price of a related good*. Put another way,

Cross-price elasticity of demand shows the responsiveness of demand to changes in prices of related goods.

$$\text{Cross-price elasticity of demand} = \frac{\text{Percentage change in demand}}{\text{Percentage change in price of a related good}}$$

EMPIRICALLY MEASURING ELASTICITIES

Applying the Tools

In the text, the discussion of determining elasticity concentrates on the technical aspects of the calculation. It assumes we know at what point on the supply and demand curve we are. In the real world, economists don't have the luxury of that knowledge. The data points they use involve interactions of supply and demand, and they must use statistical tools to ensure that they are holding "other things constant." Specifically, to determine points on a demand curve we must vary supply (and nothing else); to determine points on a supply curve we must vary demand (and nothing else).

In practice, holding everything else constant is difficult to do, which means real-world estimates of elasticity are often less than perfect. The tables presented in the text are some economists' estimates, but there are often disputes and technical issues that could lead to different estimates.

Where do firms get the information they need to calculate elasticities? Think of the grocery store where you can get a special buyer's card; you show it to the checkout clerk and you get all the discounts. And the card is free! Those grocery stores are not just being nice. When the clerk scans your purchases, the store gets information that is forwarded to a central processing unit that can see how people react to different prices. This information is valuable; it allows firms to fine-tune their pricing—raising prices on goods for which the demand is inelastic, and lowering prices on goods for which the demand is elastic.

Alternatively, think of the warranty cards that you send in when you buy a new computer or a new TV. The information goes into the firms' information bases and is used by their economists in future price-setting decisions.

These other elasticity concepts tell you how much the demand curve will shift when there is a change in a shift factor. Let's consider each separately.

INCOME ELASTICITY OF DEMAND

The most commonly used of the elasticity terms introduced above is *income elasticity of demand*. Income elasticity of demand tells us how much demand will change with a change in income. An increase in income generally increases one's consumption of almost all goods, although the increase may be greater for some goods than for others. **Normal goods**—*goods whose consumption increases with an increase in income*—have income elasticities greater than zero.

Normal goods are sometimes divided into luxuries and necessities. **Luxuries** are *goods that have an income elasticity greater than 1*—their percentage increase in demand is greater than the percentage increase in income. For example, say your income goes up 10 percent and your consumption of DVDs goes up 20 percent. The income elasticity of DVDs is 2; thus, DVDs are a luxury good. Alternatively, say your income goes up by 100 percent and your demand for shoes goes up by 50 percent. Your income elasticity for shoes would be 0.5. Shoes are a **necessity**—*a good that has an income elasticity less than 1*. The consumption of a necessity rises by a smaller proportion than the rise in income.

Q-8 If a good's consumption increases with an increase in income, what type of good would you call it?

It is even possible that an increase in income can affect relative preferences so much that an increase in income can cause a *decrease* in the consumption of a particular good. These goods have a negative income elasticity of demand. The term applied to such goods is **inferior goods**—*goods whose consumption decreases when income increases*. In some circumstances, potatoes could be an example of an inferior good. As income goes up, people might so significantly shift their consumption toward meat and away from potatoes that their total consumption of potatoes decreases. A study by a Stanford economist also found tortillas to be an inferior good in Mexico.

Web Note 6.2
Inferior Goods

Table 6-2 presents income elasticities measured for some groups of goods. Notice a few things about this table. In the short run, people often save high proportions of their

Table 6-2 Income Elasticities for Selected Goods

Commodity	Income Elasticity Short-Run	Long-Run
Motion pictures	0.81	3.41
Foreign travel	0.24	3.09
Tobacco products	0.21	0.86
Food produced and consumed on farms	−0.61	—
Furniture	2.60	0.53
Jewelry and watches	1.00	1.64
Beer	—	0.84
Hard liquor	—	2.5
Dental services	—	1.6
Private university tuition	—	1.1

Sources: Hendrik S. Houthakker and Lester D. Taylor, *Consumer Demand in the United States: Analyses and Projections,* 2nd ed. (Cambridge, Mass.: Harvard University Press, 1970); E. A. Selvanthan, "Cross-Country Alcohol Consumption: An Application of the Rotterdam Demand System," *Applied Economics* 23 (1991); Shermon Folland, Allen C. Goodman, and Miron Stano, *The Economics of Health Care* (New York: Macmillan, 1993); Yu Hsing and Hui S. Chang, "Testing Increasing Sensitivity of Enrollment at Private Institutions to Tuition and Other Costs," *The American Economist* 41, no. 1 (Spring 1996).

increases in income, so most goods, other than impulse goods, such as furniture, have low short-run income elasticities. To avoid this problem, economists generally focus on long-run income elasticities. Notice which goods are necessities (the ones with long-run income elasticities less than 1). Notice also which goods are luxuries (the ones with elasticities greater than 1).

Finally, notice the one good with a negative income elasticity—food produced and consumed on farms. As mentioned above, such goods are called inferior goods. As income rises, people buy proportionately less of such goods.

Cross-Price Elasticity of Demand

Cross-price elasticity of demand is another frequently used elasticity concept. Let's consider an example. Say the price of Toyotas rises. What is likely to happen to the demand for Fords? It is likely to rise, so the cross-price elasticity between the two is positive. Positive cross-price elasticities of demand mean the goods are **substitutes**—*goods that can be used in place of one another.* When the price of a good goes up, the demand for the substitute goes up.

Most goods have substitutes, so most cross-price elasticities are positive. But not all. To see that, let's consider another example: Say the price of hot dogs rises; what is likely to happen to the demand for ketchup? If you're like me and use lots of ketchup on your hot dogs, as I cut my consumption of hot dogs I will also cut my consumption of ketchup. Ketchup and hot dogs are not substitutes but rather complements. **Complements** are *goods that are used in conjunction with other goods*. A fall in the price of a good will increase the demand for its complement. The cross-price elasticity of complements is negative.

Substitutes have positive cross-price elasticities; complements have negative cross-price elasticities.

Some estimates of cross-price elasticities of demand are shown in Table 6-3. You can see that the strongest substitutes are European autos for U.S. and Asian autos. A 10 percent fall in the price of U.S. and Asian autos leads to a 6 percent fall in the demand for European autos. Hard liquor and beer are complements. If the price of beer falls by 10 percent, the demand for hard liquor increases by 1.1 percent.

Table 6-3 Cross-Price Elasticities

Commodities	Cross-Price Elasticity
Beef in response to price changes in pork	0.11
Beef in response to price changes in chicken	0.02
U.S. automobiles in response to price changes in European and Asian automobiles	0.28
European automobiles in response to price changes in U.S. and Asian automobiles	0.61
Beer in response to price changes in wine	0.23
Hard liquor in response to price changes in beer	−0.11

Sources: J. A. Johnson and E. H. Oksanen, "Socioeconomic Determinants of the Consumption of Alcoholic Beverages," *Applied Economics* (1974); Patrick S. McCarthy, "Market Price and Income Elasticities of New Vehicle Demand," *Review of Economics and Statistics* (August 1996); Kuo S. Huang, "Nutrient Elasticities in a Complete Food Demand System," *American Journal of Agricultural Economics* (February 1996).

Some Examples

To make sure you've got these concepts down, see Figure 6-5, which demonstrates two examples. In Figure 6-5(a), income has risen by 20 percent, increasing demand at price P_0 from 20 to 26. To determine the income elasticity we must first determine the percentage change in demand. We calculate the percentage demand to be $6/[(20 + 26)/2] = (6/23) \times 100 = 26$ percent. The percentage change in income is 20, so the income elasticity is 26/20, or 1.3.

In Figure 6-5(b), a 33 percent fall in the price of pork has caused the demand for beef to fall by 3.8 percent—from 108 to 104 at a price of P_0. The cross-price elasticity of demand is $3.8/33 = 0.12$.

The Power of Supply/Demand Analysis

Now that you've got the elasticity terms down, let's consider some examples that demonstrate the power of supply/demand analysis when it is combined with the concept of elasticity. Let's start with some easy cases.

Figure 6-5 (a and b) Calculating Elasticities
Shift factors, such as income or price of another good, shift the entire demand curve. To calculate these elasticities, we see how much demand will shift at a constant price and then calculate the relevant elasticities.

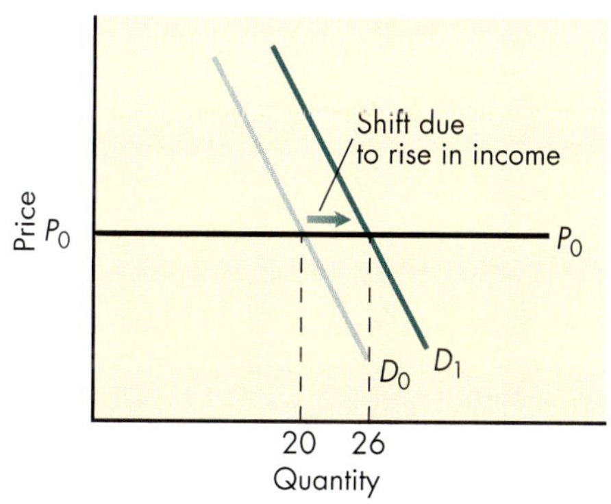

(a) Calculating income elasticity

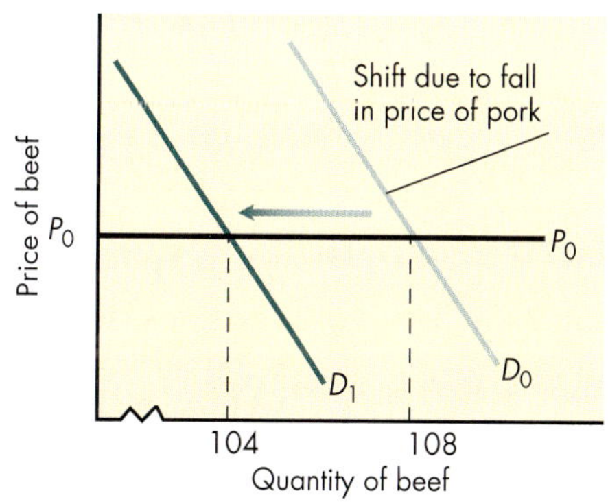

(b) Calculating cross-price elasticity

A Review of the Alternative Elasticity Terms

Knowing the Tools

Income elasticity of demand is defined as *the percentage change in demand divided by the percentage change in income.*

$$\text{Income elasticity of demand} = \frac{\text{Percentage change in demand}}{\text{Percentage change in income}}$$

Cross-price elasticity of demand is defined as *the percentage change in demand divided by the percentage change in the price of a related good.*

$$\text{Cross-price elasticity of demand} = \frac{\text{Percentage change in demand}}{\text{Percentage change in price of a related good}}$$

Complement: Cross-price elasticity of demand is negative.

Substitute: Cross-price elasticity of demand is positive.

Normal good: Income elasticity of demand is positive.

Luxury: Income elasticity is greater than 1.

Necessity: Income elasticity is less than 1.

Inferior good: Income elasticity of demand is negative.

When Should a Supplier Not Raise Price?

Q.9 A firm faces an elastic demand for its product. It has come to an economist to advise it on whether to lower its price. The answer she gives is: Maybe. Why is this the right answer?

First, let's say a firm is trying to increase its profits and hires you to tell it whether it should raise or lower its price. The firm knows that it faces an inelastic demand. Should it raise its price?

I hope your answer was: Definitely yes. How can I be so sure the correct answer is yes? Because I remembered the discussion of the relationship between price elasticity of demand with total revenue. With an inelastic demand the percentage change in quantity is less than the percentage change in price, so total revenue must increase with an increase in price. Total costs will also decrease, so profits—total revenues minus total costs—must also increase.

Along those same lines, consider a university president thinking of raising tuition. Say that raising tuition by 10 percent will decrease the number of students by 1 percent. What's the price elasticity? The percentage change in quantity is 1 percent; the percentage change in price is 10. Dividing the percentage change in quantity by the percentage change in price, we have an elasticity of 0.1. That's an inelastic demand ($E_D < 1$), so raising tuition will increase the university's total revenue.

But if a 10 percent rise in tuition will decrease the enrollment by 25 percent, the elasticity will be large (2.5). In response to an increase in tuition, the university's total revenue will decrease significantly. When you have an elastic demand, you should hesitate to increase price. To make sure you're following the argument, explain the likely effect an elastic demand will have on lowering tuition. (Your argument should involve the possibility of increasing profit.) If you're not following the argument, go back to the section on elasticity and total revenue, especially Figure 6-3.

When the long-run and short-run elasticities differ, the analysis becomes somewhat more complicated. Consider the case of a local transit authority that, faced with a budget crisis, increased its fares from $1.50 to $1.75. The rise in revenue during the first

Figure 6-6 (a and b) Effects of Shifts in Supply on Price and Quantity
In both (**a**) and (**b**) the supply shifts out from S_0 to S_1. Initial price is P_0 and quantity is Q_0. The new equilibrium is P_1 and Q_1. In (**a**), supply intersects demand where demand is inelastic and the quantity effects are relatively small. In (**b**), the demand is more elastic and the quantity effects are much larger. In general the effects of shifts in supply on equilibrium quantity and price are determined by the elasticity of demand. When demand is inelastic, price changes are large and quantity changes are small. A useful exercise is to go through the same two cases for demand shifts, showing how the quantity effect is determined by the elasticity of supply.

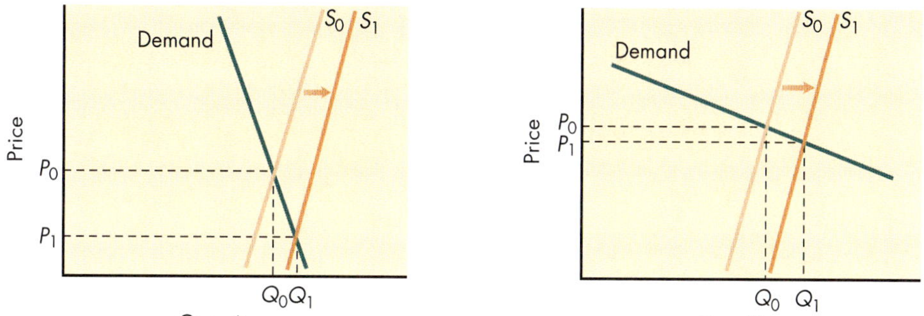

(a) Inelastic supply and inelastic demand **(b) Inelastic supply and elastic demand**

year helped the authority balance its books. But in the two years following, ridership declined so much that total revenue fell. What happened? In the short-run, commuters had few substitutes to taking the bus—demand was relatively inelastic so that total revenue rose when fares were increased. But, as time went on, commuters found alternative ways to get to work. Long-run demand was more elastic in this case, so much so that total revenue declined.

Elasticity and Shifting Supply and Demand

Let's now turn to shifts in supply and demand. Knowing the elasticity of the supply and demand curves allows us to be more specific about the effects of shifts in supply and demand.

Figure 6-6 demonstrates the relative effects of supply shifts on equilibrium price and quantity under different assumptions about elasticity. As you can see, the more elastic the demand, the greater the effect of a supply shift on quantity, and the smaller the effect on price. Going through a similar exercise for demand shifts with various supply elasticities is also a useful exercise. If you do so, you will see that the more elastic the supply, the greater the effect of a demand shift on quantity, and the smaller the effect on price.

We can be even more precise with regard to the percentage change in price. Specifically, when demand shifts,

$$\text{Percentage change in price} = \frac{\text{Percentage change in demand}}{E_D + E_S}$$

When supply shifts,

$$\text{Percentage change in price} = \frac{\text{Percentage change in supply}}{E_D + E_S}$$

Let's consider two examples. Suppose demand shifts out to the right by 5 percent, the elasticity of demand is 0.8, and the elasticity of supply is 2. Price will rise by 5%/2.8, or 1.8 percent. Alternatively, if supply shifts out to the right by 33 percent and the

Q.10 The elasticity of supply is 1 and the elasticity of demand is 2. If demand increases by 10 percent, by what percent will price change?

elasticity of demand and supply are both 1, price will fall by 33%/2, or 16.5 percent. In general, the more elastic supply and demand, the less price will change for a given percentage change in either demand or supply.

To be sure that you have understood elasticity, consider the following three observations about price and quantity and match them with the three descriptions of supply and demand:

a. Price rises significantly; quantity hardly changes at all.
b. Price remains almost constant; quantity increases enormously.
c. Price falls significantly; quantity hardly changes at all.

1. Demand highly elastic; supply shifts out.
2. Supply highly inelastic; demand shifts out.
3. Demand is highly inelastic; supply shifts out.

The answers are a–2; b–1; c–3.

Conclusion

I'll stop the exercises here. As you can see, the elasticity concept is important. Economists use it all the time when discussing supply and demand.

However, the elasticity concept is not easy to remember, or to calculate, so working with it takes some practice. It becomes a bit less forbidding if you remember that elasticity is what your shorts lose when they've been through the washer and drier too many times. If a relationship is elastic, price (for price elasticity) exerts a strong pull on quantity. If it's inelastic, there's little pull on quantity.

Summary

- Elasticity is defined as percentage change in quantity divided by percentage change in some variable that affects demand (or supply) or quantity demanded (or supplied). The most common elasticity concept used is price elasticity.
- Elasticity is a better descriptor than is slope because it is independent of units of measurement.
- To calculate percentage changes in prices and quantities use the average of the end values:

$$E_D = \frac{\text{Percentage change in quantity demanded}}{\text{Percentage change in price}}$$

$$E_S - \frac{\text{Percentage change in quantity supplied}}{\text{Percentage change in price}}$$

- Five elasticity terms are: *elastic* ($E > 1$); *inelastic* ($E < 1$); *unit elastic* ($E = 1$); *perfectly inelastic* ($E = 0$); and *perfectly elastic* ($E = \infty$).
- The more substitutes a good has, the greater its elasticity.
- Factors affecting the number of substitutes in demand are (1) time period considered, (2) the degree to which the good is a luxury, (3) the market definition, and (4) the importance of the good in one's budget.
- The most important factor affecting the number of substitutes in supply is time. As the time interval lengthens, supply becomes more elastic.
- Elasticity changes along straight-line demand and supply curves. Demand becomes less elastic as we move down along a demand curve.
- When a supplier raises price, if demand is inelastic total revenue increases; if demand is elastic, total revenue decreases; if demand is unit elastic total revenue remains constant.

- Other important elasticity concepts are income elasticity and cross-price elasticity of demand.
- $$\text{Income elasticity of demand} = \frac{\text{Percentage change in demand}}{\text{Percentage change in income}}$$
- $$\text{Cross-price elasticity of demand} = \frac{\text{Percentage change in demand}}{\text{Percentage change in price of a related good}}$$
- Knowing elasticities allows us to be more precise about the qualitative effects that shifts in demand and supply have on prices and quantities.
- When demand shifts, percentage change in price $= \dfrac{\text{percentage change in demand}}{E_D + E_S}$
- When supply shifts, percentage change in price $= \dfrac{\text{percentage change in supply}}{E_D + E_S}$

Key Terms

complement *(148)*
cross-price elasticity of demand *(146)*
elastic *(133)*
income elasticity of demand *(146)*
inelastic *(133)*
inferior good *(147)*
luxury *(147)*
necessity *(147)*
normal good *(147)*
perfectly elastic *(137)*
perfectly inelastic *(137)*
price elasticity of demand *(132)*
price elasticity of supply *(133)*
substitute *(148)*
unit elastic *(137)*

Questions for Thought and Review

1. Determine the price elasticity of demand if, in response to an increase in price of 10 percent, quantity demanded decreases by 20 percent. Is demand elastic or inelastic?
2. A firm has just increased its price by 5 percent over last year's price, and it found that quantity sold remained the same. The firm comes to you and wants to know its price elasticity of demand. How would you calculate it? What additional information would you search for before you did your calculation?
3. When tolls on the Dulles Airport Greenway were reduced from $1.75 to $1.00, traffic increased from 10,000 to 26,000 trips a day. Assuming all changes in quantity were due to the change in price, what is the price elasticity of demand for the Dulles Airport Greenway?
4. In 1999 Domino's Pizza, a corporate sponsor of the Washington Redskins (a football team) offered to reduce the price of its medium-size pizza by $1 for every touchdown scored by the Redskins during the previous week. Until that year, the Redskins weren't scoring many touchdowns. Much to the surprise of Domino's, in one week in 1999, the Redskins scored six touchdowns. (Maybe they like pizza.) Domino's pizzas were selling for $2 a pie! The quantity of pizzas demanded soared the following week from 1 pie an hour to 100 pies an hour. What was price elasticity of demand for Domino's pizza?
5. Which of the pairs of goods would you expect to have a greater price elasticity of demand?
   a. Cars, transportation.
   b. Housing, leisure travel.
   c. Rubber during World War II, rubber during the 20th century.
6. Which has greater elasticity: a supply curve that goes through the origin with slope of 1 or a supply curve that goes through the origin with slope of 4?
7. Why would an economist be more hesitant about making an elastic estimate of the effect of an increase in price of 1 percent rather than an increase in price of 50 percent?
8. Demand for "prestige" college education is generally considered to be highly inelastic. What does this suggest about tuition increases at prestige schools in the future? Why don't colleges raise tuition by amounts even greater than they already do?
9. Once a book has been written, would an author facing an inelastic demand curve for the book prefer to raise or lower the book's price? Why?
10. Colleges have increasingly used price sensitivity to formulate financial aid. The more eager the student, the less aid he or she can expect to get. Use elasticity to explain this phenomenon. Is this practice justified?

11. In the discussion of elasticity and raising and lowering prices, the text states that if you have an elastic demand you should hesitate to raise your price, and that lowering price can *possibly* increase profits (total revenue minus total cost). Why is the word *possibly* used?
12. For each of the following goods, state whether it is a normal good, a luxury, a necessity, or an inferior good. Explain your answers.
    a. Vodka.
    b. Table salt.
    c. Furniture.
    d. Perfume.
    e. Beer.
    f. Sugar.
13. For each of the following pairs of goods, state whether the cross-price elasticity is likely positive, negative, or zero. Explain your answers.
    a. Lettuce, carrots.
    b. Housing, furniture.
    c. Nike sneakers, LA Gear sneakers.
    d. Jeans, formal suits.
14. If there were only two goods in the world, can you say whether they would be complements or substitutes? Explain your answer.
15. How is elasticity related to the revenue from a sales tax?

Problems and Exercises

1. A major cereal producer decides to lower price from \$3.60 to \$3 per 15-ounce box.
    a. If quantity demanded increases by 18 percent, what is the price elasticity of demand?
    b. What if, instead of lowering its price, the cereal producer had increased the size of the box from 15 to 17.8 ounces? What would you expect that the response would have been? Why?
2. In the 1960s coffee came in 1-pound cans. Today, most coffee comes in 11-ounce cans.
    a. Can you think of an explanation why?
    b. Can you think of other products besides coffee whose standard size has shrunk? (Often the standard size is supplemented by a "super-size" alternative.)
3. The president of a liberal arts college in Pennsylvania asked economist Paul Heise about the effect of a particular proposal on net income, enrollment, and student GPA. The proposal was the following: "For the incoming class: (1) cut tuition for students in the top 10 percent of their high school class by 50 percent; (2) cut tuition for students in the 10th to 20th percentiles of their high school class by 33 percent; (3) cut tuition for students in the 20th to 30th percentiles of their high school class by 25 percent; (4) leave tuition the same for all others." He believed the demand was highly elastic.
    a. What was Professor Heise's response?
    b. What would his response have been if the demand had been highly inelastic?
4. Economists William Hunter and Mary Rosenbaum wrote an article in which they estimated the demand elasticity for motor fuel to be between 0.4 and 0.85.
    a. If the price rises 10 percent and the initial quantity sold is 10 million gallons, what is the range of estimates of the new quantity demanded?
    b. In carrying out their estimates they came up with different elasticity estimates for rises in price than for falls in price, with an increase in price having a larger elasticity than a decrease in price. What hypothesis might you propose for their findings?
5. In the box "Geometric Tricks for Estimating Price Elasticity," there are three statements about the elasticities of straight-line supply curves. One of those statements is that supply curves intersecting the quantity axis are inelastic. Can you prove that that is true by algebraic manipulation of the elasticity formula?
6. Calculate the price elasticities of the designated points on the following graph. (Reread the box "Calculating Elasticity at a Point.")

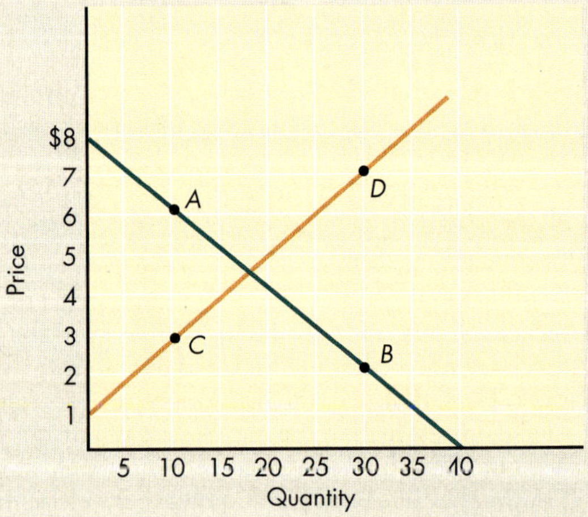

7. Calculate the elasticity of the designated ranges of supply and demand curves on the following graph.

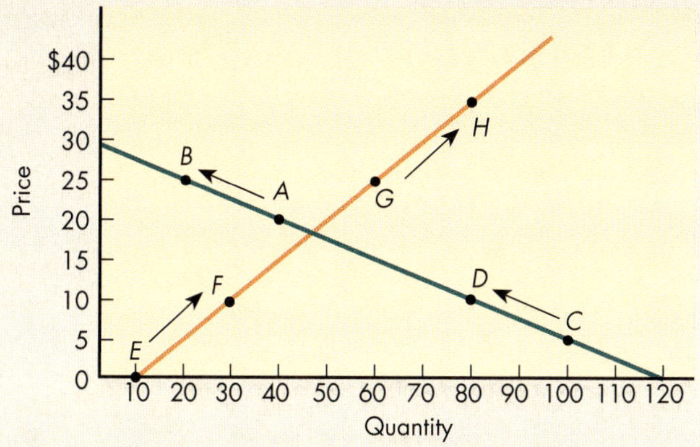

8. Calculate the income elasticities of demand for the following:
   a. Income rises by 20 percent; demand rises by 10 percent.
   b. Income rises from $30,000 to $40,000; demand increases (at a constant price) from 16 to 19.
9. When the price of ketchup rises by 15 percent, the demand for hot dogs falls by 1 percent.
   a. Calculate the cross-price elasticity of demand.
   b. Are the goods complements or substitutes?
   c. By how much would the demand have to rise for the goods to switch from complements to substitutes, or vice versa?
10. According to *The Wall Street Journal*, in the 1990s the going price for live worms was $1.17 a dozen. Then a drought hit.
    a. Demonstrate graphically what happened to the price and quantity of worms sold.
    b. If the price rose to $1.75 and the quantity sold fell from 90,000 to 60,000, what would your estimate of the elasticity of demand be?
11. What will be the percentage change in price in the following instances?
    a. Demand shifts to the right by 10 percent, elasticity of demand is 1, elasticity of supply is 2.
    b. Demand shifts to the right by 10 percent, elasticity of demand is 0.2, elasticity of supply is 0.5.
    c. Supply shifts to the right by 25 percent, elasticity of demand is 3, elasticity of supply is 2.
12. Economists have estimated the following transportation elasticities. For each pair, explain possible reasons why the elasticities differ.
    a. Elasticity of demand for buses is 0.23 during peak hours and 0.42 during off-peak hours.
    b. Elasticity of demand for buses is 0.7 in the short run and 1.5 in the long run.
    c. Elasticity of demand for toll roads is 4.7 for low-income commuters and 0.63 for high-income commuters.

WEB QUESTIONS

1. Cigarette smoking is widely recognized as the number one cause of cancer in the United States. One method the government can use to reduce cigarette smoking is to tax cigarettes. Read "The Impact of Proposed Cigarette Price Increases" by Frank J. Chaloupka at www.advocacy.org/publications/mtc/priceincreases.htm to answer the following questions about the effect of taxation on cigarette smoking.
   a. Who is likely to be more affected by tax increases on cigarettes—all adults or young adults? Cite specific elasticity of demand estimates from the article to support your answer.
   b. To have the greatest effect on reducing cancer from tobacco use, what other products should government tax?
   c. What is the long-run elasticity of demand for cigarette smoking? What does this mean for the likely impact of taxes on long-run cigarette use?
2. The effect of the minimum wage on employers and employees depends on the elasticity of demand and supply for labor. Go to the Employment Policies Institute at www.epionline.org/study_MacphersonFlo_6-2002.pdf to read an article by David A. McPherson, "The Employment Impact of a Comprehensive Minimum Wage Law," and answer the following questions:
   a. What was the percentage increase in the minimum wage in Oregon from 1998 to 1999?
   b. What is the elasticity of demand for labor used in the study? Is demand elastic or inelastic?
   c. What is the effect of the increase in the minimum wage on labor costs for Oregon firms? Is this consistent with the elasticity of demand for labor? How would the effect on labor costs change if elasticity of demand for labor were greater than 1?
   d. In the long run what will happen to the change in labor costs compared to the change in labor costs in the short run? What accounts for the difference?

Answers to Margin Questions

1. Price elasticity of supply = Percentage change in quantity supplied divided by percentage change in price = 8/4 = 2. *(133)*
2. If price elasticity of demand is greater than 1, by definition demand is elastic. *(133)*
3. The percentage change in quantity is 100 (8/8 × 100) and the percentage change in price is 100 (2/2 × 100). Elasticity, therefore, is approximately 1 (100/100). *(137)*
4. I tell her that she is partially right (for the bottom part of the curve), but that elasticity on a straight-line demand curve changes from perfectly elastic at the vertical axis intersection to perfectly inelastic at the horizontal axis intersection. *(137)*
5. Four factors affecting the number of substitutes in demand are (1) time period considered, (2) the degree to which the good is a luxury, (3) the market definition, and (4) importance of the good in one's budget. *(140)*
6. Supply is generally more elastic in the long run because there are more alternative goods and services for producers to produce. *(141)*
7. If demand is inelastic, total revenue increases with an increase in price. *(144)*
8. If consumption increases with an increase in income, the good is a normal good. *(147)*
9. With an elastic demand, lowering price will increase total revenue because it will increase sales. But producing more will increase costs, so information about total revenue is not enough to answer the question. *(150)*
10. Price increases 3⅓ percent. Percentage change in price is the percentage change in demand (10) divided by the sum of the elasticities of supply and demand (1 + 2). *(151)*

TAXATION AND GOVERNMENT INTERVENTION

7

Collecting more taxes than is absolutely necessary is legalized robbery.

—*Calvin Coolidge*

After reading this chapter, you should be able to:

- Show how equilibrium maximizes producer and consumer surplus.
- Demonstrate the cost of taxation to consumers and producers.
- Distinguish between the benefit principle and the ability-to-pay principle.
- Explain why the person who physically pays the tax is not necessarily the person who bears the burden of the tax.
- Demonstrate how an effective price ceiling is the equivalent of a tax on producers and a subsidy to consumers.
- Define rent seeking and show how it is related to elasticity.

Chapter 6 introduced you to the term *elasticity*. In this chapter we will have a chance to apply what you learned. As we do that you'll see that when combined with the concept of elasticity, the supply and demand tools become even more useful. We'll see why by considering two policy issues: taxation and government intervention into markets.

PRODUCER AND CONSUMER SURPLUS

We begin our discussion of the effects of taxation and government intervention by showing how economists measure the benefits of the market to consumers and producers. That benefit can be seen by considering what the supply and demand curves are telling us. Each of these curves tells us how much individuals will be willing to pay (in the case of demand) or accept (in the case of supply) for a good. Thus, in Figure 7-1(a) a consumer would be willing to pay $8 each for 2 units of the good. The supplier is willing to sell 2 units for $2 apiece.

If the consumer pays less than what he's willing to pay, he walks away better off. Thus, the distance between the demand curve and the price he pays is a net gain for the consumer. Economists call this net benefit **consumer surplus**—*the value the consumer gets from buying a product less its price*. It is represented by the area underneath the demand curve and above the price that an individual pays. Thus, with the price at equilibrium ($5), consumer surplus is represented by the blue area.

Similarly, if a producer receives more than the price she would be willing to sell it for, she too receives a net benefit. Economists call this gain **producer surplus**—*the price the producer sells a product for less the cost of producing it*. It is represented by the area above the supply curve but below the price the producer receives. Thus, with the price at equilibrium ($5), producer surplus is represented by the red area.

What's good about market equilibrium is that it makes the combination of consumer and producer surpluses as large as it can be. To see this, say that for some reason the equilibrium price is held at $6. Consumers will demand only 4 units of

Figure 7-1 (a and b) Consumer and Producer Surplus
Market equilibrium price and quantity maximizes the combination of consumer surplus (shown in blue) and producer surplus (shown in red) as demonstrated in (a). When price deviates from its equilibrium, as in (b), combined consumer and producer surplus falls. The gray shaded region shows the loss of total surplus when price is $1 higher than equilibrium price.

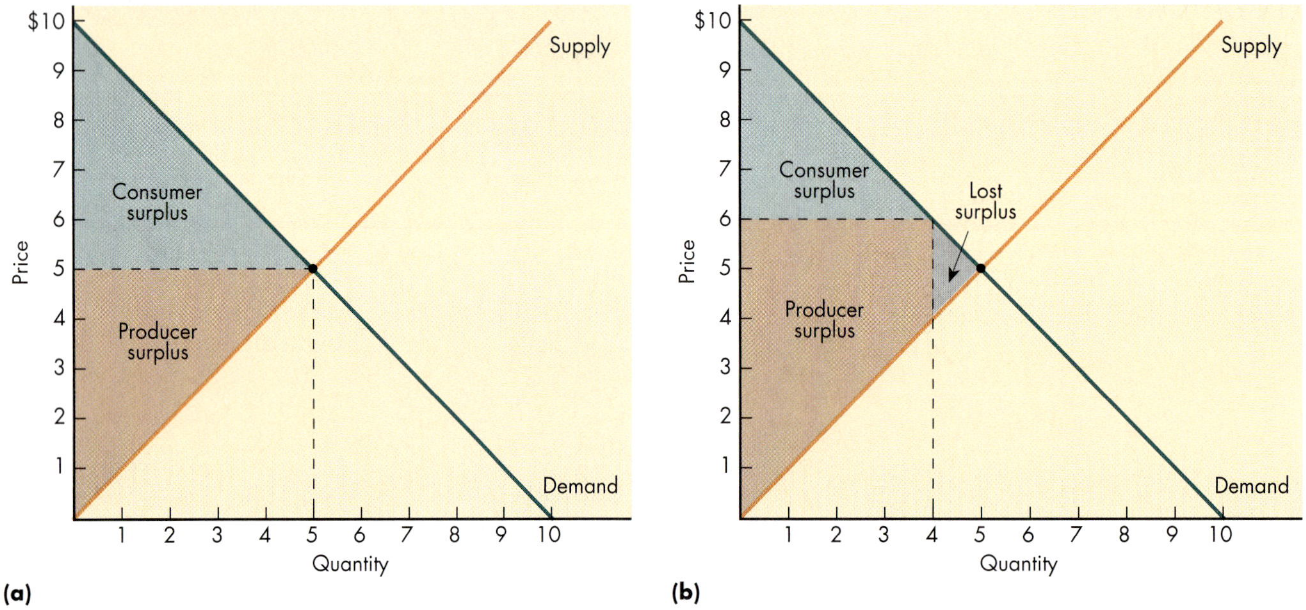

Q-1 If price moves from disequilibrium to equilibrium, what happens to the combination of producer and consumer surplus in the market?

the good, and some suppliers are not able to sell all the goods they would like. The combined producer and consumer surplus will decrease, as shown in Figure 7-1(b). The gray triangle represents lost consumer and producer surplus. In general, a deviation of price from equilibrium lowers the combination of producer and consumer surplus. This is one of the reasons economists support markets and why we teach the supply/demand model. It gives us a visual sense of what is good about markets: By allowing trade, markets maximize the combination of consumer and producer surplus.

To fix the ideas of consumer and producer surplus in your mind, let's consider a couple of real-world examples. Think about the water you drink. What does it cost? Almost nothing. Given that water is readily available, it has a low price. But since you'd die from thirst if you had no water, you are getting an enormous amount of consumer surplus from that water. Next, consider a ballet dancer who loves the ballet so much he'd dance for free. But he finds that people are willing to pay to see him and that he can receive $4,000 a performance. He is receiving producer surplus.

Taxation and Government

Taxes are a pain, but some taxes are necessary.

Now that we've seen how market equilibrium maximizes consumer and producer surplus, we're in a position to explore the costs and benefits of government intervention and taxation. An old saying goes, "The only things in life that are certain are death and taxes." And if you ask individuals what they dislike most about government, many would say taxes. Unfortunately, the government needs taxes to function, and the market likewise needs government. When governments do not have a well-functioning tax system, as is the case in some developing and transitional economies such as Russia's, the government is unable to provide the institutional structure markets need to work

The Ambiguity of Total Surplus

Beyond the Tools

To talk about consumer and producer surplus we must figure out a way of taking into account people's valuation of surplus. The market does that—it allows each person to vote with their income in the buying of goods. This means that whoever has the income plays a role in determining how we measure total surplus. This presents a circular reasoning problem in moving from total surplus to social welfare, and in talking about efficiency as if it involves maximizing total surplus. If the distribution of income is one of society's goals, then efficiency cannot unambiguously be defined without also specifying distributional goals.

Let's consider an extreme example to show the problems this can present. Say we start with two individuals, Jules and Jim, and two goods, apples and oranges. Jules likes only oranges and Jim likes only apples. If Jim has all the income, only apples count for determining total output because Jim likes only apples. Since no oranges are traded, oranges are given no weight because Jules has no income. Now, say that Jules has all the income. In that case only oranges contribute to total output. More generally, when two individuals have different tastes, the way in which income is distributed can change the contribution of goods to the valuation of total output.

Economists get around part of the problem theoretically either by assuming individuals have the same tastes or by assuming that income can be costlessly redistributed. This separates the issue of equity from the issue of efficiency. In practice, economists recognize that these conditions do not hold. They know that in the real world it is extraordinarily difficult to redistribute income. You can't go up to Bill Gates and tell him, "Hey, you need to give $10 billion to some poor people." For this reason economists are careful to apply the producer and consumer surplus analysis only to those cases where the conditions are "reasonable" approximations of reality—where distributional and taste issues do not play a big role in a policy recommendation. Of course, economists may disagree on what are "reasonable" approximations of reality. That is why economic policy is an art, not a science.

effectively. The connection between taxes and the roles of government led American jurist Oliver Wendell Holmes, Jr., to state that taxes are the price we pay for civilization.

Tax rates depend on what goods and services government provides. Having more government-provided goods and services means having higher taxes. The taxes can be low if government plays a minor role in the market—simply providing an institutional framework—or they can be high if government plays a major role such as providing free education and free health care to all citizens. Figure 7-2 gives you a sense of tax rates

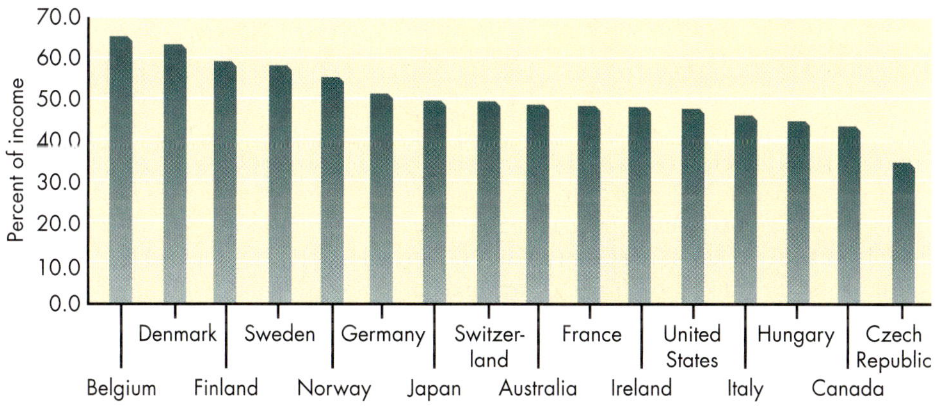

Figure 7-2 Highest Tax Rates on Wage Income (2001)

As you can see from this figure that shows the highest tax rates on wage income for various countries, the United States is one of the lower tax-rate countries.

Source: OECD.

Figure 7-3 The Costs of Taxation
A per unit tax *t* paid by the supplier shifts the supply curve up from S_0 to S_1. Equilibrium price rises from P_0 to P_1, and equilibrium quantity falls from Q_0 to Q_1. Consumer surplus is represented by areas A, B, and C before the tax and area A after the tax. Producer surplus is represented by areas *D*, *E*, and *F* before the tax and area *F* after the tax. Government collects tax shown by areas *B* and *D*. The tax imposes a deadweight loss, represented by the welfare loss triangle of areas C and *E*.

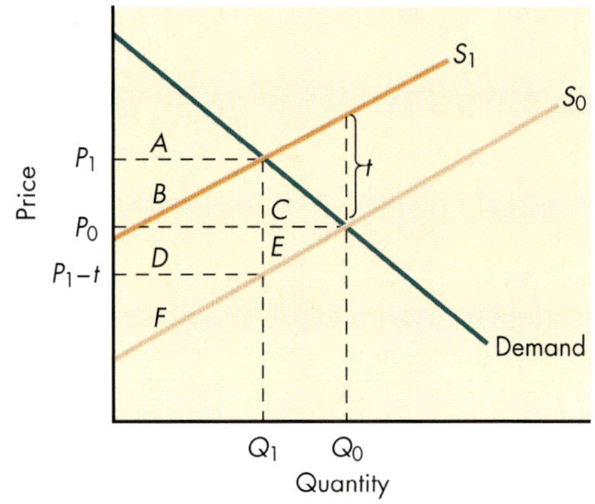

in various countries. As you can see, the United States is one of the lower tax-rate countries.

How Much Should Government Tax?

How should a country decide how much to tax? An economist would answer that question by asking another question: What are the costs and the benefits of taxation?

A tax paid by the supplier shifts the supply curve up by the amount of the tax.

The Costs of Taxation[1] The costs of taxation to society include the direct cost of the revenue paid to government, the loss of consumer and producer surplus caused by the tax, and the cost of administering the tax codes. Figure 7-3 provides the basic framework for understanding the costs of taxation. For a given good, a per unit tax *t* paid by the supplier increases the price at which suppliers are willing to sell that good. The increase in price is shown by a shift upward of the supply curve from S_0 to S_1. The equilibrium price of the good rises and the quantity sold declines.

Before the tax, consumers pay P_0 and producers keep P_0. Consumer surplus is represented by areas $A + B + C$, and producer surplus is represented by areas $D + E + F$. With the tax *t*, equilibrium price rises to P_1 and equilibrium quantity falls to Q_1. Consumers now pay P_1, but producers keep only $P_1 - t$. Tax revenue paid equals the tax *t* times equilibrium quantity Q_1, or areas B and *D*.

Q-2 Demonstrate the welfare loss of a tax when the supply is highly elastic and the demand is highly inelastic.

The total cost to consumers and producers is more than tax revenue. Consumers pay area *B* in tax revenue and also lose area C in consumer surplus. Producers pay area *D* in tax revenue and lose area *E* in producer surplus. The triangular area $C + E$ represents a cost of taxation in excess of the revenue paid to government. It is lost consumer and producer surplus that is not gained by government. *The loss of consumer and producer surplus from a tax* is known as **deadweight loss.** Deadweight loss is shown graphically by the **welfare loss triangle**—*a geometric representation of the welfare cost in terms of misallocated resources caused by a deviation from a supply/demand equilibrium.* Keep in mind that with the tax, quantity sold declines. The loss of welfare therefore represents a loss for those consumers and producers who would have traded without the tax but do not trade with the tax.

[1]The analysis presented here is highly simplified. Numerous points can be added to the analysis, some of which will be discussed in later chapters. Despite its limitations, the visual sense of the costs and benefits that the producer and consumer surplus concepts convey is a fundamental building block of the economic way of thinking.

The costs of taxation don't end there. Resources must be devoted by government to administer the tax code and by individuals to comply with it. Firms and individuals either spend hours filling out income tax forms or pay others to do so. Firms hire accountants and lawyers to take full advantage of any tax-code allowances. Administration costs can be as much as 5 percent of the total tax revenue paid to government. Like the tax itself, these costs increase the price at which producers are willing to sell their goods, reducing quantity sold and further increasing welfare loss.

The cost of taxation includes the direct cost of revenue paid, lost surplus, and administrative cost.

The Benefits of Taxation The benefits of taxes are the gains to society that result from the goods and services government provides when fulfilling the six roles in a market economy discussed in Chapter 2:

Web Note 7.1
What Taxes Buy

1. Provide a stable set of institutions and rules.
2. Promote effective and workable competition.
3. Correct for externalities.
4. Ensure economic stability and growth.
5. Provide public goods.
6. Adjust for undesired market results.

Some government-provided goods are part of the basic institutional structure of a market economy and must be supplied if the market is to function effectively. The basic legal system is an example. Other goods are provided by government because they have the qualities of a public good; national defense is an example.

Still other goods are provided by government for reasons of equity or because they create positive externalities. Private markets will provide these goods but perhaps not distribute them equitably or in sufficient quantities. Education up through high school is an example; it is publicly supplied even though it could be privately supplied. A number of governments supply health care publicly. In the United States most health care is supplied privately, although portions of it are paid for by government through Medicare and Medicaid.

The policy debate about the benefits of taxation generally focuses on goods that could be supplied by the market or by government. The various elements of health care, such as prescription drug insurance, are examples that have recently been much in the news. Some people want the government to provide greater amounts of health care free to individuals. Others oppose such plans because they would require higher taxes.

Another policy debate that has been much in the news is the use of voucher systems to fund education. In a voucher system each student would be given a certain amount of money, in the form of a voucher, to be used to attend the school of his or her choice. Although a voucher system would likely decrease the amount of education government supplies, it would not reduce taxes, since taxes would still have to be collected to fund the vouchers. Private supply of education would have each family paying for their education without any vouchers.

Measuring the benefits of government-supplied goods is difficult, mainly because they are not provided in a market setting. Because of this difficulty, along with the problem of deciding whether certain goods should be provided by government at all, the task of choosing which goods and services to provide and how to finance them is always surrounded by debate.

Two Principles of Taxation

I'll discuss the problems government faces in choosing what goods to provide in Chapter 18. In this chapter I will focus on the taxes needed to pay for the goods that government does provide. In making decisions about taxes, government follows two general principles: the *benefit principle*, and the *ability-to-pay principle*.

The Benefit Principle The **benefit principle** of taxation follows the same principle as the market: *The individuals who receive the benefit of a good or service should pay the tax necessary to supply that good.* An example of a tax based on the benefit principle is the gasoline tax levied to finance road construction in the United States. Since those who buy gasoline are using the roads, there is a connection between use and payment; however, unlike a toll, the tax is not direct—people do not pay each time they use the road. Another example is airport use taxes, which provide funding for the building of airports.

With government-supplied goods individuals do not reveal their preference for the good.

The difference between paying for goods through taxes and paying for them in a market is that, with government-supplied goods, consumers aren't directly paying for the goods and consequently do not reveal their preference for the good. The connection between benefit and cost in the decision to buy a publicly provided good is looser than it is with a privately supplied good.

The Ability-to-Pay Principle The **ability-to-pay principle** of taxation does not make any connection between use and payment but simply states: *The individuals who are most able to bear the burden of the tax should pay the tax.* Generally this principle is interpreted as supporting a progressive tax—one whose rate increases with increases in income. With a progressive tax, the tax on the first $10,000 a person earns might be 14 percent and the tax on the next $10,000 might be 20 percent. (A person earning $20,000 would pay an average rate of 17 percent.) During World War II the United States had a highly progressive tax, with the top rate reaching 95 percent; it has declined since then, and the top federal income tax rate is now 38.6 percent. (State income taxes can add another 10 percent.)

Q-3 If the tax on the first $20,000 is zero and thereafter the tax is 20 percent, what average tax rate would a person earning $30,000 pay?

The reasoning behind the ability-to-pay principle is that similar tax rates represent a smaller sacrifice for those with higher incomes compared to those with lower incomes. The wealthy should pay more because they can. Since the ability-to-pay principle of taxation makes no attempt to relate the benefit to the tax, the income tax revenue is used to finance a wide variety of government activities such as welfare and defense.

Difficulty of Applying the Principles of Taxation The two principles of taxation discussed above are the ones that economists and policymakers use most often to assess tax structures. Unfortunately, they are not easy to apply and often conflict. For example, the benefits of the goods that government supplies are often difficult to assign, making the benefit principle ambiguous. Consider education; it benefits not only the recipient but also the general public. How much does each benefit? (If you asked many high school students whether they would be willing to pay the $8,000 a year it costs to educate them in public school, I suspect many would say no.) Or consider funding health insurance for poor individuals. Under the benefit principle the poor would pay the majority of the costs. Under the ability-to-pay principle the rich would pay.

The two principles of taxation, the benefit principle and the ability-to-pay principle, are often in conflict with each other.

When taxes are based on the ability-to-pay principle, many high-income individuals ask why they should pay disproportionately more for goods such as income-support programs that are benefiting others, not them. The conflict between these two principles, combined with people's general desire to have "the other person" pay the taxes while they receive the benefits, often leads to significant debates about what to tax. Thus, we see debates about whether education should be financed by a *property tax*—a tax on houses and land—or by a *sales tax*—a tax on goods and services sold to consumers. Should income be taxed, or should only specific goods, like gasoline, be taxed? Should we use a corporate income tax or the general income tax?

What Goods Should Be Taxed?

Applying the Tools

What goods should be taxed depends on the goal of government. If the goal is to fund a program with as little loss as possible in consumer and producer surplus, then the government should tax a good whose supply or demand is inelastic. If the goal is to change behavior, taxes will be most effective if demand or supply is elastic. As a quick review, use the following table:

Goal of Government	Most Effective When
Raise revenue, limit deadweight loss	Demand or supply is inelastic
Change behavior	Demand or supply is elastic

Distributional issues must also be considered when determining what goods are to be taxed. In general, the group with the relatively more inelastic supply or demand will bear a greater portion of the tax. The following table reviews these conclusions:

Elasticity	Who Bears the Burden?
Demand inelastic and supply elastic	Consumers
Supply inelastic and demand elastic	Producers
Both supply and demand elastic	Shared; but the group whose supply or demand is more inelastic

The elasticity concept helps provide insight into the above debates. One of the facts you learned about elasticity is that the more broadly the good is defined, the more inelastic is the demand. Thus, the demand for all goods is much more inelastic than the demand for a particular good, since individuals cannot switch their consumption out of all goods but can switch from one specific good to another. This means that if government, given its targeted revenue, wants to have as little effect on individual actions as possible—or, in the language of consumer and producer surplus, if government wants to minimize the welfare loss—then it should tax goods with inelastic supplies or demands. Broad-based taxes such as income and sales taxes—which represent over 50 percent of state, local, and federal tax revenue—do just that. Most countries use a broad-based income tax, value-added tax, or general sales tax as their primary source of tax revenue.

If the government wants to minimize the welfare loss it should tax goods with inelastic supplies and demands.

Who Bears the Burden of a Tax?

Taxes are like hot potatoes: Everyone wants to pass them on to someone else. Nobody wants to pay taxes, and there are usually large political fights about whom government should tax. For example, should the Social Security tax (mandated by the Federal Insurance Contributions Act, or FICA) be placed on workers or on the company that hires them? Or does it matter? The supply/demand framework gives an unexpected answer to this question.

Burden Depends on Relative Elasticity Let's consider the issue of who bears the burden of a tax by looking at the example involving excise taxes introduced in Chapter 5. There I defined an **excise tax** as *a tax levied on a specific good* and gave the example of a luxury tax on expensive boats that the United States imposed in 1990. An excise tax can be levied (who will physically pay the tax) on the consumer or on the seller.

The person who *physically pays* the tax, however, is not necessarily the person who *bears the burden* of the tax. Who bears the burden of the tax (also known as tax

Figure 7-4 (a, b, and c) Who Bears the Burden of a Tax?
In the general case the burden of a tax is determined by the relative elasticities of supply and demand. The blue shaded area shows the burden on the consumer; the red shaded area shows the burden on the supplier. This split occurs regardless of who actually pays the tax, as can be seen by noticing that the burden of the tax is equal in (**a**), where the supplier pays the tax, and in (**c**), where the consumer pays the tax. In (**b**) you can see how consumers with an inelastic demand bear a greater burden of the tax. The blue shaded area represents the burden paid by consumers; the red area shows the burden on suppliers.

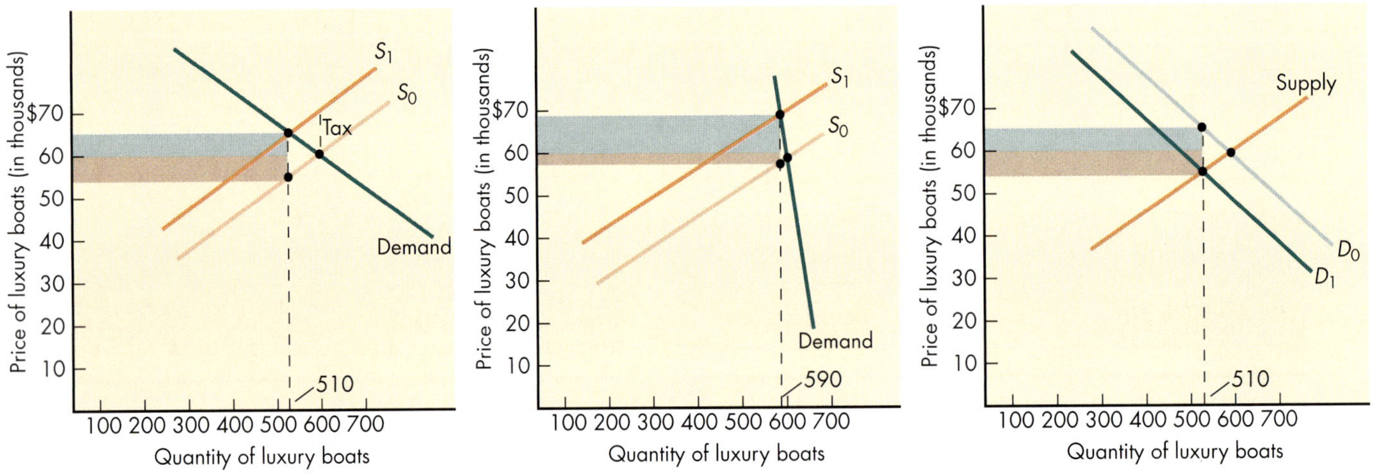

(a) **Supplier pays tax** (b) **Demand is inelastic** (c) **Consumer pays tax**

incidence) depends on who is best able to change his or her behavior in response to the tax, or who has the greater elasticity. Elasticity and supply/demand analysis lets us answer the question "Who will end up bearing the burden of the tax?" (More technically: "What is the incidence of the tax?")

Figure 7-4(a) shows the case I considered in Chapter 5. A $10,000 per unit tax levied on the supplier shifts the supply curve up from S_0 to S_1. That reduces quantity supplied and quantity demanded by 90—from 600 to 510. The equilibrium price rises from $60,000 to $65,000. Suppliers are able to shift $5,000 of the total $10,000 per unit tax onto consumers, leaving the suppliers the burden of the remaining $5,000.

Had we known elasticities at the market equilibrium, we could have stated, without additional calculations, that the tax burden would be shared equally. Specifically, suppliers sold and consumers purchased 90 fewer boats, an approximate 15 percent reduction. The suppliers' price fell by about 8 percent while the consumers' price rose by about 8 percent, meaning the elasticity of both supply and demand was approximately 1.9.[2] With equal elasticities, the tax burden will be divided equally.

In reality the tax burden is rarely shared equally because elasticities are rarely equal. The relative burden of the tax follows this general rule: *The more inelastic one's relative supply and demand, the larger the burden of the tax one will bear.* If demand were more inelastic, sellers would have been able to sell the boats at a higher price and could have passed more of the tax along to the buyers.

Figure 7-4(b) shows what the divisions would have been had the demand curve been highly inelastic. In this case the price would rise more, the supplier would pay a lower proportion of the tax (the red area), and the consumer would pay a much larger

[2]There will be slight variations in the measured elasticities depending on how they are calculated. The precise equality holds only for point elasticities. (See Chapter 6.)

proportion (the blue area). The general rule about elasticities and the tax burden is this: If demand is more inelastic than supply, consumers will pay a higher percentage of the tax; if supply is more inelastic than demand, suppliers will pay a higher share. This rule makes sense—*elasticity is a measure of how easy it is for the supplier and consumer to change behavior and substitute another good.*

Tax burden is allocated by relative elasticities.

More specifically, we can calculate the percentage of the tax actually borne by the demander by dividing the price elasticity of supply by the sum of the price elasticities of supply and demand and multiplying by 100. Similarly, we can calculate the percentage of the tax borne by the supplier by dividing the price elasticity of demand by the sum of the price elasticities of supply and demand and multiplying by 100. For example, say the price elasticity of supply is 1 and the price elasticity of demand is 3. In that case the consumer will pay one-fourth [1/(1 + 3)] of the tax and the supplier will pay three-fourths [3/(1 + 3)] of the tax.

Q.4 How much of a $100 tax would a consumer pay if elasticity of demand is .2 and price elasticity of supply is 1.8?

The rule about the elasticities and the tax burden can lead to some unexpected consequences of taxation. For example, the U.S. luxury tax on boats was initially implemented as a way to tax the wealthy. It turned out, however, that the wealthy found substitutes for American-made boats; their demand was relatively elastic. They either purchased other luxury items or purchased their boats from foreign firms. U.S. boat manufacturers, however, couldn't easily switch to producing other products. Their supply was inelastic. As a result, they tried to pass on the cost increase to consumers, but they saw their sales plummet. They had to lower their price by almost as much as the tax, which meant that they were bearing most of the burden of the tax. As noted in Chapter 5, pressured by boat manufacturers, the government repealed the luxury tax on boats three years after it was instituted.

Who Pays a Tax Is Not Necessarily Who Bears the Burden The allocation of tax burden by relative elasticity means that it doesn't matter who actually pays the tax and that, as I said earlier, the person who bears the burden can differ from the person who pays. To assure yourself that it doesn't matter who pays the tax, ask yourself how your answer would have differed if the tax of $10,000 had been paid by the consumer. Figure 7-4(c) shows this case. Because the tax is paid by the consumer, the demand curve shifts down by the amount of the tax. As you can see, the results of the tax are identical. The percentage of the tax paid by the supplier and the consumer, after adjusting for the changes in supply and demand price, is independent of who actually makes the physical payment of the tax.

The burden is independent of who physically pays the tax.

Tax Incidence and Current Policy Debates

Now let's consider two policy questions in relation to what we have learned about tax incidence.

Social Security Taxes The first policy question concerns the Social Security (or payroll) tax, which accounts for 36 percent of federal government revenue. In 2003, the Social Security tax rate was 12.4 percent on wages up to an annual maximum wage of $87,000, and another 2.9 percent on all wages, no matter how high, designed to finance Medicare. As a political compromise, half of Social Security taxes are placed on the employee and half on the employer. But the fact that the law places the tax equally on both does not mean that the burden of the tax is shared equally between employees and employers. On average, labor supply tends to be less elastic than labor demand. This means that the Social Security tax burden is primarily on the employees, even though employees see only their own statutory portion of the Social Security tax on their pay stub.

Q.5 If Social Security taxes were paid only by employees, what would likely happen to workers' pretax pay?

Web Note 7.2
Pensions

Now, let's say that you are advising a person running for Congress who has come up with the idea to place the entire tax on the employer and eliminate the tax on the employee. What will the effect of that be? Our tax incidence analysis tells us that, ultimately, it will have no effect. Wages paid to employees will fall to compensate employers for the cost of the tax. This example shows that who is assessed the tax can be quite different than who actually bears the burden, or incidence, of the tax. The burden will be borne by those with the most inelastic supply or demand, because they have no way of getting out of paying the tax by substitution.

So what do you tell the candidate? Is the idea a good one or not? Although economically it will not make a difference who pays the tax, politically it may be a popular proposal because individuals generally look at statutory assessment, not incidence. The candidate may gain significant support from workers, since they would no longer see a Social Security tax on their pay stub. The moral, then, is this: Politics often focuses on surface appearance; economics tries to get under the surface, and what is good economics is not always good politics.

What makes sense politically is not always what makes sense economically.

Sales Taxes Our second policy question concerns sales taxes paid by retailers on the basis of their sales revenue. In my state the general sales tax is 5 cents on the dollar. Since sales taxes are broadly defined, consumers have little ability to substitute. Demand is inelastic and consumers bear the greater burden of the tax. Although stores could simply incorporate the tax into the price of their goods, most stores add the tax onto the bill after the initial sale is calculated, to make you aware of the tax. Again, it doesn't matter whether the tax is assessed on the store or on you.

Recently, however, the Internet has given consumers a substitute to shopping at actual retail stores. Retail sales over the Internet are over $36 billion annually and are continuing to grow. States have found it very difficult to tax Internet sales because the supplier has no retail address. The point of sale is in cyberspace. Technically in these cases, the buyer is required to pay the tax to the state where he or she lives, but in practice that seldom happens. How to tax Internet sales will be heavily debated over the next few years. The federal government has placed a moratorium on new Internet sales taxes until 2003. As Internet sales grow, states will lose more and more sales tax revenue and retail shops will bear a larger portion of the tax levied on their sales, which together will invite strong pressure to end the moratorium.

Government Intervention

Taxes are not the only way government affects our lives. For example, government establishes laws that dictate what we can do, what prices we can charge for goods, and what working conditions are and are not acceptable. This second part of the chapter continues the discussion of such issues, which began in Chapter 5. I show how the elasticity concept can help us talk about such interventions and how, using the producer and consumer surplus framework, such interventions can be seen as a combination of tax and subsidy that does not show up on government books.

Government Intervention as Implicit Taxation

To see how government intervention in the market can be seen as a combination tax and subsidy, let's first consider the two types of price controls mentioned in Chapter 5: price ceilings and price floors.

Price Ceilings and Floors As I discussed in Chapter 5, a **price ceiling** is a government-set price below the market equilibrium price. It is in essence an implicit tax

Figure 7-5 (a and b) Effect of Price Controls on Consumer and Producer Surplus
Price floors and price ceilings create deadweight loss just as taxes do. In (a) we see how a price ceiling, P_1, transfers surplus D from producers to consumers. Price ceilings are equivalent to a tax on producers and a subsidy to consumers. In (b) we see how a price floor, P_2, transfers surplus B from consumers to producers. With both a price floor and a price ceiling, areas C and E represent the welfare loss triangle.

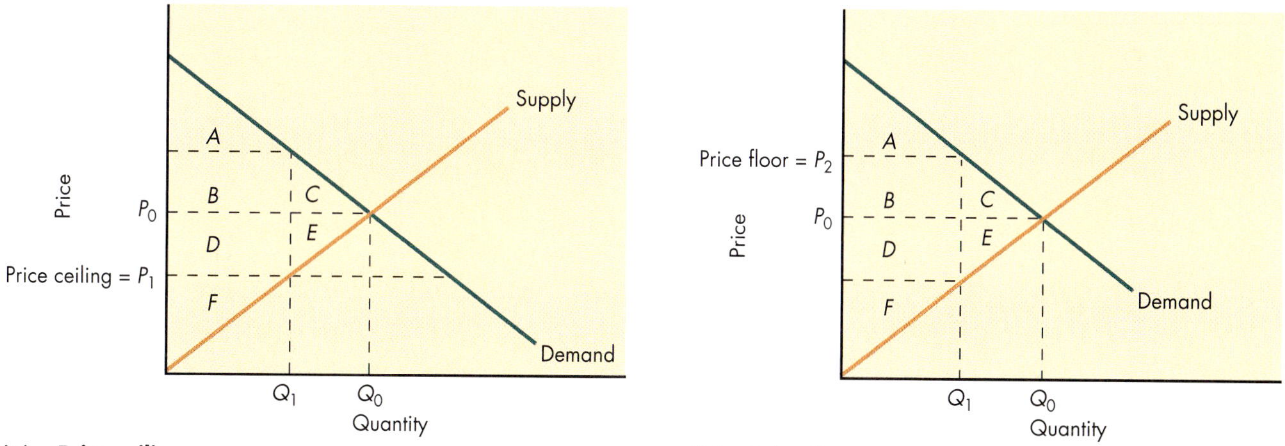

(a) Price ceiling **(b) Price floor**

on producers and an implicit subsidy to consumers. Consider the effect of a price ceiling on producer and consumer surplus, shown in Figure 7-5(a).

Q-6 Demonstrate the effect of an effective price ceiling on producer and consumer surplus when both supply and demand are highly inelastic.

If the price were at the market equilibrium price, the total surplus would be the combination of the areas A through F. But with an effective price ceiling P_1, the quantity supplied falls from Q_0 to Q_1. The combined producer and consumer surplus is reduced by triangles C and E. The loss of surplus represents those individuals who would like to make trades—the individuals represented by the demand and supply curves between Q_1 and Q_0—but cannot do so because of the price ceiling.

This loss of consumer and producer surplus is identical to the welfare loss from taxation.[3] That is not a coincidence. The price ceiling is a combination implicit tax on suppliers, shown by area D, and implicit subsidy to consumers of that same area. It is as if government places a tax on suppliers when they buy the good, and then gives that tax revenue to consumers when they consume the good.

A price ceiling is a combination implicit tax on suppliers and implicit subsidy to consumers.

Price floors have the opposite effect on the distribution of consumer and producer surplus. **Price floors**—*government-set prices above equilibrium price*—transfer consumer surplus to producers. They can be seen as a tax on consumers of area B and a subsidy to producers of that same area, as shown in Figure 7-5(b). Price floors also impose a deadweight loss, shown by the welfare loss triangle, areas C and E.

The Difference between Taxes and Price Controls While the effects of taxation and controls are similar, there is an important difference: *Price ceilings create shortages; taxes do not.* The reason is that taxes leave people free to choose how much they want to supply and consume as long as they pay the tax. Thus, taxes create a wedge between the price the consumers pay and the price the suppliers receive. That difference is just enough to equate quantity demanded with quantity supplied.

Price ceilings create shortages; taxes do not.

[3]As I will discuss below, for price controls the welfare triangle provides a minimum amount of loss in consumer and producer surplus; the actual loss may be greater.

Web Note 7.3
Sin Taxes

Since with price ceilings the price consumers pay is the same as the price suppliers receive, as long as the price ceiling is below equilibrium price the desired quantity demanded will not be equal to the desired quantity supplied. Some method of rationing—limiting the demand or increasing the supply in the case of price ceilings, and limiting the supply and increasing the demand in the case of price floors—must be found. In the examples of price ceilings so far, we have assumed that suppliers can choose to supply how much or how little they want. Thus, there are shortages. Such shortages create black markets—markets in which individuals buy or sell illegally. (Black markets may also be created by taxes if buyers and sellers attempt to evade the tax.)

A Price Ceiling with Forced Supply: The Draft There are other ways of dealing with shortages. For example, there could be "forced supply"—that is, suppliers could be required by law to supply all the goods demanded at the ceiling price. The military draft is an example. A draft is a law that requires some people to serve a set period in the armed forces at whatever pay the government chooses. It has often been used as a way of meeting the military's need for soldiers. The draft is a price ceiling combined with forced supply. (This case study may become highly relevant because, in recent years, the military has been falling short of the number of recruits it needs and some members of Congress have been suggesting that the United States reinstitute the draft. The legislative authority to do so already exists, and currently all men are legally required to register for the draft when they turn 18.)[4]

The draft is a price ceiling combined with forced supply.

The effects of a draft are shown in Figure 7-6. A draft must be imposed when the wage offered by the army is below equilibrium because the quantity of soldiers demanded exceeds the quantity supplied. In Figure 7-6 the offered wage W_0 is below the equilibrium wage W_e. The market answer to the shortage would be to increase the wage to W_e, which would both reduce the quantity of soldiers demanded by government and increase the quantity of men willing to become soldiers. How much the wage would need to be increased to bring about equilibrium depends on the elasticity of supply and demand. If both supply and demand are inelastic, then the pay will need to be increased enormously; if both are elastic, the pay will need to be increased only slightly.

The people who are proposing the draft suspect that both supply and demand are inelastic, in which case the market solution would be very expensive to the government, requiring large increases in taxes. They argue that a draft is much cheaper, and requires lower taxes.

Our supply/demand analysis reveals the fallacy in that reasoning. Government interventions, such as the draft, transfer surplus from one set of individuals to another. Any intervention is the equivalent of a tax on the one from whom the surplus is taken and a subsidy to the one to whom the surplus is given. So the draft imposes a tax, but it is a tax that doesn't show up on the government books. Rather, the tax is on all individuals drafted (young men), and the subsidy is given to those who demand defense services. So, yes, with a draft the government does not have to collect as much revenue as it would if it raised the wage to a market-clearing wage, but the draft places the equivalent of an explicit tax on young men. Instead of being able to do what they want, they must serve in the armed forces.

Q-7 Does a draft allow the government to have lower taxes?

Courtesy Selective Service System

By paying a lower-than-equilibrium wage, the government is transferring surplus from those drafted to itself. To get around the shortage, the draft requires men to serve whether they want to or not. The effective supply curve becomes the horizontal line W_0. The quantity supplied is forced to meet the quantity demanded at the price ceiling.

[4]Women are not, which raises some questions that will likely be much discussed if the draft is reinstituted.

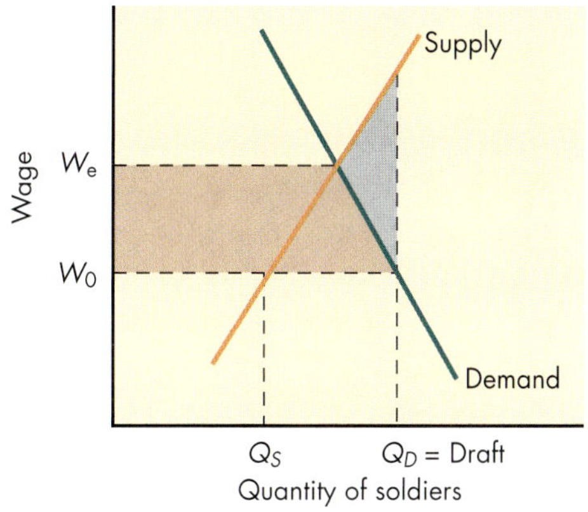

Figure 7-6 Effect of a Draft on Surplus
The military draft is one solution to the shortage that occurs when wages are below the equilibrium wage. The market solution to the shortage of soldiers is for the army to offer soldiers a higher wage. This, however, would require government to raise taxes on the general public. The draft solution would not require an increase in explicit taxes. Instead, it forces young men to supply the quantity demanded by the army. Those who are drafted will accept a lower wage than they could get in the market, which is a transfer of surplus to government. The amount of the transferred surplus is shown by the red shaded region. The gray shaded region shows the deadweight loss associated with the draft.

In this case of forced supply even more surplus is transferred than in the previous cases we considered. Specifically, in Figure 7-6 the red shaded area is transferred from suppliers to consumers of national defense. In this case the welfare loss triangle is the shaded triangle to the right of the market equilibrium. It is the opportunities that the suppliers lose but that the demanders do not receive.

The above analysis of welfare loss due to the price ceiling is the minimum loss that the ceiling will create. The analysis assumes that the individuals drafted will be those whose opportunity cost of being drafted is lowest. In fact, that is not the case. The actual amount of loss depends on how the draft selects individuals. If it selects individuals totally randomly (which in principle is how drafts are structured), it will draft some into the armed forces who would not consider serving even at the equilibrium wage. (For example, Elvis Presley was drafted; when he entered the army he gave up millions of dollars of income, so his opportunity cost was extremely high.) Thus, the welfare loss is larger for interferences in the market such as the draft than it is for an equivalent tax, although it is difficult to specify how much larger it is.

Generally, the welfare loss is larger for controls than for an equivalent tax.

Rent Seeking, Politics, and Elasticities

If price controls reduce total producer and consumer surplus, why do governments institute them? The answer is that *people care more about their own surplus than they do about total surplus*. As we have seen, price ceilings redistribute surplus from producers to consumers, so if the consumers have the political power there will be strong pressures to create price ceilings. Alternatively, if the suppliers have the political power, there will be strong pressures to create price floors.

The possibility of transferring surplus from one set of individuals to another causes people to spend time and resources on doing so. For example, if criminals know that \$1 million ransoms are commonly paid for executives, it will be worthwhile for them to figure out ways to kidnap executives—which happens in some developing and transitional economies. (That's why all countries state that they will never pay ransoms; however, not all countries follow their stated policies.)

The possibility of kidnapping, in turn, causes executives to hire bodyguards, which in turn causes kidnappers to think of ingenious ways to kidnap (which in turn . . .). The result is that, as one group attempts to appropriate surplus from another group, enormous amounts of resources are spent on activities that benefit no one.

The same reasoning holds for lobbying government. Individuals have an incentive to spend resources to lobby government to institute policies that increase their own surplus. Others have an incentive to spend money to counteract those lobbying efforts.

Figure 7-7 Inelastic Demand and the Incentive to Restrict Supply
When demand is inelastic, increases in productivity that shift the supply curve to the right result in lower revenue for suppliers. Although suppliers gain area *B*, they lose the much larger area A. Suppliers have an incentive to restrict supply when demand is inelastic because, by doing so, they will increase their revenues.

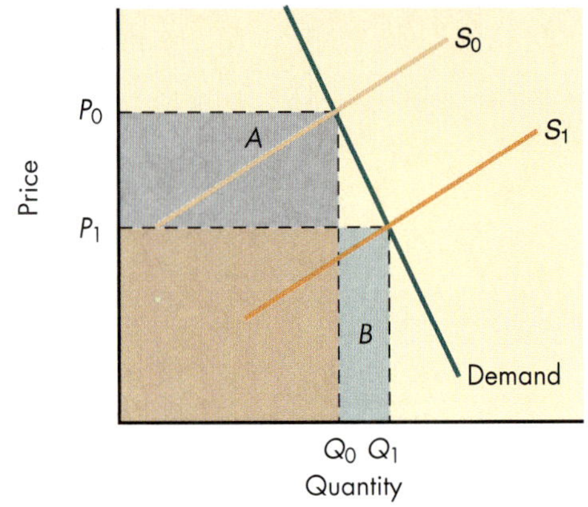

Q-8 Would a firm's research and development expenditures be classified as rent seeking?

Activities designed to transfer surplus from one group to another are called **rent-seeking activities.** Rent-seeking activities require resources, and the net result is unproductive. **Public choice economists**—*economists who integrate an economic analysis of politics with their analysis of the economy*—argue that rent seeking through government is significant, and that much of the transfer of surplus that occurs through government intervention creates an enormous waste of resources. They argue that the taxes and the benefits of government programs offset each other and do not help society significantly, but they do cost resources. These economists point out that much of the redistribution through government is from one group of the middle class to another group of the middle class.

Q-9 How can an increase in productivity harm suppliers?

Inelastic Demand and Incentives to Restrict Supply To understand the rent-seeking process a bit better, let's look more carefully at the incentives that consumers and producers have to lobby government to intervene in the market. We'll begin with suppliers. A classic example of the political pressures to limit supply is found in agricultural markets. Within the past century new machinery, new methods of farming, and hybrid seeds have increased the productivity of farmers tremendously. You might think that because farmers can now produce more at a lower cost, they'd be better off. But if you think that, you're ignoring the interaction of supply and demand. As advances in productivity increase supply they do increase the quantity sold, but they also result in lower prices. Farmers sell more but they get less for each unit they sell. Because food is a necessity and has few substitutes, the demand for many agricultural goods is inelastic. Since demand is inelastic the price declines by a greater proportion than the rise in quantity sold, meaning that total revenue declines and the farmers are actually worse off. The situation is shown in Figure 7-7.

Web Note 7.4
Professional Licensing

Because of the increase in supply, price declines from P_0 to P_1 and quantity sold increases from Q_0 to Q_1. The farmer's revenue rises by area *B* but also falls by larger area *A*. To counteract this trend, farmers have an incentive to get government to restrict supply or create a price floor, thereby raising their revenue. In fact, that's what they did in the 1930s. Farmers then were instrumental in getting the government to establish the Farm Board, a federal agency whose job was to manage productivity of agricultural goods. The benefits of limiting competition are greatest for suppliers when demand is inelastic because price will rise proportionately more than quantity will fall.

This simple example provides us with an important insight about how markets work and how the politics of government intervention work. Inelastic demand creates an enormous incentive for suppliers either to pressure government to limit the quantity

Elasticity and Whether a Price Increase Is Significant

Knowing the Tools

When talking about price increases in the text, I mean percentage price increases, which is what the elasticity concept relates to the percentage changes in quantity. A $20 price increase on a $20,000 car is insignificant, because it is such a small percentage of the total price (0.1 percent). So remember, when deciding whether a price increase is significant or not, think of the price increase in percentage, not absolute, terms.

The difference between percentage change and absolute change is a source of constant confusion. Consider the discussions of fluctuations in the Dow Jones Industrial Average. On March 16, 2000, the Dow Jones Industrial Average rose 499 points—its biggest point gain in a single day and 118 points more than the next-largest single-day gain. In percentage terms, however, the Dow had risen 4.93 percent—a less-than-historical gain. It was not even large enough to make the top 35 list of largest single-day percentage gains. The day that holds the record for the largest percentage gain the Dow is October 6, 1931, when it rose by 99.34 points. But, because the day's beginning the Dow was 668, the 99-point rise represented a whopping 14.87 percent single-day gain.

Another way to look at it is this: A movement of 100 when the Dow was 600 is a 16.7 percent change in the value of the stocks. A movement of 100 when the Dow is 10,000 is a 1 percent change. So remember to think percentages when deciding whether a change in price (or in anything) is large or small.

supplied or to get together and look for other ways to limit the quantity supplied. The more inelastic demand is, the more farmers have to gain by restricting supply. By limiting quantity supplied they can raise the price, increasing total revenue.

Sometimes sellers can get government to limit quantity supplied through licensing; other times the existing suppliers can limit supply by force. A well-placed threat ("If you enter this market, I will blow up your store") is often effective. In some transitional economies, such threats are common. What stops existing suppliers from making good on such threats? Government. But the government also creates opportunities for individuals to prevent others from entering the market. Therein lies a central problem of political economy. You need government to see that competition works—to ensure that existing suppliers don't prevent others from entering the market—but government can also be used to prevent competition and protect existing suppliers. Hence, the point that we will return to throughout this book: Government is part of both the problem and the solution.

The central problem of political economy is that you need government to ensure that competition works, but government can also be used to prevent competition.

Inelastic Supplies and Incentives to Restrict Prices Firms aren't the only ones who can lobby government to intervene. Consider consumers. When supply is inelastic, consumers can face significant price increases if their demand increases. Thus, when the supply of a good is inelastic and the demand for that good rises, prices will rise significantly and consumers will scream for price controls.

This is what happened in the New York City rent-control example (price ceilings imposed on apartments) in Chapter 5. During World War II an influx of short-term workers into New York City increased demand for apartments. Because supply was inelastic, rents rose tremendously. To keep apartments affordable, the city capped rents.

Such controls are not costless. One of the results of rent control was to create an ongoing shortage of apartments. As we noted earlier, effective price ceilings will cause a shortage unless suppliers are forced to supply a market-clearing quantity. With the knowledge of elasticities you also know whether a large or small shortage will develop with a price ceiling and whether a large or small surplus will develop with a price floor.

Figure 7-8 (a, b, and c) Price Floors and Elasticity of Demand and Supply
A price floor above equilibrium market price will always create a surplus. The extent of the surplus created depends on the elasticity of the curves. With elastic curves, a large surplus is created by price controls; with inelastic curves, a small surplus is created. Thus, in (a) the intersection of supply and demand occurs where the curves are most elastic and the result is the largest surplus. In (b) demand and supply intersect where the demand curve is less elastic and the surplus declines. In (c) demand and supply intersect where supply and demand are most inelastic and the result is the smallest surplus.

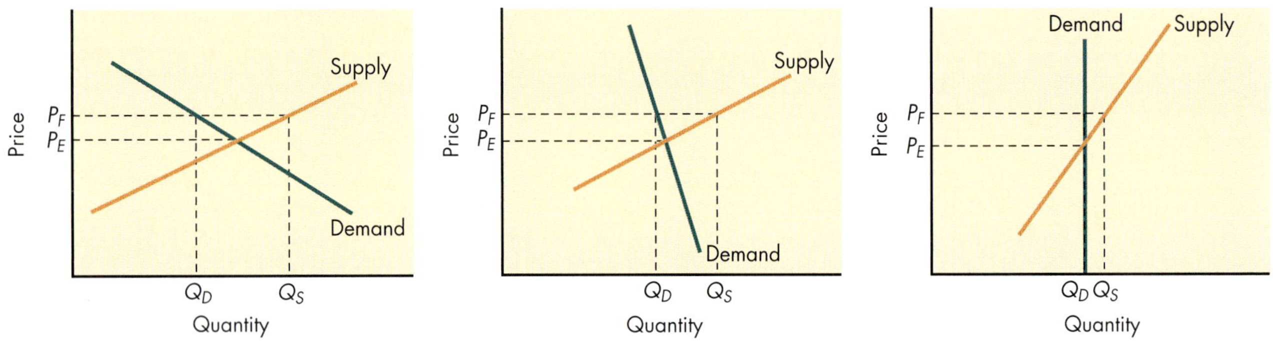

(a) Price floor with elastic supply and demand

(b) Price floor with elastic supply and inelastic demand

(c) Price floor with inelastic supply and demand

To make sure you understand how elasticity can tell you the relative size of a surplus or shortage when there are price controls, look at Figure 7-8, which shows three cases of price floors, each with different elasticities of supply and demand.

The more elastic supply and demand, the larger the surplus or shortage created by price controls.

As you can see, all three cases create excess supply—surpluses—but the proportional amount of excess supply depends on the elasticity. In Figure 7-8(a), supply and demand intersect at P_E, where they are relatively elastic. There, the price floor, P_F, leads to a relatively large surplus. Figure 7-8(b) represents an intermediate case: The intersection is where supply is elastic and demand is highly inelastic, and a relatively smaller surplus is created by the price floor. In Figure 7-8(c), where the demand and supply curves intersect at relatively inelastic portions, the surplus created by the price floor is relatively small. A good exercise is to go through the same analysis for price ceilings.

The Long-Run/Short-Run Problem of Price Controls Now let's combine our analysis of price controls with another insight from the elasticity chapter—that in the long run, supply and demand tend to be much more elastic than in the short run. This means that price controls will cause only relatively small shortages or surpluses in the short run, but large ones in the long run. Let's consider how this would play out in our rent-control example—see Figure 7-9. In the short run, both supply and demand are inelastic; thus, if the government allows landlords to charge the price they want and demand shifts from D_0 to D_1, they will raise their price significantly, from P_0 to P_1.

In the long run, however, additional apartments will be built and other existing buildings will be converted into apartments. Supply becomes more elastic, rotating from S_0 to S_1. Faced with additional competition, landlords will lower their price to P_2. In the long run price will fall and the number of apartments rented will increase.

Q-10 Why do price controls tend to create ongoing shortages or surpluses in the long run?

Herein lies another political policy problem. In large part, it is the rise in price that brings in new competitors and increases in output. But if the government imposes price controls, the long-run incentives for competitors to enter the market will be eliminated. The political problems arise because politics generally responds to short-run pressures. In the short run demand and supply are generally inelastic, making it look like the price

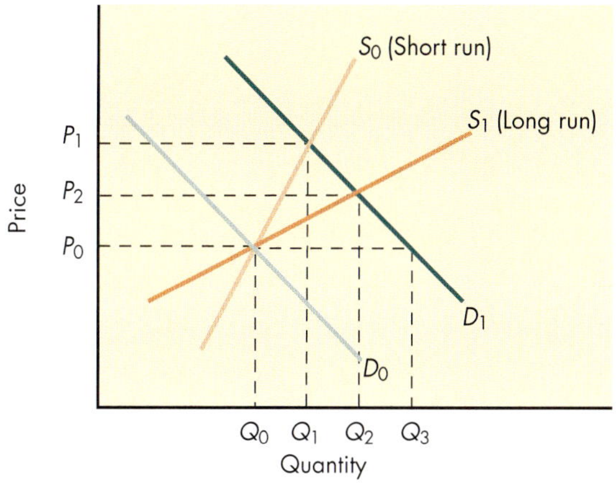

Figure 7-9 Long-Run and Short-Run Effects of Price Controls This exhibit shows how an increase in demand from D_0 to D_1 raises equilibrium price from P_0 to P_1. As time progresses, the supply curve becomes flatter, which is shown as a rotation of the supply curve from S_0 to S_1. Equilibrium price falls to P_2. If a price ceiling of P_0 had been imposed, the incentive for suppliers to build more apartments would be eliminated. Instead, landlords would convert their apartments to different uses and potential landlords would choose to build fewer apartments, and the shortage resulting from the price control ($Q_3 - Q_0$) would remain.

ceiling will not create significant problems. But in the long run, supply is usually elastic. Landlords will convert their rent-controlled apartments to different uses, fewer resources will be spent keeping up existing apartments, and fewer new apartments will be built. In the long run, the shortage becomes even more severe. As we noted in Chapter 5, the rent-control laws in New York City were initially written to be effective whenever the vacancy rate was below 5 percent, which was the vacancy rate at the time. But the rent controls stopped new apartments from being built and old ones from being maintained. Today, the vacancy rate is less than 4 percent and many rent-controlled apartments have deteriorated. The government's imposition of a price ceiling prevents the market from achieving a more desirable long-run equilibrium, at which output has expanded and price has fallen from its initially high level.

Conclusion

Government is a part of our life and, therefore, so too are taxes. Economic theory doesn't say government should or shouldn't play any particular role in the economy or what the taxes should be. Those decisions depend on normative judgments and the relevant costs and benefits. What economic theory does is to help point out the costs and benefits. For example, in the case of taxes economists can show that the cost of taxation in terms of lost surplus is independent of who physically pays the tax.

In thinking about taxes and government involvement the public often perceives economic theory and economists as suggesting the best policy is one of laissez-faire, or government noninvolvement in the economy. Many economists do suggest a laissez-faire policy, but that suggestion is based on empirical observations of government's role in the past, not on economic theory.

Economists as a group favor less government than does the general public.

Still, economists as a group generally favor less government involvement than does the general public. I suspect this is because economists are taught to look below the surface at the long-run effect of government actions. They've discovered that the effects often aren't the intended effects, and that programs frequently have long-run consequences that make the problems worse, not better. Economists, both liberal and conservative, speak in the voice of reason: "Look at all the costs; look at all the benefits. Then decide whether government should or should not intervene." The supply/demand framework and the elasticity concept are extremely useful tools in making those assessments.

Summary

- Equilibrium maximizes the combination of consumer surplus and producer surplus. Consumer surplus is the net benefit a consumer gets from purchasing a good, while producer surplus is the net benefit a producer gets from selling a good.
- Government taxes firms and individuals in order to carry out its six roles in a market economy. A government will maximize benefits to society only if it chooses to tax when the marginal benefit of the goods and services provided with the revenue of the tax exceeds the cost of the tax.
- Taxes create a loss of consumer and producer surplus known as deadweight loss, which graphically is represented by the welfare loss triangle.
- The cost of taxation to consumers and producers includes the actual tax paid, the deadweight loss, and the costs of administering the tax.
- Government follows both the benefit principle (individuals who receive the benefit should pay the tax) and the ability-to-pay principle (individuals who are most able to pay should pay the tax) when deciding on whom to levy taxes.
- Who bears the burden of the tax depends on the relative elasticities of demand and supply. The more inelastic one's relative supply and demand, the larger the burden of the tax one will bear.
- Although Social Security taxes are levied equally on employers and employees, the supply of labor tends to be more inelastic than the demand for labor, so workers bear the greater burden of these taxes.
- Price ceilings and price floors, like taxes, result in loss of consumer and producer surplus.
- Price ceilings transfer producer surplus to consumers and therefore are equivalent to a tax on producers and a subsidy to consumers. Price floors have the opposite effect; they are a tax on consumers and a subsidy to producers.
- Rent-seeking activities are designed to transfer surplus from one group to another. Producers facing inelastic demand for their product will benefit more from rent-seeking activities than producers facing elastic demand. Consumers facing inelastic supply for a product benefit more from rent-seeking activities such as lobbying for price ceilings than consumers facing an elastic supply.
- The more elastic supply and/or demand is, the greater the surplus is with an effective price floor and the greater the shortage is with an effective price ceiling.
- Price controls worsen as the length of time considered rises because elasticity rises as time progresses.

Key Terms

ability-to-pay principle *(162)*
benefit principle *(162)*
consumer surplus *(157)*
deadweight loss *(160)*
excise tax *(163)*
price ceiling *(166)*
price floor *(167)*
producer surplus *(157)*
public choice economist *(170)*
rent-seeking activity *(170)*
welfare loss triangle *(160)*

Questions for Thought and Review

1. Explain why the combination of consumer and producer surplus is not maximized if there is either excess demand or supply.
2. Use economic reasoning to explain why nearly every purchase you make provides you with consumer surplus.
3. Name one local tax that is based on the ability-to-pay principle and one local tax that is based on the benefit principle. State your reason for categorizing the taxes as you did.
4. How is elasticity related to the revenue from a sales tax?
5. If the federal government wanted to tax a good and suppliers were strong lobbyists, but consumers were not, would government prefer supply or demand to be more inelastic? Why?
6. What types of goods would you recommend government tax if it wants the tax to result in no welfare loss? Name a few examples.

7. Suppose demand for cigarettes is inelastic and the supply of cigarettes is elastic. Who would bear the larger burden of a tax placed on cigarettes?
8. If the demand for a good is perfectly elastic and the supply is elastic, who will bear the burden of a tax on the good paid by consumers?
9. What percent of a tax will the demander pay if price elasticity of supply is .3 and price elasticity of demand is .7? What percent will the supplier pay?
10. Which good would an economist normally recommend taxing if government wanted to minimize welfare loss and maximize revenue: a good with an elastic or inelastic supply? Why?
11. Should tenants who rent apartments worry that increases in property taxes will increase their rent? Does your answer change when considering the long run?
12. Can you explain the tax system that led to this building style, which was common in old Eastern European cities?

13. In which case would the shortage resulting from a price ceiling be greater—when supply is inelastic or elastic? Explain your answer.
14. Define rent seeking. Do firms have a greater incentive to engage in rent-seeking behavior when demand is elastic or when it is inelastic?

Problems and Exercises

1. A political leader comes to you and wonders from whom she will get the most complaints if she institutes a price ceiling when demand is inelastic and supply is elastic.
   a. How do you respond?
   b. Demonstrate why your answer is correct.
2. Suppose the government established a requirement that everyone consume 10 percent more beets than he or she is currently consuming.
   a. Show graphically the welfare loss that would occur.
   b. If someone shows you that the welfare loss is small, say 0.5 percent of the cost of beets, and that eating beets improves people's health, would you support a beet-eating requirement? Why or why not?
3. Demonstrate the welfare loss of:
   a. A restriction on output when supply is perfectly elastic.
   b. A tax *t* placed on suppliers that shifts up a supply curve.
   c. A subsidy *s* given to suppliers that shifts down a supply curve.
   d. A restriction on output when demand is perfectly elastic.
4. Because of the negative incentive effect that taxes have on goods with elastic supply, in the late 1980s Margaret Thatcher (then prime minister of Great Britain) changed the property tax to a poll tax (a tax at a set rate that every individual must pay).
   a. Show why the poll tax is preferable to a property tax in terms of consumer and producer surplus.
   b. What do you think the real-life consequences of the poll tax were?
5. Demonstrate how a price floor is like a tax on consumers and a subsidy to suppliers.
   a. Who gets the revenue in the case of a tax? Label the area that illustrates the tax.
   b. Who gets the revenue in the case of a price floor? Label the transfer of surplus from consumers to suppliers.
   c. Label welfare loss of the tax and the price floor.
6. Suppose government imposed a minimum wage above equilibrium wage.
   a. What do you expect to happen to the resulting shortage of jobs as time progresses? (Assume that inflation and economic growth are both zero.)
   b. What do you expect to happen to the producer surplus transferred to minimum wage earners as time progresses?
7. Use the graph below to answer the following questions:

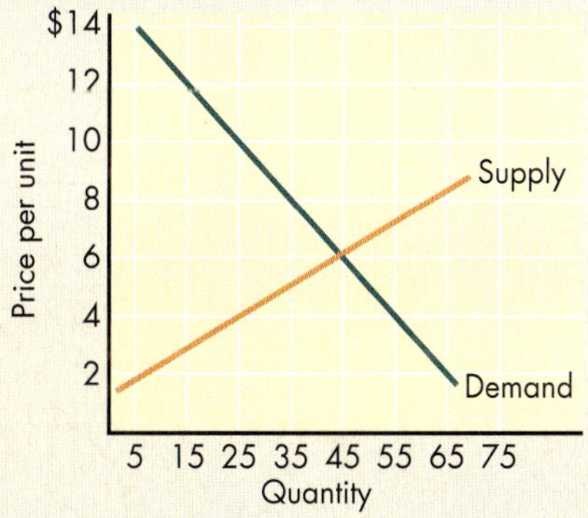

a. What is equilibrium price and quantity?
b. What is producer surplus when the market is in equilibrium?
c. What is consumer surplus when the market is in equilibrium?
d. If price were held at $10 a unit, what is consumer and producer surplus?

8. Use the graph below that shows the effect of a $4 per unit tax on suppliers to answer the following questions:

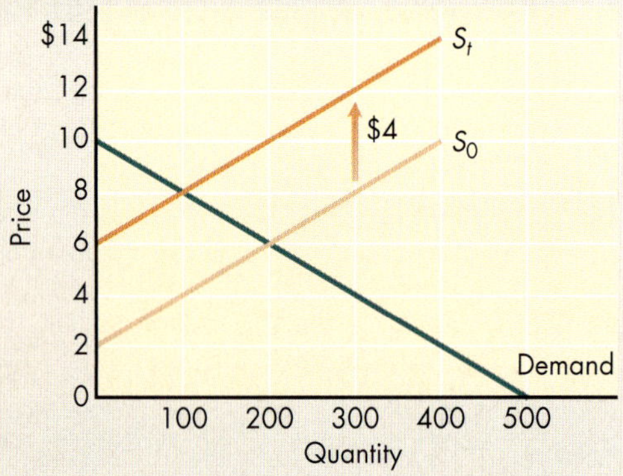

a. What is equilibrium price and quantity before the tax? After the tax?
b. What is producer surplus when the market is in equilibrium before the tax? After the tax?
c. What is consumer surplus when the market is in equilibrium before the tax? After the tax?
d. What is total tax revenue collected after the tax is implemented?

9. Calculate the percent of the tax borne by the demander and supplier in each of the following cases:
a. $E_D = .3, E_S = 1.2$
b. $E_D = 3, E_S = 2$
c. $E_D = .5, E_S = 1$
d. $E_D = .5, E_S = .5$
e. Summarize your findings regarding relative elasticity and tax burden.

WEB QUESTIONS

1. Gasoline taxes are commonly used to fund transportation-related expenditures. Cal-Tax is an advocacy group in California whose mission is to protect taxpayers from unnecessary taxes and to promote efficient, quality government services. Read their analysis of gasoline taxes in California at www.caltax.org/research/gastax.htm to answer the following questions:
a. How does California rank relative to other states in terms of taxes per gallon?
b. How does California rank in transportation expenditures relative to other states?
c. Is the gas tax in California based on the benefit principle, the ability-to-pay principle, or some other principle?
d. What has happened to revenue from gas taxes on a revenue-per-mile basis over the past few years? What accounts for this change?
e. Is the gas tax in California a progressive or a regressive tax? (*Regressive* means that the tax rate falls with income.)

2. Henry George, an American economist living in the 1800s, had very specific views on taxation. Read about these by clicking on *Taxation* on the Henry George Institute's home page at www.henrygeorge.org and answer the following questions:
a. What are the four criteria of a good tax according to Classical economists?
b. In what way do broad-based taxes fulfill those criteria? In what way do they fail to fulfill those criteria?
c. What good in our economy, according to Henry George, best fits the four criteria?
d. Demonstrate the welfare loss associated with the taxation of the good Henry George believes should be taxed. Who will bear the burden of the tax?

3. Go to www.ecommercetimes.com. Using its search engine, find recent articles about taxes on Internet sales to answer the following:
a. What is the current status of the Federal government moratorium on new Internet taxes?
b. What do analysts say will be the impact of new taxes on Internet sales? What does this imply about their estimates of the elasticity of demand for online purchases?
c. What argument can you give to support taxing Internet sales?

ANSWERS TO MARGIN QUESTIONS

1. The combination of consumer and producer surplus will increase since there will be no lost surplus at the equilibrium price. *(158)*
2. Welfare loss when supply is highly elastic and demand is highly inelastic is shown by the shaded triangle in the graph below. The supply curve shifts up by the amount of the tax. Since equilibrium quantity changes very little, from Q_0 to Q_1, welfare loss is very small. *(160)*

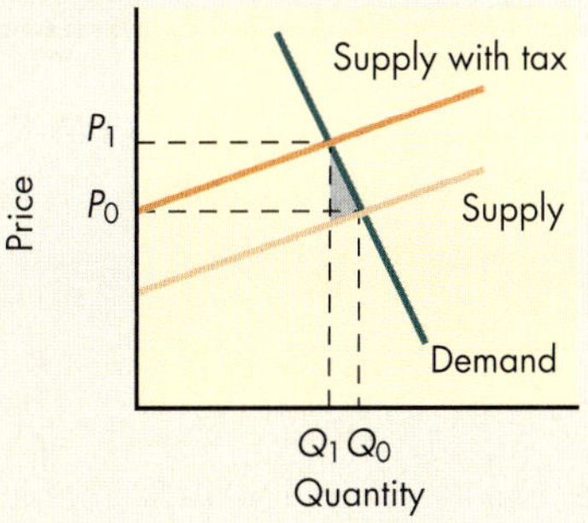

3. The average tax would be total tax divided by total income, or $2,000 (20% of $10,000) divided by $30,000 = 6.7%. *(162)*
4. The percentage of the tax borne by the consumer equals price elasticity of supply divided by the sum of the price elasticities of demand and supply, or

$$\frac{1.8}{(0.2 + 1.8)} = 0.9.$$

   The consumer pays $90 of the tax. *(165)*
5. If the entire amount of the tax were levied on employees, their before-tax income would rise because employers would have to compensate their employees for the increased taxes they would have to physically pay. The burden of the taxation does not depend on who pays the tax. It depends on relative elasticities. *(165)*
6. The effect of a price ceiling below equilibrium price when demand and supply are inelastic is shown in the following graph. Quantity demanded exceeds quantity supplied, but because demand and supply are both inelastic, the shortage is not big. Likewise, the welfare loss triangle, shown by the shaded area in the graph, is not large. *(167)*

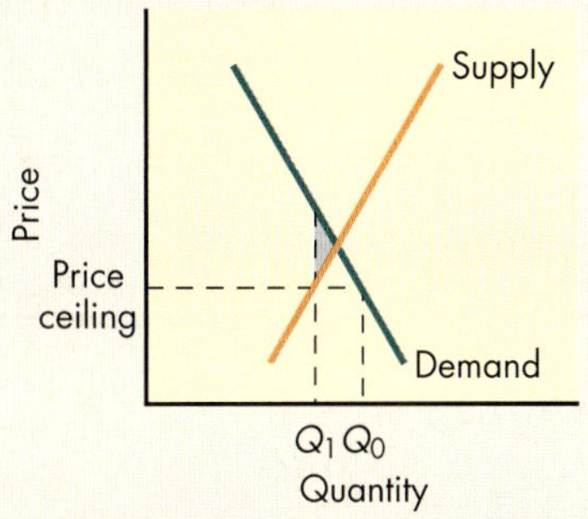

7. Yes and no. A draft, by reducing the taxes needed to pay wages to soldiers, lowers taxes that show up in government coffers, but does place an implicit tax on young men. Those who are drafted must accept the below-equilibrium wage, and give up the wage they could have made in the marketplace. The difference can be considered a tax paid to government. *(168)*
8. No. Research and development expenditures are an effort to increase technology to either lower production costs or discover a new product that can be marketed. If the firm can get a patent on that new product, the firm will have a monopoly and be able to restrict supply, transferring surplus from consumers to themselves, but this is not rent seeking. Rent-seeking activities are designed to transfer surplus from one group to another given current technology. They are unproductive. *(170)*
9. If suppliers are selling a product for which demand is inelastic, increases in productivity would result in a drop in price that would be proportionately greater than the rise in equilibrium quantity. Total revenue would decline for suppliers. *(170)*
10. Price controls tend to create ongoing shortages and surpluses in the long run because they prevent market forces from working. *(172)*

8 The Logic of Individual Choice: The Foundation of Supply and Demand

After reading this chapter, you should be able to:

- Discuss the principle of diminishing marginal utility.
- Summarize the principle of rational choice.
- Explain the relationship between marginal utility and price when a consumer is maximizing total utility.
- Explain how the principle of rational choice accounts for the laws of demand and supply.
- Explain why economists can believe there are many explanations of individual choice but nonetheless focus on self-interest.

The theory of economics must begin with a correct theory of consumption.

—*Stanley Jevons*

The analysis of how individuals make choices is central to microeconomics. It is the foundation of economic reasoning and it gives economics much of its power. The first part of this chapter shows you that foundation and leads you through some exercises to make sure you understand the reasoning. The second part of the chapter relates that analysis to the real world, giving you a sense of when the model is useful and when it's not.

As you go through this chapter, think back to Chapter 1, which set out the goals for this book. One goal was to get you to think like an economist. This chapter, which formally develops the reasoning process behind economists' cost/benefit approach to problems, examines the underpinnings of how to think like an economist.

Utility Theory and Individual Choice

Different sciences have various explanations for why people do what they do. For example, Freudian psychology tells us we do what we do because of an internal fight between the id, ego, and superego plus some hangups we have about our bodies. Other psychologists tell us it's a search for approval by our peers; we want to be OK. Economists agree that these are important reasons but argue that if we want an analysis that's simple enough to apply to problems, these heavy psychological explanations are likely to get us all mixed up. At least to start with, we need an easier underlying psychological foundation. And economists have one—self-interest. People do what they do because it's in their self-interest.

Economists' analysis of individual choice doesn't deny that most of us have our quirks. That's obvious in what we buy. On certain items we're penny-pinchers; on others we're big spenders. For example, how many of you or your parents clip coupons to save 40 cents on cereal but then spend $40 on a haircut? How many save 50 cents a pound by buying a low grade of meat but then spend $20 on a bottle of wine, $75 on dinner at a restaurant, or $60 for a concert ticket?

But through it all comes a certain rationality. Much of what people do reflects their rational self-interest. That's why economists start their analysis of individual choice with a relatively simple, but powerful, underlying psychological foundation.

Using that simple theory, two things determine what people do: the pleasure people get from doing or consuming something, and the price of doing or consuming that something. Price is the tool the market uses to bring the quantity supplied equal to the quantity demanded. Changes in price provide incentives for people to change what they're doing. Through those incentives the invisible hand guides us all. To understand economics you must understand how price affects our choices. That's why we focus on the effect of price on the quantity demanded. We want to understand the way in which a change in price will affect what we do.

In summary, economists' theory of rational choice is a simple, but powerful, theory that shows how these two things—pleasure and price—are related.

Measuring Pleasure

Let's start with an analysis of what we buy. Why do we buy what we buy? Economists' analysis of individual choice starts with the proposition that individuals try to get as much pleasure as possible out of life. To analyze the choice formally we must measure pleasure.

How does one measure pleasure? I don't know the answer to that, but back in the 1800s economists such as Jeremy Bentham thought that eventually they would be able to measure pleasure by measuring brain waves. In the expectation of this discovery they even developed a measure of pleasure they called a *util*. They predicted that someday a machine that could measure utils would be developed. Not surprisingly they called this machine a *utilometer*. This utilometer was to be connected to people's heads and an economist would read it as people went through their daily activities. Eating broccoli might give 10 utils; eating a hot fudge sundae might give 10,000 utils.

Web Note 8.1
Pleasure and Pain

Eventually these 19th-century economists gave up hope of developing a utilometer, but economists still use a quaint shorthand term, **utility,** for *the pleasure or satisfaction that one expects to get from consuming a good or service*. (And you thought that economists didn't have a sense of humor.) Utility serves as the basis of economists' analysis of individual choice.

Utility refers to the satisfaction one gets from consuming a good or service.

Economists initially used actual numbers to represent utility. But no economist today believes that the actual numbers given to utility have meaning. Economists have gone to great lengths to show that all you need is a relative ranking of goods that people reveal when they choose one good over another.

It's important to keep in the back of your mind that economists don't need actual numbers to discuss utility, especially if you're going on in economics. In introductory economics there's nothing quite as useful as a unit of utility. It gives us real numbers to work with rather than all kinds of fancy measure theories. So here's the deal: I'll use real numbers in discussing utility and you promise that you'll remember they're not really needed. (If you don't accept this deal, see Appendix A, where I go through the same analysis without using actual numbers.)

Q-1 One of the assumptions of economists' theory of choice is that utility must be measured. True or false? Why?

Total Utility and Marginal Utility

In thinking about utility, it's important to distinguish between *total utility* and *marginal utility*. **Total utility** refers to *the total satisfaction one gets from consuming a product*. **Marginal utility** refers to *the satisfaction one gets from consuming one additional unit of a product above and beyond what one has consumed up to that point*. For example, eating a whole pound of Beluga caviar might give you 4,700 units of utility.[1] Consuming the first 15

It is important to distinguish between marginal and total utility.

[1]Throughout the book I choose specific numbers to make the examples more understandable and to make the points I want to make. A useful exercise is for you to choose different numbers and reason your way through the same analysis.

ounces may have given you 4,697 units of utility. Consuming the last ounce of caviar might give you an additional 3 units of utility. The 4,700 is total utility; the 3 is the marginal utility of eating that last ounce of caviar.

An example of the relationship between total utility and marginal utility is given in Figure 8-1. Let's say that the marginal utility of the 1st slice of pizza is 14, and since you've eaten only 1 slice, the total utility is also 14. Let's also say that the marginal utility of the 2nd slice of pizza is 12, which means that the total utility of 2 slices of pizza is 26 (14 + 12). Similarly for the 3rd, 4th, and 5th slices of pizza, whose marginal utilities are 10, 8, and 6, respectively. The total utility of your eating those 5 pieces of pizza is the sum of the marginal utilities you get from eating each of the 5 slices. The fifth row of column 2 of Figure 8-1(a) shows that sum.

Notice that marginal utility shows up between the lines. It is the utility of changing consumption levels. For example, the marginal utility of changing from 1 to 2 slices of pizza is 12. The relationship between total and marginal utility can also be seen graphically. In Figure 8-1(b) we graph total utility (column 2 of the utility table) on the vertical axis, and the number of slices of pizza (column 1 of the utility table) on the horizontal axis. As you can see, total utility increases up to 7 slices of pizza; after 8 slices it starts decreasing—after 8 pieces of pizza you're so stuffed that you can't stand to look at another slice.

Q-2 If the total utility curve is a straight line—that is, does not exhibit diminishing marginal utility—what will the marginal utility curve look like?

In Figure 8-1(c) we graph marginal utility (column 3 of the utility table) on the vertical axis and slices of pizza (column 1) on the horizontal axis. Notice how marginal utility decreases while total utility increases. When total utility stops increasing (between 7 and 8 slices), marginal utility is zero. Beyond this point total utility decreases and marginal utility is negative. An additional slice of pizza will actually make you worse off.

Diminishing Marginal Utility

Now let's consider the shapes of these curves a bit more carefully: What are they telling us about people's choices? As we've drawn the curves, the marginal utility that a person gets from each additional slice of pizza decreases with each slice of pizza eaten. Economists believe that the shapes of these curves is generally a reasonable description of the pattern of people's enjoyment. They call that pattern the **principle of diminishing marginal utility:**

The principle of diminishing marginal utility states that, after some point, the marginal utility received from each additional unit of a good decreases with each additional unit consumed, other things equal.

> *As you consume more of a good, after some point the marginal utility received from each additional unit of a good decreases with each additional unit consumed, other things equal.*

As individuals increase their consumption of a good, at some point consuming another unit of the product will simply not yield as much additional pleasure as did consuming the preceding unit.

Consider, for example, that late-night craving for a double-cheese-and-pepperoni pizza. You order one and bite into it. Ah, pleasure! But if you've ordered a large pizza and you're eating it all by yourself, eventually you'll get less additional enjoyment from eating additional slices. In other words, the marginal utility you get is going to decrease with each additional slice of pizza you consume. That's the principle of diminishing marginal utility.

Notice that the principle of diminishing marginal utility does not say that you don't enjoy consuming more of a good; it simply states that as you consume more of the good, you enjoy the additional units less than you did the initial units. A fourth slice of pizza still tastes good, but it doesn't match the taste of the third slice. At some point, however, marginal utility can become negative. Say you had two large pizzas and only two hours in which to eat them. Eating the last slice could be pure torture. But in most

Q-3 Consuming more of a good generally increases its marginal utility. True or false? Why?

Figure 8-1 (a, b, and c) Marginal and Total Utility
Marginal utility tends to decrease as consumption of a good increases. Notice how the information in the table (**a**) can be presented graphically in two different ways. The two different ways are, however, related. The downward slope of the marginal utility curve (**c**) is reflected in the total utility curve bowed downward in (**b**). Notice that marginal utility relates to changes in quantity so the marginal utility line is graphed at the halfway point. For example, in (**c**), between 7 and 8, marginal utility becomes zero.

Number of pizza slices	Total utility	Marginal utility
		14
1	14	
		12
2	26	
		10
3	36	
		8
4	44	
		6
5	50	
		4
6	54	
		2
7	56	
		0
8	56	
		−2
9	54	

(a) Utility table

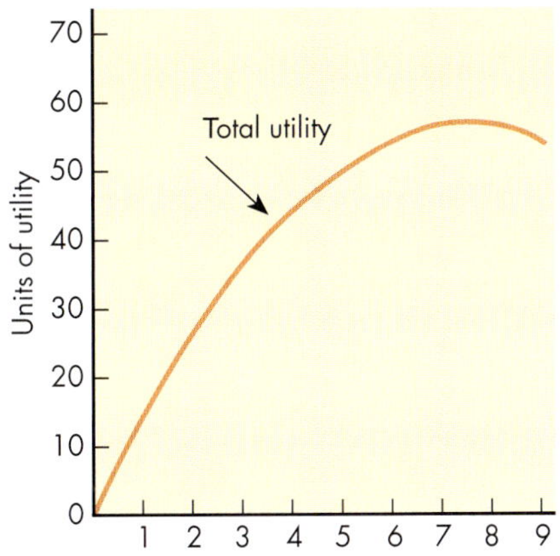

(b) Total utility

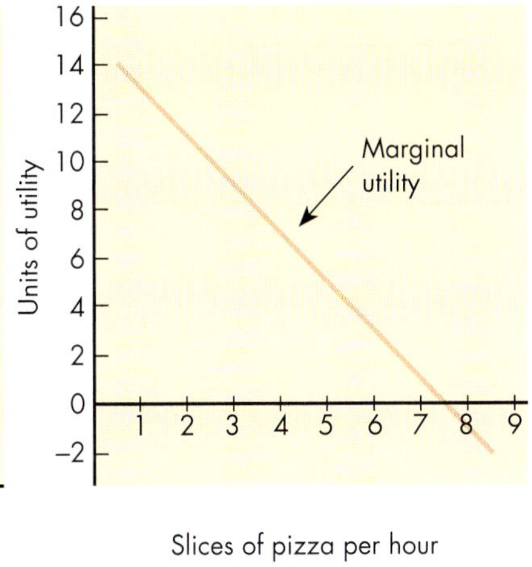

(c) Marginal utility

situations you have the option *not* to consume any more of a good. When consuming a good becomes torture (meaning its utility is negative), you simply don't consume any more of it. If you eat a slice of pizza (or consume an additional unit of a good), that's a good indication that its marginal utility is still positive.

Rational Choice and Marginal Utility

The analysis of rational choice is the analysis of how individuals choose goods within their budget in order to maximize total utility, and how maximizing total utility can be accomplished by considering marginal utility. That analysis begins with the premise that rational individuals want as much satisfaction as they can get from their available resources. The term *rational* in economics means, specifically, that people prefer more to less and will make choices that give them as much satisfaction as possible. The problem is that people face a budget constraint. They must choose among the alternatives. How do they do that?

Because people face a budget constraint, they must choose among alternatives.

Some Choices

Let's start by considering three choices. (Answer each choice as you read it.)[2]

Web Note 8.2
Tastes and Choices

Choice 1: Between spending another dollar on a slice of pizza that gives you an additional 41 units of utility or spending another dollar on a hero sandwich that gives you an additional 30 units of utility.

Choice 2: Between reading an additional chapter in this book that gives you an additional 200 units of utility at a cost of one hour of your time, or reading an

[2]To keep the analysis simple in this example, I consider either/or decisions. Below, I show how to extend the analysis to marginal choices.

Psychology and Economics

Beyond the Tools

More and more psychology is being integrated into economics and economic reasoning. Instead of just assuming that individuals act rationally, modern economists are conducting experiments to determine how individuals act. In 2002 the Nobel Prize Committee recognized this change when it awarded the Nobel Prize in Economics to a professor of psychology, Danny Kahneman, and to an economist, Vernon Smith.

Smith was given the award for being a leader in experimental economics. He has played a central role in getting economists to test their theories with laboratory experiments, in which one can observe, rather than assume, how people behave. In these experiments economists have found that individuals have a sense of fairness along with economic rationality that guides their decisions.

Kahneman, together with Amos Tversky (who died in 1996), developed the theory of behavioral economics and argued that people aren't as calculating as economists often assume and that they repeatedly make errors in judgment that can be predicted and categorized. For example, a principle of economic rationality is that a sunk cost is a sunk cost, and should not be taken into account in decisions. But consistently individuals take sunk costs into account. He found that people are far less likely to sell a share of stock that they bought for $90 for $70 than they are to sell a share of stock for $70 that they bought for $50, even though economic rationality says that a rational person will not take into account the purchase price of a stock when deciding whether to sell it; they will only take into account future stock prices. Such insights are changing the face of modern economics, but they should be seen as complements to, rather than substitutes for, standard economic reasoning.

additional chapter in psychology that gives you an additional 100 units of utility at a cost of 40 minutes of your time.

Choice 3: Between having your next date with that awesome guy Jerry, which gives you an additional 2,000 units of utility and costs you $70, or taking out plain Jeff on your next date, which gives you an additional 200 units of utility and costs you $10.

The correct choices, in terms of marginal utility, are (1) the pizza, (2) a chapter of this book, and (3) Jerry.

If you answered all three correctly, either you're lucky or you have a good intuitive understanding of the principle of rational choice. Now let's explore the principle of rational choice more thoroughly by considering each of the three examples.

Choice 1 Since the slice of pizza and the hero sandwich both cost $1, and the pizza gives you more units of utility than the hero, the pizza is the rational choice. If you spend $1 on the hero rather than the pizza, you're losing 11 units of utility and not making yourself as happy as you could be. You're being irrational. Any choice (for the same amount of money) that doesn't give you as much utility as possible is an irrational choice.

But now let's say that the price of heroes falls to 50 cents so that you can buy two heroes for the same price you previously had to pay for only one. Let's also say that two heroes would give you 56 units of utility (not $2 \times 30 = 60$—remember the principle of diminishing marginal utility). Which would now be the more rational choice? The two heroes, because their 56 units of utility are 15 more than you would get from that dollar spent on one slice of pizza.

Another way of thinking about your choice is to recognize that essentially what you're doing is buying units of utility. Obviously you want to get the most for your money, so you choose goods that have the highest units of utility per unit of cost. Let's see how this way of thinking about a decision works by considering our second choice.

Q-4 Which is the rational choice—watching one hour of MTV that gives you 20 units of utility or watching a two-hour movie that gives you 30 units of utility?

Choice 2 Here the two alternatives have a cost in time, not money. The analysis, however, is the same. You calculate the marginal utility (additional units of utility) of the choice facing you, and divide that by the costs of the activity; that gives you the marginal utility per unit of cost. Then choose the activity that has the highest marginal utility per unit of cost or lowest cost per unit of utility. When you do that, you see that this chapter gives you 3⅓ units of utility per minute (200/60 = 3⅓), while the psychology chapter gives you 2½ units of utility per minute. So you choose to read another chapter in this book.[3]

Choice 3 Taking out Jerry gives you 28½ units of utility per dollar (2,000/$70), while taking out Jeff gives you 20 units of utility per dollar (200/$10). So you choose to take out Jerry.[4]

The Principle of Rational Choice

The principle of rational choice tells us to spend our money on those goods that give us the most marginal utility per dollar.

The **principle of rational choice** is as follows: *Spend your money on those goods that give you the most marginal utility (MU) per dollar.* The principle of rational choice is important enough for us to restate.

$$\text{If } \frac{MU_x}{P_x} > \frac{MU_y}{P_y}, \text{ choose to consume an additional unit of good } x.$$

$$\text{If } \frac{MU_x}{P_x} < \frac{MU_y}{P_y}, \text{ choose to consume an additional unit of good } y.$$

By substituting the marginal utilities and prices of goods into these formulas, you can always decide which good it makes more sense to consume. Consume the one with the highest marginal utility per dollar.

Simultaneous Decisions

So far in discussing our examples, we've considered the choices separately. But in real life, choices aren't so neatly separated. Say you were presented with all three choices simultaneously. If you make all three of the decisions given in the examples, are you being rational? The answer is no. Why? The pizza gives you 41 units of utility per dollar; taking out Jerry gives you 28½ units of utility per dollar. You aren't being rational; you aren't maximizing your utility. It would clearly make sense to eat more pizza, paying for it by cutting the date with Jerry short. (Skip the coffee at the end of the meal.)

But what about the other choice: studying psychology or economics? We can't compare the costs of studying to the costs of the other goods because, as I noted earlier, the costs of both studying alternatives are expressed in terms of time, not money. If we can assign a money value to the time, however, we can make the comparison. Let's say you can earn $6 per hour, so the value of your time is 10 cents per minute. This allows us to think about both alternatives in terms of dollars and cents. Since a chapter in economics takes an hour to read, the cost in money of reading a chapter is

[3]As I've pointed out before, I choose the numbers to make the points I want to make. A good exercise for you is to choose different numbers that reflect your estimate of the marginal utility you get from choice, and see what your rational choices are. And remember our deal.

[4]In these examples I am implicitly assuming that the "goods" are divisible. Technically, this assumption is needed for marginal utilities to be fully specified.

Q.5 True or false? You are maximizing total utility only when the marginal utility of all goods is zero. Explain your answer.

60 minutes × 10 cents = \$6. Similarly, the cost of the 40 minutes you'd take to read the psychology chapter is \$4.

With these values we can compare our studying decisions with our other decisions. The value in units of utility per dollar of reading a chapter of this book is:

$$\frac{200}{\$6} = 33\tfrac{1}{3} \text{ units of utility per dollar}$$

So forget about dating Jerry with its 28½ units of utility per dollar. Your rational choice is to study this chapter while stuffing yourself with pizza.

But wait. Remember that, according to the principle of diminishing marginal utility, as you consume more of something, the marginal utility you get from it falls. So as you consume more pizza and spend more time reading this book, the marginal utilities of these activities will fall. Thus, as you vary your consumption, the marginal utilities you get from the goods are changing.

Maximizing Utility and Equilibrium

When do you stop changing your consumption? The principle of rational choice says you should keep adjusting your spending within your budget if the marginal utility per dollar (MU/P) of two goods differs. The only time you don't adjust your spending is when there is no clear winner. *When the ratios of the marginal utility to price of the two goods are equal*, you're maximizing utility; this is the **utility-maximizing rule:**

The utility maximizing rule: $\frac{MU_x}{P_x} = \frac{MU_y}{P_y}$

$$\text{If } \frac{MU_x}{P_x} = \frac{MU_y}{P_y}, \text{ you're maximizing utility.}$$

When you're maximizing utility, you're in equilibrium. To understand how, by adjusting your spending, you can achieve equilibrium, it's important to remember the principle of diminishing marginal utility. As we consume more of an item, the marginal utility we get from the last unit consumed decreases. Conversely, as we consume *less* of an item, the marginal utility we get from the last unit consumed *increases*. (The principle of diminishing marginal utility operates in reverse.)

Achieving equilibrium by maximizing utility (juggling your choices, adding a bit more of one and choosing a bit less of another) requires more information than I've so far presented. We need to know the marginal utility of alternative amounts of consumption for each choice and how much we have to spend on all those items. With that information we can choose among alternatives, given our available resources.

An Example of Maximizing Utility

Table 8-1 offers an example in which we have the necessary information to make simultaneous decisions and maximize utility. In this example, we have \$7 to spend on ice cream cones and Big Macs. The choice is between ice cream at \$1 a cone and Big Macs at \$2 apiece. In the table you can see the principle of diminishing marginal utility in action. The marginal utility (*MU*) we get from either good decreases as we consume more of it. Marginal utility (*MU*) becomes negative after 5 Big Macs or 6 ice cream cones.

The key columns for your decision are the *MU/P* columns. They tell you the *MU* per dollar spent on each of the items. By following the rule that we choose the good with the higher marginal utility per dollar, we can quickly determine the optimal choice.

Let's start by considering what we'd do with our first \$2. Clearly we'd only eat ice cream. Doing so would give us 29 + 17 = 46 units of utility, compared to 20 units of utility if we spent the \$2 on a Big Mac. How about our next \$2? Again the choice is

Table 8-1 Maximizing Utility
This table provides the information needed to make simultaneous decisions. Notice that the marginal utility we get from another good declines as we consume more of it. To maximize utility, adjust your choices until the marginal utility of all goods is equal.

Big Macs (P = $2)				Ice Cream (P = $1)			
Q	*TU*	*MU*	*MU/P*	*Q*	*TU*	*MU*	*MU/P*
0	0			0	0		
		20	10			29	29
1	20			1	29		
		14	7			17	17
2	34			2	46		
		10	5			7	7
3	44			3	53		
		3	1.5			2	2
4	47			4	55		
		0	0			1	1
5	47			5	56		
		−5	−2.5			0	0
6	42			6	56		
		−10	−5			−4	−4
7	32			7	52		

clear; the 10 units of utility per dollar from the Big Mac are plainly better than the 7 units of utility per dollar we can get from ice cream cones. So we buy 1 Big Mac and 2 ice cream cones with our first $4.

Now let's consider our fifth and sixth dollars. The *MU/P* for a second Big Mac is 7. The *MU/P* for a third ice cream cone is also 7, so we could spend the fifth dollar on either—if McDonald's will sell us half a Big Mac. We ask them if they will, and they tell us no, so we must make a choice between either two additional ice cream cones or another Big Mac for our fifth and sixth dollars. Since the marginal utility per dollar of the fourth ice cream cone is only 2, it makes sense to spend our fifth and sixth dollars on another Big Mac. So now we're up to 2 Big Macs and 2 ice cream cones and we have one more dollar to spend.

Now how about our last dollar? If we spend it on a third ice cream cone we get 7 additional units of utility. If McDonald's maintains its position and only sells whole Big Macs, this is our sole choice since we only have a dollar and Big Macs sell for $2. But let's say that McDonald's wants the sale and this time offers to sell us half a Big Mac for $1. Would we take it? The answer is no. One-half of the next Big Mac gives us only 5 units of utility per dollar whereas the third ice cream cone gives us 7 units of utility per dollar. So we spend the seventh dollar on a third ice cream cone.

With these choices and $7 to spend we've arrived at equilibrium—the marginal utilities per dollar are the same for both goods and we're maximizing total utility. Our total utility is 34 from 2 Big Macs and 53 units of utility from the 3 ice cream cones, making a total utility of 87.

Why do these two choices make sense? Because they give us the most total utility for the $7 we have to spend. We've followed the utility-maximizing rule: Maximize utility by adjusting your choices until the marginal utilities per dollar are the same. These choices make the marginal utility per dollar between the last Big Mac and the last ice cream cone equal. The marginal utility per dollar we get from our last Big Mac is:

$$\frac{MU}{P} = \frac{14}{\$2} = 7$$

The marginal utility per dollar we get from our last ice cream cone is:

$$\frac{MU}{P} = \frac{7}{\$1} = 7$$

The marginal utility per dollar of each choice is equal, so we know we can't do any better. For any other choice we would get less total utility, so we could increase our total utility by switching to one of these two choices.

Extending the Principle of Rational Choice

Our example involved only two goods, but the reasoning can be extended to the choice among many goods. Our analysis has shown us that the principle of rational choice among many goods is simply an extension of the principle of rational choice applied to two goods. That general principle of rational choice is to consume more of the good that provides a higher marginal utility per dollar.

When $\frac{MU_x}{P_x} > \frac{MU_z}{P_z}$, consume more of good *x*.

When $\frac{MU_y}{P_y} > \frac{MU_z}{P_z}$, consume more of good *y*.

Stop adjusting your consumption when the marginal utilities per dollar are equal.

So the general utility-maximizing rule is that you are maximizing utility when the marginal utilities per dollar of the goods consumed are equal.

When $\frac{MU_x}{P_x} = \frac{MU_y}{P_y} = \frac{MU_z}{P_z}$ you are maximizing utility.

When this rule is met, the consumer is in equilibrium; the cost per additional unit of utility is equal for all goods and the consumer is as well off as it is possible to be.

Q-6 If you are initially in equilibrium and the price of one good rises, how would you adjust your consumption to return to equilibrium?

Notice that the rule does not say that the rational consumer should consume a good until its marginal utility reaches zero. The reason is that consumers don't have enough money to buy all they want. They face a budget constraint and do the best they can under that constraint—that is, they maximize utility. To buy more goods a person has to work more, so she should work until the marginal utility of another dollar earned just equals the marginal utility of goods purchased with another dollar. According to economists' analysis of rational choice, a person's choice of how much to work is made simultaneously with the person's decision of how much to consume. So when you say you want a Porsche but can't afford one, economists ask whether you're working two jobs and saving all your money to buy a Porsche. If you aren't, you're demonstrating that you don't really want a Porsche, given what you would have to do to get it.

Rational Choice and the Laws of Demand and Supply

Now that you know the rule for maximizing utility, let's see how it relates to the laws of demand and supply. We begin with demand. The law of demand says that the quantity demanded of a good is inversely related to its price. That is, when the price of a good goes up, the quantity we consume of it goes down.

Income and Substitution Effects

Knowing the Tools

In the discussion of the law of demand I didn't say precisely how much the quantity demanded would decrease with an increase in the price of an ice cream cone from $1 to $2. I didn't because of a certain ambiguity that arises when one talks about changes in nominal prices. To understand the cause of this ambiguity, notice that if the price of an ice cream cone has risen to $2, with $7 we can no longer consume 2 Big Macs and 3 ice cream cones. We've got to cut back for two reasons: First, we're poorer due to the rise in price. The reduction in quantity demanded because we're poorer is called the *income effect.* Second, the *relative* prices have changed. The price of ice cream has risen relative to the price of Big Macs. The reduction in quantity demanded because relative price has risen is called a *substitution effect.* Technically the law of demand is based only on the substitution effect.

To separate the two effects, let's assume that somebody compensates us for the rise in price of ice cream cones. Since it would cost $10 [(2 × $2 = $4) + (3 × $2 = $6)] to buy what $7 bought previously, we'll assume that someone gives us an extra $3 to compensate us for the rise in price. Since we are not any poorer because of the price change, this eliminates the income effect. We now have $10, so we can buy 2 Big Macs and the 3 ice cream cones as we did before. If we do so, our total utility is once again 87 (34 units of utility from 2 Big Macs and 53 units of utility from 3 ice cream cones.) But will we do so? We can answer that with the table.

Big Macs (*P* = $2)				Ice Cream (*P* = $2)			
Q	*TU*	*MU*	*MU/P*	*Q*	*TU*	*MU*	*MU/P*
0	0			0	0		
		20	10			29	14.5
1	20			1	29		
		14	7			17	8.5
2	34			2	46		
		10	5			7	3.5
3	44			3	53		

We see that Big Macs give us more *MU* per dollar. What happens if we exchange an ice cream cone for an additional Big Mac, so instead of buying 3 ice cream cones and 2 Big Macs, we buy 3 Big Macs and 2 ice cream cones? The *MU* per dollar of Big Macs falls from 7 to 5 and the *MU* per dollar of the ice cream cone (whose price is now $2) rises from 3.5 to 8.5. Our total utility rises to 44 from 3 Big Macs and 46 from 2 ice cream cones, for a total of 90 units of utility rather than the previous 87. We've increased our total utility by shifting our consumption out of ice cream, the good whose price has risen. The price of ice cream went up and, even though we were given more money so we could buy the same amount as before, we did not; we bought fewer ice cream cones. That's the substitution effect in action: It tells us that when the relative price of a good goes up, the quantity purchased of that good decreases, *even if you're given money to compensate you for the rise.*

Now let's consider the law of demand in relation to our principle of rational choice. When the price of a good goes up, the marginal utility *per dollar* we get from that good goes down. So when the price of a good goes up, if we were initially in equilibrium, we no longer are. Therefore, we choose to consume less of that good. The principle of rational choice shows us formally that following the law of demand is the rational thing to do.

According to the principle of rational choice, if there is diminishing marginal utility and the price of a good goes up, we consume less of that good. Hence, the principle of rational choice leads to the law of demand.

Let's see how. If:

$$\frac{MU_x}{P_x} = \frac{MU_y}{P_y}$$

and the price of good y goes up, then:

$$\frac{MU_x}{P_x} > \frac{MU_y}{P_y}$$

Our utility-maximizing rule is no longer satisfied. Consider the preceding example, in which we were in equilibrium with 87 units of utility (34 from 2 Big Macs and 53 from 3 ice cream cones) with the utility-maximizing rule fulfilled:

$$\begin{array}{ccc} \text{Big Mac} & & \text{Ice cream} \\ \dfrac{14 \text{ units of utility}}{\$2} & = & \dfrac{7 \text{ units of utility}}{\$1} = 7 \end{array}$$

If the price of an ice cream cone rises from \$1 to \$2, the marginal utility per dollar for Big Macs (whose price hasn't changed) exceeds the marginal utility per dollar of ice cream cones:

$$\begin{array}{ccc} \text{Big Mac} & > & \text{Ice cream} \\ \dfrac{14}{\$2} & > & \dfrac{7}{\$2} \end{array}$$

To satisfy our utility-maximizing rule so that our choice will be rational, we must somehow raise the marginal utility we get from the good whose price has risen. Following the principle of diminishing marginal utility, we can increase marginal utility only by *decreasing* our consumption of the good whose price has risen. As we consume fewer ice cream cones and more Big Macs, the marginal utility of ice cream rises and the marginal utility of a Big Mac falls.

This example can be extended to a general rule: If the price of a good rises, you'll increase your total utility by consuming less of it. When the price of a good goes up, consumption of that good will go down. Our principle of rational choice underlies the law of demand:

Quantity demanded rises as price falls, other things constant.

Or alternatively:

Quantity demanded falls as price rises, other things constant.

This discussion of marginal utility and rational choice shows the relationship between marginal utility and the price we're willing to pay. When marginal utility is high, as it is with diamonds, the price we're willing to pay is high. When marginal utility is low, as it is with tap water, the price we're willing to pay is low. Since our demand for a good is an expression of our willingness to pay for it, quantity demanded is related to marginal utility.

THE LAW OF SUPPLY

According to the principle of rational choice, if there is diminishing marginal utility and the price of supplying a good goes up, you supply more of that good.

The above discussion focused on demand and goods we consume, but this analysis of choice holds for the law of supply of factors of production, such as labor, that individuals supply to the market, as well as for demand. In supply decisions you are giving up something—your time, land, or some other factor of production—and getting money in return. To show you how this works, let's consider one final example—how much labor you should supply to the market.

Say that working another hour at your part-time job pays you another \$5 and that you currently work 20 hours per week. That additional income from the final hour of work gives you an additional 24 units of utility. Also assume that your best alternative use of that hour—studying economics—gives you another 24 units of utility. (You didn't know economics gave you so much pleasure, did you?) So what should you do when your boss asks you to work an extra hour? Tell her no, you are already satisfying the utility-maximum rule $MU_w/W = MU_s/W$.

$$\begin{array}{ccc} \text{Studying} & & \text{Working} \\ \dfrac{24 \text{ units of utility}}{\$5} & = & \dfrac{24 \text{ units of utility}}{\$5} \end{array}$$

The price of studying an additional hour is also your wage per hour because that wage is the opportunity cost of studying.

But now say that your boss offers to raise your wage to $5.50 per hour for work you do over 20 hours. That means that both your wage at work and the price of studying have increased. But now you can get more goods for working that additional hour. Let's say that those additional goods raise the marginal utility you get from an additional hour of work to 32 additional units of utility. Now the marginal utility of working an additional hour exceeds the marginal utility of studying an additional hour:

$$\begin{array}{ccc} \text{Studying} & & \text{Working} \\ \dfrac{24 \text{ units of utility}}{\$5.50} & < & \dfrac{32 \text{ units of utility}}{\$5.50} \end{array}$$

So you work the extra hour.

Now say your boss comes to you and asks what it would take to get you to work five hours more per week. After running the numbers through your computer-mind, you solve the utility-maximizing rule and tell her, "$8.00 an hour for overtime work and you've got your worker." Combining these hours and wages gives you the supply curve shown in Figure 8-2, which demonstrates the law of supply.

Q-7 Use the principle of rational choice to explain how you would change your quantity of work supplied if your employer raised your wage by $1 per hour.

To see that you have the reasoning down, say that an exam is coming, and you haven't studied. This will likely raise the marginal utility of studying sufficiently, so you will choose to work less, if you have a choice. What will that change do to the supply curve?

If you answered that it will shift it to the left, you're in good shape.

Opportunity Cost

Before we leave the principle of rational choice, let's consider how it relates to the opportunity cost concept that I presented in earlier chapters. *Opportunity cost* was the benefit forgone of the next-best alternative. Now that you've been through the principle of rational choice, you have a better sense of what is meant by opportunity cost of a forgone opportunity—it is essentially the marginal utility per dollar you forgo from the consumption of the next-best alternative.

To say $MU_x/P_x > MU_y/P_y$ is to say that the opportunity cost of not consuming good x is greater than the opportunity cost of not consuming good y. So you consume x.

The principle of rational choice states that, to maximize utility, choose goods until the opportunity costs of all alternatives are equal.

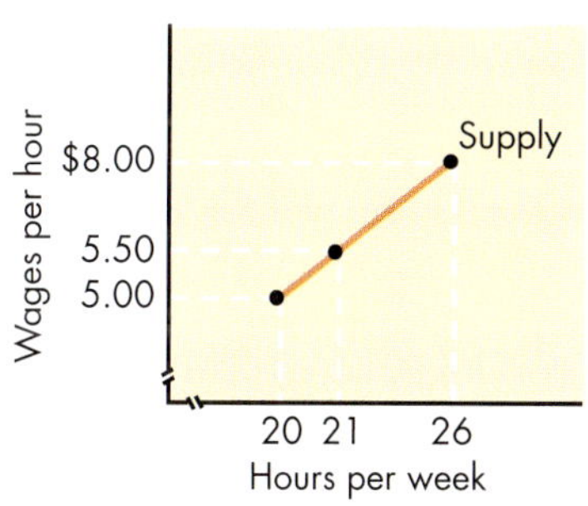

Figure 8-2 Deriving Labor Supply from Marginal Utility
Factor supply curves can be derived from a comparison of marginal utilities for various activities in relation to work. In this example the higher the wage, the higher the marginal utility of the goods you can get for the wage relative to the next-best alternative, giving you an upward-sloping labor supply curve.

Q-8 If the opportunity cost of consuming good *x* is greater than the opportunity cost of consuming good *y*, which good has the higher marginal utility per dollar?

When the marginal utilities per dollar spent are equal, the opportunity cost of the alternatives are equal. In reality people don't use the utility terminology, and, indeed, a specific measure of utility doesn't exist. But the choice based on the price of goods relative to the benefit they provide is used all the time. Instead of utility terminology, people use the "really need" terminology. They say they will work the extra hour rather than study because they *really need* the money. To say you are working because you "really need" the money is the equivalent of saying the marginal utility of working is higher than the opportunity cost of other choices. So the general rule fits decisions about supply, even if most people don't use the word *utility*. The more you "really, really need" something, the higher its marginal utility.

Applying Economists' Theory of Choice to the Real World

Understanding a theory involves more than understanding how a theory works; it also involves understanding the limits the assumptions underlying the theory place on the use of the theory. So let's consider some of the assumptions on which economists' analysis of choice is based. The first assumption we'll consider is the implicit assumption that decisions can be made costlessly.

The Cost of Decision Making

The principle of rational choice makes reasonably good intuitive sense when we limit our examples to two or three choices, as I did in this chapter. But in reality, we make hundreds of thousands of choices simultaneously. It simply doesn't make intuitive sense that we're going to apply rational choice to all those choices at once—that would exceed our decision-making abilities. This cost of decision making means that it is only rational to be somewhat irrational—to do things without applying the principle of rational choice. Thinking about decisions is one of the things we all economize on.

Q-9 Bounded rationality violates the principle of rational choice. True or false?

How real-world people make decisions in real-world situations is an open question that modern economists are spending a lot of time researching. Following the work of Nobel Prize winner Herbert Simon, a number of economists have come to believe that, to make real-world decisions, most people use *bounded rationality*—rationality based on rules of thumb—rather than using the principle of rational choice. They argue that many of our decisions are made with our minds on automatic pilot. This view of rationality has significant implications for interpreting and predicting economic events. For example, one rule of thumb is "You get what you pay for," which means that something with a high price is better than something with a low price. Put technically, we rely on price to convey information about quality. This reliance on price for information changes the inferences one can draw from the analysis, and can lead to upward-sloping demand curves.

A second rule of thumb that people sometimes use is "Follow the leader." If you don't know what to do, do what you think smart people are doing. Consider the clothes you're wearing. I suspect many of your choices of what to wear reflect this and the previous rules of thumb. Suppliers of clothing certainly think so and spend enormous amounts of money to exploit these rules of thumb. They try to steer your automatic pilot toward their goods. The suppliers emphasize these two rules ("You get what you pay for" and "Follow the leader") to convince people their product is the "in" thing to buy. If they succeed, they've got a gold mine; if they fail, they've got a flop. Advertising is designed to mine these rules of thumb.

Advertising is designed to mine rules of thumb.

In technical terms, the "Follow the leader" rule leads to *focal point equilibria,* in which a set of goods is consumed, not because the goods are objectively preferred to all other goods, but simply because, through luck, or advertising, they have become focal points to which people have gravitated. Once some people started consuming a good, others followed.

Given Tastes

A second assumption implicit in economists' theory of rational choice is that our preferences are given, and are not shaped by society. In reality our preferences are determined not only by nature but also by our experiences—by nurture. Let's consider an example: Forty percent of major league baseball players chew tobacco, but close to zero percent of college professors chew tobacco. Why? Are major league baseball players somehow born with a tobacco-chewing gene while college professors are not? I doubt it. Tastes often are significantly influenced by society.

Conspicuous Consumption

Another aspect of taste that has been described by economists is **conspicuous consumption**—*the consumption of goods not for one's direct pleasure, but simply to show off to others*. The term was created approximately 100 years ago by Thornstein Veblen. Veblen argued that, just as some animals strut around to show their abilities, humans consume to show that they can "afford it." For Veblen, mansions, designer clothing, and $300 appetizers were all examples of conspicuous consumption. He further argued that male industrialists (which were all industrialists at the time) were so busy with business that they didn't have time to show off enough, so they married a trophy spouse whose purpose was to show off for them in the most ostentatious manner possible.

Tastes and Individual Choice

Web Note 8.3
Veblen Goods

One way in which economists integrate the above insights into economics is by emphasizing that the analysis is conducted on the assumption of "given tastes." As discussed above, in reality, economists agree that often forces besides price and marginal utility play a role in determining what people demand. They fully recognize that a whole other analysis is necessary to supplement theirs—an analysis of what determines taste.

Ask yourself what you ate today. Was it health food? Pizza? Candy? Whatever it was, it was probably not the most efficient way to satisfy your nutritional needs. The most efficient way to do that would be to eat only soybean mush and vitamin supplements at a cost of about $300 per year. That's less than one-tenth of what the average individual today spends on food per year. Most of us turn up our noses at soybean mush. Why? Because tastes are important.

I emphasize this point because some economists have been guilty of forgetting their simplifying assumption. Some economists in the 1800s thought that society's economic needs eventually would be fully met and that we would enter a golden age of affluence where all our material wants would be satisfied. They thought there would be surpluses of everything. Clearly that hasn't happened. Somehow it seems that whenever a need is met, it's replaced by a want, which soon becomes another need.

Somehow, whenever a need is met, it's replaced by a want, which soon becomes another need.

There are, of course, examples of wants being temporarily satisfied, as a U.S. company on a small island in the Caribbean is reported to have discovered. Employees weren't showing up for work. The company sent in a team of efficiency experts who discovered the cause of their problem: The firm had recently raised wages, and workers had decided they could get all they wanted (warm weather, a gorgeous beach, plenty of food, and a little bit of spending money) by showing up for work once, maybe twice, a week. Such a situation was clearly not good for business, but the firm found a solution. It sent

Making Stupid Decisions

Applying the Tools

It is hard to make good decisions. You need lots of training—in math, in economics, in logic. Think of kids—do five-year-olds make rational decisions? Some dyed-in-the-wool utilitarians might argue that whatever decision one makes must, by definition, be rational, but such usage makes the concept tautological—true by definition.

When applying the theory of rational choice, most economists agree that some decisions people make can be irrational. For example, they will concede that five-year-olds make a lot of what most parents would call stupid (or irrational) decisions. By a stupid decision they mean a decision with expected consequences that, if the child had logically thought about them, would have caused the child not to make that particular decision. But five-year-olds often haven't learned how to think logically about expected consequences, so economists don't assume decisions made by five-year-olds reflect the rational choice model.

In the real world, parents and teachers spend enormous effort to teach children what is rational, reasonable, and "appropriate." Children's decision-making process reflects that teaching. But parents and teachers teach more than a decision-making process; they also teach children a moral code that often includes the value of honor and the value of selflessness. These teachings shape their children's decision-making process (although not always in the way that parents or teachers think or hope) and modify their preferences. So our decision-making process and our preferences are, to some degree, taught to us.

Recognizing that preferences and decision-making processes are, to some degree, taught, not inherent, eliminates the fixed point by which to judge people's decisions: Are they making decisions that reflect their true needs, or are they simply reflecting what they have been taught? Eliminating that fixed point makes it difficult to draw unambiguous policy implications from economists' model of rational choice.

---

in thousands of Sears catalogs (back when Sears sent catalogs), and suddenly the workers were no longer satisfied with what they already had. They wanted more and went back to work to get it. When they were presented with new possibilities, their wants increased. Companies know that tastes aren't constant, and they spend significant amounts of money on advertising to make consumers have a taste for their goods. It works, too.

Q-10 Using the principle of rational choice, explain why a change in tastes will shift a demand curve.

Tastes are also important in explaining differences in consumption between countries. For example, a Japanese person wouldn't consider having a meal without rice. Rice has a ceremonial, almost mystical value in Japan. In many parts of the United States supper means meat and potatoes. In Germany, carp (a large goldfish) is a delicacy; in the United States many people consider carp inedible. In the United States corn is a desirable vegetable; in parts of Europe, until recently, it was considered pig food.

Economists take into account changes in tastes as shift factors of demand.

To say we don't analyze tastes in the core of economic theory doesn't mean that we don't take them into account. Think back to Chapter 4, when we distinguished shifts in demand (the entire demand schedule shifts) from movements along the demand curve. Those movements along the demand curve were the effect of price. Tastes were one of the shift factors of demand. So economists do include tastes in their analysis; a change in tastes makes the demand curve shift.

Conclusion

We began this chapter with a discussion of the simplifying nature of the economists' analysis of rational choice. Now that you've been through it, you may be wondering if it's all that simple. In any case, I'm sure most of you would agree that it's complicated enough. When we're talking about formal analysis, I'm in total agreement.

But if you're talking about informal analysis and applying the analysis to the real world, most economists would also agree that this theory of choice is in no way acceptable. Economists believe that there's more to life than maximizing utility. We believe in love, anger, and doing crazy things just for the sake of doing crazy things. We're real people.

But, we argue, simplicity has its virtue, and often people hide their selfish motivations. Few people like to go around and say, "I did this because I'm a self-interested, calculating person who cares primarily about myself." Instead they usually emphasize other motives. "Society conditioned me to do it"; "I'm doing this to achieve fairness"; "It's my upbringing." And they're probably partially right, but often they hide and obscure their self-interested motives in their psychological explanations. The beauty of economists' simple psychological assumption is that it cuts through many obfuscations (that's an obfuscating word meaning "smokescreens") and, in doing so, often captures a part of reality that others miss. Let's consider a couple of examples.

Economists use their simple self-interest theory of choice because it cuts through many obfuscations, and in doing so, often captures a part of reality that others miss.

Why does government have restrictions on who's allowed to practice law? The typical layperson's answer is that these restrictions exist to protect the public. The economists' answer is that many of the restrictions do little to protect the public. Instead their primary function is to restrict the number of lawyers and thereby increase the marginal utility of existing lawyers and the price they can charge.

Why do museum directors almost always want to increase the size of their collections? The layperson's (and museum directors') answer is that they're out to preserve our artistic heritage. The economists' answer is that it often has more to do with maximizing the utility of the museum staff. (Economist William Grampp made this argument in a book about the economics of art. He supported his argument by pointing out that more than half of museums' art is in storage and not accessible to the public. Acquiring more art will simply lead to more art going into storage.)

Now in no way am I claiming that the economic answer based on pure self-interest is always the correct one. But I am arguing that approaching problems by asking the question "What's in it for the people making the decisions?" is a useful approach that will give you more insight into what's going on than many other approaches. It gets people to ask tough, rather than easy, questions. After you've asked the tough questions, then you can see how to modify the conclusions by looking deeply into the real-world institutions.

Approaching problems by asking the question "What's in it for the people making the decision?" is a useful approach that will give you more insight than many other approaches.

All too often students think of economics and economic reasoning as establishment reasoning. That's not true. Economic reasoning can be extremely subversive to existing establishments. But whatever it is, it is not subversive in order to be subversive, or proestablishment to be proestablishment. It's simply a logical application of a simple idea—individual choice theory—to a variety of problems.

SUMMARY

- Total utility is the satisfaction obtained from consuming a product; marginal utility is the satisfaction obtained from consuming one additional unit of a product.
- The principle of diminishing marginal utility states that after some point, the marginal utility of consuming more of the good will fall.

- The principle of rational choice is:

  If $\frac{MU_x}{P_x} > \frac{MU_y}{P_y}$, choose to consume more of good x.

  If $\frac{MU_x}{P_x} < \frac{MU_y}{P_y}$, choose to consume more of good y.

- The utility-maximizing rule says:

  If $\frac{MU_x}{P_x} = \frac{MU_y}{P_y}$, you're maximizing utility; you're indifferent between good x and good y.

- Unless $MU_x/P_x = MU_y/P_y$, an individual can rearrange his or her consumption to increase total utility.
- Opportunity cost is essentially the marginal utility per dollar one forgoes from the consumption of the next-best alternative.
- The law of demand can be derived from the principle of rational choice.
- If you're in equilibrium and the price of a good rises, you'll reduce your consumption of that good to reestablish equilibrium.
- The law of supply can be derived from the principle of rational choice.
- If your wage rises, the marginal utility of the goods you can buy with that wage will rise and you will work more to satisfy the utility-maximizing rule.
- To apply economists' analysis of choice to the real world, we must carefully consider, and adjust for, the underlying assumptions, such as costlessness of decision making and given tastes.

Key Terms

conspicuous consumption *(191)*
marginal utility *(179)*
principle of diminishing marginal utility *(180)*
principle of rational choice *(183)*
total utility *(179)*
utility *(179)*
utility-maximizing rule *(184)*

Questions for Thought and Review

1. Explain how marginal utility differs from total utility.
2. According to the principle of diminishing marginal utility, how does marginal utility change as more of a good is consumed? As less of a good is consumed?
3. How would the world be different than it is if the principle of diminishing marginal utility seldom held true?
4. It is sometimes said that an economist is a person who knows the price of everything but the value of nothing. Is this statement true or false? Why?
5. Assign a measure of utility to your studying for various courses. Do your study habits follow the principle of rational choice?
6. What key psychological assumptions do economists make in their theory of individual choice?
7. Explain your motivation for four personal decisions you have made in the past year, using economists' model of individual choice.
8. State the law of demand and explain how it relates to the principle of rational choice.
9. State the law of supply and explain how it relates to opportunity cost.
10. If the supply curve is perfectly inelastic, what is the opportunity cost of the supplier?
11. There is a small but growing movement known as "voluntary simplicity," which is founded on the belief in a simple life of working less and spending less. Do Americans who belong to this movement follow the principle of rational choice?
12. Although the share of Americans who say they are "very happy" hasn't changed much in the last five decades, the number of products produced and consumed per person has risen tremendously. How can this be?
13. Early Classical economists found the following "diamond/water" paradox perplexing: "Why is water, which is so useful and necessary, so cheap, when diamonds, which are so useless and unnecessary, so expensive?" Using the utility concept, explain why it is not really a paradox.

14. Give an example of a recent purchase for which you used a rule of thumb in your decision-making process. Did your decision follow the principle of rational choice? Explain.

15. According to Thorstein Veblen what is the purpose of conspicuous consumption? Does the utility derived from the consumption of these goods come from their price or functionality? Give an example of such a good.

Problems and Exercises

1. Complete the following table of Scout's utility from drinking cans of soda and answer the questions below.

Cans of Soda	Total Utility	Marginal Utility
0	___	
		10
1	___	
		12
2	22	
		___
3	32	
		8
4	___	
		4
5	___	
		___
6	44	
		___
7	42	

   a. At what point does marginal utility begin to fall?
   b. Will Scout consume the 7th can of soda? Explain your answer.
   c. True or false? Scout will be following the utility-maximizing rule by consuming 2 cans of soda. Explain your answer.

2. The following table gives the price and total units of three goods: A, B, and C.

Good	Price	Total Utility							
		1	2	3	4	5	6	7	8
A	$10	200	380	530	630	680	700	630	430
B	2	20	34	46	56	64	72	78	82
C	6	50	60	70	80	90	100	90	80

   As closely as possible, determine how much of the three goods you would buy with $20. Explain why you chose what you did.

3. The following table gives the marginal utility of John's consumption of three goods: A, B, and C.

Units of Consumption	*MU* of A	*MU* of B	*MU* of C
1			
	20	25	45
2			
	18	20	30
3			
	16	15	24
4			
	14	10	18
5			
	12	8	15
6			
	10	6	12

   a. Good A costs $2 per unit, good B costs $1, and good C costs $3. How many units of each should a consumer with $12 buy to maximize his or her utility?
   b. How will the answer change if the price of B rises to $2?
   c. How about if the price of C is 50 cents but the other prices are as in *a*?

4. The total utility of your consumption of widgets is 40; it changes by 2 with each change in widgets consumed. The total utility of your consumption of wadgets is also 40 but changes by 3 with each change in wadgets consumed. The price of widgets is $2 and the price of wadgets is $3. How many widgets and wadgets should you consume?

5. Nobel Prize–winning economist George Stigler explains how the famous British economist Phillip Wicksteed decided where to live. His two loves were fresh farm eggs, which were more easily obtained the farther from London he was, and visits from friends, which decreased the farther he moved away from London. Given these two loves, describe the decision rule that you would have expected Wicksteed to follow.

6. You are buying your spouse, significant other, or close friend a ring. You decide to show your reasonableness, and buy a cubic zirconium ring that sells at 1/50 the cost of a mined diamond and that any normal person could not tell from a mined diamond just by looking at it. In fact, the zirconium will have more brilliance and fewer occlusions (imperfections) than a mined diamond.

a. How will your spouse (significant other, close friend) likely react?
b. Why?
c. Is this reaction justified?

7. Suppose Charlie Parker CDs cost $10 apiece and Lester Young CDs cost $5 apiece. You have $40 to spend on CDs. The marginal utility that you derive from additional CDs is as follows:

Number of CDs	Charlie Parker	Lester Young
0		
	60	30
1		
	40	28
2		
	30	24
3		
	20	20
4		
	10	10
5		

How many of each CD would you buy? Suppose the price of a Lester Young CD rises to $10. How many of each CDs would you buy? Use this to show how the principle of rational choice leads to the law of demand.

Web Questions

1. Go to www.travelocity.com.
   a. Find a selection of prices of airline fares between two cities for a period of one month ahead of time and staying over a Saturday night. If there are differences in the prices explain why they likely differ.
   b. Now shorten your stay, and do not include a Saturday-night stay. What happens to the prices? Explain why.
   c. Now find the price of the same flight you had in *a*, only this time booking only three days ahead. What happens to prices? Explain why.
2. Go to www.iwon.com.
   a. What does this site do?
   b. Why do they give out a $10,000 daily prize and a $25 million yearly prize for using the site?
   c. What advertisements were shown there?
   d. What does the existence of these advertisements suggest about economists' assumption that tastes are fixed?

Answers to Margin Questions

1. False. Economists' theory of choice does not require them to measure utility. It only requires that the marginal utility of one good be compared to the marginal utility of another. *(179)*
2. If the total utility curve is a straight line, the marginal utility curve will be flat with a slope of zero since marginal utility would not change with additional units. *(180)*
3. False. The principle of diminishing marginal utility is that as one increases consumption of a good, the good's marginal utility decreases. *(180)*
4. Given a choice between the two, the rational choice is to watch MTV for one hour since it provides the highest marginal utility per hour. *(183)*
5. False. You are maximizing total utility when the marginal utilities per dollar are the same for all goods. This does not have to be where marginal utility is zero. *(184)*
6. If I am currently in equilibrium, then $MU_x/P_x = MU_y/P_y = MU_z/P_z$ for all goods I consume. If the price of one good goes up, I will decrease my consumption of that good and increase the consumption of other goods until the equilibrium is met again where $MU_x/P_x = MU_y/P_y = MU_z/P_z$. *(186)*
7. If offered one more dollar per hour, I would choose to substitute labor for leisure since the price of leisure (pay per hour of work) has increased. Following the principle of rational choice, I would work more to lower the marginal utility of work so that $MU_w/P_w = MU_l/P_l$. *(189)*

8. Good y has the higher marginal utility per dollar since the opportunity cost of consuming good x is the marginal utility per dollar of consuming good y. *(190)*
9. This could be true or false. It depends on how you interpret bounded rationality. If it is interpreted within a costless decision-making environment, it does violate the principle of rational choice since there is no reason to be less than rational. If, however, it is interpreted within a costly decision-making environment, then you can be making decisions within a range because the marginal cost of increasing the range of choices exceeds the marginal benefit of doing so, and in that case bounded rationality is consistent with the principle of rational choice. Information is not costless. *(190)*
10. If a person is in equilibrium and a change in tastes leads to an increase in the marginal utility for one good, he will increase consumption of that good to reestablish equilibrium. A change in tastes will shift a demand curve because it will cause a change in quantity consumed without a change in the good's price. *(192)*

APPENDIX A

Indifference Curve Analysis

As I stated in the chapter, analyzing individual choice using actual numbers is unnecessary. In the chapter, I asked you to make a deal with me: You'd remember that actual numbers are unnecessary and I'd use them anyway. This appendix is for those who didn't accept my deal (and for those whose professors want them to get some practice in Graphish). It presents an example of a more formal analysis of individual choice.

Figure A8-1 Graphing the Budget Constraint

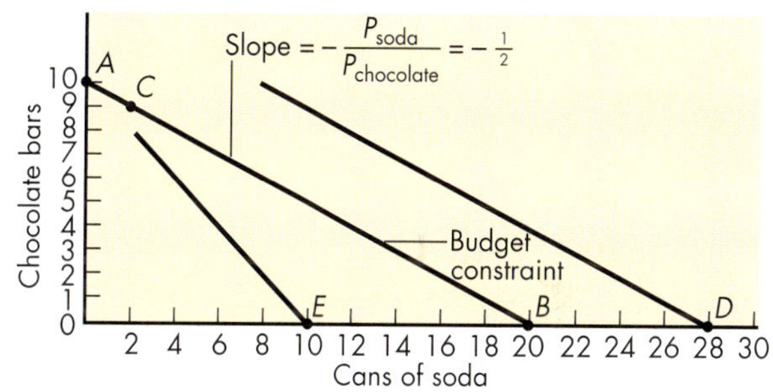

SOPHIE'S CHOICE

Sophie is a junk food devotee. She lives on two goods: chocolate bars, which cost \$1 each, and cans of soda, which sell for 50 cents apiece. Sophie is trying to get as much pleasure as possible, given her resources. Alternatively expressed, Sophie is trying to maximize her utility, given a budget constraint.

By translating this statement of Sophie's choice into graphs, I can demonstrate the principle of rational choice without ever mentioning any specific amount of utility.

The graph we'll use will have chocolate bars on the vertical axis and cans of soda on the horizontal axis, as in Figure A8-1.

GRAPHING THE BUDGET CONSTRAINT

Let's begin by asking: How can we translate her budget constraint (the \$10 maximum she has to spend) into Graphish? The easiest way to do that is to ask what would happen if she spends her \$10 all on chocolate bars or all on cans of soda. Since a chocolate bar costs \$1, if she spends it all on chocolate bars she can get 10 bars (point *A* in Figure A8-1). If she spends it all on cans of soda, she can get 20 cans of soda (point *B*). This gives us two points.

But what if she wants some combination of soda and chocolate bars? If we draw a line between points *A* and *B*, we'll have a graphical picture of her budget constraint and can answer that question because a **budget constraint** is *a curve that shows us the various combinations of goods an individual can buy with a given amount of money*. The line is her budget constraint in Graphish.

To see that it is, say Sophie is spending all her money on chocolate bars. She then decides to buy one fewer chocolate bar. That gives her \$1 to spend on soda, which, since those cans cost 50 cents each, allows her to buy 2 cans. Point C (9 chocolate bars and 2 cans of soda) represents that decision. Notice how point C is on the budget constraint. Repeat this exercise from various starting points until you're comfortable with the fact that the line does indeed represent the various combinations of soda and chocolate bars Sophie can buy with the $10. It's a line with a slope of −½ and intersects the chocolate-bars-axis at 10 and the cans-of-soda axis at 20.

To be sure that you've got it, ask yourself what would happen to the budget constraint if Sophie got another $4 to spend on the two goods. Going through the same reasoning should lead you to the conclusion that the budget constraint will shift to the right so that it will intersect the cans-of-soda axis at 28 (point *D*), but its slope won't change. (I started the new line for you.) Make sure you can explain why.

Now what if the price of a can of soda goes up to $1? What happens to the budget line? (This is a question many people miss.) If you said the budget line becomes steeper, shifting in along the cans-of-soda axis to point E while remaining anchored along the chocolate-bars-axis until the slope equals −1, you've got it. If you didn't say that, go through the same reasoning we went through at first (if Sophie buys only cans of soda . . .) and then draw the new line. You'll see it becomes steeper. Put another way, the absolute value of the slope of the curve is the ratio of the price of cans of soda to the price of chocolate bars; the absolute value of the slope becomes greater with a rise in the price of cans of soda.

Figure A8-2 Sophie's Indifference Curve

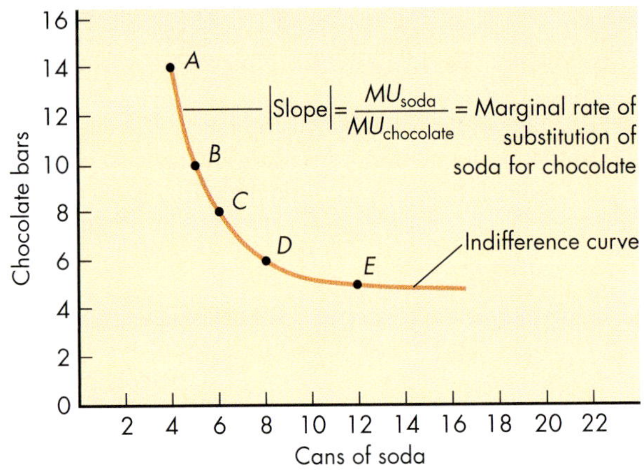

Chocolate bars	Cans of soda	
14	4	*A*
10	5	*B*
8	6	*C*
6	8	*D*
5	12	*E*

Graphing the Indifference Curve

Now let's consider the second part of Sophie's choice: the pleasure part. Sophie is trying to get as much pleasure as she can from her $10. How do we deal with this in Graphish?

To see, let's go through a thought experiment. Say Sophie had 14 chocolate bars and 4 cans of soda (point A in Figure A8-2). Let's ask her, "Say you didn't know the price of either good and we took away 4 of those chocolate bars (so you had 10). How many cans of soda would we have to give you so that you would be just as happy as before we took away the 4 chocolate bars?"

Since she's got lots of chocolate bars and few cans of soda, her answer is probably "Not too many; say, 1 can of soda." This means that she would be just as happy to have 10 chocolate bars and 5 cans of soda (point *B*) as she would to have 14 chocolate bars and 4 cans of soda (point *A*). Connect those points and you have the beginning of a "just-as-happy" curve. But that doesn't sound impressive enough, so, following economists' terminology, we'll call it an **indifference curve**—*a curve that shows combinations of goods among which an individual is indifferent.* She's indifferent between points A and B.

If you continue our thought experiment, you'll get a set of combinations of chocolate bars and cans of soda like that shown in the table in Figure A8-2.

If you plot each of these combinations of points on the graph in Figure A8-2 and connect all these points, you have one of Sophie's indifference curves: a curve representing combinations of cans of soda and chocolate bars among which Sophie is indifferent.

Let's consider the shape of this curve. First, it's downward-sloping. That's reasonable; it simply says that if you take something away from Sophie, you've got to give her something in return if you want to keep her indifferent between what she had before and what she has now. The absolute value of the slope of an indifference curve is the **marginal rate of substitution**—*the rate at which one good must be added when the other is taken away in order to keep the individual indifferent between the two combinations.*

Second, it's bowed inward. That's because as Sophie gets more and more of one good, it takes fewer and fewer of another good to compensate for the loss of the good she incurred in order to get more of the other good. The underlying reasoning is similar to that in our discussion of the law of diminishing marginal utility, but notice we haven't even mentioned utility. Technically the reasoning for the indifference curve being bowed inward is called the

Figure A8-3 A Group of Indifference Curves

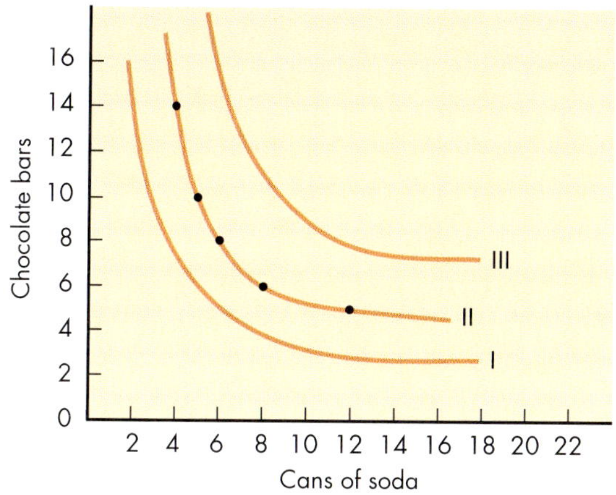

Figure A8-4 Why Indifference Curves Cannot Cross

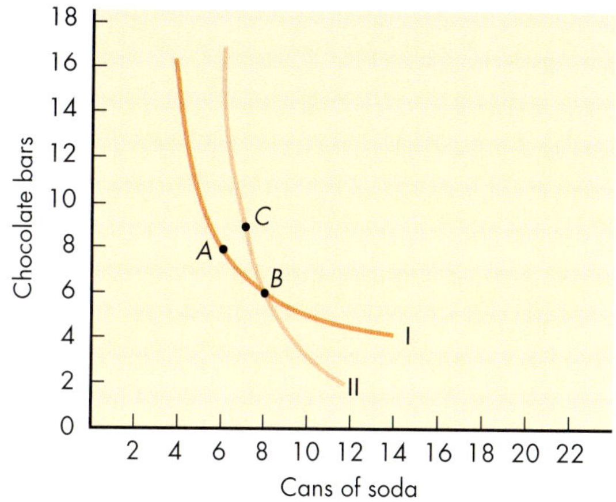

law of diminishing marginal rate of substitution—which tells us that *as you get more and more of a good, if some of that good is taken away, then the marginal addition of another good you need to keep you on your indifference curve gets less and less*.

Even more technically we can say that the absolute value of the slope of the indifference curve equals the ratio of the marginal utility of cans of soda to the marginal utility of chocolate bars:

$$\left| \text{Slope} \right| = \frac{MU_{\text{soda}}}{MU_{\text{chocolate}}} = \text{Marginal rate of substitution}$$

That ratio equals the marginal rate of substitution of cans of soda for chocolate bars. Let's consider an example. Say that in Figure A8-2 Sophie is at point A and that the marginal utility she gets from an increase from 4 to 5 cans of soda is 10. Since we know that she was willing to give up 4 chocolate bars to get that 1 can of soda (and thereby move from point *A* to point *B*), that 10 must equal the loss of utility she gets from the loss of 4 chocolate bars out of the 14 she originally had. So the marginal rate of substitution of cans of soda for chocolate bars between points *A* and *B* must be 4. That's the absolute value of the slope of that curve. Therefore, her *MU* of a chocolate bar must be about 2.5 (10 for 4 chocolate bars).

You can continue this same reasoning, starting with various combinations of goods. If you do so, you can get a whole group of indifference curves like that in Figure A8-3. Each curve represents a different level of happiness. Assuming she prefers more to less, Sophie is better off if she's on Curve II than if she's on Curve I, and even better off if she's on Curve III. Her goal in life is to get out to the furthest indifference curve she can.

To see whether you've followed the reasoning, ask yourself the following question: "Assuming Sophie prefers more of a good to less (which seems reasonable), can any two of Sophie's indifference curves cross each other as the ones in Figure A8-4 do?"

The answer is no, no, no! Why? Because they're indifference curves. If the curves were to cross, the "prefer-more-to-less" principle would be violated. Say we start at point A: Sophie has 8 chocolate bars and 6 cans of soda. We know that since *A* (8 chocolate bars and 6 sodas) and *B* (6 chocolate bars and 8 cans of soda) are on the same indifference curve, Sophie is indifferent between *A* and *B*. Similarly with points *B* and *C*: Sophie would just as soon have 9 chocolate bars and 7 cans of soda as she would 6 chocolate bars and 8 cans of soda.

It follows by logical deduction that point *A* must be indifferent to C. But consider points A and C carefully. At point C, Sophie has 7 cans of soda and 9 chocolate bars. At point *A* she has 6 cans of soda and 8 chocolate bars. At point C she has more of both goods than she has at point A, so to say she's indifferent between these two points violates the "prefer-more-to-less" criterion. Ergo (that's Latin, meaning "therefore"), two indifference curves cannot intersect. That's why we drew the group of indifference curves in Figure A8-3 so that they do not intersect.

Combining Indifference Curves and Budget Constraints

Now let's put the budget constraint and the indifference curves together and ask how many chocolate bars and cans of soda Sophie will buy if she has $10, given the

Figure A8-5 Combining Indifference Curves and Budget Constraint

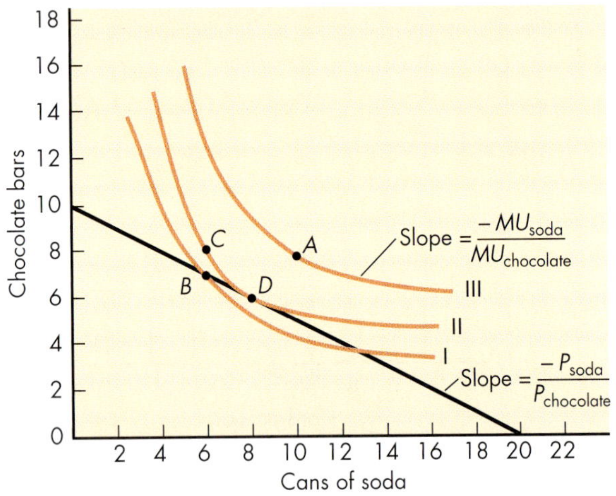

psychological makeup described by the indifference curves in Figure A8-3.

To answer that question, we must put the budget line of Figure A8-1 and the indifference curves of Figure A8-3 together, as we do in Figure A8-5.

As we discussed, Sophie's problem is to get to as high an indifference curve as possible, given her budget constraint. Let's first ask if she should move to point A (8 chocolate bars and 10 cans of soda). That looks like a good point. But you should quickly recognize that she can't get to point A; her budget line won't let her. (She doesn't have enough money.) Well then, how about point B (7 chocolate bars and 6 cans of soda)? She can afford that combination; it's on her budget constraint. The problem with point B is the following: She'd rather be at point C since point C has more chocolate bars and the same amount of soda (8 chocolate bars and 6 cans of soda). But, you say, she can't reach point C. Yes, that's true, but she can reach point D. And, by the definition of indifference curve, she's indifferent between point C and point D, so point D (6 chocolate bars and 8 cans of soda), which she can reach given her budget constraint, is preferred to point B.

The same reasoning holds for all other points. The reason is that the combination of chocolate bars and cans of soda represented by point D is the best she can do. It is the point where the indifference curve and the budget line are tangent—the point at which the slope of the budget line ($-P_s/P_c$) equals the slope of the indifference curve ($-MU_s/MU_c$). Equating those slopes gives $P_s/P_c = (MU_s/MU_c)$, or:

$$MU_c/P_c = MU_s/P_s$$

This equation, you may remember from the chapter, is the equilibrium condition of our principle of rational choice. So by our Graphish analysis we arrived at the same conclusion we arrived at in the chapter, only this time we did it without using actual numbers. This means that even without a utilometer, economists' principle of rational choice is internally logical.

Deriving a Demand Curve from the Indifference Curve

Not only can we derive the principle of rational choice with indifference curve/budget line analysis, we can also derive a demand curve. To do so, ask yourself what a demand curve is. It's the quantity of a good that a person will buy at various prices. Since the budget line gives us the relative price of a good, and the point of tangency of the indifference curve gives us the quantity that a person would buy at that price, we can derive a demand curve from the indifference curves and budget lines. To derive a demand curve we go through a set of thought experiments asking how many cans of soda Sophie would buy at various prices. We'll go through one of those experiments.

We start with the analysis we used before when Sophie started with $10 and chose to buy 8 cans of soda when the price of a can of soda was 50 cents (point A in Figure A8-6(a)). That analysis provides us with one point on the demand curve. I represent that by point A in Figure A8-6(b). At a price of 50 cents, Sophie buys 8 cans of soda.

Now say the price of a can of soda rises to $1. That rotates the budget line in, from budget line 1 to budget line 2 as in Figure A8-6(a). She can't buy as much as she could before. But we can determine how much she'll buy by the same reasoning we used previously. She'll choose a point at which her lower indifference curve is tangent to her new budget line. As you can see, she'll choose point B, which means that she buys 6 cans of soda when the price of a can of soda is $1. Graphing that point (6 cans of soda at $1 each) on our price/quantity axis in Figure A8-6(b), we have another point on our demand curve, point B. Connect these two together and you can see we're getting a downward-sloping demand curve, just as the law of

Figure A8-6 (a and b) From Indifference Curves to Demand Curves

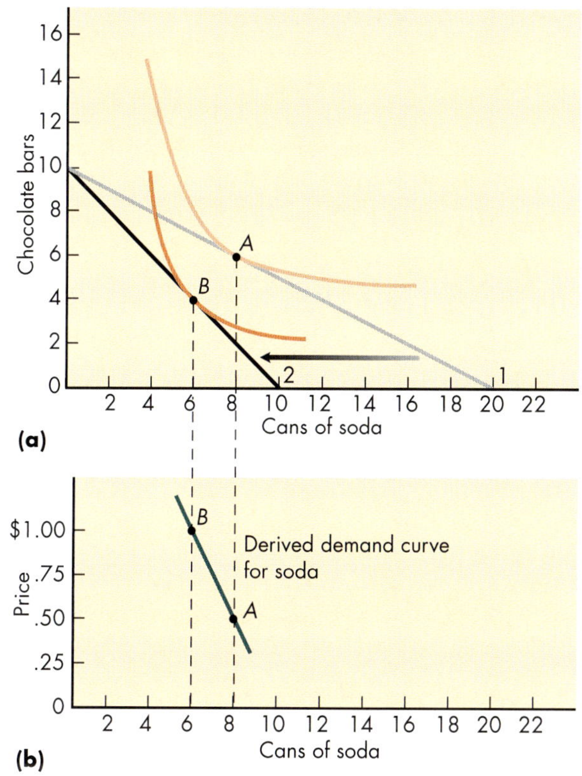

demand said we would. To make sure you understand, continue the analysis for a couple of additional price changes. You'll see that the demand curve you derive will be downward-sloping.

There's much more we can do with indifference curves. We can distinguish income effects and substitution effects. (Remember, when the price of a can of soda rose, Sophie was worse off. So to be as well off as before, as is required by the substitution effect, she'd have to be compensated for that rise in price by an offsetting fall in the price of chocolate bars.) But let's make a deal. You tentatively believe me when I say that all kinds of stuff can be done with indifference curves and budget constraints, and I'll leave the further demonstration and the proofs for you to experience in the intermediate microeconomics courses.

KEY TERMS

budget constraint *(197)*
indifference curve *(198)*
law of diminishing marginal rate of substitution *(199)*
marginal rate of substitution *(198)*

QUESTIONS FOR THOUGHT AND REVIEW

1. Zachary has $5 to spend on two goods: video games and hot dogs. Hot dogs cost $1 apiece while video games cost 50 cents apiece.
   a. Draw a graph of Zachary's budget constraint, placing videos on the Y axis.
   b. Suppose the price of hot dogs falls to 50 cents apiece. Draw the new budget constraint.
   c. Suppose Zachary now has $8 to spend. Draw the new budget constraint using the prices from *b*.
2. Zachary's indifference curves are shown in the following graph. Determine on which indifference curve Zachary will be, given the budget constraints and prices in *a*, *b*, and *c* from problem 1.

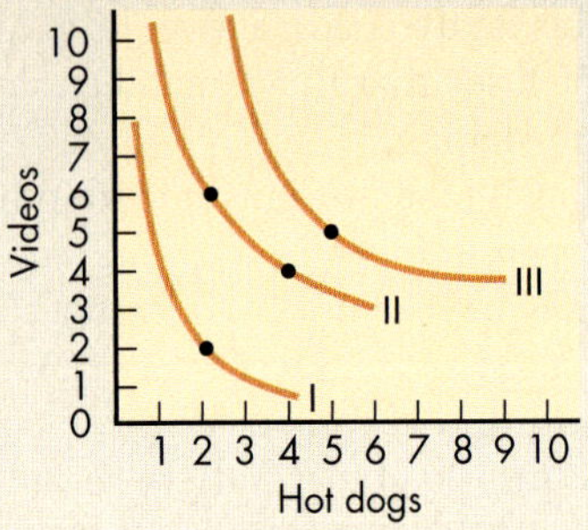

a. Given a choice, which budget constraint would Zachary prefer most? Least?
b. What is the marginal rate of substitution of hot dogs for videos at each of the combinations chosen with budget constraints *a*, *b*, and *c* in problem 1?

3. What would an indifference curve look like if the marginal rate of substitution were zero? If it were constant?
4. What might an indifference curve look like if the law of diminishing marginal utility did not hold?

PRODUCTION AND COST ANALYSIS I

9

Production is not the application of tools
to materials, but logic to work.

—*Peter Drucker*

After reading this chapter, you should be able to:

- Differentiate economic profit from accounting profit.
- Distinguish between long-run and short-run production.
- State the law of diminishing marginal productivity.
- Calculate fixed costs, variable costs, marginal costs, total costs, average fixed costs, average variable costs, and average total costs, given the appropriate information.
- Distinguish the various kinds of cost curves and describe the relationships among them.
- Explain why the marginal and average cost curves are U-shaped.
- Explain why the marginal cost curve always goes through the minimum point of an average cost curve.

The ability of market economies to supply material goods and services to members of their societies makes them the envy of many other societies and is one of the strongest arguments for using the market as a means of organizing society. Somehow markets are able to channel individuals' imagination, creativity, and drive into the production of material goods and services that other people want. They do this by giving people incentives to supply goods and services to the market.

Ultimately all supply comes from individuals. Individuals control the factors of production such as land, labor, and capital. Why do individuals supply these factors to the market? Because they want something in return. This means that industry's ability to supply goods is dependent on individuals' willingness to supply the factors of production they control. This connection became obvious in the formerly socialist countries in the late 1980s and early 1990s when consumer goods were often unavailable. People in those countries stopped working (supplying their labor). They reasoned: Why supply our labor if there's nothing to get in return?

The analysis of supply is more complicated than the analysis of demand. In the supply process, people first offer their factors of production to the market. Then the factors are transformed by firms, such as GM or IBM, into goods that consumers want. **Production** is the name given to that *transformation of factors into goods and services*.

To make it simple for you, I separate out the analysis of the supply of factors of production (considered in detail in later chapters) from the supply of produced goods. This allows us to assume that the prices of factors of production are constant, which simplifies the analysis of the supply of produced goods enormously. There's no problem with doing this as long as you remember that behind any produced good are individuals' factor supplies. Ultimately people, not firms, are responsible for supply.

Even with the analysis so simplified, there's still a lot to cover—so much, in fact, that we devote two chapters (this chapter and the next) to considering production, costs, and supply. In this chapter I introduce you to the production process and short-run cost analysis. Then, in the next chapter, I focus on long-run costs and how cost analysis is used in the real world.

THE ROLE OF THE FIRM

Web Note 9.1
Virtual Firms

With goods that already exist, like housing and labor, the law of supply is rather intuitive. Their supply to the market depends on people's opportunity costs of keeping them for themselves and of supplying them to the market. But many of the things we buy (such as VCRs, cars, and jackets) don't automatically exist; they must be produced. The supply of such goods depends on production.

Firms:
1. Organize factors of production,
2. produce goods and services, and/or
3. sell produced goods and services.

A key concept in production is the firm. A **firm** is *an economic institution that transforms factors of production into goods and services*. A firm (1) organizes factors of production; and/or (2) produces goods; and/or (3) sells produced goods to individuals, businesses, or government.

Which combination of activities a firm will undertake depends on the cost of undertaking each activity relative to the cost of subcontracting the work out to another firm. When the firm only organizes production, it is called a *virtual firm*. Virtual firms organize the factors of production and subcontract out all production. Let's consider an example—a "psychic superline" that provides super psychic advice to individuals. If it is a virtual firm, it hires individuals to act as psychics, an advertising company to convince gullible people to call in, a phone routing company to route incoming calls, and a billing company to bill callers (the telephone company does this for them). The firm's sole role is organization. While most firms are not totally virtual, more and more of the organizational structure of businesses is being separated from the production process. As cost structures change because of technological advances such as the Internet, an increasing number of well-known firms will likely concentrate on organizational instead of production activities.

More and more of the organizational structure of business is being separated from the production process.

THE FIRM AND THE MARKET

Firms replace the market with command and control.

The firm operates within a market, but, simultaneously, it is a negation of the market in the sense that it replaces the market with command and control. How an economy operates—which activities are organized through markets, and which activities are organized through firms—depends on *transactions costs* (costs of undertaking trades through the market) and the rent or command over resources that organizers can appropriate to themselves by organizing production in a certain way. Ronald Coase won a Nobel Prize in 1991 for pathbreaking work on the nature of the firm and transactions costs.

In Chapter 3 we discussed the types of firms that exist in real life. They include sole proprietorships, partnerships, corporations, for-profit firms, nonprofit firms, and cooperatives. These various firms are the production organizations that translate factors of production into consumer goods.

FIRMS MAXIMIZE PROFIT

The firm plays the same role in the theory of supply that the individual does in the theory of demand. The difference is that whereas individuals maximize utility, firms maximize profit. Profit is defined as follows:

Profit = *Total revenue* − *Total cost*

In accounting, total revenue equals total sales times price; if a firm sells 1,000 pairs of earrings at $5 each, its total revenue is $5,000. For an accountant, total costs are the

Value Added and the Calculation of Total Production

Applying the Tools

This book (like all economics textbooks) treats production as if it were a one-stage process—as if a single firm transformed a factor of production into a consumer good. Economists write like that to keep the analysis manageable. (Believe me, it's complicated enough.) But you should keep in mind that reality is more complicated. Most goods go through a variety of stages of production.

For example, consider the production of desks. One firm transforms raw materials into usable raw materials (iron ore into steel); another firm transforms usable raw materials into more usable inputs (steel into steel rods, bolts, and nuts); another firm transforms those inputs into desks, which it sells wholesale to a general distributor, which then sells them to a retailer, which sells them to consumers. Many goods go through five or six stages of production and distribution. As a result, if you added up all the sales of all the firms you would overstate how much total production was taking place.

To figure out how much total production is actually taking place, economists use the concept *value added*. Value added is the contribution that each stage of production makes to the final value of a good. A firm's value added is determined by subtracting from the firm's total output the cost of the inputs bought from other firms. For example, if a desk assembly firm spends $4,000 of its revenue on component parts and sells its output for $6,000, its value added is $2,000, or 33⅓ percent of its revenue.

When you add up all the stages of production, the value added of all the firms involved must equal 100 percent, and no more, of the total output. When I discuss "a firm's" production of a good in this book, to relate that discussion to reality, you should think of that firm as a composite firm consisting of all the firms contributing to the production and distribution of that product.

Why is it important to remember that there are various stages of production? Because it brings home to you how complicated producing a good is. If any one stage gets messed up, the good doesn't get to the consumer. Producing a better mousetrap isn't enough. The firm must also be able to get it out to consumers and let them know that it's a better mousetrap. The standard economic model doesn't bring home this point. But if you're ever planning to go into business for yourself, you'd better remember it. Many people's dreams of supplying a better product to the market have been squashed by this reality.

wages paid to labor, rent paid to owners of capital, interest paid to lenders, and actual payments to other factors of production. If the firm paid $2,000 to employees to make the earrings and $1,000 for the materials, total cost is $3,000.

In determining what to include in total revenue and total costs, accountants focus on such explicit revenues and explicit costs. That's because they must have quantifiable measures that go into a firm's income statement. For this reason, you can think of *accounting profit* as explicit revenue less explicit cost. The accounting profit for the earring firm is $2,000.

Economists have different measures of revenues and costs and hence have a different measure of profit. Economists include in revenue and costs both explicit and implicit costs and revenues. Their measure of profit is both explicit and implicit revenue less both explicit and implicit costs.

What are implicit costs and implicit revenue? Implicit costs include the opportunity costs of the factors of production provided by the owners of the business. Say that the owner of our earring firm could have earned $1,500 working elsewhere if he did not own the earring firm. The opportunity cost of working in his own business is $1,500. It is an implicit cost of doing business and would be included as a cost. For economists, **total cost** is *explicit payments to the factors of production plus the opportunity cost of the factors provided by the owners of the firm*. Total cost of the earring firm is $3,000 in explicit cost and $1,500 in implicit cost, or $4,500. Generally implicit costs must be estimated and are not directly measurable, which is why accountants do not include them.

Accounting focuses on explicit costs and revenues; economics focuses on both explicit and implicit costs and revenues.

Enron, Accounting Gimmicks, and the Theory of the Firm

Applying the Tools

Issues of accounting were much in the news in 2002 when Enron Corporation went into bankruptcy and its accounting practices were questioned. What Enron did was to use accounting gimmicks to record implicit revenue on its books while keeping implicit costs off its books, thereby inflating profits. (Its accounting firm, Arthur Andersen, should have disallowed the practice, but did not and was convicted for failing to do so.) To understand why Enron wanted to overstate profits requires us to go beyond the standard theory of the firm. Standard theory assumes that the owner of the firm is the person making the decisions, so he gets the profit he maximizes. It is economic profit that he wants to maximize; accounting, for him, is simply a way of figuring out what he is earning.

As discussed in Chapter 3, corporations do the great majority of business in the real world. In corporations owners of the business (whose interest is in economic profits) do not make decisions; instead corporate managers, whose compensation is often tied to accounting profits, not economic profits, do. This can give managers an incentive to overstate accounting profits, which is what Enron did. The result, in this case, was bankruptcy.

Implicit revenues include the increase in the value of assets. Say the earring firm owns a kiosk whose market value rises from \$10,000 to \$11,000. The economic concept of revenue would include the \$1,000 increase in the value of the kiosk as part of total revenue. For economists, **total revenue** is *the amount a firm receives for selling its product or service plus any increase in the value of the assets owned by the firm*. Total revenue of the earring firm is \$5,000 in explicit revenue plus \$1,000 in implicit revenue, or \$6,000. For economists,

Economic profit = *(Explicit and implicit revenue)* − *(Explicit and implicit cost)*

So in this case, economic profit is (\$5,000 + \$1,000) − (\$3,000 + \$1,500) = \$1,500. The difference really has to do with measurability. Implicit costs must be estimated, and the estimations can sometimes be inexact. General accounting rules do not permit such inexactness because it might allow firms to misstate their profit, something accounting rules are designed to avoid.

The Production Process

As I stated at the beginning of the chapter, supply is the key to the market's ability to provide the goods people want. Underlying supply is production; firms are important because they control the production process.

The Long Run and the Short Run

The production process is generally divided into a *long-run* planning decision, in which a firm chooses the least expensive method of producing from among all possible methods, and a *short-run* adjustment decision, in which a firm adjusts its long-run planning decision to reflect new information.

A long-run decision is a decision in which the firm can choose among all possible production techniques.

A short-run decision is a decision in which the firm is constrained in regard to what production decisions it can make.

In a **long-run decision** *a firm chooses among all possible production techniques*. This means that it can choose the size of the plant it wants, the type of machines it wants, and the location it wants. The firm has fewer options in a **short-run decision,** in which *the firm is constrained in regard to what production decisions it can make*.

The terms *long run* and *short run* do not necessarily refer to specific periods of time independent of the nature of the production process. They refer to the degree of flexibility the firm has in changing the level of output. In the long run, by definition, the firm can vary the inputs as much as it wants. In the short run some of the flexibility that existed in the long run no longer exists. In the short run some inputs are so costly to adjust that they are treated as fixed. *So in the long run all inputs are variable; in the short run some inputs are fixed.*

Production Tables and Production Functions

How a firm combines factors of production to produce goods and services can be presented in a **production table** *(a table showing the output resulting from various combinations of factors of production or inputs)*.

Real-world production tables are complicated. They often involve hundreds of inputs, hundreds of outputs, and millions of possible combinations of inputs and outputs. Studying these various combinations and determining which is best requires expertise and experience. Business schools devote entire courses to it (operations research and production analysis); engineering schools devote entire specialties to it (industrial engineering).

Studying the problems and answering the questions that surround production make up much of what a firm does: What combination of outputs should it produce? What combination of inputs should it use? What combination of techniques should it use? What new techniques should it explore? To answer these questions, the managers of a firm look at a production table.

Production tables are so complicated that in introductory economics we concentrate on short-run production analysis in which one of the factors is fixed. Doing so allows us to capture some important technical relationships of production without getting too tied up in numbers. The relevant part of a production table of earrings appears in Figure 9-1(c). In it the number of the assumed fixed inputs (machines) has already been determined. Columns 1 and 2 of the table tell us how output of earrings varies as the variable input (the number of workers) changes. For example, you can see that with 3 workers the firm can produce 17 pairs of earrings. Column 3 tells us workers' **marginal product** *(the additional output that will be forthcoming from an additional worker, other inputs constant)*. Column 4 tells us workers' **average product** *(output per worker)*.

The marginal product is the additional output forthcoming from an additional input, other inputs constant; the average product is the total output divided by the quantity of the input.

It is important to distinguish marginal product from average product. Workers' average product is the total output divided by the number of workers. For example, let's consider the case of 5 workers. Total output is 28, so average product is 5.6 (28 divided by 5). To find the marginal product we must ask how much additional output will be forthcoming if we change the number of workers. For example, if we change from 4 to 5 workers, the additional worker's marginal product will be 5; if we change from 5 to 6, the additional worker's marginal product will be 3. That's why the marginal products are written between each level of output.

The information in a production table is often summarized in a production function. A **production function** is *the relationship between the inputs (factors of production) and outputs*. Specifically, the production function tells the maximum amount of output that can be derived from a given number of inputs. Figure 9-1(a) is the production function that displays the information in the production table in Figure 9-1(c). The number of workers is on the horizontal axis and the output of earrings is on the vertical axis.

The Law of Diminishing Marginal Productivity

Figure 9-1(b) graphs the workers' average and marginal productivities from the production function in Figure 9-1(a). (Alternatively you can determine those graphs by plotting columns 3 and 4 from the table in Figure 9-1(c).) Notice that both marginal and average productivities are initially increasing, but that eventually they both

Figure 9-1 (a, b, and c) A Production Table and Production Function

The production function in (a) is a graph of the production table in (c). Its shape reflects the underlying production technology. The graph in (b) shows the marginal and average product. Notice that when marginal product is increasing, the production function is bowed upward; when marginal product is decreasing, the production function is bowed downward, and when marginal product is zero, the production function is at its highest point. Firms are interested in producing where both average product and marginal product are positive and falling, which starts at 4 workers and ends at 7.5 workers.

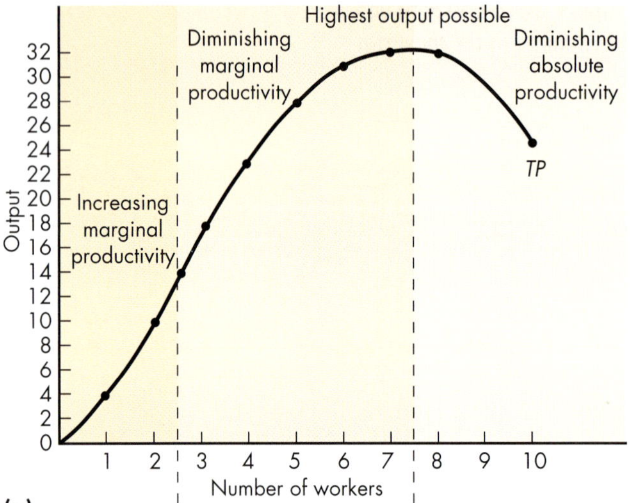

(a)

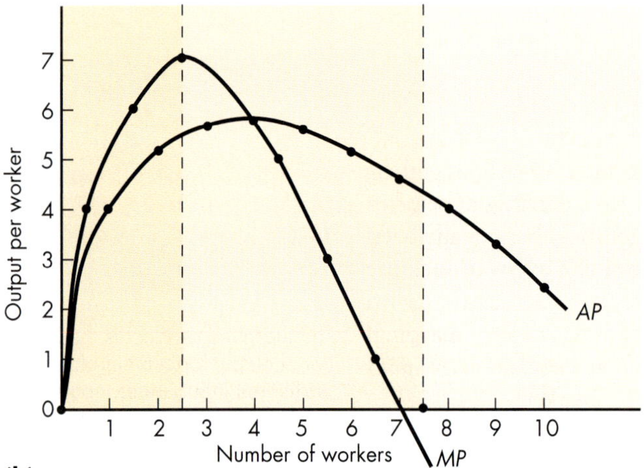

(b)

Number of workers	Total output	Marginal product (change in total output)	Average product (total product/ number of workers)	
1	4	4	4	Increasing marginal productivity
2	10	6	5	
3	17	7	5.7	
4	23	6	5.8	Diminishing marginal productivity
5	28	5	5.6	
6	31	3	5.2	
7	32	1	4.6	
8	32	0	4.0	Diminishing absolute productivity
9	30	−2	3.3	
10	25	−5	2.5	

(c)

decrease. Between 7 and 8 workers, the marginal productivity of workers actually becomes negative.

Q-1 What are the normal shapes of marginal productivity and average productivity curves?

This means that initially this production function exhibits increasing marginal productivity and then it exhibits *diminishing marginal productivity*. Eventually it exhibits negative marginal productivity.

The same information can be gathered from Figure 9-1(a), but it's a bit harder to interpret.[1] Notice that initially the production function is bowed upward. Where it's bowed upward there is increasing marginal productivity, as you can see if you extend a line down to Figure 9-1(b). Then, between 2.5 and 7.5 workers, the production function is bowed downward but is still rising. In this range there's diminishing marginal productivity, as you can see by extending a line down to Figure 9-1(b). Finally marginal productivity is negative.

[1]Technically the marginal productivity curve is a graph of the slope of the total product curve.

The most important area of these relationships is the area of diminishing marginal productivity and falling average product (between 4 and 7.5 workers). Why? Because that's the most likely area for a firm to operate in. For example, if it's in the first range and marginal productivity is increasing, a firm can increase its existing workers' output by hiring more workers; it will have a strong incentive to do so and get out of that range. Similarly, if hiring an additional worker actually cuts total output (as it does when marginal productivity is negative), the firm would be crazy to hire that worker. So it stays out of that range.

Q-2 Firms are likely to operate on what portion of the marginal productivity curve?

This range of the relationship between fixed and variable inputs is so important that economists have formulated a law that describes what happens in production processes when firms reach this range—when more and more of one input is added to a fixed amount of another input. The **law of diminishing marginal productivity** states that *as more and more of a variable input is added to an existing fixed input, eventually the additional output one gets from that additional input is going to fall.*

The law of diminishing marginal productivity states that as more and more of a variable input is added to an existing fixed input, after some point the additional output one gets from the additional input will fall.

As I stated in Chapter 2, the law of diminishing marginal productivity is sometimes called the *flowerpot law* because if it didn't hold true, the world's entire food supply could be grown in one flowerpot. In the absence of diminishing marginal productivity, we could take a flowerpot and keep adding seeds to it, getting more and more food per seed until we had enough to feed the world. In reality, however, a given flowerpot is capable of producing only so much food no matter how many seeds we add to it. At some point, as we add more and more seeds, each additional seed will produce less food than did the seed before it. Eventually the pot reaches a stage of diminishing absolute productivity, in which the total output, not simply the output per unit of input, decreases as inputs are increased.

The Costs of Production

In any given firm, owners and managers probably discuss costs far more than anything else. Invariably costs are too high and the firm is trying to figure out ways to lower them. But the concept *costs* is ambiguous; there are many different types of costs and it's important to know what they are. Let's consider some of the most important categories of costs in reference to Table 9-1, which shows costs associated with making between 3 and 32 pairs of earrings.

Fixed Costs, Variable Costs, and Total Costs

Fixed costs are *costs that are spent and cannot be changed in the period of time under consideration.* There are no fixed costs in the long run since all inputs are variable and hence their costs are variable. In the short run, however, a number of costs will be fixed. For example, say you make earrings. You buy a machine for working with silver, but suddenly there's no demand for silver earrings. Assuming that machine can't be modified and used for other purposes, the money you spent on it is a fixed cost. So within the model, all fixed costs are assumed to be sunk costs.

Web Note 9.2
What's Fixed? What's Variable?

Fixed costs are shown in column 2 of Table 9-1. Notice that fixed costs remain the same ($50) regardless of the level of production. As you can see, it doesn't matter whether output is 15 or 20; fixed costs are always $50.

Besides buying the machine, the silversmith must also hire workers. These workers are the earring firm's **variable costs**—*costs that change as output changes.* The earring firm's variable costs are shown in column 3. Notice that as output increases, variable costs increase. For example, when the firm produces 10 pairs of earrings, variable costs are $108; when it produces 16, variable costs rise to $150.

Table 9-1 The Cost of Producing Earrings

1 Output	2 Fixed Costs (*FC*)	3 Variable Costs (*VC*)	4 Total Costs (*TC*) (*FC* + *VC*)	5 Marginal Costs (*MC*) (Change in total costs/ Change in output)	6 Average Fixed Costs (*AFC*) (*FC*/Output)	7 Average Variable Costs (*AVC*) (*VC*/Output)	8 Average Total Costs (*ATC*) (*AFC* + *AVC*)
3	$50	$ 38	$ 88	$12	$16.67	$12.66	$29.33
4	50	50	100		12.50	12.50	25.00
9	50	100	150	8	5.56	11.11	16.67
10	50	108	158		5.00	10.80	15.80
16	50	150	200	7	3.13	9.38	12.50
17	50	157	207		2.94	9.24	12.18
22	50	200	250	10	2.27	9.09	11.36
23	50	210	260		2.17	9.13	11.30
27	50	255	305	15	1.85	9.44	11.30
28	50	270	320		1.79	9.64	11.43
32	50	400	450		1.56	12.50	14.06

All costs are either fixed or variable in the standard model, so the *total cost* is the sum of the fixed and variable costs:

TC = FC + VC

$$TC = FC + VC$$

The earring firm's total costs are presented in column 4. Each entry in column 4 is the sum of the entries in columns 2 and 3 in the same row. For example, to produce 16 pairs of earrings, fixed costs are $50 and variable costs are $150, so total cost is $200.

AVERAGE TOTAL COST, AVERAGE FIXED COST, AND AVERAGE VARIABLE COST

Total cost, fixed cost, and variable cost are important, but much of a firm's discussion is about average cost. So the next distinction we want to make is between total cost and average cost. To arrive at the earring firm's average cost, we simply divide the total amount of whatever cost we're talking about by the quantity produced. Each of the three costs we've discussed has a corresponding average cost.

Average cost equals total cost divided by quantity.

For example, **average total cost** (often called average cost) equals *total cost divided by the quantity produced.* Thus:

$$ATC = TC/Q$$

Average fixed cost equals *fixed cost divided by quantity produced:*

$$AFC = FC/Q$$

Q-3 If total costs are 400, fixed costs are 0, and output is 10, what are average variable costs?

Average variable cost equals *variable cost divided by quantity produced:*

$$AVC = VC/Q$$

Average fixed cost and average variable cost are shown in columns 6 and 7 of Table 9-1. The most important average cost concept, average total cost, is shown in column 8. Average total cost can also be thought of as the sum of average fixed cost and average variable cost:

$$ATC = AFC + AVC$$

As you can see, the average total cost of producing 16 pairs of earrings is $12.50. It can be calculated by dividing total cost ($200) by output (16).

Marginal Cost

All these costs are important to our earring firm, but they are not the most important cost it considers when deciding how many pairs of earrings to produce. That distinction goes to marginal cost, which appears in column 5.[2] **Marginal cost** is *the increase (decrease) in total cost from increasing (or decreasing) the level of output by one unit*. Let's find marginal cost by considering what happens if our earring firm increases production by one unit—from 9 to 10. Looking again at Table 9-1, we see that the total cost rises from $150 to $158. In this case the marginal cost of producing the 10th unit is $8.

Graphing Cost Curves

Let's say that the owner of the earring firm is a visually oriented person who asks you (an economic consultant) to show her what all those numbers in Table 9-1 mean. To do so, you first draw a graph, putting quantity on the horizontal axis and a dollar measure of various costs on the vertical axis.

Total Cost Curves

Figure 9-2(a) graphs the total cost, total fixed cost, and total variable costs of all the levels of output given in Table 9-1.[3] The total cost curve is determined by plotting the entries in column 1 and the corresponding entries in column 4. For example, point *L* corresponds to a quantity of 10 and a total cost of $158. Notice that the curve is upward-sloping: Increasing output increases total cost.

The total fixed cost curve is determined by plotting column 1 and column 2 on the graph. The total variable cost curve is determined by plotting column 1 and column 3.

As you can see, the total variable cost curve has the same shape as the total cost curve: Increasing output increases variable cost. This isn't surprising, since the total cost curve is the vertical summation of total fixed cost and total variable cost. For example, at output 10, total fixed cost equals $50 (point M); total variable cost equals $108 (point O); and total cost equals $158 (point *L*).

Average and Marginal Cost Curves

Figure 9-2(b) presents the average fixed cost curve, average total cost curve (or average cost curve, as it's generally called), average variable cost curve, and marginal cost curve associated with the cost figures in Table 9-1. Each point on the four curves represents a combination of two corresponding entries in Table 9-1. Points on the average variable cost curve are determined by plotting the entries in column 1 and the corresponding entries in column 7. Points on the average fixed cost curve are determined by entries in column 1 and the corresponding entries in column 6. Points on the average total cost curve are determined by entries in column 1 and the corresponding entries in column 8. Finally, the marginal cost curve is determined by plotting the entries in column 1 and the corresponding entries in column 5. As was the case with the total cost curves, all

The marginal cost curve goes through the minimum point of the average total cost curve and average variable cost curve; each of these curves is U-shaped. The average fixed cost curve slopes down continuously.

[2]Since only selected output levels are shown, not all entries have marginal costs. For a marginal cost to exist, there must be a marginal change, a change by only one unit.

[3]To keep the presentation simple, we focus only on the most important part of the total cost curve, that part that follows the simplest rules. Other areas of the total cost curve can be bowed downward rather than bowed upward.

Figure 9-2 (a and b) Total and per Unit Output Cost Curves
Total fixed costs, shown in (**a**), are always constant; they don't change with output. All other total costs increase with output. As output gets high, the rate of increase has a tendency to increase. The average fixed cost curve shown in (**b**), is downward-sloping; the average variable cost curve and average total cost curve are U-shaped. The U-shaped *MC* curve goes through the minimum points of the *AVC* and *ATC* curves. (The *AFC* curve is often not drawn since *AFC* is also represented by the distance between the *AVC* and *ATC*.)

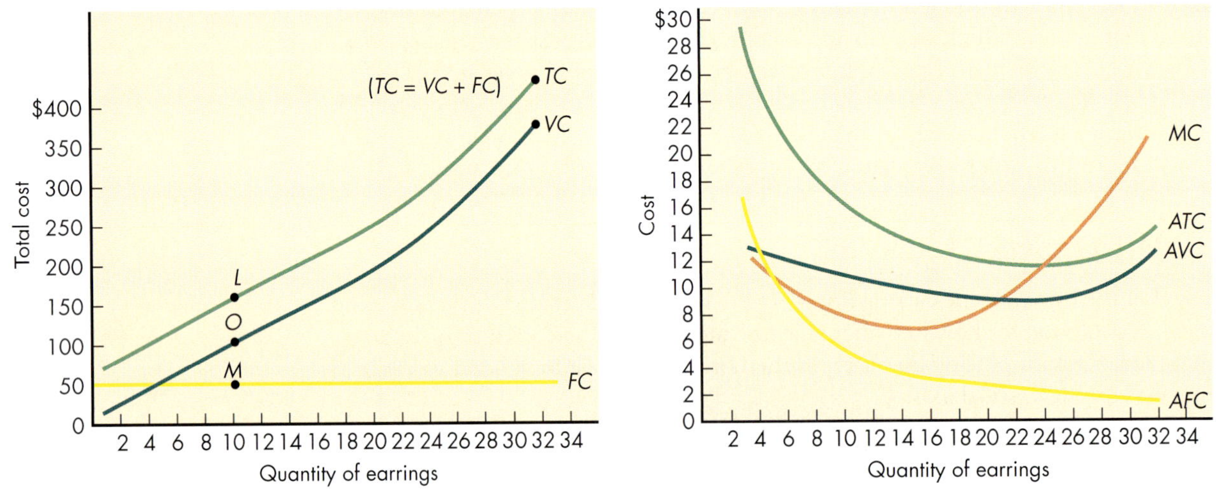

(a) Total cost curves **(b) Per unit output cost curves**

the firm's owner need do is look at this graph to find the various costs associated with different levels of output.

One reason the graphical visualization of cost curves is important is that the graphs of the curves give us a good sense of what happens to costs as we change output.

Downward-Sloping Shape of the Average Fixed Cost Curve

Let's start our consideration with average fixed cost. Average fixed cost is decreasing throughout. The average fixed cost curve looks like a child's slide: It starts out with a steep decline; then it becomes flatter and flatter. What this tells us about production is straightforward: As output increases, the same fixed cost can be spread over a wider range of output, so average fixed cost falls. Average fixed cost initially falls quickly but then falls more and more slowly. As the denominator gets bigger while the numerator stays the same, the increase has a smaller and smaller effect.

The U Shape of the Average and Marginal Cost Curves

Q-4 Draw a graph of both the marginal cost curve and the average cost curve.

Let's now move on to the average and marginal cost curves. Why do they have the shapes they do? Or, expressed another way, how does our analysis of production relate to our analysis of costs? You may have already gotten an idea of how production and costs relate if you remembered Figure 9-1 and recognized the output numbers that we presented there were similar output numbers to those that we used in the cost analysis. Cost analysis is simply another way of considering production analysis. The laws governing costs are the same laws governing productivity that we just saw in our consideration of production.

In the short run, output can be raised only by increasing the variable input. But as more and more of a variable input is added to a fixed input, the law of diminishing marginal productivity enters in. Marginal and average productivities fall. The key insight here is that when marginal productivity falls, marginal cost must rise, and when average productivity of the variable input falls, average variable cost must rise. So to say that productivity falls is equivalent to saying that cost rises.

As more and more of a variable input is added to a fixed input, the law of diminishing marginal productivity causes marginal and average productivities to fall. As these fall, marginal and average costs rise.

It follows that if eventually the law of diminishing marginal productivity holds true, then eventually both the marginal cost curve and the average cost curve must be upward-sloping. And, indeed, in our examples they are. It's also generally held that at low levels of production, marginal and average productivities are increasing. This means that marginal cost and average variable cost are initially falling. If they're falling initially and rising eventually, at some point they must be neither rising nor falling. This means that both the marginal cost curve and the average variable cost curve are U-shaped.

As you can see in Figure 9-2(b), the average total cost curve has the same general U shape as the average variable cost curve. It has the same U shape because it is the vertical summation of the average fixed cost curve and the average variable cost curve. Its minimum, however, is to the right of the minimum of the average variable cost curve. We'll discuss why after we cover the shape of the average variable cost curve.

Q.5 What determines the distance between the average total cost and the average variable cost?

Average total cost initially falls faster and then rises more slowly than average variable cost. If we increased output enormously, the average variable cost curve and the average total cost curve would almost meet. Average total cost is of key importance to the firm's owner. She wants to keep it low.

Q.6 If you increase output enormously, what two cost curves would almost meet?

The Relationship between the Marginal Productivity and Marginal Cost Curves

Let's now consider the relationship between marginal product and marginal cost. In Figure 9-3(a), I draw a marginal cost curve and average variable cost curve. Notice their U shape. Initially costs are falling. Then there's some minimum point. After that, costs are rising.

In Figure 9-3(b), I graph the average and marginal productivity curves similar to those that I presented in Figure 9-1(b), although this time I relate average and marginal productivities to output, rather than to the number of workers. This allows us to relate output per worker and output. Say, for example that we know that the average product of 2 workers is 5, and that 2 workers can produce an output of 10. This means that when output is 10, the workers' average productivity is 5. By continuing this reasoning we can construct the curves. Point A corresponds to an output of 10 and average productivity of 5.

If $MP > AP$, then AP is rising.
If $MP < AP$, then AP is falling.

Now let's compare the graphs in Figure 9-3 (a and b). If you look at the two graphs carefully, you'll see that one is simply the mirror image of the other. The minimum point of the average variable cost curve (output = 21) is the same level of output as the maximum point of the average productivity curve; the minimum point of the marginal cost curve (output = 12) is at the same level of output as the maximum point on the marginal productivity curve. When the productivity curves are falling, the corresponding cost curves are rising. Why is that the case? Because as productivity falls, costs per unit increase; and as productivity increases, costs per unit decrease.

Q.7 When the marginal cost equals the minimum point of the average variable cost, what is true about the average productivity and marginal productivity of workers?

When the productivity curves are falling, the corresponding cost curves are rising.

The Relationship between the Marginal Cost and Average Cost Curves

Now that we've considered the shapes of each cost curve, let's consider some of the important relationships among them—specifically the relationships between the marginal

Web Note 9.3
Marginal Costs in the Information Economy

Figure 9-3 (a and b) The Relationship between Productivity and Costs

The shapes of the cost curves are mirror-image reflections of the shapes of the corresponding productivity curves. (The corresponding productivity curve is an implicit function in which marginal productivity is related to output rather than inputs. At each output there is an implicit number of workers who would supply that output.) When one is increasing, the other is decreasing; when one is at a minimum, the other is at a maximum.

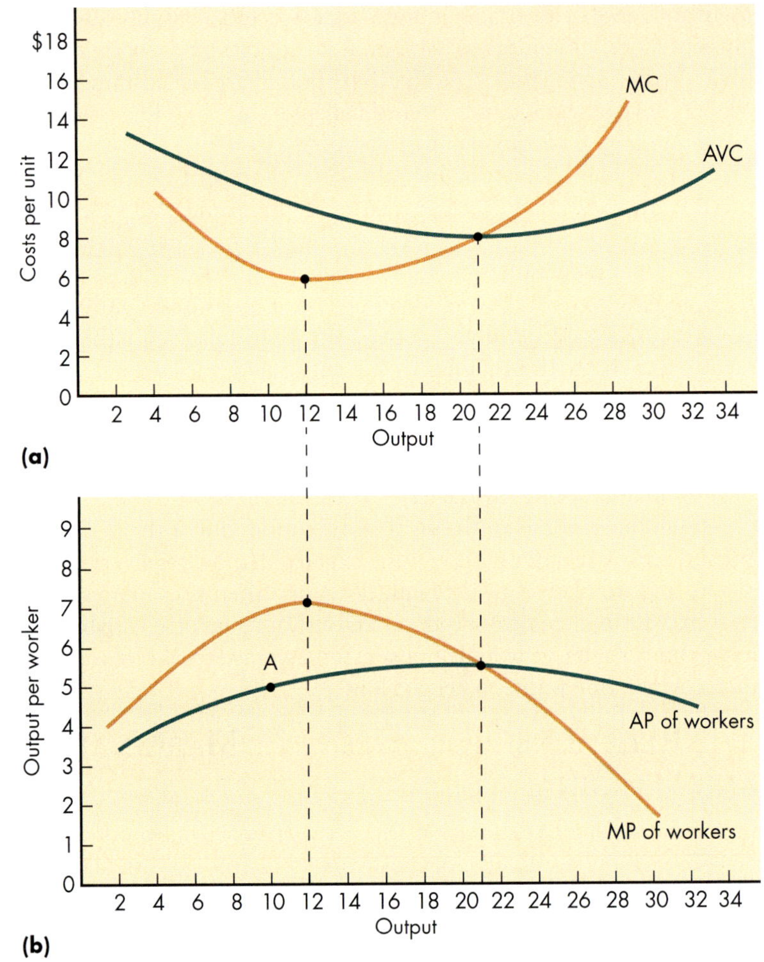

cost curve on the one hand and the average variable cost and average total cost curves on the other. These relationships are shown graphically for a different production process in Figure 9-4.

Let's first look at the relationship between marginal cost and average total cost. In areas A and B at output below 5, even though marginal cost is rising, average total cost is falling. Why? Because in areas A and B the marginal cost curve is below the average total cost curve. At point B, where average total cost is at its lowest, the marginal cost curve intersects the average total cost curve. In area C, above output 5, where average total cost is rising, the marginal cost curve is above the *ATC* curve.

When marginal cost exceeds average cost, average cost must be rising. When marginal cost is less than average cost, average cost must be falling. This relationship explains why marginal cost curves always intersect the average cost curve at the minimum of the average cost curve.

The positioning of the marginal cost curve is not happenstance. The position of marginal cost relative to average total cost tells us whether average total cost is rising or falling.

If MC > *ATC*, then *ATC* is rising.

If MC = *ATC*, then *ATC* is at its low point.

If MC < *ATC*, then *ATC* is falling.

To understand why this is, think of it in terms of your grade point average. If you have a B average and you get a C on the next test (that is, your marginal grade is a C),

Review of Costs

Knowing the Tools

We've covered a lot of costs and cost curves quickly, so a review is in order. First, let's list the cost concepts and their definitions.

1. Marginal cost: the additional cost resulting from a one-unit increase in output.
2. Total cost: the sum of all costs.
3. Average total cost: total cost divided by total output (*TC/Q*).
4. Fixed cost: cost that is already spent and cannot be recovered. (It exists only in the short run.)
5. Average fixed cost: fixed cost divided by total output (*FC/Q*).
6. Variable cost: cost of variable inputs. Variable cost does not include fixed cost.
7. Average variable cost: variable cost divided by total output (*VC/Q*).

Each of these costs can be represented by a curve. A number of these curves have specific relationships to the other cost curves.

1. *MC: MC* intersects *AVC* and *ATC* at their minimum points.
2. If *MC* > *AVC*, then *AVC* is rising. If *MC* < *AVC*, then *AVC* is falling.
3. If *MC* > *ATC*, then *ATC* is rising. If *MC* < *ATC*, then *ATC* is falling.
4. *ATC:* a U-shaped curve higher than the *AVC*.
5. *AVC:* a U-shaped curve lower than the *ATC*, with the minimum point slightly to the left.
6. *AFC:* a downward-sloping curve that starts high, initially decreases rapidly, and then decreases slowly.

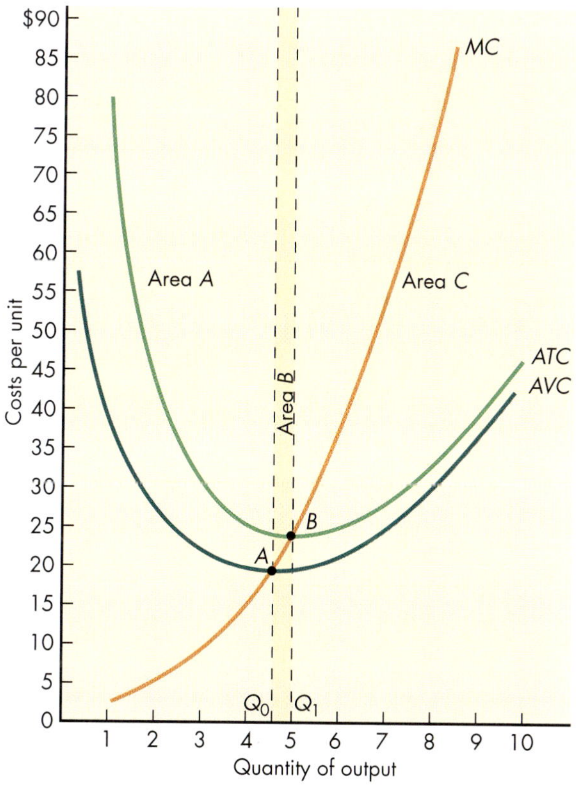

Figure 9-4 The Relationship of Marginal Cost Curve to Average Variable Cost and Average Total Cost Curves
The marginal cost curve goes through the minimum point of both the average variable cost curve and the average total cost curve. Thus, there is a small range where average total costs are falling and average variable costs are rising.

Q-8 If marginal costs are increasing, what is happening to average total costs?

Q-9 If marginal costs are decreasing, what must be happening to average variable costs?

Q-10 Why does the marginal cost curve intersect the average total cost curve at the minimum point?

Dr. Seuss books are often more interesting than economics books. From HORTON HATCHES THE EGG by Dr. Seuss, TM & Copyright © by Dr. Seuss Enterprises, L. P. 1940. Renewed 1968. Used by permission of Random House Children's Books, a Division of Random House, Inc.

your grade point average will fall below a B. Your marginal grade is below your average grade, so your average grade is falling. If you get a C+ on the next exam (that is, your marginal grade is a C+), *even though your marginal grade has risen from a C to a C+*, your grade point average will fall. Why? Because your marginal grade is still below your average grade. To make sure you understand the concept, explain the next two cases:

1. If your marginal grade is above your average grade, your average grade will rise.
2. If your marginal grade and average grade are equal, the average grade will remain unchanged.

Marginal and average reflect a general relationship that also holds for marginal cost and average variable cost.

If MC > AVC, then AVC is rising.

If MC = AVC, then AVC is at its low point.

If MC < AVC, then AVC is falling.

This relationship is best seen in area *B* of Figure 9-4, when output is between Q_0 and Q_1. In this area the marginal cost curve is above the average variable cost curve, so average variable cost is rising; but the MC curve is below the average total cost curve, so average total cost is falling.

The intuitive explanation for what is represented in this area is that average total cost includes average variable cost, but it also includes average fixed cost, which is falling. As long as short-run marginal cost is only slightly above average variable cost, the average total cost will continue to fall. Put another way: Once marginal cost is above average variable cost, as long as average variable cost doesn't rise by more than average fixed cost falls, average total cost will still fall.

Intermission

At this point I'm going to cut off the chapter, not because we're finished with the subject, but because there's only so much that anyone can absorb in one chapter. It's time for a break.

Those of you with significant others, go out and do something significant. Those of you with parents bearing the cost of this education, give them a call and tell them that you appreciate their expenditure on your education. Think of the opportunity cost of that education to them; it's not peanuts. Those of you who are married should go out and give your spouse a big kiss; tell him or her that the opportunity cost of being away for another minute was so high that you couldn't control yourself. Those of you with kids, go out and read them a Dr. Seuss book. (My favorite is about Horton.) Let's face it—Seuss is a better writer than I, and if you've been conscientious about this course, you may not have paid your kids enough attention. We'll return to the grind in the next chapter.

Summary

- Accounting profit is explicit revenue less explicit cost. Economists include implicit revenue and cost in their determination of profit.
- Implicit revenue includes the increases in the value of assets owned by the firm. Implicit costs include opportunity cost of time and capital provided by the owners of the firm.

- In the long run a firm can choose among all possible production techniques; in the short run it is constrained in its choices.
- The law of diminishing marginal productivity states that as more and more of a variable input is added to a fixed input, the additional output the firm gets will eventually be decreasing.
- Costs are generally divided into fixed costs, variable costs, and total costs.
- $TC = FC + VC$; MC = change in TC; $AFC = FC/Q$; $AVC = VC/Q$; $ATC = AFC + AVC$.
- The average variable cost curve and marginal cost curve are mirror images of the average product curve and the marginal product curve, respectively.
- The law of diminishing marginal productivity causes marginal and average costs to rise.
- If $MC > ATC$, then ATC is rising.
  If $MC = ATC$, then ATC is constant.
  If $MC < ATC$, then ATC is falling.
- The marginal cost curve goes through the minimum points of the average variable cost curve and average total cost curve.

Key Terms

average fixed cost *(210)*
average product *(207)*
average total cost *(210)*
average variable cost *(210)*
economic profit *(206)*
firm *(204)*
fixed costs *(209)*
law of diminishing marginal productivity *(209)*
long-run decision *(206)*
marginal cost *(211)*
marginal product *(207)*
production *(203)*
production function *(207)*
production table *(207)*
profit *(204)*
short-run decision *(206)*
total cost *(205)*
total revenue *(206)*
variable costs *(209)*

Questions for Thought and Review

1. What costs and revenues do economists include when calculating profit that accountants don't include? Give an example of each.
2. "There is no long run; there are only short and shorter runs." Evaluate that statement.
3. What is the difference between marginal product and average product?
4. If average product is falling, what is happening to short-run average variable cost?
5. If marginal cost is increasing, what do we know about average cost?
6. If average productivity falls, will marginal cost necessarily rise? How about average cost?
7. Say that neither labor nor machines are fixed but that there is a 50 percent quick-order premium paid to both workers and machines for delivery of them in the short run. Once you buy them, they cannot be returned, however. What do your short-run marginal cost and short-run average total cost curves look like?
8. If machines are variable and labor fixed, how will the general shapes of the short-run average cost curve and marginal cost curve change?
9. If you increase production to an infinitely large level, the average variable cost and the average total cost will merge. Why?
10. Explain whether the following statements are true or false: Supplying labor depends on opportunity costs because labor already exists. Supplying goods that need to be produced does not depend on opportunity costs since they do not already exist.
11. Explain how studying for an exam is subject to the law of diminishing marginal productivity.
12. Labor costs are 17.5 percent of revenue per vehicle for General Motors. In union negotiations in the late 1990s, GM attempted to cut its workforce to increase productivity. Together with the reductions they expected in jobs, GM officials hoped to make its North American operations fully competitive with its U.S. and Japanese rivals on total costs. Why are productivity gains so important to GM?
13. It is obvious that all for-profit businesses in the United States will maximize profit. True or false? Why? (Requires reading "Applying the Tools: Enron, Accounting Gimmicks, and the Theory of the Firm")

PROBLEMS AND EXERCISES

1. Peggy-Sue's cookies are the best in the world, or so I hear. She has been offered a job by Cookie Monster, Inc., to come to work for them at $125,000 per year. Currently, she is producing her own cookies, and she has revenues of $260,000 per year. Her costs are $40,000 for labor, $10,000 for rent, $35,000 for ingredients, and $5,000 for utilities. She has $100,000 of her own money invested in the operation, which, if she leaves, can be sold for $40,000 that she can invest at 10 percent per year.
   a. Calculate her accounting and economic profits.
   b. Advise her as to what she should do.
2. Economan has been infected by the free enterprise bug. He sets up a firm on extraterrestrial affairs. The rent of the building is $4,000, the cost of the two secretaries is $40,000, and the cost of electricity and gas comes to $5,000. There's a great demand for his information, and his total revenue amounts to $100,000. By working in the firm, though, Economan forfeits the $50,000 he could earn by working for the Friendly Space Agency and the $4,000 he could have earned as interest had he saved his funds instead of putting them in this business. Is he making a profit or loss by an accountant's definitions of profit and loss? How about by an economist's definition?
3. Find and graph the *TC*, *AFC*, *AVC*, *AC*, and MC from the following table.

Units	*FC*	*VC*
0	$100	$ 0
1	100	40
2	100	60
3	100	70
4	100	85
5	100	130

4. An economic consultant is presented with the following total product table and asked to derive a table for average variable costs. The price of labor is $15 per hour.

Labor	*TP*
1	5
2	15
3	30
4	36
5	40

   a. Help him do so.
   b. Show that the graph of the average productivity curve and average variable cost curve are mirror images of each other.
   c. Show the marginal productivity curve for labor inputs between 1 and 5.
   d. Show that the marginal productivity curve and marginal cost curve are mirror images of each other.
5. A firm has fixed costs of $100 and variable costs of the following:

Output	1	2	3	4	5	6	7	8	9
Variable costs	$35	75	110	140	175	215	260	315	390

   a. Graph the *AFC*, *ATC*, *AVC*, and MC curves.
   b. Explain the relationship between the MC curve and the two average cost curves.
   c. Say fixed costs dropped to $50. Graph the new *AFC*, *ATC*, *AVC*, and MC curves.
   d. Which curves shifted in *c*? Why?
6. Say that a firm has fixed costs of $100 and constant average variable costs of $25.
   a. Graph the *AFC*, *ATC*, *AVC*, and MC curves.
   b. Explain why the curves have the shapes they do.
   c. What law is not operative for this firm?
   d. Say that instead of remaining a constant $25, average variable costs increase by $5 for each unit, so that the cost of 1 is $25, the cost of 2 is $30, the cost of 3 is $35, and so on. Graph the *AFC*, *ATC*, *AVC*, and MC curves associated with these costs.
   e. Explain how costs would have to increase in *d* in order for the curves to have the "normal" shapes of the curves presented in the text.
7. Explain how each of the following will affect the average fixed cost, average variable cost, average total cost, and marginal cost curves faced by a steel manufacturer:
   a. New union agreement increases hourly pay.
   b. Local government imposes an annual lump-sum tax per plant.
   c. Federal government imposes a "stack tax" on emission of air pollutants by steel mills.
   d. New steel-making technology increases productivity of every worker.

Web Questions

1. Go to the Avis Rent A Car, Inc., home page at www.avis.com, and find out how much it costs to rent a car for a week, driving from your city to a city in another state.
   a. Fill in the following cost table:

Miles	Total Cost	Marginal Cost	Average Fixed Cost	Average Variable Cost
0	_____	_____	_____	_____
500	_____	_____	_____	_____
1,000	_____	_____	_____	_____
1,500	_____	_____	_____	_____
2,500	_____	_____	_____	_____

   b. How does average fixed cost change as total number of miles driven increases?
   c. How does marginal cost change as total number of miles driven increases?
2. Go to www.ers.usda.gov. Click on the "data" button, look for cost data on corn, and answer the following questions:
   a. What is the cost of producing an acre of corn?
   b. State two major components of the variable (operating) costs of corn production.
   c. State two major components of fixed (allocated overhead) costs of corn production.
   d. What price of corn was needed to cover operating costs?
   e. What price of corn was needed to cover corn's total operating costs?

Answers to Margin Questions

1. Normally the marginal productivity curve and average productivity curve are both inverted U shapes. *(208)*
2. Firms are likely to operate on the downward-sloping portion of the marginal productivity curve because on the upward-sloping portion, firms could increase workers' output by hiring more workers. It will continue to hire more workers at least to the point where diminishing marginal productivity sets in. *(209)*
3. Average variable costs would be 40. *(210)*
4. As you can see in the graph, both these curves are U-shaped and the marginal cost curve goes through the average cost curve at the minimum point of the average cost curve. *(212)*

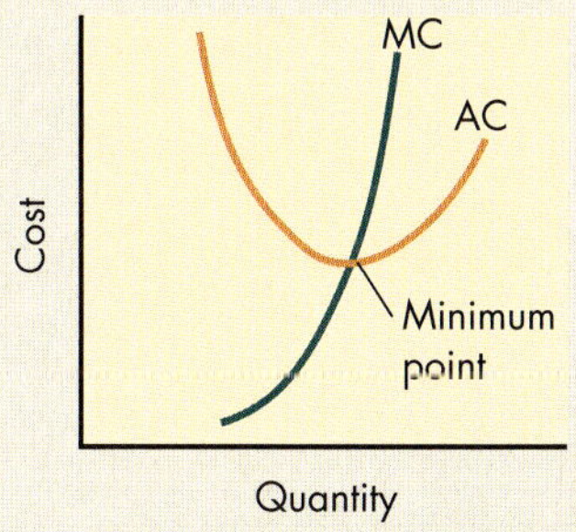

5. The distance between the average total cost and the average variable cost is determined by the average fixed cost at that quantity. As quantity increases, the average fixed cost decreases, so the two curves get closer and closer together. *(213)*
6. As output increases, the average total costs and average variable costs come closer and closer together. *(213)*
7. Since the average productivity and marginal productivity of workers are the mirror images of average costs and marginal costs, and when the marginal costs and average costs intersect the two are equal, it follows that the average productivity and marginal productivity of workers must be equal at that point. *(213)*
8. It is impossible to say what is happening to average total costs on the basis of what is happening to marginal costs. It is the magnitude of marginal costs relative to average total costs that is important. *(216)*
9. It is impossible to say because it is the magnitude of marginal cost relative to average variable cost that determines what is happening to average variable cost. *(216)*
10. The marginal cost curve intersects the average total cost curve at the minimum point because once the marginal cost exceeds average total costs, the average total costs must necessarily begin to rise, and vice versa. *(216)*

10 PRODUCTION AND COST ANALYSIS II

After reading this chapter, you should be able to:

- Distinguish technical efficiency from economic efficiency.
- Explain how economies and diseconomies of scale influence the shape of long-run cost curves.
- State the envelope relationship between short-run cost curves and long-run cost curves.
- Explain the role of the entrepreneur in translating cost of production to supply.
- Discuss some of the problems of using cost analysis in the real world.

Economic efficiency consists of making things that are worth more than they cost.

—*J. M. Clark*

Welcome back. I hope you've reestablished your relationship with the real world and are ready to return, with renewed vigor, to the world of economics. When we took our intermission last chapter, we had worked our way through the various short-run costs. That short run is a time period in which some inputs are fixed. In the first part of this chapter we consider firms' long-run decisions and the determinants of the long-run cost curves. Then in the second part we'll talk about applying cost analysis to the real world.

MAKING LONG-RUN PRODUCTION DECISIONS

Firms have many more options in the long run than they do in the short run. They can change any input they want. Plant size is not given; neither is the technology available given.

To make their long-run decisions, firms look at the costs of the various inputs and the technologies available for combining those inputs, and then decide which combination offers the lowest cost.

Say you're opening a hamburger stand. One decision you'll have to make is what type of stove to buy. You'll quickly discover that many different types are available. Some use more gas than others but cost less to buy; some are electric; some are self-cleaning and hence use less labor; some are big; some are little; some use microwaves; some use convection. Some have long-term guarantees; some have no guarantees. Each has a colorful brochure telling you how wonderful it is. After studying the various detailed specifications and aspects of the production technology, you choose the stove that has the combination of characteristics that you believe best fits your needs.

Next you decide on workers. Do you want bilingual workers, college-educated workers, part-time workers, experienced workers . . . ? You get the idea: Even simple production decisions involve complicated questions. These decisions are made on the basis of the expected costs, and expected usefulness, of inputs.

Technical Efficiency and Economic Efficiency

When choosing among existing technologies in the long run, firms are interested in the lowest cost, or most economically efficient, methods of production. They consider all technically efficient methods and compare their costs. The terms *economically efficient* and *technically efficient* differ in meaning. Here's how: **Technical efficiency** in production means that *as few inputs as possible are used to produce a given output*.

Web Note 10.1
Cheap Labor

Many different production processes can be technically efficient. For example, say you know that to produce 100 tons of wheat you can use 10 workers and 1 acre or use 1 worker and 100 acres. Which of these two production techniques is more efficient? Both can be technically efficient since neither involves the use of more of both inputs than the other technique. But that doesn't mean that both are equally economically efficient. That question can't be answered unless you know the relative costs of the two inputs. If an acre of land rents for $1 million and each worker costs $10 a day, our answer likely will be different than if land rents for $40 an acre and each worker costs $100 a day. The **economically efficient** method of production is *the method that produces a given level of output at the lowest possible cost*.

Q-1 True or false? If a process is economically efficient it is also technically efficient. Explain your answer.

In long-run production decisions, firms will look at all available production technologies and choose the technology that, given the available inputs and their prices, is the economically efficient way to produce. These choices will reflect the prices of the various factors of production. Those prices, in turn, will reflect the factors' relative scarcities.

Consider the use of land by firms in the United States and in Japan. The United States has large amounts of land (8 acres) per person, so the price of land is lower than in Japan, which has only 0.74 acre per person. An acre of rural land in the United States might cost about $700; in Japan it costs over $10,000. Because of this difference in the price of inputs, production techniques use land much more intensively in Japan than in the United States. Similarly with China: Labor is more abundant and capital is scarcer, so production techniques in China use capital much more intensively than it is used in the United States. Whereas China would use hundreds of workers, and very little machinery, to build a road, the United States would use three or four people along with three machines. Both countries are being economically efficient, but because costs of inputs differ, the economically efficient method of production differs. Thus, the economically efficient method of production is the technically efficient method of production that has the lowest cost. (For a further, graphical analysis of economic efficiency, see Appendix A.)

Q-2 Why does China use production techniques that require more workers per acre of land than does the United States?

Determinants of the Shape of the Long-Run Cost Curve

In Chapter 9 we saw that the law of diminishing marginal productivity accounted for the shape of the short-run average cost curve. The firm was adding more of a variable input to a fixed input. The law of diminishing marginal productivity doesn't apply to the long run since in the long run all inputs are variable. The most important determinants of what is economically efficient in the long run are economies and diseconomies of scale. Let's consider each of these in turn and see what effect they will have on the shape of the long-run average cost curve.

The shape of the long-run cost curve is due to the existence of economies and diseconomies of scale.

Economies of Scale

We say that production exhibits **economies of scale** *when long-run average total costs decrease as output increases*. For example, if producing 40,000 VCRs costs a firm

Producing the Mazda Miata

Applying the Tools

In the late 1980s the normal production run of a U.S. automobile was 200,000 units per year. Why was it so high? Because of indivisible setup costs of the then-current production technology. In order to reduce those indivisible setup costs to an acceptable level, the production level per year had to equal at least 200,000 or the car was considered an economic failure. The Pontiac Fiero, a sporty two-seater, was dropped in 1988 because it didn't sell well enough to sustain that production level.

But what is an indivisible setup cost depends on the structure of production. Japanese companies structured production differently from U.S. companies and had a much lower level of indivisible setup costs. For example, at just about the same time as Pontiac dropped the Fiero, a Japanese company, Mazda, entered the market with the Miata, another sporty two-seater. Because Mazda's assembly line was designed to handle different sizes and shapes of vehicles (which permits economies of scope, discussed later in the chapter), its minimum profitable production level for the Miata was about 30,000, not 200,000. This alternative structure of production made it possible for the Miata to do well in a market that buys a total of about 40,000 two-seater sports coupes annually. In response to this competition, U.S. companies followed suit and in the early 2000s they changed production methods. Now, indivisible setup costs make up a smaller portion of the total costs, thereby lowering their minimum efficient level of production. That's why you have seen an increase in the number of sporty two-seaters you can buy.

$16 million ($400 each), but producing 200,000 VCRs costs the firm $40 million ($200 each), between 40,000 and 200,000 units, the production of VCRs exhibits significant economies of scale. One can also say that there are increasing returns to scale.

In real-world production processes, at low levels of production economies of scale are extremely important because many production techniques require a certain minimum level of output to be useful. For example, say you want to produce a pound of steel. You can't just build a mini blast furnace, stick in some coke and iron ore, and come out with a single pound of steel. The smallest technically efficient blast furnaces have a production capacity measured in tons per hour, not pounds per year. The cost of the blast furnace is said to be an **indivisible setup cost** (*the cost of an indivisible input for which a certain minimum amount of production must be undertaken before the input becomes economically feasible to use*).

In the production of steel, the cost of a blast furnace is an indivisible setup cost that requires a minimum level of production to be economically feasible.

Indivisible setup costs are important because they create many real-world economies of scale: As output increases, the costs per unit of output decrease. As an example, consider this book. Setting the type for it is an indivisible setup cost; it is a cost that must be incurred if any production is to take place, but it is not a cost that increases with the number of books produced. That means that the more copies of the book that are produced, the lower the typesetting cost per book. That's why it costs more per book to produce a textbook for an upper-level, low-enrollment course than it does for a lower-level, high-enrollment course. The same amount of work goes into both (both need to be written, edited, and set into type), and the printing costs differ only slightly. The actual print-run costs of printing a book are only about $3 to $8 per book. The other costs are indivisible setup costs. Prices of produced goods, including books, reflect their costs of production. As you move to upper-level academic courses, where print runs are smaller, you'll likely discover that the books are smaller and less colorful but are priced the same as, or more than, this introductory text.

Q-3 Why are larger production runs often cheaper per unit than smaller production runs?

In the long-run planning decisions about the cost of producing this book, the expected number of copies to be sold was an important element. That figure influenced the number of books produced, which in turn affected the expected cost per unit. This

Figure 10-1 (a and b) A Typical Long-Run Average Total Cost Table and Curve
In the long run, average costs initially fall because of economies of scale; then they are constant for a while, and finally they tend to rise due to diseconomies of scale.

Quantity	Total Costs of Labor	Total Costs of Machines	Total Costs = $TC_L + TC_M$	Average Total Costs = TC/Q
11	$381	$254	$ 635	$58
12	390	260	650	54
13	402	268	670	52
14	420	280	700	50
15	450	300	750	50
16	480	320	800	50
17	510	340	850	50
18	549	366	915	51
19	600	400	1,000	53
20	666	444	1,110	56

(a) Long-run production table

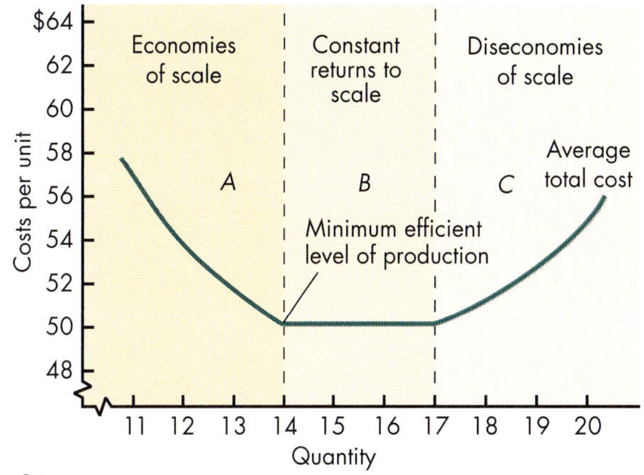

(b) Long-run average cost curve

will be the case anytime there are economies of scale. With economies of scale, cost per unit of a small production run is higher than cost per unit of a large production run.

Figure 10-1(a) demonstrates a normal long-run production table; Figure 10-1(b) shows the related typical shape of a long-run average cost curve. (Notice that there are no fixed costs. Because we're in the long run, all costs are variable.) Economies of scale account for the downward-sloping part. Cost per unit of output is decreasing.

In the longer run all inputs are variable, so only economies of scale can influence the shape of the long-run cost curve.

Because of the importance of economies of scale, businesspeople often talk of a minimum efficient level of production. What they mean by minimum efficient level of production is that, given the price at which they expect to be able to sell a good, the indivisible setup costs are so high that production runs of less than a certain size don't make economic sense. Thus, the **minimum efficient level of production** is *the amount of production that spreads setup costs out sufficiently for a firm to undertake production profitably*. At this point, the market has expanded to a size large enough for firms to take advantage of all economies of scale. The minimum efficient level of production is where the average total costs are at a minimum.

Diseconomies of Scale

Notice that on the right side of Figure 10-1(b) the long-run average cost curve is upward-sloping. Average cost is increasing. We say that production exhibits **diseconomies of scale** *when long-run average total costs increase as output increases*. For example, if producing 200,000 VCRs costs the firm $40 million ($200 each) and producing 400,000 VCRs costs the firm $100 million ($250 each), there are diseconomies of scale associated with choosing to produce 400,000 rather than 200,000. One can also say there are decreasing returns to scale. Diseconomies of scale usually, but not always, start occurring as firms get large.

Diminishing marginal productivity refers to the decline in productivity caused by increasing units of a variable input being added to a fixed input. Diseconomies of scale refer to the decreases in productivity that occur when there are equal increases of all inputs (no input is fixed).

Diseconomies of scale could not occur if production relationships were only technical relationships. If that were the case, the same technical process could be used over and over again at the same cost. In reality, however, production relationships have social dimensions, which introduce the potential for important diseconomies of scale into the production process in two ways:

Q-4 If production involved only technical relationships and had no social dimension, what would the long-run average total cost curve look like?

1. As the size of the firm increases, monitoring costs generally increase.
2. As the size of the firm increases, team spirit or morale generally decreases.

Monitoring costs are *the costs incurred by the organizer of production in seeing to it that the employees do what they're supposed to do.* If you're producing something yourself, the job gets done the way you want it done; monitoring costs are zero. However, as the scale of production increases, you have to hire people to help you produce. This means that if the job is to be done the way you want it done, you have to monitor (supervise) your employees' performance. The cost of monitoring can increase significantly as output increases; it's a major contributor to diseconomies of scale. Most big firms have several layers of bureaucracy devoted simply to monitoring employees. The job of middle managers is, to a large extent, monitoring.

As firms become larger, monitoring costs increase and achieving team spirit is more difficult.

The other social dimension that can contribute to diseconomies of scale is the loss of **team spirit** (*the feelings of friendship and being part of a team that bring out people's best efforts*). Most types of production are highly dependent on team spirit. When the team spirit or morale is lost, production slows considerably. The larger the firm is, the more difficult it is to maintain team spirit.

An important reason diseconomies of scale can come about is that the bigger things get, the more checks and balances are needed to ensure that the right hand and the left hand are coordinated. The larger the organization, the more checks and balances and the more paperwork.

Some large firms manage to solve these problems and avoid diseconomies of scale. But problems of monitoring and loss of team spirit often limit the size of firms. They underlie diseconomies of scale in which relatively less output is produced for a given increase in inputs, so that per-unit costs of output increase.

Constant Returns to Scale

Sometimes in a range of output a firm does not experience either economies of scale or diseconomies of scale. In this range there are **constant returns to scale** *where long-run average total costs do not change with an increase in output.* Constant returns to scale are shown by the flat portion of the average total cost curve in Figure 10-1(b). Constant returns to scale occur when production techniques can be replicated again and again to increase output. This occurs before monitoring costs rise and team spirit is lost.

The Importance of Economies and Diseconomies of Scale

Economies and diseconomies of scale play important roles in real-world long-run production decisions.

Economies and diseconomies of scale play important roles in real-world long-run production decisions. Economies of scale underlie firms' attempts to expand their markets either at home or abroad. If they can make and sell more at lower per-unit costs, they will make more profits. Diseconomies of scale prevent a firm from expanding and can lead corporate raiders to buy the firm and break it up in the hope that the smaller production units will be more efficient, thus eliminating some of the diseconomies of scale.

Q-5 Why is the short-run average cost curve a U-shaped curve?

Q-6 Why is the long-run average total cost curve generally considered to be a U-shaped curve?

The long-run and the short-run average cost curves have the same U shape. But it's important to remember that the reasons why they have this U shape are quite different. The assumption of initially increasing and then eventually diminishing marginal productivity (as a variable input is added to a fixed input) accounts for the shape of the short-run average cost curve. Economies and diseconomies of scale account for the shape of the long-run average total cost curve. (See the box "Distinguishing Diseconomies of Scale from Diminishing Marginal Productivity" for a review of why.)

Distinguishing Diseconomies of Scale from Diminishing Marginal Productivity

Knowing the Tools

As pointed out in the text, the shapes of the short-run average cost curve and the long-run average cost curve are similar. But the reasons underlying those shapes are quite different. It is important to reemphasize that difference. In the short run, some inputs are fixed; in the long run, all inputs vary.

Let's first review why the short-run average cost curve is U-shaped. What accounts for its shape is what's happening to marginal productivity of each additional unit of input *keeping all other inputs fixed.* Since costs are based on inputs, how much an input contributes to output directly affects the costs of production. Average total costs in the short run fall initially because of the assumption of increasing marginal productivity: Additional inputs are able to produce increasing increments of output. An example of increasing marginal productivity is a 5 percent increase in the quantity of labor, holding capital constant, leading to a 5 percent increase in output, and the next 5 percent increase leading to a 10 percent increase in output.

Eventually, marginal productivity falls and the short-run average cost curve slopes upward. Adding more of *one* factor of production, holding the others constant, contributes less and less to output, causing marginal costs, and eventually average costs, to rise. An example of diminishing marginal productivity is a 5 percent increase in the quantity of labor, holding capital constant, leading to a 2 percent increase in output and the next 5 percent increase, holding capital constant, leading to a 1 percent increase in output. The assumption of initially increasing marginal productivity and eventually diminishing marginal productivity leads to the U shape of the short-run average cost curve.

Now consider the long-run average cost curve. Its shape is determined by what's happening to returns to scale. Returns to scale are not about how changes in one input affect output. Instead, they involve changing *all inputs equally.* If there are economies of scale, increasing all factors of production equally, say by 5 percent, leads to a greater increase in output, say by 8 percent.

The assumption economists make in the long run is that initially economies of scale cause the long-run average total cost curve to slope downward. Eventually, however, there are diseconomies of scale. That is, increasing all inputs equally, say by 5 percent, leads to a smaller increase in output, say by 3 percent. Diseconomies of scale cause average total costs to rise and the long-run average total cost curve to slope upward. If there are neither economies of scale nor diseconomies of scale, the average total cost curve is flat because inputs and output both are changing by equal proportions. An example of constant returns to scale is a 5 percent increase in all inputs leading to a 5 percent increase in output. With constant returns to scale, average costs do not change.

The assumption we make about production in the long run is that there are first increasing, then constant, and finally decreasing returns to scale. That assumption about returns to scale accounts for the U shape of the long-run average cost curve.

Envelope Relationship

Since in the long run all inputs are flexible, while in the short run some inputs are not flexible, long-run cost will always be less than or equal to short-run cost at the same level of output. To see this, let's consider a firm that had planned to produce 100 but now adjusts its plan to produce more than 100. We know that in the long run the firm chooses the lowest-cost method of production. In the short run it faces an additional constraint: All expansion must be done by increasing only the variable input. That constraint must increase average cost (or at least not decrease it) compared to what average cost would have been had the firm planned to produce that level to begin with. If it didn't, the firm would have chosen that new combination of inputs in the long run. Additional constraints increase cost. The *envelope relationship* is the relationship between long-run and short-run average total costs. It is shown in Figure 10-2.

The envelope relationship is the relationship explaining that, at the planned output level, short-run average total cost equals long-run average total cost, but at all other levels of output, short-run average total cost is higher than long-run average total cost.

Why it's called an envelope relationship should be clear from the figure. Each short-run average total cost curve touches (is tangent to) the long-run average total cost

Figure 10-2 Envelope of Short-Run Average Total Cost Curves

The long-run average total cost curve is an envelope of the short-run average total cost curves. Each short-run average total cost curve touches the long-run average total cost curve at only one point. (*SR* stands for short run; *LR* stands for long run.)

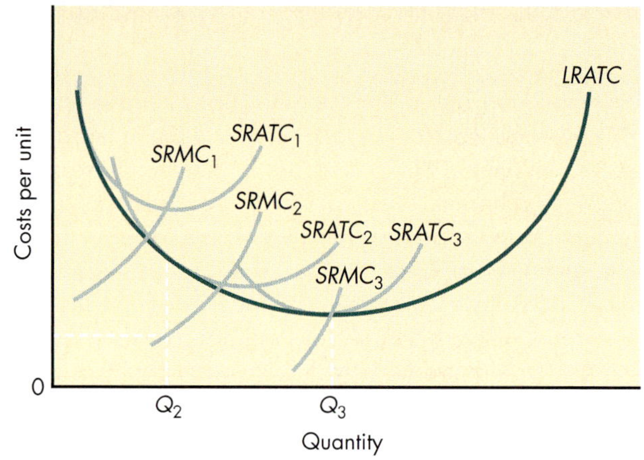

curve at one, and only one, output level; at all other output levels, short-run average cost exceeds long-run average cost. The long-run average total cost curve is an envelope of short-run average total cost curves.

The intuitive reason why the short-run average total cost curves always lie above the long-run average cost curve is simple. In the short run, you have chosen a plant; that plant is fixed, and its costs for that period are part of your average fixed costs. Changes must be made within the confines of that plant. In the long run you can change everything, choosing the combination of inputs in the most efficient manner. The more options you have to choose from, the lower the costs of production. Put another way: Constraints always raise costs (or at least won't lower them). So in the long run, costs must be the same or lower.

Another insight to note about this envelope relationship is the following: When there are economies of scale and you have chosen a plant size that is efficient, given output, your short-run average costs will fall as you increase production. Technically, this must be the case because the short-run marginal cost (*SRMC*) curve goes through the minimum point of the short-run average total cost (*SRATC*) curve, and the minimum point of the *SRATC* curve is to the right of the efficient level of production in the long run. That means that at output Q_2, $SRMC_2$ has to be below $SRATC_2$ and short-run average total cost is falling. Intuitively, what's happening is that at output Q_2, your fixed costs are high. Now demand increases and you increase production. Your average fixed costs are high; your marginal costs are low; and initially the fall in average fixed costs more than offsets the increased marginal cost. Once marginal cost exceeds *SRATC*, that no longer is the case.[1]

Only when the firm is at the minimum point of the long-run average total cost (*LRATC*) curve (at output Q_3) is the $SRATC_3$ curve tangent to the *LRATC* curve at a

[1]The above reasoning is dependent on the curves being smooth (i.e., having no kinks). This smoothness is a standard assumption of the model. If we give up the smoothness assumption, the *SRATC* curve could be kinked and the *SRMC* curve could be discontinuous. In that case, the *SRATC* curve might be tangent to the *LRATC* curve from the left, but not from the right, and it might not decrease. This would make movement from the long to the short run a discrete jump, whereas the existing model and smoothness assumption make it a smooth continuous movement. So if your intuition doesn't lead you to understand the model, you are probably thinking of a model with different assumptions. You'll be in good company, too. When an economist by the name of Jacob Viner first created this model, his intuition led him to a different result because his intuition was basing the analysis on different assumptions than he was using in his formal model.

WHY ARE TEXTBOOKS SO LONG?

Applying the Tools

Understanding costs and their structure will help you understand why intro economics textbooks are so long—and why their length is to your advantage.

The majority of the costs of a book are fixed costs in relation to the length of the book. The initial costs in terms of length are about 20 percent of the total price of the book. So increasing the length of the book increases costs slightly. But the longer length allows the writer to include more issues that some professors want, and many professors will not consider using the book unless it does include these issues. That means that greater length can allow publishers to sell more books, allowing the fixed costs to be divided over more output. This decrease in fixed cost per unit can lower average total cost more than increasing the length of the book increases average total costs per unit. So if the added length increases the number of users, the additional length can lower the average cost of the book.

It does lower the costs of the book—up to a point. Textbook publishers are continually looking for that point. They direct authors to shorten their books but also to include almost all issues that various groups want. The latter direction—in favor of inclusion—often takes precedence, which is why textbooks are so long. This doesn't mean that textbooks will always be longer. Recently, economics textbooks have become smaller because students began to complain that the texts were getting too heavy to carry.

point where the *SRMC* curve intersects both the curves. For large markets, this point is the least-cost production level of a firm.

ENTREPRENEURIAL ACTIVITY AND THE SUPPLY DECISION

In this chapter and the preceding one we have discussed the technical nature of costs and production. In the next chapter we will formally relate costs of production to the supply of goods. As a bridge between the two chapters, let's consider the entrepreneur, who establishes the relationship between costs and the supply decision, and discuss some of the problems of using cost analysis in the real world.

In thinking about the connection between cost and supply, one fundamental insight is that the revenue received for a good must be greater than the planned cost of producing it. Otherwise why would anyone supply it? The difference between the expected price of a good and the expected average total cost of producing it is the supplier's expected economic profit per unit. It's profit that underlies the dynamics of production in a market economy.

The expected price must exceed the opportunity cost of supplying the good for a good to be supplied.

Cost curves do not become supply curves through some magic process. To move from cost to supply, entrepreneurial initiative is needed. An **entrepreneur** is *an individual who sees an opportunity to sell an item at a price higher than the average cost of producing it*. The entrepreneur is the organizer of production and the one who visualizes the demand and convinces the individuals who own the factors of production that they want to produce that good. Businesses work hard at maintaining the entrepreneurial spirit in their employees. The greater the difference between price and average total cost, the greater the entrepreneur's incentive to tackle the organizational problems and supply the good.

Q-7 Why is the role of the entrepreneur central to the production process in the economy?

USING COST ANALYSIS IN THE REAL WORLD

All too often students walk away from an introductory economics course thinking that cost analysis is a relatively easy topic. Memorize the names, shapes, and relationships of the curves, and you're home free. In the textbook model, that's right. In real life, it's not, because actual production processes are marked by economies of scope, learning by doing and technological change, many dimensions, unmeasured costs, joint costs, indivisible costs, uncertainty, asymmetries, and multiple planning and adjustment periods with many different short runs. And this is a short list!

Economies of Scope

Web Note 10.2
Increasing the Scope

The cost of production of one product often depends on what other products a firm is producing. Economists say that in the production of two goods there are **economies of scope** *when the costs of producing products are interdependent so that it's less costly for a firm to produce one good when it's already producing another.* For example, once a firm has set up a large marketing department to sell cereal, the department might be able to use its expertise in marketing a different product—say, dog food. A firm that sells gasoline can simultaneously use its gas station attendants to sell soda, milk, and incidentals. The minimarts so common along our highways and neighborhood streets developed because gasoline companies became aware of economies of scope.

Q-8 What is the difference between an economy of scope and an economy of scale?

Economies of scope play an important role in firms' decisions about what combination of goods to produce. They look for both economies of scope and economies of scale. When you read about firms' mergers, think about whether the combination of their products will generate economies of scope. Many otherwise unexplainable mergers between seemingly incompatible firms can be explained by economies of scope.

By allowing firms to segment the production process, globalization has made economies of scope even more important to firms in their production decisions. Low-cost labor in other countries has led U.S. firms to locate their manufacturing processes in those countries and to concentrate domestic activities on other aspects of production. As I have stressed throughout this book, production is more than simply manufacturing; the costs of marketing, advertising, and distribution are often larger

Production then: The nature of production has changed considerably in the last 70 years. This picture shows a 1933 production line in which people did the work as the goods moved along the line.
Bettmann/CORBIS.

components of the cost of a good than are manufacturing costs. Each of these involves special knowledge and expertise, and the U.S. companies are specializing in the marketing, advertising, and distribution aspects of the production process. By concentrating on those aspects, and by making themselves highly competitive by taking advantage of low-cost manufacturing elsewhere, U.S. firms become more competitive and expand, increasing demand for U.S. labor. Often they expand into new areas, taking advantage of economies of scope in distribution and marketing.

Consider Nike—it produces shoes, right? Wrong. It is a U.S. marketing and distribution company; it outsources all its production to affiliate companies. Nike is expanding, but not in the production of shoes. It is expanding into leisure clothing, where it hopes economies of scope in its marketing and distribution specialties will bring it success.

Nike is only one of many examples. The large wage differentials in the global economy are causing firms to continually reinvent themselves—to shed aspects of their business where they do not have a comparative advantage, and to add new businesses where their abilities can achieve synergies and economies of scope.

Learning by Doing and Technological Change

The production terminology that we've been discussing is central to the standard economic models. In the real world, however, other terms and concepts are also important. The production techniques available to real-world firms are constantly changing because of *learning by doing* and *technological change*. These changes occur over time and cannot be accurately predicted.

Unlike events in the standard economic model, all events in the real world are influenced by the past. That's why learning by doing is important in the real world, but isn't a part of the standard economic model. **Learning by doing** simply means that *as we do something, we learn what works and what doesn't, and over time we become more proficient at it*. Practice may not make perfect, but it certainly makes better and more efficient.

Q.9 Does learning by doing cause the cost curve to be downward-sloping?

Production now: The nature of production has changed considerably in the last 70 years. This picture shows a modern production line. Robots do much of the work.

Many firms estimate worker productivity to grow 1 to 2 percent a year because of learning by doing.

Many firms estimate that output per unit input will increase by 1 or 2 percent a year, even if no changes in inputs or technologies occur, as employees learn by doing.

The concept of learning by doing emphasizes the importance of the past in trying to predict performance. Let's say a firm is deciding between two applicants for the job of managing its restaurant. One was a highly successful student but has never run a restaurant; the other was an OK student who has run a restaurant that failed. Which one does the firm hire? The answer is unclear. The first applicant may be brighter, but the lack of experience will likely mean that the person won't be hired. Businesses give enormous weight to experience. So this firm may reason that in failing, the second applicant will have learned lessons that make her the better candidate. U.S. firms faced such a choice when they were invited to expand into the new market economies of Eastern Europe in the early 1990s. Should they hire the former communist managers who had failed to produce efficiently, or should they hire the reformers? (Generally they decided on the former communist managers, hoping they had learned by failing.)

Technological change is *an increase in the range of production techniques that leads to more efficient ways of producing goods as well as the production of new and better goods*. That is, technological change offers an increase in the known range of production. For example, at one point automobile tires were made from rubber, clothing was made from cotton and wool, and buildings were made of wood. As a result of technological change, many tires are now made from petroleum distillates, much clothing is made from synthetic fibers (which in turn are made from petroleum distillates), and many buildings are constructed from steel.

Technological change can fundamentally alter the nature of production costs.

The standard long-run model takes technology as a given. From our experience, we know that technological change affects firms' decisions and production. Technological change can fundamentally alter the nature of production costs.

In some industries technological change is occurring so fast that it overwhelms all other cost issues. The computer industry is a good example. The expectation of technological change has been built into the plans of firms in that industry. The industry has followed Moore's law, which states that the cost of computing will fall by half every 18 months. Indeed, that has happened since the 1980s. With costs falling that fast because of learning by doing and technological change, all other cost components are overwhelmed, and, instead of costs increasing as output rises significantly, as might be predicted because of diseconomies of scale, costs keep going down.

Web Note 10.3
Moore's Law

The fall in the cost of computer chips has affected other industries as well. All types of household goods that use computer technology—including telephones, refrigerators, automobiles, TVs and VCRs, and compact disc players—are undergoing enormous change. For instance, in Asia, VCRs are now almost extinct; they have been replaced by digital video disc (DVD) players—where all images are transmitted digitally. The same is happening in the United States. Another change is that mass-stamped CDs will soon be replaced by individual CDs created by downloading files from the Internet using MP3 technology. In a few years, CDs may not be used at all—music will be stored in music memory banks that will be modified computer hard drives. Computer technology has also revolutionized automobiles, making them more reliable and cheaper. In the 1960s, I could work on my own car, changing the points or modifying the carburetor. Modern cars have no such parts; they have been replaced by electronic parts. When a car isn't running right its owner must now take it to a garage. My point, however, is that automobiles have fundamentally changed; they are much more efficient and reliable and their price has fallen because of the introduction of computer technology. Technological change drives costs down, and can overwhelm diseconomies of scale, causing prices to fall more and more.

Technological change occurs in all industries, not only high-tech industries.

Don't think of technological change as occurring only in high-tech industries. Consider chicken production. The price of chickens has fallen enormously over the past

50 years. Why? Because of technological change. At one time chickens were raised in farmyards. They walked around, ate scraps and feed, and generally led a chicken's life. Walking around had definite drawbacks—it took space (which cost money); it made standardization (a requirement of taking advantage of economies of scale) difficult, which prevented lowering costs; it used energy, which meant more feed per pound of chicken; and sometimes it led to disease, since chickens walked in their own manure.

The technological change was to put the chickens in wire cages so that the manure falls through to a conveyor belt and is transferred outside. Another conveyor belt feeds the chickens food laced with antibiotics to prevent disease. Soft music is played to keep them calm (they burn fewer calories). Once they reach the proper weight, they are slaughtered in a similar automated process. Perdue Farms Inc., which led the way in developing this new technology, does not grow any chickens itself. It outsources this approach to chicken farms. Farmers bid for the right to grow the chickens for Perdue. Perdue then puts its label on the chickens, ships them to the supermarkets, and advertises the plump chickens with its name on them. How the chickens feel about this technological change is not clear. (When I asked them, all they had to say was *cluck*.)

This method of raising chickens will likely be replaced in the next couple of decades by another technological change—genetic engineering that will allow chicken parts to be produced directly from single cells. Only the breasts and drumsticks will be produced (and wings if you live in Buffalo). All low-efficiency, low-profit-margin parts such as necks, feet, and heads will be eliminated.

In many businesses the effect of learning by doing and technological change on prices is built into the firm's pricing structure. If they expect their costs to fall with more experience, or if they expect technological advances to lower costs in the future, they might bid low for a big order to give themselves the chance to lower their costs through learning by doing or technological change.

Technological change and learning by doing are intricately related. The efficient chicken production we now have did not come about overnight. It occurred over a 20-year period as firms learned how to do it. Chickens respond to Mozart better than to hip-hop. That had to be learned. Similarly, genetic reproduction of chicken parts will evolve as scientists and firms learn more about cloning and DNA.

Technological change and learning by doing are intricately related.

Many Dimensions

The only dimension of output in the standard model is how much to produce. Many, if not most, decisions that firms make are not the one-dimensional decisions of the standard model, such as "Should we produce more or less?" They're multidimensional questions like "Should we change the quality? Should we change the wrapper? Should we improve our shipping speed? Should we increase our inventory?" Each of these questions relates to a different dimension of the production decision and each has its own marginal costs. Thus, there isn't just one marginal cost; there are 10 or 20 of them. Good economic decisions take all relevant margins into account.

Good economic decisions take all relevant margins into account.

The reason that the standard model is important is that each of these questions can be analyzed by applying the same reasoning used in the standard model. But you must remember, *in applying the analysis, it's the reasoning, not the specific model, that's important*.

Unmeasured Costs

If asked, "In what area of decision making do businesses most often fail to use economic insights?" most economists would say costs. The relevant costs are generally not the costs you'll find in a firm's accounts.

Why the difference? Economists operate conceptually; they include in costs exactly what their theory says they should. They include all opportunity costs. Accountants who have to measure firms' costs in practice and provide the actual dollar figures take a much more pragmatic approach; their concepts of costs must reflect only explicit costs—those costs that are reasonably precisely measurable.

Here I review the difference between explicit and implicit costs (discussed in Chapter 9) and introduce another difference—how economists and accountants measure depreciation of capital.

Economists Include Opportunity Cost First, say that a business produces 1,000 widgets[2] that sell at $3 each for a total revenue of $3,000. To produce these widgets the business had to buy $1,000 worth of widgetgoo, which the owner has hand-shaped into widgets. An accountant would say that the total cost of producing 1,000 widgets was $1,000 and that the firm's profit was $2,000. That's because an accountant uses explicit costs that can be measured.

Economic profit is different. An economist, looking at that same example, would point out that the accountant's calculation doesn't take into account the time and effort that the owner put into making the widgets. While a person's time involves no explicit cost in money, it does involve an opportunity cost, the forgone income that the owner could have made by spending that time working in another job. If the business takes 400 hours of the person's time and the person could have earned $6 an hour working for someone else, then the person is forgoing $2,400 in income. Economists include that implicit cost in their concept of cost. When that implicit cost is included, what looks like a $2,000 profit becomes a $400 economic loss.

Q-10 As the owner of the firm, Jim pays himself $1,000. All other expenses of the firm add up to $2,000. What would an economist say are the total costs for Jim's firm?

Economic Depreciation versus Accounting Depreciation Now let's take depreciation. Say a firm buys a machine for $10,000 that's meant to last 10 years. After 1 year, machines like that become in short supply, so instead of falling, its value rises to $12,000. An accountant, looking at the firm's costs that year, would use historical cost (what the machine cost in terms of money actually spent) depreciated at, say, 10 percent per year, so the machine's cost for each of its 10 years of existence would be $1,000. An economist would say that since the value of the machine is rising, the machine has no cost; in fact, it provides a revenue of $2,000 to the firm. The standard model avoids such messy, real-world issues of measuring costs and instead assumes that all costs are measurable in a single time period.

The Standard Model as a Framework

Despite its limitations the standard model provides a good framework for cost analysis.

The standard model can be expanded to include these real-world complications. I don't do so because I suspect that even with its simplifications, the standard model has been more than enough to learn in an introductory course. Learning the standard model, however, provides you with only the rudiments of cost analysis, in the same way that learning the rules of mechanics provides you with only the basics of mechanical engineering. In addition to a knowledge of the laws of mechanics, building a machine requires years of experience. Similarly for economics and cost analysis. Introductory economics provides you with a superb framework for starting to think about real-world cost measurement, but it can't make you an expert cost analyst.

---

[2]What's a widget? It's a wonderful little gadget that's the opposite of a wadget. (No one knows what they look like or what they are used for.) Why discuss widgets? For the same reason that scientists discuss fruit flies—their production process is simple, unlike most real-world production processes.

New Approaches in Cost Analysis

Applying the Tools

> Factories run by numbers. Numbers to calculate profit and losses; to analyze the costs of new products; and to chart corporate strategy. But a lot of managers are relying on the wrong numbers.
>
> As they adopt new manufacturing techniques like computer-aided design, just-in-time stock management, and total quality control, many firms are discovering that their existing account systems also need dragging into the 1990s. Unless the bean-counters join the manufacturing revolution, traditional cost accounting will have little place in the factory of the future.

The above quote introduced an article in *The Economist* (March 3, 1990, p. 61) describing a conference on strategic manufacturing. This conference focused on managerial or cost accounting (the application of cost analysis to managerial decisions). Unlike *financial accounting* (which involves keeping track of income, assets, and liabilities), managerial accounting is used to help managers determine the cost of producing products and plan future investment. It's the direct application of microeconomics to production.

In the 1980s and 1990s cost accounting changed enormously. The leaders of this change—such as Robert Kaplan of the Harvard Business School—argue that cost accounting systems based on traditional concepts of fixed and variable costs lead firms consistently to make the wrong decisions. They argue that in today's manufacturing, direct labor costs have fallen substantially—in many industries to only 2 or 3 percent of the total cost—and overhead costs have risen substantially. This change in costs facing firms requires a much more careful division among types of overhead costs, and a recognition that what should and should not be assigned as a cost to a particular product differs with each decision.

These developments in managerial accounting require an even deeper understanding of costs than accountants have previously needed. As one firm's director of manufacturing was quoted in *The Economist* article, "Unless management accountants move fast [to incorporate these new concepts], they will be almost without use to the manufacturing manager."

Conclusion and a Look Ahead

We've come to the end of our discussion of production, cost, and supply. The two chapters we spent on them weren't easy; there's tons of material here, and, quite frankly, it will likely require at least two or three reads and careful attention to your professor's lecture before your mind can absorb it. So if you're planning to sleep through a lecture, the ones on these chapters aren't the ones for that.

These chapters, in combination with our discussion of individual choice, will provide the framework for most of the later chapters, which really do get into interesting real-world issues. But you've got to know the basics to truly understand those issues. So, now that you've come to the end of these two chapters, unless you really feel comfortable with the analysis, it's probably time to review them from the beginning. (Sorry, but remember, there ain't no such thing as a free lunch.)

Summary

- An economically efficient production process must be technically efficient, but a technically efficient process need not be economically efficient.
- The long-run average total cost curve is U-shaped. Economies of scale initially cause average total cost to decrease; diseconomies eventually cause average total cost to increase.

- Production is a social, as well as a technical, phenomenon; that's why concepts like team spirit are important—and that's why diseconomies of scale occur.
- The marginal cost and short-run average cost curves slope upward because of diminishing marginal productivity. The long-run average cost curve slopes upward because of diseconomies of scale.
- There is an envelope relationship between short-run average cost curves and long-run average cost curves. The short-run average cost curves are always above the long-run average cost curve.
- An entrepreneur is an individual who sees an opportunity to sell an item at a price higher than the average cost of producing it.
- Once we start applying cost analysis to the real world, we must include a variety of other dimensions of costs that the standard model does not cover.
- Costs in the real world are affected by economies of scope, learning by doing and technological change, the many dimensions to output, and unmeasured costs such as opportunity costs.

Key Terms

constant returns to scale *(224)*
diseconomies of scale *(223)*
economically efficient *(221)*
economies of scale *(221)*
economies of scope *(228)*
entrepreneur *(227)*
indivisible setup cost *(222)*
learning by doing *(229)*
minimum efficient level of production *(223)*
monitoring costs *(224)*
team spirit *(224)*
technical efficiency *(221)*
technological change *(230)*

Questions for Thought and Review

1. Distinguish technical efficiency from economic efficiency.
2. A student has just written on an exam that in the long run fixed cost will make the average total cost curve slope downward. Why will the professor mark it incorrect?
3. What inputs do you use in studying this book? What would the long-run average total cost and marginal cost curves for studying look like? Why?
4. Why could diseconomies of scale never occur if production relationships were only technical relationships?
5. When economist Jacob Viner first developed the envelope relationship, he told his draftsman to make sure that all the marginal cost curves went through both (1) the minimum point of the short-run average cost curve and (2) the point where the short-run average total cost curve was tangent to the long-run average total cost curve. The draftsman told him it couldn't be done. Viner told him to do it anyhow. Why was the draftsman right?
6. What is the role of the entrepreneur in translating cost of production into supply?
7. Your average total cost is $40; the price you receive for the good is $12. Should you keep on producing the good? Why?
8. A student has just written on an exam that technological change will mean that the cost curve is downward-sloping. Why did the teacher mark it wrong?
9. If you were describing the marginal cost of an additional car driving on a road, what costs would you look at? What is the likely shape of the marginal cost curve?
10. The cost of setting up a steel mill is enormous. For example, a Gary, Indiana, hot-strip mill would cost an estimated $1.5 billion to build. Using this information and the cost concepts from the chapter, explain the following quotation: "To make operations even marginally profitable, big steelmakers must run full-out. It's like a car that is more efficient at 55 miles an hour than in stop-and-go traffic at 25."
11. One farmer can grow 1,000 bushels of corn on 1 acre of land with 200 hours of labor and 20 pounds of seed. Another farmer can grow 1,000 bushels of corn on 1 acre of land with 100 hours of labor and 20 pounds of seed. Could both methods be technically efficient? Is it possible that both of these production processes are economically efficient?

Problems and Exercises

1. Visit a nearby company and ask it what would happen to its per-unit costs if sales increased by 10 percent. Try to figure out how its answer relates to the concepts in this and the preceding chapter, remembering especially the discussion about using cost analysis in the real world.
2. A pair of shoes that wholesale for $28.79 has approximately the following costs:

Manufacturing labor	$ 2.25
Materials	4.95
Factory overhead, operating expenses, and profit	8.50
Sales costs	4.50
Advertising	2.93
Research and development	2.00
Interest	.33
Net income	3.33
Total	$28.79

   a. Which of these costs would likely be a variable cost?
   b. Which would likely be a fixed cost?
   c. If output were to rise, what would likely happen to average total costs? Why?
3. Find out the total budget of your college or university. (It often takes a bit of sleuthing, but almost all college and university budgets are in the public record.) Find out the number of students. What is the total cost per student? What is the relevant marginal cost of an additional student?

   Now say you're on a planning committee charged with eliminating an expected 2 percent budget deficit next year. Using the budget figures, make some suggestions. Have a college administrator (preferably the treasurer or comptroller) visit your class and react to those suggestions. Explain why presidents of universities and colleges don't last long.
4. Draw a long-run cost curve.
   a. Why does it slope downward initially?
   b. Why does it eventually slope upward?
   c. How would your answers to *a* and *b* differ if you had drawn a short-run cost curve?
   d. How large is the fixed-cost component of the long-run cost curve?
   e. If there were constant returns to scale everywhere, what would the long-run cost curve look like?
5. A major issue of contention at many colleges concerns the cost of meals that is rebated when a student does not sign up for the meal plan. The administration usually says that it should rebate only the marginal cost of the food alone, which it calculates at, say, $1.25 per meal. Students say that the marginal cost should include more costs, such as the saved space from fewer students using the facilities and the reduced labor expenses on food preparation. This can raise the marginal cost to $6.00.
   a. Who is correct, the administration or the students?
   b. How might your answer to *a* differ if this argument were being conducted in the planning stage, before the dining hall is built?
   c. If you accept the $1.25 figure of a person not eating, how could you justify using a higher figure of about $6.00 for the cost of feeding a guest at the dining hall, as many schools do?
6. A dressmaker can sew 800 garments with 160 bolts of fabric and 3,000 hours of labor. Another dressmaker can sew 800 garments with 200 bolts of fabric and 2,000 hours of identical labor. Fabric costs $100 a bolt and labor costs $10 an hour.
   a. Is it possible that both methods are technically efficient? Why or why not?
   b. Is it possible that both methods are economically efficient?

Web Questions

1. Go to the Internet site About.com (www.about.com) and answer the following questions:
   a. What services does About.com provide? What does it charge for those services?
   b. What are the fixed costs associated with running About.com? What is the marginal cost of providing About.com to one additional person?
   c. List the advertising you saw while visiting About.com.
   d. Under what circumstances will an entrepreneur supply a good to the market? What incentives do the owners of About.com have to supply this product on the Internet? (Hint: Look at your answer to *c*).
2. Go to the business section of *The Guardian Unlimited* at www.guardian.co.uk/business, the website of a British newspaper, and search for the article, "Drug Cocktail Is a Downer" to answer the following questions:
   a. What are possible reasons Glaxo and SmithKline merged?
   b. What problems is the combined company facing?
   c. How do the problems you mentioned in *b* relate to diseconomies of scale?

ANSWERS TO MARGIN QUESTIONS

1. True. Since an economically efficient method of production is that method that produces a given level of output at the lowest possible cost, it must also use as few inputs as possible. It is also technically efficient. *(221)*
2. China uses more labor-intensive techniques than does the United States because the price of labor is much lower in China relative to the United States. Both countries are producing economically efficiently. *(221)*
3. Larger production runs are generally cheaper per unit than smaller production runs because of indivisible setup costs, which do not vary with the size of the run. *(222)*
4. Because the same technical process could be used over and over again at the same cost, the long-run average cost curve would never become upward-sloping. *(224)*
5. The short-run average total cost curve initially slopes downward because of increasing marginal productivity and large average fixed costs, then begins sloping upward because of diminishing marginal productivity, giving it a U shape. *(224)*
6. The long-run average total cost curve is generally considered to be U-shaped because initially there are economies of scale and, for large amounts of production, there are diseconomies of scale. *(224)*
7. Economic activity does not just happen. Some dynamic, driven individual must instigate production. That dynamic individual is called an entrepreneur. *(227)*
8. Economies of scale are economies that occur because of increases in the amount of one good a firm is producing. Economies of scope occur when producing different types of goods lowers the cost of each of those goods. *(228)*
9. Learning by doing causes a shift in the cost curve because it is a change in the technical characteristics of production. It does not cause the cost curve to be downward-sloping—it causes it to shift downward. *(229)*
10. An economist would say that he doesn't know what total cost is without knowing what Jim could have earned if he had undertaken another activity besides running his business. Just because he paid himself $1,000 doesn't mean that $1,000 is his opportunity cost. *(232)*

APPENDIX A

Isocost/Isoquant Analysis

In the long run, a firm can vary more than one factor of production. One of the decisions firms face in this long run is which combination of factors of production to use. Economic efficiency involves choosing those factors so that the cost of production is at a minimum.

In analyzing this choice of which combination of factors to use, economists have developed a graphical technique called *isocost/isoquant analysis*. In this technique the analyst creates a graph placing one factor of production, say labor, on one axis and another factor, say machines, on the other axis, as I have done in Figure A10-1. Any point on that graph represents a combination of machines and labor that can produce a certain amount of output, say pairs of earrings. For example, point A represents 3 machines and 4 units of labor being used to produce 8 pairs of earrings. Any point in the blue shaded area represents more of one or both factors and any point in the red shaded area represents less of one or both factors.

Figure A10-1 The Isocost/Isoquant Graph

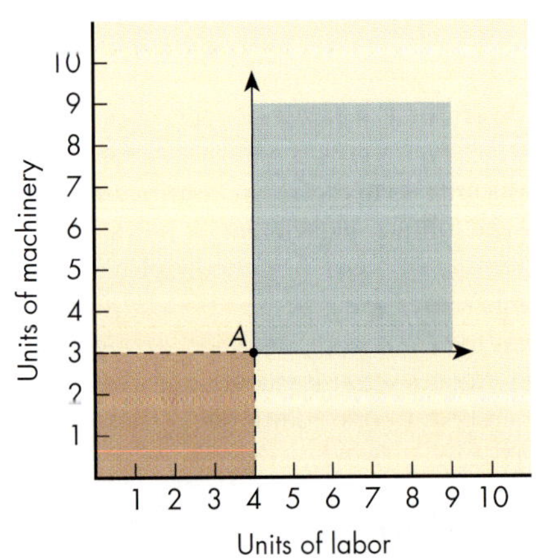

THE ISOQUANT CURVE

The firm's problem is to figure out how to produce its output—let's say it has chosen an output of 60 pairs of earrings—at as low a cost as possible. That means somehow we must show graphically the combinations of machines and labor that can produce 60 pairs of earrings as cheaply as possible. We do so with what is called an isoquant curve. An **isoquant curve** is *a curve that represents combinations of factors of production that result in equal amounts of output.* (*Isoquant* is a big name for an "equal quantity.") At all points on an isoquant curve the firm can produce the same amount of output. So, given a level of output, a firm can find out what combinations of the factors of production will produce that output. Suppose a firm can produce 60 pairs of earrings with the following combination of labor and machines:

	Labor	Machines	Pairs of Earrings
A	3	20	60
B	4	15	60
C	6	10	60
D	10	6	60
E	15	4	60
F	20	3	60

This table shows the technical limits of production. It shows that the firm can use, for example, 3 units of labor and 20 machines or 20 units of labor and 3 machines to produce 60 pairs of earrings. The isoquant curve is a graphical representation of the table. I show the isoquant curve for producing 60 pairs in Figure A10-2. Points A to F represent rows A to F in the table.

To be sure you understand it, let's consider some points on the curve. Let's start at point A. At point A the firm is producing 60 pairs of earrings using 20 machines and 3 workers. If the firm wants to reduce the number of machines by 5, it must increase the number of units of labor by 1 to keep output constant. Doing so moves the firm to point B. At point B the firm is also producing 60 pairs of earrings, but is doing it with 15 machines and 4 workers. Alternatively, if the firm were at point D, and it wants to reduce the number of machines from 6 to 4, it must increase the number of units of labor from 10 to 15 to keep output constant at 60. At any point on this isoquant curve the firm is being technically efficient—it is using as few resources as possible to produce 60 pairs of earrings. Thus, it would never want to produce 60 at a point like G, because that point uses more inputs. It is a technically inefficient method of production.

Figure A10-2 Isoquant Curve for 60 Earrings

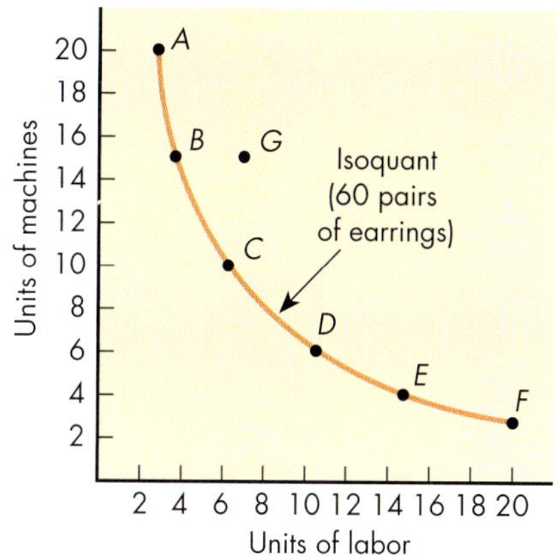

The numbers in the production table and the shape of the curve were not chosen randomly. They were chosen to be consistent with the law of diminishing marginal productivity, which means the curve is bowed inward. That is because as the firm increases the use of one factor more and more, it must use fewer and fewer units of the other factor to keep output constant. This reflects the technical considerations embodied in the law of diminishing marginal productivity. Thus, the chosen numbers tell us that if a firm wants to keep output constant, as it adds more and more of one factor (and less of the other factor), it has to use relatively more of that factor. For example, initially it might add 1 machine to replace 1 worker, holding output constant. If it continues it will have to use 1.5 machines, then 2 machines, and so on.

The rate at which one factor must be added to compensate for the loss of another factor, to keep output constant, is called the **marginal rate of substitution.** To say that there is diminishing marginal productivity is to say that there is a diminishing marginal rate of substitution. It is because the table assumes a diminishing marginal rate of substitution that the isoquant curve is bowed inward.

Graphically, the slope of the isoquant curve is the marginal rate of substitution. To be exact, the absolute value of the slope at a point on the isoquant curve equals the ratio of the marginal productivity of labor to the marginal productivity of machines:

$$|\text{Slope}| = MP_{\text{labor}}/MP_{\text{machines}}$$
$$= \text{Marginal rate of substitution}$$

With this equation, you can really see why the isoquant is downward sloping. As the firm moves from point A to point F it is using more labor and fewer machines. Because of the law of diminishing marginal productivity, as the

Figure A10-3 An Isoquant Map

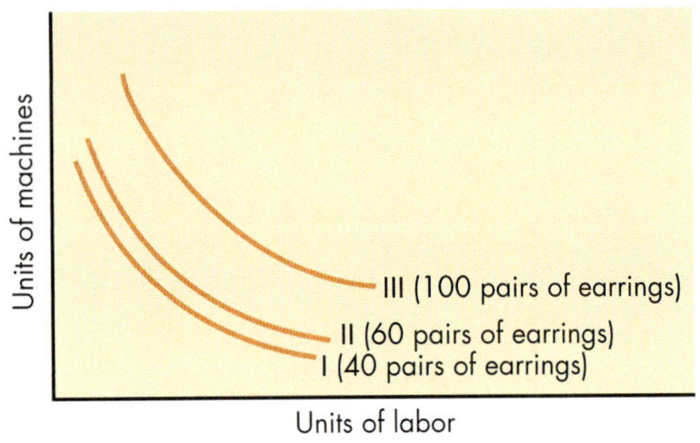

firm moves from A to F, the marginal productivity of labor decreases and the marginal productivity of machines increases. The slope of the isoquant falls since the marginal rate of substitution is decreasing.

Let's consider a specific example. Say in Figure A10-2 the firm is producing at point *B*. If it cuts its input by 5 machines but also wants to keep output constant, it must increase labor by 2 (move from point *B* to point C). So the marginal rate of substitution of labor for machines between points B and C must be 5/2 or 2.5.

The firm can complete this exercise for many different levels of output. Doing so will result in an **isoquant map,** *a set of isoquant curves that show technically efficient combinations of inputs that can produce different levels of output*. Such a map for output levels of 40, 60, and 100 is shown in Figure A10-3.

Each curve represents a different level of output. Isoquant I is the lower level of output, 40, and the isoquant III is the highest level of output. When a firm chooses an output level it is choosing one of those isoquants. The chosen isoquant represents the technically efficient combinations of resources that can produce the desired output.

THE ISOCOST LINE

So far I have only talked about technical efficiency. To move to economic efficiency, we have to bring in the costs of production. We do so with the **isocost line**—*a line that represents alternative combinations of factors of production that have the same costs*. (*Isocost* is a fancy name for "equal cost.") Each point on the isocost line represents a combination of factors of production which, in total, cost the firm an equal amount.

To draw the isocost line you must know the cost per unit of each input as well as the amount the firm has chosen to spend on production. Say labor costs $5 a unit and machinery costs $3 a unit and that the firm has chosen to

Figure A10-4 Isocost Curves

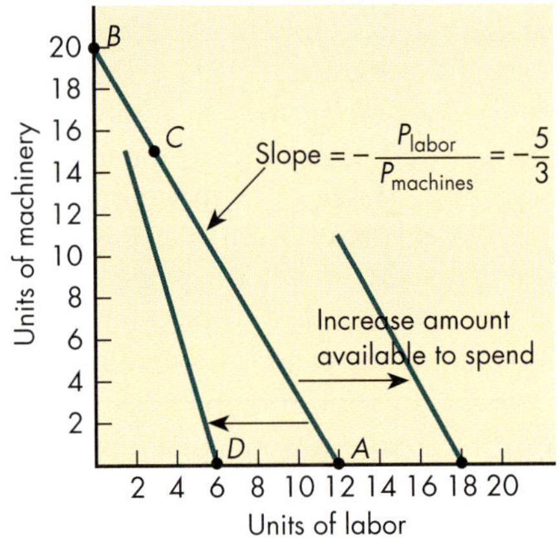

spend $60. What is the greatest number of earrings it can produce with that $60? To answer that question, we need to create a curve representing the various amounts of inputs a firm can get with that $60. We do so in the following manner. Say the firm decides to spend the entire $60 on labor. Since labor costs $5 a unit, if the firm spends all of the $60 on labor it can buy 12 units of labor. This alternative is represented by point A in Figure A10-4.

Alternatively, since machines cost $3 a unit, if the firm chooses to spend all of the $60 on machines it can buy 20 machines (point *B* in Figure A10-4). This gives us two points on the isocost curve. Of course, the assumption of diminishing marginal rates of substitutions makes it highly unlikely that firm would want to produce at either of these points. Instead, it would likely use some combination of inputs. But these extreme points are useful nonetheless, because by connecting them (the line that goes from A to B in Figure A10-4), we can see the various combinations of inputs that also cost $60.

To see that this is indeed the case, say the firm starts with 20 machines and no labor. If the firm wants to use some combination of labor and machinery, it can give up some machines and use the money it saves by using fewer machines to purchase units of labor. Let's say it gives up 5 machines, leaving it with 15. That means it has $15 to spend on labor, for which it can buy 3 units of labor. That means 15 machines and 3 units of labor is another combination of labor and machines that cost the firm $60. This means that point C is also a point on the isocost line. You can continue with this exercise to prove to yourself that the line connecting points *A* and *B* does represent various combinations of labor and machinery the firm can buy with $60. Thus, the line connecting *A* and *B* is the $60 isocost line.

To see that you understand the isocost line, it is useful to go through a couple of examples that would make it shift. For example, what would happen to the isocost line if the firm chooses to increase its spending on production to \$90? To see the effect we go through the same exercise as before: If it spent it all on labor, it could buy 18 units of labor. If it spent it all on machines, it could buy 30 units of machinery. Connecting these points will give us a curve to the right of and parallel to the original curve. It has the same slope because the relative prices of the factors of production, which determines the slope, have not changed.

Now ask yourself, What happens to the isocost line if the price of labor rises to \$10 a unit? If you said the isocost curve becomes steeper, shifting along the labor axis to point *D* while remaining anchored along the machinery axis until the slope is −10/3, you've got it. In general, the absolute value of the slope of the isocost curve is the ratio of the price of the factor of production on the *x*-axis to the price of the factor of production on the *y*-axis. That means that as the price of a factor rises, the end point of the isocost curve shifts in on the axis on which that factor is measured.

Choosing the Economically Efficient Point of Production

Now let's move on to a consideration of the economically efficient combination of resources to produce 60 pairs of earrings with \$60. To do that we must put the isoquant cost curve from Figure A10-2 and the isocost curve from Figure A10-4 together. We do so in Figure A10-5.

The problem for the firm is to produce as many pairs of earrings as possible with the \$60 it has to spend. Or, put another way, given a level of production it has chosen, it wants to produce at the least-cost combination of the factors of production.

Let's now find the least-cost combination of inputs to produce 60 pairs of earrings. Let's say that, initially, the firm chooses point A on its isoquant curve—that's at 15 machines and 4 workers. That produces 60 pairs of earrings, but has a cost of \$45 + \$20 = \$65. The firm can't produce 60 pairs of earrings unless it is willing to spend more than \$60. If it fires a worker to bring its cost in line, moving it to point *B*, it moves down to a lower isoquant—it is producing only 40 pairs.

If the firm has a less-than-competent manager, that manager will conclude that you can't produce 60 for \$60. But say the firm has an efficient manager—one who has taken introductory economics. As opposed to *reducing* the number of workers as the other manager did, she *increases* the number of workers to 6 and reduces the number of

Figure A10-5 Combining Isoquant and Isocost Curves

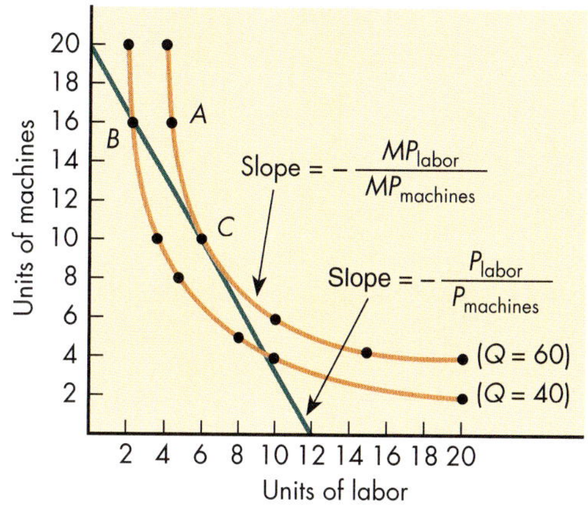

machines to 10. Doing so still produces 60 pairs of earrings, since C is a point on the isoquant curve, but the strategy reduces the cost from \$65 at point A to \$60 (10 machines at \$3 = \$30, and 6 workers at \$5 = \$30). So she is producing 60 pairs of earrings at a cost of \$60. She is operating at the economic efficient point—point C.

Let's talk about the characteristics of Point C. Point C is the point where the isoquant curve is tangent to the isocost curve—the point at which the slope of the isoquant curve ($-MP_L/MP_M$) equals the slope of the isocost curve ($-P_L/P_M$). That is, $-MP_L/MP_M = -P_L/P_M$. This can be rewritten as:

$$MP_L/P_L = MP_M/P_M$$

What this equation says is that when the additional output per dollar spent on labor equals the additional output per dollar spent on machines, the firm is operating efficiently. It makes sense. If the additional output per dollar spent on labor exceeded the additional output per dollar spent on machines, the firm would do better by increasing its use of labor and decreasing its use of machines.

Point C represents the combination of labor and machines that will result in the highest output given the isocost curve facing the firm. To put it in technical terms, the firm is operating at an economically efficient point where marginal rate of substitution equals the ratio of the factor prices. Any point other than C on the isocost curve will cost \$60 but produce fewer than 60 pairs of earrings. Any other point than C on the isoquant curve will produce 60 pairs of earrings but cost more than \$60. Only C is the economically efficient point given the factor costs.

To see that you understand the analysis, say that the price of labor falls to \$3 and you still want to produce 60. What will happen to the amount of labor and machines you hire? Alternatively, say that the price of machines rises to $5 and you want to spend only $60. What will happen to the amount of labor and machines you hire?

If your answers are (1) you hire more workers and fewer machines, and (2) you reduce production using fewer machines and, maybe, less labor, you've got the analyses down. If you didn't give those answers, I suggest rereading this appendix, if it is to be on the exam, and working through the questions for thought and review.

Key Terms

isocost line *(238)*
isoquant curve *(237)*
isoquant map *(238)*
marginal rate of substitution *(237)*

Questions for Thought and Review

1. What happens to the marginal rate of substitution as a firm increases the use of one input, keeping output constant? What accounts for this?
2. Draw an isocost curve for a firm that has $100 to spend on producing jeans. Input includes labor and materials. Labor costs $8 and materials cost $4 a unit. How does each of the following affect the isocost curve? Show your answer graphically.
   a. Production budget doubles.
   b. Cost of materials rises to $10 a unit.
   c. Costs of labor and materials each rise by 25 percent.
3. Show, using isocost/isoquant analysis, how firms in the United States use relatively less labor and relatively more land than Japan for the production of similar goods, yet both are behaving economically efficiently.
4. Demonstrate the difference between economic efficiency and technical efficiency, using the isocost/isoquant analysis.
5. Draw a hypothetical isocost curve and an isoquant curve tangent to the isocost curve. Label the combination of inputs that represents an efficient use of resources.
   a. How does a technological innovation affect your analysis?
   b. How does the increase in the price of the input on the *x*-axis affect your analysis?
6. Show graphically the analysis of the example in Figure A10-5 if the price of labor falls to $3. Demonstrate that the firm can increase production given the same budget.
7. Show graphically the analysis of the example in Figure A10-5 if the price of machines rises to $5. Demonstrate that the firm must reduce production if it keeps the same budget.

PERFECT COMPETITION

11

There's no resting place for an enterprise in a competitive economy.

—Alfred P. Sloan

After reading this chapter, you should be able to:

- List the six conditions for a perfectly competitive market.
- Explain why producing an output at which marginal cost equals price maximizes total profit for a perfect competitor.
- Demonstrate why the marginal cost curve is the supply curve for a perfectly competitive firm.
- Determine the output and profit of a perfect competitor graphically and numerically.
- Construct a market supply curve by adding together individual firms' marginal cost curves.
- Explain why perfectly competitive firms make zero economic profit in the long run.
- Explain the adjustment process from short-run equilibrium to long-run equilibrium.

The concept *competition* is used in two ways in economics. One way is as a process. *Competition as a process* is a rivalry among firms and is prevalent throughout our economy. It involves one firm trying to figure out how to take away market share from another firm. An example is my publishing firm giving me a contract to write a great book like this in order for the firm to take market share away from other publishing firms that are also selling economics textbooks. The other use of *competition* is as a *perfectly competitive market structure*. It is this use that is the subject of this chapter. Although perfect competition has highly restrictive assumptions, it provides us with a reference point we can use to think about various market structures and competitive processes. Why is such a reference point important? Think of the following analogy.

In physics when you study the laws of gravity, you initially study what would happen in a vacuum. Perfect vacuums don't exist, but talking about what would happen if you dropped an object in a perfect vacuum makes the analysis easier. So too with economics. Our equivalent of a perfect vacuum is perfect competition. In perfect competition the invisible hand of the market operates unimpeded. In this chapter we'll consider how perfectly competitive markets work and see how to apply the cost analysis developed in Chapters 9 and 10.

A PERFECTLY COMPETITIVE MARKET

A **perfectly competitive market** is *a market in which economic forces operate unimpeded.* For a market to be called *perfectly competitive*, it must meet some stringent conditions:

1. Both buyers and sellers are price takers.
2. The number of firms is large.
3. There are no barriers to entry.
4. Firms' products are identical.
5. There is complete information.
6. Selling firms are profit-maximizing entrepreneurial firms.

These conditions are needed to ensure that economic forces operate instantaneously and are unimpeded by political and social forces. For example, if there weren't a large number of firms, the few firms in the industry would have an incentive to get together and limit output so they could get a higher price. They would stop the invisible hand from working. Similarly for the other conditions, although the reasoning why they're necessary can get rather complicated.

THE NECESSARY CONDITIONS FOR PERFECT COMPETITION

To give you a sense of these conditions, let's consider each a bit more carefully.

1. *Both buyers and sellers are price takers.* A **price taker** is *a firm or individual who takes the price determined by market supply and demand as given.* When you buy, say, toothpaste, you go to the store and find that the price of toothpaste is, say, $2.33 for the medium-size tube; you're a price taker. The firm, however, is a price maker since it set the price at $2.33. So even though the toothpaste industry is highly competitive, it's not a perfectly competitive market. In a perfectly competitive market, market supply and demand determine the price; both firms and consumers take the market price as given.
2. *The number of firms is large.* This is almost self-explanatory. *Large* means sufficiently large so that any one firm's output compared to the market output is imperceptible, and what one firm does has no influence on what other firms do.

Q.1 Why is the assumption of no barriers to entry necessary for the existence of perfect competition?

3. *There are no barriers to entry.* **Barriers to entry** are *social, political, or economic impediments that prevent firms from entering a market.* They might be legal barriers such as exist when firms acquire a patent to produce a certain product. Barriers might be technological, such as when the minimum efficient scale of production allows only one firm to produce at the lowest average total cost. Or barriers might be created by social forces, such as when bankers will lend only to individuals with specific racial characteristics. Perfect competition can have no barriers to entry.
4. *Firms' products are identical.* This requirement means that each firm's output is indistinguishable from any other firm's output. Corn bought by the bushel is relatively homogeneous. One kernel is indistinguishable from any other kernel. In contrast, you can buy 30 different brands of many goods—soft drinks, for instance: Pepsi, Coke, 7UP, and so on. They are all slightly different from one another and thus not identical.
5. *There is complete information.* In a perfectly competitive market, firms and consumers know all there is to know about the market—prices, products, and available technology, to name a few aspects. If any firm experiences a technological breakthrough, all firms know about it and are able to use the same technology instantaneously. No firm or consumer has a competitive edge over another.
6. *Selling firms are profit-maximizing entrepreneurial firms.* Firms can have many goals and be organized in a variety of ways. For perfect competition to exist, firms must seek maximum profit and only profit, and the people who make the decisions must receive only profits and no other form of income from the firms.

THE DEFINITION OF SUPPLY AND PERFECT COMPETITION

These are enormously strong conditions and are seldom met simultaneously. But they are necessary for a perfectly competitive market to exist. Combined, they create an

The Internet and the Perfectly Competitive Model

Applying the Tools

Recent technological developments are making the perfectly competitive model more directly relevant to our economy. Specifically, the Internet has eliminated the spatial dimension of competition (except for shipping), allowing individuals to compete globally rather than locally. When you see a bid on the Internet, you don't care where the supplier is (as long as you do not have to pay shipping fees). Because it allows access to so many buyers and sellers, the Internet reduces the number of seller-set posted price markets (such as found in retail stores), and replaces them with auction markets.

The Internet has had its biggest impact in firms' buying practices. Today, when firms want to buy standardized products, they will often post their technical requirements for desired components on the Net and allow suppliers from all over the world to bid to fill their orders. Firms have found that buying in this fashion over the Internet has on average lowered the prices they pay by over 10 percent.

Similar changes are occurring in consumer markets. With sites like Priceline.com, individuals can set the price they are willing to pay for goods and services (such as hotel rooms and airline tickets) and see if anyone wants to supply them. (Recently, I successfully bid $120 for a $460 retail price hotel room in New York City.) With sites such as eBay you can buy and sell almost anything. The Internet is even developing its own payment systems, such as PayPal.

In short, with the Internet, entry and exit are much easier than in traditional brick-and-mortar business, and that makes the market more like a perfectly competitive market. As Internet search engines become better designed for commerce, and as more people become Internet savvy, the economy will more and more closely resemble the perfectly competitive model.

environment in which each firm, following its own self-interest, will offer goods to the market in a predictable way. If these conditions hold, we can talk formally about the supply of a produced good and how it relates to costs. This follows from the definition of supply we gave in Chapter 4:

> *Supply* is a schedule of quantities of goods that will be offered to the market at various prices.

This definition requires the supplier to be a price taker (our first condition). In almost all other market structures (frameworks within which firms interact economically), firms are not price takers; they are price makers. They don't ask, "How much should I supply, given the market price?" Instead they ask, "Given a demand curve, how much should I produce and what price should I charge?" In other market structures, the supplier sets the quantity and price, based on costs, at whatever level is best for it.[1]

The second condition—that the number of firms is large—is necessary so that firms have no ability to *collude* (to operate in concert so that they can get more for themselves). Conditions 3 through 5 are closely related to the first two; they make it impossible for any firm to forget about the hundreds of other firms out there just waiting to replace their supply. Condition 6 tells us a firm's goals. If we didn't know the goals, we wouldn't know how firms would react when faced with the given price.

What's nice about these conditions is that they allow us to formally relate supply to the cost concept we developed in Chapters 9 and 10: marginal cost. If the conditions

[1]A firm's ability to set price doesn't mean that it can choose just any price it pleases. Other market structures can be highly competitive, so the range of prices a firm can charge and still stay in business is often limited. Such highly competitive firms are not perfectly competitive—they still set price rather than supply a certain quantity and accept whatever price they get.

Figure 11-1 (a and b) Market Demand Curve versus Individual Firm Demand Curve
Even though the demand curve for the market is downward-sloping, the perceived demand curve of an individual firm is perfectly elastic because each firm is so small relative to the market.

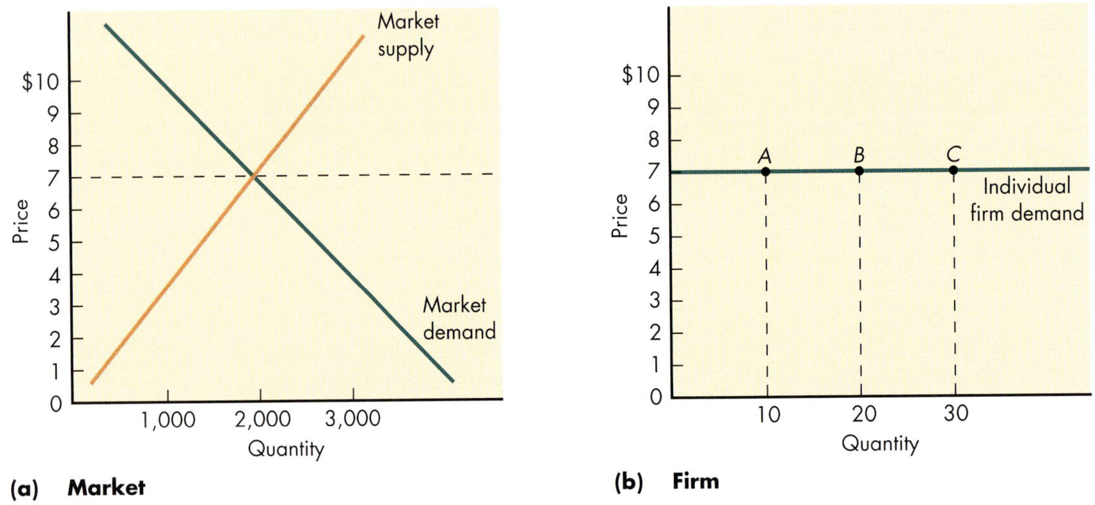

hold, a firm's supply curve will be that portion of the firm's short-run marginal cost curve above the average variable cost curve, as we'll see shortly.

Web Note 11.1
Barriers to Entry

If the conditions for perfect competition aren't met, then we can't use our formal concept of supply and how it relates to cost; we can still talk informally about the supply of produced goods and cost conditions. We generally talk informally about perfect competition, keeping in the back of our minds which conditions aren't met and modifying the analysis accordingly. Even if the conditions for perfect competition don't fully exist, supply forces are still strong and many of the insights of the competitive model can be applied to firm behavior in other market structures.

Even if we can't technically specify a supply curve, supply forces are still strong and many of the insights of the competitive model carry over.

Demand Curves for the Firm and the Industry

Now that we've considered the competitive supply curve for the firm, let's turn our attention to the competitive demand curve for the firm. Here we must recognize that the demand curve for the industry is downward-sloping as in Figure 11-1(a), but the perceived demand curve for the firm is horizontal (perfectly elastic), as in Figure 11-1(b).

Q-2 How can the demand curve for the market be downward-sloping but the demand curve for a competitive firm be perfectly elastic?

Why the difference? It's a difference in perception. Each firm in a competitive industry is so small that it perceives that its actions will not affect the price it can get for its product. Price is the same no matter how much the firm produces. Think of an individual firm's actions as removing one piece of sand from a beach. Does that lower the level of the beach? For all practical, and even most impractical, purposes, we can assume it doesn't. Similarly for a perfectly competitive firm. That is why we consider the demand curve facing the firm to be horizontal.

The price the firm can get is determined by the market supply and demand curves shown in Figure 11-1(a). Market price is $7, and the firm represented in Figure 11-1(b) will get $7 for each unit of its product whether it produces 10 units (point *A*), 20 units (point *B*), or 30 units (point *C*). Its demand curve is perfectly elastic even though the demand curve for the market is downward sloping.

This difference in perception is extremely important. It means that firms will increase their output in response to an increase in market demand even though that

Figure 11-2 (a and b) Marginal Cost, Marginal Revenue, and Price
The profit-maximizing output for a firm occurs where marginal cost equals marginal revenue. Since for a competitive firm $P = MR$, its profit-maximizing output is where $MC = P$. At any other output it is forgoing profit.

Price = *MR*	Quantity Produced	Marginal Cost
$35.00	0	
		$28.00
35.00	1	
		20.00
35.00	2	
		16.00
35.00	3	
		14.00
35.00	4	
		12.00
35.00	5	
		17.00
35.00	6	
		22.00
35.00	7	
		30.00
35.00	8	
		40.00
35.00	9	
		54.00
35.00	10	

(a) MC/Price table

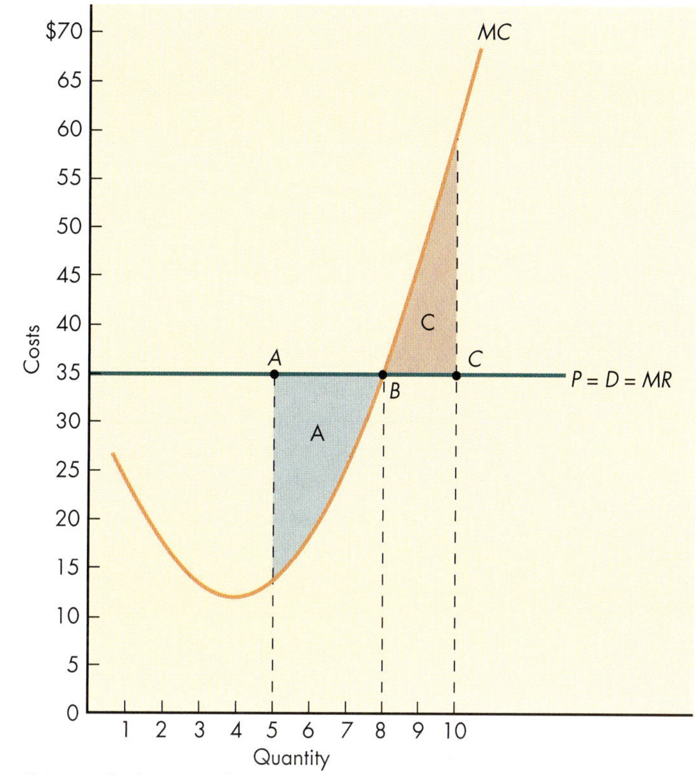

(b) MC/Price graph

increase in output will cause price to fall and can make all firms collectively worse off. But since, by the assumptions of perfect competition, they don't act collectively, each firm follows its self-interest. Let's now consider that self-interest in more detail.

The Profit-Maximizing Level of Output

The goal of a firm is to maximize profits—to get as much for itself as possible. So when it decides what quantity to produce, it will continually ask the question "What will changes in how much I produce do to profit?" Since profit is the difference between total revenue and total cost, what happens to profit in response to a change in output is determined by **marginal revenue (MR),** *the change in total revenue associated with a change in quantity*, and **marginal cost (MC),** *the change in total cost associated with a change in quantity*. That's why marginal revenue and marginal cost are key concepts in determining the profit-maximizing or loss-minimizing level of output of any firm.

To determine the profit-maximizing output, all you need to know is *MC* and *MR*.

To emphasize the importance of *MR* and MC, those are the only cost and revenue figures shown in Figure 11-2. Notice that we don't illustrate profit at all. We'll calculate profit later. All we want to determine now is the profit-maximizing level of output. To do this you need only know MC and *MR*. Specifically, a firm maximizes profit when MC = *MR*. To see why, let's first look at MC and *MR* more closely.

Marginal Revenue

For a competitive firm, $MR = P$.

Let's first consider marginal revenue. Since a perfect competitor accepts the market price as given, marginal revenue is simply the market price. In the example shown in Figure 11-2, if the firm increases output from 2 to 3, its revenue rises by $35 (from $70 to $105). So its marginal revenue is $35, the price of the good. Since at a price of $35 it can sell as much as it wants, for a competitive firm, $MR = P$.

Marginal revenue is given in column 1 of Figure 11-2(a). As you can see, *MR* equals $35 for all levels of output. But that's what we saw in Figure 11-1, which showed that the demand curve for a perfect competitor is perfectly elastic at the market price. For a perfect competitor, the marginal revenue curve and demand curve it faces are the same.

Marginal Cost

Now let's move on to marginal cost. I'll be brief since I discussed marginal cost in detail in Chapter 9. Marginal cost is that change in total cost that accompanies a change in output. Figure 11-2(a) shows marginal cost in column 3. Notice that initially in this example, marginal cost is falling, but by the fifth unit of output, it's increasing. This is consistent with our discussion in earlier chapters.

Notice also that the marginal cost figures are given for movements from one quantity to another. That's because marginal concepts tell us what happens when there's a change in something, so marginal concepts are best defined between numbers. The numbers in the shaded rows are the marginal costs. So the marginal cost of increasing output from 1 to 2 is $20, and the marginal cost of increasing output from 2 to 3 is $16. The marginal cost right at 2 (which the marginal cost graph shows) would be between $20 and $16 at approximately $18.

Profit Maximization: MC = MR

Q-3 What are the two things you must know to determine the profit-maximizing output?

As I noted above, to maximize profit, a firm should produce where marginal cost equals marginal revenue. Looking at Figure 11-2(b), we see that a firm following that rule should produce at an output of 8, where $MC = MR = \$35$. Now let me try to convince you that 8 is indeed the profit-maximizing output. To do so, let's consider three different possible quantities the firm might look at.

Let's say that initially the firm decides to produce 5 widgets, placing it at point A in Figure 11-2(b). At output A, the firm gets $35 for each widget but its marginal cost of increasing output is $17. We don't yet know the firm's total profit, but we do know how changing output will affect profit. For example, say the firm increases production from 5 to 6. Its revenue will rise by $35. (In other words, its marginal revenue is $35.) Its marginal cost of increasing output is $17. Since profit increases by $18 (the difference between *MR*, $35, and MC, $17), it makes sense (meaning the firm can increase its profit) to increase output from 5 to 6 units. It makes sense to increase output as long as the marginal cost is below the marginal revenue. The blue shaded area (A) represents the entire increase in profit the firm can get by increasing output.

Now let's say that the firm decides to produce 10 widgets, placing it at point C. Here the firm gets $35 for each widget. The marginal cost of producing that 10th unit is $54. So, MC > *MR*. If the firm decreases production by one unit, its cost decreases by $54 and its revenue decreases by $35. Profit increases by $19 ($54 − $35 = $19), so at point C, it makes sense to decrease output. This reasoning holds true as long as the marginal cost is above the marginal revenue. The red shaded area (C) represents the increase in profits the firm can get by decreasing output.

At point *B* (output = 8) the firm gets $35 for each widget, and its marginal cost is $35, as you can see in Figure 11-2(b). The marginal cost of increasing output by one unit is $40 and the marginal revenue of selling one more unit is $35, so its profit falls by $5. If the firm decreases output by one unit, its MC is $30 and its *MR* is $35, so its profit falls by $5. Either increasing or decreasing production will decrease profit, so at point *B*, an output of 8, the firm is maximizing profit.

Since *MR* is just market price, we can state the **profit-maximizing condition** of a competitive firm as MC = *MR* = *P*.

Profit-maximizing condition for a competitive firm: *MC* = *MR* = *P*.

You should commit this profit-maximizing condition to memory. You should also be sure that you understand the intuition behind it. If marginal revenue isn't equal to marginal cost, a firm obviously can increase profit by changing output. If that isn't obvious, the marginal benefit of an additional hour of thinking about this condition will exceed the marginal cost (whatever it is), meaning that you should . . . right, you guessed it . . . study some more.

If marginal revenue does not equal marginal cost, a firm can increase profit by changing output.

The Marginal Cost Curve Is the Supply Curve

Now let's consider again the definition of the supply curve as a schedule of quantities of goods that will be offered to the market at various prices. Notice that the marginal cost curve fits that definition. It tells how much the firm will supply at a given price. Figure 11-3 shows the various quantities the firm will supply at different market prices. If the price is $35, we showed that the firm would supply 8 (point *A*). If the price had been $19.50, the firm would have supplied 6 (point *B*); if the price had been $61, the firm would have supplied 10 (point *C*). Because the marginal cost curve tells us how much of a produced good a firm will supply at a given price, *the marginal cost curve is the firm's supply curve*. The MC curve tells the competitive firm how much it should produce at a given price. (As you'll see later, there's an addendum to this statement. Specifically, the marginal cost curve is the firm's supply curve only if price exceeds average variable cost.)

Because the marginal cost curve tells us how much of a produced good a firm will supply at a given price, the marginal cost curve is the firm's supply curve.

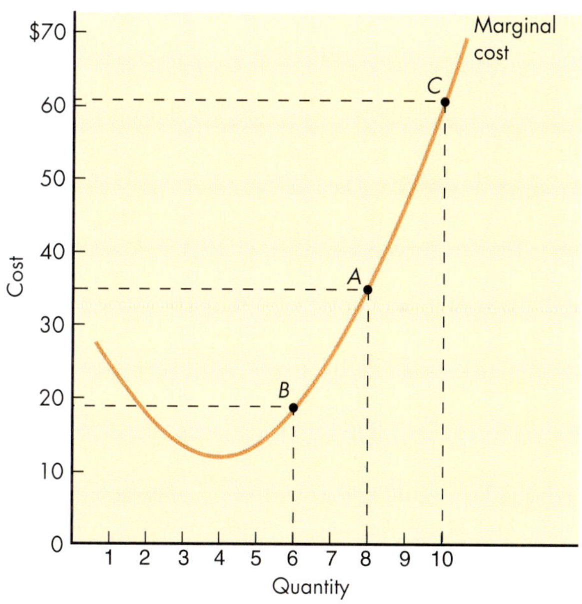

Figure 11-3 The Marginal Cost Curve Is a Firm's Supply Curve
Since the marginal cost curve tells the firm how much to produce, the marginal cost curve is the perfectly competitive firm's supply curve. This exhibit shows three points on a firm's supply curve; as you can see the quantity the firm chooses to supply depends on the price. For example, if market price is $19.50 the firm produces 6 units.

THE BROADER IMPORTANCE OF THE MR = MC EQUILIBRIUM CONDITION

Applying the Tools

This Marginal revenue = Marginal cost equilibrium condition is simple, but it's enormously powerful. As we'll see, it carries over to other market structures. If you replace revenue with benefits, it also forms the basis of economic reasoning. With whom should you go out? What's the marginal benefit? What's the marginal cost? Should you marry Pat? What's the marginal benefit? What's the marginal cost? As we discussed in Chapter 1, thinking like an economist requires thinking in these marginal terms and applying this marginal reasoning to a wide variety of activities. Understanding this condition is to economics what understanding gravity is to physics. It gives you a sense of if, how, and why prices and quantities will move.

FIRMS MAXIMIZE TOTAL PROFIT

Q-4 Why do firms maximize total profit rather than profit per unit?

Notice that when you talk about maximizing profit, you're talking about maximizing *total profit*, not profit per unit. Profit per unit would be maximized at a much lower output level than is total profit. Firms don't care about profit per unit; as long as an increase in output will increase total profits, a profit-maximizing firm should increase output. That's difficult to grasp, so let's consider a concrete example.

Say two people are selling T-shirts that cost $4 each. One sells 2 T-shirts at a price of $6 each and makes a profit per shirt of $2. His total profit is $4. The second person sells 8 T-shirts at $5 each, making a profit per unit of only $1 but selling 8. Her total profit is $8, twice as much as the fellow who had the $2 profit per unit. In this case, $5 (the price with the lower profit per unit), not $6, yields more total profit.

PROFIT MAXIMIZATION USING TOTAL REVENUE AND TOTAL COST

An alternative method of determining the profit-maximizing level of output is to look at the total revenue and total cost curves directly. Figure 11-4 shows total cost and total revenue for the firm we're considering so far. The table in Figure 11-4(a) shows total revenue in column 2, which is just the number of units sold times market price. Total cost is in column 3. Total cost is the cumulative sum of the marginal costs from Figure 11-2(a) plus a fixed cost of $40. Total profit (column 4) is the difference between total revenue and total cost. The firm is interested in maximizing total profit. Looking down column 4 of Figure 11-4(a), you can quickly see that the profit-maximizing level of output is 8, as it was using the *MR* = MC rule, since total profit is highest at an output of 8.

In Figure 11-4(b) we plot the firm's total revenue and total cost curves from the table in Figure 11-4(a). The total revenue curve is a straight line; each additional unit sold increases revenue by the same amount, $35. The total cost curve is bowed upward at most quantities, reflecting the increasing marginal cost at different levels of output. The firm's profit is represented by the distance between the total revenue curve and the total cost curve. For example, at output 5, the firm makes $45 in profit.

Total profit is maximized where the vertical distance between total revenue and total cost is greatest. In this example total profit is maximized at output 8, just as in the alternative approach. At that output, marginal revenue (the slope of the total revenue curve) and marginal cost (the slope of the total cost curve) are equal.

Figure 11-4 (a and b) Determination of Profits by Total Cost and Total Revenue Curves
The profit-maximizing output level can also be seen by considering the total cost curve and the total revenue curve. Profit is maximized at the output where total revenue exceeds total cost by the largest amount. This occurs at an output of 8.

Quantity	Total Revenue	Total Cost	Total Profit
0	$ 0	$ 40	$−40
1	35	68	−33
2	70	88	−18
3	105	104	1
4	140	118	22
5	175	130	45
6	210	147	63
7	245	169	76
8	280	199	81
9	315	239	76
10	350	293	57

(a) Total revenue and total cost table

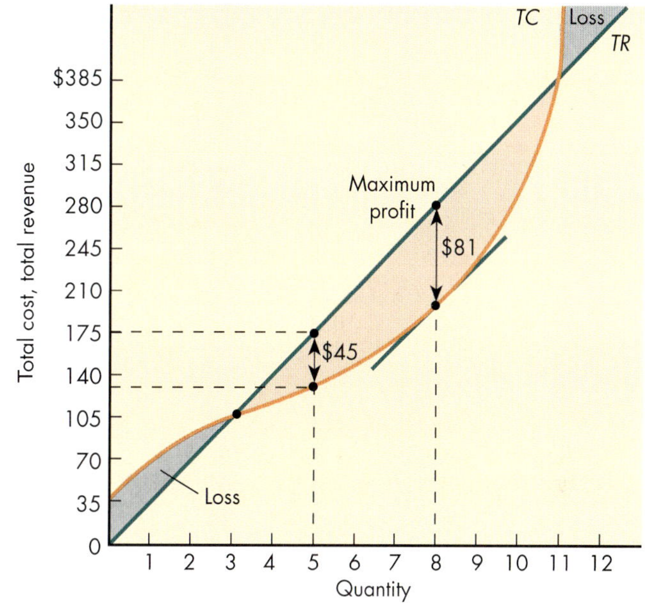

(b) Total revenue and total cost curves

Total Profit at the Profit-Maximizing Level of Output

In the initial discussion of the firm's choice of output, given price, I carefully presented only marginal cost and price. We talked about maximizing profit, but nowhere did I mention what profit, average total cost, average variable cost, or average fixed cost is. I mentioned only marginal cost and price to emphasize that marginal cost is all that's needed to determine a competitive firm's supply curve (and a competitive firm is the only firm that has a supply curve) and the output that will maximize profit. Now that you know that, let's turn our attention more closely to profit.

Marginal cost is all that is needed to determine a competitive firm's supply curve.

Determining Profit from a Table of Costs and Revenue

The $P = MR = MC$ condition tells us how much output a competitive firm should produce to maximize profit. It does not tell us the profit the firm makes. Profit is determined by total revenue minus total cost. Table 11-1 expands Figure 11-2(a) and presents a table of all the costs relevant to the firm. Going through the columns and reminding yourself of the definition of each is a good review of Chapters 9 and 10. If the definitions don't come to mind immediately, you need a review. If you don't know the definitions of *MC*, *AVC*, *ATC*, *FC*, and *AFC*, go back and reread Chapters 9 and 10.

The firm is interested in maximizing profit. Looking at Table 11-1, you can quickly see that the profit-maximizing position is 8, as it was before, since at an output of 8, total profit is highest.

Table 11-1 Costs Relevant to a Firm

Price = Marginal Revenue	1 Quantity Produced	2 Total Fixed Cost	3 Average Fixed Cost	4 Total Variable Cost	5 Average Variable Cost	6 Total Cost	7 Marginal Cost	8 Average Total Cost	9 Total Revenue	10 Total Profit
$35.00	0	$40.00	—	0	—	$ 40.00		—	0	$−40.00
							$28.00			
35.00	1	40.00	$40.00	$ 28.00	$28.00	68.00		$68.00	$ 35.00	−33.00
							20.00			
35.00	2	40.00	20.00	48.00	24.00	88.00		44.00	70.00	−18.00
							16.00			
35.00	3	40.00	13.33	64.00	21.33	104.00		34.67	105.00	1.00
							14.00			
35.00	4	40.00	10.00	78.00	19.50	118.00		29.50	140.00	22.00
							12.00			
35.00	5	40.00	8.00	90.00	18.00	130.00		26.00	175.00	45.00
							17.00			
35.00	6	40.00	6.67	107.00	17.83	147.00		24.50	210.00	63.00
							22.00			
35.00	7	40.00	5.71	129.00	18.43	169.00		24.14	245.00	76.00
							30.00			
35.00	8	40.00	5.00	159.00	19.88	199.00		24.88	280.00	81.00
							40.00			
35.00	9	40.00	4.44	199.00	22.11	239.00		26.56	315.00	76.00
							54.00			
35.00	10	40.00	4.00	253.00	25.30	293.00		29.30	350.00	57.00

Using the MC = *MR* = *P* rule, you can also see that the profit-maximizing level of output is 8. Increasing output from 7 to 8 has a marginal cost of $30, which is less than $35, so it makes sense to do so. Increasing output from 8 to 9 has a marginal cost of $40, which is more than $35, so it does not make sense to do so. The output 8 is the profit-maximizing output. At that profit-maximizing level of output, the profit the firm earns is $81, which is calculated by subtracting total cost of $199 from total revenue of $280. Notice also that average total cost is lowest at an output of about 7, and the average variable cost is lowest at an output of about 6.[2] Thus, the profit-maximizing position (which is 8) is *not* necessarily a position that minimizes either average variable cost or average total cost. It is only the position that maximizes total profit.

Determining Profit from a Graph

The profit-maximizing output can be determined in a table (as in Table 11-1) or in a graph (as in Figure 11-5).

These relationships can be seen in a graph. In Figure 11-5(a) I add the average total cost and average variable cost curves to the graph of marginal cost and price first presented in Figure 11-2. Notice that the marginal cost curve goes through the lowest points of both average cost curves. (If you don't know why, it would be a good idea to go back and review Chapter 9.)

---

[2] I say "about 6" and "about 7" because the table gives only whole numbers. The actual minimum point occurs at 5.55 for average variable cost and 6.55 for average total cost. The nearest whole numbers to these are 6 and 7.

Figure 11-5 (a, b, and c) Determining Profits Graphically
The profit-maximizing output depends *only* on where the MC and *MR* curves intersect. The total amount of profit or loss that a firm makes depends on the price it receives and its average total cost of producing the profit-maximizing output. This exhibit shows the case of (**a**) a profit, (**b**) zero profit, and (**c**) a loss.

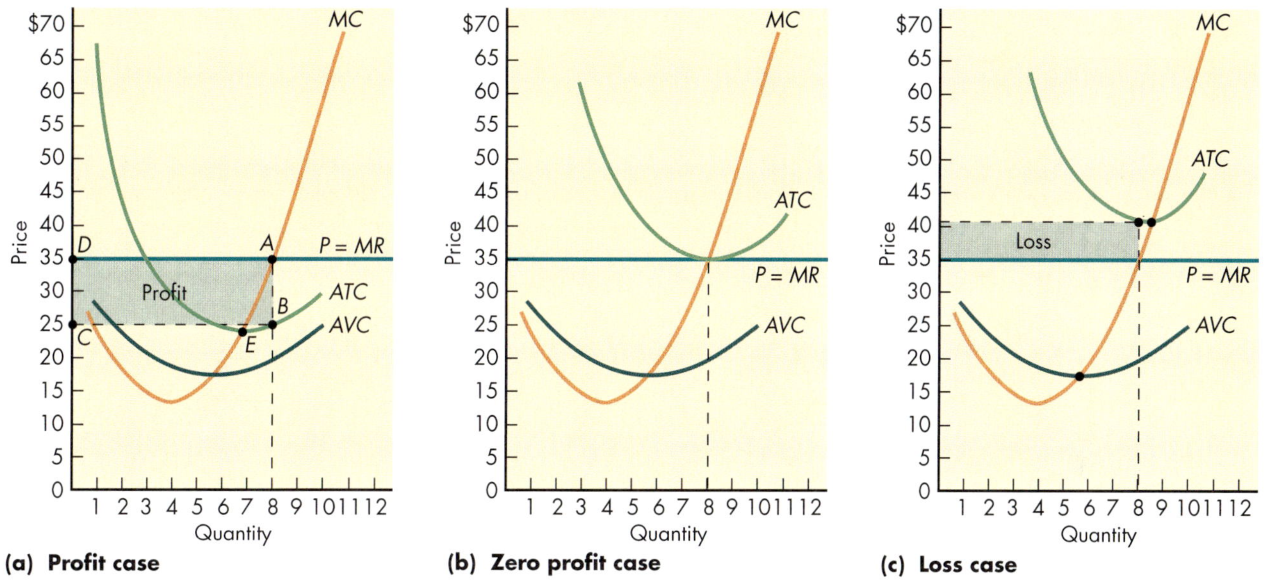

Find Output Where MC = MR The way you find profit graphically is first to find the point where MC = *MR* (point *A*). That intersection determines the quantity the firm will produce if it wants to maximize profit. Why? Because the vertical distance between a point on the marginal cost curve and a point on the marginal revenue curve represents the additional profit the firm can make by changing output. For example, if it increases production from 6 to 7, its marginal cost is $22 and its marginal revenue is $35. By increasing output it can increase profit by $13 (from $63 to $76). The same reasoning holds true for any output less than 8. For outputs higher than 8, the opposite reasoning holds true. Marginal cost exceeds marginal revenue, so it pays to decrease output. So, to maximize profit, the firm must see that there is no distance between the two curves—it must see where they intersect.

Q-5 If the firm described in Figure 11-5 is producing 4 units, what would you advise it to do, and why?

Find Profit per Unit Where MC = MR After having determined the profit-maximizing quantity, drop a vertical line down to the horizontal axis and see what average total cost is at that output level (point *B*). Doing so determines the profit per unit at the profit-maximizing output because it's the difference between the price the firm receives (its average revenue) and its average cost. Since the firm will earn that profit on each unit sold, you next extend a line back to the vertical axis (point C). That tells us that the average total costs per unit are $25. Next go up the price axis to the price that the firm receives (point *D*). For a competitive firm, that price is the marginal revenue. Connecting these points gives us the shaded rectangle, *ABCD*, which is the total profit earned by the firm (the total quantity times the profit per unit).

When the *ATC* curve is below the marginal revenue curve, the firm makes a profit. When the *ATC* curve is above the marginal revenue curve, the firm incurs a loss.

Notice that at the profit-maximizing position, the profit per unit isn't at its highest because average total cost is *not* at its minimum point. Profit per unit of output would be highest at point *E*. A common mistake that students make is to draw a line up from point *E* when they are finding profits. That is wrong. It is important to remember: *To*

Profit Maximization and Real-World Firms

Applying the Tools

Most real-world firms do not have profit as their only goal. The reason is that, in the real world, the decision maker's income is part of the cost of production. For example, a paid manager has an incentive to hold down costs, but has little incentive to hold down his income which, for the firm, is a cost. Alternatively, say that a firm is a worker-managed firm. If workers receive a share of the profits, they'll push for higher profits, but they'll also see to it that in the process of maximizing profits they don't hurt their own interest—maximizing their wages.

A manager-managed firm will push for high profits but will see to it that it doesn't achieve those profits by hurting the manager's interests. Managers' pay will be high. In short, real-world firms will hold down the costs of factors of production *except* the cost of the decision maker.

In real life, this problem of the lack of incentives to hold down costs is important. For example, firms' managerial expenses often balloon even as firms are cutting "costs." Similarly, CEOs and other high-ranking officers of the firm often have enormously high salaries. How and why the lack of incentives to hold down costs affects the economy is best seen by first considering the nature of an economy with incentives to hold down all costs. That's why we use as our standard model the profit-maximizing firm. (*Standard model* means the model that economists use as our basis of reasoning; from it, we branch out.)

To determine maximum profit, you must first determine what output the firm will choose to produce by seeing where *MC* equals *MR*, and then dropping a line down to the *ATC* curve.

determine maximum profit you must first determine what output the firm will choose to produce by seeing where MC *equals* MR *and then determine the average total cost at that quantity by dropping a line down to the* ATC *curve*. Only then can you determine what maximum profit will be.

Zero Profit or Loss Where MC = MR Notice also that as the curves in Figure 11-5(a) are drawn, *ATC* at the profit-maximizing position is below the price, and the firm makes a profit per unit of a little over $10. The choice of short-run average total cost curves was arbitrary and doesn't affect the firm's profit-maximizing condition: MC = MR. It could have been assumed that fixed cost was higher, which would have shifted the *ATC* curve up. In Figure 11-5(b) it's assumed that fixed cost is $81 higher than in Figure 11-5(a). Instead of $40, it's $121. The appropriate average total cost curve for a fixed cost of $121 is drawn in Figure 11-5(b). Notice that in this case economic profit is zero and the marginal cost curve intersects the minimum point of the average total cost curve at an output of 8 and a price of $35. In this case, the firm is making zero economic profit. (Remember from Chapter 10 that even though economic profit is zero, all resources, including entrepreneurs, are being paid their opportunity cost.)

Q-6 What is wrong with the following diagram?

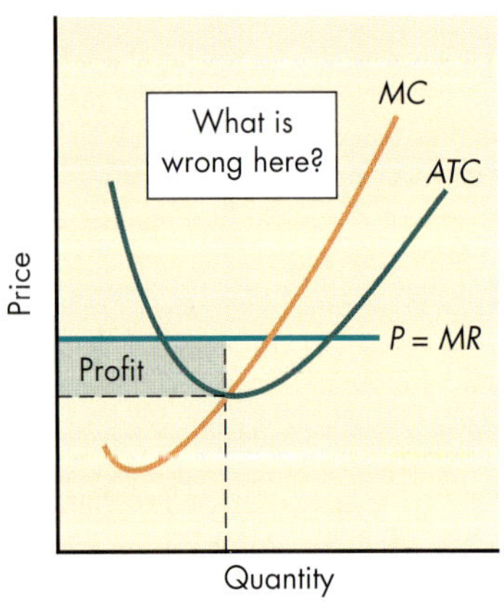

In Figure 11-5(c), fixed cost is much higher—$169. Profit-maximizing output is still 8, but now at an output of 8, the firm is making an economic loss of $6 on each unit sold, since its average total cost is $41. The loss is given by the shaded rectangle. In this case, the profit-maximizing condition is actually a loss-minimizing condition. So MC = MR = *P* is both a *profit-maximizing condition* and a *loss-minimizing condition*.

I draw these three cases to emphasize to you that determining the profit-maximizing output level doesn't depend on fixed cost or average total cost. It depends only on where marginal cost equals price.

The Shutdown Point

Earlier I stated the supply curve of a competitive firm is its marginal cost curve. More specifically, the supply curve is the part of the marginal cost curve that is above the

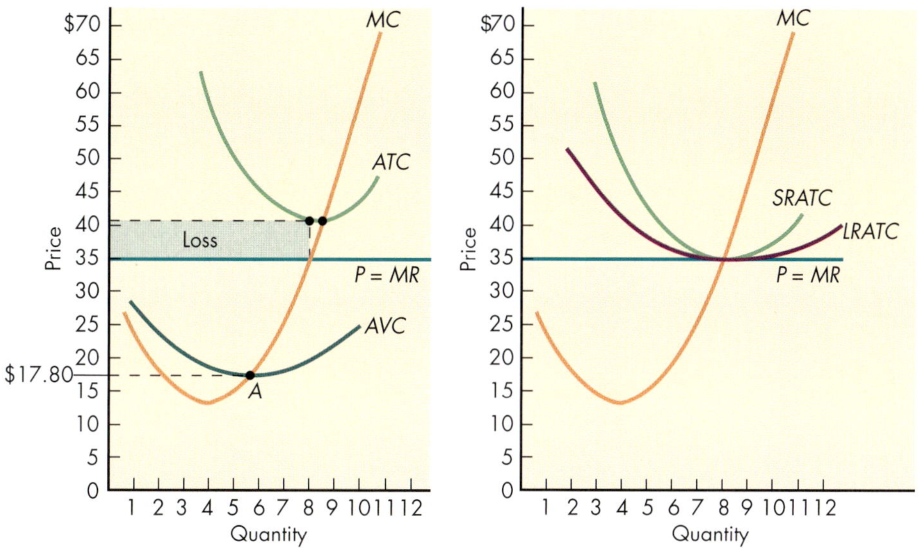

(a) The shutdown decision **(b) Long-run equilibrium**

Figure 11-6 The Shutdown Decision and Long-Run Equilibrium
A firm should continue to produce as long as price exceeds average variable cost. Once price falls below that, it will do better by temporarily shutting down and saving the variable costs. This occurs at point A in (**a**). In (**b**), the long-run equilibrium position for a marginal firm in an industry is shown. In that long-run equilibrium, only normal profits are made.

average variable cost curve. Considering why this is the case should help the analysis stick in your mind.

Q-7 In the early 2000s, many airlines were making losses, yet they continued to operate. Why?

Let's consider Figure 11-6(a)—a reproduction of Figure 11-5(c)—and the firm's decision at various prices. At a price of $35, it's incurring a loss of $6 per unit. If it's making a loss, why doesn't it shut down? The answer lies in the fixed costs. There's no use crying over spilt milk. In the short run a firm knows these fixed costs are sunk costs; it must pay them regardless of whether or not it produces. The firm considers only the costs it can save by stopping production, and those costs are its variable costs. As long as a firm is covering its variable costs, it pays to keep on producing. By producing, its loss is $48; if it stopped producing, its loss would be all the fixed costs ($169). So it makes a smaller loss by producing.

However, once the price falls below average variable costs (below $17.80), it will pay to shut down (point A in Figure 11-6(a)). In that case the firm's loss from producing would be more than $169, and it would do better to simply stop producing temporarily and avoid paying the variable cost. Thus, the point at which price equals *AVC* is the **shutdown point** (*that point at which the firm will be better off if it temporarily shuts down than it will if it stays in business*). When price falls below the shutdown point, the average variable costs the firm can avoid paying by shutting down exceed the price it would get for selling the good. When price is above average variable cost, in the short run a firm should keep on producing even though it's making a loss. As long as a firm's total revenue is covering its total variable cost, temporarily producing at a loss is the firm's best strategy because it's making a smaller loss than it would make if it were to shut down.

The shutdown point is the point at which the firm will be better off if it shuts down than it will if it stays in business.

If *P* > minimum of *AVC*, the firm will continue to produce in the short run. If *P* < minimum of *AVC*, the firm will shut down.

Short-Run Market Supply and Demand

Most of the preceding discussion has focused on supply and demand analysis of a firm. Now let's consider supply and demand in an industry. We've already discussed industry

FINDING OUTPUT, PRICE, AND PROFIT

Knowing the Tools

To find a competitive firm's price, level of output, and profit given a firm's marginal cost curve and average total cost curve, use the following three steps:

1. Determine the market price at which market supply and demand curves intersect. This is the price the competitive firm accepts for its products. Draw the horizontal marginal revenue (*MR*) curve at the market price.
2. Determine the profit-maximizing level of output by finding the level of output where the *MR* and *MC* curves intersect.
3. Determine profit by subtracting average total costs at the profit-maximizing level of output from the price and multiplying by the firm's output.

If you are demonstrating profit graphically, find the point at which *MC* = *MR*. Extend a line down to the *ATC* curve. Extend a line from this point to the vertical axis. To complete the box indicating profit, go up the vertical axis to the market price.

---

demand. Even though the demand curve faced by the firm is perfectly elastic, the industry demand curve is downward sloping.

How about the industry supply curve? We previously demonstrated that the supply curve for a competitive firm is that firm's marginal cost curve (above the average variable cost curve). To discuss the industry supply curve, we must use a market supply curve. In the short run when the number of firms in the market is fixed, the **market supply curve** is just the *horizontal sum of all the firms' marginal cost curves, taking account of any changes in input prices that might occur.* To move from individual firms' marginal cost curves or supply curves to the market supply curve we add the quantities all firms will supply at each possible price. Since all firms have identical marginal cost curves, a quick way of summing the quantities is to multiply the quantities from the marginal cost curve of a representative firm at each price by the number of firms in the market. As the short run evolves into the long run, the number of firms in the market can change. As more firms enter the market, the market supply curve shifts to the right because more firms are supplying the quantity indicated by the representative marginal cost curve. Likewise, as the number of firms in the market declines, the market supply curve shifts to the left. Knowing how the number of firms in the market affects the market supply curve is important to understanding long-run equilibrium in perfectly competitive markets.

The market supply curve is the horizontal sum of all the firms' marginal cost curves, taking account of any changes in input prices that might occur.

LONG-RUN COMPETITIVE EQUILIBRIUM

The analysis of the competitive firm consists of two parts: the short-run analysis just presented and the long-run analysis. In the short run the number of firms is fixed and the firm can either earn economic profit or incur economic loss. In the long run, firms enter and exit the market and neither economic profits nor economic losses are possible. In the long run, firms make zero economic profit. Thus, in the long run, only the zero profit equilibrium shown in Figure 11-6(b) is possible. As you can see, at that long-run equilibrium, the firm is at the minimum of both the short-run and the long-run average total cost curves.

Why can't firms earn economic profit or make economic losses in the long run? Because of the entry and exit of firms: If there are economic profits, firms will enter the

The Shutdown Decision and the Relevant Costs

Applying the Tools

Chapters 9 and 10 emphasized that it is vital to choose the relevant costs to the decision at hand. Discussing the shutdown decision gives us a chance to demonstrate the importance of those choices. Say the firm leases a large computer it needs to operate. The rental cost of that computer is a fixed cost for most decisions, if, as long as the firm keeps the computer, the rent must be paid whether or not the computer is used. However, if the firm can end the rental contract at any time, and thereby save the rental cost, the computer is not a fixed cost. But neither is it your normal variable cost. Since the firm can end the rental contract and save the cost only if it shuts down, that rental cost of the computer is an *indivisible setup cost.* For the shutdown decision, the computer cost is a variable cost. For other decisions about changing quantity, it's a fixed cost.

The moral: The relevant cost can change with the decision at hand, so when you apply the analysis to real-world situations, be sure to think carefully about what the *relevant cost* is.

---

market, shifting the market supply curve to the right. As market supply increases, the market price will decline and reduce profits for each firm. Firms will continue to enter the market and the market price will continue to decline until the incentive of economic profits is eliminated. At that price, all firms are earning zero profit. Similarly, if the price is lower than the price necessary to earn a profit, firms incurring losses will leave the market and the market supply curve will shift to the left. As market supply shifts to the left, market price will rise. Firms will continue to exit the market and market price will continue to rise until all remaining firms no longer incur losses and earn zero profit. Only at zero profit do entry and exit stop.

Since profits create incentives for new firms to enter, output will increase, and the price will fall until zero profits are being made.

Zero profit does not mean that entrepreneurs don't get anything for their efforts. The entrepreneur is an input to production just like any other factor of production. In order to stay in the business the entrepreneur must receive the opportunity cost, or **normal profit** (*the amount the owners of business would have received in the next-best alternative*). That normal profit is built into the costs of the firm; economic profits are profits above normal profits.

Web Note 11.2
Barriers to Exit

Another aspect of the zero profit position deserves mentioning. What if one firm has superefficient workers or machinery? Won't the firm make a profit in the long run? The answer is, again, no. In a long-run competitive market, other firms will see the value of those workers and machines and will compete to get them for themselves. As firms compete for the superefficient factors of production, the price of those specialized inputs will rise until all profits are eliminated. Those factors will receive what are called rents to their specialized ability. For example, say the average worker receives $400 per week, but Sarah, because she's such a good worker, receives $600. So $200 of the $600 she receives is a rent to her specialized ability. Either her existing firm matches that $600 wage or she will change employment.

Q-8 If a competitive firm makes zero profit, why does it stay in business?

The zero profit condition is enormously powerful; it makes the analysis of competitive markets far more applicable to the real world than can a strict application of the assumption of perfect competition. If economic profit is being made, firms will enter and compete that profit away. Price will be pushed down to the average total cost of production as long as there are no barriers to entry. As we'll see in later chapters, in their analysis of whether markets are competitive, many economists focus primarily on whether barriers to entry exist.

The zero profit condition is enormously powerful; it makes the analysis of competitive markets far more applicable to the real world than would otherwise be the case.

Figure 11-7 (a and b) Market Response to an Increase in Demand
Faced with an increase in demand, which it sees as an increase in price and hence profits, a competitive firm will respond by increasing output (from A to B) in order to maximize profit. The market response is shown in (**a**); the firm's response is shown in (**b**). As all firms increase output and as new firms enter, price will fall until all profit is competed away. Thus the long-run market supply curve will be perfectly elastic, as is S_{LR} in (**a**). The final equilibrium will be the original price but a higher output. The original firms return to their original output (A), but since there are more firms in the market, the market output increases to C.

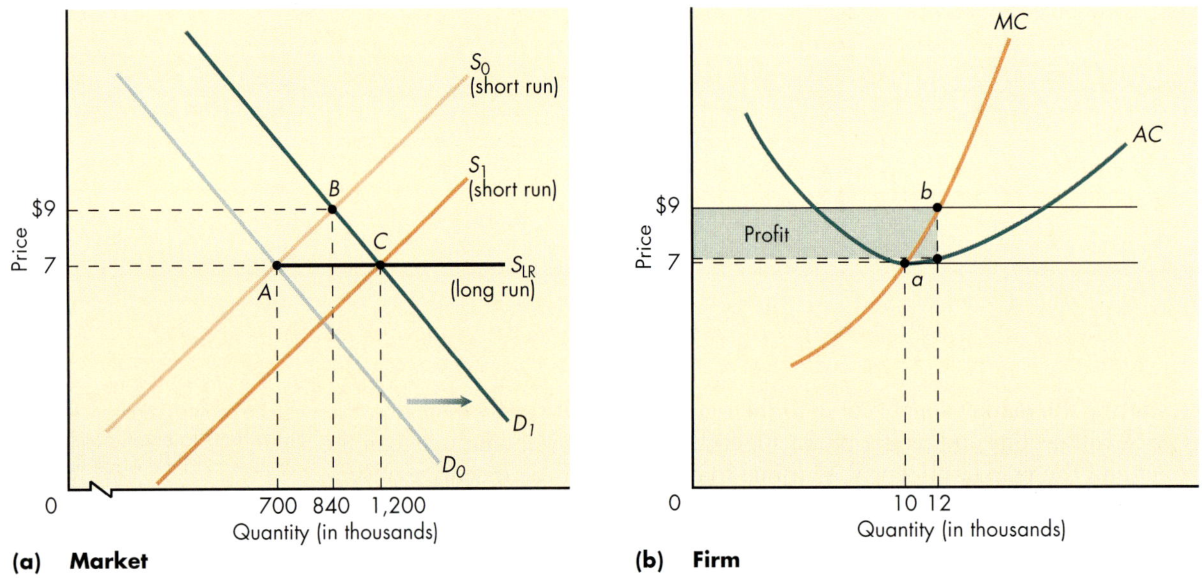

Adjustment from the Short Run to the Long Run

Now that we've been through the basics of the perfectly competitive supply and demand curves, we're ready to consider the two together and to see how the adjustment to long-run equilibrium will likely take place in the firm and in the market.

An Increase in Demand

Q-9 If berets suddenly became the "in" thing to wear, what would you expect to happen to the price in the short run? In the long run?

First, in Figure 11-7(a and b), let's consider a market that's in equilibrium but that suddenly experiences an increase in demand. Figure 11-7(a) shows the market reaction. Figure 11-7(b) shows a representative firm's reaction. Originally market equilibrium occurs at a price of $7 and market quantity supplied of 700 thousand units (point A in (a)), with each of 70 firms producing 10 thousand units (point *a* in (b)). Firms are making zero profit because they're in long-run equilibrium. If demand increases from D_0 to D_1, the firms will see the market price increasing and will increase their output until they're once again at a position where MC = *P*. This occurs at point *B* at a market output of 840 thousand units in (a) and at point *b* at a firm output of 12 in (b). In the short run the 70 existing firms each make an economic profit (the shaded area in Figure 11-7(b)). Price has risen to $9, but average cost is only $7.10, so if the price remains $9 each firm is making a profit of $1.90 per unit. But price cannot remain at $9 since each firm will have an incentive to expand output and new firms will have an incentive to enter the market.

As existing firms expand and new firms enter, if input prices remain constant, the short-run market supply curve shifts from S_0 to S_1 and the market price returns to $7.

A Summary of a Perfectly Competitive Industry

Knowing the Tools

Four things to remember when considering a perfectly competitive industry are

1. The profit-maximizing condition for perfectly competitive firms is $MC = MR = P$.
2. To determine profit or loss at the profit-maximizing level of output, subtract the average total cost at that level of output from the price and multiply the result by the output level.
3. Firms will shut down production if price is equal to or falls below the minimum of their average variable costs.
4. A perfectly competitive firm is in long-run equilibrium only when it is earning zero economic profit, or when price equals the minimum of long-run average total costs.

The entry of 50 new firms provides the additional output in this example, bringing market output to 1.2 million units sold for $7 apiece. The final equilibrium will be at a higher market output but the same price.

Long-Run Market Supply

The long-run market supply curve is a schedule of quantities supplied when firms are no longer entering or exiting the market. This occurs when firms are earning zero profit. In this case, the long-run supply curve is created by extending to the right the line connecting points A and C. Since equilibrium price remains at $7, the long-run supply curve is perfectly elastic. The long-run supply curve is horizontal because factor prices are constant. That is, factor prices do not increase as industry output increases. Economists call this market a *constant-cost industry*. Two other possibilities exist: an *increasing-cost industry* (in which factor prices rise as more firms enter the market and existing firms expand production) and a *decreasing-cost industry* (in which factor prices fall as industry output expands).

In the long run firms earn zero profits.

Factor prices are likely to rise when industry output increases if the factors of production are specialized. An increase in the demand for the factors of production that accompanies an increase in output, in this case, will bid up factor prices. The effect on long-run supply is the following: The rise in factor prices forces costs up for each individual firm and increases the price at which firms earn zero profit. Firms will stop entering the market and expanding production at a higher equilibrium price since the price at which zero profit is made has risen. Therefore, in increasing-cost industries, the long-run supply curve is upward sloping. In the extreme case, in which all firms in an industry are competitively supplying a perfectly inelastic resource or factor input, the long-run market supply curve is perfectly inelastic (vertical). Any increase in demand would increase the price of that factor. Costs would rise in response to the increase in demand; output would not. Input costs would also rise if there are diseconomies of scale. In both cases, the long-run equilibrium price would have been higher and output would have been lower than if input prices remained constant.[3]

Q-10 In 2001, demand for burkhas (the garment the Taliban required all Afghani women to wear) declined when the Taliban was ousted. In the short run, what would you expect to happen to the price of burkhas? How about in the long run?

[3]To check your understanding, ask yourself the following question: What if there had been economies of scale? If you answered, "There couldn't have been," you're really into economic thinking. (For those of you who aren't all that heavily into economic thinking, the reason is that if there had been economies of scale, the market structure would not have been perfectly competitive. One firm would have kept expanding and expanding and, as it did, its costs would have kept falling.)

The other possibility is a decreasing-cost industry. If factor prices decline when industry output expands, individual firms' cost curves shift down. As they do, the price at which the zero profit condition falls and the price at which firms cease to enter the market also falls. In this case, the long-run market supply curve is downward sloping. Factor prices may decline as output rises when new entrants make it more cost-effective for other firms to provide services to all firms in the area. The supply of factors of production expands and reduces the price of inputs to production.

In the short run, the price does more of the adjusting. In the long run, more of the adjustment is done by quantity.

Notice that in the long-run equilibrium, once again zero profit is being made. Long-run equilibrium is defined by zero economic profit. Notice also that the long-run supply curve is more elastic than the short-run supply curve. That's because output changes are much less costly in the long run than in the short run. *In the short run, the price does more of the adjusting. In the long run, more of the adjustment is done by quantity.*

An Example in the Real World

The perfectly competitive model and the reasoning underlying it are extremely powerful. With them you have a simple model to use as a first approach to predict the effect of an event, or to explain why an event occurred. For example, consider the decision of the owners of the Kmart chain of department stores to close nearly 300 stores after experiencing two years of losses.

Tim Boyle/Getty Images.

Figure 11-8 shows what happened. Initially, Kmart saw the losses it was suffering as temporary. In the two years prior to the shutdown decision, Kmart's cost curves looked like those in Figure 11-8. Since price exceeded average variable cost, Kmart continued to produce even though it was making a loss.

But after two years of losses Kmart's perspective changed. The company moved from the short run to the long run. Kmart began to believe that the demand wasn't temporarily low but rather permanently low. It began to ask: What costs are truly fixed and what costs are simply indivisible costs that we can save if we close down completely, selling our buildings and reducing our overhead? Since in the long run all costs are variable, the *ATC* became its relevant *AVC*. Kmart recognized that demand had fallen below these long-run average costs. At that point, it shut down those stores for which $P < AVC$.

There are hundreds of other real-world examples to which the perfectly competitive model adds insight. That's one reason why it's important to keep it in the back of your mind.

Figure 11-8 A Real-World Example: A Shutdown Decision
Supply/demand analysis can be applied to a wide variety of real-world examples. This exhibit shows one, but there are many more. As you experience life today, a good exercise is to put on your supply/demand glasses and interpret everything you see in a supply/demand framework.

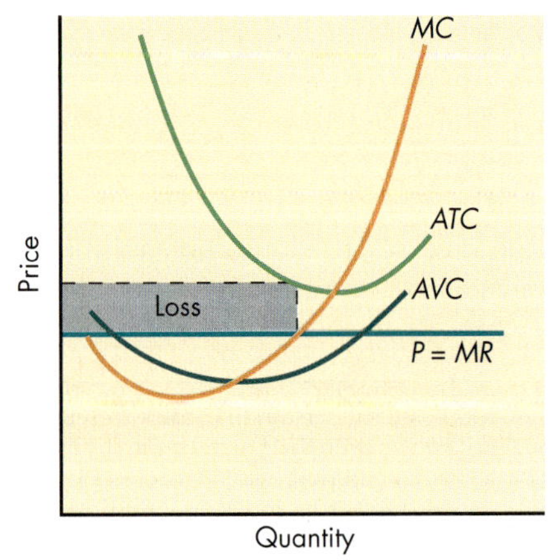

Conclusion

We've come to the end of the presentation of perfect competition. It was tough going, but if you went through it carefully, it will serve you well, both as a basis for later chapters and as a reference point for how real-world economies work. But like many good things, a complete understanding of the chapter doesn't come easy.

Summary

- The necessary conditions for perfect competition are that buyers and sellers be price takers, the number of firms be large, there be no barriers to entry, firms' products be identical, there be complete information, and sellers be profit-maximizing entrepreneurial firms.
- The profit-maximizing position of a competitive firm is where marginal revenue equals marginal cost.
- The supply curve of a competitive firm is its marginal cost curve. Only competitive firms have supply curves.
- To find the profit-maximizing level of output for a perfect competitor, find that level of output where *MC* = *MR*. Profit is price less average total cost times output at the profit-maximizing level of output.
- In the short run, competitive firms can make a profit or loss. In the long run, they make zero profits.
- The shutdown price for a perfectly competitive firm is a price below the minimum point of the average variable cost curve.
- The short-run market supply curve is the horizontal summation of the marginal cost curves for all firms in the market. An increase in the number of firms in the market shifts the market supply curve to the right, while a decrease shifts it to the left.
- Perfectly competitive firms make zero profit in the long run because if profit were being made, new firms would enter and the market price would decline, eliminating the profit. If losses were being made, firms would exit and the market price would rise, eliminating the loss.
- The long-run supply curve is a schedule of quantities supplied where firms are making zero profit. The slope of the long-run supply curve depends on what happens to factor prices when output increases. Constant-cost industries have horizontal long-run supply curves. Increasing-cost industries have upward-sloping long-run supply curves, and decreasing-cost industries have downward-sloping long-run supply curves.

Key Terms

barriers to entry *(242)*
marginal cost (MC) *(245)*
marginal revenue (MR) *(245)*
market supply curve *(254)*
normal profit *(255)*
perfectly competitive market *(241)*
price taker *(242)*
profit-maximizing condition *(247)*
shutdown point *(253)*

Questions for Thought and Review

1. Why must buyers and sellers be price takers for a market to be perfectly competitive?
2. Draw marginal cost, marginal revenue, and average total cost curves for a typical perfectly competitive firm and indicate the profit-maximizing level of output and total profit for that firm. Is the firm in long-run equilibrium? Why or why not?
3. Draw marginal cost, marginal revenue, and average total cost curves for a typical perfectly competitive firm in long-run equilibrium and indicate the profit-maximizing level of output and total profit for that firm.
4. What portion of the marginal cost curve is the firm's supply curve? How is a firm's marginal cost curve related to the market supply curve?

5. Draw the *ATC*, *AVC*, and MC curves for a typical firm. Label the price at which the firm would shut down temporarily and the price at which the firm would exit the market in the long run.

6. Under what cost condition is the shutdown point the same as the point at which a firm exits the market?

7. Why is long-run market supply curve upward-sloping in an increasing-cost industry, downward-sloping in a decreasing-cost industry, and horizontal in a constant-cost industry?

8. What will be the effect of a technological development that reduces marginal costs in a competitive market on short-run price, quantity, and profit?

9. If a firm is owned by its workers but otherwise meets all the qualifications for a perfectly competitive firm, will its price and output decisions differ from the price and output decisions of a perfectly competitive firm? Why?

10. You're thinking of buying one of two firms. One has a profit margin of $8 per unit; the other has a profit margin of $4 per unit. Which should you buy? Why?

11. If marginal cost is four times the quantity produced and the price is $20, how much should the firm produce? Why?

12. Find three events in the newspaper that can be explained or interpreted with supply/demand analysis.

13. State what is *wrong* with each of the graphs.

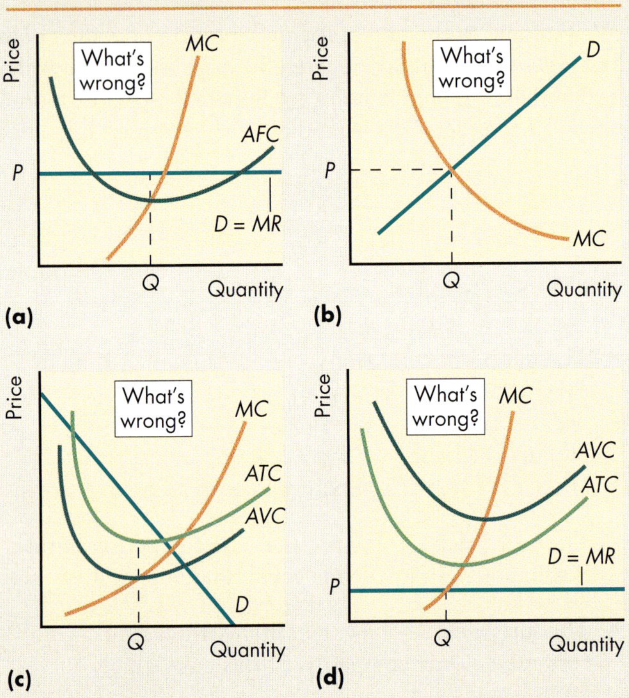

14. In the late 1990s and early 2000s, hundreds of music stores closed in the face of stagnant demand for CDs and new competitors—online music vendors and discount retailers. Explain how price competition from these new sources would cause a retail store to close. In the long run, what effect will new entrants have on the price of CDs?

PROBLEMS AND EXERCISES

1. a. Based on the following table, what is the profit-maximizing output?

Output	Price	Total Costs
0	$10	$ 31
1	10	40
2	10	45
3	10	48
4	10	55
5	10	65
6	10	80
7	10	100
8	10	140
9	10	220
10	10	340

   b. How would your answer change if, in response to an increase in demand, the price of the good increased to $15?

2. A profit-maximizing firm has an average total cost of $4, but it gets a price of $3 for each good it sells.
   a. What would you advise the firm to do?
   b. What would you advise the firm to do if you knew average variable costs were $3.50?

3. Say that half of the cost of producing wheat is the rental cost of land (a fixed cost) and half is the cost of labor and machines (a variable cost). If the average total cost of producing wheat is $8 and the price of wheat is $6, what would you advise the farmer to do? ("Grow something else" is not allowed.)

4. Use the accompanying graph, which shows the marginal cost and average total cost curves for the shoe store Zapateria, a perfectly competitive firm.
   a. How many pairs of shoes will Zapateria produce if the market price of shoes is $70 a pair?
   b. What is the total profit Zapateria will earn if the market price of shoes is $70 a pair?
   c. Should Zapateria expect more shoe stores to enter this market? Why or why not?

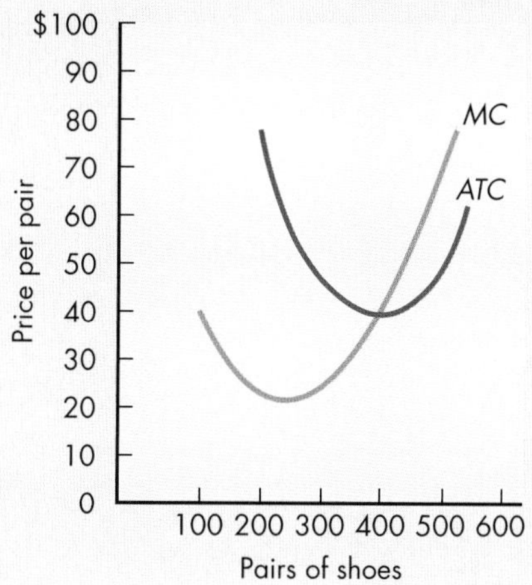

   d. What is the long-run equilibrium price in the shoe market assuming it is a constant-cost industry?

5. Each of 10 firms in a given industry has the costs given in the left-hand table. The market demand schedule is given in the right-hand table.

Quantity	Total Cost
0	12
1	24
2	27
3	31
4	39
5	53
6	73
7	99

Price	Quantity Demanded
2	110
4	100
6	90
8	80
10	70
12	60
14	50
16	40

   a. What is the market equilibrium price and the price each firm gets for its product?
   b. What is the equilibrium market quantity and the quantity each firm produces?
   c. What profit is each firm making?
   d. Below what price will firms begin to exit the market?

6. Suppose an increasing-cost industry is in both long-run and short-run equilibrium. Explain what will happen to the following in the long run if the demand for that product declines:
   a. Price.
   b. Quantity.
   c. Number of firms in the market.
   d. Profit.

7. Graphically demonstrate the quantity and price of a perfectly competitive firm.
   a. Explain why a slightly larger quantity would not be preferred.
   b. Explain why a slightly lower quantity would not be preferred.
   c. Label the shutdown point in your diagram.
   d. You have just discovered that shutting down means that you would lose your land zoning permit which is required to start operating again. How does that change your answer to *c*?

8. A California biotechnology firm submitted a tomato that will not rot for weeks to the U.S. Food and Drug Administration. It designed such a fruit by changing the genetic structure of the tomato. What effect will this technological change have:
   a. On the price of tomatoes?
   b. On farmers who grow tomatoes?
   c. On the geographic areas where tomatoes are grown?
   d. On where tomatoes are generally placed on salad bars in winter?

9. Currently central banks (banks of governments) hold 35,000 tons of gold—one-third of the world's supply. This is the equivalent of 17 years' production. In the 1990s there was discussion about the central banks selling off their gold, since it is no longer tied to money supplies. Assuming they did sell it:
   a. Demonstrate, using supply/demand analysis, the effect on the price of gold in the long run and the short run.
   b. If you were an economist advising the central banks and you believed that selling off the gold made sense, would you advise them to do it quickly or slowly? Why?

10. The milk industry has a number of interesting aspects. Provide economic explanations for the following:
    a. Fluid milk is 87 percent water. It can be dried and reconstituted so that it is almost indistinguishable from fresh milk. What is a likely reason that such reconstituted milk is not produced?
    b. The United States has regional milk-marketing regulations whose goals are to make each of the regions self-sufficient in milk. What is a likely reason for this?
    c. A U.S. senator from a milk-producing state has been quoted as saying, "I am absolutely convinced . . . that simply bringing down dairy price supports is not a way to cut production." Is it likely that he is correct? What is a probable reason for his statement?

11. Subtle changes in the tax laws often mean enormous amounts of money to individuals and groups. Consider the case of whiskey, as did economists Jack High and Clayton Coppin. Whiskey is distilled grain. The distilling process produces poisonous impurities, called fusel oil, that must be removed before the whiskey is drinkable. One way to remove these impurities is by aging the whiskey in wooden barrels. Whiskey produced in this manner is "straight whiskey." The second method is distillation—removing the fusel oil through additional distilling. The latter method removes more impurities and is cheaper, but it results in a whiskey with little taste. However, taste can be added back through flavorings or blending with aged whiskey. Up until 1868 distilled or blended whiskey predominated, but in that year a law was passed that allowed straight-whiskey producers who stored their whiskey in government warehouses to defer their taxes on it until it was fully aged.
    a. What advantage would this law have for straight-whiskey producers?
    b. After the tax was paid the whiskey received a tax stamp, certifying that its producers had paid the tax and that their straight whiskey had been stored in a "bonded government warehouse." If you were a straight-whiskey producer, how might you try to use that tax stamp to your advantage in advertising?
    c. How might competing producers of distilled whiskey certify the quality of their product?

Web Questions

1. A number of markets are developing on the Internet. One of those markets is eBay. Check out eBay at www.ebay.com and explain whether you believe that the eBay Internet auction market is perfectly competitive. Be sure to explain which of the six conditions are met and how.
2. Find 60-month new auto loans in five different states using a loan information center on the Internet such as www.bankrate.com and answer the following questions:
    a. By how much did the interest rates differ among those institutions you sampled?
    b. Which of the six conditions for perfect competition does the auto loan market meet?
    c. Is your answer to *b* consistent with your answer to *a*? Why or why not?

Answers to Margin Questions

1. Without the assumption of no barriers to entry, firms could make a profit by raising price; hence, their demand curve would not be perfectly elastic and, hence, perfect competition would not exist. *(242)*
2. The competitive firm is such a small portion of the total market that it can have no effect on price. Consequently it takes the price as given, and hence its perceived demand curve is perfectly elastic. *(244)*
3. To determine the profit-maximizing output of a competitive firm, you must know price and marginal cost. *(246)*
4. Firms are interested in getting as much for themselves as they possibly can. Maximizing total profit does this. Maximizing profit per unit might yield very small total profits. *(248)*
5. If the firm in Figure 11-5 were producing 4 units, I would explain to it that the marginal cost of increasing output is only $12 and the marginal revenue is $35, so it should significantly expand output until 8, where the marginal cost equals the marginal revenue, or price. *(251)*
6. The diagram is drawn with the wrong profit-maximizing output and hence the wrong profit. Output is determined where marginal cost equals price and profit is the difference between the average total cost and price at that output, not at the output where marginal cost equals average total cost. The correct diagram is shown here. *(252)*

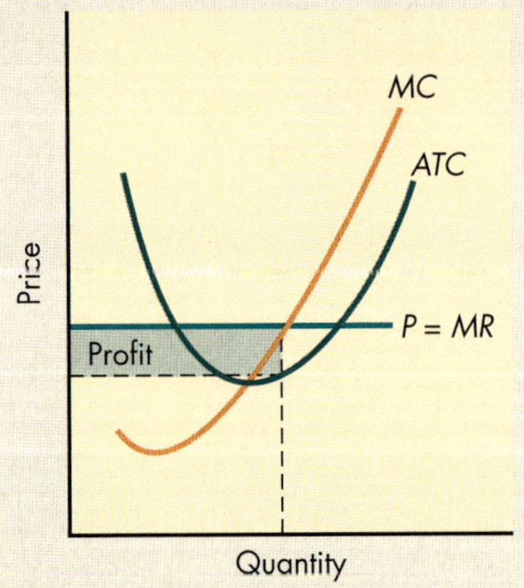

7. The marginal cost for airlines is significantly below average total cost. Since they're recovering their average variable cost, they continue to operate. In the long run, if this continues, some airlines will be forced out of business. *(253)*

8. The costs for a firm include the normal costs, which in turn include a return for all factors. Thus it is worthwhile for a competitive firm to stay in business, since it is doing better, or at least as well, as it could in any other activity. *(255)*
9. Suddenly becoming the "in" thing to wear would cause the demand for berets to shift out to the right, pushing the price up in the short run. In the long run it would probably push the price down, as there probably are considerable economies of scale in the production of berets. *(256)*
10. A decline in demand pushed the short-run price of these burkhas down. In the long run, however, once a number of burkha makers go out of business, the price of burkhas should eventually move back to approximately where it was before the decline, assuming constant returns to scale. *(257)*

12 MONOPOLY

After reading this chapter, you should be able to:

- Summarize how and why the decisions facing a monopolist differ from the collective decisions of competing firms.
- Explain why *MC* = *MR* maximizes total profit for a monopolist.
- Determine a monopolist's price, output, and profit graphically and numerically.
- Show graphically the welfare loss from monopoly.
- Explain why a price-discriminating monopolist will earn more profit than a normal monopolist.
- Explain why there would be no monopoly without barriers to entry.
- List three normative arguments against monopoly.

Monopoly is business at the end of its journey.

—*Henry Demarest Lloyd*

In Chapter 11 we considered perfect competition. We now move to the other end of the spectrum: monopoly. **Monopoly** is *a market structure in which one firm makes up the entire market*. It is the polar opposite to competition. It is a market structure in which the firm faces no competitive pressure from other firms.

Monopolies exist because of barriers to entry into a market that prevent competition. These can be legal barriers (as in the case where a firm has a patent that prevents other firms from entering), sociological barriers where entry is prevented by custom or tradition, natural barriers where the firm has a unique ability to produce what other firms can't duplicate, or technological barriers where the size of the market can support only one firm.

THE KEY DIFFERENCE BETWEEN A MONOPOLIST AND A PERFECT COMPETITOR

A key question we want to answer in this chapter is: How does a monopolist's decision differ from the collective decision of competing firms (i.e., from the competitive solution)? Answering that question brings out a key difference between a competitive firm and a monopoly. Since a competitive firm is too small to affect the price, it does not take into account the effect of its output decision on the price it receives. A competitive firm's marginal revenue (the additional revenue it receives from selling an additional unit of output) is the given market price. A monopolistic firm takes into account that its output decision can affect price; its marginal revenue is not its price. A monopolistic firm will reason: "If I increase production, the price I can get for each unit sold will fall, so I had better be careful about how much I increase production."

Let's consider an example. Say your drawings in the margins of this book are seen by a traveling art critic who decides you're the greatest thing since Rembrandt, or at least since Andy Warhol. Carefully he tears each page out of the book, mounts them on special paper, and numbers them: Doodle Number 1 (Doodle While Contemplating Demand), Doodle Number 2 (Doodle While Contemplating Production), and so on.

Doodle Number 27: Contemplating Costs

All told, he has 100. He figures, with the right advertising and if you're a hit on the art circuit, he'll have a monopoly in your doodles. He plans to sell them for $20,000 each: He gets 50 percent, you get 50 percent. That's $1 million for you. You tell him, "Hey, man! I can doodle my way through the entire book. I'll get you 500 doodles. Then I get $5 million and you get $5 million."

Q-1 Why should you study rather than doodle?

The art critic has a pained look on his face. He says, "You've been doodling when you should have been studying. Your doodles are worth $20,000 each only if they're rare. If there are 500, they're worth $1,000 each. And if it becomes known that you can turn them out that fast, they'll be worth nothing. I won't be able to limit quantity at all, and my monopoly will be lost. So obviously we must figure out some way that you won't doodle anymore—and study instead. Oh, by the way, did you know that the price of an artist's work goes up significantly when he or she dies? Hmm?" At that point you decide to forget doodling and to start studying, and to remember always that increasing production doesn't necessarily make suppliers better off.

As we saw in Chapter 11, competitive firms do not take advantage of that insight. Each individual competitive firm, responding to its self-interest, is not doing what is in the interest of the firms collectively. In competitive markets, as one supplier is pitted against another, consumers benefit. In monopolistic markets, the firm faces no competitors and does what is in its best interest. Monopolists can see to it that the monopolists, not the consumers, benefit; perfectly competitive firms cannot.

Monopolists see to it that monopolists, not consumers, benefit.

A Model of Monopoly

How much should the monopolistic firm choose to produce if it wants to maximize profit? To answer that we have to consider more carefully the effect that changing output has on the total profit of the monopolist. That's what we do in this section. First, we consider a numerical example; then we consider that same example graphically. The relevant information for our example is presented in Table 12-1.

Determining the Monopolist's Price and Output Numerically

Table 12-1 shows the price, total revenue, marginal revenue, total cost, marginal cost, average total cost, and profit at various levels of production. It's similar to the table in Chapter 11 where we determined a competitive firm's output. The big difference is that marginal revenue changes as output changes and is not equal to the price. Why?

First, let's remember the definition of marginal revenue: Marginal revenue is the change in total revenue associated with a change in quantity. In this example, if a

Table 12-1 Monopolistic Profit Maximization

1 Quantity	2 Price	3 Total Revenue	4 Marginal Revenue	5 Total Cost	6 Marginal Cost	7 Average Total Cost	8 Profit
0	$36	$ 0		$ 47			$−47
			$33		$ 1		
1	33	33		48		$48.00	−15
			27		2		
2	30	60		50		25.00	10
			21		4		
3	27	81		54		18.00	27
			15		8		
4	24	96		62		15.50	34
			9		16		
5	21	105		78		15.60	27
			3		24		
6	18	108		102		17.00	6
			−3		40		
7	15	105		142		20.29	−37
			−9		56		
8	12	96		198		24.75	−102
			−15		80		
9	9	81		278		30.89	−197

monopolist increases output from 4 to 5, the price it can charge falls from $24 to $21 and its revenue increases from $96 to $105, so marginal revenue is $9. Marginal revenue of increasing output from 4 to 5 for the monopolist reflects two changes: a $21 gain in revenue from selling the 5th unit and a $12 decline in revenue because the monopolist must lower the price on the previous 4 units it produces by $3 a unit, from $24 to $21. This highlights the key characteristic of a monopolist—its output decision affects its price. Because an increase in output lowers the price on all previous units, a monopolist's marginal revenue is always below its price. Comparing columns 2 and 4, you can confirm that this is true.

A monopolist's marginal revenue is always below its price.

Now let's see if the monopolist will increase production from 4 to 5 units. The marginal revenue of increasing output from 4 to 5 is $9, and the marginal cost of doing so is $13. Since marginal cost exceeds marginal revenue, increasing production from 4 to 5 will reduce total profit and the monopolist will not increase production. If it decreases output from 4 to 3, where $MC < MR$, the revenue it loses ($15) exceeds the reduction in costs ($8). It will not reduce output from 4 to 3. Since it cannot increase total profit by increasing output to 5 or decreasing output to 3, it is maximizing output at 4 units.

Q-2 In Table 12-1, explain why 4 is the profit-maximizing output.

As you can tell from the table, profits are highest ($34) at 4 units of output and a price of $24. At 3 units of output and a price of $27, the firm has total revenue of $81 and total cost of $54, yielding a profit of $27. At 5 units of output and a price of $21, the firm has a total revenue of $105 and a total cost of $78, also for a profit of $27. The highest profit it can make is $34, which the firm earns when it produces 4 units. This is its profit-maximizing level.

A Trick in Graphing the Marginal Revenue Curve

Knowing the Tools

Here's a trick to help you graph the marginal revenue curve. The *MR* line starts at the same point on the price axis as does a linear demand curve, but it intersects the quantity axis at a point half the distance from where the demand curve intersects the quantity axis. (If the demand curve isn't linear, you can use the same trick if you use lines tangent to the curved demand curve.) So you can extend the demand curve to the two axes and measure halfway on the quantity axis (3 in the graph below). Then draw a line from where the demand curve intersects the price axis to that halfway mark. That line is the marginal revenue curve.

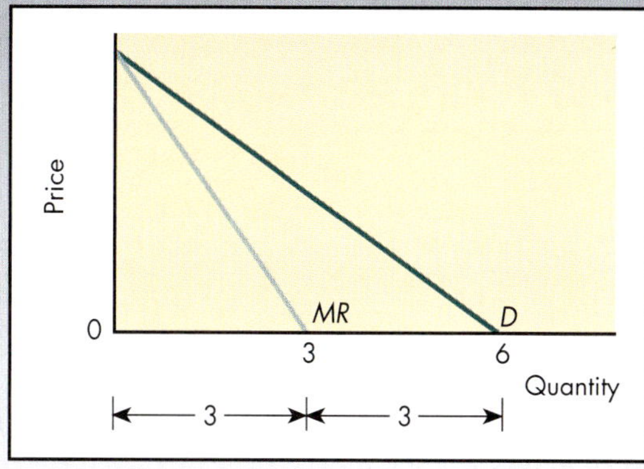

Determining the Monopolist's Price and Output Graphically

The monopolist's output decision can also be seen graphically. Figure 12-1 graphs the table's information into a demand curve, a marginal revenue curve, and a marginal cost curve. The marginal cost curve is a graph of the change in the firm's total cost as it changes output. It's the same curve as we saw in our discussion of perfect competition. The marginal revenue curve tells us the change in total revenue when quantity changes. It is graphed by plotting and connecting the points given by quantity and marginal revenue in Table 12-1.

The marginal revenue curve for a monopolist is new, so let's consider it a bit more carefully. It tells us the additional revenue the firm will get by expanding output. It is a downward-sloping curve that begins at the same point as the demand curve but has a steeper slope. In this example, marginal revenue is positive up until the firm produces 6 units. Then marginal revenue is negative; after 6 units the firm's total revenue decreases when it increases output.

Q-3 In the graph below, indicate the monopolist's profit-maximizing level of output and the price it would charge.

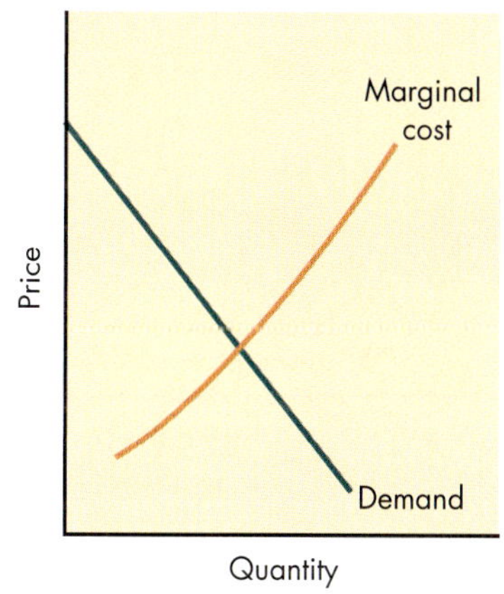

Notice specifically the relationship between the demand curve (which is the average revenue curve) and the marginal revenue curve. Since the demand curve is downward-sloping, the marginal revenue curve is below the average revenue curve. (Remember, if the average curve is falling, the marginal curve must be below it.)

Having plotted these curves, let's ask the same questions as we did before: What output should the monopolist produce, and what price can it charge? In answering those questions, the key curves to look at are the marginal cost curve and the marginal revenue curve.

MR = MC *Determines the Profit-Maximizing Output* The monopolist uses the general rule that any firm must follow to maximize profit: Produce the quantity at which MC = *MR*. If you think about it, it makes sense that the point where marginal revenue equals marginal cost determines the profit-maximizing output. If the marginal revenue is below the marginal cost, it makes sense to reduce production. Doing so decreases marginal cost and increases marginal revenue. When *MR* < MC, reducing output increases total profit. If marginal cost is below marginal revenue, you should

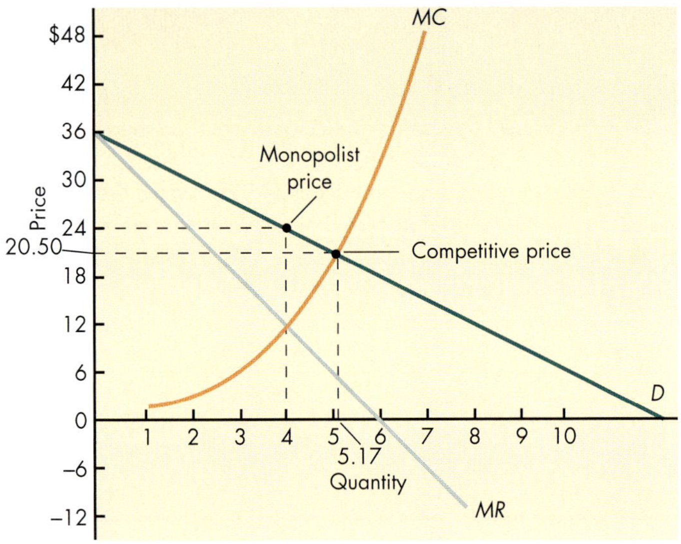

Figure 12-1 Determining the Monopolist's Price and Output Graphically
The profit-maximizing output is determined where the MC curve intersects the *MR* curve. To determine the price (at which MC = *MR*) that would be charged if this industry were a monopolist with the same cost structure, we first find that output and then extend a line to the demand curve, in this case finding a price of \$24. This price is higher than the competitive price, \$20.50, and the quantity, 4, is lower than the competitor's quantity, 5.17.

increase production because total profit will rise. If the marginal revenue is equal to marginal cost, it does not make sense to increase or reduce production. So the monopolist should produce at the output level where MC = *MR*. As you can see, the output the monopolist chooses is 4 units, the same output that we determined numerically.[1] This leads to the following insights:

The general rule that any firm must follow to maximize profit is: Produce at an output level at which *MC* = *MR*.

If *MR* > MC, the monopolist gains profit by increasing output.

If *MR* < MC, the monopolist gains profit by decreasing output.

If MC = *MR*, the monopolist is maximizing profit.

Thus, *MR* = MC is the profit-maximizing rule for a monopolist.

The Price a Monopolist Will Charge The *MR* = MC condition determines the quantity a monopolist produces; in turn, that quantity determines the price the firm will charge. A monopolist will charge the maximum price consumers are willing to pay for that quantity. Since the demand curve tells us what consumers will pay for a given quantity, to find the price a monopolist will charge you must extend the quantity line up to the demand curve. We do so in Figure 12-1 and see that the profit-maximizing output level of 4 allows a monopolist to charge a price of \$24.

Comparing Monopoly and Perfect Competition

Q-4 Why does a monopolist produce less output than would perfectly competitive firms in the same industry?

For a competitive industry, the horizontal summation of firms' marginal cost curves is the market supply curve.[2] Output for a perfectly competitive industry would be 5.17, and price would be \$20.50, as Figure 12-1 shows. The monopolist's output was 4 and its

[1]This could not be seen precisely in Table 12-1 since the table is for discrete jumps and does not tell us the marginal cost and marginal revenue exactly at 4; it only tells us the marginal cost and marginal revenue (\$8 and \$15, respectively) of moving from 3 to 4 and the marginal cost and marginal revenue (\$16 and \$9, respectively) of moving from 4 to 5. If small adjustments (1/100 of a unit or so) were possible, the marginal cost and marginal revenue precisely at 4 would be \$12. Because drawing the curve implicitly assumes we can make very small changes, the graphs of the marginal revenue curve and marginal cost curve will intersect at an output of 4 and a marginal cost and marginal revenue of \$12.
[2]The above statement has some qualifications best left to intermediate classes.

Figure 12-2 (a, b, c, and d) Finding the Monopolist's Price and Output
Determining a monopolist's price and output can be tricky. The text discusses the steps shown in this exhibit. To make sure you understand, try to go through the steps on your own, and then check your work with the text.

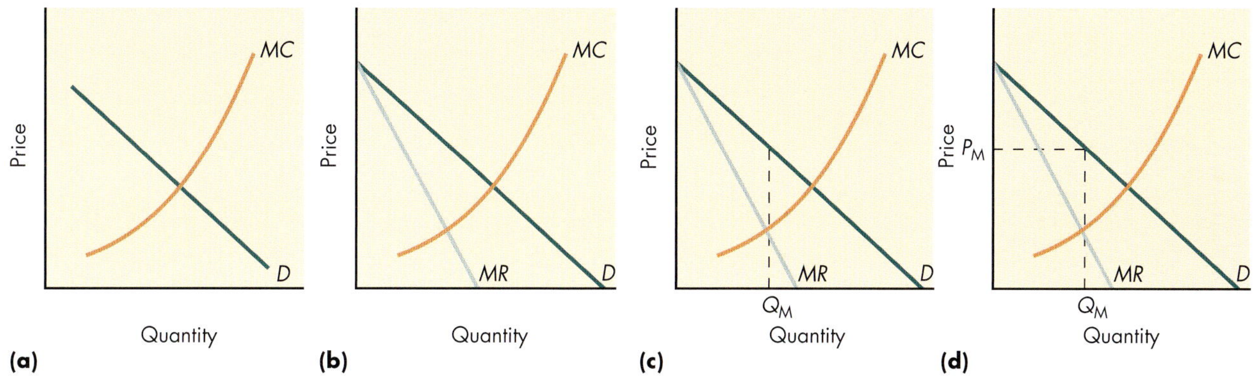

price was $24. So, if a competitive market is made into a monopoly, you can see that output would be lower and price would be higher. The reason is that the monopolist takes into account the effect that restricting output has on price.

Equilibrium output for the monopolist, like equilibrium output for the competitor, is determined by the MC = *MR* condition, but because the monopolist's marginal revenue is below its price, its equilibrium output is different from a competitive market.

An Example of Finding Output and Price

We've covered a lot of material quickly, so it's probably helpful to go through an example slowly and carefully review the reasoning process. Here's the problem:

> Say that a monopolist with marginal cost curve MC faces a demand curve *D* in Figure 12-2(a). Determine the price and output the monopolist would choose.

The first step is to draw the marginal revenue curve, since we know that a monopolist's profit-maximizing output level is determined where MC = *MR*. We do that in Figure 12-2(b), remembering the trick in the box on page 267 of extending our demand curve back to the vertical and horizontal axes and then bisecting the horizontal axis.

The second step is to determine where MC = *MR*. Having found that point, we extend a line up to the demand curve and down to the quantity axis to determine the output the monopolist chooses, Q_M. We do this in Figure 12-2(c).

Finally we see where the quantity line intersects the demand curve. Then we extend a horizontal line from that point to the price axis, as in Figure 12-2(d). This determines the price the monopolist will charge, P_M.

Profits and Monopoly

The monopolist's profit can be determined only by comparing average total cost to price. So before we can determine profit, we need to add another curve: the average total cost curve. As we saw with a perfect competitor, it's important to follow the correct sequence when finding profit:

- First, draw the firm's marginal revenue curve.
- Second, determine the output the monopolist will produce by the intersection of the marginal cost and marginal revenue curves.

Figure 12-3 (a, b, and c) The Monopolist Makes a Profit

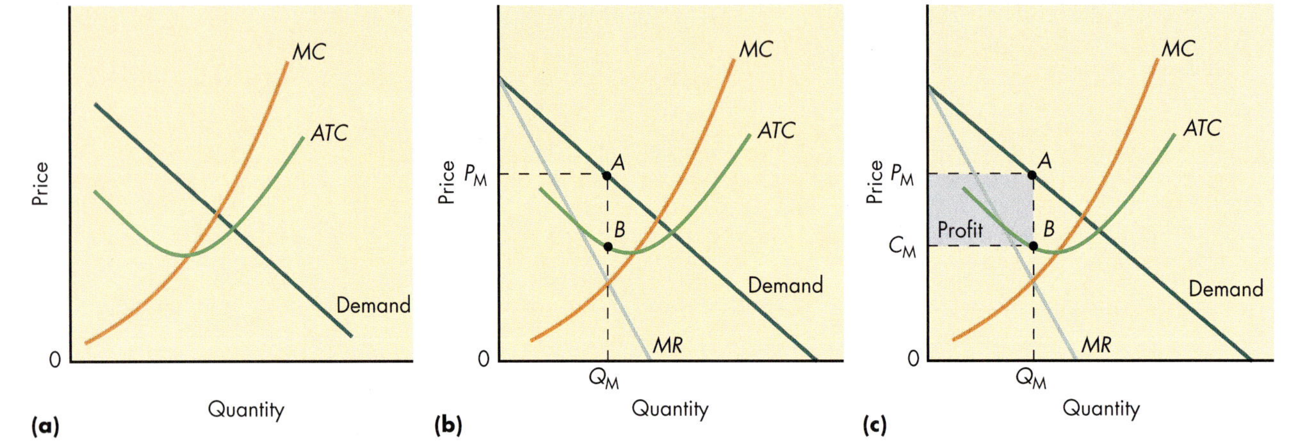

- Third, determine the price the monopolist will charge for that output. (Remember, the price it will charge depends on the demand curve.)
- Fourth, determine the monopolist's profit (loss) by subtracting average total cost from average revenue (P) at that level of output and multiplying by the chosen output.

Q.5 Indicate the profit that the monopolist shown in the graph below earns.

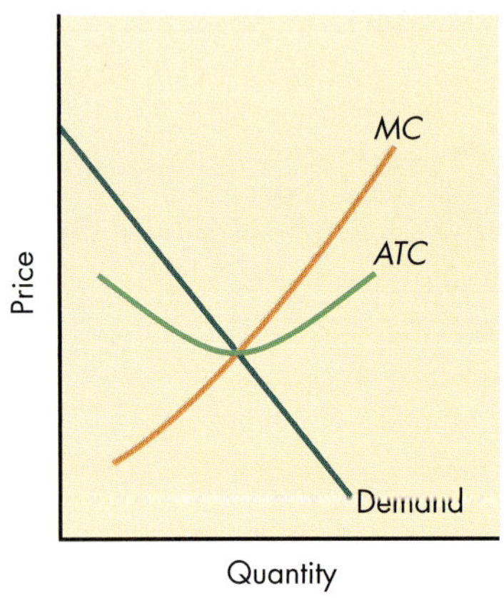

If price exceeds average total cost at the output it chooses, the monopolist will make a profit. If price equals average total cost, the monopolist will make no profit (but it will make a normal return). If price is less than average cost, the monopolist will incur a loss: Total cost exceeds total revenue.

A Monopolist Making a Profit

I consider the case of a profit in Figure 12-3, going through the steps slowly. The monopolist's demand, marginal cost, and average total cost curves are presented in Figure 12-3(a). Our first step is to draw the marginal revenue curve, which has been added in Figure 12-3(b). The second step is to find the output level at which marginal cost equals marginal revenue. From that point draw a vertical line to the horizontal (quantity) axis. That intersection tells us the monopolist's output, Q_M in Figure 12-3(b). The third step is to find what price the monopolist will charge at that output. We do so by extending the vertical line to the demand curve (point A) and then extending a horizontal line over to the price axis. Doing so gives price, P_M. Our fourth step is to determine the average total cost at that quantity. We do so by seeing where our vertical line at the chosen output intersects the average total cost curve (point B). That tells us the monopolist's average cost at its chosen output.

To determine profit, we extend lines from where the quantity line intersects the demand curve (point A) and the average total cost curve (point B) to the price axis in Figure 12-3(c). The resulting shaded rectangle in Figure 12-3(c) represents the monopolist's profit.

A Monopolist Breaking Even and Making a Loss

In Figure 12-4 we consider two other average total cost curves to show you that a monopolist may make a loss or no profit as well as an economic profit. In Figure 12-4(a)

Finding a Monopolist's Output, Price, and Profit

Knowing the Tools

To find a monopolist's level of output, price, and profit, follow these four steps:

1. Draw the marginal revenue curve.
2. Determine the output the monopolist will produce: The profit-maximizing level of output is where *MR* and *MC* curves intersect.
3. Determine the price the monopolist will charge: Extend a line from where *MR* = *MC* up to the demand curve. Where this line intersects the demand curve is the monopolist's price.
4. Determine the profit the monopolist will earn: Subtract the *ATC* from price at the profit-maximizing level of output to get profit per unit. Multiply profit per unit by quantity of output to get total profit.

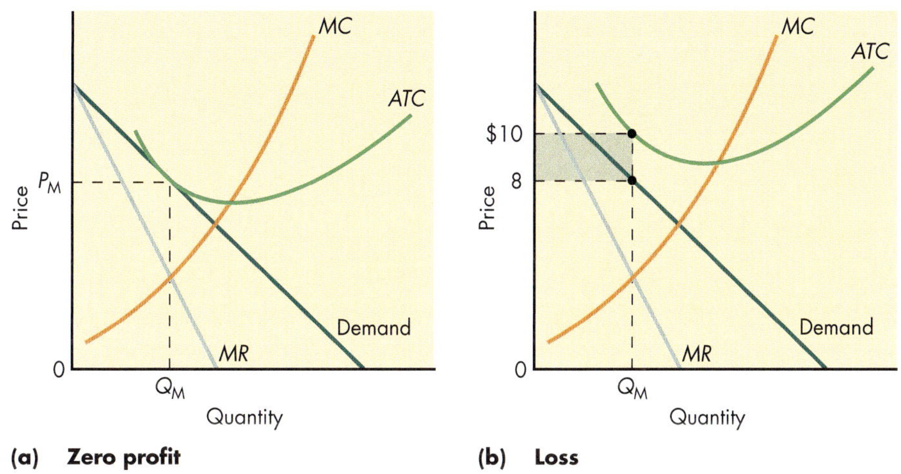

Figure 12-4 (a and b) Other Monopoly Cases Depending on where the *ATC* curve falls, a monopolist can make a profit, break even (as in (**a**)), or make a loss (as in (**b**)) in the short run. In the long run, a monopolist who is making a loss will get out of business.

the monopolist is making zero profit; in Figure 12-4(b) it's making a loss. Whether a firm is making a profit, zero profit, or a loss depends on average total costs relative to price. So clearly in the short run a monopolist can be making either a profit or a loss, or it can be breaking even.

Most of you, if you've been paying attention, will say, "Sure, in the model monopolists might not make a profit, but in the real world monopolists are making a killing." And it is true that numerous monopolists make a killing. But many more monopolists just break even or lose money. Each year the U.S. Patent Office issues about 175,000 patents. A **patent** is *legal protection of a technical innovation that gives the person holding it sole right to use that innovation*—in other words, it gives the holder a monopoly to produce a good. Most patented goods make a loss; in fact, the cost of getting the patent often exceeds the revenues from selling the product.

Each year the Home Shopping Network (HSN) considers thousands of products, and only a very few actually make it onto the network. Let's consider an example—the self-stirring pot. It was a pot with a battery-operated stirrer attached to its lid. The stirrer was designed to prevent the bottom of the pot from burning. Unfortunately for the inventor, HSN considered the cost (even after economies of scale were taken into account) far more than what people would be willing to pay and therefore decided not to

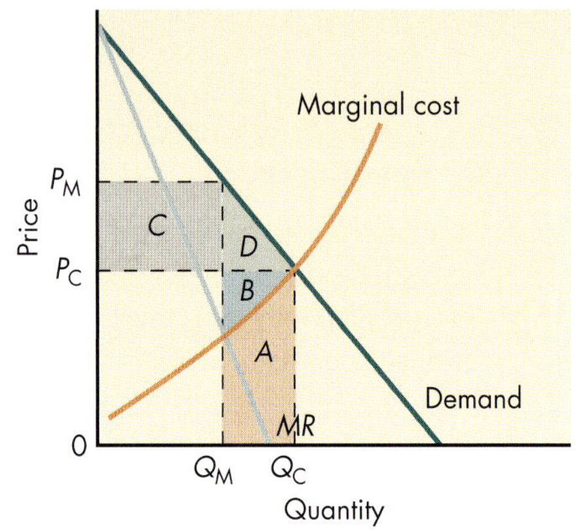

Figure 12-5 The Welfare Loss from Monopoly
The welfare loss from a monopoly is represented by the triangles *B* and *D*. The rectangle C is a transfer from consumer surplus to the monopolist. The area *A* represents the opportunity cost of diverted resources. This is not a loss to society since the resources will be used in producing other goods.

include the pot in its offerings. The inventor had a monopoly on the production and sale of the self-stirring pot, but only a loss to show. Examples like this can be multiplied by the thousands. The reality for many monopolies is that their costs exceed their revenues, so they make a loss.

The Welfare Loss from Monopoly

As we saw above, there is no necessary reason to believe that a monopolist is guaranteed a profit. Thus, profits can't be the primary reason that the economic model we're using sees monopoly as bad. If not because of profits, then what standard is the economic model using to conclude that monopoly is undesirable?

Q-6 Why is area *C* in Figure 12-5 not considered a loss from monopoly?

The welfare loss from monopoly is a triangle, as in the graph below. It is not the loss that most people consider. They are often interested in normative losses that the graph does not capture.

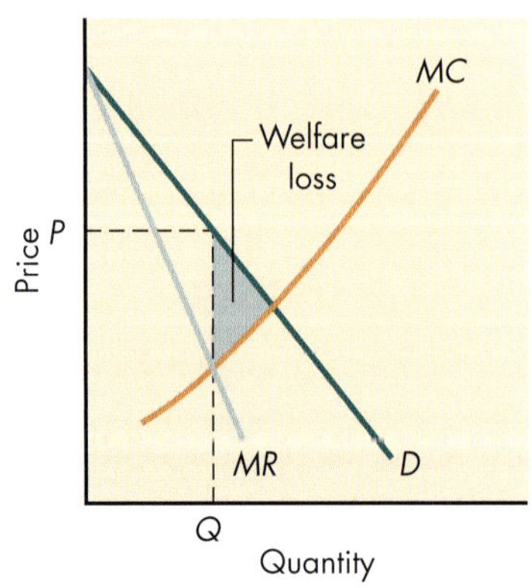

One reason can be seen by reconsidering graphically the normal monopolist equilibrium and perfectly competitive equilibrium in reference to producer and consumer surplus. This we do in Figure 12-5. In a competitive equilibrium, the total consumer and producer surplus is the area between the demand curve and the marginal cost curve up to market equilibrium quantity Q_C. The monopolist reduces output to Q_M and raises price to P_M. The benefit lost to society from reducing output from Q_C to Q_M is measured by the area under the demand curve between output levels Q_C and Q_M. That area is represented by the shaded areas labeled *A*, *B*, and *D*. Some of that loss is regained. Society gains the opportunity cost of the resources that are freed up from reducing production—the value of the resources in their next-best use indicated by the shaded area *A*. So the net cost to society of decreasing output from Q_C to Q_M is represented by areas *B* and *D*. (Area C is the monopolist's profit. It is neither a gain nor a loss to society. It represents a transfer of income from the consumer to the monopolist that would occur with a rise in price. Since both monopolist and consumer are members of society, the gain and loss net out.) The triangular areas *B* and *D* are the net cost to society from the existence of monopoly.

As discussed in Chapter 7, this area designated by *B* and *D* is often called the *deadweight loss* or *welfare loss triangle*. That welfare cost of monopoly is one of the reasons economists oppose monopoly. That cost can be summarized as follows: Because monopolies charge a price higher than marginal cost, people's decisions don't reflect the true cost to society. Price exceeds marginal cost. Because price exceeds marginal cost, people's choices are distorted; they choose to consume less of the monopolist's output and more of some other output than they would if markets were competitive. That

Monopsony

Beyond the Tools

Monopoly occurs when there is a single seller; there are also markets in which there is a single buyer. Such markets are called monopsonies. An example of a monopsony is a "company town" in which a single firm is the only employer. Whereas a monopolist takes into account the fact that if it sells more it will lower the market price, a monopsonist takes into account the fact that it will raise the market prices if it buys more. Thus, it buys less and pays less than would a market with an equivalent number of competitive buyers.

distinction means that the marginal cost of increasing output is lower than the marginal benefit of increasing output, so there's a welfare loss.

The Price-Discriminating Monopolist

So far we've considered monopolists that charge the same price to all consumers. Let's consider what would happen if our monopolist suddenly gained the ability to **price-discriminate**—*to charge different prices to different individuals or groups of individuals* (for example, students as compared to businesspeople). If a monopolist can identify groups of customers who have different elasticities of demand, separate them in some way, and limit their ability to resell its product between groups, it can charge each group a different price. Specifically, it could charge consumers with less elastic demands a higher price and individuals with more elastic demands a lower price. By doing so, it will increase total profit. Suppose, for instance, Megamovie knew that at $6 it would sell 1,000 movie tickets and at $3 a ticket it would sell 1,500 tickets. Assuming Megamovie could show the film without cost, it would maximize profits by charging $6 to 1,000 moviegoers, earning a total profit of $6,000. If, however, it could somehow attract the additional 500 viewers at $3 a ticket without reducing the price to the first 1,000 moviegoers, it could raise its profit by $1,500, to $7,500. As you can see, a price-discriminating monopolist increases its profit.

When a monopolist price-discriminates, it charges individuals high up on the demand curve higher prices and those low on the demand curve lower prices.

Web Note 12.1
Divide and Conquer

We see many examples of price discrimination in the real world:

1. *Movie theaters give discounts to senior citizens and children*. Movie theaters charge senior citizens and children a lower price because they have a more elastic demand for movies.
2. *Airline Super Saver fares include Saturday-night stayovers*. This is a method of price discrimination. Businesspeople who have highly inelastic demands generally aren't willing to stay over a Saturday night, so they're charged a high price while tourists and leisure travelers who have a far more elastic demands and who are willing to stay over a Saturday night are charged a lower price.
3. *Automobiles are seldom sold at list price*. Once again we have an example of price discrimination. Salespeople can size up the customer and determine the customer's elasticity. People who haven't done the research and don't know that selling at 10 percent off list is normal (i.e., people with inelastic demands) pay higher prices than people who search out all the alternatives (people with elastic demand).

Automobiles are seldom sold at list price.
Vincent Hobbs/Superstock.

To see whether you are following the reasoning, try to provide a price discrimination explanation for the following:

Q-7 Why does a price-discriminating monopolist make a higher profit than a normal monopolist?

1. Theaters have special rates on Monday and Tuesday nights.
2. Retail tire companies run special sales about half the time.
3. Restaurants generally make most of their profit on alcoholic drinks and just break even on food.
4. College-town stores often give students discounts.

Now that you've answered those, see if you can extend your understanding by listing the central characteristics of markets that make them highly susceptible to price discrimination.

If you answered, "The market demand is made up of distinguishable individuals who have different demand elasticities," you've got it.

Barriers to Entry and Monopoly

The standard model of monopoly just presented is simple, but, like many things simple, it hides some issues. One issue the standard model of monopoly hides is in this question: What prevents other firms from entering the monopolist's market? You should be able to answer that question relatively quickly. If a monopolist exists, it must exist due to some type of barrier to entry (a social, political, or economic impediment that prevents firms from entering the market). Three important barriers to entry are natural ability, economies of scale, and government restrictions. In the absence of barriers to entry, the monopoly would face competition from other firms, which would erode its monopoly.

If there were no barriers to entry, profit-maximizing firms would always compete away monopoly profits.

This recognition is one of the main reasons why economists generally support free international trade and oppose tariffs. Tariffs are a barrier to entry to foreign firms and thus provide monopoly power to U.S. firms, allowing them to charge the consumer more than they otherwise could.

Web Note 12.2
Diamonds are Forever

Studying how these barriers to entry are established enriches the standard model and lets us distinguish different types of monopoly.

Natural Ability

A barrier to entry that might exist is that a firm is better at producing a good than anyone else. It has unique abilities that make it more efficient than all other firms. The barrier to entry in such a case is the firm's natural ability. The defense attorneys in the Microsoft antitrust case argued that it was Microsoft's superior products that led to its capture of 90 percent of the market.

Monopolies based on ability usually don't provoke the public's ire. Often in the public's mind such monopolies are "just monopolies." The standard economic model doesn't distinguish between a "just" and an "unjust" monopoly. The just/unjust distinction raises the question of whether a firm has acquired a monopoly based on its ability or on certain unfair tactics such as initially pricing low to force competitive companies out of business but then pricing high. Many public debates over monopoly focus on such normative issues, about which the economists' standard model has nothing to say.

Economies of Scale

An alternative reason why a barrier to entry might exist is that there are significant economies of scale. If sufficiently large economies of scale exist, it would be inefficient to have two producers since if each produced half of the output, neither could take advantage of the economies of scale. Such industries are called natural monopolies. A **natural monopoly** is *an industry in which a single firm can produce at a lower cost than*

In a natural monopoly a single firm can produce at a lower cost than can two or more firms.

Can Price Controls Increase Output and Lower Market Price?

Applying the Tools

In Chapter 7 you learned how effective price ceilings increase market price, reduce output, and reduce the welfare of society. With any type of price control in a competitive market, some trades that individuals would like to have made are prevented. Thus, with competitive markets, price controls of any type are seen as generally bad (though they might have some desirable income distribution effects).

When there is monopoly the argument is not so simple. The monopoly price is higher than the marginal cost and society loses out; monopolies create their own deadweight loss. In the monopoly case price controls can actually lower price, increase output, and reduce deadweight loss. Going through the reasoning why provides a good review of the tools.

The exhibit below shows you the argument.

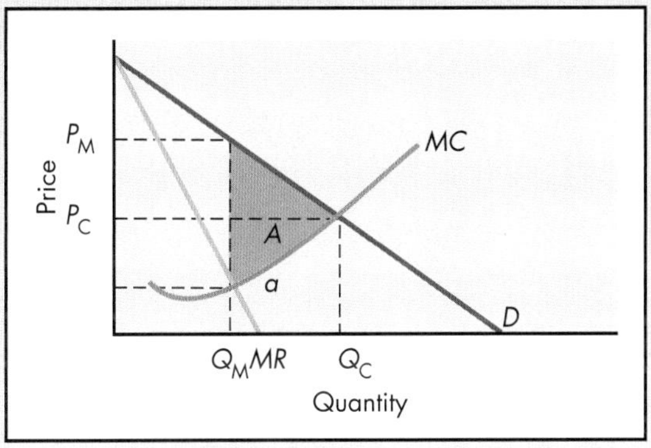

The monopoly sets its quantity where $MR = MC$. Output is Q_M and price is P_M; the welfare loss is the blue shaded triangle *A*. Now say that the government comes in and places a price ceiling on the monopolist at the competitive price, P_C. Since the monopolist is compelled by law to charge price P_C, it no longer has an incentive to restrict output. Put another way, the price ceiling—the dashed line P_C—becomes the monopolist's demand curve and marginal revenue curve. (Remember, when the demand curve is horizontal, the marginal revenue curve is identical to the demand curve.) Given the law, the monopolist's best option still is to produce where $MC = MR$, but that means charging price P_C and increasing output to Q_C. As you can see from the exhibit, the price ceiling causes output to rise and price to fall.

If, when there is monopoly, price controls can increase efficiency, why don't economists advocate price controls more than they do? Let's review four reasons why.

1. For price controls to increase output and lower price, the price has to be set within the right price range—below the monopolist's price and above the price where the monopolist's marginal cost and marginal revenue curves intersect. It is unclear politically that such a price will be chosen. Even if regulators could pick the right price initially, markets may change. Demand may increase or decrease, putting the controlled price outside the desired range.
2. All markets are dynamic. The very existence of monopoly profits will encourage other firms in other industries to try to break into that market, keeping the existing monopolist on its toes. Because of this dynamic element, in some sense no market is ever a pure textbook monopoly.
3. Price controls create their own deadweight loss in the form of rent seeking. Price controls do not eliminate monopoly pressures. The monopolist has a big incentive to regain its ability to set its own price and will lobby hard to remove price controls. Economists see resources spent to regain their monopoly price as socially wasteful.
4. Economists distrust government. Governments have their own political agendas—there is no general belief among economists that governments will try to set the price at the competitive level. Once one opens up the price control gates in cases of monopoly, it will be difficult to stop government from using price controls in competitive markets.

The arguments are, of course, more complicated, and will be discussed in more detail, but this should give you a good preview of some of the policy arguments to come in later chapters.

can two or more firms. A natural monopoly will occur when the technology is such that indivisible setup costs are so large that average total costs fall within the range of possible outputs. I demonstrate that case in Figure 12-6(a).

Figure 12-6 (a and b) A Natural Monopolist
This graph in (**a**) shows the average cost curve for a natural monopoly. One firm producing Q_1 would have average cost of C_1. If total production remains at Q_1 and another firm enters the market, sharing quantity produced, each firm would produce $Q_{1/2}$ goods at average cost C_2. If three firms each produced $Q_{1/3}$, the average cost for each would be C_3. In a case of a natural monopoly, as the number of firms in the industry increases, the average cost of producing a fixed number of units increases.

The graph in (**b**) shows that a natural monopolist would produce Q_M and charge a price P_M. It will earn a profit shown by the orange shaded box. If the monopolist were required to charge a price equal to marginal cost, P_C, it would incur a loss shown by the blue shaded box.

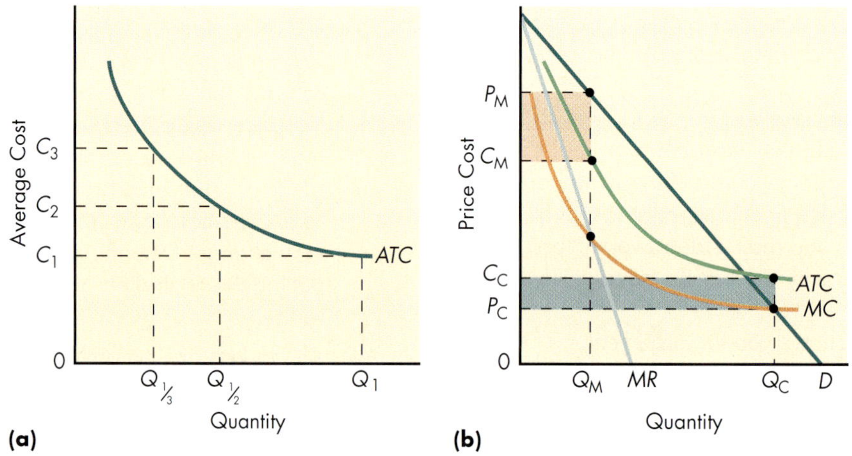

Q-8 Why is the competitive price impossible for an industry that exhibits strong economies of scale?

If one firm produces Q_1, its cost per unit is C_1. If two firms each produce half that amount, $Q_{1/2}$, so that their total production is Q_1, the cost per unit will be C_2, which is significantly higher than C_1. In cases of natural monopoly, as the number of firms in the industry increases, the average total cost of producing a fixed number of units increases. For example, if there were three firms in the industry and they each had a third of the market, each firm would have an average cost of C_3.

Until the 1990s local telephone service was a real-world example of such a natural monopoly. It made little sense to have two sets of telephone lines going into people's houses. I say "until recently" because technology changes and now, with wireless communications and cable connections, the technical conditions that made local telephone service a natural monopoly are changing. Such change is typical; natural monopolies are only natural given a technology.

A natural monopoly can also occur when a single industry standard is more efficient than multiple standards, even when that standard is owned by one firm. An example is the operating system for computers. It is much more efficient (because the communication among users is easier) for there to be a single standard rather than multiple standards.

From a welfare standpoint natural monopolies are different from other types of monopolies. In the case of a natural monopoly, even if a single firm makes some monopoly profit, the price it charges may still be lower than the price two firms making normal profit would charge because its average total costs will be lower. In the case of a natural monopoly not only is there no welfare loss from monopoly but there can actually be a welfare gain since a single firm producing is so much more efficient than many firms producing. Such natural monopolies are often organized as public utilities. For example, most towns have a single water department supplying water to residents.

Figure 12-6(b) shows the profit-maximizing level of output and price that a natural monopolist would choose. To show the profit-maximizing level of output, I've added a marginal cost curve that is below the average total cost curve and also falling. (If you don't know why this must be the case, a review of costs is in order.) A natural monopolist uses the same $MC = MR$ rule that a monopolist uses to determine output. The monopolist will produce Q_M and charge a price P_M. Average total costs are C_M and the natural monopolist earns a profit shown by the orange shaded box.

Where natural monopoly exists, the perfectly competitive solution is impossible, since average total costs are not covered where $MC = P$. A monopolist required by government to charge the competitive price P_C, where $P = MC$, will incur a loss shown by the blue shaded box because marginal cost is always below average total cost. Some output restriction is necessary in order for production to be feasible. In such cases monopolies are often preferred by the public as long as they are regulated by government. I will discuss the issues of regulating natural monopolies in Chapter 14.

Government-Created Monopolies

A third reason monopolies can exist is that they're created by government. The support of laissez-faire by Classical economists such as Adam Smith and their opposition to monopoly arose in large part in reaction to those government-created monopolies, not in reaction to any formal analysis of welfare loss from monopoly.

Normative Views of Monopoly

Many laypeople's views of government-created monopoly reflect the same normative judgments that Classical economists made. Classical economists considered, and much of the lay public considers, such monopolies unfair and inconsistent with liberty. Monopolies prevent people from being free to enter whatever business they want and are undesirable on normative grounds. In this view, government-created monopolies are simply wrong.

This normative argument against government-created monopoly doesn't extend to all types of government-created monopolies. The public accepts certain types of government-created monopoly that it believes have overriding social value. An example is patents. To encourage research and development of new products, government gives out patents for a wide variety of innovations, such as genetic engineering, Xerox machines, and cans that can be opened without a can opener.

Q-9 If a patent is a monopoly, why does the government give out patents?

A second normative argument against monopoly is that the public doesn't like the income distributional effects of monopoly. Although, as we saw in our discussion of monopoly, monopolists do not always earn an economic profit, they often do, which means that the monopoly might transfer income in a way that the public (whose normative views help determine society's policy toward monopoly) doesn't like. This distributional effect of monopoly based on normative views of who deserves income is another reason many laypeople oppose monopoly: They believe it transfers income from "deserving" consumers to "undeserving" monopolists.

A third normative reason people oppose government-created monopoly that isn't captured by the standard model of monopoly is that the possibility of government-created monopoly encourages people to spend a lot of their time in political pursuits trying to get the government to favor them with a monopoly, and less time doing "productive" things. It causes *rent-seeking* activities in which people spend resources to gain monopolies for themselves.

Possible economic profits from monopoly lead potential monopolists to spend money to get government to give them a monopoly.

Each of these arguments probably plays a role in the public's dislike of monopoly. As you can see, these real-world arguments blend normative judgments with objective analysis, making it difficult to arrive at definite conclusions. Most real-world problems require this blending, making applied economic analysis difficult. The economist must interpret the normative judgments about what people want to achieve and explain how public policy can be designed to achieve those desired ends.

Let's now consider how economic theory might be used to analyze monopoly and to suggest how government might deal with that monopoly.

Government Policy and Monopoly: AIDS Drugs

Let's consider the problem of acquired immune deficiency syndrome (AIDS) and the combination of medicinal drugs, including azidothymidine (AZT), used to treat it. AZT, used in combination with other drugs in mixtures called cocktails, is believed to arrest AIDS completely. These drugs were developed by a small group of pharmaceutical companies, which own patents on them, giving them a monopoly. Patents are given on medicine to encourage firms to find cures for various diseases. The monopoly the patent gives them lets them charge a high price so that the firms can expect to make a profit from their research. Whether such patents are in the public interest isn't an issue, since the patent has already been granted.

Q-10 The medicinal drug tetracycline sold for animals costs about 1/20 as much as the same drug sold for human beings. What is the likely explanation?

What is an issue is what to do about these drugs. Currently demand for them is highly inelastic, so the price pharmaceutical companies can charge is high even though their marginal cost of producing them is low. Whether they are making a profit depends on their cost of development. But since that cost is already spent, that's irrelevant to the current marginal cost; development cost affects their *ATC* curve, not their marginal cost curve. Thus, the pharmaceutical companies are charging an enormously high price for drugs that may help save people's lives and that cost them a very small amount to produce.

What, if anything, should the government do? Some people have suggested that the government regulate the price of the drugs, requiring the firms to charge only their marginal cost. This would make society better off. But most economists have a problem with that policy. They point out that doing so will significantly reduce the incentives for drug companies to research new drugs. One reason drug companies spend billions of dollars for drug research is their expectation that they'll be able to make large profits if they're successful. If drug companies expect the government to come in and take away their monopoly when they're successful, they won't search for cures. So forcing these pharmaceuticals to charge a low price for their drugs would help AIDS victims, but it would hurt people suffering from diseases that are currently being researched and that might be researched in the future. So there's a strong argument not to regulate.

But the thought of people dying when a cheap cure—or at least a partially effective treatment—is available is repulsive to me and to many others. African countries, where 70 percent of all people infected with the virus that causes AIDS live, have threatened to license production of these drugs to local manufacturers and make them available at cost. U.S. pharmaceutical companies pressured the United States to cut off foreign aid if the African countries carried out their threat. That did not provide them with good public relations and the major drug companies felt the pressure, leading them to make drugs for AIDS available to AIDS patients in poor nations at a much lower price than they do to others (an example of price discrimination).

An alternative policy suggested by economic theory is for the government to buy the patents and allow anyone to make the drugs so their price would approach their marginal cost. Admittedly, this would be expensive. It would cause negative incentive effects, as the government would have to increase taxes to cover the buyout's costs. But this approach would avoid the problem of the regulatory approach and achieve the same ends. However, it would also introduce new problems, such as determining which patents the government should buy.

Whether such a buyout policy makes sense remains to be seen, but in debating such issues the power of the simple monopoly model becomes apparent.

Conclusion

We've come to the end of the presentation of the formal models of perfect competition and monopoly. Working through the models takes a lot of effort, but it's effort well spent. In Chapter 1, I quoted Einstein: "A theory should be as simple as possible, but not more so." This chapter's analysis isn't simple; it takes repetition, working through models, and doing thought experiments to get it down pat. But it's as simple as possible. Even so, it's extremely easy to make a foolish mistake, as I did in my Ph.D. oral examination when I was outlining an argument on the blackboard. ["*What* did you say the output would be for this monopolist, Mr. Colander?"] As I learned then, it takes long hours of working through the models again and again to get them right.

Summary

- The price a monopolist charges is higher than that of a competitive market due to the restriction of output; a monopolist can make a profit in the long run.
- A monopolist's profit-maximizing output is where marginal revenue equals marginal cost.
- A monopolist can charge the maximum price consumers are willing to pay for the quantity the monopolist produces.
- To determine a monopolist's profit, first determine its output (where MC = MR). Then determine its price and average total cost at that output level. The difference between price and average total cost at the profit-maximizing level of output is profit per unit. Multiply this by output to find total profit.
- Because monopolists reduce output and charge a price that is higher than marginal cost, monopolies create a welfare loss to society.
- If a monopolist can (1) identify groups of customers who have different elasticities of demand, (2) separate them in some way, and (3) limit their ability to resell its product between groups, it can price discriminate.
- A price-discriminating monopolist earns more profit than a normal monopolist because it can charge a higher price to those with less elastic demands and a lower price to those with more elastic demands.
- Three important barriers to entry are natural ability, increasing returns to scale, and government restrictions.
- Natural monopolies exist in industries with strong economies of scale. Because their average total costs are always falling, it is more efficient for one firm to produce all the output.
- The competitive price is impossible in a natural monopoly because marginal cost is always below average total cost. No firm would enter an industry where not even normal (zero economic) profit can be made.
- Normative arguments against monopoly include the following: (1) monopolies are inconsistent with freedom, (2) the distributional effects of monopoly are unfair, and (3) monopolies encourage people to waste time and money trying to get monopolies.

Key Terms

monopoly *(264)*
natural monopoly *(274)*
patent *(271)*
price-discriminate *(273)*

Questions for Thought and Review

1. Demonstrate graphically the profit-maximizing positions for a perfect competitor and a monopolist. How do they differ?
2. Monopolists differ from perfect competitors because monopolists make a profit. True or false? Why?
3. Why is marginal revenue below average revenue for a monopolist?
4. Explain the effects on college education of the development of a teaching machine that you plug into a student's brain and that makes the student understand everything. How would your answer differ if a college could monopolize production of this machine?
5. Say you place a lump sum tax (a tax that is treated as a fixed cost) on a monopolist. How will that affect her output and pricing decisions?
6. A monopolist is selling fish. But if the fish don't sell, they rot. What will be the likely elasticity at the point on the demand curve at which the monopolist sets the price?
7. When you buy a cheap computer printer or home fax you can sometimes get it for free after the rebate. Why would a firm sell you something for a zero price? (The answer isn't that it wants to be nice.)
8. In late 2001, the U.S. government threatened to disregard Bayer's patent of ciprofloxacin, the most effective drug to fight anthrax, and license the production of the drug to American drug companies to stockpile the drug in case of an anthrax epidemic. While the policy would lower costs to the U.S. government of stockpiling the drug, it also would have other costs. What are those costs?
9. Provide a price discrimination argument for the existence of the four unexplained examples of price discrimination in the text.
10. Airlines are always running sales. On closer look, however, existing fares can be cheaper than restricted flights. What accounts for the practice of advertising "bargain" fares that may not be the lowest fare available? What conditions in the airline market make this practice possible?
11. Demonstrate the welfare loss created by a monopoly.
12. Will the welfare loss from a monopolist with a perfectly elastic marginal cost curve be greater or less than the welfare loss from a monopolist with an upward-sloping marginal cost curve?
13. In the late 1990s, the Government Accounting Office reported that airlines block new carriers at major airports. What effect does this have on fares and the number of flights at those airports? How much are airlines willing to spend to control the use of gates to block new carriers?
14. Copyrights provide authors with a monopoly. What effect would eliminating copyrights have on the price and output of textbooks? Should copyrights be eliminated?
15. How is efficiency related to the number of firms in an industry characterized by strong economies of scale?

Problems and Exercises

1. A monopolist with a straight-line demand curve finds that it can sell two units at $12 each or 12 units at $2 each. Its fixed cost is $20 and its marginal cost is constant at $3 per unit.
   a. Draw the MC, *ATC*, *MR*, and demand curves for this monopolist.
   b. At what output level would the monopolist produce?
   c. At what output level would a perfectly competitive firm produce?
2. State what's wrong with the following graphs:

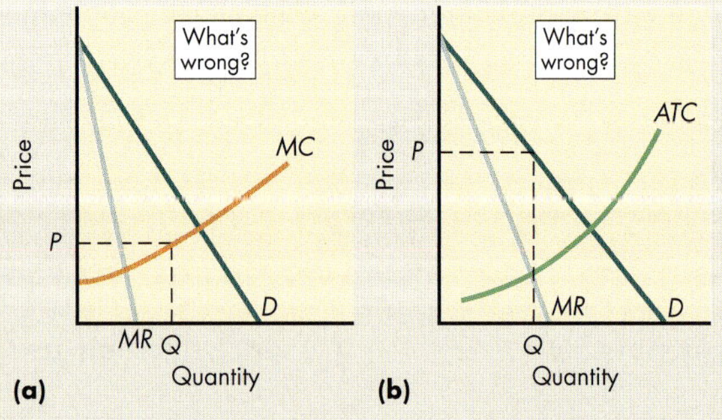

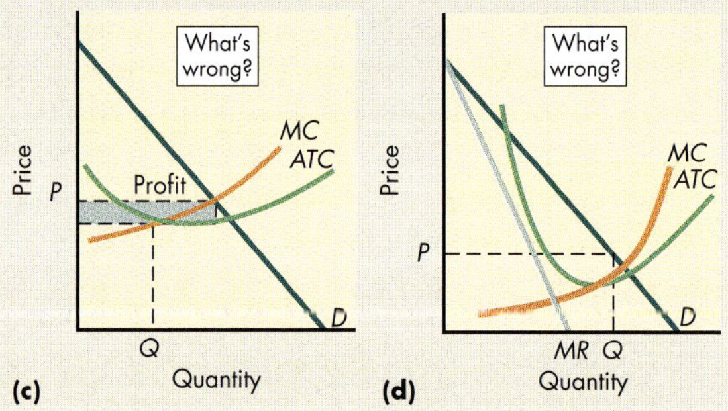

3. Wyeth-Ayerst Laboratories developed Norplant, a long-acting contraceptive, in the early 1990s. In the United States, the firm priced the contraceptive at $350, and in other countries, the firm priced it at $23.
   a. Why would the firm price it differently in different countries?
   b. Was the pricing fair?
   c. What do you think will happen to the price over time? Why?

4. Assume your city government has been contracting with a single garbage collection firm that has been granted an exclusive franchise, or sole right to pick up trash within the entire city limits. However, it has been proposed that the companies be allowed to compete for business with residents on an individual basis. The city government has estimated the price residents are willing to pay for various numbers of garbage collections per month and the total costs per resident as shown in the following table.

Pickup (*Q*)	Price per Pickup (Demand)	Total Revenue (*TR*)	Marginal Revenue (*MR*)	Total Cost (*TC*)	Marginal Cost (*MC*)	Average Total Cost (*ATC*)
0	$4.20	0	—	$ 3.20	—	—
1	3.80	____	____	4.20	____	____
2	3.40	____	____	5.60	____	____
3	3.00	____	____	7.80	____	____
4	2.60	____	____	10.40	____	____
5	2.20	____	____	13.40	____	____
6	1.90	____	____	16.80	____	____

a. What are the fixed costs per month of garbage collection per resident?
b. Considering that the current garbage collection firm the city has contracted with has a monopoly in garbage collection services, what is the current number of collections residents receive per month and the price charged residents for each collection? What is the economic profit received from each resident by the monopoly firm?
c. If competitive bidding were allowed and therefore a competitive market for garbage collection services developed, what would be the number of collections per month and the price charged residents per collection? What is the economic profit received from each resident by the competitive firms?
d. Based on the above analysis, should the city government allow competitive bidding? Why? Would you expect there to be any quality differences between the monopolistic and competitive trash collection firms?

5. Econocompany is under investigation by the U.S. Department of Justice for violating antitrust laws. The government decides that Econocompany has a natural monopoly and that, if it is to keep its business, it must sell at a price equal to marginal cost. Econocompany says that it can't do that and hires you to explain to the government why it can't.
a. You do so in reference to the following graph.
b. What price would it charge if it were unregulated?
c. What price would you advise that it should be allowed to charge?

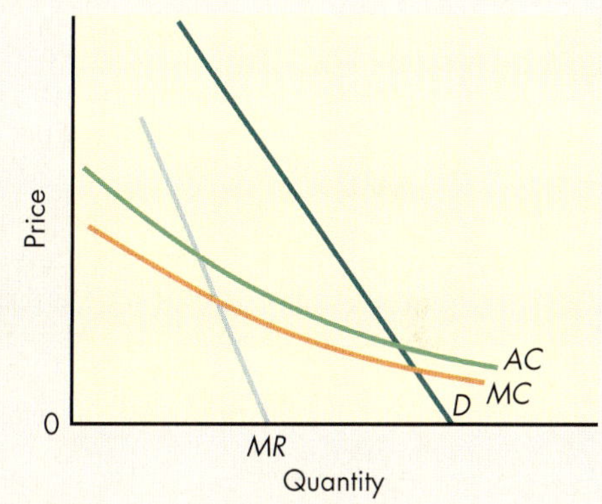

6. New York City has issued 12,000 taxi licenses, called *medallions*, and has not changed that number since 1937.
a. What does that limitation likely do to the price of taxi medallions?
b. In the early 1990s, the New York City Taxi Commission promulgated a rule that required single-cab medallion owners to drive their cabs full-time. What will that rule do to the price of the medallion?
c. If New York City increased the number of medallions by 1,000, selling the additional 1,000 at the market rate, and gave half the proceeds to owners of existing medallions, what would happen to the price of medallions?
d. What would happen to the wealth of existing medallion owners?

WEB QUESTIONS

1. The Federal Communications Commission regulates interstate and international communications, including merger activity within industry. Go to the FCC website at www.fcc.gov and search for "monopoly." Select one document in support of and another opposed to a proposed merger between communication companies.
a. What reasons do consumers have for opposing the merger?
b. What reasons do consumers have for supporting the merger?
c. Does the theory of a monopolist found in the chapter support the reasons stated in your answers to *a* and *b*. Explain.

2. Go to the U.S. Patent and Trademark Office's homepage at www.ustpo.gov to answer the following questions:

a. What right does a patent give the holder of a patent? Can inventors produce and sell their inventions without patents?
b. What can a patent-holder expect to pay the Patent and Trademark office over the lifetime of the patent?
c. What is the length of a patent? Why do you believe government sets expiration dates for patents?

ANSWERS TO MARGIN QUESTIONS

1. If you doodle too much, your doodles will become worthless. Besides, if you want to pass the next test you have to study. *(265)*
2. At output 4, the marginal cost of \$12 (between \$8 and \$16) equals the marginal revenue of \$12 (between \$15 and \$9), making it the profit-maximizing output. It has the highest total profit, \$34. *(266)*
3. To determine the profit-maximizing price and output, one must determine where the marginal revenue curve equals marginal cost. So one must first draw the marginal revenue curve and see where it intersects marginal cost. That intersection determines the quantity, as in the graph below. Carrying the line up to the demand curve determines the price. *(267)*

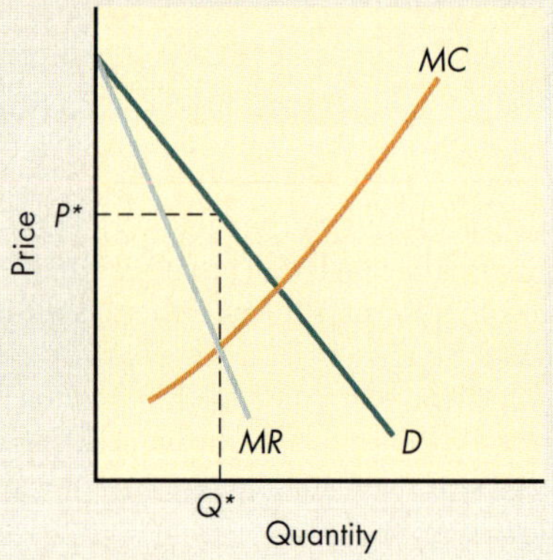

4. A monopolist produces less output than a perfectly competitive firm because it takes into account the fact that increasing output will lower the price of all previous units. *(268)*
5. To determine profit, follow the following four steps: (1) draw the marginal revenue curve, (2) find the level of output where MC = *MR* indicated in the graph in the next column by Q^*, (3) find the price the monopolist would charge indicated by P^* and extend a horizontal line from the demand curve at that price to the price axis, (4) determine the average total cost at Q^* shown by C^* and extend a horizontal line from the *ATC* curve at that cost to the price axis. The box created is the monopolist's profit. The profit is the shaded box shown in the graph below. *(270)*

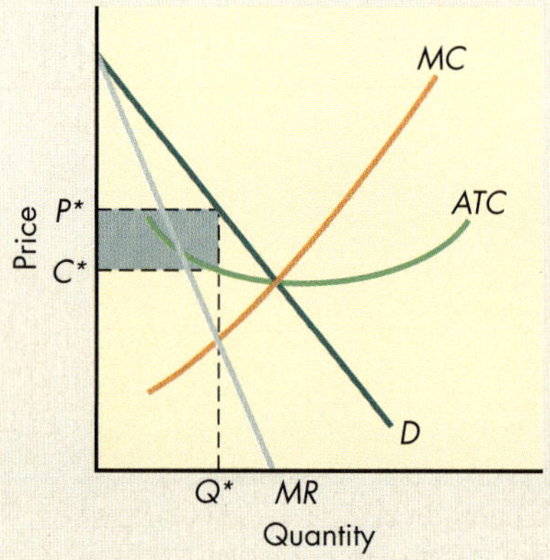

6. Area C represents the profit going to a monopolist. It is not considered a loss since, while consumers lose it, monopolists gain it. It is a redistribution of resources rather than an efficiency loss. *(272)*
7. A price-discriminating monopolist makes a greater profit than a normal monopolist because a price-discriminating monopolist is able to charge a higher price to those consumers who have less elastic demands. *(274)*
8. The marginal cost curve for an industry that exhibits strong economies of scale is always below average total costs. Therefore, the competitive price, where *P* = MC, will always result in losses for firms. Firms would not enter into such an industry and there would be no supply. *(276)*
9. The government gives out patents to encourage research and development of new products. This suggests that the public and government believe that certain monopolies have overriding social value. *(277)*
10. A likely explanation for medicinal drugs being sold at a much lower cost for animals than for human beings is differing elasticities of demand. The demand for drugs for human beings is highly inelastic, whereas the demand for medicinal drugs for animals is elastic. When there is a price-discriminating monopolist for these drugs, those with more inelastic demands are charged higher prices. *(278)*

APPENDIX A

The Algebra of Competitive and Monopolistic Firms

In the Appendix to Chapter 5, I presented the algebra relevant to supply and demand. To relate that algebra to competitive firms, all you must remember is that the market supply curve equals the marginal cost curve for the competitive industry. Let's review it briefly.

Say that marginal costs, and thus market supply, for the industry is given by

$$P = 2Q_S + 4$$

Let's also say that the market demand curve is

$$Q_D = 28 - \tfrac{1}{4}P$$

To determine equilibrium price and quantity in a competitive market, you must equate quantity supplied and quantity demanded and solve for price. First, rewrite the marginal cost equation with quantity supplied on the left:

$$Q_S = \tfrac{1}{2}MC - 2$$

Then set quantity demanded equal to quantity supplied and MC = P. Then solve for equilibrium price:

$$\begin{aligned} Q_S = Q_D \Rightarrow 28 - \tfrac{1}{4}P &= \tfrac{1}{2}P - 2 \\ 112 - P &= 2P - 8 \\ 3P &= 120 \\ P &= 40 \end{aligned}$$

Thus, the equilibrium price is \$40. Competitive firms take this price as given and produce up until their marginal cost equals price. The industry as a whole produces 18 units.

Now let's consider the algebra relevant for a monopolistic firm. In the monopolistic case, supply and demand are not enough to determine where the monopolist will produce. The monopolist will produce where marginal revenue equals marginal cost. But, for the monopolist, the industry demand curve is the demand curve, which means that in order to determine where the monopolist will produce, we must determine the marginal revenue curve that goes along with the above demand curve. There are two ways to do that.

First, if you know calculus you can determine the marginal revenue curve in the following manner: Since marginal revenue tells us how much total revenue will change with each additional unit produced, you first specify the demand curve in terms of quantity produced.

$$P = 112 - 4Q$$

Since $TR = PQ$ we can multiply this by Q to get total revenue. Doing so gives us:

$$TR = PQ = 112Q - 4Q^2$$

To find marginal revenue, take the first derivative of total revenue with respect to Q.

$$P = 112 - 8Q$$

Second, if you don't know calculus, all you need to remember is the trick shown in a box in the chapter on how to graph the marginal revenue curve. Remember, the marginal revenue curve starts at the same price as the demand curve and bisects the quantity axis at one-half the value of the quantity axis intercept of the demand curve. The marginal revenue curve, because it bisects the quantity axis at one-half the value of the quantity axis intercept of the accompanying demand curve, must fall twice as fast as the market demand curve. That is, its slope is twice the slope of the market demand curve.

Knowing that its slope is twice the market demand curve slope, you can write the marginal revenue curve with the same price axis intercept as the demand curve and a slope of two times the slope of the demand curve. (Warning: this only works with linear demand curves.) The price-axis intercept of the demand curve is the value of P where Q equals 0: 112. The quantity-axis intercept of the demand curve is the value of Q where P equals 0: 28. So, the marginal revenue curve has a price-axis intercept at 112 and a quantity-axis intercept at 14. Mathematically, such a curve is represented by

$$P = 112 - (112/14)\mathrm{P}$$

or

$$P = 112 - 8Q$$

Now that we've determined the monopolist's marginal revenue curve, we can determine its equilibrium quantity by setting $MR = MC$ and solving for Q. Doing so gives us:

$$\begin{aligned} 112 - 8Q &= 2Q + 4 \\ -10Q &= -108 \\ Q &= 10.8 \end{aligned}$$

The monopolist then charges the price consumers are willing to pay for that quantity. Mathematically, substitute 10.8 into the demand equation and solve for price:

$$P = 112 - 4(10.8)$$
$$P = \$68.80$$

Comparing the price and quantity produced by a monopolist and those of a competitive industry shows that the monopolist charges a higher price and produces a lower output.

QUESTIONS FOR THOUGHT AND REVIEW

1. The market demand curve is $Q_D = 50 - P$. The marginal cost curve is $MC = 4Q + 6$.
   a. Assuming the marginal cost curve is for a competitive industry as a whole, find the profit-maximizing level of output and price.
   b. Assuming the marginal cost curve is for only one firm which comprises the entire market, find the profit-maximizing level of output and price.
   c. Compare the two results.
2. The market demand curve is $Q_D = 160 - 4P$. A monopolist's total cost curve is $TC = 6Q^2 + 15Q + 50$.
   a. Find the profit-maximizing level of output and price for a monopolist.
   b. Find its average cost at that level of output.
   c. Find its profit at that level of output.
3. Suppose fixed costs for the monopolist in question 2 increases by 52.
   a. Find the profit-maximizing level of output and price for a monopolist.
   b. Find its average cost at that level of output.
   c. Find its profit at that level of output.
4. The market demand curve is $Q_D = 12 - \frac{1}{3}P$. Costs do not vary with output.
   a. Find the profit-maximizing level of output and price for a monopolist.
   b. Find the profit-maximizing level of output and price for a competitive industry.

MONOPOLISTIC COMPETITION, OLIGOPOLY, AND STRATEGIC PRICING

13

Competition, you know, is a lot like chastity.
It is widely praised, but alas, too little practiced.

—*Carol Tucker*

After reading this chapter, you should be able to:

- Describe two methods of determining market structure.
- List the four distinguishing characteristics of monopolistic competition.
- Demonstrate graphically the equilibrium of a monopolistic competitor.
- State the central element of oligopoly.
- Explain why decisions in the cartel model depend on market share and decisions in the contestable market model depend on barriers to entry.
- Illustrate a strategic decision facing a duopolist using the prisoner's dilemma.

As soon as economists start talking about real-world competition, market structure becomes a focus of the discussion. **Market structure** refers to *the physical characteristics of the market within which firms interact*. It involves the number of firms in the market and the barriers to entry. Monopoly and competition are the two polar cases of market structure. Real-world markets generally fall in between, and it is essential to introduce briefly two market structures between perfect competition and monopoly: monopolistic competition and oligopoly. They not only provide you with a sense of how the models can apply to the real world but also help cement in your mind the concepts introduced in Chapter 12.

Perfect competition has an almost infinite number of firms; monopoly has one firm. **Monopolistic competition** is *a market structure in which there are many firms selling differentiated products; there are few barriers to entry*. **Oligopoly** is *a market structure in which there are only a few firms; there are often significant barriers to entry*.

THE PROBLEMS OF DETERMINING MARKET STRUCTURE

Any estimate of the distribution of market structures must be treated with care. Defining an industry is a complicated task—inevitably, numerous arbitrary decisions must be made. Similarly, defining the relevant market of a given industry is complicated. For example, there are fewer than 10,000 banks in the United States, and banking is considered reasonably competitive. However, a particular small town may have only one or two banks, so there will be a monopoly or oligopoly with respect to banks in that town. Is the United States or the town the relevant market? The same argument exists when we think of international competition. Many firms sell in international markets and, while a group of firms may compose an oligopoly in the United States, the international market might be more accurately characterized by monopolistic competition.

Another dimension of the definitional problem concerns deciding what is to be included in an industry. If you define the industry as "the transportation industry," there are many firms. If you define it as "the urban transit industry," there are fewer firms; if you define it as "the commuter rail industry," there are still fewer firms. Similarly with the geographic dimension of industry. There's more competition in the global market than in the local market. The narrower the definition, the fewer the firms.

Classifying Industries

One of the ways in which economists classify markets is by cross-price elasticities (the responsiveness of the change in the demand for a good to change in the price of a related good). Industrial organization economist F. M. Sherer has suggested the following rule of thumb: When two goods have a cross-price elasticity greater than or equal to 3, they can be regarded as belonging to the same market.

The **North American Industry Classification System (NAICS)** is *an industry classification that categorizes firms by type of economic activity and groups firms with like production processes*. It was adopted by the United States, Mexico, and Canada in 1997 and replaces the Standardized Industrial Classification (SIC) codes developed in the 1930s. All firms are placed into 20 broadly defined two-digit sectors. These two-digit sectors are further subdivided into three-digit subsectors, four-digit industry groupings, five-digit industries, and six-digit national industry groupings. Each subgrouping becomes more and more narrowly defined. Table 13-1 lists the 20 sectors and shows the subgroupings for one sector, Information, to give you an idea of what's included in each.

Q-1 Which would have more output: the two-digit industry 21 or the four-digit industry 2111? Explain your reasoning.

When economists talk about industry structure, they generally talk about industries in the four- to six-digit subsector groupings in the United States. This is a convention. Economists are often called on to give expert testimony in court cases, and if an

Table 13-1 Industry Groupings in the North American Industry Classification System

Two-Digit Sectors		Three- to Six-Digit Subsectors
11	Agriculture, forestry, fishing, and hunting	
21	Mining	
22	Utilities	
23	Construction	
31–33	Manufacturing	
42	Wholesale trade	
44–45	Retail trade	
48–49	Transportation and warehousing	513 Broadcasting and telecommunications
51	Information	5133 Telecommunications
52	Finance and insurance	51332 Wireless telecommunications carriers, except satellite
53	Real estate and rental and leasing	513321 Paging
54	Professional, scientific, and technical services	
55	Management of companies and enterprises	
56	Administrative and support, and waste management and remediation services	
61	Education services	
62	Health care and social assistance	
71	Arts, entertainment, and recreation	
72	Accommodation and food services	
81	Other services (except public administration)	
92	Public administration	

Source: U.S. Census Bureau (www.census.gov/epcd/www/naics.html).

economist wants to argue that an industry is more competitive than its opponents say it is, he or she challenges this convention of using a four- to six-digit classification of industry, asserting that the classification is arbitrary (which it is) and that the relevant market should be the two- to three-digit classification.

Determining Industry Structure

To measure industry structure, economists use one of two methods: the concentration ratio or the Herfindahl index.

A **concentration ratio** is *the value of sales by the top firms of an industry stated as a percentage of total industry sales*. The most commonly used concentration ratio is the four-firm concentration ratio. For example, a four-firm concentration ratio of 60 tells you that the top four firms in the industry produce 60 percent of the industry's output. The higher the ratio, the closer the industry is to an oligopolistic or monopolistic type of market structure.

The **Herfindahl index** is *an index of market concentration calculated by adding the squared value of the individual market shares of all the firms in the industry*. For example, say that 10 firms in the industry each have 10 percent of the market:

The Herfindahl index is a method used by economists to classify how competitive an industry is.

$$\text{Herfindahl index} = 10^2+10^2+10^2+10^2+10^2+10^2+10^2+10^2+10^2+10^2 = 1{,}000$$

The Herfindahl index gives higher weights to the largest firms in the industry because it squares market shares.

Because it squares market shares, the Herfindahl index gives more weight to firms with large market shares than does the concentration ratio measure.

The two measures can differ because of their construction, but generally if the concentration ratio is high, so is the Herfindahl index. Table 13-2 presents the four-firm concentration ratio and the Herfindahl index of selected industries.

The Herfindahl index plays an important role in government policy; it is used as a rule of thumb by the U.S. Department of Justice in determining whether an industry is sufficiently competitive to allow a merger between two large firms. If the Herfindahl index is less than 1,000, the Department of Justice generally assumes the industry is sufficiently competitive, and it doesn't look more closely at the merger. We'll discuss this in more detail in Chapter 15.

Table 13-2 Concentration Ratios and the Herfindahl Index

Industry	Four-Firm Concentration Ratio	Herfindahl Index
Meat products	35	393
Fruit and vegetable canning	24	259
Breakfast cereal	82	2,445
Women's and misses' dresses	13	76
Book printing	32	364
Stationery	56	1,128
Soap and detergent	66	1,619
Men's footwear	50	857
Women's footwear	50	795
Bolts, nuts, rivets, and washers	9	40
Electronic computer	45	728
Radio, TV, wireless broadcasting	49	972
Burial caskets	74	2,965

Source: *Census of Manufacturers*, (factfinder.census.gov).

Conglomerate Firms and Bigness

Q-2 If the four-firm concentration ratio of an industry is 60 percent, what is the highest Herfindahl index that industry could have? What is the lowest?

Neither the four-firm concentration ratio nor the Herfindahl index gives us a picture of corporations' bigness. That's because many corporations are conglomerates—companies that span a variety of unrelated industries. For example, a conglomerate might produce both shoes and automobiles.

To see that concentration ratios are not an index of bigness, say there were only 11 firms in the entire United States, each with a 9 percent share of each industry. Both indexes would classify the U.S. economy as unconcentrated, but many people would seriously doubt whether that were the case. Little work has been done on classifying conglomerates or in determining whether they have any effect on an industry's performance.

The Importance of Classifying Industry Structure

A basic rule of economics is that less concentrated industries are more likely to resemble perfectly competitive markets. In terms of formal modeling it's important to classify industries because the number of firms in an industry plays an important role in determining whether firms will tend to explicitly take other firms' actions into account. In monopolistic competition, there are so many firms that individual firms tend not to explicitly take into account rival firms' likely responses to their decisions. Collusion is difficult. In oligopoly there are fewer firms, and each firm is more likely to explicitly engage in **strategic decision making**—*taking explicit account of a rival's expected response to a decision you are making*. In oligopolies all decisions, including pricing decisions, are strategic decisions. Collusion is much easier. Thus, one distinguishes between monopolistic competition and oligopoly by whether or not firms explicitly take into account competitors' reactions to their decisions.

Oligopolies take into account the reactions of other firms; monopolistic competitors do not.

Q-3 Your study partner, Jean, has just said that monopolistic competitors use strategic decision making. How would you respond?

Why is the distinction important? Because it determines whether economists can model and predict the price and output of an industry. Nonstrategic decision making can be predicted relatively accurately if individuals behave rationally. Strategic decision making is much more difficult to predict, even if people behave rationally. What one person does depends on what he or she expects other people to do, which in turn depends on what others expect the one person to do. Consistent with this distinction, economists' model of monopolistic competition has a definite prediction. A model of monopolistic competition will tell us: Here's how much will be produced and here's how much will be charged. Economists' models of oligopoly don't have a definite prediction. There are no unique price and output decisions at which an oligopoly will rationally arrive; there are a variety of rational oligopoly decisions, and a variety of oligopoly models.

Characteristics of Monopolistic Competition

The four distinguishing characteristics of monopolistic competition are:

1. Many sellers.
2. Differentiated products.
3. Multiple dimensions of competition.
4. Easy entry of new firms in the long run.

Let's consider each in turn.

Foreign Competitive Oligopolies

Applying the Tools

Market structures change over time. Take, for instance, the automobile industry, which has always been used as the classic oligopoly model. Starting in the 1970s, however, foreign automakers have made large inroads into the U.S. market and have added new competition to it. Foreign companies such as Honda, Nissan, and Toyota have entered the U.S. market, as seen in the accompanying pie chart, which lists major automobile companies and their market shares.

The four-firm concentration ratio is over 75 percent, so the industry is still classified as an oligopoly. GM still considers what Ford's and Chrysler's reactions will be, but with the addition of foreign competition, there are getting to be too many firms for one firm to consider the reactions of all the other firms. The auto industry is becoming more monopolistically competitive.

Such change in industry structure is to be expected. Monopoly and oligopoly create the possibility that firms can make above-normal profits. Above-normal profits invite entry, and unless there are entry barriers, the result will likely be a breakdown in that monopoly or oligopoly.

Market Shares in the Automotive Industry

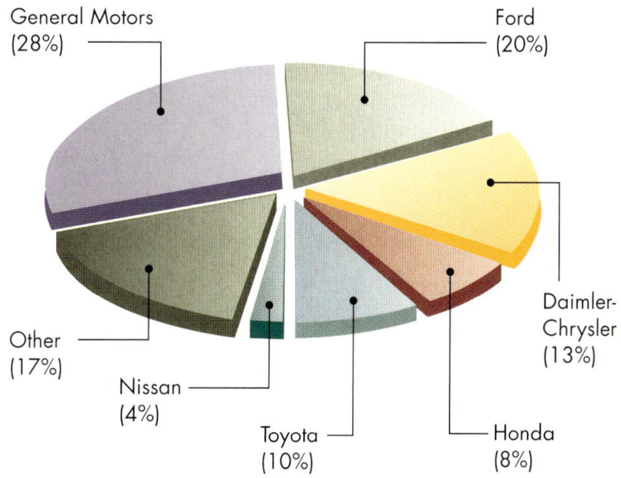

Source: *Automotive News*, 2002.

Many Sellers

When there are only a few sellers, it's reasonable to explicitly take into account your competitors' reaction to the price you set. When there are many sellers, it isn't. In monopolistic competition firms don't take into account rivals' reactions. Here's an example. There are many types of soap: Ivory, Irish Spring, Yardley's Old English, and so on. So when Ivory decides to run a sale, it won't spend a lot of time thinking about Old English's reaction. There are so many firms that one firm can't concern itself with the reaction of any specific firm. The soap industry is characterized by monopolistic competition. In contrast, there are only a few major automobile firms, so when GM sets its price, it will explicitly consider what Ford's reaction may be. If GM raises its price, will Ford go along and also raise price? Or will it hold its price at its current level and try to sell its cars on the basis of lower prices? The automobile industry is an oligopoly.

The fact that there are many sellers in monopolistic competition also makes collusion difficult since, when there are many firms, getting all of them to act as one is difficult. In economists' models monopolistically competitive firms are assumed to act independently.

Product Differentiation

The "many sellers" characteristic gives monopolistic competition its competitive aspect. Product differentiation gives it its monopolistic aspect. In a monopolistically competitive market, the goods that are sold aren't homogeneous, as in perfect competition; they are differentiated slightly. Irish Spring soap is slightly different from Ivory, which in turn is slightly different from Yardley's Old English.

Web Note 13.1
Product Differentiation

So in one sense each firm has a monopoly in the good it sells. But that monopoly is fleeting; it is based on advertising to convince people that one firm's good is different from the goods of competitors. The good may or may not really be different. Bleach differs little from one brand to another, yet buying Clorox makes many people feel that they're getting pure bleach. I generally don't buy it; I generally buy generic bleach. Ketchup, however, while made from the same basic ingredients, differs among brands (in my view). For me, only Heinz ketchup is real ketchup.

Because a monopolistic competitor has some monopoly power, advertising to increase that monopoly power (and hence increase the firm's profits) makes sense as long as the marginal benefit of advertising exceeds the marginal cost. Despite the fact that their goods are similar but differentiated, to fit economists' monopolistically competitive model, firms must make their decisions as if they had no effect on other firms.

Multiple Dimensions of Competition

In monopolistic competition, competition takes many forms.

In perfect competition, price is the only dimension on which firms compete; in monopolistic competition, competition takes many forms. Product differentiation reflects firms' attempt to compete on perceived attributes; advertising is another form competition takes. Other dimensions of competition include service and distribution outlets. These multiple dimensions of competition make it much harder to analyze a specific industry, but the alternative methods of competition follow the same two general decision rules as price competition:

- Compare marginal costs and marginal benefits; and
- Change that dimension of competition until marginal costs equal marginal benefits.

Ease of Entry of New Firms in the Long Run

The last condition a monopolistically competitive market must meet is that entry must be relatively easy; that is, there must be no significant entry barriers. Barriers to entry create the potential for long-run economic profit and prevent competitive pressures from pushing price down to average total cost. In monopolistic competition if there were long-run economic profits, other firms would enter until no economic profit existed.

Output, Price, and Profit of a Monopolistic Competitor

Although a full analysis of the multiple dimensions of monopolistic competition cannot be compressed into two dimensions, a good introduction can be gained by considering it within the standard two-dimensional (price, quantity) graph.

To do so we simply consider the four characteristics of monopolistic competition and see what implication they have for the analysis. First, we recognize that the firm has some monopoly power; therefore, a monopolistic competitor faces a downward-sloping demand curve. The downward-sloping demand curve means that in making decisions about output, the monopolistic competitor will, as will a monopolist, use a marginal revenue curve that is below price. At its profit-maximizing output, marginal cost will be less than price (not equal to price as it would be for a perfect competitor). We consider that case in Figure 13-1(a).

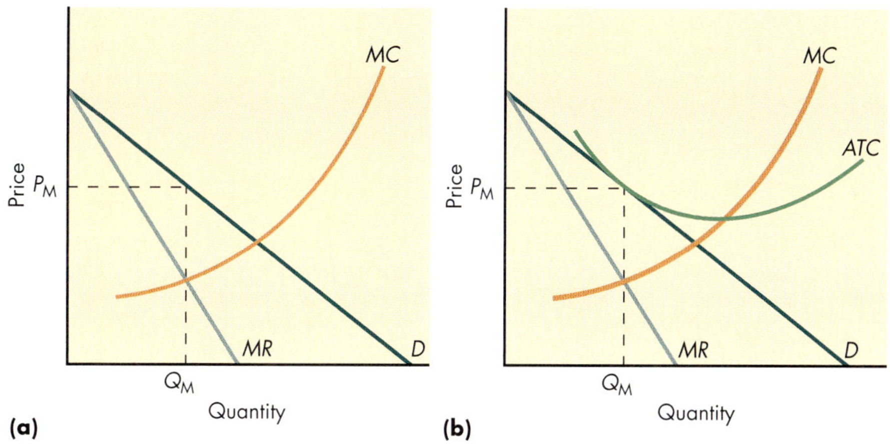

Figure 13-1 (a and b) Monopolistic Competition
In (**a**) you can see that a monopolistically competitive firm prices in the same manner as a monopolist. It sets quantity where marginal revenue equals marginal cost. In (**b**) you can see that the monopolistic competitor is not only a monopolist but also a competitor. Competition implies zero economic profit in the long run.

The monopolistic competitor faces the demand curve *D*, marginal revenue curve *MR*, and marginal cost curve MC. This demand curve is its portion of the total market demand curve. Using the MC = *MR* rule discussed in Chapter 12, you can see that the firm will choose output level Q_M (because that's the level of output at which marginal revenue intersects marginal cost). Having determined output, we extend a dotted line up to the demand curve and see that the firm will set a price equal to P_M. This price exceeds marginal cost. So far all we've done is reproduce the monopolist's decision.

Where does the competition come in? Competition implies zero economic profit in the long run. (If there's profit, a new competitor will enter the market, decreasing the existing firms' demand [shifting it to the left].) In long-run equilibrium a perfect competitor makes only a normal profit. Economic profits are determined by *ATC*, not by MC, so the competition part of monopolistic competition tells us where the average total cost curve must be at the long-run equilibrium output. It must be equal to price, and it will be equal to price only if the *ATC* curve is tangent to the demand curve at the output the firm chooses. We add that average total cost curve to the MC, *MR*, and demand curves in Figure 13-1(b). Profit or loss, I hope you remember, is determined by the difference between price and average total cost at the quantity the firm chooses.

Q-4 How do the equilibrium for a monopoly and for a monopolistic competitor differ?

To give this condition a little more intuitive meaning, let's say, for instance, that the monopolistically competitive firm is making a profit. This profit would set two adjustments in motion. First, it would attract new entrants. Some of the firm's customers would then defect, and its portion of the market demand curve would decrease. Second, to try to protect its profits the firm would likely increase expenditures on product differentiation and advertising to offset that entry. (There would be an All New, Really New, Widget campaign.) These expenditures would shift its average total cost curve up. These two adjustments would continue until the profits disappeared and the new demand curve is tangent to the new average total cost curve. A monopolistically competitive firm can make no long-run economic profit.

Comparing Monopolistic Competition with Perfect Competition

If both the monopolistic competitor and the perfect competitor make zero economic profit in the long run, it might seem that, in the long run at least, they're identical. They aren't, however. The perfect competitor perceives its demand curve as perfectly elastic, and the zero economic profit condition means that it produces at the minimum

The difference between a monopolist and a monopolistic competitor is in the position of the average total cost curve in long-run equilibrium.

Figure 13-2 (a and b) A Comparison of Perfect and Monopolistic Competition
The perfect competitor perceives its demand curve as perfectly elastic, and zero economic profit means that it produces at the minimum of the *ATC* curve, as represented in **(a)**. A monopolistic competitor, on the other hand, faces a downward-sloping demand curve and produces where marginal cost equals marginal revenue, as represented in **(b)**. In long-run equilibrium the *ATC* curve is tangent to the demand curve at that level, which is *not* at the minimum point of the *ATC* curve. The monopolistic competitor produces Q_M at price P_M. A perfect competitor with the same marginal cost curve would produce Q_C at price P_C.

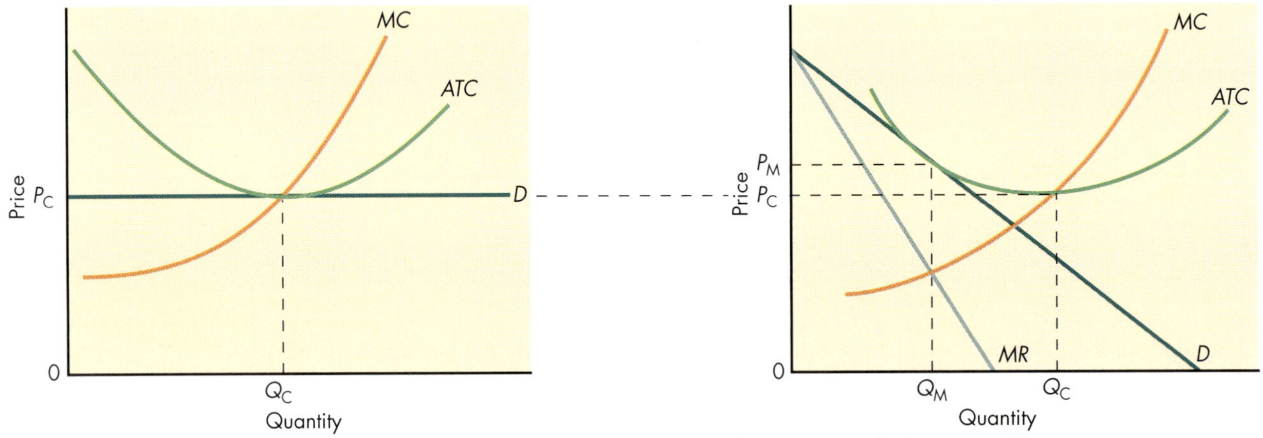

(a) Perfect competition

(b) Monopolistic competition

of the average total cost curve where the marginal cost curve equals price. We demonstrate that case in Figure 13-2(a).

The monopolistic competitor faces a downward-sloping demand curve for its differentiated product. It produces where the marginal cost curve equals the marginal revenue curve, and not where MC equals price. In equilibrium, price exceeds marginal cost. The average total cost curve of a monopolistic competitor is tangent to the demand curve at that output level, which cannot be at the minimum point of the average total cost curve since the demand curve is sloping downward. The minimum point of the average total cost curve (where a perfect competitor produces) is at a higher output (Q_C) than that of the monopolistic competitor (Q_M). I demonstrate the monopolistically competitive equilibrium in Figure 13-2(b) to allow you to compare monopolistic competition with perfect competition.

For a monopolistic competitor in long-run equilibrium, $(P = ATC) \geq (MC = MR)$.

The perfect competitor in long-run equilibrium produces at a point where MC = P = ATC. At that point, ATC is at its minimum. A monopolistic competitor produces at a point where MC = *MR*. Price is higher than marginal cost. For a monopolistic competitor in long-run equilibrium:

$$(P = ATC) \geq (MC = MR)$$

At that point, *ATC* is *not* at its minimum.

What does this distinction between a monopolistically competitive industry and a perfectly competitive industry mean in practice? It means that for a monopolistic competitor, since increasing output lowers average cost, increasing market share is a relevant concern. If only the monopolistic competitor could expand its market, it could do better. For a perfect competitor, increasing output offers no benefit in the form of lower average cost. A perfect competitor would have no concern about market share (the firm's percentage of total sales in the market).

Comparing Monopolistic Competition with Monopoly

An important difference between a monopolist and a monopolistic competitor is in the position of the average total cost curve in long-run equilibrium. For a monopolist, the average total cost curve can be, but need not be, at a position below price so that the monopolist makes a long-run economic profit. The average total cost curve of a monopolistic competitor must be tangent to the demand curve at the price and output chosen by the monopolistic competitor. No long-run economic profit is possible.

Advertising and Monopolistic Competition

While firms in a perfectly competitive market have no incentive to advertise (since they can sell all they want at the market price), monopolistic competitors have a strong incentive. That's because their products are differentiated from the others; advertising plays an important role in providing that differentiation.

Goals of Advertising Goals of advertising include shifting the firm's demand curve to the right and making it more inelastic. Advertising works by providing consumers with information about the firm's product and by making people want only a specific brand. That allows the firm to sell more, to charge a higher price, or to enjoy a combination of the two. It is advantageous to the firm if the marginal revenue of advertising exceeds the marginal cost of advertising. Advertising has two effects: It shifts the demand curve to the right, and it shifts the average total cost curve up.

Goals of advertising include shifting the firm's demand curve to the right and making it more inelastic.

When many firms are advertising, the advertising might be done less to shift the demand curve out than to keep the demand curve where it is—to stop consumers from shifting to a competitor's product. In either case, firms advertise to move the demand curve further out and to make it more inelastic than it would be if the firms weren't advertising.

Q-5 Why do monopolistically competitive firms advertise and perfect competitors do not?

Does Advertising Help or Hurt Society? Our perception of products (the degree of trust we put in them) is significantly influenced by advertising. Think of the following pairs of goods:

Rolex	Cheerios	Clorox bleach	Bayer
Timex	Oat Circles	generic bleach	generic aspirin

Web Note 13.2 Brand Names

Each of these names conveys a sense of what it is and how much trust we put in the product, and that determines how much we're willing to pay for it. For example, most people would pay more for Cheerios than for Oat Circles. Each year firms in the United States spend more than $150 billion on advertising. A 30-second commercial during the Super Bowl can cost as much as $3 million. That advertising increases firms' costs but also differentiates their products.

Are we as consumers better off or worse off with differentiated products? That's difficult to say. There's a certain waste in much of the differentiation that occurs. It shows up in the graph by the fact that monopolistic competitors don't produce at the minimum point of their average total cost curve. But there's also a sense of trust that we get from buying names we know and in having goods that are slightly different from one another. I'm a sophisticated consumer who knows that there's little difference between generic aspirin and Bayer aspirin. Yet sometimes I buy Bayer aspirin even though it costs more.

Edward Chamberlin, who, together with Joan Robinson, was the originator of the description of monopolistic competition, believed that the difference between the cost of a perfect competitor and the cost of a monopolistic competitor was the cost of what he called "differentness."[1] If consumers are willing to pay that cost, then it's not a waste but, rather, it's a benefit to them.

We must be careful about drawing any implications from this analysis. Average total cost for a monopolistically competitive firm includes advertising and costs of differentiating a product. It's debatable whether we as consumers are better off with as much differentiation as we have, or whether we'd all be better off if all firms produced a generic product at a lower cost.

Characteristics of Oligopoly

Oligopolistic firms are mutually interdependent.

The central element of oligopoly is that there are a small number of firms in an industry so that, in any decision it makes, each firm must take into account the expected reaction of other firms. Oligopolistic firms are mutually interdependent and can be collusive or noncollusive.

Most industries in the United States have some oligopolistic elements. If you ask almost any businessperson whether he or she directly takes into account rivals' likely response, the answer you'll get is "In certain cases, yes; in others, no."

Most retail stores that you deal with are oligopolistic in your neighborhood or town, although by national standards they may be quite competitive. For example, how many grocery stores do you shop at? Do you think they keep track of what their competitors are doing? You bet. They keep a close eye on their competitors' prices and set their own accordingly.

Models of Oligopoly Behavior

No single general model of oligopoly behavior exists. The reason is that an oligopolist can decide on pricing and output strategy in many possible ways, and there are no compelling grounds to characterize any of them as *the* oligopoly strategy. Although there are five or six formal models, I'll focus on two informal models of oligopoly behavior that give you insight into real-world problems rather than exercise your reasoning and modeling abilities as my earlier discussion did. The two models we'll consider are the cartel model and the contestable market model. These should give you a sense of how real-world oligopolistic pricing takes place.

Why, you ask, can't economists develop a simple formal model of oligopoly? The reason lies in the interdependence of oligopolists. Since there are few competitors, what one firm does specifically influences what other firms do, so an oligopolist's plan must always be a contingency or strategic plan. If my competitors act one way, I'll do X, but if they act another way, I'll do Y. Strategic interactions have a variety of potential outcomes rather than a single outcome such as shown in the formal models we discussed. An oligopolist spends enormous amounts of time guessing what its competitors will do, and it develops a strategy of how it will act accordingly.

The Cartel Model

If oligopolies can limit the entry of other firms and form a cartel, they increase the profits going to the combination of firms in the cartel.

A **cartel** is *a combination of firms that acts as if it were a single firm;* a cartel is a shared monopoly. If oligopolies can limit entry by other firms, they have a strong incentive to cartelize the industry and to act as a monopolist would, restricting output to a level that maximizes profit to the combination of firms. Thus, the **cartel model of oligopoly** is *a model that assumes that oligopolies act as if they were monopolists that have assigned output*

[1]Joan Robinson, a Cambridge, England, economist, called this the theory of imperfect competition, rather than the theory of monopolistic competition.

quotas to individual member firms of the oligopoly so that total output is consistent with joint profit maximization. All firms follow a uniform pricing policy that serves their collective interest.

Web Note 13.3
Price-Fixing

Since a monopolist makes the most profit that can be squeezed from a market, cartelization is the best strategy for an oligopoly. It requires each oligopolist to hold its production below what would be in its own interest were it not to collude with the others. Such explicit formal collusion is against the law in the United States, but informal collusion is allowed and oligopolies have developed a variety of methods to collude implicitly. Thus, the cartel model has some relevance.

Q-6 Why is it difficult for firms in an industry to maintain a cartel?

The model has some problems, however. For example, various firms' interests often differ, so it isn't clear what the collective interest of the firms in the industry is. In many cases a single firm, often the largest or dominant firm, takes the lead in pricing and output decisions, and the other firms (which are often called *fringe firms*) follow suit, even though they might have preferred to adopt a different strategy.

This dominant-firm cartel model works only if the smaller firms face barriers to entry, or the dominant firm has significantly lower cost conditions. If that were not the case, the smaller firms would pick up an increasing share of the market, eliminating the dominant firm's monopoly. An example of such a dominant-firm market was the copier market in the 1960s and 1970s, in which Xerox set the price and other firms followed. That copier market also shows the temporary nature of such a market. As the firms became more competitive on cost and quality, Xerox's market share fell and the company lost its dominant position. The copier market is far more competitive today than it used to be.

In other cases the various firms meet—sometimes only by happenstance, at the golf course or at a trade association gathering—and arrive at a collective decision. In the United States meetings for this purpose are illegal, but they do occur. In yet other cases the firms engage in **implicit collusion**—*multiple firms make the same pricing decisions even though they have not explicitly consulted with one another.* They "just happen" to come to a collective decision.

In some cases firms collude implicitly—they just happen to make the same pricing decisions. This is not illegal.

Implicit Price Collusion

Implicit price collusion, in which firms just happen to charge the same price but didn't meet to discuss price strategy, isn't against the law. Oligopolies often operate as close to the fine edge of the law as they can. For example, many oligopolistic industries allow a price leader to set the price, and then the others follow suit. The airline and steel industries take that route. Firms just happen to charge the same price or very close to the same price.

It isn't only in major industries that you see such implicit collusion. In small towns, you'll notice that most independent carpenters charge the same price. There's no explicit collusion, but were a carpenter to offer to work for less than the others, he or she would feel unwelcome at the local breakfast restaurant.

Or let's take another example: the Miami fish market where sport fishermen sell their catch at the dock. When I lived in Miami I often went to the docks to buy fresh fish. There were about 20 stands, all charging the same price. Price fluctuated, but it was by subtle agreement, and close to the end of the day the word would go out that the price could be reduced.

I got to know some of the sellers and asked them why they priced like that when it would be in their individual interest to set their own price. Their answer: "We like our boat and don't want it burned." They may have been talking in hyperbole, but social pressures play an important role in stabilizing prices in an oligopoly.

Cartels and Technological Change

Even if all firms in the industry cooperate, other firms, unless they are prevented from doing so, can always enter the market with a technologically superior new product at the same price or with the same good at a lower price. It is important to remember that technological changes are constantly occurring, and that a successful cartel with high profits will provide incentives for significant technological change, which can eliminate demand for its monopolized product.

Why Are Prices Sticky? Informal collusion happens all the time in U.S. businesses. One characteristic of informal collusive behavior is that prices tend to be sticky. They don't change frequently, so the existence of informal collusion is an important reason why prices are sticky. But it's not the only reason.

Another reason is that firms don't explicitly collude, but they have certain expectations of other firms' reactions, which changes their perceived demand curves. Specifically, they perceive a kinked demand curve facing them. This kinked demand curve is used especially to explain why firms often do not use lower-price strategies to increase sales.

Let's go through the reasoning behind the kinked demand curve. If a firm increases its price, and the firm believes that other firms won't go along, its perceived demand curve for increasing price will be very elastic (D_1 in Figure 13-3). It will lose lots of business to the other firms that haven't raised their price. The relevant portions of its demand curve and its marginal revenue curve are shown in blue in Figure 13-3.

Q-7 Is the demand curve as perceived by an oligopolist likely to be more or less elastic for a price increase or a price decrease?

If it decreased its price, however, the firm assumes that all other firms would immediately match that decrease, so it would gain very few, if any, additional sales. A large fall in price would result in only a small increase in sales, so its demand is very inelastic (D_2 in Figure 13-3). This less elastic portion of the demand curve and the corresponding marginal revenue curve are shown in orange in Figure 13-3.

Notice that when you put these two curves together you get a rather strange demand curve (it's kinked) and an even stranger marginal revenue curve (one with a gap). I didn't make a mistake in drawing the curves; that's the way they come out given the assumptions. When the demand curve has a kink, the marginal revenue curve must have a gap.

When the demand curve has a kink, the marginal revenue curve must have a gap.

If firms do indeed perceive their demand curves to be kinked at the market price, we have another explanation of why prices tend to be sticky. Shifts in marginal cost (such as MC_0 to MC_1) will not change the firm's profit maximization position. A large shift in marginal cost is required before firms will change their price. Why should this be the case? The intuitive answer lies in the reason behind the kink. If the firm raises its price, other firms won't go along, so it will lose lots of market share. However, when the firm

Figure 13-3 The Kinked Demand Curve
One explanation of why prices are sticky is that firms face a kinked demand curve. When we draw the relevant marginal revenue curve for the kinked demand we see that the corresponding *MR* curve is discontinuous. It has a gap in it. Shifts in marginal costs between *c* and *d* will not change the price or the output that maximizes profits.

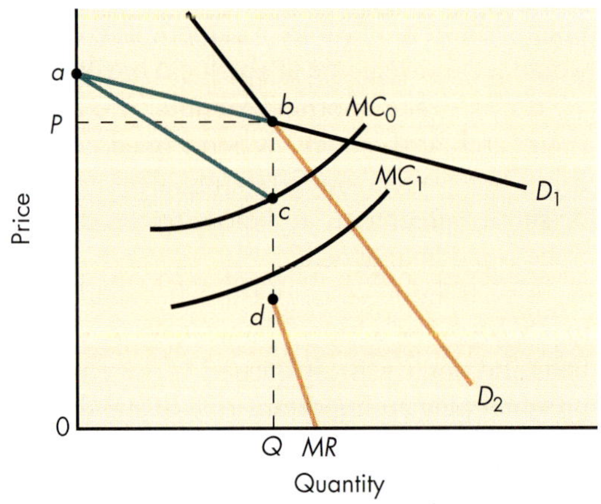

lowers price, other firms will go along and the firm won't gain market share. Thus, the firm has strong reasons not to change its price in either direction.

I should emphasize that the kinked demand curve is not a theory of oligopoly pricing. It does not say why the original price is what it is; the kinked demand curve is simply a theory of sticky prices.

The Contestable Market Model

A second model of oligopoly is the *contestable market model*. The **contestable market model** is *a model of oligopoly in which barriers to entry and barriers to exit, not the structure of the market, determine a firm's price and output decisions*. Thus, it emphasizes entry and exit conditions, and says that the price that an oligopoly will charge will exceed the cost of production only if new firms cannot exit and enter the market. The higher the barriers, the more the price exceeds cost. Without barriers to entry or exit, the price an oligopolist sets will be equivalent to the competitive price. Thus, an industry that structurally looks like an oligopoly could set competitive prices and output levels.

In the contestable market model of oligopoly, pricing and entry decisions are based only on barriers to entry and exit, not on market structure. Thus, even if the industry contains only one firm, it could still be a competitive market if entry is open.

Comparison of the Contestable Market Model and the Cartel Model

Because of the importance of social pressures in determining strategies of oligopolies, no one "oligopolistic model" exists. Oligopolies with a stronger ability to collude (i.e., more social pressures to prevent entry) are able to get closer to a monopolist solution. Equilibrium of oligopolies with weaker social pressures and less ability to prevent new entry is closer to the perfectly competitive solution. That's as explicit as we can be.

An oligopoly model can take two extremes: (1) the cartel model, in which an oligopoly sets a monopoly price; and (2) the contestable market model, in which an oligopoly with no barriers to entry sets a competitive price. Thus, we can say that an oligopoly's price will be somewhere between the competitive price and the monopolistic price. Other models of oligopolies give results in between these two.

Q-8 What are the two extremes an oligopoly model can take?

Much of what happens in oligopoly pricing is highly dependent on the specific legal structure within which firms interact. In Japan, where large firms are specifically allowed to collude, we see Japanese goods selling for a much higher price than those same Japanese goods sell for in the United States. For example, you may well pay twice as much for a Japanese television in Japan as you would in the United States. From the behavior of Japanese firms, we get a sense of what pricing strategy U.S. oligopolists would follow in the absence of the restrictions placed on them by law.

Strategic Pricing and Oligopoly

Notice that both the cartel model and the contestable market model use **strategic pricing** decisions—*firms set their price based on the expected reactions of other firms*. Strategic pricing and interdependence are central characteristics of oligopoly.

Strategic pricing and interdependence are central characteristics of an oligopoly.

One can see the results of strategic decision making all the time. For example, consider a firm that announces that it will not be undersold—that it will match any competitor's lower price and will even go under it. Is that a pro-competitive strategy, leading to a low price? Or is it a strategy to increase collusive information and thereby prevent other firms from breaking implicit pricing agreements? Recent work in economics suggests that it is the latter.

Guaranteed price matches are a way for firms to implicitly collude on prices. Tony Freeman/Photoedit.

Let's now see how a specific consideration of strategic pricing decisions shows that the cartel model and the contestable market model are related.

New Entry as a Limit on the Cartelization Strategy

One of the things that limits oligopolies from acting as a cartel is the threat from outside competition. The threat will tend to be more effective if this outside competitor is much larger than the firms in the oligopoly.

For example, small-town banks have a tendency to collude (implicitly, of course), offering lower interest to savers and charging higher interest to borrowers than big banks charge, even though their average costs aren't significantly higher. When I ask small-town banks why this is, they tell me that my perceptions are faulty and that I should mind my own business. But if a big bank, which couldn't care less about increasing the wealth of a small-town banker, enters the town and establishes a branch office, interest rates to savers seem to go up and interest rates to borrowers seem to go down. The big bank can add significant competition—competition that couldn't come from within the town.

On a national scale, the outside competition often comes from international firms. For example, implicit collusion among U.S. automobile firms led to foreign firms' entry into the U.S. automobile market. There are many such examples of this outside competition breaking down cartels with no barriers to entry. Thus, a cartel with no barriers to entry faces a long-run demand curve that's very elastic. This means that its price will be very close to its marginal cost and average cost. This is the same prediction that came from the contestable market theory.

Price Wars Whenever there's strategic decision making there's the possibility of a price war. Price wars are the result of strategic pricing decisions gone wild. Thus, in any oligopoly it's possible that firms can enter into a price war where prices fall below average total cost.

The reasons for such wars are varied. Since oligopolistic firms know their competitors, they can personally dislike them; sometimes a firm's goal can be simply to drive a disliked competitor out of business, even if that process hurts the firm itself. Passion and anger play roles in oligopoly pricing because interpersonal and interfirm relations are important.

Alternatively, a firm might follow a predatory pricing strategy—a strategy of pushing the price down temporarily to drive the other firm out of business to increase long-term profits. Some argue that Microsoft followed a predatory pricing strategy by virtually giving away its Office Suite on new computer systems to make its software the industry standard. If the predatory pricing strategy is successful, the firm can charge an even higher price because potential entrants know that the existing firm will drive them out if they try to enter. It's this continual possibility that strategies can change that makes oligopoly prices so hard to predict.

Game Theory, Oligopoly, and Strategic Decision Making

The inability to come to an explicit conclusion about what price and quantity an oligopoly will choose doesn't mean that economic reasoning and principles don't apply to oligopoly. They do. Most oligopolistic strategic decision making is carried out with the implicit or explicit use of **game theory** *(an application of economic principles in which players make interdependent choices)*. Game theory is economic reasoning applied to decision making.

To give you a sense of game theory, I'll present the **prisoner's dilemma**, *a well-known game that demonstrates the difficulty of cooperative behavior in certain circumstances*. The standard prisoner's dilemma can be seen in the following example: Two suspects are caught and are interrogated separately. Each prisoner is offered the following options:

A Beautiful Mind

Applying the Tools

Despite the fact that almost all economists are suave, debonair, exciting people, it isn't often that one is the main character in an Oscar-winning movie, but John Nash was. The movie is *A Beautiful Mind.* It tells the story of John Nash, a mathematician who won the Nobel Prize in economics for his work in game theory. Nash's contribution was the development of an equilibrium concept in noncooperative games (games in which individuals do not collude), which goes by the name Nash equilibrium. A Nash equilibrium is one in which individuals follow their best strategy, assuming that all other people in the game will do the same. You already know one Nash equilibrium: the prisoner's dilemma game presented in the text. (Al Tucker, who was Nash's mentor at Princeton, invented the prisoner's dilemma.)

Now, many economists make similar important contributions to economic thinking, and the Nobel Prize for game theory could have been given to a number of different economists, and in fact was shared by two other economists (John Harsanyi and Reinhard Selten). What made Nash's story compelling enough for a movie was his fight with schizophrenia, which after his initial professional success caused him to resign his position at the Massachusetts Institute of Technology and be placed in a mental institution by his wife. After being released, he walked the Princeton campus, where he'd been a graduate student, and was helped by his former colleagues. The story became perfect for Hollywood when in the 1990s Nash gained control over the disease and was able to get back to work and accept the prize.

The movie gives you a sense of John Nash's life and work, but Sylvia Nasar's book, *A Beautiful Mind,* upon which the movie is based, provides a much more accurate depiction of his life. Actually, both the book and the movie employ a certain amount of artistic discretion in presenting the story, but both not only show how much of the work in economic theory today is mathematical and technical but also provide a fun introduction to game theory.

- If neither prisoner confesses, each will be given a 6-month sentence on a minor charge.
- If one prisoner confesses and the other does not, the one who confesses will go free and the other will be given a 10-year sentence.
- If they both confess, they'll each get a 5-year sentence.

What strategy will each choose? If neither can count on the other not to confess, the optimal strategy (the one that maximizes expected benefits) will be for each to confess, because each must assume the other will do the same. Confessing is the rational thing for each prisoner to do. That's why it's called the *prisoner's dilemma.* Trust gets one out of the prisoner's dilemma. If the prisoners can trust each other, the optimal strategy is not to confess, and they both get only a light sentence. But trust is a hard commodity to come by without an explicit enforcement mechanism.

In the prisoner's dilemma, where mutual trust gets each one out of the dilemma, confessing is the rational choice.

Prisoner's Dilemma and a Duopoly Example

The prisoner's dilemma has its simplest application to oligopoly when the oligopoly consists of only two firms. So let us consider the strategic decisions facing a "foam peanut" (packing material) **duopoly**—*an oligopoly with only two firms.* Let us assume that the average total cost and marginal cost of producing foam peanuts are the same for both firms, and are such that only two firms can exist in the industry. These costs are shown in Figure 13-4(a).

Web Note 13.4
The Prisoner's Dilemma

Assume that a production facility with a minimum efficient scale of 4,000 tons is the smallest that can be built. In Figure 13-4(b), the marginal costs are summed and the industry demand curve is drawn in a way that the competitive price is $500 per ton and

Figure 13-4 (a and b) Firm and Industry Duopoly Cooperative Equilibrium
In (**a**) I show the marginal and average total cost curve for either firm in the duopoly. Thus to get the average and marginal cost for the industry, you double each. In (**b**) the industry marginal cost curve (the horizontal sum of the individual firms' marginal cost curves) is combined with the industry demand and marginal revenue curves. At the competitive solution for the industry, output is 8,000 and price is \$500. As you can see in (**a**), at that price economic profits are zero. At the monopolistic solution, output is 6,000 and price is \$600. As you can see in (**a**), *ATC* is \$575 at an industry output of 6,000 (firm output of 3,000), so each firm's profit is 25 × \$3,000 = \$75,000 (the shaded area in (**a**)).

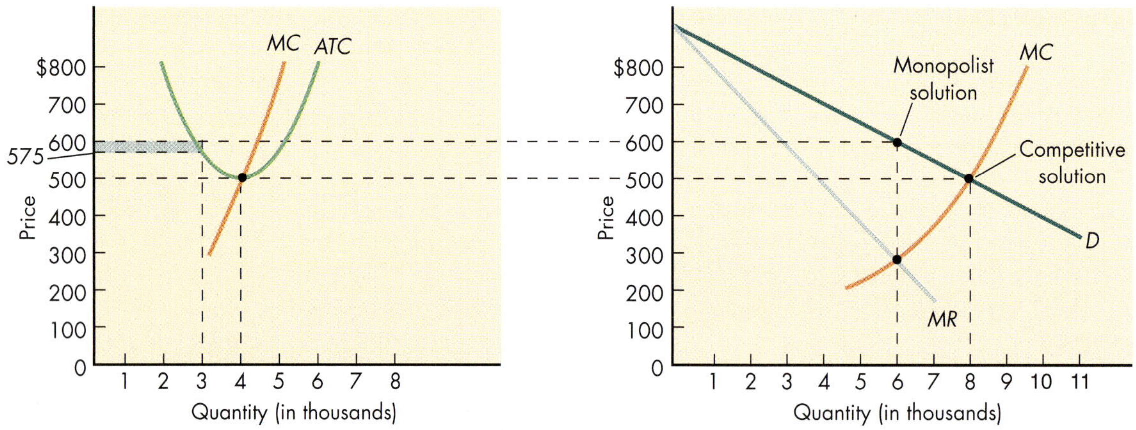

(a) Firm's cost curves **(b) Industry: Competitive and monopolist solution**

the competitive output is 8,000 tons. The relevant industry marginal revenue curve is also drawn.

If the firms collude fully, they will act as a joint monopolist setting total output at 6,000 tons where *MR* = MC (3,000 tons each). This gives them a price of \$600 with a cost of \$575 per ton, for a joint economic profit of \$150,000, or \$75,000 each. The firms prefer this equilibrium to the competitive equilibrium where they earn zero economic profit.

If they can ensure that they will both abide by the agreement, the monopolist output will be the joint profit-maximizing output. But what if one firm cheats? What if one firm produces 4,000 tons (1,000 tons under the counter)? The additional 1,000 tons in output will cause the price to fall to \$550 per ton. The cheating firm's average total costs fall to \$500 as its output rises to 4,000, so its profit rises to \$200,000. The noncheating firm's profit moves in the opposite direction. Its average total costs remain \$575, but the price it receives falls to \$550, so it loses \$75,000 instead of making \$75,000. This gives it a large incentive to cheat also. The division of profits and output split is shown in Figure 13-5. If the noncheating firm decides to become a cheating firm, it eliminates its loss and the other firm's profit, and the duopoly moves to a zero profit position.

In Figure 13-5(a), you can see that the firm that abides by the agreement and produces 3,000 units makes a loss of \$75,000; its average total costs are \$575 and the price it receives is \$550. In Figure 13-5(b) you can see that the cheating firm makes a profit of \$200,000; its average costs are \$500, so it is doing much better than when it did not cheat. The combined profit of the cheating and the noncheating firms is \$200,000 − \$75,000 = \$125,000, which is lower than if they cooperated. By cheating, the firm has essentially transferred \$125,000 of the other firm's profit to itself and has reduced their combined profit by \$25,000. Figure 13-5(c) shows how output is split between the two firms. If both firms cheat, the equilibrium output moves to the competitive output, 8,000, and both of the firms make zero profit.

Figure 13-5 (a, b, and c) Firm and Industry Duopoly Equilibrium When One Firm Cheats
In this figure I demonstrate the three different outcomes. Figures (a) and (b) show the noncheating and the cheating firms' output and profit, respectively, while (c) shows the industry output and price.

Say they both cheat. The price is $500 and output is 8,000 (4,000 per firm) (point *A* in (c)). Both firms make zero profit since their average total costs of $500 equal the price they receive.

If neither cheats, the industry output is 6,000, the price is $600, and their *ATC* is $575. This outcome gives them a profit of $75,000 each and would place them at point C in (c). This outcome was considered in Figure 13-4.

If one firm cheats and the other does not, the output is 7,000 and the industry price is $550 (point *B* in (c)). The noncheating firm's loss is shown by the shaded area in (a); its costs are $575, its output is 3,000, the price it receives is $550, and its loss is $75,000. The cheating firm's profit is shown by the shaded area in (b). Its average total costs are $500, the price it receives is $550, and its output is 4,000, so its profit is $200,000. So if one firm is cheating, it pays to be that firm; it doesn't pay to be honest when the other firm cheats.

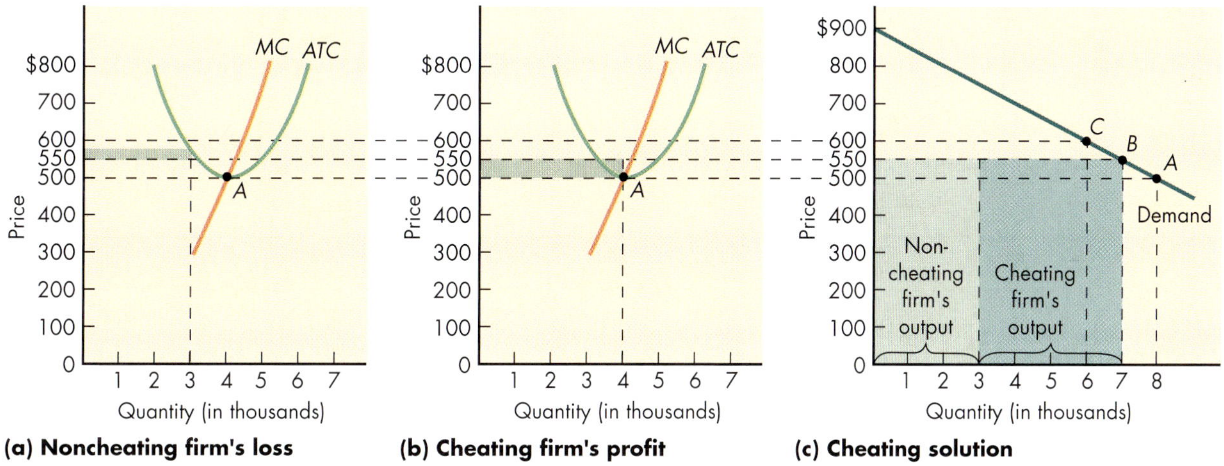

It is precisely to provide insight into this type of strategic situation that game theory was developed. It does so by analyzing the strategies of both firms under all circumstances and placing the combination in a payoff matrix—a box that contains the outcomes of a strategic game under various circumstances.

Duopoly and a Payoff Matrix

The duopoly presented above is a variation of the prisoner's dilemma game. The results can also be presented in a payoff matrix that captures the essence of the prisoner's dilemma. In Figure 13-6, each square shows the payoff from a pair of decisions listed in the columns and rows. The blue triangles show A's profit; the gold triangles show B's profit. For example, if neither cheats, the result for both is shown in the upper left-hand square, and if they both cheat, the result is shown in the lower right-hand square.

Notice the dilemma they are in if detecting cheating is impossible. If they can't detect whether the other one cheated and each believes the other is maximizing profit, each must expect the other one to cheat. But if firm A expects firm B to cheat, the relevant payoffs are in the second row. Given this expectation, if firm A doesn't cheat, it loses $75,000. So firm A's optimal strategy is to cheat. Similarly for firm B. If it expects firm A to cheat, its relevant payoffs are in the second column. Firm B's optimal strategy is to cheat. But if they both cheat, they end up in the lower right-hand square with zero profit.

In reality, of course, cheating is partially detectable, and even though explicit collusion and enforceable contracts are illegal in the United States, implicit collusive contracts are not. Moreover, in markets where similar conditions hold time after time, the cooperative solution is more likely since each firm will acquire a reputation based on its

Game Theory and Experimental Economics

Beyond the Tools

Game theory has offered significant insight into the structure of economic problems but arrives at the conclusion that a number of alternative solutions are possible. A new branch of economics—*experimental economics*—has developed that offers insight into which outcome will be forthcoming. Let's consider an example.

When game theorists have done experiments, they have found that people believe that the others in the game will work toward a cooperative solution. Thus, when the gains from cheating are not too great, often people do not choose the individual profit-maximizing position but instead choose a more cooperative strategy, at least initially. Such cooperative solutions tend to break down, however, as the benefits of cheating become larger. Additionally, as the number of participants gets larger, the less likely it is that the cooperative solution will be chosen and the more likely it is that competitive solutions will be chosen.

Experimental economists have also found that the structure of the game plays an important role in deciding the solution. For example, posted-price markets, in which the prices are explicitly announced, are more likely to reach a collusive result than are nonposted or uncertain-price markets, where actual sale prices are not known. Experiments in game theory are used extensively in designing auctions for allocating such things as telecom licenses.

Figure 13-6 The Payoff Matrix of Strategic Pricing Duopoly

The strategic dilemma facing each firm in a duopoly can be shown in a payoff matrix that captures the four possible outcomes. **A**'s strategies are listed horizontally; **B**'s strategies are listed vertically. The payoffs of the combined strategies for both firms are shown in the four boxes of the matrix, with **B**'s payoff shown in the gold shaded triangles and **A**'s payoff shown in the blue shaded triangles. For example, if **A** cheats but **B** doesn't, **A** makes a profit of $200,000 but **B** loses $75,000.

Their combined optimal strategy is to cartelize and achieve the monopoly payoff, with both firms receiving a profit of $75,000. However, each must expect that if it doesn't cheat and the other does cheat, it will lose $75,000. To avoid losing that $75,000, both firms will cheat, which leads them to the payoff in the lower right-hand corner—the competitive solution with zero profit for each firm.

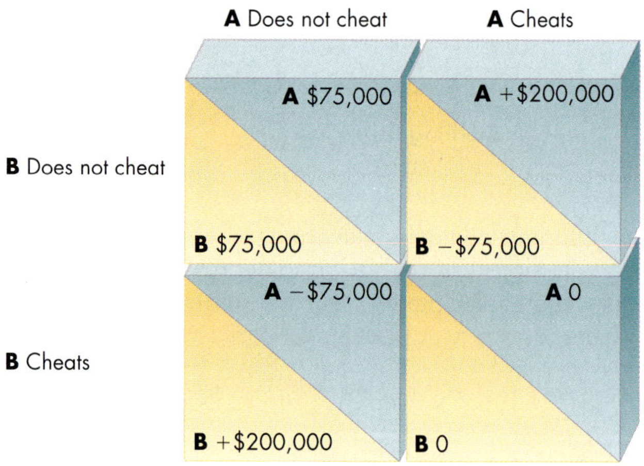

past actions, and firms can retaliate against other firms that cheat. But the basic dilemma remains for firms and tends to push oligopolies toward a zero profit competitive solution.

The push toward a zero profit equilibrium can be seen in the price war between Amazon.com and Buy.com in 2002. When Amazon.com lowered its threshold for free shipping from $99 to $49, Buy.com responded by offering free shipping on all sales the very next day and then added to that an offer to beat Amazon.com prices by 10 percent.

Oligopoly Models, Structure, and Performance

The fourfold division of markets that I've considered so far has all been based on the structure of the markets. By *structure* I mean the number, size, and interrelationship of firms in an industry. A monopoly (one firm) is the least competitive; perfectly competitive industries (an almost infinite number of firms) are the most competitive.

A Comparison of Various Market Structures

Knowing the Tools

Characteristics \ Structure	Monopoly	Oligopoly	Monopolistic Competition	Perfect Competition
Number of Firms	One	Few	Many	Almost infinite
Barriers to Entry	Significant	Significant	Few	None
Pricing Decisions	$MC = MR$	Strategic pricing, between monopoly and perfect competition	$MC = MR$	$MC = MR = P$
Output Decisions	Most output restriction	Output somewhat restricted	Output restricted somewhat by product differentiation	No output restriction
Interdependence	Only firm in market, not concerned about competitors	Interdependent strategic pricing and output decision	Each firm acts independently	Each firm acts independently
Profit	Possibility of long-run economic profit	Some long-run economic profit possible	No long-run economic profit possible	No long-run economic profit possible
P* and *MC	$P > MC$	$P > MC$	$P > MC$	$P = MC$

Classification by structure is easy for students to learn and accords nicely with intuition. The cartelization model fits best with this classification system because it assumes the structure of the market (the number of firms) is directly related to the price a firm charges. It predicts that oligopolies charge higher prices than do monopolistic competitors.

The contestable market model gives far less weight to market structure. According to it, markets that structurally look highly oligopolistic could actually be highly competitive—much more so than markets that structurally look less competitive. This contestable market model view of judging markets by performance, not structure, has had many reincarnations. Close relatives of it have previously been called the *barriers-to-entry* model, the *stay-out pricing* model, and the *limit-pricing* model. These models provide a view of competition that doesn't depend on market structure.

Q-9 The Herfindahl index is 1,500. Using a contestable market approach, what would you conclude about this industry?

Q-10 The Herfindahl index is 1,500. Using a structural analysis of markets approach, what would you conclude about this industry?

To see the implications of the contestable market approach, let's consider an oligopoly with a four-firm concentration ratio of 60 percent and a Herfindahl index of 1,500. Using the structural approach we would say that, because of the multiplicity of oligopoly models, we're not quite sure what price firms in this industry would charge, but that it seems reasonable to assume that there would be some implicit collusion and that the price would be closer to a monopolist price than to a competitive price. If that same market had a four-firm concentration ratio of 30 percent and a Herfindahl index of 700, the industry would be more likely to have a competitive price.

A contestable market model advocate would disagree, arguing that barriers to entry and exit are what's important. If no significant barriers to entry exist in the first case but significant barriers to entry exist in the second case, the second case would be more monopolistic than the first. An example is the Miami fish market mentioned earlier, where there were 20 sellers (none with a large percentage of the market) and significant barriers to entry (only fishers from the pier were allowed to sell fish there and the slots at the pier were limited). Because of those entry limitations, the pricing and output decisions would be close to the monopolistic price. If you took that same structure but had free entry, you'd get much closer to competitive decisions.

As I presented the two views, I emphasized the differences in order to make the distinction clear. However, I must also point out that there's a similarity in the two views. Often barriers to entry are the reason there are only a few firms in an industry. And when there are many firms, that suggests that there are few barriers to entry. In such situations, which make up the majority of cases, the two approaches come to the same conclusion.

Conclusion

As you can see, the real world gets very complicated very quickly. I'll show you just how complicated in Chapter 14. But don't let the complicated real world get you down on the theories presented here. It's precisely because the real world is so complicated that we need some framework, like the one presented in this chapter. That framework lets us focus on specific issues—and hopefully the most important. Because the framework is so important, as a conclusion to this chapter I have summarized the primary market structures in the box "A Comparison of Various Market Structures" on page 303.

Summary

- Industries are classified by economic activity in the North American Industry Classification System (NAICS). Industry structures are measured by concentration ratios and Herfindahl indexes.
- A concentration ratio is the sum of the market shares of individual firms with the largest shares in an industry.
- A Herfindahl index is the sum of the squares of the individual market shares of all firms in an industry.
- Conglomerates operate in a variety of different industries. Industry concentration measures do not assess the bigness of these conglomerates.
- Monopolistic competition is characterized by (1) many sellers, (2) differentiated products, (3) multiple dimensions of competition, and (4) ease of entry for new firms.
- The central characteristic of oligopoly is that there are a small number of interdependent firms.

- In monopolistic competition firms act independently; in an oligopoly they take account of each other's actions.
- Monopolistic competitors differ from perfect competitors in that the former face a downward-sloping demand curve.
- A monopolistic competitor differs from a monopolist in that a monopolistic competitor makes zero economic profit in long-run equilibrium.
- An oligopolist's price will be somewhere between the competitive price and the monopolistic price.
- Game theory and the prisoner's dilemma can shed light on strategic pricing decisions.
- A contestable market theory of oligopoly judges an industry's competitiveness more by performance and barriers to entry than by structure. Cartel models of oligopoly concentrate on market structure.

KEY TERMS

cartel *(294)*
cartel model of oligopoly *(294)*
concentration ratio *(287)*
contestable market model *(297)*
duopoly *(299)*
game theory *(298)*
Herfindahl index *(287)*
implicit collusion *(295)*
market structure *(285)*
monopolistic competition *(285)*
North American Industry Classification System (NAICS) *(286)*
oligopoly *(285)*
prisoner's dilemma *(298)*
strategic decision making *(288)*
strategic pricing *(297)*

QUESTIONS FOR THOUGHT AND REVIEW

1. Which industry is more highly concentrated: one with a Herfindahl index of 1,200 or one with a four-firm concentration ratio of 55 percent?
2. What are the ways in which a firm can differentiate its product from that of its competitors? What is the overriding objective of product differentiation?
3. What are the "monopolistic" and the "competitive" elements of monopolistic competition?
4. Does the product differentiation in monopolistic competition make us better or worse off? Why?
5. Both a perfect competitor and a monopolistic competitor choose output where $MC = MR$, and neither makes a profit in the long run. How is it, then, that the monopolistic competitor produces less than a perfect competitor?
6. If a monopolistic competitor is able to restrict output, why doesn't it earn economic profits?
7. What are some of the barriers to entry in the restaurant industry? In the automobile industry?
8. Is an oligopolist more or less likely to engage in strategic pricing compared to a monopolistic competitor?
9. What is the difference between the contestable market model and the cartel model of oligopoly? How are they related?
10. Is a contestable model or cartel model more likely to judge an industry by performance? Explain your answer.
11. What did Adam Smith mean when he wrote, "Seldom do businessmen of the same trade get together but that it results in some detriment to the general public"?
12. Private colleges of the same caliber generally charge roughly the same tuition. Would you characterize these colleges as a cartel type of oligopoly?
13. Describe a situation you have faced in your lifetime that can be characterized as a prisoner's dilemma.
14. In the late 1990s, Kellogg's, which controlled 32 percent of the breakfast cereal market, cut the prices of some of its best-selling brands of cereal to regain market share lost to Post, which controlled 20 percent of the market. General Mills had 24 percent of the market. The price cuts were expected to trigger a price war. Based on this information, what market structure best characterizes the market for breakfast cereal?

PROBLEMS AND EXERCISES

1. Suppose a monopolistic competitor in long-run equilibrium has a constant marginal cost of $6 and faces the demand curve given in the following table:

Q	20	18	16	14	12	10	8	6
P	$ 2	4	6	8	10	12	14	16

   a. What output will the firm choose?
   b. What will be the monopolistic competitor's average fixed cost at the output it chooses?

2. A firm is convinced that if it lowers its price, no other firm in the industry will change price; however, it believes that if it raises its price, some other firms will match its increase, making its demand curve more inelastic. The current price is $8 and its marginal cost is constant at $4.
   a. Sketch the general shape of the firm's *MR*, *MC*, and demand curves and show why there are two possible equilibria.
   b. If there are two equilibria, which of the two do you think the firms will arrive at? Why?
   c. If the marginal cost falls to $3, what would you predict would happen to price?
   d. If the marginal cost rises to $5, what would you predict would happen to price?
   e. Do a survey of five or six firms in your area. Ask them how they believe other firms would respond to their increasing or decreasing price. Based on that survey, discuss the relevance of this kinked demand model compared to the one presented in the book.

3. You're the manager of a firm that has constant marginal cost of $6. Fixed cost is zero. The market structure is monopolistically competitive. You're faced with the following demand curve:

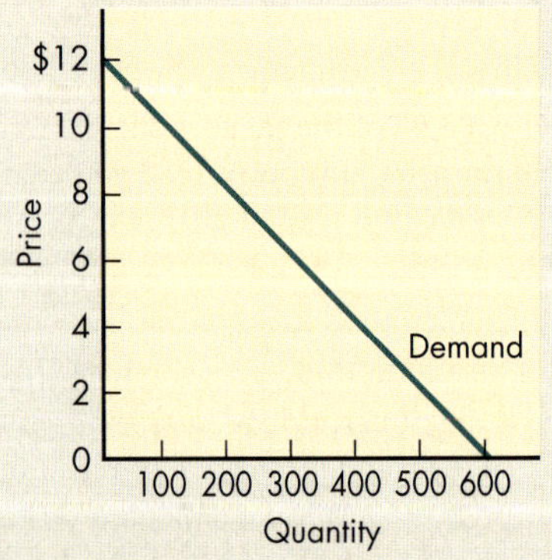

   a. Determine graphically the profit-maximizing price and output for your firm in the short run. Demonstrate what profit or loss you'll be making.
   b. Do the same for the long run.
   c. Thanks to a technological innovation, you have zero marginal cost. Demonstrate the new profit-maximizing price and output in the short run. Demonstrate graphically the short-run profit at that new profit-maximizing output.

4. The pizza market is divided as follows:

Pizza Hut	20.7%
Domino's	17.0
Little Caesars	6.7
Pizza Inn/Pantera's	2.2
Round Table	2.0
All others	51.4

   a. How would you describe its market structure?
   b. What is the approximate Herfindahl index?
   c. What is the four-firm concentration ratio?

5. In 1982 Robert Crandell, CEO of American Airlines, phoned the Braniff Airways CEO and said, "Raise your fares 20 percent and I'll raise mine the next morning."
   a. Why would he do this?
   b. If you were the Braniff Airways CEO, would you have gone along?
   c. Why should Crandell not have done this?

6. Two firms, TwiddleDee and TwiddleDum, make up the entire market for wodgets. They have identical costs. They are currently colluding explicitly and are making $2 million each. TwiddleDee has a new CEO, Mr. Notsonice, who is considering cheating. He has been informed by his able assistant that if he cheats he can increase the firm's profit to $3 million, but that cheating will reduce TwiddleDum's profit to $1 million. You have been hired to advise Mr. Notsonice.
   a. Construct a payoff matrix for him that captures the essence of the decision.
   b. If the game is only played once, what strategy would you advise?
   c. How would your answer to *b* change if the game were to be played many times?
   d. What change in the profit made when colluding (currently $2 million) would be needed to change your advice in *b*?

7. In 1993, the infant/preschool toy market four-firm concentration ratio was 72 percent. With 8 percent of the market, Mattel was the fourth largest firm in that market. Mattel proposed to buy Fisher-Price, the market leader with 27 percent. At this time the new Clinton administration was trying to develop a set of rules dealing with such mergers. Your assignment is to help it decide by answering questions *a* through *d*.

a. Why would Mattel want to buy Fisher-Price?
b. What arguments can you think of in favor of allowing this acquisition?
c. What arguments can you think of against allowing this acquisition?
d. How do you think the four-firm concentration ratio for the entire toy industry would compare to this infant/preschool toy market concentration ratio?
e. What did the Clinton administration decide? (Requires library or online research.)

8. The text recounts how Amazon.com cut its free-shipping threshold from $99 to $49 and how, the very next day, Buy.com offered free shipping on everything and promised to beat any Amazon.com price by 10 percent.
   a. Construct a hypothetical payoff matrix for the decision of whether to offer free shipping or not.
   b. In what solution is Buy.com better off?
   c. In what solution is Amazon.com better off?
   d. In what solution are joint profits maximized?
   e. What are Amazon's and Buy.com's current rates for shipping?

Web Questions

1. Go to the electronic reading room of the U.S. Department of Justice (DOJ) at www.usdoj.gov and search to find the document "Horizontal Merger Guidelines." Use the table of contents to find the sections "Product Market Definition" and "Concentration and Market Shares."
   a. How does the DOJ determine the relevant product market?
   b. Explain how the definition of market depends on cross-price elasticity of demand.
   c. What measure of market concentration does the DOJ use?
   d. Above what level for the market concentration measure does the DOJ believe the market to be highly concentrated?
2. Go to the U.S. Census Bureau's home page at www.census.gov and "Business" click on NAICS to answer the following questions:
   a. What are the industry codes for potato farming, tire manufacturing, and family clothing stores?
   b. The NAICS replaced the Standard Industrial Classification (SIC). How did the SIC classify industries? How does the NAICS classify industries?
   c. Why did the Census Bureau change its method of classification? Will the new classification be more or less helpful than the SIC when classifying firms to determine market structure? Explain.
3. The Organization of Petroleum Exporting Countries (OPEC) is an international cartel. Go to its home page at www.opec.org to answer the following questions:
   a. What are OPEC's objectives? How does it meet those objectives?
   b. What countries are members of OPEC? What percentage of world oil production comes from these nations? In what way is OPEC a cartel?
   c. What significant oil-exporting countries are not members? What has OPEC done to limit the effect of nonmember production on its pricing decisions?

Answers to Margin Questions

1. The smaller the number of digits, the more inclusive the classification. Therefore, the two-digit industry would have significantly more output. *(286)*
2. The highest Herfindahl index for this industry would occur if one firm had the entire 60 percent, and all other firms had an infinitesimal amount, making the Herfindahl index slightly over 3,600. The lowest Herfindahl index this industry could have would occur if each of the top four firms had 15 percent of the market, yielding a Herfindahl index of 900. *(288)*
3. I would respond that monopolistic competitors, by definition, do not take into account the expected reactions of competitors to their decisions; therefore, they cannot use strategic decision making. I would tell Jean she probably meant, "*Oligopolies* use strategic decision making." *(288)*
4. Both a monopoly and a monopolistic competitor produce where marginal cost equals marginal revenue. The difference is in the positioning of the average total cost curve. For a monopolistic competitor, that average total cost curve must be tangent to the demand curve because a monopolistic competitor makes no profits in the long run. A monopoly can make profits in the long run, so its average total cost can be below the price. *(291)*
5. Monopolistically competitive firms advertise because their products are differentiated from others. Advertising can convince people that a firm's product is better than that of other firms and increase the demand curve it faces. Perfect competitors, in contrast, have no incentive to advertise since their products are the same as every other firm's product and they can sell all they want at the market price. *(293)*

6. Maintaining a cartel requires firms to make decisions that are not in their individual best interests. Such decisions are hard to enforce unless there is an explicit enforcement mechanism, which is difficult in a cartel. *(295)*
7. The demand curve perceived by an oligopolist is more elastic above the current price because it believes that others will not follow price increases. If it increased price, it would see quantity demanded fall by a lot. The opposite is true below the current price. The demand curve below current price is less elastic. Price declines would be matched by competitors and the oligopolist would see little change in quantity demanded with a price decline. *(296)*
8. The two extremes an oligopoly model can take are: (1) a cartel model, which is the equivalent of a monopoly; and (2) a contestable market model, which, if there are no barriers to entry, is the equivalent of a competitive industry. *(297)*
9. The contestable markets approach looks at barriers to entry, not structure. Therefore, we can conclude nothing about the industry from the Herfindahl index. *(303)*
10. In a market with a Herfindahl index of 1,500, the largest firm would have, at most, slightly under 38 percent of the market. The least concentrated such an industry could be would be if seven firms each had between 14 and 15 percent of the market. In either of these two cases, the industry would probably be an oligopolistic industry and could border on monopoly. *(304)*

14

Real-World Competition and Technology

It is ridiculous to call this an industry. This is rat eat rat; dog eat dog. I'll kill 'em, and I'm going to kill 'em before they kill me. You're talking about the American way of survival of the fittest.

—*Ray Kroc (founder of McDonald's)*

After reading this chapter, you should be able to:

- Define the monitoring problem and state its implications for economics.
- Explain how corporate takeovers can limit X-inefficiency.
- Discuss why competition should be seen as a process, not a state.
- List two actions firms take to break down monopoly and three they take to protect monopoly.
- Discuss why oligopoly is the best market structure for technological change.

In earlier chapters we've seen some nice, neat models, but as we discussed in Chapter 13, often these models don't fit reality directly. Real-world markets aren't perfectly monopolistic; they aren't perfectly competitive either. They're somewhere between the two. The monopolistic competition and oligopoly models in Chapter 13 come closer to reality and provide some important insights into the "in-between" markets, but, like any abstraction, they, too, fail to capture aspects of the actual nature of competition. In this chapter I remedy that shortcoming and give you a sense of what actual firms, markets, and competition are like. This chapter also discusses an issue that is very much in the news—technology—and relates it to the models we developed earlier.

When reading this chapter, think about the two uses of competition discussed in Chapter 11: competition as a process, the end state of which is zero profits, and competition as a market structure. In this chapter the focus is on competition as a process—it is a rivalry between firms and between individuals. This competitive process is active in all market forms and is key to understanding real-world competition.

The Goals of Real-World Firms and the Monitoring Problem

Maybe the best place to start is with the assumption that firms are profit maximizers. There's a certain reasonableness to this assumption; firms definitely are concerned about profit, but are they trying to maximize profit? The answer is: It depends.

Short-Run versus Long-Run Profit

The first insight is that if firms are profit maximizers, they aren't just concerned with short-run profit; most are concerned with long-run profit. Thus, even if they can, they may not take full advantage of a potential monopolistic situation now, to strengthen their long-run position. For example, many stores have liberal return policies: "If you don't like it, you can return it for a full refund." Similarly, many firms spend millions of dollars improving their reputations. Most firms want to be known as good citizens. Such expenditures on reputation and goodwill can increase long-run profit, even if they reduce short-run profit.

Q-1 What are two reasons why real-world firms are not pure profit maximizers?

The Problem with Profit Maximization

A second insight into how real-world firms differ from the model is that the decision makers' income is often a cost of the firm. Most real-world production doesn't take place in owner-operated businesses; it takes place in large corporations with eight or nine levels of management, thousands of stockholders whose stock is often held in trust for them, and a board of directors, chosen by management, overseeing the company by meeting two or three times a year. Signing a proxy statement is as close as most stockowners get to directing "their company" to maximize profit.

Most real-world production doesn't take place in owner-operated businesses; it takes place in large corporations.

Managers' Incentives Why is the structure of the firm important to the analysis? Because economic theory tells us that, unless someone is seeing to it that they do, self-interested decision makers have little incentive to hold down their pay. But their pay is a cost of the firm. And if their pay isn't held down, the firm's profit will be lower than otherwise. Most firms manage to put some pressure on managers to make at least a predesignated level of profit. (If you ask managers, they'll tell you that they face enormous pressure.) So the profit motive certainly plays a role—but to say that profit plays a role is not to say that firms maximize profit. Having dealt with many companies, I'll go out on a limb and say that there are enormous wastes and inefficiencies in many U.S. businesses.

This structure presents a problem in applying the model to the real world. The general economic model assumes that individuals are utility maximizers—that they're motivated by self-interest. Then, in the standard model of the firm, the assumption is made that firms, composed of self-interest-seeking individuals, are profit-seeking firms, without explaining how self-interest-seeking individuals who manage real-world corporations will find it in their interest to maximize profit for the firm. Economists recognize this problem, which was introduced in an earlier chapter. It's an example of the **monitoring problem**—*the need to oversee employees to ensure that their actions are in the best interest of the firm*.

The monitoring problem is that employees' incentives differ from the owner's incentives.

Need for Monitoring Monitoring is required because employees' incentives differ from the owner's incentives, and it's costly to see that the employee does the owner's bidding. The monitoring problem is now a central problem focused on by economists who specialize in industrial organization. They study internal structures of firms and look for a contract that managers can be given: an **incentive-compatible contract** in which *the incentives of each of the two parties to the contract are made to correspond as closely as possible*. The specific monitoring problem relevant to firm structure is that often owners find it too costly to monitor the managers to ensure that managers do what's in the owners' interest. And self-interested managers are interested in maximizing the firm's profit only if the structure of the firm requires them to do so.

Self-interested managers are interested in maximizing firm profit only if the structure of the firm requires them to do so.

When appropriate monitoring doesn't take place, high-level managers can pay themselves very well. As can be seen in Table 14-1, many U.S. managers receive multimillion-dollar salaries. But are these salaries too high? That's a difficult question.

One way to get an idea about an answer is to compare U.S. managers' salaries with those in Japan, where the control of firms is different. Banks in Japan have significant

Who Controls Corporations?

Applying the Tools

When a corporation is formed, it issues stock, which is sold or given to individuals. Ownership of stock entitles you to vote in the election of a corporation's directors, so in theory holders of stock control the company. In practice, however, in most large corporations, ownership is separated from control of the firm. Most stockholders have little input into the decisions a corporation makes. Instead, corporations are often controlled by their managers, who often run them for their own benefit as well as for the owners'. The reason is that the owners' control of management is limited.

A large percentage of most corporations' stock is not even controlled by the owners; instead, it is controlled by financial institutions such as mutual funds (financial institutions that invest individuals' money for them) and by pension funds (financial institutions that hold people's money for them until it is to be paid out to them upon their retirement). Thus, ownership of corporations is another step removed from individuals. Studies have shown that 80 percent of the largest 200 corporations in the United States are essentially controlled by managers and have little effective stockholder control.

Why is the question of who controls a firm important? Because economic theory assumes the goal of business owners is to maximize profits, which would be true of corporations if stockholders made the decisions. Managers don't have the same incentives to maximize profits that owners do. There's pressure on managers to maximize profits, but that pressure can often be weak or ineffective. An example of how firms deal with this problem involves stock options. Many companies give their managers stock options—rights to buy stock at a low price—to encourage them to worry about the price of their company's stock. But these stock options dilute the value of company ownership and decrease profits per share and can give managers an incentive to overstate profits through accounting gimmicks, as happened at Enron, Xerox, and a number of other firms in the early 2000s.

Table 14-1 Compensation of CEOs of Selected Companies (base pay plus bonuses and stock options)

Company	Salary in 2001
Abbott Laboratories	$ 26,517,797
AMR Corp	7,188,511
Cisco Systems, Inc.	131,858,597
Citigroup Inc.	30,328,821
Coca-Cola Co.	105,186,544
Dow Jones & Co., Inc.	5,062,286
Gap Inc.	9,026,929
Hewlett-Packard	14,767,854
Home Depot	41,105,409
Lucent Technologies	21,567,312
U.S. Airways	4,816,561
Walt Disney	1,004,020

Source: AFL-CIO (www.paywatch.org).

Web Note 14.1
Executive Compensation

control over the operations of firms, and they closely monitor their performance. The result is that, in Japan, high-level managers on average earn about one-fourth of what their U.S. counterparts make, while wages of low-level workers are comparable to those of low-level workers in the United States. Given Japanese companies' success in competing with U.S. companies, this suggests that high managerial pay in the United States

Q-2 Why would most economists be concerned about third-party-payer systems in which the consumer and the payer are different?

reflects a monitoring problem inherent in the structure of corporations. There are, of course, other perspectives. Considering what some sports, film, and music stars receive places the high salaries of U.S. managers in a different light.

What Do Real-World Firms Maximize?

If firms don't maximize profit, what do they maximize? What are their goals? The answer again is: It depends.

Real-world firms often have a set of complicated goals that reflect the organizational structure and incentives built into the system. Clearly, profit is one of their goals. Firms spend a lot of time designing incentives to get managers to focus on profit.

Although profit is one goal of a firm, often firms focus on other intermediate goals such as cost and sales.

But often intermediate goals become the focus of firms. For example, many real-world firms focus on growth in sales; at other times they institute a cost-reduction program to increase long-run profit. At still other times they may simply take it easy and not push hard at all, enjoying the position they find themselves in—being what British economist Joan Robinson called **lazy monopolists**—*firms that do not push for efficiency, but merely enjoy the position they are already in*. This term describes many, but not all, real-world corporations. When Robinson coined the term, firms faced mostly domestic competition. Today, with firms facing more and more global competition, firms are a bit less lazy than they were—as we'll discuss later in this chapter.

The Lazy Monopolist and X-Inefficiency

Lazy monopolists are not profit maximizers; they see to it that they make enough profit so that the stockholders aren't squealing, but they don't push as hard as they could to hold their costs down. They perform as efficiently as is consistent with keeping their jobs. The result is what economists call **X-inefficiency** *(firms operating far less efficiently than they could technically)*. Such firms have monopoly positions, but they don't make large monopoly profits. Instead, their costs rise because of inefficiency; they may simply make a normal level of profit or, if X-inefficiency becomes bad enough, a loss.

Q-3 Why doesn't a manager have the same incentive to hold costs down as an owner does?

The standard model avoids dealing with the monitoring problem by assuming that the owner of the firm makes all the decisions. The owners of firms who receive the profit, and only the profit, would like to see that all the firm's costs are held down. Unfortunately, very few real-world firms operate that way. In reality owners seldom make operating decisions. They hire or appoint managers to make those decisions. The managers they hire don't have that same incentive to hold costs down. Therefore, it isn't surprising to many economists that managers' pay is usually high and that high-level managers see to it that they have "perks" such as chauffeurs, jet planes, ritzy offices, and assistants to do as much of their work as possible.

The equilibrium of a lazy monopolist is presented in Figure 14-1. A monopolist would produce at price P_M and quantity Q_M. Average total cost would be C_M, so the monopolist's profit would be the entire shaded rectangle (areas A and B). The lazy monopolist would allow costs to increase until the firm reached its normal level of profit. In Figure 14-1, costs rise to C_{LM}. The profit of the lazy monopolist is area B. The remainder of the potential profit is eaten up in cost inefficiencies.

The competitive pressures a firm faces limit its laziness.

What places a limit on firms' laziness is the degree of competitive pressures they face. All economic institutions must have sufficient revenue coming in to cover costs, so all economic institutions have a limit on how lazy and inefficient they can get—a limit imposed by their monopoly position. They can translate the monopoly profit into X-inefficiency, thereby benefiting the managers and workers in the firm, but once they've done so, they can't be more inefficient. They would go out of business.

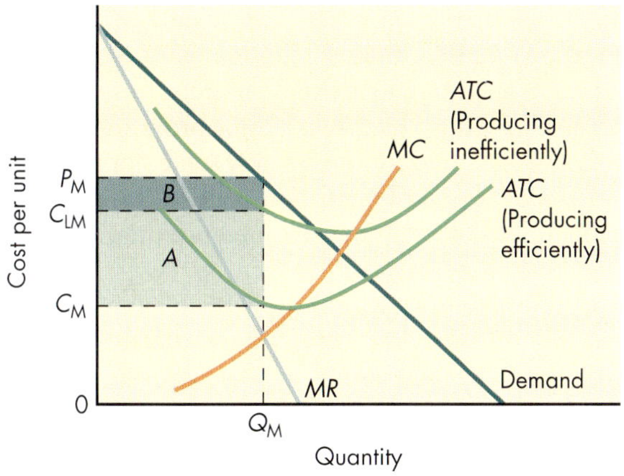

Figure 14-1 True Cost Efficiency and the Lazy Monopolist
A monopolist producing efficiently would have costs C_M and would produce at price P_M and quantity Q_M. A lazy monopolist, in contrast, would let costs rise until the minimum level of profit is reached, at C_{LM}. Profit for the monopolist is represented by the entire shaded area, whereas profit for the lazy monopolist is squeezed down to area *B*.

How Competition Limits the Lazy Monopolist

If all individuals in the industry are lazy, then laziness becomes the norm and competitive pressures don't reduce their profits. Laziness is relative, not absolute. But if a new firm comes in all gung-ho and hardworking, or if an industry is opened up to international competition, the lazy monopolists can be squeezed and must undertake massive restructuring to make themselves competitive. Many U.S. firms have been undergoing such restructuring in order to make themselves internationally competitive.

A second way in which competitive pressure is placed on a lazy monopolist is by a **corporate takeover**, in which *another firm or a group of individuals issues a tender offer (that is, offers to buy up the stock of a company to gain control and to install its own managers)*. Usually such tender offers are financed by large amounts of debt, which means that if the takeover is successful, the firm will need to make large profits just to cover the interest payments on the debt.

A corporate takeover, or simply the threat of a takeover, can improve a firm's efficiency.

Managers don't like takeovers. A takeover may cost them their jobs and the perks that go along with those jobs, so they'll often restructure the company on their own as a preventive measure. Such restructuring frequently means incurring large amounts of debt to finance a large payment to stockholders. These payments put more pressure on management to operate efficiently. Thus, the threat of a corporate takeover places competitive pressure on firms to maximize profits.

Q-4 In what way does the threat of a corporate takeover place competitive pressures on a firm?

Were profit not a motive at all, one would expect the lazy monopolist syndrome to take precedence. In fact, it's not surprising that nonprofit organizations often display lazy monopolist tendencies. For example, some colleges, schools, libraries, jails, and nonprofit hospitals have a number of rules and ways of doing things that, upon reflection, benefit the employees of the institution rather than the customers. At most colleges, students aren't polled about what time they would prefer classes to meet; instead, the professors and administrators decide when they want to teach. I leave it to you to figure out whether your college exhibits these tendencies and whether you'd prefer that your college, library, or hospital change to a for-profit institution. Studying these incentive-compatible problems is what management courses are all about.

Web Note 14.2
Creative Destruction

Motivations for Efficiency Other than the Profit Incentive

I'm not going to discuss management theory here other than to stimulate your thinking about the problem. However, I'd be remiss in presenting you this broad outline of the monitoring problem without mentioning that the drive for profit isn't the only drive that pushes for efficiency. Some individuals derive pleasure from efficiently run organizations. Such individuals don't need to be monitored. Thus, if administrators are well intentioned, they'll hold down costs even if they aren't profit maximizers. In such cases, monitoring (creating an organization and structure that gives people profit incentives) can actually reduce efficiency! It's amazing to some economists how some nonprofit organizations operate as efficiently as they do—some libraries and colleges fall into that category. Their success is built on their employees' pride in their jobs, not on their profit motive.

Individuals have complicated motives; some simply have a taste for efficiency.

Most economists don't deny that such inherently efficient individuals exist, and that most people derive some pleasure from efficiency, but they believe that it's hard to maintain that push for efficiency year in, year out, when some of your colleagues are lazy monopolists enjoying the fruits of your efficiency. Most people derive some pleasure from efficiency, but, based on their observation of people's actions, economists believe that holding down costs without the profit motive takes stronger willpower than most people have.

THE FIGHT BETWEEN COMPETITIVE AND MONOPOLISTIC FORCES

Even if all the assumptions for perfect competition could hold true, it's unlikely that real-world markets would be perfectly competitive. The reason is that perfect competition assumes that individuals accept a competitive institutional structure, even though changing that structure could result in significant gains for sellers or buyers. The simple fact is that *self-interest-seeking individuals don't like competition for themselves* (although they do like it for others), and when competitive pressures get strong and the invisible hand's push turns to shove, individuals often shove back, using either social or political means. That's why you can understand real-world competition only if you understand how the invisible hand, social forces, and political pressures push against each other to create real-world economic institutions. Real-world competition should be seen as a process—a fight between the forces of monopolization and the forces of competition.

Competition is a process—a fight between the forces of monopolization and the forces of competition.

HOW MONOPOLISTIC FORCES AFFECT PERFECT COMPETITION

Let's consider some examples. During the Depression of the 1930s, competition was pushing down prices and wages. What was the result? Individuals socially condemned firms for unfair competition, and numerous laws were passed to prevent it. Unions were strengthened politically and given monopoly powers so they could resist the pressure to push down wages. The Robinson-Patman Act was passed, which made it illegal for many firms to lower prices. Individual states passed similar laws, and it was under one of these that Wal-Mart lost a 1993 court case in which it was accused of charging too-low prices in its pharmacies.

The United States has a myriad of laws, regulations, and programs that prevent agricultural markets from working competitively.

Q-5 Explain, using supply and demand curves, why most agricultural markets are not perfectly competitive.

As another example, consider agricultural markets, which have many of the conditions for almost perfect competition. To my knowledge, not one country in the world allows a competitive agricultural market to exist. As you'll see in Chapter 19, the United States has myriad laws, regulations, and programs that prevent agricultural markets from working competitively. U.S. agricultural markets are characterized by price supports, acreage limitations, and quota systems. Thus, where perfectly competitive markets could exist, they aren't allowed to. An almost infinite number of other examples can be found. Our laws and social values and customs simply do not allow perfect competition to work because government emphasizes other social goals besides efficiency. When competition negatively affects these other goals (which may or may not be goals that most people in society hold), government prevents competition from operating.

Economic Insights and Real-World Competition

The extreme rarity of perfectly competitive markets *should not* make you think that economics is irrelevant to the real world. Far from it. In fact, the movement away from perfectly competitive markets could have been predicted by economic theory.

Consider Figure 14-2. Competitive markets will exist only if suppliers or consumers don't collude. If the suppliers producing *0L* can get together and restrict entry, preventing suppliers who would produce *LM* from entering the industry, the remaining suppliers can raise their price from P_M to P_L, giving them the shaded area *A* in additional income. If the cost of their colluding and preventing entry is less than that amount, economic theory predicts that these individuals will collude. The suppliers kept out of the market lose only area *C*, so they don't have much incentive to fight the restrictions on entry. Consumers lose the areas *A* plus *B*, so they have a strong incentive to fight. However, often their cost of organizing a protest is higher than the suppliers' cost of collusion, so consumers accept the restrictions.

Suppliers introducing restrictions on entry seldom claim that the reason for the restrictions is to increase their incomes. Usually they couch the argument for restrictions in terms of the general good but, while their reasons are debatable, the net effect of restricting entry into a market is to increase suppliers' income to the detriment of consumers.

How Competitive Forces Affect Monopoly

Q-6 Why is it almost impossible for a perfect monopoly to exist?

Don't think that because perfect competition doesn't exist, competition doesn't exist. In the real world, competition is fierce; the invisible hand is no weakling. It holds its own against other forces in the economy.

Competition is so strong that it makes the other extreme (perfect monopolies) as rare as perfect competition. For a monopoly to last, other firms must be prevented from entering the market. In reality it's almost impossible to prevent entry, and therefore it's almost impossible for perfect monopoly to exist. Monopoly profits send out signals to other firms who want to get some of that profit for themselves.

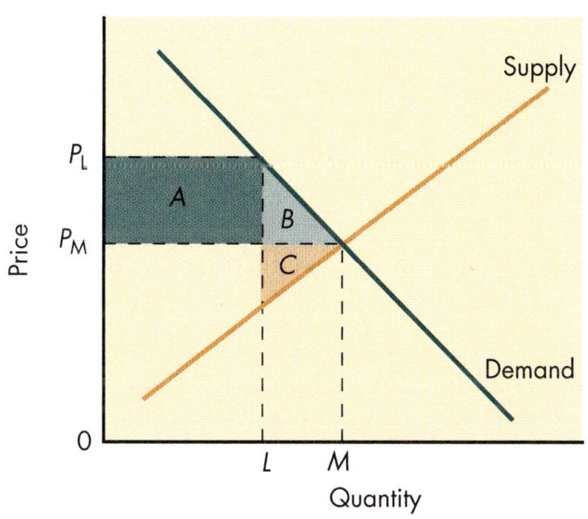

Figure 14-2 Movement Away from Competitive Markets
In the case where suppliers of *0L* can restrict suppliers of *LM* from entering the market, they can raise the price of the good from P_M to P_L, giving the suppliers of *0L* area A in additional income. The suppliers kept out of the market lose area C. The consumers, however, lose both areas A and B, giving them strong incentive to fight collusion. Often the costs of organizing for consumers are higher than the costs for the suppliers, so consumers accept the market restrictions.

Breaking Down Monopoly To get some of the profit, firms will break down a monopoly through political or economic means. If the monopoly is a legal monopoly, high profit will lead potential competitors to lobby to change the law underpinning that monopoly. If the law can't be changed—say, the monopolist has a patent (which, I discussed in Chapter 12, is a legal right to be the sole supplier of a good)—potential competitors will generally get around the obstacle by developing a slightly different product or by working on a new technology that avoids the monopoly but satisfies the relevant need.

Establishing an initial presence in a market can be more effective than obtaining a patent when trying to extract monopoly profit.

Say, for example, that you've just discovered the proverbial better mousetrap. You patent it and prepare to enjoy the life of a monopolist. But to patent your mousetrap, you must submit to the patent office the technical drawings of how your better mousetrap works. That gives all potential competitors (some of whom have better financing and already existing distribution systems) a chance to study your idea and see if they can think of a slightly different way (a way sufficiently different to avoid being accused of infringing on your patent) to achieve the same end. They often succeed—so often, in fact, that many firms don't apply for patents on new products because the information in the patent application spells out what's unique about the product. That information can help competitors more than the monopoly provided by the patent would hurt them. Instead many firms try to establish an initial presence in the market and rely on inertia to protect what little monopoly profit they can extract.

Reverse Engineering Going to the patent office isn't the only way competitors gather information about competing products. One of the other ways routinely used by firms is called **reverse engineering**—*the process of a firm buying other firms' products, disassembling them, figuring out what's special about them, and then copying them within the limits of the law.*

Variations on reverse engineering go on in all industries. Consider the clothing industry. One firm I know of directs its secretaries to go to top department stores on their lunch hour and buy the latest fashions. The secretaries bring the clothes back and, that afternoon, the seamstresses and tailors dismantle each garment into its component parts, make a pattern of each part, and sew the original up again. The next day the secretary who chose that garment returns it to the department store, saying "I don't really like it."

Meanwhile the firm has express-mailed the patterns to its Hong Kong office, and two weeks later its shipment of garments comes in—garments that are almost, but not perfectly, identical to the ones the secretaries bought. The firm sells this shipment to other department stores at half the cost of the original.

If you ask businesspeople, they'll tell you that competition is fierce and that profit opportunities are fleeting—which is a good sign that competition does indeed exist in the U.S. economy.

Competition and Natural Monopoly

The view one takes of the fight between competitive and monopolistic forces influences one's view of what government policy should be in relation to natural monopolies—industries whose average total cost is falling as output increases. We saw in Chapter 12 that natural monopolies can make large profits and that consequently there have been significant calls for government regulation of these monopolies to prevent their "exploitation" of the consumer.

Over the past decade economists and policymakers have become less supportive of such regulation. They argue that even in these cases of natural monopoly, competition works in other ways. High monopoly profits lead to research on alternative ways of supplying the product, such as sending TV signals through electrical lines or sending phone messages by satellite. New technologies provide competition to existing firms. When this competition doesn't work fast enough, people direct their efforts toward government, and political pressure is brought to bear either to control the monopoly through regulation or to break up the monopoly.

New technologies can compete with and undermine natural monopolies.

Regulating Natural Monopolies In the past, the pressure to regulate natural monopolies has been stronger than competitive pressure that lowers prices. Regulated natural monopolies have been given the exclusive right to operate in an industry but, in return, they've had to agree to have the price they charge and the services they provide regulated. Regulatory boards control the price that natural monopolies charge so that it will be a "fair price," which they generally define as a price that includes all costs plus a normal return on capital investment (a normal profit, but no economic profit). Most states have a number of regulatory boards.

Web Note 14.3
Regulating Natural Monopolies

When firms are allowed to pass on all cost increases to earn a normal profit on those costs, they have little or no incentive to hold down costs. In such cases, X-inefficiency develops with a passion, and such monopolies look for capital-intensive projects that will increase their rate bases. To fight such tendencies, regulatory boards must screen every cost and determine which costs are appropriate and which aren't—an almost impossible job. For example, nuclear power is an extremely capital-intensive method of producing electric power, and regulated electric companies favored nuclear power plants until they were told that some nuclear power plant construction costs could not be passed on.

When firms are allowed to pass on all cost increases to earn a normal profit on those costs, they have little or no incentive to hold down costs.

Once regulation gets so specific that it's scrutinizing every cost, the regulatory process becomes extremely bureaucratic, which itself increases the cost. Moreover, to regulate effectively, the regulators must have independent information and must have a sophisticated understanding of economics, cost accounting, and engineering. Often regulatory boards are made up of volunteer laypeople who start with little expertise; they are exhausted or co-opted by the political infighting they have had to endure by the time they develop some of the expertise they need. As is often the case in economics, there's no easy answer to the problem.

Q-7 What is the problem with regulations that set prices relative to costs?

It is because of the problems with regulation that more and more economists argue that even in the case of natural monopoly, no explicit regulation is desirable, and that society would be better off relying on direct competitive forces guided by broader regulatory guidelines emphasizing free entry into the industry. They argue that regulated monopolies inevitably inflate their costs so much and are so inefficient and lazy that a monopoly right should never be granted.

Deregulating Natural Monopolies In the 1980s and 1990s such views led to the deregulation and competitive supply of both electric power and telephone services.[1] Regulators are making these markets competitive by breaking down the layers of the industry into subindustries and deregulating those subindustries that can be competitive. For example, the phone industry can be divided into the phone line industry, the caller service industry, the pay phone industry, and the directory information industry. By dividing up the industry, regulators can carve out that part that has the characteristics of a natural monopoly and open the remaining parts to competition.

Let's take a closer look at the electrical industry. It used to be that electricity was supplied by independent firms, each providing electricity for its own customers. Today, however, electricity is supplied through a large grid that connects to many regions of

[1]Telephone regulation will be discussed more fully in Chapter 15, on antitrust regulation.

the country. (This grid was developed to provide backup power to different sections of the country.) Given this grid, electricity generated in one area can easily be sent all over the country. Now that many suppliers can compete for customers, a reasonable competition in power supply is feasible. Many states have adopted provisions to open their electricity markets to multiple providers.

Economies of scale can create natural monopolies.

The power line industry, however, cannot be competitive. It would be extremely costly for each company to run a separate power line into your house. That is, the power line industry exhibits *economies of scale*. Because of the economies of scale, the power line industry is the natural monopoly aspect of electrical power supply. The deregulation of electricity involves splitting off the production of electricity from the maintenance of the line—and choosing an appropriate charge for electric line maintenance. While in the newspapers you will likely read that the electrical power industry is being deregulated, that is not quite correct. Only those portions of the market where competition is likely to exist are being deregulated.

How Firms Protect Their Monopolies

The image I've presented of competition being motivated by profits is a useful one. It shows how a market economy adjusts to ever-changing technology and demands in the real world. Competition is a dynamic, not a static, force.

Firms do not sit idly by and accept competition. They fight it.

Firms do not sit idly by and accept competition. They fight it. How do monopolies fight real-world competition? By spending money on maintaining their monopoly. By advertising. By lobbying. By producing products that are difficult to copy. By not taking full advantage of their monopoly position, which means charging a low price that discourages entry. Often firms could make higher short-run profits by charging a higher price, but they forgo the short-run profits in order to strengthen their long-run position in the industry.

Cost/Benefit Analysis of Creating and Maintaining Monopolies

Q-8 What decision rule does a firm use when deciding whether to create or maintain a monopoly?

Preventing real-world competition costs money. Monopolies are expensive to create and maintain. Economic theory predicts that if firms have to spend money on creating and protecting their monopoly, they're going to "buy" less monopoly power than if it were free. How much will they buy? They will buy monopoly power until the marginal cost of such power equals the marginal benefit. Thus, they'll reason:

- Does it makes sense for us to hire a lobbyist to fight against this law that will reduce our monopoly power? Here is the probability that a lobbyist will be effective, here is the marginal cost, and here is the marginal benefit.
- Does it make sense for us to buy this machine? If we do, we'll be the only one to have it and are likely to get this much business. Here is the marginal cost, and here is the marginal benefit.
- Does it make sense for us to advertise to further our market penetration? Here are the likely various marginal benefits; here are the likely marginal costs.

Examples of firms spending money to protect or create monopolies are in the news all the time. The farm lobby fights to keep quotas and farm support programs. Drug companies spend a lot of resources to discover new drugs they can patent. A vivid example of the length to which firms will go to create a monopoly position is Owens Corning's fight to trademark its hue of pink Fiberglas. Owens Corning spent more than

Branding

Applying the Tools

One of the important ways in which firms try to differentiate their product and maintain a monopoly position is called branding. U.S. firms spend over $200 billion on advertising their products, trying to produce brand names and create a pleasant image in the minds of consumers. Here are a few food-related brand names. I'm sure you know about most, but a couple are still in the process for forming brand recognition.

- *Coffee.* When you think of coffee, you think of Starbucks and inexpensive extravagance. You might not be able to afford a Lexus, but you can afford a Starbucks cup of coffee.
- *Chicken.* Perdue doesn't produce any chicken, but it does do a lot of advertising, and it brands the chicken it sells, so when you think of chicken you think of Perdue. You also think Perdue when you see Kevin Harvick race, because he has a big Perdue logo on his racecar.
- *Bananas.* A banana is a banana is a banana, but only if you haven't been influenced by Miss Chiquita. At its peak the Chiquita banana jingle was played 376 times a day on radio stations across the United States.
- *Steak.* Most steaks are currently sold generically. Firms such as Omaha Steaks are now trying to change that. Don't just buy a steak—buy an Omaha steak.
- *Water.* Firms take water from the tap (or possibly from a spring), run it through some filters, and sell the image of purity by creating a nice-sounding name—Dasani, Vermont Pure . . . Well, it's better for you than soda.
- *Pork.* Pork tends to be associated with pigs and does not carry a "good-for-you" image. A national association of pork producers is trying to change that image: "Pork—the other white meat."

$200 million to advertise and promote its color "pink" and millions more in the court to protect its right to sole use of that hue. Owens Corning has weighed the costs and benefits and believes that its pink provides sufficient brand recognition to warrant spending millions to protect it.

Establishing Market Position

Some economists, such as Robert Frank, have argued that today's economy is becoming more and more like a monopoly economy. Modern competition, he argues, is a winner-take-all competition. In such a competition, the winner (established because of brand loyalty, patent protection, or simply consumer laziness) achieves a monopoly and can charge significantly higher prices than its costs without facing competition. The initial competition, focusing on establishing market position, is intense.

In winner-take-all markets, the initial competition is on establishing market position.

To see how important establishing a market position is in today's economy, consider the initial public offering (IPO) of the new firms that were so highly valued by Wall Street in the late 1990s. Many of these new firms had no profits and no likelihood of profits for a number of years, but they were selling at extraordinarily high stock prices. Why? The reasoning was that these companies were spending money to establish brand names. As their names became better known, they would establish a monopoly position, and eventually their monopoly positions would be so strong that they couldn't help but make a profit. With the dot-com stock market crash in the early 2000s, this argument was shown to be wrong for most of these firms. For one or two lucky firms that established their brands, it will be true. The problem is that for other firms, it will not be true—in any competitive process there are winners and losers, and I, like most people, have no way of differentiating between the two.

TECHNOLOGY

Technological development—*the discovery of new or improved products or methods of production*—has been a driving force in the economy in recent years. As we saw in Chapter 10, technological advance lowers the costs of production and makes economies more efficient—producing more output with the same number of inputs.

Technological advance is a natural outcome of specialization because it requires large investments of time and money in very specialized areas. Specialization allows producers to learn more about the particular aspects of production in which they specialize. As they learn more, they become not only more productive but also more likely to produce technological advances because they gain a deeper understanding of their specialty.

For example, instead of producing an entire line of clothing, companies might specialize in the production of certain types of carbon-based fibers and explore ways of making more useful material. The result of such specialization can be a technological advance, such as Gore-Tex—a material that insulates but also "breathes" and thus keeps individuals dry and cool on warm rainy days, and dry and warm on cold rainy or snowy days. Instead of spreading resources to the entire process of making a jacket, a company can concentrate on just one aspect—fibers.

TECHNOLOGY, EFFICIENCY, AND MARKET STRUCTURE

Given the significance of technology, an important question is: What causes technology to grow? Market incentives are an important part of the answer. Before markets existed, economies grew slowly. After markets came into existence in the 1700s, technology advanced more rapidly because individuals gained incentives, in the form of profits, to discover new and cheaper ways of doing things. Globalization of our economy provides an even greater incentive to develop new technologies because the revenue that can be captured from a global market with over 6 billion people (world population) is much greater than the revenue that can be generated from 290 million people (U.S. population).

Are some market structures more conducive to growth than others? The answer economists have come to is a tentative yes, and it is an answer that makes certain market structures look better than the way they were presented earlier. Let's review what we've learned about market structure. In the basic supply/demand framework, perfect competition is seen as the benchmark—it leads to efficient outcomes. All other market structures lead to some deadweight loss. But the supply/demand framework does not consider technological issues. It implicitly assumes that technology is unchanging or is unaffected by market structure. If market structure does affect technological advance, another type of efficiency must be considered. This efficiency might be called dynamic efficiency. **Dynamic efficiency** refers to *a market's ability to promote cost-reducing or product-enhancing technological change*. Market structures that best promote technological change are dynamically efficient. Oligopoly provides the best market structure for technological advance. To see why, let's look at the four market structures: perfect competition, monopolistic competition, monopoly, and oligopoly.

In considering market structures, dynamic efficiency must be considered as well as static efficiency.

PERFECT COMPETITION AND TECHNOLOGY

Q-9 Why isn't perfect competition a good market structure for technological advance?

Perfectly competitive firms have no incentive to develop new technologies. Moreover, perfect competitors earn no profits and consequently may not be able to acquire the funds to devote to research and development that leads to technological change. Even if they did, they would gain little from it. A perfectly competitive market would quickly transfer the gains of the innovation to other firms, making it difficult for the innovating firm to recoup the costs of developing the new technology.

Monopolistic Competition and Technology

Monopolistic competition is somewhat more conducive to technological change because firms have some market power. The promise of gaining additional market power provides the incentive to fund research in new technologies. But, as we learned earlier, monopolistic competitors also lack long-run profits. Easy entry limits their ability to recoup their investment in technological innovation. Eventually, their increased market share will deteriorate and they will return to earning normal profits.

Through its support of patents, the United States does provide incentives to innovate. Patents allow the development of new products through the promise of monopoly profits for a specified period of time. Of course, a firm with a patent will change the market structure into a monopoly.

Monopoly and Technology

On the other end of the spectrum is pure monopoly. Monopolies may earn the profits needed for research and development, but they seldom have the incentive to innovate. Since a monopolist's market is protected from entry, the easiest path is the lazy monopolist path. Since almost all monopolies are created by government (the government gives a monopoly to a specific company), pure monopolists don't face the threat of new competitors. Until recently, European telephone companies and European domestic airlines were monopolies. These industries developed far fewer innovations than did the equivalent U.S. firms that faced more competition, and European industry prices were much higher than those in the United States. A European phone call, for instance, could cost five times more than a U.S. phone call.

In response to these observations, European governments have moved toward privatization and more competition. Both telecommunications and domestic airlines have been privatized, and their monopolies are slowly being removed. The result has been a fall in prices of their products and expanding new technologies in the telecommunications industries.

Oligopoly and Technology

That leaves oligopoly. Oligopoly is the market structure that is most conducive to technological change. Since the typical oligopolist realizes ongoing economic profit, it has the funds to carry out research and development. Moreover, the belief that its competitors are innovating also forces it to do so. Oligopolists are constantly searching for ways to get an edge on competitors, so most technological advance takes place in oligopolistic industries.

Oligopoly tends to be most conducive to technological change.

Q-10 Why is oligopoly the best market structure for technological advance?

The computer industry is an example of an oligopolistic market that has demonstrated tremendous innovation. Technological progress has been rapid, following *Moore's law*—every 18 months the cost of computer speed is cut by half. Another example is the telecommunications industry, which has been oligopolistic since the breakup of AT&T and which has been experiencing enormous technological change.

Some economists, especially those who favor a model in which the threat of competition is enough to keep a firm behaving competitively (a contestable market approach), argue that market structure does not matter for technological progress. It is the conditions of entry that matter. They argue that it is primarily developments in pure science that lead to technological advance. Businesses sample technological advances and develop those that have market potential. They argue that technological advances lead to the formation of oligopolies; oligopolies don't necessarily lead to technological advances. The cigarette industry and the aluminum industry are highly oligopolistic but have had little technological advance. In the steel industry, companies outside the group of existing producers started minimills that led to technological advance. The process did not originate with the oligopolistic steel companies.

Network Externalities, Standards, and Technological Lock-In

Web Note 14.4
Network Economies

In support of the view that technology determines market structure, economists have focused on those aspects of production that involve *network* externalities. An externality, as explained in Chapter 2, is an effect of a decision on a third party that is not taken into account by the decision maker. A **network externality** occurs *when greater use of a product increases the benefit of that product to everyone*. Telephones exhibit network externalities. If you were the only person in the world with a telephone, it would be pretty useless. As the number of people with telephones increases, the telephone's value to communication grows enormously. Another example of a product with network externalities is the Windows operating system. It is of much more use to you if many other people use it too, because you can then communicate with other Windows users and purchase software based on that platform.

Network externalities lead to market standards and affect market structure.

Network externalities are important to market structure because they lead to the development of industry standards. Standards become important because network externalities involve the interaction among individuals and processes. Many examples of the development of industry standards exist. Some are television broadcast standards (they differ in the United States and Europe, which is why U.S. TVs cannot be used in Europe), building standards (there is a standard size of doors), and electrical current standards (220 or 110; AC or DC).

Standards and Winner-Takes-All Industries Network externalities have two implications for the economic process. First, they increase the likelihood that an industry becomes a winner-takes-all industry. Early in the development of new products, there may be two or three competing standards, any one of which could be a significant improvement over what existed before. As network externalities broaden the use of a product, the need for a single standard becomes more important and eventually one standard wins out. The firm that gets its standard accepted as the industry standard gains an enormous advantage over the other firms. This firm will dominate the market. Microsoft and its Windows operating system is an example of how getting your product accepted as the standard can do wonders for the firm. Once a standard develops, even if the other firms try to enter with a better technological standard, they will have a hard time competing because everyone is already committed to the existing industry standard. Deviating from that standard will reduce the benefits of the network externality.

The first-mover advantage helps explain the high stock prices of start-up technology companies.

First-Mover Advantage Firms in an industry developing a standard will have a strong incentive to be the first to market with the product; they will be willing to have large losses initially in their attempt to set the industry standard. The "first-mover advantage" helps explain why the stock of small technology companies sold for extremely high prices even though they were having large losses. The large losses were created because the firms were spending money to gain market share so that their products would become the industry standard. If the firm is successful in getting its product accepted as the standard, the demand for the product will rise and it will have enormous profits in the future.

Technological Lock-In The second implication of network externalities is that the market might not gravitate toward the most efficient standard. Economists debate how standards can be inefficient and yet be maintained by the first-mover advantage. Some economists argue that the inefficiency can be quite large; others argue that it is small. One aspect of the debate has centered around the QWERTY keyboard on computers. Research by Paul David showed that the arrangement of the keys in the QWERTY keyboard was designed to slow people's typing down so that the keys would not stick on the early mechanical typewriters. As the technology of typewriters improved, the need to slow down typing soon ended, but because the QWERTY keyboard was introduced first, it had become the standard. Other, more efficient keyboards have been proposed but not adopted. The QWERTY keyboard has remained, even with its built-in inefficiencies. David suggested that QWERTY is a metaphor for **technological lock-in**—*when prior use of a technology makes the adoption of subsequent technologies difficult*.

QWERTY is a metaphor for technological lock-in.

David's technological lock-in argument suggests that many of our institutions and technologies may be inefficient. Other economists argue that the QWERTY keyboard was not that inefficient and if it had been, other keyboards would have been adopted. I am not sure who is right in this debate, but it may soon be made obsolete by another technological development: voice recognition software, which will make keyboarding a relic of the past.

The QWERTY debate is a part of a larger debate about the competitive process and government involvement in that process. The issues are somewhat the same as they were in the earlier discussion of government regulation of natural monopolies. Many economists see government involvement as necessary to protect the economy and the consumer. They advocate what economist Brian Arthur calls "a nudging hand" approach, in which the government keeps the initial competition fair.

Other economists see monopoly as part of the competitive process—something that will be eliminated as competitive forces act against it. Standards will develop, but they will be temporary. If the standards are sufficiently inefficient, they will be replaced, or an entirely new product will come along that makes the old standard irrelevant. For such economists, neither natural monopoly nor technological lock-in is a reason for government interference. Government interference, even the nudging hand, would stop the competitive process and make the society worse off.

Modern debates about policy regarding competition take dynamic issues into account, but still leave open a debate about what the role of government should be.

Who is right? My own view leans toward the competitive process view with a nudge here or there, but one cannot be dogmatic about it; each case must be decided on its own merits. Moreover, even in those cases where explicit regulation is not called for, the government must set up appropriate rules and property rights to see that the competitive playing field is reasonably level.

An example of what I mean by setting appropriate rules can be seen in the ongoing process of ending local telephone service monopolies and allowing consumers choice in both local and long-distance carriers. Whether this process will be a success depends on the charge the local telephone firms are allowed to make for access to their phone lines into individuals' houses. Government must determine the charge and set up fair initial rules. Unless it does, the competitive process won't work properly.

Conclusion

The stories of competition and monopoly have no end. Both are continuous processes. Monopolies create competition. Out of the competitive struggle, other monopolies emerge, only to be beaten down by competition. Technology is a big part of that struggle. Individuals and firms, motivated by self-interest, try to use the changes brought by technology to their benefit. By doing so they change both the nature of the economy and the direction of technological change itself.

Summary

- The goals of real-world firms are many. Profit plays a role, but the actual goals depend on the incentive structure embodied in the structure of the firm.
- The monitoring problem arises because the incentives faced by managers are not always to maximize the profit of the firm. Economists have helped design incentive-compatible contracts to help alleviate the monitoring problem.
- Monopolists facing no competition can become lazy and not hold down costs as much as they can. X-inefficiency refers to firms operating less efficiently than they could technically.
- X-inefficiency can be limited by the threat of competition or takeovers. Corporate takeovers often mean change in management.
- The competitive process involves a continual fight between monopolization and competition. Suppliers are willing to pay an amount equal to the additional profit gained from the restriction. Consumers are willing to pay an amount equal to the additional cost of products to avoid a restriction. Consumers, however, face a higher cost of organizing their efforts.
- Firms compete against patents that create monopolies by making slight modifications to existing patents and engaging in reverse engineering to copy other firms' products within the limits of the law.
- The U.S. government is deregulating natural monopolies by dividing the firms into various subindustries, carving out that part that exhibits the characteristics of a natural monopoly, and opening the remaining parts to competition.
- Firms protect their monopolies by such means as advertising, lobbying, and producing products that are difficult for other firms to copy.
- Firms will spend money on monopolization until the marginal cost equals the marginal benefit.
- Oligopoly provides the best market structure for technological advance because oligopolists have an incentive to innovate in the form of additional profits and because they have the profits to devote to investing in the research and development of new technologies.

Key Terms

corporate takeover *(313)*
dynamic efficiency *(320)*
incentive-compatible contract *(310)*
lazy monopolist *(312)*
monitoring problem *(310)*
network externality *(322)*
reverse engineering *(316)*
technological development *(320)*
technological lock-in *(323)*
X-inefficiency *(312)*

Questions for Thought and Review

1. Describe the monitoring problem. How does an incentive-compatible contract address the monitoring problem?
2. It is obvious that all for-profit businesses in the United States will maximize profit. True or false? Why?
3. Are managers and high-level company officials paid high salaries because they're worth it to the firm, or because they're simply extracting profit from the company to give themselves? How would you tell whether you're correct?

4. Define *X-inefficiency*. Can a perfect competitor be X-inefficient? Explain why or why not.
5. Some analysts have argued that competition will eliminate X-inefficiency from firms. Will it? Why?
6. Nonprofit colleges must be operating relatively efficiently. Otherwise for-profit colleges would develop and force existing colleges out of business. True or false? Why?
7. If it were easier for consumers to collude than for suppliers to collude, there would often be shortages of goods. True or false? Why?
8. If it were easier for consumers to collude than for suppliers to collude, the price of goods would be lower than the competitive price. True or false? Why?
9. Monopolies are bad; patents give firms monopoly; therefore, patents are bad. True or false? Why?
10. Natural monopolies should be broken up to improve competition. True or false? Why?
11. Technically competent firms will succeed. True or false? Why?
12. Monsanto Corporation lost its U.S. patent protection for its highly successful herbicide Roundup in the year 2000. What do you suppose was Monsanto's strategy for Roundup in the short run? In the long run?
13. Why would a company want to sacrifice short-run profits to establish market position?
14. What two characteristics does a market structure need to have for firms in that industry to engage in technological advance?
15. Taking into consideration changing technologies, why might the basic supply/demand framework not lead to the most efficient outcome?
16. How do network externalities increase the winner-take-all nature of a market?

Problems and Exercises

1. The title of an article in *The Wall Street Journal* was "Pricing of Products Is Still an Art, Often Having Little Link to Costs." In the article, the following cases were cited:
   - Vodka pricing: All vodkas are essentially indistinguishable—colorless, tasteless, and odorless—and the cost of producing vodka is independent of brand name, yet prices differ substantially.
   - Perfume: A $100 bottle of perfume may contain $4 to $6 worth of ingredients.
   - Jean and "alligator/animal" shirts: The "plain pocket" jeans and the Lacoste knockoffs often cost 40 percent less than the brand-name items, yet the knockoffs are essentially identical to the brand-name items.

   a. Discuss whether these differences undermine economists' analysis of pricing.
   b. What do each of these examples likely imply about fixed costs and variable costs?
   c. What do they likely imply about costs of production versus costs of selling?
   d. As what type of market would you characterize each of the above examples?
2. Demonstrate graphically the net gain to producers and the net loss to consumers if suppliers are able to restrict their output to Q_r in the graph in the next column. Demonstrate the net deadweight loss to society.

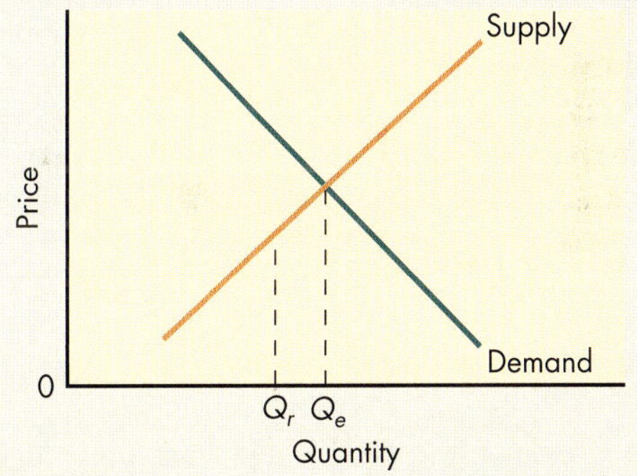

3. Airlines and hotels have many frequent-flier and frequent-visitor programs in which individuals who fly the airline or stay at the hotel receive bonuses that are the equivalent of discounts.
   a. Give two reasons why these companies have such programs rather than simply offer lower prices.
   b. Can you give other examples of such programs?
   c. What is a likely reason why firms don't monitor these programs?
   d. Should the benefits of these programs be taxable?

4. Up to how much is the monopolist depicted in the accompanying graph willing to spend to protect its market position? Demonstrate your answer graphically.

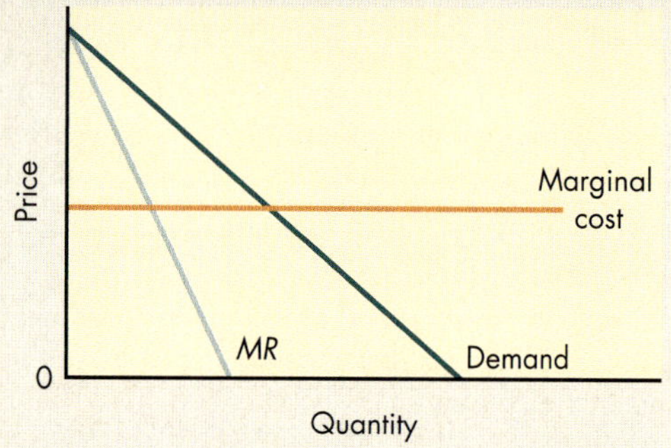

5. Discuss each of the following market structures in terms of static and dynamic efficiency.
   a. Perfect competition.
   b. Monopolistic competition.
   c. Oligopoly.
   d. Monopoly.

Web Questions

1. Go to the AFL-CIO's www.paywatch.org, play the game Greed!, and then answer the following questions:
   a. What are three of the compensation issues facing CEOs?
   b. What are two of the compensation issues facing workers?
   c. What is the perspective of the organization that hosts this game?
2. Go to www.forbes.com and look at Forbes's list of highly compensated CEOs. Select a CEO in the top 10 and answer the following questions:
   a. How has the CEO's firm performed relative to its competitors?
   b. What is the average pay of a CEO in that industry?
   c. Based on your answer to *a*, do you believe that the CEO's compensation is fair? What additional information would you need to support your answer?

Answers to Margin Questions

1. Firms are not interested in just short-run profits. They are also interested in long-run profits. So a firm might sacrifice short-run profits for higher long-run profits. Also, those making the decisions for the firm are not always those who own the firm. *(310)*
2. Most economists are concerned about third-party-payer systems because of the problems of monitoring. It is the consumers who have the strongest incentive to make sure that they are getting value for their money. Any third-party-payer system reduces the consumers' vigilance and therefore puts less pressure on holding costs down. *(311)*
3. A manager does not have the same incentive to hold costs down as an owner does because when an owner holds costs down, the owner's profits are increased, but when a manager holds costs down, the increased profits accrue to the owner, not the manager. Thus the manager has less direct motivation to hold costs down than an owner does. This is especially true if the costs being held down are the manager's perks and pay. *(312)*
4. The threat of a corporate takeover places competitive pressures on firms because it creates the possibility of the managers being replaced and losing all their perks and above-market-equilibrium pay. *(313)*
5. Most agricultural markets are not perfectly competitive because the gains from moving away from competitive markets are fairly large and, for small deviations from competitive markets, the costs are fairly small to those suppliers and consumers who are kept out. This can be seen in the graph on the next page.

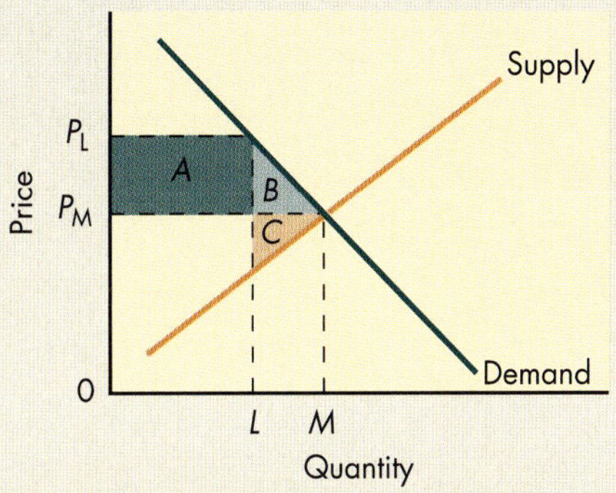

If suppliers producing $0L$ got together and limited supply to L, they could push the price up to P_L and could gain the rectangle A for themselves. Consumers and suppliers who are kept out of the market lose triangles B and C respectively, which, in the diagram, are not only each smaller than A, but also B and C combined are smaller than A. Of course, the area A is lost to the consumers, but the costs of organizing those consumers to fight and protect competition are often prohibitively large. *(314)*

6. It is almost impossible for perfect monopoly to exist because preventing entry is nearly impossible. Monopoly rents are a signal to potential entrants to get the barriers of entry removed. *(315)*
7. The problem with cost-based regulation that sets prices relative to costs is that this removes the incentive for firms to hold down costs and can lead to X-inefficiency. While, in theory, regulators could scrutinize every cost, in practice that is impossible—there would have to be a regulatory board duplicating the work that a firm facing direct market pressure undertakes in its normal activities. *(317)*
8. If the additional benefits of creating or maintaining a monopoly exceed the cost of doing so, do it. If it doesn't, don't. *(318)*
9. Perfect competition is not conducive to technological advance because firms don't earn the profits needed to invest in research and development. It also doesn't have the promise of future above-normal profits needed to motivate researchers to innovate. *(320)*
10. Oligopoly is the best market structure for technological advance because oligopolists have the profits to devote to research and development and have the incentive to innovate. Innovation may provide the oligopolist with a way to increase market share. *(321)*

15 ANTITRUST POLICY AND REGULATION

After reading this chapter, you should be able to:

- Explain the difference between the structure and the performance methods of judging competition.
- Give a brief history of U.S. antitrust policy.
- State the resolution of the IBM, AT&T, and Microsoft antitrust cases.
- Differentiate among horizontal, vertical, and conglomerate mergers.
- List five reasons why unrelated firms would want to merge.
- Compare U.S. antitrust policy with antitrust policy of other countries.
- List three alternatives to antitrust policy that government can use to affect the competitive process.

We have always known that heedless self-interest was bad morals; we now know that it is bad economics.

—*Franklin Delano Roosevelt*

In the courtroom everyone waits for the Microsoft star witness, an economist who is arguing that Microsoft does not have a monopoly. On the stand he testifies, "The market is too dynamic, too much in flux for a monopoly to exist."

"But how about the fact that Microsoft intentionally tied its Web browser to its Windows operating system in order to harm Netscape's ability to compete?" the government lawyer asks.

"Those were technical decisions," the economist answers, "necessary to make the Web browser operate efficiently."

"Yeah, right," replies the government lawyer.

The above is a paraphrase of what was said in a federal court in an antitrust case the government brought against Microsoft. It captures a very real aspect of all theoretical discussions of market structure and policy. Once theory is translated into policy, market structure and behavior play an important role in how the economy functions. One way in which theory is translated into policy is through antitrust policy and regulation. In this chapter we consider both.

ANTITRUST POLICY: JUDGMENT BY PERFORMANCE OR STRUCTURE?

Antitrust policy is *the government's policy toward the competitive process*. It's the government's rulebook for carrying out its role as referee. In volleyball, for instance, the rulebook would answer such questions as: When should a foul be called? When has a person caught and thrown rather than hit the ball over the net? In business a referee is needed for such questions as: When can two companies merge? What competitive practices are legal? When is a company too big? To what extent is it fair for two companies to coordinate their pricing policies? When is a market sufficiently competitive or too monopolistic?

The United States has seen wide swings in economists' prescriptions concerning such questions, depending on which of the two views of competition has held sway. The two competing views are:

1. **Judgment by performance:** *We should judge the competitiveness of markets by the* performance *(behavior) of firms in that market.*
2. **Judgment by structure:** *We should judge the competitiveness of markets by the* structure *of the industry.*

Judgment by performance is the view that competitiveness of a market should be judged by the behavior of firms in that market.

Judgment by structure is the view that competitiveness of a market should be judged by the structure of that market.

To show how the U.S. government has applied these two views of competition in promoting workable and effective competition, this chapter considers government's application of antitrust laws to regulate business. It then considers how recent structural changes in the economy are altering the government's role in refereeing the market.

History of U.S. Antitrust Laws

Although U.S. ideology has always been strongly in favor of laissez-faire and government noninvolvement in business, there has simultaneously been a populist (pro-people) sensibility that fears bigness and monopoly. These fears of bigness and monopoly burst forth in the late 1800s as many firms were merging or organizing together to form trusts or cartels. As stated in Chapter 13, a *cartel*—or, as we'll use the term in this chapter, a *trust*—is a combination of firms in which the firms haven't actually merged but nonetheless act essentially as a single entity. A trust sets common prices and governs the output of individual member firms. A trust can, and often does, act like a monopolist.

In the 1870s and 1880s, trusts were forming in a number of industries, including railroads, steel, tobacco, and oil. Some of these trusts' actions are typified by John D. Rockefeller's Standard Oil. Standard Oil demanded that railroads pay it kickbacks on freight rates. These payments allowed Standard Oil to set lower prices for its products than other companies, which had to pay the railroads full price on freight. Standard Oil thus could sell at lower prices than its competitors.

Bettmann/Corbis.

If prices had remained low, this would have had a positive effect on consumers and a negative effect on Standard Oil's competitors. But prices didn't remain low. By 1882, Standard Oil had driven many of its competitors out of business, and the writing was on the wall for those competitors that remained. At that time, Standard Oil created a trust and "invited" its few surviving competitors to join. Then Standard Oil Trust used the monopoly power it had gained to close down refineries, raise prices, and limit the production of oil. The price of oil rose from a competitive level to a monopolistic level, and the consumer, as well as Standard Oil's competitors, ended up suffering.

The Sherman Antitrust Act

Public outrage against trusts like Standard Oil's was high. The organizers of the trusts were widely known as *robber barons* because of their exploitation of natural resources and their other unethical behavior. The trusts were seen as making enormous profits, preventing competition, and in general bullying everyone in sight. In response the U.S. Congress passed the **Sherman Antitrust Act** of 1890—*a law designed to regulate the competitive process.*

Public outrage at the formation and activities of trusts such as Standard Oil led to the passage of the Sherman Act, the Clayton Act, and the Federal Trade Commission Act.

The Sherman Act contained two main sections:

> Section 1: Every contract, combination in the form of trust or otherwise, or conspiracy in restraint of trade or commerce among the several States, or with foreign nations, is hereby declared to be illegal.
>
> Section 2: Every person who shall monopolize, or attempt to monopolize, or combine or conspire with any other person or persons, to monopolize any part of the trade or commerce among the several States, or with foreign nations, shall be deemed guilty of a misdemeanor, and, on conviction thereof, shall be punished by a

Q-1 What were the two provisions of the Sherman Antitrust Act?

fine not exceeding five thousand dollars, or by imprisonment not exceeding one year, or by both said punishments, in the discretion of the court.

The Sherman Act was broad and sweeping, but vague.

The Sherman Act was meant to be as sweeping and broad as its language sounds. After all, it was passed in response to a public outcry against trusts. But if you look at it carefully, in some respects it is vague and weak. For example, offenses under Section 2 were initially only misdemeanors, not felonies.[1] It's unclear what constitutes "restraint of trade." Moreover, although the act prohibits monopolization, it does not explicitly prohibit monopolies. In short, with the Sherman Act, Congress passed the buck to the courts, letting them decide U.S. antitrust policy.[2]

The following story summarizes the courts' role in antitrust policy. Three umpires are describing their job. The youngest of the three says, "I call them as I see them." The middle-aged umpire says, "No, that's not what an umpire does. An umpire calls them the way they are." The senior umpire says, "You're both wrong. They're nothing until I call them." And that's how it is with the courts and monopoly. Whether a firm is behaving monopolistically isn't known until the court makes its decision.

As Congress was passing the Sherman Act, economists too were debating the implications of trusts and whether it was in the public interest to restrict them. Part of the debate concerned whether the mergers reflected technological changes in production and expanding transportation systems that made increased economies of scale more important (in which case restricting trusts might not be in the public interest since doing so might prevent firms from taking advantage of economies of scale), or whether trusts simply represented attempts at monopolization to restrict output and generate monopoly profits (in which case restricting trusts would more likely be in the public interest since doing so would reduce monopoly).

Economists reflecting the performance viewpoint argued that competition was strong and would ultimately limit monopolies.

A second part of the debate concerned how fast economic forces would operate and how fragile competition was. Some economists argued that competition was strong and that it would limit the profit trusts and monopolies made and force them to charge the competitive price (in which case restricting trusts might not be in the public interest). These economists were reflecting the performance viewpoint—that competition should be relied on to break down the monopolies. They argued that bigness doesn't imply the absence of market competition and that the government's role should merely be to make sure that no significant barriers to entry are created.

Economists reflecting the structure viewpoint argued that trusts should be broken up by government.

Other economists, reflecting the structure viewpoint, argued that competition was fragile and that it wouldn't operate unless there were a large number of small firms. They argued that trusts and monopolies (even if they don't charge monopolistic prices) are bad, that the trusts should be broken up by government, and that laws should not allow new monopolies or trusts to be formed. However, the debate was for the courts, not economists, to settle.

The Standard Oil and American Tobacco Cases: Judging Market Competitiveness by Performance

Web Note 15.1
The Trusts

In 1911, the U.S. Supreme Court established its interpretation of the Sherman Act by handing down its opinions in cases involving Standard Oil and the American Tobacco Company. The Court determined that both companies were structural monopolies; each company controlled 90 percent of its market. However, the Court decided that the monopolistic structure of the markets did not violate the Sherman Antitrust Act. A

[1]Under federal law, a misdemeanor is any misconduct punishable by only a fine or by a jail sentence of a year or less. A felony requires a sentence of more than a year.
[2]Subsequent amendments to the Sherman Act have strengthened it. For example, offenses under Section 2 are now felonies, not misdemeanors.

company's violation of the act was determined not by the structure of the industry but by the particular firm's performance—that is, by whether or not the firm engaged in "unfair business practices." This judgment by performance, not judgment by structure, is often called the *abuse theory* because a firm is legally considered a monopoly only if it commits monopolistic abuses.

Standard Oil and the American Tobacco Company were judged guilty, not because of their structure, but because of their performance.

In these two cases the distinction was academic. Both Standard Oil and American Tobacco were judged guilty (very guilty) of unfair business practices and were broken up. But the academic distinction played an important role in determining the industrial structure of the United States. It allowed structural monopolies to continue to exist, but it prohibited them from using certain monopolistic practices, such as demanding kickbacks.

In 1920, this structure/performance distinction was important in a case involving U.S. Steel. Here the Supreme Court ruled that, while U.S. Steel was a structural monopoly, it was not a monopoly in performance. That is, the firm had not used unfair business practices to become a monopolist and thus was not in violation of antitrust law. Unlike Standard Oil, U.S. Steel was not required to break up into a group of smaller companies.

Q-2 What was the resolution of the Standard Oil case?

The Clayton Act and the Federal Trade Commission Act

In an attempt to give more guidance to the courts and to provide for more vigorous enforcement of the antitrust provisions, in 1914 Congress passed the Clayton Antitrust Act and the Federal Trade Commission Act.

The **Clayton Antitrust Act** is *a law that made four specific monopolistic practices illegal* when their effect was to lessen competition:

1. Price discrimination, that is, selling identical goods to different customers at different prices.
2. Tie-in contracts, in which the buyer must agree to deal exclusively with one seller and not to purchase goods from competing sellers.
3. Interlocking directorships, in which memberships of boards of directors of two or more firms are almost identical.
4. Buying stock in a competitor's company when the purpose of buying that stock is to reduce competition.

The Clayton Antitrust Act made four specific monopolistic practices illegal:

1. Price discrimination.
2. Tie-in contracts.
3. Interlocking directorships.
4. Purchase of a competitor's stock.

In establishing the Federal Trade Commission (FTC) in 1914, Congress gave it the power to regulate competition and police markets. The **Federal Trade Commission Act** is *a law that made it illegal for firms to use "unfair methods of competition" and to engage in "unfair or deceptive acts or practices,"* whether or not those actions had any impact on competition. Other than that broad mandate, Congress gave the FTC little direction as to what rules it was to use to regulate trade and police markets. As a result, for more than 20 years the commission was rather ineffective. In 1938, however, it was given the job of preventing false and deceptive advertising, which remains one of its primary roles.

The ALCOA Case: Judging Market Competitiveness by Structure

Judgment by performance was the primary criterion governing U.S. antitrust policy until 1945. In 1945 the U.S. courts changed their interpretation of the law with the Aluminum Company of America (ALCOA) case. In the ALCOA case, the company was found guilty of violating the antitrust statutes even though the court did not rule that

Q-3 What was the resolution of the ALCOA case?

Web Note 15.2
Predatory Pricing

ALCOA had been guilty of unfair practices. What ALCOA had done was to use its knowledge of the market to expand its capacity before any competitors had a chance to enter the market. In addition, it had kept its prices low to prevent potential entry by competitors, an activity known as *predatory pricing*. It showed no signs of exploiting its monopoly power to charge high prices or to force competing firms out of business. Thus, on performance standards, it was not violating the law. But in the ALCOA case, the structure of the market, not the company's performance, was used to determine whether ALCOA was in violation of antitrust law.

Judging Markets by Structure and Performance: The Reality

Judgment by structure seems unfair on a gut level. After all, in economics the purpose of competition is to motivate firms to produce better goods than their competitors are producing, and to do so at lower cost. If a firm is competing so successfully that all the other firms leave the industry, the successful firm will be a monopolist, and on the basis of judgment by structure will be guilty of antitrust violations. Under the judgment-by-structure criterion, a firm is breaking the law if it does what it's supposed to be doing: producing the best product it can at the lowest possible cost.

An important reason supporting the structure criterion is practicality.

Supporters of the judgment-by-structure criterion recognize this problem but nonetheless favor the structure criterion. An important reason for this is practicality.

Contextual Judgments and the Capabilities of the Courts

Judgment by performance requires that each action of a firm be analyzed on a case-by-case basis. Doing that is enormously time-consuming and expensive. In some interpretations, actions of a firm might be considered appropriate competitive behavior; in other interpretations, the same actions might be considered inappropriate. For example, say that an automobile company requires that in order for its warranty to hold, owners of its warranted vehicles must use only the company's parts and service centers. Is this requirement of the automobile company intended to create a monopoly position for its parts and service center divisions or to ensure proper maintenance? The answer depends on the context of the action.

But judging each case contextually is beyond the courts' capabilities. There are so many firms and so many actions that the courts can't judge all industries on their performance. They must devise a way to limit the issues they look at. In order to apply the performance criterion reasonably, the Supreme Court must set out certain guidelines to tell firms in what situations the Court will take a closer look at their performance. Because the available information concerns structure, those guidelines inevitably refer to market structure, even though it is firms' performance that will ultimately be judged. So even though judging by structure may have problems, it is necessary.

It's very much like the procedure college admissions offices use in deciding which applicants to accept. They judge applicants on their "total performance," not just on their quantitative scores on standardized tests. However, they often use a certain quantitative score as a cutoff point in order to reduce applications to a manageable number. Applicants below the cutoff point are automatically rejected; applicants above it are considered one by one.

Another argument in favor of judging competitiveness by structure is that structure can be a predictor of future performance. Advocates of the structure criterion argue that a monopolist may be pricing low now, but it is, after all, a monopolist, and it won't price low in the future. The low price will eliminate competition now, and, once the

Wal-Mart, State Laws, and Competition

Applying the Tools

It isn't only the federal government that has laws on competition. States have a variety of laws that govern competitive practices. One such state law is Arkansas's Unfair Practices Act, which prohibits selling, or advertising for sale, items below cost "for the purpose of injuring competitors and destroying competition." In the early 1990s, three Arkansas pharmacies sued Wal-Mart for violating this law by selling its goods at "too low" a price. The background of the case is the following.

Wal-Mart had been expanding aggressively throughout the United States reaching a total of about 3,000 stores in the mid 1990s. It does not deny that it, like many other stores, sells some goods below cost. But it argues that when it sells below cost it does not do so to "destroy competition" or "injure competitors," but rather to maintain low prices for consumers. It claims that its pricing policies promote, not destroy, competition.

In principle, most economists agree with Wal-Mart; new competition, by its very nature, hurts existing businesses—that's the way the market competitive process works. Those who don't sell for the lowest price lose, and those who sell for the lowest price gain. But most economists also recognize that Wal-Mart's brand of competition can have externalities affecting the social fabric of small-town economies. A new Wal-Mart store can undermine the town centers and replace them with commercial sprawl on the outskirts of these towns. Whether these externalities are a reason to limit Wal-Mart's aggressive pricing policies is a debatable question.

Wal-Mart initially lost its suit in Arkansas; however, in 1995 the Arkansas Supreme Court overturned the lower court decision and held that Wal-Mart's pricing was not part of a strategy to price below cost over a prolonged period. While Wal-Mart won this suit, the threat of other suits discouraged the company from following quite as aggressive a pricing policy as it otherwise would have.

---

competition is gone, the firm will not be able to resist the temptation to use its monopoly power.

Determining the Relevant Market and Industry Supporters of the performance criterion admit that this standard has problems, but they point out that the structure criterion also has problems. As you saw in Chapter 13, it's difficult to determine the relevant market (local, national, or international) and the relevant industry (three-digit or five-digit NAICS code) necessary to identify the structural competitiveness of any industry.

Choosing the relevant market when evaluating competitiveness is difficult to do.

Such questions have been the center of many antitrust court cases. For example, in the ALCOA case, the company argued that metals such as copper and steel were interchangeable with aluminum, and that therefore the relevant industry to consider was the metals industry. If the Court had chosen metals, not aluminum, as the relevant industry, ALCOA wouldn't have been found to have a monopoly. The Court decided, however, that aluminum had sufficiently unique properties to constitute its own market. Since it determined that ALCOA had 90 percent of the aluminum market, ALCOA was declared a monopoly and was broken up.

Q-4 What was the resolution of the Du Pont case?

The arguments in the Du Pont case (1956) again centered on the definition of *industry*. The Supreme Court found that Du Pont was innocent of monopolizing the production of cellophane even though Du Pont was the only producer of cellophane. The Court reasoned that the relevant industry was not the cellophane industry but rather the flexible wrap industry, which also included aluminum foil and wax paper. Du Pont did not have a monopoly of the flexible wrap industry and thus, the Court said, was not in violation of the antitrust laws.

More recently, in 1993, the Department of Justice opposed a merger between Gillette and Parker Pens, arguing that the combined firm would control about 40 percent of the premium-fountain-pen market. The Court, however, allowed the merger, arguing that the relevant market was much larger—the market for premium writing instruments, which also included mechanical pencils, ballpoint pens, rollerballs, and fountain pens. The premium-writing-instruments market had many more competitors than the premium-fountain-pen market.

Similar ambiguities exist with the decision about the relevant geographic market. In the Pabst Brewing case (1966), the definition of the market played a key role. Pabst wanted to merge with the Blatz Brewing Company. On a national scale, both companies were relatively small, accounting together for about 4.5 percent of beer sales in the United States as a whole. Pabst argued that the United States was the relevant market. The Court, however, decided that Wisconsin, where Pabst had its headquarters, was the relevant market, and since the two firms held a 24 percent share of that market, the merger was not allowed.

Both structure and performance criteria have ambiguities, and in the real world there are no definitive criteria for judging whether a firm has violated the antitrust statutes.

What should one make of debates regarding relevant markets? The bottom line is that both structure and performance criteria have ambiguities, and in the real world there are no definitive criteria for judging whether a firm has violated the antitrust statutes. A firm isn't at fault or in the clear until the courts make the call.

Recent Antitrust Enforcement

In recent years, few mergers have been challenged by the government. In 2000, for example, the Department of Justice challenged only 48 of the more than 9,500 mergers that took place among U.S. companies. Most of the mergers that were challenged were settled, abandoned, or restructured. Only one went to court. Despite the fact that few recent mergers have been challenged, antitrust law still works mainly through its deterrent effect. Many potential mergers are never even proposed because firms know they would not be allowed. Few major antitrust cases have been brought, in part because a century of experience has taught business what the law allows, and in part because the government has been lenient in its interpretation of the antitrust laws. That leniency has three interrelated causes. The first is a change in the American ideology. Whereas in the 1950s and 1960s the prevailing ideology saw big business as "bad," by the 1980s the view became more complex—big business was seen as a combination of good and bad. In this new ideological framework, the political pressure to push antitrust enforcement waned.

Since the 1980s the United States has been more lenient in antitrust cases because of a change in ideology, the globalization of the U.S. economy, and the increasing complexity of technology.

Second, as the United States became more integrated into the global economy, big business faced significant international competition and hence competition created by U.S. market structure became less important.

Third, as technologies became more complicated, the issues in antitrust enforcement also became more complicated for the courts to handle. By the time the legal system had resolved a case, the technology would have changed so much that the issues in that case were no longer relevant.

Three Modern Antitrust Cases

The modern era of antitrust policy has been marked by important cases in the computer and telecommunications markets. One such case was against IBM.

The IBM Case

In 1967 the U.S. Department of Justice sued IBM for violating the antitrust laws. The department argued that the company had a 72 percent share of the general-purpose

Nefarious Business Practices

Applying the Tools

In a secretly recorded comment during a price-fixing meeting, the former president of ADM stated, "Our competitors are our friends and our customers are our enemies."

The U.S. antitrust laws concern far more than mergers and market structure; they also place legal restrictions on certain practices of businesses such as price-fixing. By law, firms are not allowed to *explicitly* collude in order to fix prices above the competitive level. A key aspect of the law is the explicit nature of the collusion that is disallowed. Airlines, gas stations, and firms in many other industries have prices that generally move in tandem—when one firm changes its price, others seem to follow. Such practices would suggest that these firms are implicitly colluding, but they are not violating the law unless there is explicit collusion.

To prove explicit collusion is difficult—there must be a smoking gun, and there is seldom sufficient evidence of explicit collusion to prosecute businesses. There are exceptions, however. In 1996, Archer Daniels Midland (ADM), a major supplier of food and grains, was caught red-handed when one of its former officials gave prosecutors tapes of meetings in which price-fixing occurred. Meeting secretly around the world, in countries like Mexico, France, Canada, and Japan, ADM executives tried to set prices of Lysine, a feed additive, and citric acid. One of ADM's officials, working undercover for the FBI, secretly recorded these meetings. Faced with the taped evidence against them, ADM agreed to pay $100 million in fines—the largest criminal antitrust fine in history up to that year. Since 1996 four other companies have been fined even greater sums, with Roche Holding paying a fine of $500 million.

Company	Fine (in millions)
Roche Holding	$500
BASF	225
SGL Carbon	135
Ucar International	110
ADM	100

electronic digital computing industry, and that it had acquired that market share because of unfair business practices such as bundling of hardware, software, and maintenance services at a single price (that is, requiring customers to buy all three together). If you wanted IBM equipment (hardware), you also had to take IBM service and software whether you wanted them or not. When you bought an IBM machine you bought everything, so other companies had little chance to compete. Moreover, the department argued that IBM constantly redesigned its computers, making it impossible for other companies to keep up and compete fairly on the sale of any IBM mainframe-compatible item.

In technology industries the market is continually changing.

IBM argued that the relevant market was broader, that it included all types of computers such as military computers, programmable calculators, and other information-processing products. It further claimed that its so-called unfair practices were simply a reflection of efficient computer technology. Fast-moving technological developments required it to continually redesign its products merely to provide its customers with the latest, best equipment. And, it said, the only way to provide the best level of service to its customers was to include its maintenance services in the price of its products. The case dragged on for years until finally, in 1982, the government withdrew its case.

The reason it did so was that the market had changed. Many of the government's objections had become moot; mainframe computers were being replaced with personal computers, a market in which Apple and DEC had become serious competitors, and the globalization of the computer industry made IBM's dominance in the United States far less important.

IBM may have triumphed in the antitrust case against it, but in doing so it may have lost the war. Here's why.

Q-5 What was the resolution of the IBM case?

About the same time as the case was at its height, IBM was negotiating with an upstart company about an operating system for a small part of its market—the personal computer (PC) market, which was just developing. Bill Gates, the president of the young company, offered to sell its disk operating system (DOS) to IBM for $75,000. IBM refused to buy it; to have bought DOS would have given IBM greater control over the PC market, and would have made a court-ordered breakup of IBM more likely. Instead, IBM left Bill Gates to license DOS to IBM and everyone else, while IBM concentrated on mainframe computers and the production of PCs.

The IBM case was dropped by the United States, but the prosecution likely led to IBM's problems in the 1990s. It won but it also lost.

By the early 1990s, the cost of that decision was clear. The mainframe market was dying, and IBM was hemorrhaging losses. Meanwhile, Bill Gates had become a multibillionaire, and his company—Microsoft—had become a controlling force in the PC market. Now the tables were turned and in 1994 it was Microsoft that was being pursued by the U.S. government for violating antitrust laws.

The losses at IBM ended in the mid-1990s and its competitive position improved. Thus, ultimately it weathered the antitrust case, but its history was forever changed by it.

The AT&T Case

The other major antitrust case of the 1980s, the AT&T case, demonstrates another aspect of U.S. antitrust policy and shows how technological change plays an important role in competition and questions of industrial market structure.

AT&T as a Regulated Monopoly Up until 1982, AT&T was what was called a *regulated monopoly*. It had the exclusive right to provide telephone service in the United States. AT&T controlled 90 percent of the telecommunications market: long-distance and local telephone service, and the production of telephones themselves as well as other communications equipment.

A natural monopoly is an industry in which significant economies of scale make the existence of more than one firm inefficient.

Why was it given that right? Because it was felt that economies of scale and network externalities made supplying telephone service a **natural monopoly** *(an industry in which significant economies of scale make the existence of more than one firm inefficient)*. Telephone service required every house to be connected with lines, which had to be buried underground or strung overhead on poles. It made little sense to have more than one company stringing competing lines. Moreover, the government decided that universal telephone service was socially desirable, and AT&T was required to provide universal service. Unregulated companies likely would have practiced *cream skimming* (providing service to low-cost areas and avoiding high-cost areas).

In return for its monopoly, AT&T was subjected to regulatory control by the Federal Communications Commission and state utility commissions. This government regulation was designed to limit the company's profit to a fair level and prevent it from abusing its monopoly.

Under AT&T's monopoly, phone service in the United States was the best and cheapest in the world, although some believed it could and should have been even cheaper. Some economists argued that AT&T's guarantee of a "fair" return on its investment gave it a strong incentive to act as a lazy monopolist and to invest heavily, thereby increasing costs. If a company knows it can pass its costs on to customers (and add a profit margin as well), it has little incentive to hold down costs. But even if service was more expensive than it needed to be, on the whole most agreed that the system worked well.

Technological Change and Competition In the 1970s technological changes fundamentally altered the nature of the long-distance telephone industry. The development of satellite transmission and fiber optics made physical line connections no longer the only option, so long-distance telephone service was no longer a natural monopoly. In fact, significant competition began to develop, and AT&T's new competitors claimed that they weren't being allowed reasonable access to the AT&T-controlled local telephone network. AT&T charged competing firms high fees for access to all their local lines—fees that competitors argued were unfair.

The issue was complicated by the fact that the regulatory commissions had set local charges low and long-distance rates high (implicitly subsidizing local service with AT&T's long-distance profits). As long as AT&T controlled both local and long-distance calling its revenues were unaffected by this rule. But when competitors began to undercharge AT&T on long-distance service, AT&T grew increasingly concerned. AT&T's high access charges were an attempt to see that the competitors used some of their own profits to help subsidize local rates.

As a result of these claims and counterclaims, the Department of Justice introduced an antitrust suit against AT&T in 1978, alleging that potential competitors were not being allowed reasonable access to AT&T's local telephone network. The case had merit, but so did AT&T's defense: How could a firm provide high-cost local service at a low price with no way to pay for it? As is now usual for any contested antitrust case, the case went on and on, and no conclusion was in sight.

Q-6 What was the resolution of the AT&T case?

Resolution of the AT&T Case In January 1982, AT&T and the Department of Justice announced that they had settled the case and that AT&T had agreed to be broken up. Specifically, AT&T agreed that by January 1, 1984, it would divest itself of 22 local operating companies, which accounted for more than 75 percent of AT&T's assets. These companies quickly merged into seven local operating companies that became known as the *Baby Bells*. AT&T kept its long-distance telephone service, its manufacturing division, and its research facilities. In return, AT&T was subject to far less regulation. After the settlement, AT&T could enter any unregulated business it desired, such as data transmission and computers. The Baby Bells, alternatively, were restricted to the local telephone market.

The AT&T case was settled by AT&T agreeing to be split up into regional companies handling local service, and AT&T itself competing in the long-distance market.

The result of this settlement was an enormous upheaval in the telephone industry. Local rates for phone service went up twofold or even threefold, while long-distance rates fell substantially. Two major competitors, MCI and Sprint, emerged, and competition for long-distance business became fierce. (Now more than 800 firms offer long-distance service.)

Developments since the AT&T Case The breakup of AT&T was not the end of the changes. The seven Baby Bells continued merging with one another, and in 2003 only four remained—SBC Communications, Verizon, Bell South, and Qwest. In 1995, AT&T had divided itself into three companies—AT&T, Lucent Technologies, and National Cash Register. Only AT&T remained in the market for communication services, expanding its offerings into wireless communications, digital cable, cable, and long distance.

Technological innovations continued to change the nature of the telecommunications industry. Advances in wireless technology provided competition for both local and long-distance carriers, while the Internet became a larger and larger market. Simultaneously, new high-speed fiber-optic networks turned telephone lines into a potential competitor for regulated cable TV monopolies. Data, voice, and video could be transmitted by copper wire (phone lines), cable, and wireless (satellite).

Because of these changes the market divisions established by the FCC no longer made sense, and in 1996 Congress passed the Telecommunications Act, which deregulated the telecommunications industry and allowed long-distance carriers, local phone companies, and cable television companies to enter one another's markets. Cable, long-distance, local, cellular phone, and Internet were combined and seen as an "information flow" market. In exchange for being able to compete in the market for long-distance services, the Baby Bells were required to offer access to their local networks to their competitors for a fee.

The Baby Bells fought competition in the local phone market by setting difficult technical requirements for use of their lines and by taking advantage of every loophole in the 1996 act they could find. For instance, they fought pressure to open up local networks for high-speed Internet access, arguing that doing so meant sharing lines, which was not required by the 1996 act. Competing companies such as AT&T claimed that the Baby Bells' access fees were too high, precisely the charge that had been levied earlier against AT&T. The delaying tactics worked; in the early 2000s, the four Baby Bells still controlled 90 percent of the local telephone market. As they attempted to maintain control of the local market, they simultaneously expanded into long distance. Verizon, for example, won a 20 percent market share in those states where it had permission to offer long-distance service. This move by local phone companies into long-distance markets is expected to expand in the near future as the companies continue to open up their local markets to others.

The competition is not only between long-distance and local service providers. Competition has also come from wireless communication providers and international telecommunications companies. For example, wireless communications companies are attempting to be the sole providers of telephone service for households. By 2002, they had made some inroads; 3 percent of Americans relied entirely on wireless services. Similarly, international companies have entered the U.S. market just as U.S. companies have entered world markets.

The competition in telecommunications, as in most industries, takes place on both the regulatory front and the business front. On the regulatory front companies try to interpret any regulatory ruling in a manner that is most advantageous to them, and to force competitors to bring legal proceedings to achieve a different ruling. By doing so, they often win even when they lose because the delay of entry allows them to establish their position in the market and make it difficult for competitors to enter even when they are allowed to do so. With the ongoing technological developments, government antitrust policy regarding telecommunications firms is likely to stay in the news in the indefinite future.

Given the technological developments, government antitrust policy regarding telecommunications is likely to stay in the news.

The Microsoft Case

One of the most important antitrust cases brought in the 1990s was the Microsoft case. This is an extremely interesting case to consider both because of its similarities to the IBM case and because of the issues it raises about competition, the competitive process, and government's role in that competitive process.

Microsoft makes computer software. From the company's small start some 20 years ago, sales of Microsoft software have grown to account for about 50 percent of the world's software market. Its PC operating system, Windows, accounts for an even larger share—more than 90 percent—of the world's operating system software market.

Since all software must be compatible with an operating system, the widespread use of Windows gives Microsoft enormous power—power that competitors claim it has used to gain competitive advantage for its other divisions. Competitors' calls for action, and reports of monopolistically abusive acts by Microsoft, led the U.S. Department of Justice in 1998 to charge Microsoft with violating antitrust laws.

The government suit against Microsoft charged the company with being a monopoly and using that monopoly power in a predatory way. Specifically, it charged Microsoft with:

1. Possessing monopoly power in the market for personal computer operating systems.
2. Tying other Microsoft software products to its Windows operating system.
3. Entering into agreements that keep computer manufacturers that install Windows from offering competing software.

Microsoft had dominated the market for PC operating systems for about a decade. The U.S. Department of Justice argued that this long-standing monopoly position was the result of unfair business practices. Microsoft argued that Windows sold so well because it was a superior product. Microsoft further argued that, because it faced competition from technological change, it was not a monopolist.

Because of their experience with the AT&T and IBM cases, prosecutors were initially hesitant to bring charges against Microsoft. They knew that the case would be extremely complicated, contentious, and long. And they fully expected that the competitive issues would change significantly in the interim. They eventually decided to bring the case, however, because the judge granted them an expedited process—meaning that the case would be resolved much faster than previous cases—and because they felt that Microsoft had violated a 1994 consent that it had entered into following an earlier antitrust investigation.

Is Microsoft a Monopolist? The computer software industry is a market with barriers to entry that originate from two sources—network externalities and economies of scale. Network externalities exist because as the number of applications supported by a single platform increase, the value of the platform also increases. Economies of scale exist because the cost of developing a new platform and new software is significant, while the cost of producing it is minimal. It is a potential candidate for monopoly.

Is Microsoft a monopoly in the market for operating systems? Looking only at the market within a static framework, Microsoft, given its stable 90 percent share, almost definitely has a monopoly. Looking at the market from a dynamic perspective, the issue is much more complicated. Competing operating systems exist; Jaguar (developed by Apple), and Linux are both competitors to Windows.

Whether one sees Microsoft as a monopolist depends in part on whether one views it in a static or dynamic framework.

The Linux operating system is a particularly strong potential competitor because it is an "open-source" operating system. All programmers can get the code and modify it, allowing them to tailor it for their software and streamline the structure of their programs. Linux reduces the costs of software development and leads to more efficient programs.

Courtesy Microsoft Corporation.

Another potential competitive force is the merging of software and hardware. As the power of computers increases according to Moore's law, it is becoming more and more feasible to design specific chips to do specific jobs, incorporating into a single chip aspects that were previously separated into hardware and software. Within 10 years the entire PC structure—a machine to handle a multitude of tasks—could become obsolete, and instead the market may consist of $10 or $15 machines that will perform specific tasks more efficiently than can a multipurpose machine like the PC. Each of these changes could eliminate Microsoft's monopoly advantage. In this dynamic view of the market, Microsoft's monopoly is at best temporary, and will survive only if it outcompetes the other technologies.

Is Microsoft a Predatory Monopolist? The U.S. Department of Justice argued that Microsoft used its monopoly in the operating systems market to gain a larger share of the software market and engaged in unfair practices against its competitors to maintain the barriers to entry in the operating systems market. Let's first look at its actions to gain market share in the software market.

Competing software companies alleged that companies like Novell (now Corel), which had the leading word-processing software, WordPerfect, were put at a significant disadvantage because Microsoft combined its software with the Windows operating system. Not surprisingly, Microsoft's Word has become the dominant word-processing system. By directing the development of new software to favor Windows, Microsoft strengthened the barrier to entry created by network externalities. Microsoft also penalized computer manufacturers that installed Windows if they installed competing software. IBM, for example, was denied Windows 95 when it decided to pre-install its PCs with Lotus, a direct competitor to Microsoft's Excel.

Microsoft was also alleged to have engaged in unfair practices in how it addressed the threat of competition in the operating system market. Direct competitive threats came mainly from two firms—Netscape and Sun Microsystems. Netscape and Sun were developing programs that operated across multiple platforms and were developing potential rival operating systems.

Microsoft used its power in one market to give it advantages in other markets.

Netscape designed and marketed a very popular Web browser called Netscape Navigator. Navigator posed a threat to Microsoft not only because it could serve as a platform for other software applications and circumvent the need for Windows but also because Navigator could work on many operating systems, increasing the ability of software to work on systems other than Windows. In response to that threat, Microsoft attempted to get Netscape to agree to stop developing Navigator as a competing platform in exchange for a "special relationship" with Microsoft. Netscape wouldn't agree. In response, Microsoft withheld the source code Netscape needed to provide its browser on the Windows platform for three months. This gave Microsoft an advantage to offer its own Web browser, Internet Explorer, with Windows starting in 1995. Microsoft then bundled its browser to Windows (essentially offering it at no cost) and made it virtually impossible for consumers to remove the Internet Explorer icon from the PC screen. Installing Windows actually disabled competing Internet browsers. Microsoft also prohibited computer manufacturers such as Compaq from offering Netscape as an alternative browser when they sold PCs with Windows.

The government argued that this competition was unfair and predatory. Microsoft argued that Internet Explorer was a Windows program improvement; it was part of Windows. Netscape Navigator, which had been more popular than Internet Explorer and had seen its sales climbing rapidly, was in a matter of a few years nearly replaced by the Microsoft browser.

Another potential competitor was Sun Microsystems, which was developing Java, a programming language designed to create software applications on a variety of platforms, not just Windows. Sun Microsystems had entered into an agreement with Microsoft that allowed Microsoft to distribute the Java code under explicit instructions not to change it. But Microsoft created a version of Java that kept it tied to Windows and changed the platform-neutral characteristics of Java. Microsoft also instructed other companies not to cooperate with Sun. These actions stunted the development of a program that would allow software to run across multiple platforms, which would have reduced the network externality barriers to trade enjoyed by Microsoft.

Resolution of the Microsoft Case So is Microsoft a monopoly? And has it been involved in anticompetitive practices? The answer the court gave was yes. In 2000 the judge concluded that Microsoft violated Section 2 of the Sherman Act by attempting to maintain its monopoly power by anticompetitive means. He also ruled that Microsoft violated Section 1 of the Sherman Act by unlawfully tying its Web browser to its operating system. In a strongly worded decision he stated that "Microsoft mounted a deliberate assault upon entrepreneurial efforts that, left to rise or fall on their own merits, could well have enabled the introduction of competition into the market." As a remedy

Web Note 15.3
More on Microsoft

the government proposed breaking up Microsoft into two companies. Microsoft quickly appealed, and in mid-2001 the appeals court ruled that, while Microsoft was indeed a monopoly, a breakup was not necessary—instead, the case should be resolved by mediation. A few months later the federal government, nine states, and Microsoft agreed to a settlement. Microsoft agreed not to engage in contracts that prohibited PC makers from using competing products or in practices that favored PC makers that offered only Microsoft products. It also agreed to release technical information about Windows improvements to software developers. Microsoft maintained its right to keep e-mail systems and software programs such as media players bundled with Windows. Nine other states (co-plaintiffs) objected to the settlement because they believed the restrictions on Microsoft were too mild.

The nine states continued suing Microsoft, contending that software developers in applications such as media players could compete only if Microsoft made its operating system modular and provided the relevant code to competitors so they could integrate their software into the Windows operating system as seamlessly as they could integrate Microsoft products. Both sides brought in experts on whether this was easy to do or not.

In November 2002 the Court decided against the dissenting states. Thus, the agreement that Microsoft had entered into with the federal government stood. However, the judge stated that she would be following Microsoft's actions carefully to see that it abided by the agreement. (Two states appealed.) So the end result of the Microsoft case was that even though Microsoft had been declared a monopoly, it was not broken up. Instead it agreed to a set of rules of competition that required it to provide technical information to competitors and to allow firms to use software from Microsoft competitors.

Most observers believe that these limitations do not place a serious constraint on Microsoft's domination of the software industry since, for a number of its competitors, that technical information will be too late, because in the four years that had passed since the beginning of the case, Microsoft had already integrated its Windows operating system with Microsoft media players, and had developed a head start in integrating a number of other new technologies into its Windows operating system. So even if it lives up to the spirit of the agreement, it will retain a lead for years to come. And if it doesn't live up to its agreement, since any legal action against Microsoft will take additional years to litigate, the same process can be expected to continue and Microsoft will have likely established its position in even newer technologies before any limitations can be imposed on it by the government.

Assessment of Antitrust Policy

Economic scholars' overall assessment of antitrust policy is mixed. In certain cases, such as the IBM case, most agree that antitrust prosecution went too far. But most believe that other decisions (as in the 1911 Standard Oil and American Tobacco cases) set a healthy precedent by encouraging a more competitive U.S. business environment. Almost all agree that antitrust enforcement has not reduced the size of firms below the minimally efficient level, the level at which a firm can take full advantage of economies of scale. But they are mixed in their judgments as to whether the enforcement was needed. Performance advocates generally believe that it was not, while structural advocates generally believe that it was. They are also mixed in their judgment about whether any type of antitrust action is feasible in a technologically dynamic industry such as computers or telecommunications.

Economists' judgment on antitrust is mixed.

Mergers, Acquisitions, and Takeovers

Other than the Microsoft case, antitrust activity was minimal in the 1990s and early 2000s. But industrial structure has changed significantly. The nature of those changes was treated in Chapter 10, where I discussed how firms are increasingly looking for alternative ways of structuring themselves so that they can achieve economies of scope and economies of scale that go along with specialization. To do this, firms are simultaneously merging and breaking up. Firms are allowed to break up as much as they want; when they merge, however, they must see that any merger falls within the antitrust guidelines. In order to put recent merger activity into perspective, let's consider the various subcategories and types of mergers that are possible.

Acquisitions and Takeovers

Merger is *a general term meaning the act of combining two firms*. The picture it conveys is of two firms combining to form one firm. That picture isn't always appropriate, however. For example, often the firm buying another company is essentially what's called a *shell corporation*, which exists primarily to buy up other firms. A combination that is technically a merger but has distinguishing characteristics all its own is the **takeover**—*the purchase of one firm by a shell firm that then takes direct control of all the purchased firm's operations*. The term *takeover* is used to emphasize that little true merging is taking place. Takeovers change the control over the firm, but do not affect market concentration.

Another kind of merger is an **acquisition**—*a merger in which a company buys another company and the purchaser has the right of direct control over the resulting operation (but does not always exercise that right)*. It is a merger, but it is not a merger of equals, and the acquiring firm does not necessarily take over direct control of the acquired firm's operations. In a merger of equals, neither firm takes over the other, and it's not clear who'll be in charge after the merger.

Takeovers and acquisitions are said to be *friendly* or *hostile*. In a friendly takeover, one corporation is willing to be acquired by the other. A **hostile takeover** is *a merger in which the firm being taken over doesn't want to be taken over*. How can that happen?

Remember the discussion of corporations from Chapter 3. Corporations are owned by stockholders, but are managed by a different group of individuals. The two groups' interests do not necessarily coincide. When it is said that a corporation doesn't want to be taken over, that means that the corporation's managers don't want the company to be taken over. In a hostile takeover, the management of each corporation presents its side to the shareholders of both corporations. The shareholders of the corporation that is the takeover target ultimately decide whether or not to sell their shares. If enough shareholders sell, the takeover succeeds.

In a hostile takeover, the shareholders ultimately decide whether to sell their shares.

Mergers

Mergers are also classified by the types of businesses that are merging.

Horizontal mergers are companies in the same industry merging together.

Horizontal Mergers Most U.S. antitrust policy has concerned **horizontal mergers**—*the combining of two companies in the same industry*. The creation of Standard Oil is an example of a horizontal merger. The 2000 merger between pharmaceutical companies Glaxo Wellcome and SmithKline, GlaxoSmithKline, is another. Since the passage of the Cellar-Kefauver Act of 1950, almost all mergers of companies with substantial market shares in the same industry have been prohibited, even though enforcement was loosened in the 1980s. For example, in 2000 the FTC blocked a proposed merger between WorldCom and Sprint because the combined firm would have controlled 30 to 50 percent of telecommunications markets in several locations.

Exactly what is considered substantial market share has changed over time. The general guideline government used in the 1970s and early 1980s was that, in highly concentrated industries, the government would challenge all mergers involving the following combinations of market share:

Acquiring Firm	*Acquired Firm*
4%	4% or more
10%	2% or more
15%	1% or more

For less-concentrated industries, the guidelines used slightly different percentages. In 1982, the Department of Justice changed the guidelines and began looking at all mergers in which the Herfindahl index, after the merger, would be above 1,000. Special highly restrictive rules regarding mergers existed for industries with Herfindahl indexes above 1,800. Since then the rules have evolved and have become more flexible; for example, in 1997 the government issued new rules that allow some mergers if the companies can show that the merger will lower price, or will improve a product or service, even if the merger doesn't meet the guidelines.

Vertical mergers are combinations of two companies, one of which supplied inputs to the other's production.

Vertical Mergers A **vertical merger** is *a combination of two companies that are involved in different phases of producing a product,* one company being a buyer of products the other company supplies. For example, if a computer company merges with an electronic chip company, a vertical merger has taken place. Similarly, if a clothes manufacturer buys a retail boutique, that's a vertical merger. If either of the merged firms is able to limit access of other buyers or sellers to the market, such a merger is in violation of the Clayton Act.

Q-7 If Ben & Jerry's, a maker of ice cream, bought a dairy farm, what type of merger would it be?

A famous vertical merger case is the Du Pont/General Motors case (1961), in which Du Pont was required to sell its 23 percent share of General Motors because Du Pont was a major supplier to the automobile industry. The Supreme Court felt Du Pont's ownership share of GM was restricting competition. Similarly in the Brown Shoe/Kinney Shoe case (1962), Brown Shoe, primarily a wholesaler, was forbidden to buy Kinney Shoe, which was a chain of shoe retailers.

Web Note 15.4
Vertical Power

In most of the 1980s, the U.S. government challenged any vertical merger in which the supplying firm had a 10 percent or more market share and the buyer company purchased 6 percent or more of the market. This rule was loosened some as the 1980s progressed, but specific new guidelines were not developed. Although today few vertical mergers are challenged, in 1994, Silicon Graphics, a producer of computer workstations, was not allowed to purchase Alias Research or Wavefront Technologies, which produced three-dimensional graphics software that ran on their workstations, because Silicon Graphics controlled 90 percent of the workstation market. The FTC believed that after the purchase Silicon Graphics could potentially limit the software's compatibility on rival stations, reducing competition in the workstation market even further.

Conglomerate mergers are combinations of unrelated businesses. Five reasons why unrelated firms merge are:

1. To achieve economies of scope.
2. To get a good buy.
3. To diversify.
4. To ward off a takeover bid.
5. To strengthen their political-economic influence.

Conglomerate Mergers A third type of merger is a conglomerate merger. **Conglomerate mergers** involve *the merging of relatively unrelated businesses.* Conglomerate mergers are generally approved by the U.S. antitrust laws under the assumption that they do not significantly restrict competition. Thus, when Tyco acquired nine firms in 2001 in the health care, finance, personal care, and security industries, no antitrust action was taken to prevent the mergers because the firms were unrelated.

Why would unrelated firms want to merge? Or why would one firm want to be bought out by another? There are five general reasons:

1. *To achieve economies of scope.* Although the businesses are unrelated, some overlap is almost inevitable, so economies of scope are likely. For example, one firm's technical or marketing expertise may be helpful to the other firm, or the conglomerate's increased size may give it better bargaining power with its suppliers.

2. *To get a good buy*. Firms are always on the lookout for good buys. If a firm believes that another firm's stock is significantly undervalued, it can buy that stock at its low price and then sell it at a profit later when the stock is no longer undervalued.
3. *To diversify*. Many industries have a cyclical nature. In some parts of the business cycle they do poorly; in other parts of the business cycle they do just fine. Buying an unrelated company allows a firm to diversify and thereby to even out the cyclical fluctuation in its profits.
4. *To ward off a takeover bid*. Firms are always susceptible to being bought out by someone else. Sometimes they prevent an unwanted buyout by merging with another firm in order to become so large that they're indigestible. For example, in 1989 Time, Inc., merged with Warner Communications to reduce the likelihood that Time would be taken over by a third firm, Paramount. (Since then Time Warner has merged with America Online for other reasons.)
5. *To strengthen their political-economic influence*. The bigger you are, the more influence you have. Individuals who run companies like to have and use influence. Merging can increase their net influence considerably.

Q-8 When the long-distance phone company AT&T merged with the cellular phone company McCaw to create AT&T Wireless Services, what type of merger was it?

Recent Merger Activity and Deacquisitions

Figure 15-1 presents the number of mergers in the United States each year since 1892. As you can see mergers rose significantly in the late 1990s and into the early 2000s. The primary reasons for the increase in the number of mergers are globalization, deregulation, and technological change. Globalization leads to mergers because firms can gain instant foreign distribution networks and knowledge of local markets from mergers. They can also lower costs by restructuring production to low-cost areas. Deregulation of the telecommunications, electricity, and financial industries has encouraged mergers that take advantage of economies of scale and scope. Bank mergers and phone company mergers are examples.

The acceleration of technological change in recent years is another contributor to merger activity. Firms are looking for ways to develop new technologies or take advantage of new technologies, and merging with another company is one way to acquire a

Figure 15-1 Mergers in the United States since 1892
The number of mergers in the United States has fluctuated substantially in the last 100 years. Source of data changed in 1962, accounting for the break in the series.

Source: Federal Trade Commission, national press, Mergerstat.com, and author extrapolations.

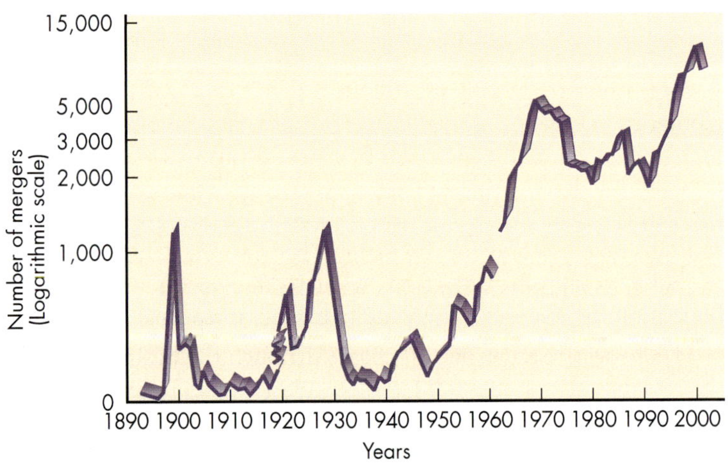

new technology. The merger of America Online and Time Warner is an example of an Internet (technology) company combining with a "content" company.

At the same time that these mergers are taking place, firms are also engaging in **deacquisitions**—*one company's sale of parts of either another company it has bought, or parts of itself.* Sometimes regulators require such deacquisitions as a condition of a merger. Deacquisition also occurs as firms focus on those areas where they have comparative advantage and where growth is highest, and sell off aspects of their firms that are not part of their core business. Automobile firms are breaking off their component manufacturing operations. In the late 1990s Hewlett-Packard voluntarily split into two companies—Hewlett-Packard, which focuses on computers, and Agilent, which focuses on noncomputer aspects of the business. Then, in 2002 H-P combined with Compaq. The motto of the 2000s is that firms have to continually reinvent themselves.

As I mentioned at the beginning of this section, voluntarily breaking up companies is becoming much more prominent as firms try to find their niche in the global marketplace. Companies are continually spinning off portions of their business where they do not believe they have a comparative advantage, and buying businesses where they think they do have a comparative advantage. This process is likely to continue, making the U.S. market structure a continually changing landscape.

The U.S. market structure is a continually changing landscape.

Assessment of Mergers and Acquisitions

I've introduced a lot of terms in this section and, ideally, started you thinking about the issues involved in deciding on a merger and acquisition policy. This chapter does not arrive at definite conclusions, and in this it reflects the economics profession, which has no one position on what policy the United States should follow toward mergers.

But the economics profession's failure to come to an undivided view on mergers isn't necessarily a failing of economists. Mergers have both costs and benefits, and reasonable people will assess them differently.

International Competition and Antitrust Policy in Other Countries

As I discussed in Chapter 14, the nature of competition is changing in the United States. Ten or twenty years ago, when people talked about competition, they meant competition among U.S. firms. Now, however, they often mean international competition.

Because of this internationalization of competition, the political climate in the United States is changing. More and more, U.S. antitrust policymakers see the international market as the relevant market. The policy focus of government is shifting from "Is U.S. industry internally competitive so that it does not take advantage of the consumer?" to "Is U.S. industry internationally competitive so that it can compete effectively in the world economy?"

Other countries' approaches toward antitrust are a likely harbinger of future U.S. antitrust policy. The reason is that other countries, because most are smaller than the United States, have consistently seen the international market as the relevant market and have designed their antitrust laws accordingly. Their domestic markets were simply too small to take advantage of economies of scale.

Q-9 Does Japan have stricter or less strict antitrust laws than the United States has?

What's interesting about other countries' antitrust laws is how lax they are when compared to U.S. laws. No other country forces companies to break up for antitrust violations, although some push for price rollbacks in cases of extreme monopolization. Even when, for example, the United States tried to export its stringent antitrust laws during its military occupation of Germany and Japan after World War II, those laws were repealed by those nations soon after the occupation ended.

Antitrust Agencies in Some Other Countries

Applying the Tools

***Britain:* British Monopoly Commission**

While it has the power to recommend structural reorganization, the British Monopoly Commission generally has not done so. Instead, it has pushed for price reductions in certain industries. After World War II, a number of major industries were nationalized, putting the government in direct control of prices, but many of these industries have been privatized in the past few years.

***Japan:* Fair Trade Commission**

The Japanese Fair Trade Commission is weak and subordinated to the Ministry of International Trade and Industry and other government agencies. In retailing, small firms continue to dominate with the support of government. But the 1980s saw the beginnings of a retailing system with large stores, like the system in the United States. The Fair Trade Commission may take a role in suppressing that development.

***Germany:* Federal Cartel Office**

The Federal Cartel Office is relatively small. Often it allows and even encourages cartels. It does have the authority to push for price reductions if it determines that the cartel has abused its power.

***France:* Commission on Competition**

The Commission on Competition has been very weak and has often advocated mergers. In the 1960s, France actively promoted large-scale mergers, and during that period the government nationalized large industries without hearing objections from the Commission on Competition.

***European Union:* The European Commission**

Starting in 1990, the EU's rules regarding mergers officially took precedence over member nations' local rules in those cases in which the merger involved significant activities in more than one member state. There were many such mergers; as expected, the expansion of the market that was made possible by the integration of the EU economies in 1992 generated significant merger activity as firms consolidated and tried to take advantage of new trading possibilities.

It wasn't only EU member firms that were merging. The largest percentage of growth in EU merger activity has been between EU firms and non-EU, especially U.S., firms. At times this has resulted in conflict between the European Commission (EC) and other countries' antitrust agencies. For instance, the EC had serious concerns regarding the 1997 merger between Boeing and McDonnell Douglas, but backed down after the United States pressured them to allow the merger. This case was unusual; for the most part the EC has been very lenient in allowing mergers and, from 1991 to 1998, the EC disallowed only 10 mergers. In the early 2000s, it has started to be less lenient to non-European firms.

In 2002, the EC started to actively promote mergers when the European Court ruled in favor of the EC's fight against "golden shares"—shares held by government with special voting rights. Specifically, these golden shares allowed governments that held these golden shares to block any mergers they wanted to. The courts ruled that mergers could be disallowed only for reasons of national security.

Other countries oppose antitrust laws because of economies of scale, lack of strong ideology supporting competition, and strong cultural ties between government and business.

One important reason other countries oppose antitrust regulation is that they recognize the importance of economies of scale. In many countries that have only small markets, the minimum efficient production level requires high concentration.

A second reason is their history. Most countries don't have the same populist worldview that exists in the United States. The ideological and cultural underpinning of strong antitrust laws (individualistic competition based on small producers) fits in nicely with the American populist worldview. In the United States, many people believe that bigness is bad. That belief is not as prevalent in other countries.

A third reason that other countries don't have strong antitrust laws is cultural. In the United States, government and business are often seen as enemies of each other. In cultures such as Japan's or Germany's, government and business are seen as allies, working together to increase exports and compete internationally.

Accounting, Fraud, and Government Regulation

Applying the Tools

In the early 2000s, serious accounting irregularities came to light in firms such as Enron and WorldCom. These firms, and many others, had used various accounting procedures—some legal, some not—to make their profits appear higher than they actually were. When the irregularities were revealed, these companies' stock values fell precipitously. In the case of Enron and WorldCom, the decline took the companies into bankruptcy.

Why would firms lie about profits? An important reason is that higher profits lead to higher stock prices—and top managers' pay (which includes stock options) depends on the price of the stock. *Options* are rights to buy a stock at a set price regardless of what happens to the price of the stock. If the stock price rises above the option price, those who exercise their options pocket the difference. Enough options and a high enough price can amount to tens or hundreds of millions of dollars. The high reported profits drive share prices high and, assuming the managers sell the stock before the accounting irregularity is discovered, they make a fortune even as the company is left in ruins.

In response to stories like these, the U.S. government increased regulation of company accounting rules, created a new board to oversee those rules, and required CEOs to sign off on the accuracy of the accounting figures provided to investors.

Will the new laws help? Perhaps somewhat, but problems remain. For example, despite most economists' suggestion that firms report stock options on the books as a cost, which would lessen the incentive of companies to give stock options to managers, the new government regulation does not require that. So there will remain an incentive on the part of managers to overstate profits and run. However, the New York Stock Exchange, a private company that oversees trading of many stocks, now requires including stock options as costs for companies listed on the exchange, so we will likely see this change taking place at many large companies.

Despite the fact that the antitrust laws are generally weaker abroad than in the United States sometimes they disallow mergers allowed in the United States and present another hurdle for global companies. For example, in the early 2000s General Electric attempted to merge with Honeywell. The merger was approved by U.S. authorities, and since both were U.S.-based companies, it seemed like the merger would go through. The European Commission, however, blocked the merger because the combined revenues were more than $4.2 billion, more than $212 million of which was from Europe, which meant they fell under EU as well as U.S. jurisdiction.

Regulation, Government Ownership, and Industrial Policies

Antitrust policy is not the only way in which governments affect the competitive process. Other ways include (1) regulating the activities of firms, (2) government ownership—taking charge of the firms and operating them directly, and (3) industrial policy—influencing firms with laws and taxes. While I consider these issues in other parts of the book, here I want to briefly discuss some of the central elements of these three means of affecting the competitive process.

The government can also affect the competitive process by (1) regulation, (2) government ownership, and (3) industrial policy.

Regulation

Regulation involves the setting of the rules that firms must follow if they are to conduct business. There are two types of regulation—price regulation and social regulation. *Price regulation* is regulation directed at industries that have natural monopoly elements. In order to allow them to take advantage of the economies of scale, firms are given an

Two types of regulation are price regulation and social regulation.

exclusive right to conduct business, but are subject to pricing controls. Examples include the Federal Energy Regulatory Commission (FERC), which regulates gas and oil pipelines and other energy-related areas; the Federal Communications Commission (FCC), which regulates cable television, telephones, television, and other communications areas; and the Securities and Exchange Commission (SEC), which regulates financial markets. *Social regulation* is concerned with the conditions under which goods and services are produced, the safety of those goods, and the side effects of production on society. Examples of social regulatory bodies include the Food and Drug Administration (FDA), the Environmental Protection Agency (EPA), and the Equal Employment Opportunity Commission (EEOC).

Price Regulation Price regulation is usually imposed in those industries where there seems to be a natural monopoly, as discussed in Chapter 12. In such cases, a single producer is most efficient because two firms could not take advantage of the economies of scale. But if the firm is to have the monopoly, it will be able to charge high prices to consumers and transfer the consumer surplus into its profit. Thus, when government grants such monopolies, it must also regulate the price they charge. Usually this has taken the form of requiring the firm to charge its average total cost plus a profit margin.

Price regulated firms often do not have an incentive to hold down costs.

That sounds reasonable in theory, but the practice has problems. The first is that the regulated firm does not have an incentive to hold down costs. Cost increases lead directly to price increases. X-inefficiency will exist. Regulatory boards have tried to counteract that tendency of rising costs by permitting firms to pass on only "legitimate" costs, but generally the people on the regulatory boards do not have the accounting expertise to review costs and determine whether they are legitimate or not, especially when the companies have a strong incentive to make all costs look legitimate.

The problem is worsened by the fact that the boards are often made up of individuals from the industry that is being regulated. This gives the commission necessary expertise, but it also creates a potentially unhealthy connection between the regulatory commission and the firms being regulated. Some economists have argued that the connection is so close that the regulatory board simply reflects the regulated firms' interests, and that it protects them from competition arising from technological change.

Another problem raised by critics is that, once established, regulation may tend to extend far beyond natural monopolies and be introduced into industries where competition could work. Still another problem is that regulation continues even after technological change has created competitive market conditions. For example, the trucking and airline industries remained regulated industries for years after they became industries with significant competition. Often the regulatory boards simply function as a way of allowing an industry to operate as a legal cartel, holding prices up rather than keeping them down.

Problems with price regulation have led to deregulation in recent years.

The above criticisms have led to significant deregulation over the last 20 years. Trucking, airlines, and aspects of phone service have all been deregulated, and electric power generation is currently being deregulated, as discussed in Chapter 14. In general, most economists' assessments of the results of this deregulation have been positive and some economists have estimated that deregulation saves consumers approximately $50 billion annually.

Social Regulation[3] Whereas most economists are skeptical of pricing regulation, they are far more divided on social regulation. Social regulation differs from pricing regulation in that:

---

[3]Social regulation is discussed more fully in Chapter 20.

1. Social regulation applies to most firms and is not designed specifically for a natural monopoly. For example, when the Occupational Safety and Health Administration (OSHA) issues a requirement that all workers have a periodic break from work, it applies to all firms in the United States that fall under OSHA's control.
2. Social regulation affects large aspects of business: working conditions, the quality of the products, and the production processes firms are allowed to use.

Whereas pricing regulation has declined in the last 20 years, social regulation has increased substantially. Economists debate whether this is good or bad. Critics of social regulation point out that regulation has high administrative and compliance costs and that those costs hurt consumers more than the regulation benefits them. They believe that this occurs because the social regulation laws are too often poorly written and ambiguous, and put into law without information on what is reasonable and feasible. The result is higher prices, far less technical progress than there otherwise would have been, and fewer new entrants into a field as the regulatory burdens become unbearable for small firms.

Advocates of social regulation agree with some of the above but argue that the benefits of social regulation are worth the costs, and that the objections are simply a call for better regulation. They argue that social regulation has made manufacturing much safer in the United States, has improved the quality of life and the environment enormously, introduced far more justice into the economy, and reduced discrimination against minorities.

Judging between these two views is difficult because measurement of both the costs and benefits is difficult or impossible. In such cases, the economic cost/benefit framework cannot provide a definitive answer.

Government Ownership

Instead of regulation, an alternative way of dealing with the problems of natural monopolies is for the government to own the firms itself. European countries have used this approach much more often than has the United States. Instead of regulating the telephone (or other natural monopoly) industry, governments took it over and ran it with state employees. Since the 1980s most countries have been selling off government-owned businesses to private owners. Why? Most governments have found that government-owned firms did not have an incentive to hold costs down or to introduce new technology. Workers in government-owned firms, who were guaranteed jobs, used political threats to hold their wages high. Since the government firms faced little competition, they could raise prices and pass on the higher costs to consumers. The result was that European prices for telephone service, airline travel, and electricity were much higher than in the United States. Economic integration in Europe has been accompanied by privatization of many of the formerly government-owned industries, and a fall in prices in many of these industries.

Government-owned firms tend not to have an incentive to hold costs down.

Q-10 Why have European countries recently privatized many government-owned firms in the telecommunications, electricity, and airline industries?

Industrial Policies

In the 1980s and 1990s, a rallying cry for many politicians was that the U.S. economy needed an industrial policy. An **industrial policy** is *a formal policy that government takes toward business*. These politicians wanted the United States to follow a policy like Japan's, where a branch of government—the Ministry of International Trade and Industry (MITI)—played an active role in guiding business decisions. Economists generally opposed such a policy, and when the Japanese economy faltered in the 1990s, the calls went away.

An industrial policy is a formal policy that government takes toward business.

Web Note 15.5
Military-Industrial Policy

In thinking about government's relation with business, it is important to remember that, in actual fact, the United States has always had, and always will have, a type of industrial policy. That policy is embodied in its tax code, its laws, and its regulatory structure, and in the positions the government takes in international negotiations about tariffs and trade. An example is the U.S. government's strong support of international copyrights and patents, which prevent foreign firms from making "knockoffs" without paying a royalty to the U.S. firm. The policy is, however, an implicit policy of working with business, not an explicit policy of directing business.

Many close connections between government and business have developed. For example, the military works closely with its suppliers, and the relationship between them has been called a *military-industrial complex.* This combination of business and government plays important roles in making decisions about what is produced. For example, when Congress seemed about to cut production of the B-2 Stealth bomber, Northrup, the plane's manufacturer, took out full-page newspaper ads, pointing out that parts of the B-2 were produced in 48 states and that thousands of jobs would be lost if the government canceled the contract. Congress gave in, as it has done on many other defense items that are widely regarded as nonessential to national security. Many other business–government alliances exist in the United States, and there are similar government-drug complexes, government–higher-education complexes and government–high-tech complexes. In a democracy where politicians are dependent on business for funding their campaigns, such complexes are inevitable.

Conclusion

We've come to the end of our discussion of market structure and government policy toward the competitive process. What conclusion should we come to? That's a tough question because the problem has so many dimensions. What we can say is that market structure is important, and generally more competition is preferred to less competition. We can also say that, based on experience, government-created and protected monopolies have not been the optimal solution, especially when industries are experiencing technological change. But how government should deal with monopolies that develop as part of the competitive process is less clear. Competition has both dynamic elements and market structure elements, and often monopolies that develop as part of the competitive process are temporary—and they will be overwhelmed by other monopolies. Thus the debate about government entering into the market to protect competition has no single answer, which makes cases like the Microsoft antitrust case difficult to resolve.

Summary

- Antitrust policy is the government's policy toward the competitive process.
- Judgment by performance means judging the competitiveness of markets by the behavior of firms in that market. Judgment by structure means judging the competitiveness of markets by how many firms operate in the industry and their market shares.
- There is a debate on whether markets should be judged on the basis of structure or on the basis of performance.
- Important antitrust laws include the Sherman Antitrust Act, the Clayton Act, and the Federal Trade Commission Act.

- The antitrust suit against IBM filed in 1967 was withdrawn in 1982 because the computer market had changed, making the charges against IBM moot.
- The antitrust suit against AT&T ended in a settlement that required AT&T to be broken up. AT&T has both divided itself and merged with other companies.
- In 2000 the courts found that Microsoft had a monopoly that was protected by barriers to entry and that Microsoft engaged in practices to maintain that monopoly power. Microsoft agreed to stop some practices.
- Three types of mergers are horizontal, vertical, and conglomerate.
- A horizontal merger is the combination of two companies in the same industry, a vertical merger is the combination of two companies in different industries, and a conglomerate merger is the combination of two companies in relatively unrelated industries.
- Five reasons that two unrelated firms would want to merge are economies of scope, a good buy, diversification, warding off a takeover bid, and strengthening political-economic influence.
- The increasing internationalization of the U.S. market has changed U.S. antitrust policy from looking at just domestic competition to considering international competition.
- Antitrust laws in other countries are generally more lenient than in the United Sates.
- Three ways other than antitrust policy that government affects the competitive process are regulation, government ownership, and industrial policy.

Key Terms

acquisition *(342)*
antitrust policy *(328)*
Clayton Antitrust Act *(331)*
conglomerate merger *(343)*
deacquisition *(345)*
Federal Trade Commission Act *(331)*
horizontal merger *(342)*
hostile takeover *(342)*
industrial policy *(349)*
judgment by performance *(329)*
judgment by structure *(329)*
merger *(342)*
natural monopoly *(336)*
Sherman Antitrust Act *(329)*
takeover *(342)*
vertical merger *(343)*

Questions for Thought and Review

1. What is the difference between judgment by performance and judgment by structure?
2. Distinguish the basis of judgment for the Standard Oil and the ALCOA cases.
3. How would the U.S. economy likely differ today if Standard Oil had not been broken up?
4. How did the Clayton Antitrust Act clarify the Sherman Antitrust Act?
5. Colleges require that students take certain courses at that college in order to get a degree. Is that an example of a tie-in contract that limits consumers' choices? If so, should it be against the law?
6. Colleges give financial aid to certain students. Is this price discrimination? If so, should it be against the law?
7. Should interlocking directorships be against the law? Why or why not?
8. If you were an economist for a firm that wanted to merge, would you argue that the three-digit or five-digit NAICS industry is the relevant market? Why?
9. If you were an economist for Mattel, manufacturer of the doll Barbie, which was making an unsolicited bid to take over Hasbro, manufacturer of G.I. Joe, would you argue that the relevant market is dolls, preschool toys, or all toys including video games? Why? Would your answer change if you were working for Hasbro?
10. Has telephone service improved since AT&T was broken up? What does this imply about antitrust laws?
11. How did the antitrust suit against IBM affect IBM's future business?
12. In what market did Microsoft have a monopoly in the late 1990s? What technological advances threatened that monopoly?
13. Under the 1997 Department of Justice guidelines, would a merger be allowed between the number three firm in an industry and a firm with 2 percent of the market? The number four firm in the industry has 11 percent of the market.
14. Should the United States have a policy against conglomerate mergers? Why or why not?

15. How has the globalization of the U.S. economy changed U.S. antitrust policy?
16. What two methods does government have for dealing with natural monopolies? What problems are associated with each?
17. How would you design an industrial policy to avoid the problems inherent in industrial policies?

PROBLEMS AND EXERCISES

1. You're working at the Department of Justice. Ms. Ecofame has just brought in a new index, the Ecofame index, which she argues is preferable to the Herfindahl index. The Ecofame index is calculated by cubing the market share of the top 10 firms in the industry.
   a. Calculate an Ecofame guideline that would correspond to the 1997 Department of Justice guidelines.
   b. State the advantages and disadvantages of the Ecofame index as compared to the Herfindahl index.
2. Using a monopolistic competition model, a cartel model of oligopoly, and a contestable market of oligopoly, discuss and demonstrate graphically, where possible, the effect of antitrust policy.
3. In 1993 Mattel proposed acquiring Fisher-Price for $1.2 billion. In the toy industry, Mattel is a major player with 11 percent of the market. Fisher-Price has 4 percent. The other two large firms are Tyco, with a 5 percent share, and Hasbro, with a 15 percent share. In the infant/preschool toy market, Mattel has an 8 percent share and Fisher-Price has a 27 percent share, the largest. The other two large firms are Hasbro, with a 25 percent share, and Rubbermaid, with a 12 percent share.
   a. What are the approximate Herfindahl and four-firm concentration ratios for these firms in each industry?
   b. If you were Mattel's economist, which industry definition would you suggest using in court if you were challenged by the government?
   c. Give an argument why the merger might decrease competition.
   d. Give an argument why the merger might increase competition.
4. In 1992 American Airlines offered a 50-percent-off sale and cut fares. In 1993 Continental Airlines and Northwest Airlines sued American Airlines over this action.
   a. What was the likely basis of the suit?
   b. How does the knowledge that Continental and Northwest were in serious financial trouble play a role in the suit?
5. Demonstrate graphically how regulating the price of a monopolist can both increase quantity and decrease price.
   a. Why did the regulation have the effect it did?
   b. How relevant to the real world do you believe this result is in the "contestable markets" view of the competitive process?
   c. How relevant to the real world do you believe this result is in the "cartel" view of the competitive process?

WEB QUESTIONS

1. Go to AT&T's corporate website at www.att.com to find out recent corporate events.
   a. What companies has AT&T acquired recently?
   b. How do those acquisitions affect AT&T's business?
   c. What antitrust issues might the mergers present?
   d. Is the FCC contesting the acquisition? (Search the FCC website at www.fcc.gov to find out.)
2. The Antitrust Division of the U.S. Department of Justice maintains a summary of its antitrust activities at www.usdoj.gov/atr. Go to this site, click on "Overview" and "Brochure: Antitrust Enforcement and the Consumer" to answer the following questions.
   a. According to this brochure, how does collusion among firms harm consumers and the economy?
   b. What type of collaboration, if any, does the Department of Justice recognize as legal?
   c. What are the three ways antitrust laws are enforced?
   d. How did vitamin producers worldwide in the 1990s violate U.S. antitrust laws? Was the U.S. Department of Justice able to impose penalties on non-U.S. entities?

Answers to Margin Questions

1. The Sherman Antitrust Act contained two main sections. The first stated that every contract, combination, or conspiracy in restraint of trade was illegal. The second stated that every person who shall monopolize or attempt to monopolize shall be deemed guilty of a misdemeanor. These provisions, while sounding strong, were so broad that they were almost unenforceable, and the interpretation was left to the courts. *(329)*
2. In the Standard Oil case, the Court determined that Standard Oil controlled 90 percent of the market. It said that this monopolistic structure of the market did not necessarily violate the Sherman Antitrust Act. However, the Court also decided that Standard Oil had engaged in systematic abuse and unfair business practices, and therefore was guilty of antitrust violations and must be broken up. *(331)*
3. In the ALCOA case, the Supreme Court changed the interpretation of the law. Here it found ALCOA was not guilty of any unfair practices. It agreed that ALCOA had simply used its knowledge of the market to expand capacity before any competitors had a chance to enter, and had kept its price low to prevent other entry. Thus, on performance standards, it was not violating the law. But the Court decided the structure of the market, not the company's performance, was the appropriate standard by which to judge cases, and, therefore, ALCOA was in violation of the antitrust law. *(331)*
4. In the 1956 Du Pont case, the Supreme Court found that Du Pont was innocent of monopolizing the production of cellophane, even though it was the only producer. The Court's reasoning was that the relevant market was the entire flexible wrap industry, not just cellophane. Since Du Pont did not dominate the flexible wrap industry, it was not in violation of antitrust law. *(333)*
5. In the late 1960s, the Department of Justice filed suit against IBM for violating the antitrust laws. It alleged that IBM had a monopoly of the general-purpose electronic digital computing industry and that it had acquired its market share because of unfair business practices. The case dragged on for 13 years but never went to court. In 1982, the government withdrew its lawsuit. The antitrust case, however, had significant effects on IBM. It is likely that the experience caused IBM to shy away from the then-small personal computer market. This decision by IBM very likely was the beginning of the serious problems that IBM faced in the 1990s. *(335)*
6. In 1978, the Department of Justice sued AT&T, alleging that its potential competitors were not being allowed reasonable access to AT&T's local telephone network. The case was resolved in January 1982, when AT&T agreed to let itself be broken up. Specifically, AT&T divested itself of 22 operating companies and focused thereafter only on long-distance telephone service, manufacturing, and research and development. This settlement left AT&T free to enter into any unregulated business it desired, and in the 1990s AT&T expanded with fiber-optic networks. Ironically, these expansions placed it in direct competition with the still-regulated Baby Bells, which had inherited AT&T's monopoly rights. *(337)*
7. If Ben & Jerry's bought a dairy farm, it would be a vertical merger because Ben & Jerry's would be buying one of its suppliers. *(343)*
8. AT&T's merger with McCaw was a mixture of a horizontal merger and a conglomerate merger. It is a horizontal merger to the degree that one interprets the industry broadly as a "communications industry." It is a conglomerate merger if one interprets the industry narrowly and distinguishes the wireless communications industry from the wire communications industry. *(344)*
9. Japan has antitrust laws that are significantly less strict than those of the United States. *(345)*
10. European countries have been privatizing firms in telecommunications, electricity, and airline industries because the government-owned firms were inefficient, resulting in higher costs for consumers and less innovation. *(349)*

16 WORK AND THE LABOR MARKET

After reading this chapter, you should be able to:

- Use the theory of rational choice to explain why an increase in the marginal tax rate is likely to reduce the quantity of labor supplied.
- List four factors that influence the elasticity of market labor supply.
- Explain how the demand for labor is a derived demand.
- List four factors that influence the elasticity of market labor demand.
- Define *monopsony* and *bilateral monopoly.*
- Discuss real-world characteristics of labor markets in terms of market, political, and social forces.
- List three types of discrimination.

Work banishes those three great evils:
boredom, vice, and poverty.

—*Voltaire*

Most of us earn our living by working. We supply labor (get a job) and get paid for doing things that other people tell us they want done. Even before we get a job, work is very much a part of our lives. We spend a large portion of our school years preparing for work. Probably many of you are taking this economics course because you've been told that it will help prepare you for a job—or that it will get you more pay than you're getting in your present job. For you, this course is investment in human capital (skills embodied in workers through experience, education, and on-the-job training). If work in the marketplace isn't already familiar to you, once you get out of school it will become so (unless you're sitting on a hefty trust fund or marry somebody who is).

Your job will occupy at least a third of your waking hours. To a great extent, it will define you. When someone asks, "What do you do?" you won't answer, "I clip coupons, go out on dates, visit my children . . ." Instead you'll answer, "I work for the Blank Company" or "I'm an economist" or "I'm a teacher." Defining ourselves by our work means that work is more than the way we get income. It's a part of our social and cultural makeup. If we lose our jobs, we lose part of our identity.

There's no way I can discuss all the social, political, cultural, and economic dimensions of work and labor in one chapter, but it's important to begin by at least pointing them out in order to put my discussion of labor markets in perspective. A **labor market** is *a factor market in which individuals supply labor services for wages to other individuals and to firms that need (demand) labor services*. Because social and political pressures are particularly strong in labor markets, we can understand the nature of such markets only by considering how social and political forces interact with economic forces to determine our economic situation.

If the invisible hand were the only force operating, wages would be determined entirely by supply and demand. There's more to it than that, as you'll see, but it shouldn't be surprising to you that my discussion of the invisible hand and the labor market is organized around the concepts of supply and demand.

The Supply of Labor

The labor supply choice facing an individual (that is, the decisions of whether, how, and how much to work) can be seen as a choice between nonmarket activities and legal market activities. Nonmarket activities include sleeping, dating, studying, playing, cooking, cleaning, gardening, and black market trading. Legal market activities include taking some type of paid job or working for oneself, directly supplying products or services to consumers.

Many considerations are involved in individuals' choices of whether and how much to work and what kind of job to work at. Social background and conditioning are especially important, but the factor economists focus on is the **incentive effect** (*how much a person will change his or her hours worked in response to a change in the wage rate*). The incentive effect is determined by the value of supplying one's time to legal market activities relative to the value of supplying one's time to nonmarket activities. The normal relationship is:

Economists focus on the incentive effect when considering an individual's choice of whether and how much to work.

The higher the wage, the higher the quantity of labor supplied.

Applying rational choice theory to the supply of labor tells us that the higher the wage, the higher the quantity of labor supplied.

This relationship between the wage rate and the quantity of labor supplied is shown in Figure 16-1. The wage rate is measured on the vertical axis; the quantity of labor supplied is measured on the horizontal axis. As you can see, the supply curve's upward slope indicates that as the wage rate increases, the quantity of labor supplied increases. Why is that the normal relationship? Because work involves opportunity cost. By working one hour more, you have one hour less to devote to nonmarket activities. Alternatively, if you devote the hour to nonmarket activities, you lose one hour's worth of income from working.

Q-1 Under the usual conditions of supply, what would you expect would happen to the amount of time you study if the wage of your part-time job rises?

Say, for example, that by working you would have made $10 per hour. If you decide to work two hours less, you'll have $20 less to spend but two hours more available for other activities (including spending the smaller amount of money). When the wage rises, say to $12 per hour, an hour of leisure has a higher opportunity cost. As the cost of leisure goes up, you buy less of it, meaning that you work more.

As I noted in my general discussions of supply and demand, the incentive effects represented by the market supply curve come from individuals' either/or decisions to enter, or leave, the labor market; and from individuals' decisions to work more, or fewer, hours. Given the institutional constraints in the labor market, which require many people to work a fixed set of hours if they work at all, much of the incentive effect of higher wages influences the either/or decisions of individuals. This affects the labor force participation rate (the number of people employed or looking for work as a percentage of

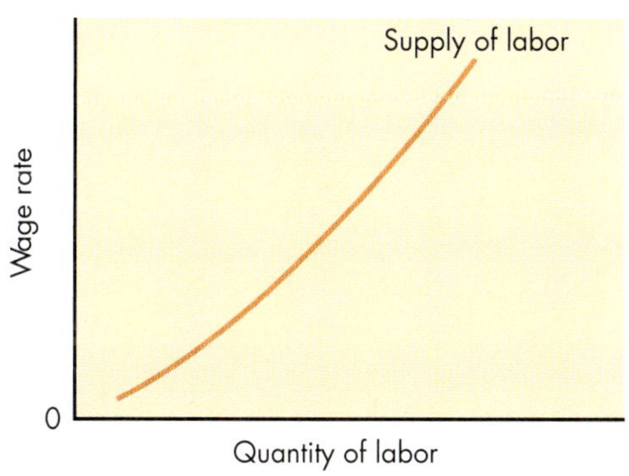

Figure 16-1 The Supply of Labor The supply of labor is generally considered to be upward-sloping because the opportunity cost of not working increases as wages get higher.

INCOME AND SUBSTITUTION EFFECTS

Knowing the Tools

Because labor income is such an important component of most people's total income, when wages change other things often do not stay equal, and at times the effect can seem strange. For example, say that you earn $10 an hour and you decide to work eight hours per day. Suddenly demand for your services goes up and you find that you can receive $40 an hour. Will you decide to work more hours? According to the rational choice rule, you will, but you might also decide that at $40 an hour you'll work only six hours a day—$240 a day is enough; the rest of the day you want leisure time to spend your money. In such a case a higher wage means working less.

Does this violate the rational choice rule? The answer is no, because other things—specifically your income—do not remain equal. The higher wage makes you decide to work more—as the rational choice rule says; but the effect of the higher wage is overwhelmed by the effect of the higher income that allows you to decide to work less.

To distinguish between these two effects, economists have given them names. The decision, based on the rational choice rule, to work more hours when your pay goes up is called the *substitution effect.* You substitute work for leisure because the price of leisure has risen. The decision to work fewer hours when your pay goes up, based on the fact that you're richer and therefore can live a better life, is called the *income effect.*

It's possible that the income effect can exceed the substitution effect, and a wage increase can cause a person to work less, but that possibility does not violate the rational choice rule, which refers to the substitution effect only. For those of you who didn't make a deal with me in Chapter 8, on individual choice, a good exercise is to show the income and substitution effects with indifference curves and to demonstrate how it might be possible for an increase in the wage to lead to a decline in hours of work.

people able to work) rather than adjusting the number of hours worked. For example, when wages rise, retired workers may find it worthwhile to go back to work, and many teenagers may choose to find part-time jobs.

REAL WAGES AND THE OPPORTUNITY COST OF WORK

The upward-sloping supply curve of labor tells you that, other things equal, as wages go up, the quantity of labor supplied goes up. But if you look at the historical record, you will see that over the last century real wages in the United States increased substantially but the average number of hours worked per person fell. This difference is partly explained by the income effect. (See the box "Income and Substitution Effects.") Higher incomes make people richer, and richer people choose more leisure.

Given that people are far richer today than they were 50 or 100 years ago, it isn't surprising that they work less. What's surprising is that they work as much as they do—eight hours a day rather than the four or so hours a day that would be enough to give people the same income they had a century ago.

The explanation of why people haven't reduced their hours of work more substantially can be found in how leisure has changed. A century ago, conversation was an art. People could use their time for long, leisurely conversations. Letter writing was a skill all educated people had, and cooking dinner was a three-hour event. If today people were satisfied with leisure consisting of long conversations, whittling, and spending quality time with their families rather than skiing, golfing, or traveling, they could get by with working perhaps only four or five hours per day instead of eight hours. But that isn't the case.

Modern gadgets increase the efficiency of leisure but cost money, which means people must work more to enjoy their leisure.

Today leisurely dinners, conversations about good books, and witty letters have been replaced by "efficient" leisure: a fast-food supper, a home video, and the instant analysis of current events. Microwave ovens, frozen dinners, Pop-Tarts, cellular telephones, the Internet—the list of gadgets and products designed to save time is endless. All these gadgets that increase the "efficiency" of leisure (increase the marginal utility per hour of leisure spent) cost money, which means people today must work more to enjoy their leisure! In the United States, one reason people work hard is so that they can play hard (and expensively).

The fast pace of modern society has led a number of people to question whether we, as a society, are better off working hard to play hard. Are we better off or simply more harried? Most economists don't try to answer this normative question; but they do point out that people are choosing their harried lifestyle, so to argue that people are worse off, one must argue that people are choosing something they don't really want. That may be true, but it's a tough argument to prove.

Economists do not try to answer the normative question of whether people are better off today, working hard to play hard, or simply are more harried.

The Supply of Labor and Nonmarket Activities

In addition to leisure, labor supply issues and market incentives play an important role in other nonmarket activities. For example, there's a whole set of illegal activities, such as selling illegal drugs, that are alternatives to taking a legal job.

Web Note 16.1
Who Works?

Let's say that an 18-year-old street kid figures he has only two options: Either he can work at a minimum wage job or he can deal drugs illegally. Dealing drugs involves enormous risks of getting arrested or shot, but it also means earning $50 or $75 an hour. Given that choice, many risk takers opt to sell drugs. When an emergency room doctor asked a shooting victim in New York City why he got involved in selling drugs, he responded, "I'm not going to work for chump change. I make $3,000 a week, tax-free. What do they pay you, sucker?" The doctor had to admit that even he wasn't making that kind of money.

For middle-class individuals who have prospects for good jobs, the cost of being arrested can be high—an arrest can destroy their future prospects. For poor street kids with little chance of getting a good job, an arrest makes little difference to their future. For them the choice is heavily weighted toward selling drugs. This is especially true for the entrepreneurial types—the risk takers—the movers and shakers who might have become the business leaders of the future. I've asked myself what decision I would have made had I been in their position. And I suspect I know the answer.

Prohibiting certain drugs leads to potentially high income from selling those drugs and has significant labor market effects. The incentive effects that prohibition has on the choices of jobs facing poor teenagers is a central reason why some economists support the legalization of currently illegal drugs.

Income Taxation, Work, and Leisure

Q-2 Why do income taxes reduce your incentive to work?

It is after-tax income, not before-tax income, that determines how much you work. Why? Because after-tax income is what you give up by not working. The government, not you, forgoes what you would have paid in taxes if you had worked. This means that when the government raises your marginal rate (the tax you pay on an additional dollar), it reduces your incentive to work. When the marginal tax rate gets really high—say 60 or 70 percent—it can significantly reduce individuals' incentive to work and earn income.

One main reason why the U.S. government reduced marginal income tax rates in the 1980s was to reduce the negative incentive effects of high taxes. Whereas in the 1950s and 1960s the highest U.S. marginal income tax rate was 70 percent, today the highest marginal income tax rate is about 40 percent. European countries, which have significantly higher marginal tax rates than the United States, are currently struggling with the problem of providing incentives for people to work.

European countries, which have relatively high marginal tax rates, are struggling with the problem of providing incentives for people to work.

Reducing the marginal tax rate in the United States hasn't completely eliminated the problem of negative incentive effects on individuals' work effort. The reason is that the amounts people receive from many other government programs are tied to earned income. When your earned income goes up, your benefits from these other programs go down.

Say, for example, that you're getting welfare and you're deciding whether to take a $6-an-hour job. Income taxes and Social Security taxes reduce the amount you take home from the job by 20 percent, to $4.80 an hour. But you also know that the Welfare Department will reduce your welfare benefits by 50 cents for every dollar you take home. This means that you lose another $2.40 per hour, so the marginal tax rate on your $6-an-hour job isn't 20 percent; it's 60 percent. By working an hour, you've increased your net income by only $2.40. When you consider the transportation cost of getting to and from work, the expense of getting new clothes to wear to work, the cost of child care, and other job-associated expenses, the net gain in income is often minimal. Your implicit marginal tax rate is almost 100 percent! At such rates, there's an enormous incentive either not to work or to work off the books (get paid in cash so you have no recorded income that the tax agent can trace).

Q.3 What is the irony of any need-based program?

The negative incentive effect can sometimes be even more indirect. For example, college scholarships are generally given on the basis of need. A family that earns more gets less in scholarship aid; the amount by which the scholarship is reduced as a family's income increases acts as a marginal tax on individuals' income. Why work hard to provide for yourself if a program will take care of you if you don't work hard? Hence, the irony in any need-based assistance program is that it reduces the people's incentive to prevent themselves from being needy. These negative incentive effects on labor supply that accompany any need-based program present a public policy dilemma for which there is no easy answer.

The Elasticity of the Supply of Labor

Exactly how these various incentives affect the amount of labor an individual supplies is determined by the elasticity of the individual's labor supply curve.

Elasticity of market supply depends on:

1. Individuals' opportunity cost of working.
2. The type of market being discussed.
3. The elasticity of individuals' supply curves.
4. Individuals entering and leaving the labor market.

The elasticity of the market supply curve is determined by the elasticity of individuals' supply curves and by individuals entering and leaving the labor force. Both of these, in turn, are determined by individuals' opportunity cost of working. If a large number of people are willing to enter the labor market when wages rise, then the market labor supply will be highly elastic even if individuals' supply curves are inelastic.

The elasticity of supply also depends on the type of market being discussed. For example, the elasticity of the labor supply facing one firm of many in a small town will likely be far greater than the elasticity of the labor supply facing all firms combined in that town. If only one firm raises its wage, it will attract workers away from other firms; if all the firms in town raise their wages, any increase in labor must come from increases in labor force participation, increases in hours worked per person, or in-migration (the movement of new workers into the town's labor market).

Existing workers prefer inelastic labor supplies because that means an increase in demand for labor will raise their wage by more. Employers prefer elastic supplies because that means an increase in demand for labor doesn't require large wage increases. These preferences can be seen in news reports about U.S. immigration laws, their effects, and their enforcement. Businesses such as hotels and restaurants often oppose strict immigration laws. Their reason is that jobs such as janitor, chambermaid, and busperson are frequently filled by new immigrants or illegal aliens who have comparatively low expectations.

Because of the importance of the elasticity of labor supply, economists have spent a great deal of time and effort estimating it. Their best estimates of labor supply elasticities to market activities are about 0.1 for heads of households and 1.1 for secondary workers in households. These elasticity figures mean that a wage increase of 10 percent will increase the quantity of labor supplied by 1 percent for heads of households (an inelastic supply) and 11 percent for secondary workers in households (an elastic supply). Why the difference? Institutional factors. Hours of work are only slightly flexible. Since most heads of households are employed, they cannot significantly change their hours worked. Many secondary workers in households are not employed, and the higher elasticity reflects new secondary workers entering the labor market.

Immigration and the International Supply of Labor

Web Note 16.2
Leaving Home

International limitations on the flow of people, and hence on the flow of labor, play an important role in elasticities of labor supply. In many industries, wages in developing countries are 1/10 or 1/20 the rate of wages in the United States. This large wage differential means that many people from those low-wage countries would like to move to the United States to earn the higher wages. Because they cannot always meet the legal immigration restrictions that limit the flow, many people come into the United States illegally. In addition to about 800,000 legal immigrants per year, more than 400,000 people per year come illegally. Illegal immigrants take a variety of jobs at lower wages and worse conditions than U.S. citizens and legal immigrants are willing to take. The result is that the actual supply of labor is more elastic than the measured supply, especially in those jobs that cannot be easily policed.

In the early 1990s, the European Union introduced open borders among member countries. That institutional change has brought about a more open flow of individuals into higher-wage EU countries from lower-wage EU countries, although other institutionalized restrictions on flows of people, such as language and culture barriers, prevented the EU from being a unified labor market through the early 2000s.

The Derived Demand for Labor

The demand for labor follows the basic law of demand:

> The higher the wage, the lower the quantity of labor demanded.

This relationship between the wage rate and the quantity of labor demanded is shown by the blue line in Figure 16-2. Its downward slope states that as the wage rate falls the quantity of labor demanded rises. The reason for this relationship differs between the demand for labor by self-employed individuals and by firms.

When individuals are self-employed (work for themselves), the demand for their labor is the demand for the product or service they supply—be it cutting hair, shampooing rugs, or filling teeth. You have an ability to do something, you offer to do it at a certain price, and you see who calls. You determine how many hours you work, what price you charge, and what jobs you take. The income you receive depends on the demand for the good or service you supply and your decision about how much labor you want to supply. In analyzing self-employed individuals, we can move directly from demand for the product to demand for labor.

When a person is not self-employed, determining the demand for labor isn't as direct. It's a two-step process: Consumers demand products from firms; firms, in turn, demand labor and other factors of production. The demand for labor by firms is a **derived demand**—*the demand for factors of production by firms, which depends on consumers' demands*. In other words, it's derived from consumers' demand for the goods that the firm sells. Thus, you can't think of demand for a factor of production such as labor separately

Derived demand is the demand for factors of production by firms, which depends on consumers' demands.

Figure 16-2 Equilibrium in the Labor Market
When the supply and demand curves for labor are placed on the same graph, the equilibrium wage, W_e, is where the quantity supplied equals quantity demanded. At this wage, Q_e laborers are supplied.

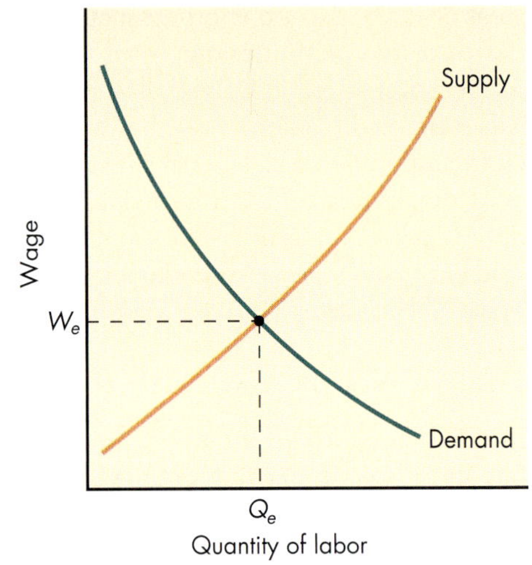

from demand for goods. Firms translate consumers' demands into a demand for factors of production.

Factors Influencing the Elasticity of Demand for Labor

Q-4 Name at least two factors that influence the elasticity of a firm's derived demand for labor.

The elasticity of the derived demand for labor, or for any other input, depends on a number of factors. One of the most important is (1) *the elasticity of demand for the firm's good*. The more elastic the final demand, the more elastic the derived demand. Other factors influencing the elasticity of derived demand include (2) *the relative importance of the factor in the production process* (the more important the factor, the less elastic is the derived demand); (3) *the possibility of, and cost of, substitution in production* (the easier substitution is, the more elastic is the derived demand); and (4) *the degree to which the marginal productivity falls with an increase in the factor* (the faster productivity falls, the less elastic is the derived demand).

Four factors that influence the elasticity of demand for labor are:

1. The elasticity of demand for the firm's good.
2. The relative importance of labor in the production process.
3. The possibility of, and cost of, substitution in production.
4. The degree to which marginal productivity falls with an increase in labor.

Each of these relationships follows from the definition of *elasticity* (the percentage change in quantity divided by the percentage change in price) and a knowledge of production. To be sure you understand, ask yourself the following question: If all I knew about two firms was that one was a perfect competitor and the other was a monopolist, which firm would I say is likely to have the more elastic derived demand for labor? If your answer wasn't automatically "the competitive firm" (because its demand curve is perfectly elastic and hence more elastic than a monopolist's), I would suggest that at this point you review the discussion of factors influencing demand elasticity in Chapter 6 and relate that to this discussion. The two discussions are similar and serve as good reviews for each other.

Labor as a Factor of Production

The traditional factors of production are land, labor, capital, and entrepreneurship. When economists talk of the labor market, they're talking about two of these factors: labor and entrepreneurship. **Entrepreneurship** is *labor services that involve high degrees of organizational skills, concern, oversight responsibility, and creativity*. It is a type of creative labor.

Entrepreneurship is labor services that involve high degrees of organizational skills, concern, oversight responsibility, and creativity.

The reason for distinguishing between labor and entrepreneurship is that an hour of work is not simply an hour of work. If high degrees of organizational skill, concern, oversight responsibility, and creativity are exerted (which is what economists mean by *entrepreneurship*), one hour of such work can be the equivalent of days, weeks, or even years of simple labor. That's one reason that pay often differs between workers doing what seems to be the same job. It's also why one of the important decisions a firm makes is what type of labor to hire. Should the firm try to hire high-wage entrepreneurial labor or low-wage nonentrepreneurial labor?

In the appendix to this chapter, I formally develop the firm's derived demand. Here in the chapter itself I will simply point out that the demand for labor follows the basic law of demand—the lower the price, the higher the quantity demanded. Figure 16-2 shows a demand-for-labor curve combined with a supply-of-labor curve. As you would expect, equilibrium is at wage W_e and quantity supplied Q_e.

Shift Factors of Demand

Factors that shift the demand curve for labor will put pressure on the equilibrium price to change. Let's consider some examples. Say the cost of a competing factor of supply, such as a machine that also could do the job, rises. That would shift the demand for this factor (labor) out, and in doing so put pressure on the wage to rise.

Alternatively, say a new technology develops that requires skills different from those currently being used—for instance, requiring knowing how to use a computer rather than knowing how to use a slide rule. The demand for individuals knowing how to use slide rules will decrease, and their wage will tend to fall.

Another example: Say an industry becomes more monopolistic. What will that do to the demand for labor in that industry? Since monopolies produce less output, the answer is that it would decrease the demand for workers, since the industry would hire fewer of them. The demand for workers would shift in and wages would tend to fall.

Finally, say the demand for the firm's good increases. Then it's clear that the firm's demand for labor will also increase. The way in which these shift factors work is developed in more detail in the appendix to this chapter.

Q.5 What would happen to the demand for labor if a firm's product became more popular?

Technology and the Demand for Labor What effect will a change in technology have on the demand for labor? This question has often been debated, and it has no unambiguous answer. What economists do know is that the simple reasoning often used by laypeople when they argue that the development of new technology will decrease the demand for labor is wrong. That simple reasoning is as follows: "Technology makes it possible to replace workers with machines, so it will decrease the demand for labor." This is sometimes called *Luddite reasoning* because it's what drove the Luddites to go around smashing machines in early-19th-century England.

What's wrong with Luddite reasoning? First, look at history. Technology has increased enormously, yet the demand for labor has not decreased; instead it has increased as output has increased. In other words, Luddite reasoning doesn't take into account the fact that total output can change. A second problem with Luddite reasoning is that labor is necessary for building and maintaining the machines, so increased demand for machines increases the demand for labor.

Web Note 16.3
Productivity Studies

Luddite reasoning isn't *all* wrong. Technology can sometimes decrease the demand for certain types of skills. The computer has decreased demand for calligraphers; the automobile reduced demand for carriage makers. New technology changes the types of labor demanded. If you have the type of labor that will be made technologically obsolete, you can be hurt by technological change. However, technological change hasn't reduced the overall demand for labor; it has instead led to an increase in total output and a need for even more laborers to produce that output.

In the 21st century we're likely to see a continued increase in the use of robots to do many repetitive tasks that blue-collar workers formerly did. Thus, demand for manufacturing labor will likely continue to decline, but it will be accompanied by an increase in demand for service industry labor—designing and repairing robots and designing activities that will fill up people's free time.

International Competitiveness and a Country's Demand for Labor Many of the issues in the demand for labor concern one firm's or industry's demand for labor relative to another firm's or industry's demand. When we're talking about the demand for labor by the country as a whole—an issue fundamentally important to many of the policy issues being discussed today—we have to consider the country's overall international competitiveness. A central determinant of a country's competitiveness is the relative wage of labor in that country compared to the relative wage of labor in other countries.

Wages vary considerably among countries. For example, in 2001 workers in the manufacturing industry earned an average $20.32 an hour in the United States, $22.86 an hour in Germany, and $2.34 an hour in Mexico. Multinational corporations are continually making decisions about where to place production facilities, and labor costs—wage rates—play an important role in these decisions. That means the country's exchange rate plays an important role in determining the demand for labor in a country. For example, in the early 1990s many Japanese automobile companies switched their production of cars to be sold in the United States from production facilities in Japan to facilities in the United States. Why? Because the rise in value of the yen, and fall in value of the dollar, meant that the hourly rate of labor in the United States was about $16 and the hourly rate in Japan was about $20.

Wages aren't the only consideration when a firm decides where to locate production. Other factors include worker productivity, transportation costs, trade restrictions, and social institutions.

But why produce in the United States when the hourly rate in Taiwan, for example, was only 1/4 that in the United States? Or in Mexico, where the hourly rate was only 1/10 that in the United States? The reasons are complicated, but include (1) differences in workers—U.S. workers may be more productive; (2) transportation costs—producing in the country to which you're selling keeps transportation costs down; (3) potential trade restrictions—Japan was under enormous pressure from the U.S. government to reduce its trade surplus with the United States, and producing in the United States helped it avoid future trade restrictions; and (4) compatibility of production techniques with social institutions—production techniques must fit with a society's social institutions. If they don't, production will fall significantly. Number (5) is the *focal point phenomenon*—a situation where a company chooses to move, or expand, production to another country because other companies have already moved or expanded there. A company can't consider all places, and it costs a lot of money to explore a country's potential as a possible host country. Japanese businesses know what to expect when they open a plant in the United States; they don't know in many other countries. So the United States and other countries that Japanese businesses have knowledge about become focal points. They are considered as potential sites for business, while other, possibly equally good, countries are not. Combined, these reasons lead to a "follow-the-leader" system in which countries fall in and out of global companies' production plans. The focal-point countries expand and develop; the others don't.

Q-6 Name two factors besides relative wages that determine the demand for labor in one country compared to another.

THE ROLE OF OTHER FORCES IN WAGE DETERMINATION

Supply and demand forces strongly influence wages, but they do not fully determine wages.

Supply and demand forces strongly influence wages, but they do not fully determine wages. Real-world labor markets are filled with examples of individuals or firms who resist these supply and demand pressures through organizations such as labor unions,

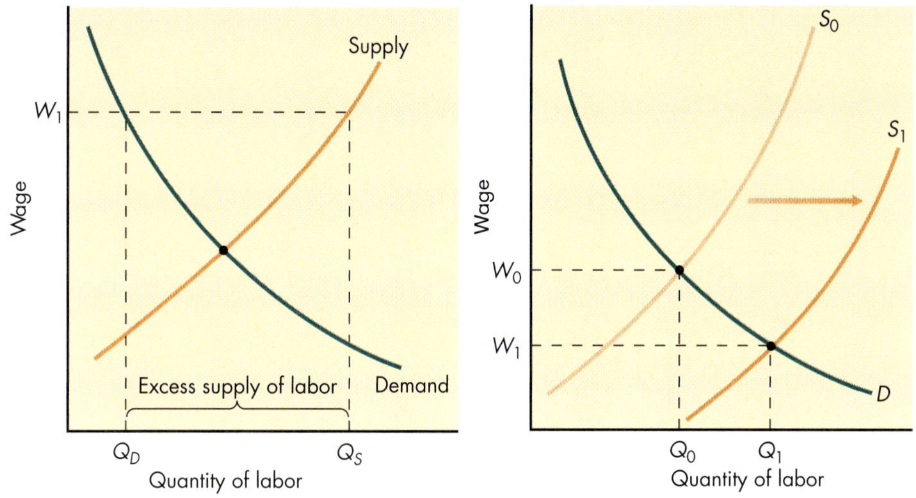

(a) Maintaining excess supply **(b) An increase in supply**

Figure 16-3 The Labor Market in Action
In (**a**) you can see the effect of an above-equilibrium wage: If workers force the firm to pay them a wage of W_1, more workers will be supplied (Q_S) than demanded (Q_D). With an excess supply of labor, jobs must be rationed. In (**b**) you can see the effect of an increase in the supply of labor. Assuming the demand for labor remains the same, the increase in the supply of labor will cause the wage level to drop from W_0 to W_1.

professional associations, and agreements among employers. But, as I've emphasized throughout the book, supply/demand analysis is a useful framework for considering such resistance.

For example, say that you're advising a firm's workers on how to raise their wages. You point out that if workers want to increase their wages, they must figure out some way either to increase the demand for their services or to limit the labor supplied to the firm. One way to limit the number of workers the firm will hire (and thus keep existing workers' wages high) is to force the firm to pay an above-equilibrium wage, as in Figure 16-3(a). Say that in their contract negotiations the workers get the firm to agree to pay a wage of W_1. At wage W_1, the quantity of labor supplied is Q_S and the quantity of labor demanded is Q_D. The difference, $Q_S - Q_D$, represents the number of people who want jobs at wage W_1 compared to the number who have them. In such a case, jobs must be rationed. Whom you know, where you come from, or the color of your skin may play a role in whether you get a job with that firm.

As a second example, consider what would happen if U.S. immigration laws were liberalized. If you say the supply curve of labor would shift outward and the wage level would drop, you're right, as shown in Figure 16-3(b). In it the supply of labor increases from S_0 to S_1. In response, the wage falls from W_0 to W_1 and the quantity of labor demanded increases from Q_0 to Q_1.

Q-7 How could an increase in the supply of labor lead to an increase in the demand for labor?

In analyzing the effect of such a major change in the labor supply, however, remember that the supply and demand framework is relevant only if the change in the supply of labor doesn't also affect the demand for labor. In reality, a liberalization of U.S. immigration laws might increase the demand for products, thereby increasing the demand for labor and raising wages. When you look at the overall effect of a change, you will often find that the final result is less clear-cut. That's why it's important always to remember the assumptions behind the model you're using. Those assumptions often add qualifications to the simple "right" answer.

Looking at the overall effects of a change, rather than just the partial equilibrium effects, often makes the final result less clear-cut.

IMPERFECT COMPETITION AND THE LABOR MARKET

Just as product markets can be imperfectly competitive, so too can labor markets. For example, there might be a **monopsony** (*a market in which a single firm is the only buyer*).

A monopsony is a market in which a single firm is the only buyer.

Alternatively, laborers might have organized together in a union that allows workers to operate as if there were only a single seller. In effect, the union could operate as a monopoly. Alternatively again, there might be a **bilateral monopoly** (*a market with only a single seller and a single buyer*). Let's briefly consider these three types of market imperfections.

Monopsony

A monopsonist takes into account the fact that hiring another worker will increase the wage rate it must pay all workers.

When there's only one buyer of labor services, it makes sense for that buyer to take into account the fact that if it hires another worker, the equilibrium wage will rise and it will have to pay more for all workers. The choice facing a monopsonist can be seen in Figure 16-4, in which the supply curve of labor is upward sloping so that the **marginal factor cost** (*the additional cost to a firm of hiring another worker*) is above the supply curve since the monopsonist takes into account the fact that hiring another worker will increase the wage rate it must pay to all workers.

Instead of hiring Q_c workers at a wage of W_c, as would happen in a competitive labor market, the monopsonist hires Q_m workers and pays them a wage of W_m. (A good exercise to see that you understand the argument is to show that where there's a monopsonist, a minimum wage simultaneously can increase employment and raise the wage.)

Union Monopoly Power

When a union exists, it will have an incentive to act as a monopolist, restricting supply to increase its members' wages. To do so it must have the power to restrict both supply and union membership. A union would have a strong tendency to act like a monopolist and to move to an equilibrium somewhat similar to the monopsonist case, except for one important difference. The wage the union would set wouldn't be set below the competitive wage; instead, the wage would be above the competitive wage at W_u, as in Figure 16-4. Faced with a wage of W_u, competitive firms will hire Q_u workers. Thus, with union monopoly power, the benefits of restricting supply accrue to the union members, not to the firm as in the monopsonist case.

Figure 16-4 Monopsony, Union Power, and the Labor Market A monopsonist hires fewer workers and pays them less than would a set of competitive firms. The monopsonist determines the quantity of labor, Q_m, to hire at the point where the marginal factor cost curve intersects the demand curve. The monopsonist pays a wage of W_m. A union has a tendency to push for a higher wage, W_u, and a lower quantity of workers, Q_u.

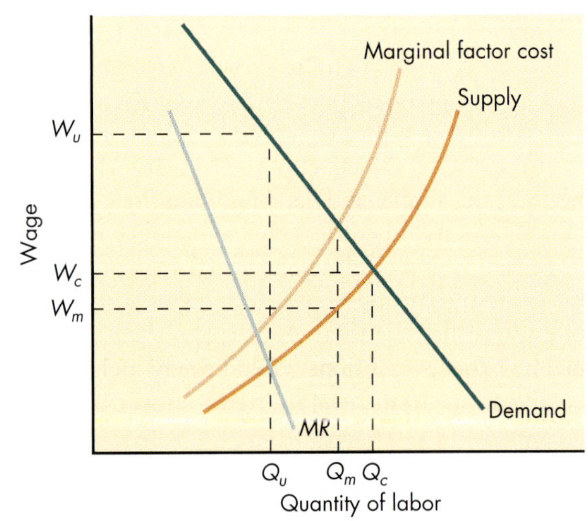

Bilateral Monopoly

As our final case, let's consider a bilateral monopoly in which a monopsonist faces a union with monopoly power. In this case, we can say that the equilibrium wage will be somewhere between the monopsonist wage W_m and the union monopoly power wage W_u. The equilibrium quantity will be somewhere between Q_u and Q_m in Figure 16-4. Where in that range the wage and equilibrium quantity will be depends on the two sides' negotiating skills and other noneconomic forces.

A bilateral monopoly is a market in which a single seller faces a single buyer.

Downsizing, Upsizing, and X-Inefficiency

From 1992 to 2003, employment rose in the United States by over 20 million jobs. At the same time there was much concern in the nation about **downsizing**—*a reduction in the workforce*—of major corporations, especially at the level of middle management. Considering these two issues—increased total employment and the downsizing at particular firms—gives us a good sense of how supply/demand analysis carries over into the real world.

Q-8 How is it that in the late 1990s and early 2000s total U.S. employment grew and companies downsized at the same time?

First let's consider the increase in employment during this time period. What were the reasons total employment grew? First, the U.S. economy grew—that growth increased demand for goods and hence for labor. Second, the value of the dollar remained low relative to the value of the currencies of other major industrial countries. Demand for U.S. exports increased, and hence the demand for U.S. labor increased. Third, union power in the United States declined, lowering overall wages (adjusted for inflation) in unionized industries, thereby increasing the quantity of labor demanded. Combined, these three forces accounted for the rise in employment.

The downsizing was, in part, a way by which union power was reduced. Firms producing with a high-wage workforce had an incentive to shift their production to firms that had low-wage workforces—that is, to low-wage firms abroad and to low-wage U.S. firms. The term developed for this is **outsourcing**—*a firm shifting production from its own plant to other firms, either in the United States or abroad, where wages are lower*. Firms' outsourcing increased the demand for low-wage labor; they *upsized* as firms with high-wage labor downsized.

Some reasons employment grew in the 1990s and early 2000s include:

1. Economic growth.
2. Low value of the dollar.
3. Declining union power.

Why didn't high-wage firms simply cut wages? To some degree they did, but cutting wages often leads to bitter fights within a firm. Downsizing keeps the angry workers out of the production process and makes the workers who are not laid off feel lucky that they have kept their jobs.

Such outsourcing was only part of the cause of downsizing. A second part was a reduction in X-inefficiency. As discussed in Chapter 14, for a variety of reasons, such as the monitoring problem, managers have a tendency to become lazy and produce inefficiently. When faced with significant international and domestic competition, as firms have been in recent years, they must reduce that inefficiency or go out of business. Thus, downsizing is a normal part of the way the competitive process works. It results from a reduction in demand for labor from inefficient firms and a transfer of demand to more efficient firms, who, it might be said, are upsizing. In this period, upsizing significantly exceeded downsizing, but it was primarily the downsizing that was reported in the press.

Downsizing is a normal part of the way the competitive process works.

Political and Social Forces and the Labor Market

Let's now consider some real-world characteristics of U.S. labor markets. For example:

Nonwage Income and Property Rights

Beyond the Tools

The four traditional categories of income are wages, rent, profits, and interest. Wages, discussed in the text, are determined by economic factors (the forces of supply and demand), with strong influences by political and social forces, which often restrict entry or hold wages at nonmarket-clearing levels. Supply and demand determine price and income, given an institutional structure that includes property rights and a contractual legal system.

The same holds true for nonwage income: rent, profits, and interest. The forces of supply and demand also determine these forms of income. But, as we have emphasized throughout the book, supply and demand are not necessarily the end of the story. Supply and demand determine price and income, given an institutional structure that includes property rights—the rights given to people to use specified property as they see fit—and the contractual legal system—the set of laws that govern economic behavior of the society. If you change property rights, you change the distribution of income. Thus, in a larger sense, supply and demand don't determine the distribution of income; the distribution of property rights does.

The system of property rights and the contractual legal system that underlie the U.S. economy evolved over many years. Many people believe that property rights were unfairly distributed to begin with; if you believe that, you'll also believe that the distribution of income and the returns to those property rights are unfair. In other words, you can favor markets but object to the underlying property rights. Many political fights about income distribution concern fights over property rights, not fights over the use of markets.

Such distributional fights have been going on for a long time. In feudal times much of the land was held communally; it belonged to everyone, or at least everyone used it. It was common land—a communally held resource. As the economy evolved into a market economy, that land was appropriated by individuals, and these individuals became landholders who could determine the use of the land and could receive rent for allowing other individuals to use that land. Supply and demand can explain how much rent will accrue to a landholder; it cannot explain the initial set of property rights.

The type of issues raised by looking at the underlying property rights are in large part academic for western societies. The property rights that exist, and the contractual legal system under which markets operate, are given. You're not going to see somebody going out and introducing a new alternative set of property rights in which the ownership of property is transferred to someone else. The government may impose shifts at the margin; for example, new zoning laws—laws that set limits on the use of one's property—will modify property rights and create fights about whether society has the right to impose such laws. But there will be no wholesale change in property rights. That's why most economic thinking simply takes property rights as given.

But taking property rights as given isn't a reasonable assumption for the developing countries or the formerly socialist countries now in the process of establishing markets. They must decide what structure of property rights they want. Who should be given what was previously government land and property? Who should own the factories? Do those societies want land to be given to individuals in perpetuity, or do they want it given to individuals for, say, 100 years? As these questions have been raised, economists have redirected their analysis to look more closely at the underlying legal and philosophical basis of supply and demand. As they do so they are extending and modifying the economic theory of income distribution.

1. English teachers are paid close to what economics teachers are paid even though the quantity of English teachers supplied significantly exceeds the quantity of English teachers demanded, while the quantity of economics teachers supplied is approximately equal to the quantity demanded.
2. On average, women earn about 85 cents for every $1 earned by men.
3. Certain types of jobs are undertaken primarily by members of a single ethnic group. For example, a large percentage of construction workers on high-rise buildings are Mohawk Indians. They have an uncanny knack for keeping their balance on high, open building frames.

4. Firms often pay higher than "market" wages.
5. Firms often don't lay off workers even when there is a decrease in the demand for their products.
6. It often seems that there are two categories of jobs: dead-end jobs and jobs with potential for career advancement. Once in a dead-end job, a person finds it almost impossible to switch to a job with potential.
7. The rate of unemployment among blacks is more than twice as high as the rate among whites.

Supply/demand analysis alone doesn't explain these phenomena. Each of them can, however, be explained as the result of market, political, and social forces. Thus, to understand real-world labor markets, it is necessary to broaden the analysis of labor markets to include other forces that limit the use of the market. These include legal and social limitations on the self-interest-seeking activities of firms and individuals. Let's consider a couple of the central issues of interaction among these forces and see how they affect the labor market.

To understand real-world labor markets, one must broaden the analysis.

Fairness and the Labor Market

People generally have an underlying view of what's fair. That view isn't always consistent among individuals, but it's often strongly held. The first lesson taught in a personnel or human resources course is that people aren't machines. They're human beings with feelings and emotions. If they feel good about a job, if they feel they're part of a team, then they will work hard; if they feel they're being taken advantage of, they can be highly disruptive.

On some assembly-line jobs, it is relatively easy to monitor effort, so individuals can be—and in the past often were—treated like machines. Their feelings and emotions were ignored. Productivity was determined by the speed of the assembly line; if workers couldn't or wouldn't keep up the pace, they were fired.

Efficiency Wages Most modern jobs, however, require workers to make decisions and to determine how best to do a task. Today's managers are aware that workers' emotional state is important to whether they make sound decisions and do a good job. So most firms, even if they don't really care about anything but profit, will try to keep their workers happy. It's in their own interest to do so. That might mean paying workers more than the going market wage, not laying them off even if layoffs would make sense economically, providing day care so the workers aren't worried about their children, or keeping wage differentials among workers small to limit internal rivalry. Such actions can often make long-run economic sense, even though they might cost the firm in the short run. They are common enough that they have acquired a name—**efficiency wages** *(wages paid above the going market wage to keep workers happy and productive)*.

Firms sometimes pay what's called efficiency wages to keep workers happy and productive.

Views of fairness also enter into wage determination through political channels. Social views of fairness influence government, which passes laws to implement those views. Minimum wage laws, comparable worth laws, and antidiscrimination laws are examples.

Comparable Worth Laws Let's consider one of those, **comparable worth laws,** which are *laws mandating comparable pay for comparable work*—that is, mandatory "fairness." The problem in implementing these laws is in defining what is comparable. Do you define comparable work by the education it requires, by the effort the worker puts out, or by other characteristics? Similarly with pay: Compensation has many dimensions

Web Note 16.4
Comparable Worth

and it is not at all clear which are the relevant ones, or whether the political system will focus on the relevant ones.

Economists who favor comparable worth laws point out that social and intrafirm political issues are often the determining factors in setting pay. In fact, firms often have their own implicit or explicit comparable worth systems built into their structure. For example, seniority, not productivity, often determines pay. Bias against women and minorities and in favor of high-level management is sometimes built into firms' pay-setting institutions. In short, within firms, pay structure is influenced by, but is not determined by, supply and demand forces. Comparable worth laws are designed to affect those institutional biases and thus are not necessarily any less compatible with supply and demand forces than are current pay-setting institutions.

The Federal government is not the only government agency that establishes labor laws. State and local government also do. For example, recently a number of local governments have established "living wage" laws, which are a type of minimum wage laws that require specified employers to pay a "living wage." "Living wage" is most often defined as that wage that would allow a worker to support a family of four at the poverty level. The analysis of these laws is similar to that of the minimum wage.

Job Discrimination and the Labor Market

Discrimination exists in all walks of life: Women are paid less than men, and blacks are often directed into lower-paying jobs. Economists have done a lot of research to understand the facts regarding discrimination and what can be done about it. The first problem is to measure the amount of discrimination and get an idea of how much discrimination is caused by what. Let's consider discrimination against women.

Q.9 Economic theory argues that discrimination should be eliminated. True or false? Why?

On average, women receive somewhere around 85 percent of the pay that men receive. That has increased from about 60 percent in the 1970s. This pay gap suggests that discrimination is occurring. The economist's job is to figure out how much of this is statistically significant and, of the portion that is caused by discrimination, what the nature of that discrimination is.

Analyzing the data, economists have found that somewhat more than half of the pay difference can be explained by causes other than discrimination, such as length of time on the job. But that still leaves a relatively large difference that can be attributed to discrimination.

Three types of discrimination are:

1. Discrimination based on individual characteristics that will affect job performance.
2. Discrimination based on correctly perceived statistical characteristics of the group.
3. Discrimination based on individual characteristics that don't affect job performance or are incorrectly perceived.

Three Types of Direct Demand-Side Discrimination In analyzing discrimination, it's important to distinguish various types. The first is discrimination based on relevant individual characteristics. Firms commonly make decisions about employees based on individual characteristics that will affect job performance. For example, restaurants might discriminate against (avoid hiring) applicants with sourpuss personalities. Another example might be a firm hiring more young salespeople because its clients like to buy from younger rather than older employees. If that characteristic can be an identifying factor for a group of individuals, the discrimination becomes more visible.

A second type of discrimination is discrimination based on group characteristics. This occurs when firms make employment decisions about individuals because they are members of a group who on average have particular characteristics that affect job performance. A firm may correctly perceive that young people in general have a lower probability of staying on a job than do older people and therefore may discriminate against younger people.

A third type of discrimination is discrimination based on irrelevant individual characteristics. This discrimination is based either on individual characteristics that do not

Democracy in the Workplace

Beyond the Tools

In the United States, slavery is illegal. You cannot sell yourself to someone else, even if you want to. It's an unenforceable contract. But work, which might be considered a form of partial slavery, is legal. You can sell your labor services for a specific, limited period of time.

Is there any inherent reason that such partial slavery should be seen as acceptable? The answer to that question is complicated. It deals with the rights of workers and is based on value judgments. You must answer it for yourself. I raise it because it's a good introduction to Karl Marx's analysis of the labor market (which deals with alienation) and to some recent arguments about democracy in the workplace.

Marx saw selling labor as immoral, just as slavery was immoral. He believed that capitalists exploited workers by alienating them from their labor. The best equivalent I can think of is the way most people today view the selling of sex. Most people see selling sex as wrong because it alienates a person from his or her own body. Marx saw all selling of labor that same way. A labor market makes workers see themselves as objects, not as human beings.

The underlying philosophical issues of Marx's concern are outside of economics. Most people in the United States don't agree with Marx's philosophical underpinnings. But it's nonetheless a useful exercise to think about this issue and ask yourself whether it helps explain why we somehow treat the labor market as different from other markets and limit by law the right of employers to discriminate in the labor market.

Some of Marx's philosophical tenets are shared by the modern democracy-in-the-workplace movement. In this view, a business isn't owned by a certain group; it is an association of individuals who have come together to produce a certain product. For one group—the owners of stock—to have all the say as to how the business is run, and for another group—the regular workers—to have no say, is immoral in the same way that not having a democratic government is immoral. According to this view, work is as large a part of people's lives as is national or local politics, and a country can call itself a democracy only if it has democracy in the workplace.

As with most grandiose ideas, this one is complicated, but it's worth considering because it's reflected in certain laws. Consider, for example, the 1989 federal law that limits firms' freedom to close plants without giving notice to their workers. The view that workers have certain inalienable rights played a role in passing that law.

For those of you who say "Right on!" to the idea of increasing workers' rights, let me add a word of caution. Increasing workers' rights has a cost. It makes it less likely that firms and individuals who can think up things that need doing will do so, and thus will decrease the number of jobs available. It will also increase firms' desire to discriminate. If you know you must let a person play a role in decisions once you hire that person, you're going to be much more careful about whom you hire.

None of these considerations mean that democracy in the workplace can't work. There are examples of somewhat democratic "firms." Universities are run as partial democracies, with the faculty deciding what policies should be set. (There is, however, serious debate about how well universities are run.) But as soon as you add worker democracy to production, more questions come up: What about consumers? Shouldn't they, too, have a voice in decisions? What about the community within which the firm is located?

Economics can't answer such questions. Economics can, however, be used to predict and analyze some of the difficulties such changes might bring about.

---

affect job performance or on incorrectly perceived statistical characteristics of groups. A firm might not hire people over 50 because the supervisor doesn't like working with older people, even though older people may be just as productive as, or even more productive than, younger people.

Of the three types, the third will be easiest to eliminate; it doesn't have an economic motivation. In fact, discrimination based on individual characteristics that don't affect job performance is costly to a firm. Competing firms will hire these people and be in a better competitive position because of it. Market forces will work toward eliminating this type of discrimination.

An example of the success of a firm's policy to reduce discrimination is the decision by McDonald's to create a special program to hire workers with learning disabilities. Individuals who are learning disabled often make good employees. They tend to have lower turnover rates and follow procedures better than do many of the more transient employees McDonald's hires. Moreover, through their advertising, McDonald's helped change some negative stereotypes about people with disabilities. So in this case market forces and political forces are working together.

Discrimination based on characteristics that affect job performance is hard to eliminate.

If the discrimination is of either of the first two types (that is, based on characteristics that do affect job performance, either directly or statistically), the discrimination will be harder to eliminate. In these cases not discriminating can be costly to the firm, so political forces to eliminate discrimination will be working against market forces to keep discrimination.

Whenever discrimination saves the firm money, the firm will have an economic incentive to use subterfuges to get around an antidiscrimination law. These subterfuges will make the firm appear to be complying with the law, even when it isn't. For example, a firm will find some other reason besides age to explain why it isn't hiring an older person.

Institutional Discrimination Institutional discrimination is discrimination in which the structure of the job makes it difficult or impossible for certain groups of individuals to succeed. Consider the policies of colleges and universities. To succeed as a professor, administrator, or other professional in the academic market, one must devote an enormous amount of effort during one's 20s and 30s. But these years are precisely the years when, given genetics and culture, many women have major family responsibilities. This makes it difficult for women to succeed in the academic market. Were academic institutions different—say, a number of positions at universities were designed for high-level, part-time work during this period—it would be easier for women to advance.

Requiring peak time commitment when women are also facing peak family responsibilities is the norm for many companies, too. Thus, women face significant institutional discrimination.

Institutions can have built-in discrimination.

Whether this discrimination is embodied in the firm's structure or in the family is an open question. For example, sociologists have found that in personal relationships women tend to move to be with their partners more than men move to be with their partners. In addition, women in two-parent relationships do much more work around the house and take a greater responsibility for child rearing than men do even when both the man and the woman are employed.

How important are these sociological observations? In discussing discrimination I ask the members of my class if they expect their personal relationships with their partners to be fully equal. The usual result is the following: 80 percent of the women expect a fully equal relationship; 20 percent expect their partner's career to come first. Eighty percent of the men expect their own careers to come first; 20 percent expect an equal relationship. I then point out that somebody's expectations aren't going to be fulfilled. Put simply, most observers believe that the institutional discrimination that occurs in interpersonal relationships is significant.

Economists have made adjustments for these sociological factors, and have found that institutional factors explain a portion of the lower pay that women receive but that other forms of workplace discrimination also explain a portion.

Whether prejudice should be allowed to affect the hiring decision is a normative question for society to settle. In answering these normative questions, our society has passed laws making it illegal for employers to discriminate on the basis of race, religion, sex, age, disability, or national origin. The reason society has made it illegal is its ethical belief in equal opportunity for all, or at least most, individuals. (Homosexuals still aren't protected by federal legislation assuring them equal opportunities.)

THE EVOLUTION OF LABOR MARKETS

Now that we've briefly considered how noneconomic forces can influence labor markets, let's turn our attention to how labor markets developed.

Labor markets as we now know them developed in the 1700s and 1800s. Given the political and social rules that operated at that time, the invisible hand was free to push wage rates down to subsistence level. Workweeks were long and working conditions were poor. Laborers began to turn to other ways—besides the market—of influencing their wage. One way was to use political power to place legal restrictions on employers in their relationship with workers. A second way was to organize together—to unionize. Let's consider each in turn.

Evolving Labor Laws Over the years, government has responded to workers' political pressure with a large number of laws that limit what can and what cannot be done in the various labor markets. For example, in many areas of production, laws limit the number of normal hours a person can work in a day to eight. The laws also prescribe the amount of extra pay an employee must receive when working more than the normal number of hours. (Generally it's time-and-a-half.) Similarly, the number and length of workers' coffee breaks are defined by law (one coffee break every four hours).

Child labor laws mandate that a person must be at least 16 years old in order to be hired. The safety and health conditions under which a person can work are regulated by laws. (For example, on a construction site all workers are required to wear hard hats.) Workers can be fired only for cause, and employers must show that they had cause to fire a worker. (For example, a 55-year-old employee cannot be fired simply because he or she is getting old.) Employers must not allow sexual harassment in the workplace. (Bosses can't make sexual advances to employees and firms must make a good-faith attempt to see that employees don't sexually harass their co-workers.)

Combined, these laws play an enormously important role in the functioning of the labor market.

Unions and Collective Bargaining Some of the most important labor laws concern workers' right to organize together in order to bargain collectively with employers. These laws also specify the tactics workers can use to achieve their ends. In the latter part of the 1800s, workers had few rights to organize themselves. The Knights of Labor was formed in 1869, and by 1886 it had approximately 800,000 members. But a labor riot in 1886 turned public opinion against these workers and led to the organization's breakup. In its place, the American Federation of Labor developed and began to organize strikes to achieve higher wages.

Web Note 16.5
Laws or Contracts?

Business opposed unions' right to strike, and initially the government supported business. Police and sometimes the army were sent in to break up strikes. Under the then-existing legal structure of the economy, unions were seen as monopolistic restraints on trade and an intrusion into management rights.

In the 1930s, society's view of unions changed (in part as a backlash to the strong-arm tactics used by firms to break up unions), and laws such as the National Labor Relations Act (also called the Wagner Act) were passed guaranteeing workers the right to form unions, to strike, and to engage in collective bargaining. As Figure 16-5 shows, from 1935 to 1980 unions grew significantly in size and importance.

Businesses weren't happy with unions' increasing strength, and in 1947 they managed to get the Taft-Hartley Act passed. That act placed limitations on union activities.

Figure 16-5 Change in Union Membership, 1895–2001

The graph shows union membership from 1895 to 2001. As can be seen, after the Depression in the 1930s, unions grew in importance. In the 1980s the importance of unions declined, even though the labor force was growing significantly.

Source: Bureau of Labor Statistics (http://stats.bls.gov).

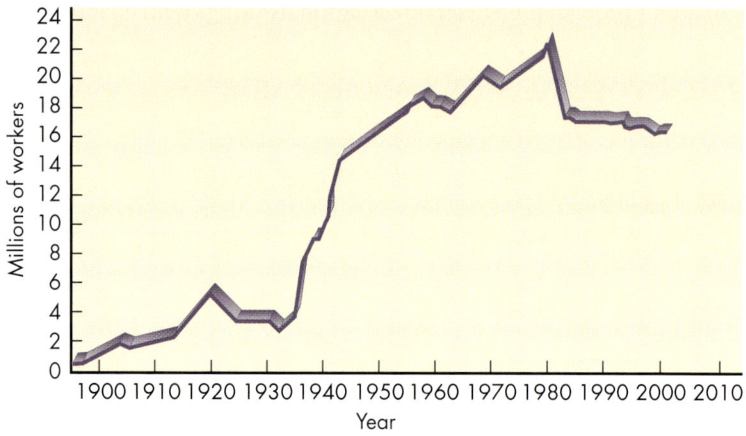

A closed shop is a firm in which the union controls hiring.

A union shop is a firm in which all workers must join the union.

It allowed states to pass "right-to-work" laws forbidding union membership to be made a requirement for continued employment. Moreover, it made **closed shops,** *firms where the union controls hiring*, illegal. Before anyone can be hired in a closed shop, he or she must be a member of the particular union. Federal law does permit **union shops**—*firms in which all workers must join the union.* Individuals are required to join a union after working for the firm for a period of time. The Taft-Hartley Act also outlawed *secondary boycotts*. In a secondary boycott, in order to strengthen its bargaining position, a union gets unions at other firms to force their firms to refuse to buy a firm's products, under threat of a strike.

Union power weakened further in 1981, when, in response to a strike by air traffic controllers, President Ronald Reagan fired all the controllers and refused to hire them back. Private firms similarly won the right to hire permanent replacements for striking workers.

Part of the reason labor union membership has declined in recent years is the unions' successes.

As Figure 16-5 shows, the number of workers in unions declined in the 1980s and has remained relatively constant since, even as the labor force has grown. Unions don't have the political or economic clout they once had. Part of the reason, ironically, is their success. By pressuring the government to pass laws that protected workers, unions made themselves less necessary. Another part of the reason is the changing nature of production in the United States. Labor unions were especially strong in manufacturing industries. As the relative number of manufacturing jobs has declined in the United States and the number of service jobs has increased, the base of union membership has been reduced. Unions have somewhat compensated for this change by pushing unionization drives among public sector workers (that is, government employees), and this sector has seen the largest increase in union membership. Today, more than 40 percent of union members work in the public sector. These unions are becoming stronger and will likely be exerting their influence.

Conclusion: The Labor Market and You

This chapter is meant to give you a sense of how the labor market works. But what does it all mean for those of you who'll soon be getting a job or are in the process of changing jobs? I'll try to answer that question in this last section.

Table 16-1 shows a variety of potentially useful statistics about the labor market. Let's consider how some of them might affect you. For example, consider relative pay of jobs requiring a college degree compared to jobs requiring only a high school diploma.

Table 16-1 Some Typical Starting Salaries

Occupation	Private or State
Budget analyst	$32,000
Management analyst	34,000
Secretary	21,000
Physician assistant	47,000
Flight attendant	28,000
Secondary school teacher	28,000
Economist	34,000
Janitor	16,000
Retail sales (salary and commission)	17,000
Insurance sales	27,000

Sources: Author's estimates based on *Occupational Outlook Handbook 02/03* and U.S. Dept. of Labor Statistics (pay varies significantly by region) (http://stats.bls.gov).

(a) Some typical starting salaries of BAs: 2002

Degree	Annual Salary*
Law (3 years)	
Large firms	$105,000
Small firms	47,000
Engineering	
Bachelor's degree	47,000
Master's degree	60,000
Business	
Bachelor's degree	36,000
Master's (MBA) degree (2 years)	60,000
M.D. (4 years and 3-year internship)	115,000
Ph.D. (5 years)	
In economics	55,000
In humanities	50,000

*These figures are rough estimates based on data from the Department of Labor and informal surveys of author.

(b) Starting salaries for selected professional degrees, 2002

Jobs requiring a college degree pay significantly more, on average, than do jobs requiring only a high school diploma. In recent years the income gap between the two groups has noticeably increased. So the answer to the question of whether it's worthwhile to stick college out for another couple of years and get a degree is probably yes.

Q.10 Ph.D.s earn less than MBAs, so therefore one should get an MBA rather than a Ph.D. True or false? Why?

Next, consider the salaries of Ph.D.s compared to the salaries of MBAs. A Ph.D. is a person who has gone to graduate school after college, usually for a number of years, and earned an advanced degree called a **D**octorate of **Ph**ilosophy—even though there are many subjects besides philosophy (such as economics) in which one can earn a Ph.D. As you can see, Ph.D.s' starting salaries are lower than salaries of MBAs (masters of business administration) and professionals with other kinds of advanced degrees. Does this mean that Ph.D.s are discriminated against? Not necessarily. It's possible that Ph.D.s' lower pay suggests that Ph.D.s derive a "psychic income" from their work in addition to the amount of money they earn.

Since Ph.D.s are often quite smart, their willingness to accept psychic income as a substitute for higher pay suggests that there's much more to consider in a job than the salary. What's most important about a job isn't the wage, but whether you like what you're doing and the life that job is consistent with. (Of course, their lower salaries also could imply that Ph.D.s really aren't so smart.)

So my suggestion to you is definitely to finish college, especially if you enjoy it. (And with books like this, how could you help but enjoy it?) But go to graduate school only if you really enjoy learning. In picking your job, first and foremost pick a job that you enjoy (as long as it pays you enough to live on). Among jobs you like, choose a job in a field in which the supply of labor is limited, or the demand for labor is significantly increasing. Either of those trends is likely to lead to higher wages. After all, if you're doing something you like, you might as well get paid as much as possible for it.

Jobs in which the supply will likely be limited are those in which social or political forces have placed restrictions on entry or those requiring special abilities. If you have some special ability, try to find a job you enjoy in which you can use that ability. You might also look for a job in which entry is restricted, but beware: Jobs that are restricted

In the late 1800s, many workers worked in sweatshops; they often had quotas that required them to work 60 or more hours a week. Fines were imposed for such indiscretions as talking or smiling.
The Bettman Archive.

in supply must be rationed, so while such jobs pay higher wages, you may need personal connections to obtain one of them.

I'm sure most of you are aware that your choice of jobs is one of the most important choices you'll be making in your life. So I'm sure you feel the pressure. But you should also know that a job, unlike marriage, isn't necessarily supposed to be for life. There's enormous flexibility in the U.S. labor market. Many people change jobs six or seven times in their lifetimes. So while the choice is important, a poor choice can be remedied; don't despair if the first job you take isn't perfect. Good luck.

Summary

- Incentive effects are important in labor supply decisions. The higher the wage, the higher the quantity supplied.
- Elasticity of market supply of labor depends on (1) individuals' opportunity cost of working, (2) the type of market being discussed, (3) the elasticity of individuals' supply curves, and (4) individuals entering and leaving the labor market.
- The demand for labor by firms is derived from the demand by consumers for goods and services. It follows the basic law of demand—the higher the wage, the lower the quantity demanded.
- Elasticity of market demand for labor depends on (1) the elasticity of demand for the firm's good, (2) the relative importance of labor in production, (3) the possibility and cost of substitution in production, and (4) the degree to which marginal productivity falls with an increase in labor.
- Technological advances and changes in international competitiveness shift the demand for labor. Both have

reduced demand for some types of labor and increased demand for other types. The net effect has been an increase in the demand for labor.

- A monopsony is a market in which a single firm is the only buyer. A monopsonist hires fewer workers at a lower wage compared to a competitive firm.
- A bilateral monopoly is a market in which there is a single seller and a single buyer. The wage and number of workers hired in a bilateral monopoly depend on the relative strength of the union and the monopsonist.
- Firms are aware of workers' well-being and will sometimes pay efficiency wages to keep workers happy and productive.
- Views of fairness in the labor market have led to laws that mandate comparable pay for comparable work.
- Discrimination may be based on (1) relevant individual characteristics, (2) group characteristics, and (3) irrelevant individual characteristics. The easiest to eliminate is discrimination based on irrelevant individual characteristics. The other two are motivated by market incentives.
- Labor laws have evolved and will continue to evolve. Since the 1980s, labor unions have been declining in importance.

KEY TERMS

bilateral monopoly *(364)*
closed shops *(372)*
comparable worth laws *(367)*
derived demand *(359)*
downsizing *(365)*
efficiency wages *(367)*
entrepreneurship *(360)*
incentive effect *(355)*
labor market *(354)*
marginal factor cost *(364)*
monopsony *(363)*
outsourcing *(365)*
union shops *(372)*

QUESTIONS FOR THOUGHT AND REVIEW

1. Why are social and political forces more active in the labor market than in most other markets?
2. "Welfare laws are bad, not for society, but for the people they are meant to help." Discuss.
3. Which would you choose: selling illegal drugs at $75 an hour (20 percent chance per year of being arrested) or a $6-an-hour factory job? Why?
4. If the wage goes up 20 percent and the quantity of labor supplied increases by 5 percent, what's the elasticity of labor supply?
5. My brother was choosing between being a carpenter and being a plumber. I advised him to take up plumbing. Why?
6. Why might it be inappropriate to discuss the effect of immigration policy using supply and demand analysis?
7. Demonstrate graphically the effect of a minimum wage law. Does economic theory tell us such a law would be a bad idea?
8. Show graphically how a minimum wage can simultaneously increase employment and raise the wage rate.
9. Comparable worth laws require employers to pay the same wage scale to workers who do comparable work or have comparable training. What likely effect would these laws have on the labor market?
10. Why is unemployment nearly twice as high among blacks as among whites? What should be done about the situation?
11. Give four reasons why women earn less than men. Which reasons do you believe are most responsible for the wage gap?

PROBLEMS AND EXERCISES

1. A study done by economists Daniel Hamermesh and Jeff Biddle found that people who are perceived as good-looking earn an average of 10 percent more than those who are perceived as homely and 5 percent more than people who are perceived as average-looking. The pay differential was found to be greater for men than for women.
   a. What conclusions can you draw from these findings?
   b. Do the findings necessarily mean that there is a "looks" discrimination?

c. What might explain the larger pay penalty for males for looks?

2. In the early 1990s a teen subminimum training wage law was passed by which employers were allowed to pay teenagers less than the minimum wage.
   a. What effect would you predict this law would have, based on standard economic theory?
   b. In analyzing the effects of the law, Professors Card and Kreuger of Princeton University found that few businesses used it and that it had little effect. Why might that have been the case?
3. Economists Mark Blaug and Ruth Towse did a study of the market for economists in Britain. They found that the quantity demanded was about 150–200 a year, and that the quantity supplied was about 300 a year.
   a. What did they predict would happen to economists' salaries?
   b. What likely happens to the excess economists?
   c. Why doesn't the price change immediately to bring the quantity supplied and the quantity demanded into equilibrium?
4. Some economists have argued against need-based scholarships because they work as an implicit tax on parents' salaries and hence discourage saving for college.
   a. If the marginal tax rate parents face is 20 percent, and 5 percent of parents' assets will be deducted from a student's financial aid each year for four years a child is in school, what is the implicit marginal tax on that portion of income that is saved? (For simplicity assume the interest rate is zero and that the parents' contribution is paid at the time the child enters college.)
   b. How would your answer differ if parents had two children with the second entering college right after the first one graduated? (How about three?) (Remember that the assets will likely decrease with each child graduating.)
   c. When parents are divorced, how should the contribution of each parent be determined? If your school has need-based scholarships, how does it determine the expected contributions of divorced parents?
   d. Given the above, would you suggest moving to an ability-based scholarship program? Why or why not?
5. Explain each of the following phenomena using the invisible hand or social or political forces:
   a. Firms often pay higher than market wages.
   b. Wages don't fluctuate much as unemployment rises.
   c. Pay among faculty in various disciplines at colleges does not vary much although market conditions among disciplines vary significantly.
6. A recent study by the International Labor Organization estimates that 250 million children in developing countries between the ages of 5 and 14 are working either full- or part-time. The estimates of the percentage of children working within countries is as high as 42 percent in Kenya. Among the reasons cited for the rise in child labor are population increases and poverty.
   a. Why do firms hire children as workers?
   b. Why do children work?
   c. What considerations should be taken into account by countries when deciding whether to implement an international ban on trade for products made with child labor?
7. Interview three married female and three married male professors at your college, asking them what percentage of work in the professor's household each adult household member does.
   a. Assuming your results can be extended to the population at large, what can you say about the existence of institutional discrimination?
   b. If gender-related salary data for individuals at your college are available, determine whether women or men of equal rank and experience receive higher average pay.
   c. Relate your findings in *a* and *b*.
   d. Does the existence of institutional discrimination suggest that no discrimination by employers exists? Why or why not?

WEB QUESTIONS

1. The National Committee on Pay Equity (NCPE) is a central clearinghouse for information on pay equity. Go to its home page at www.feminist.com/fairpay to answer the following questions.
   a. What is pay equity?
   b. What two laws protect workers against wage discrimination?
   c. Does the NCPE believe that most of the pay gap is from women earning less in the same jobs or women working in lower-paying occupations? How does this affect the enforcement of antidiscrimination laws?
2. The Cato Institute is a public policy institute that favors a laissez-faire approach to the market. One of its commentaries, "Immigration Reform Means More High-Tech Jobs," argues that immigration creates jobs in the United States. Go to Cato's home page at www.cato.org, search for the commentary using keywords immigration and reform and read it to answer the following questions:
   a. For what type of workers is the author arguing immigration should be increased?
   b. How do highly skilled immigrants create jobs for Americans?

c. What was the state of the economy when the article was written? How does this affect the results of the study?

d. Do you believe the author would argue that the number of visas for unskilled laborers should be increased as well? Why or why not?

Answers to Margin Questions

1. Under usual conditions of supply, one would expect that if the wage of my part-time job rises, the quantity of labor I supply in that part-time job also rises. Institutional constraints such as tax considerations or company rules might mean that the quantity of labor I supply doesn't change. However, under the usual conditions of supply, I will study less if the wage of my part-time job rises. *(355)*
2. Taxes reduce the opportunity cost, or relative price, of nonwork activities. So you will substitute leisure for labor as marginal tax rates increase. *(357)*
3. The irony of any need-based program is that such a program reduces people's incentive to prevent themselves from becoming needy. *(358)*
4. Some factors that influence the elasticity of a firm's derived demand for labor include (1) the elasticity of demand for the firm's good; (2) the relative importance of labor in the production process; (3) the possibility, and cost, of substitution in production; and (4) the degree to which the marginal productivity falls with an increase in labor. *(360)*
5. The demand for laborers at that firm would shift out to the right. *(361)*
6. Differences among countries in productivity, transportation costs, trade restrictions, and social institutions all determine the relative demand for labor in one country compared to another country. *(362)*
7. If the increase in labor supply leads to an increase in the demand for products in general, the increase in labor supply will also lead to an increase in labor demand. *(363)*
8. General growth in the economy, the fall in the value of the dollar, and the decline in the power of unions all led to more employment in the late 1990s and early 2000s. Nonetheless, increasing competitive pressures caused many inefficient firms to downsize. The net effect, however, was a rise in total employment. *(365)*
9. Economic theory does not argue that discrimination should be eliminated. Economic theory tries to stay positive. Discrimination is a normative issue. If one's normative views say that discrimination should be eliminated, economic theory might be useful to help do that most efficiently. *(368)*
10. There is more to life than income, so it does not necessarily follow that one should take the job that pays the highest wage. (In the author's view, a Ph.D.'s life is far more fulfilling than an MBA's life, although some MBAs may disagree with that.) Each person must decide for him- or herself how to weigh the various dimensions of a job. *(373)*

Appendix A

Derived Demand

This appendix considers the issues of derived demand in more detail. Although it focuses on the derived demand for labor, you should note that the formal analysis of the firm's derived demand for labor presented in the chapter is quite general and carries over to the derived demand for capital and for land. Firms translate consumers' demands for goods into derived demands for any and all of the factors of production. Let's start our consideration by looking at the firm's decision to hire.

The Firm's Decision to Hire

What determines a firm's decision to hire someone? The answer is simple. A profit-maximizing firm hires someone if it thinks there's money to be made by doing so. Unless there is, the firm won't hire the person. So for a firm to decide whether to hire someone, it must compare the worker's **marginal revenue product (MRP)** *(the marginal revenue it expects to earn from selling the additional worker's*

Figure A16-1 (a and b) Determining How Many Workers to Hire and the Firm's Derived Demand for Labor
The marginal revenue product is any firm's demand curve for labor. Since for a competitive firm $P = MR$, a competitive firm's derived demand curve is its value of the marginal product curve ($P \times MPP$). This curve tells us the additional revenue the firm gets from having an additional worker. From the chart in (**a**) we can see that when the firm increases from 27 to 28 workers, the marginal product per hour for each worker is 9. If the product sells for \$2, then marginal revenue product is \$18, which is one point on the demand curve for labor (point *A* in (**b**)). When the firm increases from 34 to 35 workers, the value of the marginal product decreases to \$4. This is another point on the firm's derived demand curve (point *B* in (**b**)). By connecting the two points, as I have done in (**b**), you can see that the firm's derived demand curve for labor is downward-sloping.

1 Number of Workers	2 Total Product per Hour	3 Marginal Physical Product per Hour	4 Average Product per Hour	5 Marginal Revenue Product (*MRP*)
27	270		10.00	
		9.00		\$18
28	279		9.96	
		8.00		16
29	287		9.90	
		7.00		14
30	294		9.80	
		6.00		12
31	300		9.68	
		5.00		10
32	305		9.53	
		4.00		8
33	309		9.36	
		3.00		6
34	312		9.18	
		2.00		4
35	314		8.97	

(a)

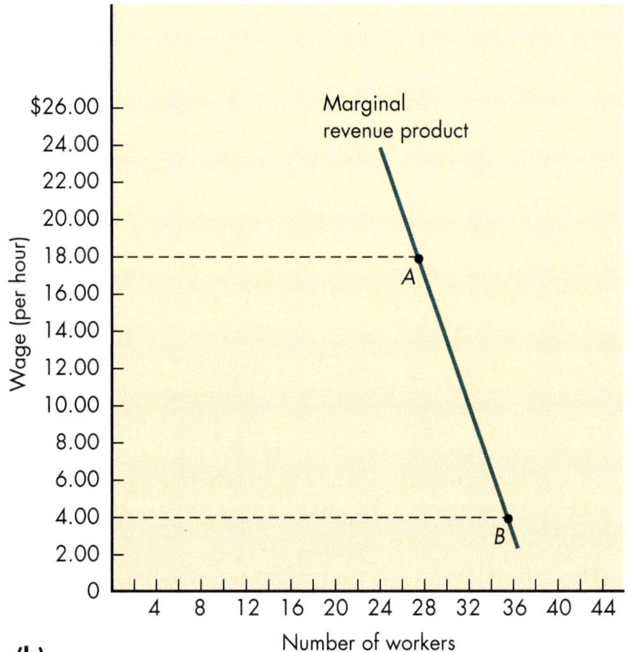

(b)

output) with the wage that it expects to pay the additional worker. For a competitive firm (for which $P = MR$), that marginal revenue product equals the worker's **value of marginal product (VMP)**—the worker's **marginal physical product (MPP)** (*the additional units of output that hiring an additional worker will bring about*) times the price (P) at which the firm can sell the additional product.

Marginal revenue product = $MPP \times P$

Say, for example, that by hiring another worker a firm can produce an additional 6 widgets an hour, which it can sell at \$2 each. That means the firm can pay up to \$12 per hour and still expect to make a profit. Notice that a key question for the firm is: How much additional product will we get from hiring another worker? A competitive firm can increase its profit by hiring another worker as long as the value of the worker's marginal product (which also equals her marginal revenue product) ($MPP \times P$) is higher than her wage.

To see whether you understand the principle, consider the example in Figure A16-1(a). Column 1 shows the number of workers, all of whom are assumed to be identical. Column 2 shows the total output of those workers. Column 3 shows the marginal physical product of an additional worker. This number is determined by looking at the change in the total product due to this person's work. For example, if the firm is currently employing 30 workers and it hires one more, the firm's total product or output will rise from 294 to 300, so the marginal product of moving from 30 to 31 workers is 6.

Notice that workers' marginal product decreases as more workers are hired. Why is this? Remember the assumption of fixed capital: More and more workers are working with the same amount of capital and there is diminishing marginal productivity.

Column 4 shows **labor productivity**—*the average output per worker*, which is a statistic commonly referred to in economic reports. It's determined by dividing the total

Difficulties in Determining Marginal Productivities

Applying the Tools

The economic model of labor markets assumes that marginal productivities can be determined relatively easily. In reality they can't. They require guesses and estimates that are often influenced by a worker's interaction with the person doing the guessing and estimating. Thus, social interaction plays a role in determining wages. If you get along with the manager, his estimate of your marginal productivity is likely to be higher than if you don't. And for some reason, managers' estimates of their own marginal productivity tend to be high. In part because of difficulties in estimating marginal productivities, actual pay can often differ substantially from marginal productivities.

output by the number of workers. Column 5 shows the additional worker's marginal revenue product, which, since the firm is assumed to be competitive, is determined by multiplying the price the firm receives for the product it sells ($2) by the worker's marginal physical product.

Column 5, the marginal revenue product, is of central importance to the firm. It tells the firm how much additional money it will make from hiring an additional worker. That marginal revenue product represents a competitive firm's demand for labor.

Figure A16-1(b) graphs the firm's derived demand for labor, based on the data in column 5 of Figure A16-1(a). The resulting curve is the firm's **derived demand curve for labor,** which *shows the maximum amount of labor, measured in labor hours, that a firm will hire*. To see this, let's assume that the wage is $9 and that the firm is hiring 30 workers. If it hires another worker so it has 31 workers, workers' marginal revenue product of $12 exceeds their wage of $9, so the firm can increase profits by doing so. It increases output and profits since the additional revenue the firm gets from increasing workers from 30 to 31 is $12 and the additional cost the firm incurs is the wage of $9.

Now say the firm has hired 4 additional workers so it has 34 workers. As the firm hires more workers, the marginal product of workers declines. As you can see from the graph in Figure A16-1(b), the marginal revenue product of decreasing from 34 to 33 workers is $6. Since the workers' marginal revenue product of $6 is less than their wage of $9, now the firm can increase profits by laying off some workers. Doing so decreases output but increases profit, because it significantly increases the average product of the remaining workers.

Only when a worker's wage of $9 equals the marginal revenue product does the firm have no incentive to change the number of employees. In this example, the wage ($9) equals workers' marginal revenue product at 32 workers. When the firm is hiring 32 workers, either hiring another worker or laying off one worker will decrease profits. Decreasing from 32 to 31 workers loses $10 in revenue, but increasing from 32 to 33 workers gains $8 in revenue, but costs $9 in wages. Since the marginal revenue product curve tells the firm, given a wage, how many workers it should hire, *the marginal revenue product curve is the firm's demand curve for labor*.

The fact that the demand curve for labor is downward sloping means that as more workers are hired, workers' marginal product falls. This might tempt you to think that the last worker hired is inherently less productive than the first worker hired. But that simply can't be because, by assumption, the workers are identical. Thus, the marginal product of any worker must be identical to the marginal product of any other worker, given that a specified number of workers are working. What the falling marginal product means is that *when 30 rather than 25 workers are working*, the marginal product of any one of those 30 workers is less than the marginal product of any one of 25 of those workers when only 25 are working. When the other inputs are constant, hiring an additional worker lowers the marginal product not only of the last worker but also of any of the other workers.

To understand what's going on here you must remember that when marginal product is calculated, all other inputs are held constant—so if a firm hires another worker, that worker will have to share machines or tools with other workers. When you share tools, you start running into significant bottlenecks, which cause production to fall. That's why the marginal product of workers goes down when a new worker is hired. This assumption that all other factors of production are held constant is an important one. If all other factors of production are increased, it is not at all clear that workers' productivity will fall as output increases.

Why does a firm hire another worker if doing so will lead to a fall in other workers' productivity and, possibly, a fall in the average productivity of all workers? Because the firm is interested in total profit, not productivity. As long as hiring an extra worker increases revenue by more than the worker costs, the firm's total profit increases. A profit-maximizing firm would be crazy not to hire another worker, even if by doing so it lowers the marginal product of the workers.

Factors Affecting the Demand for Labor

There are many technical issues that determine how the demand for products is translated through firms into a demand for labor (and other factors of production), but we need not go into them in detail. I will, however, state three general principles:

1. Changes in the demand for a firm's product will be reflected in changes in its demand for labor.
2. The structure of a firm plays an important role in determining its demand for labor.
3. A change in the other factors of production that a firm uses will change its demand for labor.

Let's consider each of these principles in turn.

Changes in the Firm's Demand

The first principle is almost self-evident. An increase in the demand for a product leads to an increase in demand for the laborers who produce that product. The increase in demand pushes the price up, raising the marginal revenue product of labor (which, you'll remember, for a competitive firm is the price of the firm's product times the marginal physical product of labor).

The implications of this first principle, however, are not so self-evident. Often people think of firms' interests and workers' interests as being counter to one another, but this principle tells us that in many ways they are not. What benefits the firm also benefits its workers. Their interests are in conflict only when it comes to deciding how to divide up the total revenues among the owners of the firm, the workers, and the other inputs. Thus, it's not uncommon to see a firm and its workers fighting each other at the bargaining table, but also working together to prevent imports that might compete with the firm's product or to support laws that may benefit the firm.

An example of such cooperation occurred when union workers at a solar energy firm helped fight for an extension of government subsidies for solar energy. Why? Because their contract included a clause that if the solar energy subsidy bill passed, the union workers' wages would be significantly higher than if it didn't. This cooperation between workers and firms has led some economists to treat firms and workers as a single entity, out to get as much as they can as a group. These economists argue that it isn't helpful to separate out factor markets and goods markets. They argue that bargaining power models, which combine factor and goods markets, are the best way to analyze at what level wages will be set. In other words, the cost of labor to a firm should be modeled as if it is determined at the same time that its price and profitability are determined, not separately.

The Structure of the Firm and Its Demand for Labor

The way in which the demand for products is translated into a demand for labor is determined by the structure of the firm. For example, let's consider the difference between a monopolistic industry and a competitive industry. For both, the decision about whether to hire is based on whether the wage is below or above the marginal revenue product. But the firms that make up the two industries calculate their marginal revenue products differently.

The price of a competitive firm's output remains constant regardless of how many units it sells. Thus, its marginal revenue product equals the value of the marginal product. To calculate its marginal revenue product we simply multiply the price of the firm's product by the worker's marginal physical product. For a competitive firm:

Marginal revenue product of a worker =
Value of the worker's marginal product =
$MPP \times$ Price of product

The price of a monopolist's product decreases as more units are sold since the monopolist faces a downward-sloping demand curve. The monopolist takes that into account. That's why it focuses on marginal revenue rather than price. As it hires more labor and produces more output, the price it charges for its product will fall. Thus, for a monopolist:

Marginal revenue product of a worker =
$MPP \times$ Marginal revenue

Since a monopolist's marginal revenue is always less than price, a monopolist industry will always hire fewer workers than a comparable competitive industry, which is consistent with the result we discussed in Chapter 12: that a monopolistic industry will always produce less than a competitive industry, other things equal.

To ensure that you understand the principle, let's consider the example in Table A16-1, a table of prices, wages, marginal revenues, marginal physical products, and marginal revenue products for a firm in a competitive industry and a monopolistic industry.

Table A16-1 The Effect of Monopoly and Firm Structure on the Demand for Labor

1	2	3	4	5	6	7
					Marginal Revenue Product	
Number of Workers	Wage	Price P	Marginal Revenue (Monopolist) MR	Marginal Physical Product MPP	Competitive ($MPP \times P$)	Monopolist ($MPP \times MR$)
5	$2.85	$1.00	$.75	5	$5.00	$3.75
6	2.85	.95	.65	3	2.85	1.95
7	2.85	.90	.55	1	.90	.55

A firm in a competitive industry will hire up to the point where the wage equals $MPP \times P$ (columns 5 × 3). This occurs at 6 workers. Hiring either fewer or more workers would mean a loss in profits for a firm in a competitive industry.

Now let's compare the competitive industry with an equivalent monopolistic industry. Whereas the firm in the competitive industry did not take into account the effect an increase in output would have on prices, the monopolist will do so. It takes into account the fact that in order to sell the additional output of an additional worker, it must lower the price of the good. The relevant marginal revenue product for the monopolist appears in column 7. At 6 workers, the worker's wage rate of $2.85 exceeds the worker's marginal revenue product of $1.95, which means that the monopolist would hire fewer than 6 workers—5 full-time workers and 1 part-time worker.

As a second example of how the nature of firms affects the translation of demand for products into demand for labor, consider what would happen if workers rather than independent profit-maximizing owners controlled the firms. You saw before that whenever another worker is hired, other inputs constant, the marginal physical product of all similar workers falls. That can contribute to a reduction in existing workers' wages. The profit-maximizing firm doesn't take into account that effect on existing workers' wages. It wants to hold its costs down. If existing workers are making the decisions about hiring, they'll take that wage decline into account. If they believe that hiring more workers will lower their own wage, they have an incentive to see that new workers aren't hired. Thus, like the monopolist, a worker-controlled firm will hire fewer workers than a competitive profit-maximizing firm.

There aren't many worker-controlled firms in the United States, but a number of firms include existing workers' welfare in their decision processes. Moreover, with the growth of the team concept, in which workers are seen as part of a team with managers, existing workers' input into managerial decision making is increasing. In many U.S. firms workers have some say in whether additional workers will be hired and at what wage they will be hired. Other firms have an implicit understanding or a written contract with existing workers that restricts hiring and firing decisions. Some firms, such as IBM, had never laid off a worker; if they had to reduce their workforce, they created early retirement incentives. Ultimately, however, if their business gets bad enough, the invisible hand wins out over the social forces, and they lay off workers. That happened for IBM, and many other large U.S. businesses, in the early 1990s.

Why do firms consider worker's welfare? They do so to be seen as a "good employer," which makes it easier for them to hire in the future. Given the strong social and legal limitations on firms' hiring and firing decisions, one cannot simply apply marginal productivity theory to the real world. One must first understand the institutional and legal structures of the labor market. However, the existence of these other forces doesn't mean that the economic forces represented by marginal productivity don't exist. Rather, it means that firms struggle to find a wage policy that accommodates both economic and social forces in their wage-setting process. For example, in the 1980s and 1990s, a number of firms (such as airline and automobile firms) negotiated two-tier wage contracts. They continued to pay their existing workers a higher wage, but paid new workers a lower wage, even though old and new workers were doing identical jobs. These two-tier wage contracts were the result of the interactions of the social and market forces.

Changes in Other Factors of Production

A third principle determining the derived demand for labor is the amount of other factors of production that the firm has. Given a technology, an increase in other factors of production will increase the marginal physical product of existing workers. For example, let's say that a firm buys more machines so that each worker has more machines with which to work. The workers' marginal physical product increases, and the cost per unit of output for the firm decreases. The net effect on the demand for labor is unclear; it depends on how much the firm increases output, how much the firm's price is affected, and how easily one type of input can be substituted for another—or whether it must be used in conjunction with others.

While we can't say what the final effect on demand will be, we can determine the firm's **cost minimization condition**—where *the ratio of marginal product to the price of an input is equal for all inputs*.[1] When a firm is using resources as efficiently as possible, and hence is minimizing costs, the marginal product of each factor of production divided by the price of that factor must equal that of all the other factors. Specifically, the *cost minimization condition* is:

$$\frac{MP_l}{w} = \frac{MP_m}{P_m} = \frac{MP_x}{P_x}$$

where

w = Wage rate

l = Labor

m = Machines

x = Any other input

[1]This condition was explicitly discussed in terms of isocost/isoquant analysis in the appendix to Chapter 10.

If this cost minimization condition is not met, the firm could hire more of the input with the higher marginal product relative to price, and less of other inputs, and produce the same amount of output at a lower cost.

Let's consider a numerical example. Say the marginal product of labor is 20 and the wage is $4, while the marginal product of machines is 30 and the rental price of machines is $4. You're called in to advise the firm. You say, "Fire one worker, which will decrease output by 20 and save $4; spend that $4 on machines, which will increase output by 30." Output has increased by 10 while costs have remained constant. As long as the marginal products divided by the prices of the various inputs are unequal, you can make such recommendations to lower cost.

Conclusion

Changes in these factors make demand for labor shift around a lot. This shifting introduces uncertainty into people's lives and into the economic system. Often people attempt to build up institutional barriers to reduce uncertainty—either through social or political forces. Thus, labor markets function under an enormous volume of regulations and rules. We need to remember that while economic factors often lurk behind the scenes to determine pay and hiring decisions, these are often only part of the picture.

Key Terms

cost minimization condition *(382)*
derived demand curve for labor *(379)*
labor productivity *(378)*
marginal physical product (MPP) *(378)*
marginal revenue product (MRP) *(377)*
value of marginal product (VMP) *(378)*

Questions for Thought and Review

1. Using the information in Figure A16-1, answer the following questions:
   a. If the market wage were $7 an hour, how many workers would the firm hire?
   b. If the price of the firm's product fell to $1, how would your answer to *a* change?
2. If firms were controlled by workers, would they likely hire more or fewer workers? Why?
3. In the 1980s and the 1990s farmers switched from small square bales, which they hired students on summer break to stack for them, to large round bales, which can be handled almost entirely by machines. What is the likely reason for the switch?
4. Should teachers be worried about the introduction of computer- and video-based teaching systems? Why or why not?

5. A competitive firm gets $3 per widget. A worker's average product is 4 and marginal product is 3. What is the maximum the firm should pay the worker?
6. How would your answer to question 5 change if the firm were a monopolist?
7. Fill in the following table for a competitive firm that has a $2 price for its goods.

Number of Workers	*TP*	*MPP*	*AP*	*MRP*
1	10		_____	
		_____		_____
2	19			
		8		_____
3	_____		_____	
				_____
4	_____		8.5	
		_____		$12
5	_____		_____	

8. Your manager comes in with three sets of proposals for a new production process. Each process uses three inputs: land, labor, and capital. Under proposal A, the firm would be producing an output where the *MPP* of land is 30, labor is 42, and capital is 36. Under proposal B, at the output produced the *MPP* would be 20 for land, 35 for labor, and 96 for capital. Under proposal C, the *MPP* would be 40 for land, 56 for labor, and 36 for capital. Inputs' cost per hour is $5 for land, $7 for labor, and $6 for capital.
   a. Which proposal would you adopt?
   b. If the price of labor rises to $14, how will your answer change?

17 Who Gets What? The Distribution of Income

After reading this chapter, you should be able to:

- State what a Lorenz curve is.
- Explain how the poverty definition is both an absolute and a relative measure.
- Discuss U.S. income inequality in a global context.
- Summarize the statistical findings on income and wealth distribution.
- State two alternative ways to describe income distribution.
- Explain three problems in determining whether an equal income distribution is fair.
- List three side effects of redistributing income.
- Summarize the U.S. tax and expenditure programs to redistribute income.

"God must love the poor," said Lincoln, "or he wouldn't have made so many of them." He must love the rich, or he wouldn't divide so much mazuma among so few of them.

—*H. L. Mencken*

In 2001, Lawrence Ellison, CEO of Oracle, earned $706 million (base pay plus stock options); that's more than $13 million per week. Assuming he worked 70 hours per week (you have to work hard to earn that kind of money), that's more than $193,000 per hour.

Today, the average doctor earns $180,000 per year; that's $3,462 per week. Assuming she works 70 hours per week (she's conscientious, makes house calls, and spends time with her hospitalized patients), that's $49 per hour.

Joe Smith, a cashier in a fast-food restaurant, earns $6.35 per hour. But to earn enough for his family to be able to eat, he works a lot of overtime, for which he is paid time-and-a-half, or $9.53 per hour. So he makes $28,079 per year, or $539 per week, by working 70 hours per week.

Nguyen, a peasant in Vietnam, earns $250 a year; that's $4.80 per week. Assuming he works 70 hours per week (you have to work hard at that rate of pay just to keep from starving), that's 7 cents per hour.

Are such major differences typical of how income is distributed among people in general? Are such differences fair? And if they're unfair, what can be done about them? This chapter addresses such issues. (I should warn you, however: If you're looking for answers, this chapter won't provide them; it will simply make the assumptions on both sides clear.)

The issues addressed in these questions play a fundamentally important role in policy debates today. The reason why is that in the last 20 years the income distribution in the United States has changed considerably. Many formerly middle-income people have moved into the upper-income levels; their wealth and their control of real assets have grown considerably. But simultaneously, lower-income people's income has stagnated or fallen. This change is bringing income distribution issues to center stage in modern policy debates.

Ways of Considering the Distribution of Income

There are several different ways to look at income distribution. In the 1800s, economists were concerned with how income was divided among the owners of businesses (for whom profits were the source of income), the owners of land (who received rent), and workers (who earned wages). That concern reflected the relatively sharp distinctions among social classes that existed in capitalist societies at that time. Landowners, workers, and owners of businesses were separate groups, and few individuals moved from one group to another.

Web Note 17.1
Rent, Profit, and Wages

Time has changed that. Today workers, through their pension plans and investments in financial institutions, are owners of over 50 percent of all the shares issued on the New York Stock Exchange. Landowners as a group receive a relatively small portion of total income. Companies are run not by capitalists, but by managers who are, in a sense, workers. In short, the social lines have blurred.

This blurring of the lines between social classes doesn't mean that we can forget the question "Who gets what?" It simply means that our interest in who gets what has a different focus. We no longer focus on classification of income by source. Instead we look at the relative distribution of total income. How much income do the top 5 percent get? How much do the top 15 percent get? How much do the bottom 10 percent get? **Share distribution of income** is the name given to *the relative division of total income among income groups*.

The share distribution of income is the relative division of total income among income groups.

A second distributional issue economists are concerned with is the **socioeconomic distribution of income** (*the allocation of income among relevant socioeconomic groupings*). How much do blacks get relative to whites? How much do the old get compared to the young? How much do women get compared to men?

The socioeconomic distribution of income is the relative division or allocation of total income among relevant socioeconomic groups.

The Share Distribution of Income

The U.S. share distribution of income measures aggregate family income, from the poorest segment of society to the richest. It ranks people by their income and tells how much the richest 20 percent (a quintile) and the poorest 20 percent receive. For example, the poorest 20 percent might get 5 percent of the income and the richest 20 percent might get 40 percent.

The Lorenz Curve

Figure 17-1(a) presents the share distribution of income for the United States in 2001. In it you can see that the 20 percent of Americans receiving the lowest level of income got 3.5 percent of the total income. The top 20 percent of Americans received 51.1 percent of the total income. The ratio of the income of the top 20 percent compared to the income of the bottom 20 percent was about 15:1.

A **Lorenz curve** is *a geometric representation of the share distribution of income among families in a given country at a given time*. It measures the cumulative percentage of *families* on the horizontal axis, arranged from poorest to richest, and the cumulative percentage of *family income* on the vertical axis. Since the figure presents cumulative percentages (all of the families with income below a certain level), both axes start at zero and end at 100 percent.

A Lorenz curve is a geometric representation of the share distribution of income among families in a given country at a given time.

Q-1 When drawing a Lorenz curve, what do you put on the two axes?

A perfectly equal distribution of income would be represented by a diagonal line like the one in Figure 17-1(b). That is, the poorest 20 percent of the families would have 20 percent of the total income (point A); the poorest 40 percent of the families would

Figure 17-1 (a and b) A Lorenz Curve of U.S. Income, 2001
If income were perfectly equally distributed, the Lorenz curve would be a diagonal line. In (**b**) we see the U.S. Lorenz curve based on the numbers in (**a**) compared to a Lorenz curve reflecting a perfectly equal distribution of income.

Income Quintile	Percentage of Total Family Income	Cumulative Percentage of Total Family Income
Lowest fifth	3.5%	3.5%
Second fifth	8.8	12.3
Third fifth	14.5	26.8
Fourth fifth	23.1	49.9
Highest fifth	50.1	100.0

(a)

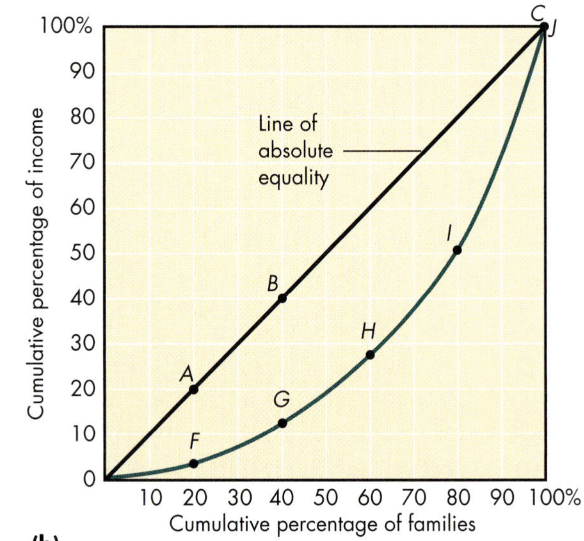

(b)

Source: *Current Population Reports*, U.S. Bureau of the Census, 2002 (www.census.gov).

have 40 percent of the income (point *B*); and 100 percent of the families would have 100 percent of the income (point C). An unequal distribution of income is represented by a Lorenz curve that's below the diagonal line. All real-world Lorenz curves are below the diagonal because income is always distributed unequally in the real world.

The green line in Figure 17-1(b) represents a Lorenz curve of the U.S. income distribution presented in Figure 17-1(a)'s table. From Figure 17-1(a) you know that, in 2001, the bottom 20 percent of the families in the United States received 3.5 percent of the income. Point *F* in Figure 17-1(b) represents that combination of percentages (20 percent and 3.5 percent). To find what the bottom 40 percent received, we must add the income percentage of the bottom 20 percent and the income percentage of the next 20 percent. Doing so gives us 12.3 percent (3.5 plus 8.8 percent from column 2 of Figure 17-1(a)). Point G in Figure 17-1(b) represents the combination of percentages (40 percent and 12.3 percent). Continuing this process for points *H*, *I*, and C, you get a Lorenz curve that shows the share distribution of income in the United States in 2001.

U.S. Income Distribution over Time

From 1929 to 1970, income inequality in the United States decreased. From 1970 to 2001, it increased.

Lorenz curves are most useful in visual comparisons of income distribution over time and between countries. Figure 17-2 presents Lorenz curves for the United States in 1929, 1970, and 2001. They show that from 1929 to 1970 the share distribution of income became more equal. (The curve for 1970 is closer to being a diagonal than the curve for 1929.) Income of the bottom fifth of families rose by a much higher proportion than did income of the top fifth. That was a continuation of a trend that had begun in the 1920s. In the 1970s that trend stopped and began to reverse. As you can see, from 1970 to 2001 income distribution became less equal. (The curve for 2001 is further from being diagonal than is the curve for 1970.) The income of the bottom fifth of families fell by over 10 percent, while the income of the top fifth rose significantly.

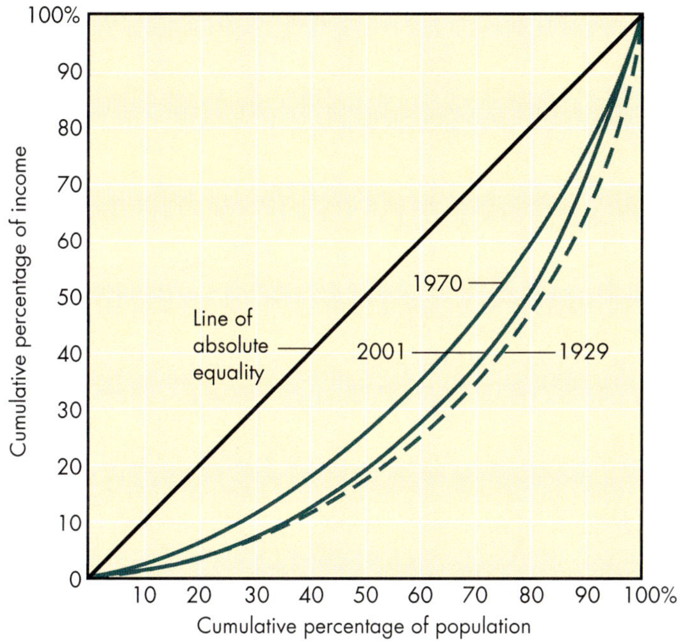

Figure 17-2 Lorenz Curves for the United States: 1929, 1970, and 2001
The amount of inequality of income distribution has fluctuated in the United States. Until about 1970, it decreased; since then it has increased.

Important reasons for the initial increase in equality are the redistribution measures instituted by the U.S. government between the 1930s and the 1970s, including welfare programs, unemployment insurance, Social Security, progressive taxation (taxation of higher income at higher rates, lower income at lower rates), and improved macroeconomic performance of the economy.

The trend back toward greater inequality starting in the 1970s was caused by a fall in the real income of the poor. This was due to wage increases that didn't keep up with price increases during that period, a movement away from progressive taxation, and a reduction in government funding for some social programs; this trend toward inequality will likely become a hot political topic in upcoming years.

The distribution of income over time is also affected by demographic factors. Many families have relatively low income in their early years, relatively higher income in their middle years, and then relatively low income again in their retirement years. The Lorenz curve reflects these differences, so even if lifetime income were equally distributed, income in any one year would not be. Moreover, when the percentages of these groups change, the Lorenz curve will change. For example, when the baby-boom generation's members retire and are no longer working, their collective income will fall. That decline in income relative to the income of the smaller number of working families will affect the Lorenz curve.

Defining Poverty

Much of the government's concern with income distribution has centered on the poorest group—those in poverty. Defining poverty is not easy. Do we want to define it as an absolute amount of real income that does not change over time? If poverty were defined as an *absolute* amount of real income, few in the United States would be in poverty today; most of today's poor have higher real incomes than did the middle class 50 or 60 years ago. Or do we want to define it as a *relative* concept that rises as the average income in the society rises? For example, anyone with an income of less than one-fifth of the average income could be defined as being in poverty. If that relative concept of poverty were chosen, then the proportion of people classified as poor would always be the same.

The Official Definition of Poverty

Q-2 Is the U.S. definition of poverty an absolute or a relative definition?

The United States uses a definition of poverty that is a combination of a relative and an absolute measure. Thus, it satisfies neither those who favor an absolute measure nor those who favor a relative measure, and there are both calls to increase and calls to decrease the **poverty threshold**—*the income below which a family is considered to live in poverty*. The official definition of poverty is the following:

Poverty is defined by the U.S. government as having an income being equal to or less than three times an average family's minimum food expenditures as calculated by the U.S. Department of Agriculture.

> A family is in poverty if it has an income equal to or less than three times an average family's minimum food expenditures as calculated by the U.S. Department of Agriculture.

The minimum weekly food budget includes 4 eggs, 1½ pounds of meat, 3 pounds of potatoes, about 4 pounds of vegetables, and other foods; the cost is about $29.00 per person per week. Tripling that amount to about $87.00 (since food is said to require one-third of a family's income) and multiplying it by 52 (the number of weeks in a year), we arrive at a poverty level of about $4,524 per person per year, or about $18,100 for a family of four.

As Table 17-1 shows, using the official poverty measure, the number of people in poverty decreased in the 1960s and then began increasing in the 1970s. The number of poor rose to over 30 million in the 1980s. Then, due to a recession in the early 1990s, it rose even more. It declined throughout the remainder of the 1990s as the U.S. economy continued to grow but rose slightly in the early 2000s as the economy slowed. In 2001, 32.9 million Americans lived below the poverty threshold.

Debates about the Definition of Poverty

The minimum food budget used to determine the poverty line was determined in the 1960s and has not been recalculated to account for rising standards of living. Thus, it is in principle an absolute measure. However, it is adjusted by the rate of inflation rather than by the rise in the price of the originally selected foods. Since food prices have risen

Table 17-1 Number and Percentage of Persons in Poverty, 1960–2001

	Number of People (in millions)	Percentage of Population	Poverty Income of Family of 4 (in current dollars)
1960	39.9	22.2%	$ 3,022
1970	24.4	12.6	3,986
1980	29.3	13.0	8,414
1990	33.6	13.5	13,359
1995	36.4	13.8	15,569
1996	36.5	13.8	16,036
1997	35.6	13.3	16,400
1998	34.5	12.7	16,660
1999	32.3	11.8	17,029
2000	31.6	11.3	17,603
2001	32.9	11.7	18,100

Source: *Current Population Reports,* U.S. Bureau of the Census, 2002 (www.census.gov).

by less than the rise in the general price level, the index of poverty has gone up by more than it would have had the fixed ratio of food to income remained constant. That means the definition includes significant aspects of relativity.

Those who favor a relative measure of poverty argue that our current poverty measure is too low. They point out that since food is now closer to a fourth of a family's total budget, it would make sense to increase the poverty threshold by multiplying food expenditures by a number a bit less than four rather than by three. Doing so would raise the poverty threshold to $21,500, and would add about 12 million people to the poverty roll.

There are arguments both that the poverty line is too high and too low.

Those who favor an absolute measure of poverty argue that the current measure is too high. They point out that U.S. poverty figures do not include in-kind (noncash) transfers, such as food stamps and housing assistance. Nor does the current poverty measure take into account underreporting of income, or the savings people have. (Many elderly people may have low incomes but significant wealth, which they could choose to spend.) If we make adjustments for in-kind transfers and underreporting of income, the official number of people in poverty decreases to about 60 percent of the official number. University of Texas economist Daniel Slesnick takes it further and points out that, since the price of food has increased at less than the rate of inflation, a much lower level of expenditures than the amount used to calculate the poverty threshold will provide a "nutritionally adequate diet." Slesnick calculated that when one takes the decrease in the relative price of food into account, the number of people in poverty would have fallen to one-seventh the official count.

The moral of this debate: Like most economic statistics, poverty statistics should be used with care.

The Costs of Poverty

People who favor policies aimed at achieving equality of income argue that poverty brings significant costs to society. One is that society suffers when some of its people are in poverty, just as the entire family suffers when one member doesn't have enough to eat. Most people derive pleasure from knowing that others are not in poverty.

Another cost of poverty is that it increases incentives for crime. In contrast, as people's incomes increase, they have more to lose by committing crimes, and therefore fewer crimes are committed. As the economy boomed in the 1990s, the crime rate decreased; it continued to decline in 2001.

Those who favor equality of income argue that the increased poverty in the late 1970s and 1980s represents a failure of the economic policies of that period. Others respond that the widening gap between rich and poor is not the result of government tax and spending policies. It has more to do with demographic changes. For example, the number of single-parent families increased dramatically during this period, while rapid growth of the labor force depressed wages for young unskilled workers.

Advocates of reducing poverty respond that this argument is unconvincing. They argue that the tax cuts of the 1980s favored the rich while decreased funding for government programs hurt the poor. To compensate, they argue, free day care should be provided for children so that single parents can work full-time, and government should supplement the low wages of the working poor. They argue that demographic changes are not a valid excuse for ducking a question of morality.

International Dimensions of Income Inequality

When considering income distribution, we usually are looking at conditions within a single country. For example, the richest 5 percent of the U.S. population gets approximately 30 times what the poorest 5 percent of the American people get.

Web Note 17.2
Income Distribution Data

The Gini Coefficient

Knowing the Tools

A second measure economists use to talk about the degree of income inequality is the Gini coefficient of inequality. The Gini coefficient is derived from the Lorenz curve by comparing the area between the (1) Lorenz curve and the diagonal (area *A*) and (2) the total area of the triangle below the diagonal (areas *A* and *B*). That is:

Gini coefficient = Area *A*/(Areas *A* + *B*)

A Gini coefficient of zero would be perfect equality, since area *A* is 0 if income is perfectly equally distributed. The highest the Gini coefficient can go is 1. So all Gini coefficients must be between 0 and 1. The lower the Gini coefficient, the closer income distribution is to being equal. The Gini coefficient for the United States was 0.47 in 2001.

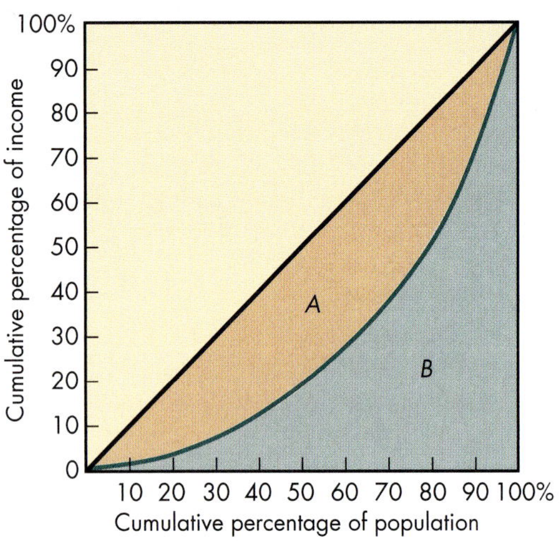

The following table gives Gini coefficients for a number of other countries. The Gini coefficients for transitional economies such as the Slovak Republic are most likely higher today because they are now market economies and their incomes are less equally distributed.

Gini Coefficients for Selected Countries	
Algeria	.353
Bangladesh	.336
Brazil	.591
Canada	.315
Czech Republic	.266
Denmark	.247
Germany	.300
Guatemala	.558
Hungary	.253
Indonesia	.317
Japan	.249
Latvia	.320
Netherlands	.326
Panama	.485
Philippines	.462
Romania	.305
Slovak Republic	.263
South Africa	.593
Thailand	.414
United Kingdom	.361
United States	.470

Source: *CIA World Factbook* 2002 (www.cia.gov)

There are other ways to look at income. We might judge income inequality in the United States relative to income inequality in other countries. Is the U.S. distribution of income more or less equal than another country's? We could also look at how income is distributed among countries. Even if income is relatively equally distributed within countries, it may be unequally distributed among countries.

Comparing Income Distribution across Countries

The United States has less income inequality than most developing countries but more income inequality than many developed countries.

Figure 17-3 gives us a sense of how the distribution of income in the United States compares to that in other countries. We see that the United States has significantly more income inequality than Sweden, but significantly less than Brazil (or most other developing and newly industrialized countries).

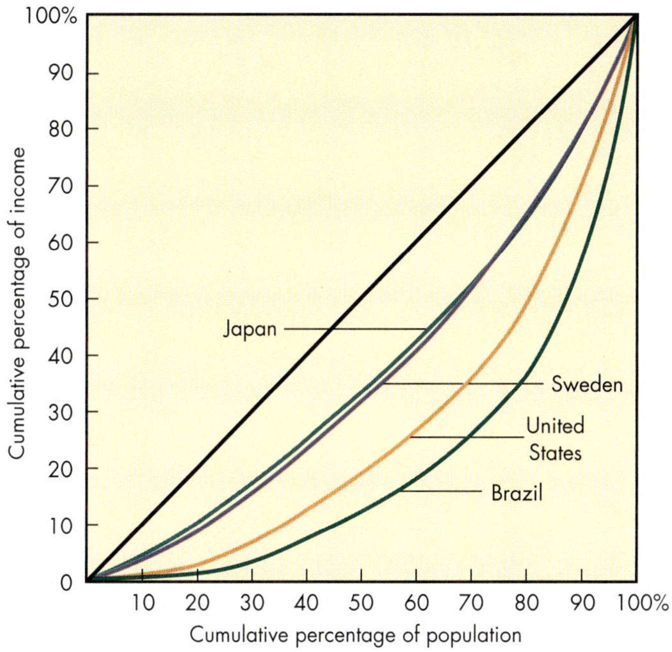

Figure 17-3 U.S. Income Distribution Compared to that of Other Countries
Among countries of the world, the United States has neither the most equal nor the most unequal distribution of income.

Source: *World Development Report*, The World Bank (www.worldbank.org).

An important reason why the United States has more income inequality than Sweden is that Sweden's tax system is more progressive. Until recently (when Sweden's socialist party lost power), the top marginal tax rate on the highest incomes in Sweden was 80 percent, compared to about 40 percent in the United States. Given this difference, it isn't surprising that Sweden has less income inequality. In a newly industrialized country like Brazil, where a few individuals earn most of the income and, to a large degree, control the government, the government is not likely to begin redistributing income to achieve equality.

Q-3 How does the income distribution in the United States compare with that in other countries?

Income Distribution among Countries

When we consider the distribution of world income, the picture becomes even more unequal than the picture we see within countries. The reason is clear: Income is highly unequally distributed among countries. The average per capita income of the richest countries in the world is approximately 100 times the average income of the poorest countries of the world. Thus, a Lorenz curve of world income would show much more inequality than the Lorenz curve for a particular country. Worldwide, income inequality is enormous. A minimum level of income in the United States would be a wealthy person's income in a poor country like Bangladesh.

The Total Amount of Income in Various Countries

To gain a better picture of income distribution problems, you need to consider not only the division of income but also the total amounts of income in various countries. Figure 17-4 presents per capita income (gross domestic product) for various countries. Looking at the enormous differences of income among countries, we must ask which is more important: the distribution of income or the absolute level of income. Which would you rather be: one of four members in a family that has an income of $3,000 a

Figure 17-4 Per Capita Income (Gross Domestic Product) in Various Countries, 2001

Income is unequally distributed among the countries of the world. These relative comparisons change considerably over time as exchange rates fluctuate. These estimates are done using purchasing power parity, which eliminates much of the fluctuation due to exchange rate variation.

Source: *CIA World Factbook*, Central Intelligence Agency, 2002 (www.ocdi.gov) and various country home pages.

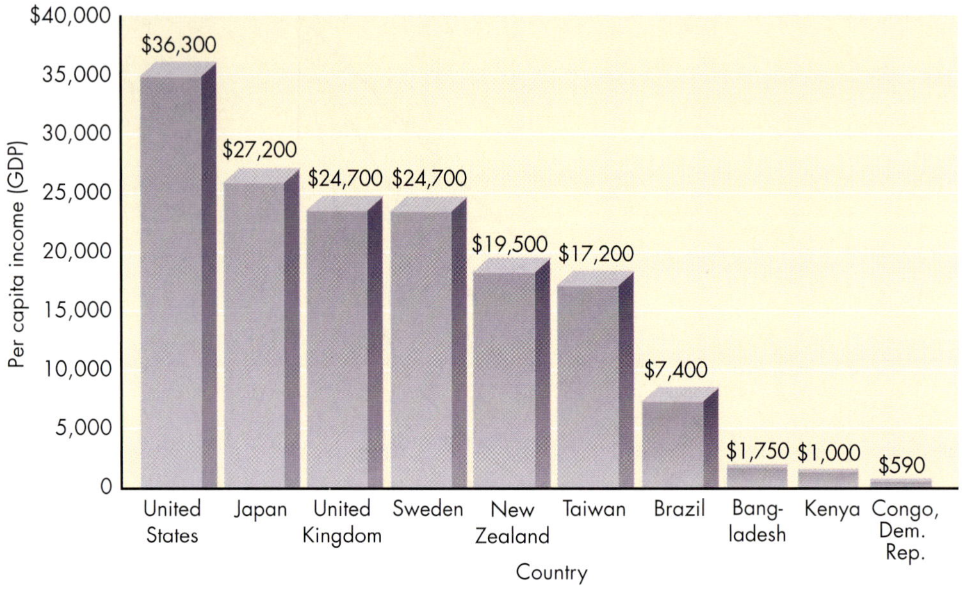

year, which places you in the top 10 percent of Bangladesh's income distribution, or one of four members of a family with an income of $12,000 (four times as much), which places you in the bottom 10 percent of the income earners in the United States?

The Distribution of Wealth

In considering equality, two measures are often used: *equality of wealth* and *equality of income*. Because of space limitations, my focus will be on income, but I want to mention wealth. **Wealth** is *the value of the things individuals own less the value of what they owe*. It is a *stock* concept representing the value of assets such as houses, buildings, and machines. For example, a farmer who owns a farm with a net worth of $1 million is wealthy compared to an investment banker with a net worth of $225,000.

Wealth is the value of assets individuals own less the value of what they owe.

Income is *payments received plus or minus changes in value in a person's assets in a specified time period*. In contrast to wealth, income is a *flow* concept. It's a stream through time. That farmer might have an income of $20,000 a year while the investment banker might have an income of $80,000 a year. The farmer, with $1 million worth of assets, is wealthier than the investment banker, but the investment banker has a higher income than the farmer.

Income is payments received plus or minus changes in value of a person's assets in a specified time period.

A Lorenz Curve of the Distribution of Wealth

Wealth is significantly more unequally distributed in the United States than is income.

Figure 17-5 compares the Lorenz curve for wealth in the United States with the Lorenz curve for income in the United States. You can see that wealth in the United States is more unequally distributed than income and that the bottom 40 percent of the U.S. population has essentially zero wealth.

How Much Wealth Do the Wealthy Have?

Billionaires often lose a billion here, gain a billion there; sometimes they even become multibillionaires. Seldom do they become poor.

Relative comparisons such as those depicted by Lorenz curves don't give you a sense of how much wealth it takes to be "wealthy." The following numbers provide you with a better sense. Bill Gates, who founded Microsoft and became the richest person in the

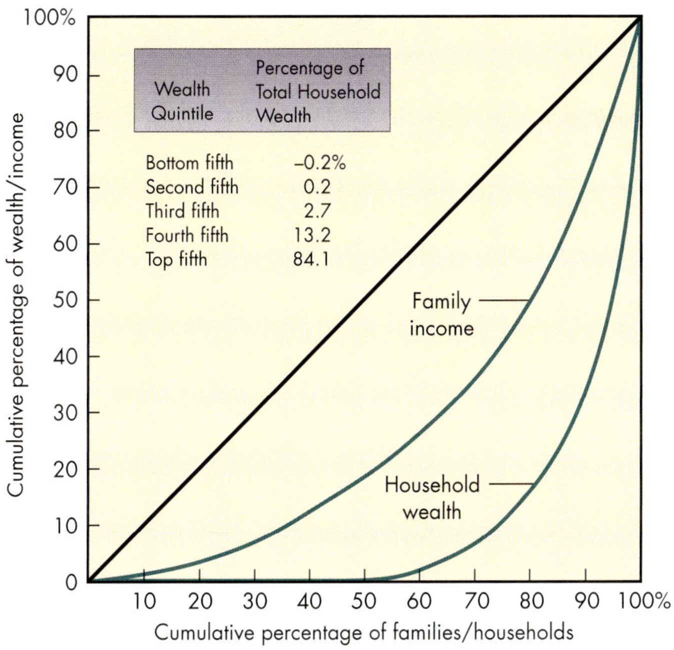

Figure 17-5 Wealth Distribution in the United States and Wealth Compared to Income

Wealth is much more unequally distributed than income in the United States. In fact, the lowest 40 percent of the population has 0 percent of the wealth; these people have borrowed as much as they own.

Source: U.S. Bureau of the Census and Edward N. Wolf, New York University (with permission).

United States, had a net worth of about $54 billion in 2001. Five of the 10 wealthiest people in the United States were from the Walton family (whose father founded Wal-Mart), each with $17 billion. Most of us have little chance of joining that group; in fact, most of us have little possibility of becoming one of the top 5 percent of the wealth-holders in the United States, which would require total wealth of at least $4 million. Once there was a time when people's ultimate financial goal was to be a millionaire. In the 2000s, the ultimate financial goal for the wealthiest people is to be a billionaire. The millionaire's club is no longer highly exclusive.

Of course, people in the club don't always stay there; the club is constantly changing. For example, a number of families who were in the club earlier are no longer in it. Many of the Japanese billionaires lost billions in the fall of the Japanese stock market and fell off the top 10 in the world list of wealthiest people. Today, some of these people and families might only be multimillionaires.

Socioeconomic Dimensions of Income Inequality

The size distribution of inequality is only one of the dimensions that inequality of income and wealth can take. As I mentioned before, the distribution of income according to source of income (wages, rents, and profits) was once considered important. Today's focus is on the distribution of income based on race, ethnic background, geographic region, and other socioeconomic factors such as gender and type of job.

Income Distribution According to Socioeconomic Characteristics

Table 17-2 gives an idea of the distribution of income according to socioeconomic characteristics.

You can see that income differs substantially by type of job, leading some economists to argue that a new professional/nonprofessional class distinction is arising in the

Table 17-2 Various Socioeconomic Income Distribution Designations

Median Income, 2001 By Occupational Category	Female	Male
Executive, administrators, and managerial	$39,217	$57,276
Professional specialists	40,930	57,628
Technical and related support	31,056	46,282
Sales	25,677	41,896
Administrative support, including clerical	26,355	32,995
Precision production, craft, and repair	26,031	35,199
Machine operators, assemblers, and inspectors	20,879	30,494
Transportation and material moving	25,095	31,908
Handlers, equipment cleaners, helpers, and lab	19,018	23,328
Service workers	17,763	25,004
Farming, forestry, and fishing	17,968	21,016

By Age, 2001	Median Household Income
Less than 25	$28,196
25–34	45,080
35–44	53,320
45–54	58,045
55–64	45,864
Over 65	23,118

By Sex	Median Income 1970	1980	1990	2001
Male	$7,537	$15,340	$27,866	$38,215
Female	3,138	6,772	19,816	29,215

By Race, 2001	Median Household Income
White	$44,517
Black	29,470
Hispanic	33,565

Source: *Current Population Reports, Consumer Income,* U.S. Bureau of the Census, 2002 (www.census.gov).

United States. Substantial differences also exist between the incomes of women and men, and between whites and blacks.

Income Distribution According to Class

As I stated above, early economists focused on the distribution of income by wages, profits, and rent because that division corresponded to their class analysis of society. Landowners received rent, capitalists received profit, and workers received wages. Tensions among these classes played an important part in economists' analyses of the economy and policy.

The United States has socioeconomic classes with some mobility among classes. This is not to say such classes should exist; it is only to say that they do exist.

Even though class divisions by income source have become blurred, other types of socioeconomic classes have taken their place. The United States has a kind of upper class. In fact, a company in the United States publishes the *Social Register,* containing the names and pedigrees of about 35,000 socially prominent people who might be categorized "upper-class." Similarly, it is possible to further divide the U.S. population into a middle class and a lower class.

Class divisions are no longer determined solely by income source. For example, upper-class people do not necessarily receive their income from rent and profits. CEOs of major companies are generally considered upper-class, and they receive much of their income as payment for their services. Today we have "upper-class" people who derive their income from wages and "lower-class" people who derive their income from profits (usually in the form of pensions, which depend on profits from the investment of pension funds in stocks and bonds). Of course, once people become rich, they earn interest and profits on their wealth as well as income.

The Importance of the Middle Class What has made the most difference in today's class structure in the United States compared to its class structure in earlier

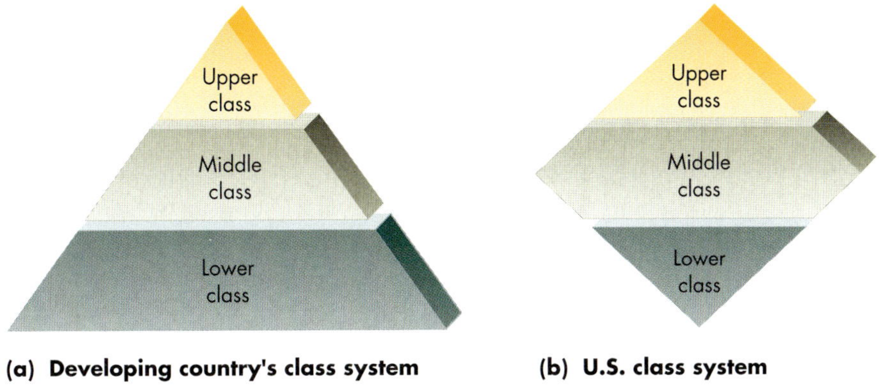

Figure 17-6 (a and b) The Class System as a Pyramid and as a Diamond
The class system in developing countries is a pyramid; in the United States the class system is more diamond-shaped.

periods and to the structure in today's developing countries is the tremendous growth in the relative size of the middle class. Economists used to see the class structure as a pyramid. From a base composed of a large lower class, the pyramid tapered upward through a medium-sized middle class to a peak occupied by the upper class (Figure 17-6(a)). The class structure is still pyramidal in developing countries. In the United States and other developed countries, the pyramid has bulged out into a diamond, as shown in Figure 17-6(b). The middle class has become the largest class, while the upper and lower classes are smaller in relative terms.

In the United States the middle class is the largest class.

This enormous increase in the relative size of the middle class in developed countries has significantly blurred the distinction between capitalists and workers. In early capitalist society, the distributional fight (the fight over relative income shares) was largely between workers and capitalists. In modern market-based societies, the distributional fight is among various types of individuals. Union workers are pitted against nonunion workers; salaried workers are pitted against workers paid by the hour. The old are pitted against the young; women are pitted against men; blacks are pitted against Hispanics and Asians, and all three groups are pitted against whites.

Q-4 How have distributional fights about income changed over time?

Distributional Questions and Tensions in Society While mainstream economists tend to focus on the size distribution of income, nonmainstream economists tend to emphasize class and group structures in their analysis. Radical economists emphasize the control that the upper class has over the decision process and the political process. Conservative economists emphasize the role of special interests of all types in shaping government policy. Both radical and conservative analyses bring out the tensions among classes in society much better than does the mainstream, classless analysis.

Both radical and conservative analyses bring out the tensions among classes in society much better than does mainstream classless analysis.

When people feel they belong to a particular class or group, they will often work to further the interests of that class or group. They also generally have stronger feelings about inequalities among classes or groups than when they lack that sense of class or group identity. Using a classless analysis means overlooking the implications of class and group solidarity in affecting the tensions in society.

Those tensions show up every day in political disputes over the tax system, in the quiet fuming of individuals as they see someone else earning more for doing the same job, and in strikes and even riots. Such tensions exist in all countries. In some transitional and developing countries they break out into the open as armed insurrections or riots over food shortages.

Those tensions have been kept to a minimum in American society. A majority of Americans believe that income distribution is sufficiently fair for them to accept their share more or less contentedly. To remedy the unfairness that does exist, they don't demand that the entire system be replaced. Instead they work for change within the present system. They look to affirmative action laws, comparable worth laws, minimum wage laws, and social welfare programs for any improvement they perceive to be necessary or desirable. There's much debate about whether these government actions have achieved the desired ends, but the process itself reduces tensions and has worked toward the maintenance of the entire system.

People's acceptance of the U.S. economic system is based not only on what the distribution of income is but also on what people think it should be, what they consider fair. It is to that question that we now turn.

Income Distribution and Fairness

Judgments about whether the distribution of income is fair or should be changed are normative ones, based on the values the analyst applies to the situation. Value judgments necessarily underlie all policy prescriptions.

Philosophical Debates about Equality and Fairness

Depending on one's values, any income distribution can be justified. For example, Friedrich Nietzsche, the 19th-century Germany philosopher, argued that society's goal should be to support its supermen—its best and brightest. Lesser individuals' duty should be to work for the well-being of these supermen. Bertram de Juvenal, a 20th-century philosopher, has argued that a high level of income inequality is necessary to sustain the arts, beauty, education, and civilization. He and others say that a world of equally distributed income would be a world without beauty. Even if we don't personally own beautiful, expensive homes or aren't devoted opera fans, these philosophers argue, our lives are improved because some people do own such homes and because opera performances exist. Inequality creates diversity in our lives, and that diversity enriches the lives of everyone.

Q-5 Is it self-evident that greater equality of income would make the society a better place to live? Why?

Other philosophers disagree strongly. They argue that equality itself is the overriding goal. That view is embodied in the Declaration of Independence: "We hold these truths to be self-evident, that all men are created equal." And for many people the inherent value of equality is not open to question—it is simply self-evident.

Believing that equality is an overriding goal does not necessarily imply that income should be equally distributed. For example, John Rawls (a Harvard University professor who believed that equality is highly desirable and that society's goal should be to maximize the welfare of the least well-off) agreed that to meet that goal some inequality is necessary. Rawls argued that if, in pursuing equality, you actually make the least well-off worse off than they otherwise would have been, then you should not pursue equality any further. For example, say under one policy there would be perfect equality and everyone would receive $10,000 per year. Under another policy, the least well-off person receives $12,000 per year and all others receive $40,000. Rawls argued that the second policy is preferable to the first even though it involves more inequality.

Economists, unlike philosophers, are not concerned about justifying any particular distribution of income. In their objective role, economists limit themselves to explaining the effects that various policies will have on the distribution of income; they let the policymakers judge whether those effects are desirable.

However, in order to judge economic policies, you, in your role as a citizen who elects policymakers, must make certain judgments about income distribution because all real-world economic policies have distribution effects. Accordingly, a brief discussion of income distribution and fairness is in order.

What Should Be the Goal of Economic Policy?

Beyond the Tools

Today, most discussions of economic policy focus on a goal of increasing income: Policies that achieve higher income are good policies; policies that do not are bad policies. Historically, that has not always been the goal. In the 1800s the economic policy focused on basic goods—distinguishing necessities from luxuries. Only policies that increased basic goods were good; the welfare implications of policies that increased luxuries were much more problematic.

The 1930s marked a major change in how economic policy was conceived. Economics began focusing much more on utility, downplaying the distinction between luxuries and basic goods. With this change the goal of economic policy became much more focused on total income, regardless of how that income was divided. The division of goods into necessities and luxuries was seen as adding a normative element to policy that was outside the purview of positive economics.

Recently, Nobel prize–winning economist Amartya Sen has argued against that utilitarian approach, pointing out that normative elements are unavoidable in policy analysis. He argues that using income as a measure of welfare is not the best approach and has suggested replacing it with a "capabilities" measure. For Sen, the goal of economic policy should be to increase a society's capabilities, which he defines as an individual's freedom within that society to achieve a particular life. For Sen, capabilities are best measured by basic indicators—such as life expectancy, literacy, and infant mortality rates—not by income. Poor ratings on such indicators impede people from leading good and happy lives. Sen's work is controversial, but it is important in reminding us that the goals of economic policy should always be kept in mind and that we should not simply accept the goal as being an increase in total income.

Fairness and Equality

The U.S. population has a strong general tendency to favor equality—equality is generally seen as fair. Most people, including me, share that view. However, in some instances equality of income is not directly related to people's view of fairness. For example, consider this distribution of income between John and Fred:

John gets $50,000 a year.

Fred gets $12,000 a year.

Think a minute. Is that fair?

Q-6 You are dividing a pie among five individuals. What would be a fair distribution of that pie?

The answer I'm hoping for is that you don't yet have enough information to make the decision.

Here's some more information. Say that John gets that $50,000 for holding down three jobs at a time, while Fred gets his $12,000 for sitting around doing nothing. At this point, many of us would argue that it's possible John should be getting even more than $50,000 and Fred should be getting less than $12,000.

Fairness has many dimensions and it is often difficult to say what is fair and what isn't.

But wait! What if we discover that Fred is an invalid and unless his income increases to $15,000 a year he will die? Most of us would change our minds again and argue that Fred deserves more, regardless of how much John works.

Three problems in determining whether an equal income distribution is fair are:

1. People don't start from equivalent positions.
2. People's needs differ.
3. People's efforts differ.

But wait! How about if, after further digging, we discover that Fred is an invalid because he squandered his health on alcohol, drugs, and fried foods? In that case some people would likely change their minds again as to whether Fred deserves more.

By now you should have gotten my point. Looking only at a person's income masks many dimensions that most people consider important in making value judgments about fairness.

Fairness as Equality of Opportunity

The concept of fairness is crucial and complicated, and it deserves deeper consideration than just a gut reaction.

When most people talk about believing in equality in income, they mean they believe in equality of opportunity for comparably endowed individuals to earn income. If equal opportunity of equals leads to inequality of income, then the inequality in income is fair. Unfortunately, there's enormous latitude for debate on what constitutes equal opportunity of equals.

In the real world, needs differ, desires differ, and abilities differ. Should these differences be considered relevant differences in equality? You must answer that question before you can judge any economic policy, because to make a judgment on whether an economic policy should or should not be adopted, you must make a judgment about whether a policy's effect on income is fair. In making those judgments, most people rely on their immediate gut reaction. I hope what you have gotten out of the discussion about John and Fred and equality of opportunity is the resolve to be cautious about trusting your gut reactions. The concept of fairness is crucial and complicated, and it deserves deeper consideration than just a gut reaction.

The Problems of Redistributing Income

Let's now say that we have considered all the issues discussed so far in this chapter and have concluded that some redistribution of income from the rich to the poor is necessary if society is to meet our ideal of fairness. How do we go about redistributing income?

First, we must consider what programs exist and what their negative side effects might be. The side effects can be substantial and can subvert the intention of the program so that far less money is available overall for redistribution and inequality is reduced less than we might expect.

Three Important Side Effects of Redistributive Programs

Three side effects of redistribution of income are:

1. The labor/leisure incentive effect.
2. The avoidance and evasion incentive effect.
3. The incentive effect to look more needy than you are.

Three important side effects that economists have found in programs to redistribute income are:

1. A tax may result in a switch from labor to leisure.
2. People may attempt to avoid or evade taxes, leading to a decrease in measured income.
3. Redistributing money may cause people to make themselves look as if they're more needy than they really are.

All economists believe that people will change their behavior in response to changes in taxation and income redistribution programs. These responses, called *incentive effects of taxation*, are important and must be taken into account in policymaking. But economists differ significantly in the importance they assign to incentive effects, and empirical evidence doesn't resolve the question. Some economists believe that incentive effects are so important that little taxation for redistribution should take place. They argue that when the rich do well, the total pie is increased so much that the spillover benefits to the poor are greater than the proceeds the poor would get from redistribution. For example, supporters of this view argue that the growth in capitalist economies was made possible by entrepreneurs. Because those entrepreneurs invested in new technology, income in society grew. Moreover, those entrepreneurs paid taxes. The benefits resulting from entrepreneurial action spilled over to the poor, making the poor

Q-7 When determining the effects of programs that redistribute income, can one reasonably assume that other things will remain equal?

far better off than any redistribution would. The fact that some of those entrepreneurs became rich is irrelevant because all society was better off due to their actions.

Other economists believe that there should be significant taxation for redistribution. While they agree that sometimes the incentive effects are substantial, they see the goal of equality overriding these effects.

Politics, Income Redistribution, and Fairness

We began this discussion of income distribution and fairness by making the assumption that our value judgments determine the taxes we pay—that if our values led us to the conclusion that the poor deserved more income, we could institute policies that would get more to the poor. Reality doesn't necessarily work that way. Often politics, not value judgments, plays a central role in determining what taxes individuals will pay. The group that can deliver the most votes will elect lawmakers who will enact tax policies that benefit that group at the expense of groups with fewer votes.

Often politics, not value judgments, plays a central role in determining what taxes an individual will pay.

On the surface, the democratic system of one person/one vote would seem to suggest that the politics of redistribution would favor the poor, but it doesn't. One would expect that the poor would use their votes to make sure income was redistributed to them from the rich. Why don't they? The answer is complicated.

One reason is that many of the poor don't vote because they assume that one vote won't make much difference. As a result, poor people's total voting strength is reduced. A second reason is that the poor aren't seen by most politicians as a solid voting bloc. There's no organization of the poor that can deliver votes to politicians. A third reason is that those poor people who do vote often cast their votes with other issues in mind. An anti-income-redistribution candidate might have a strong view on abortion as well, and for many the abortion view is the one that decides their vote.

Web Note 17.3
Macroeconomic Issues

A fourth reason is that elections require financing. Much of that financing comes from the rich. The money is used for advertising and publicity aimed at convincing the poor that it's actually in their best interests to vote for a person who supports the rich. People are often misled by that kind of biased publicity.

Reasonable-sounding arguments can be made to support just about any position, and the rich have the means to see that the arguments supporting their positions get the publicity. Of course, some of their arguments are also correct. The issues are usually sufficiently complicated that a trained economist must study them for a long time to determine which arguments make sense.

Income Redistribution Policies

The preceding discussion should have provided you with a general sense of the difficulty of redistributing income. Let's now consider briefly how income redistribution policies and programs have worked in the real world. In considering this, it is helpful to keep in mind that there are two direct methods and one indirect method through which government redistributes income. The direct methods are (1) *taxation* (policies that tax the rich more than the poor) and (2) *expenditures* (programs that help the poor more than the rich). The indirect method involves the establishment and protection of property rights. Let's first consider direct methods.

Direct methods of redistribution are taxation and expenditures programs.

Taxation to Redistribute Income

The U.S. federal government gets its revenue from a variety of taxes. The three largest sources of revenue are the personal income tax, the corporate income tax, and the Social Security tax.

State and local governments get their revenue from income taxes, sales taxes, and property taxes. The rates vary among states.

Q-8 A progressive tax is preferable to a proportional tax. True or false? Why?

As I stated in Chapter 2, tax systems can be progressive, proportional (sometimes called *flat rate*), or regressive. A **progressive tax** is one in which *the average tax rate increases with income*. It redistributes income from the rich to the poor. A **proportional tax** is one in which *the average rate of tax is constant regardless of income level*. It is neutral in regard to income distribution. A **regressive tax** is one in which *the average tax rate decreases as income increases*. It redistributes income from poor to rich.

Federal Income Taxes In the early 1940s, the federal personal income tax was made highly progressive, with a top tax rate of 90 percent on the highest incomes. The degree of progressivity went down significantly through various pieces of legislation after World War II until 1986, when the income tax system was amended to provide for an initial rate of 15 percent and a top rate of 28 percent. The changes did not reduce the actual progressivity of the personal income tax as much as they seemed to, because the 1986 reforms eliminated many of the loopholes in the U.S. Tax Code. Some loopholes had allowed rich people to legally reduce their reported incomes and to pay taxes on those lower incomes at lower rates. The top personal income tax rate on high-income individuals today is almost 40 percent.

Whereas the personal income tax is progressive, the Society Security tax is initially proportional. All individuals pay the same tax rate on wage income (7.65 percent for employer and 7.65 percent for employee; 15.3 percent for self-employed) up to a cap of about $85,000. Above that income cap, no Social Security tax is due (except for 1.45 percent for medical insurance, which has no cap on the amount to which it is applied). At this income cap the Social Security tax becomes regressive: Higher-income individuals pay a lower percentage of their total income in Social Security taxes than do lower-income individuals. (They also receive relatively less in Social Security benefits, compared to what they put in. So, while the Social Security tax is regressive, taken as a whole the Social Security system is progressive.)

State and Local Taxes State and local governments get most of their income from the following sources:

Web Note 17.4 State Lotteries

1. Income taxes, which are generally somewhat progressive.
2. Sales taxes, which tend to be proportional (all people pay the same tax rate on what they spend) or slightly regressive. (Since poor people often spend a higher percentage of their incomes than rich people, poor people pay higher average sales taxes as a percentage of their incomes than rich people.)
3. Property taxes, which are taxes paid on the value of people's property (usually real estate, but sometimes also personal property like cars). Since the value of people's property is related (although imperfectly related) to income, the property tax is considered to be roughly proportional.

When all the taxes paid by individuals to all levels of governments are combined, the conclusion that most researchers come to is that little income redistribution takes place on the tax side. The progressive taxes are offset by the regressive taxes, so the overall tax system is roughly proportional. That is, on average the tax rates individuals pay are roughly equal. Recent changes in the tax laws have increased the rate that high-income people pay and lowered the rate that lower-income people pay. These changes may make the effective tax structure slightly more progressive, but meaningful statistics won't be available for a few years.

Expenditure Programs to Redistribute Income

Taxation has not proved to be an effective means of redistributing income. However, the government expenditure system has been quite effective. The federal government's expenditures that contribute to redistribution include the following.

Expenditure programs have been more successful than taxation for redistributing income.

Social Security The program that redistributes the most money is the **Social Security** system, *a social insurance program that provides financial benefits to the elderly and disabled and to their eligible dependents and/or survivors*. Social Security also has a component called **Medicare,** which is a *multibillion-dollar medical insurance system*.

Q-9 The U.S. Social Security system is only a retirement system. True or false?

The amount of an individual's Social Security retirement, disability, or survivors' monthly cash benefits depends on a very complex formula, which is skewed in favor of lower-income workers. The program is not a pension program that pegs benefits to the amount paid in. Many people will get much more than they paid in; some who never paid anything in will get a great deal; and others who paid in for years will get nothing. (No benefits are payable if you die before you retire and leave no survivors eligible for benefits due to your work.) On the whole, the program has been successful in keeping the elderly out of poverty. In addition, Social Security benefits have helped workers' survivors and the disabled.

In the early 2000s, there were more than 45 million recipients of cash Social Security benefits, many of whom also received Medicare health insurance payments. Total benefits paid in the early 2000s, including Medicare, came to over $600 billion each year.

Public Assistance **Public assistance** programs are *means-tested social programs targeted to the poor and providing financial, nutritional, medical, and housing assistance*. (These programs are more familiarly known as *welfare payments*.) Public assistance programs exist in every state of the union, although the amount paid varies greatly from state to state. The main kinds of public assistance are:

Temporary Assistance for Needy Families (TANF). Provides temporary financial assistance to needy families with children under age 19.

Food stamps. Provide nutritional assistance in the form of coupons redeemable at most food stores.

Medicaid. Medical assistance for the poor, paid for by the individual states. It's different from, and usually more generous than, Medicare.

General assistance. State assistance to poor people when emergencies arise that aren't taken care of by any of the other programs.

By far the largest proportion of payments goes to needy families with dependent children, especially since these families are usually so poor that, in addition to qualifying for TANF, they meet the eligibility requirements for food stamps and Medicaid.

TANF was instituted by the Personal Responsibility and Work Opportunity Reconciliation Act of 1996 to replace Aid to Families with Dependent Children (AFDC). It has a number of provisions that distinguish it from earlier programs. One important provision is that it establishes a lifetime limit of 60 months (not necessarily consecutive) of benefits. The purpose of the law is to direct welfare recipients to work, and another provision in the law requires welfare recipients to take a job within two years. The law also gives states significant latitude in determining benefits and eligibility criteria. These changes are major ones; they raise many questions about job training and child care. The effects of this law are discussed in the box, "From Welfare to Work."

From Welfare to Work

Applying the Tools

In an effort to reduce the negative incentive effects of welfare, in 1996 Congress passed the Personal Responsibility and Work Opportunity Reconciliation Act. The new law requires recipients of welfare assistance to work after two years on assistance and limits welfare assistance to a total of five years over a lifetime. Part of the act was also designed to offset the taxation implicit in moving from welfare to work, which could be as high as 90 percent or more, since under the old law welfare recipients who earned income above a certain level often lost almost all their welfare benefits. The new law extended funding to the working poor; for example, it provided funding for child care to help mothers move into the workforce and extended Medicaid to include the first year of work. With the changes, the implicit tax on income was reduced to about 40 percent: For every dollar of additional income, people lost 40 cents of benefits. Congress also promised monetary rewards to states that were successful in moving people off the welfare rolls.

This new law has played an important role in reducing the number of people on welfare from 14 million in 1994 to 5 million in 2002, in reducing the average stay on welfare from over 8 to under 4 years, and in reducing the unemployment rate among single mothers from over 40 percent in the early 1990s to under 30 percent in 2002.

Critics of the law have pointed out that much of the reduction occurred in the late 1990s and early 2000, when the economy was booming and one could expect the number of welfare recipients to fall anyway. But early figures suggested that the reductions continued into the recession in 2001–2002.

Of course, the law has negative effects. Some people run out of benefits and are forced into deeper poverty. Observers are keeping a close eye on the figures and on the overall effect of the law, but the general feeling is that the law has significantly increased the incentives to get off, and stay off, welfare.

Supplemental Security Income Hundreds of thousands more people would be receiving public assistance if it weren't for **Supplemental Security Income (SSI),** *a federal program that pays benefits, based on need, to the elderly, blind, and disabled.* Although SSI is administered through the Social Security offices, it is unlike Social Security benefits because eligibility for SSI payments is based solely on the basis of need. Again unlike Social Security, the recipients pay nothing toward the cost of the program. To be eligible, though, people must have very low incomes and almost no resources except a home, if they are fortunate enough to own one, a wedding ring and engagement ring, and an automobile. In the early 2000s, over $30 billion was paid in SSI benefits each year.

Unemployment Compensation **Unemployment compensation** is *short-term financial assistance, regardless of need, to eligible individuals who are temporarily out of work.* It is limited financial assistance to people who are out of work through no fault of their own and have worked in a covered occupation for a substantial number of weeks in the period just before they became unemployed.

Normally a person can receive unemployment benefits for only about six months in any given year, and the amount of the benefit is always considerably less than the amount the person earned when working.

A person can't just quit a job and live on unemployment benefits. While receiving unemployment benefits, people are expected to actively search for work. Lower-income workers receive unemployment payments that are more nearly equal to their working wage than do higher-income workers, but there is no income eligibility test. In the early 2000s about $20 billion was paid in unemployment benefits each year.

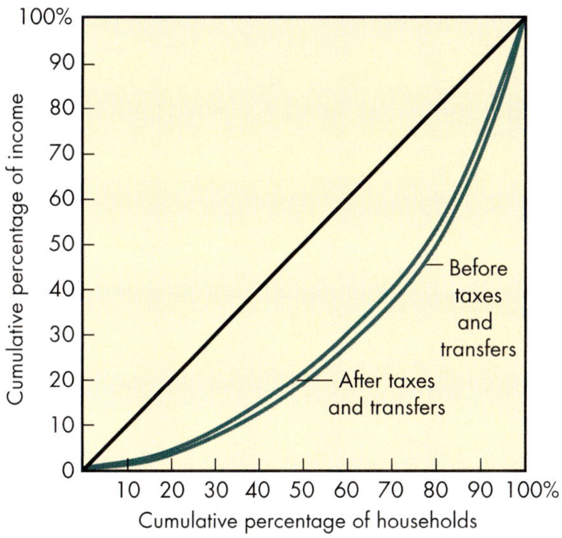

Figure 17-7 Distribution of Income before and after Taxes and Transfers, 2001

Although little redistribution takes place through the tax system, significant redistribution occurs through the transfer system, making the after-tax and transfer distribution of income more equal than the before-tax distribution of income.

Source: *Current Population Reports*, U.S. Bureau of the Census, 2002 (www.census.gov).

Housing Programs Federal and state governments have many different programs to improve housing or to provide affordable housing. While many of these programs are designed to benefit low-income persons, there are also programs for moderate-income persons and lower-income persons (people whose incomes are lower than moderate but higher than low).

The federal agency overseeing most of these programs, the Department of Housing and Urban Development (HUD), has been criticized for abuse and mismanagement. Hundreds of millions of dollars that could have benefited the poor went instead to developers of housing and other projects, to consultants, and to others who skimmed off money before—or instead of—building or rehabilitating housing. In part because of these problems, federal funding for housing was steadily reduced during the 1980s. In the early 2000s, about $30 billion was allocated to housing programs each year.

How Successful Have Income Redistribution Programs Been?

Figure 17-7 shows approximate Lorenz curves before and after analyzing the effect of both taxes and government programs on the redistribution of income. As you can see, the after-transfer income is significantly closer to being equally distributed. But because of the incentive effects of collecting and distributing the money, that redistribution has come at the cost of a reduction in the total amount of income earned by the society. The debate about whether the gain in equality of income is worth the cost in reduction of total income is likely to continue indefinitely.

Most government redistribution works through its expenditure programs, not through taxes.

While the direct methods of redistributing income get the most press and discussion, perhaps the most important redistribution decisions that the government makes involve an indirect method, the establishment and protection of property rights. Let's take an example: intellectual property rights. Intellectual property consists of things like a book you've written, a song you've composed, or a picture you've drawn. How these property rights are structured plays a fundamental role in determining the distribution of income.

Q-10 Why are property rights important in the determination of whether any particular income distribution is fair?

For example, if strict private property rights are given for, say, a design for a computer screen (e.g., a neat little trash can in the corners and windows of various files) any user other than the designer herself will have to pay for the right to use it. The designer (or the person who gets the legal right to the design) becomes very rich. If no property rights are given for the design, then no payment is made and income is much more equally distributed. Of course, without a promise of high returns to designing a computer screen device, fewer resources will be invested in finding the ideal design. While most people agree that some incentive is appropriate, there is no consensus on whether the incentives embodied in our current property rights structure are too large. I suspect that the trash can (recycling bin) design, while ingenious, would have been arrived at with a much smaller incentive.

The point of the above example is not that property rights in such ideas should not be given out. The point is that decisions on property rights issues have enormous distributional consequences that are often little discussed, even by economists. Ultimately, we can answer the question of whether income redistribution is fair only after we have answered the question of whether the initial property rights distribution is fair.

Conclusion

Much more could be said about the issues involved in income redistribution. But limitations of time and space pressure us to move on. I hope this chapter has convinced you that income redistribution is an important but difficult question. Specifically, I hope I have given you the sense that income distribution questions are integrally related to questions about the entire economic system. Supply and demand play a central role in the determination of the distribution of income, but they do so in an institutional and historical context. Thus, the analysis of income distribution must include that context as well as the analyst's ethical judgments about what is fair.

Summary

- The Lorenz curve is a measure of the distribution of income among families in a country. The farther the Lorenz curve is from the diagonal, the more unequally income is distributed.
- The official poverty measure is an absolute measure because it is based on the minimum food budget for a family. It is a relative measure because it is adjusted for average inflation.
- Income is less equally distributed in the United States than in some countries such as Sweden, but more equally distributed than in other countries such as Brazil. There is more income inequality among countries than income inequality within a country.
- Wealth is distributed less equally than income.
- Income differs substantially by class and by other socioeconomic characteristics such as age, race, and gender.
- Fairness is a philosophical question. People must judge a program's fairness for themselves.
- Income is difficult to redistribute because of incentive effects of taxes, avoidance and evasion effects of taxes, and incentive effects of redistribution programs.
- On the whole, the U.S. tax system is roughly proportional, so it is not very effective as a means of redistributing income.
- Government spending programs are more effective than tax policy in reducing income inequality in the United States.

Key Terms

income *(392)*
Lorenz curve *(385)*
Medicare *(401)*
poverty threshold *(388)*
progressive tax *(400)*
proportional tax *(400)*
public assistance *(401)*
regressive tax *(400)*
share distribution of income *(385)*
Social Security *(401)*
socioeconomic distribution of income *(385)*
Supplemental Security Income (SSI) *(402)*
unemployment compensation *(402)*
wealth *(392)*

Questions for Thought and Review

1. Why are we concerned with the distribution of income between whites and blacks, but not between redheads and blonds?
2. The Lorenz curve for Bangladesh looks like this:

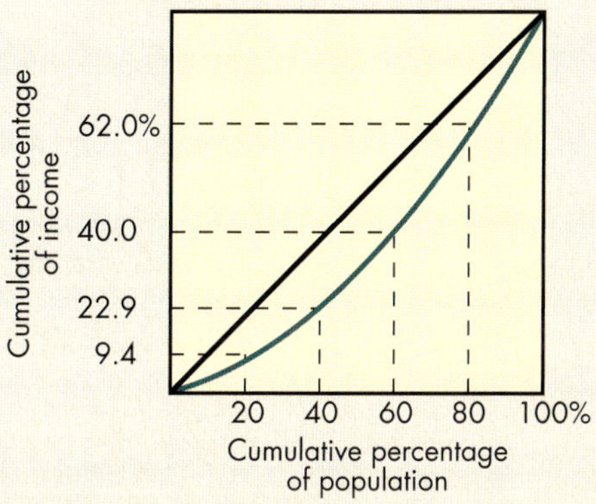

How much income do individuals in the top income quintile in Bangladesh receive?

3. If we were to draw a Lorenz curve for lawyers, what would it represent?
4. Should poverty be defined absolutely or relatively? Why?
5. Some economists argue that a class distinction should be made between managerial decision makers and other workers. Do you agree? Why or why not?
6. If a garbage collector earns more than an English teacher, does that mean something is wrong with the economy? Why or why not?
7. Is it ever appropriate for society to:
   Let someone starve?
   Let someone be homeless?
   Forbid someone to eat chocolate?
8. If you receive a paycheck, what percentage of it is withheld for taxes? What incentive effect does that have on your decision to work?
9. Which have been more successful in redistributing income—tax or expenditure programs?
10. "There are many more poor people in the United States than there are rich people. If the poor wanted to, they could exercise their power to redistribute as much money as they please to themselves. They don't do that, so they must see the income distribution system as fair." Discuss.

Problems and Exercises

1. The accompanying table shows income distribution data for three countries.

	Percentage of Total Income		
Income Quintile	India	Czech Republic	Mexico
Lowest 20%	8.5%	10.5%	4.1%
Second quintile	12.1	13.9	7.8
Third quintile	15.8	16.9	12.5
Fourth quintile	21.1	21.3	20.2
Highest 20%	42.5	37.4	55.4

   a. Using this information, draw a Lorenz curve for each country.
   b. Which country has the most equal distribution of income?
   c. Which country has the least equal?
   d. By looking at the three Lorenz curves, can you tell which country has the most progressive tax system? Why or why not?

2. "There are lies, damned lies, and statistics. Then, there are annual poverty figures." Both liberal and conservative economists believe U.S. poverty statistics are suspect. Here are some reasons:
   (1) They do not take into account in-kind benefits such as food stamps and tax credits.
   (2) They do not consider regional cost-of-living differences.
   (3) They do not take into account unreported income.

(4) Food accounts for one-fourth of a family's budget, not one-third.
(5) Ownership of assets such as homes, cars, and appliances is not taken into account.

a. What would the effect of correcting each of these be on measured poverty?
b. Would making these changes be fair?

3. The dissident Russian writer A. Amalrik has written:

> The Russian people . . . have . . . one idea that appears positive: the idea of *justice* . . . In practice, "justice" involves the desire that "nobody should live better than I do" . . . The idea of justice is motivated by hatred of everything that is outstanding, which we make no effort to imitate but, on the contrary, try to bring down to our level, by hatred of any sense of initiative, of any higher or more dynamic way of life than the life we live ourselves.

What implications would such a worldview have for the economy?

4. List four conditions you believe should hold before you would argue that two individuals should get the same amount of income.
   a. How would you apply the conditions to your views on welfare?
   b. How would you apply the conditions to your views on how progressive the income tax should be?
   c. If the income tax were made progressive in wage rates (tax rates increase as wage rates increase) rather than progressive in income, would your conditions be better met? Why?
5. In Taxland, the first $10,000 earned per year is exempt from taxation. Between $10,000.01 and $30,000, the tax rate is 25 percent. Between $30,000.01 and $50,000, it's 30 percent. Above $50,000, it's 35 percent. You're earning $75,000 a year.
   a. How much in taxes will you have to pay?
   b. What is your average tax rate? Your marginal tax rate?
   c. Taxland has just changed to a tax credit system in which, in lieu of any exemption, eligible individuals are given a check for $4,000. The two systems are designed to bring in the same amount of revenue. Would you favor or oppose the change? Why?
6. Some economists have proposed making the tax rate progressivity depend on the wage rate rather than the income level. Thus, an individual who works twice as long as another but who receives a lower wage would face a lower marginal tax rate.
   a. What effect would this change have on incentives to work?
   b. Would this system be fairer than our current system? Why or why not?
   c. If, simultaneously, the tax system were made regressive in hours worked so that individuals who work longer hours faced lower marginal tax rates, what effect would this change have on hours worked?
   d. What would be some of the administrative difficulties of instituting the above changes to our income tax code?

Web Questions

1. About.com has information about a variety of economic topics. Go to www.taxes.about.com to answer the following questions:
   a. At what rate are capital gains income taxed?
   b. What is the alternative minimum tax?
   c. What are education credits?
2. The federal government is a great source for information on the Web. Go to www.ssa.gov/pubs/10072.html. Answer the following questions:
   a. What is a Social Security credit, and how much earnings does it take to get a credit?
   b. How many credits do you need to collect benefits?
   c. What is the charge for a Social Security number?
   d. What are the eligibility requirements for Medicare?
   e. What is the difference between Part A and Part B Medicare?

Answers to Margin Questions

1. When drawing a Lorenz curve, you put the cumulative percentage of income on the vertical axis and the cumulative percentage of families (or population) on the horizontal axis. *(385)*
2. The U.S. definition of poverty is an absolute measure, but the way poverty is calculated means that some relativity is included in the definition. *(388)*
3. The United States has significantly more income inequality than Sweden and Japan, but significantly less than Brazil. *(391)*
4. In early capitalist society, the distributional fight was between workers and capitalists. In modern capitalist society, the distributional fight is more varied. For example, in the United States minorities are pitted against whites and males against females. *(395)*

5. No, it is not self-evident that greater equality of income would make society a better place to live. Unequal income distribution has its benefits. Still, most people would prefer a somewhat more equal distribution of income than currently exists. *(396)*
6. What is fair is a very difficult concept. It depends on people's needs, people's wants, to what degree people are deserving, and other factors. Still, in the absence of any more information than is given in the question, I would divide the pie equally. *(397)*
7. No, one cannot reasonably assume other things remain constant. Redistributive programs have important side effects that can change the behavior of individuals and subvert the intent of the program. Three important side effects include substituting leisure for labor, a decrease in measured income, and attempts to appear more needy. *(398)*
8. As a general statement, "A progressive tax is preferable to a proportional tax" is false. A progressive tax may well be preferable, but that is a normative judgment (just as its opposite would be). Moreover, taxes have incentive effects that must be considered. *(400)*
9. False. The U.S. Social Security system includes many other aspects, such as disability benefits and survivors' benefits. *(401)*
10. The distribution of initial property rights underlies the initial distribution of income. Those with the property rights will reap the returns from those rights. Ultimately, we can answer the question whether income distribution is fair only after we have answered whether the initial property rights distribution is fair. *(403)*

18 Government Policy and Market Failures

After reading this chapter, you should be able to:

- Explain what an externality is and show how it affects the market outcome.
- Describe three methods of dealing with externalities.
- Define *public good* and explain the problem with determining the value of a public good to society.
- Explain how informational problems can lead to market failure.
- List five reasons why government's solution to a market failure could worsen the market failure.

Web Note 18.1
The Invisible Hand

> The business of government is to keep the government out of business—that is unless business needs government aid.
>
> —*Will Rogers*

There is an ongoing (indeed unending) debate: Should the government intervene in markets such as health care or agriculture? The supply/demand framework you learned in the previous chapters was created to provide some insight into answering that question, and those chapters began exploring the issues. In this chapter we explore economic policy questions more deeply and develop a fuller understanding of some of the roles of government first presented in Chapter 2.

The economic analysis of policy is set in the economic framework, which can also be called the *invisible hand framework*. It says that if markets are perfectly competitive they will lead individuals to make voluntary choices that are in the society's interest. It is as if individuals are guided by an invisible hand to do what society wants them to do.

Market Failures

For the invisible hand to guide private actions toward the social good, a number of conditions must be met. When those conditions are not met, economists say that there is a **market failure**—*a situation in which the invisible hand pushes in such a way that individual decisions do not lead to socially desirable outcomes*. In this chapter we consider three sources of market failures: externalities, public goods, and imperfect information.

Anytime a market failure exists, there is a reason for possible government intervention to improve the outcome. But it is important to remember that even if a market failure exists, it is not clear that government action will improve the result, since the politics of implementing the solution often lead to further problems. These problems of government intervention are often called *government failures*, so after discussing the three sources of market failures, we will discuss government failures. The economic policy debate will then be framed as a matter of choosing which failure is likely to be the lesser of two evils.

Pareto Optimality and the Perfectly Competitive Benchmark

Knowing the Tools

Perfect competition serves as a benchmark for judging policies. A foundation for this benchmark is in the work of Stanford economist Kenneth Arrow, who showed that the market translates self-interest into society's interest. (Arrow was given a Nobel Prize in 1972 for this work.) Arrow's ideas are based on many assumptions that can only be touched on in an introductory book. I will, however, discuss one here—the interpretation of the term *society's welfare*. In the economic framework society's welfare is interpreted as coming as close as one can to a *Pareto optimal position*—a position from which no person can be made better off without another being made worse off. (Pareto optimal policies will be discussed more in Chapter 20.)

Let's briefly consider what Arrow proved. He showed that if the market was perfectly competitive, and if there was a complete set of markets (a market for every possible good) now and in the future, the invisible hand would guide the economy to a Pareto optimal position. If these assumptions hold true, the supply curve (which represents the marginal cost to the suppliers) would represent the marginal cost to society. Similarly, the demand curve (which represents the marginal benefit to consumers) would represent the marginal benefit to society. In a supply/demand equilibrium, not only would an individual be as well off as he or she possibly could be, given where he or she started from, but so too would society. A perfectly competitive market equilibrium would be in a Pareto optimal position.

A number of criticisms exist to using perfect competition as a benchmark:

1. *The Nirvana criticism:* A perfectly competitive equilibrium is highly unstable. It's usually in some person's interest to restrict entry by others, and, when a market is close to a competitive equilibrium, it is in few people's interest to stop such restrictions. Thus, perfect competition will never exist in the real world. Comparing reality to a situation that cannot occur (i.e., to Nirvana) is unfair and unhelpful because it leads to attempts to achieve the unachievable. A better benchmark would be a comparison with workable competition—a state of competition that one might reasonably hope could exist.
2. *The second-best criticism:* The conditions that allow the conclusion that perfect competition leads to a Pareto optimal position are so restrictive that they are never even approached in reality. If the economy deviates in hundreds of ways from perfect competition, how are we to know whether a movement toward a competitive equilibrium in one of those ways will move the economy closer to perfect competition?
3. *The normative criticism:* Even if the previous two criticisms didn't exist, the perfect competition benchmark still isn't appropriate because there is nothing necessarily wonderful about Pareto optimality. A Pareto optimal position could be a horrendous position, depending on the starting position. For example, say the starting position is the following: One person has all the world's revenues and all the other people are starving. If that rich person would be made worse off by having some money taken from him and given to the starving poor, that starting position would be Pareto optimal. By most people's normative criteria, it would also be a lousy position.

Critics of the use of the perfect competition benchmark argue that society has a variety of goals. Pareto optimality may be one of them, but it's only one. They argue that economists should take into account all of society's goals—not just Pareto optimality—when determining a benchmark for judging policies.

Externalities

An important requirement for the invisible hand to guide markets in society's interest is that market transactions have no side effects on anyone not involved in them. As I discussed in Chapter 2, such side effects are called **externalities**—*the effects of a decision on a third party that are not taken into account by the decision maker*. Externalities can be either positive or negative. Secondhand smoke and carbon monoxide emissions are examples of **negative externalities**, which occur *when the effects of a decision not taken into account by the decision maker are detrimental to others*. **Positive externalities** occur *when*

An externality is an effect of a decision on a third party not taken into account by the decision maker.

Figure 18-1 A Negative Externality
When there is a negative externality, the marginal private cost will be below the marginal social cost and the competitive price will be too low to maximize social welfare.

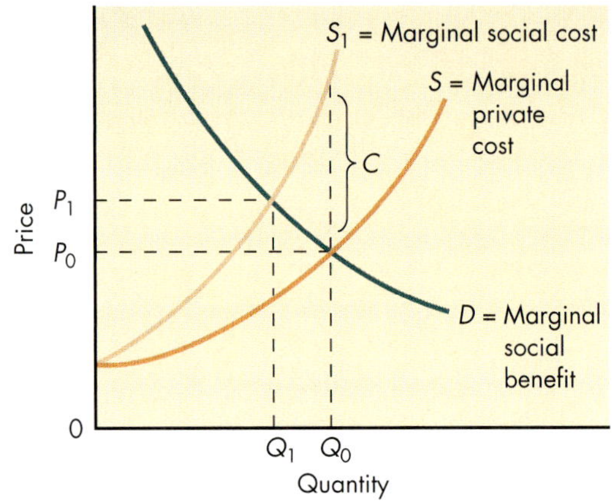

the effects of a decision not taken into account by the decision maker are beneficial to others. An example is education. When you purchase a college education, it affects not only you but others as well. Innovation is another example. The invention of the personal computer has had significant beneficial effects on society, which were not taken into account by the inventors. When there are externalities, the supply and/or demand curves no longer represent the marginal cost and marginal benefit curves to society.

A Negative Externality Example

Say that you and I agree that I'll produce steel for you. I'll build my steel plant on land I own, and start producing. We both believe our welfare will improve. But what about my plant's neighbors? The resulting smoke will pollute the air they breathe. The people involved in the market trade (you and I) are made better off, but people external to the trade are made worse off. Thus, there is a negative externality. My production of steel has a cost to society that neither you nor I take into account.

When there are externalities the marginal social cost differs from the marginal private cost.

Q-1 Why does the existence of an externality prevent the market from working properly?

The effect of a negative externality is shown in Figure 18-1. The supply curve *S* represents the marginal private cost to society of producing steel. The demand curve *D* represents the marginal social benefit of consuming the steel. When there are no externalities, the marginal private costs and benefits represent the marginal social costs and benefits, so the supply/demand equilibrium (P_0, Q_0) represents the point where the marginal social benefit equals the marginal social cost. At that point society is as well off as possible.

But now consider what happens when production results in negative externalities. In that case people not involved in production also incur costs. This means that the supply curve no longer represents both the marginal private and marginal social costs of supplying the good. Marginal social cost is greater than the marginal private cost. This case can be represented by adding a curve in Figure 18-1 called the *marginal social cost curve*. The **marginal social cost** includes all the marginal costs that society bears—or *the marginal private costs of production plus the cost of the negative externalities associated with that production.*

Since in this case the externality represents an additional cost to society, the marginal social cost curve lies above the marginal private cost curve. The distance between the two curves represents the additional marginal cost of the externality. For example, at quantity Q_0, the private marginal cost faced by the firm is P_0. The marginal cost from the externality at quantity Q_0 is shown by distance C. The externality cost is not taken

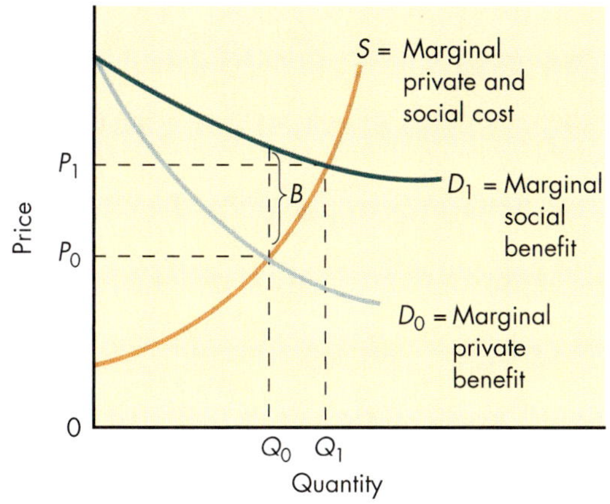

Figure 18-2 A Positive Externality
When there is a positive externality, the marginal social benefit will be above the marginal private benefit and the market price will be too low to maximize social welfare.

into account, and the supply/demand equilibrium is at too high a quantity, Q_0, and at too low a price, P_0.

Notice that the market solution results in a level of steel production that exceeds the level that equates the marginal social costs with the marginal social benefits. If the market is to maximize welfare, some type of government intervention may be needed to reduce production from Q_0 to Q_1 and raise price from P_0 to P_1.

A Positive Externality Example

Private trades can also benefit third parties not involved in the trade. These are positive externalities. Again, an example is education. Consider a person who is working and takes a class at night. He or she will bring the knowledge from class back to co-workers through day-to-day interaction on projects. The co-workers will be learning the material from the class indirectly. They are outside the initial decision to take the class, but they benefit nonetheless.

In the case of positive externalities, the market will not provide enough of the good. Let's see how. In Figure 18-2, we start again with the standard demand and supply curves. The supply curve S represents the marginal private cost of the course. The demand curve D_0 is the marginal private benefit to those who take the course. Since others not taking the course also benefit, the marginal social benefit, shown by D_1, is above the marginal private benefit. The **marginal social benefit** equals *the marginal private benefit of consuming a good plus the benefits of the positive externalities resulting from consuming that good*. The vertical distance between D_0 and D_1 is the additional benefit that others receive at each quantity. At quantity Q_0, the market equilibrium, the marginal benefit of the externality is shown by distance B. At this quantity, the marginal social benefit exceeds the marginal social cost. The market provides too little of the good. The optimal price and quantity for society are P_1 and Q_1, respectively. Again, some type of intervention to increase quantity and lower price may be warranted.

Q-2 If a positive externality exists, does that mean that the market works better than if no externality exists?

Positive externalities make the marginal private benefit below the marginal social benefit.

Alternative Methods of Dealing with Externalities

Ways to deal with externalities include (1) direct regulation, (2) incentive policies (tax incentive policies and market incentive policies), and (3) voluntary solutions.

Externalities can be dealt with via:
1. Direct regulation.
2. Incentive policies.
3. Voluntary solutions.

Common Resources and the Tragedy of the Commons

Applying the Tools

Individuals tend to overuse commonly owned goods. Let's consider an example—say that grazing land is held in common. Individuals are free to bring their sheep to graze on the land. What is likely to happen? Each grazing sheep will reduce the amount of grass for other sheep. If individuals don't have to pay for grazing, when deciding how much to graze their sheep they will not take into account the cost to others of their sheep's grazing. The result may be overgrazing—killing the grass and destroying the grazing land. This is known as the *tragedy of the commons.* A more contemporary example of the tragedy of the commons is fishing. The sea is a common resource; no one owns it, and whenever people catch fish, they reduce the number of fish that others can catch. The result will likely be overfishing.

The tragedy of the commons is an example of the problems posed by externalities. Catching fish imposes a negative externality. Because of the negative effect on others, the social cost of catching a fish is greater than the private cost. Overfishing has been a problem in the United States and throughout the world. Thus, the tragedy of the commons is caused by individuals not taking into account the negative externalities of their actions.

Why doesn't the market solve the externality problem? Some economists argue that in the tragedy of the commons examples it would, if given a chance. The problem is a lack of property rights (lack of ownership). If rights to all goods were defined, the tragedy of the commons would disappear. In the fishing example, if someone owned the sea, he or she would charge individuals to fish. By charging for fishing rights the owner would internalize the externality and thus avoid the tragedy of the commons.

Direct Regulation

In a program of **direct regulation,** *the amount of a good people are allowed to use is directly limited by the government*. Let's consider an example. Say we have two individuals, Ms. Thrifty, who uses 10 gallons of gasoline a day, and Mr. Big, who uses 20 gallons of gas a day. Say we have decided that we want to reduce total daily gas consumption by 10 percent, or 3 gallons. The regulatory solution might require both individuals to reduce consumption by some specified amount. Likely direct regulatory reduction strategies would be to require an equal quantity reduction (each consumer reducing consumption by 1.5 gallons) or an equal percentage reduction (each consumer reducing consumption by 10 percent).

Both of those strategies would work, but neither would be **efficient** *(achieving a goal at the lowest cost in total resources without consideration as to who pays those costs)*. This is because direct regulation does not take into account that the costs of reducing consumption may differ among individuals. Say, for example, that Ms. Thrifty could easily (i.e., almost costlessly) reduce consumption by 3 gallons while Mr. Big would find it very costly to reduce consumption by even 0.5 gallon. In that case, either regulatory solution would be **inefficient** *(achieving a goal in a more costly manner than necessary)*. It would be less costly (more efficient) to have Ms. Thrifty undertake most of the reduction. A policy that would automatically make the person who has the lower cost of reduction *choose* (as opposed to being *required*) to undertake the most reduction would achieve the same level of reduction at a lower cost. In this case the efficient policy would get Ms. Thrifty to choose to undertake the majority of the reduction.

Q-3 It is sometimes said that there is a trade-off between fairness and efficiency. Explain one way in which that is true and one way in which that is false.

Incentive Policies

Economists tend to like incentive policies to deal with externalities.

Two types of incentive policies would each get Ms. Thrifty to undertake the larger share of reduction. One is to create a tax incentive to achieve the desired reduction; the other

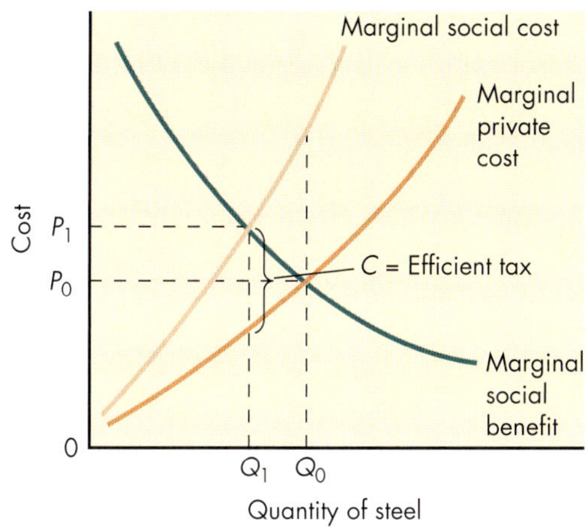

Figure 18-3 Regulation through Taxation
If the government sets a tax sufficient to take into account a negative externality, individuals will respond by reducing the quantity of the pollution-causing activity supplied to a level that individuals would have supplied had they included the negative externality in their decision.

is to create a type of property right embodied in a permit or certificate, and to allow individuals to trade those property rights freely.

Tax Incentive Policies Let's say that the government imposes a tax on gasoline consumption of 50 cents per gallon. This would be an example of a **tax incentive program** *(a program using a tax to create incentives for individuals to structure their activities in a way that is consistent with the desired ends)*. Since Ms. Thrifty can almost costlessly reduce her gasoline consumption, she will likely respond to the tax by reducing gasoline consumption, say, by 2.75 gallons. She pays only $3.63 in tax but undertakes most of the conservation. Since Mr. Big finds it very costly to reduce his consumption of gasoline, he will likely respond by reducing gasoline consumption by very little, say by 0.25 gallon. He pays $9.88 in tax but does little of the conservation.

In this example, the tax has achieved the desired end in a more efficient manner than would the regulatory solution—the person for whom the reduction is least costly cuts consumption the most. Why? Because the incentive to reduce is embodied in the price, and individuals are forced to choose how much to change their consumption. The tax has made them internalize the externality. The solution also has a significant element of fairness about it. The person who conserves the most pays the least tax.

Q-4 In what sense is the tax incentive approach fair?

Let's now consider how the tax incentive solution will solve the problem in our earlier example of steel production creating an externality. Figure 18-3 shows the situation. Say the government determines that the additional marginal social cost of producing steel equals C. If the government sets the pollution tax on steel production at C, the firm will reduce its output to Q_1 on its own. Such taxes on externalities are often called **effluent fees**—*charges imposed by government on the level of pollution created.* The efficient tax equals the additional cost imposed on society but not taken into account by the decision maker. With such a tax, the cost the suppliers face is the social cost of supplying the good. With the tax, the invisible hand guides the traders to equate the marginal social cost to the marginal social benefit and the equilibrium is socially optimal.

Market Incentive Policies A second incentive policy that gets individuals to internalize an externality is a **market incentive plan** *(a plan requiring market participants to certify that they have reduced total consumption—not necessarily their own individual consumption—by a specified amount)*. Such a program would be close to the regulatory solution but involves a major difference. If individuals choose to reduce consumption by more than the required amount, they will be given a marketable certificate that they can sell to someone who has chosen to reduce consumption by less than the required amount. By buying that certificate, the person who has not personally reduced consumption by the requisite amount will have met the program's requirements. Let's see how the program would work with Mr. Big and Ms. Thrifty.

In our example, Mr. Big finds it very costly to reduce consumption while Ms. Thrifty finds it easy. So we can expect that Mr. Big won't reduce consumption much and will instead buy certificates from Ms. Thrifty, who will choose to undertake significant reduction in her consumption to generate the certificates, assuming she can sell them to Mr. Big for a high enough price to make that reduction worth her while. So, as was the case in the tax incentive program, Ms. Thrifty undertakes most of the conservation—but she reaps a financial benefit for it.

Incentive policies are more efficient than direct regulatory policies.

Obviously there are enormous questions about the administrative feasibility of these types of proposals, but what's important to understand here is not the specifics of the proposals but the way in which incentive policies are *more efficient* than the regulatory policy. As I stated before, *more efficient* means *less costly* in terms of resources, with no consideration paid to who is bearing those costs. Incorporating the incentive into a price and then letting individuals choose how to respond to that incentive lets those who find it least costly undertake most of the adjustment.

More and more, governments are exploring incentive policies for solving problems. Sin taxes (taxes on goods government believes to be harmful) are an example of the tax incentive approach. (These will be discussed further in Chapter 20.) Marketable permits for pollution are an example of the marketable certificate approach. You can probably see more examples discussed in the news.

Voluntary Reductions

A third alternative method of dealing with externalities is to make the reduction voluntary, leaving individuals free to choose whether to follow what is socially optimal or what is privately optimal. Let's consider how a voluntary program might work in our Mr. Big and Ms. Thrifty example. Let's say that Ms. Thrifty has a social conscience and undertakes most of the reduction while Mr. Big has no social conscience and does not reduce consumption significantly. It seems that this is a reasonably efficient solution. But what if the costs were reversed and Mr. Big had the low cost of reduction and Ms. Thrifty had the high cost? Then the voluntary solution would not be so efficient. Of course, it could be argued that when people choose to do something voluntarily it makes them better off. So one could argue that even in the case where Ms. Thrifty has a high cost of reduction and voluntarily undertakes most of the reduction, she also has a high benefit from reducing her consumption.

Web Note 18.2
Union Shops

The largest problem with voluntary solutions is that a person's willingness to do things for the good of society generally depends on that person's belief that others will also be helping.

Q-5 What are two reasons to be dubious of solutions based on voluntary action that is not in people's self-interest?

If a socially conscious person comes to believe that a large number of other people won't contribute, he or she will often lose that social conscience: Why should I do what's good for society if others won't? This is an example of the **free rider problem** (*individuals' unwillingness to share in the cost of a public good*), which economists believe will often limit, and eventually undermine, social actions based on voluntary contributions. A small number of free riders will undermine the social consciousness of many in the society and eventually the voluntary policy will fail.

Economists believe that a small number of free riders will undermine the social consciousness of many in the society and that eventually a voluntary policy will fail.

There are exceptions. During times of war and extreme crisis, voluntary programs are often successful. For example, during World War II the war effort was financed in part through successful voluntary programs. But for other long-term social problems that involve individuals accepting significant changes in their actions, generally the results of voluntary programs haven't been positive.

The Optimal Policy

An **optimal policy** is *one in which the marginal cost of undertaking the policy equals the marginal benefit of that policy*. If a policy isn't optimal (that is, the marginal cost exceeds the marginal benefit or the marginal benefit exceeds the marginal cost), resources are being wasted because the savings from a reduction of expenditures on a program will be worth more than the gains that would be lost from reducing the program, or the benefit from spending more on a program will be worth more than the cost of expanding the program.

If a policy isn't optimal, resources are being wasted because the savings from reduction of expenditures on a program will be worth more than the gains that will be lost from reducing the program.

Let's consider an example of this latter case. Say the marginal benefit of a program significantly exceeds it marginal cost. That would seem good. But that would mean that we could expand the program by decreasing some other program or activity whose marginal benefit doesn't exceed its marginal cost, with a net gain in benefits to society. To spend too little on a beneficial program is as inefficient as spending too much on a nonbeneficial program.

This concept of optimality carries over to economists' view of most problems. For example, some environmentalists would like to completely rid the economy of pollution. Most economists believe that doing so is costly and that since it's costly, one would want to take into account those costs. That means that society should reduce pollution only to the point where the marginal cost of reducing pollution equals the marginal benefit. That point is called the *optimal level of pollution*—the amount of pollution at which the marginal benefit of reducing pollution equals the marginal cost. To reduce pollution below that level would make society as a whole worse off.

Some environmentalists want to rid the world of all pollution, while most economists want to reduce pollution to the point where the marginal cost of reducing pollution equals the marginal benefit.

Public Goods

A **public good** is *a good that is nonexclusive (no one can be excluded from its benefits) and nonrival (consumption by one does not preclude consumption by others)*. As I discussed in Chapter 2, in reality there is no such thing as a pure public good, but many of the goods that government provides—education, defense, roads, and legal systems—have public-good aspects to them. Probably the closest example we have of a pure public good is national defense. A single individual cannot protect himself or herself from a foreign invasion without protecting his or her neighbors as well. Protection for one person means that many others are also protected. Governments generally provide goods with significant public aspects to them because private businesses will not supply them, unless they transform the good into a mostly private good.

Web Note 18.3
Charging for Roads

What is and is not considered a public good depends on technology. Consider roads—at one point roads were often privately supplied, since with horses and buggies the road owners could charge tolls relatively easily. Then, with the increased speed of the automobile, collecting tolls on most roads became too time-consuming. At that point the nonexclusive public-good aspect of roads became dominant—once a road was built, it was most efficiently supplied to others at a zero cost—and government became the provider of most roads. Today, with modern computer technology, sensors that monitor road use can be placed on roads and in cars. Charging for roads has once again become more feasible. In the future we may again see more private provision of roads. Some economists have even called for privatization of existing roads, and private roads are being built in California and in Bangkok, Thailand.

One of the reasons that pure public goods are sufficiently interesting to warrant a separate discussion is that a modification of the supply/demand model can be used to neatly contrast the efficient supply of a private good with the efficient supply of a public good. The key to understanding the difference is to recognize that once a pure public good is supplied to one individual, it is simultaneously supplied to all, whereas a private good is supplied only to the individual who purchased it. For example, if the price of an apple is 50 cents, the efficient purchase rule is for individuals to buy apples until the marginal benefit of the last apple consumed is equal to 50 cents. The analysis focuses on the individual. If the equilibrium price is 50 cents, the marginal benefit of the last apple sold in the market is equal to 50 cents. That benefit is paid for by one individual and is enjoyed by one individual.

Now consider a public good. Say that the marginal benefit of an additional missile for national defense is 50 cents to one individual and 25 cents to another. In this case the value of providing one missile provides 75 cents (25 + 50) of total social benefit. With a public good the focus is on the group. The societal benefit in the case of a public good is the *sum* of the individual benefits (since each individual gets the benefit of the good). With private goods, we count only the benefit to the person buying the good, since only one person gets it.

The above reasoning can be translated into supply and demand curves. The market demand curve represents the marginal benefit of a good to society. As we saw in Chapter 4 in the case of a private good, the market demand curve is the *horizontal sum* of the individual demand curves. The total amount of a private good supplied is split up among many buyers. While the market demand curve for a private good is constructed by adding all the quantities demanded at every price, the market demand curve in the case of public goods is the *vertical sum* of the individual demand curves at every quantity. The quantity of the good supplied is not split up; the full benefit of the total output is received by everyone.

With private goods you sum demand curves horizontally; with public goods you sum it vertically.

Figure 18-4 gives an example of a public good. In it we assume that society consists of only two households—A and B, with demand curves D_A and D_B. To arrive at the market demand curve for the public good, we vertically add the price that each individual is willing to pay for each unit since both receive a benefit when the good is supplied. Thus, at quantity 1 we add \$0.60 to \$0.50. We arrive at \$1.10, the marginal benefit of providing the first missile. By adding together the willingness to pay by individuals A and B for quantities 2 and 3, we generate the market demand curve for missiles.

Figure 18-4 The Market Value of a Public Good
The market demand curve for a public good is constructed differently than for a private good. Since a public good is enjoyed by many people without diminishing its value to others, the market demand curve is constructed by adding the marginal benefit each individual receives from the public good at each quantity. For example, the value of the first unit to the market is \$1.10, the sum of individual A's value (\$0.50) and individual B's value (\$0.60). In other words, vertically sum the individual demand curves to construct the market demand curve for a public good.

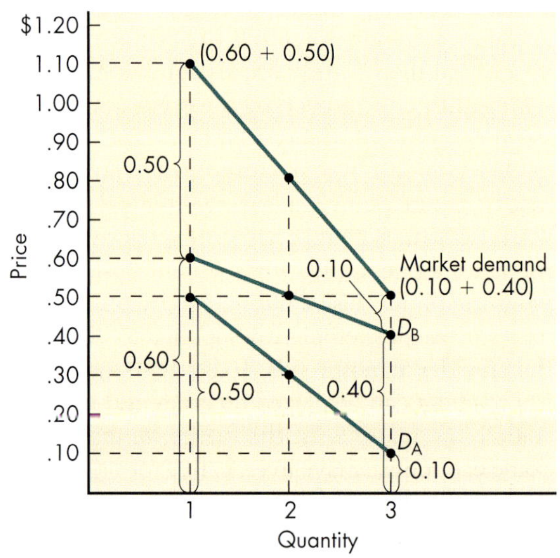

Extending this example from two individuals to the economy as a whole you can see that, even though the benefit of a public good is small to each person, the total benefit is large. With 290 million people in the United States, the benefit of that missile would be $145 million even if each person valued it on average at 50 cents.

Adding demand curves vertically is easy to do in textbooks, but not in practice. With private-good demand curves individuals reveal their demand when they buy a good. If they don't buy it, it wasn't worth the price. Since individuals do not purchase public goods, their demand is not revealed by their actions. Government must guess at it. If a public good is to be financed by a tax on the citizens who benefit from it, individuals have an incentive to conceal their willingness to pay for it. This is why in the supply of public goods we see the free rider problem. The self-interested citizen wants to benefit from the public good without bearing the cost of providing it. Similarly, if people think they will not be taxed, but will benefit from the public good, they have an incentive to exaggerate their willingness to pay.

Q-6 Why is it so difficult for government to decide the efficient quantity of a public good to provide?

Informational Problems

The final case of market failure I want to address is caused by imperfect information. The perfectly competitive model assumes that individuals have perfect information about what they are buying. So, if they voluntarily buy a good, it is a reasonable presumption that they expect that they are making themselves better off by doing so. But what happens if the buyer doesn't have perfect information? Say someone convinces you that he is selling an expensive diamond and you buy it, only to find out later that it is actually just glass. Or alternatively, say someone convinces you her used car is a cherry (in perfect condition). You buy it only to discover later that it is a lemon (faulty) and won't run no matter what you do to it.

Real-world markets often involve deception, cheating, and inaccurate information. For example, car dealers know about defects in the cars they sell but do not always reveal those defects to consumers. Another example is when consumers who want health insurance do not reveal their health problems to the insurance company. In both cases, it is in the interest of the knowledgeable person not to reveal information that the other person or firm would need to know to make an informed decision about the transaction. Hence, imperfect information can be a cause of market failure.

Imperfect information can be a cause of market failure.

When there is a lack of information, or when buyers and sellers don't have equal information, markets in some goods may not work well. Let's consider the used-car example more carefully to make the point. Let's say that owners of used cars know everything about their cars, but buyers know nothing. If sellers are profit maximizers, they will reveal as little as possible about the cars' defects; they will reveal as much as they can about the cars' good qualities.

To make the example specific, let's say also that only two types of cars exist—"lemons" that are worth $4,000 and "cherries" that are worth $8,000. The market initially consists of equal quantities of lemons and cherries. Say also that the buyers cannot distinguish between lemons and cherries. What will happen? Individuals, knowing that they have a 50 percent chance of buying a lemon, may well offer around $6,000 (the average of $4,000 and $8,000). Given that price, individuals with cherries will be very hesitant to sell, and individuals with lemons will be anxious to sell. Eventually, buyers will recognize that the sellers of cherries have left the market. In the end only lemons will be offered for sale, and buyers will offer only $4,000 with the expectation that cars offered will be lemons. When the market for cherries—good used cars—has disappeared, the result is a market failure.

Adverse selection problems can occur when buyers and sellers have different amounts of information about the good for sale.

Such a market failure is called an **adverse selection problem**—*a problem that occurs when buyers and sellers have different amounts of information about the good for sale*. In the case of adverse selection, only lemons—those with the most problems—remain in the market. Take the example of medical insurance. Insurance providers need to make a profit. To do so, they set rates that reflect their estimate of the costs of providing health care. The problem is that individuals have better information about their health than do the insurance providers. Health insurers want a diverse group to spread out the costs, but they face a greater demand among those with the worst health problems. Seeing that their customers have more health problems than average, medical insurance providers raise the rates. Those who are in good health find those charges to be too high and reduce the quantity of health insurance they purchase. The providers are therefore left with a group with an even higher incidence of health problems and higher medical costs than the general population. Less than the desired amount of low-cost insurance exists for people in good health.

Q-7 How would you expect medical insurance rates to change if medical insurers could use information contained in DNA to predict the likelihood of major medical illnesses?

Workplace safety is another example of imperfect information causing market failure. Although businesses have an incentive to provide a safe working environment to limit costs, they may not choose a level of safety that would be preferred by employees. If the employer does not disclose unsafe working conditions, and those conditions cannot be easily identified by workers, there is again an informational problem. Employees may not be adequately compensated for the risks they face.

Policies to Deal with Informational Problems

What should society do about informational problems that lead to market failures? One answer is to regulate the market and see that individuals provide the right information. Another is for the government to license individuals in the market, requiring those with licenses to reveal full information about the good being sold. Government has set up numerous regulatory commissions and passed laws that require full disclosure of information. The Federal Trade Commission, the Consumer Product Safety Commission, the Occupational Safety and Health Administration, the Food and Drug Administration, and state licensing boards are all examples of regulatory solutions designed to partially offset informational market failures.

But these regulatory solutions have problems of their own. The commissions and their regulations introduce restrictions on individuals that can slow down the economic process and prevent trades that people want to make. Consider as an example the Food and Drug Administration (FDA). It restricts what drugs may be sold until sufficient information about the drugs' effects can be disclosed. The FDA testing and approval process can take 5 or 10 years, is extraordinarily costly, and raises the price of drugs. The delays have caused some people to break the law by taking the drugs before they are approved.

A Market in Information

Information problems may be a problem of the lack of a market.

Economists who lean away from government regulation suggest that the problem presented by the information examples above are not really a problem of market failure but instead a problem of the lack of a market. Information is valuable and is an economic product in its own right. Left on their own, markets will develop to provide the information that people need and are willing to pay for. (For example, a large number of consumer magazines provide such information.) In the car example, the buyer can hire a mechanic who can test the car with sophisticated diagnostic techniques and determine whether it is likely a cherry or a lemon. Firms can offer guarantees that will provide buyers with assurance that they can either return the car or have it fixed if the car is a lemon. There are many variations of such market solutions. If the government regulates information, these markets may not develop; people might rely on government instead of markets. Thus, the informational problem is not a problem of the market; it is a problem of government regulation.

Licensing of Doctors

Let's consider another informational problem that contrasts the market approach with the regulatory approach: medical licensing.[1] Currently all doctors are required to be licensed in order to practice, but this was not always the case.

In the early 1800s, medical licenses were not required by law in the United States, so anyone who wanted to could set up shop as a physician. Today, however, it is illegal to practice medicine without a license. Licensing of doctors is justified by information problems. Since individuals often don't have an accurate way of deciding whether a doctor is good, government intervention is necessary. The information problem is solved because licensing requires that all doctors have at least a minimum competency. People have the *information* that a doctor must be competent because they see the license framed and hanging on the doctor's office wall.

Some economists argue that licensure laws were established to restrict supply, not to help the consumer.

A small number of economists, of whom Milton Friedman is the best known, have proposed that licensure laws be eliminated, leaving the medical field unlicensed. They argue that licensure was instituted as much, or more, to restrict supply as it was to help the consumer. Specifically, critics of medical licensure raise these questions:

> Why, if licensed medical training is so great, do we even need formal restrictions to keep other types of medicine from being practiced?
>
> Whom do these restrictions benefit: the general public or the doctors who practice mainstream medicine?
>
> What have the long-run effects of licensure been?

Even the strongest critics of licensure agree that, in the case of doctors, the informational argument for government intervention is strong. But the question is whether licensure is the right form of government intervention. Why doesn't the government simply provide the public with information about doctors' training and about which treatments work and which don't? That would give the freest rein to *consumer sovereignty* (the right of the individual to make choices about what is consumed and produced). If people have the necessary information but still choose to treat cancer with laetrile or treat influenza with massive doses of vitamin C, why should the government tell them they can't?

If the informational alternative is preferable to licensure, why didn't the government choose it? Friedman argues that government didn't follow that path because the licensing was done as much for the doctors as for the general public. Licensure has led to a monopoly position for doctors. They can restrict supply and increase price and thereby significantly increase their incomes.

Let's now take a closer look at the informational alternative that critics say would be preferable.

The Informational Alternative to Licensure

Web Note 18.4
Medical Information

The informational alternative is to allow anyone to practice medicine, but to have the government certify doctors' backgrounds and qualifications. The government would require that doctors' backgrounds be made public knowledge. Each doctor would have to post the following information prominently in his or her office:

1. Grades in college.
2. Grades in medical school.

[1] The arguments presented here about licensing doctors also apply to dentists, lawyers, college professors, cosmetologists (in some states, cosmetologists must be licensed), and other professional groups.

Licensure and Surgery

Applying the Tools

Surgery should be the strongest case for licensure. Would you want an untrained butcher to operate on you? Of course not. But opponents of licensure point out that it's not at all clear how effectively licensure prevents butchery. Ask a doctor, "Would you send your child to any board-certified surgeon picked at random?" The honest answer you'd get is "No way. Some of them are butchers." How do they know that? Being around hospitals, they have access to information about various surgeons' success and failure rates; they've seen them operate and know whether or not they have manual dexterity.

Advocates of the informational alternative suggest that you ask yourself, "What skill would you want in a surgeon?" A likely answer would be "Manual dexterity. Her fingers should be magic fingers." Does the existing system of licensure ensure that everyone who becomes a surgeon has magic fingers? No. To become licensed as a surgeon requires a grueling seven-year residency after four years of medical school, but manual dexterity, as such, is never explicitly tested or checked!

The informational alternative wouldn't necessarily eliminate the seven-year surgical residency. If the public believed that a seven-year residency was necessary to create skilled surgeons, many potential surgeons would choose that route. But there would be other ways to become a surgeon. For example, in high school, tests could be given for manual dexterity. Individuals with superb hand/eye coordination could go to a one-year technical college to train to be "heart technicians," who would work as part of a team doing heart surgery.

Clearly open-heart surgery is the extreme case, and most people will not be convinced that it can be performed by unlicensed medical personnel. But what about minor surgery? According to informational alternative advocates, many operations could be conducted more cheaply and better (since people with better manual dexterity would be doing the work) if restrictive licensing were ended. Or, if you don't accept the argument for human medical treatments, how about for veterinarians? For cosmetologists? For plumbers? Might the informational alternatives work in these professions?

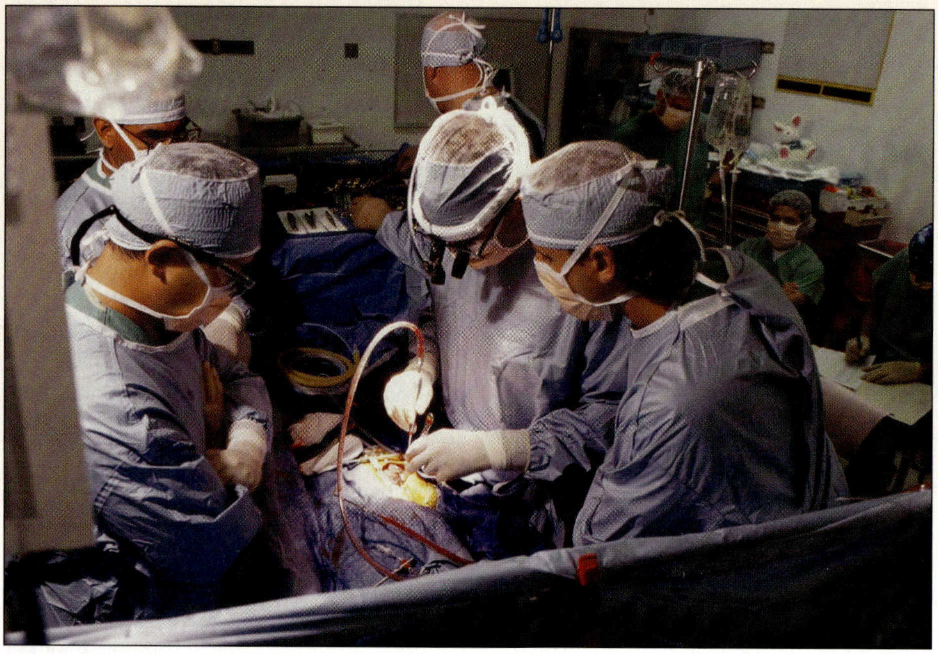

Tony Arruza/Corbis.

3. Success rate for various procedures.
4. References.
5. Medical philosophy.
6. Charges and fees.

Q-8 Who would benefit and who would lose if an informational alternative to licensing doctors were used?

According to supporters of the informational alternative, these data would allow individuals to make informed decisions about their medical care. Like all informed decisions, they would be complicated. For instance, doctors who take patients with minor problems only can show high "success rates," while doctors who are actually more skilled but who take on problem patients may have to provide more extensive information so people can see why their success rates shouldn't be compared to those of the doctors who take just easy patients. But despite the problems, supporters of the informational alternative argue that it's better than the current situation.

Current licensure laws don't provide any of this information to the public. All a patient knows is that a doctor has managed to get through medical school and has passed the medical board exams (which are, after all, only sets of multiple-choice questions). The doctor may have done all this 30 years ago, possibly by the skin of his or her teeth, but, once licensed, a doctor is a doctor for life. (A well-known doctor joke is the following: What do you call the person with the lowest passing grade point average in medical school? Answer: Doctor.) Thus, the informational alternative would provide much more useful data to the public than the current licensing procedure does.

The informational alternative relies on people having the ability to assess the information provided. Supporters of licensing argue that people do not have that ability; supporters of the informational alternative argue that they do.

Government Failure and Market Failures

The above three types of market failure—externalities, public goods, and informational problems—give you a good sense of how markets can fail. They could be extended almost infinitely; all real-world markets in some way fail. But the point was to provide you not only with a sense of the way in which markets fail but also with a sense that economists know that markets fail and many of them support markets and oppose regulation anyway. Simply to point out a market failure is not necessarily to call for government to step in and try to rectify the situation. Why? The reason can be called **government failure**—when *the government intervention in the market to improve the market failure actually makes the situation worse*.

Q-9 Would an economist necessarily believe that we should simply let the market deal with a pollution problem?

Why are there government failures? Let's briefly list some important reasons:

1. *Government doesn't have an incentive to correct the problem.* Government reflects politics, which reflects individuals' interests in trying to gain more for themselves. Political pressures to benefit some group or another will often dominate over doing the general good.
2. *Governments don't have enough information to deal with the problem.* Regulating is a difficult business. To intervene effectively, even if it wants to, government must have good information, but just as the market often lacks adequate information, so does the government. Individuals have the information and will be in a better position to decide the best plan of action.
3. *Intervention in markets is almost always more complicated than it initially seems.* Almost all actions have unintended consequences. Government attempts to offset market failures can prevent the market from dealing with the problem more effectively. The difficulty is that generally the market's ways of dealing with problems work only in the long run. As government deals with the short-run problems, it eliminates the incentives that would have brought about a long-run market solution.
4. *The bureaucratic nature of government intervention does not allow fine-tuning.* When the problems change, the government solution often responds far more slowly. An example is the Interstate Commerce Commission, which continued to exist years after its regulatory job had been eliminated.

Q-10 If one accepts the three reasons for market failure, how might one still oppose government intervention?

5. *Government intervention leads to more government intervention.* Given the nature of the political process, opening the door in one area allows government to enter into other areas where intervention is harmful. Even in those cases where government action may seem to be likely to do some good, it might be best not to intervene, if that intervention will lead to additional government action in cases where it will not likely do good.

Conclusion

As a textbook writer, I wish I could say that some conclusions can be drawn about whether the government should, or should not, enter into the economy. I certainly have views about particular instances (in case you haven't guessed, I'm a highly opinionated individual), but to lay out arguments and information that would convince a reasonable person to agree with me would take an entire book for each area in which government might intervene.

What I can do in this textbook is to stimulate your interest in discovering for yourself the information and the subtleties of the debates for and against government intervention. Just about every time you read, hear, or are asked the question "Should the government intervene in a market?" the answer is "It depends." If your first impulse is to give any answer other than that one, you may have trouble maintaining the appropriate objectivity when you start considering the costs and benefits of government intervention.

Should the government intervene in the market? It depends.

Summary

- Three sources of market failure are externalities, public goods, and imperfect information.
- An externality is the effect of a decision on a third party that is not taken into account by the decision maker. Positive externalities provide benefits to third parties. Negative externalities impose costs on third parties.
- The markets for goods with negative externalities produce too much of the good for too low of a price. The markets for goods with positive externalities produce too little of the good for too great a price.
- Economists generally prefer incentive-based programs to regulatory programs because incentive-based programs are more efficient. An example of an incentive-based program is to tax the producer of a good that results in a negative externality by the amount of the externality.
- Voluntary solutions are difficult to maintain for long periods of time because other people have an incentive to be free riders—to enjoy the benefits of others' volunteer efforts without putting forth effort themselves.
- An optimal policy is one in which the marginal cost of undertaking the policy equals its marginal benefit.
- Public goods are nonexclusive and nonrival. It is difficult to measure the benefits of public goods because people do not reveal their preferences by purchasing them in the marketplace.
- Theoretically, the market value of a public good can be calculated by summing the value that each individual places on every quantity. This is vertically summing individual demand curves.
- Individuals have an incentive to withhold information that will result in a lower price if one is a seller and a

higher price if one is a consumer. Because of this incentive to withhold information, the markets for some goods disappear. Such market failures are known as adverse selection problems.

- Licensure and full disclosure are two solutions to the information problem.
- Government intervention may worsen the problem created by the market failure. Government failure occurs because (1) governments don't have an incentive to correct the problem, (2) governments don't have enough information to deal with the problem, (3) intervention is more complicated than it initially seems, (4) the bureaucratic nature of government precludes fine-tuning, and (5) government intervention often leads to more government intervention.

KEY TERMS

adverse selection problem *(417)*
direct regulation *(412)*
efficient *(412)*
effluent fees *(413)*
externality *(409)*
free rider problem *(414)*
government failure *(421)*
inefficient *(412)*
marginal social benefit *(411)*
marginal social cost *(410)*
market failure *(408)*
market incentive plan *(413)*
negative externality *(409)*
optimal policy *(415)*
positive externality *(409)*
public good *(415)*
tax incentive program *(413)*

QUESTIONS FOR THOUGHT AND REVIEW

1. State three reasons for a potentially beneficial role of government intervention.
2. Is the marginal social benefit of a good that exhibits positive externalities greater or less than the private social benefit of that good? Why?
3. Explain why a market incentive program is more efficient than a direct regulatory program.
4. How would an economist likely respond to the statement "There is no such thing as an acceptable level of pollution"?
5. Would a high tax on oil significantly reduce the amount of pollution coming from the use of oil? Why or why not?
6. Would a high tax on oil significantly reduce the total amount of pollution in the environment?
7. More than half of 30 economists polled recently stated that the federal gasoline tax should be $1 or higher. What do you suppose were their reasons?
8. List the public-good aspects (if any) of the following goods: safety, street names, a newspaper, a steak dinner, a lighthouse.
9. If you are willing to pay $1,000 for a used stereo that is a "cherry" and $200 for a used stereo that is a "lemon," how much will you be willing to offer to purchase a stereo if there is a 50 percent chance that the stereo is a lemon? If owners of cherry stereos want $700 for their cherries, how will your estimate of the chance of getting a cherry change?
10. Define the adverse selection problem. Does your understanding of adverse selection change your view of commercial dating services? If so, how?
11. If neither buyers nor sellers could distinguish between "lemons" and "cherries" in the used-car market, what would you expect to be the mix of lemons and cherries for sale?
12. Automobile insurance companies charge lower rates to married individuals than they do to unmarried individuals. What economic reason is there for such a practice? Is it fair?
13. Should government eliminate the Food and Drug Administration's role in restricting which drugs may be marketed? Why or why not?
14. List five ways you are affected on a daily basis by government intervention in the market. For what reason might government be involved? Is that reason justified?
15. Financial analysts are currently required to be licensed. Should they be licensed? Why or why not?
16. An advanced degree is required in order to teach at most colleges. In what sense is this a form of restricting entry through licensure?
17. Who would benefit and who would lose if an informational alternative to licensing doctors were introduced?

Problems and Exercises

1. Using the table below, which shows the demand for a public good in an economy consisting of two households, A and B, answer the following questions:

Price		$0.00	$0.50	$1.00	$1.50	$2.00	$2.50	$3.00
Quantity	A	12	10	8	6	4	2	0
Demanded	B	4	3	2	1	0	0	0

   a. Graph the individual demand curves and the market demand curve.
   b. What would make you doubt that the table is an accurate reporting of the individual demand curves?
   c. If the marginal cost of providing one unit of the good is $2.00, what is the socially optimal amount of the public good?
   d. Given the free rider problem, is your answer to *c* most likely an underestimate or an overestimate?

2. There's a gas shortage in Gasland. You're presented with two proposals that will achieve the same level of reduction in the use of gas. Proposal A would force everybody to reduce their gas consumption by 5 percent. Proposal B would impose a 50-cent tax on the consumption of a gallon of gas, which would also achieve a 5 percent reduction. Demand curves for two groups are shown below.
   a. Show the effect of both proposals on each group.
   b. Which group would support a regulatory policy? Which would support a tax policy?

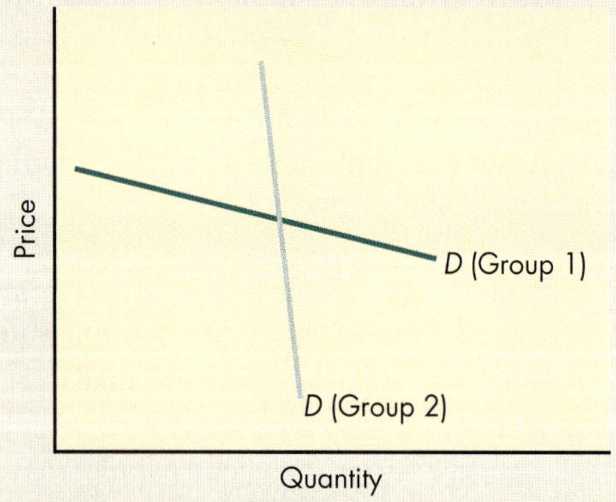

3. The marginal cost, marginal social cost, and demand for fish are represented by the curves in the graph in the following column. Suppose that there are no restrictions on fishing.
   a. Assuming perfect competition, what is the catch going to be, and at what price will it be sold?
   b. What are the socially efficient price and output?
   c. Some sports fishers propose a ban on commercial fishing. As the community's economic adviser, you're asked to comment on it at a public forum. What do you say?

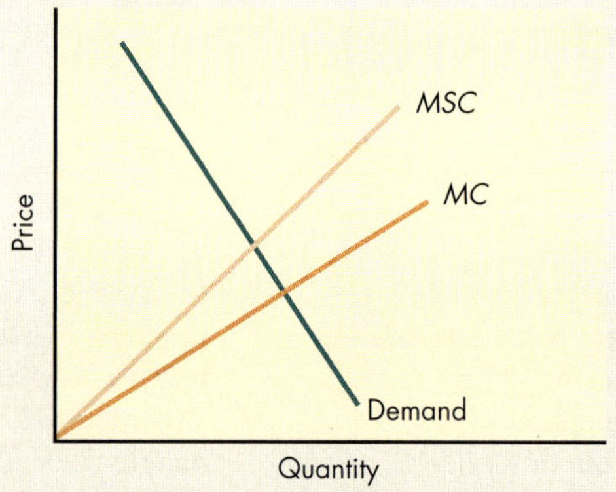

4. You are in Seattle, watching the Seattle Stomp—a dance home owners do in their trash cans.
   a. What can you say about trash fees in Seattle? Be as specific as possible.
   b. What change in fee structure might eliminate the Seattle Stomp?

5. In his book *At the Hand of Man,* Raymond Bonner argues that Africa should promote hunting, charging large fees for permits to kill animals (for example, $7,500 for a permit to shoot an elephant).
   a. What are some arguments in favor of this proposal?
   b. What are some arguments against?

6. California passed an air quality law that required 3.75 percent of all the cars sold in the state to emit zero pollution by 1998, and required 10 percent of all cars sold in the state to meet this standard by 2003.
   a. What was the likely impact of this law?
   b. Can you think of any way in which this law might actually increase pollution rather than decrease it?
   c. How might an economist suggest modifying this law to better achieve economic efficiency?

7. Economics professors Thomas Hopkins and Arthur Gosnell of the Rochester Institute of Technology estimated that in the year 2000, regulations cost the United States $662 billion, or about $5,700 per family.
   a. Do their findings mean that the United States has too many regulations?
   b. How would an economist decide which regulations to keep and which to do away with?

8. A debate about dairy products concerns the labeling of milk produced from cows who have been injected with the hormone BST, which significantly increases milk

production. Since the FDA has determined that this synthetically produced copy of a milk hormone is indistinguishable from the hormone produced naturally by the cow, and has also determined that milk from cows treated with BST is indistinguishable from milk from untreated cows, some people have argued that no labeling requirement is necessary. Others argue that the consumer has a right to know.

a. Where do you think most dairy farmers stand on this labeling issue?
b. If consumers have a right to know, should labels inform them of other drugs, such as antibiotics, normally given to cows?
c. Do you think dairy farmers who support BST labeling also support the broader labeling law that would be needed if other drugs were included? Why?

Web Questions

1. The Emissions Trading Educational Initiative (ETEI) is a project of the Environmental Defense Fund and the Emissions Marketing Association to educate the public about emissions trading. Visit the ETEI website at www.etei.org. Answer the following questions:
   a. What is "cap and trade"?
   b. What type of market failure does cap and trade address in Case Study #1? Explain your answer.
   c. Is cap and trade efficient?
   d. What is the solution to the market failure in Case #1? Has the program been successful?
2. Visit the home page for Occupational Safety and Health Administration (OSHA) at www.osha.gov. Answer the following questions:
   a. When was OSHA established and what is its mission?
   b. What market failure is OSHA designed to address?
   c. Who is covered by OSHA? Who is not covered?
   d. How does OSHA enforce its workplace standards?

Answers to Margin Questions

1. An externality is an effect of a decision not taken into account by the decision maker. When there are externalities, the private price no longer necessarily reflects the social price, and therefore the market may not work properly. *(410)*
2. No. The existence of a positive externality does not mean that the market works better than if no externality existed. It means that the market is not supplying a sufficient amount of the resource or activity, and insufficient supply can be as inefficient as an oversupply. *(411)*
3. An example of the trade-off between fairness and efficiency is whether to allow nontaxpayers to enjoy the benefits of a public park maintained through local taxes. It would cost too much to exclude them from enjoying the park, so the exclusion is inefficient, but not to exclude that person is unfair to the taxpayers who pay to maintain the park. An example of a policy that might be seen as both fair and efficient is a gas tax designed to deter pollution. Consumers choose to reduce their gas use based on the new price, so the solution is efficient. The solution has an element of fairness in it since those causing the pollution are those paying more. *(412)*
4. The tax incentive approach to pollution is fair in the following sense: Individuals whose actions result in more pollution pay more. Individuals whose actions result in less pollution pay less. In some broader sense this may not be fair if one takes into account the initial positions of those polluting. For example, the poor may have older cars that get fewer miles per gallon and have to pay a higher cost of pollution resulting from gasoline use. *(413)*
5. Voluntary actions that are not in people's self-interest may not work in large groups because individuals will rely on others to volunteer. There is also a potential lack of efficiency in voluntary solutions since the person who voluntarily reduces consumption may not be the person who faces the least cost of doing so. *(414)*
6. It is difficult for government to decide the efficient quantity of a public good because public goods are not purchased by individuals in markets. Individuals do not reveal the value they place on public goods. Individuals also face incentives to overstate the value they place on public goods if they do not have to pay for them, and to understate the value if they do have to share the cost. *(417)*
7. Since adverse selection is a problem in the medical insurance industry, with fuller information, I would expect that average medical rates would decline since the adverse selection problem would disappear. Medical insurers would be able to offer lower-cost insurance to people who are less likely to get sick and who perhaps choose not to be covered at today's high rates. *(418)*
8. If an informational alternative to licensing were introduced, existing doctors would suffer a significant monetary loss, and students who would likely go on to medical school in existing institutions would face lower potential incomes when they entered practice. Gainers would

likely be (1) those who did not want to go through an entire medical school schedule but were willing to learn a specialty that required far less education and in which they had a particular proclivity to do good, and (2) consumers, who would get more for less. *(420)*

9. An economist would not necessarily believe that we should simply let the market deal with the pollution problem. Pollution clearly involves externalities. Where economists differ from many laypeople is how they would handle the problem. An economist is likely to look more carefully into the costs, try to build price incentives into whatever program is designed, and make the marginal private cost equal the marginal social cost. *(421)*
10. One can accept all three explanations for market failure and still oppose government intervention if one believes that government intervention will cause worse problems than the market failure. *(421)*

POLITICS AND ECONOMICS: THE CASE OF AGRICULTURAL MARKETS

19

> American farmers have become welfare addicts, protected and assisted at every turn by a network of programs paid for by their fellow citizens. If Americans still believe in the virtue of self-reliance, they should tell Washington to get out of the way and let farmers practice it.
>
> —*Stephen Chapman*

After reading this chapter, you should be able to:

- Describe the competitive nature of agricultural markets.
- Explain the good/bad paradox in farming.
- State the general rule of political economy in a democracy.
- Explain how a price support system works.
- Explain, using supply and demand curves, the distributional consequences of four alternative methods of price support.
- Discuss real-world pressures politicians face when designing agricultural policy.

In May 2002 the U.S. Congress passed an agricultural support bill that authorized approximately $180 billion in price supports and other aid to farmers between 2002 and 2010. This was an increase of $80 billion over already established programs, which had been reduced six years earlier, when Congress made large payments to farmers under a Freedom to Farm Act to try to wean them off government support systems. Why did it pass this bill? The answer is that a number of farm states would be swing votes in that year's upcoming election. Both parties wanted to please those states.

Agricultural markets provide good examples of the interaction between the invisible hand and political forces. Considering the economics of agricultural markets shows us how powerful a tool supply/demand analysis is in helping us understand not only the workings of perfectly competitive markets but also the effects of government intervention in a market.

While the chapter is about agricultural markets, bear in mind that the lessons of the analysis apply to a wide variety of markets in which the invisible hand and politics interact. As you read the chapter, applying the analysis to other markets will be a useful exercise.

THE NATURE OF AGRICULTURAL MARKETS

In many ways, agricultural markets fit the classic picture of perfect competition. First, there are many independent sellers who are generally *price takers*. Second, there are many buyers. Third, the products are interchangeable: Farm A's wheat can readily be substituted for farm B's wheat. And fourth, prices can, and do, vary considerably. On the basis of these inherent characteristics, it is reasonable to talk about agricultural markets as competitive markets.

In other ways, however, agricultural markets are far from perfectly competitive. The competitiveness of many agricultural markets is influenced by

The Cost of a Box of Wheaties

Applying the Tools

When people think of agricultural products, they often think of the products they buy, like Wheaties. Doing so gives them the wrong impression of the cost of agricultural products. To see why, let's consider an 18-ounce box of Wheaties that costs you, say, $3.35.

If you look at the ingredients, you'll see that you're buying wheat, sugar, salt, malt syrup, and corn syrup. So you're buying agricultural products, right? Well, a little bit. Actually, the total cost of those agricultural ingredients is probably somewhere around 25 cents, less than 10 percent of the cost of the box of Wheaties. What are you spending the other 90 percent on? Well, there's packaging, advertising, transporting the boxes, processing the ingredients, stocking the grocery store shelves, and profits. These are important components of Wheaties, but they aren't agricultural components.

The point of this example is simple: Much of our food expenditure isn't for agricultural goods; it's for the services that transform agricultural goods into processed foods, convince us we want to eat those foods, and get those foods to us.

---

government programs. In fact, neither the United States nor any other country allows the market, unhindered, to control agricultural prices and output. For example, the U.S. government sets a minimum price for milk; buys up large quantities of wheat and stockpiles it; and licenses tobacco growers, allowing only those with licenses to grow tobacco.

Agricultural markets involve a constant struggle between political and economic forces.

I could have made the list of government programs much longer, because the government has a program for just about every major agricultural market. The point is clear, however: The competitive market in agriculture is not a story of the invisible hand alone. It's the story of a constant struggle between political and economic forces. Whenever the invisible hand pushes prices down, various coalitions of political forces generally work to push them back up. Without continued political pressure and government programs, far fewer farms would exist. Farm states know this and are strongly encouraging their farmers to engage in *value-added farming*, in which farmers take over some of the other activities that give agricultural goods their value to the consumer.

The Good/Bad Paradox in Agriculture

The good/bad paradox is the phenomenon of doing poorly because you're doing well.

Agriculture is characterized by what might be called a **good/bad paradox** *(the phenomenon of doing poorly because you're doing well)*. This good/bad paradox shows up in a variety of ways. Looking at the long run, we see that the enormous increase in agricultural productivity over the past few centuries has reduced agriculture's importance in U.S. society and has forced many farmers off the farm. Looking at the short run, we see that when harvests are good, farmers often fare badly financially; when harvests are poor, some farmers do very well financially. Let's consider these two cases in some detail.

The Long-Run Decline of Farming

Most countries, the United States included, began as predominantly agricultural societies. When the United States was founded a little more than 200 years ago, 97 percent of the labor force was engaged in farming. Today just over 2 percent of the U.S. labor force works in agriculture.

The decline in the number of farmers isn't the result of the failure of U.S. agriculture. Rather, it's the result of its tremendous success—the enormous increase in its productivity. It used to take the majority of the population to provide food for the United

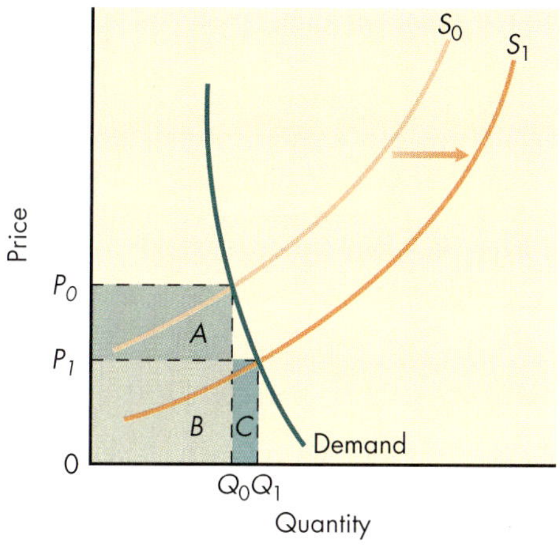

Figure 19-1 The Good/Bad Paradox
The good/bad paradox is demonstrated in this graph. At price P_0 the quantity of wheat produced is Q_0. Total income is P_0Q_0. But if the supply of wheat increases from S_0 to S_1 due to increased productivity, the price of wheat will fall from P_0 to P_1 and quantity demanded will increase from Q_0 to Q_1. The increase in farmers' income (area C) is small. The decrease in farmers' income (area A) is large. Overall, the increased productivity has led to a decrease in farmers' incomes.

States. Today it takes only a small proportion to produce more food than the U.S. population can consume.

Figure 19-1 shows how success, however, can lead to problems. In the long run the demand for wheat is inelastic (i.e., the percentage change in quantity demanded is small relative to the percentage change in price), as it is for most agricultural products, so the figure shows the equilibrium in the inelastic portion of the demand curve.

In this example, initially farmers are selling quantity Q_0 for price P_0. Their total income is P_0Q_0, shown by rectangles A and B. Now say that increases in productivity shift the supply curve out from S_0 to S_1. Output increases from Q_0 to Q_1, and price falls by a proportionately greater amount to P_1. Income falls to P_1Q_1, shown by the B and C rectangles. Farmers have gained the C rectangle but lost the A rectangle. The net effect is the difference in size between the two rectangles. So in this example, the net effect is negative.

Q-1 What is the good/bad paradox?

In short, although productivity has increased, total revenue has fallen and many farmers have stopped farming altogether. They've done good by producing a lot, but the result for themselves is bad. This good/bad paradox will occur whenever the supply curve shifts outward in the inelastic range of the demand curve.

Due to competition among farmers, most benefits of productivity increases in agriculture have gone to consumers in the form of lower prices.

Due to competition among farmers, most benefits of productivity increases in agriculture have gone to consumers in the form of lower prices. As an example, consider chicken. In the early 1930s, when Herbert Hoover was president of the United States and running for reelection, he promised prosperity to the country by saying there would be "two chickens in every pot." That promise meant a lot because, in today's money, chicken then cost \$8 a pound. In the early 2000s, the price of chicken has fallen to under \$2 a pound, only about one-quarter of its price in 1930.

The Short-Run Cyclical Problem Facing Farmers

The long-run good/bad paradox for farmers is mirrored by a short-run good/bad paradox: Good harvests often mean bad times and a fall in income; poor harvests often mean a rise in income.

A fact of life that farmers must deal with is that agricultural production tends to be highly unstable because it depends on weather and luck. Crops can be affected by too little rain, too much rain, insects, frost, heat, wind, hail—none of which can be easily controlled. Say you're an apple grower and you're having a beautiful spring—until the week that your trees are blossoming, when it rains continually. Bees don't fly when it rains, so they don't pollinate your trees. No pollination, no apple crop. There goes your apple crop for this year, and there goes your income.

The short-run demand for most agricultural goods is even more inelastic than the long-run demand. Because short-run demand is so inelastic, short-run changes in supply can have a significant effect on price. The result is that good harvests for farmers in general can lower prices significantly, while poor harvests can raise prices significantly. When the short-run price effect overwhelms the short-run quantity effect (as it does when demand is inelastic), farmers face the short-run good/bad paradox.

Marketing Poultry, *a 1936 Department of Agriculture publication, is representative of the major role government has played in agriculture.*

The Difficulty of Coordinating Farm Production

This good/bad paradox caused by inelastic demand isn't lost on farmers. They, quite naturally, aren't wild about passing on the gains to consumers instead of keeping the gains themselves. However, because agriculture is competitive, it is not in any one farmer's interest to decrease his or her supply to avoid encountering the paradox. Competitive farmers take the market price as given. That's the definition of a competitive industry. While it is in the industry's interest to have a "bad year" (to reduce total supply), it is in each individual farmer's interest to have a good year (to increase output) even if the combination of *all* farmers having a good year would cause all farmers to have a bad year (revenues would fall).

Q-2 How can it be in the interest of the agricultural industry to have a "bad year"?

It is, however, in farmers' joint interest to figure out ways to have continually "bad" years—which are, of course, actually "good" years for them. In other words, it's in their interest to figure out ways to limit the production of all farmers.

In a competitive industry, limiting production is easier said than done. It is difficult for farmers to limit production privately among themselves, because although they make up only a small percentage of the total U.S. population, there are still a lot of them—3.1 million. That's too many to coordinate easily.

Ways around the Good/Bad Paradox

Q-3 What are two ways around the good/bad paradox?

The difficulty of organizing privately to limit supply can be avoided by organizing through government. The U.S. political structure provides an alternative way for farmers (and other suppliers) to coordinate their actions and limit supply. Suppliers can organize and get government to establish programs to limit production or hold price high, thereby avoiding the good/bad paradox. And that's what farmers did, which is why so many government agricultural programs exist today. (For a history of the U.S. government farm programs, go to the Colander website: www.mhhe.com/economics/colander.) These programs have been a combination of **price stabilization programs**—*programs designed to eliminate short-run fluctuations in prices, while allowing prices to follow their long-run trend line* and **price support programs**—*programs designed to maintain prices at levels higher than the market prices.*

The General Rule of Political Economy

If farmers are helped by farm programs, who is hurt? The answer is taxpayers and consumers. One would expect that these broad groups would strongly oppose farm programs because farm programs cost them in two ways: (1) higher taxes that government requires in order to buy up surplus farm output, and (2) higher prices for food. It's not easy for a politician to tell nonfarm constituents, "I'm supporting a bill that means higher prices and higher taxes for you." Nevertheless, the farm lobby has been quite successful in seeing that these programs are retained.

Economists who specialize in the relationship between economics and politics (known as *public choice economists*) have suggested that the reasons for farm groups' success involve the nature of the benefits and costs. The groups that are hurt by agricultural subsidies are large, but the negative effect on each individual in that group is relatively small. Large groups that experience small costs per individual don't provide a strong political opposition to a small group that experiences large gains. This seems to reflect a **general rule of political economy** in a democracy: *When small groups are helped by a government action and large groups are hurt by that same action, the small group tends to lobby far more effectively than the large group; thus, policies tend to reflect the small group's interest, not the interest of the large group.*

The general rule of political economy states that small groups that are significantly affected by a government policy will lobby more effectively than large groups that are equally affected by that same policy.

This bias in favor of farm programs is strengthened by the historical representation of farmers in Congress. Right from its beginnings in 1787, the U.S. political system has reflected the importance of agriculture. The Constitution gives representation in the Senate equally to all states. Only representation in the House of Representatives is based on a state's population. Since farm states have smaller populations than urban states, this arrangement gives farmers relatively more political power per capita than nonfarmers. This political structure played an important role in making the farm states the voter swing states in 2002 and, in part, explains why farmers can lobby effectively for strong support packages.

Farmers' strong political representation in Congress establishes a core of lawmakers who favor price supports. That core is supplemented with individuals who like the countryside filled with farms rather than with suburban sprawl. Consumers and taxpayers in general, who would be hurt by price supports, generally lack the political organization necessary to make their will known and counter the pressure for price controls.

Farmers' strong political representation in Congress establishes a core of lawmakers who favor price supports.

Four Price Support Options

Let's now consider the theory underlying some alternative farm price support options. In doing so, we'll try to understand which options, given the political realities, would have the best chance of being implemented, and why.

In a price support system, the government maintains a higher-than-equilibrium price, as diagrammed in Figure 19-2. At support price P_1, the quantity people want to supply is Q_S, but the quantity demanded at that price is Q_D.

In a price support system, the government maintains a higher-than-equilibrium price.

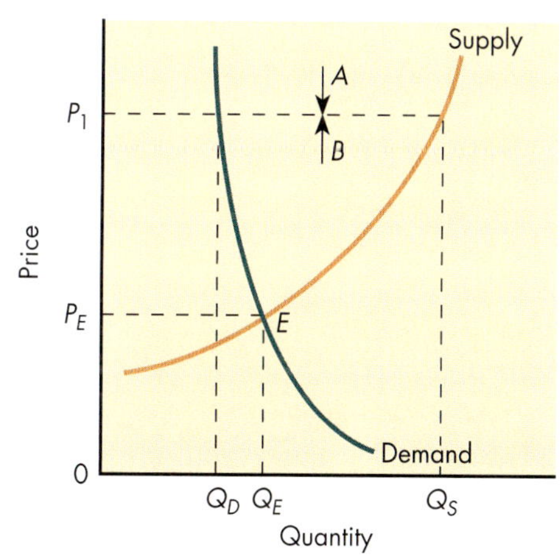

Figure 19-2 A Price Support System
In a price support system, the government maintains a higher-than-equilibrium price. At support price P_1, the quantity of product demanded is only Q_D, while the quantity supplied is Q_S. This causes downward pressures on the price, P_1, which must be offset by various government measures.

Four price support options are:

1. Regulatory force.
2. Economic incentives to reduce supply.
3. Subsidizing the sale of goods to consumers.
4. Buying up and storing, giving away, or destroying the good.

At price P_1, there's excess supply, which exerts a downward pressure on price (arrow *A*). To maintain price at P_1, some other force (arrow *B*) must be exerted; otherwise the invisible hand will force the price down.

The government has various options to offset the downward pressure on price. These include:

1. Using legal and regulatory force to prevent anyone from selling or buying at a lower price.
2. Providing economic incentives to reduce the supply enough to eliminate the downward pressure on price.
3. Subsidizing the sale of the good to consumers so that while suppliers get a high price, consumers have to pay only a low price.
4. Buying up and storing, giving away, or destroying enough of the good so that the total demand (including government's demand) increases enough to eliminate downward pressure on price.

These methods distribute the costs and benefits in slightly different ways. Let's consider each in detail.

Supporting the Price by Regulatory Measures

Suppose the government simply passes a law saying that, from now on, the price of wheat will be at least \$5 per bushel. No one may sell wheat at a lower price. If the competitive equilibrium price is higher than \$5, the law has no effect. When the competitive equilibrium is below the price floor (say the competitive equilibrium is \$3.50 per bushel), the law limits suppliers from selling their wheat at that lower price.

The price floor helps some suppliers and hurts others. Those suppliers who are lucky enough to sell their wheat benefit. Those suppliers who aren't lucky and can't find buyers for their wheat are hurt. How many suppliers will be helped and how many will be hurt depends on the elasticities of supply and demand. When supply and demand are inelastic, a large change in price brings about a small change in quantity supplied, so the hurt group is relatively small. When the supply and demand are elastic, the hurt group is larger.

In Figure 19-3(a), at \$5 suppliers would like to sell quantity Q_2 but they can sell only Q_1. They end up with a surplus of wheat, $Q_2 - Q_1$. Consumers, who must pay the higher price, \$5, and receive only Q_1 rather than Q_e, are also hurt.

With a price floor, some method of nonprice rationing must determine how the limited demand will be distributed among suppliers.

The Need for Rationing The law may or may not specify who will, and who will not, be allowed to sell, but it must establish some noneconomic method of rationing the limited demand among the suppliers. If it doesn't, buyers are likely, for example, to buy from farmers who are their friends. If individual farmers have a surplus, they'll probably try to dispose of that surplus by selling it on the black market at a price below the legal price. To maintain the support price, the government will have to arrest farmers who sell below the legal price. If the number of producers is large, such a regulatory approach is likely to break down quickly, since individual incentives to sell illegally are great and the costs of enforcing the law are accordingly high.

In understanding who benefits and who's hurt by price floors, it's useful to distinguish between two groups of farmers: the farmers who were producing before the law went into effect, and the farmers who entered the market afterward. In Figure 19-3(a), the first group supplies Q_e; the second group, which would want to enter the market when the price went up, would supply $Q_2 - Q_e$. Why must these groups be clearly identified? Because one relatively easily enforceable way to limit the quantity supplied is to

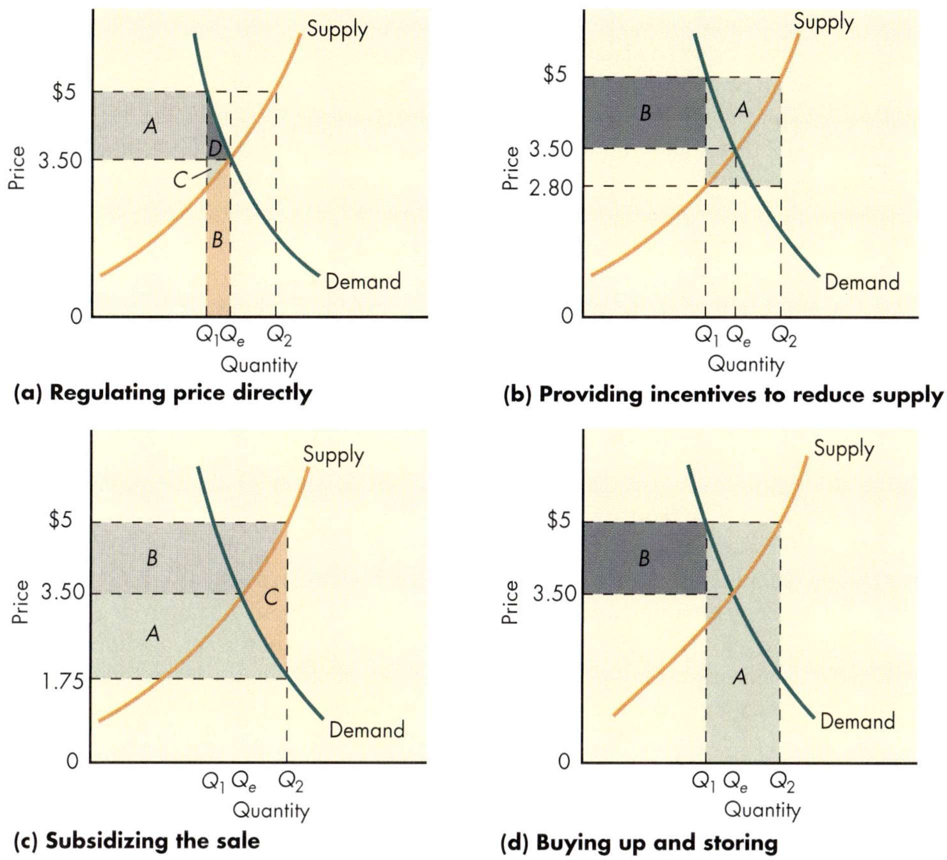

Figure 19-3 (a, b, c, and d) Alternative Methods of Government Price Supports
Alternative methods have different distributional consequences. The consequences of regulatory measures are shown in (**a**); the consequences of providing economic incentives to reduce supply in (**b**); the consequences of subsidizing the sale in (**c**); and the consequences of buying up and storing the good in (**d**).

forbid any new farmers to enter the market. Only people who were producing at the beginning of the support program will be allowed to produce, and they will be allowed to produce only as much as they did before the program went into effect. Restricting production to the existing suppliers will reduce the quantity supplied to Q_e, leaving only $Q_e - Q_1$ to be rationed among suppliers.

To use this method of restriction is to **grandfather**—*to pass a law affecting a specific group but providing that those in the group before the law was passed are exempt from some provisions of the law.* To "grandfather in" existing suppliers is one of the easiest provisions to enact into law and one of the easiest to enforce; thus, it is one of the most widely used. For example, when supply limitations were placed on tobacco, existing growers were all allowed to grow tobacco on land they were currently using for tobacco production. They could not, however, devote any new land to growing tobacco. (Later, tobacco farmers were allowed to sell their acreage allocations so that if old land was taken out of tobacco production, new land could be added.)

Grandfathering is one of the politically easiest ways of restricting supply.

When it comes to keeping groups out of production, foreign producers are perhaps the politically easiest targets. To keep the domestic price of a good up, foreign imports must be limited as well as domestic production. U.S. taxpayers might put up with subsidizing U.S. farmers, but they're likely to balk at subsidizing foreign farmers. So most farm subsidy programs are supplemented with tariffs and quotas on foreign imports of the same commodity. (See Chapter 21 for definitions and further discussion of tariffs and quotas.)

Distributional Consequences Notice that with the equilibrium in the inelastic portion of the demand curve, even though the average farmer is constrained as to how much can be sold, he or she is made better off by that constraint because the total revenue going to all farmers is higher than it would be if supply weren't constrained. The farmer's total revenue from this market increases by rectangle *A* in Figure 19-3(a) and decreases by the rectangle composed of the combined areas *B* and C. Of course, making the farmer better off is not cost-free. Consumers are made worse off because they must pay more for a smaller supply of wheat. There's no direct cost to taxpayers other than the cost of enforcing and administering the regulations.

Notice in the diagram the little triangle made up of areas C and *D*, which shows an amount of income that society loses but farmers don't get. It's simply wasted. As discussed in Chapter 7, that little triangle is the welfare loss of producer and consumer surplus to society from the restriction.

Providing Economic Incentives to Reduce Supply

A second way in which government can keep a price high is to provide farmers with economic incentives to reduce supply.

Looking at Figure 19-3(b), you see that at the support price, \$5 per bushel, the quantity of wheat supplied is Q_2 and quantity demanded is Q_1. To avoid a surplus, the government must somehow find a way to shift the quantity supplied back from Q_2 to Q_1. For example, it could pay farmers not to grow wheat, as it did in the acreage control programs established under President John F. Kennedy in the early 1960s. How much would such an economic incentive cost? Given the way the curves are drawn, to reduce the quantity supplied to Q_1, the government would have to pay farmers \$2.20 (\$5.00 − \$2.80) for each bushel of wheat they didn't grow. This payment of \$2.20 would induce suppliers producing $Q_2 - Q_1$ not to produce, reducing the quantity supplied to Q_1. The payment is shown by the *A* rectangle.

The Need for Rationing There is, however, a problem in identifying those individuals who would truly supply wheat at \$5 a bushel. Knowing that the government is paying people not to grow wheat, people who otherwise had no interest in growing wheat will pretend that at \$5 they would supply the wheat, simply to get the subsidy. To avoid this problem, often this incentive approach is combined with our first option, regulatory restrictions. Farmers who are already producing wheat at Q_e are grandfathered in; only they are given economic incentives not to produce. All others are forbidden to produce.

Q-4 Which of the four methods of price support would farmers favor least? Why?

Distributional Consequences When economic incentives are supplied, the existing farmers do very well for themselves. Their income goes up for two reasons. They get part of the *A* rectangle from the government in the form of payments not to grow wheat, and they get the *B* rectangle from consumers in the form of higher prices for the wheat they do grow. Farmers are also free to use their land for other purposes, so their income rises by the amount they can earn from using the land taken out of wheat production for something other than growing wheat. Consumers are still being hurt as before: They are paying a higher price and getting less. In addition, they're being hurt in their role as taxpayers because the lightly shaded area (rectangle A) represents the taxes they must pay to finance the government's economic incentive program. Thus, this option is much more costly to taxpayers than the regulatory option.

Subsidizing the Sale of the Good

A third option is for the government to subsidize the sale of the good to hold down the price consumers pay but keep the amount suppliers receive high. Figure 19-3(c) shows how this works. Suppliers supply quantity Q_2 and are paid \$5 per bushel. The government then turns around and sells that quantity at whatever price it can get—in this case, \$1.75. No direct transfer takes place from the consumer to the supplier. Both are made better off. Consumers get more goods at a lower price. They are benefited by area *A*. Suppliers get a higher price and can supply all they want. They are benefited by area *B*. What's the catch? The catch, of course, is that taxpayers foot the entire bill, paying the difference between the \$5 and the \$1.75 (\$3.25) for each bushel sold. The cost to taxpayers is represented by areas *A*, *B*, and *C*. This option costs taxpayers the most of any of the four options.

Q-5 Which of the four methods of price support would taxpayers favor least? Why?

Buying Up and Storing, Giving Away, or Destroying the Good

The final option is for the government to buy up all the quantity supplied that consumers don't buy at the support price. This option is shown in Figure 19-3(d). At the support price of \$5 a bushel consumers buy Q_1 and the government buys $Q_2 - Q_1$ at a total cost represented by the *A* rectangle.

Distributional Consequences In this case consumers transfer the *B* rectangle to suppliers when they pay \$5 rather than \$3.50, the competitive equilibrium price. The government (i.e., the taxpayers) pays farmers rectangle *A*. The situation is very similar to our second option, in which the government provides suppliers with economic incentives not to produce. However, this fourth option is more expensive for the government since it must pay \$5 rather than providing a \$2.20 per bushel incentive not to grow as it did in option (b). In return for this higher payment, the government is getting something in return: $Q_2 - Q_1$ of wheat.

Q-6 Which of the four methods of price support would consumers favor least? Why?

The Need to Dispose of Surplus Of course, if the government buys the surplus wheat, it takes on the problem of what to do with this surplus. Say the government decides to give it to the poor. Since the poor were already buying food, in response to a free food program they will replace some of their purchases with the free food. This replacement brings about a drop in demand—which means that the government must buy even more surplus. Instead of giving it away, though, the government can burn the surplus or store it indefinitely in warehouses and grain elevators. Burning up the surplus or storing it, at least, doesn't increase the amount government must buy.

Web Note 19.1
Food for Peace

Why, you ask, doesn't the government give the surplus to foreign countries as a type of humanitarian aid? The reason is that just as giving the surplus to our own poor creates problems in the United States, giving the surplus to the foreign poor creates problems in the countries involved. To the degree that the foreign poor have any income, they're likely to spend most of it on food. Free food would supplant some of their demand, thus lowering the price for those who previously sold food to them. Giving anything away destroys somebody's market, and when markets are destroyed someone gets upset. So when the United States has tried to give away its surplus food, other foreign countries have put enormous pressure on the United States not to "spoil the world market."

Which Group Prefers Which Option?

The four price support options I've just described can, of course, be used in various combinations. It's a useful exercise at this point to think through which of the options farmers, taxpayers, and consumers would likely favor and to relate current debates about farm programs to these options.

The U.S. House Committee on Agriculture posts information about current farm legislation at www.agriculture.house.gov.

The first option, regulation, costs the government the least, but it benefits farmers the least. Since existing farmers are likely to be the group directly pushing for price supports, government is least likely to choose this approach. If it is chosen, most of the required reduction in quantity supplied will probably come from people who might enter farming at some time in the future, not from existing farmers.

The second option, economic incentives, costs the government more than the first option but less than the third and fourth options. Farmers are benefited by economic incentive programs in two ways. They get paid not to grow a certain crop, and they can sometimes get additional income from using the land for other purposes. When farmers aren't allowed to use their land for other purposes, they usually oppose this option, preferring the third or fourth option.

The third option, subsidies on the sales to keep prices down, benefits both consumers (who get low prices) and farmers (who get high prices). Taxpayers are harmed the most by this option. They must finance the subsidy payments for all subsidized farm products.

The last option, buying up and storing or destroying the goods, costs taxpayers more than the first two options but less than the third, since consumers pay part of the cost. However, it leaves the government with a surplus to deal with. If there's a group who can take that surplus without significantly reducing their current demand, then that group is likely to support this option.

Economics, Politics, and Real-World Policies

Q-7 What two farm programs have been the most prevalent in the United States?

The two farm programs most prevalent in the United States have been the **land bank program** (in which *government supports prices by giving farmers economic incentives to reduce supply*) and the **nonrecourse loan program** (in which *government "buys" goods in the form of collateral on defaulting loans*). Programs that support prices through regulation, our first option, generally haven't been applied to existing farmers. They have, however, often been used to prevent new farmers from entering the market—which isn't surprising since the political impetus for farm programs comes from existing farmers. The third option, to subsidize the sale of the good so the farmer gets a high price and the consumer pays a low price, hasn't been used because, as discussed previously, it would be the most costly to taxpayers.

Interest Groups

The actual political debate is, of course, much more complicated than presented here. For example, other pressure groups are involved. Recently, farm groups and environmental groups have combined forces and have become more effective in shaping and supporting farm policy. Thus, recent new restrictions on supply in farming often operate in ways that environmentalists would favor, such as regulating the types of fertilizer and chemicals farmers can use.

Q-8 Are taxpayers, farmers, and consumers separate groups that are independent of each other?

Moreover, the three interest groups discussed here—farmers, taxpayers, and consumers—aren't entirely distinct one from another. Their memberships overlap. All taxpayers are also consumers, farmers are both taxpayers and consumers, and so on. Thus, much of the political debate is simply about from whose pocket the government is going to get money to help farmers. Shall it be the consumer's pocket (through higher prices)? Or the taxpayer's (through higher taxes)? That said, the political reality is that consumer and taxpayer interests and the lobbying groups that represent them generally examine only part of the picture—the part that directly affects them. Accordingly, politicians often act as if these groups had separate memberships. Politicians weigh the

Changes in U.S. Agricultural Policy

Applying the Tools

In 1996 the U.S. government voted for sweeping reforms designed to eliminate major aspects of the farm support programs by 2002. What made that politically possible was a combination of three forces: (1) the government deficit, which put pressure on government to eliminate costly programs; (2) the ability of U.S. farmers to sell abroad, which reduced the benefits of the existing farm support program to them; and (3) the general pro-market ideology that gained favor in the late 1990s and early 2000s.

When we look at the reforms more carefully, they look less sweeping than they initially appeared. There are three reasons why. First, three of the programs that most sharply limit production—peanut, sugar, and dairy programs—were left untouched because of strong lobbying efforts directed at members of Congress. Second, while in a number of areas direct price supports were eliminated, other indirect price support systems were not. The most important of these was the program that allows farmers to borrow money cheaply from the government, using the expected crop as collateral. This program allows the farmer to default on the loan, instead of paying it back, should the price of their crop be less than the prices set as collateral. This means that if agricultural prices fall significantly, the buy-up-and-store option discussed in the text will still exist and will hold prices up. This method of price support is extraordinarily costly to taxpayers.

Third, to "compensate" farmers for their elimination of direct price supports, the government gave direct grants to farmers. These grants started at $5.8 billion in 1998 and fell to $4 billion in 2002, when the law ended. With agricultural prices high, as they were at the time the law was passed, the net result of this "compensation" was that the total payments to farmers were initially higher than they were under the old price support system. As prices fell in 1999 large emergency grants were given to farmers, and as mentioned at the beginning of the chapter, in 2002 Congress passed a large farm bill that reintroduced and expanded subsidies to U.S. farmers. So the grand hopes of eliminating farm subsidies in 1996 were dashed.

options by attempting to balance their view of the general good with the power and preferences of the special interest groups that they represent or that contribute to their election campaigns.

International Issues

Web Note 19.2
EU Agricultural Policy

The final real-world complication that must be taken into account is the international dimension. If you think government is significantly involved in U.S. agriculture, you should see its role in other countries such as the members of the European Union (EU) and Japan. For example, more than half the EU's budget is devoted to farm subsidies, and most of its farms stay in business only because of protection. Our agricultural policy is, in part, determined by trade negotiations with these other countries. For example, a reduction in EU subsidies could bring about a reduction in our subsidies.

If you think government is significantly involved in U.S. agriculture, you should see its role in other countries, such as the members of the European Union and Japan.

Conclusion

This chapter has focused on agricultural markets, but it should be clear that the discussion is about much more than just agriculture; it's about the interrelationship between economics and politics. If individuals are self-interested maximizers, it's reasonable to assume that they're maximizers in all aspects of their lives. What they can't achieve in the economic sphere, they might be able to achieve in the political sphere.

To understand the economic policies that exist, we must consider how people act in both spheres. Consideration of the economics underlying government policies often leads to useful insights. For example, as discussed in Chapter 7, a military draft can be seen as a mechanism for shifting the costs of defense away from the taxpayer and onto

Q.9 Is the military draft a cheaper way of maintaining defense than a volunteer army?

a specific group of individuals—young people. The government's support for the arts can be seen as a transfer from general taxpayers to a specific group of individuals who like the arts. Government support for education can be seen as a transfer from general taxpayers to a specific group of individuals: students and instructors. These groups maintain strong lobbies to achieve their political ends, and the interaction of the various lobbying groups typically strongly influences what policies government will follow.

Q-10 Economic theory tells us that a volunteer army is preferable to an army maintained by a draft. True or false? Why?

Economics doesn't tell you whether government intervention or any particular policy is good or bad. That, you must decide for yourself. But what economics can do is pose the policy question in terms of gains and losses for particular groups. Posing the question in that framework often cuts through to the real reasons behind various groups' support for this or that policy. Often people support programs that transfer money from other taxpayers and consumers to themselves. They are, however, unlikely to say that is their motive. For example, I've seldom heard teachers say that the reason they favor government support for education is that those policies transfer money to them.

The economic framework directs you to look beyond the reasons people say they support policies; it directs you to look for the self-interest. The supply/demand framework provides a neat graphical way to picture the relative gains and losses resulting from various policies.

But as usual there's an *on the other hand*. Just because some groups may support policies for self-serving reasons, it is not necessarily the case that the policies are bad or shouldn't be adopted. Reality is complicated, with many more gray answers than black-and-white ones.

Summary

- Agricultural markets have many qualities of perfectly competitive markets: sellers are price takers, there are many buyers, products are interchangeable, and prices vary considerably. The competitiveness of agricultural markets is affected by significant government intervention.
- The good/bad paradox is the result of the inelastic demand in most agricultural markets. Increases in productivity increase supply; but, because demand is inelastic, the percentage decline in price is greater than the percentage increase in equilibrium quantity. Total revenue declines.
- A general rule of political economy in a democracy is that policies tend to reflect small groups' interests, not the interests of large groups.
- Because farmers are a small, easily identifiable group, and because farm states get larger representation relative to population in the Senate, the farm lobby is very strong.
- A price support program works by government maintaining higher-than-equilibrium prices through regulations, economic incentives, subsidies, and buying up and storing or destroying.
- Regulatory price supports cost government the least, but benefit the farmers the least.
- Economic incentive price supports cost the government and taxpayers more than regulatory price supports, but less than subsidy price supports or buying up and storing the good.
- Subsidy price supports benefit consumers, who pay lower prices, and farmers, who receive higher prices. Subsidy price supports cost taxpayers the most.
- Buying up and storing the good gives government a surplus to deal with.
- Two prevalent farm programs in the United States are the land bank program, in which government gives farmers economic incentives to reduce supply, and the

nonrecourse loan program, in which government "buys" goods in the form of collateral on defaulting loans.

- Agricultural policy is affected by interest groups (consumers, taxpayers, and farmers) and international issues (farm policies of our trading partners).

Key Terms

general rule of political economy *(431)*
good/bad paradox *(428)*
grandfather *(433)*
land bank program *(436)*
nonrecourse loan program *(436)*
price stabilization programs *(430)*
price support programs *(430)*

Questions for Thought and Review

1. If the demand for farm products were elastic rather than inelastic, would the good/bad paradox still exist? Why or why not?
2. Demonstrate, using supply and demand curves, the distributional consequences of a price support system achieved through acreage restriction.
3. Which would a taxpayers' group prefer: price support achieved through buying up the surplus or through providing economic incentives for not producing? Why?
4. What is the most costly method of price support to the taxpayer? Demonstrate graphically.
5. What is the least costly method of price support to the taxpayer? Demonstrate graphically.
6. Why do tariffs and quotas generally accompany price support systems?
7. How does the elasticity of supply affect the cost of price supports in each of the four options?
8. Why is grandfathering an attractive option for governments when they institute price supports?
9. All government intervention in markets makes society worse off. True or false? Evaluate.
10. What type of price support program is the nonrecourse loan? the land bank program?

Problems and Exercises

1. Show graphically how the effects of an increase in supply will differ according to the elasticities of supply and demand.
   a. Specifically, demonstrate the following combinations:
      (1) An inelastic supply and an inelastic demand.
      (2) An elastic supply and an inelastic demand.
      (3) An elastic supply and an elastic demand.
      (4) An inelastic supply and an inelastic demand.
   b. Demonstrate the effect of a government guarantee of the price in each of the four cases.
   c. If you were a farmer, which of the four combinations would you prefer?
2. Congratulations. You've been appointed finance minister of Farmingland. The president wants to protect her political popularity by increasing farmers' incomes. She's considering two alternatives: (a) bolstering agricultural prices by adding governmental demand to private demand; and (b) giving farmers financial incentives to restrict supply and thereby increase price. She wants to use the measure that's least costly to the government. The conditions of supply and demand are illustrated in the accompanying diagram. (S_1 is what the restricted supply curve would look like. P_s is the price that the president wants to establish.) Which measure would you advise?

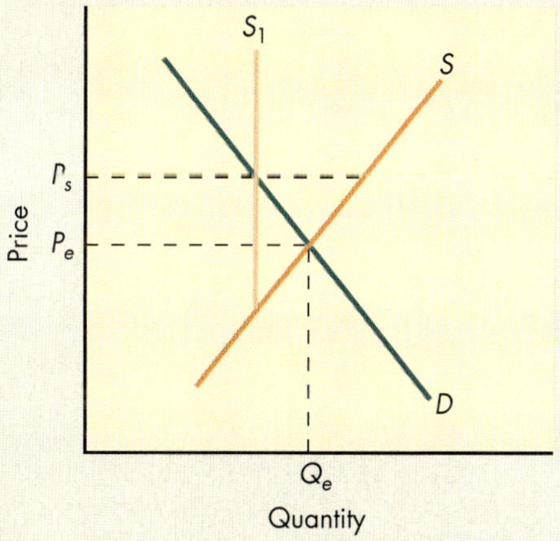

3. The Pure Food and Drug Act of 1906 is known as "Dr. Wiley's Law." It is generally regarded by non-economic historians as representing the triumph of consumer interests over producer interests.
   a. Why might an economist likely be somewhat wary of this interpretation?
   b. What evidence would a skeptical economist likely look for to determine the motives behind the passage of this law?
   c. What would be the significance of the fact that the Pure Food and Drug Act was passed in 1906, right when urbanization and technological change were fostering new products that competed significantly with existing producers' interests?
4. The U.S. government makes it against the law to grow peanuts unless the grower has been granted a government quota. It also essentially forbids peanut imports and sets a minimum U.S. price of peanuts at about 50 percent higher than the price of peanuts on the world market. This program costs the government $4 million a year in administrative costs.
   a. Are there likely any other costs associated with the program?
   b. Demonstrate graphically how to come up with about $250 million of additional costs.
   c. When "peanut land"—land with peanut quotas—is sold, what is the likely price of that land compared to equivalent land without a peanut quota?
   d. Say that, under the World Trade Organization, the United States agrees to allow open imports of peanuts into the United States and guarantees that all sellers receive the existing price. What will happen to the governmental costs of the program?
   e. Say the government limits the guaranteed high price to U.S. producers. What will it have to do to make that guarantee succeed?
5. Say that a law, if passed, will reduce Mr. A's wealth by $100,000 and increase Mr. B's wealth by $100,000.
   a. How much would Mr. A be willing to spend to stop passage of the law?
   b. How much would Mr. B be willing to spend to ensure passage of the law?
   c. What implications for social policy do your answers to *a* and *b* have?
6. The U.S. Bureau of Land Management sets a fee for ranchers who graze their animals on public land equal to $1.43 per animal unit per month—the amount of forage needed to feed one cow and its calf, or five sheep, for a month. The market rate for grazing on private land is about $14 per animal unit per month.
   a. Why do you think there is a difference?
   b. What are the advantages of setting the lower fee?
   c. Would you expect excess demand for government grazing land? Why? Demonstrate graphically.

Web Questions

1. The U.S. Department of Agriculture provides a Foreign Agriculture Service that reports prices for agricultural goods. Go to its home page at www.fas.usda.gov, look up the commodity pages, and search for recent world and domestic sugar prices. Answer the following questions:
   a. What is the cost of raw sugar on world markets? What is the cost of domestic raw sugar?
   b. What accounts for the difference between domestic and world price for raw sugar?
   c. At the Foreign Agriculture Service home page, search for and read the report "Import Requirements for Sugar and Sugar Containing Articles." How does U.S. trade policy help maintain high U.S. domestic sugar prices?
2. Go to the Council on Biotechnology Information's home page at www.whybiotech.com to answer the following questions:
   a. What are genetically engineered crops and what are their benefits to farmers?
   b. What has been the effect on farm profits in the short run?
   c. What are the possible long-term effects of genetically engineered crops on farm production? On farm income?

Answers to Margin Questions

1. The good/bad paradox is the phenomenon of doing poorly because you're doing well. It exists when demand for your product is inelastic. Specifically, as it applies to agriculture, it means that when most farmers produce a lot, prices are low and their net income drops. *(429)*
2. Because demand is inelastic, it is in the interest of the agricultural industry for the supply of agricultural goods to decline from bad weather or other supply disruptions. The percentage rise in price will be greater than the percentage decline in quantity demanded, and total revenue for the industry will rise. *(430)*
3. There are two ways around the good/bad paradox. One is for suppliers to coordinate their activity and limit supply. The second way is for suppliers to lobby and get

government to establish programs to limit production, stabilizing the price and holding it high. Because of the difficulty of coordinating the large number of farmers, it is this second track that U.S. farmers have followed. *(430)*

4. Farmers are least likely to support the regulatory method of price support, in which regulatory force is used to prevent anyone from selling or buying at a lower price. Although such a policy benefits farmers, it benefits them far less than other price support policies. *(434)*
5. Taxpayers will likely least favor the price support method of subsidizing the sale of goods to consumers, because this method costs taxpayers the most. The low price paid by consumers and the high price received by farmers together necessitate large subsidies. *(435)*
6. Consumers would least favor the price support method of providing economic incentives to reduce supply and the price support method of regulatory force. Both these methods reduce the supply and push up the price. Some consumers would benefit from the buying up, giving away, or destroying method, which suggests that consumers on average would prefer this to the regulatory or the economic incentive method. *(435)*
7. The land bank program, which gives farmers incentives to reduce supply, and the nonrecourse loan program, which buys up goods, have been the two most prevalent U.S. farm programs. *(436)*
8. While this chapter discusses taxpayers, farmers, and consumers as separate groups independent of each other, in reality they are not. Each individual is, generally, both a taxpayer and a consumer, while farmers are generally members of all three groups. It is nonetheless useful to treat them as separate groups because specific interests predominate: for example, farmers' interests as farmers significantly outweigh their interests as taxpayers or as consumers. *(436)*
9. In terms of actual money payment by the government, having a military draft likely is a cheaper way of maintaining defense than is a volunteer army. However, a military draft can be seen as a type of hidden tax on a specific group of individuals—young people who are subject to the draft—to the degree that they are paid less than the going wage. If that hidden tax is also included in the cost, the military draft is not a cheaper way of maintaining defense. Because it involves inefficiencies in who participates, it can, indeed, be seen as more expensive than an all-volunteer army. *(437)*
10. False. Economic theory tells us nothing about what is preferable. Choices about what is preferable can only be made by specifying one's value judgments. Such choices belong in normative economics and in the art of economics, where distributional effects, broader sociological issues, and value judgments are included in the analysis. *(438)*

20 Microeconomic Policy, Economic Reasoning, and Beyond

After reading this chapter, you should be able to:

- List three reasons why economists sometimes differ in their views on social policy.
- Explain why liberal and conservative economists often agree in their views on social policy.
- Explain the cost/benefit approach the typical economist takes to analyze regulations.
- Describe three types of failure of market outcomes.
- Explain why economists are doubtful government can correct failure of market outcomes.

If an economist becomes certain of the solution of any problem, he can be equally certain that his solution is wrong.

—*H. A. Innis*

One important job of economists is to give advice to politicians and other policymakers on a variety of questions relating to social policy: How should unemployment be dealt with? How can society distribute income fairly? Should the government redistribute income? Would a program of equal pay for jobs of comparable worth (a pay equity program) make economic sense? Should the minimum wage be increased? These are tough questions.

In Chapter 18 I discussed the supply/demand framework that economists use to think about such issues. In this chapter I consider economic reasoning in a broader context.

The reason for doing so is that economic reasoning, and the supply/demand model are tools, not rules. To draw policy implications from it, the supply/demand model has to be placed in context. Used in the proper context, the supply/demand model is enormously strong, something no one should be without. Used out of context, it can lead to conclusions that don't seem right, and that maybe are not right. Consider the assembly-line chicken-production example in Chapter 10. Some of you may have felt that the assembly-line production of chickens was somehow not right—that the efficiency of the production process somehow did not outweigh the chickens' suffering. Yet the economic model, which focuses on efficiency, directs production toward that assembly line. This chapter considers when you might want to use economic reasoning, and when you might not.

The chapter is divided into two parts. The first part of the chapter extends the supply/demand model to a broader cost/benefit framework, tying together the discussion we had about economic reasoning in the introductory chapters with the chapters that developed the foundations of the supply/demand model. It shows you how economic reasoning is used in practice. The second part of the chapter turns economic reasoning back upon itself, considering not only the benefits (which are considerable) but also the costs of using economic reasoning. In doing so I discuss how markets that are working perfectly may still lead to outcomes that are undesirable.

Economists' Differing Views about Social Policy

Economists have many different views on social policy because:

1. Economists' suggestions for social policy are determined by their subjective value judgments (normative views) as well as by their objective economic analyses.
2. Policy proposals must be based on imprecise empirical evidence, so there's considerable room for differences of interpretation not only about economic issues but also about how political and social institutions work. Economic policy is an art, not a science.
3. Policy proposals are based on various models that focus on different aspects of a problem.

Economists' views on social policy differ widely because (1) they have different underlying values, (2) they interpret empirical evidence differently, and (3) they use different underlying models.

All three reasons directly concern the role of ideology in economics. However, any policy proposal must embody both economic analysis and value judgments because the goals of policy reflect value judgments. When an economist makes a policy proposal, it's of this type: "If A, B, and C are your goals, then you should undertake policies D, E, and F to achieve those goals most efficiently." In making these policy suggestions, the economist's role is much the same as an engineer's: He or she is simply telling someone else how to achieve desired ends most efficiently. Ideally the economist is as objective as possible, telling someone how to achieve his or her goals (which need not be the economist's goals).

How Economists' Value Judgments Creep into Policy Proposals

Even though economists attempt to be as objective as possible, value judgments still creep into their analyses in three ways: interpretation of policymakers' values, interpretation of empirical evidence, and choice of economic models.

Interpretation of the Policymaker's Values In practice, social goals are seldom so neat that they can be specified A, B, and C; they're vaguely understood and vaguely expressed. An economist will be told, for instance, "We want to make the poor better off" or "We want to see that middle-income people get better housing." It isn't clear what *poor, better off,* and *better housing* mean. Nor is it clear how judgments should be made when a policy will benefit some individuals at the expense of others, as real-world policies inevitably do.

Faced with this problem, some academic economists have argued that economists should recommend only **Pareto optimal policies**—*policies that benefit some people and hurt no one*. The policies are named in honor of the famous Italian economist Wilfredo Pareto, who first suggested that kind of criterion for judging social change.[1] It's hard to object to the notion of Pareto optimal policies because, by definition, they improve life for some people while hurting no one.

Pareto optimal policies are policies that benefit some people and hurt no one.

Q-1 If someone suggests that economists should focus only on Pareto optimal policies, how would you respond?

I'd give you an example of a real-world Pareto optimal policy if I could, but unfortunately I don't know of any. Every policy inevitably has some side effect of hurting, or at

[1]Pareto, in his famous book *Mind and Society*, suggested this criterion as an analytic approach for theory, not as a criterion for real-world policy. He recognized the importance of the art of economics and that real-world policy has to be judged by much broader criteria.

least seeming to hurt, somebody. In the real world, Pareto optimal policies don't exist. Any economist who has advised governments on real-world problems knows that all real-world policies make some people better off and some people worse off.

But that doesn't mean that economists have no policy role. In their policy proposals, economists try to spell out the effect of a policy on the distribution of income and wealth, whether a policy will help a majority of people, who those people are, and whether the policy is consistent with the policymaker's value judgments. Doing so isn't easy because the policymaker's value judgments are often vague and must be interpreted by the economist. In that interpretation, the economist's own value judgments often slip in.

Interpretation of Empirical Evidence Value judgments creep into economic policy proposals through economists' interpretations of empirical evidence, which is almost always imprecise. For example, say an economist is assessing the elasticity of a product's demand in the relevant price range. She can't run an experiment to isolate prices and quantities demanded; instead she must look at events in which hundreds of other things changed, and do her best to identify what caused what. In selecting and interpreting empirical evidence, our values will likely show through, try as we might to be objective. People tend to focus on evidence that supports their position. Economists are trained to be as objective as they can be, but pure objectivity is impossible.

Let's consider the example of a debate in which some economists proposed that a large tax be imposed on sales of disposable diapers, citing studies that suggested disposable diapers made up between 15 and 30 percent of the garbage in a landfill. Others objected, citing studies that showed disposable diapers made up only 1 or 2 percent of the refuse going into landfills. Such differences in empirical estimates are the norm, not the exception. Inevitably, if precise estimates are wanted, more studies are necessary. (In this case, the further studies showed that the lower estimates were correct.) But policy debates don't wait for further studies. Economists' value judgments influence which incomplete study they choose to believe is more accurate.

Choice of Economic Models Similarly with the choice of models. A model, because it focuses on certain aspects of economic reality and not on others, necessarily reflects certain value judgments, so economists' choice of models must also reflect certain value judgments. Albert Einstein once said that theories should be as simple as possible, but not more so. To that we should add a maxim: Scientists should be as objective and as value-free as possible, but not more so.

This book presents the mainstream economic model. That model directs us to certain conclusions. Two other general models that some economists follow are a **Marxian (radical) model,** which is *a model that focuses on equitable distribution of power, rights, and income among social classes*, and a **public choice (conservative) model,** which is *a model that focuses on economic incentives as applied to politicians*. These two models, by emphasizing different aspects of economic interrelationships, sometimes direct us to other conclusions.

Q-2 How does a radical analysis of labor markets differ from a mainstream analysis?

Let's consider an example. Mainstream economic analysis directs us to look at how the invisible hand achieves harmony and equilibrium through the market. Thus, when mainstream economists look at labor markets, they generally see supply and demand forces leading to equilibrium. When Marxist economists look at labor markets, their model focuses on the tensions among the social classes, and they generally see exploitation of workers by capitalists. When public choice economists look at labor markets, they see individuals using government to protect their monopolies. Their model focuses on political restrictions that provide rents to various groups. Each model captures

Each model captures different aspects of reality. That's why it's important to be as familiar with as many different models as possible.

different aspects of reality. That's why it's important to be as familiar with as many different models as possible.

The Need for a Worldview

John Maynard Keynes, an economist who gained fame in the 1930s, once said that economists should be seen in the same light as dentists—as competent technicians. He was wrong, and his own experience contradicts that view. In dealing with real-world economic policy, Keynes was no mere technician. He had a definite worldview, which he shared with many of the policymakers he advised. An economist who is to play a role in policy formation must be willing to combine value judgments and technical knowledge. That worldview determines how and when the economic model will be applied.

Agreement among Economists about Social Policy

Liberal and conservative economists agree on many policy prescriptions because they use the same models, which focus on incentives and individual choice.

Despite their widely varying values, both liberal and conservative economists agree more often on policy prescriptions than most laypeople think they do. They're economists, after all, and their models focus on certain issues—specifically on incentives and individual choice. They believe economic incentives are important, and most economists tend to give significant weight to individuals' ability to choose reasonably. This leads economists, both liberal and conservative, to look at problems differently than other people do.

Many people think economists of all persuasions look at the world coldheartedly. In my view, that opinion isn't accurate, but it's understandable how people could reach it. Economists are taught to look at things in an "objective" way that takes into account a policy's long-run incentive effects as well as the short-run effects. Many of their policy proposals are based on these long-run incentive effects, which in the short run make the policy look coldhearted. The press and policymakers usually focus on short-run effects. Economists argue that they aren't being coldhearted at all, that they're simply being reasonable, and that following their advice will lead to less suffering than following others' advice will. This is not to say that all advice economists give will lead to significant benefits and less suffering in the long run. Some of it may be simply misguided.

Q-3 When can "being mean" actually be "being nice"?

The problem economists face is similar to the one parents face when they tell their children that they can't eat candy or must do their homework before they can play. Explaining how "being mean" is actually "being nice" to a six-year-old isn't easy.

A former colleague of mine, Abba Lerner, was well known for his strong liberal leanings. The government of Israel asked him what to do about unemployment. He went to Israel, studied the problem, and presented his advice: "Cut union wages." The government official responded, "But that's the same advice the conservative economist gave us." Lerner answered, "It's good advice, too." The Israeli Labor government then went and did the opposite; it raised wages, thus holding on to its union support in the short run.

Another example comes from a World Bank economist. She had to advise a hospital in a developing country to turn down the offer of a free dialysis machine because the marginal cost of the filters it would have to buy to use the machine significantly exceeded the costs of life-saving medicines that would save even more lives. Economic reasoning involves making such hard decisions.

The best way to see the consistency and the differences in economists' policy advice is to consider some examples. Let's start with a general consideration of economic views on government regulation.

Economists' Cost/Benefit Approach to Government Regulation

Say that 200 people die in a plane crash. Newspaper headlines trumpet the disaster while news magazines are filled with stories about how the accident might have been caused, citing speculation about poor maintenance and lack of government regulation. The publicity spreads the sense that "something must be done" to prevent such tragedies. Politicians quickly pick up on this, feeling that the public wants action. They introduce a bill outlawing faulty maintenance, denounce poor regulatory procedures, and demand an investigation of sleepy air controllers. In short, they strike out against likely causes of the accident and suggest improved regulations to help prevent any more such crashes.

Many regulations are formulated for political expediency and do not reflect cost/benefit considerations.

Economists differ in their views on government regulation of airlines and other businesses, but most find themselves opposing some of the supposedly problem-solving regulations proposed by politicians. They generally adopt a **cost/benefit approach** to problems—*assigning costs and benefits, and making decisions on the basis of the relevant costs and benefits*—which requires them to determine a quantitative cost and benefit for everything, including life. What's the value of a human life? All of us would like to answer, "Infinite. Each human life is beyond price." But if that's true, then in a cost/benefit framework, everything of value should be spent on preventing death. People should take no chances. They should drive at no more than 30 miles per hour with airbags, triple-cushioned bumpers, double roll bars—you get the picture.

Cost/benefit analysis is analysis in which one assigns a cost and benefit to alternatives, and draws a conclusion on the basis of those costs and benefits.

It might be possible for manufacturers to make a car in which no one would die as the result of an accident. But people don't want such cars. Many people don't buy the auto safety accessories that are already available, and many drivers ignore the present speed limit. Instead, many people want cars with style and speed.

The Value of Life

Far from regarding human life as priceless, people make decisions every day that reflect the valuations they place on their own lives. Table 20-1 presents one economist's estimates of some of these quantitative decisions. These values are calculated by looking at people's revealed preferences (the choices they make when they must pay the costs). To

Table 20-1 The Value of a Human Life
Such figures are increasingly being used in state and federal courts to support claims for loss of enjoyment of life.

Basis for Calculation	Value of Life (in 2003 dollars)
Automotive air bag purchases	$ 552,000
Smoke detector purchases	580,000
EPA requirements for sulfur scrubbers	775,000
Wage premiums for dangerous police work	1,320,000
Auto safety features	3,873,000
EPA regulations of radium content in water	3,873,000
Wage premiums for dangerous factory jobs	4,957,000
Seat belt usage	4,965,000
Premium tire usage	5,565,000
OSHA rules for workplace safety	5,577,000

Source: Stan V. Smith, Ph.D., adjunct professor, DePaul College of Law, and president, Corporate Financial Group, Chicago. Used by permission. (Updated by author.)

Car crashes are evidence human life is not beyond price.
Rick Doyle/Corbis.

find them, economists calculate how much people will pay to reduce the possibility of their death by a certain amount. If that's what people will pay to avoid death, the value of life can be calculated by multiplying the inverse of the reduction in the probability of death by the amount they pay. (What is relevant for these calculations is not the actual probabilities but the decision makers' estimate of the probabilities.)

Q-4 If Table 20-1 correctly describes the valuation individuals place on life with regard to air bag purchases and seat belt usage, how would you advise them to alter their behavior in order to maximize utility?

For example, say someone will buy a car whose air bags add up to \$500 to the vehicle's cost, but won't buy a car whose air bags add more than \$500 to its cost. Also say that the buyer believes that an air bag will reduce the chance of dying in an automobile accident by 1/720. That means that to increase the likelihood of surviving an auto accident by 1/720, the buyer will pay \$500. That also means that the buyer is implicitly valuing his or her life at roughly \$360,000 (720 × \$500 = \$360,000).

Alternatively, say that people will pay an extra \$52 for a set of premium tires that reduces the risk of death by 1/100,000. As opposed to having a 3/100,000 chance per year of dying in a skid on the highway, people with premium tires all round have a 2/100,000 chance of dying (3/100,000 − 2/100,000 = 1/100,000). Multiplying 100,000 (the inverse of the reduction in probability) by \$52, the extra cost of the set of premium tires, you find that people who buy these tires are implicitly valuing their lives at \$5,200,000.[2] Another way of determining the value that society places on life is to look at awards juries give for the loss of life. One study looking at such awards found that juries on average value life at about \$3.5 million.

No one can say whether people know what they're doing in making these valuations, although the inconsistencies in the valuations people place on their lives suggest that to some degree they don't, or that other considerations are entering into their decisions. But even given the inconsistencies, it's clear that people are placing a finite value on life. Most people are aware that in order to "live" they must take chances on losing their lives. Economists argue that individuals' revealed choices are the best estimate that society can have of the value of life, and that in making policy society shouldn't pretend that life is beyond value.

Economists argue that individuals' revealed choices are the best estimate that society can have of the value of life, and that in making policy society shouldn't pretend that life is beyond value.

Placing a value on human life allows economists to evaluate the cost of a crash. Say each life is worth \$2 million. If 200 people die in that plane accident and a \$200 million plane is destroyed, the cost of the crash is \$600 million.

Web Note 20.1
The Value of Life

Right after the accident, or even long after the accident, tell a mother and father you're valuing the life of their dead daughter at \$2 million and the plane at \$200 million, and you'll see why economists have problems with getting their views across. Even if people can agree rationally that a value must be placed on life—that they implicitly give their own lives a value—it's not something they want to deal with emotionally, especially after an accident. Using a cost/benefit approach, an economist must be willing to say, if that's the way the analysis turns out, "It's reasonable that my son dies in this accident because the cost of preventing the accident by imposing stricter government regulations would have been greater than the benefit of preventing it."

Economists take the emotional heat for making such valuations. Their cost/benefit approach requires them to do so.

Comparing Costs and Benefits of Different Dimensions

After the marginal cost and marginal benefit data have been gathered and processed, one is ready to make an informed decision. Will the cost of a new regulation outweigh the benefit, or vice versa? Here again, economists find themselves in a difficult position in evaluating a regulation about airplane safety. Many of the costs of regulation are

[2]For simplicity of exposition, I'm not considering risk preferences or other benefits of these decisions such as lowering the chance of injury.

small but occur in large numbers. Every time you lament some "bureaucratic craziness" (such as a required weekly staff meeting or a form to be signed assuring something has been done), you're experiencing a cost. But when those costs are compared to the benefits of avoiding a major accident, the dimensions of comparison are often wrong.

Cost/benefit analysis sometimes leads one to uncomfortable results.

For example, say it is discovered that a loose bolt was the probable cause of the plane crash. A regulation requiring airline mechanics to check whether that bolt is tightened and, to ensure that they do so, requiring them to fill out a form each time the check is made, might cost \$1. How can we compare \$1 to the \$600 million cost of the crash? Such a regulation obviously makes sense from the perspective of gaining a \$600 million benefit from \$1 of cost.

But wait. Each plane might have 4,000 similar bolts, each of which is equally likely to cause an accident if it isn't tightened. If it makes sense to check that one bolt, it makes sense to check all 4,000. And the bolts must be checked on each of the 4,000 flights per day. All of this increases the cost of tightening bolts to \$16 million per day. But the comparison shouldn't be between \$16 million and \$600 million. The comparison should be between the marginal cost (\$16 million) and the marginal benefit, which depends on how much tightening bolts will contribute to preventing an accident.

Let's say that having the bolts checked daily reduces the probability of having an accident by 0.001. This means that the check will prevent one out of a thousand accidents that otherwise would have happened. The marginal benefit of checking a particular bolt isn't \$600 million (which it would be if you knew a bolt was going to be loose), but is:

$$0.001 \times \$600 \text{ million} = \$600{,}000$$

That \$600,000 is the marginal benefit that must be compared to the marginal cost of \$16 million.

Given these numbers, I leave it to you to decide: Does this hypothetical regulation make sense?

Putting Cost/Benefit Analysis in Perspective

Q-5 Why should you be very careful about any cost/benefit analysis?

Web Note 20.2
Social Cost and
Social Benefit

The numbers in our plane crash example are hypothetical. The numbers used in real-world decision making are not hypothetical, but they are often ambiguous. Measuring costs, benefits, and probabilities is difficult, and economists often disagree on specific costs and benefits.

Cost/benefit analyses are often used to justify what someone already wants to do. For example, from the 1950s to the 1980s the U.S. Army Corps of Engineers always seemed to come up with conclusions that their projects—dams, canals, and the like—made sense from a cost/benefit analysis point of view. In the 1990s many of the corps' projects were reassessed, and in that reassessment many of the projects no longer made so much sense—the earlier analyses had not taken into account larger environmental costs.

Cost/benefit analysis is often biased toward quantifiable costs.

Costs have many dimensions, some more quantifiable than others. Cost/benefit analysis is often biased toward quantifiable costs and away from nonquantifiable costs, or it involves enormous ambiguity as nonquantifiable costs are quantified.

The subjectivity and ambiguity of costs are one reason why economists differ in their views of regulation. In considering any particular regulation, some economists will favor it and some will oppose it. But their reasoning process—comparing marginal costs and marginal benefits—is the same; they differ only on the estimates they calculate.

The Problem of Other Things Changing

One problem that economists have concerns the "other things equal" assumption discussed in Chapter 4. Supply/demand analysis assumes that all other things remain equal. But in a large number of issues it is obvious that other things do not remain equal.

However, it is complicated to sort out how they change, and the sorting-out process is subject to much debate. The more macro the issue, the more other things change, and hence the more debate.

Q-6 When using marginal cost/marginal benefit analysis, do "other things remain constant"? Explain.

Let's consider the minimum wage example we discussed in earlier chapters. Suppose you can estimate the supply and demand elasticities for labor. Is that enough to enable you to estimate the number of people who will be made unemployed by a minimum wage? To answer that, ask yourself: Are other things likely to remain constant? The answer is: No; a chain of possible things can change. Say the firm decides to replace these workers with machines. So it will buy some machines. But machines are made by other workers, and so the demand for workers in the machine-making industry will rise. So the decrease in employment in the first industry may be offset by an increase in employment elsewhere.

But there are issues on the other side too. For example, if other things change workers who get the higher wage may not receive a net benefit. Say you had a firm that was paying a wage lower than the minimum wage but was providing lots of training, which was preparing people for much better jobs in the future. Now the minimum wage goes into effect. The firm keeps hiring workers, but it eliminates the training. Its workers are actually worse off.

How important are such issues? That's a matter of empirical research, which is why empirical research is central to economics. Unfortunately, the data aren't very good, which is why there is so much debate about policy issues in economics.

There are many more examples of "other things changing," but the above should be sufficient to give you an idea of the problem.

The Cost/Benefit Approach in Context

Economics teaches people to be "reasonable."

Economics teaches people to be reasonable—sickeningly reasonable, some people would say. I hope that you have some sense of what I mean by that. The cost/benefit approach to problems (which pictures a world of individuals whose self-interested actions are limited only by competition) makes economists look for the self-interest behind individuals' actions, and for how competition can direct that self-interest into the public interest.

In an economist's framework,

- Well-intentioned policies often are prevented by individuals' self-interest-seeking activities.
- Policies that relieve immediate suffering often have long-run consequences that create more suffering.
- Politicians have more of an incentive to act fast—to look as if they're doing something—than to do something that makes sense from a cost/benefit point of view.

The marginal cost/marginal benefit story is embodied in the supply/demand framework.

The marginal cost/marginal benefit approach is telling a story. That story is embodied in the supply/demand framework. Supply represents the marginal costs of a trade, and demand represents the marginal benefits of a trade. Equilibrium is where quantity supplied equals quantity demanded—where marginal cost equals marginal benefit. That equilibrium maximizes the combination of consumer and producer surplus and leads to an efficient, or Pareto optimal, outcome. The argument for competitive markets within that supply/demand framework is that markets allow the society to achieve **economic efficiency**—*achieving a goal, in this case producing a specified amount of output, at the lowest possible cost*. Alternatively expressed, the story is that, given a set of resources, markets produce the greatest possible output. When the economy is efficient, it is on its production possibility curve, producing total output at its lowest opportunity cost.

Economic Efficiency and the Goals of Society

Knowing the Tools

Economic efficiency means achieving a goal at the lowest possible cost. For the definition to be meaningful, the goal must be specified. Efficiency in the pursuit of efficiency is meaningless. Thus, when we talk about economic efficiency, we must have some goal in mind. In the supply/demand framework, we *assume* the goal is to maximize total output. Each of the three failures of market outcomes that we discuss in this section represents a situation in which the goals of society cannot be captured by a single measure—where society's goal is more complicated than to maximize total output—and thus the assumed goal of efficiency (maximizing total output) is not the only goal of society.

Q-7 True or false? The goal of society is efficiency.

The supply/demand framework is logical, satisfying, and (given its definitions and assumptions) extraordinarily useful. That's why we teach it. It gives students who understand it the ability to get to the heart of many policy problems. It tells them that every policy has a cost, every policy has a benefit, and if the assumptions are met, competition sees to it that the benefits to society are achieved at the lowest possible cost. Applied to policy issues, the framework gets you to face trade-offs that you would often rather avoid, and that you likely wouldn't see if you didn't use it. It is what "thinking like an economist" is all about.

Failure of Market Outcomes

A good story emphasizes certain elements and deemphasizes others to make its point. When the moral of the story is applied, however, we have to be careful to consider all the relevant elements—especially those that the story didn't emphasize. That's why in the second part of this chapter I will discuss some implicit assumptions that the supply/demand framework pushes to the back of the analysis and that therefore often don't get addressed in principles courses. I classify these as failures of market outcomes. A **failure of market outcome** occurs *when, even though the market is functioning properly (there are no market failures), it is not achieving society's goals.*

Failure of market outcome occurs when, even though it is functioning properly, the market is not achieving society's goals.

Three separate types of failures of market outcomes will be considered:

1. *Failures due to distributional issues:* Whose surplus is the market maximizing?
2. *Failures due to rationality problems of individuals:* What if individuals don't know what is best for themselves?
3. *Failures due to violations of inalienable or at least partially inalienable rights of individuals:* Are there certain rights that should not be for sale?

I'll discuss an example of each of the three failures of market outcomes and contrast them with market failures discussed in Chapter 18. Then I will conclude with a brief discussion of why, even though most economists recognize these failures of market outcomes, they still favor the use of markets for the large majority of goods that society produces.

Distribution

Say that the result of market forces is that some people don't earn enough income to be able to survive—the demand for their labor intersects the supply for their labor at a wage of 25 cents an hour. Also assume there are no market failures, as described in

Chapter 18. (Information is perfect, trades have no negative externalities, and all goods are private goods.)

The market solution to a wage that is so low the worker can't survive is starvation—people who don't earn enough die. Not all low-wage workers must die, however. As some low-wage workers die, the supply of labor shifts back, raising the wage for the survivors. This process takes time, but eventually all remaining workers will receive a subsistence wage. This is the long-run market solution. Implicit within the supply/demand framework is a Darwinian "survival of the fittest" approach to social policy. Most people would regard the market solution—starvation—as an undesirable outcome. Even though the market is doing precisely what it is supposed to be doing—equating quantity supplied and quantity demanded—most people would not find the outcome acceptable.

Implicit within the supply/demand framework is a "survival of the fittest" approach to social policy.

Distribution of Total Surplus Let me now relate this distributional issue to the supply/demand framework by considering distribution of consumer and producer surplus. For most discussions of economic policy, an implicit assumption is that the goal of policy is to create as much total surplus as possible. In a world of only one good and one person, that goal would be clear. But with many goods and many people, what is meant by total surplus in terms of social welfare can be unclear. One reason is that society does not value all surplus equally. In the above starvation example, *the reason most people do not like the market outcome is that they care about not only the size of the total surplus but also how total surplus is distributed.* The supply/demand framework does not distinguish among those who get producer and consumer surplus, and thus avoids that distribution issue.

Examples of Distributional Issues Let's consider two real-world examples where distributional issues are likely to play a significant role in value judgments about the market outcome. Our economy produces $200-an-ounce olive oil, but it does not provide a minimum level of health care for all. This happens because income distribution is highly unequal. The high income of the wealthy means there is demand for $200-an-ounce bottles of olive oil. (It's all the rage in Silicon Valley.) Businesses establish production facilities to produce it (or any one of a million other luxury items), and it is sold on the market. Selling $200-an-ounce bottles of olive oil is efficient if one's goal is to maximize total consumer and producer surplus. However, given the distribution of income, it would be inefficient to produce health care for the poor. The poor just don't have sufficient income to demand it. Since they have little income, the poor are given little weight in the measure of consumer surplus.

A second example of where distribution of income likely makes a big difference in our normative judgments, and where we would likely not apply the consumer and producer surplus reasoning, concerns the demand for the AIDS drug cocktail. The cocktail can stop AIDS from killing people; thus, the desire for the AIDS cocktail among individuals with AIDS is high. The desire for the drug among those without AIDS is minimal.

In some African countries, almost 30 percent of the population has AIDS. Since consumer surplus reflects desire, one might think that in Africa the consumer surplus from the desire for the AIDS drug cocktail would be enormous. But it isn't. Most people in Africa have relatively little income; in fact, most have so little income that they cannot afford the cocktail at all. Since the price of the cocktail is above their total income, they get no consumer surplus from the cocktail at all in the supply/demand framework—it would be "inefficient" to supply it to them. In the supply/demand framework you can only have a demand for a good if you have the desire *and* the income to pay for it.

For many goods maximizing total surplus is a useful shorthand.

The point of these examples is not to convince you that the consumer surplus concept is useless. Far from it. For the majority of goods, it is a useful shorthand that demonstrates the power of competitive markets. The point of the examples is to show you the type of case where overriding the supply/demand framework in policy considerations may be socially desirable and efficient if society's goals include a particular distribution of consumer surplus. The sole purpose of society is not to maximize consumer and producer surplus. Society has other goals. Once these other goals are taken into account, the competitive result may not be the one that is desired.

Societies integrate other goals into market economics by establishing social safety nets (programs such as welfare, unemployment insurance, and Medicaid). When individuals are below a certain income, what they receive does not depend solely on what they earn in the market. How high to set a given social safety net is a matter of debate, but favoring the market outcome in most cases is not inconsistent with favoring a social safety net in others.

Consumer Sovereignty and Rationality Problems

John Drunk drinks more than is good for him; he just has to have another drink. He buys liquor voluntarily, so that means buying it makes him better off, right? Not necessarily. Even when they have full information, individuals sometimes do not do what is in their own best interest. If they don't do what's best for themselves, then the market solution—let people enter freely into whatever trades they want to—is not necessarily the best solution. Again, the market is working, but the outcome may be a failure.

Q-8 A cocaine addict purchases an ounce of cocaine from a drug dealer. Since this was a trade both individuals freely entered, is society better off?

This problem is sometimes called *rationality failure of individuals*. The supply/demand framework starts with the proposition that individuals are completely **rational**—that *what individuals do is in their own best interest*. Reflecting on this, however, as we did in Chapter 7, we see that that is not always the case. Most of us are irrational at times; we sometimes can "want" something that we really "don't want." Think of smoking, chocolate, or any other of our many vices.

Even if we don't have serious addictions, we may have minor ones; often we don't know what we want and we are influenced by what people tell us we want. Businesses spend lots of money on advertising to convince us that we want certain things. Individuals can be convinced they want something that, if they thought further about it, they would not want. The fact that individuals don't know what they want can be a second reason for government intervention—getting people what is good for them.

Let's look at an example: The U.S. government has taken the position that if people could be induced to stop smoking, they would be better off. **Sin taxes**—*taxes that discourage activities society believes are harmful (sinful)*—are meant to do just this. Based on the consumer surplus argument, a tax on smoking would create deadweight loss; it would reduce the combination of consumer and producer surplus. But in this case consumer surplus does not reflect individuals' welfare.

Notice the difference between the argument for taxes to change behavior (sin taxes) and the argument for taxes to raise revenue discussed in Chapter 7. When government wants to raise revenue it takes into account how much deadweight loss is created by the tax. With sin taxes, government is trying to discourage the use of the good that is being taxed. When society takes the position that individuals' demands in the marketplace do not reflect their true welfare, it is not at all clear that the market result is efficient. (See the box "Elasticity and Taxation to Change Behavior.")

Elasticity and Taxation to Change Behavior

Applying the Tools

A good way to see how economists view the difference between the effect of a sin tax and the effect of a tax to raise revenue is to ask: Would a policymaker rather have an elastic or an inelastic demand curve for the good being taxed? If the purpose is to raise revenue while creating only a minimal amount of deadweight loss, an inelastic demand is preferable. If the purpose is to change behavior, as it is in the example of an alcohol-dependent individual, a more elastic demand curve is better because a relatively small tax can cause a relatively large reduction in purchases.

Consider an example of taxation to reduce consumption. If government believes that smoking is bad for people, it can decrease the amount people smoke by placing a tax on cigarettes. If the demand for cigarettes is inelastic, then the tax will not significantly decrease smoking; but if the demand is elastic, then it will. If demand is inelastic, government may choose alternative methods of affecting behavior, such as advertising campaigns. If the purpose of taxation is to raise taxes, an inelastic demand would be better; that's why most states rely on general sales taxes for revenue—such taxes allow them to raise revenue with relatively little effect on the efficiency of the market.

The following table provides a quick review of when a tax will be most effective, given a particular goal of government.

Goal of Government	Most Effective When
Raise revenue, limit efficiency loss	Demand or supply is inelastic
Change behavior	Demand or supply is elastic

Inalienable Rights

Web Note 20.3
Markets for Body Parts

Nice Guy wants to save his son, who needs an operation that costs $300,000. He doesn't have that kind of money, but he knows that Slave Incorporated, a newly created company, has been offering $300,000 to the first person who agrees to become a slave for life. He enters into the contract, gets his money, and saves his son. Again, the market is working just as it is supposed to. There's no negative externality, and there's no information problem—Nice Guy knows what he's doing and Slave Inc. knows what it's doing. Both participants in the trade believe that it is making them better off.

Q.9 True or false? If someone chooses to sell himself into slavery, the individual, and thus society, is better off.

Many people's view of the trade will likely be different; they would regard such a market outcome—an outcome that allows slavery—as a market outcome failure. That is why governments have developed laws that make such trades illegal.

As Amartya Sen pointed out (and won a Nobel Prize for doing so), most societies regard certain rights as inalienable. By definition, inalienable rights cannot be sold or given away. There can be no weighing of costs and benefits. For example, the right to freedom is an inalienable right, so slavery is wrong, and any trade creating slavery should not be allowed, regardless of any issues of consumer and producer surplus.

The Need to Prioritize Rights To understand why market outcomes might be undesirable, we have to go back and consider markets in a broader perspective. Markets develop over time as individuals trade to make themselves better off. But markets don't just come into existence—they require the development of property rights for both suppliers and consumers. Each side must know what is being traded. So markets can exist only if there are property rights.

Property rights, in turn, are included in a broader set of rights that are part of society's constitution—the right to vote, the right to free speech, the right to the pursuit of happiness, the right to life. Property rights are subrights to the right to pursue happiness.

If that right to property rights conflicts with other rights, society must make a judgment about which right has priority. Thus, within the written or unwritten constitution of a society, rights needs to be prioritized.

Examples of Inalienable Rights Let's consider a couple of examples. Say I come up to you with a gun and offer you this deal: Your money or your life. This can be viewed as a trade. Because I have the gun, I control whether you live or die. You control the money you have. If we make the "trade," you'll be better off because I don't shoot you and I'll be better off because I'll have more money. But it is not an acceptable trade, because the right to your life was inalienable—no one but you owns it; I cannot claim to own it. So, even if the gun gave me the power over your life, it did not give me the right to it. Other moral prohibitions that are related to inalienable rights include those against prostitution, selling body parts, and selling babies.

My point is not that the moral judgment our society has made about these rights is correct; they may or may not be correct. Nor is my point that such trades should not be subjected to the market. My point is that society must make these judgments. Such issues are moral questions and therefore do not have to stand up to the consumer and producer surplus arguments. If something is wrong, it is wrong; whether it is efficient is irrelevant.

Moral judgments underlie all policy prescriptions.

Moral judgments must be made about where markets should exist, and someone might decide that the market should be allowed everywhere (that is the libertarian view), but such moral judgments can override consumer surplus arguments about markets achieving efficiency. Consider again the efficient-chicken-farming example discussed in Chapter 10. If you believe that it is immoral to treat chickens the way "efficient" farming requires them to be treated, then the fact that the farming is efficient may be irrelevant to you.

Government Failure

Distributional issues, issues of rationality, and the existence of inalienable rights are representative of the types of problems that can arise in the market. For most economists these issues play a role in interpreting the policy results that follow from the economic model presented, even when there is no market failure. But it is important to remember that even these failures of market outcomes do not necessarily call for government action. The reason is government failure.

As I discussed in Chapter 18, if the failure is to be corrected someone must formulate and enact the policy, and if we believe that government's attempt to correct it will do more harm than good, then we can still support the market as the lesser of two evils. For the government to correct the problem, it must

For the government to correct a problem it must
1. Recognize the problem.
2. Have the will to deal with it.
3. Have the ability to deal with it.

1. Recognize the problem.
2. Have *the will* to do something positive about the problem.
3. Have *the ability* to do something positive about the problem.

Government seldom can do all three of these well. Often the result is that government action is directed at the wrong problem at the wrong time.

Probably the most vocal group of economists on the subject of government failure are *public choice economists*. This group, started by James Buchanan and Gordon Tullock, has pointed out that politicians are subject to the laws of supply and demand, like everyone else. Often the result of politics is that the redistribution that takes place does not go from rich to poor, but from one group of the middle class to another group of the middle class. Public choice economists argue that when the government enters the

The Conventional Policy Wisdom among Economists

Applying the Tools

Where do economists come out on whether government can correct a failure of market outcomes? The easy answer is that they conclude that to make a policy decision we must weigh the costs of market failure against the costs of government failure. But those costs are often poorly specified and difficult to estimate. Thus, policy considerations require subjective judgments. Let me give you my interpretation of how economists fit these broader considerations into their analysis.

Most economists downplay the distribution issues for the majority of goods, and use distribution in their policy consideration only for the extreme examples, such as those I presented in the text. They believe that it is far better to be open about the distributional goals and to give money directly to individuals, rather than to hide the redistribution by changing the pricing structure through subsidizing goods. Let's take an example: The European Union's agricultural policy currently provides large amounts of price supports for European agricultural production. To keep farmers in business, the prices of agricultural goods are kept high. If the social decision were to keep farmers in business, most economists, however, would prefer to see the EU provide direct subsidies to farmers. Then the policy of redistribution is clear to everyone, and is far less costly in terms of both efficiency and implementation.

The "rights argument" plays a role in all economists' policy arguments. Almost all economists oppose selling citizenship. All oppose slavery. All see economic policy as being conducted within a constitutional setting, and that means that inalienable rights come before market efficiency.

There are, of course, areas of ambiguity—allowing the regulated sale of body parts from individuals who have died is one such area. Let's consider it. There is currently a shortage of organs for transplants. When someone dies, from a medical perspective his or her organs can usually be "harvested" and used by someone else—but only if the deceased had signed a donor card. If the family of the deceased donor were given $5,000 for burial expenses, some economists argue, the shortage of transplant organs would disappear and everyone would be better off—the family could give the deceased a much nicer funeral and people needing the organs could live. Our society is moving cautiously in that direction; Pennsylvania has recently announced that it is giving $300 in funeral expenses to the survivors of those who donate organs. My feeling is that economists are more open to such market solutions than the general public, but there is nothing in economics that requires such solutions.

The argument about problems arising from rationality issues is also accepted by most economists, but they downplay it for most nonaddictive goods. The reason is that while it is true that individuals may not know what they want, it is far less likely that the government will know better. Based on that view, on average, the acceptance of consumer sovereignty, and the market result, is probably warranted. Exceptions include children and some elderly. How to deal with addictive goods is still very much in debate among economists, and there is no conventional wisdom.

market, the incentives are not to achieve its goal in the least-cost manner; the incentives are to provide a policy that its voting constituency likes. The result is larger and larger government, with little benefit for society, and public choice economists advocate as little government intervention as possible regardless of whether there are market failures or failures of market outcomes.

Economic policy is, and must be, applied within a political context. This means that political elements must be taken into account. Politics enters into the determination of economic policy in two ways, one positive and one negative. Its positive contribution is that politicians take market failures and failures of market outcomes into account when formulating policy. Ultimately the political system decides what externalities should be adjusted for, what is a desirable distribution, what rights are above the market, and when people's demand does not reflect their true demand. To the extent that the

Q-10 In what way does government positively contribute to economic policy? In what way does it negatively contribute to economic policy?

government's political decisions reflect the will of society, government is making a positive contribution.

The negative contribution is that political decisions do not always reflect the will of society.[3] The political reality is that, in the short run, people are often governed by emotion, swayed by mass psychology, irrational, and interested in their own rather than the general good. Politicians and other policymakers know that; the laws and regulations they propose reflect such calculations. Politicians don't get elected and reelected by constantly saying that all choices have costs and benefits. What this means is that while policymakers listen to the academic economists from whom they ask advice, and with whom in private they frequently agree, in practice they often choose to ignore that advice.

Because government both adjusts for failures of market outcomes and is subject to short-run political pressures, the way in which economic reasoning influences policy can be subtle. Sometimes we see elaborate charades acted out: Politicians put forward bills that from a cost/benefit viewpoint don't make sense but that make the politicians look good. They hope the bills won't pass, but they also hope that presenting them will allow enough time to pass so that emotions can cool and a more reasonable bill can be put forward. Other times, compromise bills are proposed that incorporate as much cost/benefit policy as possible, but also appeal to voters' emotional sense. In short, economic policy made in the real world reflects a balancing of cost/benefit analysis and special interest desires.

Conclusion

Adam Smith, the creator of modern economics, was a philosopher; his economics was part of his philosophy. Before he wrote the *Wealth of Nations*, in which he set out his argument for markets, he wrote a book called *The Theory of Moral Sentiments*, in which he laid out his broader philosophy. That foundation, in turn, was part of the Scottish Enlightenment, which spelled out what was meant by a good society, and how they believed individuals' and society's rights should be considered. Any economic policy issue must be interpreted within such a broad philosophical framework. Clearly, an introductory course in economics cannot introduce you to these broader philosophical and political issues. But it can point out to you their importance, and that economic policy arguments must fit within that broader context.

Economics provides the tools, not the rules, for policy.

This chapter was written to give you a sense of that broader context—economics provides the tools, not the rules, for policy. Cost/benefit analysis and the supply/demand framework are powerful tools for analyzing issues and coming up with policy conclusions. But to apply them successfully, they must be applied in context.

Applying economics is much more than muttering "supply and demand." Economics involves the thoughtful use of economic insights and empirical evidence.

Thomas Carlyle, who, as we saw in the introductory quotation to Chapter 4, argued that all you have to do is teach a parrot the words *supply* and *demand* to create an economist, was wrong. Economics involves the thoughtful use of economic insights and empirical evidence. If this chapter gave you a sense of the nature of that thoughtful application along with the core of economic reasoning, then it succeeded in its purpose.

[3]By even discussing the "will of society" I am avoiding a very difficult problem in political philosophy of what that will is, and how it is to be determined. I leave it to your political science courses to discuss such issues.

Summary

- Economists differ because of different underlying value judgments, because empirical evidence is subject to different interpretations, and because their underlying models differ.
- Value judgments inevitably work their way into policy advice, but good economists try to be objective.
- Economists tend to agree on certain issues because their training is similar. Economists use models that focus on economic incentives and rationality.
- The economic approach to analyzing issues is a cost/benefit approach. If the marginal benefits exceed the marginal costs, do it. If the marginal costs exceed the marginal benefits, don't do it.
- People make choices every day that reveal the value that they place on their lives. The value of life is calculated by multiplying the inverse of the reduction in the probability of death by the amount individuals pay for that reduction.
- Collecting and interpreting empirical evidence is difficult, which contributes to disagreements among economists.
- Economics involves the thoughtful use of economic insights and empirical evidence.
- The cost/benefit approach and the supply/demand framework deemphasize the possibility that market outcomes may be undesirable to society.
- Three failures of market outcomes are failures due to distributional issues, failures due to rationality problems of individuals, and failures due to violations of inalienable rights.
- Although an implicit assumption in most policy discussions is that the goal of policy is to maximize consumer and producer surplus, society does care about how that total surplus is distributed.
- The supply/demand framework assumes that individuals are rational. Individuals are not always rational in practice. Their actions are swayed by addictions, advertising, and other pressures.
- Some rights, called inalienable rights, cannot be bought and sold. What rights are inalienable are moral judgments that do not have to stand up to the same cost/benefit framework.
- Economics provides the tools, not the rules, for policy.

Key Terms

cost/benefit approach *(446)*
economic efficiency *(449)*
failure of market outcome *(450)*
Marxian (radical) model *(444)*
Pareto optimal policies *(443)*
public choice (conservative) model *(444)*
rational *(452)*
sin taxes *(452)*

Questions for Thought and Review

1. Could anyone object to a Pareto optimal policy? Why?
2. Would it be wrong for economists to propose only Pareto optimal policies?
3. Would all economists oppose price controls? Why or why not?
4. Should body organs be allowed to be bought or sold? Why or why not?
5. In cost/benefit terms, explain your decision to take an economics course.
6. How much do you value your life in dollar terms? Are your decisions consistent in that valuation?
7. If someone offered you $1 million for one of your kidneys, would you sell it? Why or why not?
8. Why might an economist propose a policy that has little chance of adoption?
9. In the 1970s legislators had difficulty getting laws passed requiring people to wear seat belts. Now not only do most people wear seat belts, many cars have air bags too. Do people value their lives more now than in the 1970s?

10. Why are economists' views of politicians cynical?
11. Michael Tanner and Stephen Moore of the Cato Institute recently calculated the hourly wage equivalent of welfare for a single mother with two children for each of the 50 United States. Their estimates ranged from $17.50 an hour for Hawaii to $5.33 in Mississippi. What do you suppose were their policy recommendations? What arguments can be made to oppose those prescriptions?
12. Economist Steven D. Levitt estimated that, on average, for each additional criminal locked up in the United States, 15 crimes are eliminated. In addition, although it costs about $30,000 a year to keep a prisoner incarcerated, the average prisoner would have caused $53,900 worth of damage to society per year if free. If this estimation is correct, does it make economic sense to build more prisons?

PROBLEMS AND EXERCISES

1. Say that the cost of a car crash is $8,000. Assume further that installing a safety device in a car at a cost of $12 will reduce the probability of an accident by 0.05 percent. The plant makes 1,000 cars each day.
   a. If the preceding are the only relevant costs, would you favor or oppose the installation of the safety device?
   b. What other costs might be relevant?
2. In a study of hospital births, the single most important prediction factor of the percentage of vaginal births as opposed to Caesarean (C-section) births was ownership status of hospitals—whether they were for-profit or nonprofit.
   a. Which had more C-sections, and why?
   b. What implications about the health care debate can you draw from the above results?
   c. How might the results change if the for-profit hospital received a fixed per-patient payment as it would in a managed care system?
3. The technology is now developing so that road use can be priced by computer. A computer in the surface of the road picks up a signal from your car and automatically charges you for the use of the road.
   a. How could this technological change contribute to ending bottlenecks and rush-hour congestion? Demonstrate graphically.
   b. How will people likely try to get around the system?
   c. If people know when the prices will change, what will likely happen immediately before? How might this be avoided?
4. In the early 1990s, the 14- to 17-year-old population fell because of low birth rates in the mid-1970s. Simultaneously, aging baby boomers who decided to have kids combined to increase the number of babies and hence to increase the number of parents needing baby-sitters. What effect will these two events likely have on:
   a. The number of times parents go out without their children?
   b. The price of baby-sitters?
   c. The average age of baby-sitters?
5. As organ transplants become more successful, scientists are working on ways to transplant animal organs to humans. Pigs are the odds-on favorites as "donors" since their organs are about the same size as human organs.
   a. What would the development of such organ farms likely do to the price of pigs?
   b. If you were an economic adviser to the government, would you say that such a development would be Pareto optimal (for humans)?
   c. Currently, there is a black market in human organs. What would this development likely do to that market?
6. If one uses a willingness-to-pay measure in which life is valued at what people are willing to pay to avoid risks that might lead to death, the value of a U.S. citizen's life is $2.6 million, a Swede's life is worth $1.2 million, and a Portuguese's life is worth $20,000 (according to an article in the *Journal of Transport Economics and Policy*).
   a. What policy implications does this value schedule have?
   b. Say you operate an airline. Should you spend more on safety precautions in the United States than you do in Portugal?
   c. Should safety standards be lower in Portugal and Sweden than in the United States?
7. According to U.S. government statistics, the cost of averting a premature death differs among various regulations. Car seat belt standards cost $100,000 per premature death avoided, while hazardous waste landfill disposal bans cost $4.2 trillion per premature death avoided.
   a. If you were choosing between these two regulations, which would you choose? Why?
   b. If these figures are correct, should neither, one, the other, or both of these regulations be implemented?
8. A 29-year-old politician, Anthony Zielinski, who was a member of the Milwaukee Board of Supervisors, proposed that the county government sell the organs of dead welfare recipients to help pay off the welfare recipients' welfare costs and burial expenses.
   a. What was the likely effect of that proposal?
   b. Why was that the effect?
9. Technology will soon exist such that individuals can choose the sex of their offspring. Assume that technology has now arrived and that 70 percent of the individuals choose male offspring.

a. What effect will that have on social institutions such as families?
b. What effect will it have on dowries—payments made by the bride's family to the groom—which are still used in a number of developing countries?
c. Why might an economist suggest that if 70 percent male is the expectation, families would be wise to have daughters rather than sons?

Web Questions

1. Find out whether you could survive on the minimum wage by going to www.aflcio.org/articles/minimum_wage/paycalc.htm. (If you do not support yourself, answer the questions assuming you are the head of a household with two children.)
   a. Are you able to provide for your monthly budgeted expenses? By how much do you overspend?
   b. Compare your budget to that of the average head of a household earning the minimum wage. How would your lifestyle change if you had to adjust your budget to a minimum wage income?
2. Some groups are now lobbying local governments to institute "living wage" policies. Go to the New Party's home page at www.newparty.org/livwag to answer the following questions:
   a. What is a living wage?
   b. How does the living wage compare to the federal minimum wage?
   c. What are the New Party's arguments in favor of the living wage?
3. The U.S. Constitution spells out various rights of its citizens. Go to the Cornell Law School home page at www.law.cornell.edu and look up the U.S. Constitution.
   a. List six rights granted by the U.S. Constitution.
   b. Are all these rights inalienable?
   c. Should any of these rights be allowed to be bought and sold on a market? Why or why not?
   d. Go to the Libertarian Party's home page at www.lp.org and read its Statement of Purpose. From your reading, do Libertarians believe that individuals should have the right to buy and sell rights granted to them by the constitution? Explain your answer.

Answers to Margin Questions

1. I would respond that in the real world, Pareto optimal policies don't exist, and all real-world policies make someone better off and someone worse off. In making real-world policy judgments, one cannot avoid the difficult distributional and broader questions. It is those more difficult questions, which are value-laden, that make economic policy an art rather than a science. *(443)*
2. A radical analysis of the labor market differs from the mainstream analysis in that it emphasizes the tensions among social classes. Thus, a radical analysis will likely see exploitation built into the institutional structure. Mainstream analysis is much more likely to take the institutional structure as given and not question it. *(444)*
3. Oftentimes being "mean" in the short run can actually involve being "nice" in the long run. The reason is that often policy effects that are beneficial in the long run have short-run costs, and people focusing on those short-run costs see the policy as "mean." *(445)*
4. To maximize life, one would expect that the marginal value per dollar spent should be equal in all activities. Thus, if Table 20-1 is correct, it would suggest that you should be far less concerned about seat belt usage and far more concerned about whether your automobile has air bags or not. *(447)*
5. Costs and benefits are ambiguous; economists often disagree enormously on specific costs and benefits, or the costs and benefits are difficult or impossible to quantify. Thus, you should be extremely careful about using a cost/benefit analysis as anything more than an aid to your analysis of the situation. *(448)*
6. Other things do not always remain constant. The more macro the issue, the more things are likely to change. These changes must be brought back into the analysis, which complicates things enormously. *(449)*
7. False. Efficiency is achieving a goal as cheaply as possible. Stating efficiency as a goal does not make sense. *(450)*
8. No. The cocaine addict may be responding to the cravings created from the addiction, and not from any rational desire for more cocaine. Society may not be better off. *(452)*
9. False. Society may find that personal freedom is an inalienable right. Selling such a right would make society worse off. *(453)*
10. Government makes a positive contribution by adjusting for market failures and failures of market outcomes. Government may make a negative contribution because government is swayed by short-run political pressures. *(456)*

21 International Trade Policy

After reading this chapter, you should be able to:

- Summarize some important data of trade.
- Explain the principle of comparative advantage.
- List three determinants of the terms of trade.
- Explain three policies countries use to restrict trade.
- Discuss why countries impose trade restrictions.
- Summarize why economists generally oppose trade restrictions.
- Explain how free trade associations both help and hinder international trade.

One of the purest fallacies is that trade follows the flag. Trade follows the lowest price current. If a dealer in any colony wished to buy Union Jacks, he would order them from Britain's worst foe if he could save a sixpence.

—*Andrew Carnegie*

If economists had a mantra, it would be "Trade is good." Trade allows specialization and division of labor and thereby promotes technological growth. Consistent with that mantra, most economists oppose trade restrictions. Not everyone agrees with economists; almost every day we hear calls from some sector of the economy to restrict foreign imports to save U.S. jobs and protect U.S. workers from unfair competition. In this chapter we consider why economists generally favor free trade, and why, despite what economists tell them, countries impose trade restrictions. We begin with an overview of international trade.

Patterns of Trade

Before I consider these issues, let's look at some numbers to get a sense of the nature and dimensions of international trade.

Increasing but Fluctuating World Trade

In 1928, total world trade was about $500 billion (in today's dollars). U.S. gross domestic product (GDP) was about $830 billion, so world trade as a percentage of U.S. GDP was almost 60 percent. In 1935, that ratio had fallen to less than 30 percent. In 1950 it was 20 percent. Then it started rising. Today it is about 65 percent, with world trade amounting to nearly $8 trillion. As you can see, international trade has been growing, but with significant fluctuations in that growth. Sometimes international trade has grown rapidly; at other times it has grown slowly or has even fallen.

In part, fluctuations in world trade result from fluctuations in world output. When output rises, international trade rises; when output falls, international trade falls. Fluctuations in world trade are also in part explained by trade restrictions that countries have imposed from time to time. For example, decreases in world income during the Depression caused a large decrease in trade, but that decrease was exacerbated by a worldwide increase in trade restrictions during the 1930s.

Differences in the Importance of Trade

The importance of international trade to countries' economies differs widely, as we can see in the table below, which presents the importance of the shares of exports—the value of goods and services sold abroad—and imports—the value of goods and services purchased abroad—for various countries.

	Total Output*	Export Ratio	Import Ratio
United States	$10,082	10%	14%
Canada	875	43	38
Netherlands	413	67	62
Germany	2,174	35	33
United Kingdom	1,470	34	40
Italy	1,402	21	21
France	1,510	28	26
Japan	3,450	10	9

*Numbers in billions.

Source: *The World Factbook 2002* (www.cia.gov) and individual country web pages.

Among the countries listed, the Netherlands has the highest amount of exports compared to total output; the United States and Japan have the lowest.

Q-1 Among the countries listed in the table, which has the lowest exports and imports as a percentage of total output?

The Netherlands' imports are also the highest as a percentage of total output. Japan's are the lowest. The relationship between a country's imports and its exports is no coincidence. For most countries, imports and exports roughly equal one another, though in any particular year that equality can be rough indeed. For the United States in recent years, imports have generally significantly exceeded exports. But that situation can't continue forever, as I'll discuss.

Total trade figures provide us with only part of the international trade picture. We must also look at what types of goods are traded and with whom that trade is conducted.

What and with Whom the United States Trades

The majority of U.S. exports and imports involve significant amounts of manufactured goods. This isn't unusual, since much of international trade is in manufactured goods.

Figure 21-1 shows the regions with which the United States trades. Exports to Canada and Mexico made up the largest percentage of total U.S. exports to individual countries in 2001. The largest regions to whom the U.S. exports are the Pacific Rim and the European Union. Countries from which the United States imports major quantities include Canada and Mexico and the regions of the European Union and the Pacific Rim. Thus, the countries we export to are also the countries we import from.

The primary trading partners of the United States are Canada, Mexico, the European Union, and the Pacific Rim countries.

Notice the **balance of trade**—*the difference between the value of exports and the value of imports* in Figure 21-1. Imports far exceed exports. In economic terms this means that the U.S. economy is running a trade deficit—an excess of imports over exports. The trade deficit the United States has been running since the 1970s remained large in the early 2000s, at more than $350 billion a year.

Debtor and Creditor Nations

Running a trade deficit isn't necessarily bad. In fact, while you're doing it, it's rather nice. If you were a country, you probably would be running a trade deficit now since, most likely, you're consuming (importing) more than you're producing (exporting).

Figure 21-1 (a and b) U.S. Exports and Imports by Region, 2001
Major regions that trade with the United States include Canada, Mexico, the European Union, and the Pacific Rim.

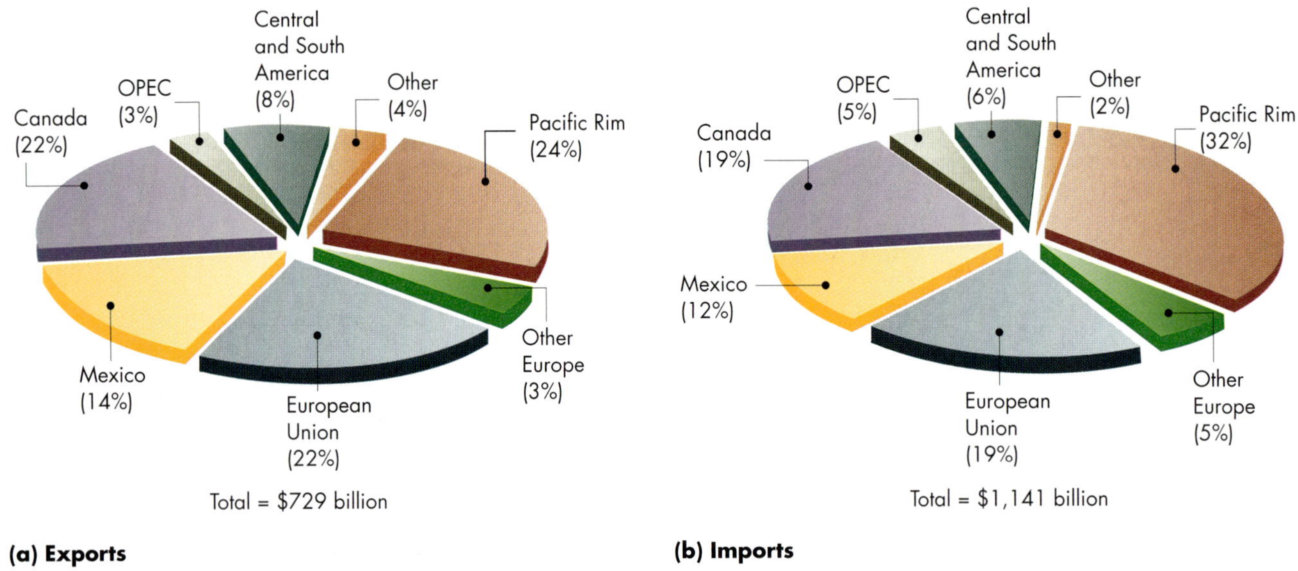

Source: FT900 U.S. International Trade in Goods and Services 2001, U.S. Census Bureau (www.census.gov).

How can you do that? By living off past savings, getting support from your parents or a spouse, or borrowing.

Countries have the same options. They can live off foreign aid, past savings, or loans. For example, the U.S. economy is currently financing its trade deficit by selling off assets—financial assets such as stocks and bonds, or real assets such as real estate and corporations. Since the assets of the United States total many trillions of dollars, it can continue to run trade deficits of a similar size for decades to come.

Q-2 Will a debtor nation necessarily be running a trade deficit?

The United States has not always run a trade deficit. Following World War II it ran trade surpluses—an excess of exports over imports—with other countries, so it was an international lender. Thus, it acquired large amounts of foreign assets. Because of the large trade deficits the United States has run since the 1980s, now the United States is a large debtor nation. The United States has borrowed more from abroad than it has lent abroad.

As the United States has gone from being a large creditor nation to being the world's biggest debtor, international considerations have been forced on the nation. The cushion of being a creditor—of having a flow of interest income—has been replaced by the trials of being a debtor and having to pay out interest every year without currently getting anything for it when they pay that interest.

THE PRINCIPLE OF COMPARATIVE ADVANTAGE

The principle of comparative advantage states that as long as the relative opportunity costs of producing goods differ among countries, then there are potential gains from trade.

The reason two countries trade is that trade can make both countries better off. The reasoning showing that this is true underlies the principle of comparative advantage to which you were introduced in Chapter 2. It is, however, important enough to warrant an in-depth review. The basic idea of the principle of **comparative advantage** is that *as long as the relative opportunity costs of producing goods (what must be given up in one good in*

International Issues in Perspective

Beyond the Tools

Over the past 20 years, international issues have become increasingly important for the U.S. economy. That statement would be correct even if the reference period went back as far as the late 1800s. From the late 1800s through the first 40 years of the 1900s, the United States was in an isolationist period in which the country turned inward in both economic and foreign policies.

The statement would not be correct if the reference period were earlier than the late 1800s. In the 1600s, 1700s, and most of the 1800s, international trade was vital to the American economy—even more vital than now. The American nation grew from colonial possessions of England, France, and Spain. These "new world" colonial possessions were valued for their gold, agricultural produce, and natural resources. From a European standpoint, international trade was the colonies' reason for being.*

A large portion of the U.S. government's income during much of the 1800s came from tariffs. Our technology was imported from abroad, and international issues played a central role in wars fought here. (Many historians believe that the most important cause of the U.S. Civil War was the difference of views about tariffs on manufactured goods. The South opposed them because it wanted cheap manufactured goods, while the North favored them because it wanted to protect its manufacturing industries.) Up until the 1900s, no one would have studied the U.S. economy independently of international issues. Not only was there significant international trade; there was also significant immigration. The United States is a country of immigrants.

Only in the late 1800s did the United States adopt an isolationist philosophy in both politics and trade. So in reference to that isolationist period, the U.S. economy has become more integrated with the world economy. However, in a broader historical perspective, that isolationist period was an anomaly, and today's economy is simply returning international issues to the key role they've usually played.

A second important insight is that international trade has social and cultural dimensions. While much of the chapter deals with specifically economic issues, we must also remember the cultural and social implications of trade.

Let's consider an example from history. In the Middle Ages, Greek ideas and philosophy were lost to Europe when hordes of barbarians swept over the continent. These ideas and that philosophy were rediscovered in the Renaissance only as a by-product of trade between the Italian merchant cities and the Middle East. (The Greek ideas that had spread to the Middle East were protected from European upheavals.) *Renaissance* means rebirth: a rebirth in Europe of Greek learning. Many of our traditions and sensibilities are based on those of the Renaissance, and that Renaissance was caused, or at least significantly influenced, by international trade. Had there been no trade, our entire philosophy of life might have been different.

Fernand Braudel, a French historian, has provided wonderful examples of the broader implications for trade. For instance, he argued that the effects of international trade, specifically Sir Walter Raleigh's introduction of the potato into England from South America in 1588, had more long-run consequences than did the celebrated 1588 battle of the English navy and Spanish Armada.

Another example is the major change in socialist countries in the 1990s. Through the 1960s China, the Soviet Union, and the Eastern European countries were relatively closed societies—behind the Iron Curtain. That changed in the 1970s and 1980s as these socialist countries opened up trade with the West as a way to speed their own economic development. That trade, and the resulting increased contact with the West, gave the people of those countries a better sense of the material goods to be had in the West. That trade also spread Western ideas of the proper organization of government and the economy to these societies. A strong argument can be made that along with trade came the seeds of discontent that changed those societies and their economies forever.

In economics courses we do not focus on these broader cultural issues but instead focus on relatively technical issues such as the reasons for trade and the implications of tariffs. But keep in the back of your mind these broader implications as you go through the various components of international economics. They add a dimension to the story that otherwise might be forgotten.

*The American Indian standpoint was, I suspect, somewhat different.

The Gains to International Traders

Applying the Tools

Trade does not take place on its own—markets and trade require entrepreneurs to bring it about. The market is not about abstract forces; it is about real people operating to improve their position. Many of the gains from trade do not go to the countries involved but rather to the trader. And the gains that traders get can be enormous.

Consider, for example, the beautifully knit Peruvian sweaters often sold at art fairs and college campuses for $75 apiece. The Peruvian women knitting those sweaters are paid only a small fraction of that $75—say $6 apiece—and the trader makes the difference. So much of the benefits of trade do not go to the producer or the consumer; they go to the trader. Another example is the high-priced sneakers ($100) that many "with-it" students wear. Those sneakers are likely made in China, and the cost of making a pair of sneakers is about $8. The trader has other costs, of course; there are, for example, costs of transportation and advertising—someone has to convince you that you need those "with-it" sneakers. (Just do it, right?) But that advertising is not done in China, and a portion of the benefits of the trade are accruing to advertising firms, which can pay more to creative people who think up those crazy ads.

order to get another good) differ among countries, then there are potential gains from trade. (If the idea is not clear to you, the appendix to this chapter goes through the reasoning and the geometry in more detail.) Let's review this principle by considering the story of I.T., an imaginary international trader, who convinces two countries to enter into trades by giving both countries some of the advantages of trade; he keeps the rest for himself.

The Gains from Trade

Here's the situation. On his trips to the United States and Saudi Arabia, I.T. noticed that no trade between the two countries was taking place. He also noticed that the opportunity cost of producing a ton of food in Saudi Arabia was 10 barrels of oil and that the opportunity cost for the United States of producing a ton of food was 1/10 of a barrel of oil. At the time, the United States' production was 60 barrels of oil and 400 tons of food, while Saudi Arabia's production was 400 barrels of oil and 60 tons of food.

I.T. made the United States and Saudi Arabia the following offer: If the United States would specialize in food, devoting the resources then being used to produce 60 barrels of oil to producing food, it could increase its food production from 400 tons to 1,000 tons. I.T. would then give the United States 120 barrels of oil in exchange for 500 of those tons. That would leave 500 tons of food to the United States (100 tons more than it had before the deal) and give it double the amount of oil—120 barrels (compared to its pre-deal 60 barrels). By accepting this deal, the United States wound up with more of both commodities without increasing the resources it expended.

Q-3 In terms of oil and food, exactly how much richer is I.T. after the trade?

He told Saudi Arabia that if it would specialize in oil, devoting the resources used to produce 60 tons of food to producing oil and thus increasing its oil production from 400 barrels to 1,000 barrels, he would give it 120 tons of food—double the amount of food it had before the deal—in exchange for 500 barrels of that oil. Like the United States, Saudi Arabia wound up with more of both commodities without increasing the resources it expended. Thus, both countries ended up with more than they initially had of both goods.

The situation is shown in the table on the next page. On the left are production and consumption totals before I.T. suggested that the countries trade. On the right is the production I.T. suggests along with the consumption of oil and food for each country after trade, along with what's left over for I.T.

	No Trade Production and Consumption		Trade Production		Trade Consumption		
	S.A.	U.S.	S.A.	U.S.	S.A.	U.S.	I.T.
Oil (barrels)	400	60	1,000	0	500	120	380
Food (tons)	60	400	0	1,000	120	500	380

As you can see, in this case I.T. benefits enormously from his insight—he ends up with 380 barrels of oil and 380 tons of food.

Dividing Up the Gains from Trade

As the above story suggests, when countries avail themselves of comparative advantage there are high gains of trade to be made. Who gets these gains is unclear. The principle of comparative advantage doesn't determine how those gains of trade will be divided up among the countries involved and among traders who make the trade possible. While there are no definitive laws determining how real-world gains from trade will be apportioned, economists have developed some insights into how those gains are likely to be divided up. The first insight concerns how much the trader gets. The general rule is:

> The more competition that exists among traders, the less likely it is that the trader gets big gains of trade; more of the gains from trade will go to the citizens in the two countries, and less will go to the traders.

Three determinants of the terms of trade are:

1. The more competition, the less the trader gets.
2. Smaller countries get a larger proportion of the gain than larger countries.
3. Countries producing goods with economies of scale get a larger gain from trade.

What this insight means is that where entry into trade is unimpaired, most of the gains of trade will pass from the trader to the countries. Thus, the trader's big gains from trade occur in markets that are newly opened.

This insight isn't lost on trading companies. Numerous import/export companies exist whose business is discovering possibilities for international trade in newly opened markets. Individuals representing trading companies go around hawking projects or goods to countries. For example, at the end of the 1999 NATO bombing campaign in Kosovo, what the business world calls the *import/export contingent* flew to Kosovo with offers of goods and services to sell. Many of these same individuals had been in Iraq and Iran in the early 1990s, in Saudi Arabia when oil prices rose in the 1970s, and in the Far East when China opened its doors to international trade in the 1980s.

A second insight is:

> Once competition prevails, smaller countries tend to get a larger percentage of the gains of trade than do larger countries.

The reason, briefly, is that more opportunities are opened up for smaller countries by trade than for larger countries. The more opportunities, the larger the relative gains. Say, for instance, that the United States begins trade with Mali, a small country in Africa. Enormous new consumption possibilities are opened up for Mali—prices of all types of goods will fall. Assuming Mali has a comparative advantage in fish, before international trade began cars were probably extraordinarily expensive in Mali, while fish was cheap. With international trade, the price of cars in Mali falls substantially, so Mali gets the gains. Because the U.S. economy is so large compared to Mali's, the U.S. price of fish doesn't change noticeably. Mali's fish are just a drop in the bucket. The price ratio of cars to fish doesn't change much for the United States, so it doesn't get much of the gains of trade. Mali gets almost all the gains from trade.

Q-4 In what circumstances would a small country not get the larger percentage of the gains from trade?

There's an important catch to this gains-from-trade argument. The argument holds only once competition among traders prevails. That means that Mali residents are sold cars at the same price (plus shipping costs) as U.S. residents. International traders in small countries often have little competition from other traders and keep large shares of the gains from trade for themselves. In the preceding example, the United States and Saudi Arabia didn't get a large share of the benefits. It was I.T. who got most of the benefits. Since the traders often come from the larger country, the smaller country doesn't get the benefits of the gains from trade; the larger country's international traders do.

A third insight is:

> Gains from trade go to the countries producing goods that exhibit economies of scale.

Trade allows an increase in production. If there are economies of scale, that increase can lower the average cost of production of a good. Hence, an increase in production can lower the price of the good in the producing country. The country producing the good with the larger economies of scale has its costs reduced by more, and hence gains more from trade than does its trading partner.

Varieties of Trade Restrictions

Let's now turn to the policies countries can use to restrict trade. These include tariffs and quotas, voluntary restraint agreements, embargoes, regulatory trade restrictions, and nationalistic appeals. I'll consider each in turn and also review the geometric analysis of each.

Tariffs and Quotas

Three policies used to restrict trade are:

1. Tariffs (taxes on internationally traded goods).
2. Quotas (quantity limits placed on imports).
3. Regulatory trade restrictions (government-imposed procedural rules that limit imports).

Tariffs are *taxes governments place on internationally traded goods*—generally imports. (Tariffs are also called *customs duties*.) Tariffs are the most-used and most-familiar type of trade restriction. Tariffs operate in the same way a tax does: They make imported goods relatively more expensive than they otherwise would have been, and thereby encourage the consumption of domestically produced goods. On average, U.S. tariffs raise the price of imported goods by about 3 percent. Figure 21-2(a) presents average tariff rates for industrial goods for a number of countries and the European Union, and Figure 21-2(b) shows the tariff rates imposed by the United States since 1920.

Probably the most infamous tariff in U.S. history is the Smoot-Hawley Tariff of 1930, which raised tariffs on imported goods to an average of 60 percent. It was passed at the height of the Great Depression in the United States in the hope of protecting American jobs. It didn't work. Other countries responded with similar tariffs. As a result of these trade wars, international trade plummeted from $60 billion in 1928 to $25 billion in 1938, unemployment worsened, and the international depression deepened. These effects of the tariff convinced many, if not most, economists that free trade is preferable to trade restrictions.

The dismal failure of the Smoot-Hawley Tariff was the main reason the **General Agreement on Tariffs and Trade (GATT),** *a regular international conference to reduce trade barriers*, was established in 1947 immediately following World War II. In 1995 GATT was replaced by the **World Trade Organization (WTO),** *an organization whose functions are generally the same as GATT's were—to promote free and fair trade among countries*. Unlike GATT, the WTO is a permanent organization with an enforcement system (albeit weak). Since its formation, rounds of negotiations have resulted in a decline in worldwide tariffs.

Quotas are *quantity limits placed on imports*. They have the same effect on equilibrium price and quantity as the quantity restrictions discussed in Chapter 5, and their

Figure 21-2 (a and b) Selected Tariff Rates
The tariff rates in **(a)** will be continually changing as the changes negotiated by the World Trade Organization come into effect. In **(b)** you see tariff rates for the United States since 1920.

Country	%	Country	%
Argentina	30.9	Norway	2.0
Australia	12.2	Peru	29.4
Canada	4.8	Philippines	22.2
Colombia	35.1	Poland	9.9
Czech Rep.	3.8	Singapore	5.1
European Union	3.6	South Africa	17.2
Hungary	6.9	Sri Lanka	28.1
India	32.4	Thailand	28.0
Indonesia	36.9	United States	3.5
Japan	1.7	Venezuela	30.9
Mexico	33.7	Zimbabwe	4.6

(a) Tariff rates by country

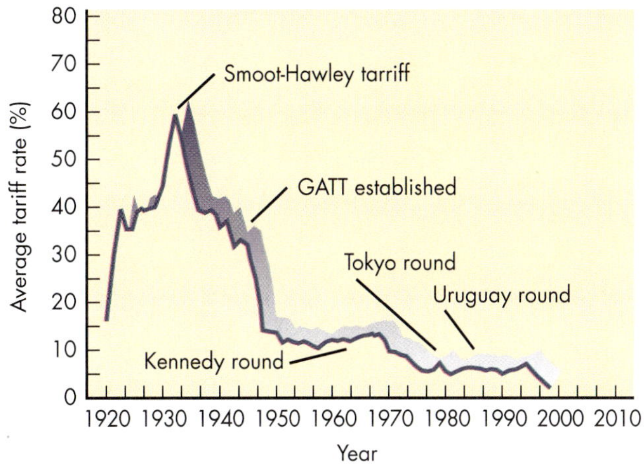

(b) U. S. Tariff rates since 1920

Source: General Agreement on Tariffs and Trade (GATT), The Results of the Uruguay Round of Multilateral Trade Negotiations, November, 1994 (www.wto.org).

effect in limiting trade is similar to the effect of a tariff. Both increase price and reduce quantity. Tariffs, like all taxes on suppliers, shift the supply curve up by the amount of the tax, as Figure 21-3 shows. A tariff, T, raises equilibrium price from P_0 to P_1 by an amount that is less than the tariff, and equilibrium quantity declines from Q_0 to Q_1. With a quota, Q_1, the equilibrium price also rises to P_1.

There is, however, a difference between tariffs and quotas. In the case of the tariff, the government collects tariff revenue represented by the shaded region. In the case of a quota, the government collects no revenue. The benefit of the increase in price goes to the importer as additional corporate revenue. So which of the two do you think import companies favor? The quota, of course—it means more profits as long as your company is the one to receive the rights to fill those quotas. In fact, once quotas are instituted, firms compete intensely to get them.

Tariffs affect trade patterns. For example, there is a U.S. tariff on light trucks from Japan, so the United States imports few light trucks from Japan. You will see Japanese-named trucks, but most of these are produced in the United States. Many similar examples exist, and by following the tariff structure, you can gain a lot of insight into patterns of trade.

Figure 21-3 The Effects of Tariffs and Quotas
A quota limiting foreign quantity supplied to Q_1 is the equivalent of a tariff of T.

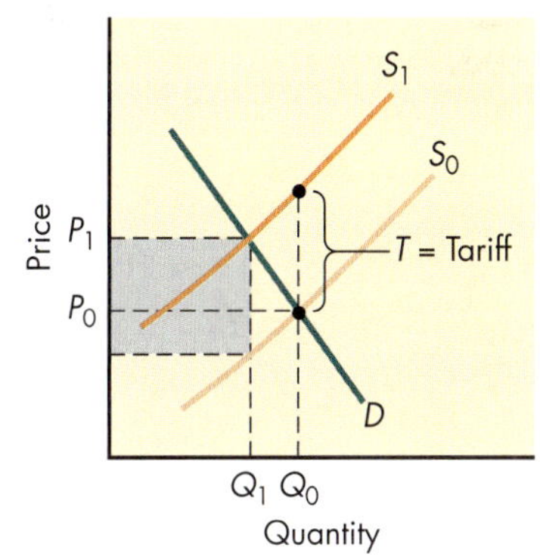

The issues involved with tariffs and quotas can be seen in a slightly different way by assuming that our country is small relative to the world economy and that imports compete with domestic producers. The small-country assumption means that the supply from the world to this country is perfectly elastic at the world price, \$2, as in Figure 21-4(a).

The world price of the good is unaffected by this country's demand. This assumption allows us to distinguish the world supply from domestic supply. In the absence of any trade restrictions, the world price of \$2 would be the domestic price. Domestic low-cost suppliers would supply 100 units of the good at \$2. The remaining 100 units demanded are being imported.

In Figure 21-4(a) I show the effect of a tariff of 50 cents placed on all imports. Since the world supply curve is perfectly elastic, all of this tax, shown by the shaded region, is

Figure 21-4 (a and b) Tariffs and Quotas When the Domestic Country Is Small
This exhibit shows the effects of a tariff in (**a**) and of a quota in (**b**) when the domestic country is small. The small-country assumption means that the world supply is perfectly elastic, in this case at $2.00 a unit. With a tariff of 50 cents, world supply shifts up by 50 cents. Domestic quantity demanded falls to 175 and domestic quantity supplied rises to 125. Foreign suppliers are left supplying the difference, 50 units. The domestic government collects revenue shown in the shaded area. The figure in (**b**) shows how the same result can be achieved with a quota of 50. Equilibrium price rises to $2.50. Domestic firms produce 125 units and consumers demand 175 units. The difference between the tariff and the quota is that, with a tariff, the domestic government collects the revenue from the higher price. With a quota, the benefits of the higher price accrue to the foreign and domestic producers.

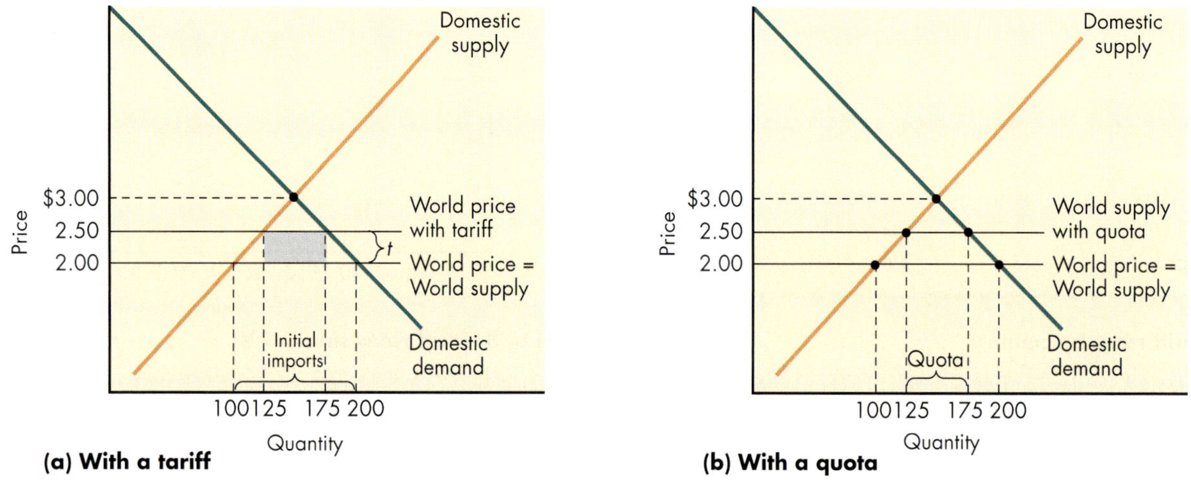

borne by domestic consumers. Price rises to $2.50 and quantity demanded falls to 175. With a tariff, the rise in price will increase domestic quantity supplied from 100 to 125, and will reduce imports to 50. Now let's compare this situation with a quota of 50, shown in Figure 21-4(b). Under a quota of 50, the final price would be the same, but higher revenue would accrue to foreign and domestic producers rather than to the government. One final difference: Any increase in demand under a quota would result in higher prices because it would have to be filled by domestic producers. Under a tariff, any increase in demand would not affect price.

VOLUNTARY RESTRAINT AGREEMENTS

Voluntary restraint agreements are often not all that voluntary.

Imposing new tariffs and quotas is specifically ruled out by the WTO, but foreign countries know that WTO rules are voluntary and that, if a domestic industry brought sufficient political pressure on its government, the WTO would be forgotten. To avoid the imposition of new tariffs on their goods, countries often voluntarily restrict their exports. That's why Japan has agreed informally to limit the number of cars it exports to the United States.

The effect of such voluntary restraint agreements is similar to the effect of quotas: They directly limit the quantity of imports, increasing the price of the good and helping domestic producers. For example, when the United States encouraged Japan to impose "voluntary" quotas on exports of its cars to the United States, Toyota benefited from the quotas because it could price its limited supply of cars higher than it could if it sent in a large number of cars, so profit per car would be high. Since they faced less competition, U.S. car companies also benefited. They could increase their prices because Toyota had done so.

Embargoes

An **embargo** is *a total restriction on import or export of a good*. Embargoes are usually established for international political reasons rather than for primarily economic reasons.

An embargo is a total restriction on import or export of a good.

An example is the U.S. embargo of trade with Iraq. The U.S. government hoped that the embargo would so severely affect Iraq's economy that Saddam Hussein would lose political power. It did make life difficult for Iraqis, but it didn't bring about the downfall of the Hussein government. The United States has also imposed embargoes on Cuba, Iran, and Libya.

Regulatory Trade Restrictions

Web Note 21.1
Regulations

Tariffs, quotas, and embargoes are the primary *direct* methods to restrict international trade. There are also indirect methods that restrict trade in not-so-obvious ways; these are called **regulatory trade restrictions** (*government-imposed procedural rules that limit imports*). One type of regulatory trade restriction has to do with protecting the health and safety of a country's residents. For example, a country might restrict imports of all vegetables grown where certain pesticides are used, knowing full well that all other countries use those pesticides. The effect of such a regulation would be to halt the import of vegetables. Another example involves building codes. U.S. building codes require that plywood have fewer than, say, three flaws per sheet. Canadian building codes require that plywood have fewer than, say, five flaws per sheet. The different building codes are a nontariff barrier that makes trade in building materials between the United States and Canada difficult.

Q-5 How might a country benefit from having an inefficient customs agency?

A second type of regulatory restriction involves making import and customs procedures so intricate and time-consuming that importers simply give up. For example, at one time France required all imported VCRs to be individually inspected in Toulouse. Since Toulouse is a provincial city, far from any port and outside the normal route for imports after they enter France, the inspection process took months.

Some regulatory restrictions are imposed for legitimate reasons; others are designed simply to make importing more difficult.

Some regulatory restrictions are imposed for legitimate reasons; others are designed simply to make importing more difficult and hence protect domestic producers from international competition. It's often hard to tell the difference. A good example of this difficulty began in 1988, when the EU disallowed all imports of meat from animals that had been fed growth-inducing hormones. As the box "Hormones and Economics" details, the debate continues.

Nationalistic Appeals

Web Note 21.2
Buy American

Finally, nationalistic appeals can help to restrict international trade. "Buy American" campaigns and Japanese xenophobia[1] are examples. Many Americans, given two products of equal appeal except that one is made in the United States and one is made in a foreign country, would buy the U.S. product. To get around this tendency, foreign and U.S. companies often go to great lengths to get a MADE IN THE U.S.A. classification on goods they sell in the United States. For example, components for many autos are made in Japan but shipped to the United States and assembled in Ohio or Tennessee so that the finished car can be called an American product.

Reasons for Trade Restrictions

Let's now turn to a different question: If trade is beneficial, as it is in our example of I.T., why do countries restrict trade? Here are some reasons why:

[1]*Xenophobia* is a Greek word meaning "fear of foreigners." Pronounce the *x* like *z*.

Hormones and Economics

Applying the Tools

Trade restrictions, in practice, are often much more complicated than they seem in textbooks. Seldom does a country say, "We're limiting imports to protect our home producers." Instead the country explains the restrictions in a more politically acceptable way. Consider the fight between the European Union (EU) and the United States over U.S. meat exports. In 1988 the EU, in line with Union-wide internal requirements, banned all imports of any meat from animals treated with growth-inducing hormones, which U.S. meat producers use extensively. The result: the EU banned the meat exported from the United States.

The EU claimed that it had imposed the ban only because of public health concerns. The United States claimed that the ban was actually a trade restriction, pointing out that its own residents ate this kind of meat with confidence because a U.S. government agency had certified that the levels of hormones in the meat were far below any danger level.

The United States retaliated against the EU by imposing 100 percent tariffs on Danish and West German hams, Italian tomatoes, and certain other foods produced by EU member nations. The EU threatened to respond by placing 100 percent tariffs on $100 million worth of U.S. walnuts and dried fruits, but instead entered into bilateral meetings with the United States. Those meetings allowed untreated meats into the EU for human consumption and treated meats that would be used as dog food. In response, the United States removed its retaliatory tariff on hams and tomato sauce, but retained its tariffs on many other goods. In the 1990s, Europe's dog population seemed to be growing exponentially as Europe's imports of "dog food" increased by leaps and bounds. In 1996 the United States asked the WTO to review the EU ban. It did so in 1997, finding in favor of the United States. The EU appealed and in 1999 the WTO stood by its earlier ruling and the United States reimposed the 100 percent tariffs. Since then, the EU has stood firm and has conducted studies that, it says, show the use of growth hormones to be unsafe, but the WTO continues to rule that they are safe.

Which side is right in this dispute? The answer is far from obvious. Both the United States and the EU have potentially justifiable positions. As I said, trade restrictions are more complicated in reality than in textbooks.

Reasons for restricting trade include:

1. Unequal internal distribution of the gains from trade.
2. Haggling by companies over the gains from trade.
3. Haggling by countries over trade restrictions.
4. Specialized production: learning by doing and economies of scale.
5. Macroeconomic aspects of trade.
6. National security.
7. International politics.
8. Increased revenue brought in by tariffs.

1. Unequal internal distribution of the gains from trade.
2. Haggling by companies over the gains from trade.
3. Haggling by countries over trade restrictions.
4. Specialized production: learning by doing and economies of scale.
5. Macroeconomic aspects of trade.
6. National security.
7. International politics.
8. Increased revenue brought in by tariffs.

Unequal Internal Distribution of the Gains from Trade

In the example of the argument for trade discussed at the beginning of the chapter, I.T. persuaded Saudi Arabia to specialize in the production of oil rather than food, and persuaded the United States to produce more food than oil. That means, of course, that some U.S. oil workers will have to become farmers, and in Saudi Arabia some farmers will have to become oil producers.

Often people don't want to make radical changes in the kind of work they do—they want to keep on producing what they're already producing. So when these people see the same kinds of goods that they produce coming into their country from abroad, they lobby to prevent the foreign competition. Sometimes they're successful. A good

Table 21-1 Cost of Saving Jobs in Selected Industries

Industry	Cost of Production (per job saved)
Footwear	$1,670,000
Dairy	1,520,000
Sugar	507,614
Frozen fruit, juice, and vegetables	175,000
Apparel	127,000
Ceramic tiles	13,432

Source: International Trade Commission, *Economic Effects of Significant Import Restraints* (www.usitc.gov), 1999.

example is the "voluntary" quotas—numerical limits—placed on Japanese cars exported to the United States in the 1980s. These quotas saved U.S. jobs but, by reducing competition, forced consumers to pay higher prices for cars. Economists have estimated that the quotas cost consumers, in higher car prices, about $100,000 for each job saved. Table 21-1 lists economists' estimates of the cost to consumers of saving a job in some other industries.

Had I.T. been open about the difficulties of trading, he would have warned the countries that change is hard. It has very real costs that I.T. didn't point out when he made his offers. But these costs of change are relatively small compared to the gains from trade. Moreover, they're short-run, temporary costs, whereas gains from trade are permanent, long-run gains. Once the adjustment has been made, the costs will be gone but the benefits will still be there.

For most goods, the benefits for the large majority of the population so outweigh the small costs to some individuals that, decided on a strict cost/benefit basis, international trade is still a deal you can't refuse. With benefits so outweighing costs, it would seem that transition costs could be forgotten. But they can't.

Benefits of trade are generally widely scattered among the entire population. In contrast, costs of free trade often fall on small groups of people who loudly oppose the particular free trade that hurts them. Though the benefits of free trade to the country at large exceed the costs of free trade to the small group of individuals, the political push from the few (who are hurt) for trade restrictions often exceeds the political push from the many (who are helped) for free trade. The result is trade restrictions on a variety of products. You'll likely see TV ads supporting such restrictions under the heading SAVING U.S. JOBS. But you'll see few ads in favor of free trade to keep prices low for consumers.

Benefits of trade are generally widely scattered among the entire population. In contrast, costs of free trade often fall on specific small groups.

It isn't only in the United States that the push for trade restrictions focuses on the small costs and not on the large benefits. For example, the European Union (EU) places large restrictions on food imports from nonmember nations. If the EU were to remove those barriers, food prices in EU countries would decline significantly—it is estimated that meat prices alone would fall by about 65 percent. Consumers would benefit, but farmers would be hurt. The farmers, however, have the political clout to see that the costs are considered and the benefits aren't. The result: The EU places high duties on foreign agricultural products.

Q-6 Why does the EU place high barriers against agricultural products?

The cost to society of relaxing trade restrictions has led to a number of programs to assist those who are hurt. Such programs are called **trade adjustment assistance programs**—*programs designed to compensate losers for reductions in trade restrictions*.

Because eliminating trade restrictions often imposes high costs on a small subgroup in society, government has instituted trade adjustment assistance programs to compensate for the losses.

The argument for these programs is the following:

> Trade will make most members of society better off, but will make a particular subgroup in society worse off. Because of the country's political dynamics, this subgroup can prevent free trade. If programs are structured so that they transfer some of society's gains to individuals who are made worse off by trade, the opposition to trade can be eliminated and society can be made better off.

Since a trade adjustment program compensates those who are hurt by trade, one might think that such programs will eliminate the opposition to free trade. Unfortunately, they generally do not.

Governments have tried to use trade adjustment assistance to facilitate free trade, but they've found that it's enormously difficult to limit the adjustment assistance to those who are actually hurt by international trade. As soon as people find that there's assistance for people injured by trade, they're likely to try to show that they too have been hurt and deserve assistance. Losses from free trade become exaggerated and magnified. Instead of only a small portion of the gains from trade being needed for trade adjustment assistance, much more is demanded—often even more than the gains.

Telling people who claim to be hurt that they aren't really being hurt isn't good politics.

Telling people who claim to be hurt that they aren't really being hurt isn't good politics. That's why offering trade adjustment assistance as a way to relieve the pressure to restrict trade is a deal many governments can refuse.

Haggling by Companies over the Gains from Trade

Many naturally advantageous bargains aren't consummated because each side is pushing for a larger share of the gains from trade than the other side thinks should be allotted.

To see how companies haggling over the gains of trade can restrict trade, let's reconsider the original deal that I.T. proposed. I.T. got 380 tons of food and 380 barrels of oil. The United States got an additional 100 tons of food and 60 barrels of oil. Saudi Arabia got an additional 100 barrels of oil and 60 tons of food.

Suppose the Saudis had said, "Why should we be getting only 100 barrels of oil and 60 tons of food when I.T. is getting 380 barrels of oil and 380 tons of food? We want an additional 300 tons of food and another 300 barrels of oil, and we won't deal unless we get them." Similarly the United States might have said, "We want an additional 300 tons of food and an additional 300 barrels of oil, and we won't go through with the deal unless we get them." If either the U.S. or the Saudi Arabian company that was involved in the trade for its country (or both) takes this position, I.T. might just walk—no deal. Tough bargaining positions can make it almost impossible to achieve gains from trade.

Strategic bargaining can lead to higher gains from trade for the side that drives the hardest bargain, but it can also make the deal fall through.

Q-7 In strategic trade bargaining, it is reasonable to be unreasonable. True or false? Explain.

The side that drives the hardest bargain gets the most gains from the bargain, but it also risks making the deal fall through. Such strategic bargaining goes on all the time. **Strategic bargaining** means *demanding a larger share of the gains from trade than you can reasonably expect*. If you're successful, you get the lion's share; if you're not successful, the deal falls apart and everyone is worse off.

Haggling by Countries over Trade Restrictions

Another type of trade bargaining that often limits trade is bargaining between countries. Trade restrictions and the threat of trade restrictions play an important role in that kind of haggling. Sometimes countries must go through with trade restrictions that they really don't want to impose, just to make their threats credible.

Once one country has imposed trade restrictions, other countries attempt to get those restrictions reduced by threatening to increase their own restrictions. Again, to make the threat credible, sometimes countries must impose or increase trade restrictions simply to show they're willing to do so. For example, in the mid-1990s China was allowing significant illegal copying of U.S. software without paying royalties on the work. The United States exerted pressure to stop such copying but felt that China was not responding effectively. To force compliance, the United States made a list of Chinese goods that it threatened with 100 percent tariffs unless China complied. The United States did not want to put on these restrictions, but felt that it would have more strategic bargaining power if it threatened to do so. Hence the name **strategic trade policies**—*threatening to implement tariffs to bring about a reduction in tariffs or some other concession from the other country.*

Strategic trade policies are threats to implement tariffs to bring about a reduction in tariffs or some other concession from the other country.

Ultimately, strategic bargaining power depends on negotiators' skills and the underlying gains from trade that a country would receive. A country that would receive only a small portion of the gains from trade is in a much stronger bargaining position than a country that would receive significant gains. It's easier for the former to walk away from trade.

The United States is currently using such a strategic trade policy in its attempt to get the European Union to lower its restrictions on imports of U.S. agricultural goods. The U.S. Congress often threatens to restrict imports from the EU significantly if the EU doesn't ease its trade restrictions against U.S. goods. For example, in 2002, the EU proposed $335 million in tariffs on a variety of U.S. goods in response to U.S. tariffs on imported steel.

The potential problem with strategic trade policies is that they can backfire. One rule of strategic bargaining is that the other side must believe that you'll go through with your threat. Thus, strategic trade policy can lead a country that actually supports free trade to impose trade restrictions, just to show how strongly it believes in free trade.

So the bottom line on strategic trade policy is that when such strategic trade policies are successful, they end up eliminating or reducing trade restrictions. When they are unsuccessful, they can lead to a trade war. Thus, in response to the United States' threat, China made a threat of its own—to put prohibitive tariffs on U.S. goods. Just before the deadline the two countries had set, they agreed to avoid a trade war. China agreed to increase copyright enforcement and the United States agreed that China's proposed increased enforcement met U.S. objections.

When should trade restrictions be used for strategic purposes? And, just as important, when should they *not* be used for strategic purposes? Economic theory does not tell us. That question is part of the practice of the art of economics. (It should be pointed out that economic game theorists are adding insights into the issue and that the area of strategic trade policies is a hot one for research.)

Specialized Production

My discussion of comparative advantage took it as a given that one country was inherently more productive than another country in producing certain goods. But when one looks at trading patterns, it's often not at all clear why particular countries have a productive advantage in certain goods. There's no inherent reason for Switzerland to specialize in the production of watches or for South Korea to specialize in the production of cars. Much in trade cannot be explained by inherent resource endowments.

If they don't have inherent advantages, why are countries and places often so good at producing what they specialize in? Two important explanations are that they *learn by doing* and that *economies of scale* exist.

Learning by doing means becoming better at a task the more you perform it.

Learning by Doing **Learning by doing** means *becoming better at a task the more often you perform it.* Take watches in Switzerland. Initially production of watches in

THE ANTIGLOBALIZATION FORCES

Applying the Tools

Often when there is a meeting of the World Trade Organization or of a similar type organization promoting free trade, protests (sometimes violent ones) are held by a loosely organized collection of groups opposing globalization. The goals of these groups are varied. Some argue that trade hurts developed countries such as the United States; others argue that it hurts developing countries by exploiting poor workers so that Westerners can get luxuries cheaply. Still others argue against a more subtle Western economic imperialism in which globalization spreads Western cultural values and undermines developing countries' social structures.

Paul Conklin/Photoedit

Each of these arguments has some appeal, although making the first two simultaneously is difficult because it says that voluntary trade hurts both parties to the trade. But the arguments have had little impact on the views of most policymakers and economists.

Supporting free trade does not mean that globalization does not have costs. It does, but many of the costs associated with free trade are really the result of technological changes. The reality is that technological developments, such as those in telecommunications and transportation, are pushing countries closer together and will involve difficult social and cultural changes, regardless of whether trade is free or not. Restricting trade might temporarily slow these changes but is unlikely to stop them.

Most empirical studies have found that, with regard to material goods, the workers in developing countries involved in trade are generally better off than those not involved in trade. That's why most developing countries work hard to encourage companies to move production facilities into their countries. From a worker's perspective, earning \$4 a day can look quite good when the alternative is earning \$3 a day. Would the worker rather earn \$10 a day? Of course, but the higher the wages in a given country, the less likely it is that firms are going to locate production there.

Many economists are sympathetic to various antiglobalization arguments, but they often become frustrated at the lack of clarity of the antiglobalization groups' views. To oppose something is not enough; to effect positive change, one must not only understand how the thing one opposes works but also have a realistic plan for a better alternative.

Switzerland may have been a coincidence; the person who started the watch business happened to live there. But then people in the area became skilled in producing watches. Their skill made it attractive for other watch companies to start up. As additional companies moved in, more and more members of the labor force became skilled at watchmaking and word went out that Swiss watches were the best in the world. That reputation attracted even more producers, so Switzerland became the watchmaking capital of the world. Had the initial watch production occurred in Austria, not Switzerland, Austria might be the watch capital of the world.

When there's learning by doing, it's much harder to attribute inherent comparative advantage to a country. One must always ask: Does country A have an inherent comparative advantage, or does it simply have more experience? Once country B gets the experience, will country A's comparative advantage disappear? If it will, then country B has a strong reason to limit trade with country A in order to give its own workers time to catch up as they learn by doing.

In economies of scale, costs per unit of output go down as output increases.

Economies of Scale In determining whether an inherent comparative advantage exists, a second complication is **economies of scale**—*the situation in which costs per unit of output fall as output increases*. Many manufacturing industries (such as steel and autos) exhibit economies of scale. The existence of significant economies of scale means that it makes sense (that is, it lowers costs) for one country to specialize in one good and another country to specialize in another good. But who should specialize in what is unclear. Producers in a country can, and generally do, argue that if only the government will establish barriers, they'll be able to lower their costs per unit and eventually sell at lower costs than foreign producers.

A number of countries follow trade strategies to allow them to take advantage of economies of scale. For example, in the 1970s and 1980s Japan's government consciously directed investment into automobiles and high-tech consumer products, and significantly promoted exports in these goods to take advantage of economies of scale.

Q-8 Is it efficient for a country to maintain a trade barrier in an industry that exhibits economies of scale?

Most countries recognize the importance of learning by doing and economies of scale. A variety of trade restrictions are based on these two phenomena. The most common expression of the learning-by-doing and economies-of-scale insights is the **infant industry argument,** which is that *with initial protection, an industry will be able to become competitive*. Countries use this argument to justify many trade restrictions. They argue, "You may now have a comparative advantage, but that's simply because you've been at it longer, or are experiencing significant economies of scale. We need trade restrictions on our ______ industry to give it a chance to catch up. Once an infant industry grows up, then we can talk about eliminating the restrictions."

The infant industry argument says that with initial protection, an industry will be able to become competitive.

Macroeconomic Aspects of Trade

The comparative advantage argument for free trade assumes that a country's resources are fully utilized. When countries don't have full employment, imports can decrease domestic aggregate demand and increase unemployment. Exports can stimulate domestic aggregate demand and decrease unemployment. Thus, when an economy is in a recession, there is a strong macroeconomic reason to limit imports and encourage exports. These macroeconomic effects of free trade play an important role in the public's view of imports and exports. When a country is in a recession, pressure to impose trade restrictions increases substantially.

National Security

Countries often justify trade restrictions on grounds of national security. These restrictions take two forms:

1. Export restrictions on strategic materials and defense-related goods.
2. Import restrictions on defense-related goods. For example, in a war we don't want to be dependent on oil from abroad.

For a number of goods, national security considerations make sense. For example, the United States restricts the sale of certain military items to countries that are likely to be fighting the United States someday. The problem is where to draw the line about goods having a national security consideration. Should countries protect domestic agriculture? All high-technology items, since they might be useful in weapons? All chemicals? Steel? The national security argument has been extended to a wide variety of goods whose importance to national security is indirect rather than direct. When a country makes a national security argument for trade, we must be careful to consider whether a domestic political reason may be lurking behind that argument.

International Politics

International politics frequently provides another reason for trade restrictions. As of 2002 the United States restricted trade with Cuba to punish that country for trying to extend its Marxist political and economic policies to other Latin American countries.

The United States also has trade restrictions on Iraq for its activities that support terrorists. The list can be extended, but you get the argument: Trade helps you, so we'll hurt you by stopping trade until you do what we want. So what if it hurts us too? It'll hurt you more than it hurts us.

Increased Revenue Brought in by Tariffs

A final argument made for one particular type of trade restriction—a tariff—is that tariffs bring in revenues. In the 19th century, tariffs were the U.S. government's primary source of revenue. They are less important as a source of revenue today for some developed countries because those countries have instituted other forms of taxes. However, tariffs remain a primary source of revenue for many developing countries. They're relatively easy to collect and are paid by people rich enough to afford imports. These countries justify many of their tariffs with the argument that they need the revenues.

Economists generally oppose trade restrictions because:

1. From a global perspective, free trade increases total output.
2. International trade provides competition for domestic companies.
3. Restrictions based on national security are often abused or evaded.
4. Trade restrictions are addictive.

Why Economists Generally Oppose Trade Restrictions

Each of the preceding arguments for trade restrictions has some validity, but most economists discount them and support free trade. The reason is that, in their considered judgment, the harm done by trade restrictions outweighs the benefits.

Free Trade Increases Total Output

Economists' first argument for free trade is that, viewed from a global perspective, free trade increases total output. From a national perspective, economists agree that particular instances of trade restriction may actually help one nation, even as most other nations are hurt. But they argue that the country imposing trade restrictions can benefit *only if the other country doesn't retaliate* with trade restrictions of its own. Retaliation is the rule, not the exception, however, and when there is retaliation, trade restrictions cause both countries to lose.

Q-9 What was the long-run effect on the steel industry of the trade restrictions on the import of steel during the 1950s and 1960s?

International Trade Provides Competition

A second reason most economists support free trade is that trade restrictions reduce international competition. International competition is desirable because it forces domestic companies to stay on their toes. If trade restrictions on imports are imposed, domestic companies don't work as hard and therefore become less efficient.

For example, in the 1950s and 1960s the United States imposed restrictions on imported steel. U.S. steel industries responded to this protection by raising their prices and channeling profits from their steel production into other activities. By the 1970s the U.S. steel industry was using outdated equipment to produce overpriced steel. Instead of making the steel industry stronger, restrictions made it a flabby, uncompetitive industry.

In the 1980s and 1990s, the U.S. steel industry became less and less profitable. Larger mills closed or consolidated, while non-union minimills, which made new steel out of scrap steel, did well. By the late 1990s, minimills accounted for 45 percent of total U.S. steel production. In 2002, it looked as if a number of larger mills were going to declare bankruptcy, and enormous pressure was placed on the federal government to bail them out by taking over their pension debt and instituting tariffs. President George W. Bush responded by calling for 20–30 percent tariffs on foreign steel imports. Most economists opposed the tariffs and pointed out that they were unlikely to lead to a rebuilding of the U.S. steel industry because other countries had a comparative advantage in steel production. Moreover, other countries would retaliate with tariffs on U.S. goods. Despite their opposition, the tariffs were instituted. Major U.S. trading partners—including EU countries, Japan, and China—responded by implementing tariffs on U.S. goods worth about $335 million.

The benefits of international competition are not restricted to mature industries like steel; they can also accrue to young industries wherever they appear. Economists dispose of the infant industry argument by reference to the historical record. In theory the argument makes sense. But very few of the infant industries protected by trade restrictions have ever grown up. What tends to happen instead is that infant industries become dependent on the trade restrictions and use political pressure to keep that protection. As a result, they often remain immature and internationally uncompetitive. Most economists would support the infant industry argument only if the trade restrictions included definite conditions under which the restrictions would end.

Very few of the infant industries protected by trade restrictions have ever grown up.

Web Note 21.3
Protection and Industrialization

Restrictions Based on National Security Are Often Abused or Evaded

Most economists agree with the national security argument for export restrictions on goods that are directly war related. Selling bombs to Iraq, with whom the United States was at war in early 1991, doesn't make much sense (although it should be noted that the United States did exactly that throughout the 1980s when the United States supported Iraq in its war with Iran).

Economists point out that the argument is often carried far beyond goods directly related to national security. For example, in the 1980s the United States restricted exports of sugar-coated cereals to the Soviet Union purportedly for reasons of national security. Sugar-frosted flakes may be great, but they were unlikely to help the Soviet Union in a war.

Another argument that economists give against the national security rationale is that trade restrictions on military sales can often be evaded. Countries simply have another country buy the goods for them. Such third-party sales—called *transshipments*—are common in international trade and limit the effectiveness of any absolute trade restrictions for national security purposes.

Economists also argue that by fostering international cooperation, international trade makes war less likely—a significant contribution to national security.

Trade Restrictions Are Addictive

Economists' final argument against trade restrictions is: Yes, some restrictions might benefit a country, but almost no country can limit its restrictions to the beneficial ones. Trade restrictions are addictive—the more you have, the more you want. Thus, a majority of economists take the position that the best response to such addictive policies is "Just say no."

Yes, some restrictions might benefit a country, but almost no country can limit its restrictions to the beneficial ones.

Institutions Supporting Free Trade

Web Note 21.4
Export Promotion

As I have stated throughout the text, economists generally like markets and favor trade being as free as possible. They argue that trade allows specialization and the division of labor. When each country follows its comparative advantage, production is more efficient and the production possibility curve shifts out. These views mean that most economists, liberal and conservative alike, generally oppose international trade restrictions.

Despite political pressures to restrict trade, governments have generally tried to follow economists' advice and have entered into a variety of international agreements and

Dumping

Applying the Tools

The WTO allows countries to impose trade restrictions on imports if they can show that the goods are being dumped. *Dumping* is selling a good in a foreign country at a lower price than in the country where it's produced. On the face of it, who could complain about someone who wants to sell you a good cheaply? Why not just take advantage of the bargain price? The first objection is the learning-by-doing argument. To stay competitive, a country must keep on producing. Dumping by another country can force domestic producers out of business. Having eliminated the competition, the foreign producer has the field to itself and can raise the price. Thus, dumping can be a form of predatory pricing.

The second argument against dumping involves the short-term macroeconomic and political effects it can have on the importing country. Even if one believes that dumping is not a preliminary to predatory pricing, it can displace workers in the importing country, causing political pressure on that government to institute trade restrictions. If that country's economy is in a recession, the resulting unemployment will have substantial macroeconomic repercussions, so pressure for trade restrictions will be amplified.

Important international economic organizations include the WTO, which took the place of GATT.

organizations. The most important is the World Trade Organization (WTO), which has about 150 members, and is the successor to the General Agreement on Tariffs and Trade (GATT). You will still occasionally see references to GATT, even though the WTO has taken its place. One of the differences between the WTO and GATT is that the WTO includes some enforcement mechanisms.

A free trade association is a group of countries that allows free trade among its members and puts up common barriers against all other countries' goods.

The push for free trade has a geographic dimension, which includes **free trade associations**—*groups of countries that have reduced or eliminated trade barriers among themselves*. The European Union (EU) is the most famous free trade association. All barriers to trade among the EU's member countries were removed in 1992. In the coming decade more European countries can be expected to join the EU. In 1993, the United States and Canada agreed to enter into a similar free trade union, and they, together with Mexico, created the North American Free Trade Association (NAFTA). Under NAFTA, tariffs and other trade barriers among these countries are being gradually reduced. Some other trading associations include Mercosur (among South American countries) and Asean (among Southeast Asian countries).

Q-10 What is economists' view of limited free trade associations such as the EU or NAFTA?

Economists have mixed reactions to free trade associations. They see free trade as beneficial, but they are concerned about the possibility that these regional free trade associations will impose significant trade restrictions on nonmember countries. They also believe that bilateral negotiations between member nations will replace multilateral efforts among members and nonmembers. Whether the net effect of these bilateral negotiations is positive or negative remains to be seen.

Groups of other countries have loose trading relationships because of cultural or historical reasons. These loose trading relationships are sometimes called trading zones. For example, many European countries maintain close trading ties with many of their former colonies in Africa where they fit into a number of overlapping trading zones. European companies tend to see that central area as their turf. The United States has close ties in Latin America, making the Western hemisphere another trading zone. Another example of a trading zone is that of Japan and its economic ties with other Far East countries; Japanese companies often see that area as their commercial domain.

These trading zones overlap, sometimes on many levels. For instance, Australia and England, Portugal and Brazil, and the United States and Saudi Arabia are tied together for historical or political reasons, and those ties lead to increased trade between them that seems to deviate from the above trading zones. Similarly, as companies become more and more global, it is harder and harder to associate companies with particular countries. Let me give an example: Do you know who the largest exporters of cars from the United States are? The answer is: Japanese automobile companies!

Thus, there is no hard-and-fast specification of trading zones, and knowing history and politics is important to understanding many of the relationships.

One way countries strengthen trading relationships among groups of countries is through a most-favored-nation status. The term **most-favored nation** refers to *a country that will be charged as low a tariff on its exports as any other country*. Thus, if the United States lowers tariffs on goods imported from Japan, which has most-favored-nation status with the United States, it must lower tariffs on those same types of goods imported from any other country with most-favored-nation status.

A most-favored nation is a country that will pay as low a tariff on its exports as will any other country.

This status is often used as a bargaining tool to gain political or economic concessions from the country desiring the most-favored-nation status. In the 1990s the United States reviewed China's most-favored-nation status almost annually in an effort to correct China's human rights violations and intellectual property rights encroachments and after agreeing to a number of conditions, China was given permanent most-favored-nation status by the United States in 2000.

Conclusion

International trade will become more and more important for the United States. With international transportation and communication becoming easier and faster, and with other countries' economies growing, the U.S. economy will inevitably become more interdependent with the other economies of the world. As international trade becomes more important, the push for trade restrictions will likely increase. Various countries' strategic trade policies will likely conflict, and the world will find itself on the verge of an international trade war that would benefit no one.

Concern about that possibility leads most economists to favor free trade. As often happens, economists advise politicians to follow a politically unpopular policy—to take the hard course of action. Whether politicians follow economists' advice or whether they follow the politically popular policy will play a key role in determining the course of the U.S. economy in the 2000s.

Summary

- International trade has fluctuated since 1928 and stands today at about $7 trillion a year. Canada and Mexico are the United States' largest trading partners.
- According to the principle of comparative advantage, as long as the relative opportunity costs of producing goods (what must be given up in one good in order to get another good) differ among countries, there are potential gains from trade, even if one country has an absolute advantage in everything.
- Three insights into the terms of trade include:
  1. The more competition exists in international trade, the less the trader gets and the more the involved countries get.
  2. Once competition prevails, smaller countries tend to get a larger percentage of the gains from trade than do larger countries.
  3. Gains from trade go to countries that produce goods that exhibit economies of scale.
- Trade restrictions include tariffs and quotas, embargoes, voluntary restraint agreements, regulatory trade restrictions, and nationalistic appeals.

- Reasons that countries impose trade restrictions include unequal internal distribution of the gains from trade, haggling by companies over the gains from trade, haggling by countries over trade restrictions, learning by doing and economies of scale, macroeconomic aspects of trade, national security, international political reasons, and increased revenue brought in by tariffs.
- Economists generally oppose trade restrictions because of the history of trade restrictions and their understanding of the advantages of free trade.
- The World Trade Organization is an international organization committed to reducing trade barriers.
- Free trade associations help trade by reducing barriers to trade among member nations. Free trade associations could hinder trade by building up barriers to trade with nations outside the association; negotiations among members could replace multilateral efforts to reduce trade restrictions among members and nonmembers.

Key Terms

balance of trade *(461)*
comparative advantage *(462)*
economies of scale *(474)*
embargo *(469)*
free trade association *(478)*
General Agreement on Tariffs and Trade (GATT) *(466)*
infant industry argument *(475)*
learning by doing *(473)*
most-favored nation *(479)*
quotas *(466)*
regulatory trade restrictions *(469)*
strategic bargaining *(472)*
strategic trade policy *(473)*
tariffs *(466)*
trade adjustment assistance programs *(471)*
World Trade Organization (WTO) *(466)*

Questions for Thought and Review

1. Will a country do better importing or exporting a good for which it has a comparative advantage? Why?
2. Widgetland has 60 workers. Each worker can produce 4 widgets or 4 wadgets. Each resident in Widgetland currently consumes 2 widgets and 2 wadgets. Wadgetland also has 60 workers. Each can produce 3 widgets or 12 wadgets. Wadgetland's residents consume 1 widget and 9 wadgets. Is there a basis for trade? If so, offer the countries a deal they can't refuse.
3. Why does competition among traders affect how much of the gains to trade are given to the countries involved in the trade?
4. Why do smaller countries usually get most of the gains from trade? What are some reasons why a small country might not get the gains of trade?
5. Which country will get the larger gain from trade—a country with economies of scale or diseconomies of scale? Explain your answer.
6. Suggest an equitable method of funding trade adjustment assistance programs. Why is it equitable? What problems might a politician have in implementing such a method?
7. If you were economic adviser to a country that was following your advice about trade restrictions and that country fell into a recession, would you change your advice? Why, or why not?
8. The U.S. trade balance improved significantly in 1991 when the U.S. economy went into recession. Is this consistent with economic predictions? Why or why not?
9. How can free trade protect national security?
10. What are two reasons economists support free trade?
11. Demonstrate graphically how the effects of a tariff differ from the effects of a quota.
12. How do the effects of voluntary restraint agreements differ from the effects of a tariff? How are they the same?
13. Mexico exports many vegetables to the United States. These vegetables are grown using chemicals that are not allowed in U.S. vegetable agriculture. Should the United States restrict imports of Mexican vegetables? Why or why not?
14. When the United States placed a temporary price floor on tomatoes imported from Mexico, U.S. trade representative Mickey Kantor said, "The agreement will provide strong relief to the tomato growers in Florida and other states, and help preserve jobs in the industry." What costs did Americans bear from the price floor?
15. A study by the World Bank on the effects of Mercosur, a regional trade pact among four Latin American countries, concluded that free trade agreements "might confer significant benefits, but there are also significant dangers." What are those benefits and dangers?
16. What is the relationship between GATT and WTO?

Problems and Exercises

1. Suppose there are two states that do not trade—Iowa and Nebraska. Each state produces the same two goods—corn and wheat. For Iowa the opportunity cost of producing 1 bushel of wheat is 3 bushels of corn. For Nebraska the opportunity cost of producing 1 bushel of corn is 3 bushels of wheat. At present, Iowa produces 20 million bushels of wheat and 120 million bushels of corn, while Nebraska produces 20 million bushels of corn and 120 million bushels of wheat.
   a. Explain how, with trade, Nebraska can end up with 40 million bushels of wheat and 120 million bushels of corn while Iowa can end up with 40 million bushels of corn and 120 million bushels of wheat.
   b. If the states ended up with the numbers given in *a*, how much would the trader get?
2. Country A can produce, at most, 40 olives or 20 pickles, or some combination of olives and pickles such as the 20 olives and 10 pickles it is currently producing. Country B can produce, at most, 120 olives or 60 pickles, or some combination of olives and pickles such as the 100 olives and 50 pickles it is currently producing.
   a. Is there a basis for trade? If so, offer the two countries a deal they can't refuse.
   b. How would your answer to *a* change if you knew that there were economies of scale in the production of pickles and olives rather than the production possibilities described in the question? Why? If your answer is yes, which country would you have produce which good?
3. The world price of textiles is P_w, as in the accompanying figure of the domestic supply and demand for textiles.

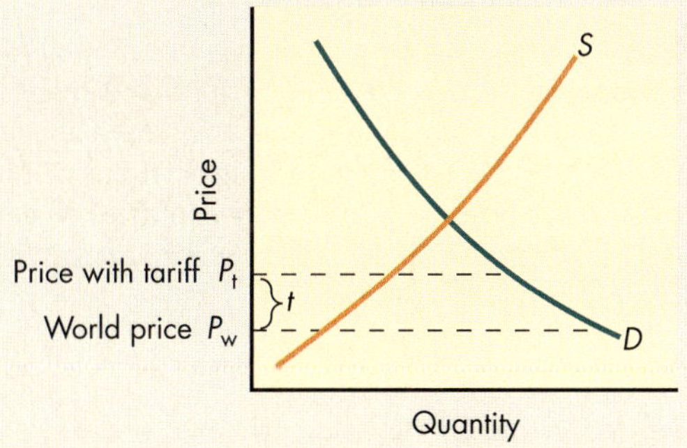

The government imposes a tariff *t*, to protect the domestic producers. For this tariff:
   a. Shade in the gains to domestic producers.
   b. Shade in the revenue to government.
   c. Shade in the costs to domestic producers.
   d. Are the gains greater than the costs? Why?
4. In 2001 the hourly cost to employers per German industrial worker was $22.86. The hourly cost to employers per U.S. industrial worker was $20.32, while the average cost per Taiwanese industrial worker was $5.70.
   a. Give three reasons why firms produce in Germany rather than in a lower-wage country.
   b. Germany has just entered into an agreement with other EU countries that allows people in any EU country, including Greece and Italy, which have lower wage rates, to travel and work in any EU country, including high-wage countries. Would you expect a significant movement of workers from Greece and Italy to Germany right away? Why or why not?
   c. Workers in Thailand are paid significantly less than workers in Taiwan. If you were a company CEO, what other information would you want before you decided where to establish a new production facility?
5. Peter Sutherland, the former director-general of GATT and WTO, published a pamphlet on the costs of trade protection. He subtitled the pamphlet "The Sting: How Governments Buy Votes on Trade with the Consumer's Money."
   a. What does he likely mean by this subtitle?
   b. If a government is out to increase votes with its trade policy, would it more likely institute tariffs or quotas? Why?
6. One of the basic economic laws is "the law of one price." It says that given certain assumptions one would expect that if free trade is allowed, the price of goods in countries should converge.
   a. Can you list what three of those assumptions likely are?
   b. Should the law of one price hold for labor also? Why or why not?
   c. Should it hold for capital more so or less so than for labor? Why or why not?

Web Questions

1. Go to the WTO's home page at www.wto.org to find out how trade disputes are settled.
   a. What is the procedure for settling disputes?
   b. What is the timetable for the settlement procedure?
   c. What happens if one of the countries does not abide by the settlement?
2. Go to the National Center for Policy Analysis website (www.ncpa.org). Select "Policy Issues," then "Trade" and

finally "Tariffs and other Trade Barriers" to answer the following:
   a. List three trade barriers mentioned in the articles.
   b. What are the reasons the trade barriers were instituted?
   c. According to the articles, what was the result of those trade barriers?
3. Go to the home page of free trade association Asean (www.aseansec.org) and answer the following questions:
   a. What countries belong to the trade association?
   b. When was the association established?
   c. What is the association's stated objective?
   d. What is the combined gross domestic product of all members?
4. Choose a country, and using *The Economist* magazine's country site (www.economist.com/countries), answer the following questions:
   a. Using export and import shares, how globalized is your country?
   b. What goods does your country export and import?
   c. What are the probable goods for which your country has a comparative advantage?

Answers to Margin Questions

1. Japan has the lowest exports and imports as a percentage of total output, followed closely by the United States. *(461)*
2. A debtor nation will not necessarily be running a trade deficit. *Debt* refers to accumulated past deficits. If a country had accumulated large deficits in the past, it could run a surplus now but still be a debtor nation. *(462)*
3. I.T. ended up with 380 tons of food and 380 barrels of oil after the trade. *(464)*
4. The percentage of gains of trade that goes to a country depends upon the change in the price of the goods being traded. If trade led to no change in prices in a small country, then that small country would get no gains from trade. Another case in which a small country gets a small percentage of the gains from trade would occur when its larger trading partner was producing a good with economies of scale and the small country was not. A third case is when the traders who extracted most of the surplus or gains from trade come from the larger country; then the small country would end up with few of the gains from trade. *(466)*
5. An inefficient customs agency can operate with the same effect as a trade restriction, and if trade restrictions would help the country then it is possible that an inefficient customs agency could also help the country. *(469)*
6. The EU places high barriers against agricultural products to protect its farmers. As in the case with many of the international trade barriers, this is primarily for political, not economic, purposes. *(471)*
7. True. In strategic trade bargaining it is reasonable to be unreasonable. The belief of the other bargainer that you will be unreasonable leads you to be able to extract larger gains from trade. Of course, this leads to the logical paradox that if "unreasonable" is "reasonable," unreasonable really is reasonable, so it is only reasonable to be reasonable. Sorting out that last statement can be left for a philosophy or logic class. *(472)*
8. Whether or not it is efficient for a country to maintain barriers to trade in an industry that exhibits economies of scale depends upon the marginal costs and marginal benefits of maintaining those barriers. Having significant economies of scale does mean that average costs of production will be lower; however, trade restrictions might mean that the industry might be able to inflate its costs. *(475)*
9. The U.S. steel industry became internationally uncompetitive and produced overpriced steel. The restrictions produced an uncompetitive industry. *(476)*
10. Most economists have a mixed view of limited free trade associations such as NAFTA or the EU. While they see free trade as beneficial, they are concerned about the possibility that these limited trade associations will impose trade restrictions on nonmember countries. Whether the net effect of these will be positive or negative is a complicated issue. *(478)*

APPENDIX A

The Geometry of Absolute Advantage and Comparative Advantage

The chapter briefly went through an example of the gains of trade. This appendix presents that same example geometrically, together with another example. In doing so it contrasts the concept of absolute advantage with the concept of comparative advantage.

WHY DO NATIONS TRADE?

International trade exists for the same reason that all trade exists: Party A has something that party B wants and party B has something that party A wants. Both parties can be made better off by trade.

THE PRINCIPLE OF ABSOLUTE ADVANTAGE

Trade between countries in different types of goods is relatively easy to explain. For example, trade in raw materials and agricultural goods for manufactured goods can be easily explained by the principle of **absolute advantage:**

> A country that can produce a good at a lower cost than another country is said to have an absolute advantage in the production of that good. When two countries have absolute advantages in different goods, there are gains of trade to be had.

The principle of absolute advantage explains trade of, say, oil from Saudi Arabia for food from the United States. Saudi Arabia has millions of barrels of easily available oil, but growing food in its desert climate and sandy soil is expensive. The United States can grow food cheaply in its temperate climate and fertile soil, but its oil isn't as easily available or as cheap to extract. Because it can produce a certain amount of oil with fewer resources, Saudi Arabia has an absolute advantage over the United States in producing oil. Because it can produce a certain amount of food with fewer resources, the United States has an absolute advantage over Saudi Arabia in producing food. When each country specializes in the good it has an absolute advantage in, both countries can gain from trade.

In Figure A21-1, I consider a hypothetical numerical example that demonstrates how the principle of absolute advantage can lead to gains from trade. For simplicity, I assume constant opportunity costs.

Figures A21-1(b) and (d) show the choices for the United States; Figures A21-1(a) and (c) show the choices for Saudi Arabia. In Figures A21-1(a) and (b) you see that the United States and Saudi Arabia can produce various combinations of food and oil by devoting differing percentages of their resources to producing each. Comparing the two tables and assuming the resources in the two countries are comparable, we see that Saudi Arabia has an absolute advantage in the production of oil and the United States has an absolute advantage in the production of food.

For example, when the United States and Saudi Arabia devote equal amounts of resources to oil production, Saudi Arabia can produce 10 times as much as the United States. Alternatively, when the United States devotes 60 percent of a given amount of resources to oil production, it gets 60 barrels of oil. But when Saudi Arabia devotes 60 percent of that same amount of resources to oil production, it gets 600 barrels of oil. The information in the tables is presented graphically in Figures A21-1(c) and (d). These graphs represent the two countries' production possibility curves without trade. Each combination of numbers in the table corresponds to a point on the curve. For example, point *B* in each graph corresponds to the entries in row *B*, columns 2 and 3, in the relevant table.

Let's assume that, without any international trade, the United States has chosen point C (production of 60 barrels of oil and 400 tons of food) and Saudi Arabia has chosen point *D* (production of 400 barrels of oil and 60 tons of food).

Now International Trader (I.T.), who understands the principle of absolute advantage, comes along and offers the following deal to Saudi Arabia:

> If you produce 1,000 barrels of oil and no food (point A) and give me 500 barrels of oil while keeping 500 barrels for yourself, I guarantee you 120 tons of food, double the amount of food you're now getting. I'll put you on point G, which is totally above your current production possibility curve. You'll get more oil and more food. It's an offer you can't refuse.

I.T. then flies off to the United States, to whom he makes the following offer:

> If you produce 1,000 tons of food and no oil (point *F*) and give me 500 tons of food while keeping 500 tons for yourself, I'll guarantee you 120 barrels of oil, double the amount you're now getting. I'll put you on point *H*, which is totally above your current

Figure A21-1 (a, b, c, and d) Absolute Advantage: The United States and Saudi Arabia
Looking at tables (**a**) and (**b**), you can see that if Saudi Arabia devotes all its resources to oil, it can produce 1,000 barrels of oil, but if it devotes all of its resources to food, it can produce only 100 tons of food. For the United States, the story is the opposite: Devoting all of its resources to oil, the United States can only produce 100 barrels of oil—10 times less than Saudi Arabia—but if it devotes all of its resources to food, it can produce 1,000 tons of food—10 times more than Saudi Arabia. Assuming resources are comparable, Saudi Arabia has an absolute advantage in the production of oil, and the United States has an absolute advantage in the production of food. The information in the tables is presented graphically in (**c**) and (**d**). These are the countries' production possibility curves without trade. Each point on each country's curve corresponds to a row on that country's table.

Percentage of Resources Devoted to Oil	Oil Produced (barrels)	Food Produced (tons)	Row
100%	1,000	0	*A*
80	800	20	*B*
60	600	40	*C*
40	400	60	*D*
20	200	80	*E*
0	0	100	*F*

(a) Saudi Arabia's production possibility table

Percentage of Resources Devoted to Oil	Oil Produced (barrels)	Food Produced (tons)	Row
100%	100	0	*A*
80	80	200	*B*
60	60	400	*C*
40	40	600	*D*
20	20	800	*E*
0	0	1,000	*F*

(b) United States' production possibility table

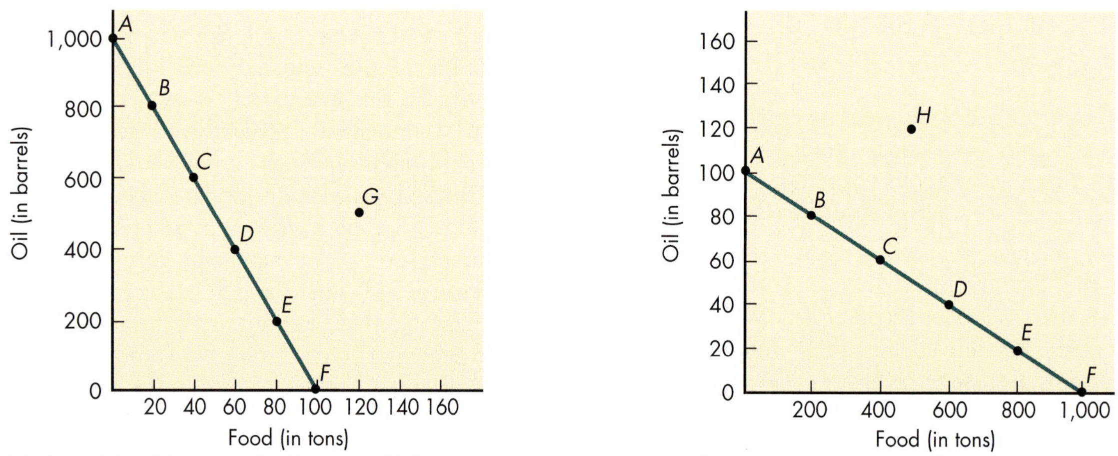

(c) Saudi Arabia's production possibility curve

(d) United States' production possibility curve

production possibility curve. You'll get more oil and have more food. It's an offer you can't refuse.

Both countries accept; they'd be foolish not to. So the two countries' final consumption positions are as follows:

	Oil (barrels)	Food (tons)
Total production	1,000	1,000
U.S. consumption	120	500
Saudi consumption	500	120
I.T.'s profit	380	380

For arranging the trade, I.T. makes a handsome profit of 380 tons of food and 380 barrels of oil.

I.T. has become rich because he understands the principle of absolute advantage. Unfortunately for I.T., the principle of absolute advantage is easy to understand, which means that he will quickly face competition. Other international traders come in and offer the countries even better deals than I.T. offered, squeezing his share. With free entry and competition in international trade, eventually I.T.'s share is squeezed down to his costs plus a normal return for his efforts.

Now obviously this hypothetical example significantly overemphasizes the gains a trader makes. Generally the person arranging the trade must compete with other traders and offer both countries a better deal than the one presented here. But the person who first recognizes a trading opportunity often makes a sizable fortune. The second

Table A21-1 Germany's Comparative Advantage over Algeria in the Production of Autos and Food

(a) Germany				(b) Algeria			
% of Resources Devoted to Autos	Autos Produced	Food Produced	Row	% of Resources Devoted to Autos	Autos Produced	Food Produced	Row
100%	100	0	*A*	100%	20	0	*A*
80	80	40	*B*	80	16	1	*B*
60	60	80	*C*	60	12	2	*C*
40	40	120	*D*	40	8	3	*D*
20	20	160	*E*	20	4	4	*E*
0	0	200	*F*	0	0	5	*F*

and third persons who recognize the opportunity make smaller fortunes. Once the insight is generally recognized, the possibility of making a fortune is gone. Traders still make their normal returns, but the instantaneous fortunes are not to be made without new insight. In the long run, benefits of trade go to the producers and consumers in the trading countries, not the traders.

I.T. realizes this and spends part of his fortune on buying a Greek island, where he retires to contemplate more deeply the nature of international trade so he can triple his remaining fortune. He marries, has a daughter whom he names I.T. Too, and dies. But before he dies he teaches his daughter about international trade and how new insights can lead to fortunes. His dying words to his daughter are "Keep searching for that new insight."

The Principle of Comparative Advantage

Many years pass. I.T. Too grows up, and one day, while walking along the beach, she contemplates the possibilities of trade between Germany and Algeria in automobiles and food. No other traders have considered trade between these two countries because Germany is so much more productive than Algeria in all goods. No trade is currently taking place because Germany has an absolute advantage in production of both autos and food. Assuming the resources in the two countries are comparable, this case can be seen in Table A21-1.

But I.T. Too is bright. She remembers what her father taught her about opportunity costs back in her first economics lesson. She reasons as follows: Germany's opportunity cost of producing an auto is 2/1. That means Germany must give up 2 tons of food to get 1 additional auto. For example, if Germany is initially producing 60 autos and 80 tons of food, if it cuts production of autos by 20, it will increase its food output by 40. For each car lost, Germany gains 2 tons of food. When Algeria cuts its production of autos by 4, it gains 1 ton of food. Algeria's opportunity cost of producing another auto is 1/4. It must give up 1 ton of food to get an additional 4 autos.

I.T. Too further reasons that if Algeria needs to give up only 1/4 unit of food to get an auto while Germany needs to give up 2 tons of food to produce 1 auto, there are potential gains to be made, which can be split up among the countries and herself. Then, like her father before her, she can make the countries offers they can't refuse. She walks the beach mulling the following: "*Absolute advantage* is not necessary for trade; *comparative advantage* is." A smile comes over her face; she understands.

Flying happily over the Mediterranean Sea, she formulates her insight precisely. She calls it the principle of **comparative advantage:** As long as the relative opportunity costs of producing goods (what must be given up in one good in order to get another good) differ among countries, there are potential gains from trade, even if one country has an absolute advantage in everything.

It is comparative advantage, not absolute advantage, that forms a basis of trade. If one country has a comparative advantage in one good, the other country must, by definition, have a comparative advantage in the other good.

Having formulated her idea, she applies it to the Germans and Algerians. She sees that, unexpectedly, Germany has a comparative advantage in producing food and Algeria has a comparative advantage in producing cars. With this insight firmly in mind, she leaves her island, flies to Germany, and makes the Germans the following offer:

> You're currently producing and consuming 60 autos and 80 tons of food (row C of Table A21-1(a)). If you'll produce only 48 autos but 104 tons of food and give me 22 tons of food, I'll guarantee you 13 autos for

those 22 tons of food. You'll have more autos (61) and more food (82). It's an offer you can't refuse.

She then goes to Algeria and presents the Algerians with the following offer:

> You're currently producing 4 tons of food and 4 automobiles (row *E* of Table A21-1(b)). If you'll produce only automobiles (row A) and turn out 20 autos, keeping 5 for yourself and giving 15 of them to me, I'll guarantee you 5 tons of food for the 15 autos. You'll have more autos (5) and more food (5). It's an offer you can't refuse.

Neither Germany nor Algeria can refuse. They both agree to I.T. Too's offer. The final position appears as follows:

	Autos	Food
Total production	68	104
Germany consumption	61	82
Algerian consumption	5	5
I.T. Too's profit	2	17

I.T. Too then proceeds to visit various other countries, making similar offers. They accept the offers because it's in their interest to accept them. Countries (and people) trade because trade benefits them.

As was the case with her father, her initial returns are the greatest. Then, as other people recognize the principle of comparative advantage and offer the countries better deals than hers, her share shrinks until her return just covers her opportunity cost and the costs of transporting the goods. But because the principle of comparative advantage is more difficult to understand than the principle of absolute advantage, the competing traders enter in much more slowly. Her above-normal returns last longer than did her father's, but eventually they're competed away. When her profits declines to only normal levels, she sells out and retires.

Competitiveness, Exchange Rates, and Comparative Advantage

The standard presentation of absolute and comparative advantage is generally conducted in real terms without reference to a numeraire (price level) or exchange rate. These financial issues are traditionally covered in higher-level courses, where the study of money and financial issues is integrated in the analysis of trade. We should, however, point out that money and financial markets are necessary to make trade and payment imbalances possible. Exchange rates play a central role in determining a country's absolute advantage. In fact, without implicit exchange rates, absolute advantage cannot be determined. In turn, absolute advantage plays a big role in whether a country can have a temporary trade surplus or trade deficit—phenomena that we ruled out by assumption in this analysis of trade so that we keep the presentation challenging, but learnable. In the analysis we presented, trade surpluses or deficits are not considered.

Generally a low exchange rate encourages exports from a country and discourages imports; a high exchange rate discourages exports and encourages imports. An example of the importance of exchange rates can be seen by considering the United States and Japan: in the mid-1980s a dollar bought 200 yen, but in the mid-1990s the dollar bought only 100 yen. That change halved the absolute advantage of Japan and significantly discouraged our consumption of Japanese products. The resurgence of the U.S. auto industry was in large part due to that change in the exchange rate.

Key Terms

absolute advantage *(483)*

comparative advantage *(485)*

QUESTIONS FOR THOUGHT AND REVIEW

1. Suppose that two countries, Machineland and Farmland, have the following production possibility curves.

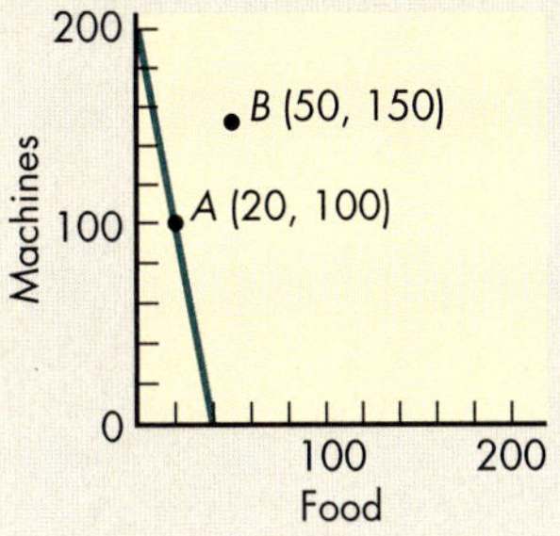

Machineland

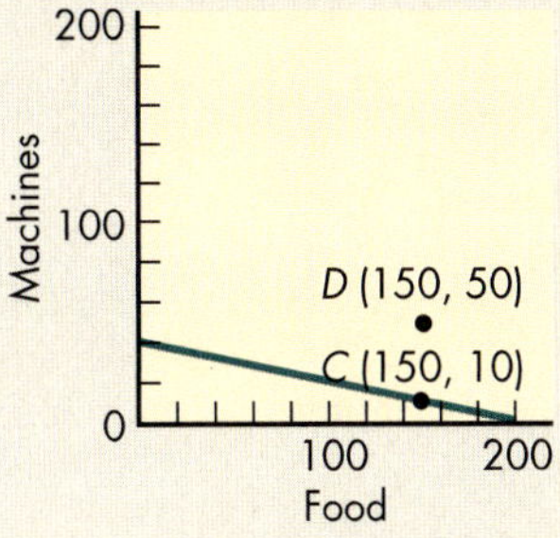

Farmland

a. Explain how these two countries can move from points *A* and *C*, where they currently are, to points *B* and *D*.

b. If possible, state by how much total production for the two countries has risen.

c. If you were a trader, how much of the gains from trade would you deserve for discovering this trade?

d. If there were economies of scale in the production of both goods, how would your analysis change?

2. Suppose Greece and France each produced only Kalamata olives and Roquefort cheese. Their production possibility curves are given in the following tables:

Greece		
% of Resources Devoted to Olives	Olives Produced (millions of olives)	Roquefort Produced (thousands of pounds)
100%	500	0
80	400	100
60	300	200
40	200	300
20	100	400
0	0	500

France		
% of Resources Devoted to Olives	Olives Produced (millions of olives)	Roquefort Produced (thousands of pounds)
100%	200	0
80	160	10
60	120	20
40	80	30
20	40	40
0	0	50

Currently, contrary to expectations, Greece produces 300 million olives and 200,000 pounds of Roquefort, while France produces 40 million olives and 40,000 pounds of Roquefort.

a. What is the opportunity cost of producing olives in each country? What is the opportunity cost of producing Roquefort in each country?

b. The European Commission rules that traditional foods have trademark protection. Only Roquefort made in France can be Roquefort and only olives produced in Greece can be Kalamata olives. Now Greece and France, following the new ruling, must each produce their respective trademarked goods and trade. Are they made better off? Why?

c. Show your answer graphically by selecting points now attainable that were previously not attainable.

3. Suppose there are two countries, Busytown and Lazyasiwannabe, with the following production possibility tables:

Busytown		
% of Resources Devoted to Cars	Cars Produced (thousands)	Gourmet Meals Produced (thousands)
100%	60	0
80	48	10
60	36	20
40	24	30
20	12	40
0	0	50

Lazyasiwannabe		
% of Resources Devoted to Cars	Cars Produced (thousands)	Gourmet Meals Produced (thousands)
100%	50	0
80	40	10
60	30	20
40	20	30
20	10	40
0	0	50

a. Draw the production possibility curves for each country.

b. Which country has the absolute advantage in producing cars? In producing gourmet meals?

c. Which country has the comparative advantage in producing cars? In producing gourmet meals?

d. Suppose each country specializes in the production of one good. Explain how Busytown can end up with 36,000 cars and 22,000 meals and Lazyasiwannabe can end up with 28,000 meals and 24,000 cars.

PART III

MACROECONOMICS

The specific focus of macroeconomics is the study of unemployment, business cycles (fluctuations in the economy), growth, and inflation. While the macroeconomic theories studied have changed considerably over the past 65 years, the focus of macroeconomics on those problems has remained. Thus, we'll define macroeconomics as the study of the economy in the aggregate with specific focus on unemployment, inflation, business cycles, and growth.

The following chapters provide you with the background necessary to discuss the modern debate about these issues. Let's begin with a little history.

Macroeconomics emerged as a separate subject within economics in the 1930s, when the U.S. economy fell into the Great Depression. Businesses collapsed and unemployment rose until 25 percent of the workforce—millions of people—were out of work.

The Depression changed the way economics was taught and the way in which economic problems were conceived. Before the 1930s, economics was microeconomics (the study of partial-equilibrium supply and demand). After the 1930s, the study of the core of economic thinking was broken into two discrete areas: microeconomics, as before, and macroeconomics (the study of the economy in the aggregate).

Macroeconomic policy debates have centered on a struggle between two groups: Keynesian (pronounced KAIN-sian) economists and Classical economists. Should the government run a budget deficit or a surplus? Should the government increase the money supply when a recession threatens? Should it decrease the money supply when inflation threatens? Can government prevent recessions? Keynesians generally answer one way; Classicals, another.

Classical economists generally oppose government intervention in the economy; they favor a laissez-faire policy.[1] Keynesians are more likely to favor government intervention in the economy. They feel a laissez-faire policy can sometimes lead to disaster. Both views represent reasonable economic positions. The differences between them are often subtle and result from their taking slightly different views of what government can do and slightly different perspectives on the economy.

In the last 10 years the differences between Keynesians and Classicals have shrunk so that now, at the turn of the century, there seems to be a consensus view of macro that captures the views held by the majority of the profession. It is that consensus view that all introductory textbooks, including this one, present. Even so, it is helpful to keep the traditional policy differences between Keynesians and Classicals in mind, because the differences often do flare up in debates about current policy. So while I will emphasize the presentation of a consensus view, I will from time to time discuss differences and difficulties in holding the consensus together.

The structure of Part III, Macroeconomics, is as follows: Section I, Macroeconomic Problems (Chapters 22 and 23), introduces the macroeconomic problems, terminology, and statistics used in tracking the economy's macroeconomic performance. Section II, The Macroeconomic Framework (Chapters 24–26), provides the long-run and short-run frameworks economists use when they discuss policy questions and presents the models for those frameworks. Section III, Money, Inflation, and Monetary Policy (Chapters 27–29), looks at how money and the financial system fits into the macro model and discusses monetary policy—the most used policy in macro today. Section IV, Macro Policy in Perspective (Chapters 30–32), ties together the models and policies and summarizes lessons economists have learned. Section V, International Policy Issues (Chapters 33 and 34), discusses policy within an international context.

[1] *Laissez-faire* (introduced to you in Chapter 2) is a French expression meaning "Leave things alone; let them go on without interference."

22 Economic Growth, Business Cycles, Unemployment, and Inflation

After reading this chapter, you should be able to:

- Explain the difference between the long-run framework and short-run framework.
- Summarize some relevant statistics about growth, business cycles, unemployment, and inflation.
- List four phases of the business cycle.
- Explain how unemployment is measured and state some microeconomic categories of unemployment.
- Relate the target rate of unemployment to potential income.
- Define inflation and distinguish a real concept from a nominal concept.
- State two important costs of inflation.

Remember that there is nothing stable in human affairs; therefore avoid undue elation in prosperity, or undue depression in adversity.

—*Socrates*

Like people, the economy has moods. Sometimes it's in wonderful shape—it's expansive; at other times, it's depressed. Like people whose moods are often associated with specific problems (headaches, sore back, itchy skin), the economy's moods are associated with various problems.

Macroeconomics is the study of the aggregate moods of the economy, with specific focus on problems associated with those moods—the problems of growth, business cycles, unemployment, and inflation. These four problems are the central concern of macroeconomics. The macroeconomic theory we'll consider is designed to explain how supply and demand forces in the aggregate interact to create these problems. The macroeconomic policy controversies we'll consider concern these four problems. So it's only appropriate that in this first macro chapter we consider an overview of these problems, their causes, their consequences, and the debate over what to do about them.[1]

Two Frameworks: The Long Run and the Short Run

In analyzing macroeconomic problems economists generally use two frameworks—a short-run and a long-run framework. Issues of growth are generally considered in a long-run framework. Business cycles are generally considered in a short-run framework. The other two problems, inflation and unemployment, fall within both frameworks. Economists use these two frameworks because the long-run forces that cause growth and the short-run forces that cause business cycles are different. Having two different frameworks allows us to consider these forces separately, making life easier for you.

[1]As I stated in the introduction to this part of the text, I present a consensus view of macroeconomics, although sometimes I distinguish between Keynesian and Classical approaches. I do so to keep the presentation at a level appropriate for a principles book. In reality, there is not always consensus among economists and many more distinctions can be made among economic viewpoints. The appendix to this chapter presents some of these viewpoints.

The Power of Compounding

Knowing the Tools

A difference in growth rates of one percentage point may not seem like much, but over a number of years, the power of compounding can turn these small differences in growth rates into large differences in income levels. Consider Eastern European countries compared to Western European countries. In 1950, average per capita income was about $3,000 in Eastern European countries, about half that in Western European countries. Over the next 50 years, income grew 1 percent a year in Eastern European countries and 1.5 percent a year in Western European countries. One-half percentage point may be small, but it meant that in those 50 years, income in Western European countries more than tripled, rising to $20,000, while income in Eastern European countries only doubled to about $6,000.

The reason small differences in growth rates can mean huge differences in income levels is *compounding*. Compounding means that growth is based not only on the original level of income but also on the accumulation of previous-year increases in income. For example, say you start at $100 and your income grows at a rate of 10 percent each year; the first year your income grows by $10, to $110. The second year the same growth rate increases income by $11, to $121. Then, the third year income grows by $12.10, which is still 10 percent but is a larger total increase. After 50 years that same 10 percent means an increase of over $70 a year.

What is the difference between the two frameworks? The long-run growth framework focuses on supply; that's why sometimes it is called supply-side economics. Because supply is so important in the long run, policies that affect production—such as incentives that promote work, capital accumulation, and technological change—are key. The short-run business cycle framework focuses on demand. Much of the policy discussion of short-run business cycles focuses on ways to increase or decrease components of aggregate expenditures, such as policies to get consumers and businesses to increase their spending.[2]

Q-1 In the 1990s, the Japanese institution of lifetime employment was deteriorating and more and more Japanese workers were getting laid off. Is this an issue best studied under the long-run framework or the short-run framework?

As an introduction to the central issues in macroeconomics, let's look briefly at each of the problems of growth, business cycles, unemployment, and inflation.

Growth

Generally the U.S. economy is growing or expanding. Economists use changes in **real gross domestic product (real GDP)**—*the market value of final goods and services produced in an economy, stated in the prices of a given year*—as the primary measurement of growth. When people produce and sell their goods, they earn income, so when an economy is growing, both total output and total income are increasing. Such growth gives most people more this year than they had last year. Since most of us prefer more to less, growth is easy to take.

The U.S. Department of Commerce traced U.S. economic growth in output since about 1890 and discovered that, on average, output of goods and services grew about 3.5 percent per year. In the 1970s and 1980s the growth was more like 2.5 percent. In the late 1990s and early 2000s it was again 3.5 percent. This 2.5 to 3.5 percent growth rate is sometimes called the *secular growth trend*. The rate at which the actual output grows

U.S. economic output has grown at an annual 2.5 to 3.5 percent rate.

[2] A short-run/long-run distinction helps make complicated issues somewhat clearer, but it obscures other issues such as: How long is the short run, and how do we move from the short run to the long run? Some economists argue that in the long run we are only in another short run, while others argue that since our actions are forward-looking, we are always in the long run.

in any one year fluctuates, but on average the U.S. economy has been growing at that long-term trend. Since population has also been growing, per capita economic growth (growth per person) has been less than 2.5 to 3.5 percent.

Q-2 Output in the United States in 2003 was about $10.5 trillion, and there were about 290 million people living in the United States. What was per capita output?

This brings us to another measure of growth—changes in per capita real output. **Per capita real output** is *real GDP divided by the total population*. Output per person is an important measure of growth because, while total output may be increasing, the population could be growing so fast that per capita real output is falling.

Global Experiences with Growth

Table 22-1 shows per capita growth for various areas of the world from 1820 to 2000. It tells us a number of important facts about growth:

1. Growth rates today are high by historical standards. For 130 years beginning in 1820, world output grew by only 0.9 percent per year. At that rate it took 82 years for world income to double. From 1950 to 2000, the world economy grew at a much faster rate, 1.8 percent per year, cutting the number of years it took income to double from 80 to 40.
2. The range in growth rates among countries is wide. From 1820 to 1950, North America led, with 1.6 percent annual growth. From 1950 to 2000, however, Japan and Western Europe were among the fastest growing, partially due to the opportunities for growth lost during World War II and the replacement of productive capital destroyed in the war. Japan's growth acceleration is the most pronounced. Japan turned from investing in military might before World War II to investing in capital destroyed by the war. This acceleration meant that these countries were catching up to other high-growth areas of the world. Japan's average income in 1950 was around one-fifth of the average income in North America. By 2000 it had grown close to equal, although with its recent slow growth it was losing ground in the early 2000s. Another country that has been catching up is China. While income in China was actually lower in 1950 than in 1820, beginning in the last part of the 20th century and continuing into the 21st century China's income has been one of the fastest growing in the world.

Table 22-1 Average Annual per Capita Income, Various Regions: 1820 to 2000

	Growth Rates			Income Levels (1990 international dollars)		
	1820–1950	1950–2000*	1820–2000*	1820	1950	2000*
The world	0.9	1.8	1.1	$ 675	$2,108	$ 5,672
Western Europe	1.1	2.5	1.5	1,269	6,546	19,846
North America	1.6	1.8	1.6	1,233	9,463	26,224
Japan	0.8	4.8	1.9	675	1,927	20,438
Eastern Europe	1.1	1.0	1.0	803	3,162	5,967
Latin America	1.0	1.4	1.1	671	2,478	6,797
China	−0.2	3.4	0.8	600	439	3,442
Other Asia	0.3	2.4	0.9	560	848	3,269
Africa	0.6	0.8	0.6	400	1,307	1,291

*Author estimated updates.

Source: Angus Maddison, *Monitoring the World Economy* (1995) and *Chinese Economic Performance in the Long Run* (1998), OECD Development Center, Paris.

3. African countries have consistently grown below the average for the world. In 1820, Africa's per capita income was 40 percent less than the world average. The gap widened to 60 percent in 1950, and to almost 80 percent in 2000.

This 180-year perspective of growth is useful, but by historical standards even 180 years is relatively short. Looking back even further shows us how high our current growth rates are. Before 1820 world income per capita grew about 0.03 percent a year. The growth trend that we now take for granted started only at the end of the 18th century, about the time that markets and democracies became the primary organizing structures of the economy and society. Thus, growth seems to be associated with the development of markets and democracy. Significant growth took off only as the market system developed, and it increased as markets increased in importance.

The growth trend we now take for granted started only at the end of the 18th century.

The Benefits and Costs of Growth

Economic growth (per capita) allows everyone in society, on average, to have more. Thus, it isn't surprising that most governments are generally searching for policies that will allow their economies to grow. Indeed, one reason market economies have been so successful is that they have consistently channeled individual efforts toward production and growth. Individuals feel a sense of accomplishment in making things grow and, if sufficient economic incentives and resources exist, individuals' actions can lead to a continually growing economy.

Politically, growth, or predictions of growth, allows governments to avoid hard distributional questions of who should get what part of our existing output: With growth there is more to go around for everyone. A growing economy generates jobs, so politicians who want to claim that their policies will create jobs generally predict those policies will create growth.

Politically, growth, or predictions of growth, allows governments to avoid hard questions.

Of course, there are also costs to material growth—pollution, resource exhaustion, and destruction of natural habitat. These costs lead some people to believe that we would be better off in a society that deemphasized material growth. (That doesn't mean we shouldn't grow emotionally, spiritually, and intellectually; it simply means we should grow out of our material goods fetish.) Many people believe these environmental costs are important, and the result is often an environmental–economic growth stalemate.

To reconcile the two goals, some have argued that spending on the environment can create growth and jobs, so the two need not be incompatible. Unfortunately, there's a problem with this argument. It confuses growth and jobs with increased material consumption—what most people are worried about. As more material goods made available by growth are used for pollution control equipment, less is available for the growth of an average individual's personal consumption, since the added material goods created by growth have already been used. What society gets, at best, from these expenditures is a better physical environment, not more of everything. Getting more of everything would violate the TANSTAAFL law.

Business Cycles

While the secular, or long-term, trend is a 2.5 to 3.5 percent increase in GDP, there are numerous fluctuations around that trend. Sometimes real GDP is above the trend; at other times GDP is below the trend. This phenomenon has given rise to the term *business cycle*. A **business cycle** is *the upward or downward movement of economic activity, or real GDP, that occurs around the growth trend*. Figure 22-1 graphs the fluctuations in GDP for the U.S. economy since 1860.

A business cycle is the upward or downward movement of economic activity that occurs around the growth trend.

Until the late 1930s, economists took such cycles as facts of life. They had no convincing theory to explain why business cycles occurred, nor did they have policy

Figure 22-1 U.S. Business Cycles
Business cycles have always been a part of the U.S. economic scene.

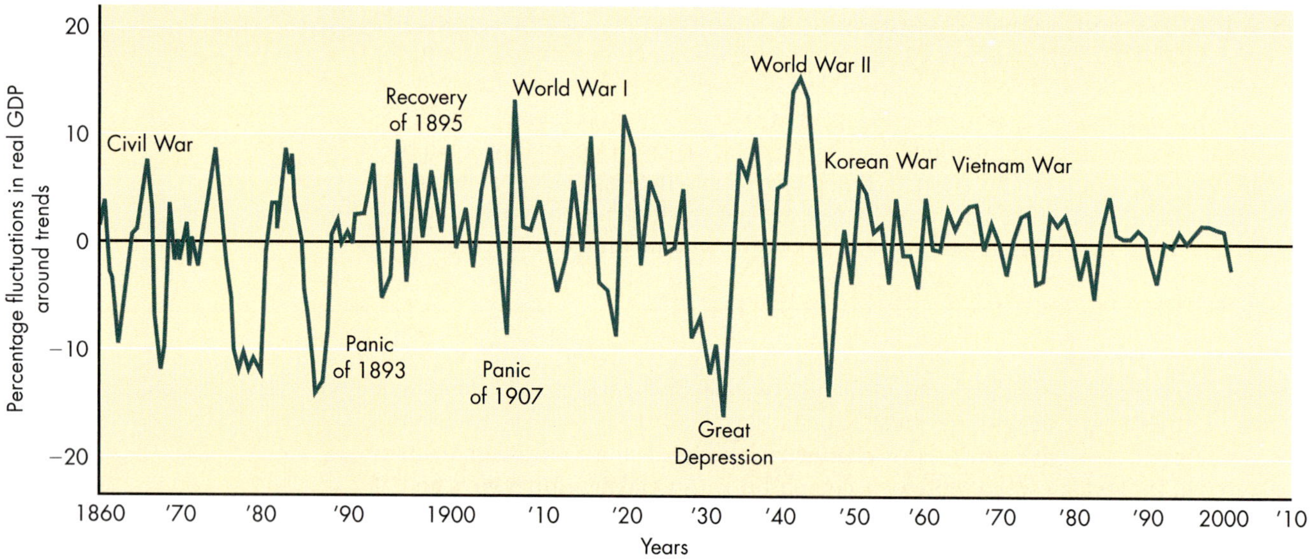

Source: *Historical Statistics of the United States, Colonial Times to 1970*, and U.S. Department of Commerce (www.doc.gov).

suggestions to smooth them out. In fact, they felt that any attempt to smooth them through government intervention would make the situation worse.

Since the 1940s, however, many economists have not taken business cycles as facts of life. They have hotly debated the nature and causes of business cycles and of the underlying growth. In this book I distinguish two groups of macroeconomists: **Keynesians** (who *generally favor activist government policies*) and **Classicals** (who *generally favor laissez-faire or nonactivist policies*). Classical economists argue that fluctuations in economic activity are to be expected in a market economy. Indeed, they say, it would be strange if fluctuations did not occur when individuals are free to decide what they want to do. We should simply accept these fluctuations as we do the seasons of the year. Keynesian economists argue that fluctuations can and should be controlled. They argue that *expansions* (the part of the business cycle above the long-term trend) and *contractions* (the part of the cycle below the long-term trend) are symptoms of underlying problems of the economy, which should be dealt with by government actions. Classical economists respond that individuals will anticipate government's reaction, thereby undermining government's attempts to control cycles. Which of these two views is correct is still a matter of debate.

The Phases of the Business Cycle

Much research has gone into measuring business cycles and setting official reference dates for the beginnings and ends of contractions and expansions. As a result of this research, business cycles have been divided into phases, and an explicit terminology has been developed. The National Bureau of Economic Research announces the government's official dates of contractions and expansions. In the postwar era (since mid-1945), the average business expansion has lasted about 59 months. A major expansion occurred from 1982 until mid-1990, when the U.S. economy fell into a recession. In

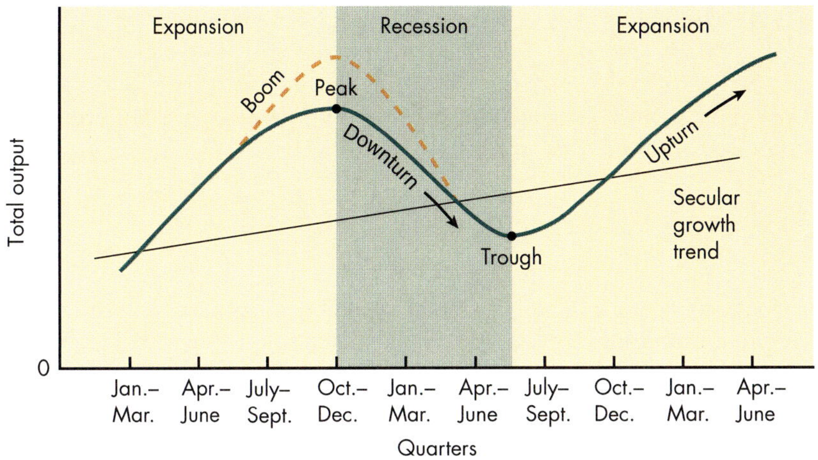

Figure 22-2 Business Cycle Phases Economists have many terms that describe the position of the economy on the business cycle. Some of them are given in this graph.

mid-1991 it slowly came out of the recession, and began the longest expansion in U.S. history, which ended in March 2001.

Business cycles have varying durations and intensities, but economists have developed a terminology to describe all business cycles and just about any position on a given business cycle. Since this terminology is often used by the press it is helpful to go over it. I do so in reference to Figure 22-2, which gives a visual representation of a business cycle.

The four phases of the business cycle are:
1. The peak.
2. The downturn.
3. The trough.
4. The upturn.

Let's start at the top. The top of a cycle is called the *peak*. A *boom* is a very high peak, representing a big jump in output. (That's when the economy is doing great. Most everyone who wants a job has one.) Eventually an expansion peaks. (At least, in the past, they always have.) A *downturn* describes the phenomenon of economic activity starting to fall from a peak. In a recession the economy isn't doing so great and many people are unemployed. A **recession** is generally considered to be *a decline in real output that persists for more than two consecutive quarters of a year.*[3]

Web Note 22.1 Depression Images

A **depression** is *a large recession*. There is no formal line indicating when a recession becomes a depression. In general, a depression is much longer and more severe than a recession. This ambiguity allows some economists to joke, "When your neighbor is unemployed, it's a recession; when you're unemployed, it's a depression." If pushed for something more specific, I'd say that if unemployment exceeds 12 percent for more than a year, the economy is in a depression.

The bottom of a recession or depression is called the *trough*. As total output begins to expand, the economy comes out of the trough; economists say it's in an *upturn*, which may turn into an **expansion**—*an upturn that lasts at least two consecutive quarters of a year.* An expansion leads us back up to the peak. And so it goes.

[3]The actual definition of a recession is more ambiguous than this generally accepted definition. Technically, an economy is in a recession only after it has been declared to be in a recession by a group of economists appointed by the National Bureau of Economic Research (NBER). Because real output is reported only quarterly and is sometimes revised substantially, the NBER Dating Committee looks at monthly data such as industrial production, employment, real income, sales, and sometimes even people's perceptions of what is happening in the economy to determine whether a recession has occurred. In 2001, for example, the committee announced that a recession had begun in March even though, according to preliminary GDP figures, real output did not fall for two consecutive quarters. (Revised figures, which came out more than six months later, showed that GDP had started falling in January of 2001 and fell for three quarters.) The fact that (1) the NBER economists include many factors when determining a recession and (2) they base their decision on preliminary data make it difficult to provide an unambiguous definition.

This terminology is important because if you're going to talk about the state of the economy, you need the words to do it. Why are businesses so interested in the state of the economy? They want to be able to predict whether it's going into a contraction or an expansion. Making the right prediction can determine whether the business will be profitable or not. That's why a large amount of economists' activity goes into trying to predict the future course of the economy.

Why Do Business Cycles Occur?

Why do business cycles occur? Are they simply random events, a bit like static on a radio, or do they have some fundamental causes that make them predictable? And if they have causes, are those causes on the supply side or demand side of the economy? These questions will be addressed in the short-run chapters on business cycles. What we will see is that the consensus view believes that fluctuations of output around the growth trend are caused by changes in the demand side of the economy. We will also see that a debate exists about whether these economic fluctuations can and should be reduced. There is far less policy debate about depressions. Most economists believe that potential depressions should be offset by economic policy. Thus, when in 1998 the Southeast Asian economies went into what people believed could lead to a depression, there were substantial calls for government to institute policies that might help offset it. (There was debate, however, about precisely what those policies should be.)

If prolonged contractions are a type of cold the economy catches, the Great Depression of the 1930s was double pneumonia.

The general view that something must be done to offset depressions was built into economics in the Great Depression of the 1930s. Production of goods and services fell by 30 percent from 1929 to 1933, leading to changes in the U.S. economy's structure. The new structure included a more active role for government in reducing the severity of cyclical fluctuations. Look back at Figure 22-1 and compare the periods before and after World War II. (World War II began in 1941 and ended in 1945.) Notice that the downturns and panics since 1945 have generally been less severe than before.

This change in the nature of business cycles can be better seen in Table 22-2. Notice that since the late 1940s cycle duration has increased but, more important, the average length of expansions has increased while the average length of contractions has decreased.

Web Note 22.2
Dating Business Cycles

Table 22-2 Duration of Business Cycles, Pre–World War II and Post–World War II

Cycles	Duration (in months) Pre–World War II (1854–1945)	Post–World War II (1945–2003)
Number	22	10
Average duration (trough to trough)	50	61
Length of longest cycle	99 (1870–79)	128 (1991–2001)
Length of shortest cycle	28 (1919–21)	28 (1980–82)
Average length of expansions	29	59
Length of shortest expansion	10 (1919–20)	12 (1980–81)
Length of longest expansion	80 (1938–45)	120 (1991–2001)
Average length of recessions	21	11
Length of shortest recession	7 (1918–19)	6 (1980)
Length of longest recession	65 (1873–79)	16 (1981–82)

Source: National Bureau of Economic Research (http://nber.org) and *Survey of Current Business* (www.bea.doc.gov).

How to interpret these statistics is the subject of much controversy. As is the case with much economic evidence, the data are subject to different interpretations. Some economists argue that a large part of the reduction in the fluctuations' severity is an illusion.

If the severity of the fluctuations has been reduced (which most economists believe has happened), one reason is that changes in institutional structure were made as a result of the Great Depression. Both the financial structure and the government taxing and spending structure were changed, giving the government a more important role in stabilizing the economy. Consideration of that stronger government role is a key element of macroeconomics.

Leading Indicators

Economists have developed a set of signs that indicate when a recession is about to occur and when the economy is in one. These signs are called *leading indicators*—indicators that tell us what's likely to happen 12 to 15 months from now, much as a barometer gives us a clue about tomorrow's weather. They include:

Q-3 List three leading indicators.

1. Average workweek for production workers in manufacturing.
2. Average weekly claims for unemployment insurance.
3. Manufacturers' new orders for consumer goods and materials.
4. Vendor performance, measured as a percentage of companies reporting slower deliveries from suppliers.
5. Index of consumer expectations.
6. New orders for nondefense capital goods.
7. Number of new building permits issued for private housing units.
8. Stock prices—500 common stocks.
9. Interest rate spread—10-year government bond less federal funds rate.
10. Money supply, M2.

These are combined into an index of leading economic indicators that is frequently reported in the popular press. (You can find the most recent index at www.conference-board.org, the home page of The Conference Board, the organization that publishes it.) Economists use leading indicators in making forecasts about the economy. They are called *indicators*, not *predictors*, because they're only rough approximations of what's likely to happen in the future. For example, before building a house, you must apply for a building permit. Usually this occurs six to nine months before the actual start of construction. By looking at the number of building permits that have been issued, you can predict how much building is likely to begin in six months or so. But the prediction might be wrong, since getting a building permit does not require someone to actually build. Business economists—who spend much of their time and effort delving deeper into these indicators, trying to see what they are really telling us, as opposed to what they seem to be telling us—joke that the leading indicators have predicted six of the past two recessions.

Unemployment

Both business cycles and growth are directly related to unemployment in the U.S. economy. Unemployment occurs when people are looking for a job and cannot find one. The **unemployment rate** is *the percentage of people in the economy who are willing and able to work but who are not working.* When an economy is growing and is in an expansion, unemployment is usually falling; when an economy is in a recession, unemployment is usually rising, although often with a lag.

The relationship between the business cycle and unemployment is obvious to most people, but often the seemingly obvious hides important insights. Just why are the business cycle and growth related to unemployment? True, aggregate income must fall in a recession, but, logically, unemployment need not result. A different result could be that everyone's income falls. Looking at the problem historically, we see that unemployment has not always been a problem associated with business cycles.

In preindustrial farming societies, unemployment wasn't a problem because preindustrial farmers didn't receive wages—they received net revenue (the income left after all costs had been paid). That means the average amount they netted per hour (the equivalent of a wage) was variable. In good years they had a high income per hour; in bad years they had a low income per hour.

The variability in people's net income per hour meant that when economic activity fluctuated, people's income rose or fell, but they kept on working. Low income was a problem; but since people didn't become unemployed, **cyclical unemployment** *(unemployment resulting from fluctuations in economic activity)* was not a problem.

Q.4 True or false? In a recession structural unemployment is expected to rise.

While cyclical unemployment did not exist in preindustrial society, **structural unemployment** *(unemployment caused by the institutional structure of an economy or by economic restructuring making some skills obsolete)* did. For example, the demand for scribes in Europe fell after the invention of the printing press in 1438. Some unemployment would likely result; that unemployment would be called *structural unemployment*. But structural unemployment wasn't much of a problem for government, or at least people did not consider it government's problem. The reason is that those in the family with income would share it with unemployed family members.

Unemployment as a Social Problem

The Industrial Revolution changed the nature of work and introduced unemployment as a problem for society. This is because the Industrial Revolution was accompanied by a shift to wage labor and to a division of responsibilities. Some individuals (capitalists) took on ownership of the means of production and *hired* others to work for them, paying them a wage per hour. This change in the nature of production marked a significant change in the nature of the unemployment problem.

First, it created the possibility of cyclical unemployment. With wages set at a certain level, when economic activity fell, workers' income per hour did not fall. Instead, factories would lay off or fire some workers. That isn't what happened on the farm; when a slack period occurred on the farm, the income per hour of all workers fell and few were laid off.

Second, the Industrial Revolution was accompanied by a change in how families dealt with unemployment. Whereas in preindustrial farm economies individuals or families took responsibility for their own slack periods, in a capitalist industrial society factory owners didn't take responsibility for their workers in slack periods. The pink slip (a common name for the notice workers get telling them they are laid off) and the problem of unemployment were born in the Industrial Revolution.

Without wage income, unemployed workers were in a pickle. They couldn't pay their rent, they couldn't eat, they couldn't put clothes on their backs. What was previously a family problem became a social problem. Not surprisingly, it was at that time—the late 1700s—that economists began paying more attention to the problem of unemployment.

Initially, economists and society still did not view unemployment as a social problem. It was the individual's problem. If people were unemployed, it was their own fault;

hunger, or at least the fear of hunger, and people's desire to maintain their lifestyle would drive them to find other jobs relatively quickly. Thus, early capitalism had an unemployment solution: the fear of hunger.

Unemployment as Government's Problem

As capitalism evolved, the fear-of-hunger solution to unemployment decreased in importance. The government developed social welfare programs such as unemployment insurance and assistance to the poor. In the Employment Act of 1946, the U.S. government specifically took responsibility for unemployment. The act assigned government the responsibility of creating *full employment,* an economic climate in which just about everyone who wants a job can have one. It was government's responsibility to offset cyclical fluctuations and thereby prevent cyclical unemployment, and to somehow deal with structural unemployment.

As capitalism evolved, capitalist societies no longer saw the fear of hunger as an acceptable answer to unemployment.

Initially government regarded 2 percent unemployment as a condition of full employment. The 2 percent was made up of **frictional unemployment** *(unemployment caused by new entrants into the job market and people quitting a job just long enough to look for and find another one)* and of a few "unemployables," such as alcoholics and drug addicts, along with a certain amount of necessary structural and seasonal unemployment resulting when the structure of the economy changed. Thus, any unemployment higher than 2 percent was considered either unnecessary structural or cyclical unemployment and was now government's responsibility; frictional and necessary structural unemployment were still the individual's problem.

By the 1950s, government had given up its view that 2 percent unemployment was consistent with full employment. It raised its definition of full employment to 3 percent, then to 4 percent, then to 5 percent unemployment. In the 1970s and early 1980s, government raised it further, to 6.5 percent unemployment. At that point the term *full employment* fell out of favor (it's hard to call 6.5 percent unemployment "full employment"), and the terminology changed. The term I will use in this book is *target rate of unemployment,* although you should note that it is sometimes called the *natural rate of unemployment.* The **target rate of unemployment** is *the lowest sustainable rate of unemployment that policymakers believe is achievable given existing demographics and the economy's institutional structure.* Since the late 1980s the appropriate target rate of unemployment has been a matter of debate, but most economists place it at somewhere around 5 percent unemployment.

The target rate of unemployment is the lowest sustainable rate of unemployment that policymakers believe is achievable under existing conditions.

Why the Target Rate of Unemployment Changed

Q.5 Why has the target rate of unemployment changed over time?

Why has the target rate of unemployment changed over time? One reason is that, in the 1970s and early 1980s, a low inflation rate, which also was a government goal, seemed to be incompatible with a low unemployment rate. I'll talk about this incompatibility later when I discuss the problem of simultaneous inflation and unemployment. A second reason is demographics: Different age groups have different unemployment rates, and as the population's age structure changes, so does the target rate of unemployment.

A third reason is our economy's changing social and institutional structure. These social and institutional changes affected the nature of the unemployment problem. For example, women's role in the workforce has changed significantly in the past 40 years. In the 1950s, the traditional view that "woman's place is in the home" remained strong. Usually only one family member—the man—had a job. If he lost his job, no money came in. In the 1970s to 1990s, more and more women entered the workforce so that today over 70 percent of all married-couple families are two-earner families. In a two-earner family, if one person loses a job, the family doesn't face immediate starvation. The other person's income carries the family over.

FROM FULL EMPLOYMENT TO THE TARGET RATE OF UNEMPLOYMENT

Beyond the Tools

As I emphasized in Chapter 1, good economists attempt to remain neutral and objective. It isn't always easy, especially since the language we use is often biased.

This problem has proved to be a difficult one for economists in their attempt to find an alternative to the concept of full employment. An early contender was the natural rate of unemployment. Economists have often used the word *natural* to describe economic concepts. For example, they've talked about "natural" rights and a "natural" rate of interest. The problem with this usage is that what's natural to one person isn't necessarily natural to another. The word *natural* often conveys a sense of "that's the way it should be." However, in describing as "natural" the rate of unemployment that an economy can achieve, economists weren't making any value judgments about whether 5.5 percent unemployment is what should, or should not, be. They simply were saying that, given the institutions in the economy, that is what is achievable. So a number of economists objected to the use of the word *natural.*

As an alternative, a number of economists started to use the term *nonaccelerating inflation rate of unemployment (NAIRU),* but even they agreed it was a horrendous term. And so many avoided its use and shifted to the relatively neutral term *target rate of unemployment.*

The target rate of unemployment is the rate that one believes is attainable without causing accelerating inflation. It is not determined theoretically; it is determined empirically. Economists look at what seems to be achievable and is historically normal, adjust that for structural and demographic changes they believe are occurring, and come up with the target rate of unemployment.

Government institutions also changed. As programs like unemployment insurance and public welfare were created to reduce suffering associated with unemployment, people's responses to unemployment changed. People today are more picky about what jobs they take than they were in the 1920s and 1930s. People don't just want any job, they want a *fulfilling* job with a decent wage. As people have become choosier about jobs, a debate has raged over the extent of government's responsibility for unemployment.

WHOSE RESPONSIBILITY IS UNEMPLOYMENT?

Differing views of individuals' responsibility and society's responsibility affect people's views on whether somebody is actually unemployed. Classical economists take the position that, generally, individuals should be responsible for finding jobs. They emphasize that an individual can always find *some* job at *some* wage rate, even if it's only selling apples on the street for 40 cents apiece. Given this view of individual responsibility, unemployment is impossible. If a person isn't working, that's his or her choice; the person simply isn't looking hard enough for a job. For an economist with this view, almost all unemployment is actually frictional unemployment.

Keynesian economists tend to say society owes people jobs commensurate with their training or past job experience. They further argue that the jobs should be close enough to home so people don't have to move. Given this view, frictional unemployment is only a small part of total unemployment. Structural and cyclical unemployment are far more common.

In the 1960s the average rate of unemployment in Europe was considerably below the average rate of unemployment in the United States. In the 1990s and early 2000s that reversed and the average unemployment rate in Europe has now significantly exceeded that in the United States. One of the reasons for this reversal is that Europe tried to create high-paying jobs, while it left a variety of taxes and social programs in place that discouraged the creation of low-paying jobs.

Categories of Unemployment

Applying the Tools

A good sense of the differing types of unemployment and the differing social views that unemployment embodies can be conveyed through three examples of unemployed individuals. As you read the following stories, ask yourself which category of unemployment each individual falls into.

Example 1 Joe is listed as unemployed and collects unemployment insurance. He's had various jobs in the past and was laid off from his last one. He spent a few weeks on household projects, believing he would be called back by his most recent employer—but he wasn't. He's grown to like being on his own schedule. He's living on his unemployment insurance (while it lasts, which usually isn't more than six months), his savings, and money he picks up by being paid cash under the table working a few hours now and then at construction sites.

The Unemployment Compensation Office requires him to make at least an attempt to find work, and he's turned up a few prospects. However, some were back-breaking laboring jobs and one would have required him to move to a distant city, so he's avoiding accepting regular work. Joe knows the unemployment payments won't last forever. When they're used up, he plans to increase his under-the-table activity. Then, when he gets good and ready, he'll really look for a job.

Example 2 Flo is a middle-aged, small-town housewife. She worked before her marriage, but when she and her husband started their family she quit her job to be a full-time housewife and mother. She never questioned her family values of hard work, independence, belief in free enterprise, and scorn of government handouts. When her youngest child left the nest, she decided to finish the college education she'd only just started when she married.

After getting her degree, she looked for a job, but found the market for middle-aged women with no recent experience to be depressed—and depressing. The state employment office where she sought listings recognized her abilities and gave her a temporary job in that very office. Because she was a "temp," however, she was the first to be laid off when the state legislature cut the local office budget—but she'd worked long enough to be eligible for unemployment insurance.

She hesitated about applying, since handouts were against her principles. But while working there she'd seen plenty of people, including her friends, applying for benefits after work histories even slimmer than hers. She decided to take the benefits. While they lasted, she found family finances on almost as sound a footing as when she was working. Although she was bringing in less money, net family income didn't suffer much since she didn't have Social Security withheld nor did she have the commuting and clothing expenses of going to a daily job.

Example 3 Tom had a good job at a manufacturing plant where he'd worked up to a wage of $450 a week. Occasionally he was laid off, but only for a few weeks, and then he'd be called back. But then the plant was bought by an out-of-state corporation that laid off half the workforce and put in automated equipment. Tom, an older worker with comparatively high wages, was one of the first to go, and he wasn't called back.

Tom had a wife, three children, a car payment, and a mortgage. He looked for other work but couldn't find anything paying close to what he'd been getting. Tom used up his unemployment insurance and his savings. He sold the house and moved his family into a trailer. Finally he heard that there were a lot of jobs in Massachusetts, 800 miles away. He moved there, found a job, and began sending money home every week. Then the Massachusetts economy faltered. Tom was laid off again, and his unemployment insurance ran out again. Relying on his $100,000 life insurance policy, unfortunately he figured he was worth more to his family dead than alive, so he killed himself.

As these three examples suggest, unemployment encompasses a wide range of cases. Unemployment is anything but a one-dimensional problem, so it's not surprising that people's views of how to deal with it differ.

The United States, in contrast, actively promoted the creation of jobs of any type. The result has been a large growth of jobs in the United States, many of which are low-paying jobs. An unemployed engineer, had he been in the United States, might well have given up engineering and become a restaurant manager.

Figure 22-3 Unemployment Rate since 1900
The unemployment rate has always fluctuated, with the average around 5 or 6 percent. Since the 1930s, fluctuations have decreased. In the mid-1940s, the United States government started focusing on the unemployment rate as a goal. Initially, it chose 3 percent, but gradually that increased to somewhere between 5 and 7 percent.

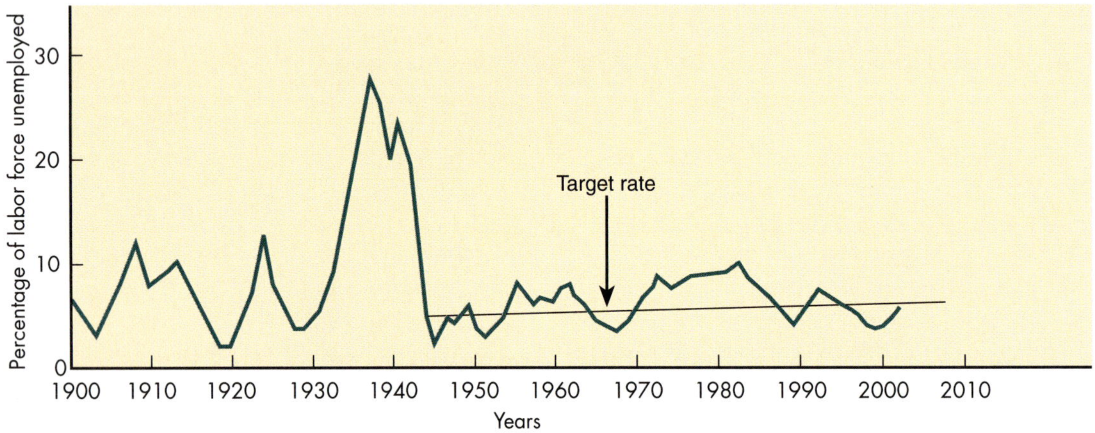

Source: U.S. Bureau of Labor Statistics (http://stats.bls.gov).

How Is Unemployment Measured?

When there's debate about what the unemployment problem is, it isn't surprising that there's also a debate about how to measure it. When talking about unemployment, economists usually refer to the "unemployment rate" published by the U.S. Department of Labor's Bureau of Labor Statistics. Fluctuations in the official unemployment rate since 1900 appear in Figure 22-3. In it you can see that during World War II (1941–45) unemployment fell from the high rates of the 1930s Depression to an extremely low rate, only 1.2 percent. You can also see that while the rate started back up in the 1950s, reaching 4 or 5 percent, it remained low until the 1970s, when the rate began gradually to rise again. After peaking in the early 1980s it began to fall again. In 1990 it was about 5 percent; then in 1991 the economy fell into recession and unemployment rates rose to over 7 percent in 1992. During the expansion that followed the unemployment rate returned to slightly above 4 percent by 2000, but it rose again to nearly 6 percent during the 2002 recession.

The unemployment rate is measured by dividing the number of unemployed individuals by the number of people in the civilian labor force and multiplying by 100.

Calculating the Unemployment Rate The U.S. unemployment rate is determined by dividing the number of unemployed individuals by the number of people in the **labor force**—*those people in an economy who are willing and able to work*—and multiplying by 100. For example, if the total unemployed stands at 8 million and the labor force stands at 140 million, the unemployment rate is:

$$\frac{8 \text{ million}}{140 \text{ million}} = 0.57 \times 100 = 5.7\%$$

Q-6 During some months, the unemployment rate declines, but the number of unemployed rises. How can this happen?

To determine the labor force, start with the total civilian population and subtract all persons incapable of working, such as inmates of institutions and people under 16 years of age. (The civilian population excludes about 2 million individuals who are in the armed forces.) From that figure subtract the number of people not in the labor force, including homemakers, students, retirees, the voluntarily idle, and the disabled. The

Figure 22-4 Unemployment/Employment Figures (in millions)
This exhibit shows you how the unemployment rate is calculated. Notice that the labor force is not the entire population.

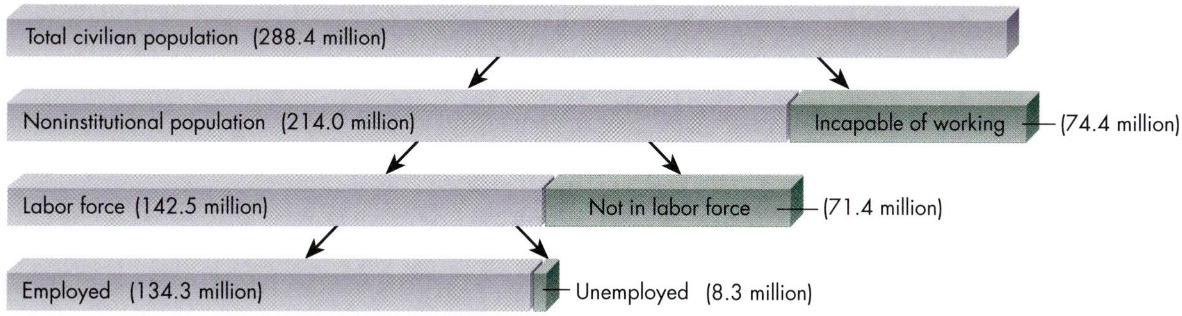

Source: *Employment and Earnings 2003*. Bureau of Labor Statistics (http://stats.bls.gov). Data may not add up due to rounding.

result is the potential workforce, which is about 140 million people, or about 50 percent of the civilian population (see Figure 22-4).

The civilian labor force can be divided into employed and unemployed. The Bureau of Labor Statistics (BLS) defines people as *employed* if they work at a paid job (including part-time jobs) or if they are unpaid workers in an enterprise operated by a family member. The BLS's definition of *employed* includes all those who were temporarily absent from their jobs that week because of illness, bad weather, vacation, labor–management dispute, or personal reasons, whether or not they were paid by their employers for the time off.

Web Note 22.3
Defining
Unemployment

In 2002 the number of unemployed individuals was about 8.3 million. Dividing this number by the labor force (142.5 million) gives us an unemployment rate of 5.8 percent.

How Accurate Is the Official Unemployment Rate? The BLS measures unemployment using a number of assumptions that have been the source of debate. For example, should *discouraged workers*—people who do not look for a job because they feel they don't have a chance of finding one—be counted as unemployed? Some Keynesian economists believe these individuals should be considered unemployed. Moreover they question whether part-time workers who would prefer full-time work, the *underemployed*, should be classified as employed.

The Keynesian argument is that there is such a lack of decent jobs and of affordable transportation to get to the jobs that do exist that many people become very discouraged and have simply stopped trying. Because BLS statisticians define these people as voluntarily idle, and do not count them as unemployed, Keynesians argue that the BLS undercounts unemployment significantly.

Q-7 In what way is the very concept of unemployment dependent on the value judgments made by the individual?

The Classical argument about unemployment is that being without a job often is voluntary. People may say they are looking for a job when they're not really looking. Many are working "off the books"; others are simply vacationing. Some Classicals contend that the way the BLS measures unemployment exaggerates the number of those who are truly unemployed. A person is defined as unemployed if he or she is not employed and is actively seeking work.

To help overcome these problems, economists use supplemental measures to give them insight into the state of the labor market; these include the **labor force participation rate,** which *measures the labor force as a percentage of the total population at least 16 years old* and the **employment rate**—*the number of people who are working as a percentage of the labor force*.

Despite problems, the unemployment rate statistic still gives us useful information about changes in the economy.

Despite problems, the unemployment rate statistic still gives us useful information about changes in the economy. The measurement problems themselves are little changed from year to year, so in comparing one year to another, those problems are not an issue. Keynesian and Classical economists agree that a changing unemployment rate generally tells us something about the economy, especially if interpreted in the light of other statistics. That's why the unemployment rate is used as a measure of the state of the economy.

Unemployment and Potential Output

The unemployment rate gives a good indication of how much labor is available to increase production and thus provides a good idea of how fast the economy could grow. Capital is the second major input to production. Thus, the *capacity utilization rate*—the rate at which factories and machines are operating compared to the maximum sustainable rate at which they could be used—indicates how much capital is available for economic growth.

Table 22-3 shows the unemployment rates and the capacity utilization rates for selected countries over the last 25 years. Generally U.S. economists today feel that unemployment rates of about 5 percent and capacity utilization rates between 80 and 85 percent are about as much as we should expect from the economy. To push the economy beyond that would be like driving your car 90 miles an hour. True, the marks on your speedometer might go up to 130, but 90 is a more realistic top speed. Beyond 120 (assuming that's where your car is red-lined), the engine is likely to blow up (unless you have a Maserati).

Potential output is defined as the output that will be achieved at the target rate of unemployment and the target level of capacity utilization.

Economists translate the target unemployment rate and target capacity utilization rate into the target level of potential output, or simply potential output (or *potential income,* because output creates income). **Potential output** is *the output that would materialize at the target rate of unemployment and the target rate of capacity utilization*. It is the rate of output beyond which the economy would experience accelerating inflation. Potential output grows at the secular (long-term) trend rate of 2.5 to 3.5 percent per year. When the economy is in a downturn or recession, actual output is below potential output. As you will see throughout the rest of the book, there is much debate about what the appropriate target rates of unemployment, capacity utilization, and potential output actually are.

Table 22-3 Unemployment and Capacity Utilization Rates for Selected Countries (percentages)

	Capacity Utilization			Unemployment			Annual Growth in Real Output
	1975	1985	2000**	1975	1985	2000	1975–2000
United States	74.6	79.8	80.4	8.5	7.2	4.0	3.2
Japan	81.4	82.5	74.6	1.9	2.6	4.8	2.6
Germany	76.9	79.6	85.1	3.4	8.2	9.1	3.0
United Kingdom	81.9	81.1	81.8	4.6	11.2	5.5	2.2
Canada	83.1	82.5	85.8	6.9	10.5	6.1	2.5
Mexico	85.0	92.0	85.7	*	*	2.2	1.6
Republic of Korea	86.4	74.6	83.3	*	10.9	3.9	7.7

*Unavailable.

**Capacity utilization rates are for most recent year available.

Source: Organization for Economic Cooperation and Development (www.oecd.org).

To determine what effect changes in the unemployment rate will have on output we use **Okun's rule of thumb,** which states that *a 1 percentage point change in the unemployment rate will be associated with a 2 percent change in output in the opposite direction.*[4] For example, if unemployment rises from 5 percent to 6 percent, total output of $10 trillion will fall by 2 percent, or $200 billion, to $9.8 trillion. In terms of number of workers, a 1 percent increase in the unemployment rate means about 1.4 million additional people are out of work.

Okun's rule of thumb states that a 1 percentage point change in the unemployment rate will be associated with a 2 percent change in output in the opposite direction.

These figures are rough, but they give you a sense of the implications of a change. For example, say unemployment falls 0.2 percentage point, from 4.5 to 4.3 percent. That means about 285,000 more people have jobs and that output will be $40 billion higher than otherwise would have occurred if the increase holds for the entire year.

Notice I said "will be $40 billion higher than otherwise would have occurred" rather than simply saying "will increase by $40 billion." That's because generally the economy is growing as a result of increases in productivity or increases in the number of people choosing to work. Changes in either of these can cause output and employment to grow, even if there's no change in the unemployment rate. We must point this out because in the 1980s the number of people choosing to work increased substantially, significantly increasing the labor participation rate. Then, in the mid-1990s, as many large firms structurally adjusted their production methods to increase their productivity, unemployment sometimes rose even as output rose. Thus, when the labor participation rate and productivity change, an increase in unemployment doesn't necessarily mean a decrease in employment or a decrease in output.

Microeconomic Categories of Unemployment

In the post–World War II period, unemployment was seen primarily as cyclical unemployment, and the focus of macroeconomic policy was on how to eliminate that unemployment through a specific set of macroeconomic policies. Understanding those macroeconomic policies is important, but today it's not enough. Unemployment has many dimensions, so different types of unemployment are susceptible to different types of policies.

Today's view is that you don't use a sledgehammer to pound in finishing nails, and you don't use macro policies to deal with certain types of unemployment; instead you use micro policies. To determine where microeconomic policies are appropriate as a supplement to macroeconomic policies, economists break unemployment down into a number of categories and analyze each category separately. These categories include how people become unemployed, demographic characteristics, duration of unemployment, and industry (see Figure 22-5).

Some microeconomic categories of unemployment are reasons for unemployment, demographic unemployment, duration of unemployment, and unemployment by industry.

Inflation

Inflation is *a continual rise in the price level.* The price level is an index of all prices in the economy. Even when inflation itself isn't a problem, the fear of inflation guides macroeconomic policy. Fear of inflation prevents governments from expanding the economy and reducing unemployment. It prevents governments from using macroeconomic policies to lower interest rates. It gets some political parties booted out of office and others elected.

Inflation is a continual rise in the price level.

A one-time rise in the price level is not inflation. Unfortunately, it's often hard to tell if a one-time rise in the price level is going to stop, so the distinction blurs in

[4]The precise specification of Okun's rule of thumb has changed over time. Earlier estimates placed it at a 1 to 2.5 ratio.

Figure 22-5 Unemployment by Microeconomic Subcategories, 2002
Unemployment isn't all the same. This figure gives you a sense of some of the subcategories of unemployment.

*Figures for Black adjusted to include estimates of the number of Hispanics.

Source: *Employment and Earnings 2003*, Bureau of Labor Statistics (http://stats.bls.gov).

practice, but we must understand the distinction. If the price level goes up 10 percent in a month, but then remains constant, the economy doesn't have an inflation problem. Inflation is an *ongoing rise* in the price level.

From 1800 until World War II the U.S. inflation rate and price level fluctuated; sometimes the price level would rise, and sometimes the price level would fall—there would be deflation. Since World War II the price level has continually risen, which means the inflation rate (the measure of the change in prices over time) has been positive, as can be seen in Figure 22-6. The rate fluctuates, but the movement of the price level has been consistently upward.

Measurement of Inflation

Since inflation is a sustained rise in the general price level, we must first determine what the general price level was at a given time by creating a **price index,** *a number that summarizes what happens to a weighted composite of prices of a selection of goods (often called a market basket of goods) over time*. An index converts prices relative to base year prices. Price indexes are important. Many people lament the high cost of goods and services today. They complain, for example, that an automobile that costs $15,000 today cost only $3,000 in the "good old days." But that comparison is meaningless, because the price level has changed. Today, the average wage is more than five times what it was when cars cost only $3,000. To relate the two prices, we need a price index. There are a number of different measures of the price level. The most often used are the producer

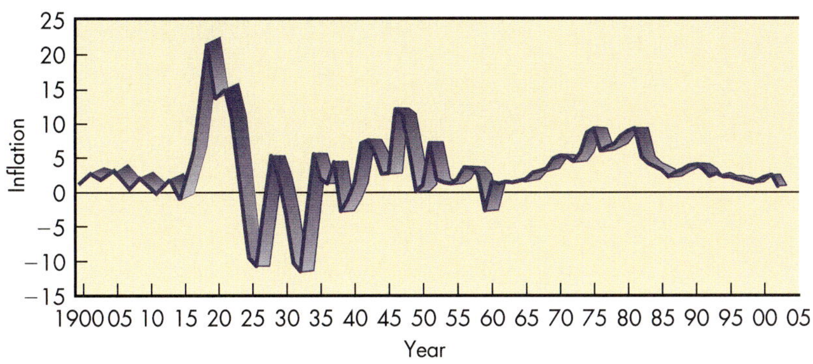

Figure 22-6 Inflation since 1900
Until 1940, rises in the price level were followed by falls in the price level, keeping the price level relatively constant. Since the 1940s, inflation has almost always been positive, which means that the price level has been continually rising.

Source: U.S. Department of Commerce (www.doc.gov).

price index, the GDP deflator, and the consumer price index. Each has certain advantages and disadvantages.

Creating a Price Index Before introducing the official price indexes, let's work through the creation of a fictitious price index—the Colander price index—and calculate the associated inflation. I'll do so for 2003 and 2004, using 2003 as the base year. A price index is calculated by dividing the current price of a basket of goods by the base price of a basket of goods. Table 22-4 lists a market basket of goods I consume in a base year and their associated prices in 2003 and 2004. The market basket of goods is listed in column 1 and represents the quantity of each item purchased in the base year.

The price of the market basket in each year is the sum of the expenditures on each item—the quantity of each good purchased times its market price. The market basket remains the same in each year; only the prices change. The price of the market basket in 2003 is $540 and in 2004 is $675. To calculate the Colander price index, divide the price of the market basket by the price of the market basket in the base year and multiply it by 100. In this case 2003 is the base year, so the price index in 2004 is

Q-8 Health care costs make up 15 percent of total expenditures. Say they rise by 10 percent, while the other components of the price index remain constant. By how much does the price index rise?

$$\$675/\$540 \times 100 = 125$$

To make sure you are following this example, calculate the Colander price index in 2003.

The answer is 100. The base year index is always 100 since you are dividing base years by the base year prices and multiplying by 100.

Inflation in 2004, then, is the percent change in the price index. This is calculated in 2004 as

$$(125/100 - 1) \times 100 = 25\%$$

Table 22-4 A Simple Year-to-Year Market Basket Comparison

(1)	(2)	(3)	(4)	(5)
	Prices		Expenditures	
Basket of Goods	2003	2004	2003	2004
10 pairs jeans	$20.00/pr.	$25.00/pr.	$200	$250
12 flannel shirts	15.00/shirt	20.00/shirt	180	240
100 lbs. apples	0.80/lb.	1.05/lb.	80	105
80 lbs. oranges	1.00/lb.	1.00/lb.	80	80
Total expenditures			$540	$675

Measurement Problems with the Consumer Price Index

Knowing the Tools

You may have wondered about the fixed basket of goods used to calculate our fictitious price index and the CPI. The basket of goods was fixed in the base year. But buying habits change. The further in time that fixed basket is from the current basket, the worse any fixed-basket price index is at measuring inflation. Four biases that have existed in the past are the substitution bias, the quality improvement bias, the new product bias, and the discounting bias.

- **Substitution bias.** First of all, changes in prices will change consumption patterns. In our fictitious price index example, the price of apples rose, but the price of oranges did not. It is likely that the basket of goods in 2004 included more oranges and fewer apples than in the base year basket, in which case total expenditures in 2004 would have been less and measured inflation would have been less. Any fixed-basket price index has a substitution bias because it does not take into account the fact that when the price of one good rises, consumers substitute a cheaper item.
- **Quality improvement bias.** The fixed basket of goods is assumed to accurately represent similar products in later years. For example, a car in 1982 is assumed to be the same as a car in 1992. But in 1992 many cars had airbags as a standard feature. Some of the price increase for cars reflected this quality improvement, but the CPI treated it as if it were a price increase for a comparable product sold in 1982.
- **New product bias.** A fixed basket of goods leaves no room for the introduction of new products. This would not be a problem if the prices of new products changed at about the same rate as prices of other goods in the basket, but in the 1970s this was not true. For years, the CPI did not include the price of computers, whose prices were declining at a 17 percent annual rate! This resulted in the CPI overstating inflation during this period.
- **Discounting bias.** Ever since World War II, consumers have shifted consumption toward discount purchases. The Bureau of Labor Statistics, however, treats a product sold at a discount store as different from products sold at retail stores. Products sold at discount stores are assumed to be of lower quality. To the extent that they are not different, however, changes in the CPI overstate true inflation.

These and other problems arise because of the choices we must make when constructing a price index. The choices are what to name as the base year, what products to include in the basket, the relative importance to assign each product, and how to account for changes in the quality and for the introduction of new products. In the late 1990s a commission of economists suggested that, because of these biases, the CPI overstated inflation by about 1 percentage point per year, and some adjustments were made to offset the biases.

The Bureau of Labor Statistics (BLS), the government agency that constructs the CPI, has been dealing with each of these issues to eliminate the biases. For example, the BLS currently updates the basket of goods every two years and rotates new products into its sample procedures. The BLS believes its methods address the problems, while critics argue that they have only partially done so.

But enough on price indexes in general. Let's now discuss the price indexes most commonly used when talking about inflation.

The *GDP deflator* is an index of the price level of aggregate output or the average price of the components in GDP relative to a base year.

Real-World Price Indexes The total output deflator, or **GDP deflator** (gross domestic product deflator), is *an index of the price level of aggregate output, or the average price of the components in total output (or GDP), relative to a base year.* (Recently, another price index, the chain-type price index for GDP, has become more popular; it is a GDP deflator with a constantly moving base year.) GDP is a measure of the total market value of aggregate production of goods and services produced in an economy in a year. (We'll discuss the calculation of GDP in more detail in Chapter 23.) A deflator is an adjustment for "too much air." In this context, it is an adjustment for inflation—so that we know how much total output would have risen if there were no inflation.

The GDP deflator is the inflation index economists generally favor because it includes the widest number of goods. As of 1995, the base period used to calculate the GDP deflator changes yearly. (Before 1995 it changed every 5 years.) Unfortunately, since it's difficult to compute, it's published only quarterly and with a fairly substantial lag. That is, by the time the figures come out, the period the figures measure has been over for quite a while.

Published monthly, the **consumer price index (CPI)** *measures the prices of a fixed basket of consumer goods, weighted according to each component's share of an average consumer's expenditures*. It measures the price of a fixed basket of goods rather than measuring the prices of all goods. It is the index of inflation most often used in news reports about the economy and is the index most relevant to consumers. In reality, there are consumer price indexes for two population groups: (1) for all urban consumers (the urban CPI)—about 80 percent of the U.S. population—and (2) for urban wage earners and clerical workers (the wage-earner CPI)—about 32 percent of the U.S. population. The numbers that compose the CPI are collected at 87 separate locations and include prices from over 7,000 rental units and 23,000 business establishments.

The *consumer price index (CPI)* is an index of inflation measuring prices of a fixed basket of consumer goods, weighted according to each component's share of an average consumer's expenditures.

Figure 22-7 shows the relative percentages of the basket's components. As you see, housing, transportation, and food make up the largest percentages of the CPI. To give you an idea of what effect the rise in price of a component of the CPI will have on the CPI as a whole, let's say food prices rise 10 percent in a year and all other prices remain constant. Since food is about 15 percent of the total, the CPI will rise 15% × 10% = 1.5%. The CPI and GDP deflator indexes roughly equal each other when averaged over an entire year.

In the mid-1990s many economists believed that the CPI overstated inflation by about 1 percentage point a year, and the Bureau of Labor Statistics has implemented a number of changes that address some of those problems. In order to avoid some of the problems with the CPI, some policymakers have recently been focusing on another measure of consumer prices—the **personal consumption expenditure (PCE) deflator.** The PCE is *a measure of prices of goods that consumers buy that allows yearly changes in the basket of goods that reflect actual consumer purchasing habits*. The measure smoothes out some of the problems associated with the CPI. Why are there different measures for consumer price changes? Indexes are simply composite measures; they cannot be perfect. (See the box "Measurement Problems with the Consumer Price Index.")

The **producer price index (PPI)** is *an index of prices that measures average change in the selling prices received by domestic producers of goods and services over time*. This index includes many goods that most consumers do not purchase. It measures price change

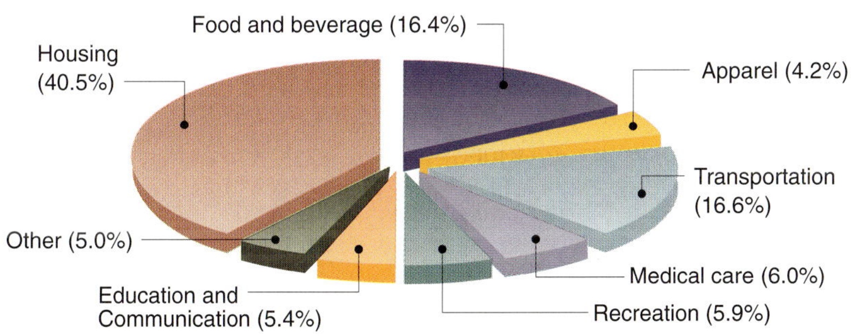

Figure 22-7 Composition of CPI
The consumer price index is determined by looking at the prices of goods in the categories listed in this exhibit. These categories represent the rough percentages of people's expenditures.

Source: *CPI Detailed Reports*, Bureau of Labor Statistics, 2003 (http://stats.bls.gov).

from the perspective of the sellers, which may differ from the purchaser's price because of subsidies, taxes, and distribution costs. There are actually three different producer price indexes for goods at various stages of production. Even though the PPI doesn't directly measure the prices consumers pay, it is important. Because it includes intermediate goods at early stages of production it serves as an early predictor of inflation since when firms' costs go up, they often raise their prices. (For more on the PPI go to stats.bls.gov/ppi/ppifaq.htm.)

Real and Nominal Concepts

One important way in which inflation indexes are used is to separate changes in real output from changes in nominal output. Economists use the term *real* when talking about concepts that are adjusted for inflation. **Real output** is *the total amount of goods and services produced, adjusted for price-level changes*. It is the measure of output that would exist if the price level had remained constant. **Nominal output** is *the total amount of goods and services measured at current prices*. For example, say total output rises from $8 trillion to $10 trillion. Nominal output has risen by

$$\frac{\$10 \text{ trillion} - \$8 \text{ trillion}}{\$8 \text{ trillion}} = \frac{\$2 \text{ trillion}}{\$8 \text{ trillion}} \times 100 = 25\%$$

Q-9 Nominal output has increased from $5 trillion to $6 trillion. The GDP deflator has risen by 15 percent. By how much has real output risen?

Let's say, however, the price level has risen 20 percent, from 100 percent to 120 percent. The price index is 120. Because the price index has increased, real output (nominal output adjusted for inflation) hasn't risen by 25 percent; it has risen by less than the increase in nominal output. To determine how much less, we use a formula to adjust the nominal figures to account for inflation. This is called *deflating* the nominal figures. To deflate we divide the most recent nominal figure, $10 trillion, by the price index of 120 percent and multiply by 100:

$$\text{Real output} = \frac{\text{Nominal output}}{120} \times 100 = \frac{\$10 \text{ trillion}}{1.2} \approx \$8.3 \text{ trillion}$$

That $8.3 trillion is the measure of output that would have existed if the price level had not changed, that is, the measure of real output. Real output has increased from $8 trillion to $8.3 trillion, or by $300 billion.

When you consider price indexes, you mustn't lose sight of the forest for the trees. Keep in mind the general distinction between real and nominal output. The concepts *real* and *nominal* and the process of adjusting from nominal to real by dividing the nominal amount by a price index will come up again and again. So whenever you see the word *real*, remember:

The "real" amount is the nominal amount divided by the price index. It is the nominal amount adjusted for inflation.

The "real" amount is the nominal amount divided by the price index. It is the nominal amount adjusted for inflation.

Expected and Unexpected Inflation

An important distinction to make when talking about inflation is between expected and unexpected inflation. **Expected inflation** is *inflation people expect to occur*. **Unexpected inflation** is *inflation that surprises people*.

When an individual sets a price (for goods or labor) he or she is actually setting a relative price—relative to other prices in the economy. The money price is the good's nominal price. The laws of supply and demand affect relative prices, not nominal prices.

Now let's say that everyone suddenly expects the price level to rise 10 percent. Let's also say that all individual sellers want a ½ percent raise in their relative price. They're not greedy; they just want a little bit more than what they're currently getting. The relative price increase people want must be tacked onto the inflation they expect. In this case, they have to raise their money price by 10½ percent—10 percent to keep up and ½ percent to get ahead. Ten percent of the inflation is caused by expectations of inflation; ½ percent of the inflation is caused by pressures from suppliers wanting to increase profits. Thus, whether or not inflation is expected makes a big difference in individuals' behavior.

Since prices and wages are often set for periods of two months to three years ahead, whether inflation is expected can play an important role in the inflation process. In the early 1970s people didn't expect the high inflation rates that did occur. When inflation hit, people just tried to keep up with it. By the end of the 1970s, people expected more inflation than actually occurred and raised their prices—and, in doing so, caused the inflation rate to increase.

Expectations of inflation play an important role in any ongoing inflation. They can snowball a small inflationary pressure into an accelerating large inflation. Individuals keep raising their prices because they expect inflation, and inflation keeps on growing because individuals keep raising their prices. That's why expectations of inflation are of central concern to economic policymakers.

Costs of Inflation

Inflation has costs, but not the costs that noneconomists often associate with it. Specifically, inflation doesn't make the nation poorer. True, whenever prices go up somebody (the person paying the higher price) is worse off, but the person to whom the higher price is paid is better off. The two offset each other. So inflation does not make society on average any poorer. Inflation does, however, redistribute income from people who cannot or do not raise their prices to people who can and do raise their prices. This often creates feelings of injustice about the economic system. Thus, inflation can have significant distributional or equity effects.

While inflation may not make the nation poorer, it does cause income to be redistributed, and it can reduce the amount of information that prices are supposed to convey.

A second cost of inflation is its effect on the information prices convey to people. Consider an individual who laments the high cost of housing, pointing out that it has doubled in 10 years. But if inflation averaged 7 percent a year over the past 10 years, a doubling of housing prices should be expected. In fact, with 7 percent inflation, on average *all* prices double every 10 years. That means the individual's wages have probably also doubled, so he or she is no better off and no worse off than 10 years ago. The price of housing relative to other goods, which is the relevant price for making decisions, hasn't changed. When there's inflation it's hard for people to know what is and what isn't a relative price. People's minds aren't computers, so inflation reduces the amount of information that prices can convey and causes people to make choices that do not reflect relative prices.

Q-10 True or false? Inflation makes everyone in an economy worse off because everyone is paying higher prices.

Despite these costs, inflation is usually accepted by governments as long as it stays at a low rate. What scares economists is inflationary pressures above and beyond expectations of inflation. In that case, expectations of higher inflation can cause inflation to build up and compound itself. A 3 percent inflation becomes a 6 percent inflation, which in turn becomes a 12 percent inflation. Once inflation hits 5 percent or 6 percent, it's definitely no longer a little thing. Inflation of 10 percent or more is significant. While there is no precise definition, we may reasonably say that inflation has become **hyperinflation** *when inflation hits triple digits—100 percent or more per year.*

Hyperinflation is exceptionally high inflation of, say, 100 percent or more per year.

The United States has been either relatively lucky or wise because it has not experienced hyperinflation since the Civil War (1861–65). Other countries, such as Brazil, Israel, and Argentina, have not been so lucky (or have not followed the same policies the United States has). These countries have frequently had hyperinflation. But even with inflation at these levels, economies have continued to operate and, in some cases, continued to do well.

Web Note 22.4
Living with
Hyperinflation

In hyperinflation people try to spend their money quickly, but they still use the money. Let's say the U.S. price level is increasing 1 percent a day, which is a yearly inflation rate of about 4,000 percent.[5] Is an expected decrease in value of 1 percent per day going to cause you to stop using dollars? Probably not, unless you have a good alternative. You will, however, avoid putting your money into a savings account unless that savings account somehow compensates you for the expected inflation (the expected fall in the value of the dollar), and you will try to ensure that your wage is adjusted for inflation. In hyperinflation, wages, the prices firms receive, and individual savings are all in some way adjusted for inflation. Hyperinflation leads to economic institutions with built-in expectations of inflation. For example, usually in a hyperinflation the government issues indexed bonds whose value keeps pace with inflation.

Once these adjustments have been made, substantial inflation will not destroy an economy, but it certainly is not good for it. Such inflation tends to break down confidence in the monetary system, the economy, and the government.

Conclusion

This chapter has talked about growth, unemployment, and inflation. The interrelationship among these three concepts centers on trade-offs between inflation on the one hand and growth and unemployment on the other. If the government could attack inflation without worrying about unemployment or growth, it probably would have solved the problem of inflation by now. Unfortunately, when the government tries to stop inflation, it often causes a recession—increasing unemployment and slowing growth. Similarly, reducing unemployment by stimulating growth tends to increase inflation. To the degree that inflation and unemployment are opposite sides of the coin, the opportunity cost of reducing unemployment is inflation. The government must make a trade-off between low unemployment and slow growth on the one hand and inflation on the other. Opportunity costs must be faced in macro as well as in micro. The models you will learn in later chapters will help clarify the choices policymakers face.

---

[5]Why about 4,000 percent and not 365 percent? Because of compounding. In the second day the increase is on the initial price level *and* the 1 percent rise in price level that occurred the first day. When you carry out this compounding for all 365 days, you get almost 4,000 percent.

Summary

- Economists use two frameworks to analyze macroeconomic problems. The long-run growth framework focuses on supply, while the short-run business-cycle framework focuses on demand.
- Growth is measured by the change in real gross domestic product (real GDP) and by the change in per capita real GDP. Per capita real GDP is real GDP divided by the total population.
- The secular trend growth rate of the economy is 2.5 to 3.5 percent. Fluctuations of real output around the secular trend growth rate are called *business cycles*.
- Phases of the business cycle include peak, trough, upturn, and downturn.
- Unemployment is calculated as the number of unemployed individuals divided by the labor force. Unemployment rises during a recession and falls during an expansion.

- The target rate of unemployment is the lowest sustainable rate of unemployment possible under existing institutions. It's associated with an economy's potential output. The lower the target rate of unemployment, the higher an economy's potential output.
- The microeconomic approach to unemployment subdivides unemployment into categories and looks at those individual components.
- A real concept is a nominal concept adjusted for inflation. Real output equals nominal output divided by the price index.
- Inflation is a continual rise in the price level. The CPI, the PPI, and the GDP deflator are all price indexes used to measure inflation.
- The GDP deflator is the broadest price index. It measures inflation of all goods produced in an economy. The CPI measures inflation faced by consumers. The PPI measures inflation faced by producers.
- Expectations of inflation can provide pressure for an inflation to continue even when other causes don't exist.
- Inflation redistributes income from people who do not raise their prices to people who do raise their prices. Inflation also reduces the information that prices convey.

Key Terms

business cycle *(493)*
Classicals *(494)*
consumer price index (CPI) *(509)*
cyclical unemployment *(498)*
depression *(495)*
employment rate *(503)*
expansion *(495)*
expected inflation *(510)*
frictional unemployment *(499)*
GDP deflator *(508)*
hyperinflation *(511)*
inflation *(505)*
Keynesians *(494)*
labor force *(502)*
labor force participation rate *(503)*
nominal output *(510)*
Okun's rule of thumb *(505)*
per capita real output *(492)*
personal consumption expenditure deflator (PCE) *(509)*
potential output *(504)*
price index *(506)*
producer price index (PPI) *(509)*
real gross domestic product (real GDP) *(491)*
real output *(510)*
recession *(495)*
structural unemployment *(498)*
target rate of unemployment *(499)*
unemployment rate *(497)*
unexpected inflation *(510)*

Questions for Thought and Review

1. What are two ways in which long-term economic growth is measured?
2. How does the U.S. per capita growth rate of 1.5 to 2 percent a year since 1950 compare to growth rates in other areas around the world?
3. What is the difference between real output and potential output?
4. Draw a representative business cycle, and label each of the four phases.
5. The index of leading indicators has predicted all past recessions. Nonetheless it's not especially useful for predicting recessions. Explain.
6. If unemployment fell to 1.2 percent in World War II, why couldn't it be reduced to 1.2 percent today?
7. Distinguish between structural unemployment and cyclical unemployment.
8. What type of unemployment is best studied within the long-run framework? What type is best studied under the short-run framework?
9. Does the unemployment rate underestimate or overestimate the unemployment problem? Explain.
10. If unemployment rises by 2 percentage points, what will likely happen to output in the United States?
11. Why are expectations central to understanding inflation?
12. Inflation, on average, makes people neither richer nor poorer. Therefore it has no cost. True or false? Explain.
13. Would you expect that inflation would generally be associated with low unemployment? Why?

Problems and Exercises

1. The Bureau of Labor Statistics reported that in December 2002 the total labor force was 142,542,000 of a possible 214,967,000 working-age adults. The total number of unemployed was 8,590,000. From this information, calculate the following for December 2002:
   a. Labor force participation rate.
   b. Unemployment rate.
   c. Employment rate.
2. Answer the following questions about real output, nominal output, and inflation:
   a. The price level of a basket of goods in 2002 was $64. The price level of that same basket of goods in 2003 was $68. If 2002 is the base year, what was the price index in 2003?
   b. If nominal output is $300 billion and the price index is 115, what is real output?
   c. Inflation is 5 percent; real output rises 2 percent. What would you expect to happen to nominal output?
   d. Real output rose 3 percent and nominal output rose 7 percent. What happened to inflation?
3. In H. G. Wells's *Time Machine*, a late-Victorian time traveler arrives in England some time in the future to find a new race of people, the Eloi, in their idleness. Their idleness is, however, supported by another race, the Morlocks, underground slaves who produce the output. If technology were such that the Elois' lifestyle could be sustained by machines, not slaves, is it a lifestyle that would be desirable? What implications does the above discussion have for unemployment?
4. In 1991, Japanese workers' average tenure with a firm was 10.9 years; in 1991 in the United States the average tenure of workers was 6.7 years.
   a. What are two possible explanations for these differences?
   b. Which system is better?
   c. In the mid-1990s Japan experienced a recession while the United States economy grew. What effect did this likely have on these ratios?
5. Assume that nominal output rises from $12.5 billion in 2005 to $13 billion in 2006. Assume also that the GDP deflator rises from 100 to 105.
   a. What is the percentage increase in nominal output?
   b. What is the percentage increase in the price index?
   c. How much has real output increased?
   d. What is the percentage increase in real output?
   e. By how much would the price index have had to rise for real income to remain constant?

Web Questions

1. Use the Economic Statistics Briefing Room at the White House's home page (www.whitehouse.gov) and the Philadelphia Federal Reserve Bank's Livingston Survey (www.phil.frb.org/econ/liv) to answer the following questions:
   a. What are the current unemployment rate and inflation rate?
   b. What do forecasters predict for these variables according to the Livingston Survey?
   c. Are these predictions consistent with your predictions?
2. Go to Economagic.com to answer the following:
   a. Graph quarterly real GDP since 1989. Mark a peak and a trough of a business cycle.
   b. What phase of the business cycle is the economy currently in?
   c. For how many quarters has the economy been in this phase?
   d. How long ago was the last recession?

Answers to Margin Questions

1. This is both a long-run and a short-run issue. It is a short-run issue because the Japanese economy was in a severe recession and aggregate expenditures had declined. It is a long-run issue because the recession put in motion institutional changes that makes it easier for Japanese firms to lay off workers so that the average unemployment rate may be higher during times of expansion too. *(491)*
2. To calculate per capita output, divide real output ($10.5 trillion) by the total population (290 million). This equals $36,207. *(492)*
3. Three leading indicators are the average workweek, the layoff rate, and changes in the money supply. There are others. *(497)*
4. False. Structural unemployment is determined by the institutional structure of an economy, not fluctuations in economic activity. *(498)*
5. The target rate of unemployment changed over time because (1) low inflation was incompatible with what people thought was the target rate of unemployment, and (2) demographics—the age structure of the population—

changed, and people of different ages have different rates of unemployment. *(499)*

6. The unemployment rate is the number of unemployed divided by the labor force. The unemployment rate can fall while the number of unemployed rises if the labor force rises by a proportionately greater amount than the rise in the number of unemployed. *(502)*
7. Since people can always sell apples on the street, one can always get a job. So the value judgment is what type of job and at what wage society owes individuals jobs. *(503)*
8. The price index will rise by $0.15 \times 0.1 = 0.015 = 1.5\%$. *(507)*
9. Real output equals the nominal amount divided by the price index. Since the price index has risen by 15 percent, real output has risen to $5.22 trillion ($6 trillion divided by 1.15). Real output has risen by $220 billion. *(510)*
10. False. Inflation does not make everyone worse off because, although some people are paying higher prices, others are receiving higher prices. *(511)*

Appendix A

Nonmainstream Approaches to Macro

An introductory book necessarily focuses on mainstream views, leaving out many of the other views of economists. But you should be aware that there are many more views of macroeconomics out there than those of the Classicals and Keynesians. Not only are there many subdivisions of Classicals and Keynesians, but many economists don't fit into either group. They're called nonmainstream or heterodox economists.

A characteristic of nonmainstream, or heterodox, economists is that they are far more open to discuss major institutional changes than are mainstream economists. More specifically, a **heterodox economist,** or nonmainstream economist, is *one who doesn't accept the basic underlying model used by a majority of economists as the most useful model for analyzing the economy. Economists who do accept that model* are called **mainstream economists.**

In this appendix I will briefly introduce four heterodox macroeconomists' approaches to give you a sense of how their analyses differ from the mainstream analysis presented in this book. The four heterodox approaches are Austrian, Post-Keynesian, Institutionalist, and Radical.

Austrians

Austrian economists are *economists who believe in the liberty of all individuals first and social goals second.* They oppose state intrusion into private property and private activities. They are not all economists from Austria; rather, they are economists from anywhere who follow the ideas of Ludwig von Mises and Friedrich von Hayek, two economists who were from Austria. Austrian economists are sometimes classified as conservative, but they are more appropriately classified as **libertarians,** who *believe in liberty of individuals first and in other social goals second.* Consistent with their views, they are often willing to support what are sometimes considered radical ideas, such as legalizing addictive drugs or eliminating our current monetary system—ideas that conservative economists would oppose.

In macroeconomics, Austrian economists emphasize the uncertainty in the economy and the inability of a government controlled by self-interested politicians to undertake socially beneficial policy. Well-known Austrian macroeconomists include Murray Rothbard, Peter Boettke, and Mario Rizzo.

One proposal of Austrian economists will give you a flavor of their approach. That proposal is to eliminate the Federal Reserve System and to establish a **free market in money**—*a policy that would leave people free to use any money they want, and would significantly reduce banking regulation.* In a sense, their proposal carries the Classical argument in favor of laissez-faire to its logical conclusions. Why should the government have a monopoly of the money supply? Why shouldn't people be free to use whatever money they desire, denominated in whatever unit they want? Why don't we rely upon competition to prevent inflation? Why don't we have a free market in money?

A sub-group of Austrian economists is *public choice* economists. They use the mainstream supply and demand approach, but apply it much more broadly than do mainstream economists. Specifically, they see government decisions as reflecting economic forces rather than attempts by government to do good. Well-known public choice economists include Gordon Tullock, James Buchanan, and Robert Tollison.

Post-Keynesians

Post-Keynesian macroeconomists are *economists who believe that uncertainty is a central issue in macroeconomics*. They follow Keynes's approach more so than do mainstream economists. They agree with Austrians about the importance of uncertainty in understanding the macro economy, but their policy response to that uncertainty is not to have government get out of the macro economy; it is for the government to take a larger role in guiding the economy.

One of their policy proposals that gives you a flavor of their approach is **tax-based incomes policies**—*policies in which the government tries to directly affect the nominal wage- and price-setting institutions*. Under a tax-based incomes policy, any firm raising its wage or price would be subject to a tax, and any firm lowering its wage or price would get a subsidy. Such a plan, they argue, would reduce the upward pressure on the nominal price level, and reduce the rate of unemployment necessary to hold down inflation. Well-known Post-Keynesian economists include Paul Davidson, Barkley Rosser, and John Cornwall.

Institutionalists

Institutionalist economists are *economists who argue that any economic analysis must involve specific considerations of institutions*. Institutionalists have a long history in economics; their lineage goes back to the early 1930s and the writings of Thorstein Veblen, J. M. Clarke, and John R. Commons. Institutionalists were early supporters of welfare capitalism, and they helped set up many of the institutions of welfare capitalism, such as Social Security, which we now take for granted. Institutionalists are very close to Post-Keynesians in their approach to macroeconomics, but they give stronger emphasis to the role of institutions, and to the role of government in establishing new institutions, than do Post-Keynesians.

You can get a sense of their policy approach from one of the policies many Institutionalists support: **indicative planning**—*a macroeconomic policy in which the government sets up an overall plan for various industries and selectively directs credit to certain industries*. Thus for Institutionalists political forces direct the invisible hand. Well-known Institutionalists include James Peach, Ronnie Phillips, and Anne Mayhew.

Radicals

Radical economists are *economists who believe substantial equality-preferring institutional changes should be implemented to our economic system*. Radical economists evolved out of Marxian economics. Compared to mainstream economists, Radicals are far more willing to consider major institutional changes in our macro economy. They focus on the lack of equity in our current economic system, and their political discussions focus on institutional changes that might bring about a more equitable system. Specifically, they see the current economic system as one in which a few people—capitalists and high-level managers—benefit enormously, while others—minority groups such as African Americans and Hispanics—are left out, without a job. To incorporate such issues, Radical economists often use a class-oriented analysis and are much more willing to talk about social conflict and tensions in our society than are mainstream economists.

Compared to mainstream economists, Radical economists' analysis focuses much more on distributional fights between capitalists and workers and their different savings propensities. According to one important branch of radical theory, when profits are high, because capitalists save a large portion of their income, aggregate demand will be too low, and the economy goes into a recession; then government must run a deficit to bail out the economy. Mainstream economists agree that such distributional effects exist, but they consider them too small to worry about. Mainstream economists focus on fluctuations in business investment and consumers' spending decisions, not on differences in people's consumption.

Policy proposals some Radicals favor and that give you a sense of their approach are policies to establish worker cooperatives to replace the corporation. Radicals argue that such worker cooperatives would see that the income of the firm was more equitably allocated. Well-known Radical economists include Samuel Bowles, Herbert Gintis, and Howard Sherman.

Consistency of the Various Approaches

A characteristic of almost all heterodox economists of all types is that their analyses tend to be less formal than mainstream analysis. *Less formal* doesn't mean better or worse. There are advantages and disadvantages to formality, but *less formal* does mean that there's more potential for ambiguity in interpretation. It's easy to say whether the logic in a formal model is right or wrong. It's much harder to say whether the logic in an informal model is right or wrong because it's often hard to see precisely what the logic is. The advantage of an informal model is that it can include many more variables and can be made more realistic, so you can discuss real-world problems more easily with that model. Nonmainstream economists often want to talk about the real world, which is why they use informal models.

Often, after I discuss the mainstream and nonmainstream approaches, some student asks which is right. I respond with a story told by a former colleague of mine, Abba Lerner; the story goes as follows:

> "But look," the rabbi's wife remonstrated, "when one party to the dispute presented their case to you, you said, 'You are quite right,' and then when the other party presented their case you again said, 'You are quite right.' Surely they cannot both be right?" To which the Rabbi answered, "My dear, you are quite right!"

The moral of the story is that there's nothing necessarily inconsistent among mainstream and heterodox economists' approaches. They are simply different ways of looking at the same event. Which approach is most useful depends on what issues and events you are analyzing. The class analysis used by radicals is often more appropriate to developing countries than it is to the United States, and, in analyzing developing countries, many mainstream economists also include class fights in their approach. Similarly, Austrian analysis provides more insight into the role of the entrepreneur and individual in the economy than does mainstream analysis, while Post-Keynesian and Institutionalist analyses are useful when considering major institutional changes.

The distinctions between nonmainstream and mainstream economists can be overdone. One economist may well fall into two or three different groupings and use a combination of various analyses.

Key Terms

Austrian economists *(515)*
free market in money *(515)*
heterodox economists *(515)*
indicative planning *(516)*
Institutionalist economists *(516)*
libertarian *(515)*
mainstream economists *(515)*
Post-Keynesian macroeconomists *(516)*
Radical economists *(516)*
tax-based incomes policy *(516)*

23 National Income Accounting

After reading this chapter, you should be able to:

- State why national income accounting is important.
- Define GDP and calculate it in a simple example, avoiding double counting.
- Explain why GDP can be calculated using either the income approach or the expenditures approach.
- List the four expenditure components of GDP.
- Distinguish between real GDP and nominal GDP.
- State some limitations of national income accounting.
- Describe the shortcomings of using GDP to compare standards of living among countries.

The government is very keen on amassing statistics . . . They collect them, add them, raise them to the nth power, take the cube root and prepare wonderful diagrams. But you must never forget that every one of these figures comes in the first instance from the village watchman, who just puts down what he damn pleases.

—*Sir Josiah Stamp (head of Britain's revenue department in the late 19th century)*

Before you can talk about macroeconomics in depth, you need to be introduced to some terminology used in macroeconomics. That terminology can be divided into two parts. The first part deals with the macroeconomic statistics you are likely to see in the newspaper—GDP and its components. The second part discusses problems of using GDP figures. Among other things it distinguishes between real and nominal (or money) concepts, which are used to differentiate and compare goods and services over time. These concepts play a central role in interpreting the movement in components of the national income accounts.

National Income Accounting

In the 1930s, it was impossible for macroeconomics to exist in the form we know it today because many aggregate concepts we now take for granted either had not yet been formulated or were so poorly formulated that it was useless to talk rigorously about them. This lack of aggregate terminology was consistent with the Classical economists' lack of interest in the aggregate approach to studying the economy in the 1930s; they preferred to focus on microeconomics.

With the advent of Keynesian macroeconomics in the mid-1930s, development of a terminology to describe macroeconomic aggregates became crucial. Measurement is a necessary step toward rigor. A group of Keynesian economists set out to develop an aggregate terminology and to measure the aggregate concepts they defined so that people would have concrete terms to use when talking about macroeconomic problems. Their work (for which two of them, Simon Kuznets and Richard Stone, received the Nobel Prize) is called **national income accounting**—*a set of rules and definitions for measuring economic activity in the aggregate economy*, that is, in the economy as a whole.

National income accounting provides a way of measuring total, or aggregate, production. In national income accounting, aggregate economic production is broken down into subaggregates (such as consumption, investment, and personal income); national income accounting defines the relationship among these subaggregates. In short, national income accounting enables us to measure and analyze how much the nation is producing and consuming.

Measuring Total Economic Output of Goods and Services

The previous chapter introduced economists' primary measure of domestic output: real gross domestic product (real GDP). **Gross domestic product (GDP)** is *the total market value of all final goods and services produced in an economy in a one-year period.* GDP is probably the single most-used economic measure. When economists, journalists, and other analysts talk about the economy, they continually discuss GDP, how much it has increased or decreased, and what it's likely to do.

Gross domestic product (GDP) is the aggregate final output of residents and businesses in an economy in a one-year period.

Until 1992, the United States (unlike the rest of the world) used gross national product as its primary measure of aggregate output. As economic issues have become internationalized, national income accounting has been affected. In 1992, the United States followed the rest of the world and switched to gross domestic product as its primary measure of aggregate output.

Whereas gross domestic product measures the economic activity that occurs within a country, the economic activity of the citizens and businesses of a country is measured by **gross national product (GNP)**—*the aggregate final output of citizens and businesses of an economy in a one-year period.* So the economic activity of U.S. citizens working abroad is counted in U.S. GNP but isn't counted in U.S. GDP. Similarly for the foreign economic activity of U.S. companies. However, the income of a Mexican or German person or business working in the United States isn't counted in U.S. GNP but is counted in U.S. GDP. Thus, GDP describes the economic output within the physical borders of a country while GNP describes the economic output produced by the citizens of a country. To move from GDP to GNP we must add *net foreign factor income* to GDP. **Net foreign factor income** is defined as *the income from foreign domestic factor sources minus foreign factor income earned domestically.* Put another way, we must add the foreign income of our citizens and subtract the income of residents who are not citizens.

GDP is output produced within a country's borders; GNP is output produced by a country's citizens.

For many countries there's a significant difference between GNP and GDP. For example, consider Kuwait. Its citizens have significant foreign income—income that far exceeds the income of the foreigners in Kuwait. This means that Kuwait's GNP (the income of its citizens) far exceeds its GDP (the income of its residents). For the United States, however, foreign output of U.S. businesses and people for the most part offsets the output of foreign businesses and people within the United States. Kuwait's net foreign factor income has been large and positive, while that of the United States has been minimal. This chapter focuses on GDP, since it is the primary measure presented in government statistics.

Q.1 Which is higher: Kuwait's GDP or its GNP? Why?

Calculating GDP

Aggregate final output (GDP) consists of millions of different services and products: apples, oranges, computers, haircuts, financial advice, and so on. To arrive at total output, somehow we've got to add them all together into a composite measure. Say we produced 7 oranges plus 6 apples plus 12 computers. We have not produced 25 comapplorgs. You can't add apples and oranges and computers. You can only add like things (things that are measured in the same units). For example, 2 apples + 4 apples = 6 apples. If we want to add unlike things, we must convert them into like things. We do that by multiplying each good by its *price*. Economists call this *weighting the importance of each good by its price*. For example, if you have 4 pigs and 4 horses and you price pigs at $200 each and horses at $400 each, the horses are weighted as being twice as important as the pigs.

Multiplying the quantity of each good by its market price changes the terms in which we discuss each good from a quantity of a specific product to a *value* measure of that good. For example, when we multiply 6 apples by their price, 25 cents each, we get $1.50; $1.50 is a value measure. Once all goods are expressed in that value measure, they can be added together.

Take the example of 7 oranges and 6 apples. (For simplicity let's forget the computers, haircuts, and financial advice.) If the oranges cost 50 cents each, their total value is $3.50; if the apples cost 25 cents each, their total value is $1.50. Their values are expressed in identical measures, so we can add them together. When we do so, we don't get 13 orples; we get $5 worth of apples and oranges.

If we follow that same procedure with all the final goods and services produced in the economy in the entire year, multiplying the quantity produced by the market price per unit, we have all the economy's outputs expressed in units of value. If we then add up all these units of value, we have that year's gross domestic product.

Two important aspects to remember about GDP are:

1. GDP represents a flow.
2. GDP represents the market value of final output.

There are two important aspects to remember about GDP. First, GDP represents a flow (an amount per year), not a stock (an amount at a particular moment of time). Second, GDP refers to the market value of *final* output. Let's consider these statements separately.

GDP Is a Flow Concept

In economics it's important to distinguish between flows and stocks. Say a student just out of college tells you she earns $8,000. You'd probably think, "Wow! She's got a low-paying job!" That's because you implicitly assume she means $8,000 per year. If you later learned that she earns $8,000 per week, you'd quickly change your mind. The confusion occurred because how much you earn is a flow concept; it has meaning only when a time period is associated with it: so much per week, per month, per year. A stock concept is the amount of something at a given point in time. No time interval is associated with it. Your weight is a stock concept. You weigh 150 pounds; you don't weigh 150 pounds per week.

GDP is a flow concept, the amount of total final output a country produces per year. The *per year* is often left unstated, but it is important to keep in your mind that it's essential. GDP is usually reported quarterly or every three months, but it is reported on an *annualized basis*, meaning the U.S. Department of Commerce, which compiles GDP figures, uses quarterly figures to estimate total output for the whole year.

Q-2 How do wealth accounts differ from national income accounts?

The store of wealth, in contrast, is a stock concept. The stock equivalent to national income accounts is the **wealth accounts**—*a balance sheet of an economy's stock of assets and liabilities*. These accounts have recently been developed for the United States, making the U.S. national income accounts consistent with the United Nations' system of national accounts, which uses an integrated system of income and wealth accounts. Table 23-1 shows a summary account of U.S. net worth from the wealth accounts for the United States in 2001. These are stock measures; they exist at a moment of time. For example, on December 31, 2001, the accounting date for these accounts, U.S. private net worth was $41.1 trillion.

GDP Measures Final Output

As a student in my first economics class, I was asked how to calculate GDP. I said, "Add up the value of the goods and services produced by all the companies in the United States to arrive at GDP." I was wrong (which is why I remember it). Many goods produced by one firm are sold to other firms, which use those goods to make other goods. GDP doesn't measure total transactions in an economy; it measures **final output**—*goods and services purchased for final use*. When one firm sells products to another firm for use in production of yet another good, the first

Table 23-1 U.S. National Wealth Accounts in 2001 (net worth)

	Dollars (in trillions)			Percentage of Component	
Private net worth	$41.1				110%
Tangible wealth		$16.7			
Owner-occupied real estate			$13.8	37	
Consumer durables			2.8	8	
Other			0.1	0	
Financial wealth		24.4			
Corporate equities			9.0	24	
Noncorporate equities			4.9	13	
Other (pension reserves, life insurance, etc.)			10.5	28	
Government net financial assets	−3.7				−10
Federal		−3.1		−8	
State and local		−0.6		−2	
Total net worth	37.4			100	

Source: *Flow of Funds Accounts,* Board of Governors, Federal Reserve (www.federalreserve.gov). The value of the government's financial liabilities is greater than the value of its financial assets, which is why it shows up as a negative percentage.

firm's products aren't considered final output. They're **intermediate products**—*products used as input in the production of some other product.* To count intermediate goods as well as final goods as part of GDP would be to double-count them. An example of an intermediate good would be wheat sold to a cereal company. If we counted both the wheat (the intermediate good) and the cereal (the final good) made from that wheat, the wheat would be double-counted. Double counting would significantly overestimate final output.

If we did not eliminate intermediate goods, a change in organization would look like a change in output. Say a firm that produced steel merged with a firm that produced cars. Both together then produce exactly what each did separately before the merger. Final output hasn't changed, nor has intermediate output. The only difference is that the intermediate output of steel is now internal to the firm. Using only each firm's sales of goods to final consumers (and not sales to other firms) as the measure of GDP prevents mere changes in organization from affecting the measure of output.

Two Ways of Eliminating Intermediate Goods There are two ways to eliminate intermediate goods from the measure of GDP. One is to calculate only final sales. To do so, firms would have to separate goods they sold to consumers from intermediate goods used to produce other goods. For example, each firm would report how much of its product it sold to consumers and how much it sold to other producers for use that year in production of other goods; we would eliminate the latter to exclude double counting.

A second way to eliminate double counting is to follow the value added approach. **Value added** is *the increase in value that a firm contributes to a product or service.* It is calculated by subtracting intermediate goods (the cost of materials that a firm uses to produce a good or service) from the value of its sales. For instance, if a firm buys $100 worth of thread and $10,000 worth of cloth and uses them in making a thousand pairs of jeans that are sold for $20,000, the firm's value added is not $20,000; it is $9,900 ($20,000 in sales minus the $10,100 in intermediate goods that the firm bought).

To avoid double counting, you must eliminate intermediate goods, either by calculating only final output (expenditures approach), or by calculating only final income (income approach) by using the value added approach.

Table 23-2 provides another example. It gives the cost of materials (intermediate goods) and the value of sales in the following scenario: Say we want to measure the contribution to GDP made by a vendor who sells 200 ice cream cones at $2.50 each for

Table 23-2 Value Added Approach Eliminates Double Counting

Participants	I Cost of Materials	II Value of Sales	III Value Added	Row
Farmer	$ 0	$ 100	$100	1
Cone factory and ice cream maker	100	250	150	2
Middleperson (final sales)	250	400	150	3
Vendor	400	500	100	4
Totals	$750	$1,250	$500	5

total sales of $500. The vendor bought his cones and ice cream at a cost of $400 from a middleperson, who in turn paid the cone factory and ice cream maker a total of $250. The farmer who sold the cream to the factory got $100. Adding up all these transactions, we get $1,250, but that includes intermediate goods. Either by counting only the final value of the vendor's sales, $500, or by adding the value added at each stage of production (column III), we eliminate intermediate sales and arrive at the vendor's contribution to GDP of $500.

Value added is calculated by subtracting the cost of materials from the value of sales at each stage of production. The aggregate value added at each stage of production is, by definition, precisely equal to the value of final sales, since it excludes all intermediate products. In Table 23-2, the equality of the value added approach and the final sales approach can be seen by comparing the vendor's final sales of $500 (row 4, column II) with the $500 value added (row 5, column III).

Q-3 If a used-car dealer buys a car for $2,000 and resells it for $2,500, how much has been added to GDP?

Calculating GDP: Some Examples To make sure you understand what value added is and what makes up GDP, let's consider some sample transactions and determine what value they add and whether they should be included in GDP. Let's first consider secondhand sales: When you sell your two-year-old car, how much value has been added? The answer is none. The sale involves no current output, so there's no value added. If, however, you sold the car to a used-car dealer for $2,000 and he or she resold it for $2,500, $500 of value has been added—the used-car dealer's efforts transferred the car from someone who didn't want it to someone who did. I point this out to remind you that GDP is not only a measure of the production of goods; it is a measure of the production of goods *and services*.

Now let's consider a financial transaction. Say you sell a bond (with a face value of $1,000) that you bought last year. You sell it for $1,250 and pay $100 commission to the dealer through whom you sell it. What value is added to final output? You might be tempted to say that $250 of value has been added, since the value of the bond has increased by $250. GDP, however, refers only to value that is added as the result of production or services, not to changes in the values of financial assets. Therefore, the price at which you buy or sell the bond is irrelevant to the question at hand. The only value that is added by the sale is the transfer of that bond from someone who doesn't want it to someone who does. Thus, the only value added as a result of economic activity is the dealer's commission, $100. The remaining $1,150 (the $1,250 you got from the bond minus the $100 commission you paid) is a transfer of an asset from one individual to another but such transfers do not enter into GDP calculations. Only production of goods and services enters into GDP.

Is GDP Biased against Women?

Beyond the Tools

Although in the example in the book the housespouse is a man, the reality is that most housespouses are women. The fact that GDP doesn't include the work of housespouses is seen, by some, as a type of discrimination against women who work at home since their work is not counted as part of the domestic product. One answer for why it is not counted is that housework does not involve a market transaction and hence could not be measured. That makes some sense, but it does not explain why the services houses provide to homeowners are estimated and included in GDP. Why can't housework also be estimated?

The answer is that it can be estimated, and my suspicion is that not including housespouses' services in GDP does represent the latent discrimination against women that was built into the culture in the 1930s. That latent discrimination against women was so deep that it wasn't even noticed. Anyone who has seen the movie *Rosie the Riveter,* which shows government programs to get women out from wartime employment and back into their role in the home, will have a good sense of the cultural views of people in the mid-1900s and earlier.

In thinking about whether GDP is biased against women it is important to remember that the concepts we use are culturally determined and, over time, as cultural views change, the concepts no longer match our changed views. There is no escaping the fact that language is value-loaded. But so, too, is our attempt to point out the values in language. There are many other ways in which GDP makes arbitrary choices and discriminates against groups. The major discussion of the fact that latent discrimination against women was embodied in GDP accounting itself reflects our current values, just as not including housespouses' work reflected earlier values.

Let's consider a different type of financial transaction: The government pays an individual Social Security benefits. What value is added? Clearly no production has taken place, but money has been transferred. As in the case of the bond, only the cost of transferring it—not the amount that gets transferred—is included in GDP. This is accomplished by including in GDP government expenditures on goods and services, but not the value of government transfer payments. Thus, Social Security payments, welfare payments, and veterans' benefits do not enter into calculations of GDP. That's why the government can have a $2 trillion budget but only $600 billion ($2 trillion minus $1,400 billion of transfer payments) is included in GDP.

Q-4 How can the government have a $2 trillion budget but only have $600 billion of that included in GDP?

Finally, let's consider the work of a housespouse. (See the box "Is GDP Biased against Women?" for further discussion of this issue.) How much value does it add to economic activity in a year? Clearly if the housespouse is any good at what he or she does, a lot of value is added. Taking care of the house and children is hard work. Estimates of the yearly value of a housespouse's services often range from $35,000 to $45,000. Even though much value is added and hence, in principle, housespouse services should be part of GDP, by convention a housespouse contributes nothing to GDP. GDP measures only *market activities;* since housespouses are not paid, their value added is not included in GDP. This leads to some problems in measurement. For example, suppose a woman divorces her housespouse and then hires him to continue cleaning her house for $20,000 per year. Then he will be contributing $20,000 value added. That, since it is a market transaction, is included in GDP.

The housespouse example shows that the GDP measure has some problems. There are other areas in which it also has problems, but these are best left for intermediate courses. What's important for an introductory economics student to remember is that numerous decisions about how to handle various types of transactions had to be made to get a workable measure. Overall, the terminology of national income accounting is a model of consistency. It focuses on measuring final market output for the entire economy. So, in summary, GDP measures production. Secondhand sales, changes in the value of financial assets, transfer payments, and nonmarket activities are not included in GDP.

Two Methods of Calculating GDP

GDP can be calculated in two ways: the expenditures method and the income method. This is because of the national income accounting identity.

The National Income Accounting Identity

National income accounting is a form of accounting. Accounting is a way of keeping track of things. It is based on certain identities; for a firm, cost plus profit equals revenues because cost plus profit is identical to revenues. National income accounting is no different. It too is based on an identity. By definition, whenever a good or service (output) is produced, somebody receives an income for producing it. The equality of output and income is an accounting identity in the national income accounts. The identity can be seen in Figure 23-1, which illustrates the circular flow of income in an economy.[1]

Figure 23-1 shows the overall flows of income and expenditures in the economy. The top half of the flows (flow 1) shows the income households receive for supplying their factor services. The bottom half shows the outflow of expenditures individuals make to firms for the goods and services they buy. The two sides of the flow suggest that there might be two approaches to calculating GDP, and there are; there is the *expenditures approach* and the *income approach*. In the expenditures approach, we look at the bottom flow. In the income approach, we look at the top flow.

The Expenditures Approach

GDP = $C + I + G + (X - M)$ is an accounting identity because it is defined as true.

The bottom half of Figure 23-1 gives us a picture (flows 2–5) of the components of expenditures. Specifically, gross domestic product is equal to the sum of four expenditure categories: consumption (C), investment (I), government expenditures (G), and net exports ($X - M$). A shorthand way of saying this is: GDP = $C + I + G + (X - M)$. Let's consider each of these categories in relation to the flows in Figure 23-1.

This 17th-century engraving, "The Money Lender," shows that careful bookkeeping and accounting have been around for a long time.
Bleichroeder Print Collection, Baker Library, Harvard Business School.

Consumption When individuals receive income, they can either spend it on domestic goods, save it, pay taxes, or spend it on foreign goods. These four alternatives are the channels through which income is brought back into the spending stream. The largest and most important of the flows is **personal consumption expenditures**—*payments by households for goods and services* (flow 4). It is also the most obvious way in which income received is returned to firms. The other three flows are slightly more complicated.

Investment The saving/investment flow through the financial sector (flow 3) is the portion of income that individuals save. This money leaves the spending stream and goes into financial markets. If the financial markets are working properly, they translate that saving back into the spending flow by lending it to individuals who want to spend. *Business spending on equipment, structures, and inventories and household spending on new owner-occupied housing* are counted as part of **gross private investment.**

---

[1]An *identity* is a statement of equality that's true by definition. In algebra, an identity is sometimes written as a triple equal sign (≡). It is more equal than simply equal. How something can be more equal than equal is beyond me, too, but I'm no mathematician.

Figure 23-1 The Circular Flow
One of the most important insights about the aggregate economy is that it is a circular flow in which output and input are interrelated. Households' expenditures (consumption and saving) are firms' income; firms' expenditures (wages, rent, etc.) are households' income.

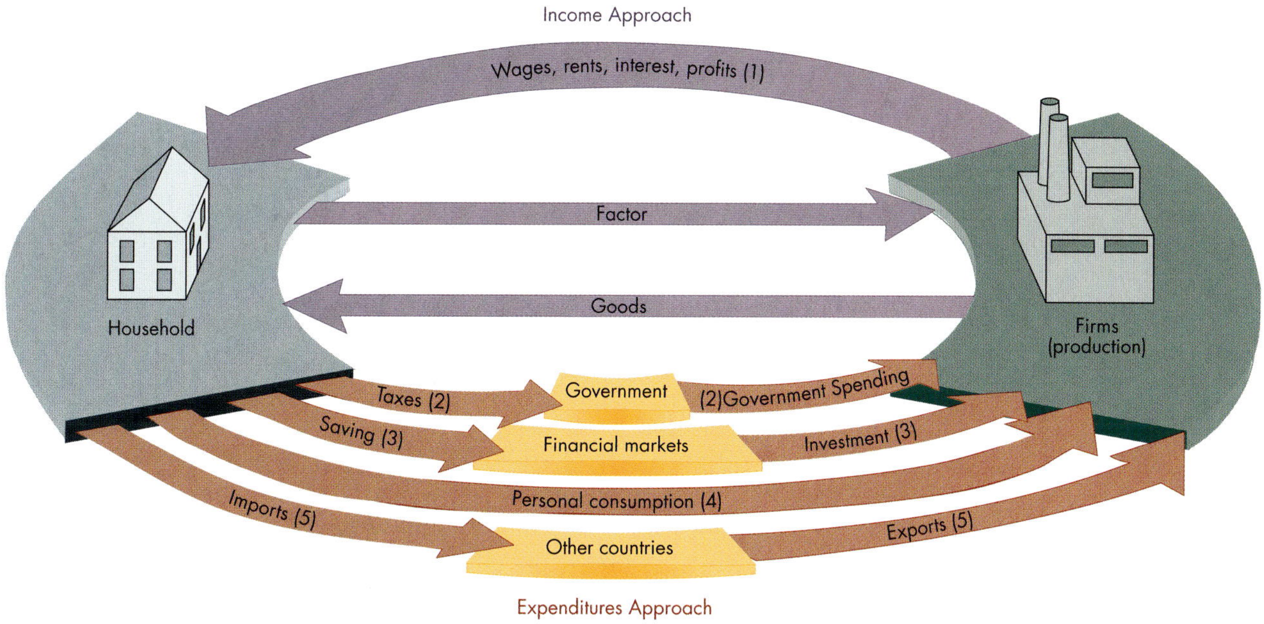

Housing, tractors, steel mills, and wine barrels are examples of gross private investment. Thus, when economists speak of investment they don't mean the kind of activity taking place when individuals buy stocks or bonds—economists consider that saving, not investing.

Sooner or later, assets such as plants and equipment wear out or become technologically obsolete. Economists call this wearing out process **depreciation**—*the decrease in an asset's value*. Depreciation is part of the cost of producing a good; it is the amount by which plants and equipment decrease in value as they grow older. Much of each year's private investment involves expenditures to replace assets that have worn out. For example, as you drive your car, it wears out. A car with 80,000 miles on it is worth less than the same type of car with only 1,000 miles on it. The difference in value is attributed to depreciation.

To differentiate between total or gross private domestic investment and the new investment that's above and beyond replacement investment, economists use the term **net private investment**—*gross private domestic investment minus depreciation*. In 2001, gross investment was $1,586 billion and depreciation was $1,106.8 billion, so net investment was $479.2 billion. Economists pay close attention to net private investment because it gives an estimate of the increase in the country's productive capacity.

Q-5 Calculate GDP with the information below:

- Consumption = 60
- Gross private investment = 20
- Government purchases = 20
- Exports = 10
- Imports = 15

Government Purchases Let's next consider the taxes/transfer flow through government (flow 2). When individuals pay taxes, those taxes are either spent by government on goods and services or returned to individuals in the form of transfer payments. *Government payments for goods and services and investment in equipment and structures* are referred to as **government purchases.** The transfer payments are spent and included in consumption or saved and channeled to investment. Notice also that there is a connection drawn between the government and financial markets. That's there because if the amount government takes in does not match the amount government spends (i.e., if it runs a deficit), it must borrow from financial markets to make up the difference.

Net Exports Finally, individuals' spending on foreign goods escapes the system and does not add to domestic production. Spending on foreign goods, imports, is subtracted from total expenditures. That flow out is offset by a flow in—foreign demand for U.S. goods; that is, U.S. exports (flow 5). Exports are added in to total expenditures. Usually these flows are combined and we talk about **net exports**—*exports minus imports*.

All expenditures fall into one or another of these four divisions—consumption, investment, government purchases, or net exports—so by adding up these four categories, we get total expenditures on U.S. goods and services minus U.S. residents' expenditures on foreign goods. By definition, in national income accounting, those total expenditures on U.S. goods and services equal (with some adjustments for taxes and such) the total amount of production of goods and services (GDP). Table 23-3 gives the breakdown of GDP by expenditure category for selected countries. Notice that personal consumption expenditures is the largest component of expenditures in all countries and that there is a rough similarity of the other components in percentage terms.

GDP and NDP In the discussion of investment, I differentiated gross investment from net investment. Gross investment minus depreciation equals net investment. Economists have created another aggregate term, *net domestic product,* to reflect the adjustment to investment because of depreciation. **Net domestic product (NDP)** is *the sum of consumption expenditures, government expenditures, net foreign expenditures, and investment less depreciation*. Thus,

$$GDP = C + I + G + (X - M)$$
$$NDP = [C + I + G + (X - M)] - \text{Depreciation}$$

NDP takes depreciation into account, and depreciation is a cost of producing goods; so NDP is actually preferable to GDP as the expression of a country's domestic output. However, measuring true depreciation (the actual decrease in an asset's value) is difficult because asset values fluctuate. In fact, it's so difficult that in the real world accountants don't try to measure true depreciation, but instead use a number of conventional rules of thumb. In recognition of this reality, economists call the adjustment made to GDP to ar-

Table 23-3 Expenditure Breakdown of GDP for Selected Countries, 2001

Country	Nominal GDP (U.S. $ in billions)	=	Personal Consumption (% of GDP)	+	Gross Private Investment (% of GDP)	+	Government Purchases (% of GDP)	+	Exports (% of GDP)	−	Imports (−% of GDP)
United States	$10,082		$6,987		$1,586		$1,858		$1,034		−$1,383
			69%		16%		18%		10%		−14%
Brazil	503		60		20		19		12		−11
Germany	1,900		58		20		20		35		−33
Japan	4,200		56		36		7		10		−9
Pakistan	60		74		14		12		18		−18
Tanzania	9		83		21		13		22		−39
Tunisia	20		61		24		16		40		−41

Source: *World Development Report,* 2002, The World Bank (www.worldbank.org) and *Survey of Current Business,* Bureau of Economic Analysis. Percentages may not sum to 100 due to rounding.

rive at NDP the *capital consumption allowance* rather than *depreciation*. Since estimating depreciation is difficult, GDP rather than NDP is generally used in discussions.

The Income Approach

Now look back at the top portion of Figure 23-1. The income approach to measuring GDP adds up payments by firms to households, called *factor payments*, to arrive at **national income (NI),** or *total income earned by citizens and businesses of a country*. Firms make payments to households for supplying their services as factors of production (flow 1). These payments are broken up into employee compensation, rent, interest, and profits.

Compensation of Employees Employee compensation (the largest component of national income) consists of wages and salaries paid to individuals, along with fringe benefits and government taxes for Social Security and unemployment insurance.

Rents Rents are the income from property received by households. Rents received by firms are not included because a firm's rents are simply another source of income to the firm and hence are classified as profits. In most years the rent component of national income is small, since the depreciation owners take on buildings is close to the income they earn from those buildings.

Interest Interest is the income private businesses pay to households that have lent the businesses money, generally by purchasing bonds issued by the businesses. (Interest received by firms doesn't show up in this category for the same reason that rents received by firms don't show up in the *rent* category.) Interest payments by government and households aren't included in national income since by convention they're assumed not to flow from the production of goods and services.

Profits Profits are the amount that is left after compensation to employees, rents, and interest have been paid out. (The national income accounts use accounting profits that must be distinguished from economic profits, which are calculated on the basis of opportunity costs.)

Table 23-4 shows these components for the United States and selected countries. It lists the national income of countries and the components in absolute amounts and in percentages for the United States and in percentages for the remaining countries. As you can see, in all countries compensation of employees is the largest component of national income. The importance of employee compensation in income makes it a key

Q-6 Calculate national income with the information below:

Employee compensation = 140
Rents = 4
Interest = 12
Profits = 42

Table 23-4 National or Domestic Income Breakdown for Selected Countries, 2001

(1) Country	(2) National Income (NI) (billions of $)	=	(3) Employee Compensation (% of NI)	+	(4) Rents (% of NI)	+	(5) Interest (% of NI)	+	(6) Profits (% of NI)
United States	$8,122		$5,875		$138		$650		$1,459
			72%		2%		8%		18%
Japan	4,200		73		3		2		23
Germany	1,900		73		2		6		19
United Kingdom	1,424		64		3		7		25
Canada	695		69		8		7		16

Source: National Accounts, OECD (www.oecd.org), and embassies of countries. Percentages may not sum to 100 due to rounding.

statistic that economists focus on. A second key statistic is profits. When profits are high, firms are doing well. One final word of caution: In each country statistics are collected using slightly different methods. This makes international comparison difficult.

Equality of Income and Expenditure

The value of the employee compensation, rents, interest, and profits (the flow along the top in Figure 23-1) equals the value of goods bought (the flow along the bottom). How are these values kept exactly equal? That's the secret of double-entry bookkeeping: output must always equal income.

The definition of profit is the key to the equality. Recall that *profit* is defined as what remains after all the firm's other income (employee compensation, rent, and interest) is paid out. For example, say a firm has a total output of $800 and that it paid $400 in wages, $200 in rent, and $100 in interest. The firm's profit is total output less these payments. Profit equals $800 − $700 = $100.

The accounting identity works even if a firm incurs a loss. Say that instead of paying $400 in wages, the firm paid $700, along with its other payments of $200 in rent and $100 in interest. Total output is still $800, but total payments are $1,000. Profits, still defined as total output minus payments, are negative: $800 − $1,000 = (−$200). There's a loss of $200. Adding that loss to other income [$1,000 + (−$200)] gives total income of $800—which is identical to the firm's total output of $800. It is no surprise that total output and total income, defined in this way, are equal.

The national income accounting identity (Total output = Total income) allows us to calculate GDP either by adding up all values of final outputs (the *expenditures approach*) or by adding up the values of all earnings or income (the *income approach*).

The income accounting identity as presented so far has skipped over three qualifications. We've already discussed two of these. The first concerns the words *national* and *domestic*. National income is all income earned by citizens of a country and is equivalent to GNP. To move from domestic to national, we add net foreign factor income. I've also introduced the second qualification when talking about net domestic product (NDP). NDP is GDP less depreciation. Depreciation, though a cost of production and included in expenditures, is not paid out as income. Thus, depreciation is subtracted from GDP. The third qualification—indirect business taxes—is similar. Indirect business taxes (sales taxes, excise taxes, business property taxes, customs duties, and license fees) are reflected in all prices and, thus, in the value of total expenditures (GDP). They are not, however, paid out to owners of production as income and are not part of national income. Thus, to move from GDP to national income, we must also subtract indirect business taxes from GDP. Figure 23-2 shows these adjustments. As you can see, total expenditures (consumption, investment, government purchases, and net exports) equals GDP (column 1). GDP plus net foreign factor income equals GNP (column 2). GNP less depreciation and indirect business taxes equals national income (employee compensation, rents, interest, profit) shown in column 3.

Other National Income Terms

Two other often-used concepts deserving mention are *personal income* and *disposable personal income*. (These can be either national or domestic concepts. Since the United States still reports them as national concepts, I follow that convention here.)

Personal Income National income measures the income individuals receive for doing productive work, whereas personal income measures all income actually received by individuals. Individuals receive other income that they do not directly earn (for example, Social Security payments, welfare payments, food stamps, and veterans' bene-

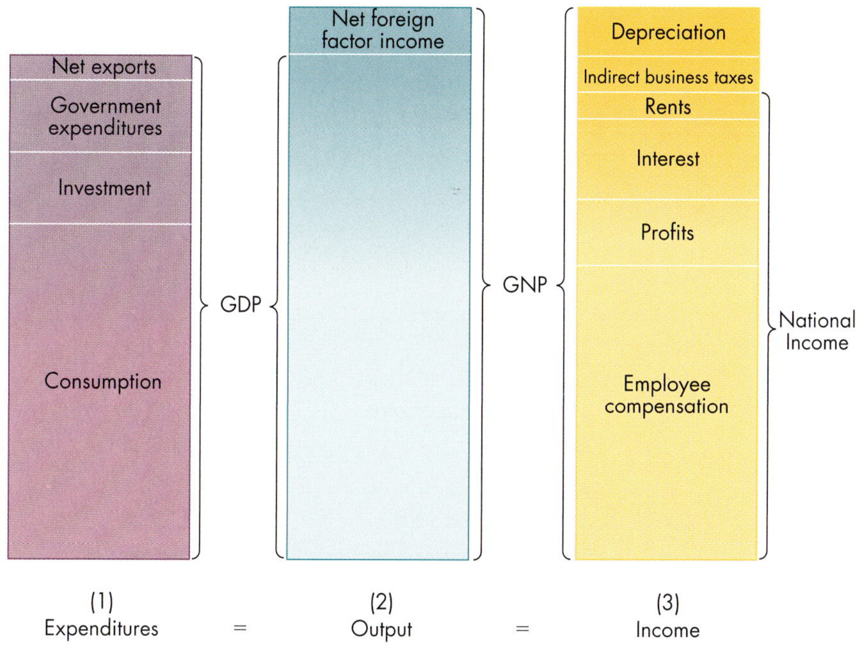

Figure 23-2 Equality of Expenditure and Income
These bars show just how total output equals total income in the national accounts. Bar 1 shows that GDP is the sum of consumption, investment, government purchases, and net exports. National income is the bracketed portion of bar 3. It equals employee compensation, rents, interest, and profit. To go from GDP to national income, we must first add net foreign factor income. This equals GNP. To get national income, then subtract depreciation and indirect business taxes (the top two items on the right-hand bar).

fits). These payments from government to individuals are not part of national income, but they are available to spend. So too are interest payments from government and individuals, which, by convention are not included in national income.

Similarly, in national income accounting, individuals are attributed income that they do not actually receive. This income includes undistributed corporate profits (retained earnings) and employers' contributions to Social Security.

If we add to national income the amounts of such payments that households receive, and subtract from national income the amounts attributed to households but not actually received by them, we arrive at **personal income (PI)**—*national income plus net transfer payments from government minus amounts attributed but not received*. Personal income can be set forth as follows:

PI = NI + Transfer payments from government
+ Net non-business interest income
− Corporate retained earnings
− Social Security taxes

Disposable Personal Income Personal income has accounted for some taxes, but not all. There's still personal income taxes and other personal taxes, which are subtracted from individuals' paychecks or paid directly by self-employed individuals. Personal income taxes and payroll taxes show up on employees' paycheck stubs, but employees don't actually get the money; the government does. Subtracting these personal income taxes from personal income, we arrive at **disposable personal income**—*personal income minus personal income taxes and other personal taxes:*

Disposable personal income = PI − Personal taxes

Disposable personal income is what people have readily available to spend. Thus, economists follow disposable personal income carefully.

Table 23-5 The Relationship between GDP and National Income and Other Measures (billions of dollars), 2001

Gross domestic product		**$10,082.2**
Plus:	Net foreign factor income	21.9
Equals:	Gross national product	10,104.1
Less:	Depreciation	1,329.3
	Indirect business taxes	817.3
	Statistical discrepancy	−164.5
Equals:	**National income**	**8,122.0**
Less:	Corporate retained earnings	323.4
	Social Security taxes	726.1
Plus:	Transfer payments	1,137.0
	Net non-business interest income	475.8
Equals:	**Personal income**	**8,685.3**
Less:	Personal taxes	1,292.1
Equals:	**Personal disposable income**	**7,393.2**

Table 23-5 shows the relationship between GDP and national income as well as personal income and personal disposable income for 2001. A good exercise for you is to review the table to be sure you understand the relationships.

USING GDP FIGURES

The most important use of GDP figures is to make comparisons of one country's production with another country's and of one year's production with another year's.

Web Note 23.1
The Human Development Index

COMPARING GDP AMONG COUNTRIES

Most countries use somewhat similar measures to calculate GDP. Thus, we can compare various countries' GDP levels and get a sense of their economic size and power.

Per capita GDP is another measure often used to compare various nations' income. To arrive at per capita GDP, we divide GDP by the country's total population. Doing so gives us a sense of the relative standards of living of the people in various countries.

Q-7 Why are national income statistics not especially good for discussing the income of developing countries?

Some of the comparisons of these measures should give you cause to wonder. For example, at existing exchange rates Bangladesh has per capita GDP of about $270, compared to U.S. per capita GDP of about $35,000. How do people in Bangladesh live? In answering that question, remember that GDP measures market transactions. In poor countries, individuals often grow their own food (subsistence farming), build their own shelter, and make their own clothes. None of those activities are market activities, and while they're sometimes estimated and included in GDP, they often aren't estimated accurately. They certainly aren't estimated at the value of what these activities would cost in the United States. Also, remember that GDP is an aggregate measure that values activities at the market price in a society. The relative prices of the products and services a consumer buys often differ substantially among countries. In New York City, $1,500 a month gets you only a small studio apartment. In Haiti, $1,500 a month might get you a mansion with four servants. Thus, GDP can be a poor measure of the relative living standards.

To avoid this problem in comparing per capita GDP, economists often calculate a different concept, *purchasing power parity*, which adjusts for the different relative prices among countries before making comparisons.

Just how much of a difference the two approaches can make can be seen in the case of China. In 1992, the International Monetary Fund (IMF) changed from calculating China's GDP using the exchange rate approach to calculating it using the purchasing power parity approach. Upon doing so, the IMF calculated that China's GDP grew over 400 percent in one year. Per capita income rose from about \$300 to well over \$1,000. When methods of calculation can make that much difference, one must use statistics very carefully.

Economic Welfare over Time

A second way in which the GDP concept is used is to compare one year with another. Using GDP figures to compare the economy's performance over time is much better than relying merely on our perceptions. Most of us have heard the phrase *the good old days*. Generally we hear it from our parents or grandparents, who are lamenting the state of the nation or economy. In comparing today to yesterday, they always seem to picture the past with greener grass, an easier life, and happier times. Compared to the good old days, today always comes out a poor second.

Using GDP figures to compare the economy's performance over time is much better than relying merely on our perceptions.

Our parents and grandparents may be right when they look back at particular events in their own lives, but if society were to follow such reasoning, it would conclude that all of history has been just one long downhill slide, worsening every year. In actuality, perceptions of the good old days are likely to be biased. It's easy to remember the nice things of yesterday while forgetting its harsh realities. Relying on past perception is not an especially helpful way of making accurate comparisons.

A preferable way is to rely on data that are not changed by emotion or anything else. Looking at GDP over time provides a way of using data to make comparisons over time. For example, say we compare U.S. GDP in 1932 (\$58 billion) to GDP in 2001 (\$10.1 trillion). Would it be correct to conclude the economy had grown 170 times larger? No. As I discussed earlier, GDP figures aren't affected by emotions, but they are affected by inflation. To make comparisons over time, we can't confine ourselves to a simple look at what has happened to GDP. We must also look at what happened to prices.

Suppose prices of all goods and hence the price level go up 25 percent in one year, but outputs of all goods remain constant. GDP will have risen 25 percent, but will society be any better off? No. To compare GDP over time, you must distinguish between increases in GDP due to inflation and increases in GDP that represent real increases in production and income.

A real concept is a nominal concept adjusted for inflation.

Real and Nominal GDP

As stated earlier, to separate increases in GDP caused by inflation from increases in GDP that represent real increases in production and income, economists distinguish between **nominal GDP** *(GDP calculated at existing prices)* and **real GDP** *(nominal GDP adjusted for inflation)*. This distinction is sufficiently important to warrant repetition in this chapter. To adjust nominal output for inflation we create a price index (a measure of how much the price level has risen from one year to the next) and divide nominal GDP by that price index and multiply by 100. That price index is the GDP deflator, introduced in the previous chapter.[2]

Real GDP is nominal GDP adjusted for inflation.

For example, say the price level rises 10 percent (from a GDP deflator of 100 to a GDP deflator of 110) and nominal GDP rises from \$9 trillion to \$10 trillion. Part of that rise in nominal GDP represents the 10 percent rise in the price level. If you divide nominal GDP, \$10 trillion, by the new GDP deflator, 110, and multiply by 100, you get

Q-8 If real income has risen from \$4 trillion to \$4.2 trillion and the price level went up by 10 percent, by how much has nominal income risen?

[2]Now you know why the total output deflator is called the *GDP deflator*. It is an index of the rise in prices of the goods and services that make up GDP.

$9.09 trillion (the amount GDP would have been if the price level had not risen). That $9.09 trillion is called real GDP. To decide whether production has increased or decreased over time, we simply compare the real incomes. In this example, real income has risen from $9 trillion to $9.09 trillion, so we can conclude that the real economy has grown by 9/900, or 1.5 percent.

The table below lists nominal GDP, the GDP deflator, and real GDP for recent years. Remember, to calculate real GDP, divide nominal GDP by the GDP deflator and multiply by 100.

	Nominal GDP	GDP Deflator	Real GDP
1999 level	$ 9,274.3	104.7	$8,859.0
% change	5.6	1.5	4.1
2000 level	$ 9,824.6	106.9	$9,191.4
% change	5.9	2.1	3.8
2001 level	$10,082.2	109.4	$9,214.5
% change	2.6	2.3	0.3

Because there was inflation in each of these years, the percent rise in real GDP was less than the percent rise in nominal GDP.

Real GDP is what is important to a society because it measures what is *really* produced. Considering nominal GDP instead of real GDP can distort what's really happening. Let's say the U.S. price level doubled tomorrow. Nominal GDP would also double, but would the United States be better off? No.

We'll use the distinction between real and nominal continually in this course, so to firm up the concepts in your mind, let's go through another example. Consider Indonesia in 1997 and 1998, when nominal GDP rose from 673 trillion to 943 trillion rupiah (their local currency units) while the GDP deflator rose from 100 to 161. Dividing nominal GDP in 1998 by the GDP deflator and multiplying by 100, we see that *real GDP* fell by over 12 percent. So not only did Indonesia's economy not grow; it actually shrank.

Some Limitations of National Income Accounting

Limitations of national income accounting include the following:

1. Measurement problems exist.
2. GDP measures economic activity, not welfare.
3. Subcategories are often interdependent.

The quotation at this chapter's start pointed out that statistics can be misleading. I want to reiterate that here. Before you can work with statistics, you need to know how they are collected and the problems they have. If you don't, the results can be disastrous.

Here's a possible scenario: A student who isn't careful looks at the data and discovers an almost perfect relationship between imports and investment occurring in a Latin American country. Whenever capital goods imports go up, investment of capital goods goes up by an equal proportion. The student develops a thesis based on that insight, only to learn after submitting the thesis that no data on investment are available for that country. Instead of gathering actual data, the foreign country's statisticians estimate investment by assuming it to be a constant percentage of imports. Since many investment goods are imported, this is reasonable, but the estimate is not a reasonable basis for an economic policy. It would be back to the drawing board for the student, whose thesis would be useless because the student didn't know how the country's statistics had been collected.

If you ever work in business as an economist, statistics will be your life's blood. Much of what economists do is based on knowing, interpreting, and drawing inferences from statistics. Statistics must be treated carefully. They don't always measure what they seem to measure. Though U.S. national income accounting statistics are among the most accurate in the world, they still have serious limitations.

GDP Measures Market Activity, Not Welfare

The first, and most important, limitation to remember is that GDP measures neither happiness nor economic welfare. GDP measures economic (market) activity. Real GDP could rise and economic welfare could fall. For example, say some Martians came down and let loose a million Martian burglars in the United States just to see what would happen. GDP would be likely to rise as individuals bought guns and locks and spent millions of dollars on protecting their property and replacing stolen items. At the same time, however, welfare would fall.

Welfare is a complicated concept. The economy's goal should not be to increase output for the sake of increasing output, but to make people better off or at least happier. But a pure happiness measure is impossible. Economists have struggled with the concept of welfare and have decided that the best they can do is to concentrate their analysis on economic activity, leaving others to consider how economic activity relates to happiness. I should warn you, however, that there is no neat correlation between increases in GDP and increases in happiness.

Measurement Errors

Q.9 How can measurement errors occur in adjusting GDP figures for inflation?

GDP figures are supposed to measure all market economic activity, but they do not. Illegal drug sales, under-the-counter sales of goods to avoid income and sales taxes, work performed and paid for in cash to avoid income tax, nonreported sales, and prostitution are all market activities, yet none of them is included in GDP figures. Estimates of the underground, nonmeasured economy range from 1.5 to 20 percent of GDP in the United States and as high as 70 percent in Nigeria. That is, if measured U.S. GDP is $10.1 trillion, inclusion of the underground, nonmeasured activity would raise it to between $10.3 trillion and $12.1 trillion. If we were able to halt underground activity and direct those efforts to the above-ground economy, GDP would rise significantly. For instance, if we legalized prostitution and marijuana sales and quadrupled tax-collection mechanisms, GDP would rise. But that rise in GDP wouldn't necessarily make us better off. See the box, "The Underground Economy" for further discussion.

Measurements of inflation can involve significant measurement errors.

A second type of measurement error occurs in adjusting GDP figures for inflation. Earlier I discussed problems using indexes. Measurement of inflation involves numerous arbitrary decisions including what base year to use, how to weight various prices, and how to adjust for changes in the quality of products. Let's take, for example, changes in the quality of products. If the price of a Toyota went up 5 percent from 2003 ($20,000) to 2004 ($21,000), that's certainly a 5 percent rise in price. But what if the 2004 Toyota had a "new, improved" 16-valve engine? Can you say that the price of cars rose 5 percent, or should you adjust for the improvement in quality? And if you adjust, how do you adjust? The people who keep track of the price indexes used to measure inflation will be the first to tell you there's no one right answer to any one of these choices. How that question, and a million other similar questions involved in measuring inflation, is answered can lead to significant differences in estimates of inflation and hence in estimates of real GDP growth.

One study for Canada argued inflation could be either 5.4 or 15 percent, depending on how the inflation index was calculated. Which inflation figure you chose would make a big difference in your estimate of how the economy was doing. The United States used to switch base years and update its price weights every five years, resulting

The Underground Economy

Applying the Tools

The U.S. government has issued over $580 billion worth of cash. That's about $2,000 for every man, woman, and child. Now ask yourself how much cash you're carrying on you. Add to that the amounts banks and businesses keep, and divide that by the number of people in the United States. The number economists get when they do that calculation is way below the total amount of cash the United States has issued. So what happens to the extra cash?

Let's switch for a minute to a Miami safehouse being raided by drug enforcement officers. They find $50 million in cash. That's what most economists believe happens to much of the extra cash that remains in the United States. It goes underground. An underground economy lurks below the real economy.

The underground economy consists of two components: (1) the production and distribution of illegal goods and services; and (2) the nonreporting of legal economic activity.

Illegal activity, such as selling illegal drugs and prostitution, generates huge amounts of cash. (Most people who buy an illegal good or service would prefer not to have the transaction appear on their monthly credit card statements.) This presents a problem for a big-time illegal business. It must explain to the Internal Revenue Service (IRS) where all that money came from. That's where money laundering comes in. Money laundering is simply making illegally gained income look as if it came from a legal business. Any business through which lots of cash moves is a good front for money laundering. Laundromats move lots of cash, which is where the term *money laundering* came from. The mob bought laundromats and claimed a much higher income from the laundromats than it actually received. The mob thus "laundered" the excess money. Today money laundering is much more sophisticated. It involves billions of dollars and international transactions in three or four different countries, but the purpose is the same: making illegally earned money look legal.

The second part of the illegal economy involves deliberately failing to report income in order to escape paying taxes on it. When people work "off the books," when restaurants don't ring up cash sales, when waiters forget to declare tips on their tax returns, they reduce their tax payments and make it look as if they have less income and as if the economy has less production than it actually does.

How important is the underground economy? That's tough to say; it is, after all, underground. A U.S. Department of Commerce economist estimated it at 1.5 percent of the total U.S. economy. The IRS estimates the underground economy at about 10 percent of the total U.S. economy. Some economists estimate it as high as 15 or 20 percent. Some countries have significant underground economies. For example, it is estimated that Nigeria's underground economy is as much as 70 percent of its above-ground economy. In other countries, more like the United States but which have higher tax rates, such as Italy, Belgium, and Spain, estimates of the underground economy range as high as 30 percent of the above-ground economy.

Web Note 23.2
The Underground Economy

in the recalculation of history every five years. In 1996, however, it began to use a new measure that updates price weights every year.

Misinterpretation of Subcategories

A third limitation of national income accounting concerns possible misinterpretation of the components. In setting up the accounts, a large number of arbitrary decisions had to be made: What to include in "investment"? What to include in "consumption"? How to treat government expenditures? The decisions made were, for the most part, reasonable, but they weren't the only ones that could have been made. Once made, however, they influence our interpretations of events. For example, when we see that investment rises, we normally think that our future productive capacity is rising, but remember that investment includes housing investment, which does not increase our future productive capacity. In fact, some types of consumption (say, purchases of personal computers by people who will become computer-literate and use their knowledge and skills to be

Q-10 How can some types of consumption increase our productive capacity by more than some types of investment?

more productive than they were before they owned computers) increase our productive capacity more than some types of investment.

Genuine Progress Indicator

Web Note 23.3
Measuring Welfare

The problems of national income accounting have led to a variety of measures of economic activity. One of the most interesting of these is the *genuine progress indicator (GPI)*, which makes a variety of adjustments to GDP so that it better measures the progress of society rather than simply economic activity. The GPI makes adjustments to GDP for changes in other social goals. For example, if pollution worsens, the GPI falls even though the GDP remains constant. Each of these adjustments requires someone to value these other social goals, and there is significant debate about how social goals should be valued. Advocates of the GPI agree that such valuations are difficult, but they argue that avoiding any such valuation, as is done with the GDP, implicitly values other social goals, such as having no pollution, at zero. Since some index will be used as an indicator of the progress of the economy, it is better to have an index that includes all social goals rather than an index of only economic activity.

Measurement is necessary, and the GDP measurements and categories have made it possible to think and talk about the aggregate economy.

By pointing out these problems, economists are not suggesting that national income accounting statistics should be thrown out. Far from it; measurement is necessary, and the GDP measurements and categories have made it possible to think and talk about the aggregate economy. I wouldn't have devoted an entire chapter of this book to national income accounting if I didn't believe it was important. I am simply arguing that national income accounting concepts should be used with sophistication, that is, with an awareness of their weaknesses as well as their strengths.

Conclusion

Used with that awareness, national income accounting is a powerful tool; you wouldn't want to be an economist without it. For those of you who aren't planning to be economists, it's still a good idea for you to understand the concepts of national income accounting. If you do, the business section of the newspaper will seem less like Greek to you. You'll be a more informed citizen and will be better able to make up your own mind about macroeconomic debates.

Summary

- National income accounting is a set of rules and definitions for measuring activity in the aggregate economy.
- GDP is the total market value of all final goods produced in an economy in one year. It's a flow, not a stock, measure of market activity.
- GDP describes the economic output produced within the physical borders of an economy, while GNP describes the economic output produced by the citizens of a country.
- Intermediate goods can be eliminated from GDP in two ways:
  1. By measuring only final sales.
  2. By measuring only value added.
- National income is directly related to national output. Whenever there's output, there's income.
- GDP is divided up into four types of expenditures:

  $$GDP = C + I + G + (X - M)$$

- NI = Compensation to employees + Rent + Interest + Profit.
- GDP plus net foreign factor income less depreciation less indirect business taxes equals national income.
- Personal income is all income received by individuals, and personal disposable income is personal income less personal taxes.
- Because GDP measures only market activities, GDP can be a poor measure of relative living standards among countries.
- To compare income over time, we must adjust for price-level changes. After adjusting for inflation, nominal measures are changed to "real" measures.
- Real GDP is the nominal GDP divided by the GDP deflator and multiplied by 100.
- National income accounting concepts are powerful tools for understanding macroeconomics, but we must recognize their limitations.
- GDP has its problems: GDP does not measure economic welfare; it does not include transactions in the underground economy; the price index used to calculate real GDP is problematic; subcategories of GDP are often interdependent.

Key Terms

depreciation *(525)*
disposable personal income *(529)*
final output *(520)*
government purchases *(525)*
gross domestic product (GDP) *(519)*
gross national product (GNP) *(519)*
gross private investment *(524)*
intermediate products *(521)*
national income (NI) *(527)*
national income accounting *(518)*
net domestic product (NDP) *(526)*
net exports *(526)*
net foreign factor income *(519)*
net private investment *(525)*
nominal GDP *(531)*
personal consumption expenditures *(524)*
personal income (PI) *(529)*
real GDP *(531)*
value added *(521)*
wealth accounts *(520)*

Questions for Thought and Review

1. Which will be larger, gross domestic product or gross national product?
2. If you add up all the transactions in an economy, do you arrive at GDP, GNP, or something else?
3. What's the relationship between a stock concept and a flow concept? Give an example that hasn't already been given in this chapter.
4. The United States is considering introducing a value added tax. What tax rate on value added is needed to get the same increase in revenue as is gotten from an income tax with a rate of 15 percent? Why?
5. If the United States introduces universal child care, what will likely happen to GDP? What are the welfare implications of that rise?
6. Economists normally talk about GDP even though they know NDP is a better measure of economic activity. Why?
7. What is the largest component of national income for most countries?
8. If the government increases transfer payments, what will happen to national income?
9. How does personal income differ from national income?
10. What is the difference between national personal income and domestic personal income?
11. If society's goal is to make people happier, and higher GDP isn't closely associated with being happier, why do economists even talk about GDP?

Problems and Exercises

1. There are three firms in an economy: A, B, and C. Firm A buys $250 worth of goods from firm B and $200 worth of goods from firm C, and produces 200 units of output, which it sells at $5 per unit. Firm B buys $100 worth of goods from firm A and $150 worth of goods from firm C, and produces 300 units of output, which it sells at $7 per unit. Firm C buys $50 worth of goods from firm A and nothing from firm B. It produces output worth $1,000. All other products are sold to consumers.
   a. Calculate GDP.
   b. If a value added tax (a tax on the total value added of each firm) of 10 percent is introduced, how much revenue will the government get?
   c. How much would government get if it introduced a 10 percent income tax?
   d. How much would government get if it introduced a 10 percent sales tax on final output?
2. State whether the following actions will increase or decrease GDP:
   a. The United States legalizes gay marriages.
   b. An individual sells her house on her own.
   c. An individual sells his house through a broker.
   d. Government increases Social Security payments.
   e. Stock prices rise by 20 percent.
   f. An unemployed worker gets a job.
3. Find personal consumption expenditures (as a percent of GDP) for the following countries. (Requires research.)
   a. Mexico
   b. Thailand
   c. Poland
   d. Nigeria
   e. Kuwait
4. You've been given the following data:

Transfer payments	$ 72
Interest paid by consumers	4
Net exports	4
Indirect business taxes	47
Net foreign factor income	2
Net non-business interest income	10
Contribution for social insurance	35
Personal taxes	91
Corporate retained earnings	51
Gross private investment	185
Government purchases	195
Personal consumption	500
Depreciation	59

   On the basis of these data calculate GDP, GNP, NDP, NI, personal income, and disposable personal income.

5. Given the following data about the economy:

Personal consumption	$700
Investment	500
Net non-business interest income	20
Government purchases	300
Profits	500
Wages	972
Net exports	275
Rents	25
Depreciation	25
Indirect business taxes	100
Corporate retained earnings	60
Net foreign factor income	−3
Interest	150
Social Security contribution	0
Transfer payments	0
Personal taxes	165

   a. Calculate GDP and GNP with both the expenditures approach and the income approach.
   b. Calculate NDP and NI.
   c. Calculate PI.
   d. Calculate disposable personal income.
6. You have been hired as a research assistant and are given the following data.

Compensation	$329
Consumption	370
Exports	55
Net foreign factor income	3
Government purchases	43
Gross investment	80
Imports	63
Indirect business taxes	27
Net interest	49
Profits	60
Rental income	1

   a. Calculate GNP, GDP, NDP, and NI.
   b. What is depreciation in this year?
   c. Right after you finish, your boss comes running in to you and tells you that she made a mistake. Imports were really $68 and compensation was $340. She tells you to get her the corrected answers to *a* and *b* immediately.

7. Below are nominal GDP and GDP deflators for four years.

Year	Nominal GDP	GDP Deflator
1998	$ 8,782	103.2
1999	9,274	104.7
2000	9,825	106.9
2001	10,082	109.4

   a. Calculate real GDP in each year.
   b. Did the percentage change in nominal GDP exceed the percentage change in real GDP in any of the last three years listed?
   c. In which year did society's welfare increase the most?

Web Questions

1. Find GDP for the most recent quarter from the home page of the Bureau of Economic Analysis at www.bea.doc.gov.
   a. What was consumption, investment, government consumption and investment, and net exports?
   b. What was nominal GDP? Real GDP?
   c. By how much did GDP increase? How much of the increase was due to an increase in the aggregate price level?
   d. Which of the components listed in *a* contributed the most to the change in GDP? Did any of the components move in opposite directions?
2. Some economists have proposed that we use the genuine progress indicator (GPI) rather than GDP as an indication of economic well-being. Using the information you find at the home page of Redefining Progress at www.rprogress.org answer the following questions:
   a. What is one category included in the GPI that suggests that GDP understates economic well-being?
   b. Name four categories included in the GPI that suggest that GDP overstates economic well-being. What is the largest of these categories?
   c. Has the GPI gone up or down during the most recent year for which there is data? What happened to GDP during that year?
3. Go to the United Nations Development Program at www.undp.org to find the most recent listing of countries' human development index (HDI) by looking at Human Development Reports to answer the following questions:
   a. What statistics are used to compose the HDI?
   b. Do the five countries with the highest HDI also have the greatest GDP per capita? Why do you think this is the case?
   c. What country has the highest discrepancy between its HDI ranking and GDP per capita? What accounts for the discrepancy?

Answers to Margin Questions

1. GDP measures the output of the residents of a country—the output within its geographical borders. GNP measures the output of the citizens and businesses of a country. Kuwait is a very rich country whose residents have a high income, much of it from investments overseas. Thus their GNP will be high. However, Kuwait also has large numbers of foreign workers who are not citizens and whose incomes would be included in GDP but not in GNP. In reality, Kuwait citizens' and businesses' foreign income exceeds foreign workers' and foreign companies' income within Kuwait, so Kuwait's GNP is greater than its GDP. *(519)*
2. Wealth accounts measure stocks—a country's assets and liabilities at a point in time. Income accounts measure flows—a country's income and expenditures over a period of time. *(520)*
3. Only the value added by the sale would be added to GDP. In this case the value added is the difference between the purchase price and the sale price, or $500. *(522)*
4. The government budget includes transfer payments, which are not included in GDP. Only those government expenditures that are for goods and services are included in GDP. *(523)*
5. GDP is the sum of consumption, gross private investment, and government purchases plus the total of exports minus imports, in this case 95. *(525)*
6. National income is the sum of employee compensation, rents, interest, and profits, in this case 198. *(527)*
7. In developing countries, individuals often grow their own food and take part in many activities that are not measured by the GDP statistics. The income figures that one

gets from the GDP statistics of developing countries do not include such activities and, thus, can be quite misleading. *(530)*

8. Nominal income must have risen $400 billion to slightly over $4.6 trillion so that, when it is adjusted for inflation, the real income will have risen to $4.2 trillion. *(531)*
9. Measurement errors occur in adjusting GDP figures for inflation because measuring inflation involves numerous arbitrary decisions such as choosing a base year, adjustment for quality changes in products, and weighting prices. *(533)*
10. Dividing goods into consumption and investment does not always capture the effect of the spending on productive capacity. For example, housing "investment" does little to expand the productive capacity. However, "consumption" of computers or books could expand the productive capacity significantly. *(534)*

24 GROWTH, PRODUCTIVITY, AND THE WEALTH OF NATIONS

After reading this chapter, you should be able to:

- Define growth and relate it to living standards.
- List five sources of growth.
- Distinguish diminishing marginal productivity from decreasing returns to scale.
- Distinguish Classical growth theory from new growth theory.
- List and discuss six government policies to promote growth.

Queen Elizabeth owned silk stockings. The capitalist achievement does not typically consist in providing more silk stockings for queens but in bringing them within the reach of factory girls in return for steadily decreasing amounts of effort.

—*Joseph Schumpeter*

Growth matters. In the long run, growth matters a lot. Thus, it is not surprising that modern economics began with a study of growth. In *The Wealth of Nations*, Adam Smith noted that what was good about market economies was that they raised society's standard of living. He argued that people's natural tendency to exchange and specialize allowed economies to grow.

As we discussed in Chapter 22, growth remained an important focus of economics through the 1920s as economists took a long-run perspective. The long-run perspective refers to the average rise in real output over a long period of time, which for the United States has been between 2.5 and 3.5 percent a year. Then, in the 1930s, the world economy fell into a serious depression. It was at that time that modern macroeconomics developed as a separate subject with a significant focus on short-run business cycles. It asked the questions "What causes depressions?" and "How does an economy get out of one?" Short-run macroeconomics became known as Keynesian economics, and remained the standard macroeconomics through the 1960s. Keynesian economics focuses on fluctuations around the growth trend and on whether those fluctuations influence that trend.

In the 1970s, as the memories of the Great Depression faded, the pendulum started to swing back again, and now, at the start of the 21st century, macroeconomists are taking a more balanced position, including both long-run growth and short-run business cycles as the core content of macro. In this chapter I consider long-run growth, and in later chapters, I examine business cycles and policies to deal with them.

GENERAL OBSERVATIONS ABOUT GROWTH

Before discussing the sources of growth, I want to make a number of general observations about growth.

Growth and the Economy's Potential Output

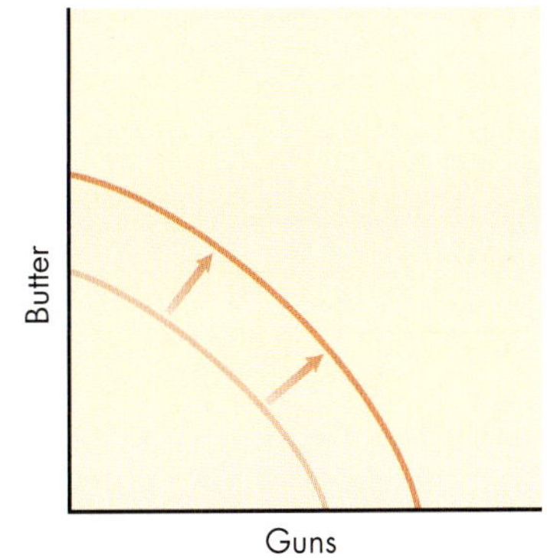

Growth is *an increase in the amount of goods and services an economy produces*. The study of growth is the study of why that increase comes about, assuming that both labor and capital are fully employed. Using the terminology from an earlier chapter, growth is an increase in **potential output**—*the highest amount of output an economy can produce from the existing production function and the existing resources*. (Recall that *potential output* can also be called *potential income* because, in the aggregate, income and output are identical.) One way to think about growth and potential output is to relate them to the production possibility curve, presented in Chapter 2. That curve gave us a picture of the choices an economy faces given available resources. When an economy is at its potential output, it is operating on its production possibility curve. When an economy is below its potential output, it is operating inside its production possibility curve. The analysis of growth focuses on the forces that shift out the production possibility curve.

The analysis of growth focuses on forces that shift out the production possibility curve.

Why do we use potential output in macro rather than the production possibility curve? Because macro focuses on aggregate output—GDP—and does not focus on the choices of dividing up GDP among alternative products as does micro and the production possibility curve. But the concept is the same. Potential output is a barrier beyond which an economy cannot expand without either increasing available factors of production or increasing **productivity** *(output per unit of input)*.

Q-1 How does long-run growth analysis justify its focus on supply?

Long-run growth analysis focuses on supply; it assumes demand is sufficient to buy whatever is supplied. That assumption is called **Say's law** *(supply creates its own demand)*, named after a French economist, Jean Baptiste Say, who first pointed it out. The reasoning behind Say's law is as follows: People work and supply goods to the market because they want other goods. The very fact that they supply goods means that they demand goods of equal value. According to Say's law, aggregate demand will always equal aggregate supply.

In the short run economists consider potential output fixed; they focus on how to get the economy operating at its potential if, for some reason, it is not. In the long run, economists consider an economy's potential output changeable. Growth analysis is a consideration of why an economy's potential shifts out, and growth policy is aimed at increasing an economy's potential output.

The Importance of Growth for Living Standards

Growth in income improves lives by fulfilling basic needs and making more goods available to more people.

Growth makes an enormous difference for living standards. Take France and Argentina as examples. In the 1950s per capita income was about $5,000 in each country, but their growth rates differed. From 1950 to 2000, France's income grew at an average rate of 3 percent per year while Argentina's grew at an average rate of 1 percent per year. Because of the differences in growth rates, France's per capita income is now over $24,000 and Argentina's per capita income is about $7,000. The difference in income levels translates into very real differences in the quality of life. For example, in France 100 percent of the people have access to safe water; in Argentina only 79 percent have such access. In France there are 546 phones per 1,000 people; in Argentina there are 174 phones per 1,000 people.

Other examples are South Korea and the Congo. In the 1950s their incomes were also nearly identical, at $150 per person. Because of differing growth rates, Korea's per capita income has multiplied more than 60 times, to about $10,000, while the Congo's per capita income is still $150. Why? Because the Congo has a zero growth rate while Korea has averaged a 9 percent annual growth rate. The moral of these stories: In the long run growth rates matter a lot.

Is Growth Good?

Beyond the Tools

The discussion in the chapter emphasizes the generally held view among economists that growth is inherently good. It increases our incomes, thereby improving our standard of living. But that does not mean that all economists support unlimited growth. Growth has costs, and economics requires us to look at both costs and benefits. For example, growth may contribute to increased pollution—reducing the quality of the air we breathe and the water we drink, and endangering the variety of species in the world. In short, the wrong type of growth may produce undesirable side effects including global warming and polluted rivers, land, and air.

New technology, upon which growth depends, also raises serious moral questions: Do we want to replace sexual reproduction with cloning? Will a brain implant be an improvement over 12 years of education? Will selecting your baby's genetic makeup be better than relying on nature? Just because growth *can* continue does not mean that it *should* continue. Moral judgments can be made against growth. For example, some argue that growth changes traditional cultures with beautiful handiwork, music, and dance into cultures of gadgets where people have lost touch with what is important. They argue that we have enough gadgets cluttering our lives and that it is time to start focusing on non-economic priorities.

This moral argument against growth carries the most weight in highly developed countries—countries with per capita incomes of at least $20,000 a year. For developing countries, where per capita income can be as low as $150 per year, the reality is the choice between growth or poverty or even between growth or starvation. In these countries it is difficult to argue against growth.

One final comment: The benefits of growth do not have to be just higher incomes and more gadgets. They could also include more leisure activities and improved working conditions. In the 19th century a 12-hour workday was common. Today the workday is eight hours, but had we been content with a lower income the workday could now be two hours, with the remainder left for free time. We'd have less growth in GDP, but we'd have a lot more time to play.

Small differences in growth rates can mean huge differences in income levels because of *compounding*. Compounding means that growth is based not only on the original level of income but also on the accumulation of previous-year increases in income. For example, say you start at $100 and your income grows at a rate of 10 percent each year; the first year your income grows by $10, to $110. The second year the same growth rate increases income by $11, to $121. Then, the third year income grows by $12.10, which is still 10 percent but is a larger total increase. After 50 years that same 10 percent means an increase of over $70 a year.

Q-2 If an economy is growing at 4 percent a year, how long will it take for its income to double?

Another way to see the effects of the difference in growth rates is to see how long it would take income to double at different growth rates. The Rule of 72 tells you that. The **Rule of 72** states: *The number of years it takes for a certain amount to double in value is equal to 72 divided by its annual rate of increase*. For example, if Argentina's income grows at a 1 percent annual rate, it will double in 72 years (72/1). If France's income grows at a 3 percent annual rate, it will double in only 24 years (72/3).

Markets, Specialization, and Growth

Specialization and the division of labor that accompany markets increase productivity and growth.

One of the facts about growth mentioned in Chapter 22 is that growth began when markets developed, and then, as markets expanded, growth accelerated. Why are markets so important to growth? To answer that question let's go back to Adam Smith's argument for markets. Smith argued that markets allow **specialization** *(the concentration of individuals on certain aspects of production)* and **division of labor** *(the splitting up of a task to allow for specialization of production)*. According to Smith, markets create an interdependent economy in which individuals can take advantage of the benefits of specialization and trade for their other needs. In doing so markets increase productivity—and, in turn, improve the standard of living.

You saw in Chapter 2 how comparative advantage and specialization increase productivity. If individuals concentrate on the production of goods for which their skills and other resources are suited, and trade for those goods for which they do not have a comparative advantage, the economy's combined production possibility curve shifts out. To see this even more clearly, consider what your life would be like without markets, trade, and specialization. You would have to grow all your food, build your own living space, and provide all your own transportation. Simply to exist under these conditions, you'd need a lot of skills, and it is unlikely that you'd become sufficiently adept in any one of them to provide yourself with anything other than the basics. You'd have all you could do to keep up.

Now consider your life today with specialization. Someone who specializes in dairy farming produces the milk you need. You don't need to know how it is produced, just where to buy it. How about transportation? You buy, not build, your car. It runs somehow—you're not quite sure how—but if it breaks down, you take it to a garage. And consider your education: Are you learning how to grow food or build a house? No, you are probably learning a specific skill that has little relevance to the production of most goods. But you'll most likely provide some good or service that will benefit the dairy farmer and auto mechanic. You get the picture—for most of the things you consume you don't have the faintest idea who makes them or how they are made, nor do you need to know.

Economic Growth, Distribution, and Markets

Markets and growth are often seen as unfair with regard to the distribution of income. Is it fair that markets give some individuals so much (billions to Bill Gates), and others so little ($5.60 an hour to Joe Wall, who has a minimum wage job and two kids)? Such questions are legitimate and need to be asked. But in answering them we should also remember the quotation from Joseph Schumpeter that opened this chapter: Even if markets and growth do not provide equality, they tend to make the poor better off. The relevant question is: Would the poor be better off with or without markets and growth?

Even though growth isn't evenly distributed, it generally raises the incomes of the poor.

There are strong arguments, based on historical evidence, that people are better off with markets. Consider the number of hours an average person must work to buy certain goods at various periods in U.S. history. A century ago it took a worker 1 hour and 41 minutes to earn enough to buy a pair of stockings; today it takes only 18 minutes of work. Figure 24-1 gives a number of other examples. As you can see from the figure, growth has made average workers significantly better off; to get the same amount, they have to work far less now than they did in the past. Growth has also made new products available. For example, before 1952 air-conditioners were not available at any price.

The reality is that, judged from an *absolute* standard, the poor benefit enormously from the growth that markets foster. Markets, through competition, make the factors of production more productive and lower the cost of goods, making more goods available to everyone. Today, the U.S. poverty level for a family of four is about $18,000. If we go back 100 years in U.S. history, and adjust for inflation, that $18,000 income would put a family in the upper middle class. Markets and growth have made that possible.

The above argument does not mean that the poor always benefit from growth; many of us judge our well-being by relative, not absolute, standards. By reducing the share of income earned by the poorest proportion of society, growth often makes the poor *relatively* worse off. So, if one uses relative standards, one could say that the poor have become worse off over certain periods. Moreover, it is not at all clear that markets require

Just because the poor benefit from growth does not mean they might not be better off if income were distributed more in their favor.

Figure 24-1 Cost of Goods in Hours of Work Growth in the U.S. economy in the past century has reduced the number of hours the average person needs to work to buy consumer goods.

Source: Federal Reserve Bank of Dallas, *Time Well Spent* (1997 annual report).

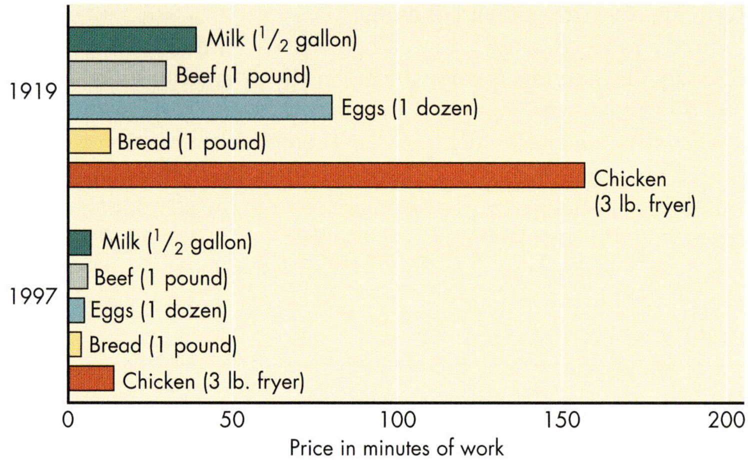

the large differentials in pay that have accompanied growth in market economies. If such large differentials did not exist, and growth had been at the same rate, the poor would be even better off than they are.

PER CAPITA GROWTH

So far the discussion of growth has focused on increases in total output. Another important measure to consider is per capita output, or total output divided by the total population. Let's look at an example. In China 1.3 billion people produce $5.6 trillion worth of goods and services. Per capita output is $4,300 ($5.6 trillion divided by 1.3 billion). The U.S. economy, producing $10.4 trillion of output, is nearly twice as large as China's economy. The United States, however, has only 290 million people. Its per capita output is over $35,000, nearly 9 times that of China. **Per capita growth** means *producing more goods and services per person*. For example, say the real output of the economy is $4 billion and that there are 1 million people. Each person, on average, has $4,000 to spend. Now say output increases by 50 percent but population also increases by 50 percent. There has been growth in output, but not in per capita output; each person still has only $4,000 to spend. The reality is that even though many developing countries' economies have grown faster than that of the United States, their populations grew even faster so their per capita output growth has been lower.

If you know the percentage change in output and percentage change in population, you can calculate per capita growth:

Per capita growth = % change in output − % change in population

Q-3 Which country has experienced higher growth per capita: country A, whose economy is growing at a 4 percent rate and whose population is growing at a 3 percent rate, or country B, whose economy is growing at a 3 percent rate and whose population is growing at a 1 percent rate?

Let's consider two examples. In 2000, the Angolan economy grew 2 percent but the population grew 3 percent. Per capita growth equaled −1 percent (2 − 3). In that same year in Hungary, output rose 5.2 percent and the population declined 0.3 percent. Per capita growth equaled 5.5 percent [5.2 − (−0.3)].

Some economists have argued that per capita output is not what we should be focusing on; they suggest that a better measure would be median income. (Remember, income and output are the same.) Per capita output measures the average, or *mean*, income. The *median* income, in contrast, is the income level that divides the population in equal halves. Half the people earn more and half the people earn less than the median income. In 2001 median income per household in the United States was $42,228. Half of all households earned less than $42,228, and half earned more.

Why focus on median income? Because it takes into account how income is distributed. If the growth in income goes to a small minority of individuals who already receive the majority of income, the mean will rise but the median will not. Let's consider an example where there is a large difference between the two measures. Say that the incomes of five people in a five-person economy are $20,000; $20,000; $30,000; $120,000; and $450,000. The median income is $30,000 (the middle income with two above and two below); the mean income is $128,000. Now say that the economy grows but that the two richest people get all the benefits, raising their incomes to $150,000 and $500,000, respectively. The median income remains $30,000; the mean income rises to $144,000. Unfortunately statistics on median income are often not collected, so I will follow convention and focus on the mean, or per capita, income.

Q-4 How would increases in income have to be distributed for the median to remain constant and the mean income to rise?

Whether you're looking at per capita or median income, growth provides more goods and services for the people in an economy, allowing society to sidestep the more difficult issues of how those goods are distributed. That's why policymakers are interested in knowing what makes an economy grow.

The Sources of Growth

Economists have determined five important sources of growth:

1. Capital accumulation—investment in productive capacity.
2. Available resources.
3. Growth-compatible institutions.
4. Technological development.
5. Entrepreneurship.

Let's consider each in turn.

Investment and Accumulated Capital

At one point, capital accumulation (where capital was thought of as just *physical capital*) and investment were seen as the key elements in growth. Physical capital includes both private capital—buildings and machines available for production—and public capital—infrastructure such as highways and water supply. The *flow* of investment leads to the growth of the *stock* of capital. While physical capital is still considered a key element in growth, it is now generally recognized that the growth recipe is far more complicated. One of the reasons for the de-emphasis on capital accumulation is that empirical evidence has suggested that capital accumulation doesn't necessarily lead to growth. For instance, the former Soviet Union invested a lot and accumulated lots of capital goods, but its economy didn't grow much because its capital was often internationally obsolete. Another reason is that products change, and buildings and machines useful in one time period may be useless in another (e.g., a six-year-old computer often is worthless). The value of the capital stock depends on its future expected earnings, which are very uncertain. Capital's role in growth is extraordinarily difficult to measure with accuracy.

A third reason for this de-emphasis on capital accumulation is that it has become clear that capital includes much more than machines. In addition to physical capital, modern economics includes **human capital** (*the skills that are embodied in workers through experience, education, and on-the-job training*, or more simply, people's knowledge) and **social capital** (*the habitual way of doing things that guides people in how they approach production*) as types of capital. The importance of human capital is obvious: A skilled labor force is far more productive than an unskilled labor force. Social capital is embodied in institutions such as the government, the legal system, and the fabric of society. In a way,

There are three types of capital:

1. Physical capital.
2. Social capital.
3. Human capital.

anything that contributes to growth can be called a type of capital, and anything that slows growth can be called a destroyer of capital. With the concept of capital including such a wide range of things, it is difficult to say what is not capital, which makes the concept of capital less useful.

Web Note 24.1
Social Capital

Despite this modern de-emphasis on investment and physical capital, all economists agree that the right kind of investment at the right time is a central element of growth. If an economy is to grow it must invest. The debate is about what kinds and what times are the right ones.

Available Resources

If an economy is to grow it will need resources. England grew in the late 1700s because it had iron and coal; the United States grew in the 20th century because it had a major supply of many natural resources, and it imported people, a resource it needed.

What is a resource depends on the production processes of an economy and technology.

Of course, you have to be careful in thinking about what is considered a resource. A resource in one time period may not be a resource in another. For example, at one time oil was simply black gooey stuff that made land unusable. When people learned that the black gooey stuff could be burned as fuel, oil became a resource. What's considered a resource depends on technology. If solar technology is ever perfected, oil will go back to being black gooey stuff. So creativity can replace resources, and if you develop new technology fast enough, you can overcome almost any lack of existing resources. Even if a country doesn't have the physical resources it needs for growth, it can import them—as did Japan following World War II.

Greater participation in the market is another means by which to increase available resources. In China at the end of the 20th century, for example, many individuals migrated into the southern provinces, which have free trade sectors. Before they migrated they were only marginally involved in the market economy. After they migrated they became employed in the market economy. This increased the labor available to the market, helping push up China's growth rate. In the United States beginning in the 1950s, the percentage of women entering the workforce increased, contributing to economic growth.

Increasing the labor force participation rate is not a totally costless way of increasing growth. We lose whatever people were doing before they joined the labor force (which was, presumably, something of value to society). Our national income accounting figures, which are measures of market activity, simply do not measure such losses.

Growth-Compatible Institutions

Throughout this book I have emphasized the importance of economic institutions, which are vitally necessary for growth. Growth-compatible institutions—institutions that foster growth—must have incentives built into them that lead people to put forth effort and discourage people from spending a lot of their time in leisure pursuits or creating impediments for others to gain income for themselves.

Q.5 Why is private property a source of growth?

When individuals get much of the gains of growth themselves, they have incentives to work harder. That's why markets and private ownership of property play an important role in growth. In the former Soviet Union, individuals didn't gain much from their own initiative and, hence, often spent their time in pursuits other than those that would foster measured economic growth. Another growth-compatible institution is the corporation, a legal institution that gives owners limited liability and thereby encourages large enterprises (because people are more willing to invest their savings when their potential losses are limited).

Many developing countries follow a type of mercantilist policy in which government must approve any new economic activity. Some government officials get a large portion of their income from bribes offered to them by individuals who want to undertake economic activity. Such policies inhibit economic growth. Many regulations, even reasonable ones, also tend to inhibit economic growth because they inhibit entrepreneurial activities. But we should recall that some regulation is necessary to ensure that the growth is of a socially desirable type. The policy problem is in deciding between necessary and unnecessary regulation.

Technological Development

Advances in technology shift the production possibility curve out by making workers more productive. Technological advances increase their ability to produce more of the things they already produce but also allow them to produce new and different products.

To think of growth as getting more of the same things is to take an incomplete view. While in some ways growth involves more of the same, a much larger aspect of growth involves changes in **technology**—changes in *the way we make goods and supply services* and changes in the goods and services we buy. Think of what this generation spends its income on—CDs, cars, computers, fast food—and compare that to what the preceding generation spent money on—LP records, cars that would now be considered obsolete, and tube and transistor radios. (When I was 11, I saved $30—the equivalent of over $100 now—so I could afford a six-transistor Motorola radio; personal computers didn't exist.)

Growth isn't just getting more of the same thing. It's also getting some things that are different.

Contrast today's goods with the goods the next generation might spend its income on: video brain implants (little gadgets in your head to receive sound and full-vision broadcasts—you simply close your eyes and tune in whatever you want, if you've paid your cellular fee for that month); fuel-cell-powered cars (gas cars will be considered quaint but polluting); and instant food (little pills that fulfill all your nutritional needs, letting your video brain implant supply all the ambiance). Just imagine! You probably can get the picture, even without a video brain implant.

How does society get people to work on developments that may change the very nature of what we do and how we think? One way is through economic incentives; another is with institutions that foster creativity and bold thinking—like this book; a third is through institutions that foster hard work. There are, of course, trade-offs. For example, the Japanese educational system, which fosters hard work and discipline, doesn't do as good a job at fostering creativity as the U.S. educational system, and vice versa. Thus, many of the new technologies of the 1980s were thought up in the United States but translated into workable products in Japan. For example, the transistor was developed in the United States, but Japan integrated it into competitive electronic products.

Still, the United States has done well on the technology front. Important developments in biotechnology, computers, and communications have occurred in the United States, and those developments helped fuel recent growth. Those new industries were much slower to develop in another important U.S. competitor, the European Union, which is one important reason why EU countries have grown far more slowly than has the United States in recent years.

Five sources of growth are:

1. Capital accumulation.
2. Available resources.
3. Growth-compatible institutions.
4. Technological development.
5. Entrepreneurship.

Entrepreneurship

Entrepreneurship is the ability to get things done. That ability involves creativity, vision, willingness to accept risk, and a talent for translating that vision into reality. Entrepreneurs have been central to growth in the United States. They have created large companies, produced new products, and transformed the landscape of the economy. Examples of entrepreneurs include Thomas Edison, who revolutionized the generation and use of electricity in the late 1800s; Henry Ford, who revolutionized transportation in the early 1900s; and Bill Gates, who led Microsoft as it transformed

Growth and Terrorism

Applying the Tools

When talking about the costs of terrorism, many focus on the short-term effects—the tremendous cost in destruction of property and loss of life. But, according to a study by the Organization for Economic Coordination and Development, there are also long-term effects on growth, which may be less dramatic but even more costly. The study points out that the reaction to the terrorist attack of September 11, 2001:

- Caused significant increases in insurance premiums, increasing costs and making firms less likely to undertake new projects.
- Made it impossible to get insurance for a number of projects, stopping these projects altogether.
- Increased transportation costs because of increased security.
- Slowed international trade because of security, making it impossible to get goods when they were needed, forcing firms to hold more inventory and increasing costs.
- Caused firms to spend more on security, lowering productivity.

Each of these effects contributed to slower growth by reducing the sources of growth. The terrorist attacks acted like sand in the wheels of trade, reduced expenditures on capital, lowered productivity, and reduced start-ups by entrepreneurs. The end result is hundreds of billions of dollars of lost output. The cost will be especially great for many Muslim countries, making it especially difficult for these countries to tie into the global economy.

and dominated the computer industry. When a country's population demonstrates entrepreneurship, it can overcome deficiencies in other ingredients that contribute to growth.

Turning the Sources of Growth into Growth

The five sources of growth cannot be taken as givens. Even if all five ingredients exist, they may not exist in the right proportions. For example, economic growth depends upon people's saving and investing rather than consuming their income. Investing now helps create machines that in the future can be used to produce more output with less effort. Growth also depends upon technological change—finding new, better ways to do things. For instance, when Nicolas Appert discovered canning (storing food in a sealed container in such a way that it wouldn't spoil) in the early 19th century, the economic possibilities of society expanded enormously. But if, when technological developments occur, the savings aren't there to finance the investment, the result will not be growth. It is finding the right combination of the sources of growth that plays a central role in the growth of any economy.

The Production Function and Theories of Growth

The production function shows the relationship between the quantity of inputs used in production and the quantity of output resulting from production.

To try to get a better handle on the sources of growth, economists have developed a number of theories of growth. These have centered around the **production function,** an abstraction that shows *the relationship between the quantity of inputs used in production and the quantity of output resulting from production*. The production function we shall use is the following:

Output = A · *f*(Labor, Capital, Land)

This production function has land, labor, and capital as factors of production, and an adjustment factor A to capture the effect of changes in technology. The adjustment factor is outside the production function since it can affect the production of all factors. (The *f* stands for "function of.") The production function emphasizes the sources of growth: entrepreneurship is captured by labor, available resources by land, capital accumulation by capital, and technology and institutions by the production function itself.

Describing Production Functions

In talking about production functions economists use a couple of important terms. The first describes what happens when all inputs increase equally—this is called *scale economies*. Scale economies describe what happens to output if all inputs increase by the same percentage. Say the amount of labor, land, and capital is doubled. What happens to output? If output also doubles, economists say that the production function exhibits **constant returns to scale,** which means that *output will rise by the same proportionate increase as all inputs*. With constant returns to scale, if all inputs rise by, say, 10 percent, output will also rise by 10 percent. When *output rises by a greater proportionate increase than all inputs*, there are **increasing returns to scale;** and, when *output rises by a smaller proportionate increase as all inputs*, there are **decreasing returns to scale.**

The second term describes what happens when more of one input is added without increasing any other inputs. This case follows the **law of diminishing marginal productivity** *(increasing one input, keeping all others constant, will lead to smaller and smaller gains in output)*. You were introduced to the law of diminishing marginal productivity in Chapter 2 when we discussed the production possibility curve. It is also known as the principle of increasing marginal opportunity cost, or the flowerpot law. (If you keep adding seeds to a flowerpot, you will, past a certain point, get fewer and fewer flowers. See page 26 for a review.)

Q-6 True or false? If you can increase production 10 percent by increasing all inputs 20 percent, the production process exhibits diminishing marginal productivity.

The law of diminishing marginal productivity applies to increases in any input, holding the others constant. As you put more and more laborers on a fixed plot of land, the increase in output contributed by each additional worker falls; eventually workers will get into each other's way and not only will the output per worker decline but so too will total output. The same goes for capital. The first computer will help a secretary prepare documents more quickly. A second might help, too, but less so than the first. A third would clutter the office.

The Standard Theory of Growth—the Classical Growth Model

Classical economists recognized that all the above factors contributed to growth, but (as mentioned earlier in this chapter) their models of growth focused on capital accumulation. The **Classical growth model** is *a model of growth that focuses on the role of capital accumulation in the growth process*. The Classical economists' major policy conclusion was: The more capital an economy has, the faster it will grow. This focus on capital is what caused market economies to be called *capitalist economies*.

Since investment leads to the increase in capital, Classical economists focused their analysis, and their policy advice, on how to increase investment. The way to do that was for people to save:

Saving → Investment → Increase in capital → Growth

Saving, investment, and capital are central to the Classical growth model.

According to the Classical growth model, if an economy wants to grow, it has to save; the more saving, the better. Saving was good for both private individuals and

Figure 24-2 Diminishing Returns and Population Growth
This production function exhibits diminishing marginal productivity of labor. Because of diminishing marginal productivity, per capita income declines as the labor supply increases. As output per person declines, at some point output available per person is no longer sufficient to feed the population.

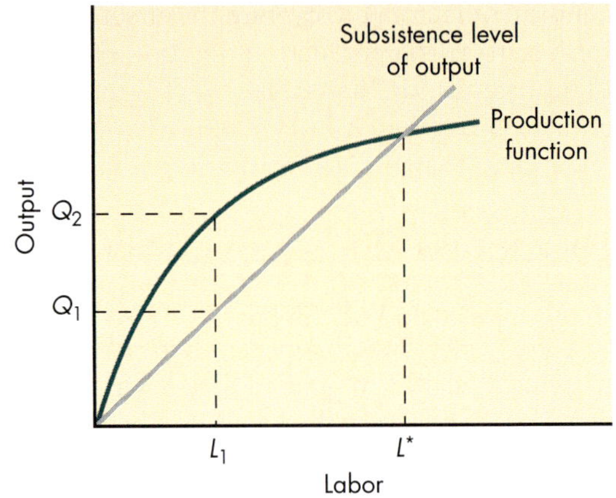

governments. Thus, Classical economists objected to government deficits, which occur when government spends more than it collects in taxes. (This view of deficits and saving was directly challenged by Keynes in the 1930s, as we will see in the next chapter.)

Focus on Diminishing Marginal Productivity of Labor The early economists also focused on the law of diminishing marginal productivity. In the 1800s, when farming was the major activity of the economy, economists such as Thomas Malthus emphasized the limitations land placed on growth. They predicted that since land was relatively fixed, as the population grew diminishing marginal productivity would set in. Figure 24-2 shows a production function exhibiting diminishing marginal productivity.

Since each additional worker adds less output to production than the individual before, the production function is bowed downward. Output rises as the number of laborers increases, but it does not keep pace with increases in labor. Because of diminishing marginal productivity, per capita income declines as the labor supply increases. As output per person declines, at some point output available is no longer sufficient to feed the population.

Q-7 If individuals suddenly needed less food to subsist, what would happen, according to the Classical growth model?

In Figure 24-2 the straight line, labeled *subsistence level of output*, shows the minimum amount of output necessary to feed the labor force L. For example, at L_1, output is Q_2 and the minimum level of income for subsistence is Q_1. There is a surplus of $Q_2 - Q_1$. At L^* output is at its subsistence level. There is no surplus. Beyond L^* income falls below subsistence. If the population grows beyond L^*, some people would starve to death and the population would decline. Classical economists argued that the economy would be driven to point L^* in the long run, because whenever there was a surplus, workers would have more children, increasing the labor supply. This belief, called the *iron law of wages*, combined with the diminishing marginal productivity, led to the conclusion that in the long run there was no surplus and no growth. They called the long run the *stationary state*.

Technological progress and increases in capital have overwhelmed diminishing marginal productivity of labor.

Focus on Diminishing Marginal Productivity of Capital The Classical economists' predictions were wrong. Per capita output did grow because of technological progress and increases in capital. Increases in technology and capital overwhelmed the law of diminishing marginal productivity and eventually economists no longer saw land as a constraint. Modern economists, such as Robert Solow, then changed the focus of the law of diminishing marginal productivity from land to capital. They argued that as capital grew faster than labor, capital would become less productive and lead to slower and slower growth; eventually the per capita growth of our economy would stagnate. The economy could still grow if labor increased at the same rate as capital, but output would not grow any faster than the growth of the population. That is, per capita income would not grow.

The Classical growth model also predicted that as countries get more capital and become richer, their growth rates would slow down. Thus, poorer countries with little capital (such as the Latin American countries) should grow faster than richer countries with lots of capital (such as the United States). Why? Because diminishing marginal productivity would be stronger for richer countries with lots of capital than for poorer countries with little capital. Eventually per capita incomes among countries should converge.

These predictions have not come true either. As we saw in an earlier chapter, growth rates have increased, not decreased, and relative income levels of rich and poor countries have in many cases diverged, not converged. This difference between the observed reality and the predictions of the model caused economists to study the growth process empirically. Why doesn't the theory match the reality? Economists came up with two answers: ambiguity in the definition of the factors of production, and technological progress.

Ambiguities in the Definition of the Factors of Production On the surface the terms in the production function seem relatively straightforward, but in reality they involve enormous ambiguity. I will focus on one important ambiguity—precisely what we mean by *labor*. As an input in production, labor may seem rather simple—it is the hours of work that go into production. As a first approximation that is what economists use as their measure of labor input. But labor is much more than the number of hours worked or the number of people working. The measure of labor needs adjustments to capture the skills, education, experience, and effort that laborers bring to production. These adjustments mean that measuring labor, and comparing the measurements among different countries, is difficult.

Here's an example of the type of problem that develops: Both Bangladesh and Japan have populations of about 130 million, but the average worker in Japan has more education than the average worker in Bangladesh. Do we increase the labor measured in Japan to account for that country's higher education? Generally, economists do so by separating labor into two components: standard labor (the actual number of workers or hours worked) and human capital (the skills that are embodied in workers through experience, education, and on-the-job training). Human capital gives us a measure for comparing the relative productivity of different workers. Thus, for example, when a society increases the amount of education it provides its workers, the country's human capital increases, even though labor hours may not increase.

Notice how modifying the definition of *labor* to emphasize human capital provides a possible answer for the Classical growth model's incorrect predictions. If labor skills can be continually increasing, there is no need for physical capital to exhibit diminishing marginal productivity. The labor force might be growing at 5 percent, and capital at 7 percent, but the human capital measure of labor may be also increasing at 2 percent, so no diminishing marginal productivity should be expected and per capita output will rise. A variation of this argument can be used to explain why incomes between poor and rich countries have not converged. If skills in rich countries are increasing at a faster rate than skills in poor countries, incomes would not be expected to converge.

Increases in human capital have allowed labor to keep pace with capital, allowing economies to avoid the diminishing productivity of capital.

Technology An additional explanation for the failure of the Classical growth model to accurately predict our growth experience is that we are continually finding new and better ways of doing things. Technology has developed, and is growing, faster in rich

Is the 21st Century the Age of Technology or One of Many Ages of Technology?

Applying the Tools

Sometimes newspapers write as if the importance of technology to the economy in the 21st century is a new phenomenon. It is not. Technology has been changing our society for the last two centuries, and it is not at all clear that the technological changes we are currently experiencing are any more revolutionary than those experienced by other generations in the last 200 years. For example, in terms of its impact on people's lives and communications in general, the Internet is small potatoes compared to the phone system.

One economist who recognized the importance of technology was Joseph Schumpeter. Schumpeter emphasized the role of the entrepreneur. He argued that entrepreneurs create major technological changes that drive the economy forward.

According to Schumpeter, the economy's growth depends on these entrepreneurs, and the industries they are in will be the leading industries, pulling the rest of the economy along after them. The accompanying figure lists five waves of technological innovation that have driven our economy. As you can see, in the late 1700s steam power and iron manufacturing were the driving forces. In the 1860s, railroads were the dynamic industry. Later, electronics, automobiles, and chemicals drove our economy. In the 1980s through the early 21st century, computers and biotechnology have been the leading industries.

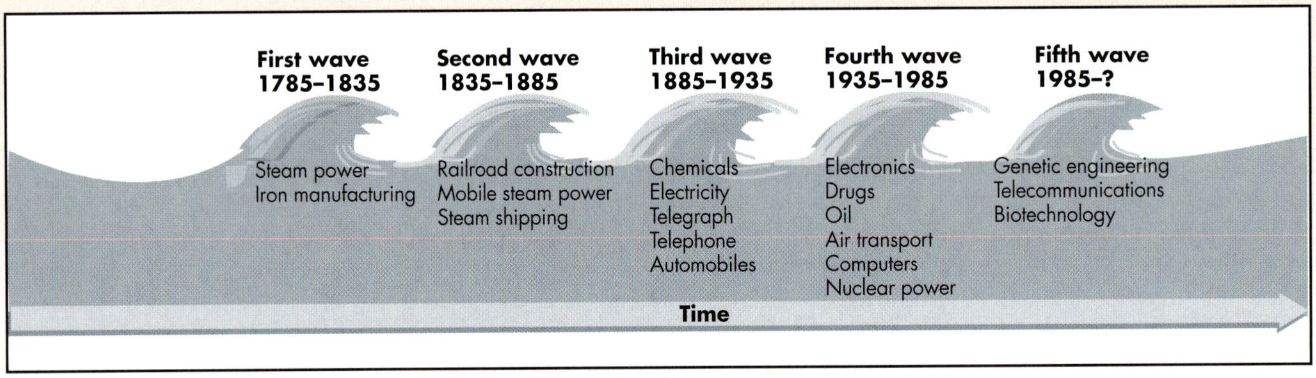

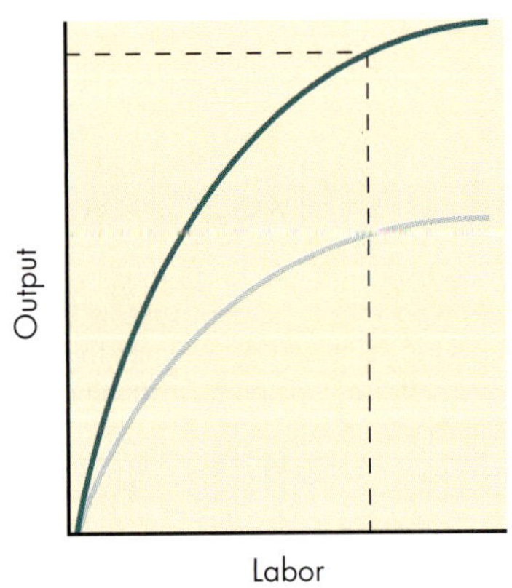

Technological growth shifts the production function up.

countries than in poor countries. If technology grows, it increases the productivity of all inputs and allows growth to continue. In terms of the production function, technology shifts the production function up, as shown in the margin here, so that more can be produced at every quantity of labor. If technology grows faster than the diminishing marginal productivity of new capital, and grows faster over time, growth for all practical purposes has no limit. Technology overwhelms diminishing marginal productivity and growth rates increase over time: the economy gets richer and richer. Although the Classical model acknowledged the role of technology in growth, it took technology as given—determined outside the model. It did not explain what causes technology to grow.

Empirical Estimates of Factor Contribution to Growth To determine which of these explanations was most probable, economist Edward Denison estimated the importance of each of the sources of growth for many countries, including the United States.

These estimates, shown in Figure 24-3, suggest that increases in labor account for 33 percent, increases in physical capital account for 19 percent, increases in human

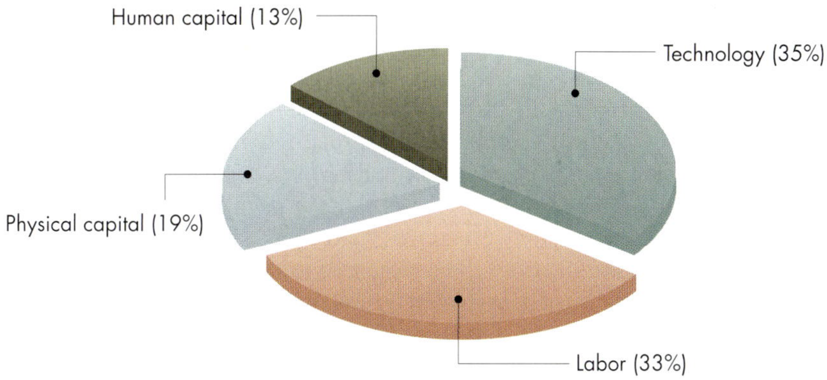

Figure 24-3 Sources of Real U.S. GDP Growth, 1928–2000
Technology accounts for the majority of growth in the United States, followed closely by increases in labor.

Source: Edward F. Denison, *Trends in Economic Growth, 1928–82* (Washington, D.C.: The Brookings Institution, 1985), and author estimates.

capital account for 13 percent, and advances in technology account for the remaining 35 percent of growth. (Land does not appear in Denison's estimates; countries are assumed to be endowed with a given amount of land and natural resources.) While the specific percentages are at best rough, the importance of technology to growth is not. It is for that reason that modern economic thinking about growth has focused more and more on technology.

New Growth Theory

Modern growth theory goes under the name *new growth theory*. Because technology is now recognized as an important ingredient to growth, modern growth theorists have made technology central to their analysis. They look for what makes technology grow. Thus, **new growth theory** is *a theory that emphasizes the role of technology rather than capital in the growth process*. Increases in technology shift the production possibility curve out, and thus make the choices an economy faces a bit easier to make—they allow the society to get more of everything. Unlike Classical growth theory, which left technology outside of economic analysis, new growth theory focuses its analysis on technology.

New growth theory emphasizes technology as the primary source of growth.

Web Note 24.2
A New Growth Theorist

Technology New growth theory's central argument is that increases in technology do not just happen. Technological advance is the result of what the economy does—it invests in research and development (e.g., drug companies researching new ways to fight disease); makes advances in pure science (e.g., the human genome project); and works out new ways to organize production (e.g., just-in-time inventory techniques). Thus, in a sense, investment in technology increases the technological stock of an economy just as investment in capital increases the capital stock of an economy. Investment in technology is called research and development; firms hire researchers to explore options. Some of those options pay off and others do not, but the net return of that investment in technology is an increase in technology.

If investment in technology is similar to investment in capital, why does new growth theory separate the two? The reason is twofold. First, increases in technology are not as directly linked to investment as capital is. Increases in investment require increases in saving, that is, building the capital. Increases in technology can occur with little investment and saving if the proverbial light bulb goes off in someone's head and that person sees a new way of doing something.

Second, increases in technology often have enormous positive spillover effects, especially if the new technology involves common knowledge and is freely available to all. A technological gain in one sector of production gives other sectors of production new ideas on how to change what they are doing, which gives other people new ideas. Ideas spread like pool balls after the break. One hits another, and soon all the nearby balls have moved. Put in technical economic terms, technological change often has significant **positive externalities**—*positive effects on others not taken into account by the decision maker.* Through those externalities, what is called general purpose technological change can have a much larger effect on growth than can an increase in capital.

The common knowledge aspect of technology creates positive externalities, which new growth theory sees as the key to growth.

The positive externalities result from the *common knowledge* aspect of technology because the idea behind the technology can often be used by others without payment to the developer. Using the same assembly line for different car models is just one example of a technological advance that has become incorporated into common knowledge. Any car manufacturer can use it.

Basic research is not always freely available; it is often protected by **patents**—*legal ownership of a technological innovation that gives the owner of the patent sole rights to its use and distribution for a limited time.* (If the development is an idea rather than a good, it can be copyrighted rather than patented, but the general concept is the same.) Patents turn innovations into private property. The Windows operating system is an example of a technology that is owned, and hence is not common knowledge. The ideas in technologies that are covered by patents, however, often have common knowledge elements. Once people have seen the new technology, they figure out sufficiently different ways of achieving the same end while avoiding the patent.

Learning by Doing As the new growth theory has analyzed technology, it has focused economic thinking on another aspect of economic processes—an individual's tendency to **learn by doing,** or to *improve the methods of production through experience*. As people do something, they become better and better at it, sometimes because of new technologies, and sometimes simply because they learned better ways to do it just from practice. Thus, as production increases, costs of production tend to decrease over time. The introduction of new technology is sometimes the result of learning by doing.

Learning by doing overcomes the law of diminishing marginal productivity because learning by doing increases the productivity of workers.

Learning by doing changes the laws of economics enormously. It suggests that production has positive externalities in learning. If these positive externalities overwhelm diminishing marginal productivity, as new growth theory suggests they do, the predictions about growth change. In the Classical theory, growth is limited by diminishing marginal productivity; in the new theory, growth potential is unlimited and can accelerate over time. It's a whole new world out there—one in which, holding wants constant, scarcity decreases over time.

We can see in Figure 24-4 new growth theory's predictions for future growth. All inputs are on the horizontal axis, and the production function exhibits increasing returns to scale. (As more inputs are added, the additional output per combination of inputs increases.) With this curve, per capita income can grow forever and the dismal science of economics becomes the optimistic science.

Technological Lock-In One of the questions new growth theory raises is: Does the economy always use the "best" technology available? Some say no and point to examples of technologies that have become entrenched in the market, or locked in to new products despite the availability of more efficient technologies. This is known as *technological lock-in*.

One proposed example of technological lock-in goes under the name QWERTY, which is the upper-left five keys on the standard computer keyboard. Economist Paul David argues that the design of this keyboard was chosen to slow people's typing down

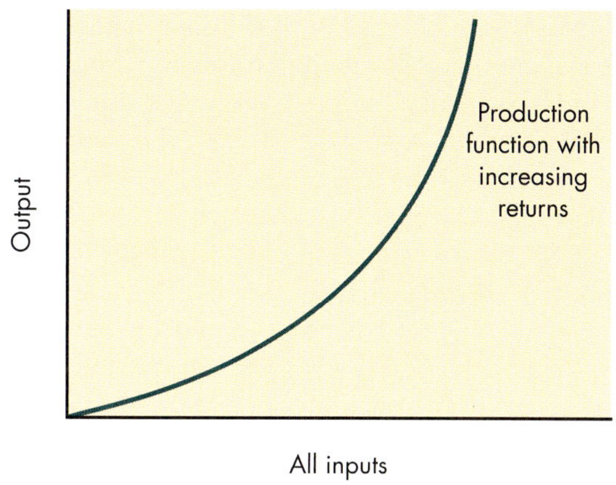

Figure 24-4 Increasing Returns to Scale
With increasing returns, increases in inputs lead to proportionately greater increases in output. New growth theory focuses on increasing returns to scale. With increasing returns, output per person can rise forever.

so that the keys in old-style mechanical typewriters would not lock up. He further argues that developments in word processing have since eliminated the problem the QWERTY keyboard was designed to solve (we don't use mechanical typewriters any more). But once people started choosing this keyboard, it was too costly for them to develop another.

This interpretation of history has been disputed by other economists, who argue that the QWERTY keyboard is not significantly less efficient than other keyboard arrangements and that, if it were, competition would have eliminated it. Sometimes this counterargument almost seems to state that the very fact that a technology exists means that it is the most efficient. Most economists do not go that far; they argue that even if the QWERTY keyboard is not a highly inefficient technology, other examples of lock-in exist—beta format videos were preferable to VHS, the Windows operating system is inferior to many alternatives, the English language doesn't compare to Esperanto, and English measurement systems are quite inefficient compared to metric.

One reason for technological lock-in is the existence of *network externalities*—an externality in which the use of a good by one individual makes that technology more valuable to other people. Telephones exhibit network externalities. A single telephone is pretty useless. Who would you call? Two telephones are more useful, but as more and more people get telephones, the possible interactions (and the benefits of telephones) increases exponentially. Network externalities can make switching to a superior technology expensive or nearly impossible. The Windows operating system is another example of a product that exhibits network externalities, and makes it difficult for other operating systems to develop.

Q-8 In what way does the Internet demonstrate network externalities?

Economic Policies to Encourage per Capita Growth

General pronouncements about growth are nice, but society is most interested in growth policies, not growth theories. What policies lead to higher growth rates? This section discusses six different policy options that have been used to increase the per capita growth rate.

Policies to Encourage Saving and Investment

Although new growth theory has downplayed the central role of capital in the growth process, new growth theorists agree that capital and investment are still important. So policymakers interested in increasing growth are always looking for ways to encourage both saving and investment. One of the plans they have used in the United States is tax incentives for saving. Thus, our income tax laws have individual retirement accounts (IRAs) and 401(k) plans (another form of investment retirement accounts) that allow individuals to save without incurring taxes. Some economists have even proposed switching from an income tax to a consumption tax, which taxes individuals only when they consume and therefore exempts all saving from taxation.

Developed countries can generate saving and investment far more easily than can developing countries. The problem in poorer countries is that the poor don't have much discretionary income, and hence can't save much, and the rich are concerned about confiscation of their wealth, and hence save abroad, either legally or illegally. Moreover, the small middle class that does exist can find few financial instruments to effectively channel saving into investment. For developing countries, generating saving and investment often requires creating new financial institutions. Let's consider a case study that gives some insight into a success story.

Developing countries have a much harder time designing saving policies than do developed countries.

A Case Study: Micro Credit Our case study considers the development of a financial institution in one of the poorest countries of the world—Bangladesh. There, Mohammed Yunus, a U.S.-trained economist, created a bank—the Grameen Bank—that made loans to poor village women at market interest rates. Even though the bank loaned to individuals with little or no collateral, the bank has had excellent payback ratios, far exceeding what most people thought possible.[1]

How did he do it? Most banks in developing countries are internationally oriented. They use the same structure that Western banks use. This leaves the traditional part of many developing countries' economies without an effective way to translate saving into investment, stranding many entrepreneurial individuals without ways to develop their ideas. Yunus reconsidered the fundamental role of banking in an economy—to make it possible for people with good ideas to develop those ideas by providing them with funds and to devise a structure that allowed such lending to take place.

With a loan from the Grameen Bank (www.grameenbank.org), these women purchased the raw materials to weave baskets whose sale will provide a source of income.
John Van Hasselt/Corbis.

He saw that Western banking institutions did not provide the answer for Bangladesh. By basing their lending decisions on the amount of collateral a borrower had, they essentially made it impossible for most people in Bangladesh to get loans. But Yunus also recognized that the collateral function served a useful purpose: it forced people to make the difficult decision about whether they really needed the loans, and to work hard to see that they could pay the loans back, even if the going got tough. If you eliminate collateral, something else must replace it.

Yunus's ingenious solution was the *borrowing circle*—a credit system that replaces traditional collateral with guarantees by friends of the borrower. Recognizing that social pressures were extremely strong in Bangladesh, Yunus offered to make loans to any woman who could find four friends who would agree to help her pay the loan back if necessary. If the borrower defaulted, the others could not borrow until the loan was repaid.

Web Note 24.3
The Grameen Bank

This simple concept worked. Today the Grameen Bank has more than 2.4 million borrowers and lends $17 million every month. The loans are taken out to buy such things as a cow or material to make a fishing net—not large items, but items to use in the types of activity that generate bottom-up growth. Other microcredit banks—banks that make small loans to poor people using alternative forms of collateral—have developed similar plans.

[1]Recently some observers have questioned whether the bank has overstated the payback ratios, but even if they are lower than reported, they are still higher than most people thought possible before the bank was created.

Even developed countries are looking into the borrowing circle concept as a way of getting credit to the poor. While the concept is extraordinarily simple, it made use of economic insights that simultaneously reflected an understanding of the cultural and social dimensions of the economy.

Growth through Foreign Investment If developing countries don't generate sufficient saving domestically, they must turn to foreign sources for saving. They can borrow from either the International Monetary Fund (IMF), the World Bank, or private sources. All have their problems. IMF and World Bank loans usually come with strict requirements on the country's fiscal and monetary policy, and private investment can leave the country exposed to capital flight and exchange rate problems. (We'll consider these issues in more detail in later chapters.)

Policies to Control Population Growth

Population control policies in developing countries have played an important role in discussions of increasing per capita growth rates. Population among low-income countries has grown an average 1.9 percent a year since 1980, compared to 0.6 percent for high-income countries. The reason high population growth presents a problem for economic growth is that it makes providing sufficient capital and education for everyone difficult. The factors of production have to be shared among more people and the law of diminishing productivity sets in. Workers cannot produce as much as before and per capita growth falls. For some low-income countries, population growth has meant an increase in the relative number of dependents (people too old or too young to work). For these countries, each worker must support a larger number of people.

Developing countries whose populations are rapidly growing have difficulty providing enough capital and education for everyone. Consequently, income per capita is low.

Policies that reduce population growth include setting up free family-planning services, increasing the availability of contraceptives, and allowing only one child per family. China, which has one-fifth of the world's population, adopted the latter policy in 1980 and enforced it by harsh penalties, such as job loss, for those who did not comply. Although it has backed off in enforcing the law in parts of the country, the policy reduced population growth from over 2 percent in the 1970s to just over 1 percent today.

Some economists argue that the best way to reduce population growth is to grow. They argue that as income and work opportunities, especially for women, rise, the opportunity cost of having children rises and families will choose to have fewer children. In most industrialized countries, population growth has not been a problem. Economic growth has led many people to have fewer children and to want other things instead—more income, more vacations, more cars, and so on.

In the United States, where the birth rate is below replacement levels, immigration has provided one source of growth in population and total output. Immigration in the United States was substantial in the 1990s and early 2000s, in some years approaching 1 million per year. This has increased the labor force and output. However, there is a debate about whether greater immigration has increased or decreased output per capita.

Policies to Increase the Level of Education

Another way to increase output per capita is to increase human capital. Increasing the educational level and skills of the workforce increases labor productivity. In the United States, government policies to increase education include free mandatory education for students through high school, financial support for students going on to higher education (for example, Pell grants), and direct subsidies of teaching colleges to help keep tuition down.

Q-9 Why would increases in education likely have a greater return in terms of increased output in developing countries than in developed countries?

In developing countries, basic skills—reading, writing, and arithmetic—are very important for economic growth. For these countries, the return on investment in education is much higher than it is for the United States, where the level of human capital is already high. In the United States, an additional year of education increases a worker's wages by an average of 10 percent, whereas in developing countries, an additional year of education will increase wages by 15 to 20 percent.

Of course by *education*, I mean the right kind of education. For developing countries the majority of jobs require only a primary education, so spending on general education is important. Technical training in improved farming methods or construction is also important; studying movements in postmodern philosophy is significantly less relevant to growth. Unfortunately, politics often guides developing countries' education policies to place more emphasis on higher education than on basic education.

Policies to Create Institutions That Encourage Technological Innovation

As we saw in Figure 24-3, the largest source of growth is technology. Thus, it is not surprising that economic policies focus on technology. The policy problem is that while all agree that technology is important, no one is sure what the best technological growth policies are.

Unlike capital, technological innovation can occur without investment; conversely, investment in technology can also result in no technological innovation.

The reason is that technological development is inherently uncertain. New technologies could result intentionally from research and development, or unintentionally from some other activity, or simply from a wandering mind. (Is your mind wandering now—are you developing the next new big idea that will reshape the world?) No one really knows when another innovation will be discovered. Some investments take years to pay off.

Not only is the nature of research uncertain, but so is its application. Individuals have not been especially good at deciding which technologies will work and which will not. Consider some famous examples of poor guesses. In 1877, Western Union turned down the opportunity to buy the patent on Alexander Graham Bell's telephone for $100,000 because it believed that the telegraph was superior. In the 1940s, the chairman of IBM, Thomas Watson Sr., could see no commercial demand for computers and felt that the IBM computer at the company's New York headquarters "could solve all the important scientific problems in the world involving scientific calculations." Perhaps the poorest guess came in 1899 from the commissioner of patents, who argued that the U.S. Patent Office should be closed because "everything that can be invented has been invented." We could list many more examples, but the idea is clear: When it comes to technology, few have done well in predicting what would succeed and what would fail.

Create Patents and Protect Property Rights Government can reduce the risks faced by innovators and entrepreneurs by creating and protecting property rights, creating institutions that limit the risk to investing in R&D, and providing a stable government. Consider patents. By holding a patent, a firm can be the sole supplier, and charge higher prices for its product than it could otherwise. The promise of higher profit that comes with a patent provides an incentive to innovate.

Q-10 Which has the possibility for a greater payoff to growth—an idea that is patented or common knowledge? Which does an individual have a greater incentive to discover?

Patents, however, are not costless to society. While patents provide an incentive to innovators, patented innovations will be priced high and thus fewer people will benefit from them. As we noted earlier, it is the common knowledge aspect of technology that leads to positive externalities and, thus, to the highest payoff in terms of growth. Our decimal number system is an example of a nonpatented idea. The Arabians developed a system of counting based on the decimal system; it was far more efficient than the

Roman numeral system. (Have you ever tried multiplying IV times VI?) Had that idea been copyrighted (and if that copyright could be enforced), every time you multiply using the Arabic numeral system, you would have to make a small payment to the holder of the copyright. Currently the U.S. is struggling with questions such as: Should general Internet business methods, such as providing a virtual shopping cart to purchase items over the Internet, be patentable?

In assigning copyrights, patents, and property rights all agree that societies must find a middle ground between giving individuals appropriate incentives to create new technologies by giving them monopoly rights to those developments and allowing everyone to take advantage of the benefits of technology. There is far less agreement on what the appropriate middle ground is.

Pharmaceuticals provide an example of the type of debate that develops. Since pharmaceutical products save lives, an argument can be made that any patent that results in higher drug prices and thereby limits use is immoral. The problem is that without the patent, fewer drugs will be developed. What happens in practice is that drugs are given a patent for a limited period, after which the drugs become "generically reproducible," and their price goes down considerably. The policy debate is over what the length of that period should be.

Patents and Developing Countries Developing countries face an even more complicated issue. Should they accept U.S. patent laws, which would limit distribution of that technology, or should they allow much freer use of new technological developments? The United States naturally wants them to accept and enforce U.S. patents and copyrights, and has made that acceptance a requirement for open trade relations. This puts great pressure on the other countries to comply in theory, but to enforce the laws as weakly as possible in practice. For example, the United States and China have been engaged in an ongoing fight on the enforcement of U.S. copyrights on computer software. You can buy the latest Windows CD in many of the open markets in China for under $2; that's below the copyright cost, so it is a good bet that those CDs are "bootlegged"—produced out of copyright.

Finding a middle ground between allowing patents which create incentives for developing countries' new technologies and exploiting the common knowledge aspect of technology is a difficult policy problem.

The Corporation and Financial Institutions Along with providing incentives for investment through patents, governments have also developed institutions that limit the risk to investors. As noted earlier in this chapter the corporation was developed to limit liability to investors. In a corporation, an investor's only risk is his or her investment in that corporation. This encourages investors to pool their funds. The corporate form of organization is important to the growth of technology because bringing technological innovation to market often requires large amounts of investment over a number of years. Consider railroads or telephones, which both required huge investments to make them available.

Well-developed financial institutions such as the stock market also help drive technological development. The stock market allows initial investors to sell their investment to others so that they are not tied into one company alone. Consider whether you would invest in Amazon.com if you couldn't sell the shares to someone else. Put in technical terms, the stock market makes investments more liquid (changeable into other types of assets) and thereby encourages investment in general.

Policies to Provide Funding for Basic Research

As I discussed above, it is technology's "common knowledge" aspect that has the greatest positive effect on growth but that gives firms little incentive to do research. By funding basic research the government can create the seeds for growth. The U.S.

U.S. government agencies provide about 60 percent of all research and development funds for basic research.

Demand, Keynesian Economics, and Growth

Beyond the Tools

The presentation in this chapter is the generally accepted analysis of growth. It focuses on the supply-side sources of growth. But because empirical relationships in growth are so difficult to discern, there are a variety of different issues that groups of economists raise. One such group, which has its origins in Keynesian ideas, argues that demand and supply are so interrelated in macro that demand has to be considered as a source of growth. The argument goes as follows: Firms produce only if they expect there to be demand for their product. If they expect demand to be high, they will try new projects and in the process will learn by doing and develop new technology. Both of these activities shift the production function out and thereby create growth. So while it looks like a supply-side issue, it is the demand side that leads the supply side: By increasing demand, one can increase long-run supply.

True, they argue, increasing aggregate demand is only a short-run phenomenon, but since the long run is simply a set of successive short runs, the short run influences the long-run path that the economy follows. They are not separable, and under the right conditions demand-side policies should be considered as one way to increase supply. As Joan Robinson, one of the early Keynesian advocates of this view, has put it, in the long run we are simply in another short run.

government funds 60 percent of basic research in the United States. Much of this funding is channeled through universities. Thus, it is not surprising that many of the high-tech businesses that have led the recent growth spurt are clustered around universities. For example, Silicon Valley is near Stanford, and the Route 128 corridor in Boston is near Harvard and MIT. Because basic research creates spin-offs and leads to pockets of growth, communities are willing to subsidize universities in their area and give tax relief to new-technology firms.

Many professors doing basic research for universities are also working for for-profit start-up companies. Their dual roles create a conflict of allegiances. Wearing their university hat, they want to make their discoveries widely available; wearing the for-profit hat, they want to keep their discoveries proprietary.

Policies to Increase the Economy's Openness to Trade

At the beginning of this chapter I emphasized that growth is associated with the development of markets. Markets allow individuals and firms to specialize, and specialization allows firms and workers to become more productive. In specialization, the bigger the market, the better. You have to be able to sell your specialized product to large numbers of people—that is, you need a large market.

Large markets allow firms to take advantage of economies of scale. The effect of markets on growth is an important reason economists generally support policies that encourage international free trade. Most economists believe that policies allowing free trade increase growth by increasing competition. (For example, relaxation of import tariffs on Japanese automobile imports made U.S. producers change their production methods and improve the quality of American-made cars.) That's why they generally support the creation of free trade areas such as NAFTA and the EU, as well as the World Trade Organization.

Stating a policy rule is easy; applying it to specific cases is difficult.

Domestically, being open to trade means opposing regulations whose primary function is to protect vested interests. The problem is that most regulations have multiple functions—some preventing trade, and some providing necessary protections. My town, for example, recently passed a strict zoning law that made the construction of new hotels here almost impossible. This protected existing hotel owners (who were major supporters) and thus represents a limit to free trade, but it also helps protect the cozy Vermont image that attracts tourists. (Tourism is a major industry here.) So, as usual, stating the policy rule is easy; applying it to specific cases is difficult.

Conclusion

Growth happens, or at least it generally has happened in market economies. But that doesn't mean it happens on its own. While saying precisely why growth happens is beyond economists at this point, economists have identified important sources of growth. These include capital accumulation, available resources, growth-compatible institutions, technological development, and entrepreneurship. What economists haven't been able to determine yet is how they all fit together to bring about growth, and the general feeling is that there is no single way of putting them together—what works likely changes over time. This makes developing an actual growth policy prescription difficult, though no less important.

Policies that economists have recommended to encourage growth include tax and institutional changes to encourage saving and thereby encourage investment, control population growth, increase the level of education, encourage technological innovation, subsidize research and development, and foster open trade. Because these are long-run policies whose effects come often years, and even decades, after they are implemented, they generally do not get a lot of press. Politicians and the press tend to focus on policies whose effect is more immediate. Thus, much real-world macro policy discussion focuses on short-run issues—issues that affect the economy within a year or two, such as how to keep an economy out of a recession or how to moderate a boom. Ultimately, however, the economic position of one nation's economy relative to others in the global economy will be determined more by growth policy than by these more-discussed policies, and thus the need for growth policies is something that policymakers should keep in the back of the mind—and bring to the front when facing short-run issues.

Summary

- Growth is an increase in the amount of goods and services an economy can produce when both labor and capital are fully employed.
- Growth increases potential output and shifts the production possibility curve out, allowing an economy to produce more goods.
- Per capita growth means producing more goods and services per person. It can be calculated by subtracting the percentage change in the population from the percentage change in output.
- Five sources of growth are (1) investment in accumulated capital, (2) available resources, (3) growth-compatible institutions, (4) technological development, and (5) entrepreneurship.
- The production function shows the relationship between the quantity of labor, capital, and land used in production and the quantity of output resulting from production.
- The law of diminishing marginal productivity states that increasing one input, keeping all others constant, will lead to smaller and smaller gains in output.
- Returns to scale describes what happens to output when all inputs increase equally.
- The Classical growth model focuses on the role of capital accumulation in the growth process. The law of diminishing productivity limits growth of per capita income.

- New growth theory emphasizes the role of technology in the growth process. Increasing returns to scale means output per person can rise forever.
- Advances in technology, which account for 35 percent of growth, have overwhelmed the effects of diminishing returns.
- Six government policies to promote growth are (1) encourage saving and investment, (2) control population growth, (3) increase the level of education, (4) create institutions that encourage technological innovation, (5) fund basic research, and (6) increase openness to trade.

Key Terms

Classical growth model *(549)*
constant returns to scale *(549)*
decreasing returns to scale *(549)*
division of labor *(542)*
growth *(541)*
human capital *(545)*
increasing returns to scale *(549)*
law of diminishing marginal productivity *(549)*
learn by doing *(554)*
new growth theory *(553)*
patents *(554)*
per capita growth *(544)*
positive externality *(554)*
potential output *(541)*
production function *(548)*
productivity *(541)*
Rule of 72 *(542)*
Say's law *(541)*
social capital *(545)*
specialization *(542)*
technology *(547)*

Questions for Thought and Review

1. a. If you suddenly found yourself living as a poor person in a developing country, what are some things that you now do that you would no longer be able to do? What new things would you have to do?
   b. Answer the questions again assuming that you are living in the United States 100 years ago.
2. Who most likely worked longer to buy a dozen eggs: a person living in 1990 or a person living in 1910? Why?
3. Have the poor benefited more or less from economic growth than the rich?
4. What roles do specialization and division of labor play in economists' support of free trade?
5. How can an increase in the U.S. saving rate lead to higher living standards? What problem would a politician face when promoting policies to encourage saving?
6. Name three types of capital and explain the differences among them.
7. Name two ways in which growth through technology differs from growth through the accumulation of physical capital.
8. What are two actions government can take to promote the development of new technologies?
9. On what law of production did Thomas Malthus base his prediction that population growth would exceed growth in goods and services? Why hasn't his prediction come true?
10. If individuals suddenly needed more food to subsist, what would the Classical growth model predict would happen to labor and output? Demonstrate graphically.
11. What are network externalities and how do they lead to growth?
12. List three ways in which growth can be undesirable. Can growth itself address those problems?
13. *Credentialism* occurs when a person's degrees become more important than his or her actual knowledge. How can credentialism hurt economic growth?
14. In what ways can competition promote technological advance? In what ways can competition harm technological advance?
15. If you were designing a development plan for Pakistan, would you suggest the country accept or reject Western copyright and patent law? Why?
16. Explain why communities are willing to give tax relief to new-technology firms that locate in their community.

Problems and Exercises

1. Income in the world economy grew an average of 2 percent per year since 1950. If this growth continues, how many years will it take for income to double?
2. If output increases by 20 percent when one of two inputs increases by 20 percent, are there constant returns to scale? Why or why not?

3. Per capita income is growing at different rates in the following countries: Nepal, 1.1 percent; Kenya, 1.7 percent; Singapore, 7.2 percent; Egypt, 3.9 percent. How long will it take for each country to double its income per person?
4. Calculate real growth per capita from 1994 to 2003 in the following countries:
   a. Democratic Republic of Congo: population growth = 3.0 percent; real output growth = −1.8 percent.
   b. Estonia: population growth = −0.4 percent; real output growth = 4.2 percent.
   c. India: population growth = 2.0 percent; real output growth = 6 percent.
   d. United States: population growth = 0.5 percent; real output growth = 2.5 percent.
5. Say that you have been hired to design an education system for a developing country.
   a. What skills will you want it to emphasize?
   b. How might it differ from an ideal educational system here in the United States?
6. Could the borrowing circle concept be adopted for use in the United States?
   a. Why or why not?
   b. What modifications would you suggest if it were to be adopted?
   c. Minorities in the United States often do not use banks. In what ways are U.S. minorities' problems similar to those of people in developing countries?
7. The graph below shows a production function and the subsistence level of output.
   a. Does the production function exhibit increasing or decreasing marginal productivity?
   b. Label a level of population at which the population is expected to grow. What is the surplus output at that population level?
   c. Label a level of population at which the population is expected to decline. Why is the population declining at this point?
   d. Label the population at which the economy is in a steady state. Why is this a steady state?

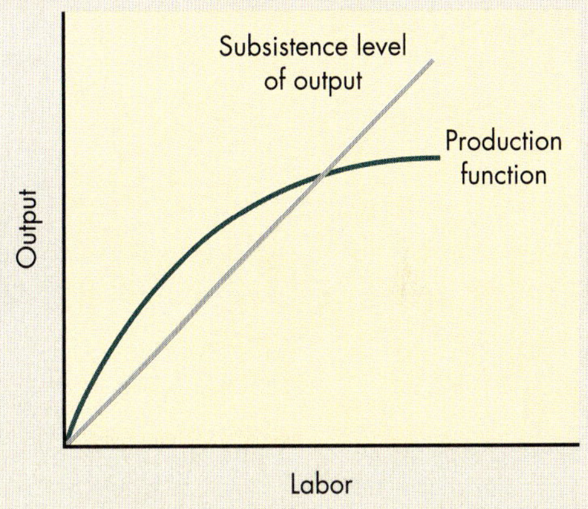

WEB QUESTIONS

1. Go to the World Bank's home page (www.worldbank.org) and look up Kenya, Mexico, the United States, and Japan.
   a. What is the per capita growth rate of income for each country over the past 20 years?
   b. What is the population growth for each country over the past 20 years?
   c. What is investment as a percent of output for each country?
2. The Heritage Foundation and *The Wall Street Journal* copublish an Index of Economic Freedom designed to measure the extent to which markets are allowed to operate freely in a country. Go to the home page of the Heritage Foundation (www.index.heritage.org) and look up the index for two of the top-rated countries and two of the bottom-rated countries.
   a. What are the reasons for their ratings?
   b. Compare the recent per capita growth rates of each country. Is economic freedom related to growth? If so, how?
3. Go to the U.S. patent office website (www.uspto.gov) and find out for how long patents are granted in the United States.
   a. What are the advantages of shortening the length of patents?
   b. What are the disadvantages of shortening the length of patents?

ANSWERS TO MARGIN QUESTIONS

1. The long-run growth analysis justifies its focus on supply by assuming that aggregate supply will create an equal level of aggregate demand. This is known as Say's law. *(541)*
2. Using the Rule of 72 (divide 72 by the growth rate of income) we can calculate that it will take 18 years for income to double when its growth rate is 4 percent a year. *(542)*

3. Country B is experiencing the higher growth in income per capita. To calculate this, subtract the population growth rates from the income growth rates for each country. Country A's per capita growth rate is 1 percent (4 − 3) and country B's per capita growth rate is 2 percent (3 − 1). *(544)*
4. The increases would have to be distributed so that no one whose income is below the median receives enough to bring their income above the median. *(545)*
5. Private property provides an incentive for people to produce by creating the possibility of benefiting from their efforts. *(546)*
6. False. A 20 percent increase in production that results from a 10 percent increase in all inputs means the production process exhibits decreasing *returns to scale*. A key part of the statement is that all inputs are changing. If one input were being kept fixed, the production function would be exhibiting diminishing marginal productivity. *(549)*
7. If individuals suddenly needed less food, the subsistence level line would rotate down. The number of laborers the economy could sustain would rise, and output would rise as well. *(550)*
8. The Internet connects hundreds of millions of people around the globe and reduces communication costs. The benefit of one person using the Internet is virtually nonexistent. The benefit of the Internet rises as more people use it, because the higher usage increases the amount of information available on the Internet and increases the ability of each user to communicate. *(555)*
9. Because the level of education is higher in the United States compared to developing countries, the law of diminishing marginal productivity of education is stronger in the United States. The benefit of additional education in the United States is lower compared to that in developing countries. *(558)*
10. Because common knowledge has greater positive externalities, common knowledge has a greater possibility of payoff in terms of growth. People have a greater incentive to discover an idea that can be patented because a patent gives the innovator the sole right to sell the idea. *(558)*

Aggregate Demand, Aggregate Supply, and Modern Macroeconomics

25

> The Theory of Economics . . . is a method rather than a doctrine, an apparatus of the mind, a technique of thinking which helps its possessor to draw correct conclusions.
>
> —*J. M. Keynes*

After reading this chapter, you should be able to:

- Discuss the historical development of modern macroeconomics.
- Explain the shape of the aggregate demand curve and what factors shift the curve.
- Explain the shape of the short-run aggregate supply curve and what factors shift the curve.
- Explain the shape of the long-run aggregate supply curve.
- Show the effects of shifts of the aggregate demand and aggregate supply curves on price level and output in both the short run and long run.
- Discuss the limitations of the macro policy model.

Chapter 24's discussion of growth and markets focused on the positive side of markets; we saw that markets unleash individual incentives, increase supply, and bring about growth. But markets can run into serious problems—markets can create recessions, inflation, and unemployment. Japan in the late 1990s and early 2000s is a good example. After a number of years of substantial growth, Japan's economy fell into recession. Policymakers had to decide whether to intervene in the market or simply hope the recession would end on its own.

The macro intervention tools—monetary and fiscal policy—are tools governments use on the aggregate demand side of the economy to deal with recessions, inflation, and unemployment. Thus, whereas the last chapter's policy focus was on production (the supply side) and individual incentives, this chapter and the next focus on expenditures (the demand side).

Economists debate the effectiveness of monetary and fiscal policy. Some favor intervention; some don't. While the problems of a recession are serious, so too are the problems with government policies. The debate among economists is about whether the cure (intervention) is worse than the disease.

Even if the non-interventionist economists were to convince all other economists that government should not intervene with monetary and fiscal policy, the odds are that government would still intervene. As I've said before, the reality is that politicians make policy; they listen to economists only when they want to. And whenever the economy faces the threat of a recession, politicians' focus inevitably changes from long-run supply issues and growth to short-run demand issues and stabilization.

Consider September 2001. After the terrorist attacks on the World Trade Center and the Pentagon, the U.S. government turned its attention away from concern about inflation, growth, and supply-side policies to the aggregate demand-side policies—both monetary and fiscal policy—that would keep the economy from going into a deep recession. It worked, at least temporarily, and the recession that followed the attacks was the shortest on record.

The Historical Development of Modern Macro

Web Note 25.1
The Great Depression

An important reason for politicians' initial interest in short-run stabilization is the Great Depression of the 1930s, a deep recession that lasted for 10 years. It was that experience that led to the development of macroeconomics as a separate course, and to the development of aggregate demand tools to deal with recurring recessions.

During the Depression unemployment lines were enormously long.
Photodisc.

Most of you only think of the Great Depression as something your grandparents and great-grandparents experienced. But it was a defining event that undermined people's faith in markets and was the beginning of modern macro's focus on the demand side of the economy. It is also where our story of modern macroeconomics begins.

During the Depression, output fell by 30 percent and unemployment rose to 25 percent. Not only was the deadbeat up the street unemployed but so were your brother, your mother, your uncle—the hardworking backbone of the country. These people wanted to work, and eventually decided that if the market wasn't creating jobs for them, the market system was at fault.

Q-1 Distinguish a Classical economist from a Keynesian economist.

From Classical to Keynesian Economics As I discussed in an earlier chapter, economists before the Depression focused on the long run and the problem of growth. Their policy recommendations were designed to lead to long-run growth, and they avoided discussing policies that would affect the economy in the short run. In the 1930s macroeconomists started focusing their discussion of macroeconomic policy on short-run issues. To distinguish the two types of economics, the earlier economists who focused on long-run issues such as growth were called *Classical economists* and economists who focused on the short run were called *Keynesian economists*. Keynesian economists were named because a leading advocate of the short-run focus was John Maynard Keynes, the author of *The General Theory of Employment, Interest and Money*, and the originator of modern macroeconomics.

Classical Economists

Classical economists believed in the market's ability to be self-regulating through the invisible hand (the pricing mechanism of the market). Short-run problems were seen as temporary glitches; the Classical framework said that the economy would always return to its potential output and its target (or natural) rate of unemployment in the long run. Thus, the essence of Classical economists' approach to problems was laissez-faire (leave the market alone).

Classical economists support laissez-faire policies.

As long as the economy was operating relatively smoothly, the Classical analysis of the aggregate economy met no serious opposition. But when the Great Depression hit and unemployment became a serious problem, most Classical economists avoided the issue (as most people tend to do when they don't have a good answer). When pushed by curious students to explain how the invisible hand, if it was so wonderful, could have allowed the Depression, Classical economists used microeconomic supply and demand arguments. They argued that labor unions and government policies kept prices and wages from falling. The problem, they said, was that the invisible hand was not being allowed to coordinate economic activity.

Their laissez-faire policy prescription followed from their analysis: Eliminate labor unions and change government policies that held wages too high. If government did so, the wage rate would fall, unemployment would be eliminated, and the Depression would end.

THE LAYPERSON'S EXPLANATION FOR UNEMPLOYMENT

Laypeople (average citizens) weren't pleased with this argument. (Remember, economists don't try to present pleasing arguments—only arguments they believe are correct.) But laypeople couldn't point to anything wrong with it. It made sense, but it wasn't satisfying. People thought, "Gee, Uncle Joe, who's unemployed, would take a job at half the going wage. But he can't find one—there just aren't enough jobs to go around at any wage." So most laypeople developed different explanations. One popular explanation of the Depression was that an oversupply of goods had glutted the market. All that was needed to eliminate unemployment was for government to hire the unemployed, even if only to dig ditches and fill them back up. The people who got the new jobs would spend their money, creating even more jobs. Pretty soon, the United States would be out of the Depression.

Classical economists argued against this lay view. They felt that money to hire people would have to be borrowed. Such borrowing would use money that would have financed private economic activity and jobs, and would thus reduce private economic activity even further. The net effect would be essentially zero. Their advice was simply to have faith in markets.

THE ESSENCE OF KEYNESIAN ECONOMICS

As the Depression deepened, the Classical "have-faith" solution lost its support. Everyone was interested in the short run, not the long run. John Maynard Keynes put the concern most eloquently: "In the long run, we're all dead."

Keynes focused on the short run, not the long run.

Keynes stopped asking whether the economy would eventually get out of the Depression on its own, and started asking what short-run forces were causing the Depression and what society could do to counteract them. By taking this approach he created the macroeconomic framework that focuses on stabilization.

While Keynes's ideas had many dimensions, the essence was that as wages and the price level adjusted to sudden changes in expenditures (such as an unexpected decrease in investment demand), the economy could get stuck in a rut.

Web Note 25.2
John Maynard Keynes

If, for some reason, people stopped buying—decreased their demand in the aggregate—firms would decrease production, causing people to be laid off; these people would, in turn, buy less—causing other firms to further decrease production, which would cause more workers to be laid off, and so on. Firms' supply decisions would be affected by consumers' buying decisions, and the economy would end up in a cumulative cycle of declining production that would end with the economy stuck at a low level of income. In developing this line of reasoning Keynes provided the theoretical foundation for the view that unemployment could be caused by too little spending. The issue was not whether a more desirable equilibrium existed; it was whether a market economy, once it had fallen into a depression, and was caught in a cumulative cycle, could get out of it on its own in an acceptable period of time.

In making his argument Keynes carefully distinguished the adjustment process for a single market (a micro issue) from the adjustment process for the aggregate economy (a macro issue), arguing that the effects differ significantly when everyone does something versus when only one person does it. This difference has a number of names: the public goods problem, the tragedy of the commons, the fallacy of composition, and the multiperson dilemma.

The problem is neatly seen by considering an analogy to a football game. If everyone is standing, and you sit down, you can't see. Everyone is better off standing. No one has an incentive to sit down. However, if somehow all individuals could be enticed to

In the Long Run, We're All Dead

Knowing the Tools

When Keynes said, "In the long run, we're all dead," he didn't mean that we can forget the long run. What he meant was that if the long run is so long that short-run forces do not let it come about, then for all practical purposes there is no long run. In that case, the short-run problem must be focused on.

Keynes believed that voters would not be satisfied waiting for market forces to bring about full employment. If something were not done in the short run to alleviate unemployment, he felt, voters would opt for fascism (as had the Germans) or communism (as had the Russians). He saw both alternatives as undesirable. For him, what would happen in the long run was academic.

Classicals, in contrast, argued that the short-run problems were not as bad as Keynes made them out to be and therefore should not be focused on to the exclusion of long-run problems.

Modern-day Classicals argue that while Keynes is dead, we are not, and the result of his short-run focus was long-run problems—specifically an inflationary bias in the economy. It is only by giving up Keynesian policies that we eliminated that bias.

sit down, all individuals would be even better off. Sitting down is a public good—a good that benefits others but one that nobody on his or her own will do. Keynesians argued that, in times of recession, spending is a public good because it benefits everyone, so government should spend or find ways of inducing private individuals to spend. This difference between individual and economywide reactions to spending decisions creates a possibility for government to exercise control over aggregate expenditures and thereby over aggregate output and income. *Government's attempt to control the aggregate level of spending in the economy* is called **aggregate demand management.**

Keynesians argued that, in times of recession, spending is a public good that benefits everyone.

Equilibrium Income Fluctuates The key idea of the Keynesian model is that, in the short run, equilibrium income is not fixed at the economy's long-run potential income; it fluctuates. Thus, for Keynes, there was a difference between **equilibrium income** *(the level of income toward which the economy gravitates in the short run because of the cumulative cycles of declining or increasing production)* and **potential income** *(the level of income that the economy technically is capable of producing without generating accelerating inflation)*. Keynes believed that at certain times the economy needed some help in reaching its potential income.

The key idea in Keynesian economics is that equilibrium income fluctuates and can differ from potential income.

He argued that market forces that are supposed to bring the economy back to long-run potential income don't work fast, and at times will not be strong enough to get the economy out of a recession; the economy could get stuck in a low-income, high-unemployment rut. As the economy adjusts to fluctuations of supply and demand in the aggregate, the equilibrium income toward which the economy would gravitate would change. The economy would not naturally gravitate to potential income in the short run.

The Paradox of Thrift Let's say that a large portion of the people in the economy suddenly decide to save more and consume less. Expenditures would decrease and saving would increase. If that saving is not immediately transferred into investment, and hence back into expenditures (as the Classicals assumed it would be), investment demand will not increase by enough to offset the fall in consumption demand, and total demand will fall. There will be excess supply. Faced with this excess supply, firms will likely cut back production, which will decrease income. People will be laid off. As people's incomes fall, both their consumption and saving will decrease. (When you're laid off, you don't save.) Eventually income will fall far enough so that once again saving and investment will be in equilibrium, but then the economy could be at an almost permanent recession, with ongoing unemployment. Keynesians believed that in this case the economy would need government's help to hold up aggregate expenditures. That is the essence of macro demand-side expansionary policy.

Keynesian economists advocated an activist demand management policy.

Notice that the Keynesian framework gives a quite different view of saving than did the growth framework in Chapter 24. There, saving was seen as something good; more saving leads to more investment, which leads to more growth. In the Keynesian framework there is a *paradox of thrift*—an increase in saving can lead to a decrease in expenditures, decreasing output and causing a recession.

Q-2 How does the short-run view of saving differ from the long-run view?

By the 1950s Keynesian economics had been accepted by most of the profession. It was taught almost everywhere in the United States. The terminology of national income accounting developed, which is closely tied to Keynesian concepts. The model that eventually developed from these early debates is called the *aggregate demand/aggregate supply* (AS/AD) *model*. Aggregate supply captures production and pricing decisions by firms, and aggregate demand captures aggregate spending decisions. Even though economists still debate how fluctuations in an economy arise, this model, which focuses on aggregate expenditures as the primary determinant of short-run income, is used by most real-world economists to discuss short-run fluctuations in output and unemployment.

The AS/AD Model

The *AS/AD* model consists of three curves. The curve describing the supply side of the aggregate economy in the short run is the short-run aggregate supply curve (*SAS*), the curve describing the demand side of the economy is the aggregate demand curve, and the curve describing the highest sustainable level of output is the long-run aggregate supply curve (*LAS*).

The first thing to note about the *AS/AD* model is that it is fundamentally different from the microeconomic supply/demand model. In microeconomics the price of a single good is on the vertical axis and the quantity of a single good on the horizontal axis. The reasoning for the shapes of the micro supply and demand curves is based on the concepts of substitution and opportunity cost. In the macro *AS/AD* model, the price level of all goods, not just the price of one good, is on the vertical axis and aggregate output, not a single good, is on the horizontal axis. The shapes of the curves have nothing to do with opportunity cost or substitution.

Knowing the difference between microeconomic supply and demand curves and macroeconomic aggregate demand and supply curves is very important.

The second thing to note about the *AS/AD* model is that it is a *historical model*. A historical model is a model that starts at a point in time and says what will likely happen when changes affect the economy. It does not try to explain how the economy got to its starting point; the macroeconomy is too complicated for that. Instead, the model starts from a historically given price and output levels and, given the institutional structure of the economy, considers how changes in the economy are likely to affect those levels. What this means is that much of the discussion in this chapter is based on the economy's institutional realities and observed empirical regularities.

Let's now consider the three central components of the *AS/AD* model—the aggregate demand (*AD*) curve, the short-run aggregate supply (*SAS*) curve, and the long-run aggregate supply curve (*LAS*).

The Aggregate Demand Curve

The **aggregate demand (*AD*) curve** is *a curve that shows how a change in the price level will change aggregate expenditures on all goods and services in an economy*. A standard *AD* curve

Take the time to draw an *AD* curve, making sure to label the axes correctly.

Figure 25-1 The Aggregate Demand Curve
The *AD* curve is a downward-sloping curve that looks like a typical demand curve, but it is important to remember that it is quite a different curve. The reason it slopes downward is not the substitution effect, but instead the wealth effect, the interest rate effect, and the international effect. The multiplier effect strengthens each of these effects.

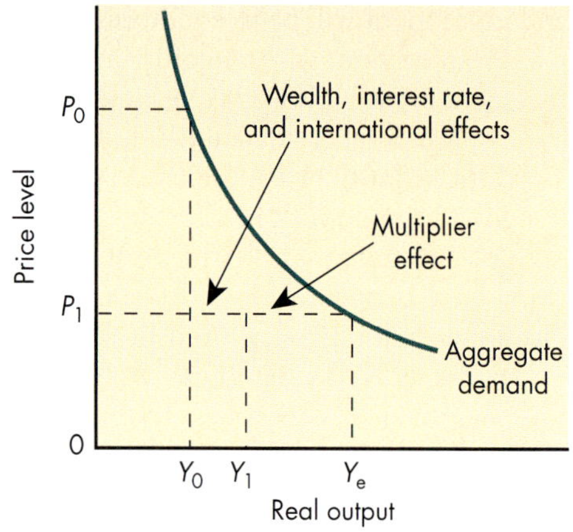

is shown in Figure 25-1. Although the curve is called an aggregate demand curve, let me repeat that it is not the same as a microeconomic demand curve. The *AD* curve is more an equilibrium curve.[1] It shows the level of expenditures at every price level, taking into account interactions among all producers and consumers in an economy.

THE SLOPE OF THE AD CURVE

As you can see, the *AD* curve is downward-sloping. A good place to begin understanding why it is downward-sloping is to remember what aggregate demand is composed of. As I discussed in Chapter 23, aggregate expenditures (demand) is the sum of consumption, investment, government spending, and net exports. The slope of the *AD* curve depends on how these components respond to changes in the price level. In particular, expenditures on consumption, investment, and net exports rise when the price level falls. A number of explanations have been suggested for why a falling price level increases aggregate expenditures. I'll discuss three of them: the wealth effect, the interest-rate effect, and the international effect.

The Wealth Effect

Let's start at price P_0 and output Y_0 in Figure 25-1. (Remember, as I said above, in a historical model we start at a given price and output and determine what would happen if the price level rises or falls from that level.) Now, say that the price level falls to P_1. How will this affect the total amount of goods and services that people demand? Let's first consider what is called the **wealth effect** (sometimes called the real balance effect), which tells us that *a fall in the price level will make the holders of money and of other financial assets richer, so they buy more*. In other words, if the price level falls, the dollar bill in your pocket will buy more than before; as you get richer, you will buy more goods and services. Since consumption expenditures are a component of aggregate demand, the quantity of aggregate demand will increase. Most economists do not see the wealth effect as strong; they do, however, accept the logic of the argument.

The Interest Rate Effect

A second explanation for why the aggregate demand curve slopes downward is called the **interest rate effect**—*the effect that a lower price level*

[1]In a number of articles and in previous editions I tried to change the terminology so that students would not be misled into thinking that the *AD* curve was a normal demand curve. But my changes did not catch on. In this edition I follow standard terminology. Students who want to consider the issue more deeply should see my website (www.mhhe.com/economics/colander).

has on investment expenditures through the effect that a change in the price level has on interest rates. The interest rate effect works as follows: a decrease in the price level will increase real cash on hand (called *money balances*), as in the wealth effect. But the path of the interest rate effect is not through making holders of cash richer. The interest rate effect focuses on the effect that changes in real money balances have on interest rates. The increase in the real money supply will give banks more money to loan out. As they make more loans, interest rates will fall, which, in turn, will increase investment expenditures. Why? Because at lower interest rates businesses will undertake more investment projects. Since investment is one component of aggregate demand, the quantity of aggregate demand will increase when the price level falls.

The International Effect A third reason why aggregate quantity demanded increases with a fall in the price level is the **international effect,** which tells us that *as the price level falls (assuming the exchange rate does not change), net exports will rise*. As the price level in the United States falls, the price of U.S. goods relative to foreign goods goes down and U.S. goods become more competitive than foreign goods; thus, U.S. exports increase and U.S. imports decrease. Let's consider an example. In the mid-1990s the Bulgarian currency was fixed to the German mark. Bulgaria's price level rose enormously, increasing the demand for German imports and reducing the quantity of aggregate demand in Bulgaria.

So, in Figure 25-1 when we include the international effect, the interest rate effect, and the wealth effect, a fall in the price level from P_0 to P_1 causes the quantity of aggregate demand to increase to Y_1.

The Multiplier Effect The wealth effect, the interest rate effect, and the international effect tell us that the quantity of aggregate demand will increase with a fall in the price level, and will decrease with an increase in the price level. But the story about the slope of the aggregate demand curve doesn't end there. It also takes into account the **multiplier effect**—*the amplification of initial changes in expenditures*. It is important to recognize that when considering the demand curve in micro, we can reasonably assume that other things remain constant; in macro, other things change. Whereas the demand curve in micro includes only the initial change, the aggregate demand curve includes the repercussions that these initial changes have throughout the economy. What I mean by *repercussions* is that the initial changes in expenditures set in motion a process in the economy that amplifies these initial effects.

The slope of the *AD* curve is determined by the wealth effect, the interest rate effect, the international effect, and the multiplier effect.

In micro other things can be assumed to remain constant, whereas in macro other things change.

To see how these repercussions will likely work in the real world, imagine that the price level in the United States rises. U.S. citizens will reduce their purchases of U.S. goods and increase their purchases of foreign goods. (That's the international effect.) U.S. firms will see the demand for their goods and services fall and will decrease their output. Profits will fall and people will be laid off. Both these effects will cause income to fall, and as income falls, people will demand still fewer goods and services. (If you're unemployed, you cut back your purchases.) Again production and income fall, which again leads to a drop in expenditures. This secondary cutback is an example of a repercussion. These repercussions *multiply* the initial effect that a change in the price level has on expenditures.

The multiplier effect amplifies the initial wealth, interest rate, and international effects, thereby making the slope of the *AD* curve flatter than it would have been. You can see this in Figure 25-1. The three effects discussed above increase output from Y_0 to Y_1. The repercussions multiply that effect so that output increases to Y_e.

Economists have suggested other reasons why changes in the price level affect the quantity of aggregate demand, but these four should be sufficient to give you an initial understanding. Going through the same exercise that I did above for the wealth, interest rate, international, and multiplier effects for a fall (rather than a rise) in the price level is a useful exercise.

Q-3 True or false? As the price level falls from 110 to 100, the international effect increases output by 10. Therefore, the slope of the *AD* curve will be −1.

Let's conclude this section with an example that brings out the importance of the multiplier effect in determining the slope of the *AD* curve. Say that the multiplier effect amplifies the wealth, interest rate, and international effects by a factor of 2 and that the international, wealth, and interest rate effects reduce output by 4 when the price level rises from 100 to 110. What will be the slope of the *AD* curve? Since the multiplier effect is 2, the total decline in output will be $2 \times 4 = 8$, so the slope will be -1.25 or (10/8).

How Steep Is the AD Curve? While all economists agree about the logic of the wealth effect, the interest rate effect, and the international effect, most also agree that for small changes in the price level, the net effect is relatively small, so, even after the effect has been expanded by the multiplier, the *AD* curve has a very steep slope.[2] Unfortunately, statistically separating out the effects determining the slope of the *AD* curve from shifts in the *AD* curve is difficult because there is much noise—random unexplained movements—in the relationship between the price level and aggregate expenditures. It is that noise on the aggregate level that makes the economy so hard to predict and accounts for the description of economic forecasting as "driving a car blindfolded while following directions given by a person who is looking out of the back window." In order to make the graphs easy to follow, they show an *AD* curve with more slope than it probably has in reality.

Shifts in the *AD* Curve

Next, let's consider what causes the *AD* curve to shift. A shift in the *AD* curve means that at every price level, total expenditures have changed. Anything other than the price level that changes the components of aggregate demand (consumption, investment, government spending, and net exports) will shift the *AD* curve. Five important shift factors of aggregate demand are foreign income, expectations, exchange rate fluctuations, the distribution of income, and government policies.

Foreign Income A country is not an island unto itself. U.S. economic output is closely tied to the income of its major world trading partners. When our trading partners go into a recession, the demand for U.S. goods, and hence U.S. exports, will fall, causing the U.S. *AD* curve to shift in to the left. Similarly, a rise in foreign income leads to an increase in U.S. exports and a rightward shift of the U.S. *AD* curve.

Q-4 If a country's exchange rate rises, what happens to its *AD* curve?

Exchange Rates The currencies of various countries are connected through exchange rates. When a country's currency loses value relative to other currencies, its goods become more competitive compared to foreign goods. Foreign demand for domestic goods increases and domestic demand for foreign goods decreases as individuals shift their spending to domestic goods at home. Both these effects increase net exports and shift the *AD* curve to the right. By the same reasoning, when a country's currency gains value, the *AD* curve shifts in the opposite direction. You can see these effects on the U.S.–Canadian border. In the early 1990s the Canadian dollar had a high value relative to the U.S. dollar. This caused many Canadians near the border to make buying trips to the United States. Then, when the Canadian dollar fell in value, those buying trips decreased, and the Canadian *AD* curve shifted right.

[2]Of the three, the international effect is probably the strongest, but its strength depends on whether fluctuations in the exchange rate offset it; exchange rates determination will be discussed in depth in a later chapter.

Expectations Another important shift factor of aggregate demand is expectations. Many different types of expectations can affect the *AD* curve. To give you an idea of the role of expectations, let's consider two expectational shift factors—expectations of future output and future prices. When businesspeople expect demand to be high in the future, they will want to increase their production capacity; their investment demand, a component of aggregate demand, will increase. Thus, positive expectations about future demand will shift the *AD* curve to the right.

Expectations of higher future income increase expenditures and shift the *AD* curve out.

Similarly, when consumers expect the economy to do well, they will be less worried about saving for the future, and they will spend more now—the *AD* curve will shift to the right. Alternatively, if consumers expect the future to be gloomy, they will likely try to save for the future and will decrease the consumption expenditures. The *AD* curve will shift to the left.

Another type of expectation that shifts the *AD* curve concerns expectations of future prices. If you expect the prices of goods to rise in the future, it pays to buy goods now that you might want in the future—before their prices rise. The current price level hasn't changed, but aggregate quantity demanded at that price level has increased, indicating a shift of the *AD* curve to the right.

Expectations of a rising price level in the future increase expenditures and shift the *AD* curve out to the right.

The effect of expectations of future price levels is seen more clearly in hyperinflation. In most cases of hyperinflation, people rush out to spend their money quickly—to buy whatever they can to beat the price increase. So even though prices are rising, aggregate demand stays high because the rise in price creates an expectation of even higher prices, and thus the current high price is seen as a low price relative to the future. I said that an increase in expectations of inflation will "have a tendency to" rather than "definitely" shift the *AD* curve to the right because those expectations of inflation are interrelated with a variety of other expectations. For example, an expectation of a rise in the price of goods you buy could be accompanied by an expectation of a fall in income, and that fall in income would work in the opposite direction, decreasing aggregate demand.

This interrelation of various types of expectations makes it very difficult to specify precisely what effect certain types of expectations have on the *AD* curve. But it does not eliminate the importance of expectations as shift factors. It simply means that we often aren't sure what the net effect of a change in expectations on aggregate demand will be.

Distribution of Income Some people save more than others, and everyone's spending habits differ. Thus, as income distribution changes, so too will aggregate demand. One of the most important of these distributional effects concerns the distribution of income between wages and profits. Workers receive wage income and are more likely to spend the income they receive; firms' profits are distributed to stockholders or are retained by the firm. Since stockholders in the United States tend to be wealthy, and the wealthy save a greater portion of their income than the poor do, a higher portion of income received as profits will likely be saved. Assuming all saving is not translated into investment, as the real wage decreases but total income remains constant, it is likely that consumption expenditures will fall and the aggregate demand will shift to the left. Similarly, as the real wage increases, it is likely that aggregate demand will shift to the right.

Monetary and Fiscal Policies One of the most important reasons why the aggregate demand curve has been so important in macro policy analysis is that often macro policymakers think that they can control it, at least to some degree. For example, if the government spends lots of money without increasing taxes, it shifts the *AD* curve to the right; if the government raises taxes significantly and holds spending constant,

Five important shift factors of *AD* are:

1. Foreign income.
2. Exchange rates.
3. Expectations.
4. The distribution of income.
5. Monetary and fiscal policies.

Figure 25-2 Effect of a Shift Factor on the AD Curve
The *AD* curve shifts out by more than the initial change in expenditures. In this example, exports increase by 100. The multiplier magnifies this shift, and the *AD* curve shifts to the right by a multiple of 100, in this case by 300.

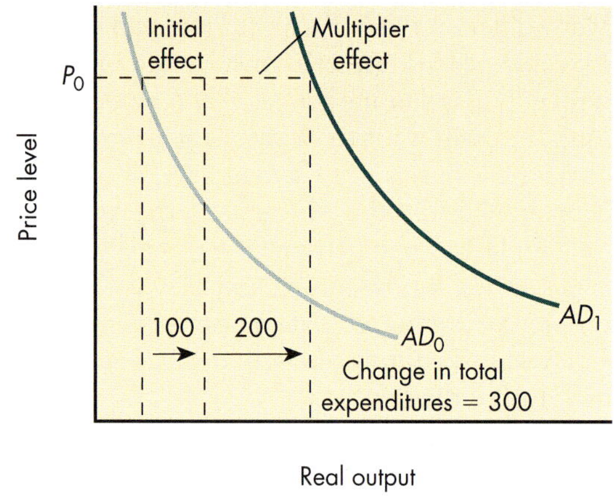

consumers will have less disposable income and will reduce their expenditures, shifting the *AD* curve to the left. Similarly, when the Federal Reserve Bank, the U.S. economy's central bank, expands the money supply it can often lower interest rates, making it easier for both consumers and investors to borrow, increasing their spending, and thereby shifting the *AD* curve to the right. This deliberate increase in aggregate demand to influence the level of income in the economy is what most policymakers mean by the term *macro policy*. Expansionary macro policy shifts the *AD* curve to the right; contractionary macro policy shifts it to the left.

Deliberate shifting of the *AD* curve is what most policymakers mean by macro policy.

Multiplier Effects of Shift Factors As I emphasized when I introduced the *AD* curve, you cannot treat the *AD* curve like a micro demand curve. This comes out most clearly when considering shifts in the curve caused by shift factors. The aggregate demand curve may shift by more than the amount of the initial shift factor because of the multiplier effect. The explanation is the same as when I introduced the multiplier effect. When government increases its spending, firms increase production, which leads to higher income. A fraction of that increase in income is spent on more goods and services, shifting the *AD* curve even further to the right. This leads firms to increase production again; income and expenditures also rise. Each round, the increase gets smaller and smaller until the increase becomes negligible. In the end the *AD* curve will have shifted by a multiple of the initial shift. Just how large that multiple is depends on how much of the change in income affects spending in each round. Thus, in Figure 25-2, when an initial shift factor of aggregate demand is 100 and the multiplier is 3, the *AD* curve will shift to the right by 300, three times the initial shift. The extra 200 shift is due to the multiplier effect.

Q.5 If government spending increases by 20, by how much does the *AD* curve shift out?

To see that you are following the argument, consider the following two shifts: (1) a fall in the U.S. exchange rate, increasing net exports by 50; and (2) an increase in government spending of 100. Explain how the *AD* curve will shift in each of these cases, and why that shift will be larger than the initial shift. If you are not sure about these explanations, review the multiplier effect discussion above.

The *AD* curve holds all shift factors constant, so the slope of the *AD* curve reflects only the effects of a change in the price level (including multiplier effects).

The Short-Run Aggregate Supply Curve

The second component of the *AS/AD* model is the **short-run aggregate supply (*SAS*) curve**—*a curve that specifies how a shift in the aggregate demand curve affects the price level*

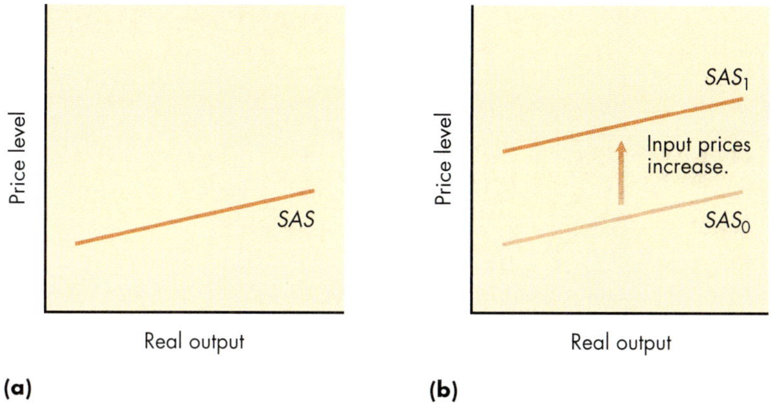

Figure 25-3 (a and b) The Short-Run Aggregate Supply Curve

The *SAS* curve shows how changes in aggregate demand affect output and the price level. As you can see in (**a**), the *SAS* curve is generally thought to be slightly upward-sloping in the short run; (**b**) shows an upward shift in the *SAS* curve caused by an increase in input prices.

and real output in the short run, other things constant. A standard *SAS* curve is shown in Figure 25-3(a).

The Slope of the SAS Curve

As you can see, the *SAS* curve is upward-sloping, which means that in the short run, other things constant, an increase in output is accompanied by a rise in the price level. That is, when aggregate demand increases, the price level—the composite of all prices—rises. The shape of the *SAS* curve reflects two different types of microeconomic markets in our economy—auction markets (which are the markets represented by the supply/demand model) and posted-price markets (in which prices are set by the producers and change only infrequently).

In auction markets, there is little question why prices rise when demand increases—as long as the supply curve in the market is upward-sloping, it is what we would expect with an increase in demand. But these auction markets make up only a small percentage of final output markets. (They are much more common in markets for resources.) Posted-price markets are a larger segment of the final output market; some estimate that posted-price markets comprise 90 percent of the total final product markets. In posted-price markets, firms set prices as a markup over costs. For example, if the markup is 40 percent and the cost of production is $10 per unit, the firm would set a price of $14.

Posted-price markets are often called **quantity-adjusting markets**—*markets in which firms respond to changes in demand primarily by modifying their output instead of changing their prices*. It would be wrong, however, to assume that prices in these markets are totally unresponsive to changes in demand. Prices change for two reasons. First, the markups in posted-price markets are not totally fixed; when demand increases, some firms will take the opportunity to raise their prices slightly, increasing their markup, and when demand falls, firms have a tendency to lower their prices slightly, decreasing their markup. This tendency to change markups as aggregate demand changes contributes to the upward slope of the *SAS* curve.

Second, input prices may change when aggregate demand shifts because, for the aggregate economy, a shift in demand for final output means that there will be an equivalent shift in demand for inputs. Raw material markets are often auction markets, and raw material costs for firms can vary directly with increases in aggregate demand because the increase in demand for resources by all firms tends to push up the price of raw materials. Increases in input prices are not, however, a reason why the *SAS* curve slopes upward. Along an *SAS* curve, all other things, including input prices, are assumed to remain constant. Increases in input prices shift the *SAS* curve. Input prices are assumed

WHY ARE PRICES INFLEXIBLE?

Knowing the Tools

Why do firms adjust production instead of price? A number of reasons have been put forward by economists, and recently a group of economists, led by Princeton economist Alan Blinder, surveyed firms to find out which reasons firms believed were most important. The survey choices were coordination failure, cost-based pricing rules, the use of variables other than prices to clear markets, and implicit contracts.

Coordination Failure and Strategic Pricing

About 90 percent of final-goods markets in the United States are oligopolistic with cost-determined prices. These are markets in which there are a few major firms that take each other's reactions into account in their decisions. Oligopolistic markets can be highly competitive, but the competition is strategic. Strategic competition has a number of implications for pricing. Under U.S. law, firms cannot directly collude—get together and decide on a pricing strategy for the industry—but they can informally coordinate their pricing procedures. If all firms can implicitly agree to act in a coordinated fashion and hold their prices up when faced with generalized decreased demand, they are not violating the law and will be better off than they would be if they acted in an uncoordinated fashion.

They also follow that strategy when they experience an increase in demand. In Blinder's survey, firms stated that they are also hesitant to raise prices on the up side when demand increases. They fear that if they increase their price they will undermine the coordinated pricing strategy with other firms, or that other firms will not follow their move and they will lose market share.

To say that the U.S. economy is oligopolistic is not to say that it is not competitive. Ask any businessperson and he or she will tell you that it is highly competitive. But firms now often compete on fronts other than price.

Cost-Based Pricing Rules

The pricing coordination strategy discussed above is maintained by firms' tendency to use cost-based pricing rules. In a cost-plus-markup pricing procedure, firms determine their direct costs and then set price in relation to those costs. Costs play a central role in determining price, and for most firms the most important costs are labor costs, which tend to be fixed by long-term wage contracts between workers and employers. (Unions, for example, typically negotiate wage contracts for three-year periods.) Thus, costs do not change with changes in demand, and, following a cost-plus-markup strategy, neither do prices.

Other Methods to Clear Markets

The use of cost-plus or markup pricing rules does not mean that markets do not clear. If firms set the price in the market too high, and therefore don't sell all they were planning to sell, they will hold that price and, initially, build up inventory before changing the quantity of goods they are producing. If inventory gets too high, firms may run sales, temporarily lowering price to eliminate excess inventory, but they will also tie production to sales. Alternatively, firms may increase their advertising when sales fall, or they may provide higher bonuses for salespeople. So when demand changes, output changes to match demand at the price determined in the firm's long-run pricing strategy. So markets can clear even when prices are inflexible.

Implicit Contracts

Most firms have ongoing relationships with their customers. That means that they don't want to antagonize them. They have found that one way to avoid antagonizing customers is not to take advantage of them even when they could. In the Blinder survey firms felt that they had implicit contracts with their customers to raise prices only when their costs changed, or when market conditions changed substantially.

Conclusion

The combination of these reasons leads to our having a large segment of the economy in which the prices do not significantly change as demand changes. For that reason, as demand increased in the 1990s, there was little pressure on prices. Of course, if costs, especially labor costs, start rising, then prices will rise. To the degree that demand changes affect costs, prices will respond, but as a first approximation it is generally acceptable to say that the price level does not significantly move in response to demand. That's why the short-run aggregate supply curve is not very steep.

to be constant along an *SAS* curve for two reasons. First, wages (the largest component of the inputs into the production of most goods) tend to be set by contract and do not vary immediately with shifts in demand. Second, in real-world posted-price markets, firms initially absorb these changes in input costs by changing their markup rather than their product prices. Changing prices is costly—both in terms of physically reticketing items and in terms of maintaining good customer relations.

Let me summarize: In macro we are talking about a composite price, so to talk about the price level we have to put these two sets of markets together, giving us the following two reasons for the upward-sloping *SAS* curve:

- In auction markets, prices rise automatically because the higher prices lead to higher profits, which cause firms to increase the quantity of the good supplied.
- In posted-price markets, prices rise somewhat because, when they experience an increase in demand, firms find they can increase their posted price and continue to maintain their competitive position relative to other firms.

Putting these two markets together we see that as aggregate demand changes, the price level changes in the same direction, meaning that the *SAS* curve is upward-sloping.

Shifts in the *SAS* Curve

Notice that in the definition of the *SAS* curve, we have assumed that other things remain constant. As discussed above, this does not mean that other things *will* remain constant. It simply means that changes in other things, such as input prices, shift the *SAS* curve. For example, if input prices rise, the *SAS* curve shifts up; if input prices fall, the *SAS* curve shifts down. So a change in input prices, such as wages, is a shift factor of supply. An important reason why money wages change is expectations of inflation. If workers expect prices to be rising by 2 percent, they are likely to ask for at least a 2 percent rise in wages simply to keep up with inflation and maintain their real wage. If they expect the price level to fall by 2 percent, they are far more likely to be happy with their current wage. So the expectation of inflation is a shift factor that works through wages.

Another shift factor of aggregate supply is a change in factor productivity. An increase in productivity, by reducing the amount of inputs required for a given amount of output, reduces input costs per unit output and shifts the *SAS* curve down. A fall in productivity shifts the *SAS* curve up.

Two other shift factors that often enter into policy discussions are changes in import prices of final goods, and excise and sales taxes. Import prices are a shift factor because they are a component of an economy's price level. When import prices rise, the *SAS* curve shifts up; when import prices fall, the *SAS* curve shifts down. Similarly, higher sales taxes shift the *SAS* curve up, and lower sales taxes shift the *SAS* curve down.

In summary, anything that changes factor costs will be a shift factor of supply. Such factors include:

- Changes in input prices.
- Changes in expectations of inflation.
- Excise and sales taxes.
- Productivity.
- Import prices.

Economists spend a lot of time tracking these shift factors because they are central to whether the economy will have an inflation problem. Two of these—the wage component of input prices and labor productivity—are followed with special care because labor costs make up about two-thirds of total production costs. The rule of thumb economists use when estimating how much the *SAS* curve will shift is that it will shift by the percentage change in wages and other factor prices minus changes in productivity. For example, if productivity rises by 3 percent and wages rise by 7 percent, we can expect the price level to rise by 4 percent for a given level of output. I show a shift up in the *SAS* curve in Figure 25-3(b). If wages and productivity rise by equal percentages, the price level would remain constant. If wages and other factors prices rise by less than the increase in productivity, the price level can fall, as recently happened in Japan. The relationship can be written as follows:

% change in the price level = % change in wages − % change in productivity

In the real world, we see shifts in the *SAS* curve in many areas. In the 1970s, for example, oil prices shot up enormously. That led to a sharp rise in the producer price index and a significant rise in factor prices, causing the *SAS* curve to shift up. Another example occurred in Argentina in early 2002 when the value of its currency, the peso, fell drastically. That caused the price of imports measured in pesos to increase substantially, which shifted its *SAS* curve up.

The Long-Run Aggregate Supply Curve

The final curve that makes up the *AS/AD* model is the **long-run aggregate supply (*LAS*) curve**—*a curve that shows the long-run relationship between output and the price level.* Whereas the *SAS* curve holds input prices constant, no prices are assumed held constant on the *LAS* curve. The position of the *LAS* curve is determined by potential output—the amount of goods and services an economy can produce when both labor and capital are fully employed. Figure 25-4(a) shows an *LAS* curve.

Notice that the *LAS* curve is vertical. Since at potential output all resources are being fully utilized, a rise in the price level means that the price of goods and factors of production, including wages, rise. Consider it this way: If all prices doubled, including

Figure 25-4 (a and b) The Long-Run Aggregate Supply Curve
The long-run aggregate supply curve shows the output that an economy can produce when both labor and capital are fully employed. It is vertical because at potential output a rise in the price level means that all prices, including input prices, rise. Available resources do not rise and thus neither does potential output.

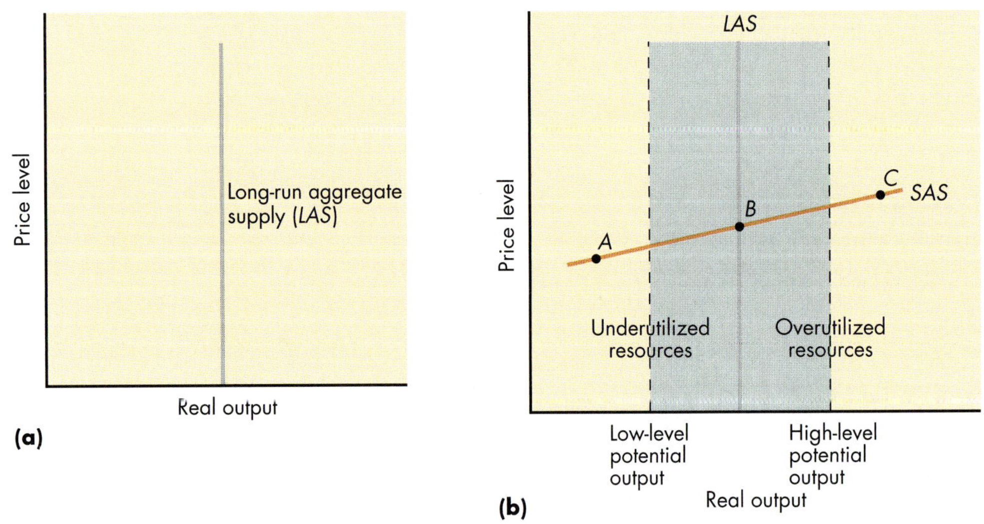

your wage, your real income would not change. Since potential output is unaffected by the price level, the *LAS* curve is vertical.

A Range for Potential Output and the *LAS* Curve

The position of the *LAS* curve is determined by potential output. Because our estimates of potential output are inexact, precisely where to draw the *LAS* curve is generally somewhat in debate. To understand policy debates, it is helpful to consider potential output to be a range of values. This range is bounded by a high level of potential output and a low level of potential output, as Figure 25-4(b) shows. The *LAS* curve can be thought of as being in the middle of that range.

This range is important because how close actual output (where the economy is along the *SAS* curve) is to potential output is a key determinant of what prediction one will make about whether the *SAS* curve will be shifting up or down. At points on the *SAS* curve to the left of the *LAS* curve (such as point *A*), resources are likely to be underutilized and we would expect there to be pressure for factor prices to fall and, other things equal, the *SAS* curve to shift down. At points to the right of the *LAS* curve (such as point *C*), we would expect factor prices to be bid up and, other things equal, pressure to be put on the *SAS* curve to shift up. Moreover, the further actual output is from potential output, the greater the pressure we would expect on factor prices to rise or fall. At the point of intersection between the *SAS* curve and the *LAS* curve (point *B*), other things equal, factor prices have no pressure to rise or fall.

In reality there are often debates about whether we will expect factor prices to rise or fall in response to a change in demand, other things equal. That debate reflects the different estimates of where potential output is. Given the uncertainty of measured potential output, we would expect there to be a debate about whether the *SAS* curve will be shifting up or down. We will discuss these issues later. For now, all I want you to remember is that the *LAS* curve is an abstraction that reduces what is actually a range of potential output into a single value.

Shifts in the *LAS* Curve

Because the position of the *LAS* curve is determined by potential output, it shifts for the same reasons that potential output shifts. As discussed in Chapter 24, those reasons are changes in capital, available resources, growth-compatible institutions, technological development, and entrepreneurship. Increases in any of these increase potential output and shift the *LAS* curve out. Decreases in any of these reduce potential output and shift the *LAS* curve in. The position of the *LAS* curve plays an important role in determining long-run equilibrium and in determining whether policy should focus on long-run or short-run issues.

Equilibrium in the Aggregate Economy

Now that we have introduced the *SAS*, *AD*, and *LAS* curves, we'll consider short-run and long-run equilibrium and how changes in the curves affect those equilibria. I start with the short run.

Short-Run Equilibrium

In the short run the intersection of the short-run aggregate supply curve and the aggregate demand curve determines equilibrium of the economy. Thus, short-run equilibrium is shown by point *E* in Figure 25-5(a). If the *AD* curve shifts to the right, from AD_0 to AD_1, equilibrium will shift from point *E* to point *F*. The price level will rise to P_1 and

Figure 25-5 (a and b) Short-Run Equilibrium
Short-run equilibrium is where the short-run aggregate supply and aggregate demand curves intersect. Point E in (**a**) is equilibrium; (**a**) also shows how a shift in the aggregate demand curve to the right changes equilibrium from E to F, increasing output from Y_0 to Y_1 and increasing price level from P_0 to P_1. In (**b**) you can see how a shift up in the short-run aggregate supply curve changes equilibrium from E to G, reducing output from Y_0 to Y_2 and increasing the price level from P_0 to P_2.

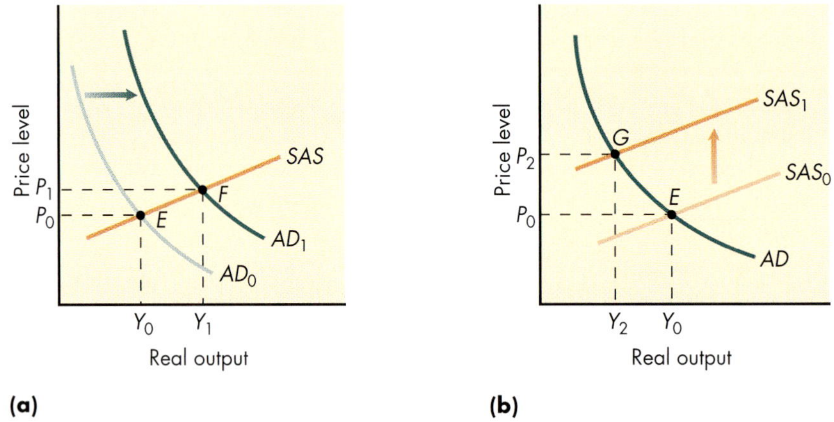

output will increase to Y_1. A decrease in aggregate demand will shift output and the price level down.

Figure 25-5(b) shows the effect on equilibrium of a shift up in the *SAS* curve. Initially equilibrium is at point E. An upward shift in the *SAS* curve from SAS_0 to SAS_1 increases the price level from P_0 to P_2 and reduces equilibrium output from Y_0 to Y_2.

Long-Run Equilibrium

Long-run equilibrium is determined by the intersection of the *AD* curve and the *LAS* curve.

Long-run equilibrium is determined by the intersection of the *AD* curve and the *LAS* curve, as shown by point E in Figure 25-6(a). Since in the long run output is determined by the position of the *LAS* curve, which is at potential output Y_P, the aggregate demand curve can determine only the price level; it does not affect the level of real output. Thus, as shown in Figure 25-6(b), when aggregate demand increases from AD_0 to AD_1, the price level rises (from P_0 to P_1) but output does not change. When aggregate demand decreases, the price level falls and output remains at potential. In the long run, output is fixed and the price level is variable, so aggregate output is determined not by aggregate demand but by potential output. Aggregate demand determines the price level.

Integrating the Short-Run and Long-Run Frameworks

To complete our analysis we have to relate the long run and short run. We start with the economy in both long-run and short-run equilibrium, as in Figure 25-7(a). As you can see at point E, with output Y_P, and price level P_0, the economy is in both a long-run equilibrium and a short-run equilibrium, since at point E the *AD* curve and *SAS* curve intersect at the economy's *LAS* curve. That is the situation economists hope for—that aggregate demand grows at just the same rate as potential output, so that growth and unemployment are at their target rates, with no, or minimal, inflation. In the late 1990s the U.S. economy was in just such a position—potential output was increasing at the same rate that aggregate demand was increasing; unemployment was low, as was inflation.

Figure 25-6 (a and b) Long-Run Equilibrium
Long-run equilibrium is where the *LAS* curve and *AD* curves intersect. Point *E* in (**a**) is long-run equilibrium. In (**b**) you can see how a shift in the aggregate demand curve changes equilibrium from *E* to *H*, increasing the price level from P_0 to P_1 but leaving output unchanged.

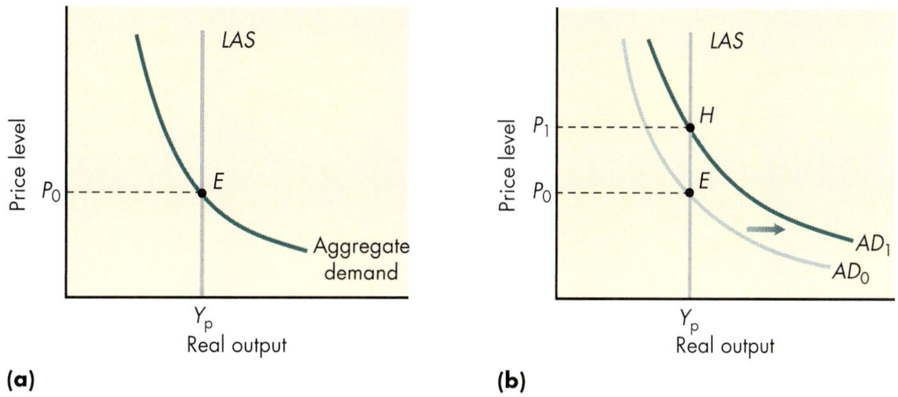

Figure 25-7 (a, b, and c) Short- and Long-Run Frameworks
The economy is in both short-run and long-run equilibrium when all three curves intersect in the same location. When the economy is in short-run equilibrium but not long-run equilibrium, the position of the *SAS* curve is determined by the relationship between output and potential output. If output is below potential, the *SAS* curve is pulled down by falling input prices, as shown in (**b**). If output is above potential, the *SAS* curve is pulled up by rising input prices, as shown in (**c**).

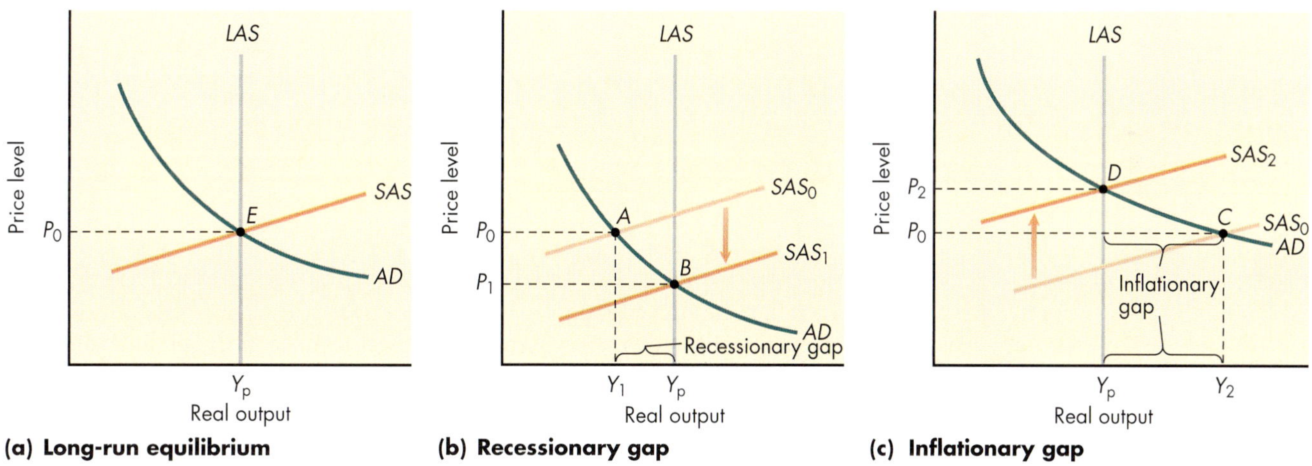

The Recessionary Gap Alas, the economy is not always at that point *E*. An economy at point *A* in Figure 25-7(b) is in a situation where the quantity of aggregate demand is below potential output and not all the resources in the economy are being fully used. The distance $Y_P - Y_1$ shows the amount of output that is not being produced but could be. This distance is often referred to as a **recessionary gap,** *the amount by which equilibrium output is below potential output*.

Q-6 If the *SAS*, *AD*, and *LAS* curves, intersect at the same point and wages are constant, what is likely to happen to output and the price level?

If the economy remains at this level of output for a long time, costs and wages would tend to fall because there would be an excess supply of factors of production. As costs and wages fall, the price level also falls. The short-run aggregate supply curve would shift down (from SAS_0 to SAS_1) until eventually the long-run and short-run equilibrium

A REVIEW OF THE AS/AD MODEL

Knowing the Tools

	What Shape Is It?	What Determines Its Shape?	What Shifts the Curve?
Aggregate demand	Downward sloping: As the price level declines expenditures rise.	The wealth effect, the interest rate effect, the international effect, and the multiplier effect.	Sudden changes in *C*, *I*, (*X*–*M*), or G caused by changes in foreign income, expectations about future income or prices, exchange rates, monetary policy, fiscal policy.
Short-run aggregate supply	Upward-sloping: The price level increases as output increases.	Firm behavior. Most firms change production instead of price when demand changes. Some firms will raise prices when output increases.	Increases in input prices shift the *SAS* curve up. Decreases in input prices shift the *SAS* curve down.
Long-run aggregate supply	Vertical: Changes in the price level have no effect on output.	Potential output is output that the economy can produce when labor and capital are fully utilized. It is not affected by prices.	Anything that increases potential output, such as increases in available resources and technological innovation.

Q-7 Demonstrate graphically both the short-run and long-run *AS/AD* equilibrium with a recessionary gap.

would be reached at point *B*. But generally in our economy that does not happen.[3] Long before costs fall, either the economy picks up on its own or the government introduces policies to expand output. That's why we seldom see declines in the price level. If the government expands aggregate demand, or some other shift factor expands aggregate demand, the *AD* curve shifts to the right, eliminating the recessionary gap and keeping the price level constant.

The Inflationary Gap An economy at point C in Figure 25-7(c) demonstrates a case where the short-run equilibrium is at a higher income than the economy's potential output. In this case economists say that the economy has an **inflationary gap** shown by $Y_2 - Y_0$—*aggregate expenditures above potential output that exist at the current price level.* Output cannot remain at Y_2 for long because the economy's resources are being used beyond their potential. Factor prices will rise and the *SAS* curve will shift up from SAS_0 to SAS_2; the new equilibrium is at point *D*.

[3]If, as happened in the Great Depression in the 1930s and in Japan in the early 2000s, the economy stays below its potential output long enough, we would see the price level fall.

The Economy beyond Potential How can resources be used beyond potential? By overutilizing resources. Consider the resources you put into classwork. Suppose that your potential is a B+. If you stay up all night studying and cram in extra reading during mealtimes, you could earn an A. But eventually you'll get tired. You can't keep up that amount of effort for long. The same is true for production. Extra shifts can be added and machinery can be run longer periods, but eventually the workers will become exhausted and the machinery will wear out. Output will have to return to its potential.

If aggregate expenditures are above potential output, then increased demand for labor would put upward pressure on wages and subsequently the overall level of prices.

The result of this inflationary gap will be a bidding up of factor prices and a rise in costs for firms. When an economy is below potential, firms can hire additional factors of production to increase production without increasing production costs. Once the economy reaches its potential output, however, that is no longer possible. If a firm is to increase its factors of production, it must lure resources away from other firms. It will do so by offering higher wages and prices. But the firm facing a loss of its resources will likely respond by increasing its wages and other prices it pays to its employees and other suppliers.

As firms compete for resources, their costs rise beyond increases in productivity, shifting up the *SAS* curve. This means that once an economy's potential output is reached, the price level tends to rise. In fact, economists sometimes look to see whether the price level has begun to rise before deciding where potential output is. Thus, in the 1990s economists kept increasing their estimates of potential output because the price level did not rise even as the economy approached, and exceeded, what they previously thought was its potential output.

If the economy is operating above potential, the *SAS* curve will shift up until the inflationary gap is eliminated. Again, that is usually not what happens. Either the economy slows down on its own or the government introduces aggregate demand policy to contract output and eliminate the inflationary gap.

Aggregate Demand Policy

A primary reason for government policymakers' interest in the *AS/AD* model is their ability to shift the *AD* curve with policy. As I mentioned above, they can do this with monetary or fiscal policy. Monetary policy involves the Federal Reserve Bank's changing the money supply and interest rates, and understanding it requires a knowledge of the financial sector. This will be discussed at length in later chapters. In this chapter I'll concentrate on **fiscal policy**—*the deliberate change in either government spending or taxes to stimulate or slow down the economy*. Fiscal policy is often discussed in terms of the government budget deficit (government expenditures less government revenue). If aggregate income is too low (actual income is below potential income), the appropriate fiscal policy is expansionary fiscal policy: increase the deficit by decreasing taxes or increasing government spending. Expansionary fiscal policy shifts the *AD* curve out to the right. If aggregate income is too high (actual income is above potential income), the appropriate fiscal policy is contractionary fiscal policy: decrease the deficit by increasing taxes or decreasing government spending. Contractionary fiscal policy shifts the *AD* curve to the left.

Q-8 If politicians suddenly raise government expenditures, and the economy is well below potential output, what will happen to prices and real income?

Let's go through a couple of examples. Say the economy is in a recessionary gap at point A in Figure 25-8(a). To eliminate the recessionary gap, government needs to implement expansionary fiscal policy. The appropriate fiscal policy would be to cut taxes or increase government spending, letting the multiplier augment those effects so that the *AD* curve shifts out to AD_1. This would raise the price level slightly but would eliminate the recessionary gap. Alternatively, say the economy is in an inflationary gap at point *B* in Figure 25-8(b). To prevent the inflation caused by the upward shift of the

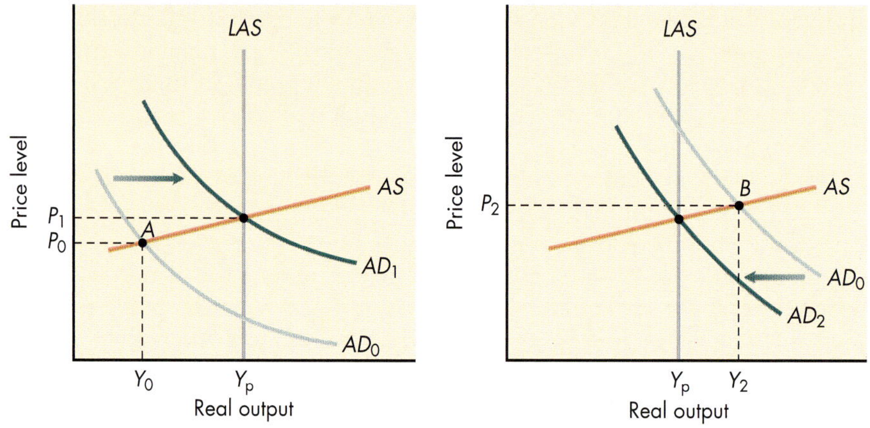

(a) Expansionary fiscal policy **(b) Contractionary fiscal policy**

Figure 25-8 (a and b) Fiscal Policy
Expansionary fiscal policy can bring an economy out of a recessionary gap, as shown in (**a**). If an economy is in an inflationary gap, contractionary fiscal policy can reduce real output to prevent inflation, as shown in (**b**).

SAS curve, the appropriate fiscal policy is to increase taxes or cut government spending. Either of these actions will shift the *AD* curve in to AD_2. This lowers the price level slightly and eliminates the inflationary gap. So the best way to picture fiscal policy is as a policy designed to shift the *AD* curve to keep output at potential.

Some Additional Policy Examples

Now that we've been through the model, let's give you some practice with it by making you an adviser to the president. He comes to you for some advice. Unemployment is 12 percent and there is no inflation. History suggests that the economy is well below its potential output, so there is no need to worry about increasing factor prices. What policy would you recommend?

Pause for answer

The answer I hope you gave was expansionary fiscal policy, shifting the *AD* curve out to its potential income, as in Figure 25-9(a).

Now let's try a different scenario. Unemployment is 5 percent and it is believed that that 5 percent is the *target rate if unemployment*—the rate of unemployment that is consistent with potential output. But measures of consumer optimism suggest that a large rise in consumer expenditures is likely. What policy would you recommend?

Pause for answer

The answer I hope you gave is contractionary fiscal policy to counteract the expected rise in the *AD* curve before it occurs and prevent the economy from creating an inflationary gap. What would happen without that fiscal policy is shown in Figure 25-9(b). The economy is initially at point C, where the price level is P_0 and output is Y_P. In the absence of offsetting policy, the increase in expenditures along with the multiplier would move the economy to point *D* at a level of output (Y_1) above potential, creating an inflationary gap. If left alone, factor prices will rise, shifting the *SAS* curve up until it reaches SAS_1. The price level would rise to P_1 and the real output would return to Y_P, point *E*. But of course that didn't happen, because you recommended a policy of cutting government spending or raising taxes so that the *AD* curve shifts back to AD_0, making the equilibrium at point C, not point *E* and avoiding any rise in prices. The economy remains at potential output at a constant price level, P_0.

Figure 25-9 (a and b) Shifting AD and SAS Curves

In (**a**) you can see what happens when the economy is below potential and aggregate demand increases just enough to bring output to its potential. In (**b**) you can see what happens when the economy begins at potential and aggregate expenditures rise. The *AD* curve shifts to the right by a multiple of the initial shift and output increases beyond potential output. Since the economy is above potential, input prices begin to rise and the *SAS* curve shifts up. Input prices continue to rise and output falls until output returns to its potential. The price level rises to P_1.

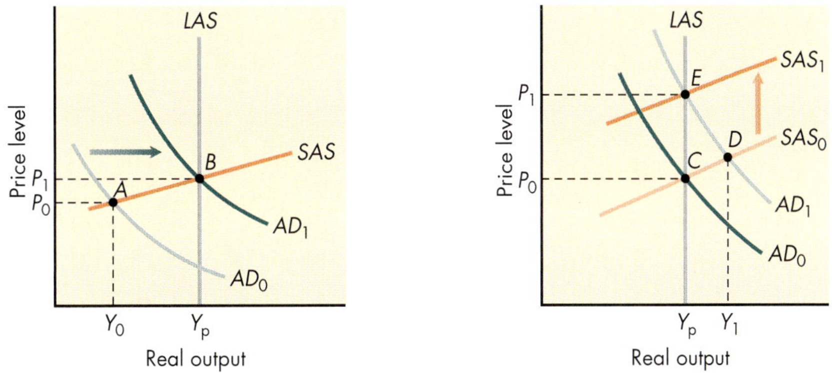

(a) Expansionary fiscal policy **(b) Economy above potential**

To give you an idea of how fiscal policy has worked in the real world, we'll look at two examples—the effect of wartime spending in the 1940s and the prolonged expansion of the mid-1990s to early 2000s.

Fiscal Policy in World War II In the 1940s the focus of U.S. policy switched from the Depression to fighting World War II. Fighting a war requires transferring civilian production to war production, so economists' attention turned to how to do so. Taxes went up enormously, but government expenditures rose far more. The result can be seen in Figure 25-10(a), which tabulates GDP, the deficit (government expenditures less taxes), and unemployment data for the wartime time span 1937–1946. As you can see, the deficit increased greatly and real GDP rose by more than the increase in the deficit. Figure 25-10(b) shows the effect in the *AS/AD* model. The *AD* curve shifts to the right by more than the increase in the deficit. As predicted, the U.S. economy expanded enormously in response to the expansionary fiscal policy that accompanied the war. One thing should bother you about this episode: If the economy exceeded its potential output, shouldn't the short-run aggregate supply curve have started to shift up, causing a serious inflation problem? It didn't because the wartime expansion was accompanied by wage and price controls, which prevented significant price-level increases, and by rationing.

During the war, economic output was expanded as far as anyone dared hope it could be. This expansion was also accompanied by an expansionary monetary policy, so we must be careful about drawing too strong an inference about the effect of fiscal policy from the episode. (The importance of monetary policy will be discussed in a later chapter.)

Web Note 25.3
War Bonds

It might seem from the example of World War II, when the U.S. economy expanded sharply, that wars are good for the economy. They certainly do bring about expansionary policy, increase GDP, and decrease unemployment. But remember, GDP is *not* welfare and a decrease in unemployment is not necessarily good. In World War II people went without many goods; production of guns and bombs increased, but production of

Figure 25-10 (a and b) War Finance: Expansionary Fiscal Policy
During wars, government budget deficits have risen significantly. As they have, unemployment has fallen and GDP has risen enormously. You can see the effect in the table in (**a**), which presents the U.S. government budget deficit and unemployment rate during World War II. The graph in (**b**) shows that this is what would be predicted in the *AS/AD* model.

Year	GDP (billions of 1958 dollars)	Deficit (billions of dollars)	Unemployment rate
1937	$ 90	$ -2.8	14.3%
1938	84	-1.0	19.0
1939	90	-2.9	17.2
1940	99	-2.7	14.6
1941	124	-4.8	9.9
1942	157	-19.4	4.7
1943	191	-53.8	1.9
1944	210	-46.1	1.2
1945	211	-45.0	1.9
1946	208	-18.2	3.9

(a)

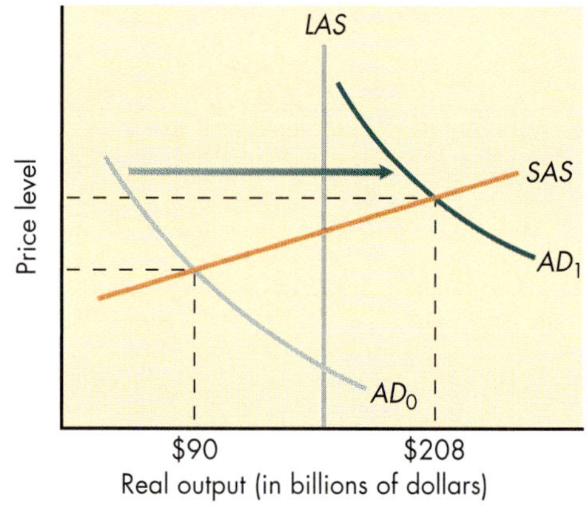

(b)

Source: *Historical Statistics of the United Stated: Colonial Times to 1970.*

butter decreased. Many people were killed or permanently disabled, which decreases unemployment but can hardly be called a good way to expand the economy.

U.S. Economic Expansion As a second example, let's consider the government budget picture in the early 2000s. In the late 1990s and early 2000s the budget went from a large deficit to a large surplus, so it would seem as if government fiscal policy was slowing the economy down. But the economy was booming. There are two explanations for this seeming paradox. The first is that, yes, the surplus was slowing the economy, but the contractionary effect of the surplus was offset by significant increases in consumer and investment spending. The private saving rate actually fell to zero at times and consumption increased enormously. Had the government budget not been in surplus, the economy would have likely exceeded potential output and inflation would have accelerated.

The second explanation for the paradox is that much of the surplus was the result of the booming economy, not contractionary fiscal policy. In fact, much of the deficit reduction, and movement into budget surplus, resulted from unexpected increases in income. When an economy is booming, as income rises, tax revenues rise and expenditures on income-support programs decline automatically. Much of the unexpected decline in the deficit was a result of tax revenue surprises.

Despite pressures in 2000 and 2001 by most economists to maintain the budget surplus (when tax revenues exceed expenditures), political pressures led to decreasing it, both by increasing government spending and by decreasing taxes. Then in mid-2001, the economy started to slow down. That slowdown was exacerbated by the terrorist attacks of September 11, following which investment and consumption fell, throwing the economy into a recession. Because of the recession, government had far less reason to run a surplus to slow the economy. In fact, the tax cut came at just the right time, keeping the recession very mild by helping hold up consumer spending. So here we have a case of expansionary fiscal policy working to prevent a recession. However, it is important to remember that the tax cuts were not proposed for their expansionary fiscal policy effects. Sometimes dumb luck is an important part of good economic policy.

Why Macro Policy Is More Complicated Than the *AS/AD* Model Makes It Look

The *AS/AD* model makes the analysis of the aggregate economy look easy. All you do is determine where the economy is relative to its potential output and, based on that, choose the appropriate policy to shift the *AD* curve. Alas, it's much harder than that.

The Problem of Implementing Fiscal Policy

First, implementing fiscal policy—changing government spending and taxes—is a slow legislative process. Government spending and taxing decisions are generally made for political, not economic, reasons. Thus, there is no guarantee that government will do what economists say is necessary. And even if it does, the changes often cannot be completed in a timely fashion.

The Problem of Estimating Potential Output

A second problem is that we have no way of measuring potential output, so when we increase aggregate demand, we can't determine whether or not the *SAS* curve will be shifting up. Thus, the key to applying the policy is to know the location of the *LAS* curve, which is vertical at the economy's potential output. Unfortunately, we have no way of knowing that with certainty. Fortunately, we do have ways to get a rough idea of where it is.

Web Note 25.4
Unemployed Machines

Because inflation accelerates when an economy is operating above potential, one way of estimating potential output is to estimate the rate of unemployment below which inflation has begun to accelerate in the past. This is the target rate of unemployment. We can then estimate potential output by calculating output at the target rate of unemployment and adjusting for productivity growth. Unfortunately the target rate of unemployment fluctuates and is difficult to predict.

Q-9 Why is it so important for policymakers to know what potential output is?

The problem can be made clearer by relating it to an earlier chapter's discussion of cyclical and structural unemployment. There I stated that cyclical unemployment occurs when output is below potential output. Workers have been laid off, and it is relatively easy to call them back to work to increase production. Structural unemployment is unemployment that remains when the economy is at its potential output. The problem isn't layoffs; it's lack of appropriate skills for the existing jobs. Differentiating these two is difficult, making it hard to estimate the target rate of unemployment.

Another way to determine potential output is to take the economy's previous income level and add the normal growth factor of 3 percent (the trend growth rate). This gives us a very rough estimate. Unfortunately regulations, technology, institutions, available resources, and expectations are always changing. Estimating potential income from past growth rates can be problematic if these shift factors are changing quickly or dramatically.

Q-10 If politicians suddenly raise government expenditures and the economy is above potential income, what will happen to prices and real income?

In some cases, the economy can be undergoing significant structural readjustment, in which it is not trying to repeat what it did in the past but trying to change from what it has been doing to something new. If that is true, potential output may have declined and what looks like cyclical unemployment is actually structural unemployment.

The Questionable Effectiveness of Fiscal Policy

In summary, there are two ways to think about the effectiveness of fiscal policy—in the model, and in reality. Models are great, and simple models, like the one I've presented in this book, that you can understand intuitively are even greater. You put in the numbers, and out comes the answer. Questions based on such models make great exam questions. But don't think that policies that work in a model will necessarily work in the real world.

The effectiveness of fiscal policy in reality depends on the government's ability to perceive a problem and to react appropriately to it. The essence of fiscal policy is government changing its taxes and its spending to offset any fluctuation that would occur in other autonomous expenditures, thereby keeping the economy at its potential level of income. If the model is a correct description of the economy, and if the government can act fast enough and change its taxes and spending in a *countercyclical* way, recessions can be prevented. This type of management of the economy is called **countercyclical fiscal policy**—*fiscal policy in which the government offsets any change in aggregate expenditures that would create a business cycle*. The term **fine tuning** is used to describe such *fiscal policy designed to keep the economy always at its target or potential level of income*. Today most economists believe that fine tuning the economy is beyond our capabilities.

A countercyclical fiscal policy designed to keep the economy always at its target or potential level of income is called fine tuning.

Almost all economists agree the government is not up to fine-tuning the economy.

As I will discuss below, today almost all economists agree the government is not up to fine-tuning the economy. The modern debate is whether it is up to any tuning of the economy at all. The reason is that the dynamic adjustment in the economy is extraordinarily complicated and that, once you take into account reasonable expectations of future policy, the formal model becomes hopelessly complex. Graduate students in economics get Ph.D.s for worrying about such hopeless complexities. At the introductory level, all we require is that you (1) know this simple *AS/AD* model and (2) remember that, in the real world, it cannot be used in a mechanistic manner; it must be used with judgment.

Conclusion

Let's conclude the chapter with a brief summary. In the 1930s modern macroeconomics developed as Classical economists' interest in growth and supply-side issues shifted to Keynesian economists' interest in business cycles and demand-side issues. To capture the issues about the effect of aggregate demand on the economy, economists have developed an *AS/AD* model.

The model summarizes the expected effects that shifts in aggregate supply and aggregate demand have on output and the price level. In the short run, outward shifts in the *AD* curve cause real output and the price level to rise. Inward shifts cause the opposite. If the economy is beyond potential output and the *LAS* curve, the *SAS* curve will shift up, causing the price level to increase and real output to decrease, until real output falls back to potential and the equilibrium is where aggregate demand intersects the *LAS* curve. In the model the government can, through fiscal policy, shift the *AD* curve in or out, thereby achieving the desired level of real output, as long as that desired level does not exceed potential output.

Unfortunately, potential output is hard to estimate, and implementing fiscal policy in a timely fashion is difficult, making macroeconomic policy more an art than a science.

SUMMARY

- The Depression marked a significant change in U.S. economic institutions. Keynesian economics developed.
- Classical economists focus on the long run and use a laissez-faire approach.
- Keynesian economists focus on short-run fluctuations and use an activist government approach.
- The *AS/AD* model consists of the aggregate demand curve, the short-run aggregate supply curve, and the long-run aggregate supply curve.
- The aggregate demand curve slopes downward because of the wealth effect, the interest rate effect, the international effect, and the multiplier effect.
- The short-run aggregate supply (*SAS*) curve is upward-sloping because, while for the most part firms in the United States adjust production to meet demand instead of changing price, some firms will raise prices when demand increases.
- The long-run aggregate supply (*LAS*) curve is vertical at potential output.
- The *LAS* curve shifts out when available resources, capital, labor, technology, and growth-compatible institutions increase.
- Short-run equilibrium is where the *SAS* and *AD* curves intersect. Long-run equilibrium is where the *AD* and *LAS* curves intersect.
- When the economy is in a short-run equilibrium but not long-run equilibrium, the *SAS* curve will shift up or down to bring the economy back to long-run equilibrium unless government policy shifts the *AD* curve first.
- When output exceeds potential, there is an inflationary gap and the *SAS* curve will shift up to eliminate the gap. When output is below potential, there is a recessionary gap and the *SAS* curve will shift down to eliminate the gap.
- Aggregate demand management policy attempts to influence the level of output in the economy by influencing aggregate demand and relying on the multiplier to expand any policy-induced change in aggregate demand.
- Fiscal policy—the change in government spending or taxes—works by providing a deliberate countershock to offset unexpected shocks to the economy.
- Macroeconomic policy is difficult to conduct because implementing fiscal policy is a slow process and we don't really know where potential output is.
- We must estimate potential output by looking at past levels of potential output and by looking at where the price level begins to rise.

KEY TERMS

aggregate demand (*AD*) curve (569)
aggregate demand management (*568*)
countercyclical fiscal policy (588)
equilibrium income (568)
fine tuning (588)
fiscal policy (583)
inflationary gap (582)
interest rate effect (*570*)
international effect (*571*)
long-run aggregate supply (*LAS*) curve (*578*)
multiplier effect (*571*)
potential income (568)
quantity-adjusting markets (*575*)
recessionary gap (*581*)
short-run aggregate supply (*SAS*) curve (*574*)
wealth effect (*570*)

QUESTIONS FOR THOUGHT AND REVIEW

1. Distinguish between a laissez-faire economist and an activist economist.
2. Classicals saw the Depression as a political problem, not an economic problem. Why?

3. What are five factors that cause the *AD* curve to shift?
4. Use the wealth, interest rate, international, and multiplier effects to explain how a rise in the price level affects aggregate quantity demanded.
5. What are two factors that cause the *SAS* curve to shift?
6. If an economy is in short-run equilibrium that is below potential, what forces will bring the economy to long-run equilibrium?
7. Moore's law states that every 18 months, the computing speed of a microchip doubles. What effect does this likely have on the economy? Explain your answer using the *AS/AD* model.
8. If the economy were close to high potential output, would policymakers present their policy prescriptions to increase real output any differently than if the economy were far from potential output? Why?
9. Why is countercyclical fiscal policy difficult to implement?
10. Why is knowing the level of potential output important to designing appropriate fiscal policy?
11. In the late 1990s a growing number of economists argued that world policymakers were focusing too much on fighting inflation. The economists also argued that the technical level of potential output had risen. Show their argument using the *AS/AD* model.
12. Explain why macro policy is more difficult than the simple model suggests.

Problems and Exercises

1. Explain what will likely happen to the *SAS* curve in each of the following instances:
   a. Productivity rises 3 percent; wages rise 4 percent.
   b. Productivity rises 3 percent; wages rise 1 percent.
   c. Productivity declines 1 percent; wages rise 1 percent.
   d. Productivity rises 2 percent; wages rise 2 percent.
2. The opening quotation of the chapter refers to Keynes's view of theory.
   a. What do you think he meant by it?
   b. How does it relate to the emphasis on the "other things constant" assumption?
   c. Do you think Keynes's interest was mainly in positive economics, the art of economics, or normative economics? Why?
3. Explain what will likely happen to the slope or position of the *AD* curve in the following circumstances:
   a. The exchange rate changes from fixed to flexible.
   b. A fall in the price level doesn't make people feel richer.
   c. A fall in the price level creates expectations of a further-falling price level.
   d. Income is redistributed from rich people to poor people.
   e. Autonomous exports increase by 20.
   f. Government spending decreases by 10.
4. Explain what will happen to the position of the *SAS* curve and/or *LAS* curve in the following circumstances:
   a. Available factors of production increase.
   b. A civil war occurs.
   c. The price of oil quadruples.
   d. Wages that were fixed become flexible, and aggregate demand increases.
5. Congratulations! You have been appointed an economic policy adviser to the United States. You are told that the economy is significantly below its potential output, and that the following will happen next year: World income will fall significantly; and the price of oil will rise significantly. (The United States is an oil importer.)
   a. What will happen to the price level and real output? Using the *AS/AD* model, demonstrate your predictions graphically.
   b. What policy might you suggest to the government?
   c. How would a real business cycle economist likely criticize the policy you suggest?
6. What fiscal policy actions would you recommend in the following instances?
   a. The economy begins at potential, but foreign economies slow dramatically.
   b. The economy has been operating above potential output and inflationary pressures rise.
   c. A new technology is invented that significantly raises potential output.

Web Questions

1. Go to the Bureau of Labor Statistics' home page (http://stats.bls.gov) and look up the recent changes in the consumer price index. Using that information answer the following:
   a. Where do you think the economy is relative to potential?
   b. How does your answer to *a* determine what policy you would suggest the government should follow?

2. Go to the Council of Economic Advisers' home page (www.whitehouse.gov/cea) and look in the *Economic Report of the President*.
   a. Find the U.S. price level and the level of output (GDP) over the last 10 years.
   b. Graph the data with price level on the vertical axis and the level of GDP on the horizontal axis.
   c. Is the curve you have drawn a supply curve, a demand curve, or neither? Why?
3. Go to the Conference Board's home page (www.conferenceboard.org) and read the press release of the consumer confidence index. Based on this release, what do you think will happen to the *AD* curve? How will this affect the price level and equilibrium output? Demonstrate your answer graphically.

Answers to Margin Questions

1. A Classical economist takes a laissez-faire approach. Classical economists believe the economy is self-regulating. A Keynesian economist takes an interventionist approach. Keynesian economists believe that equilibrium output can remain below potential output. (566)
2. In the short run, saving can lead to a decrease in expenditures and reduce equilibrium output. In the long run saving leads to the accumulation of capital and an increase in potential output. In the long run saving increases equilibrium output. (569)
3. False. The multiplier magnifies the initial effect. The rise in expenditures will be greater than 10, making the *AD* curve flatter than a slope of −1. (572)
4. A rise in a country's exchange rate will make domestic goods more expensive to foreigners and foreign goods less expensive to domestic residents. It will shift the *AD* curve in to the left because net exports will fall. (572)
5. The *AD* curve will shift out by more than 20 because of the multiplier. (574)
6. If the *AD*, *SAS*, and *LAS* curves intersect at the same point, the economy is in both long-run and short-run equilibrium. Nothing will happen to the price level and output. (581)
7. If there is a recessionary gap, the *SAS* and *AD* curves intersect to the left of potential output at a point such as A in the figure in the next column. At that level of output there will be pressure for factor prices to fall, pushing the *SAS* curve down. Unless the *AD* curve shifts out (as it usually does) the *SAS* curve will shift down and output will rise until output equals potential output and the economy is in both long-run and short-run equilibrium at a point such as *B*. (582)

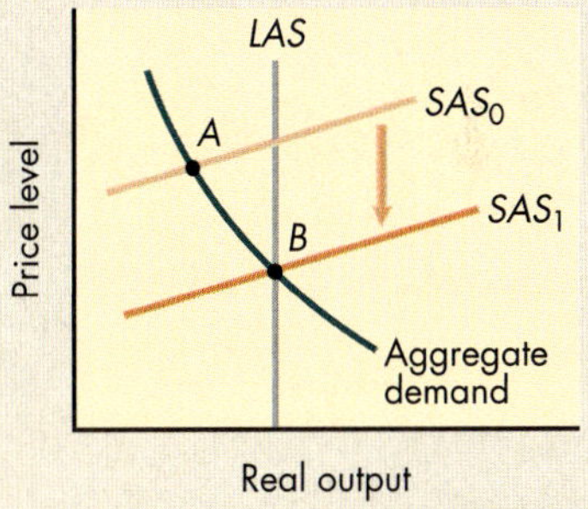

8. If the economy is well below potential, I would predict that output will rise and the price level will rise only slightly. (583)
9. Where the economy is relative to potential will determine whether the price level will rise (inflationary gap) or fall (recessionary gap) and determine the type of fiscal policy needed. (587)
10. If the economy is above potential output, I would predict that factor prices will rise, shifting the *AS* curve up. The expansion in government expenditures will shift the *AD* curve out further, putting even more pressure on factor prices to rise. My answer, therefore, is that the price level will rise very quickly and output will fall until it equals potential output. (587)

26 THE MULTIPLIER MODEL

After reading this chapter, you should be able to:

- Explain the difference between induced and autonomous expenditures.
- Show how the level of income is graphically determined in the multiplier model.
- Use the multiplier equation to determine equilibrium income.
- Explain how the multiplier process amplifies shifts in autonomous expenditures.
- Demonstrate how fiscal policy can eliminate recessionary and inflationary gaps.
- List six reasons why the multiplier model might be misleading.

Keynes stirred the stale economic frog pond to its depth.

—*Gottfried Haberler*

Policymakers want numbers. The *AS/AD* model of the last chapter didn't give them numbers; it talked about the multiplier and about how an initial shift in aggregate expenditures (other things equal) would have a multiplied effect on income. In this chapter I present a model—the multiplier model—that provides numbers. Even though it is a highly simplified model, it forms an important element of most modern econometric models (computer models that economists use to make forecasts about the economy). Such models—which include the Fed econometric model, or the DRI-WEFA model—are used to guide economic policymakers. (See the box "Econometric Models.")

THE MULTIPLIER MODEL

The multiplier model assumes that the price level remains constant. (The short-run aggregate supply curve is assumed to be horizontal, and factor prices are assumed not to change.) This assumption means that we don't have to differentiate between real and nominal income in our discussion. The model explores what happens when aggregate expenditures expand by a certain number, say, 20. In terms of the *AS/AD* model, the question it explores (shown in Figure 26-1) is: When a shift factor of aggregate demand increases by 20, how much will the *AD* curve shift out? Whereas the *AS/AD* model gives us insights into the general *qualitative* effects of these shifts, the multiplier model tells about their *quantitative* effects. For example, say that the economists at the Federal Reserve Bank (the Fed) have determined that the multiplier effect of a shift in expenditures will be 2. Their research department informs them that investment and consumption have suddenly fallen by 1 percent of GDP because a stock market bubble has burst. The Fed economists would then predict that output would fall by 2 percent.

It was just such a precipitous fall in income that the multiplier model was initially designed to explain. As I discussed in the last chapter, in the 1930s income decreased enormously and the economy fell into a depression. The multiplier model was designed to show how an initial drop in investment could have led to such a large drop in income.

Econometric Models

Beyond the Tools

The models presented in this chapter are a major simplification of econometric models. Two well-known econometric models are the Fed (Federal Reserve Bank) econometric model, the DRI–WEFA model. In econometric models, economists find standard relationships among aspects of the macroeconomy and use those relationships to predict what will happen to inflation, unemployment, and growth under certain conditions. In the 2000 presidential election, when candidate George W. Bush wanted to know the effect his proposed tax cut would have on the economy, he went to economists who entered the tax cut into their econometric models and estimated the effect.

While econometric models are much more complicated than the models presented here, they have the same structure—a short-run aggregate supply component with essentially fixed prices, an aggregate demand component, and a potential output component.

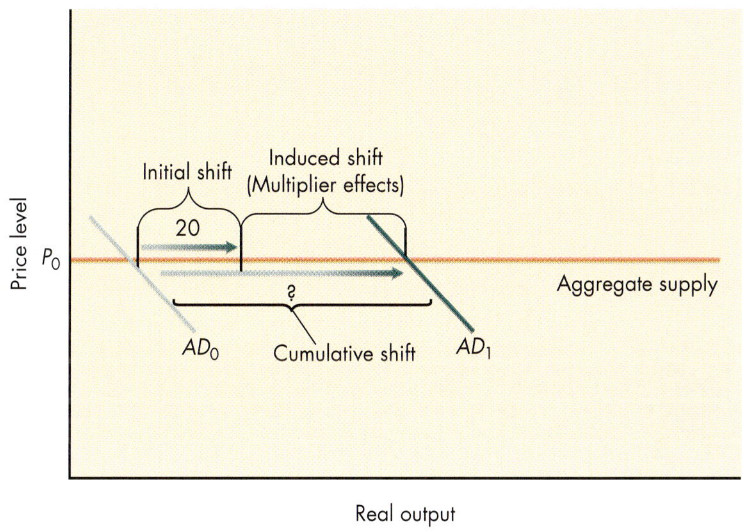

Figure 26-1 The AS/AD Model When Prices Are Fixed
The multiplier model was designed to explain how an initial shift in expenditures changes equilibrium output when the price level is fixed. It is designed to fill in the question mark in this figure. When an expenditure shift of 20 hits the economy, that shift causes additional induced effects. These shifts are called multiplier effects.

We'll start our discussion of the multiplier model by looking separately at production decisions and expenditure decisions.

Aggregate Production

Aggregate production is *the total amount of final goods and services produced in every industry in an economy*. It is at the center of the multiplier model. As I noted in Chapter 23, production creates an equal amount of income, so actual income and actual production are always equal; the terms can be used interchangeably.

Graphically, aggregate production in the multiplier model is represented by a 45° line on a graph, with real income in dollars measured on the horizontal axis and real production measured in dollars on the vertical axis, as in Figure 26-2. Given the definition of the axes, connecting all the points at which real production equals real income produces a 45° line through the origin. Since, by definition, production creates an amount of income equal to the amount of production or output, this 45° line can be thought of as an *aggregate production curve*, or alternatively the *aggregate income curve*.

Graphically, aggregate production in the multiplier model is represented by a 45° line through the origin.

Figure 26-2 The Aggregate Production Curve
Since, by definition, real output equals real income, on each point of the aggregate production curve income must equal production. This equality holds true only on the 45° line.

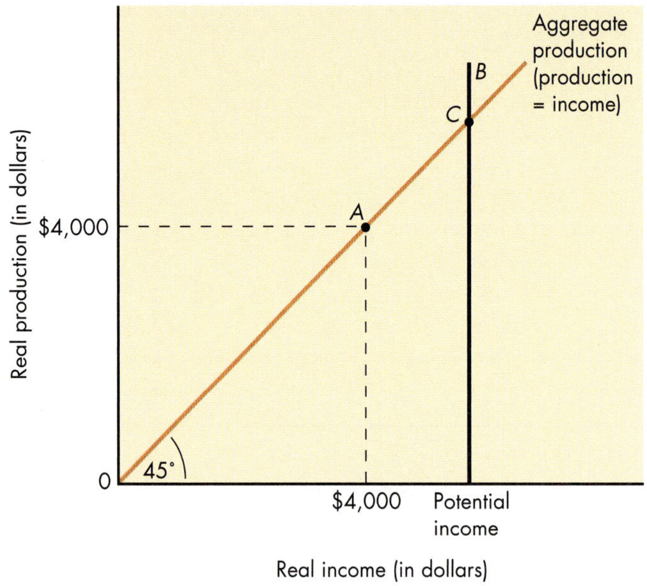

Q-1 What is true about the relationship between income and production on the aggregate production curve?

At all points on the aggregate production curve, income equals production. For example, consider point A in Figure 26-2, where real income (measured on the horizontal axis) is $4,000 and real production (measured on the vertical axis) is also $4,000. That identity between real production and real income is true only on the 45° line. Output and income, however, cannot expand without limit. The model is most relevant when output is below its potential. Once production expands to the capacity constraint of the existing institutional structure—to potential income (line *B*)—any increase beyond that can only be temporary.

Aggregate Expenditures

Aggregate expenditures in an economy (*AE*) equals *C* + *I* + *G* + (*X* − *M*).

The term **aggregate expenditures** refers to *the total amount of spending on final goods and services in the economy*. This amount consists of four main expenditure classifications: consumption (spending by consumers), investment (spending by business), spending by government, and net foreign spending on U.S. goods (the difference between U.S. exports and U.S. imports). These four components were presented in our earlier discussion of national income accounting, which isn't surprising since the national income accounts were designed around the multiplier model. Each component, in turn, is influenced by various elements in the economy. In the multiplier model we focus on their relationship to income. The multiplier model asks the question "How do each of these change as income changes?" To keep the exposition as simple but as general as possible, we focus in this chapter on the aggregate relationship between all expenditure components combined and income, that is, on the relationship between aggregate expenditures and income. (In Appendix A at the end of this chapter we present a disaggregated discussion.)

Autonomous and Induced Expenditures

Autonomous expenditures are expenditures that change because something other than income changes.

For purposes of the multiplier model, all forms of expenditures are classified as either autonomous or induced. **Autonomous expenditures** are *expenditures that do not systematically vary with income*. **Induced expenditures** are *expenditures that change as income*

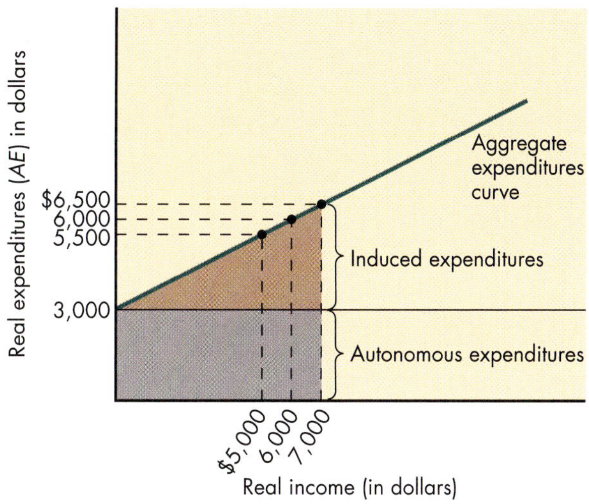

Figure 26-3 Aggregate Expenditures Curve
The *AE* curve depicted here has a slope of .5, the *mpe*, and an intercept of $3,000, the level of autonomous expenditures. The shaded area represents induced expenditures. Aggregate expenditures is the sum of these two components.

changes. Say that each time income rises by 100, expenditures increase by 60. The induced expenditures would be 60.

This assumed empirical relationship between income and aggregate expenditures can be represented graphically with the aggregate expenditure (*AE*) curve. To keep the analysis simple, the *AE* curve is usually estimated to be a linear relationship (a straight line) for incomes near current income. To make the graphical exposition easier, we will also assume that the linear relationship continues for all levels of income. This allows us to draw a linear aggregate expenditures curve such as the one shown in Figure 26-3.

Notice that when income is $6,000 aggregate expenditures are also $6,000; but when income rises by $1,000 to $7,000, aggregate expenditures rise by $500 to $6,500. The reason is that only induced expenditures change as income changes. When income falls to $5,000 expenditures fall to $5,500. Along this *AE* curve, induced expenditures fall by $500 when income falls by $1,000.

To figure out autonomous expenditures, we have to extend the *AE* curve to the left, to the point where income is zero (where the *AE* curve intersects the vertical axis). Doing so, you can see that when income is zero, aggregate expenditures are $3,000. So, autonomous expenditures are $3,000. Consumption, investment, government spending, and net exports each have an autonomous component. Autonomous expenditures is the sum of all of them. It is the level of expenditures that would exist at zero income, assuming the *AE* curve is linear. (Again, it is important to recognize that this linear extension is just for expositional purposes. In reality, income is not expected to fall to zero and the model is used to describe changes around the existing level of income.) The point to remember about autonomous expenditures is that they remain constant at all levels of income; therefore, a graph of autonomous expenditures is a straight, horizontal line as shown in Figure 26-3.

Autonomous expenditures are unrelated to income; induced expenditures are directly related to income.

To summarize, aggregate expenditures are comprised of two components—autonomous expenditures that do not vary with income, and induced expenditures that vary with income. The blue shaded region in Figure 26-3 represents autonomous expenditures; the red shaded region represents induced expenditures. So, at income $7,000, aggregate expenditures of $6,500 are comprised of $3,000 of autonomous expenditures and $3,500 of induced expenditures.

Q-2 What is the difference between induced expenditures and autonomous expenditures?

$$mpe = \frac{\text{Change in expenditures}}{\text{Change in income}}$$

Q-3 If expenditures change by $60 when income changes by $100, what is the *mpe*?

The Marginal Propensity to Expend The slope of an aggregate expenditures curve is equal to the **marginal propensity to expend (*mpe*)**—*the ratio of the change in aggregate expenditures to a change in income*. The expenditures function I have drawn has a slope of .5, which means that for every $1,000 increase income, aggregate expenditures rise by $500. If the *mpe* were .4, the slope of the *AE* curve would be .4 and aggregate expenditures would rise by $400 for every $1,000 increase in income.

The marginal propensity to expend is assumed to be greater than 0 and less than 1. Therefore, the aggregate expenditures curve will have a slope that is less than a 45-degree *AP* curve and greater than a horizontal line (like autonomous expenditures). Economists estimate the slope of the *AE* curve by looking at how much aggregate expenditures have changed with a change in income around past income and then use that information to estimate the relationship for current levels of income.

The marginal propensity to expend is an aggregation of the various relationships between each component of aggregate expenditures (consumption, investment, government spending, exports, and imports) and aggregate income. There is a marginal propensity to consume, a marginal propensity to import, and, in more complicated models, a variety of other marginal propensities. (Appendix A at the end of the chapter provides a disaggregated presentation of these components.) But it is the aggregate of these—the *mpe*—that is the key to the multiplier model.

While the presentation will focus on the aggregate *mpe*, let me briefly discuss its components. The most important determinant of the marginal propensity to expend is the marginal propensity to consume (*mpc*)—the change in consumption that occurs with a change in income.[1] It is less than 1 because individuals tend to save a portion of their income, so when income goes up by 100 their spending will go up by, say, only 80. In that case the marginal propensity to consume would be .8. If induced consumption were the only component, the marginal propensity to expend would be .8.

While the marginal propensity to consume is important to expenditures, other important, policy-relevant factors also affect how expenditures change with income. One of these factors is the income tax. As income rises, people pay higher income tax, which means that they have less income at their disposal to spend, which lowers their expenditures. Thinking back to the national income classifications, remember that disposable income is less than GDP. So taxes reduce the size of the marginal propensity to expend from what it would have been if all income were available to households to spend. In the United States taxes that vary with income are approximately 20 percent of total income. Another important determinant of the marginal propensity to expend is the marginal propensity to import—the change in imports that occurs with a change in income. With increasing globalization, individuals spend an increasing portion of their income on imports. That portion is not part of aggregate expenditures on domestic goods. Instead, it is part of the aggregate expenditures of other countries, so the fact that imports increase as income increases also reduces the size of the marginal propensity to expend. Americans spend about 15 percent of increases of their income on imports. In some countries, such as the Netherlands, that fraction can be as high as 50 or 60 percent.

---

[1]The importance of this component has led some to concentrate the multiplier model presented in principles books on consumption and the marginal propensity to consume. However, to keep the analysis simple, this focus generally requires them to assume that the other components do not vary with income. I focus on a broader concept—marginal propensity to expend—because it is more inclusive, requires less algebraic manipulation, and incorporates two other primary reasons why income may not get translated into expenditures. This allows us to talk more about policy and less about the model.

History of the Multiplier Model

Beyond the Tools

Policy fights in economics occur on many levels. Keynes fought on most of them. But it wasn't Keynes who convinced U.S. policymakers to accept his ideas. (Indeed, President Franklin D. Roosevelt met Keynes only once and thought he was a pompous academic.) Instead, it was Alvin Hansen, a textbook writer and policy adviser to government who was hired away from the University of Wisconsin by Harvard in the mid-1930s, who played the key role in getting Keynesian economic policies introduced into the United States.

The story of how Hansen converted to Keynes's ideas is somewhat mysterious. At the time, almost all economists were Classicals, and Hansen was no exception. (Otherwise it's doubtful Harvard would have recruited him.) But, somehow, on the train trip from Wisconsin to Massachusetts, Hansen metamorphosed from a Classical to a Keynesian. His graduate seminar at Harvard in the late 1930s and the 1940s became the U.S. breeding ground for Keynesian economics.

What made Hansen and other economists switch from Classical to Keynesian economics? It was the Depression; the Keynesian story explained it much better than did the Classical story, which centered on the real wage being too high.

Hansen quickly realized that talking about interdependencies of supply and demand decisions didn't work for policymakers and businesspeople. They wanted numbers—specifics—and Keynes's work had no specifics. So Alvin Hansen and his students, especially Paul Samuelson, set about to develop specifics. They developed what is now called the textbook model of Keynesian economics.

The Aggregate Expenditures Function The relationship between aggregate expenditures and income that is depicted by the *AE* curve can be written mathematically as follows:

$$AE = \underbrace{AE_0}_{\text{autonomous}} + \underbrace{mpeY}_{\text{induced}}$$

It consists of the same two components that make up the *AE* curve—autonomous expenditures (the AE_0—the subscript zero tells you it is autonomous) and induced expenditures (the *mpeY*). The aggregate expenditures function depicted by the *AE* curve we've discussed so far and shown in Figure 26-3 is $AE = \$3{,}000 + .5Y$. Autonomous expenditures are \$3,000 and the *mpe* is .5. Just like the *AE* curve, the aggregate expenditures function takes into account all components of aggregate spending. Therefore autonomous expenditures is the sum of the autonomous components of expenditures $[AE_0 = C_0 + I_0 + G_0 + (X_0 - M_0)]$ and induced expenditures is the sum of the induced components of expenditures. These induced expenditures are determined by the marginal propensity to consume, the marginal propensity to import, and taxes that vary with income.

In Figure 26-4, I graph three expenditures functions. For practice, determine which of the *AE* curves (*a*, *b*, or *c*) is associated with which expenditures function described by the following situations:

- *Situation 1*. Autonomous consumption is 100; autonomous investment is 40; autonomous net exports is 30, autonomous spending by government is 20, and the marginal propensity to expend is .6.
- *Situation 2*. Autonomous consumption is 100; autonomous investment is 40; autonomous net exports is 30, autonomous spending by government is 30, and the marginal propensity to expend is .5.

Figure 26-4 Three Aggregate Expenditure Functions

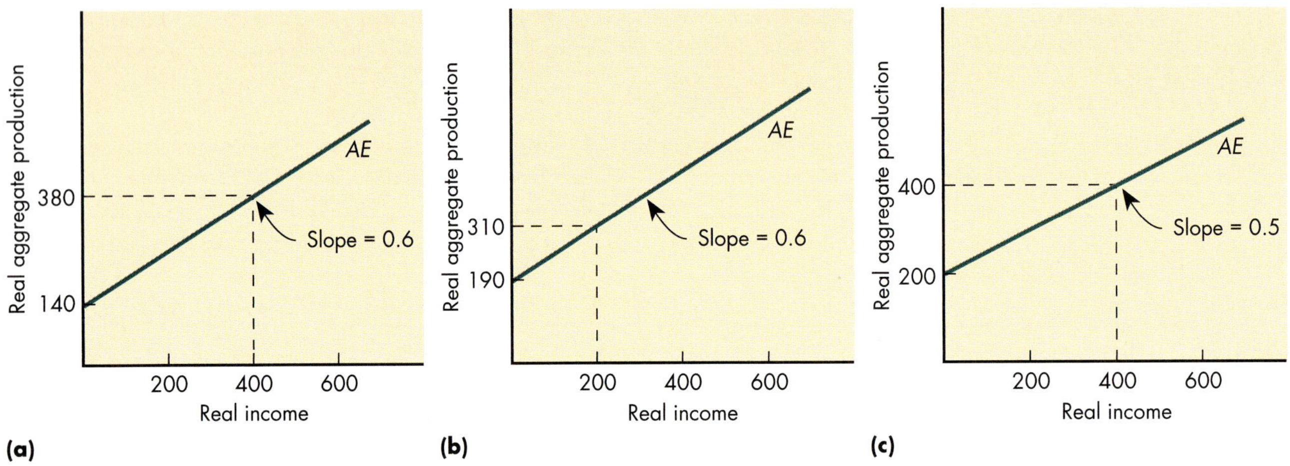

- *Situation 3*. Autonomous expenditures is 140 and the marginal propensity to expend is .6.

The answers are 1-*b*, 2-*c*, and 3-*a*. There are a number of ways you could have associated each of these situations with the graphs. Since the marginal propensity to expend in Situation 2 was .5, its slope had to be .5. Thus only graph *c* is consistent with it. Situations 1 and 3 have the same marginal propensity to expend, so we have to differentiate them by their autonomous expenditures component. Adding up autonomous expenditures in Situation 1 gives us 190, so the intercept (the level of expenditures at zero income) must be 190. That is the case for *b*. Checking, graph *a* has an intercept of 140, and a slope of .6, which means that it is consistent with Situation 3.

The aggregate expenditures function is important because once you have estimated an expenditures function for the economy, you can predict what expenditures will be at any income. Say you have estimated an aggregate expenditures function to be $AE = 240 + .4Y$. If income is \$500, you would estimate aggregate expenditures to be \$440 [240 + .4(500)]. Estimating aggregate expenditures is fundamental to predicting whether the economy will grow or fall into a recession.

Web Note 26.1
Keynes on Investment

Shifts in the Expenditures Function A key element of the expenditures function for our purposes concerns changes in autonomous expenditures. These changes are usually classified by which of the four subcomponent of autonomous expenditures changed—autonomous consumption, autonomous investment, autonomous government spending, or autonomous net exports. All of these can change suddenly, and, when one or more do, the *AE* curve shifts up or down. For example, if autonomous consumption rises by \$200, and autonomous investment falls by \$80, autonomous expenditures will rise by \$120 (\$200 − \$80).

Economists keep close tabs on these autonomous components as they develop their forecasts of the economy. For example, imagine that consumer confidence suddenly decreases, perhaps because of a terrorist threat. Consumers figure they had better save more to prepare themselves for the upcoming recession, so they cut back expenditures; autonomous consumption falls and the expenditures function shifts down. Alternatively, imagine that businesses come to believe that the economy will grow faster than they expected. To prepare, they will increase investment, increasing autonomous investment and shifting the aggregate expenditures curve up.

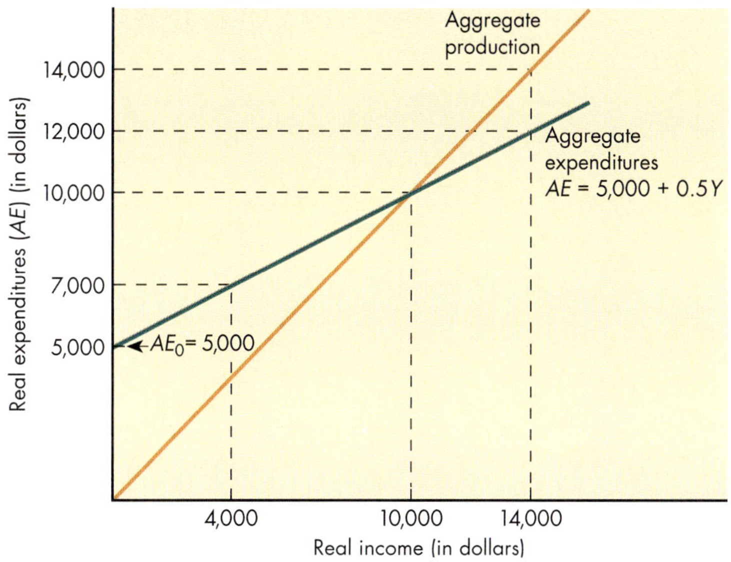

Figure 26-5 Comparing AE to AP and Solving for Equilibrium Graphically

Equilibrium in the multiplier model is determined where the *AE* and *AP* curves intersect. That equilibrium is at $10,000. At income levels higher or lower than that, planned production will not equal planned expenditures.

I'll let you work these final two examples by yourself. The first is that the government enters into a major war, and the second is that the country's exchange rate suddenly falls, causing the price of the country's exports to fall and the price of imports to rise. If you answered that they both shift the expenditures function up, you've got the reasoning down.

The reason it is important to focus on shifts is that the multiplier model is an historical model. It can be used to analyze shifts in aggregate expenditures from an historically given income level, but not to determine income independent of the economy's historical position. Notice how I discussed the model in the examples—some shift in autonomous expenditures occurred and that shift led to a change in income from its existing level.

As I mentioned above, while economists speak of what expenditures would be at zero income, or while we say the *mpe* is constant over all ranges of income, that is done simply to make the geometric portrayal of the model easier. What is actually assumed is that within the relevant range around existing income—say a 5 percent increase or decrease—the *mpe* remains constant, and the autonomous portion of the expenditures is the intercept that would occur if we extended the expenditures function.

Determining the Equilibrium Level of Aggregate Income

Now that we've developed the graphical framework for the multiplier model, we can put the aggregate production and aggregate expenditures together and see how the level of aggregate income is determined. We begin by considering the relationship between the aggregate expenditures curve and the aggregate production curve more carefully. We do so in Figure 26-5.

The aggregate production (*AP*) curve is a 45° line up until the economy reaches potential income. Its slope is 1, so at all points on it, aggregate expenditures equal aggregate income. It tells you the level of aggregate production and also the level of aggregate income since, by definition, real income equals real production when the price level does not change. Expenditures are shown by the *AE* curve. Planned expenditures

Solving for Equilibrium Income Algebraically

Knowing the Tools

For those of you who are mathematically inclined, the multiplier equation can be derived by combining the equations presented in the text algebraically to arrive at the equation for income. Rewriting the expenditures relationship, we have:

$$AE = AE_0 + mpeY$$

Aggregate production, by definition, equals aggregate income (Y) and, in equilibrium, aggregate income must equal the four components of aggregate expenditures. Beginning with the national income accounting identity, we have

$$Y = AE$$

Substituting the terms from the first equation, we have

$$Y = AE_0 + mpeY$$

Subtracting $mpeY$ from both sides,

$$Y - mpeY = AE_0$$

To arrive at the multiplier equation we factor out Y:

$$Y(1 - mpe) = AE_0$$

Now solve for Y by dividing both sides by $(1 - mpe)$:

$$Y = \left[\frac{1}{(1 - mpe)}\right] \times [AE_0]$$

This is the multiplier equation.

To determine income graphically in the multiplier model, you find the income level at which aggregate expenditures equals planned aggregate production.

(expenditures as calculated using the expenditures function) do not necessarily equal production or income. In equilibrium, however, planned expenditures must equal production. Why is that the case?

Let's first say that production, and hence income, is $14,000. As you can see, at income of $14,000, planned expenditures are $12,000. Aggregate production exceeds planned aggregate expenditures. Firms are producing more goods than are bought, and inventories are rising by more than firms want. This is true for any income level above $10,000. Similarly, at all income levels below $10,000, aggregate production is less than planned aggregate expenditures and inventories are falling below levels desired by firms. For example, at a production level of $4,000, planned aggregate expenditures are $7,000. Inventories are falling by $3,000.

The only income level at which aggregate production equals planned aggregate expenditures is $10,000. Since we know that, in equilibrium, planned aggregate expenditures must equal planned aggregate production, $10,000 is the equilibrium level of income in the economy. It is the level of income at which neither producers nor consumers have any reason to change what they are doing. At any other level of income, since there is either a shortage or a surplus of goods, or firms' inventory is greater than or less than desired, there will be incentive to change production. Thus, you can use the aggregate production curve and the aggregate expenditures curve to determine the level of income at which the economy will be in equilibrium.

The Multiplier Equation

The multiplier equation is an equation showing the relationship between autonomous expenditures and the equilibrium level of income. Y = Multiplier × Autonomous expenditures.

Another useful way to determine the level of income in the multiplier model is through the **multiplier equation,** *an equation that tells us that income equals the multiplier times autonomous expenditures.*[2]

Y = Multiplier × Autonomous expenditures

[2]The multiplier equation does not come out of thin air. It comes from combining the set of equations underlying the graphical presentation of the multiplier model into the two brackets. The multiplier equation is derived in the accompanying box.

The **expenditures multiplier** is *a number that tells us how much income will change in response to a change in autonomous expenditures*. To calculate the expenditures multiplier, you divide 1 by (1 minus the marginal propensity to expend). Thus:

The expenditures multiplier is a number that tells us how much income will change in response to a change in autonomous expenditures: $[1/(1 - mpe)]$.

$$\text{Multiplier} = \frac{1}{(1 - mpe)}$$

Once you know the value of the marginal propensity to expend, you can calculate the expenditures multiplier by reducing $[1/(1 - mpe)]$ to a simple number. For example, if $mpe = .8$, the multiplier is

$$\frac{1}{(1 - .8)} = \frac{1}{.2} = 5$$

Since the expenditures multiplier tells you the relationship between autonomous expenditures and income, once you know the multiplier and the level of autonomous expenditures, calculating the equilibrium level of income is easy. All you do is multiply autonomous expenditures by the multiplier. For example, using the autonomous expenditures of $5,000 and a multiplier of 2, from Figure 26-5, we can calculate equilibrium income in the economy to be $10,000. This is the same equilibrium income we got from the graphical exercise.

Let's see how the equation works by considering another example. Say the *mpe* is .4. Subtracting .4 from 1 gives .6. Dividing 1 by .6 gives approximately 1.7. Say, also, that autonomous expenditures (AE_0) are $750. The multiplier equation tells us to calculate income multiply autonomous expenditures, $750, by 1.7. Doing so gives 1.7 × $750 = $1,275.

To determine equilibrium income using the multiplier equation, you determine the expenditures multiplier and multiply it by the level of autonomous expenditures.

The multiplier equation gives you a simple way to determine equilibrium income in the multiplier model. Five different marginal propensities to expend and the multiplier associated with each (I round off to the nearest 10th) are shown in the table below.

mpe	Multiplier = 1/(1 − *mpe*)
.3	1.4
.4	1.7
.5	2
.75	4
.8	5

Q-4 If the *mpe* = .5, what is the expenditures multiplier?

Notice as *mpe* increases, the multiplier increases. The reason is that as the *mpe* gets larger, the induced effects of any initial shift in income also get larger. Knowing the multiplier associated with each marginal propensity to expend gives you an easy way to determine equilibrium income in the economy.

Let's look at one more example of the multiplier. Say that the *mpe* is .4 and that autonomous expenditures rise by $250 so they are $1,000 instead of $750. What is the level of equilibrium income? Multiplying autonomous expenditures, $1,000, by 1.7 tells us that equilibrium income is $1,700. With a multiplier of 1.7, income rises by $425 (250 × 1.7) because of the $250 increase in autonomous expenditures.

Q-5 If autonomous expenditures are $2,000 and the *mpe* = .4, what is the level of equilibrium income in the economy?

THE MULTIPLIER PROCESS

Let's now look more carefully at the forces that are pushing the economy toward equilibrium. What happens when the macroeconomy is in disequilibrium—when the

Figure 26-6 The Multiplier Process
At income levels A and B, the economy is in disequilibrium. Depending on which direction the disequilibrium goes, it generates increases or decreases in planned production and expenditures until the economy reaches income level C, where planned aggregate expenditures equal aggregate production.

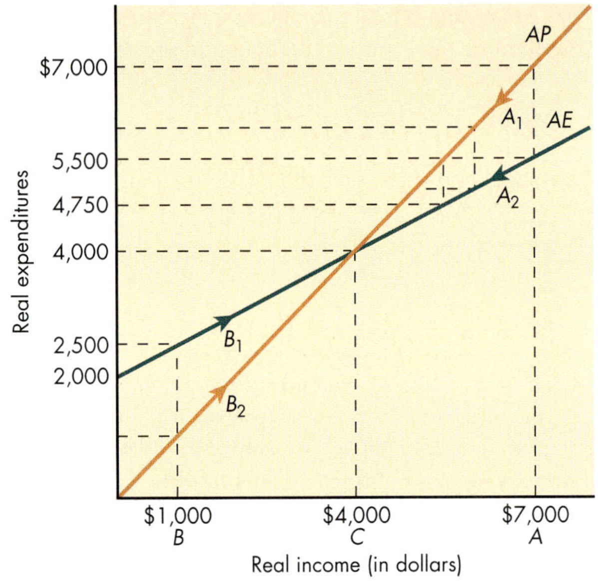

amount being injected into the economy does not equal the amount leaking from the economy? Put another way, what happens when aggregate production does not equal aggregate expenditures? Figure 26-6 shows us.

Let's first consider the economy at income level A, where aggregate production equals $7,000 and planned aggregate expenditures equal $5,500. Since production exceeds planned expenditures by $1,500 at income level A, firms can't sell all they produce; inventories pile up. In response, firms make an adjustment. They decrease aggregate production and hence income. As businesses slow production, the economy moves inward along the aggregate production curve, as shown by arrow A_1. As income falls, people's expenditures fall, and the gap between aggregate production and aggregate expenditures decreases. For example, say businesses decrease aggregate production to $5,500. Aggregate income also falls to $5,500, which causes aggregate expenditures to fall, as indicated by arrow A_2, to $4,750. Production still exceeds planned expenditures, but the gap has been reduced by $750, from $1,500 to $750.

Since a gap still remains, production and income keep falling. A good exercise is to go through two more steps. With each step, the economy moves closer to equilibrium.

Q-6 When inventories fall below planned inventories, what is likely happening to the economy?

Now let's consider the economy at income level B ($1,000) and expenditures level $2,500. Here production is less than planned expenditures. Firms find their inventory is running down. (Their investment in inventory is far less than they'd planned.) In response, they increase aggregate production and hence income. The economy starts to expand as aggregate production moves along arrow B_2 and aggregate expenditures move along arrow B_1. As individuals' income increases, their expenditures also increase, but by less than the increase in income, so the gap between aggregate expenditures and aggregate production decreases. But as long as expenditures exceed production, production and hence income keep rising.

Finally, let's consider the economy at income level C, $4,000. At point C, production is $4,000 and planned expenditures are $4,000. Firms are selling all they produce, so they have no reason to change their production levels. The aggregate economy is in equilibrium. This discussion should give you insight into what's behind the arithmetic of those earlier models.

The Circular Flow Model and the Intuition behind the Multiplier Process

Now let's think about the intuition behind the multiplier. You know from the circular flow diagram that when all individuals spend all their income (which they derive from production), the aggregate economy is in equilibrium. The circular flow diagram shown in the margin expresses the national income identity: aggregate income equals aggregate output. The flow of expenditures equals the flow of income (production). How, if not all income is spent (the *mpe* is less than 1), can expenditures equal income? The answer is that the withdrawals (income that is not spent on domestic goods) are offset by injections of autonomous expenditures.

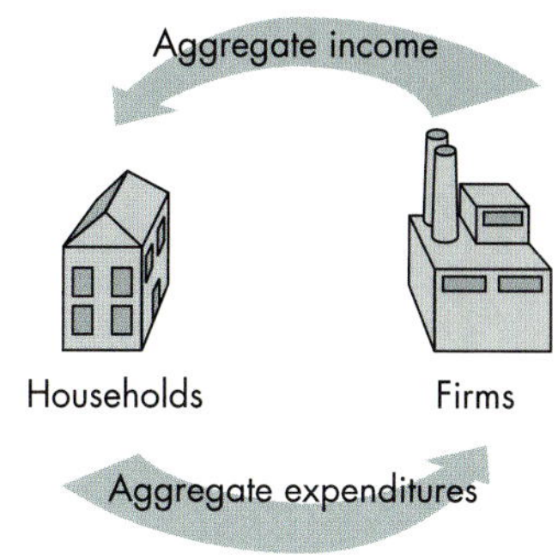

Circular flow diagram.

When thinking about the multiplier process, I picture a leaking bathtub. Withdrawals are leaks out of the bathtub. Injections are people dumping buckets of water into the tub. When the water leaking out of the bathtub just equals the water being poured in, the level of water in the tub will remain constant; the bathtub will be in equilibrium. If the amount being poured in is either more or less than the amount leaking out, the level of the water in the bathtub will be either increasing or decreasing. Thus, equilibrium in the economy requires the withdrawals from the spending stream to equal injections into the spending stream. If they don't, the economy will not be in equilibrium and will be either expanding or contracting.

To see this let's consider what happens if injections and withdrawals are not equal. Say that withdrawals exceed injections (more water is leaking out than is being poured in). In that case, the income in the economy (the level of water in the bathtub) will be declining. As income declines, so will withdrawals. Income will continue to decline until the autonomous injections flowing in (the buckets of water) just equal the withdrawals flowing out (the water leaks).

Web Note 26.2
Local Multipliers

The Multiplier Model in Action

Determining the equilibrium level of income using the multiplier is an important first step in understanding the multiplier analysis. The second step is to modify that analysis to answer a question that is of much more interest to policymakers: How much would a change in autonomous expenditures change the equilibrium level of income? This second step is important since it is precisely those sudden changes in autonomous expenditures that can cause a recession. That is why we discussed shifts in autonomous expenditures above.

It is because autonomous expenditures are subject to sudden shifts that I was careful to point out *autonomous* means "determined outside the model and not affected by income." Autonomous expenditures can, and do, shift for a variety of reasons. When they do, the multiplier process is continually being called into play.

The Steps of the Multiplier Process

Any initial change in autonomous aggregate expenditures is amplified in the multiplier process. Let's see how this works in the example in Figure 26-7, which will also serve as a review. Assume that trade negotiations between the United States and other countries have fallen apart and U.S. exports decrease by \$20. This is shown in the *AE* curve's downward shift from AE_0 to AE_1.

How far must income fall until equilibrium is reached? To answer that question, we need to know the initial change, $\Delta AE = -\$20$, and the size of the multiplier, $[1/(1 - mpe)]$. In this example, $mpe = .8$, so the multiplier is 5. That means the final

Q-7 If exports fall by \$30 and the *mpe* = .9, what happens to equilibrium income?

Figure 26-7 (a and b) Shifts in the Aggregate Expenditures Curve
Graph (**a**) shows the effect of a shift of the aggregate expenditures curve. When expenditures decrease by \$20, the aggregate expenditures curve shifts downward from AE_0 to AE_1. In response, income falls by a multiple of the shift, in this case by \$100.

Graph (**b**) shows the multiplier process under a microscope. In it the adjustment process is broken into discrete steps. For example, when income falls by \$20 (shift *B*), expenditures fall by \$16 (shift C). In response to that fall of expenditures, producers reduce output by \$16, which decreases income by \$16 (shift *D*). The lower income causes expenditures to fall further (shift *E*) and the process continues.

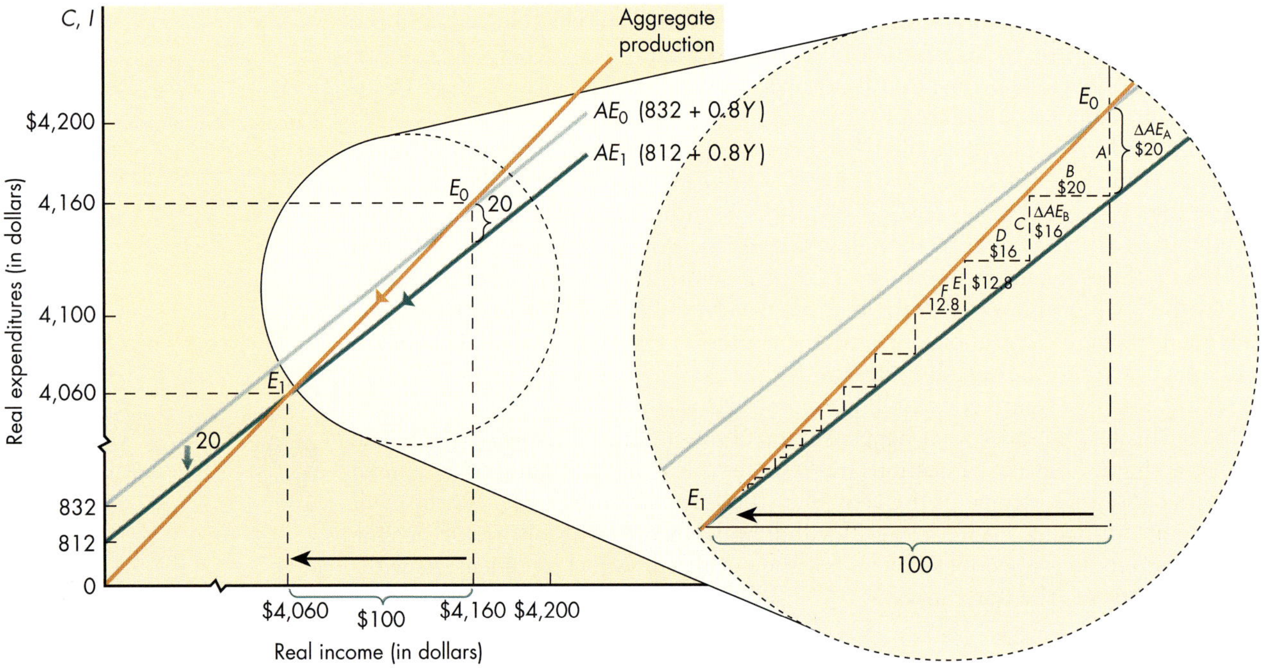

(a) The adjustment process **(b) Blowup of the adjustment process**

decrease in income that brings about equilibrium is \$100 (five times as large as the initial shift of \$20).

Figure 26-7(b), a blowup of the circled area in Figure 26-7(a), shows the detailed steps of the multiplier process so you can see how it works. Initially, autonomous expenditures fall by \$20 (shift A), causing firms to decrease production by \$20 (shift *B*). But that decrease in income causes expenditures to decrease by another \$16 (.8 × \$20) (shift C). Again firms respond by cutting production, this time by \$16 (shift *D*). Again income falls (shift *E*), causing production to fall (shift *F*). The process continues again and again (the remaining steps) until equilibrium income falls by \$100, five times the amount of the initial change. The *mpe* tells how much closer at each step aggregate expenditures will be to aggregate production. You can see this adjustment process in Figure 26-8, which shows the first steps with multipliers of various sizes.

Examples of the Effect of Shifts in Aggregate Expenditures

There are many reasons for shifts in autonomous expenditures that can affect the economy: natural disasters, changes in investment caused by technological developments, shifts in government expenditures, large changes in the exchange rate, and so on. As I discussed above, in order to focus on these shift factors autonomous expenditures are often broken up into their component parts—autonomous consumption (C_0),

Figure 26-8 The First Five Steps of Four Multipliers
The larger the marginal propensity to expend, the more steps are required before the shifts become small.

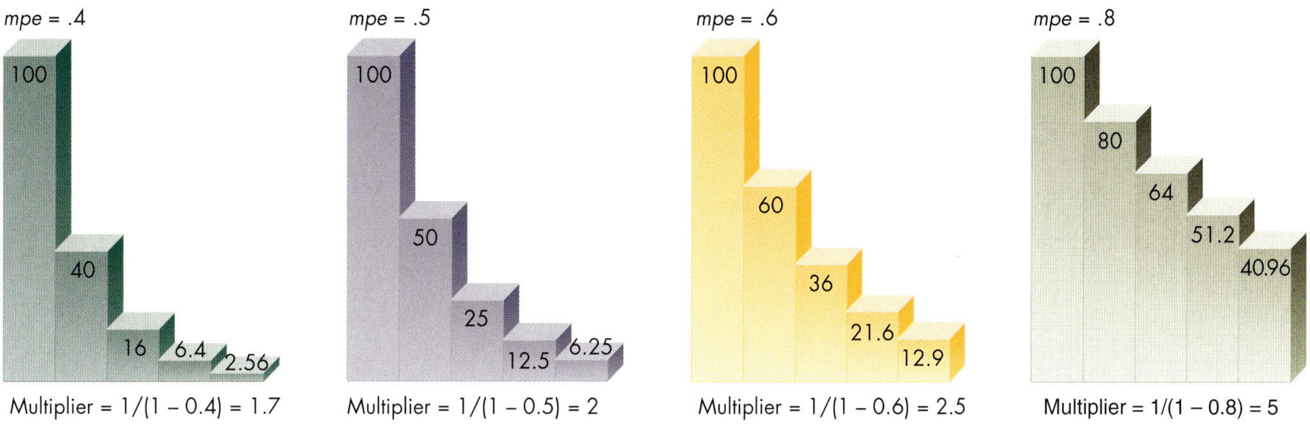

autonomous investment (I_0), autonomous government spending (G_0), and autonomous net exports ($X_0 - M_0$) (the difference between autonomous exports and autonomous imports). Changes in consumer sentiment affect C_0; major technological breakthroughs affect I_0; changes in government's spending decisions affect G_0; and changes in foreign income and exchange rates affect ($X_0 - M_0$).

Learning to work with the multiplier model requires practice, so in Figure 26-9 (a and b) I present two different expenditures functions and two different shifts in autonomous expenditures. Below each model is the equation representing how much aggregate income changes in terms of the multiplier and autonomous expenditures. As you see, the multiplier equation calculates the shift, while the graph determines it in a visual way. Now let's turn to some real-world examples.

The United States at the Turn of the Millennium In the United States in 1998, consumer confidence rose substantially, causing autonomous consumption expenditures to increase by about $200 billion more than economists had predicted. Assuming a multiplier of 2, that increase meant that income rose $400 billion higher than expected. Economists had expected the economy to grow slowly; instead it boomed. In 2001 business confidence started falling and the boom slowed. Then in September 2001, following the terrorist attacks, both consumer spending and investment fell, sending the economy into a recession.

Japan in the 1990s A dramatic appreciation of the Japanese exchange rate in 1995 cut Japanese exports, decreasing aggregate expenditures so that aggregate production was greater than planned aggregate expenditures. Then, simultaneously, consumers became worried and autonomous consumption fell. Suppliers could not sell all that they produced. Their reaction was to lay off workers and decrease output. That response would have solved the problem if only one firm had been affected. But since all firms (or at least a large majority) were affected the fallacy of composition came into play. As all producers responded in this fashion, aggregate income, and hence aggregate expenditures, also fell. The suppliers' cutback started what is sometimes called a vicious cycle. Aggregate expenditures and production spiraled downward, which is what the multiplier process explains.

Figure 26-9 (a and b) Two Different Expenditures Functions and Two Different Shifts in Autonomous Expenditures
The steeper the slope of the *AE* curve, the greater the effect of a shift in the *AE* curve on equilibrium income. In (**a**) the slope of the *AE* curve is .75 and a shift of $30 of autonomous expenditures causes a shift in income of $120. In (**b**), the slope of the *AE* curve is .66 and a shift of $30 of autonomous expenditures causes a shift in income of $90.

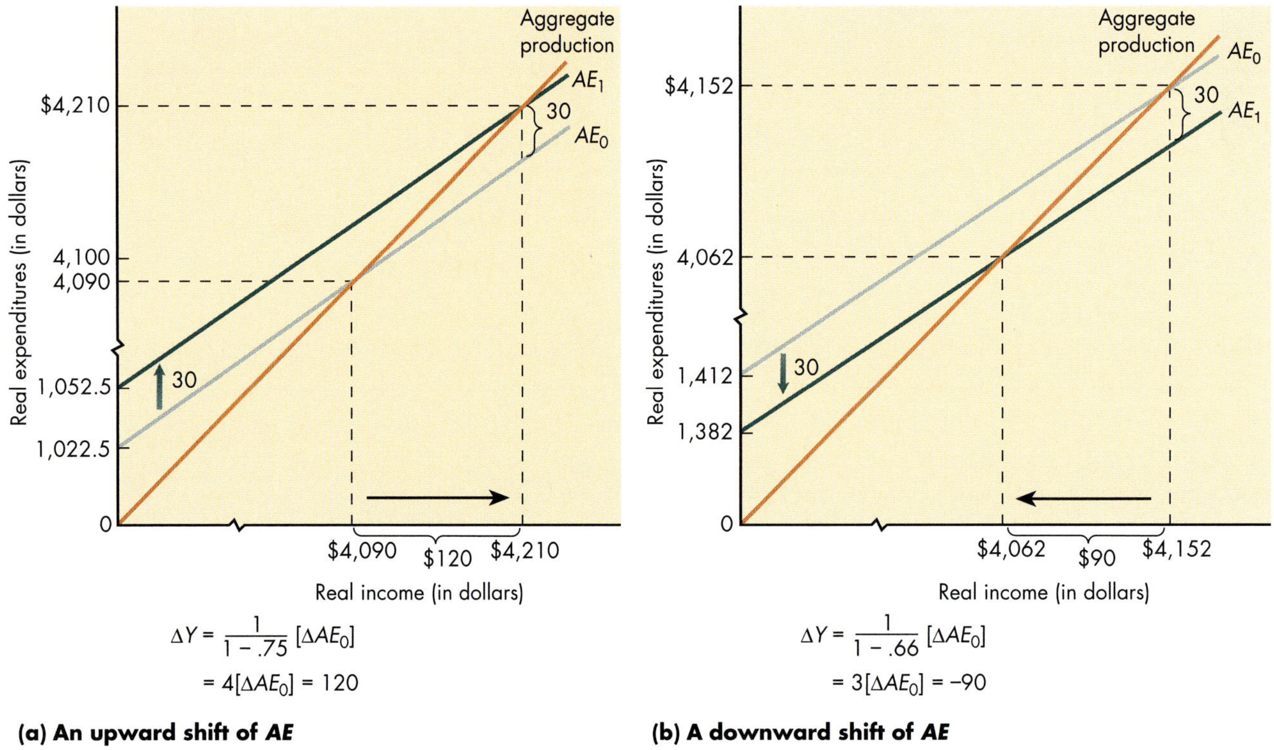

Fiscal Policy in the Multiplier Model

The multiplier model is of such interest to policymakers not only because it allows them to predict the effects of shifts in autonomous expenditures but also because they believe that it allows them to control it with countershifts of their own. By implementing policies affecting autonomous spending, governments can shift the *AE* curve up or down and, in the model at least, achieve the desired level of output.

Fighting Recession: Expansionary Fiscal Policy

To see how this is done, let's consider how government policy can get an economy out of a recession with fiscal policy. I consider this case in both the *AS/AD* model with a fixed price level and the multiplier model in Figure 26-10(a). The top panel shows fiscal policy in the multiplier model. The bottom part shows fiscal policy in the *AS/AD* model. Initially the economy is at equilibrium at income level $1,000, which is below potential income ($1,180). The economy is in a recessionary gap. This is what ideally happens: The government recognizes this recessionary gap in aggregate income of, say, $180 and responds with expansionary fiscal policy by increasing government expenditures by $60.

Assuming the price level is constant (the *SAS* curve is flat) the increased government spending shifts the *AE* curve from AE_0 upward to AE_1. Businesses that receive government contracts hire the workers who have been laid off by other firms and open

Figure 26-10 Fiscal Policy
In **(a)** if the economy is below its potential income level, the government can increase government spending to stimulate the economy. Doing so shifts the *AD* curve to the right and the *AE* curve shifts up. Income expands by a multiple of that increase. In **(b)** we see appropriate government policy for an inflationary gap. In the absence of any policy, shortages and accelerating inflation will occur. To prevent this, government must use contractionary fiscal policy, shifting the *AE* curve downward from AE_0 to AE_1 and reduce equilibrium income from \$5,000 to \$4,000. The bottom part of **(b)** shows this policy in the *AS/AD* model.

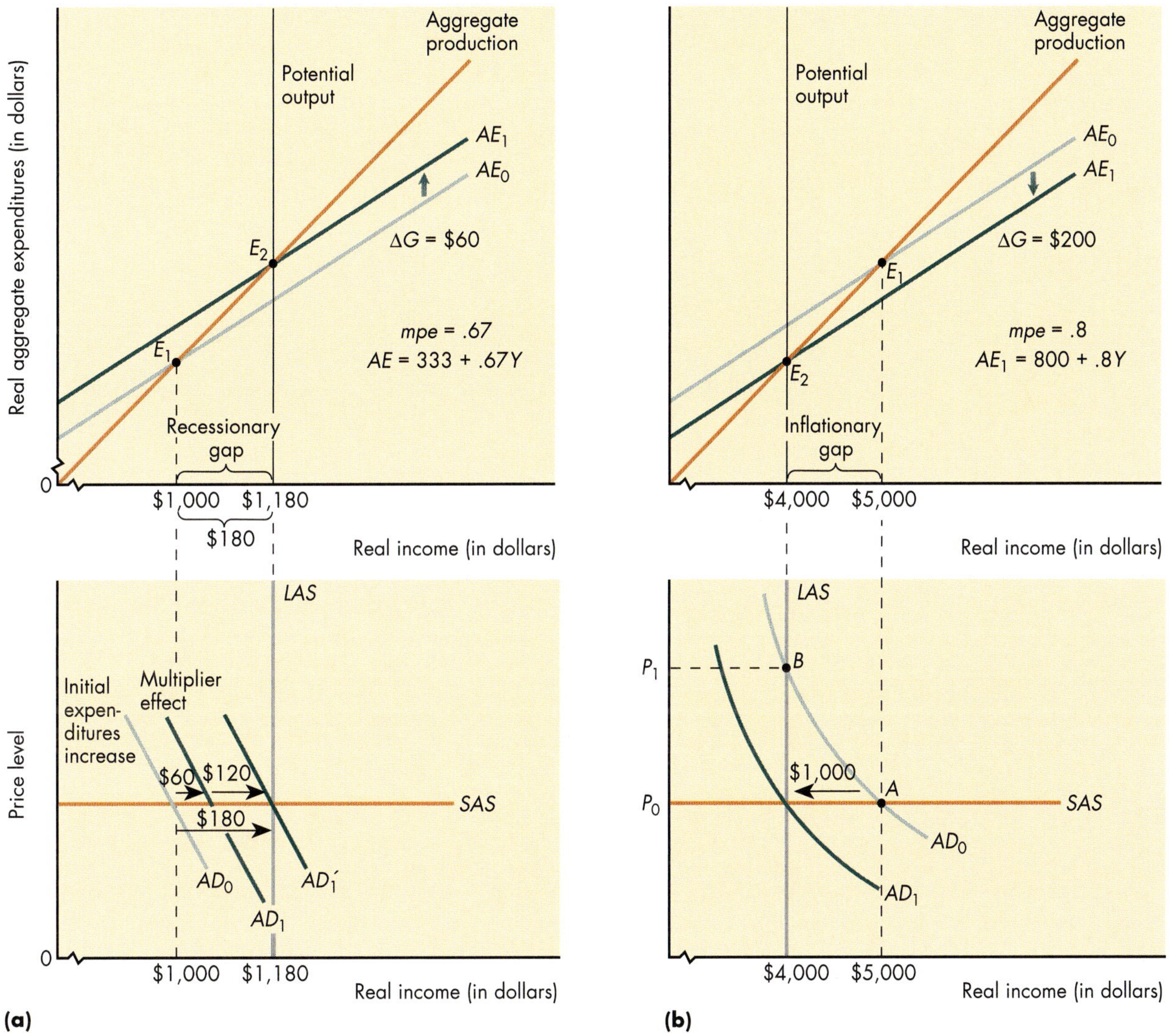

new plants; output increases by the initial expenditure of \$60. But the process doesn't stop there. At this point, the multiplier process sets in. As the newly employed workers spend more, other businesses find that their demand increases. They hire more workers, who spend an additional \$40 (since their $mpe = .67$). This increases income further. The same process occurs again and again. By the time the process had ended, income has risen by \$180 to \$1,180, the potential level of income.

The effects are shown in the *AS/AD* model in the bottom part of Figure 26-10(a). The *AD* curve shifts to the right by three times the increase in government expenditures, or by \$180. The initial shock shifts the *AD* curve to the right by \$60; the \$120 shift is due to the multiplier effects that the initial shift brings about.

Using Taxes Rather than Expenditures as the Tool of Fiscal Policy

Applying the Tools

As a brain teaser you might try to figure out what you would have advised the government to do if it had wanted to increase taxes rather than decrease expenditures to get the economy out of the inflationary gap in Figure 26-10(b). By how much should it increase taxes? If you said by $200 since the multiplier is 5, you're on the right wave length, but not quite right. True, the multiplier, 1/(1 − *mpe*), is 5, but taxes affect total expenditures in a slightly different way than does the initial change in expenditures. Specifically, expenditures will not decrease by the full amount of the tax increase. The reason why is that people will likely reduce their saving in order to hold up their expenditures. Expenditures will initially fall by that portion of the decrease in their disposable income that consumers spend on U.S. goods, which, as I stated in the text, is measured by consumer's marginal propensity to consume (*mpc*). For simplicity, let's assume that the marginal propensity to consume equals the marginal propensity to expend. Then, initially, the decrease in expenditures from the tax cut will be (.8 × $200) = $160, rather than $200. To get the initial shift of $200 from increasing taxes, the government must increase taxes by $200/.8, or $250. Then when people reduce spending by .8 of that, their expenditures will fall by $200.

How did the government economists know to increase spending by $60? By backward induction. They empirically estimated that the *mpe*—the slope of the aggregate expenditures curve—was .67, which meant that the multiplier was 1/(1 − .67) = 1/.33 = 3. They divided the multiplier, 3, into the recessionary gap, $180, and determined that if they increased spending by $60, income would increase by $180.

If the *SAS* curve had been upward-sloping, and the price level had not remained constant, predicting the precise level of increase in real income would have been harder because the increase would have been split between a change in real income and a change in nominal income. The increase in real income would have been less than it was with a flat *SAS* curve. The precise amount would depend on the degree of upward slope of the *SAS* curve.[3] The steeper the slope of the *SAS* curve, the less real income would have changed.

Fighting Inflation: Contractionary Fiscal Policy

Q-8 Demonstrate graphically the effect of contractionary fiscal policy.

Q-9 The marginal propensity to expend is .33, and there is an inflationary gap of $100. What fiscal policy would you recommend?

Fiscal policy can also work in reverse, decreasing expenditures that are too high. Expenditures are "too high" when the economy temporarily exceeds its potential output. An economy operating above potential will generate accelerating inflation.

Figure 26-10(b) shows contractionary fiscal policy in the multiplier and *AS/AD* models. Potential income is $4,000, but the equilibrium level of income is $5,000. The difference between the two, $1,000, is the inflationary gap. This inflationary gap causes upward pressure on wages and prices with no additional lasting increase in output. If the government wants to avoid inflation, it can use contractionary policy. By how much should government reduce government expenditures? To determine that, it had to calculate the multiplier. In this example, the marginal propensity to expend is assumed to be .8, which means that the multiplier would be 5. So a cut in autonomous expenditures

[3]You can determine the approximate percentage reduction in the multiplier effect on real income by writing the reciprocal of the slope of the *SAS* curve as a fraction and then placing the numerator of that fraction over the sum of the numerator and the denominator. The result is the approximate decrease in the size of the multiplier effect on real income. For example, if the slope of the *SAS* curve is 8, the multiplier effect on real income will be reduced by about 1/9 [1/(1 + 8)] from what it would have been had the *SAS* curve been horizontal.

Keynes and Fiscal Policy

Beyond the Tools

One of the themes of this book is that economic thought and policy are more complicated than an introductory book must necessarily make them seem. Fiscal policy is a good case in point. In the early 1930s, before Keynes wrote *The General Theory,* he was advocating public works programs and deficits (government spending in excess of tax revenues) as a way to get the British economy out of the Depression. He came upon what we now call the *Keynesian theory* as he tried to explain to Classical economists why he supported deficits. After arriving at his new theory, however, he spent little time advocating fiscal policy and, in fact, never mentions fiscal policy in *The General Theory.* The book's primary policy recommendation is the need to socialize investments—for the government to take over the investment decisions from private individuals. When one of his followers, Abba Lerner, advocated expansionary fiscal policy at a seminar Keynes attended, Keynes strongly objected, leading Evsey Domar, another Keynesian follower, to whisper to a friend, "Keynes should read *The General Theory.*"

What's going on here? There are many interpretations, but the one I find most convincing is the one presented by historian Peter Clarke. He argues that, while working on *The General Theory,* Keynes turned his interest from a policy revolution to a theoretical revolution. He believed he had found a serious flaw in Classical economic theory. The Classicals assumed that an economy in equilibrium was at full employment, but they did not show how the economy could move to that equilibrium from a disequilibrium. That's when Keynes's interest changed from a policy to a theoretical revolution.

His followers, such as Lerner, carried out the policy implications of his theory. Why did Keynes sometimes oppose these policy implications? Because he was also a student of politics and he recognized that economic theory can often lead to politically unacceptable policies. In a letter to a friend he later said Lerner was right in his logic, but he hoped the opposition didn't discover what Lerner was saying. Keynes was more than an economist; he was a politician as well.

of $200 would shift the *AE* curve down by $200 and decrease equilibrium income by $1,000.

The bottom part of Figure 26-10(b) shows the effects of a $200 cut in government expenditures in the *AS/AD* model. With a multiplier of 5, the *AD* curve shifts to the left by $1,000. Because the *SAS* curve is flat, equilibrium output declines to $4,000.

Limitations of the Multiplier Model

On the surface the multiplier model makes a lot of intuitive sense. However, surface sense can often be misleading. Some of the model's limitations are discussed below.

The Multiplier Model Is Not a Complete Model of the Economy

The multiplier model provides a technical method of determining equilibrium income. But in reality the model doesn't do what it purports to do—determine equilibrium income from scratch. Why? Because it doesn't tell us where those autonomous expenditures come from or how we would go about measuring them.

At best, what we can measure, or at least estimate, are directions and rough sizes of autonomous demand shifts, and we can determine the direction and possible overadjustment the economy might make in response to those changes. If you think back to our initial discussion of the multiplier model, this is how I introduced it—as an explanation of forces affecting the adjustment process, not as a determinant of the final equilibrium independent of where the economy started. It is a historical, not an analytical,

At best, what we can estimate are directions and rough sizes of autonomous demand or supply shifts.

model. Without some additional information about where the economy started from, or what is the desired level of output, the multiplier model is incomplete.

Shifts Are Not as Great as Intuition Suggests

A second problem with the multiplier model is that it leads people to overemphasize the shifts that would occur in aggregate expenditures in response to a shift in autonomous expenditures. Say people decide to save some more. You might think that it would lead to a fall in expenditures. But wait, that saving will go into the financial sector and be translated back into the expenditures sector as loans to other consumers or as loans to businesses funding investment. So if you take a broad view of aggregate expenditures, many of the shifts in expenditures are simply rearrangements from one group of expenditures to another.

The Price Level Will Often Change in Response to Shifts in Demand

One of the assumptions of the multiplier model is that the price level is fixed—that makes aggregate production a 45° line. But in reality the price level can change as aggregate demand changes because price markups and labor market conditions change. These changes in the price level reduce the effect of the multiplier on real income. Some adjustment must be made for changes in the price level when the price level changes in response to changes in aggregate demand. That adjustment is usually made by shifting the *AE* curve up (in the case of a falling price level) or down (in the case of a rising price level). The quantitative amount of that shift is uncertain, making the quantitative effect of policy on real income uncertain when the price level changes. (These adjustments are discussed in Appendix B.)

People's Forward-Looking Expectations Make the Adjustment Process Much More Complicated

People's forward-looking expectations make the adjustment process much more complicated. The multiplier model presented here assumes that people respond to current changes in income. Most people, however, act on the basis of expectations of the future. Consider the assumed response of businesses to changes in expenditures. They lay off workers and cut production at the slightest fall in demand. In reality, their response is far more complicated. They may well see the fall as a temporary blip. They will allow their inventory to rise in the expectation that the next month another temporary blip will offset the previous fall. Business decisions about production are forward looking, and do not respond simply to current changes. As a contrast to the simple multiplier model, some modern economists have put forward a **rational expectations model** of the macroeconomy in which *all decisions are based on the expected equilibrium in the economy*. Some economists go so far as to argue that since people rationally expect the economy to achieve its potential income, it will do so.

Shifts in Expenditures Might Reflect Desired Shifts in Supply and Demand

There is an implicit assumption in the multiplier model that shifts in demand are not reflections of shifts in desired production or supply. Reality is much more complicated. Shifts can occur for many reasons, and many shifts can reflect desired shifts in aggregate production, which are accompanied by shifts in aggregate expenditures. An example of such a change occurred in Japan in the 1990s as Japan's industries lost their competitive edge to Korean, Chinese, and Taiwanese industries. The Japanese economy faltered, but the problem was not simply a fall in aggregate demand, and therefore the solution to it was not simply to increase aggregate demand. There was a simultaneous shift in aggregate supply that had to be dealt with.

Suppliers operate in the future—shifting supply, not to existing demand, but to expected demand, making the relationship between aggregate production and current demand far more complicated than it seems in the multiplier model. Expansion of this line of thought has led some economists (in an earlier chapter called *real-business-cycle economists*) to develop the **real-business-cycle theory** of the economy: *the theory that fluctuations in the economy reflect real phenomena—simultaneous shifts in supply and demand, not simply supply responses to demand shifts*. Let's consider an example—the expansion of the U.S. economy in the late 1990s. The *AS/AD* model would attribute that to a shift of the *AD* curve to the right, combined with a relatively fixed *SAS* curve that did not shift up as output expanded. The real-business-cycle theory would attribute that shift in income to businesses' decision to increase supply due to technological developments, and a subsequent increase in demand via Say's law.

Expenditures Depend on Much More than Current Income

Let's say your income goes down 10 percent. The multiplier model says that your expenditures will go down by some specific percentage of that. But will they? If you are rational, it seems reasonable to base your consumption on more than one year's income—say, instead, on your permanent or lifetime income. What happens to your income in a particular year has little effect on your lifetime income. If it is true that people base their spending primarily on lifetime income, not yearly income, the marginal propensity to consume out of changes in current income could be very low, approaching zero. In that case, the expenditures function would essentially be a flat line, and the multiplier would be 1. There would be no secondary effects of an initial shift in expenditures. This set of arguments is called the **permanent income hypothesis**—*the hypothesis that expenditures are determined by permanent or lifetime income*. It undermines the reasoning of much of the specific results of the simple multiplier model.

Q-10 What effect would expenditures being dependent on permanent income have on the size of the multiplier?

Conclusion

While each of the above criticisms has some validity, most macro policymakers still use some variation of the multiplier model as the basis for their policy decisions. They don't see it as a *mechanistic model*—a model that pictures the economy as representable by a mechanically determined, timeless model with a determinant equilibrium. Modern economists have come to the conclusion that there is no simple way to understand the aggregate economy. Any mechanistic interpretation of an aggregate model is doomed to fail. The hope of economists to have a model that would give them a specific numeric guide to policy has not been met.

The model is still useful if it is seen as an interpretive model or an aid in understanding complicated disequilibrium dynamics. The specific results of the multiplier model are a guide to common sense, enabling us to emphasize a particular important dynamic interdependency while keeping others in mind. With that addendum—that it is not meant to be taken literally but only as an aid to intuition—the simple multiplier model deals with the issues that concern today's highest-level macro theorists.

The Moniac used flows of colored water to simulate income and expenditures. It was used as a teaching tool.
Science Museum/Science & Society Picture Library, London.

Summary

- The multiplier model focuses on the induced effect that a change in production has on expenditures, which affects production, and so on.
- The multiplier model is made up of the aggregate production and aggregate expenditures curves. In equilibrium, aggregate production must equal planned aggregate expenditures.
- The aggregate production curve is a line along which real income equals real production. It is a 45° line.
- Aggregate expenditures (*AE*) are made up of consumption, investment, government spending, and net exports:

  $$AE = C + I + G + (X - M)$$
- Expenditure depends on the level of income; the marginal propensity to expend (*mpe*) tells us the change in expenditures that occurs with a change in income.
- The *AE* curve shows aggregate expenditures graphically. Its slope is the *mpe* and its *y*-intercept equals autonomous expenditures.
- Equilibrium output, or income, is where the *AP* and *AE* curves intersect.
- Equilibrium output can be calculated using the multiplier equation. It is:

  $$Y = \text{Multiplier} \times \text{Autonomous expenditures}$$
- The multiplier tells us how much a change in autonomous expenditures will change equilibrium income. The multiplier equals $1/(1 - mpe)$.
- When an economy is in equilibrium, withdrawals from the spending stream equal injections into the spending stream (autonomous expenditures).
- Shifts in autonomous expenditures can be the initial change that begins the multiplier process. The multiplier process expands that initial shift to a much larger decrease or increase in production and income.
- Expansionary fiscal policy, increasing government expenditures or decreasing taxes, is represented graphically as an upward shift of the aggregate expenditures curve or a rightward shift in the *AD* curve.
- Contractionary fiscal policy, decreasing government expenditures or increasing taxes, is represented graphically as a downward shift of the aggregate expenditures curve or a leftward shift in the *AD* curve.
- The multiplier model has limitations: (1) it is incomplete without information about where the economy started and what is the desired level of output, (2) it overemphasizes shifts that occur in aggregate expenditures, (3) it assumes that the price level is fixed when in reality it isn't, (4) it doesn't take expectations into account, (5) it ignores the possibility that shifts in expenditures are desired, and (6) it ignores the possibility that consumption is based on lifetime income, not annual income.
- Macroeconomic models cannot be applied mechanistically; they are only guides to common sense.

Key Terms

aggregate expenditures (594)
aggregate production (593)
autonomous expenditures (594)
expenditures multiplier (601)
induced expenditures (594)
marginal propensity to expend (*mpe*) (596)
multiplier equation (600)
permanent income hypothesis (611)
rational expectations model (610)
real-business-cycle theory (611)

Questions for Thought and Review

1. If planned expenditures are below actual production, what will happen to income? Explain the process by which this happens.
2. Are inventories building up at levels of output above or below equilibrium output? Explain your answer.
3. What happens to the aggregate expenditures curve when autonomous expenditures fall?
4. What happens to equilibrium income when the marginal propensity to expend rises?
5. If saving were instantaneously translated into investment, what would be the multiplier's size? What would be the level of autonomous expenditures?
6. Name some forces that might cause shocks to aggregate expenditures.
7. What is the current state of U.S. fiscal policy? Would you advise the United States to change its fiscal policy? Why?
8. The marginal propensity to expend is .5 and there is a recessionary gap of $200. What fiscal policy would you recommend?
9. Why does cutting taxes by $100 have a smaller effect on GDP than increasing expenditures by $100?
10. Mr. Whammo has just invented a magic pill. Take it and it transports you anywhere. Explain his invention's effects on the economy.
11. Why is the circular flow diagram of the economy an only partially correct conception of the multiplier model?
12. How do mechanistic models differ from interpretive models?
13. Charlie Black, a GOP strategist, was once quoted as stating, "I can't tell you why this happens, but there's a lag time (before people tune into good economic news)." What is the effect of this delay in the adjustment of expectations by consumers on the dynamics of the multiplier model?

Problems and Exercises

1. The marginal propensity to expend is .8. Autonomous expenditures are $4,200. What is the level of equilibrium income in the economy? Demonstrate graphically.
2. The marginal propensity to expend is .66 and autonomous expenditures have just fallen by $20.
   a. What will likely happen to equilibrium income?
   b. Demonstrate graphically.
3. Congratulations. You've been appointed economic adviser to Happyland. Your research assistant says the country's *mpe* is .8 and autonomous expenditures have just risen by $20.
   a. What will happen to income?
   b. Your research assistant comes in and says he's sorry but the *mpe* wasn't .8; it was .5. How does your answer change?
   c. He runs in again and says exports have fallen by $10 and investment has risen by $10. How does your answer change?
   d. You now have to present your analysis to the president, who wants to see it all graphically. Naturally you oblige.
4. Congratulations again. You've just been appointed economic adviser to Examland. The *mpe* is .6; autonomous investment is $1,000; autonomous government spending is $8,000; autonomous consumption is $10,000; and autonomous net exports are $1,000.
   a. What is the level of income in the country?
   b. Autonomous net exports increase by $2,000. What will happen to income?
   c. What will happen to unemployment? (Remember Okun's rule of thumb.)
   d. You've just learned the *mpe* changed from .6 to .5. How will this information change your answers in *a*, *b*, and *c*?
5. In 1992, as President George H. W. Bush was running (unsuccessfully) for reelection, the economy slowed down; then in late 1993, after President Bill Clinton's election, the economy picked up steam.
   a. Demonstrate graphically with the multiplier model a shift in the *AE* curve that would have caused the slowdown. Which component of aggregate expenditures was the likely culprit?
   b. Demonstrate graphically with the multiplier model a shift in the *AE* curve that would have caused the improvement. Which component of aggregate expenditures was likely responsible?

c. What policies do you think President Bush could have used to stop the slowdown?
d. What policies do you think President Clinton used to try to speed up the economy?

6. Congratulations yet again. You've just been appointed chairman to the Council of Economic Advisers in Textland. You must rely on your research assistant for the specific numbers. He says income is $50,000, *mpe* is .75, and the president wants to lower unemployment from 8 to 6 percent. (Remember Okun's rule of thumb.)
   a. Advise him.
   b. Your research assistant comes in and says "Sorry, I meant that the *mpe* is .67." You redo your calculations.
   c. You're just about to see the president when your research assistant comes running, saying, "Sorry, sorry, I meant that the *mpe* is .5." Redo your calculations.
7. State what fiscal policy you would recommend to eliminate the inflationary or recessionary gap in the following scenarios:
   a. Recessionary gap of $800; *mpe* = .5.
   b. Inflationary gap of $1,500; *mpe* = .8.
   c. Real GDP = $10,200; Potential GDP = $9,000; *mpe* = .2.
   d. Real GDP = $40,500; Potential GDP = $42,000; *mpe* = .7.
8. Congratulations one more time. You have been appointed chair of Economic Advisers in Fantasyland. Income is currently $600,000, unemployment is 5 percent, and there are signs of coming inflation. You rely on your research assistant for specific numbers. He tells you that potential income is $564,000 and the *mpe* is .5.
   a. The government wants to eliminate the inflationary gap by changing expenditures. What policy do you suggest?
   b. By how much will unemployment change after your policy has taken effect?
   c. Your research assistant comes in and says "Sorry, I meant that the *mpe* is .8." Redo your calculations to parts *a* and *b*.

Web Questions

1. The Conference Board publishes a report detailing consumer attitudes and buying plans and compiles the consumer confidence index. It also reports on business executives' expectations. Go to the Conference Board's home page (www.conferenceboard.org) and read the most recent reports on consumer confidence and business executives' expectations to answer the following questions:
   a. What has happened to the consumer confidence index in the past few months?
   b. Using the multiplier model, show the likely effect of the change in consumer confidence on equilibrium output.
   c. What has happened to expectations of business executives over the past few months?
   d. Do the consumer confidence and business executives' expectations match? If not, what do you expect to happen to inventories in the coming months?
2. The White House reports data about recent economic events in its electronic briefing room. Go to the White House's home page (www.whitehouse.gov) and find the Economics Statistics Briefing Room to answer the following questions:
   a. What has happened to inventories during the past six months?
   b. What does the change in inventories suggest about the direction of the economy in the coming months? Explain your answer using the multiplier model.

Answers to Margin Questions

1. Income equals production on the aggregate production curve. (*594*)
2. Induced expenditures change as income changes. Autonomous expenditures are independent of income. (*595*)
3. The *mpe* is .6. (*596*)
4. The multiplier is 2 when the *mpe* = .5. (*601*)
5. The level of income is $3,333. (*601*)
6. When inventories fall below planned inventories the economy is probably expanding; firms will likely increase production, which will cause expenditures to increase, which will further draw down inventories. (*602*)
7. Equilibrium income falls by $300. (*603*)
8. As you can see in the graph on the next page, contractionary fiscal policy shifts the *AD* curve to the left. The multiplier then takes over to shift the *AD* curve to the left by a multiple of the initial decline in aggregate expenditures. Assuming a flat *SAS* curve, income falls by a multiple of the initial shift. In the multiplier model the *AE* curve shifts down and equilibrium income falls by a multiple of the decline in government expenditures. (*608*)

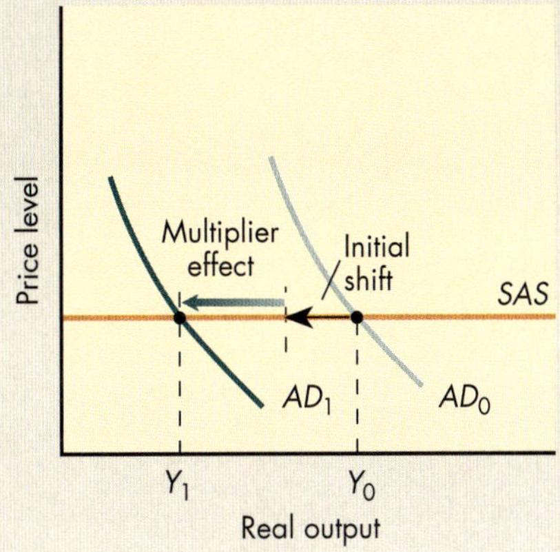

9. Since there is an inflationary gap, I would recommend contractionary fiscal policy. Since the multiplier is 1.5 (given the marginal propensity to expend of .33), I would recommend decreasing government spending by $66. (*608*)
10. If expenditures are dependent on permanent income, not current income, expenditures would not change as much with a change in current income and the multiplier would get smaller. (*611*)

Appendix A

An Algebraic Presentation of the Expanded Multiplier Model

In the chapter I developed the basic multiplier model, focusing on the *mpe*. In this appendix I briefly outline a fuller presentation in which consumption, taxes, and imports are related to income. That means that instead of having a single expenditures curve, we have a separate curve for each component of aggregate expenditures: consumption, investment, government spending, and net exports.

The Consumption Function Model

I begin with a model in which only consumption varies with income. The table in Figure A26-1(a) shows the components of the model as they are usually presented at the introductory level and Figure A26-1(b) graphs them. Notice that the only expenditure that is assumed to vary with income is consumption, which varies linearly with income and has a slope equal to the marginal propensity to consume (*mpc*)—the additional consumption that results from additional income. In this case the *mpc* is assumed to be .5, so the slope of the consumption function is .5. All other expenditures are assumed to be autonomous. The summation of expenditures, aggregate expenditures, is in column 5.

To arrive at an aggregate expenditures function, we add up the curves vertically. I do this in Figure A26-2(a). Because we have assumed that consumption is the only expenditure that varies with income, the aggregate expenditure curve has the same slope as the aggregate consumption function. Notice that the aggregate expenditures curve crosses the vertical axis at a point that's the sum of all four autonomous expenditures: $C_0 + I_0 + G_0 + (X_0 - M_0) = \$4,000$. A good exercise to help you visualize the relationships involved here is to compare the data in the columns with points on the graph to see how they correspond.

As was discussed in the text, aggregate equilibrium is where the aggregate expenditures function intersects the aggregate production curve—at point A in the Figure A26-2(b). If any of the autonomous expenditures increase, the aggregate equilibrium will change. Say that autonomous investment increased by 2,000. That shifts up the *AE* curve by 2,000 and, as you can see, increases the equilibrium income by 4,000. Why by 4,000? Because of the multiplier discussed in the chapter. With only consumption varying with income, the marginal propensity to expend is determined by the marginal propensity to consume. Since in this case *mpe* = *mpc*, the multiplier is 1/(1 − *mpc*).

A More Complete Model

More generally, the various components of aggregate expenditures will depend on income in varying degrees,

Figure A26-1 (a and b) Expenditure Components

(1) C	+	(2) I	+	(3) G	+	(4) X-M	=	(5) AE	(6) Y	(7) ΔAE	(8) ΔY	ROW
1,000		1,000		1,000		1,000		4,000	0			A
1,500		1,000		1,000		1,000		4,500	1,000	500	1,000	B
2,000		1,000		1,000		1,000		5,000	2,000	500	1,000	C
2,500		1,000		1,000		1,000		5,500	3,000	500	1,000	D
3,000		1,000		1,000		1,000		6,000	4,000	500	1,000	E
3,500		1,000		1,000		1,000		6,500	5,000	500	1,000	F
4,000		1,000		1,000		1,000		7,000	6,000	500	1,000	G
4,500		1,000		1,000		1,000		7,500	7,000	500	1,000	H
5,000		1,000		1,000		1,000		8,000	8,000	500	1,000	I
5,500		1,000		1,000		1,000		8,500	9,000	500	1,000	J
6,000		1,000		1,000		1,000		9,000	10,000	500	1,000	K
6,500		1,000		1,000		1,000		9,500	11,000	500	1,000	L
7,000		1,000		1,000		1,000		10,000	12,000	500	1,000	M

(a)

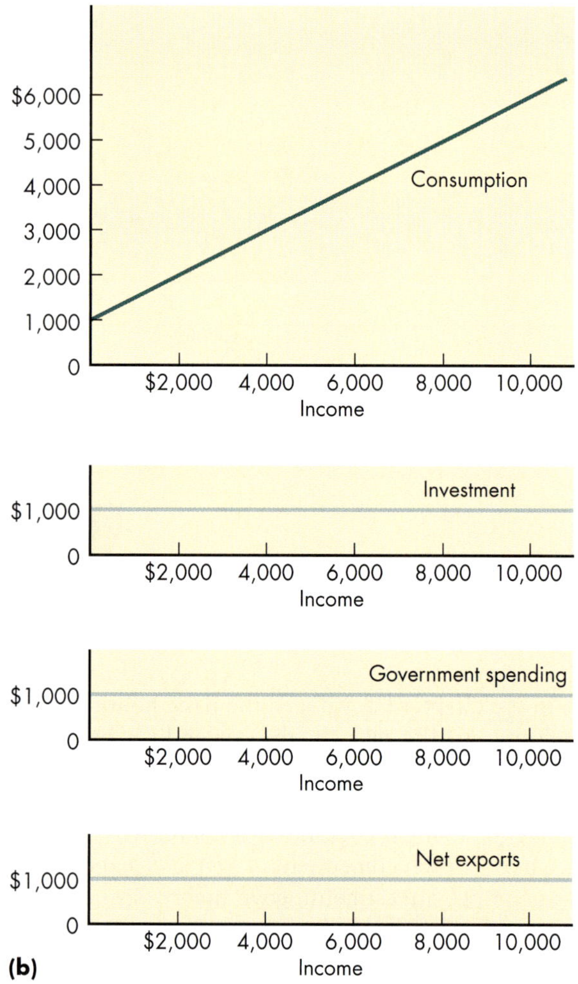

(b)

which will mean that the components each will have some slope—they will have both an induced and an autonomous component. The slope of the aggregate expenditures curve will be the composite of all these slopes. Presenting that case geometrically becomes quite messy, so we will switch to an algebraic presentation.

In this fuller presentation we break up the *mpe* into its component parts so that there is a *mpc*, specified as *c* in the equations; a marginal propensity to import, specified as *m* in the equations; and a marginal tax rate, specified as *t* in the equations.

This more complete multiplier model consists of the following equations:

(1) $C = C_0 + cY_d$

(2) $Y_d = Y - T + R$

(3) $I = I_0$

(4) $G = G_0$

(5) $R = R_0$

(6) $T = T_0 + tY$

(7) $X = X_0$

(8) $M = M_0 + mY$

(9) $C + I + G + (X - M) = Y$

Equation (1) is the consumption function. C_0 is autonomous consumption; *c* is the marginal propensity to consume; cY_d is the *mpc* multiplied by disposable income.

Equation (2) defines disposable income as a function of income minus taxes plus government transfers, *R*.

Equation (3) is the investment function. I_0 is autonomous investment.

Figure A26-2 (a and b) Summation of Aggregate Expenditures

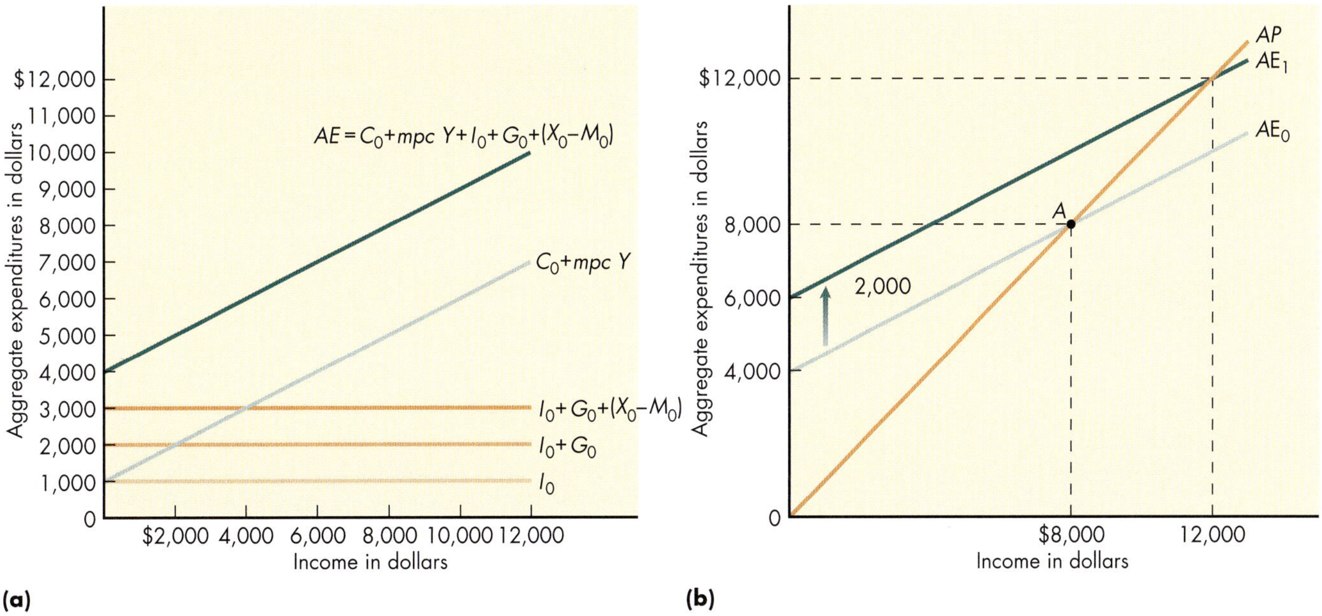

Equation (4) is the government expenditures function. G_0 is autonomous spending.

Equation (5) is the government transfer function. R_0 is autonomous transfer payments.

Equation (6) is the tax function. Taxes are composed of two parts. The autonomous component, T_0, is unaffected by income. The induced portion of taxes is tY. The tax rate is represented by t.

Equation (7) is the exogenous export function.

Equation (8) is the import function. Imports are composed of two parts. M_0 is the autonomous portion. The induced portion is mY. The marginal propensity to import is represented by m.

Equation (9) is the national income accounting identity: Total expenditures = income.

To use this model meaningfully, we must combine all these equations into a single equation, called a *reduced-form equation*, which will neatly show the effect of various shifts on the equilibrium level of income. To do so we first substitute Equation (2) into Equation (1) giving us:

$$\text{(1a) } C = C_0 + c(Y - T + R)$$

We then substitute (1a), (3), (4), (5), (6), (7), and (8) into Equation (9), giving:

$$C_0 + c[Y - (T_0 + tY) + R_0] + I_0 + G_0 + [X_0 - (M_0 + mY)] = Y$$

Removing the parentheses:

$$C_0 + cY - cT_0 - ctY + cR_0 + I_0 + G_0 + X_0 - M_0 - mY = Y$$

Moving all of the Y terms to the right side:

$$C_0 - cT_0 + cR_0 + I_0 + G_0 + X_0 - M_0 = Y - cY + ctY + mY$$

Factoring out Y on the right side:

$$C_0 - cT_0 - cR_0 + I_0 + G_0 + X_0 - M_0 = Y(1 - c + ct + m)$$

Dividing by $(1 - c + ct + m)$ gives:

$$[C_0 - cT_0 - cR_0 + I_0 + G_0 + X_0 - M_0]\left[\frac{1}{(1 - c + ct + m)}\right] = Y$$

$1/(1 - c + ct + m)$ is the multiplier for a simple multiplier model with endogenous taxes and endogenous imports.

We can relate this multiplier to the multiplier presented in the text $[1/(1 - mpe)]$ by recognizing that the marginal propensity to expend is

- Composed of the marginal propensity to consume, the marginal propensity to consume times the tax rate, and the marginal propensity to import, and
- Equal to $c - ct - m$

Thus, $mpe = c - ct - m$. We can see that the two are the same by collecting terms and rewriting the multiplier as

$1/[1 - (c - ct - m)]$. We can then by replacing the $c - ct - m$ with *mpe*. In the geometric case presented initially, the income tax, t, and the marginal propensity to import, m, were assumed to be zero, which reduces the multiplier to $1/(1 - c)$.

To see whether you follow the math, let's try a numerical example. Say you want to increase income (Y) by 100. Assume $c = .8$, $t = .2$, and $m = .14$. Substituting in these numbers you find that the multiplier is 2. (The approximate multiplier for the United States is usually around 2. Having calculated the multiplier, we can now determine how much to change autonomous expenditures to affect income. For example, to increase income by 100, we must increase autonomous expenditures by $(100/2) = 50$.

Questions for Thought and Review

1. You have just been made our nation's adviser. The president wants output to increase by 400 by decreasing taxes. Your research assistant tells you that the *mpc* is .8, and all other components of aggregate expenditures are determined outside the model. What policy would you suggest?
2. The president returns to you and tells you that instead of changing taxes, he wants to achieve the same result by increasing government expenditures. What policy would you recommend?
3. Your research assistant has a worried look on her face. "What's the problem?" you ask. "I goofed," she confesses. "I thought taxes were exogenous when actually there's a marginal tax rate of .1." Before she can utter another word, you say, "No problem. I'll simply recalculate my answers to questions 1 and 2 and change them before I send them in." What are your corrected answers?
4. She still has a pained expression. "What's wrong?" you ask. "You didn't let me finish," she says. "Not only was there a marginal tax rate of .1; there's also a marginal propensity to import of .2." Again you interrupt to make sure she doesn't feel guilty. Again you say, "No problem. I'll simply recalculate my answers to questions 1 and 2 to account for the new information." What are your new answers?
5. Explain, using the words *expenditures* and *leakages*, why making taxes and imports endogenous reduces the multiplier.
6. Suppose imports were a function of disposable income instead of income. What would be the new multiplier? How does it compare with the multiplier when imports were a function of income?

Appendix B

The Multiplier Model and the *AS/AD* Model

In Chapter 25, I emphasized that the *AD* curve was quite different from a micro demand curve; it was an equilibrium curve—a curve that told us the relationship between different price levels and different equilibria in the goods market. It has traditionally been derived from the multiplier model, and thus it has implicitly accepted the dynamics of that model. To see how it is derived from the multiplier model we must first recall how the AE curve shifts as the price level rises and falls.

In Figure B26-1(a) I draw three *AE* curves—one for each of the price levels P_0, P_1, and P_2, where $P_0 > P_1 > P_2$. How a change in the price level affects the *AE* curve can be explained by the wealth, interest rate, and international effects. A rise in the price level will shift the *AE* curve down. Similarly, a fall in the price level will shift the *AE* curve up. (A much more detailed discussion of the relationship between the price level and expenditures can be found in Chapter 25.)

The initial equilibrium is at point A. Notice that as the price level falls, aggregate expenditures rise. This initial increase causes induced expenditures to change. Production shifts because of these induced effects, increasing output further than the initial shift in aggregate expenditures and the initial increase in output to Y_1'. The new equilibrium output at P_1 is Y_1 (point B), and at P_2 the new equilibrium output is Y_2 (point C).

In Figure B26-1(b) I show the equilibrium price levels and outputs on a graph, with price level on the vertical

Figure B26-1 (a–d) Relationship between the AS/AD Model and the AP/AE Model

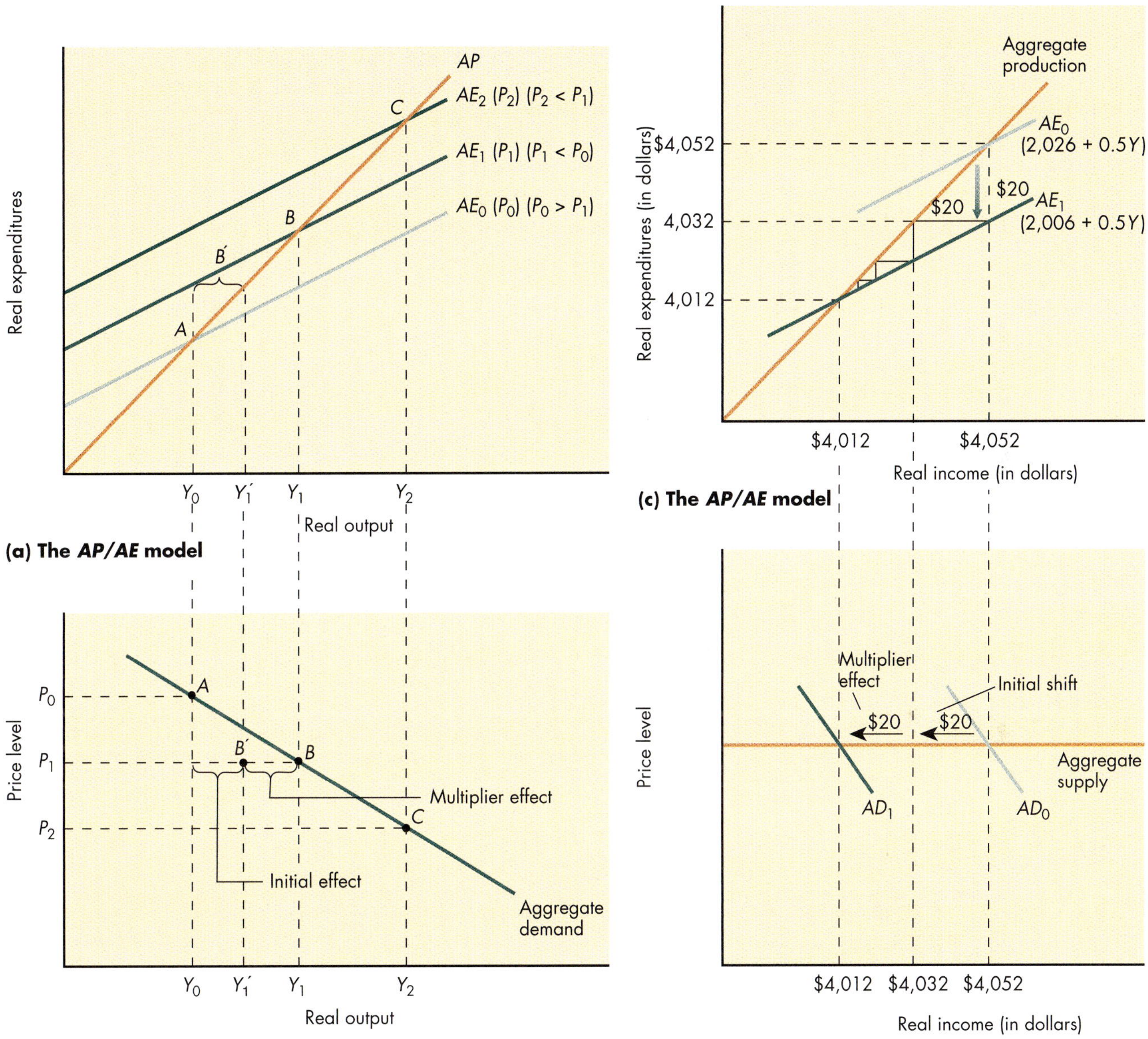

axis and real output on the horizontal axis. That gives us points A, B, and C, which correspond to points A, B, and C in Figure B26-1(a). Drawing a line through these points gives us the aggregate demand curve: a curve that shows how a change in the price level will affect quantity of aggregate demand. Notice that the slope of the *AD* curve includes both the effect of the initial shift in aggregate expenditures from a change in the price level and the multiplier effects as production and expenditures move to equilibrium. The initial shift in aggregate expenditures is shown by point *B′*. If there were no multiplier effects, the *AD* curve would go through points A and *B′*.

The first thing to note when considering the two models is that the multiplier model assumes that the price level is constant, so it assumes that the aggregate supply curve is flat. This means that the multiplier model tells us precisely how much the *AD* curve will shift when autonomous expenditures shift by a specified amount. The difference between the shift in autonomous expenditures and the *AD* curve shift is due to the multiplier.

The relationship between a shift in autonomous expenditures in the *AS/AD* model and the multiplier model can be seen in Figure B26-1(c) and (d). These consider a fall in autonomous expenditures of $20 when the multiplier is 2. In Figure B26-1(c) you can see that, in the multiplier model, a fall in expenditures of $20 will cause income to fall by $40, from $4,052, to $4,012.

Figure B26-1(d) shows that same adjustment in the *AS/AD* model. Initially expenditures fall by $20, but the *AD* curve shifts back not by $20, but by $40—the initial shift multiplied by the multiplier. That's because the *AD* curves take into account the interdependent shifts between supply and demand decisions that are set in motion by the initial shift. Thus we need the multiplier model, or some alternative model of induced effects, before we can draw an *AD* curve. (I make the qualification "or some other model" to emphasize that the interdependent shifts assumed in the multiplier model are not the only interdependent shifts that could occur. Had we assumed a different dynamic adjustment process, we would have had a different *AD* curve.)

A good test of your understanding here is to ask yourself what happens in the long run if the economy is operating above its potential where prices are perfectly flexible. (In that case, the rise in aggregate demand is fully offset by a rise in the price level, and the *AE* curve shifts right back where it started.)

Much of the modern debate in macro concerns the dynamic adjustment process that the multiplier model is meant to describe. We won't go into that debate here since it quickly becomes very complicated, but I do want to point out to you that the multiplier model is not the end of the analysis; it is simply the beginning—one of the simplest cases of dynamic adjustment. The real-world dynamic adjustment is more complicated, which is one of the reasons why there is so much debate about macroeconomic issues.

Questions for Thought and Review

1. Demonstrate graphically the effect of an increase in autonomous expenditures when the *mpe* = .5 and the *SAS* curve is flat:
   a. In the multiplier model.
   b. In the *AS/AD* model.
   c. Do the same thing as in *a* and *b*, only this time assume that the *SAS* curve is upward-sloping.
2. State how the following information changes the slope of the *AD* curve discussed in the previous chapter.
   a. The effect of price level changes on autonomous expenditures is reduced.
   b. The size of the multiplier increases.
   c. Autonomous expenditures increase by $20.
   d. Falls in the price level disrupt financial markets, which offset the normally assumed effects of a change in the price level.

MONEY, BANKING, AND THE FINANCIAL SECTOR

27

The process by which banks create money is so simple that the mind is repelled.

—*John Kenneth Galbraith*

After reading this chapter, you should be able to:

- Explain why the financial sector is central to almost all macroeconomic debates.
- Explain what money is.
- Enumerate the three functions of money.
- State the alternative measures of money and their primary components.
- Explain how banks create money.
- Calculate both the simple and the approximate real-world money multiplier.
- Explain how a financial panic can occur and the potential problem with government guarantees to prevent such panics.

Financial institutions are central to almost all macroeconomic debates. This central role is often not immediately obvious to students. In thinking about the economy, they often focus on the *real sector*—the market for the production and exchange of goods and services. In the real sector, real goods or services such as shoes, operas, automobiles, and textbooks are exchanged. That's an incomplete view of the economy. The *financial sector*—the market for the creation and exchange of financial assets such as money, stocks, and bonds—plays a central role in organizing and coordinating our economy; it makes modern economic society possible. A car won't run without oil; a modern economy won't operate without a financial sector.

As I've noted throughout this book, markets make specialization and trade possible and thereby make the economy far more efficient than it otherwise would be. But the efficient use of markets requires a financial sector that facilitates and lubricates those trades. Let's consider an example of how the financial sector facilitates trade. Say you walk into a store and buy a CD. You shell out a 20-dollar bill and the salesperson hands you the CD. Easy, right? Right—but why did the salesperson give you a CD for a little piece of paper? The answer to that question is: Because the economy has a financial system that has convinced him that that piece of paper has value. To convince him (and you) of that requires an enormous structural system, called the financial sector, underlying the CD transaction and all other transactions. That financial system makes the transaction possible; without it the economy as we know it would not exist.

As long as the financial system is operating smoothly, you hardly know it's there; but should that system break down, the entire economy would be disrupted and would either stagnate or go into a recession. That's why it is necessary to give you an overview of the financial sector as part of your foundation of macroeconomics.

In thinking about the financial sector's role, remember the following insight: *For every real transaction there is a financial transaction that mirrors it.* For example, when you buy an apple, the person selling the apple is buying 35 cents from you by spending his apple. The financial transaction is the transfer of 35 cents; the real transaction is the transfer of the apple.

The financial sector is central to almost all macroeconomic debates because behind every real transaction, there is a financial transaction that mirrors it.

For larger items, the financial transaction behind the real transaction can be somewhat complicated. When you buy a house, you'll probably pay for part of that house with a mortgage, which requires that you borrow money from a bank. The bank, in turn, borrows from individuals the money it lends to you. There's a similar financial transaction when you buy a car, or even a book, on credit.

Because there's a financial transaction reflecting every real transaction, the financial sector is important for the real sector. If you think back to the circular flow diagram, you can see the importance of the financial sector. Every time there is a flow of either goods and services or factors from one sector to another, there is financial flow in the opposite direction. If the financial sector doesn't work, the real sector doesn't work. All trade involves both the real sector and the financial sector. Thus, in this book I don't have a separate section on the steel sector or even the computer sector of the economy, but I do have a separate section on money, banking, and the financial sector of the economy.

Q-1 Joe, your study partner, says that since goods and services are produced only in the real sector, the financial sector is not important to the macroeconomy. How do you respond?

Why Is the Financial Sector Important to Macro?

The financial sector is important in macroeconomics because of its role in channeling flows out of the circular flow—such as saving—back into the circular flow, either in the form of consumer loans (such as you get when you buy something with your credit card), business loans (loans that finance business investment), or loans to government. Think of the financial sector as a gigantic channeling device, something like that shown in Figure 27-1.

The financial sector channels saving back into spending.

The financial sector—financial markets and institutions—channels or transfers saving—outflows from the spending stream in hundreds of different forms—back into spending. This channeling device is extraordinarily complicated and requires years of study to understand fully. However, you don't need that extensive study to understand that what's interesting for macro involves the aggregates—the total amount of flows coming out of, and the total amount of flows returning to, the spending stream—and how well the financial sector does at keeping these aggregate flows matched, or expanding sufficiently to allow for real growth. If the financial sector expands the flow too much, you get inflationary pressures. If it contracts the flow too much, you get a recession. And if it transfers just the right amount, you get a smoothly running economy.

Figure 27-1 The Financial Sector as a Conduit for Savings

Financial institutions channel saving—outflows from the spending stream from various entities (government, households, and corporations)—back into the spending stream as loans to various entities (government, households, and corporations). To emphasize the fact that savings take many forms, a breakdown of the type of savings for one entity, households, is shown on the left. The same is done for loans on the right, but for corporations. Each of these loans can itself be broken down again and again until each particular loan is identified individually. The lending process is an individualistic process, and each loan is different in some way from each other loan.

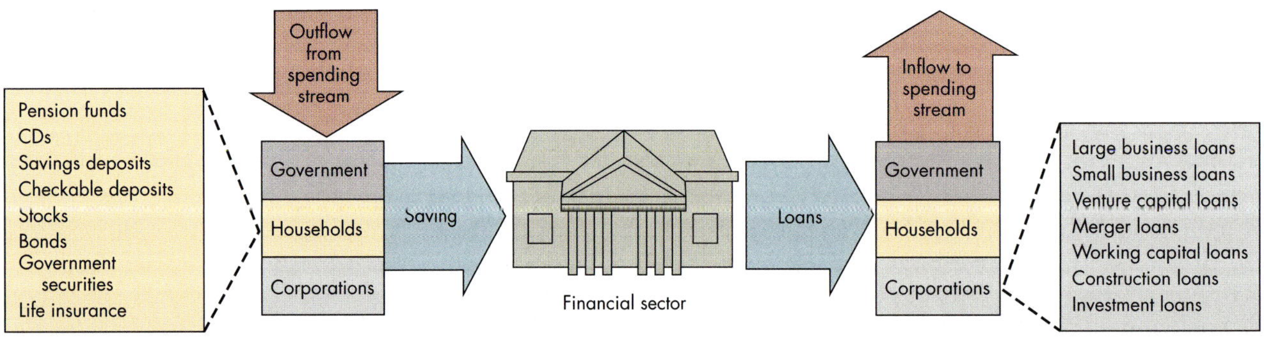

Flow from the spending stream is channeled into the financial sector as saving when individuals buy **financial assets**—*assets such as stocks or bonds, whose benefit to the owner depends on the issuer of the asset meeting certain obligations*. These obligations by the issuer of the financial asset are called financial liabilities. For every financial asset there is a corresponding financial liability. (Financial assets and liabilities are discussed in detail in Appendix A to this chapter.)

For every financial asset there is a financial liability.

THE ROLE OF INTEREST RATES IN THE FINANCIAL SECTOR

Web Note 27.1
Interest Rates

Price is the mechanism that equilibrates supply and demand in the real sector. Interest rates are the mechanism that equilibrates supply and demand in the financial sector. Both the channeling of saving into financial assets and the willingness of individuals to incur financial liabilities are strongly influenced by the interest rate on those financial assets and liabilities. In simple terms, the **interest rate** is the *price paid for the use of a financial asset*. When you deposit cash into an account, the bank pays you interest for the use of your financial asset. When the interest rate rises, people are less likely to borrow (sell a financial asset) and more likely to save (buy an additional financial asset). Thus, when interest rates fall, you often see more borrowing. The funds acquired from the sale of a financial asset reenter the spending stream as consumption and investment.

The price of bonds varies inversely with the interest rate.

When financial assets make fixed interest payments, as do most **bonds**—*promises to pay a certain amount plus interest in the future*—the price of the financial asset is determined by the market interest rate. As the market interest rate goes up, the price of the bond goes down. When the market interest rate goes down, the price of the bond goes up. Why does this relationship exist? Because when the interest rate rises, the value of the flow of payments from fixed-interest-rate bonds goes down since you can earn more on new bonds that pay the new, higher interest. The only way anyone will buy the old, lower-interest-rate bonds is if their price falls. This gives us the following general relationship between bond prices and interest rates:

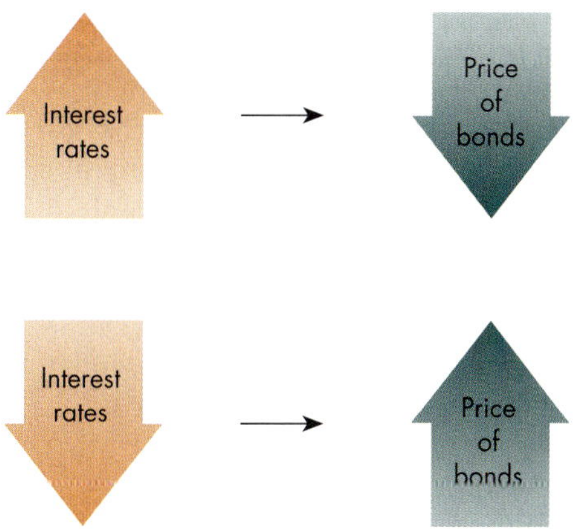

As an example, say that you buy a $1,000, one-year bond with a coupon rate of 4 percent when the economy's interest rate is 4 percent. Since the bond's interest rate is the same as the interest rate for other savings instruments, you pay $1,000 for that bond. Now say that the economy's interest rate falls to 2 percent so that all new bonds being offered pay only 2 percent. That makes your bond especially desirable since it pays a higher interest rate. People would be willing to pay up to $1,019.61. Alternatively, if the economy's interest rate rises to 6 percent, your bond will be less desirable and people would be willing to pay only $981.13. So when the interest rate falls, the price of existing bonds rise, and when the interest rate rises, the price of existing bonds falls.

The longer the length of the bond to maturity, the more the price varies with the change in the interest rate. (For a further discussion of this inverse relationship between bond prices and current interest rates, see the present value discussion in Appendix A to this chapter.)

Saving That Escapes the Circular Flow

Some economists argue that the interest rate does not perfectly translate saving back into the spending stream. They don't believe that the interest rate equilibrates demand and supply for saving. When it does not, macroeconomic problems can arise.

To get at the problems that can develop, macroeconomics simplifies the flows into two types of financial assets. One type works its way back into the system: bonds, loans, and stocks. These are translated back into investment by financial intermediaries. The other type of financial asset, when held by individuals, is not necessarily assumed to work its way back into the flow—we'll call this financial asset "money."

What's important about money from a macroeconomic perspective is that when a person holds money as opposed to holding some other financial asset, the saving that is held in the form of money is assumed to escape the circular flow. Saving held in the form of other financial assets is assumed to work its way back into the circular flow. Compared to the complicated maze of interconnected flows that exists in reality, this is an enormous simplification, but it captures a potentially serious problem and possible cause of fluctuations in the economy.

So let's now turn our attention to money.

The Definition and Functions of Money

Money is a financial asset that makes the real economy function smoothly by serving as a medium of exchange, a unit of account, and a store of wealth.

At this point you're probably saying, "I know what money is; it's currency—the dollar bills I carry around." In one sense you're right: currency is money. But in another sense you're wrong. In fact, a number of short-term financial assets are included as money. To see why, let's consider the definition of money: **Money** is *a highly liquid financial asset that's generally accepted in exchange for other goods, is used as a reference in valuing other goods, and can be stored as wealth.*

To be *liquid* means to be easily changeable into another asset or good. When you buy something with money you are exchanging money for another asset. So any of your assets that are easily spendable are money. Social customs and standard practices are central to the liquidity of money. The reason you are willing to hold money is that you know someone else will accept it in trade for something else. Its value is determined by its general acceptability to others. If you don't believe that, try spending yuan (Chinese money) in the United States. If you try to buy dinner with 100 yuan, you will be told, "No way—give me money."

The U.S. Central Bank: The Fed

So is there any characteristic other than general acceptability that gives value to money? Consider the dollar bill that you know is money. Look at it. It states right on the bill that it is a Federal Reserve note, which means that it is an IOU (a liability) of the **Federal Reserve Bank (the Fed)**—*the U.S. central bank whose liabilities (Federal Reserve notes) serve as cash in the United States.* Individuals are willing to accept the Fed's IOUs in return for real goods and services, which means that Fed notes are money.

What, you ask, is a central bank? To answer that question we had better first consider what a bank is. A **bank** is *a financial institution whose primary function is accepting deposits for, and lending money to, individuals and firms.* (There are more complicated definitions and many types of banks, but that will do for now; the issues are discussed more fully in Appendix A to this chapter.) You got extra currency? Take it to the bank and it will "hold" the extra for you, giving you a piece of paper (or a computer entry) that says you have that much currency held here ("hold" is in quotation marks because the bank does not actually hold the currency). What the bank used to give you was a bank note, and what you used to bring in to the bank was gold, but those days are gone forever. These days what you bring is that Federal Reserve note described above, and what you get is a paper receipt and a computer entry in your checking or savings account. Individuals' deposits in these accounts serve the same purpose as does currency and are also considered money.

Which brings us back to the Federal Reserve Bank, the U.S. central bank. It is a bank that has the right to issue notes (IOUs). By law these Federal Reserve Bank notes are acceptable payment for people's taxes, and by convention these notes are acceptable payment to all people in the United States, and to many people outside the United States. IOUs of the Fed are what most of you think of as cash.

To understand why money is more than just cash, it is helpful to consider the functions of money in more detail. Having done so, we will consider which financial assets are included in various measures of money.

Functions of Money

As I stated above, money is an asset that can be quickly exchanged for any other asset or good. This definition says money serves three functions:

1. It serves as a medium of exchange.
2. It serves as a unit of account.
3. It serves as a store of wealth.

To get a better understanding of what money is, let's consider each of its functions in turn.

The three functions of money are:
1. Medium of exchange,
2. Unit of account, and
3. Store of wealth.

Money as a Medium of Exchange The easiest way to understand money's medium-of-exchange use is to imagine what an economy would be like without money. Say you want something to eat at a restaurant. Without money you'd have to barter with the restaurant owner for your meal. *Barter* is a direct exchange of goods and/or services. You might suggest bartering one of your papers or the shirt in the sack that you'd be forced to carry with you to trade for things you want. Not liking to carry big sacks around, you'd probably decide to fix your own meal and forgo eating out. Bartering is simply too difficult. Money makes many more trades possible because it does not require a double coincidence of wants by two individuals, as simple barter does.

The use of money as a medium of exchange makes it possible to trade real goods and services without bartering. It facilitates exchange by reducing the cost of trading. Instead of carrying around a sack full of diverse goods, all you need to carry around is a billfold full of money. You go into the restaurant and pay for your meal with money; the restaurant owner can spend (trade) that money for anything she wants.

Money doesn't have to have any inherent value to function as a medium of exchange. All that's necessary is that everyone believes that other people will accept it in exchange for their goods. This neat social convention makes the economy more efficient.

Money doesn't have to have any inherent value to function as a medium of exchange.

That social convention depends on there not being too much or too little money. If there's too much money compared to the goods and services offered at existing prices, the goods and services will sell out, and money won't buy you anything. The social convention will break down, or prices will rise. If there's too little money compared to the goods and services offered at the existing prices, there will be a shortage of money and people will have to resort to barter, or prices will fall. Since the Federal Reserve Bank, or Fed, controls the supply of money, it also controls the value of money as a medium of exchange.

Q-2 Even though it costs only 4.2 cents per note to produce U.S. currency, why doesn't the Fed print up lots of money?

People accept money in payment and agree to hold money because they believe the Fed, and the banks the Fed regulates, will issue neither too little nor too much money. This explains why the Fed doesn't freely issue large amounts of money and why it controls (or at least tries to control) the amount of money banks issue. To issue money without restraint would destroy the social convention that gives money its value.

Money as a Unit of Account A second use of money is as a unit of account. Money prices are actually relative prices. A nominal price, say 25 cents, for a pencil conveys the information of a relative price: 1 pencil = ¼ of 1 dollar because money is both our unit of account and our medium of exchange. When you think of 25 cents you think of ¼ of a dollar and of what a dollar will buy. The 25 cents a pencil costs only has meaning relative to the information you've stored in your mind about what it can buy. If a hamburger costs $1.50, you can compare hamburgers and pencils (1 pencil = ⅙ of a hamburger) without making the relative price calculations explicitly.

Having a unit of account makes life much easier. For example, say we had no unit of account and you had to remember the relative prices of all goods. For instance, with three goods you'd have to memorize that an airplane ticket to Miami costs 6 lobster dinners in Boston or 4 pairs of running shoes, which makes a pair of shoes worth 1½ lobster dinners.

Memorizing even a few relationships is hard enough, so it isn't surprising that societies began using a single unit of account. If you don't have a single unit of account, all combinations of 100 goods will require that you remember thousands of relative prices. If you have a single unit of account, you need know only 100 prices. A single unit of account saves our limited memories and helps us make reasonable decisions based on relative costs.

Money is a useful unit of account only as long as its value relative to other prices doesn't change too quickly.

Money is a useful unit of account only as long as its value relative to the average of all other prices doesn't change too quickly. That's because it's not only used as a unit of account at a point in time, it's also a unit of account *over time*. Money is a standard of deferred payment. The value of payments that will be made in the future (such as the college loan payments many of you will be making in the future) is determined by the future value of money. Again, the Fed plays a central role in money's usefulness as a unit of account. If the Fed printed excessive currency to pay all the government's expenses, money's relative price would fall quickly (an increase in supply lowers price), which is another way of saying that the price level would explode and the unit-of-account function of money would be seriously undermined.

Maintaining the unit-of-account usefulness of money is a second reason the Fed doesn't pay all the government's bills by printing money. Consider a college loan. Hyperinflation would significantly reduce the value of what you have to pay back. So hyperinflation would help you, right? Actually, probably not—because hyperinflation would also rapidly destroy money's usefulness as a store of value and unit of account, thereby destroying the U.S. economy.

In hyperinflation, all prices rise so much that our frame of reference is lost.

As described in an earlier chapter, in hyperinflation all prices rise so much that our frame of reference for making relative price comparisons is lost. Is 25 cents for a pencil high or low? If the price level increased 33,000 percent (as it did in 1988 in Nicaragua) or over 100,000 percent (as it did in 1993 in Serbia), 25 cents for a pencil would definitely be low, but would $100 be low? Without a lot of calculations we can't answer that question. A relatively stable unit of account makes it easy to answer.

Given the advantages to society of having a unit of account, it's not surprising that a monetary unit of account develops even in societies with no central bank or government. For example, in a prisoner of war camp during World War II, prisoners had no money, so they used cigarettes as their unit of account. Everything traded was given a price in cigarettes. The exchange rates on December 1, 1944, were:

1 bar of soap: 2 cigarettes

1 candy bar: 4 cigarettes

1 razor blade: 6 cigarettes

1 can of fruit: 8 cigarettes

1 can of cookies: 20 cigarettes

As you can see, all prices were in cigarettes. If candy bars rose to 6 cigarettes and the normal price was 4 cigarettes, you'd know the price of candy bars was high.

Money as a Store of Wealth When you save, you forgo consumption now so that you can consume in the future. To bridge the gap between now and the future, you must acquire a financial asset. This is true even if you squirrel away currency under the mattress. In that case, the financial asset you've acquired is simply the currency itself. Money is a financial asset. (It's simply a bond that pays no interest.) So a third use of money is as a store of wealth. As long as money is serving as a medium of exchange, it automatically also serves as a store of wealth. The restaurant owner can accept your money and hold it for as long as she wants before she spends it. (But had you paid her in fish, she'd be wise not to hold it more than a few hours.)

As long as money is serving as a medium of exchange, it automatically also serves as a store of wealth.

Money's usefulness as a store of wealth also depends on how well it maintains its value. If prices are going up 100,000 percent per year, the value of a stated amount of money is shrinking fast. People want to spend their money as quickly as possible before prices rise any more. Thus, once again, money's usefulness as a social convention depends on the Fed not issuing too much money.

Even if prices aren't rising, you might wonder why people would hold money that pays no interest. Put another way: Why do people hold a government bond that pays no interest? The reason is that money, by definition, is highly liquid—it is more easily translated into other goods than are other financial assets. Since money is also the medium of exchange, it can be spent instantaneously (as long as there's a shop open nearby). Our ability to spend money for goods makes money worthwhile to hold even if it doesn't pay interest.

Q-3 Why do people hold money rather than bonds when bonds pay higher interest than money?

Alternative Measures of Money

According to the definition of *money*, what people believe is money and what people will accept as money are determining factors in deciding whether a financial asset is money. Consequently, it's difficult to measure *money* unambiguously. A number of different financial assets serve some of the functions of money and thus have claims to being called *money*. To handle this ambiguity, economists have developed different measures of money and have called them M_1, M_2, and L. Each is a reasonable concept of money. Let's consider their components.

M_1

M_1 consists of *currency in the hands of the public, checking account balances, and traveler's checks*. Clearly, currency in the hands of the public (the dollar bills and coins you carry around with you) are money, but how about your checking account deposits? The reason they're included in this measure of money is that just about anything you can do with currency, you can do with a check. You can store your wealth in your checking account; you can use a check as a medium of exchange (indeed, for some transactions you

M_1 is the component of the money supply that consists of currency in the hands of the public plus checking accounts and traveler's checks.

Characteristics of a Good Money

Knowing the Tools

The characteristics of a good money are that its supply be relatively constant, that it be limited in supply (sand wouldn't make good money), that it be difficult to counterfeit, that it be divisible (have you ever tried to spend half a horse?), that it be durable (raspberries wouldn't make good money), and that it be relatively small and light compared to its value (watermelon wouldn't make good money either). All these characteristics were reasonably (but not perfectly) embodied in gold. Many other goods have served as units of account (shells, wampum, rocks, cattle, horses, silver), but gold historically became the most important money, and in the 17th and 18th centuries gold was synonymous with money.

But gold has flaws as money. It's relatively heavy, easy to counterfeit with coins made only partly of gold, and, when new gold fields are discovered, subject to fluctuations in supply. These flaws led to gold's replacement by paper currency backed only by trust that the government would keep its commitment to limit its supply.

Paper money can be a good money if somehow people can trust the government to limit its supply and guarantee that its supply will be limited in the future. That trust has not always been well placed.

have no choice but to use a check), and your checking account balance is denominated in the same unit of account (dollars) as is currency. If it looks like money, acts like money, and functions as money, it's a good bet it's money. Indeed, checking account deposits are included in all measures of money.

The same arguments can be made about traveler's checks. (Some advertisements even claim that traveler's checks are better than money because you can get them replaced.) Currency, checking account deposits, and traveler's checks make up the components of M_1, the narrowest measure of money. Figure 27-2 presents the relative sizes of M_1's components.

M_2

M_2 is the component of the money supply that consists of M_1 plus other relatively liquid assets.

M_2 is made up of M_1 *plus savings deposits, small-denomination time deposits, and money market mutual fund shares*. The relative sizes of the components of M_2 are given in Figure 27-2.

The money in savings accounts (savings deposits) is counted as money because it is readily spendable—all you need do is go to the bank and draw it out. Small-denomination time deposits are also called *certificates of deposit* (*CDs*).

Q-4 Which would be a larger number, M_1 or M_2? Why?

M_2's components include more financial assets than M_1. All its components are highly liquid and play an important role in providing reserves and lending capacity for commercial banks. What makes the M_2 measure important is that economic research has shown that M_2 is the measure of money often most closely correlated with the price level and economic activity.

Beyond M_2: L

The broadest definition of the money supply is L (which stands for liquidity). It consists of almost all short-term financial assets.

An even wider variety of short-term financial assets (assets whose maturity is less than one year) also have some of the attributes of money. They're liquid and can be "spent" relatively easily. For that reason they're included in some measures of money. There are measures for M_3, M_4, and beyond. Most economists concern themselves only with the first two measures (M_1 and M_2) and the broadest measure, which is called L (for liquidity—the ability to change an asset into an immediately spendable asset). **L** is *the*

Figure 27-2 Components of M_2 and M_1
The two most-used measures of the money supply are M_1 and M_2. The two primary components of M_1 are currency in the hands of the public and checking accounts. M_2 includes all of M_1, plus savings deposits, time deposits, and money market mutual funds.

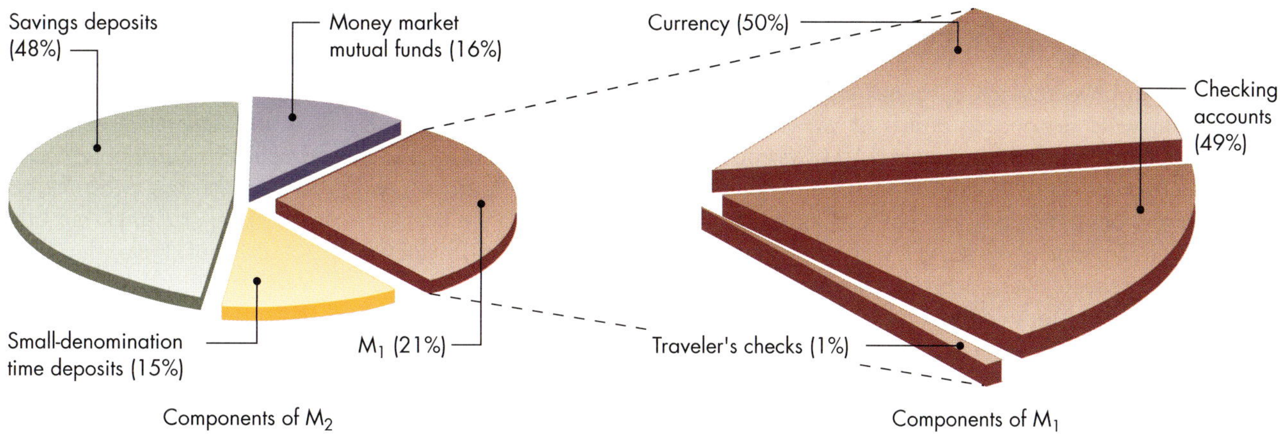

Source: *Federal Reserve Bulletin, 2003* (www.federalreserve.gov).

broadest measure of money and includes almost all short-term assets. Financial innovation has made it difficult to come up with an unchanging measure of money. Because of that difficulty, measures of money have lost some of their appeal and broader concepts of asset liquidity have gained greater appeal.

Distinguishing between Money and Credit

You might have thought that credit cards would be included in one of the measures of *money*. But I didn't include them. In fact, credit cards are nowhere to be seen in a list of financial assets. Credit cards aren't a financial liability of the bank that issues them. Instead credit cards create a liability for their users (money owed to the company or bank that issued the card) and the banks have a financial asset as a result.

Credit card balances cannot be money since they are assets of a bank. In a sense, they are the opposite of money.

Let's consider how a credit card works. You go into a store and buy something with your credit card. You have a real asset—the item you bought. The store has a financial asset—an account receivable. The store sells that financial asset at a slight discount to the bank and gets cash in return. Either the bank collects cash when you pay off your financial liability or, if you don't pay it off, the bank earns interest on its financial asset (often at a high rate, from 12 to 18 percent per year). Credit cards are essentially prearranged loans.

This distinction between credit and money should be kept in mind. Money is a financial asset of individuals and a financial liability of banks. Credit is savings made available to be borrowed. Credit is not an asset of the borrowing public.

Credit cards and credit impact the amount of money people hold. When preapproved loan credit is instantly available (as it is with a credit card) there's less need to hold money. (If you didn't have a credit card, you'd carry a lot more currency.) With credit immediately available, liquidity is less valuable to people. So credit and credit cards do make a difference in how much money people hold, but because they are not financial assets, they are not money.

Now that we've considered what money is, both in theory and in practice, let's consider the banking system's role in creating money, and what happens if individuals start

Checking and Money Market Accounts

Applying the Tools

At one time the only checking accounts were those of commercial banks. You put your money in a commercial bank and wrote a check. Then savings banks (banks allowed only to have savings accounts) started allowing individuals to write negotiable orders of withdrawal on their savings accounts. So if you held $10,000 in a savings account you could write an IOU to someone and the savings bank promised to pay it. That IOU looked like a check, and for all practical purposes it was a check. But unlike a checking account, these accounts paid interest on depositors' balances. Many people started shifting from checking accounts to savings bank accounts, and soon commercial banks complained of unfair competition by savings banks. These complaints led to commercial banks being allowed to pay interest on their checking accounts.

Mutual funds saw how nicely these accounts worked and decided to imitate them. The mutual fund invested depositors' money in the money market (short-term bills, commercial paper, and CDs) and allowed individuals to write checks on these accounts. Such brokerage accounts pay slightly higher interest than checking accounts but have check-writing restrictions and do not have the same guarantees.

So today people have a choice of depository institutions, which is nice for people but tough for textbook writers and for students who have to learn more divisions.

holding their assets as some form of money rather than as bonds or as some other financial asset.

Banks and the Creation of Money

Banks are financial institutions that borrow from people (take in deposits) and use the money they borrow to make loans to other individuals. Banks make a profit by charging a higher interest on the money they lend out than they pay for the money they borrow. Individuals keep their money in banks, accepting lower interest rates, because doing so is safer and more convenient than the alternatives.

Banking is generally analyzed from the perspective of **asset management** (*how a bank handles its loans and other assets*) and **liability management** (*how a bank attracts deposits and what it pays for them*). When banks offer people "free checking" and special money market accounts paying 4 percent, they do so after carefully considering the costs of those liabilities to them.

It is important to think of banks as both borrowers and lenders.

To think of banks as borrowers as well as lenders may seem a bit unusual, but borrowing is what they do. When you own a savings account or a checking account, the bank is borrowing from you, paying you a zero (or low) interest rate. It then lends your money to other people at a higher interest rate.

How Banks Create Money

Banks are centrally important to macroeconomics because they create money. How do banks create money? As John Kenneth Galbraith's epigram at the start of this chapter suggests, the process is simple—so simple it seems almost magical to many.

Banks "create" money because a bank's liabilities are defined as money. So when a bank incurs liabilities it creates money.

The key to understanding how banks create money is to remember the nature of financial assets: Financial assets can be created from nothing as long as an offsetting financial liability is simultaneously created. Since money is any financial asset that can be used as a medium of exchange, unit of account, and store of value, money can be created rather easily. The asset just needs to serve the functions of money. Seeing how dollar bills are created is the easiest way to begin examining the process. Whenever the Fed issues an IOU, it creates money.[1] Similarly, other banks create money by creating financial assets that serve the functions of money. As we saw when we considered the measures of money, bank checking accounts serve those functions, so they are money, just as currency is money. When a bank places the proceeds of a loan it makes to you in your checking account, it is creating money. You have a financial asset that did not previously exist.

The First Step in the Creation of Money To see how banks create money, let's consider what would happen if you were given a freshly printed $100 bill. Remember, the Fed created that $100 bill simply by printing it. The $100 bill is a $100 financial asset of yours and a financial liability of the Fed, which issued it.

If the process of creating money stopped there, it wouldn't be particularly mysterious. But it doesn't stop there. Let's consider what happens next as you use that money.

About 95 percent of all bills printed each year replace worn-out notes. The remaining 5 percent represent new currency in circulation.
Doug Mills/AP Wide World Photos

The Second Step in the Creation of Money The second step in the creation of money involves the transfer of money from one form to another—from currency to a bank deposit. Say you decide to put the $100 bill in your checking account. To make the analysis easier, let's assume that your bank is a branch of the country's only bank, Big Bank. All money deposited in branch banks goes into Big Bank. After you make your deposit, Big Bank is holding $100 currency for you, and you have $100 more in your checking account. You can spend it whenever you want simply by writing a check. So Big Bank is performing a service for you (holding your money and keeping track of your expenditures) for free. Neat, huh? Big Bank must be run by a bunch of nice people.

But wait. You and I know that bankers, while they may be nice, aren't as nice as all that. There ain't no such thing as a free lunch. Let's see why the bank is being so nice.

Banking and Goldsmiths To see why banks are so nice, let's go way back in history to when banks first developed.[2] At that time, gold was used for money and people carried around gold to make their payments. But gold is rather heavy, so if they had to make a big purchase, it was difficult to pay for the purchase. Moreover, carrying around a lot of gold left them vulnerable to being robbed by the likes of Robin Hood. So they looked for a place to store their gold until they needed some of it.

Web Note 27.2
Gold

From Gold to Gold Receipts The natural place to store gold was the goldsmith shop, which already had a vault. For a small fee, the goldsmith shop would hold your gold, giving you a receipt for it. Whenever you needed your gold, you'd go to the goldsmith and exchange the receipt for gold.

Pretty soon most people kept their gold at the goldsmith's, and they began to wonder: Why go through the bother of getting my gold out to buy something when all that happens is that the seller takes the gold I pay and puts it right back into the goldsmith's vault. That's two extra trips.

Consequently, people began using the receipts the goldsmith gave them to certify that they had deposited $100 worth (or whatever) of gold in his vault. At that point gold was no longer the only money—gold receipts were also money since they were accepted in exchange for goods. However, as long as the total amount in the gold receipts directly represented the total amount of gold, it was still reasonable to say, since the receipts were 100 percent backed by gold, that gold was the money supply.

---

[1]As we'll see when we discuss the Fed in more detail, dollar bills aren't the Fed's only IOUs.
[2]The banking history reported here is, according to historians, apocryphal (more myth than reality). But it so nicely makes the point that I repeat it anyhow.

Q-5 Most banks prefer to have many depositors rather than one big depositor. Why?

Gold Receipts Become Money Once this process of using the receipts rather than the gold became generally accepted, the goldsmith found that he had substantial amounts of gold in his vault. All that gold, just sitting there! On a normal day only 1 percent of the gold was claimed by "depositors" and had to be given out. Usually on the same day an amount at least equal to that 1 percent came in from other depositors. What a waste! Gold sitting around doing nothing! So when a good friend came in, needing a loan, the goldsmith said, "Sure, I'll lend you some gold receipts as long as you pay me some interest." When the goldsmith made this loan, he created more gold receipts than he had covered in gold in his vault. He created money.

Pretty soon the goldsmith realized he could earn more from the interest he received on loans than he could earn from goldsmithing. So he stopped goldsmithing and went full-time into making loans of gold receipts. At that point the number of gold receipts outstanding significantly exceeded the amount of gold in the goldsmith's vaults. But not to worry; since everyone was willing to accept gold receipts rather than gold, the goldsmith had plenty of gold for those few who wanted actual gold.

Money is whatever meets the definition of money.

It was, however, no longer accurate to say that gold was the country's money or currency. Gold receipts were the money. They met the definition of *money*. These gold receipts were backed partially by gold and partially by people's trust that the goldsmiths would pay off their deposits on demand. The goldsmith shops had become banks.

Banking Is Profitable The banking business was very profitable for goldsmiths. Soon other people started competing with them, offering to hold gold for free. After all, if they could store gold, they could make a profit on the loans to other people (with the first people's money). Some even offered to pay people to store their gold.

The goldsmith story is directly relevant to banks. People store their currency in banks and the banks issue receipts—checking accounts—that become a second form of money. When people place their currency in banks and use their receipts from the bank as money, those receipts also become money because they meet the definition of *money:* They serve as a medium of exchange, a unit of account, and a store of wealth. So money includes both currency that people hold and their deposits in the bank.

Which brings us back to why banks hold your currency for free. They do it not because they're nice, but because when you deposit currency in the bank, your deposit allows banks to make profitable loans they otherwise couldn't make.

The Money Multiplier

With that background, let's go back to your \$100, which the bank is now holding for you. You have a checking account balance of \$100 and the bank has \$100 currency. As long as other people are willing to accept your check in payment for \$100 worth of goods, your check is as good as money. In fact it is money in the same way gold receipts were money. But when you deposit \$100, no additional money has been created yet. The form of the money has simply been changed from currency to a checking account or demand deposit.

Now let's say Big Bank lends out 90 percent of the currency you deposit, keeping only 10 percent as **reserves**—*currency and deposits a bank keeps on hand or at the Fed or central bank, enough to manage the normal cash inflows and outflows*. This 10 percent is the **reserve ratio** (*the ratio of reserves to total deposits)*. Banks are required by the Fed to hold a percentage of deposits; that percentage is called the required reserve ratio. Banks may also choose to hold an additional percentage, called the excess reserve ratio. The reserve ratio is the sum of the required reserve ratio and the excess reserve ratio. Thus, it is at least as large as the required reserved ratio, but it can be larger.

The reserve ratio is the ratio of currency (or deposits at the central bank) to deposits a bank keeps as a reserve against currency withdrawals.

So, like the goldsmith, Big Bank lends out $90 to someone who qualifies for a loan. That person the bank loaned the money to now has $90 currency and you have $100 in a demand deposit, so now there's $190 of money, rather than just $100 of money. The $10 in currency the bank holds in reserve isn't counted as money since the bank must keep it as reserves and may not use it as long as it's backing loans. Only currency held by the public, not currency held by banks, is counted as money. By making the loan, the bank has created $90 in money.

Of course, no one borrows money just to hold it. The borrower spends the money, say on a new sweater, and the sweater store owner now has the $90 in currency. The store owner doesn't want to hold it either. She'll deposit it back into the bank. Since there's only one bank, Big Bank discovers that the $90 it has loaned out is once again in its coffers. The money operates like a boomerang: Big Bank loans $90 out and gets the $90 back again.

The same process occurs again. The bank doesn't earn interest income by holding $90, so if the bank can find additional credible borrowers, it lends out $81, keeping $9 (10 percent of $90) in reserve. The story repeats and repeats itself, with a slightly smaller amount coming back to the bank each time. At each step in the process, money (in the form of checking account deposits) is being created.

Determining How Many Demand Deposits Will Be Created What's the total amount of demand deposits that will ultimately be created from your $100 when individuals hold no currency? To answer that question, we continue the process over and over: 100 + 90 + 81 + 72.9 + 65.6 + 59 + 53.1 + 47.8 + 43.0 + 38.7 + 34.9. Adding up these numbers gives us $686. Adding up $686 plus the numbers from the next 20 rounds gives us $961.08.

As you can see, that's a lot of adding. Luckily there's an easier way. Economists have shown that you can determine the amount of money that will eventually be created by such a process by multiplying the initial $100 in money that was printed by the Fed and deposited by $1/r$, where r is the reserve ratio (the percentage banks keep out of each round). In this case the reserve ratio is 10 percent.

Dividing,

$$\frac{1}{r} = \frac{1}{.10} = 10$$

so the amount of demand deposits that will ultimately exist at the end of the process is

$$(10 \times \$100) = \$1{,}000$$

The $1,000 is in the form of checking account deposits (demand deposits). The entire $100 in currency that you were given, and that started the whole process, is in the bank as reserves, which means that $900 ($1,000 − $100) of money has been created by the process.

Calculating the Money Multiplier The ratio $1/r$ is called the **simple money multiplier**—*the measure of the amount of money ultimately created per dollar deposited in the banking system, when people hold no currency*. It tells us how much money will ultimately be created by the banking system from an initial inflow of money. In our example, $1/.10 = 10$. Had the bank kept out 20 percent each time, the money multiplier would have been $1/.20 = 5$. If the reserve ratio were 5 percent, the money multiplier would have been $1/.05 = 20$. The higher the reserve ratio, the smaller the money multiplier, and the less money will be created.

The money multiplier is the measure of the amount of money ultimately created per dollar deposited by the banking system. When people hold no currency it equals $1/r$.

Table 27-1 The Money-Creating Process
In the money-creating process, the currency keeps coming back to the banking system like a boomerang. With a 20 percent reserve requirement ultimately (1/.2) × $10,000 = $50,000 will be created. In this example you can see that after 10 rounds, most of the creation of deposits will have taken place. As you carry out the analysis further, the money creation will approach the $50,000 shown in the last line.

Bank Gets	Bank Keeps (reserve ratio: 20%)		Bank Loans (80%) = Person Borrows
$10,000	$ 2,000		$ 8,000
8,000	1,600		6,400
6,400	1,280		5,120
5,120	1,024		4,096
4,096	819		3,277
3,277	656		2,621
2,621	524		2,097
2,097	419		1,678
1,678	336		1,342
1,342	268		1,074
$44,631 (total deposits)	$ 8,926	+	$35,705
Total money existing (after 10 rounds) = $44,631			
Eventual total money creation (after infinite rounds)			
$50,000 (total deposits)	$10,000	+	$40,000

An Example of the Creation of Money[3] To make sure you understand the process, let's consider an example. Say that the reserve ratio is 20 percent and that John Finder finds $10,000 in currency, which he deposits in the bank. Thus, he has $10,000 in his checking account and the bank has $8,000 ($10,000 − $2,000 in reserves) to lend out. Once it lends that money to Fred Baker, there is $8,000 of additional money in the economy. Fred Baker uses the money to buy a new oven from Mary Builder, who, in turn, deposits the money back into the banking system. Big Bank lends out $6,400 ($8,000 − $1,600 in reserves).

Now the process occurs again. Table 27-1 shows the effects of the process for 10 rounds, starting with the initial $10,000. Each time it lends the money out, the money returns like a boomerang and serves as reserves for more loans. After 10 rounds we reach a point where total demand deposits are $44,631, and the bank has $8,926 in reserves. This is approaching the $50,000 we'd arrive at using the money multiplier:

$$\frac{1}{r}(\$10,000) = \frac{1}{.2}(\$10,000) = 5(\$10,000) = \$50,000$$

If we carried it out for more rounds, we'd actually reach what the formula predicted.

[3]The first three rounds of this example are shown in Appendix B to this chapter, using T-accounts.

Note that the process ends only when the bank holds all the currency in the economy, and the only money held by the public is in the form of demand deposits. Notice also that the total amount of money created depends on the amount banks hold in reserve.

To see that you understand the process, say that banks suddenly get concerned about the safety of their loans, and they decide to keep **excess reserves**—*reserves held by banks in excess of what banks are required to hold.* What will happen to the money multiplier? If you answered that it will decrease, you've got it. Excess reserves decrease the money multiplier as much as required reserves do. I mention this example because this is precisely what happened to the banking system in the early 1990s. Banks became concerned about the safety of their loans; they held large excess reserves, and the money multiplier decreased.

In summary, the process of money creation isn't difficult to understand as long as you remember that money is simply a bank's financial liability held by the public. Whenever banks create financial liabilities for themselves, they create financial assets for individuals, and those financial assets are money.

Calculating the Approximate Real-World Money Multiplier In the example I assumed that only banks hold currency. The simple money multiplier reflects that assumption. In reality banks are not the only holders of currency. Firms and individuals hold currency too, so in each round we must also make an adjustment in the multiplier for what people and firms hold. The math you need to calculate the money multiplier formally gets a bit complicated when firms and people hold currency. Since for our purposes a rough calculation is all we need, we will use an approximate money multiplier in which individuals' currency holdings are treated the same as reserves of banks. Thus, the **approximate real-world money multiplier** in the economy is:

When people hold currency the approximate money multiplier is $1/(r + c)$.

Q-6 If banks hold 20 percent of their deposits as reserves, and the ratio of money people hold as currency to deposits is 20 percent, what is the approximate money multiplier?

$$\frac{1}{(r + c)}$$

where r is *the percentage of deposits banks hold in reserve* and c is *the ratio of money people hold in currency to the money they hold as deposits*.[4] Let's consider an example. Say the banks keep 10 percent in reserve and the ratio of individuals' currency holdings to their deposits is 25 percent. This means the approximate real-world money multiplier will be

Q-7 If people suddenly decide to hold more currency, what happens to the size of the approximate money multiplier?

$$\frac{1}{(.1 + .25)} = \frac{1}{.35} = 2.9$$

Faith as the Backing of Our Money Supply

Web Note 27.3 Paper Money

The creation of money and the money multiplier are easy to understand if you remember that money held in the form of a checking account (the financial asset created) is offset by an equal amount of financial liabilities of the bank. The bank owes its depositors the amount in their checking accounts. Its financial liabilities to depositors, in turn, are secured by the loans (the bank's financial assets) and by the financial liabilities of people to whom the loans were made. Promises to pay underlie any modern financial system.

The initial money in the story about the goldsmiths was gold, but it quickly became apparent that it was far more reasonable to use gold certificates as money. Therefore, gold certificates backed by gold soon replaced gold itself as the money supply. Then, as goldsmiths made more loans than they had gold, the gold certificates were no longer

[4]The precise money multiplier when individuals hold currency is $(1 + c)/(r + c)$.

The Real-World Money Multiplier and Recent Banking Reforms

Applying the Tools

Life keeps getting tougher. In the old days economics students only had to learn the simple money multiplier. Recent reforms in the U.S. banking system have made that impossible. The Depository Institutions Deregulation Act of 1980 extended the reserve requirement to a wide variety of financial institutions besides banks, but it also lowered the reserve requirement for most deposits. In the early 2000s, the average reserve requirement for all types of bank deposits was under 2 percent and banks held very few excess reserves. (The U.S. reserve requirement on checking accounts is between 3 and 10 percent. In Great Britain, there are no reserve requirements.)

If you insert that low average ratio into the simple money multiplier, you get a multiplier of 50! The real-world money multiplier is much lower than that because of people's holding of currency; the ratio of money people hold as currency, *c*, is over 40 percent. (For each person in the United States there's about $2,000 in currency, although it is estimated that two-thirds of currency in circulation is held abroad. That still leaves about $700 for each person in the United States. Don't ask me where that currency is, but according to the data it's out there.) Thus, despite the fact that it makes calculating the approximate real-world money multiplier a bit more difficult, these holdings must be included in the story. Otherwise you won't have a sense of how the real-world system works.

backed by gold. They were backed by promises to get gold if the person wanted gold in exchange for the gold certificate. Eventually the percentage of gold supposedly backing the money became so small that it was clear to everyone that the promises, not the gold, underlay the money supply.

All that backs the modern money supply are bank loan customers' promises to pay and government guarantees of banks' liabilities to individuals.

The same holds true with banks. Initially currency (Federal Reserve IOUs) was backed by gold, and banks' demand deposits were in turn backed by Federal Reserve IOUs. But by the 1930s the percentage of gold backing money grew so small that even the illusion of the money being backed by anything but promises was removed. All that backs the modern money supply are bank loan customers' promises to pay and the guarantee of the government to see that the banks' liabilities to individuals will be met.

Regulation of Banks and the Financial Sector

You just saw how easy it is to create money. The banking system and money make the economy operate more efficiently, but they also present potential problems. For example, say that for some reason suddenly there's an increase in money (that is, in promises to pay) without any corresponding increase in real goods and services. As the money supply increases without an increase in real goods and services to buy with that money, more money is chasing the same number of goods. The result will be a fall in the value of money (inflation), meaning real trade will be more complicated. Alternatively, if there's an increase in real goods and services but not a corresponding increase in money, there will be a shortage of money, which will hamper the economy. Either the price level will fall (deflation) or there will be a recession.

Financial Panics

Societies have continually experienced these problems, and the financial history of the world is filled with stories of financial upheavals and monetary problems. For example, there are numerous instances of private financial firms that have promised the world, but whose promises have been nothing but hot air. One instance occurred in the 1800s in the United States, when banks were allowed to issue their own notes (their own promises to pay). These notes served as part of the U.S. money supply. Sharp financial operators soon got into the process and created "wildcat banks," so called because they were situated in places where only a wildcat would go. These wildcat banks issued notes even though they had no deposits, hoping that no one would cash the notes in. Many such banks defaulted on their promises, leaving holders of the notes with only worthless pieces of paper. Merchants quickly caught on, and soon they began checking in a "book of notes" that told whether the notes the buyer was offering were probably good or not.

Anatomy of a Financial Panic

Banking and financial systems are based on promises and trust. People exchange their currency for other financial assets (such as demand deposits) and believe that these demand deposits are as good as currency. In normal times, demand deposits really are as good as currency. When times get bad, people become concerned about the financial firms' ability to keep those promises and they call on the firms to redeem the checking account promises. But banks have only their reserves (a small percentage of their total deposits) to give depositors. Most of the depositors' assets are loaned out and cannot be collectively gotten back quickly, even though the banks have promised depositors that their deposits will be given back "on demand." Put another way, banks' borrowing is short-term while its lending is long-term; banks borrow short and lend long.

Financial systems are based on trust that expectations will be fulfilled. Banks borrow short and lend long, which means that if people lose faith in banks, the banks cannot keep their promises.

Q-8 Why does borrowing short and lending long present a potential problem for banks?

When a lot of depositors lose faith in a bank and, all at one time, call on the bank to keep its promise to provide currency in exchange for their checking account balances, the bank cannot do so. The result is that the bank fails when depositors lose faith, even though the bank might be financially sound for the long run. Fear underlies financial panics and can undermine financial institutions unless the banks can convert their earning assets into currency quickly.

Government Policy to Prevent Panic

To prevent such panics, the U.S. government has guaranteed the obligations of various financial institutions. The most important guaranteeing program is the Federal Deposit Insurance Corporation (FDIC), but there are also a variety of government-guaranteed bonds. These guarantees work as follows: The financial institutions pay a small premium for each dollar of deposit to the government-organized insurance company. That company puts the premium into a fund used to bail out banks experiencing a run on deposits. These guarantees have two effects:

Q-9 What are two effects that a government guarantee of financial institutions can have?

1. They prevent the unwarranted fear that causes financial crises. Depositors know that the government will see that they can get their currency back even if the bank fails. This knowledge stops them from responding to a rumor and trying to get their money out of a suspect financial institution before anyone else does.
2. They prevent warranted fears. Why should people worry about whether or not a financial institution is making reasonable loans on the basis of their deposits if the government guarantees the financial institutions' promises to pay regardless of what kind of loans the institutions make?

The Benefits and Problems of Guarantees

Government guarantees prevent unwarranted fears. The illusion on which banks depend (that people can get their money in the short run, even though it's only in the long run that they can *all* get it) can be met by temporary loans from the government.

Guarantees can prevent unwarranted fears from becoming financial panics. The guarantee makes the illusion a reality. If people can indeed get their money in the long run, seeing to it that this illusion is reality isn't expensive to the government. As long as the bank has sufficient long-term assets to cover its deposits, the government will be repaid its temporary loan.

The fact that deposits are guaranteed doesn't serve to inspire banks to make certain deposits are covered by loans in the long run.

Unfortunately, covering the unwarranted fear can also mean preventing the warranted fear from putting an effective restraint or discipline on banks' lending policies. If deposit liabilities are guaranteed, why should depositors worry whether banks have adequate earning assets to cover their deposits in the long run? Thus, when the short-run illusion is also a long-run illusion, and depositors can't get their money even in the long run because of excess loan defaults (that is, their fears were warranted), guaranteeing deposits can be expensive indeed for the taxpayers who must bear the cost of the guaranteed payouts to bank depositors.

The Savings and Loan Bailout

The U.S. government found this out in the late 1980s. It had guaranteed federal savings and loan (S&L) institutions' deposits during a period when savings and loan institutions were highly regulated. In 1982, S&Ls were deregulated. In this new deregulated environment they made bad loans and a number of them failed; they didn't have enough money to pay back depositors. The U.S. government, which had guaranteed those deposits, had to bail out the S&Ls by paying back depositors.

Banks and Bad Loans How, you ask, can banks make so many bad loans that they don't have enough money to pay back depositors? A small part of the answer is fraud—bank officials made loans to friends that they knew were more like gifts than loans. Part of the answer is that it doesn't take many bad loans to pull a bank under. Remember, banks take deposits in and lend those deposits out, hoping to make a profit from the *spread* (the difference between their costs and the interest they pay out, and the interest they take in minus bad loans). If, on average, more loans go bad than expected and the banks' costs are higher than expected, banks' profit can evaporate, leaving a loss. When that happens, deposits must be covered by the banks' net worth, which can be small, so there isn't much room for many bad loans. As was just pointed out, the S&Ls paid high interest rates and made many risky loans.

This 18th-century etching by Robert Goez, "The Speculator," captures a popular view of financial activities. It shows a man reduced to rags by bad speculation.
Bleichroeder Print Collection, Baker Library, Harvard Business School.

Another part of the answer is that it isn't hard to make a bad loan. Making loans is inherently risky. A person walks in with a grand idea for a mall—all she needs is a $10 million loan. The mall is needed by the community and will be worth $30 million once it's built. She has investors willing to put up $2 million of their own money and she is willing to pay 12 percent interest and give the mall as collateral. She's built successful malls before. So the bank makes the loan.

The building starts, only to have the builder discover there's a stone ledge beneath the site. Blasting is required—costs go up 12 percent. A builders' strike delays construction—costs go up 4 percent. When things are ready to proceed once the strike is settled, it rains daily, slowing construction—costs go up another 8 percent. The economy goes into a recession and one store that had promised to rent space in the mall pulls out. Let's say the store that pulled out was an "anchor" store (that is, the mall relied on that store's presence to attract large numbers of shoppers, who would then wander around and shop in the mall's smaller stores). Now the major industry in town shuts down. The mall's finished value falls 40 percent. You get the picture.

Making loans requires taking chances and, when you take chances, once in a while you lose. S&Ls bet that there would be no recession. When a recession started, they lost their bet, and a number of their loans went bad.

The last part of the answer is the government guarantee. Had the government not guaranteed the S&Ls' deposits, depositors (not the government) would have incurred the loss. They likely would have become alarmed as they saw troubles coming to their S&Ls and would have withdrawn their money before the situation became a disaster. But they didn't watch carefully and had no reason to be alarmed, because they knew the government had guaranteed their deposits (at least, up to $100,000).

Should Government Guarantee Deposits? Should the government have guaranteed S&L deposits? That's an open question. The guarantees did serve their purpose; they prevented unwarranted runs on S&Ls. But the guarantee program had serious flaws. If the government were going to guarantee deposits, it should have charged banks much higher fees. Government then would have had enough money to cover the losses resulting from bad loans. Or government should have maintained a strong regulatory presence, limiting the risks the S&Ls undertook.

The S&L crisis didn't answer the debate between the two goals: avoiding unwarranted fears while not limiting warranted fears. Some economists blame the crisis on the bank deregulation that let S&Ls make risky loans and investments. They claim the S&Ls' crisis showed the need for regulation. Others blame government guarantees that stopped the market forces from operating. As usual, both have reasonable arguments.

Q-10 Should governments guarantee deposits?

Conclusion

We'll stop our consideration of money and the financial sector there. As you can see, money is central to the operation of the macroeconomy. If money functions smoothly, it keeps the outflow from the expenditure stream (saving) and the flow back into the expenditure stream at a level that reflects people's desires. Money can be treated simply as a mirror of people's real desires.

When money doesn't function smoothly, it can influence the flows, sometimes creating too large a flow back into the expenditures stream, causing inflationary pressures, and other times creating too small a flow back in, causing a recession.

Summary

- The financial sector is the market where financial assets are created and exchanged. It channels flows out of the circular flow and back into the circular flow.
- Every financial asset has a corresponding financial liability.
- Money is a highly liquid financial asset that serves as a unit of account, a medium of exchange, and a store of wealth.
- There are various measures of money: M_1, M_2, and L. M_1 consists of currency in the hands of the public, checking account balances, and traveler's checks. M_2 is M_1 plus savings deposits, small-denomination time deposits, and money market mutual fund shares. L includes almost all short-term assets.
- Since money is what people believe money to be, creating money out of thin air is easy. How banks create money out of thin air is easily understood if you remember that money is simply a financial liability of a bank. Banks create money by loaning out deposits.
- The simple money multiplier is $1/r$. It tells you the amount of money ultimately created per dollar deposited in the banking system.
- The approximate real-world multiplier is $1/(r + c)$.
- Financial panics are based on fear. They can be prevented by government guaranteeing deposits but only at a cost.

Key Terms

approximate real-world money multiplier (635)
asset management (630)
bank (624)
bond (623)
excess reserves (635)
Federal Reserve Bank (the Fed) (624)
financial assets (623)
interest rate (623)
L (628)
liability management (630)
M_1 (627)
M_2 (628)
money (624)
reserve ratio (632)
reserves (632)
simple money multiplier (633)

Questions for Thought and Review

1. If financial institutions don't produce any tangible real assets, why are they considered a vital part of the U.S. economy?
2. Money is to the economy as oil is to an engine. Explain.
3. List the three functions of money.
4. Why doesn't the government pay for all its goods simply by printing money?
5. What are two components of M_2 that are not components of M_1?
6. Write the equations for the simple and the approximate real-world multipliers. Which multiplier is most likely to be larger?
7. If dollar bills (Federal Reserve notes) are backed by nothing but promises and are in real terms worthless, why do people accept them?
8. If the U.S. government were to raise the reserve requirement to 100 percent, what would likely happen to the interest rate banks pay on deposits? Why?
9. Name one benefit and one cost of government's guarantee of bank deposits.
10. What was the cause of the S&L crisis? What role did government guarantees play in that crisis?
11. Is the current U.S. banking system susceptible to panic? If so, how might a panic occur?
12. About 30 U.S. localities circulate their own currency with names like "Ithaca Hours" and "Dillo Hours." Doing so is perfectly legal (although by law they are subject to a 10 percent federal tax, which currently the government is not collecting). These currencies are used as payment for rent, wages, goods, and so on. Are these currencies money? Explain.

Problems and Exercises

1. Calculate the money multipliers below:
   a. Assuming individuals hold no currency, calculate the simple money multiplier for each of the following: 5%, 10%, 20%, 25%, 50%, 75%, 100%.
   b. Assuming individuals hold 20 percent of their money in the form of currency, recalculate the approximate real-world money multipliers in *a*.
2. While Jon is walking to school one morning, a helicopter flying overhead drops a $100 bill. Not knowing how to return it, Jon keeps the money and deposits it in his bank. (No one in this economy holds currency.) If the bank keeps 5 percent of its money in reserves:
   a. How much money can the bank now lend out?
   b. After this initial transaction, by how much is the money in the economy changed?
   c. What's the money multiplier?
   d. How much money will eventually be created by the banking system from Jon's $100?
3. Categorize the following as components of M_1, M_2, both, or neither.
   a. State and local government bonds.
   b. Checking accounts.
   c. Money market mutual funds.
   d. Currency.
   e. Stocks.
   f. Corporate bonds.
   g. Traveler's checks.
4. For each of the following, state whether it is considered money in the United States. Explain why or why not.
   a. A check you write against deposits you have at Bank USA.
   b. Brazilian reals.
   c. The available credit you have on your MasterCard.
   d. Reserves held by banks at the Federal Reserve Bank.
   e. Federal Reserve notes in your wallet.
   f. Gold bullion.
   g. Grocery store coupons.

5. State the immediate effect of each of the following actions on M_1 and M_2:
   a. Barry writes his plumber a check for $200. The plumber takes the check to the bank, keeps $50 in cash, and deposits the remainder in his savings account.
   b. Maureen deposits the $1,000 from her CD in a money market mutual fund.
   c. Sylvia withdraws $50 in cash from her savings account.
   d. Paulo cashes a $100 traveler's check issued in his Ohio bank at a New York bank.

Web Questions

1. Evocash is advertised as the Web's currency. But is it money? Go to www.evocash.com and check it out.
   a. What is evocash? How do you acquire it and how do you spend it?
   b. Does evocash fulfill the three functions of money? Explain your answer.
   c. Are evos money?
2. The Federal Reserve publishes a number of pamphlets describing its activities and the financial market. Go to the New York Fed's home page to read Fed Point #1 at www.ny.frb.org/pihome/fedpoint, and answer the following questions:
   a. How much currency is in circulation today? How much is that per person?
   b. What days during the week is there more cash in circulation?
   c. What's the life expectancy of a $1 bill?
   d. What collateral does the Fed put up when accepting currency from the Treasury?
   e. Which agency pays for the printing of Federal Reserve notes?

Answers to Margin Questions

1. I would respond by saying that the financial sector is central to the macroeconomy. It facilitates the trades that occur in the real sector. (*622*)
2. For money to have value, it must be in limited supply. People will use paper money as a medium of exchange, unit of account, and store of value only as long as it retains its value, which requires that be limited in supply. This means that the Fed cannot print up lots of money and maintain its use as money. (*626*)
3. Money provides liquidity and ease of payment. People hold money rather than bonds to get this liquidity and hold down transactions costs. (*627*)
4. M_2 would be the larger number, since it includes all of the components of M_1 plus additional components. (*628*)
5. Banks operate on the law of large numbers—which says that, on average, many fluctuations will affect each other, and hence their effect will be much smaller than the sum of all fluctuations—so that they will have some money flowing in and some money flowing out at all times. This allows them to make loans on the "float," the average amount that they are holding. If there is one big depositor at a bank, the law of large numbers does not necessarily hold, and the bank must hold larger reserves in case that big depositor withdraws that money. (*632*)
6. The approximate money multiplier is $1/(r + c)$, which is equal to $1/.4 = 2.5$. (*635*)
7. The approximate real-world money multiplier would decrease since individuals holding cash makes the denominator of the money multiplier larger. (*635*)
8. When banks borrow short and lend long, they are susceptible to a financial panic. Unless they have a place where they can borrow, they may not have the liquidity to pay off depositors immediately. (*637*)
9. Government guarantees of financial institutions can prevent unwarranted fears that cause financial crises, but they can also prevent warranted fears and thereby undermine financial institutions. (*637*)
10. It depends; government guarantees have both costs (they eliminate warranted fears) and benefits (they eliminate unwarranted fears). (*639*)

APPENDIX A

A Closer Look at Financial Institutions and Financial Markets

FINANCIAL ASSETS AND FINANCIAL LIABILITIES

To understand the financial sector and its relation to the real sector, you must understand how financial assets and liabilities work and how they affect the real economy.

An *asset* is something that provides its owner with expected future benefits. There are two types of assets: real assets and financial assets. Real assets are assets whose services provide direct benefits to their owners, either now or in the future. A house is a real asset—you can live in it. A machine is a real asset—you can produce goods with it.

Financial assets are *assets, such as stocks or bonds, whose benefit to the owner depends on the issuer of the asset meeting certain obligations*. **Financial liabilities** are *liabilities incurred by the issuer of a financial asset to stand behind the issued asset*. It's important to remember that *every financial asset has a corresponding financial liability;* it's that financial liability that gives the financial asset its value. In the case of bonds, for example, a company's agreement to pay interest and repay the principal gives bonds their value. If the company goes bankrupt and reneges on its liability to pay interest and repay the principal, the asset becomes worthless. The corresponding liability gives the financial asset its value.

For example, a **stock** is *a financial asset that conveys ownership rights in a corporation*. It is a liability of the firm; it gives the holder ownership rights that are spelled out in the financial asset. An equity liability, such as a stock, usually conveys a general right to dividends, but only if the company's board of directors decides to pay them.

A debt liability conveys no ownership right. It's a type of loan. An example of a debt liability is a bond that a firm issues. A **bond** is *a promise to pay a certain amount of money plus interest in the future*. A bond is a liability of the firm but an asset of the individual who holds the bond. A debt liability, such as a bond, usually conveys legal rights to interest payments and repayment of principal.

Real assets are created by real economic activity. For example, a house or a machine must be built. Financial assets are created whenever somebody takes on a financial liability or establishes an ownership claim. For example, say I promise to pay you $1 billion in the future. You now have a financial asset and I have a financial liability. Understanding that financial assets can be created by a simple agreement of two people is fundamentally important to understanding how the financial sector works.

VALUING STOCKS AND BONDS

A financial asset's worth comes from the stream of income it will pay in the future. With financial assets like bonds, that stream of income can be calculated rather precisely. With stocks, where the stream of income is a percentage of the firm's profits, which fluctuate significantly, the stream of future income is uncertain and valuations depends significantly on expectations.

Let's start by considering some generally held beliefs among economists and financial experts. The first is that an average share of stock in a company in a mature industry sells for somewhere between 15 and 20 times its normal profits. The second is that bond prices rise as market interest rates fall, and fall as market interest rates rise. The first step in understanding where the beliefs come from is to recognize that $1 today is not equal to $1 next year. Why? Because if I have $1 today I can invest it and earn interest (say 10 percent per year), and next year I will have $1.10, not $1. So if the annual interest rate in 10 percent, $1.10 next year is worth $1 today; alternatively, $1 next year is worth roughly 91 cents today. A dollar two years in the future is worth even less today, and dollars 30 years in the future are worth very little today.

Present value is *a method of translating a flow of future income or savings into its current worth*. For example, say a smooth-talking, high-pressure salesperson is wining and dining you. "Isn't that amazing?" the salesman says. "My company will pay $10 a year not only to you, but also to your great-great-great-grandchildren, and more, for 500 years—thousands of dollars in all. And I will sell this annuity—this promise to pay money at periodic intervals in the future—to you for a payment to me now of only $800, but you must act fast. After tonight the price will rise to $2,000."

Do you buy it? My rhetoric suggests that the answer should be no—but can you explain why? And what price *would* you be willing to pay?

To decide how much an annuity is worth, you need some way of valuing that $10 per year. *You can't simply add up the $10 five hundred times*. Doing so is wrong. Instead you must *discount* all future dollars by the interest rate in the economy. Discounting is required because a dollar in the future is not worth a dollar now.

If you have $1 now, you can take that dollar, put it in the bank, and in a year you will have that dollar plus interest. If the interest rate you can get from the bank is 5 percent, that dollar will grow to $1.05 a year from now. That means also that if the interest rate in the economy is 5 percent, if you have 95 cents now, in a year it will be worth $.9975 (5% × $.95 = $.0475). Reversing the reasoning, $1 one year in the future is worth 95 cents today. So the present value of $1 one year in the future at a 5 percent interest rate is 95 cents.

A dollar *two* years from now is worth even less today. Carry out that same reasoning and you'll find that if the interest rate is 5 percent, $1 two years from now is worth approximately 90 cents today. Why? Because you could take 90 cents now, put it in the bank at 5 percent interest, and in two years have $1.

THE PRESENT VALUE FORMULA

Carrying out such reasoning for every case would be a real pain. But luckily, there's a formula and a table that can be used to determine the present value (PV) of future income. The formula is:

$$PV = A_1/(1 + i) + A_2/(1 + i)^2 + \ldots + A_n/(1 + i)^n$$

where

A_n = the amount of money received n periods in the future

i = the interest rate in the economy (assumed constant)

Solving this formula for any time period longer than one or two years is complicated. To deal with it, people either use a business calculator or a present value table like that in Table A27-1.

Table A27-1(a) gives the present value of a single dollar at some time in the future at various interest rates. Notice a couple of things about the chart. First, the further into the future one goes, the lower the present value. Second, the higher the interest rate, the lower the present value. At a 12 percent interest rate, $1 fifty years from now has a present value of essentially zero.

Table A27-1(b) is an annuity table; it tells us how much a constant stream of income for a specific number of years is worth. Notice that as the interest rate rises, the value of an annuity falls. At an 18 percent interest rate, $1 per year for 50 years has a present value of $5.55. To get the value of amounts other than $1, one simply multiplies the entry in the table by the amount. For example, $10 per

Table A27-1 (a and b) Sample Present Value and Annuity Tables

	Interest Rate						
Year	3%	4%	6%	9%	12%	15%	18%
1	$0.97	$0.96	$0.94	$0.92	$0.89	$0.87	$0.85
2	0.94	0.92	0.89	0.84	0.80	0.76	0.72
3	0.92	0.89	0.84	0.77	0.71	0.66	0.61
4	0.89	0.85	0.79	0.71	0.64	0.57	0.52
5	0.86	0.82	0.75	0.65	0.57	0.50	0.44
6	0.84	0.79	0.70	0.60	0.51	0.43	0.37
7	0.81	0.76	0.67	0.55	0.45	0.38	0.31
8	0.79	0.73	0.63	0.50	0.40	0.33	0.27
9	0.77	0.70	0.59	0.46	0.36	0.28	0.23
10	0.74	0.68	0.56	0.42	0.32	0.25	0.19
15	0.64	0.56	0.42	0.27	0.18	0.12	0.08
20	0.55	0.46	0.31	0.18	0.10	0.06	0.04
30	0.41	0.31	0.17	0.08	0.03	0.02	0.01
40	0.31	0.21	0.10	0.03	0.01	0.00	0.00
50	0.23	0.14	0.05	0.01	0.00	0.00	0.00

(a) Present value table (value now of $1 to be received *x* years in the future)
The present value table converts a future amount into a present amount.

	Interest Rate						
Number of Years	3%	4%	6%	9%	12%	15%	18%
1	$ 0.97	$ 0.96	$ 0.94	$ 0.92	$0.89	$0.87	$0.85
2	1.91	1.89	1.83	1.76	1.69	1.63	1.57
3	2.83	2.78	2.67	2.53	2.40	2.28	2.17
4	3.72	3.63	3.47	3.24	3.04	2.85	2.69
5	4.58	4.45	4.21	3.89	3.60	3.35	3.13
6	5.42	5.24	4.92	4.49	4.11	3.78	3.50
7	6.23	6.00	5.58	5.03	4.56	4.16	3.81
8	7.02	6.73	6.21	5.53	4.97	4.49	4.08
9	7.79	7.44	6.80	6.00	5.33	4.77	4.30
10	8.53	8.11	7.36	6.42	5.65	5.02	4.49
15	11.94	11.12	9.71	8.06	6.81	5.85	5.09
20	14.88	13.59	11.47	9.13	7.47	6.26	5.35
30	19.60	17.29	13.76	10.27	8.06	6.57	5.52
40	23.11	19.79	15.05	10.76	8.24	6.64	5.55
50	25.73	21.48	15.76	10.96	8.30	6.66	5.55

(b) Annuity table (value now of $1 per year to be received for *x* years)
The annuity table converts a known stream of income into a present amount.

THE PRESS AND PRESENT VALUE

Applying the Tools

The failure to understand the concept of present value often shows up in the popular press. Here are three examples.

Headline: **COURT SETTLEMENT IS $40,000,000.**

Inside story: The money will be paid out over a 40-year period.

Actual value: $11,925,000 (8 percent interest rate).

Headline: **DISABLED WIDOW WINS $25 MILLION LOTTERY**

Inside story: The money will be paid over 20 years.

Actual value: $13,254,499 (8 percent interest rate).

Headline: **BOND ISSUE TO COST TAXPAYERS $68 MILLION**

Inside story: The $68 million is the total of interest and principal payments. The interest is paid yearly; the principal won't be paid back to the bond purchasers until 30 years from now.

Actual value: $20,000,000 (8 percent interest rate).

Such stories are common. Be on the lookout for them as you read the newspaper or watch the evening news.

---

year for 50 years at 18 percent interest is 10 × $5.55, or $55.50.

As you can see, the interest rate in the economy is a key to present value. *You must know the interest rate to know the value of money over time.* The higher the current (and assumed constant) interest rate, the more a given amount of money in the present will be worth in the future. Or, alternatively, the higher the current interest rate, the less a given amount of money in the future will be worth in the present.

SOME RULES OF THUMB FOR DETERMINING PRESENT VALUE

Sometimes you don't have a present value table or a business calculator handy. For those time, there are a few rules of thumb and simplified formulas for which you don't need either a present value table or a calculator. Let's consider two of them: the infinite annuity rule and the Rule of 72.

The Annuity Rule To find the present value of an annuity that will pay $1 for an infinite number of years in the future when the interest rate is 5 percent, we simply divide $1 by 5 percent (.05). Doing so gives us $20. So at 5 percent, $1 a year paid to you forever has a present value of $20. The **annuity rule** is that *the present value of any annuity is the annual income it yields divided by the interest rate.* Our general annuity rule for any annuity is expressed as:

$$PV = X/i$$

That is, the present value of an infinite flow in income, X, is that income divided by the interest rate, i.

Most of the time, people don't offer to sell you annuities for the infinite future. A typical annuity runs for 30, 40, or 50 years. However, the annuity rule is still useful. As you can see from the present value table, in 30 years at a 9 percent interest rate, the present value of $1 isn't much (it's 8 cents), so we can use this infinite flow formula as an approximation of long-lasting, but less than infinite, flows of future income. We simply subtract a little bit from what we get with our formula. The longer the time period, the less we subtract. For example, say you are wondering what $200 a year for 40 years is worth when the interest rate is 8 percent. Dividing $200 by .08 gives $2,500, so we know the annuity must be worth a bit less than $2,500. (It's actually worth $2,411.)

The annuity rule allows us to answer the question posed at the beginning of this section: How much is $10 a year for 500 years worth right now? The answer is that it depends on the interest rate you could earn on a specified amount of money now. If the interest rate is 10 percent, the maximum you should be willing to pay for that 500-year $10 annuity is $100:

$$\$10/.10 = \$100$$

If the interest rate is 5 percent, the most you should pay is $200 ($10/.05 = $200). So now you know why you should have said no to that supersalesman who offered it to you for $800.

The Rule of 72 A second rule of thumb for determining present values of shorter time periods is the **Rule of 72,** which states:

The number of years it takes for a certain amount to double in value is equal to 72 divided by the rate of interest.

Say, for example, that the interest rate is 4 percent. How long will it take for your $100 to become $200? Dividing 72 by 4 gives 18, so the answer is 18 years. Conversely, the present value of $200 at a 4 percent interest rate 18 years in the future is about $100. (Actually it's $102.67.)

Alternatively, say that you will receive $1,000 in 10 years. Is it worth paying $500 for that amount now if the interest rate is 9 percent? Using the rule of 72, we know that at a 9 percent interest rate it will take about eight years for $500 to double:

$$72/9 = 8$$

so the future value of $500 in 10 years is more than $1,000. It's probably about $1,200. (Actually it's $1,184.) So if the interest rate in the economy is 9 percent, it's not worth paying $500 now in order to get that $1,000 in 10 years. By investing that same $500 today at 9 percent, you can have $1,184 in 10 years.

The Importance of Present Value

Many business decisions require such present value calculations. In almost any business, you'll be looking at flows of income in the future and comparing them to present costs or to other flows of money in the future.

Generally, however, when most people calculate present value they don't use any of the formulas. They pull out a handy business calculator, press in the numbers to calculate the present value, and watch while the calculator graphically displays the results.

Let's now use our knowledge of present value to explain the two observations at the beginning of this section. Since all financial assets can be broken down into promises to pay certain amounts at certain times in the future, we can determine their value with the present value formula. If the asset is a bond, it consists of a stream of income payments over a number of years and the repayment of the face value of the bond. Each year's interest payment and the eventual repayment of the face value must be calculated separately, and then the results must be added together. If the financial asset is a share of stock, the valuation is a bit less clear since a stock does not guarantee the payment of anything definite—just a share of the profits. No profits, no payment. So, with stocks, expectations of profits are of central importance. Let's consider an example: Say a share of stock is earning $1 per share per year and is expected to continue to earn that long into the future. Using the annuity rule and an interest rate of 6.5 percent, the present value of that future stream of expected earnings is about 1/.065, or a bit more than $15. Assuming profits are expected to grow slightly, that would mean that the stock should sell for somewhere around $20, or 20 times its profit per share, which is the explanation to economists' view that an average stock sells for about 15 times normal profits.

To see the answer to the second—bond prices and interest rates are inversely related—say the interest rate rises to 10 percent. Then the value of the stock or bond that is earning a fixed amount—in this case $1 per share—will go down to $10. Interest rate up, value of stock or bond down. This is the explanation of the second observation.

There is nothing immutable in the above reasoning. For example, if promises to pay aren't trustworthy, you don't put the amount that's promised into your calculation; you put in the amount you actually expect to receive. That's why when a company or a country looks as if it's going to default on loans or stop paying dividends, the value of its bonds and stock will fall considerably. For example, in the early 2000s many people thought Argentina would default on its bonds. That expectation caused the price of Argentinean bonds to fall and interest rates to rise more than 30 percentage points.

Of course, the expectations could go in the opposite direction. Say that the interest rate is 10 percent, and that you expect a company's profit, which is now $1 per share, to grow by 10 percent per year. In that case, since expected profit growth is as high as the interest rate, the current value of the stock in infinite. It is such expectations of future profit growth that fueled the Internet stock craze and caused the valuation of firms with no current profits (indeed, many were experiencing significant losses) at multiples of sales of 300 or more. Financial valuations based on such optimistic expectations are the reason most economists considered the stock market in Internet stocks to be significantly overvalued in the late 1990s and predicted the fall in prices that occurred in 2001 and 2002.

Financial Institutions

A **financial institution** is *a business whose primary activity is buying, selling, or holding financial assets*. For example, some financial institutions (depository institutions and investment intermediaries) sell promises to pay in the future. These promises can be their own promises or someone else's promises. When you open a savings account at a bank, the bank is selling you its own promise that you can withdraw your money, plus interest, at some unspecified time in the future. Such a bank is a **depository institution**—*a financial institution whose primary financial liability is deposits in checking or savings accounts*. When you buy a newly issued government bond or security from a

Table A27-2 2002 Holdings of Selected Financial Institutions

Financial Institutions	Percentage of Total Financial Assets	Primary Assets (uses of funds)	Primary Liabilities (sources of funds)
Depository institutions:			
Commercial banks	36%	Business and consumer loans, mortgages, U.S. government securities, and municipal bonds	Checkable deposits and savings deposits
Savings and loan associations and mutual savings banks	4	Mortgages	Savings deposits (and checkable deposits
Credit unions	2	Consumer loans	Savings deposits (and checkable deposits)
Contractual intermediaries:			
Pension funds	20	Corporate bonds and stock	Employer and employee contributions
Life insurance companies	10	Corporate bonds and mortgages	Policy obligations
Fire and casualty insurance companies	3	Municipal bonds, corporate bonds and stocks, and U.S. government securities	Policy obligations
Investment intermediaries:			
Money market mutual funds	6	Money market instruments	Shares
Mutual funds	12	Stocks and bonds	Shares
Finance companies	3	Consumer and business loans	Commercial paper, stocks, and bonds
Financial brokers:			
Investment banks	0	None	None
Brokerage houses	4	Credit market instruments	Security RPS

Source: *Flow of Funds Accounts of the United States,* Federal Reserve System, 2002 (www.federalreserve.gov).

securities firm, it's also selling you a promise to pay in the future. But in this case, it's a third party's promise. So a securities firm is a financial broker that sells third parties' promises to pay. It's a type of marketing firm for financial IOUs.

As financial institutions sell financial assets, they channel savings from savers (individuals who give other people money now in return for promises to pay it back with interest later) to borrowers (investors or consumers who get the money now in return for their promise to pay it and the interest later).

As economists use the term, to save is to buy a financial asset. To invest (in economic terminology) is to buy real, not financial, assets that you hope will yield a return in the future.[1] How do you get funds to invest if you don't already have them? You borrow them. That means you create a financial asset that you sell to someone else who saves.

Some financial institutions serve several purposes and their various functions may have various names. For example, a depository institution, such as a commercial bank, may also serve as a **contractual intermediary**—*a financial institution that holds and stores individuals' financial assets*. Contractual intermediaries intermediate (serve as a go-between) between savers and investors. For example, a pension fund is a financial institution that takes in individuals' savings, relends those savings, and ultimately pays back those savings plus interest after the individuals retire. It uses individuals' savings to buy financial assets from people and firms who want to borrow. Similarly, a commercial bank is a financial institution that relends an individual's checking account deposits. A checking deposit is a financial asset of an individual and a financial liability of the bank.

[1]This terminology isn't the terminology most laypeople use. When a person buys a stock, in economic terms that person is saving, though most laypeople call that *investing*.

Types of Financial Institutions

Table A27-2 lists four types of financial institutions and shows the percentage of total U.S. financial assets each holds, along with the sources and uses of funds for each. These percentages give you an idea of the institution's importance, but institutions' importance can come in other ways. For example, although investment banks hold no

Do Financial Assets Make Society Richer?

Knowing the Tools

Financial assets are neat. You can call them into existence simply by getting someone to accept your IOU. *Remember, every financial asset has a corresponding financial liability equal to it.* So when you say a country has $1 trillion of financial assets, you're also saying that the country has $1 trillion of financial liabilities. An optimist would say a country is rich. A pessimist would say it's poor. An economist would say that financial assets and financial liabilities are simply opposite sides of the ledger and don't indicate whether a country is rich or poor.

To find out whether a country is rich or poor, you must look at its *real assets.* If financial assets increase the economy's efficiency and thereby increase the amount of real assets, they make society better off. This is most economists' view of financial assets. If, however, they decrease the efficiency of the economy (as some economists have suggested some financial assets do because they focus productive effort on financial gamesmanship), financial assets make society worse off.

The same correspondence between a financial asset and its liability exists when a financial asset's value changes. Say stock prices fall significantly. Is society poorer? The answer is: It depends on the reason for the change. Let's say there is no known reason. Then, while the people who own the stock are poorer, the people who might want to buy stock in the future are richer since the price of assets has fallen. So in a pure accounting sense, society is neither richer nor poorer when the prices of stocks rise or fall for no reason.

But there are ways in which changes in the value of financial assets might signify that society is richer or poorer. For example, the changes in the values of financial assets might *reflect* (rather than cause) real changes. If suddenly a company finds a cure for cancer, its stock prices will rise and society will be richer. But the rise in the price of the stock doesn't cause society to be richer. It reflects the discovery that made society richer. Society would be richer because of the discovery even if the stock's price didn't rise.

There's significant debate about how well the stock market reflects real changes in the economy. Classical economists believe it closely reflects real changes; Keynesian economists believe it doesn't. But both sides agree that the changes in the real economy, not the changes in the price of financial assets, underlie what makes an economy richer or poorer.

---

financial assets, they're important because they facilitate buying and selling such assets. Let's consider each grouping separately.

Depository Institutions

Depository institutions, the first category listed, are financial institutions whose primary financial liability is deposits in checking accounts. They hold approximately 36 percent of all the financial assets in the United States. This category includes commercial banks, savings banks, savings and loan associations (S&Ls), and credit unions. The primary financial liability of each is deposits. For example, the amount in your checking account or savings account is a financial asset for you and a financial liability for the bank holding your deposit.

Banks make money by lending your deposits (primarily in the form of business and commercial loans), charging the borrower a higher interest rate than they pay the depositor. Those loans from banks to borrowers are financial assets of the bank and financial liabilities of the borrower.

Laws governing financial institutions changed significantly in the 1980s and early 1990s. In the 1970s, each financial institution was restricted to specific types of financial transactions. Savings banks and S&Ls handled savings accounts and mortgages; they were not allowed to issue checking accounts. Commercial banks were not allowed to hold or sell stock; they did, however, issue checking accounts. These restrictions allowed us to make sharp, clear distinctions among financial institutions. Changes in the laws have eliminated many of these restrictions, blurring the distinctions among the various types of financial institutions. Now all depository institutions can issue checking accounts. Over the next decade, more changes are likely.

Some differences remain that reflect their history. Commercial banks' primary assets are loans, and their loans include business loans, mortgages, and consumer loans. Savings banks' and S&Ls' primary assets are the same kind as those of commercial banks, but their loans are primarily mortgage loans.

Contractual Intermediaries

The most important contractual intermediaries are insurance companies and pension funds. These institutions promise, for a fee, to pay an individual a certain amount of money in the future, either when some event happens (a fire or death) or, in the case of pension funds and some kinds of life insurance, when the individual reaches a certain age or dies. Insurance policies and pensions are a form of individual savings. Contractual intermediaries lend those savings. As the average age of the U.S. population increases, as it will throughout the early 21st century, the share of assets held by these contractual intermediaries will increase.

Investment Intermediaries

Investment intermediaries provide a mechanism through which small savers pool funds to purchase a variety of financial assets rather than just one or two. An example of how pooling works can be seen by considering a mutual fund company, which is one type of investment intermediary.

A mutual fund enables a small saver to diversify (spread out) his or her savings (for a fee, of course). Savers buy shares in the mutual fund, which in turn holds stocks or bonds of many different companies. When a fund holds many different companies' shares or bonds, it spreads the risk so a saver won't lose everything if one company goes broke. This is called **diversification**—*spreading the risks by holding many different types of financial assets*.

A finance company is another type of investment intermediary. Finance companies make loans to individuals and businesses, as do banks, but instead of holding deposits, as banks do, finance companies borrow the money they lend. They borrow from individuals by selling them bonds and commercial paper. **Commercial paper** is *a short-term promissory note that a certain amount of money plus interest will be paid back on demand*.

Finance companies charge borrowers higher interest than banks do, in part because their cost of funds (the interest rate they pay to depositors) is higher than banks' cost of funds. (The interest rate banks pay on savings and checking accounts is the cost of their funds.) As was the case with depository institutions, a finance company's profit reflects the difference between the interest rate it charges on its loans and the interest rate it pays for the funds it borrows.

Why do people go to finance companies if finance companies charge higher interest than banks? Because of convenience and because finance companies' loan qualifications are easier to meet than banks'.

The market for financial instruments is sometimes rather hectic, as suggested by this famous painting, "The Bulls and Bears on Wall Street."
© New York Historical Society.

Financial Brokers

Financial brokers are of two main types: investment banks and brokerage houses. Investment banks assist companies in selling financial assets such as stocks and bonds. They provide advice, expertise, and the sales force to sell the stocks or bonds. They handle such things as *mergers* and *takeovers* of companies. A merger occurs when two or more companies join to form one new company. A takeover occurs when one company buys out another company. Investment banks do not hold individuals' deposits and do not make loans to consumers. That's why in Table A27-2 they have no assets and hence no liabilities. They are nonetheless financial institutions because they assist others in buying and selling financial assets.

Brokerage houses assist individuals in selling previously issued financial assets. Brokerage houses create a secondary market in financial assets, as we'll see shortly. A **secondary financial market** is *a market in which previously issued financial assets can be bought and sold*.

Financial Markets

A **financial market** is *a market where financial assets and financial liabilities are bought and sold*. The stock market, the bond market, and bank activities are all examples of financial markets.

Financial institutions buy and sell financial assets in financial markets. Sometimes these markets are actual places, like the New York Stock Exchange, but generally a market simply exists in the form of a broker's Rolodex files, computer networks, telephone lines, and lists of people who sometimes want to buy and sell. When individuals want to sell, they call their broker and their broker calls potential buyers; when individuals want to buy, the broker calls potential sellers.

Primary and Secondary Financial Markets

There are various types of financial markets. A **primary financial market** is *a market in which newly issued financial assets are sold.* These markets transfer savings to borrowers who want to invest (buy real assets). Sellers in this market include *venture capital firms* (which sell part ownerships in new companies) and *investment banks* (which sell new stock and new bonds for existing companies). Whereas investment banks only assist firms in selling their stock, venture capital firms often are partnerships that invest their own money in return for part ownership of a new firm.

Many new businesses will turn to venture capital firms for financing because only established firms can sell stock through an investment bank. Risks are enormous for venture capital firms since most new businesses fail. But potential gains are huge. A company that's already established will most likely use an investment bank to get additional funds. Investment banks know people and institutions who buy stocks; with a new stock offering they use those contacts. They telephone those leads to try to *place* (sell) the new issue.

Generally new offerings are too large for one investment bank to sell. So the bank contracts with other investment banks and brokerage houses to sell portions of the new stock or bond issue. Figure A27-1(a) shows an advertisement announcing a stock offering. In this advertisement, a group of investment banks announces it's selling 1,550,000 shares of stock for Inergy at $31.25 per share. Figure A27-1(b) shows a tombstone ad announcing the successful completion of a sale.

There are many different types of buyers for newly issued financial assets. They include rich individuals and financial institutions, such as life insurance companies, pension funds, and mutual funds.

A secondary financial market transfers existing financial assets from one saver to another. (Remember, in economics, when an individual buys a financial asset such as a stock or bond, he or she is a saver. In economics, investment occurs only when savings are used to buy items such as machines or a factory.) A transfer on a secondary market does not represent any new saving; it is saving for one person and dissaving for another. One cancels out the other. The New York Stock Exchange is probably the best-known secondary financial market. It transfers stocks from one stockholder to another.

The floor of the New York Stock Exchange often is chaotic.
Bettmann/CORBIS.

The secondary market does, however, have an important role to play in new saving. The existence of a secondary market lets the individual buyer of a financial asset know that she can resell it, transferring the asset back into cash at whatever price the secondary market sets. **Liquidity** is this *ability to turn an asset into cash quickly.* Secondary markets provide liquidity for financial assets holders and thereby encourage them to hold financial assets. If no secondary market existed, most people would hesitate to buy a stock or a 30-year bond. What if they needed their money in, say, 10 years? Or 10 weeks?

The two secondary markets one hears the most about are the New York Stock Exchange and the National Association of Security Dealers Automated Quotations (Nasdaq). These stock exchange markets are undergoing significant change as the Internet eliminates the need for a place-specific stock market and replaces it with a virtual stock market that simply exists in the computer. More and

Figure A27-1 (a and b) Stock Offering Announcements
An advertisement (**a**) announcing the availability of a new stock issue notes that it is *not* a "solicitation of an offer to buy," but that a formal prospectus containing all the details is available from the listed investment banks. When the shares have been sold, a second advertisement (**b**) announces completion of the stock or bond offering. The second, self-congratulatory ad is called a *tombstone advertisement*.

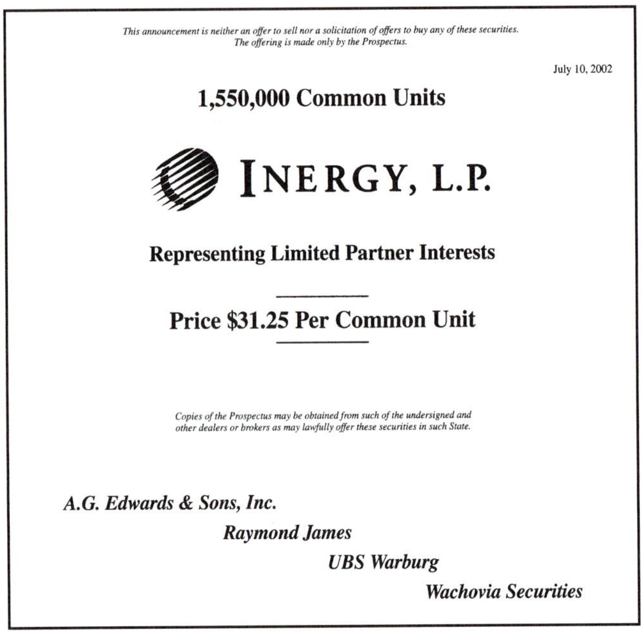

(a) Announcement of sale

(b) Tombstone ad

more people are buying and selling stocks on the Internet because they can do so quickly and at low costs. (A thousand shares can be bought or sold for less than $10.) Large stockholders can now easily bypass the stock market and trade directly with others, eliminating the intermediaries. As that happens the stock markets are changing too. Trading hours are expanding; soon 24-hour trading will be the norm. Both exchanges will likely become private companies over the next few years.

Money Markets and Capital Markets

Financial markets can also be divided into two other categories: **money markets** *(in which financial assets having a maturity of less than one year are bought and sold)* and **capital markets** *(in which financial assets having a maturity of more than one year are bought and sold)*. *Maturity* refers to the date the issuer must pay back the money that was

Figure A27-2 Principal Money Market Instruments
These pie charts show the growth and relative importance of money market instruments over time. The increasing size of the pies reflects the increasing value over time.

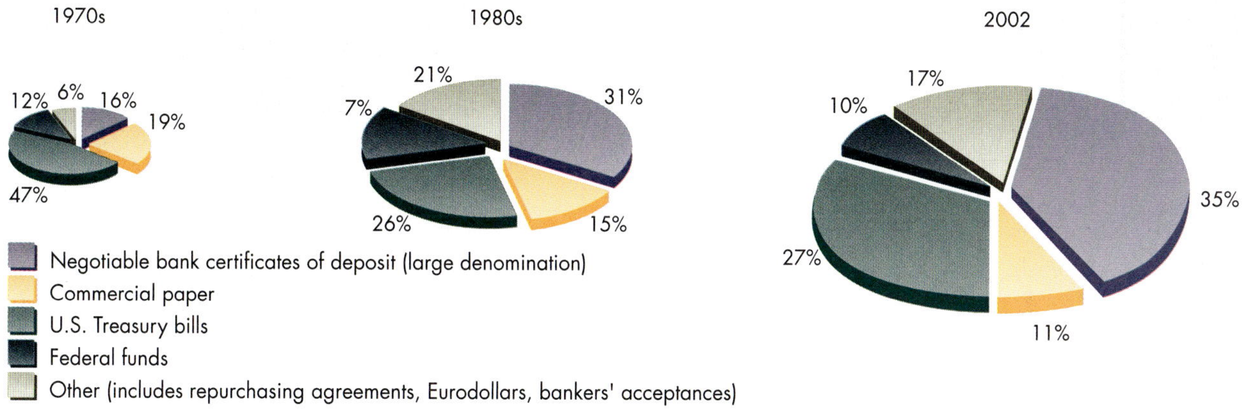

Source: Federal Reserve Bank and author extrapolations.

borrowed plus any remaining interest, as agreed when the asset was issued.) For example, say the U.S. government issues an IOU (sometimes called a *Treasury bill*) that comes due in three months. This will be sold in the money market because its maturity is less than a year. Or say the government or a corporation issues an IOU that comes due in 20 years. This IOU, which is called a *bond*, will be sold in a capital market.

Types of Financial Assets

Now that you've been introduced to financial institutions and markets, we can consider some specific financial assets. Financial assets are generally divided into money market assets and capital market assets.

Money Market Assets

Money market assets are financial assets that mature in less than one year. They usually pay lower interest rates than do longer-term capital assets because they offer the buyer more liquidity. A general rule of thumb is: The more liquid the asset, the lower the return. As in the over-the-counter market, money market and capital market transactions are made over the phone lines using computers. Newly issued money market assets are sold through an investment bank or a securities dealer. Figure A27-2 gives you a visual sense of some of the most important money market assets and their growth over time. Notice how the relative importance of various assets changes over time.

Some of the most important money market assets are negotiable CDs, commercial paper, and U.S. Treasury bills.

Negotiable CDs

A **certificate of deposit (CD)** is *a piece of paper certifying that you have a sum of money in a savings account in the bank for a specified period of time*. Think of it as a large amount of savings you agree to hold in an account at the bank for a specified period of time. But what if you need cash before the time is up? That's where the "negotiable" comes in. (Not all CDs are negotiable.) You can sell a negotiable CD in a secondary market and get cash for it if you need cash. The new owner can either sell it again on the secondary market or simply withdraw the money from the bank that issued it, including interest, when the required time is up (when the CD matures).

Commercial Paper

Why borrow from a bank if you can borrow directly from the public? Why not cut out the intermediary? Large corporations often do precisely that. The borrowings are called *commercial paper*. Commercial paper is a short-term IOU of a large corporation. Commercial paper pays a higher interest rate than U.S. Treasury bills, but a lower interest rate than banks would charge the corporation. The same reasoning holds for a person who buys commercial paper. Commercial paper generally pays a higher interest rate than a CD, which is why people are willing to

Figure A27-3 Principal Capital Market Instruments
These pie charts show the relative importance of capital market instruments since the 1970s. The increasing size of the pies reflects the increasing value over time.

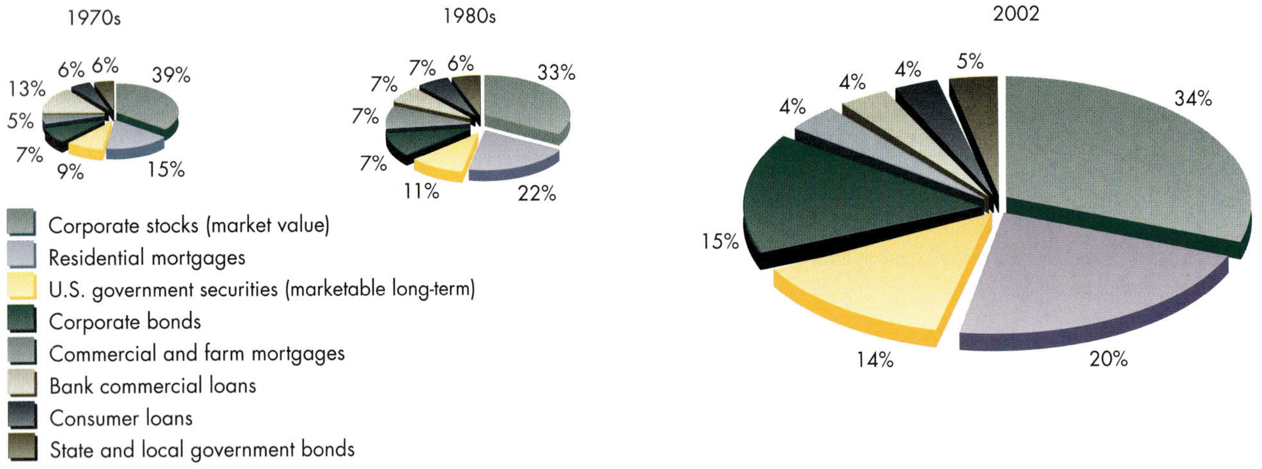

Source: Federal Reserve Bank and author extrapolations.

lend directly to the firm. Since the bank is an intermediary between the lender of funds and the borrower, the firm's action in this case is called **disintermediation**—*the process of lending directly and not going through a financial intermediary*.

U.S. Treasury Bills

U.S. Treasury bills are government IOUs that mature in less than a year. Since it's unlikely the U.S. government will go broke, IOUs of the U.S. government are very secure, so U.S. Treasury bills pay a relatively low rate of interest.

Where do these government IOUs come from? Think of what happens when the government spends more than it takes in in revenues; it runs a deficit, as we will discuss in detail in Chapter 31. That deficit must be financed by borrowing. Selling U.S. Treasury bills is one way the U.S. government borrows money.

Differences among Money Market Assets

Money market assets differ slightly from each other. For example, Treasury bills are safer than commercial paper and pay slightly lower interest. For the most part, however, they are interchangeable, and the interest rates paid on them tend to increase or decrease together.

Capital Market Assets

Capital market assets have a maturity of over one year. Figure A27-3 gives you a visual sense of the principal capital market instruments and their relative importance over time. As you can see, the most important are stocks, bonds, and mortgages.

Stocks

A stock is a partial ownership right to a company. A stock owner can vote on company policy and can attend stockholder meetings. Stocks have no maturity date, nor do they necessarily pay dividends (periodic payments to stockholders). People buy stocks because it gives them ownership rights to a percentage of the profits of the company. Firms issue stock to raise the cash necessary to invest in production. Stockholders can sell their stocks on secondary markets.

Bonds

A bond is an IOU, of either the government or a firm, that matures in more than one year. Unlike a stock, a bond must be repaid at maturity. Some bonds, called zero-coupon bonds, do not pay interest at periodic intervals. Most bonds, however, do pay a certain amount of interest at specified intervals. Like stocks, bonds can be bought and sold on the secondary market.

Leading You Through Two Financial Transactions

We've covered a lot of material quickly, so the institutions discussed may be a bit of a blur in your mind. To get a better idea of how these financial markets work, let's follow two transactions you'll likely make in your lifetime and see how they work their way through the financial system.

Insuring Your Car

You want to drive. The law requires you to have insurance, so you go to two or three insurance companies, get quotes of their rates, and choose the one offering the lowest rate. Say it costs you $800 for the year. You write a check for $800 and hand the check to the insurance agent, who keeps a commission (let's say $80) and then sends her check for $720 to the insurance company. The insurance company has $720 more sitting in the bank than it had before you paid your insurance premium.

The insurance company earns income in two ways: (1) in the difference between the money it receives in payments and the claims it pays out, and (2) in the interest it makes on its financial assets. What does the company use to buy these financial assets? It has payments from its customers (your $720, for example) available because payments come in long before claims are paid out.

Because earnings on financial assets are an important source of an insurance company's income, your $720 doesn't stay in the insurance company's bank for long. The insurance company has a financial assets division that chooses financial assets it believes have the highest returns for the risk involved. Bond salespeople telephone the financial assets division offering to sell bonds. Similarly, developers who want to build shopping malls or ski resorts go to the financial assets division, offering an opportunity to participate (really asking to borrow money).

The financial assets division might decide to lend your $720 (along with $10 million more) to a mall developer who builds in suburban locations. The division transfers the $720 to the mall developer and receives a four-year, 12 percent promissory note (a promise to pay the $720 back in four years along with $86.40 per year in interest payments). The promissory note is a financial asset of the insurance company and a financial liability of the developer. When the developer spends the money, the $720 leaves the financial sector and reenters the spending stream in the real economy. At that point it becomes investment in the economic sense.

Buying a House

Most people, when they buy a house, don't go out and pay the thousands of dollars it costs in cash. Instead they go to a bank or similar financial institution and borrow a large portion of the sales price, taking out a mortgage on the house. A **mortgage** is simply *a special name for a secured loan on real estate*. By mortgaging a house, you are creating a financial liability for yourself and a financial asset for someone else. This financial asset is secured by the house. If you default on the loan, the mortgage holder (who, as you will see, may or may not be the bank) can foreclose on the mortgage and take title to the house.

The funds available in banks come primarily from depositors who keep their savings in the bank in the form of savings accounts or checking accounts. Balances in these accounts are often small, but with lots of depositors they add up and provide banks with money to lend out. If you're planning to buy a house, you'll most likely go to a bank.

The bank's loan officer will have you fill in a lengthy form, and the bank will send an appraiser out to the house to assess its value. The appraiser asks questions about the house: Does it meet the electrical code? What kind of pipes does it have? What kind of windows does it have? All this information about you and the house is transferred onto a master form that the loan officer uses to decide whether to make the loan. (Contrary to what many laypeople believe, in normal times a loan officer wants to make the loan. Remember, a bank's profits are the difference between what it pays in interest and what it receives in interest; it needs to make loans to make profits. So the loan officer often looks at hazy answers on the form and puts an interpretation on them that's favorable to making the loan.)

In a month or so, depending on how busy the bank is, you hear back that the loan is approved for, say, $80,000 at 9 percent interest and two points. A point is 1 percent of the loan; it is a charge the bank makes for the loan. So two points means the bank is charging you $1,600 for making you a loan of $80,000 at 9 percent interest. (And you wondered why the bank was anxious to make you a loan!) The bank credits your account with $78,400, which allows you to write a check to the seller of the house at a meeting called the *closing*.

The bank gets a lot of money in deposits, but generally it doesn't have anywhere near enough deposits to cover all the mortgages it would like to make. So the process doesn't stop there. Instead the bank generally sells your mortgage on the secondary market to the Federal National Mortgage Association (FNMA or, popularly, Fannie Mae) or the Government National Mortgage Association (GNMA, or Ginnie Mae), which pay, say, $80,400 for the $80,000 mortgage. They're buying your mortgage (which you paid $1,600 in points to be allowed to get) for $400 more than its amount. The bank makes money both ways; when it makes the loan and when it sells the loan.

Fannie Mae and Ginnie Mae are nonprofit companies organized by the government to encourage home ownership. They do this by easing the flow of savings into mortgages. They take your mortgage and a number of similar ones from different areas and make them into a bond package: a $100 million bond fund secured by a group of mortgages. (Remember the long forms and the questions the appraiser asked? Those forms and answers allow Fannie Mae and Ginnie Mae to classify the mortgage and put it in a group with similar mortgages.) They then sell shares in that bond fund to some other institution that gives Fannie Mae and Ginnie Mae money in return. The Maes use that money to buy more mortgages, thereby channeling more savings into financing home ownership.

Who buys Fannie Mae and Ginnie Mae bonds? Let's go back and consider our insurance company. If the insurance company hadn't made the loan to the developer, the company might have decided that Ginnie Mae bonds were the best investment it could make. So who knows? Your insurance company may hold the mortgage to your house.

You, of course, don't know any of this. You simply keep making your mortgage payment to the bank, which, for a fee, forwards it to Ginnie Mae, which uses it to pay the interest on the bond it sold to the insurance company.

SUMMARY

We could go through other transactions, but these two should give you a sense of how real-world financial transactions work their way through financial institutions. Financial institutions make money by the fees and commissions they charge for buying and selling loans, and on the difference between the interest they pay to get the money and the interest they receive when they lend the money out.

KEY TERMS

annuity rule (644)
bond (642)
capital markets (650)
certificate of deposit (CD) (651)
commercial paper (648)
contractual intermediary (646)
depository institution (645)
disintermediation (652)
diversification (648)
financial assets (642)
financial institution (645)
financial liabilities (642)
financial market (648)
liquidity (649)
money markets (650)
mortgage (653)
present value (642)
primary financial market (649)
Rule of 72 (644)
secondary financial market (648)
stock (642)

QUESTIONS FOR THOUGHT AND REVIEW

1. If the government prints new $1,000 bills and gives them to all introductory students who are using the Colander text, who incurs a financial liability and who gains a financial asset?
2. Is the currency in your pocketbook or wallet a real or a financial asset? Why?
3. Joe, your study partner, has just said that, in economic terminology, when he buys a bond he is investing. Is he correct? Why?
4. Joan, your study partner, has just made the following statement: "A loan is a loan and therefore cannot be an asset." Is she correct? Why or why not?
5. How much is $50 to be received 50 years from now worth if the interest rate is 6 percent? (Use Table A27-1.)
6. How much is $50 to be received 50 years from now worth if the interest rate is 9 percent? (Use Table A27-1.)
7. Your employer offers you a choice of two bonus packages: $1,400 today or $2,000 five years from now. Assuming a 6 percent rate of interest, which is the better value? Assuming an interest rate of 10 percent, which is the better value?
8. Suppose the price of a one-year 10 percent coupon bond with a $100 face value is $98.

a. Are market interest rates likely to be above or below 10 percent? Explain.
b. What is the bond's yield or return?
c. If market interest rates fell, what would happen to the price of the bond?

9. Explain in words why the present value of $100 to be received in 10 years would decline as the interest rate rises.
10. A 6 percent bond will pay you $1,060 one year from now. The interest rate in the economy is 10 percent. How much is that bond worth now?
11. You are to receive $100 a year for the next 40 years. How much is it worth now if the current interest rate in the economy is 6 percent? (Use Table A27-1.)
12. You are to receive $200 in 30 years. About how much is it worth now? (The interest rate is 3 percent.)
13. A salesperson calls you up and offers you $200 a year for life. If the interest rate is 9 percent, how much should you be willing to pay for that annuity?
14. The same salesperson offers you a lump sum of $20,000 in 10 years. How much should you be willing to pay? (The interest rate is still 9 percent.)
15. What is the present value of a cash flow of $100 per year forever (a perpetuity), assuming:

    The interest rate is 10 percent.

    The interest rate is 5 percent.

    The interest rate is 20 percent.

    a. Working with those same three interest rates, what are the future values of $100 today in one year? How about in two years?
    b. Working with those same three interest rates, how long will it take you to double your money?
16. What is the difference between an investment bank and a commercial bank?
17. The difference between primary and secondary financial markets is that the primary markets are more important. True or false? Why or why not?
18. A company's stock is selling for three times earnings. How is the market valuing the prospects of that company?
19. Which market, the primary or secondary, contributes more to the production of tangible real assets? Explain why.
20. Why do money market assets generally yield lower interest payments than capital assets?
21. For the following financial instruments, state for whom it is a liability and for whom it is an asset. Also state, if appropriate, whether the transaction occurred on the capital or money markets.
    a. Lamar purchases a $100 CD at his credit union.
    b. First Bank grants a mortgage to Sandra. The bank then sells the mortgage to Fannie Mae, who packages the mortgage in a fund and sells shares of that fund to Pension USA.
    c. Sean purchases a $100 jacket using his credit card with First Bank.
    d. City of Providence issues $1 billion in municipal bonds, most of which were purchased by Providence residents, to build a community center.
    e. Investment broker sells 100 shares of existing stock to Lanier.
    f. Investment broker sells 1,000 shares of new-issue stock to Lanier.
22. State whether you agree or disagree with the following statements:
    a. If stock market prices go up, the economy is richer.
    b. A real asset worth $1 million is more valuable to an individual than a financial asset worth $1 million.
    c. Financial assets have no value to society since each has a corresponding liability.
    d. The United States has much more land than does Japan. Therefore, the value of all U.S. land should significantly exceed the value of land in Japan.
    e. U.S. GDP exceeds Japan's GDP; therefore, the stock market valuation of U.S.-based companies should exceed that of Japan-based companies.

Appendix B

Creation of Money Using T-Accounts

In this appendix I use T-accounts to demonstrate the example of the creation of money given in the text of the chapter.

The basis of financial accounting is the T-account presentation of balance sheets. The balance sheet is made up of assets on one side and liabilities and net worth on the other. By definition the two sides are equal; they balance (just as the T-account must).

To cement the money creation process in your mind, let's discuss how banks create money using transactions

Table B27-1 Textland Bank Balance Sheet

Beginning Balance			
Assets		**Liabilities and Net Worth**	
Currency	$ 30,000	Checking deposits	$150,000
Loans	300,000	Net worth	350,000
Property	170,000		
Total assets	$500,000	Total liabilities and net worth	$500,000

Table B27-1 (continued)

Transaction 1					
Assets			**Liabilities and Net Worth**		
Currency (beginning balance)	$30,000		Checking deposits (beginning balance)	$150,000	
Currency from John	10,000		John's deposit	10,000	
Total currency		$ 40,000	Total demand deposits		$160,000
Loans		300,000	Net worth		350,000
Property		170,000			
Total assets		$510,000	Total liabilities and net worth		$510,000

that affect the balance sheet. To keep the analysis simple, we limit the example to the case where only banks create money.

Table B27-1 shows the initial balance sheet of an imaginary Textland Bank, which we assume is the only bank in the country. As you can see, Textland has $500,000 in assets: $30,000 in cash, $300,000 in loans, and $170,000 in property. On the liabilities side, it has $150,000 in checking deposits and $350,000 in net worth. The two sides of the balance sheet are equal.

The first thing to notice about this balance sheet is that if all holders of checking accounts (demand deposits) wanted their currency, the bank couldn't give it to them. The currency it holds is only a portion—20 percent—of the total deposits:

$$\frac{\$30{,}000}{\$150{,}000} = 0.20$$

Banks rely on statistical averages and assume that not all people will want their money at the same time. Let's assume that Textland Bank has decided 20 percent is an appropriate reserve ratio.

Now let's say that John Finder finds $10,000 in currency. He deposits that $10,000 into Textland Bank. After he does so, what will happen to the money supply? The first step is seen in Transaction 1, which shows the effect of John Finder's deposit on the bank's account. The bank gains $10,000 in currency, but its liabilities also increase by $10,000, so, as you can see, the two sides of the balance sheet are still equal. At this point no additional money has been created; $10,000 currency has simply been changed to a $10,000 checking deposit.

Now let's assume the bank uses a reserve ratio of 20 percent, meaning it lends out 80 percent of the currency it receives in new deposits. Say it lends out 80% × $10,000 = $8,000 to Fred Baker, keeping 20 percent × $10,000 = $2,000 in reserve. The change in the bank's balance sheet is seen in Transaction 2. This step creates $8,000 in money. Why? Because John Finder still has $10,000 in his checking account, while Fred Baker has $8,000 currency, so, combining John's checking account balance with Fred's currency, the public has $8,000 in money. As you can see, loans have increased by $8,000 and currency in Textland Bank has decreased by $8,000.

Fred Baker didn't borrow the money to hold onto it. He spends it buying a new oven from Mary Builder, who, in turn, deposits the $8,000 into Textland Bank (the only bank according to our assumptions). Textland's balance sheet now looks like Transaction 3.

Mary Builder has a demand deposit of $8,000 and John Finder has a demand deposit of $10,000. But Textland

Table B27-1 (continued)

Transaction 2				
Assets			**Liabilities and Net Worth**	
Currency (after Trans. 1)	$ 40,000		Checking deposits (after Trans. 1)	$160,000
Currency loaned to Fred	− 8,000		Net worth	350,000
Total currency		$ 32,000		
Loans (beginning balance)	300,000			
Loans to Fred	8,000			
Total loans		308,000		
Property		170,000		
Total assets		$510,000	Total liabilities and net worth	$510,000

Table B27-1 (continued)

Transaction 3					
Assets			**Liabilities and Net Worth**		
Currency (after Trans. 2)	$32,000		Checking deposits	$160,000	
Currency from Mary	8,000		Mary's deposit	8,000	
Total currency		$ 40,000	Total demand deposits		$168,000
Loans		308,000	Net worth		350,000
Property		170,000			
Total assets		$518,000	Total liabilities and net worth		$518,000

bank has excess reserves of $6,400, since it must keep only $1,600 of Mary's $8,000 deposit as reserves:

80% × $8,000 = $6,400

So the bank is looking to make a loan.

At this point the process continues in the fashion described in the chapter text. A good exercise to see that you understand T-accounts is to use T-accounts to demonstrate the next two rounds of the process.

Questions for Thought and Review

1. Assume that there's only one bank in the country, that the reserve requirement is 10 percent, and that the ratio of individuals' currency holdings to their bank deposits is 20 percent. The bank begins with $20,000 in currency, $225,000 in loans, $105,000 in physical assets, $200,000 in demand deposits, and $150,000 in net worth.
   a. An immigrant comes into the country and deposits $10,000 in the bank. Show this deposit's effect on the bank's balance sheet.
   b. The bank keeps enough of this money to satisfy its reserve requirement, and loans out the rest to Ms. Entrepreneur. Show the effect on the bank's balance sheet.
   c. Ms. Entrepreneur uses the money to pay Mr. Carpenter, who deposits 80 percent of what he gets in the bank. Show the effect on the bank's balance sheet.
   d. Show the bank's balance sheet after the money multiplier is all through multiplying (based on the appendix).
2. Assume there is one bank in the country whose reserve requirement is 20 percent. It has $10,000 in currency;

$100,000 in loans; $50,000 in physical assets; $50,000 in demand deposits; and $110,000 in net worth. Mr. Aged withdraws $1,000 from the bank and dies on the way home without spending a penny. He is buried with the currency still in his pocket.

a. Show this withdrawal's effect on the bank's balance sheet.
b. What happened to the bank's reserve ratio and what must the bank do to meet reserve requirements?
c. What is the money multiplier? (Assume no currency holdings.)
d. What will happen to total money supply because of this event after the money multiplier is through multiplying?

3. Assume reserve requirements are 15 percent. Textland Bank's balance sheet looks like this:

Assets		Liabilities	
Currency	$ 30,000	Deposits	$150,000
Loans	320,000	Net worth	550,000
Property	350,000		
Total	$700,000	Total	$700,000

a. How much is the bank holding in excess reserves?
b. If the bank eliminates excess reserves by making new loans, how much new money would be created (assuming no currency holdings)? Show using T-accounts.

Monetary Policy and the Debate about Macro Policy

28

There have been three great inventions since the beginning of time: fire, the wheel and central banking.

—Will Rogers

After reading this chapter, you should be able to:

- Summarize the structure and duties of the Fed.
- List the three tools of monetary policy and explain how they work.
- Define the Federal funds rate and discuss how the Fed uses it as an intermediate target.
- State the Taylor rule and explain its relevance to monetary policy.
- Explain how monetary policy works in the *AS/AD* model.
- List six problems often encountered in conducting monetary policy.

Monetary policy is *a policy of influencing the economy through changes in the banking system's reserves that influence the money supply and credit availability in the economy*. Unlike fiscal policy, which is controlled by the government directly, monetary policy is controlled by the central bank in the United States, the Federal Reserve Bank (the Fed). We'll discuss the Fed in more detail later in this chapter when we discuss the specific tools through which monetary policy is conducted. For now let me give you a sense of monetary policy and how it fits into our macro model.

Our familiar macro policy model is shown in Figure 28-1. What is the effect of monetary policy in the *AS/AD* model? As shown in Figure 28-1(a) expansionary monetary policy shifts the *AD* curve to the right and contractionary monetary policy shifts it to the left. Changes in nominal income will be split between changes in real income and changes in the price level.

If the economy is significantly above potential, once long-run equilibrium is reached, monetary policy affects only nominal income and the price level, as in Figure 28-1(b). The economy begins at potential output Y_P (point A) and expansionary monetary policy shifts the *AD* curve to AD_1. Because the economy is beyond potential, rising factor cost pressures very quickly shift the *SAS* curve up from SAS_0 to SAS_1. Once the long-run equilibrium has been reached the price level rises from P_0 to P_1 and real output has returned to potential output (point B).

The general rule is: Expansionary monetary policy increases nominal income. Its effect on real income depends on how the price level responds:

$$\%\Delta\text{Real income} = \%\Delta\text{Nominal income} - \%\Delta\text{Price level}$$

Thus, if nominal income rises by 5 percent and the price level rises by 2 percent, real income will rise by 3 percent.

Duties and Structure of the Fed

Monetary policy is conducted by a **central bank**—*a type of bankers' bank*. If banks need to borrow money, they go to the central bank, just as when you need to borrow money, you go to a neighborhood bank. As we explained in the last chapter,

Figure 28-1 (a and b) The Effect of Monetary Policy in the AS/AD Model
Expansionary monetary policy shifts the *AD* curve to the right; contractionary monetary policy shifts the *AD* curve to the left. In (**a**) we see how monetary policy affects both real output and the price level. If the economy is at or above potential, as in (**b**), expansionary monetary policy will cause input costs to rise, which will eventually shift the *SAS* curve up enough so that real output remains unchanged. The only long-run effect of expansionary monetary policy when the economy is above potential is to increase the price level.

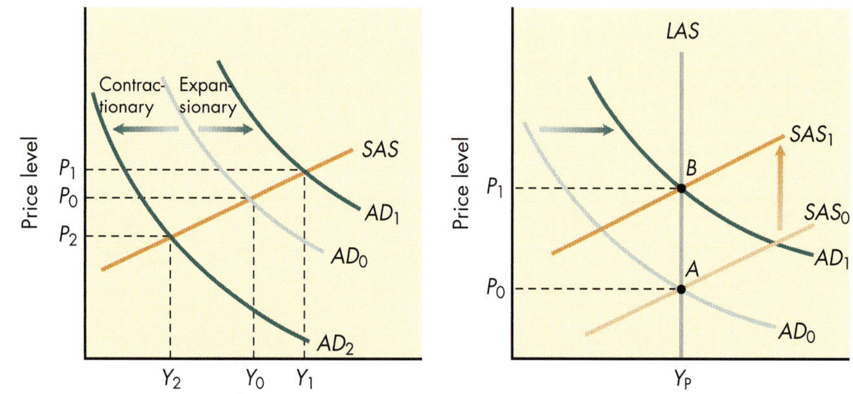

(a) Monetary policy

(b) Expansionary monetary policy beyond potential output

if there's a financial panic and a run on banks, the central bank is there to make loans to the banks until the panic goes away. Since its IOUs are cash, simply by issuing an IOU it can create money. It is this ability to create money that gives the central bank the power to control monetary policy. A central bank also serves as a financial adviser to government. As is often the case with financial advisers, the government sometimes doesn't like the advice and doesn't follow it.

It is the bank's ability to create money that gives the central bank the power to control monetary policy.

In many countries, such as Great Britain, the central bank is a part of the government, just as this country's Department of the Treasury and the Department of Commerce are part of the U.S. government. In the United States the central bank is not part of the government in the same way it is in some European countries.

STRUCTURE OF THE FED

Because of political infighting about how much autonomy the central bank should have in controlling the economy, the Federal Reserve Bank was created as a semiautonomous organization. The bank is privately owned by the member banks. However, member banks have few privileges of ownership. For example, the Board of Governors of the Federal Reserve is appointed by the U.S. president, not by the owners. Also, almost all the profits of the Fed go to the government, not to the owners. In short, the Fed is owned by the member banks in form only. In practice the Fed is an agency of the U.S. federal government.

The Fed is a semiautonomous organization composed of 12 regional banks. It is run by the Board of Governors.

Web Note 28.1
Other Central Banks

Although it is an agency of the federal government, the Fed has much more independence than most agencies. One reason is that creating money is profitable, and while the Fed returns its income after expenses to Congress, it is not dependent on Congress for appropriations. A second reason is that once appointed by the U.S. president and confirmed by the Senate for a term of 14 years, Fed governors cannot be removed from office, nor can they be reappointed. Because they cannot be removed and because they have little incentive to try to get reappointed, they feel little political pressure. If the president doesn't like what they do, tough luck, until their appointments expire or one of them decides to resign or retire.

There are seven governors of the Federal Reserve Bank. In practice, since pay at the Federal Reserve is much lower than at private banks and consulting firms, many appointees stay less than 14 years. When your job résumé includes "Governor of the Federal Reserve," private organizations are eager to hire you and pay you five or six times as much as you earned at the Fed. This means that none of the Federal Reserve Governors is hard up for a job. So while they are at the Federal Reserve, they can pretty much follow the policies they believe are best without being concerned about political retaliation, even if their terms aren't for life.

Q-1 Who appoints the chairman of the Board of Governors of the Federal Reserve System?

The president appoints one of the seven members to be chairman of the Board of Governors for a four-year term. The chairman has enormous influence and power, and is often called the second most powerful person in the United States. This is a bit of an exaggeration, but the chairman's statements are more widely reported in the financial press than any other government official's.

The Fed's general structure reflects its political history. Figure 28-2 demonstrates that structure. Notice in Figure 28-2(a) that most component banks are in the East and Midwest. The South and West have only three banks: Atlanta, Dallas, and San Francisco. The reason is that in 1913, when the Fed was established, the West and South were less populated and less important economically than the rest of the country, so fewer banks were established there.

As these regions grew, the original structure remained because no one wanted to go through the political wrangling that restructuring would bring about. Instead, the southern and western regional Feds established a number of branches to handle their banking needs.

Duties of the Fed

In legislation establishing the Fed, Congress gave it six explicit functions:

1. Conducting monetary policy (influencing the supply of money and credit in the economy).
2. Supervising and regulating financial institutions.
3. Serving as a lender of last resort to financial institutions.
4. Providing banking services to the U.S. government.
5. Issuing coin and currency.
6. Providing financial services (such as check clearing) to commercial banks, savings and loan associations, savings banks, and credit unions.

Of these functions, the most important one is conducting monetary policy, which is why I presented that first and will spend most of the chapter discussing it.

The Federal Reserve banks process millions of checks every day through automated machines, such as this one. Federal Reserve Bank of Boston.

The Importance of Monetary Policy

Not only is monetary policy the most important function of the Fed, it is probably the most-used policy in macroeconomics. The Fed conducts and controls monetary policy, whereas fiscal policy is conducted directly by the government. Both policies are directed toward the same end: influencing the level of aggregate economic activity, hopefully in a beneficial manner. (In many other countries institutional arrangements are different; the central bank is a part of government, so both monetary and fiscal policy are directly conducted by the government, albeit by different branches of government.)

Q-2 What is the difference between monetary policy and fiscal policy?

Actual decisions about monetary policy are made by the **Federal Open Market Committee (FOMC),** *the Fed's chief policymaking body.* All seven members of the Board

Figure 28-2 (a and b) The Federal Reserve System
The Federal Reserve System is composed of 12 regional banks. It is run by the Board of Governors. The Federal Open Market Committee (FOMC) is the most important policymaking body.

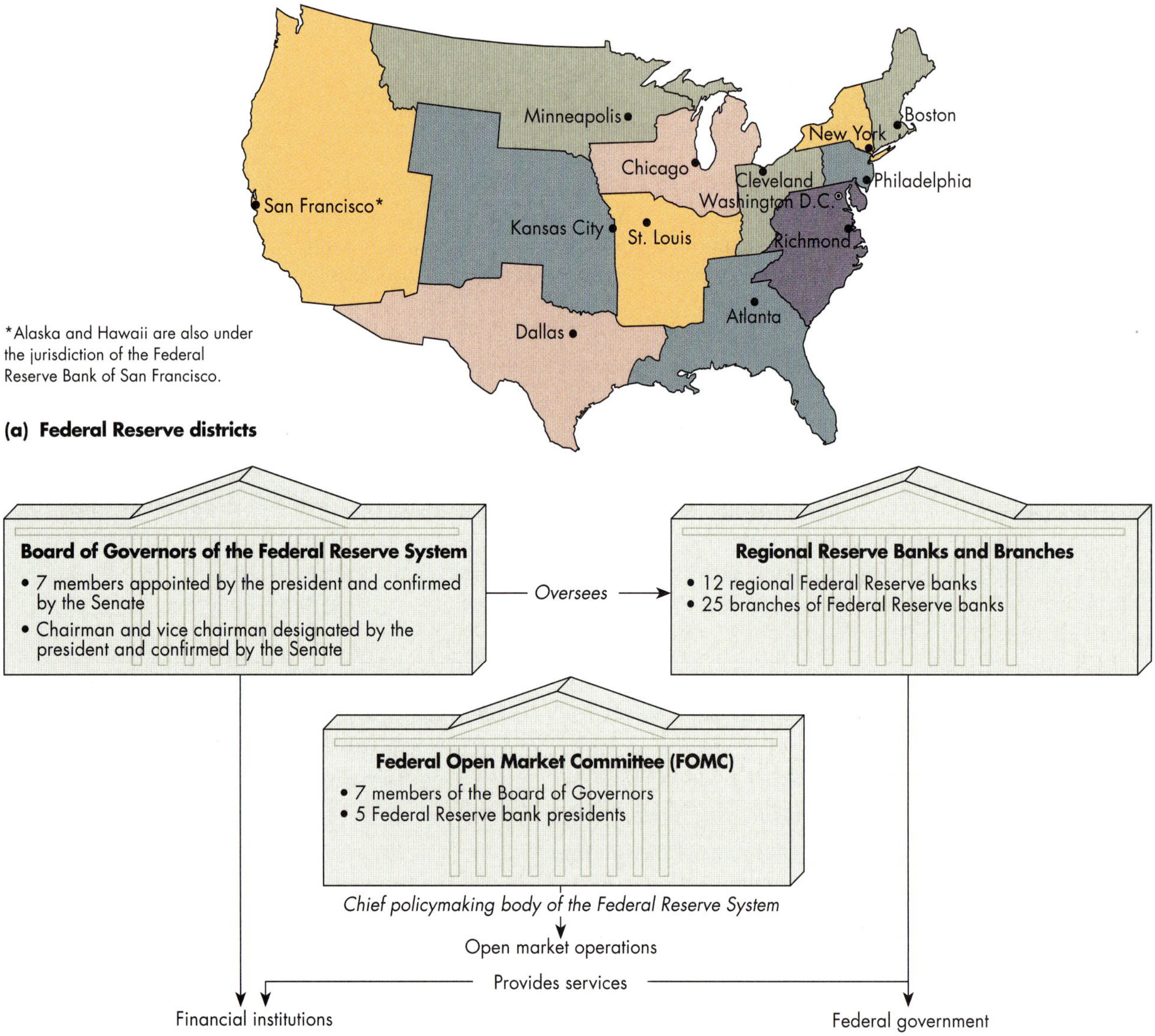

(b) Federal Reserve structure

Source: The Federal Reserve System (www.federalreserve.gov).

of Governors, together with the president of the New York Fed and a rotating group of four of the presidents of the other regional banks, vote on the FOMC. All 12 regional bank presidents attend and can speak at FOMC meetings. The financial press and business community follow their discussions closely. There are even Fed watchers whose sole occupation is to follow what the Fed is doing and to tell people what it will likely do.

CENTRAL BANKS IN OTHER COUNTRIES

Applying the Tools

In the United States, the central bank is the Fed, and much of this chapter is about its structure. But the Fed is only one of many central banks. Let's briefly introduce you to some of the others.

Bundesbank

In Germany, the central bank is called the *Bundesbank*. It has a reputation as a fierce inflation fighter, in large part because of the historical legacy of the German hyperinflation of the late 1920s and early 1930s. To fight inflation in the mid-1990s, it maintained high interest rates relative to the rest of the world, causing international monetary disruption. In the late 1990s it gave up most of its policymaking power to the European Central Bank as Germany entered the European Union and adopted the euro as its currency.

European Central Bank

In the late 1990s a number of European Union countries formed a monetary union, creating a common currency called the euro, and a new central bank called the European Central Bank (ECB). It has 12 governors, one from each individual country's central bank. These governors hold a majority of the 18 seats on the ECB General Council, which decides monetary policy for the member countries.

The primary objective of the ECB is different from the Fed's; the ECB is focused solely on maintaining price stability, as was the German Bundesbank. Its tools and its directives are similar to the Bundesbank's, and some economists have considered it as an expansion of the Bundesbank for the entire EU.

Most economists hold a wait-and-see attitude about the bank. They point out that the ECB is a new bank and it will take time for its operating procedures to become established. We can expect significant political infighting as the various countries attempt to influence the decisions of the ECB to favor them.

The Bank of England

The Bank of England is sometimes called the Old Lady of Threadneedle Street (because it's located on that street, and the British like such quaint characterizations). It does not use a required reserve mechanism. Instead, individual banks determine their own needed reserves, so any reserves they have would, in a sense, be excess reserves. Needless to say, bank reserves are much lower in England than they are in the United States.

How does the Old Lady control the money supply? With the equivalent of open market operations and with what might be called "tea control." Since there are only a few large banks in England, the Old Lady simply passes on the word at tea as to which direction she thinks the money supply should be going. Alas for sentimentalists, "tea control" is fading in England, as are many of the quaint English ways.

The Bank of Japan

Of the four banks I discuss here, the Bank of Japan is most similar to the Fed. It uses primarily open market operations to control the money supply. Reserve requirements are similar to the Fed's, but because it allows banks a longer period in which to do their averaging, and Japan does not have the many small banks that the United States does—banks that often hold excess reserves—excess reserves are much lower in Japan than in the United States. Until the early 1990s the Bank of Japan held the Japanese interest rate far below the world rate, which caused an international outflow of savings and a corresponding trade surplus. In 1990 the Japanese interest rate increased substantially, in part due to the actions of the Bank of Japan, but by the mid-1990s and into the early 2000s the Japanese interest rate was once again very low.

Clearly, there's more to be said about each of these central banks, but this brief introduction should give you a sense of both the similarities and the diversities among the central banks of the world.

History of the U.S. Banking System

Beyond the Tools

In Chapter 27, which introduced you to financial institutions, there was a discussion of financial panics that can occur when people lose faith in one financial asset and want to shift to another. Financial panics are no stranger to banking. In the 1800s the United States suffered a financial panic every 20 years or so. Initially, a few people would suddenly fear they wouldn't be able to get their money out of their bank. They'd run down to the bank to get it. Others would see them getting their money and would do likewise. This was referred to as *a run on the bank*. As a result, their bank would have to close. If a bank closed, people would worry about other banks closing, and they'd run to *their* banks. That process could spread uncontrollably; banks would close and there would be a general financial panic. These panics led to considerable debate about what government should do to regulate and control the banking system.

Much of the initial debate about the U.S. banking industry concerned whether there should be a central bank (a bank that could make loans to other banks in times of crisis and could limit those banks' expansionary loans at other times). Supporters of a central bank argued that a central bank would create financial stability. Opponents argued that it would cause recessions and favor industrial interests over farming interests, and increase centralized power in the economy.

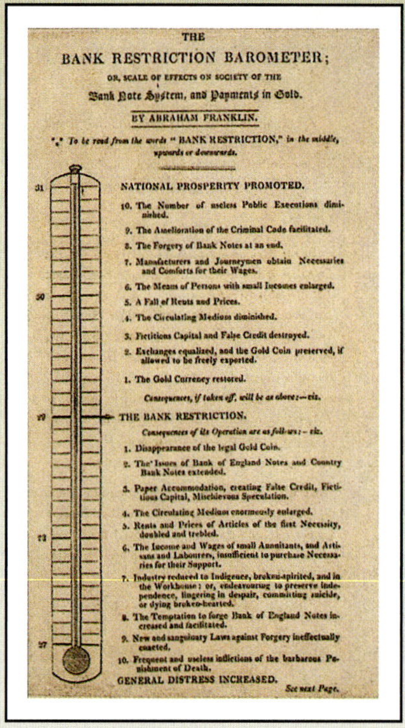

The issue of regulating banks has been at the forefront of economic policy discussions for centuries, as can be seen in this 19th-century English print of unknown origin, "The Bank Restriction Barometer." Bleichroeder Print Collection, Baker Library, Harvard Business School.

Initially central bank supporters predominated, and it wasn't long before the Bank of the United States, the first central U.S. bank chartered by the U.S. government, was established. Debates about the bank were rancorous and in 1811 its charter was not renewed. It went out of existence.

Five years later in 1816, the political forces changed and the Second Bank of the United States was chartered. Its attempt to stop the inflationary spiral of 1817 and 1818 caused a depression. The bank was blamed. Political forces once again changed, and in 1832 the Second Bank was dismantled.

The next hundred years were marked by periodic financial crises and recessions—every 10 or 20 years. These crises led to arguments that the country needed a central bank to help prevent future crises, but when a particular crisis ended, the argument would fade away. In 1907, however, there was a major financial panic. In response the government established the Federal Reserve Bank (the Fed) in 1913. Congress empowered the Fed to supply reserve assets to eliminate the incentive for depositors to panic and start a run on banks. The Fed failed to use these powers effectively during the 1929–1933 period and thus bears some of the responsibility for the depth of the Great Depression. Despite this failure, the Federal Reserve Bank has remained in existence ever since and is now the U.S. central bank.

The Conduct of Monetary Policy

You've already seen that monetary policy shifts the *AD* curve. Let's now consider how it does so. We need to look more specifically at the institutional structure of the banking system and the role of the Fed in that institutional structure.

Think back to our discussion of the banking system. Banks take in deposits, make loans, and buy other financial assets, keeping a certain percentage of reserves for those transactions. Those reserves are IOUs of the Fed—either vault cash or deposits at the Fed. *Vault cash, deposits of the Fed, plus currency in circulation* make up the **monetary base.** The monetary base held at banks serves as legal reserves of the banking system. By

Allowable reserves are either vault cash or deposits at the Fed.

Three Letters

Applying the Tools

The relationship between the U.S. president and the Fed is often more friendly than appears in the press. The president and the Fed sometimes play good cop/bad cop. The Fed undertakes a politically tough decision. The president screams and yells to the press about how awful the Fed is, while privately encouraging the Fed. The Fed takes the political heat since it doesn't have to face elections, while the president seems like a nice guy.

It's White House folklore that each president who takes up residence there receives three letters from the outgoing president. The letters are to be opened only in a dire economic emergency. Letter Number 1 says, "Blame it on Congress." Letter Number 2, to be opened only if Letter Number 1 doesn't work, says, "Blame it on the Fed." If Letter Number 2 doesn't work either, Letter Number 3 is to be opened. It says, "Prepare three letters!"

controlling the monetary base, the Fed can influence the amount of money in the economy and the activities of banks.

The actual tools of monetary policy will affect the amount of reserves in the system. In turn, the amount of reserves in the system will affect the interest rate. Other things equal, as reserves decline, the interest rate will rise; and as reserves increase, the interest rate will decline. So monetary policy will also be associated with interest rates.

Let's now turn to the three tools of monetary policy and see precisely how they influence the amount of reserves in the system.

Tools of Monetary Policy

The three tools of monetary policy are:

1. Changing the reserve requirement.
2. Changing the discount rate.
3. Executing open market operations (buying and selling bonds) and thereby affecting the Fed funds rate.

The three tools of monetary policy are:
1. Changing the reserve requirement.
2. Changing the discount rate.
3. Open market operations.

Changing the Reserve Requirement

As we said in the previous chapter, the total amount of money created from a given amount of cash depends on the percentage of deposits that a bank keeps in reserves (the bank's reserve ratio). By law, the Fed controls the minimum percentage of deposits banks keep in reserve by controlling the reserve requirement of all U.S. banks. That minimum is called the **reserve requirement**—*the percentage the Federal Reserve System sets as the minimum amount of reserves a bank must have*.

Required Reserves and Excess Reserves For checking accounts (also called *demand deposits*), the amount banks keep in reserves depends partly on the Federal Reserve requirements and partly on how much banks feel they need for safety (the cash they need to keep on hand at any time to give to depositors who claim some of their deposits in the form of cash). The amount most banks need for safety is much smaller than what the Fed requires. For them, it's the Fed's reserve requirement that determines the amount they hold as reserves.

Banks hold as little in reserves as possible. Why? Because reserves earn no interest for a bank. And we all know that banks are in business to earn profits. How much is as little as possible? That depends on the type of liabilities the bank has. In the early 2000s, required reserves for large banks for their checking accounts were about 10 percent. The reserve requirement for all other accounts was zero, making the reserve requirement for total liabilities somewhat under 2 percent.

In the early 2000s, total reserves were about $41 billion and required reserves were about $40 billion. This means excess reserves (reserves in excess of requirements) were about $1 billion.

The Reserve Requirement and the Money Supply By changing the reserve requirements, the Fed can increase or decrease the money supply. If the Fed increases the reserve requirement, it contracts the money supply; banks have to keep more reserves so they have less money to lend out; the decreased money multiplier contracts the money supply. If the Fed decreases the reserve requirement, it expands the money supply; banks have more money to lend out; the increased money multiplier further expands the money supply.

The total effect on the money supply of changing the reserve requirement can be determined by thinking back to the approximate real-world money multiplier, which, as you saw in the previous chapter, equals $1/(r + c)$ [1 divided by the sum of r (the percentage of each dollar that banks hold in reserves) plus c (the ratio of people's cash to deposits)]. When banks hold no excess reserves and face a reserve requirement of 15 percent, and people's cash-to-deposit ratio is 25 percent, the approximate money multiplier will be $1/0.4 = 2.5$, so $1 million in reserves will support a total $2.5 million money supply. In reality the cash-to-deposit ratio is about 0.4 ($c = 0.4$), the average reserve requirement for demand deposits is about 0.1 ($r = 0.1$), and banks hold little in the way of excess reserves. So the realistic approximate money multiplier for demand deposits (M_1) is

The approximate real-world money multiplier is $1/(r + c)$.

$$\frac{1}{(0.1 + 0.4)} = \frac{1}{0.5} = 2$$

A $100 increase of reserves will support a $200 increase in demand deposits.[1] For other deposits the reserve requirement is zero, so the money multiplier is larger for those.

What does a bank do if it comes up short of reserves? It can borrow from another bank that has excess reserves in what's called the Federal funds market. (The rate of interest at which these reserves can be borrowed is called the Fed funds rate. As I will discuss below, this Fed funds rate is a significant indicator of monetary policy.) But if the entire banking system is short of reserves, that option won't work since there's no one to borrow from. Another option is to stop making new loans and to keep as reserves the proceeds of loans that are paid off. Still another option is to sell Treasury bonds to get the needed reserves. (Banks often hold some of their assets in Treasury bonds so that they can get additional reserves relatively easily if they need them.) Treasury bonds are sometimes called *secondary reserves*. They do not count as bank reserves—only IOUs of the Fed count as reserves. But Treasury bonds can be easily sold and transferred into cash that does count as reserves. Banks use all these options.

[1]As c, the cash-to-deposit ratio, increases, the approximation becomes less exact. The actual multiplier is $(1 + c)/(r + c) = 1.4/0.5 = 2.8$. Since the marginal amount held varies rather substantially, and various measures of money are used, this difference between our approximation and the actual cash multiplier is not of operational significance. In estimating the effect of policy on the different measures of the money supply, analysts use only very rough estimates of the money supply.

Using the Multiplier in Practice

Applying the Tools

The money multiplier has been a staple of the macro principles course since its inception, and it remains an important concept in understanding how the monetary base is related to the aggregate supply of money in the economy. But recent changes in the financial system have made the operational use of it less important. For the most part central banks don't determine how much to change the monetary base to get a desired change in the money supply using an assumed fixed multiplier. Instead, they adjust the monetary base to target a desired amount of bank credit in the economy and short-term interest rate, and then adjust the monetary base to fit that.

The money multiplier relationship continues to be true by definition, but it is not the operational concept that it once was. The reasons include the decrease in the reserve requirement (in many countries, required reserves are zero); financial innovations that have increased the ways in which individuals can hold money; the increase in the amount of cash that individuals hold; and the decline in the stability of the relationship between the money supply and output. Each of these makes it harder to use the money multiplier as an operational variable, which is why much of the monetary policy discussion today focuses more on the interest rate than on the money supply.

Changing the Discount Rate

A second tool of monetary policy concerns another alternative banks have to get reserves needed to maintain their required reserves. A bank can also go to the Federal Reserve (the banker's bank) and take out a loan.

Q-3 True or false? The discount rate is determined by market forces.

The **discount rate** is *the rate of interest the Fed charges for loans it makes to banks*. An increase in the discount rate makes it more expensive for banks to borrow from the Fed. A discount rate decrease makes it less expensive for banks to borrow. Therefore, changing the discount rate is a second way the Fed can expand or contract the money supply.

Up until 2002 the Fed set the discount rate slightly lower than the cost of reserves for banks from other sources, relying on moral suasion to stop banks from borrowing unless they really needed it. Beginning in 2003, the Fed changed this policy and now it sets the discount rate slightly higher than the bank's other costs of funds. An increase in the discount rate discourages banks from borrowing and contracts the money supply; a decrease in the discount rate encourages the banks to borrow and increases the money supply.

Executing Open Market Operations

Changes in the discount rate and the reserve requirement are not used in day-to-day Fed operations. They're used mainly for major changes. For day-to-day operations, the Fed uses a third tool: **open market operations**—*the Fed's buying and selling of government securities* (the only type of asset the Fed is allowed by law to hold in any appreciable quantity). These open market operations are the primary tool of monetary policy.

When the Fed buys Treasury bills or bonds (government securities), it pays for them with IOUs that serve as reserve assets for banks. This IOU doesn't have to be a written piece of paper. It may be simply a computer entry credited to the bank's account, say $1 billion. An IOU of the Fed is money.

Web Note 28.2
The FOMC

Because the IOU the Fed uses to buy a government security serves as reserves to the banking system, with the simple act of buying a Treasury bond and paying for it with its IOU the Fed can increase the money supply (since this creates reserves for the bank). To increase the money supply, the Fed goes to the bond market, buys a bond, and pays for it with its IOU. The individual or firm that sold the bond now has an IOU of the

The Fed's buying and selling of government securities is called open market operations.

Inside an FOMC Meeting

Knowing the Tools

Let's go inside one of the eight regular Federal Open Market Committee (FOMC) meetings to gain some insight into how the Fed actually conducts monetary policy. The meeting consists of FOMC members and top Fed staff sitting around a large table debating what should be done. There's been enormous preparation for the meeting. The economists on the Federal Reserve staff have tracked the economy, and have made economic forecasts. Based on their studies, they've briefed the FOMC members, and the high-level staff gets to sit in on the meeting. (Getting to sit in on the meeting is seen as a real perk of the job.)

The information they've put together is gathered in three books, which are distinguished by colors. The Beige Book is prepared by each of the 12 regional Federal Reserve banks and summarizes regional business conditions based on local surveys and conversations with local businesspeople. The Green Book is prepared by the staff of the Federal Reserve in Washington, D.C.; it presents a two-year forecast of the U.S. economy as a whole. The Blue Book, also prepared by the Fed staff in Washington, analyzes three possible monetary policy options. This Blue Book is the central policy document, and one of the three options it presents will be selected by the FOMC.

The meeting begins with a summary of monetary policy actions since the committee last met, followed by a forecast of the economy. The Fed governors and regional bank presidents also present their forecasts. Once current economic conditions and forecasts are discussed, the director of monetary affairs presents the three monetary policy proposals in the Blue Book. Then there is open discussion of the various policy proposals. The committee meeting ends with a vote on what policy to follow, along with a policy directive on what open market operations to execute. At that point the FOMC also makes a public announcement regarding current policy actions as well as what future actions they may take. For example, on November 6, 2002, the FOMC issued the following statement:

> The Federal Open Market Committee decided today to lower its target for the federal funds rate by 50 basis points to 1¼ percent. In a related action, the Board of Governors approved a 50 basis point reduction in the discount rate to ¾ percent.

Notice that the statement refers to changes in interest rates as changes in basis points. A basis point is simply 1/100 of 1 percent, so 25 basis points is just ¼ of 1 percent. In many bond markets the minimum change in interest rates is 1 basis point. That might not look like much to you, but multiply any 1-basis-point change in interest rates by a large amount of money, and you've got a tidy sum. Would you rather receive 7.00 percent or 7.01 percent interest on principal of $1 billion?

Q-4 Besides open market operations, what are two tools of monetary policy?

Fed. When the individual or firm deposits the IOU in a bank—presto!—the reserves of the banking system are increased. If the Fed buys $1 million worth of bonds, it increases reserves by $1 million and the total money supply by $1 million times the money multiplier.

When the Fed sells Treasury bonds, it collects back some of its IOUs, reducing banking system reserves and decreasing the money supply. Thus,

> To expand the money supply, the Fed buys bonds.
>
> To contract the money supply, the Fed sells bonds.

Examples of Open Market Operations Understanding open market operations is essential to understanding monetary policy as it is actually practiced in the United States. So let's go through some examples.[2]

Open market operations involve the purchase or sale of federal government securities (bonds). When the Fed buys bonds, it deposits the funds in federal government

[2]A discussion of the effects of open market operations on the supply of money using T-accounts is presented in Appendix A of this chapter.

Figure 28-3 (a and b) Open Market Operations
In (**a**) you can see that an open market purchase raises existing bond prices. That increase in bond price is the equivalent to a decrease in the interest rate. In (**b**) you can see that an open market sale reduces existing bond prices. That reduction means that the interest rate rises.

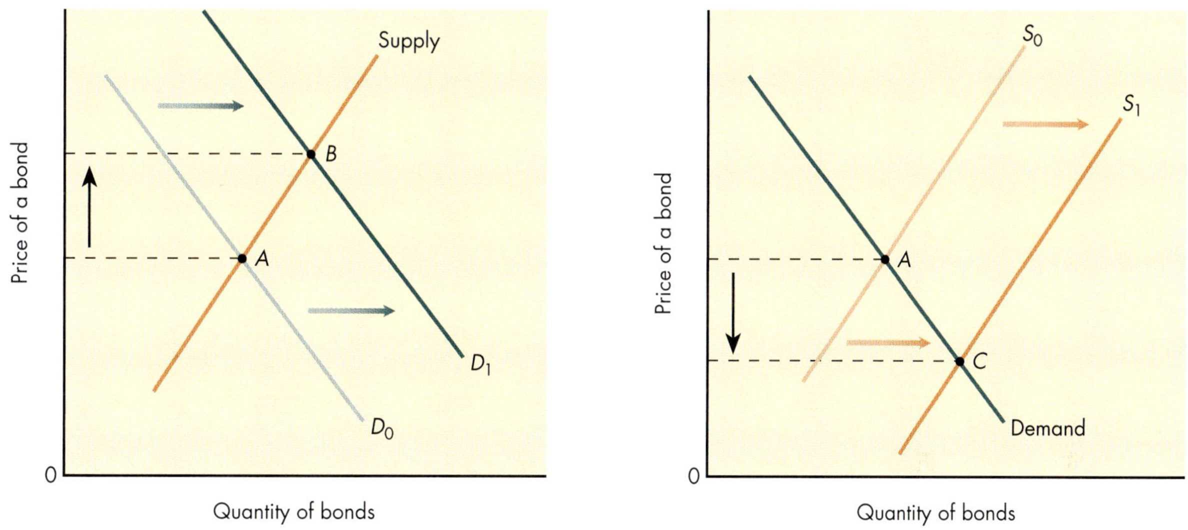

(a) An open market purchase **(b) An open market sale**

accounts at a bank. Bank cash reserves rise. Banks don't like to hold excess reserves, so they lend out the excess, thereby expanding the deposit base of the economy. The money supply rises. Thus, an open market purchase is an example of **expansionary monetary policy** (*monetary policy that tends to reduce interest rates and raise income*), since it raises the money supply (as long as the banks strive to minimize their excess reserves).

Expansionary monetary policy is monetary policy aimed at reducing interest rates and raising the level of aggregate demand.

An open market sale has the opposite effect. Here, the Fed sells bonds. In return for the bond, the Fed receives a check drawn against a bank. The bank's reserve assets are reduced (since the Fed "cashes" the check and takes the money away from the bank), and the money supply falls. That's an example of **contractionary monetary policy** (*monetary policy that tends to raise interest rates and lower income*).

Contractionary monetary policy is monetary policy aimed at increasing interest rates and thereby restraining aggregate demand.

What happens to bond prices and interest rates during this process? Figure 28-3(a) illustrates the effects of an open market purchase in which the Fed buys bonds, thereby raising the demand for bonds. Bond prices rise, and interest rates fall. To see why a rise in bond prices means a fall in interest rates, let's consider bonds more closely. Most bonds pay the bondholder a certain amount each year. If you pay $100 for a bond that pays $10 a year, you will be getting a 10 percent return on your $100. That return is the interest rate. If you had paid $200 for the bond for a $10 payment a year, your return would fall. The interest rate would fall to 5 percent [(10/200) × 100]. When the price of the bond rises, the interest rate falls.

If you were to pay less, your return would rise. When the price of a bond falls, the interest rate rises. If you paid $50 for a bond that yielded a $10 payment a year, the interest rate would be 20 percent [(10/50) × 100]. Thus, saying that the price of a bond has fallen is the same as saying that the interest rate has risen and vice versa.

In Figure 28-3(a), then, as the Fed buys bonds, the price of the bond rises and the interest rate falls. That's what we'd expect of an expansionary monetary policy.

Figure 28-3(b) shows us what happens to bond prices in an open market sale. From that you can figure out the change in interest rates. As the Fed sells bonds, the supply of bonds shifts right, leading to lower bond prices. What happens to interest rates? If you said they go up, you're on track.

Web Note 28.3
Fed Funds

The Fed Funds Market To get an even better sense of the way monetary policy works, let's look at it from the perspective of a bank. The bank will review its books, determine how many reserves it needs to meet its reserve requirement, and see if it has excess reserves or a shortage of reserves.

Say your bank didn't make as many loans as it expected to, so it has a surplus of reserves (excess reserves). Say also that another bank has made a few loans it didn't expect to make, so it has a shortage of reserves. The bank with surplus reserves can lend money to the bank with a shortage, and it can lend it overnight as **Fed funds**—*loans of excess reserves banks make to one another.* At the end of a day, a bank will look at its balances and see whether it has a shortage or surplus of reserves. If it has a surplus, it will call a Federal funds dealer to learn the **Federal funds rate**—*the interest rate banks charge one another for Fed funds*. Say the rate is 6 percent. The bank will then agree to lend its excess reserves overnight to the other bank for the daily equivalent of 6 percent per year. It's all simply done electronically, so there's no need actually to transfer funds. In the morning the money (plus overnight interest) is returned. The one-day interest rate is low, but when you're dealing with millions or billions, it adds up.

The Federal funds rate is the interest rate banks charge one another for overnight reserve loans.

The **Federal funds market,** *the market in which banks lend and borrow reserves*, is highly efficient. The Fed can reduce reserves, and thereby increase the Fed funds rate, by selling bonds. Alternatively, when the Fed buys bonds, it increases reserves, causing the Fed funds rate to fall. Generally, large city banks are borrowers of Fed funds; small country banks are lenders of Fed funds.

Figure 28-4 shows the Fed funds rate since 1990. As you can see, in 2001 and 2002 the Fed funds rate fell from 6 to 1.25 percent. I've also included the discount rate. There, you can see that until 2003 the discount rate was kept slightly lower than the Fed funds rate. In 2003 that changed and now it is kept slightly higher.

Figure 28-4 The Fed Funds Rate and the Discount Rate since 1990
The Federal Reserve Bank follows expansionary or contractionary monetary policy by targeting a lower or higher Fed funds rate. The discount rate generally follows the Fed funds rate closely.

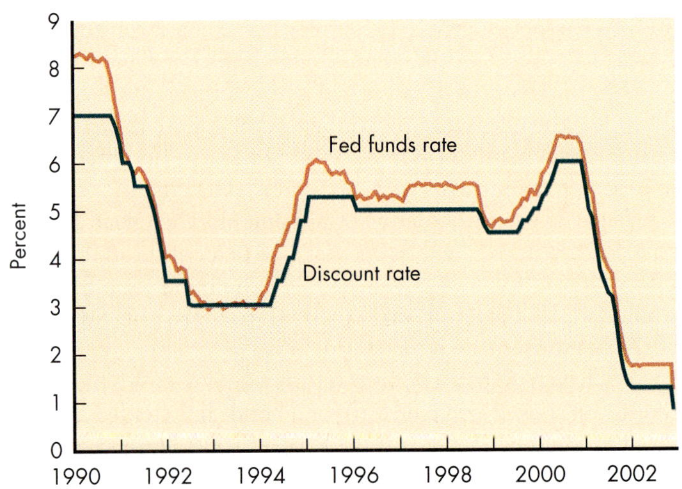

Offensive and Defensive Actions Economists keep a close eye on the Federal funds rate in determining the state of monetary policy. I mention the Federal funds rate because it is an important intermediate target of the Fed in determining what monetary policy to conduct. Remember, the Fed sets minimum reserve requirements, but the actual amount of reserves available to banks is influenced by the amount of cash people hold and excess reserves that banks may choose to hold. That changes daily. For example, say there's a storm, and businesses don't make it to the bank with their cash. Bank reserves will fall even though the Fed didn't do anything. The Fed can, and does, offset such changes—by buying and selling bonds. Such actions are called *defensive actions*. They are designed to maintain the current monetary policy. These defensive actions are to be contrasted with *offensive actions*, which are actions meant to make monetary policy have expansionary or contractionary effects on the economy.

Q-5 There's been a big storm and cash held by individuals has increased. Should the Fed buy or sell bonds? Why?

The Fed Funds Rate as an Operating Target How does the Fed decide whether its buying and selling of bonds is having the desired effect? It has to look at intermediate targets—and in recent years the Federal funds rate has been the operating target of the Fed. Thus, the Fed determines whether monetary policy is tight or loose depending on what is happening to the Federal funds rate. In practice it targets a range for that rate, and it buys and sells bonds to keep the Federal funds rate within that range. If the Federal funds rate goes above the Fed's target range, it buys bonds, which increases reserves and lowers the Federal funds rate. If the Federal funds rate goes below the Fed's target range, it sells bonds, which decreases reserves and raises the Federal funds rate.

Monetary policy affects interest rates such as the Federal funds rate. The Fed looks at the Federal funds rate to determine whether monetary policy is tight or loose.

The Complex Nature of Monetary Policy While the Fed focuses on the Fed funds rate as its operating target, it also has its eye on its ultimate targets—stable prices, acceptable employment, sustainable growth, and moderate long-term interest rates. But those ultimate targets are only indirectly affected by changes in the Fed funds rate, so the Fed watches what are called intermediate targets—consumer confidence, stock prices, interest rate spreads, housing starts, and a host of others. Thus, you can think of monetary policy as a complicated game of dominoes in which the Fed affects one variable (its operating target) to affect another set of variables (its intermediate targets) to affect yet another set of variables (its ultimate targets). Small wonder that the Fed often doesn't have the precise effect it wants.

The following diagram summarizes the tools and targets of the Fed:

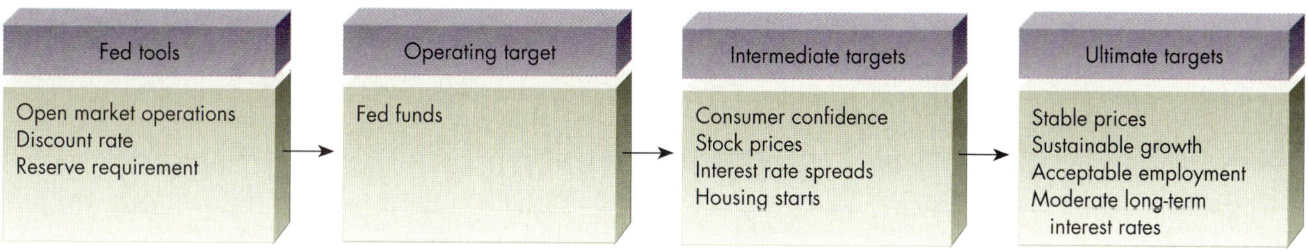

The Taylor Rule Stanford economist John Taylor has summarized a rule that, in the late 1990s and early 2000s, described Fed policy relatively well. The rule, which has become known as the **Taylor rule,** can be stated as follows: *Set the Fed funds rate at 2 percent plus current inflation if the economy is at desired output and desired inflation. If the inflation rate is higher than desired, increase the Fed funds rate by .5 times the difference between desired and actual inflation. Similarly, if output is higher than desired, increase the Fed funds rate by .5 times the percentage deviation.*

Q-6 If inflation is 1 percent and the Fed wants 2 percent inflation and output is 2 percent below potential, what would the Taylor rule predict for a Fed funds rate target?

Formally the Taylor rule is

Fed funds rate = 2 percent + Current inflation
+ 0.5 × (actual inflation less desired inflation)
+ 0.5 × (percent deviation of aggregate output from potential)

Let's consider an example. Say that inflation is 2 percent and that the Fed wants 0 percent inflation, and that aggregate output exceeds potential by 1 percent. That means that the Fed would set the Fed funds rate at 5.5 percent [2 + 2 + .5(2 − 0) + .5(1)]. As another example, say that the economy is 1 percent over potential output, inflation is 2 percent, which is equal to the target rate, as it was in late 2000 and early 2001. The Taylor rule predicted that the Fed would set the Fed funds rate at 4.5 percent. Instead, it targeted a 6 percent rate. Then, in 2001, the Fed lowered the Fed funds rate significantly, even though inflation was on target, and output was only slightly below potential output, as the Fed attempted to avoid a recession. As these examples show, Fed policy is much more complicated than the Taylor rule, but the rule is a useful first approximation for predicting Fed policy.

Fed Response to September 11

The Fed's response to the September 11, 2001, terrorist attacks illustrates Fed operations well. The attacks on the World Trade Center and the Pentagon disrupted the U.S. payment and financial systems and threatened U.S. economic well-being. The Fed acted both defensively and offensively. In defensive actions, it provided needed short-term liquidity. On September 12, to make sure banks had the cash they needed for their customers, the Fed (1) doubled its holdings of repurchase agreements to $61 billion; (2) increased discount window lending to $45 billion (nearly 1,000 times the average daily lending), urged banks to restructure loans, and promised additional funds if needed; and (3) established "swap lines" with foreign banks to temporarily exchange currencies to ensure foreign currency liquidity.

In offensive actions to address the longer-term economic effects of the attacks, on September 17 the FOMC directed the open market desk to reduce the Fed funds rate by ½ percentage point to 3 percent. It did so by buying bonds, which added reserves to the market. The Fed continued to cut the Fed funds rate by 1¼ percentage points by the end of 2001. Expansionary monetary policy lessened the negative impact of the attacks on an economy already in recession.

Monetary Policy in the *AS/AD* Model

In the *AS/AD* model, monetary policy works primarily through its effect on interest rates. As the Fed changes the monetary base, the interest rate changes. Increasing reserves increases the amount of money banks have to lend. To attract borrowers, banks offer lower interest rates. Lower interest rates lead businesses to borrow more, expanding investment expenditures, which increases aggregate demand. Decreasing reserves reduces the amount of money banks have available for loans and increases the interest rate. Higher interest rates lead businesses to borrow less, and to decrease investment expenditures, which decreases aggregate demand.

Through the multiplier effects, aggregate demand and equilibrium income decrease by a multiple of the decrease in investment. Figure 28-5(a) shows the effect of a fall in investment on equilibrium income. A decrease in investment shifts the *AD* curve to the

Figure 28-5 (a and b) Contractionary and Expansionary Monetary Policy
With a decrease in the money supply, the interest rate will rise, decreasing investment. The fall in investment shifts the aggregate demand curve from AD_0 to AD_1. Income decreases from Y_0 to Y_1, as shown in (**a**), which decreases savings sufficiently so that savings equal investment. In (**b**), expansionary monetary policy is shown working the opposite way. It shifts the *AD* curve to the right, from AD_0 to AD_1. Income increases from Y_0 to Y_1.

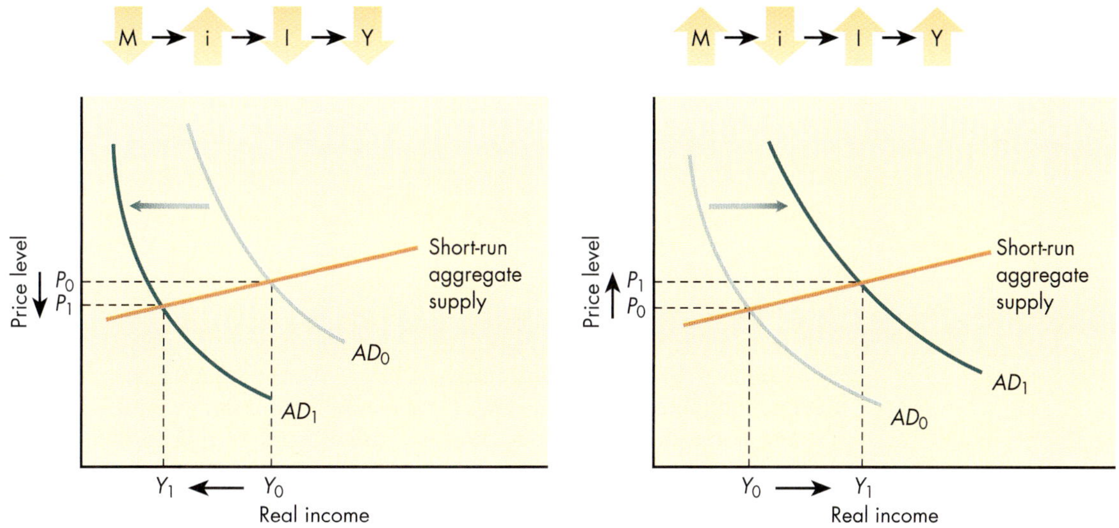

(a) Contractionary monetary policy **(b) Expansionary monetary policy**

left by a multiple of the decline in investment. Thus, *contractionary monetary policy* tends to *decrease* the money supply, *increase* the interest rate, *decrease* investment, and *decrease* income and output:

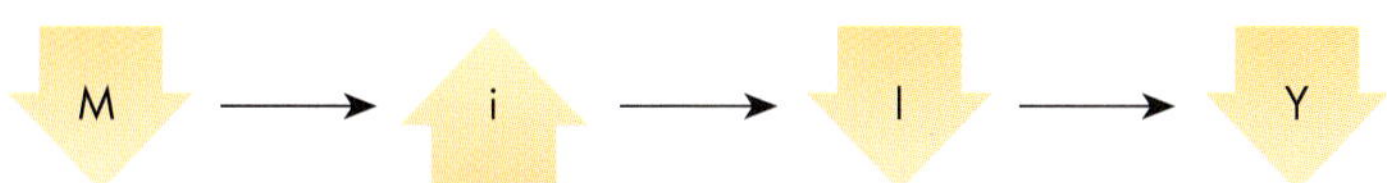

Expansionary monetary policy works in the opposite manner, as Figure 28-5(b) shows. *Expansionary* monetary policy tends to *increase* the money supply, *decrease* the interest rate, *increase* investment, and *increase* income and output:

Q-7 Demonstrate the effect of expansionary monetary policy in the *AS/AD* model.

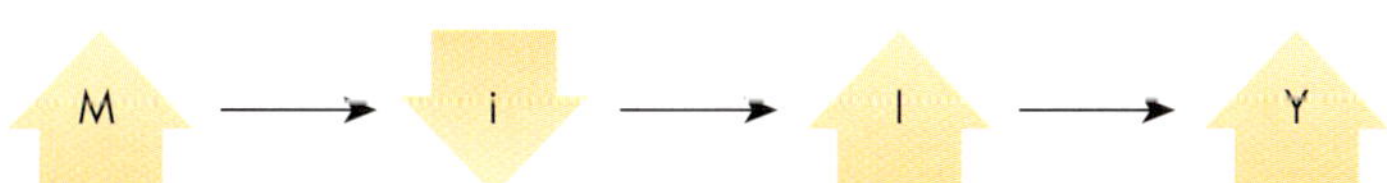

To be sure you've got it, let's try an example of monetary policy with numbers. In this scenario, we want to determine what open market operation the Fed should execute to increase output by $750 billion. You know it must increase the money supply, but to figure out how much requires knowing the relationship between the variables involved. Suppose the reserve requirement is .2, people do not hold cash, and banks have no excess reserves. Further, suppose that for every $250 billion increase in the money supply, the interest rate falls 1 percentage point and investment expenditures rise by $100 billion for every percentage-point drop in interest rates. Finally, the expenditures multiplier is 3 and the economy is far below potential. To achieve its ultimate target (increase output by $750), the Fed uses one of its tools (open market operations) to change an intermediate target (interest rates). Let's see how.

Working backward, because the expenditures multiplier is 3, the Fed wants investment expenditures to rise by $250 billion (750/3). For investment expenditures to rise by that much, the interest rate must fall by 2.5 percentage points (250/100). The Fed must increase the money supply by $625 billion (2.5 × 250). To calculate how many bonds to sell, it divides the desired increase in the money supply ($625) by the multiplier, 5, (1/.2) to arrive at an open market sale of bonds worth $125 billion.

Let's go through the reasoning again, only this time focusing on trying to provide an intuitive feel for what is happening. Say the Fed uses open market operations. As the Fed either injects or pulls out reserves, it influences the amount of money banks have to lend and the interest rate at which they can lend it. When banks have more reserves than required, they want to lend. (That's how they make their profit.) To get people to borrow more from them, banks will decrease the interest rate they charge on loans. So expansionary monetary policy tends to decrease the interest rate banks charge their customers; contractionary policy tends to increase the interest rate banks charge customers. Expansionary monetary policy increases the amount of money banks have to lend, which tends to increase investment and leads to an increase in income. Contractionary monetary policy decreases the amount of money banks have to lend, which tends to decrease investment and leads to a decrease in income.

Monetary Policy in the Circular Flow

Figure 28-6's familiar circular flow diagram shows how monetary policy works in the *AS/AD* model. It works inside the financial sector to help equate the flow of saving with investment. When the economy is operating at too low a level of income and when saving exceeds investment, in the absence of monetary policy, income will fall. Expansionary monetary policy tries to channel more saving into investment so the fall in income is stopped. It does so by increasing the available credit, lowering the interest rate, and increasing investment and hence income.

Contractionary monetary policy is called for when saving is smaller than investment and the economy is operating at too high a level of income, causing inflationary pressures. In this case, monetary policy tries to restrict the demand for investment and consumer loans.

The Emphasis on the Interest Rate

Because in the *AS/AD* model monetary policy works through the effect of interest rates on investment, our analysis focuses on the interest rate in judging monetary policy. A rising interest rate indicates a tightening of monetary policy. A falling interest rate indicates a loosening of monetary policy.

A natural conclusion is that the Fed should target interest rates in setting monetary policy. For example, if the interest rate is currently 6 percent and the Fed wants to loosen monetary policy, it should buy bonds until the interest rate falls to, say, 5.5 percent. If it wants to tighten monetary policy, it should sell bonds to make the interest rate go up to, say, 6.5 percent.

There is a problem in using interest rates to measure whether monetary policy is contractionary or expansionary. That problem is the real/nominal interest rate problem.

Figure 28-6 Monetary Policy in the Circular Flow
If monetary and fiscal policy are needed, it is because the financial sector is, in some ways, clogged and is not correctly translating saving into investment. Monetary policy works to unclog the financial sector. Fiscal policy provides an alternative route for saving around the financial sector. A government deficit absorbs excess saving and translates it back into the spending stream. A surplus supplements the shortage of saving and reduces the flow back into the spending stream.

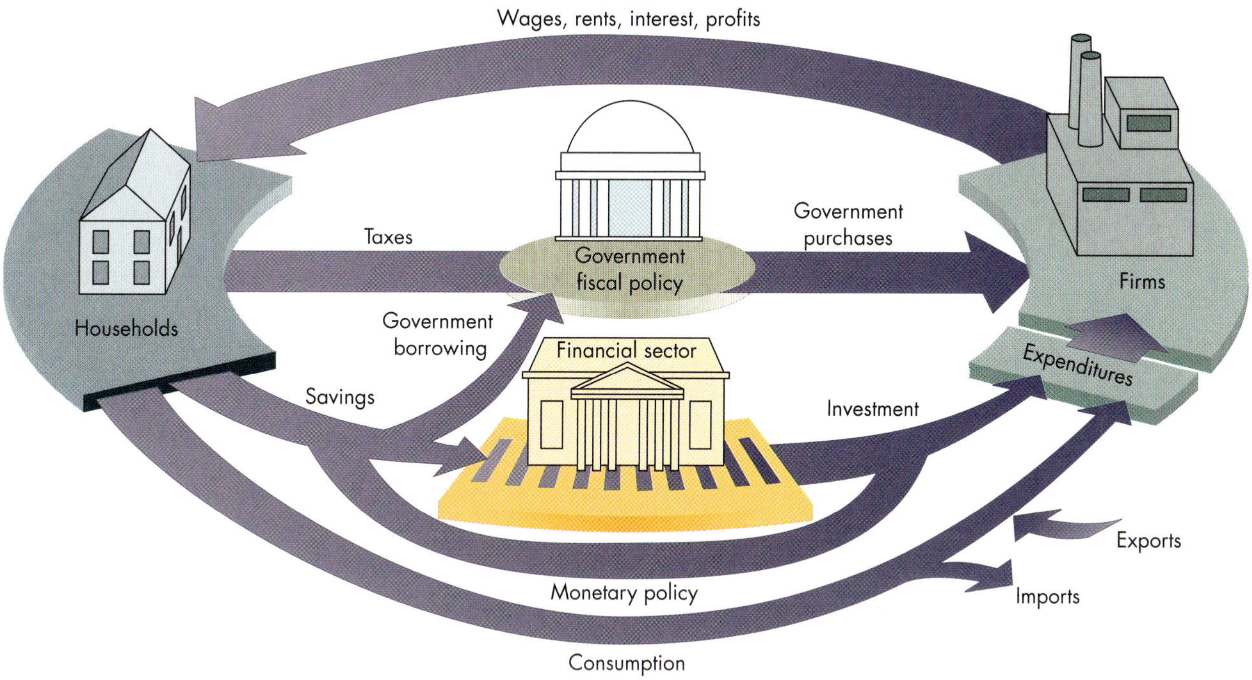

Nominal interest rates are *the rates you actually see and pay*. When a bank pays 7 percent interest, that 7 percent is a nominal interest rate. What affects the economy is the real interest rate. **Real interest rates** are *nominal interest rates adjusted for expected inflation*.

For example, say you get 7 percent interest from the bank, but the price level goes up 7 percent. At the end of the year you have $107 instead of $100, but you're no better off than before because the price level has risen—on average, things cost 7 percent more. What you would have paid $100 for last year now costs $107. (That's the definition of *inflation*.) Had the price level remained constant, and had you received 0 percent interest, you'd be in the equivalent position to receiving 7 percent interest on your $100 when the price level rises by 7 percent. That 0 percent is the *real interest rate*. It is the interest rate you would expect to receive if the price level remains constant.

Q-8 If the nominal interest rate is 10 percent and expected inflation is 3 percent, what is the real interest rate?

The real interest rate cannot be observed because it depends on expected inflation. To calculate the real interest rate, you must subtract what you believe to be the expected rate of inflation from the nominal interest rate. For example, if the nominal interest rate is 7 percent and expected inflation is 4 percent, the real interest rate is 3 percent. The relationship between real and nominal interest rates is important both for your study of economics and for your own personal finances:

Nominal interest rate = Real interest rate + Expected inflation rate

Real and Nominal Interest Rates and Monetary Policy

Q.9 How does the distinction between nominal and real interest rates add uncertainty to the effect of monetary policy on the economy?

What does this distinction between nominal and real interest rates mean for monetary policy? It adds yet another uncertainty to the effect of monetary policy. In the *AS/AD* model we assumed that expansionary monetary policy lowers the interest rate and contractionary monetary policy increases the interest rate. However, if the expansionary monetary policy leads to expectations of increased inflation, expansionary monetary policy can increase nominal interest rates (the ones you see) and leave real interest rates (the ones that affect borrowing decisions) unchanged. Why? Because of expectations of increasing inflation. Lenders will want to be compensated for the inflation (which will decrease the value of the money they receive back) and will push the nominal interest rate up to get the desired real rate of interest.

The distinction between nominal and real interest rates and the possible effect of monetary policy on expectations of inflation has led most economists to conclude that a monetary regime, not a monetary policy, is the best approach to policy. A **monetary regime** is *a predetermined statement of the policy that will be followed in various situations*. A monetary policy, in contrast, is a response to events; it is chosen without a predetermined framework.

Monetary regimes are now favored because rules can help generate the expectations that even though in certain instances the Fed is increasing the money supply, that increase is not a signal that monetary expansion and inflation are imminent. The monetary regime that the Fed currently uses involves feedback rules that center on the Federal funds rate. If inflation is above its target, the Fed raises the Federal funds rate (by selling bonds, thereby decreasing the money supply) in an attempt to slow inflation down. If inflation is below its target, and if the economy is going into a recession, the Fed lowers the Fed funds rate (by buying bonds, thereby increasing the money supply). The Taylor rule discussed above is a quantification of this general feedback rule.

Problems in the Conduct of Monetary Policy

Six problems of monetary policy:

1. Knowing what policy to use.
2. Understanding what policy you're using.
3. Lags in monetary policy.
4. Liquidity traps.
5. Political pressure.
6. Conflicting international goals.

Now that you've been through the structure and mechanics of monetary policy, let's consider the problems with using it. These include knowing what policy to use, understanding what policy you're using, lags in monetary policy, liquidity traps, political pressure, and conflicting international goals.

Knowing What Policy to Use

Web Note 28.4
The Beige Book

To use monetary policy effectively, you must know the potential level of income. Otherwise you won't know whether to use expansionary or contractionary monetary policy. Let's consider an example: mid-1991. The economy seemed to be coming out of a recession. The Fed had to figure out whether to use expansionary monetary policy to speed up and guarantee the recovery, or use contractionary monetary policy and make sure inflation didn't start up again. Initially the Fed tried to fight inflation, only to discover that the economy wasn't coming out of the recession. In early 1992, the Fed switched from contractionary to expansionary monetary policy. It continued that policy through 1994, when fears of inflation caused it to start tightening the money supply slightly. In early 2000 the Fed was again trying to decide whether to follow expansionary or contractionary policy. It decided to contract the money supply but quickly changed its stance when the economy slowed in 2001. It stood ready to return to a more contractionary monetary policy stance at the first sign of inflationary pressures. As these examples show, monetary policy is an art. The need for expansionary or contractionary policy can change quickly.

Understanding the Policy You're Using

To use monetary policy effectively, you must know whether the monetary policy you're using is expansionary or contractionary. You might think that's rather easy, but it isn't. In our consideration of monetary policy tools, you saw that the Fed doesn't directly control the money supply. It indirectly controls it, generally through open market operations by changing the *monetary base* (the vault cash and reserves banks have at the Fed). Then the money multiplier determines the amounts of M_1, M_2, and other monetary measures in the economy.

The Fed only indirectly controls the monetary base.

That money multiplier is influenced by the amount of cash that people hold as well as the lending process at the bank. Neither of those is the stable number that we used in calculating the money multipliers. They change from day to day and week to week, so even if you control the monetary base, you can never be sure exactly what will happen to M_1 and M_2 in the short run. Moreover, the effects on M_1 and M_2 can differ; one measure is telling you that you're expanding the money supply and the other measure is telling you you're contracting it.

Because money aggregates as a measure of monetary policy have become unreliable, the Fed officially stopped targeting them in 2000. Instead, it focuses on interest rates. Interest rates, however, have problems of their own. If interest rates rise, is it because of expected inflation (which is adding an inflation premium to the nominal interest rate) or is it the real interest rate that is going up? There is frequent debate over which it is. Combined, these measurement problems make the Fed often wonder not only about what policy it should follow but also what policy it is following.

Lags in Monetary Policy

Monetary policy, like fiscal policy, takes time to work its way through the economic system. First the Fed must recognize what the situation in the economy is. That isn't easy because often the data are ambiguous. Some statistics suggest the economy is expanding; some statistics suggest it is contracting. Then, the FOMC must develop a consensus for action, and change the Fed funds target. The Fed funds rate only affects overnight loans, the interest rates that affect the economy are longer-term interest rates such as mortgage rates, business loan rates, and long-term bond rates. These change more slowly, adding more time to the lag. Once the long-term rates have changed, businesses and individuals have to change their plans in response to the interest rate change; such changes are often difficult, adding yet another lag to the process. So it can often be months before the monetary policy affects spending significantly.

Liquidity Trap

Another problem in the use of monetary policy is known as a **liquidity trap**—*a situation in which increasing reserves does not increase the money supply, but simply leads to excess reserves*. A liquidity trap occurs when individuals believe that interest rates are much more likely to rise than to fall. If interest rates rise, bond prices fall, which means that bond holders lose money, so individuals want to hold cash rather than bonds. This means that increases in reserves do not affect interest rates, and do not affect borrowing. This is what happened in Japan in the late 1990s and early 2000s. The Bank of Japan (the Japanese central bank) lowered the interest rate (the one similar to the Fed funds rate in the United States) to 0.01 percent with little effect on investment spending. The belief that increases in the money supply would be ineffective in the 1930s led early Keynesians to focus on fiscal policy rather than monetary policy as a way of expanding the economy. They likened expansionary monetary policy to pushing on a string. The same problem exists with using contractionary monetary policy. Banks have been very good at figuring out ways to circumvent cuts in the money supply, making the intended results of contractionary monetary policy difficult to achieve.

Political Pressure

While the Fed is partially insulated from political pressure by its structure, it's not totally insulated. Presidents place enormous pressure on the Fed to use expansionary monetary policy (especially during an election year) and blame the Fed for any recession. When interest rates rise, the Fed takes the pressure, and if any members of the Board of Governors are politically aligned with the president, they find it difficult to persist in contractionary policy when the economy is in a recession.

One way central banks have tried to avoid that political pressure is through inflation targeting, where they set an inflation target they are required to meet. This means that their reaction to events is prescribed before the event, and the central banks can blame the inflation targeting rule they have to follow, rather than taking the blame themselves. The hope is that setting the target will add credibility to the policy and convince people that inflation will not occur, thereby reducing inflationary expectations and inflationary pressures. The problem is that if the policy is not believed, or if the wrong inflation target is chosen, the existence of the target can either limit the central banks' response or force the central banks to abandon their target, which can reduce rather than enhance credibility.

Conflicting International Goals

Q-10 What are six problems in the conduct of monetary policy?

Monetary policy is not conducted in a vacuum. It is conducted in an international arena and must be coordinated with other governments' monetary policy. Similarly, as we'll see in Chapter 34, monetary policy affects the exchange rate and trade balance. Often the desired monetary policy for its international effects is the opposite of the desired monetary policy for its domestic effects.

Conclusion

The Fed can influence, not steer, the economy.

I could continue with a discussion of the problems of using monetary policy, but the above should give you a good sense that conducting monetary policy is not a piece of cake. It takes not only a sense of the theory but also a feel for the economy. In short, the conduct of monetary policy is not a science. It does not allow the Fed to steer the economy as it might steer a car. It does work well enough to allow the Fed to *influence* the economy—much as an expert rodeo rider rides a bronco bull.

Summary

- Monetary policy is the policy of influencing the economy through changes in the banking system's reserves that affect the money supply and credit availability in the economy.

- The Fed is a central bank; it conducts monetary policy for the United States and regulates financial institutions.
- The three tools of monetary policy are:
    1. Changing the reserve requirement.
    2. Changing the discount rate.
    3. Open market operations.
- A change in reserves changes the money supply by the change in reserves times the money multiplier.
- Open market operations are the Fed's most important tool:
  To expand the money supply, the Fed buys bonds.
  To contract the money supply, the Fed sells bonds.
- The Federal Open Market Committee (FOMC) makes the actual decisions about monetary policy.
- When the Fed buys bonds, the price of bonds rises and interest rates fall. When the Fed sells bonds, the price of bonds falls and interest rates rise.
- The Taylor rule is a feedback rule that states: Set the Fed funds rate at 2 plus current inflation plus one-half the difference between actual and desired inflation plus one-half the percent difference between actual and potential output.
- In the *AS/AD* model, contractionary monetary policy works as follows:
  $M\downarrow \rightarrow i\uparrow \rightarrow I\downarrow \rightarrow Y\downarrow$
- Expansionary monetary policy works as follows:
  $M\uparrow \rightarrow i\downarrow \rightarrow I\uparrow \rightarrow Y\uparrow$
- Because in the *AS/AD* model, monetary policy affects the economy through the effect of a change in the interest rate on investment, the interest rate is an indication of the direction of monetary policy. A higher interest rate indicates contractionary monetary policy; a lower interest rate indicates expansionary monetary policy.
- Nominal interest rates are the interest rates we see and pay. Real interest rates are nominal interest rates adjusted for expected inflation: Nominal interest rate = Real interest rate + Expected inflation.
- Because monetary policy can affect inflation expectations as well as nominal interest rates, the effect of monetary policy on interest rates can be uncertain. This uncertainty has led the Fed to follow monetary regimes.
- Problems of monetary policy include knowing what policy to use, knowing what policy you are using, lags, liquidity traps, political pressure, and conflicting international goals.

Key Terms

central bank *(659)*
contractionary monetary policy *(669)*
discount rate *(667)*
expansionary monetary policy *(669)*
Fed funds *(670)*
Federal funds market *(670)*
Federal funds rate *(670)*
Federal Open Market Committee (FOMC) *(661)*
liquidity trap *(677)*
monetary base *(664)*
monetary policy *(659)*
monetary regime *(676)*
nominal interest rates *(675)*
open market operations *(667)*
real interest rates *(675)*
reserve requirement *(665)*
Taylor rule *(671)*

Questions for Thought and Review

1. Is the Fed a private or a public agency?
2. Why are there few regional Fed banks in the western part of the United States?
3. What are the six explicit functions of the Fed?
4. Name the three tools the Fed has to affect the money supply and explain how the Fed would use each tool to increase the money supply.
5. What happens to interest rates and the price of bonds when the Fed buys bonds?
6. Define the *Federal funds rate* and explain why it is the interest rate that the Fed most directly controls.
7. If the Federal Reserve announces a change in the direction of monetary policy, is it describing an offensive or defensive action? Explain your answer.
8. You can lead a horse to water, but you can't make it drink. How might this adage be relevant to expansionary (as opposed to contractionary) monetary policy?
9. Investment increases by 20 for each interest rate drop of 1 percent. The expenditures multiplier is 3. If the money

multiplier is 4, and each change of 5 in the money supply changes the interest rate by 1 percent, what open market policy would you recommend to increase income by 240?

10. If the nominal interest rate is 6 percent and inflation is 5 percent, what's the real interest rate?
11. "The effects of open market operations are somewhat like a stone cast in a pond." After the splash, discuss the first three ripples.
12. Why would a bank hold Treasury bills as secondary reserves when it could simply hold primary reserves—cash?
13. The table below gives the Fed funds rate target at the end of each year shown.

Year	Federal Funds Target Rate
1999	5.5%
2000	6.0
2001	1.75
2002	1.25

Using these figures, describe how the monetary policy directions changed from 1999 through 2002.

14. Target inflation is 2 percent; actual inflation is 3 percent. Output equals potential output. What does the Taylor rule predict will be the Fed funds rate?
15. Explain the relationship between tools, operating targets, intermediate targets, and ultimate targets. Give examples of each.

Problems and Exercises

1. Demonstrate the effect of expansionary monetary policy in the *AS*/*AD* model when the economy is:
   a. Below potential output.
   b. Significantly above potential output.
2. The Fed wants to increase the money supply (which is currently 4,000) by 200. The money multiplier is 3 and people hold no cash. For each 1 percentage point the discount rate falls, banks borrow an additional 20. Explain how the Fed can achieve its goals using the following tools:
   a. Change the reserve requirement.
   b. Change the discount rate.
   c. Use open market operations.
3. Suppose the Fed decides it needs to pursue an expansionary policy. Assume people hold no cash, the reserve requirement is 20 percent, and there are no excess reserves.
   a. Show how the Fed would increase the money supply by $2 million by changing the reserve requirement.
   b. Show how the Fed would increase the money supply by $2 million through open market operations.
4. Suppose the Fed decides that it needs to pursue a contractionary policy. It wants to decrease the money supply by $2 million. Assume people hold 20 percent of their money in the form of cash balances, the reserve requirement is 20 percent, and there are no excess reserves.
   a. Show how the Fed would decrease the money supply by $2 million by changing the reserve requirement.
   b. Show how the Fed would decrease the money supply by $2 million through open market operations.
   c. Go to your local bank and find out how much excess reserves it holds. Recalculate *a* and *b* assuming all banks held that percentage in excess reserves.
5. Some individuals have suggested raising the required reserve ratio for banks to 100 percent.
   a. What would the money multiplier be if this change were made?
   b. What effect would such a change have on the money supply?
   c. How could that effect be offset?
   d. Would banks likely favor or oppose this proposal? Why?
6. One of the proposals to reform monetary policy has been to have the central bank pay interest on reserves held at the bank.
   a. What effect would that proposal have on excess reserves?
   b. Would banks generally favor or oppose this proposal? Why?
   c. Would central banks generally favor or oppose this proposal? Why?
   d. What effect would this proposal probably have on interest rates paid by banks?
7. State the Taylor rule. What does the rule predict will happen to the Fed funds rate in each of the following situations?

a. Inflation is 2 percent, the inflation target is 3 percent, and output is 2 percent below potential.
b. Inflation is 4 percent, the inflation target is 2 percent, and output is 3 percent above potential.
c. Inflation is 4 percent, the inflation target is 3 percent, and output is 2 percent below potential.

8. Congratulations! You have been approved adviser to the Federal Reserve Bank.
   a. The Federal Open Market Committee decides that it must increase the money supply by 60. Committee members tell you the reserve ratio is .1 and the cash-to-deposit ratio is .3. They ask you what directive they should give to the open market desk. You tell them, being as specific as possible, using the real-world money multiplier.
   b. They ask you for two other ways they could have achieved the same end. You tell them.
   c. Based on the quantity theory of money, tell them what you think the effect on the price level of your policy will be.

Web Questions

1. Go to the Federal Reserve's home page at www.federalreserve.gov.
   a. Who is the chairman of the board? For how long has he or she served?
   b. Who are the governors of the board?
   c. The site publishes a short biography for each governor. What experience and/or degrees do all members have? What experiences and/or degrees differ among members?
2. The Federal Reserve Bank publishes a report called the Beige Book eight times a year that summarizes the current economic conditions in each of the 12 bank districts. This report is used by the Federal Open Market Committee when deciding on monetary policy. Go to www.federalreserve.gov/fomc to read the most recent Beige Book and answer the following questions:
   a. Report the recent conditions of consumer spending, labor markets, wages and prices, and industrial activity.
   b. What is the most recent monetary policy action taken by the FOMC?
   c. Based on your answer to *a* and *b*, what monetary policy action do you recommend the FOMC take at its next meeting?

Answers to Margin Questions

1. The president of the United States appoints the chairman of the Board of Governors of the Federal Reserve System. *(661)*
2. Monetary policy is conducted by the Fed and involves changing the money supply or interest rates. Fiscal policy is conducted by the U.S. Treasury, or government, and involves running a surplus or deficit. *(661)*
3. False. The Fed sets the discount rate. *(667)*
4. The other tools of monetary policy are changing the discount rate and changing the reserve requirement. *(668)*
5. The Fed should buy bonds to offset the unintended decline in reserves. *(671)*
6. The Taylor rule predicts a Fed funds rate target of 1.5 percent. *(672)*
7. Expansionary monetary policy makes more money available to banks for loan. Banks lower their interest rates to attract more borrowers. With lower interest rates businesses will borrow more money and increase investment expenditures. The multiplier shifts the *AD* curve to the right by a multiple of the increase in investment expenditures. Real output increases to Y_1, and the price level rises to P_1. What ultimately happens to output and the price level depends on where the economy is relative to potential. *(673)*

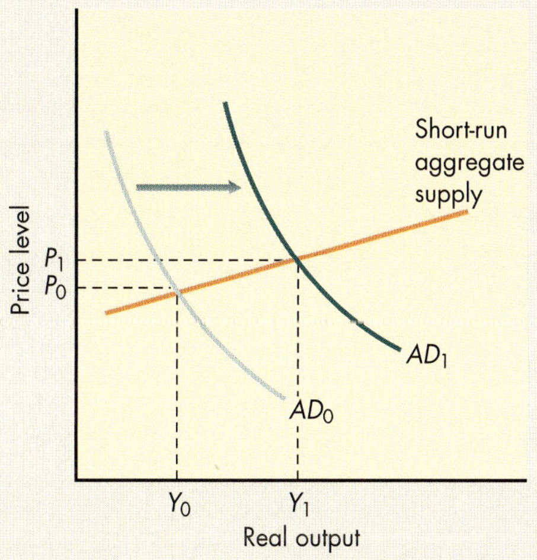

8. The real interest rate is 7 percent, the nominal interest rate (10) less expected inflation (3). *(675)*

9. Because expansionary monetary policy can lead to expectations of higher inflation, expansionary monetary policy can lead to higher nominal interest rates. Because real interest rates cannot be observed directly, interest rates are not always a good guide for the direction of monetary policy. *(676)*
10. Six problems of monetary policy are:
    1. Knowing what policy to use.
    2. Understanding what policy you're using.
    3. The lags in monetary policy.
    4. Liquidity traps.
    5. Political pressure.
    6. Conflicting international goals. *(678)*

APPENDIX A

The Effect of Monetary Policy Using T-Accounts

The Fed uses the discount rate, the reserve requirement, and open market operations to change the money supply. Each of these tools works initially by affecting the amount of reserves in the banking system. Here I will show you exactly how the Fed changes the money supply using T-accounts. To simplify things, say there's only one bank, Textland Bank, with branches all over the country. Textland is fully loaned out at a 10 percent reserve requirement. For simplicity, assume people hold no cash. Textland's beginning balance sheet is presented below in Table A28-1.

Now say the Fed sells $10,000 worth of Treasury bonds to individuals. The person who buys them pays with a check to the Fed for $10,000. The Fed, in turn, presents that check to the bank, getting $10,000 in cash from the bank. This step is shown in Table A28-2.

Table A28-1 Textland Bank Balance Sheet

Beginning Balance			
Assets		Liabilities and Net Worth	
Cash (reserves)	$ 300,000	Demand deposits	$3,000,000
Loans	2,000,000	Net worth	1,000,000
Treasury bonds	400,000		
Property	1,300,000		
Total assets	$4,000,000	Total liabilities and net worth	$4,000,000

Table A28-2

Transaction 1					
Assets			Liabilities and Net Worth		
Cash (reserves)	$ 300,000		Demand deposits	$3,000,000	
Payment to Fed (person's Treasury purchase)	(10,000)		Deposits for cash (person's check)	(10,000)	
Total cash		$ 290,000	Total deposits		$2,990,000
Loans		2,000,000	Net worth		1,000,000
Treasury bonds		400,000			
Property		1,300,000			
Total assets		$3,990,000	Total liabilities and net worth		$3,990,000

Table A28-3

Transaction 2				
Assets			**Liabilities and Net Worth**	
Cash (reserves)	$ 290,000		Demand deposits	$2,990,000
Loans (repaid)	9,000		Net worth	1,000,000
Total cash		$ 299,000		
Loans	2,000,000			
Loans called in	(9,000)			
Total loans		1,991,000		
Treasury bonds		400,000		
Property		1,300,000		
Total assets		$3,990,000	Total liabilities and net worth	$3,990,000

As you can see, bank reserves are now $290,000, which is too low to meet requirements on demand deposits of $2,990,000. With a 10 percent reserve requirement, $2,990,000 in deposits would require $\frac{1}{10} \times \$2,990,000 = \$299,000$, so the bank is $9,000 short of reserves. It must figure out a way to meet its reserve requirement. Let's say that it calls in $9,000 of its loans. After doing so it has assets of $299,000 in cash and $2,990,000 in demand deposits, so it looks as if the bank has met its reserve requirement.

If the bank could meet its reserve requirement that way, its balance sheet would be as shown in Table A28-3. Loans would decrease by $9,000 and cash would increase by the $9,000 necessary to meet the reserve requirement.

Unfortunately for the bank, meeting its reserve requirement isn't that easy. That $9,000 in cash had to come from somewhere. Most likely, the person who paid off the loans in cash did it partly by running down her checking account, borrowing all the cash she could from others, and using whatever other options she had. Since by assumption in this example, people don't hold cash, the banking system was initially fully loaned out, and Textland Bank was the only bank, the only cash in the economy was in Textland Bank's vaults! So that $9,000 in cash had to come from its vaults. Calling in the loans cannot directly solve its reserve problem. It still has reserves of only $290,000.

But calling in its loans did *indirectly* help solve the problem. Calling in loans decreased investment which, because it decreased aggregate demand, decreased the income in the economy. (If you're not sure why this is the case, think back to the macro policy model.) That decrease in income decreases the amount of demand deposits people want to hold. As demand deposits decrease, the bank's need for reserves decreases.

Contraction of the money supply in this example works in the opposite way to an expansion of the money supply. Banks keep trying to meet their reserve requirement by getting cash, only to find that for the banking system as a whole the total cash is limited. Thus, the banking system as a whole must continue to call in loans until that decline in loans causes income to fall sufficiently to cause demand deposits to fall to a level that can be supported by the smaller reserves. In this example, with a money multiplier of 10, when demand deposits have fallen by $100,000 to $2.9 million, total reserves available to the system ($290,000) will be sufficient to meet the reserve requirement.

Questions for Thought and Review

1. Demonstrate, using T-accounts, the effect of the Fed selling $1 million of Treasury bonds when the reserve requirement is 10 percent and people hold no cash.
2. Demonstrate, using T-accounts, the effect of the Fed buying $2 million of Treasury bonds when the reserve requirement is 10 percent and people hold no cash.

29 INFLATION AND ITS RELATIONSHIP TO UNEMPLOYMENT AND GROWTH

After reading this chapter, you should be able to:

- State some of the distributional effects of inflation.
- Explain how inflation expectations are formed.
- Outline the quantity theory of money and its theory of inflation.
- Outline the institutionalist theory of inflation.
- Differentiate between long-run and short-run Phillips curves.
- Explain the different views on the relationship between inflation and growth.

The first few months or years of inflation, like the first few drinks, seem just fine. Everyone has more money to spend and prices aren't rising quite as fast as the money that's available. The hangover comes when prices start to catch up.

—*Milton Friedman*

Politicians tend to get reelected when the economy is doing well. Thus, it should not surprise you that political pressures exert a strong bias toward expansionary policy. What prevents politicians from implementing the expansionary policies is inflation, or at least the fear of generating an accelerating inflation. It is for that reason that inflation and its relationship to unemployment and growth come to center stage in any discussion of macro policy. Hence this chapter. It extends our earlier consideration of inflation and considers the trade-offs between inflation, unemployment, and growth.

SOME BASICS ABOUT INFLATION

I introduced you to inflation in an earlier chapter. There, you saw the definition of *inflation* (a continuous rise in the price level) and how inflation is measured (with price indexes). I also explained that expectations of inflation can become built into individuals' behavior and economic institutions and cause a small inflation to accelerate, and that inflation creates feelings of injustice and destroys the informational value of prices and the market. (If any of those concepts seem a bit vague to you, a review might be a good idea.) I now build on that information to give you more insight into inflation.

THE DISTRIBUTIONAL EFFECTS OF INFLATION

Who wins and who loses in an inflation? The answer to that is simple: The winners are people who can raise their wages or prices and still keep their jobs or sell their goods. The losers are people who can't raise their wages or prices. Consider a worker who has entered a contract to receive 4 percent annual wage increases for three years. If the worker expected inflation to be 2 percent at the time of the agreement, she was expecting her real wage to rise 2 percent each year. If instead inflation is 6 percent, her real wage will *fall* 2 percent. The worker loses, but the firm gains because it can charge 4 percent more for its products than it anticipated. The worker's wage was fixed by contract, but the firm could raise its prices. On average, winners and losers balance out; inflation does not make the population richer or poorer. Most people, however, worry about their own position, not what happens to the average person.

Q-1 True or false? Inflation makes an economy poorer. Explain your answer.

Lenders and borrowers, because they often enter into fixed nominal contracts, are also affected by inflation. If lenders make loans at 5 percent interest and expect inflation to be 2 percent, they plan to earn a 3 percent real rate of return on their loan. If, however, inflation turns out to be 4 percent, lenders will only earn a 1 percent real rate of return, and borrowers, who were expecting to pay a real interest rate of 3 percent, end up paying only 1 percent. Lenders will lose; borrowers will gain. In other words, unexpected inflation redistributes income from lenders to borrowers.

Unexpected inflation redistributes income from lenders to borrowers.

The composition of the group winning or losing from inflation changes over time. For example, before 1975, people on Social Security and pensions lost out during inflation since Social Security and pensions were, on the whole, fixed in nominal terms. Inflation lowered recipients' real income. Starting in 1975 Social Security payments and many pensions were changed to adjust automatically for changes in the cost of living, so Social Security recipients are no longer losers. Their real income is independent of inflation. (Actually, because of the adjustment method, some say that Social Security recipients actually now gain from inflation since the adjustment more than compensates them for the rise in the price level.)

What we can say about the distributional consequences of inflation is that people who don't expect inflation and who are tied to fixed nominal contracts will likely lose during an inflationary period. However, if these people are rational, they probably won't let it happen again; they'll be prepared for a subsequent inflation. That is, they will change their expectations of inflation.

Web Note 29.1
Forecasting Inflation

Expectations of Inflation

Expectations of inflation play a key role in the inflationary process. When expectations of inflation are high, people tend to raise their wages and prices, causing inflation. Expectations can become self-fulfilling. For this reason, economists have looked carefully at how individuals form expectations. Almost all economists believe that the expectations that people have of inflation are in some sense rational, by which I mean they are based on the best information available, given the cost of that information. But economists differ on what is meant by rational and thus on how those expectations are formulated. Some economists take a strong stand and argue that rational people will expect the same inflation that is predicted by the economists' model. That is, they form **rational expectations**—*the expectations that the economists' model predicts*. If inflation was, say, 2 percent last year and is 4 percent this year but the economists' model predicts 0 percent inflation for the coming year, individuals will rationally expect 0 percent inflation.

Other economists argue that there are many different economists' models and they are imperfect, so rational expectations cannot be defined in terms of economists' models. These economists instead focus on the process by which people develop their expectations. One way people form expectations is to look at conditions that already exist, or have recently existed. Such expectations are called **adaptive expectations**—*expectations based in some way on the past*. Thus, if inflation was 2 percent last year and 4 percent this year, the prediction for inflation will be somewhere around 3 percent. Adaptive expectations aren't the only type that people use. Sometimes they use **extrapolative expectations**—*expectations that a trend will continue*. For example, say that inflation was 2 percent last year and 4 percent this year; extrapolative expectations would predict 6 percent inflation next year. There are many other types of expectations,

Q-2 Name three different types of expectations.

and individuals use various combinations of them, shifting suddenly from one type to another.

Since expectations play a key role in policy, shifts in the process of forming expectations can change the way the economy operates. It was precisely such a shift in the formation of expectations that played a key role in the expansion of the late 1990s without inflation. Sometime in the early 1990s in the United States, individuals stopped expecting high inflation and began expecting low inflation, and those expectations became self-fulfilling. The United States continued to have relatively low inflation into the early 2000s.

Productivity, Inflation, and Wages

Two key measures that policymakers use to determine whether inflation may be coming are changes in productivity and changes in wages. Together these measures determine whether or not the short-run aggregate supply curve will be shifting up. The rule of thumb is that wages can increase by the amount that productivity increases without generating any inflationary pressure:

Inflation = Nominal wage increase − Productivity growth

For example, if productivity is increasing at 2 percent, as it has been in the early 2000s, wages can go up by 2 percent without generating any inflationary pressure. Let's consider another example—the mid-1970s, when productivity growth slowed to 1 percent while wages went up by 6 percent. Inflation was 6 percent − 1 percent = 5 percent.

Deflation

The low inflation of the early 2000s brought fear of a new problem—**deflation**—*a sustained fall in the price level*. Deflation is the opposite of inflation and is associated with a number of problems in the economy. One problem is that it may prevent the central bank from lowering the real interest rate as low as it wants to, since with deflation the real interest rate is the sum of the nominal interest rate and the rate of deflation. Thus, if the nominal interest rate is 2 percent and the rate of deflation is 3 percent, the real interest rate is 5 percent. But because people can always hold money rather than bonds, the nominal interest rate cannot fall below 0 percent. Since in a deflationary economy the real interest rate is higher than the nominal interest rate, deflation places a limit on how low the Fed can push the real interest rate. For example, the Fed cannot achieve a goal of 1 percent for real interest rates when the rate of deflation is 3 percent. Even if it lowers the nominal interest rate to 0 percent—the lowest level it can, the lowest it can reduce the real rate of interest is to 3 percent—the rate of deflation. This means that it might be impossible for monetary policy to lower interest rates enough to stimulate the economy as much as desired.

Another problem of deflation is that it is often associated with large falls in asset prices—specifically stock and real estate prices. Declines in these asset prices can cause serious problems for an economy for two reasons. First, as people see their wealth evaporating, they may cut their current spending, which can decrease aggregate demand and slow the economy. Second, since these assets often serve as collateral for loans, large falls in asset prices can undermine a country's financial system, making many financial institution's liabilities exceed their assets. Thus, a fall in the value of their assets can make a financial institution insolvent. This happened in the early 2000s in Japan, making it difficult for the Japanese government to stimulate its economy. It left the Japanese government wondering how to save its banking system from large-scale defaults, because such a default would totally undermine any recovery efforts.

Theories of Inflation

Economists hold two slightly different theories of inflation: the quantity theory and institutional theory. The quantity theory emphasizes the connection between money and inflation; the institutional theory emphasizes market structure and price-setting institutions and inflation. There is significant overlap between the two theories, but because they come to different policy conclusions, it is helpful to consider them separately.

The Quantity Theory of Money and Inflation

The quantity theory of money can be summed up in one sentence: *Inflation is always and everywhere a monetary phenomenon.* If the money supply rises, the price level will rise. If the money supply doesn't rise, the price level won't rise. Forget all the other stuff—it just obscures the connection between money and inflation.

The Equation of Exchange The quantity theory of money centers on the **equation of exchange,** *an equation stating that the quantity of money times velocity of money equals the price level times the quantity of real goods sold.* This equation is:

In the quantity theory model, inflation is caused by growth in the money supply. It focuses on the equation of exchange: $MV = PQ$

$$MV = PQ$$

where:

M = Quantity of money

V = Velocity of money

P = Price level

Q = Quantity of real goods sold

Q is the real output of the economy (real GDP) and P is the price level, so PQ is the economy's nominal output (nominal GDP). V, the **velocity of money,** is *the number of times per year, on average, a dollar goes around to generate a dollar's worth of income.* Put another way, velocity is the amount of income per year generated by a dollar of money. Since $MV = PQ$, MV also equals nominal output. Thus, if there's $100 in the economy and velocity is 20, nominal GDP is $2,000. We can calculate V by dividing nominal GDP by the money supply. Let's take Canada as an example. In Canada in 2002, nominal GDP was approximately $1,600 billion and M was approximately $135 billion (using M_1), so velocity was about GDP/M = 12, meaning each dollar in the economy circulated enough to support approximately $12 in total income.

Money can affect real output (Q) in the short run, but in the long run it affects only the price level (P).

Velocity Is Constant The equation of exchange is a tautology, meaning it is true by definition. What changes it from a tautology to a theory are two assumptions. The first assumption is that velocity remains constant. Money is spent only so fast; how fast is determined by the economy's institutional structure, such as how close individuals live to stores, how people are paid (weekly, biweekly, or monthly), and what sources of credit are available. (Can you go to the store and buy something on credit, that is, without handing over cash?) This institutional structure changes slowly, quantity theorists argue, so velocity won't fluctuate very much. Next year, velocity will be approximately the same as this year.

Q-3 What's the difference between the equation of exchange and the quantity theory of money?

If velocity remains constant, the quantity theory can be used to predict how much nominal GDP will grow if we know how much the money supply grows. For example, if the money supply goes up 6 percent, the quantity theory of money predicts that nominal GDP will go up by 6 percent.

Something that is determined outside the model is called autonomous.

Real Output Is Independent of the Money Supply The second assumption is that Q is independent of the money supply. That is, Q is autonomous, meaning real output is determined by forces outside those forces in the quantity theory. If Q grows, it is because of factors that affect the real economy. Thus, policy analysis based on the quantity theory focuses on the real economy—the supply side of the economy, not the demand side.

Three assumptions of quantity theory:

1. Velocity is constant.
2. Real output is independent of money supply.
3. Causation goes from money to prices.

This assumption makes analyzing the economy a lot easier than if the financial and real sectors are interrelated and if real economic activity is influenced by financial changes. It separates two puzzles: how the real economy works, and how the price level and financial sector work. Instead of having two different jigsaw puzzles all mixed up, each puzzle can be worked separately. The quantity theory doesn't say there aren't interconnections between the real and financial sectors, but it does say that most of these interconnections involve short-run considerations. The quantity theory is primarily concerned with the long run.

With both V (velocity) and Q (quantity of output) unaffected by changes in M (money supply), the only thing that can change is P (price level). With these assumptions, the equation of exchange becomes the quantity theory of money:

$$M\overline{V} \rightarrow P\overline{Q}$$

In its simplest terms, the **quantity theory of money** says that *the price level varies in response to changes in the quantity of money*. Another way to write the quantity theory of money is: $\%\Delta M \rightarrow \%\Delta P$. If the money supply goes up 20 percent, prices go up 20 percent. If the money supply goes down 5 percent, the price level goes down 5 percent.

Examples of Money's Role in Inflation Let's consider an example of the relationship between money growth and inflation. In 1971 the Fed increased the money supply significantly. That same year government instituted wage and price controls (legal limits on prices and wages). As a result, income rose and unemployment fell, but inflation did not rise. In 1973 the wage and price controls were lifted; inflation rose from 4.2 percent in 1972 to over 9 percent in 1975, and unemployment rose from 4.9 percent in 1973 to 8.5 percent in 1975. Here's an example of expansionary monetary policy initially increasing real output as prices were slow to respond to increases in aggregate demand. In the long run, the expansionary monetary policy caused inflation.

The quantity theory view that printing money causes inflation is seen in the 18th-century satirical drawing by James Gilray showing William Pitt spewing paper money out of his mouth while gold coins are locked up in his stomach.
Bleichroeder Print Collection, Baker Library, Harvard Business School.

Another example, again from the 1970s, is when significant inflation—10 percent—had become built into the expectations of the economy. In late 1979 and the early 1980s, the Fed decreased the money supply growth significantly. This led to a leap in unemployment from 7 to 10 percent, but initially no decrease in inflation. By 1984, however, inflation had fallen to about 4 percent, and it remained low throughout the 1980s and 1990s.

Now let's consider a couple more examples. In the early 1990s, the German central bank felt Germany's inflation rate was too high. It cut the money supply growth considerably. Initially, the impact was on output, and the tight money pushed the German economy into a recession. Germany remained in that recession through early 1996, and inflation fell in the late 1990s. A second example is Russia in the early 1990s. The Russian government was short of revenue and was forced to print money to finance its debt. As a result, inflation blew up into hyperinflation, and the Russian economy continued in a serious slump.

Despite these and many other examples, the simple view connecting inflation with money supply growth lost favor in the late 1980s and early 1990s as formerly stable relationships between certain measurements of money and inflation broke down in the United States. Consider Figure 29-1, which shows the relationship between prices and the money supply for the United States.

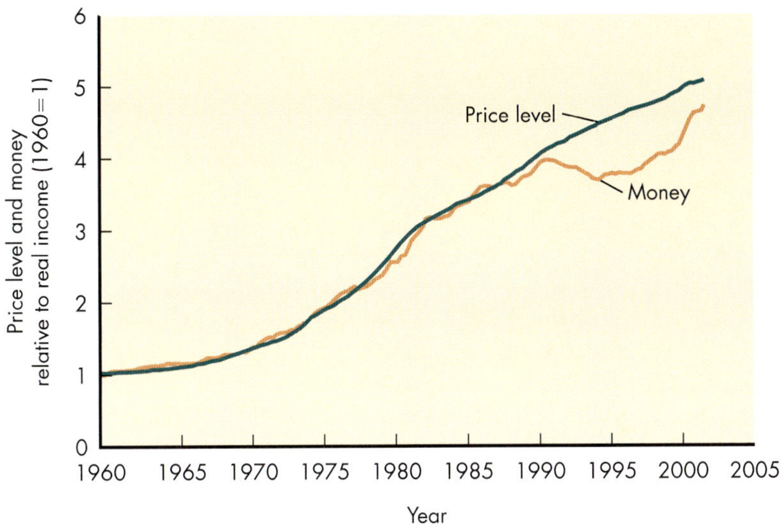

Figure 29-1 U.S. Price Level and Money Relative to Real Income
From 1960 through the 1980s, prices and the money supply were closely linked. Beginning in the 1990s, however, the relationship broke down. Whether the breakdown in the relationship is temporary or permanent is debatable. Most economists agree that enormous changes in financial institutions and the increased global interdependence of financial markets contributed to the breakdown.

Source: Federal Reserve and Bureau of Economic Analysis.

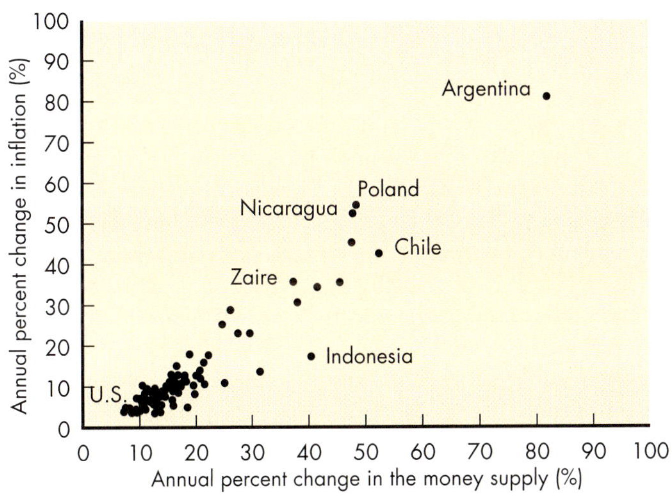

Figure 29-2 Inflation and Money Growth
The empirical evidence that supports the quantity theory of money is most convincing in countries that experience significant inflation. Argentina and Chile are examples where high money growth has accompanied high rates of inflation.

Source: Federal Reserve Bank of Minneapolis, *Quarterly Review* (3rd quarter, 1995).

Notice that in the 1990s the close relationship ended. Some economists argue that this breakdown was temporary; others argue that it was permanent. Both sides agree the breakdown was caused by (1) the enormous changes in financial institutions that were occurring because of technological changes and changing regulations, and (2) the increased global interdependence of financial markets, which increased the flow of money among countries. Where the two sides differ is in whether these changes will permanently alter the close relationship between money growth and inflation. In the 1990s it seemed that, for low inflation, the random elements (called noise) in the relationship between money and inflation overwhelmed the connection between the two.

For large inflation of the type experienced by many developing and transitional economies, the connection is still evident, and the quantity theory remains the central theory of inflation in such countries. Some empirical evidence consistent with the quantity theory's relevance for developing countries can be seen in Figure 29-2, which shows the relationship between the increase in money and the increase in prices in

The Keeper of the Classical Faith: Milton Friedman

Beyond the Tools

The quantity theory is generally associated with Classical economics, and the most famous advocate of the quantity theory was Milton Friedman. By most accounts, Milton Friedman was a headstrong student. He didn't simply accept the truths his teachers laid out. If he didn't agree, he argued strongly for his own belief. He was very bright, and his ideas were generally logical and convincing. He needed to be both persistent and intelligent to maintain and promote his views in spite of strong opposition.

Throughout the Keynesian years of the 1950s and 1960s, Friedman stood up and argued for the quantity theory, keeping it alive. During this period Classical economics was called *monetarism,* and because Friedman was such a strong advocate of the quantity theory, he was considered the leader of the monetarists.

Friedman argued that fiscal policy simply didn't work. It led to expansions in the size of government. He also opposed an activist monetary policy. The effects of monetary policy, he said, were too variable for it to be useful in guiding the economy. He called for a steady growth in the money supply, and argued consistently for a laissez-faire policy by government.

Friedman has made his mark in both microeconomics and macroeconomics. In the 1970s, his ideas caught hold and helped spawn a renewal of the quantity theory. He was awarded the Nobel Prize in economics in 1976.

110 countries from 1960 to 1990. Notice that both money and prices have increased closely together.

The Inflation Tax The reason why central banks in countries such as Argentina and Chile sometimes increase the money supply so much is complicated. The goal that most often tops their list is to keep the economy running. They are also generally far less independent of political pressures than central banks in developed countries. Finally, developing countries lack broad-based government bond markets. So if the government runs a budget deficit and is financing it domestically, the central bank often must buy the bonds to finance that deficit. If it does not, the government will default. In this case we can say that the increase in the money supply is caused by the government deficit.

Hyperinflations can make money almost worthless.
Bettmann/Corbis.

Financing the deficit by expansionary monetary policy is not costless. It causes inflation. The inflation that results from the increases in the money supply works as a type of tax on individuals and is often called an **inflation tax** *(an implicit tax on the holders of cash and the holders of any obligations specified in nominal terms)*. Inflation is considered a tax because it reduces the value of cash and other nominal obligations.

Let's consider an inflation tax in relation to the transitional economies of the former Soviet Union. With the end of central planning, the currency circulating far exceeded the amount necessary to purchase the real goods the economy could produce at market prices. Why? Most individuals had stored their financial wealth in the currency of their country. This currency represented the enormous past obligations of the former socialist governments—obligations that far exceeded the governments', or the economies', ability to meet them.

As they moved to a market economy without an acceptable tax base, these governments had no way to meet their current obligations, let alone their past obligations. The central banks generally chose to keep the governments operating (which isn't surprising, since they were often branches of the government). To do that, they increased the money supply enormously, causing hyperinflation. The hyperinflation soon took on a life of its own. The expectation of accelerating inflation created even more inflationary pressure as individuals tried to spend any money they had quickly, before the prices went up. This increased the velocity of money, the nominal demand for goods, and inflationary pressures. Eventually the hyperinflation wiped out (taxed away) the excess currency and allowed most of the transitional countries to rein in their inflation, getting it down to double digits (less than 100 percent per year). This was possible because, with the excess currency wiped out, the inflation tax only had to make up for the government budget deficit; it no longer had to be used to eliminate past obligations.

Central banks know that issuing large quantities of money will cause inflation. What they don't know, and what the policy discussions are about, is whether it's worse to have the inflation or the unpleasant alternatives of recession—or perhaps even a breakdown of the entire economy. Thus, the debate is not about whether the inflation is caused by the issuance of too much money but whether countries' budget deficits are absolutely necessary or not. Should the central bank bail out the government?

Q-4 Why do some central banks issue large quantities of money if they know that doing so will cause inflation?

Policy Implications of the Quantity Theory In terms of policy, the quantity theory says that monetary policy is powerful but unpredictable in the short run. Because of this unpredictability monetary policy cannot, and should not, be used to control the level of output in the economy. Thus, paradoxically, supporters of the quantity theory oppose an activist monetary policy. Instead they generally favor a monetary policy set by rules, not by discretionary monetary policy.

As discussed in the previous chapter, many central banks are now using monetary regimes, or feedback rules. A feedback rule might specify that the money supply will be contracted by 1 percent (or the interest rate will be raised by 1.5 percentage points) when inflation rises by 3 percent, and the money supply will be expanded by 1 percent when real output increases but remains below potential output. (This is only an example; the feedback rules can become much more complicated.) A monetary rule takes monetary policy out of the hands of politicians. Quantity theorists feel that politicians are not able to hold the money supply down because of the expansionary tendencies in politics, and thus a rule is better than discretion.

Quantity theorists favor a feedback rule because they believe that the short-run effects of monetary policy are unpredictable and the long-run effects of monetary policy are on the price level, not on real output.

The quantity theory has convinced many economists to exert pressure to create independent central banks so that politicians are separated from the control of the money supply. That way the government will not follow its political instincts and run expansionary monetary policy. Let's consider an example: New Zealand, which has legally mandated a monetary rule based on inflation. Beginning in 1989, the Reserve Bank of New Zealand was required to keep consumer price inflation between 0 and 3 percent a year, a target agreed on by the government and the central bank. After averaging 10 percent a year in the 1980s, New Zealand's inflation rate fell in the early 1990s and averaged below 3 percent per year thereafter. An important reason New Zealand instituted monetary rules was to establish credibility in its central bank's resolve to lower the inflation rate.

The U.S. Federal Reserve Bank does not have such a strict rule, but the Fed works hard to show that it is serious about fighting inflation, regardless of the consequences to unemployment or output. Many economists felt that by the mid-1990s the Fed had established its credibility, and that credibility allowed the economy to expand without generating inflation. Inflation expectations fell, lowering interest rates, which contributed to the investment boom of the late 1990s.

A final example of the importance of the quantity theory concerns the European Central Bank (ECB). The constitution states that the ECB's sole goal is to fight inflation. The hope is that this provision will significantly reduce political considerations in its policies. The euro (the European Union's currency) was introduced in 2002, so it is too early to judge the effectiveness of this approach to establishing central bank independence and low inflation.

The Institutional Theory of Inflation

Q-5 Use the equation of exchange to demonstrate the difference between quantity theory and institutional theory of inflation.

The alternative to the quantity theory is the institutional theory of inflation. Supporters of the institutional theory of inflation accept much of the quantity theory—money and inflation do move together. Where they differ is in what they see as the cause and the effect. According to the quantity theory of money, changes in the money supply cause changes in the price level. The direction of causation goes from left to right:

$$MV \rightarrow PQ$$

Institutional theorists see it the other way around. Increases in prices force government to increase the money supply or cause unemployment. The direction of causation goes from right to left:

$$MV \leftarrow PQ$$

The institutional theory of inflation focuses on the institutional and structural aspects of an economy, as well as the money supply, as important causes of inflation.

According to the institutional theory of inflation, the source of inflation is in the price-setting process of firms. When setting prices, firms and individuals find it easier to raise prices than to lower them and do not take into account the effect of their pricing decisions on the price level. To see the argument, let's consider firms' pricing decisions.

Focus on the Price-Setting Decisions of Firms Since all income is ultimately paid to individual owners of the factors of production, the revenue that firms receive is divided among profits, wages, and rent. Firms are simply intermediaries between individuals as owners of the factors of production and individuals as consumers. Given the institutional structure of our economy, it's often easier for firms to increase wages, profits, and rents to keep the peace with their employees and other owners of the factors of production than it is to try to hold those costs down. Firms then pay for that increase by raising the prices they charge consumers. That works as long as, in response to the rising price level, the government increases the money supply so that there is sufficient demand to buy the goods at the higher prices.

Let's consider an example of a lip balm company. It is happy with its competitive position in the market, and it expects 0 percent inflation. Productivity (output of lip balm per unit of input) is increasing by 2 percent, the same as the increase in productivity in the economy as a whole, so the firm can hold its nominal price of lip balm constant even if it increases wages by 2 percent. Since the price level isn't expected to change, the firm can maintain its share of the market by holding the price of its lip balm constant. The firm offers workers a 2 percent pay increase.

The firm meets with its workers to discuss the 2 percent offer. At the meeting it becomes clear to the firm that its workers will push for a 4 percent pay increase. What should the firm do? It is here where labor markets and the product market come in. Let's first consider the product market.

If the product market is highly competitive, what the firm can charge for its lip balm is set by the market; if other firms do not raise wages by 4 percent, and have a similar 2 percent productivity increase, giving in to the wage increase will ensure that the firm will incur losses and eventually go out of business. So, in a highly competitive market in which supply and demand forces alone determine prices, there's strong pressure to increase wages only 2 percent and hold the price constant. However, real-world firms generally are not in such a highly price-competitive market. They have some power to raise their price. Raising the price will make selling their goods more difficult, but not impossible. Thus, if the product market is only somewhat competitive, the lip balm firm may consider paying the 4 percent and raising the price of its product.

Whether the firm chooses this price-raising strategy depends on the state of the labor market. If the labor market is tight (unemployment is low) the firm knows that it will lose employees if it does not give the wage increase. Productivity may fall. Moreover, the firm can figure that if its workers are asking for such an increase, so too are workers of competing firms. Firms often meet workers' demands under the expectation that other firms will do so too. Meeting these demands helps maintain morale and prevents turnover of key workers. Thus, the state of the labor market plays a central role in firms' decisions on whether to give in to the wage demand or not, which is the reason economists look at unemployment to measure inflationary pressures.

Changes in the Money Supply Follow Price-Setting by Firms The institutional theory sees the nominal wage- and price-setting process as generating inflation. As one group pushes up its nominal wage or price, another group responds by doing the same. More groups follow until, finally, the first group finds that its relative wage or price hasn't increased. Then the entire process starts again. Once the nominal wage and price levels have risen, government has two options: It can either ratify the increase by increasing the money supply, thereby accepting the inflation, or it can refuse to ratify it. If it refuses to ratify it, firms will not be able to sell all they want at the higher price and will cut production and lay off workers (firms generally don't lower nominal wages). Unemployment will rise.

Institutional theorists see the nominal wage- and price-setting process as generating inflation.

Supporters of the institutional theory of inflation argue that in most sectors of the economy, competition works slowly. Social pressures, as well as the invisible hand, influence wages and prices. The result is that even when there is substantial unemployment and considerable excess supply of goods, existing workers can still put an upward push on nominal wages, and existing firms can put an upward push on nominal prices.

The Insider/Outsider Model and Inflation To get a better picture of how existing workers can push up wages despite substantial unemployment, let's consider the **insider/outsider model,** *an institutionalist story of inflation where insiders bid up wages and outsiders are unemployed.* Insiders are current business owners and workers who have good jobs with excellent long-run prospects. Outsiders are everyone else. Insiders receive above-equilibrium wages, profits, and rents. If the world were competitive, their wages, profits, and rents would be pushed down to the equilibrium level. To prevent this from happening, according to the insider/outsider model, insiders develop sociological and institutional barriers that prevent outsiders from competing away those above-equilibrium wages, profits, and rents. Such barriers include unions, laws restricting the firing of workers, and brand recognition. Because of those barriers, outsiders (often minorities) must take low-paying dead-end jobs or attempt to undertake marginal businesses that pay little return for many hours worked. Even when outsiders do find better jobs or business opportunities, they are first to be fired and their businesses are the first to suffer in a recession. Thus, outsiders have much higher unemployment rates than insiders. For example, in the United States blacks tend to be outsiders; black unemployment rates have consistently been twice as high as white unemployment rates for the same age groups.

Q-6 How would a quantity theorist likely respond to an insider/outsider model of inflation?

Institutionalists believe that, under current conditions, the costs of unemployment are borne more heavily by minorities and other outsiders.

In short, our economy is only partially competitive. The invisible hand is often thwarted by social and political forces. Such partially competitive economies are often characterized by insiders' monopolies. Insiders get the jobs and are paid monopoly wage levels. Outsiders are not employed at those higher wages. Imperfect competition allows workers (and firms) to raise nominal wages (and prices) even as unemployment (and excess supply of goods) exists. Then, as other insiders do likewise, the price level rises. This increase in the price level lowers workers' real wages. In response, workers further raise their nominal wages to protect their real wages. The result is an ongoing chase in which the insiders protect their real wages, while outsiders (the unemployed) suffer.

Dieting and Fighting Inflation

Knowing the Tools

The debate on what to do about inflation has an analogy to dieting. Fasting will cause you to lose about a pound a day. Want to lose 30 pounds? A dietitian who follows the quantity theory would say, "Fast. Thirty pounds equals 105,000 calories. When you've managed to complete a period in which you've eaten 105,000 fewer calories than are necessary to maintain your present weight, you'll have lost 30 pounds." An institutionalist dietitian would offer a variety of diets or would explore your psyche to discover why you want to overeat, and would perhaps suggest a liquid protein plan. Following the institutionalist diet, you would also take in 105,000 fewer calories than if you'd continued to overeat. But, institutionalists argue, you can't stick with a diet unless you've discovered what makes you want to overeat.

(If the ideas of nominal and real are unclear to you, a review of earlier chapters may be in order.)

Policy Implications of Institutional Theory As we saw above, the quantity theory says that monetary policy should follow a prescribed feedback rule. To stop inflation, reduce the rate of growth of the money supply. Control the money supply and you will control inflation. According to the institutional theory, governments need to institute additional policies along with those reducing the money supply to prevent inflation or stop it in its tracks. Supporters of the institutional theory agree that contractionary monetary policy will ultimately control inflation, but they argue that it will do so in an inefficient and unfair manner. They argue that tight monetary policy usually causes unemployment among those least able to handle it.

Supporters of the institutional theory ask, "Why should the unemployed and the outsiders bear the cost of fighting inflation?" Putting a brick wall in front of a speeding car will stop the car, but that doesn't mean that's how you *should* stop a car. Instead, institutional theorists suggest that contractionary monetary policies be used *in combination with* additional policies that directly slow down inflation at its source. Such an additional policy is often called an **incomes policy,** *a policy that places direct pressure on individuals to hold down their nominal wages and prices*. Formal incomes policies have been out of favor for a number of years, but informal incomes policies exist in many European countries and in many smaller countries throughout the world. In these countries the government plays an important role in the wage negotiations.

Q-7 What measures would a quantity theorist suggest government use to reduce inflation? What measures would an institutionalist suggest government use?

In Finland, for example, the government meets with the major unions and companies and attempts to convince workers to hold down wage demands and firms to hold down price increases, promising both sides certain policies if they moderate their positions. Supporters of the institutional theory argue that such an incomes policy can hold down inflation and thereby reduce the unemployment necessary to fight inflation.

Web Note 29.2
WWII Incomes Policies

Demand-Pull and Cost-Push Inflation

Quantity and institutional theories of inflation are sometimes differentiated as demand-pull inflation and cost-push inflation. When the majority of industries are at close to capacity and they experience increases in demand, we say there's demand-pull pressure. The inflation that results is called **demand-pull inflation**—*inflation that occurs when the economy is at or above potential output*. Demand-pull inflation is generally characterized by shortages of goods and shortages of workers. Because there's excess demand, firms know that if they raise their prices, they'll still be able to sell their goods and workers know if they raise their wages, they will still be employed.

When significant proportions of markets (or one very important market, such as the labor market or the oil market) experience price rises not related to demand pressure, we say that there is cost-push pressure. The resulting inflation is **cost-push inflation**—*inflation that occurs when the economy is below potential output.* In cost-push inflation, because there is no excess demand (there may actually be excess supply), firms that raise their prices are not sure demand will be sufficient to sell off their goods and workers are not sure that after raising their wage they will all be employed. But the ones who actually do the pushing are fairly sure they won't be the ones who can't sell off their goods or the ones fired. A classic cost-push example occurred in the 1970s when the Organization of Petroleum Exporting Countries raised its price on oil, triggering cost push inflation.

Notice that in much of the discussion of inflation I did not use these distinctions. The reason is that although demand-pull and cost-push pressures can be catalysts for starting inflation, they are not causes of continued inflation. The reality is that in an ongoing inflation cost-push or demand-pull forces become intertwined. As Alfred Marshall (the 19th century English economist who originated supply and demand analysis) said, it is impossible to separate the roles of supply and demand in influencing price, just as it is impossible to say which blade of the scissors is cutting a sheet of paper.

Inflation and Unemployment: The Phillips Curve

Policy discussions are usually based on a trade-off between inflation and unemployment. You saw that trade-off in the discussion of policy with the *AS/AD* model. Recall that the effect of expansionary aggregate demand depends on how close the economy is to potential output. The further beyond potential output the economy is, the more inflation expansionary aggregate demand policy would cause. Thus, the economy has a temporary trade-off between unemployment and inflation.

That trade-off can be represented graphically, as shown in Figure 29-3(a). The **short-run Phillips curve** is *a downward-sloping curve showing the relationship between inflation and unemployment when expectations of inflation are constant.* In a Phillips curve diagram, unemployment is measured on the horizontal axis; inflation is on the vertical axis. The Phillips curve shows us the possible short-run combinations of those two phenomena. It tells us that when unemployment is low, say 4 percent, inflation tends to be high, say 4 percent (point *A* in Figure 29-3(a)). It also tells us that if we want to lower inflation, say to 1 percent, we must be willing to accept high unemployment, say 7 percent (point *B* in Figure 29-3(a)).

History of the Phillips Curve

The Phillips curve began as an empirical relationship and was discovered by, you guessed it, an economist named Phillips. In the 1950s and 1960s, when unemployment was high, inflation was low; when unemployment was low, inflation was high. Figure 29-3(b) shows this empirical relationship for the United States for the years 1954–1968, when the short-run Phillips curve became part of how economists looked at the economy.

Because the short-run Phillips curve seemed to represent a relatively stable trade-off, in the 1960s the short-run Phillips curve began to play a central role in discussions of macroeconomic policy. Republicans (often advised by supporters of the quantity theory)

Figure 29-3 (a, b, c, and d) The Phillips Curve Trade-Off
Analyzing the empirical relationship between unemployment and inflation from 1954 to 1968—shown in (**b**)—led economists to believe there was the relatively stable Phillips curve which, for policy choices, could be represented by the smooth Phillips curve in (**a**). In the 1970s the empirical Phillips curve relationship between inflation and unemployment broke down, leading many economists to question the existence of any Phillips curve relationship that allowed policymakers to choose between inflation and unemployment. In (**c**) you can see how in the 1970s, no stable Phillips curve existed, while in (**d**) you can see how in the last few decades, the evidence is mixed. Specifically, from 1985 to 1992 a Phillips curve relationship seemed to exist. In the mid- to late 1990s and early 2000s, both unemployment and inflation remained low and the Phillips curve relationship once again disappeared.

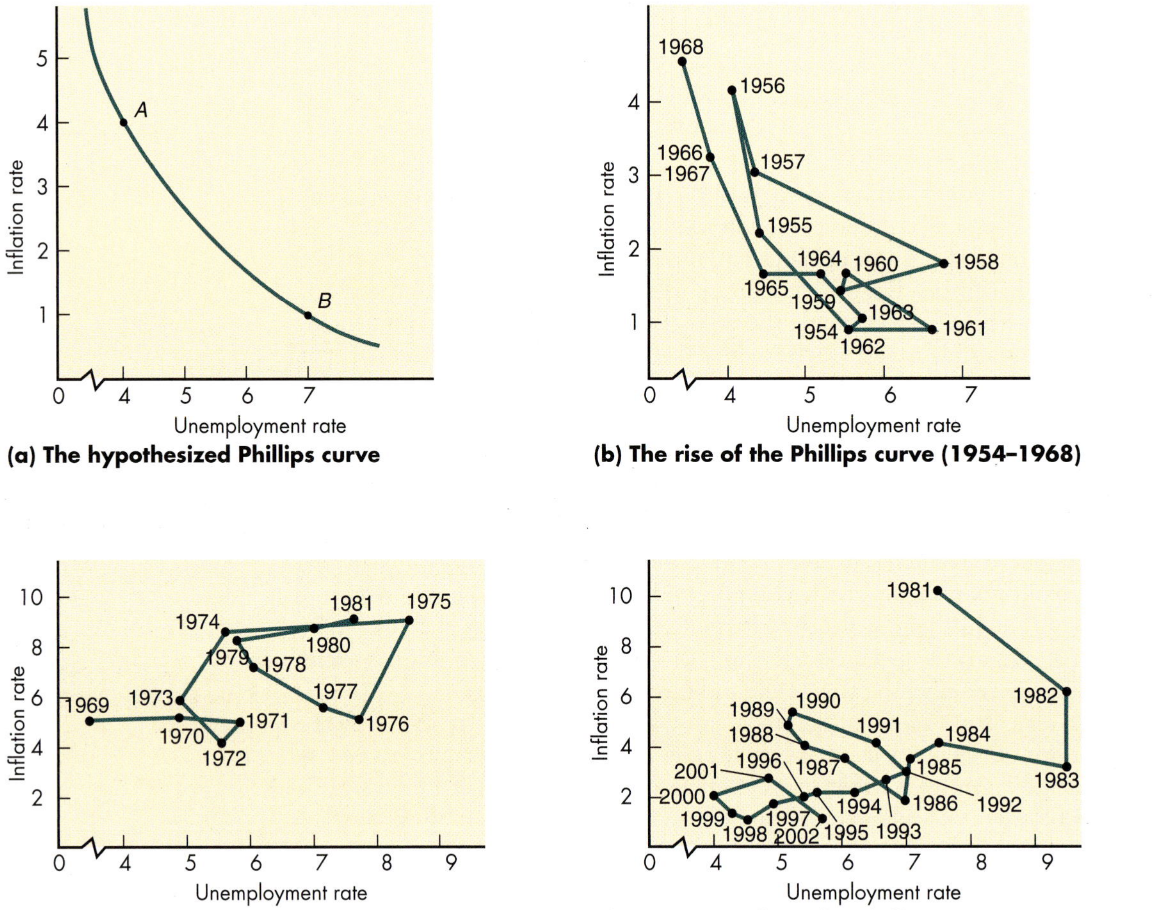

(a) The hypothesized Phillips curve

(b) The rise of the Phillips curve (1954–1968)

(c) The fall of the Phillips curve (1969–1981)

(d) Questions about the Phillips curve (1981–2002)

Source: Economic Report of the President.

generally favored contractionary monetary and fiscal policy, which maintained high unemployment and low inflation (a point like *B* in Figure 29-3(a)). Democrats (often advised by supporters of the institutional theory) generally favored expansionary monetary and fiscal policies, which brought about low unemployment but high inflation (a point like *A* in Figure 29-3(a)).

The Breakdown of the Short-Run Phillips Curve

In the early 1970s, the empirical short-run Phillips curve relationship seemed to break down. The data no longer seemed to show a trade-off between unemployment and inflation. Instead, when unemployment was high, inflation was also high. This phenomenon is termed **stagflation**—*the combination of high and accelerating inflation and high unemployment*. Figure 29-3(c) shows the empirical relationship between inflation and unemployment from 1969 to 1981.

Notice that the relatively stable relationship up until 1969 breaks down in the 1970s. In the 1970s, there doesn't seem to be any trade-off between inflation and unemployment at all. Something clearly changed in the 1970s. In the 1980s, inflation fell substantially and, beginning in 1986, a Phillips-curve-type relationship began to reappear, as can be seen in Figure 29-3(d). But then beginning in the mid- to late-1990s both inflation and unemployment remained relatively low and the trade-off once again disappeared.

The Long-Run and Short-Run Phillips Curves

This continually changing relationship between inflation and unemployment has economists somewhat perplexed. We know that a number of forces are at work, but the strength of these forces varies from one time period to another.

The Importance of Inflation Expectations One of the key forces at work is expectations of inflation. Actual inflation depends both on supply and demand forces and on how much inflation people expect. If people expect a lot of inflation, they will ask for higher nominal wage and price increases. Expectations have been incorporated into the analysis by distinguishing between a short-run Phillips curve and a long-run Phillips curve.

At all points on the short-run Phillips curve, *expectations of inflation (the rise in the price level that the average person expects) are fixed*. Thus, on the short-run Phillips curve expectations of inflation can differ from actual inflation. At all points on the long-run Phillips curve *expectations of inflation are equal to actual inflation*. The **long-run Phillips curve** is thought to be *a vertical curve at the unemployment rate consistent with potential output*. It shows the trade-off (or complete lack thereof) when expectations of inflation equal actual inflation. Economists used expectations of inflation to explain why the short-run Phillips curve relationship broke down in the 1970s.

The long-run Phillips curve is vertical; it shows the lack of a trade-off between inflation and unemployment when expectations of inflation equal actual inflation. Expectations of inflation do not change along a short-run Phillips curve.

Q-8 Draw the long-run Phillips curve. Why does it have its shape?

Let's consider how expectations of inflation can explain high inflation and high unemployment in reference to both our *AS/AD* model and the Phillips curve model. Say the economy starts out with a rate of unemployment consistent with potential output. So there is no inflation, and the economy is at its potential output. (Wages can still be going up by the rate of productivity growth, say it's 3 percent, but the price level is not rising.) Further assume that individuals are expecting zero inflation; that is, if they get a 3 percent wage increase, they expect their real income to rise by 3 percent. This starting point is represented by point A in Figure 29-4 (a and b).

In Figure 29-4(a) you can see that short-run aggregate supply and aggregate demand intersect at potential income at point A. Since the economy is in both short-run and long-run equilibrium, there are no forces moving the economy away from point A in the *AS/AD* model. Point A in Figure 29-4(b) is also on both the long-run and short-run Phillips curve. This means that point A is a sustainable combination of inflation and unemployment—the situation can continue indefinitely. The only sustainable combination of inflation and unemployment rates on the short-run Phillips curve is where it intersects the long-run Phillips curve, because that is the only unemployment rate consistent with the economy's potential income.

Moving Off the Long-Run Phillips Curve Now let's say that the government decides to increase aggregate demand, shifting the *AD* curve from AD_0 to AD_1. This pushes output above its potential, Y_P, as in Figure 29-4(a). That will increase the

Figure 29-4 (a and b) Inflation Expectations and the Phillips Curve
Both (a) and (b) show how an increase in aggregate demand can increase output initially. Eventually, however, the economy will return to potential output, but with a higher rate of inflation. The economy begins at point *A*. Initially, the aggregate demand curve moves from AD_0 to AD_1, pushing output above its potential in (a). As firms compete for labor, wages increase. To cover increasing costs, firms raise their prices. The combination of lower unemployment and higher inflation is shown by point *B* in (b). As workers realize that inflation is not 0 percent, but rather 4 percent, they will ask for further wage increases. Ultimately this process shifts the *SAS* curve to SAS_2 and the short-run Phillips curve to PC_1 (along which expected inflation equals 4 percent) and the economy to point *C*. The economy is once again in equilibrium. Unemployment has returned to 5.5 percent, but inflation is now 4 percent.

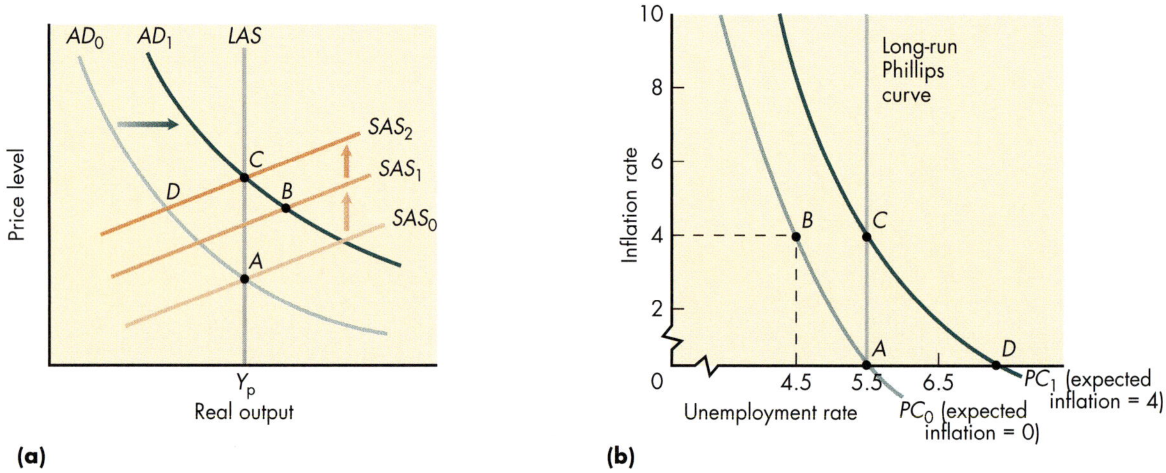

demand for labor, and that competition for labor will push wages up by more than the increase in productivity as firms compete for the small pool of unemployed workers. Say wages rise by 7 percent. Initially that increase is enough to satisfy workers who are still assumed to expect zero inflation. But notice that, unless potential output increases, there is a problem—their expectation will not be met. Since productivity is still rising by only 3 percent while wages are rising by 7 percent, the higher wage costs force firms to raise their prices by 4 percent, shifting the *SAS* curve up from SAS_0 to SAS_1. The economy moves to point *B*. This same point *B* is shown in the Phillips curve diagram where the economy is still on the short-run Phillips curve. Unemployment falls from 5.5 to 4.5 percent and inflation rises from 0 to 4 percent. But point *B* is not on the long-run Phillips curve and actual inflation exceeds expected inflation.

Moving Back onto the Long-Run Phillips Curve Point *B* is not a sustainable position. Since it is beyond potential income, Y_P, the *SAS* curve will continue to shift up. Eventually workers realize that their real wages aren't increasing by 7 percent; they are rising by only 3 percent. As workers come to expect the 4 percent inflation they ask for higher wages to compensate for that inflation. The short-run Phillips curve will shift up from PC_0 to PC_1 since each short-run Phillips curve represents the trade-off for a given level of inflationary expectation. As wages increase, the *SAS* curve shifts up to SAS_2. As the price level rises, the dollars that people hold are worth less, causing the quantity of aggregate demand to decline and the economy to move to point C. Output returns to its potential, unemployment returns to its target rate and the economy returns to a long-run equilibrium at point C on the long-run Phillips curve. Unemployment is once again at its target rate, but inflation, and expectations of inflation, are now 4 percent.

A general relationship is the following: Any time unemployment is lower than the target level of unemployment consistent with potential output, inflation and expectations of inflation will be increasing. That means that the short-run Phillips curve will be shifting up. The short-run Phillips curve will continue to shift up until output is no longer above potential. Thus, any level of inflation is consistent with the target level of unemployment if the cause of that inflation is expectations of inflation. Economists used these expectations of inflation to explain the experience in the 1970s. The economy had been pushed beyond its potential, which had caused inflation to accelerate. (This explanation was supplemented with discussions of supply-side inflationary pressures caused by the large rise in oil prices that occurred at that time.)

Stagflation and the Phillips Curve

The problem with point C is that although the economy is back at potential output, inflationary expectations are built into people's price-setting behavior. That expectational inflation can be eliminated if aggregate demand falls, pushing the economy to a higher level of unemployment that exceeds the target rate. That is how economists explained the stagflation in the late 1970s and early 1980s. Government attempted to push down the inflation through contractionary aggregate demand policy. The lower aggregate demand (shifting aggregate demand back from AD_1 to AD_0) pushed the economy to a position such as point *D* in Figure 29-4. At point *D*, unemployment exceeds the target rate. The higher unemployment puts downward pressure on wages and prices, shifting the short-run Phillips curve down.

As you can see, the long-run Phillips curve tells us whether there will be upward pressure on the price level (when the economy is to the left of the long-run Phillips curve, and unemployment is below the target rate) or downward pressure on the price level (when the economy is to the right of it and unemployment is above the target rate).

Q.9 If the economy is at point *A* on the Phillips curve below, what prediction would you make for unemployment and inflation?

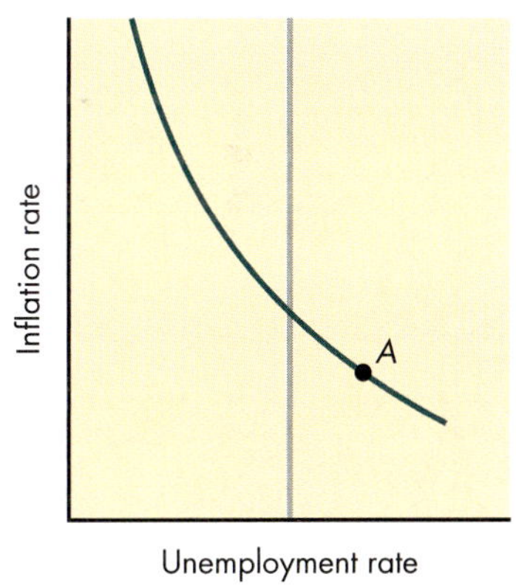

The Rise and Fall of the New Economy

The above story is the one that most economists have in the back of their mind when they give policy advice. But that story did not fit the last half of the 1990s and the early 2000s very well. During that period, output expanded significantly above what economists had predicted potential output to be, and unemployment rates were lower than most economists thought consistent with potential output. Despite this, wages did not rise significantly. Instead, productivity grew at a faster than expected rate, and inflation remained low. Everything was going better than economists had previously thought possible.

The cause of these good times was likely a combination of factors. First, the economy was experiencing a temporary positive productivity shock because Internet growth and investment were shifting potential output out. Second, competition increased because of globalization and the price comparisons made possible by e-commerce. Third, workers had become less concerned with real wages and more concerned with protecting their jobs, so firms did not raise wages even with extremely tight labor markets. What was most amazing to economists was that in 1999 oil prices increased substantially but inflation did not rise, as it did in the 1970s.

Some economists argued that this combination of factors was permanent, and that the U.S. economy was entering a new era, in which we could have both lower inflation and lower unemployment than was previously thought possible. Others argued that the forces were temporary and that the U.S. economy would come out of its "Goldilocks period."

In 2001 the economy went into a brief recession and the stock market fell. With that recession the hope of a new economy's continued high growth and low unemployment were dashed. Still, the economy did not seem to be falling back into old patterns. Although unemployment increased significantly, output continued to grow slowly, productivity growth remained positive, and inflationary pressures remained in check. In 2002 some economists feared that the U.S. economy was entering a deflationary period of slow growth, high unemployment, and falling asset price levels. The policy concern of these economists shifted from a concern about inflation to a concern of whether monetary policy would be effective in stimulating the economy.

The Relationship between Inflation and Growth

The on-going debates about macro policy can be understood by thinking back to our discussion of low and high potential output and their relation to inflationary pressure. A graph of these is shown in Figure 29-5(a). Economists generally agree that below low potential output there will be no inflationary, and possibly some deflationary, pressures. They also agree that above high potential output there will be significant inflationary pressures. The degree of inflationary pressure between these two extremes is ambiguous. Since no one knows precisely where potential output is, there is usually a debate within this range.

The government wants to choose as high an output level as possible yet keep inflation low and prevent it from accelerating. At what point it can do that is the subject of much debate. Supporters of the institutional theory of inflation tend to argue that it is best to err on the high side, with policy aiming for high potential output as in Figure 29-5(a). Economists who focus on the quantity theory tend to argue that it is best to err on the low side, with policy aiming at low potential output.

Quantity Theory and the Inflation/Growth Trade-Off

I suspect many of you will agree that erring on the high side makes the most sense. If that were the entire trade-off, such a reaction is probably right. But the quantity theory

Figure 29-5 (a and b) The Inflation/Growth Trade Off
Quantity theorists are much more likely to err on the side of preventing inflation, arguing that an ongoing inflation will begin at low potential output. They emphasize the trade-off shown in (**b**). Institutionalists are more likely to argue that the inflation threshold is at high potential output.

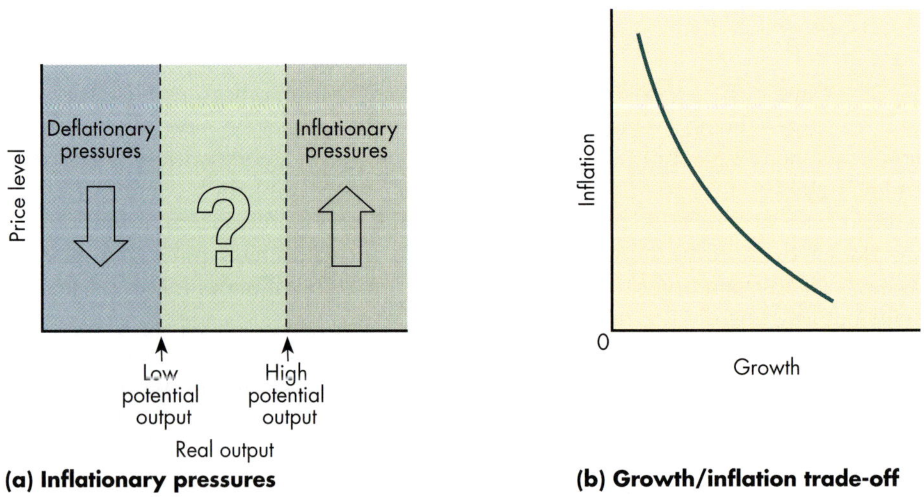

points out a problem with that reasoning, which might be called the "little bit pregnant problem." At the beginning of a pregnancy, it's true you are only a little bit pregnant, but that "little bit" has initiated a set of cellular changes that will fundamentally alter your life. Supporters of the quantity theory say it is the same with a small rise in the price level: You can't have a "little bit" of inflation. That little bit is setting in motion a series of events that will make the inflation grow and grow, unless the government gives up its attempt to achieve a high rate of output. Their solution to prevent inflation is abstinence—just say no to any rise in the price level.

Q-10 Why do quantity theorists believe that government should err on the side of lower output and a lower chance of inflation?

Those who support the quantity theory argue that erring on the low side pays off—it stops any chance of inflation. It establishes credibility of the Fed's resolve not to increase the money supply. If some inflation is allowed and the Fed loses credibility, that inflation undermines the long-run growth prospects of the economy, and hence causes future levels of potential income to be lower than they otherwise would be. Put another way, inflation undermines long-run growth; abstinence creates the environment for long-run growth. Thus, for quantity theorists, while there is no long-run trade-off between inflation and unemployment, there is a long-run trade-off between inflation and growth: High inflation leads to lower growth.

Low inflation leads to higher growth for a variety of reasons. Low inflation reduces price uncertainty, making it easier for businesses to invest in future production. Businesses can more easily enter into long-term contracts when inflation is low, which lowers the cost of doing business. Low inflation also makes using money much easier. When inflation is high, people spend more time trying to avoid the costs of inflation, which diverts their energies away from productive activities that would lead to growth.

The hypothesized relationship between inflation and growth is shown in Figure 29-5(b). For quantity theorists, even if there is a short-run relationship between inflation and unemployment, it is precarious for government to try to take advantage of it, because doing so can undermine the long-run growth potential of the economy. For quantity theorists, government policy creating an environment of price-level stability is the policy most likely to lead to high rates of growth. They suggest that the reason for the success of the economy in the late 1990s and early 2000s was that people believed that the Fed would fight inflation should it appear. Solid empirical evidence, however, does not yet exist.

Institutional Theory and the Inflation/Growth Trade-Off

Other economists, mainly supporters of the institutional theory of inflation, are less sure about this negative relationship between inflation and growth. They agree that price-level rises have the potential of generating inflation, and that high accelerating inflation undermines growth, but they do not agree that all price-level increases start an inflationary process. The lower unemployment rate accompanying the inflation is so nice, and if the government is really careful—I mean really, really careful—it can avoid reaching the point where the little bit of rise in price level starts the monster of inflation growing within the economy. And besides, if inflation gets started, the government has some medicine to give the economy that will get rid of the inflation relatively easily.

The real-world difference between the two views can be seen in the debate about monetary policy in the early 2000s, when the unemployment rate fell to around 4 percent. Until then, potential income had been estimated at an unemployment rate of 5.5 to 6 percent. So it seemed as if the economy was operating significantly beyond low-level potential output. But inflation remained low, at about 2–3 percent. Economists who focus on the quantity theory argued that inflation was just around the corner, and

Web Note 29.3
The Fed and Growth

that unless the government instituted contractionary aggregate demand policy, the seeds of inflation would be sown. Other economists argued that institutional changes in the labor market had reduced the inflation threat and that more expansionary policy was called for. The Fed followed a path between the two. Inflation did not rise, but instead fell as the economy slowed and unemployment rose. It was at that point that for some economists the policy concern changed from inflation to deflation. Whether inflation would have risen had growth continued was unclear.

Conclusion

The quantity and institutional theories of inflation, growth, and unemployment reflect two consistent but different worldviews. The institutional theorists see a world in which sociological and institutional factors interact with market forces, keeping the economy in a perpetual disequilibrium when considered in an economic framework. The quantity theorists see a world in which market forces predominate and institutional and sociological factors are insignificant. The overall economy is in continual equilibrium. These two theories carry over to economists' analyses of the central policy issue facing most governments as they decide on their monetary and fiscal policies: the trade-off between inflation and unemployment and growth. These different worldviews are an important reason why there are disagreements about policy, and the debate will likely continue for a long time.

Summary

- The winners in inflation are people who can raise their wages or prices and still keep their jobs or sell their goods. The losers are people who can't raise their wages or prices. On average, winners and losers balance out.
- Three types of inflationary expectations are rational (expectations based on economic models), adaptive (expectations based on the past), and extrapolative (expectations that a trend will continue).
- A basic rule of thumb to predict inflation is: Inflation equals nominal wage increases minus productivity growth.
- The equation of exchange is $MV = PQ$; it becomes the quantity theory when velocity is constant, real output is independent of the money supply, and causation goes from money to prices. The quantity theory says that the price level varies in direct response to changes in the quantity of money.
- The inflation tax is an implicit tax on the holders of cash and the holders of any obligations specified in nominal terms.
- Quantity theorists tend to favor a policy that relies on rules rather than on discretionary policy.
- The institutional theory of inflation sees the source of inflation in the wage-and-price setting institutions; it sees the direction of causation going from price increases to money increases.
- Institutional theorists tend to favor supplemental policies such as incomes policies to supplement tight monetary policies when fighting inflation.
- The long-run Phillips curve allows expectations of inflation to change; it is generally seen as vertical.
- The short-run Phillips curve holds expectations constant. It is generally seen as downward sloping and shifts up when expectations of inflation rise and shifts down when expectations of inflation fall.
- Quantity theorists see a long-run trade-off between inflation and growth, the higher inflation, the lower the growth rate. Institutional theorists are less sure about this trade-off.

Key Terms

adaptive expectations (685)
cost-push inflation (695)
deflation (686)
demand-pull inflation (694)
equation of exchange (687)
extrapolative expectations (685)
incomes policy (694)
inflation tax (690)
insider/outsider model (693)
long-run Phillips curve (697)
quantity theory of money (688)
rational expectations (685)
short-run Phillips curve (695)
stagflation (697)
velocity of money (687)

Questions for Thought and Review

1. Why do lenders lose out in inflation? Under what conditions would they not lose out?
2. If you base your expectations of inflation on what has happened in the past, what kind of expectations are you demonstrating?
3. If productivity growth is 3 percent and wage increases are 5 percent, what would you predict inflation would be?
4. If deflation is 3 percent and nominal interest rates are 2 percent, what are real interest rates?
5. If deflation is 2 percent and nominal interest rates are 1 percent, what is the lowest real interest rate the Fed can target?
6. What three assumptions turn the equation of exchange into the quantity theory of money?
7. What does the quantity theory predict will happen to inflation if the money supply rises 10 percent?
8. Why did the relationship between growth in the money supply and inflation break down in the 1990s?
9. For what countries is the connection between the growth in the money supply and inflation still evident? What accounts for this?
10. If governments are aware that increases in the money supply cause inflation, why do some countries increase the money supply by significant amounts anyway?
11. Define the inflation tax. Who pays it?
12. Who is more likely to support monetary rules—a quantity theorist or an institutionalist? Explain your answer.
13. What is the direction of causation between money and prices according to the institutional theory of inflation?
14. What is the insider/outsider theory of inflation? Would quantity or institutional theorists likely believe this theory?
15. How do the policy implications of the quantity theory and the institutional theory of inflation differ?
16. What would Alfred Marshall likely say about the cost-push/demand-pull distinction?
17. Draw both a short-run and a long-run Phillips curve. What does each say about the relationship between inflation and unemployment?
18. If people's expectations of inflation didn't change, would the economy move from a short-run to a long-run Phillips curve?
19. The Phillips curve is just a figment of economists' imagination. True or false?
20. What is the reasoning behind the view that there is a trade-off between inflation and growth?

Problems and Exercises

1. Assume the money supply is $500, the velocity of money is 8, and the price level is $2. Using the quantity theory of money:
   a. Determine the level of real output.
   b. Determine the level of nominal output.
   c. Assuming velocity remains constant, what will happen if the money supply rises 20 percent?
   d. If the government established price controls and also raised the money supply 20 percent, what would happen?
   e. How would you judge whether the assumption of fixed velocity is reasonable?
2. Congratulations. You've just been appointed finance minister of Inflationland. Inflation has been ongoing for the past five years at 5 percent. The target rate of unemployment, 5 percent, is also the actual rate.
   a. Demonstrate the economy's likely position on both short-run and long-run Phillips curves.
   b. The president tells you she wants to be reelected. Devise a monetary policy strategy for her that might help her accomplish her goal.
   c. Demonstrate that strategy graphically, including the likely long-run consequences.

3. In the early 1990s, Argentina stopped increasing the money supply and fixed the exchange rate of the Argentine austral at 10,000 to the dollar. It then renamed the Argentine currency the "peso" and cut off four zeros so that one peso equaled one dollar. Inflation slowed substantially. After this was done, the following observations were made. Explain why these observations did not surprise economists.
   a. The golf courses were far less crowded.
   b. The price of goods in dollar-equivalent pesos in Buenos Aires, the capital of the country, was significantly above that in New York City.
   c. Consumer prices—primarily services—rose relative to other goods.
   d. Luxury auto dealers were shutting down.
4. Grade inflation is widespread. In 1990, 81 percent of the students who took the SATs had an A or B average, but 40 percent of them scored less than 390 on the verbal SAT. Students' grades are increasing but what they are learning is decreasing. Some economists argue that grade inflation should be dealt with in the same way that price inflation should be dealt with—by creating a fixed standard and requiring all grades to be specified relative to that standard. One way to accomplish this is to index the grades professors give: specify on the grade report both the student's grade and the class average, and deflate (or inflate) the grade to some common standard. Discuss the advantages and disadvantages of such a proposal.
5. In the mid-1990s and through the early 2000s, Japan's annual money supply growth rate fell to 1–2 percent from an average annual rate of 10–11 percent in the late 1980s. What effect did this decline have on:
   a. Japanese real output?
   b. Japanese unemployment?
   c. Japanese inflation?
6. Wayne Angell, a former Fed governor, stated in an editorial, "The Federal Reserve should get back on track getting inflation rates so low that inflation would no longer be a determining factor in household and business investment decisions." Mr. Angell believes inflation lowers long-term growth.
   a. Is Wayne Angell most likely a quantity theorist or institutionalist? Explain your answer.
   b. How does inflation affect household decisions and, consequently, growth?
7. People's perception of inflation often differs from actual inflation.
   a. List five goods that you buy relatively frequently.
   b. Looking in old newspapers (found in the library on microfiche), locate sales prices for these goods since 1950, finding one price every five years or so. Determine the average annual price rise for each good from 1950 to today.
   c. Compare that price with the rise in the consumer price index.

WEB QUESTIONS

1. Economagic is a comprehensive site of free, easily available economic time series data useful for economic research, in particular economic forecasting. Go to the site www.economagic.com and find annual data for M_1 and nominal GDP from 1959 to the most recently available year. You will be able to find both by selecting the St. Louis Fed database. Use the tool called "transform this series" to calculate annual averages. Use this data to answer the following questions:
   a. Use a spreadsheet to calculate the velocity of money for each year from 1959 to the most recent year available.
   b. How much income did $1 support in 1960? In 1970? In 1980? In 1990? In 2000?
   c. What happened to the velocity of money over this time period?
   d. What implications does the variability of the velocity of money have for the quantity theory of money?
2. The Richmond Fed publishes a newsletter called *Equilibria* devoted to simple explanations of economic concepts. Go to the site of *Equilibria* (www.rich.frb.org/pubs/equilibria/issue1) and read the article "Does the Fed Drive Interest Rates?" in Issue No. 1 of *Equilibria*. Answer the following questions:
   a. What is the relationship between interest rates and inflation suggested by the article?
   b. Would you characterize the article as reflecting an institutionalist or quantity theory viewpoint? Explain your answer.
   c. What kind of feedback rule does the article suggest the Fed follows?
   d. What part of the economy could the "terrain" be referring to? (Hint: Remember the Taylor rule.)

Answers to Margin Questions

1. False. Inflation does not make an economy poorer. It redistributes income from those who do not raise their prices to those who do raise their prices. *(685)*
2. Three types of expectations are rational expectations, adaptive expectations, and extrapolative expectations. *(685)*
3. The equation of exchange, $MV = PQ$, is a tautology. What changes it to the quantity theory are assumptions about the variables, specifically that velocity remains constant, that real output is determined separately, and that the causation flows from money to prices. With these assumptions added, the equation of exchange implies that changes in the money supply are reflected in changes in the price level—which is what the quantity theory of money says. *(687)*
4. Central banks sometimes issue large quantities of money for a number of reasons. One reason is that in their estimation the benefit of doing so (avoiding a breakdown of the government and perhaps the entire economy) exceeds the cost (starting an inflation). Another reason is that some central banks lack the independence to maintain low inflation as a goal. *(691)*
5. According to the quantity theory, the direction of causation goes from money to prices ($MV \rightarrow PQ$)—increases in the money supply lead to increases in the price level. According to institutional theory, the direction of causation goes from prices to money ($MV \leftarrow PQ$)—increases in the price level are ratified by government, which increases the money supply. *(692)*
6. A quantity theorist would likely say that the insider/outsider model of inflation tends to obscure the central cause of inflation—increases in the money supply. *(693)*
7. A quantity theorist would recommend that the growth in the money supply be reduced. An institutionalist would recommend that the government hold prices down directly with an incomes policy as well as reduce the growth in the money supply. *(694)*
8. As you can see in the graph on the top of the next column, the long-run Phillips curve is perfectly vertical. Its shape is dependent on the assumption that people's expectations of inflation completely adjust to inflation in the long run, and that adjustment is not institutionally constrained. *(697)*

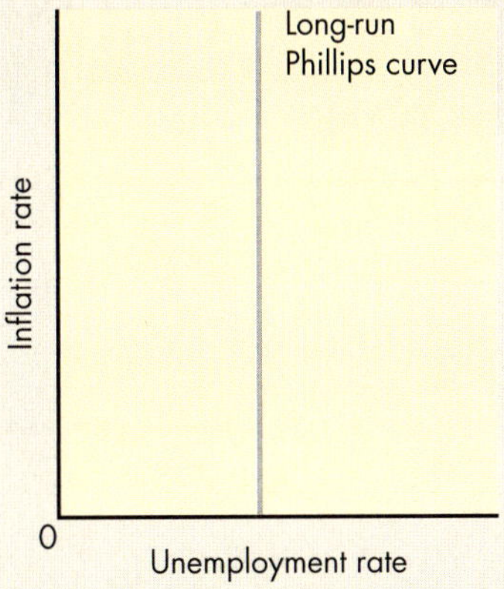

9. If the economy is at point *A* on the Phillips curve below, inflation is below expected inflation and unemployment is higher than the target rate of unemployment. If this were the only information I had about the economy, I would expect both unemployment and inflation to fall. *(699)*

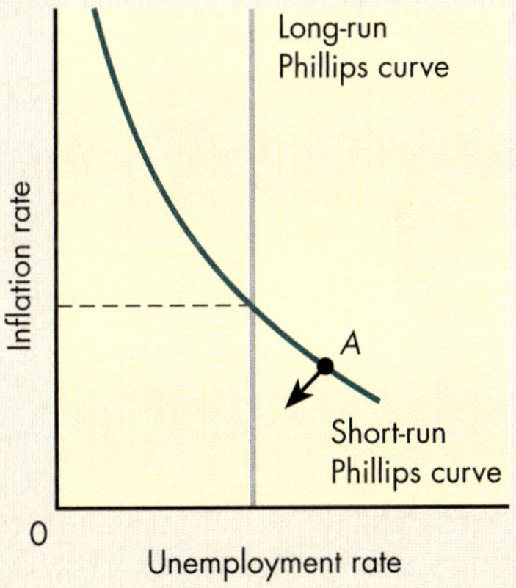

10. Quantity theorists believe that government should err on the side of low output and a lower chance of inflation because any amount of inflation sets into motion a series of changes in the economy that will likely lead to higher inflation. *(701)*

30 Aggregate Demand Policy in Perspective

After reading this chapter, you should be able to:

- List six problems with fiscal policy and explain how those problems limit its use.
- Describe how automatic stabilizers work.
- Summarize the advantages and disadvantages of using monetary and fiscal policy.
- List three alternatives to fiscal policy.
- State why economists often talk about *policy regimes* rather than simply *policy.*

An economist's lag may be a politician's catastrophe.

—*George Schultz*

There are two central tools of aggregate demand policy—monetary and fiscal policy. We've explored the problems of using monetary policy, and they were considerable. That might make you think that the other historically central tool of aggregate demand policy, fiscal policy, is the tool of choice. That would be a wrong impression. All the problems of using monetary policy are also true for fiscal policy, with some additional political problems. These additional problems are severe enough to make many say that, when talking about controlling the economy with aggregate demand policy, monetary policy is the only game in town. While most economists would agree that this characterization is a bit of an exaggeration, most would also agree that it has more than a bit of truth to it.

In this chapter I try to give you the sense of how fiscal policy and, more generally, aggregate demand policy, are thought about by policymakers. I do this by first contrasting demand-side policies with supply-side policies, and discussing the way in which the same policies may be viewed quite differently depending on whether one is looking at them from a perspective of long-run growth—their effect on the supply side—or on short-run stabilization—their effect on the demand side. Second, I discuss the problems of fiscal policy and how some of those problems have been circumvented by building desired fiscal policy into institutions. Third, I summarize the conventional wisdom about monetary and fiscal policy. Fourth, I discuss some additional policies that supplement monetary and fiscal policy. I conclude the chapter by discussing some recent critiques of monetary and fiscal policy that have led to changes in how policy is implemented.

Supply Side versus Demand Side Policies

Macro policy, by its very nature, is aggregate policy, which means that it is designed to affect the aggregate economy. But in the aggregate, supply and demand forces are interrelated. That interrelationship is captured in the circular flow diagram, which I used way back at the beginning of the course to introduce the central issues of macro. In that diagram you could see how aggregate supply—production by firms—created output but how supply simultaneously created income, and hence the potential demand to buy that output.

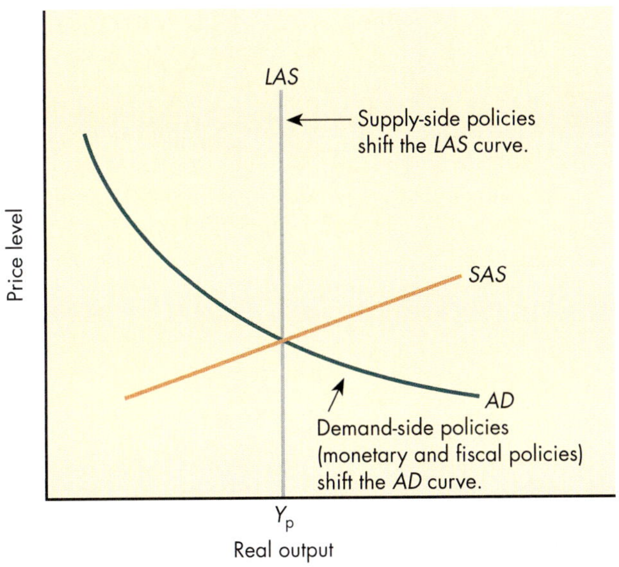

Figure 30-1 Demand-Side and Supply-Side Policies Demand-side policies (monetary and fiscal policies) shift the aggregate demand (*AD*) curve, while supply-side policies shift the long-run aggregate supply (*LAS*) curve.

Talking about policy in such an interrelated system generally becomes quite messy, which means we have to simplify. We did so in the basic *AS/AD* model. In that model we separated long-run aggregate supply forces from short-run aggregate demand forces, which allowed us to differentiate policies affecting supply and growth from policies affecting demand and stabilization. In our simplification, demand-side policies—such as monetary and fiscal policy—affect the economy by shifting the *AD* curve, increasing output as long as the economy is below potential output. Supply-side policies work by increasing potential output.

Chapter 24 discussed a variety of supply-side policies such as tax subsidies for investment, policies to encourage research and development, and policies to encourage trade. These supply-side policies were differentiated from demand-side policies, which were seen as working primarily on demand. Thus, the model abstracted from any possible interconnection between aggregate demand and long-run supply. Figure 30-1 provides the standard differentiation between demand-side policies and supply-side policies within the model.

If you are relating the model to discussions you read in the press, you have to remember that politicians are not constrained by models. They can, and do, often emphasize different interconnections. Consider the tax cut President George W. Bush pushed though in 2001. When he was first proposing it, the economy was operating at what most economists felt was beyond its potential income. So on the demand side no tax cut was needed and President Bush's arguments for it were supply-side arguments. The president argued that the lower taxes would encourage people to work harder and give firms greater incentive to invest, increasing the labor supply and thereby shifting out potential output. (He didn't emphasize another supply-side effect of the tax cut—the fact that the tax cut would reduce the budget surplus, decreasing government saving and thereby decreasing the pool of savings available for investment.)

Soon after the tax cut was passed, but before it was implemented, the economy slowed, giving rise to a demand-side reason for the tax cut. At that point President Bush shifted the argument for the tax cut, no longer emphasizing its supply-side effects but instead emphasizing its demand-side effects. Thus, in the 2002 *Economic Report of the President*, we see the following justification for the tax cut:

> The initial macroeconomic effects of tax relief have been positive, strengthening aggregate demand in the face of other downward pressures . . . The boost in aggregate demand should help provide a foundation for economy-wide recovery in 2002. (p. 45)

President Bush is not alone in emphasizing the effect that supports the policy he wanted. All politicians do. And each of the arguments has some validity since almost all policies have simultaneous supply- and demand-side effects. But usually the supply-side effects are long-term effects, while the demand-side effects are short-run effects, which is what the *AS/AD* model captures. The reality is that political rhetoric will emphasize whatever effect best supports the policy the politician wants to follow.

Problems with Fiscal Policy

Let us now return to the problems with fiscal policy. Fiscal policy sounds so easy—and in the model it is. If there's a contraction in the economy, the government runs an expansionary fiscal policy; if there's inflation, the government runs a contractionary fiscal policy, keeping the economy at the desired level of income.

In reality, that's not the way it is. A number of important problems arise that make the actual practice of fiscal policy difficult. These problems don't mean that our models of how fiscal policy works are wrong; they simply mean that for fiscal policy to work, the policy conclusions drawn from the model must be modified to reflect the real-world problems. Let's consider how the reality might not fit the model. The model assumes:

Six assumptions of the model that could lead to problems with fiscal policy are:

1. Financing the deficit doesn't have any offsetting effects.
2. The government knows what the situation is.
3. The government knows the economy's potential income level.
4. The government has flexibility in changing spending and taxes.
5. The size of the government debt doesn't matter.
6. Fiscal policy doesn't negatively affect other government goals.

1. Financing the deficit doesn't have any offsetting effect. (In reality, it often does.)
2. The government knows what the situation is—for instance, the size of the *mpe*, and other exogenous variables. (In reality, the government must estimate them.)
3. The government knows the economy's potential income level—the highest level of income that doesn't cause accelerating inflation. (In reality, the government may not know what this level is.)
4. The government has flexibility in changing spending and taxes. (In reality, government cannot change them quickly.)
5. The size of the government debt doesn't matter. (In reality, the size of the government debt often does matter.)
6. Fiscal policy doesn't negatively affect other government goals. (In reality, it often does.)

Let's consider each assumption a bit further.

1. Financing the Deficit Doesn't Have Offsetting Effects

One of the most important limitations of the multiplier model is that it assumes that financing the deficit has no offsetting effects on income. Some economists argue that that is not the case, that the government financing of deficit spending will offset the deficit's expansionary effect.

The multiplier model assumes that saving and investment can be unequal, and that the government can increase its expenditures without at the same time causing a decrease in private expenditures. Some economists object to that assumption. They believe the interest rate equilibrates saving and investment. They argue that when the government borrows to finance the deficit, that borrowing will increase interest rates and crowd out private investment.

Interest rate **crowding out**—*the offsetting of a change in government expenditures by a change in private expenditures in the opposite direction*—occurs as follows: When the government runs a deficit, it must sell bonds (that is, it must borrow) to finance that deficit. To get people to buy and hold the bonds, the government must make them attractive. That means the interest rate the bonds pay must be higher than it otherwise would have been. This tends to push up the interest rate in the economy, which makes it more expensive for private businesses to borrow, so they reduce their borrowing and their investment. That private investment is crowded out by expansionary fiscal policy. Hence the name *crowding out*. Increased government spending crowds out private spending.

Interest rate crowding out reduces the effect of increases in government expenditures.

Q-1 If interest rates had no effect on investment or consumption, how much crowding out would occur?

Crowding out is shown in Figure 30-2. Income in the economy is Y_0 and government has decided to expand that income to Y_1 by increasing its spending. If financing were not an issue, expansionary fiscal policy would shift the *AD* curve to the right by a multiple of the increase in government spending, increasing income from Y_0 to Y_1. Financing the deficit, however, increases interest rates and decreases investment by ΔI, which shifts the *AD* curve to the left to AD_2. Income falls back to Y_2.

Because of crowding out, the net expansionary effect of fiscal policy is smaller than it otherwise would have been. Some economists argue that crowding out can totally offset the expansionary effect of fiscal policy, so the net effect is zero, or even negative, since they consider private spending more productive than government spending. This is the view taken by some of those who focus on the supply-side effects of fiscal policy. Larger deficits decrease the pool of savings available for investment by raising interest rates. The result is that potential output does not increase as much as it otherwise would, and thus the policy leads to slower growth.

The crowding out effect also works in reverse with contractionary fiscal policy. Say the government runs a surplus. That surplus will slow the economy through the multiplier effect. But it also means the U.S. Treasury (a U.S. agency that issues bonds to finance the deficit) can buy back some of its outstanding bonds, which, as we discussed in earlier chapters, will have a tendency to push bond prices up and interest rates down. Lower interest rates will stimulate investment, which in turn will have an offsetting expansionary effect on the economy. So when we include financing the deficit in our consideration of fiscal policy, the net multiplier effect is reduced.

Crowding out is the offsetting effect on private expenditures caused by the government's sale of bonds to finance expansionary fiscal policy.

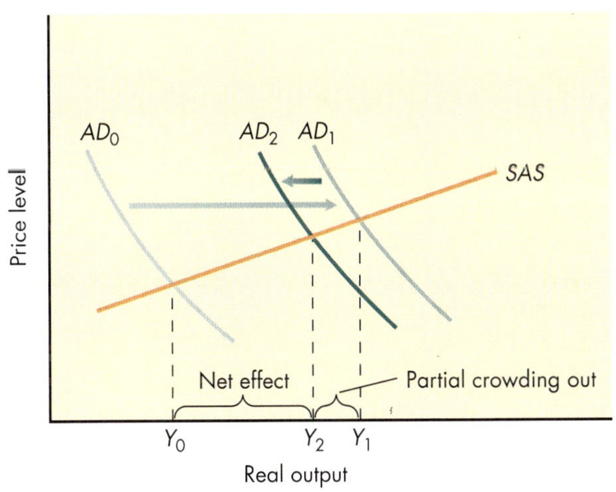

Figure 30-2 Partial Crowding Out
An increase in government spending will expand income, but will also cause interest rates to rise and thereby cause investment to decrease, which will tend to decrease income. This is called *interest rate crowding out*. The net effect of fiscal policy depends on the degree of crowding out that takes place.

Q-2 Demonstrate graphically what would happen if government expenditures policy stimulated private investment.

How large this financing offset to fiscal policy will be is a matter of debate. The empirical evidence about the degree of crowding out is mixed and has not resolved the debate. Both sides see some crowding out occurring as the debt is financed by selling bonds. The closer to the potential income level the economy is, the more crowding out is likely to occur.

2. Knowing What the Situation Is

The numbers we use to demonstrate fiscal policy in the *AS/AD* model were chosen arbitrarily. In reality, the numbers used in models must be estimated or based on preliminary figures subject to revision. Most economic data are published quarterly, and it usually takes six to nine months of data to indicate, with any degree of confidence, the state of the economy and which way it is heading. Thus, we could be halfway into a recession before we even know it is happening. For example, data revisions showed GDP fell for three consecutive quarters in 2001, whereas the preliminary figures had shown only a one-quarter decline. (Data are already three months old when published; then we need two or three quarters of such data before they compose a useful body of information to work with.)

In an attempt to deal with this problem, the government relies on large macroeconomic models and leading indicators to predict what the economy will be like six months or a year from now. As part of the input to these complex models, the government must predict economic factors that determine the size of the multiplier. These predictions are imprecise, so the forecasts are imprecise. Economic forecasting is still an art, not a science.

Economists' data problems limit the use of fiscal policy for fine tuning. There's little sense in recommending expansionary or contractionary policy until you know what policy is called for.

3. Knowing the Level of Potential Income

Web Note 30.1 What's the Speed Limit?

This problem of not knowing the level of potential income is related to the problem we just discussed. The target rate of unemployment and the potential level of income are not easy concepts to define. At one time it was thought 3 percent unemployment meant full employment. Some time later it was generally thought 6 percent unemployment meant full employment. About that time economists stopped calling the potential level of income the *full-employment* level of income.

Any variation in potential income can make an enormous difference in the policy prescription that could be recommended. To see how big a difference, let's translate a 1 percent change in unemployment into a change in income. According to *Okun's rule of thumb* (defined in an earlier chapter as the general rule of thumb economists use to translate changes in the unemployment rate into changes in income), a 1 percentage point fall in the unemployment rate is associated with a 2 percent increase in income. Thus, in 2003 with income at about \$11 trillion, a 1 percentage point fall in the unemployment rate would have increased income \$220 billion.

Now let's say one economist believes 5.5 percent is the long-run achievable target rate of unemployment, while another believes it's 4 percent. That's a 1.5 percentage point difference. Since a 1 percent decrease in the unemployment rate means an increase of about \$220 billion in national income, their views of the income level we should target differ by over \$330 billion ($1.5 \times \$220 = \$330$). Yet both views are reasonable. Looking at the same economy (the same data), one economist may call for expansionary fiscal policy while the other may call for contractionary fiscal policy.

Differences in estimates of potential income often lead to different policy recommendations.

In practice, differences in estimates of potential income often lead to different policy recommendations. Empirical estimates suggest that the size of the multiplier is somewhere between 1.5 and 2.5. Let's say it's 2.5. That means autonomous expenditures must be predicted to increase or decrease by more than $132 billion before an economist who believes the target rate of unemployment is 4 percent would agree in policy recommendation with an economist who believes the rate is 5.5 percent. Since almost all fluctuations in autonomous investment and autonomous consumption are less than this amount, there's no generally agreed-on policy prescription for most fluctuations. Some economists will call for expansionary policy; some will call for contractionary policy; and the government decision makers won't have any clear-cut policy to follow.

You might wonder why the range of potential income estimates is so large. Why not simply see whether the economy has inflation at the existing rate of unemployment and income level? Would that it were so easy. Inflation is a complicated process. Seeds of inflation are often sown years before inflation results. The main problem is that establishing a close link between the level of economic activity and inflation is a complicated statistical challenge to economists, one that has not yet been satisfactorily met. That leads to enormous debate as to what the causes are.

Almost all economists believe that outside some range (perhaps 3.5 percent unemployment on the low side and 10 percent on the high side), too much spending causes inflation and too little spending causes a recession. That 3.5 to 10 percentage point range is so large that in most cases the U.S. economy is in an ambiguous state where some economists are calling for expansionary policy and others are calling for contractionary policy.

In most cases the U.S. economy is in an ambiguous state where some economists are calling for expansionary policy and others are calling for contractionary policy.

Once the economy reaches the edge of the range of potential income or falls outside it, the economists' policy prescription becomes clearer. For example, in the Depression, when this multiplier model was developed, unemployment was 25 percent—well outside the range. Should the economy ever go into such a depression again, economists' policy prescriptions will be clear. The call will be for expansionary fiscal policy. Most times the economy is within the ambiguous range, so there are disagreements among economists.

Q-3 Why don't economists have an accurate measure of potential income?

4. The Government's Flexibility in Changing Taxes and Spending

For argument's sake, let's say economists agree that contractionary policy is needed and that's what they advise the government. Will the government implement it? And, if so, will it implement contractionary fiscal policy at the right time? The answer to both questions is: probably not. There are also problems with implementing economists' calls for expansionary fiscal policy. Even if economists are unanimous in calling for expansionary fiscal policy, putting fiscal policy in place takes time and has serious implementation problems.

Numerous political and institutional realities in the United States today make it a difficult task to implement fiscal policy. Government spending and taxes cannot be changed instantaneously. The budget process begins more than a year and a half before the government's fiscal year begins. President George W. Bush's plans for tax relief that culminated in the Economic Growth and Tax Relief Reconciliation Act were written months before the economy went into recession and many more months before the September 11, 2001, terrorist attacks, which deepened the recession. When it was first implemented, it looked to most economists as if it would be too expansionary and that it was not needed. That's why initially President Bush emphasized its supply-side effects. However, as I mentioned above, in this case the timing of the reductions in taxes was just about right—it helped boost consumer spending in a slowing economy and played an important demand-side role, even though countercyclical policy was not the motivation for passing the act.

Fighting the Vietnam War Inflation

Applying the Tools

In the chapter I described an incident in which fiscal policy worked the way it was supposed to through luck. Usually that isn't the case, and many times fiscal policy's effect comes at the wrong time and affects the economy in the wrong way. For example, one time that economists were united in their views on appropriate fiscal policy was during the Vietnam War, from the early 1960s until 1975, when the economy was pushed to its limits. About 1965, President Lyndon B. Johnson's economic advisers started to argue strongly that a tax increase was needed to slow the economy and decrease inflationary pressures. President Johnson wouldn't hear of it. He felt a tax increase would be political suicide. Finally in mid-1968, after Johnson had decided not to run for reelection, a temporary income tax increase was passed. By then, however, many economists felt that the seeds of the 1970s inflation had already been sown.

Another difficulty is that nearly two-thirds of the government budget is mandated by government programs such as Medicare and Social Security and by interest payments on the debt. Even the remaining one-third, called discretionary spending, is difficult to change. Defense programs are generally multiyear spending commitments. Discretionary spending also includes appropriations to established government agencies such as the Department of Agriculture, the Department of Transportation, and the Internal Revenue Service for their operation. Changing their budgets is politically difficult.

Politicians face intense political pressures; their other goals may conflict with the goals of fiscal policy. For example, few members of Congress who hope to be reelected would vote to raise taxes in an election year. Similarly, few members would vote to slash defense spending when military contractors are a major source of employment in their districts, even when there's little to defend against. Squabbles between Congress and the president may delay initiating appropriate fiscal policy for months, even years. By the time the fiscal policy is implemented, what may have once been the right fiscal policy may have ceased to be right, and some other policy may have become right.

Imagine trying to steer a car at 60 miles an hour when there's a five-second delay between the time you turn the steering wheel and the time the car's wheels turn. Imagining that situation will give you a good sense of how fiscal policy works in the real world.

5. Size of the Government Debt Doesn't Matter

There is no inherent reason why the adoption of activist policies should have caused the government to run deficits year after year and hence to incur ever-increasing debt—accumulated deficits less accumulated surpluses. Activist policy is consistent with running deficits some years and surpluses other years. In practice, the introduction of activist policy has been accompanied by many deficits and few surpluses, and by a large increase in government debt. If that increase in government debt hurts the economy, one can oppose policies of deficit spending, even if one believes that policy might otherwise be beneficial.

There are two reasons why activist government policies have led to an increase in government debt. First, early activist economists favored large increases in government spending as well as favoring the government's using fiscal policy. These early activist economists employed the multiplier model to justify increasing spending without increasing taxes. A second reason is political. Politically it's much easier for government to increase spending and decrease taxes than to decrease spending and increase taxes.

Due to political pressure, expansionary fiscal policy has predominated over contractionary fiscal policy.

Whether debt is a problem is an important and complicated issue, as we'll see in the next chapter. For now, all you need remember is that if one believes that the debt is harmful, then there might be a reason not to conduct expansionary fiscal policy, even when the model calls for it.

6. Fiscal Policy Doesn't Negatively Affect Other Government Goals

A society has many goals; achieving potential income is only one of those goals. So it's not surprising that those goals often conflict. When the government runs expansionary fiscal policy, the balance of trade deficit grows. As the economy expands and income rises, exports remain constant but imports rise. If a nation's international considerations do not allow a balance of trade deficit to become larger, as is true in many countries, those governments cannot run expansionary fiscal policies—unless they can somehow prevent this balance of trade deficit from becoming larger.

Summary of the Problems

So where do these six problems leave fiscal policy? While they don't eliminate its usefulness, they severely restrict it. Fiscal policy is a sledgehammer, not an instrument for fine tuning. When the economy goes into a depression, the appropriate fiscal policy is clear. Similarly when the economy has a hyperinflation, the appropriate policy is clear. But in less extreme cases, there will be debate on what the appropriate fiscal policy is—a debate economic theory can't answer conclusively.

Fiscal policy is a sledgehammer, not an instrument for fine tuning.

Building Fiscal Policies into Institutions

Economists quickly recognized the political problems with instituting direct countercyclical fiscal policy. To avoid these problems they suggested policies that built fiscal policy into U.S. institutions so that it would be put into effect without any political decisions being necessary. They called a built-in fiscal policy an **automatic stabilizer,** which is *any government program or policy that will counteract the business cycle without any new government action*. Automatic stabilizers include welfare payments, unemployment insurance, and the income tax system.

An automatic stabilizer is any government program or policy that will counteract the business cycle without any new government action.

How Automatic Stabilizers Work

Web Note 30.2 Unemployment Compensation

To see how automatic stabilizers work, consider the unemployment insurance system. When the economy is slowing down or is in a recession, the unemployment rate will rise. When people lose their jobs, they will reduce their consumption, starting the multiplier process, which decreases income. Unemployment insurance immediately helps offset the decrease in individuals' incomes as the government pays benefits to the unemployed. Thus, government spending increases, and part of the fall in income is stopped without any explicit act by the government. Automatic stabilizers also work in reverse. When income increases, government spending declines automatically.

Another automatic stabilizer is our income tax system. Tax revenue fluctuates as income fluctuates. When the economy expands tax revenues rise, slowing the economy; when the economy contracts tax revenues decline, providing a stimulus to the economy. Let's go through the reasoning why. When the economy is strong, people have more income and thus pay higher taxes. This increase in tax revenue reduces consumption expenditures from what they would have been and moderates the economy's growth. When the economy goes into a recession, the opposite occurs.

State Government Finance and Procyclical Fiscal Policy

Automatic stabilizers are sometimes offset by other institutional structures that work as a type of automatic *destabilizer*. Examples of such destabilizers are states' constitutional provisions to maintain balanced budgets. These provisions mean that whenever a recession hits, states are faced with declining tax revenue. To maintain balanced budgets, the states must cut spending, increase tax rates, or both. For example, during the 2001–2002 recession, state governments struggled to balance their budgets by cutting expenditures on education, transportation, health care, and a variety of other programs while raising income and sales taxes. These actions deepened the recession. Similarly, during the previous 10-year expansion, state revenue rose; and states increased spending and decreased tax rates. The expansionary effect of these changes further increased total income. The result is what economists call **procyclical fiscal policy**—*changes in government spending and taxes that increase the cyclical fluctuations in the economy instead of reducing them*.

To reduce the procyclical nature of state financing, economists have suggested states establish rainy-day funds—reserves kept in good times, to be used to offset declines in revenue during recessions. Large rainy-day funds (which some economists have called rainy-season funds) would decrease the destabilizing aspect of state government spending. But politics usually keep rainy-day funds small; the funds are targets that are just too tempting for spending proposals or tax cuts.

An alternative way of building countercyclical policies into institutions would be for states to use a five-year rolling-average budgeting procedure (with an underlying trend rate of increase built into it) as the budget they are required to balance. With a rolling-average budget, revenues available for spending would be determined from a growth-adjusted average of revenues for the past five years. When revenues increase substantially in a year, the surplus available to be spent would build up only slowly and would therefore be much less politically tempting to raid. When revenues fall, the measured deficit would grow much more slowly, and the constitutional budget-balancing requirements would be much less procyclical.

Balancing a rolling-average budget, rather than the current-year budget, would provide a counterweight to the balanced-budget requirement and would remove much of the procyclical aspect of current state budgeting procedures. In fact, if the federal government started using a similar five-year rolling-average budget, it too could build a more reasonable fiscal policy into its accounting procedures and reduce the need for discretionary stimulus packages in the future.

The Negative Side of Automatic Stabilizers

Q-4 What effect do automatic stabilizers have on the size of the multiplier?

Automatic stabilizers may seem like the solution to the economic woes we have discussed, but they, too, have their shortcomings. One problem is that when the economy is first starting to climb out of a recession, automatic stabilizers will slow the process, rather than help it along, for the same reason they slow the contractionary process. As income increases, automatic stabilizers increase government taxes and decrease government spending, and as they do, the discretionary policy's expansionary effects are decreased.

Figure 30-3 Decrease in Fluctuations in the Economy
Compared to the early 1900s, fluctuations in the economy have decreased; this suggests that policymakers have done something right.

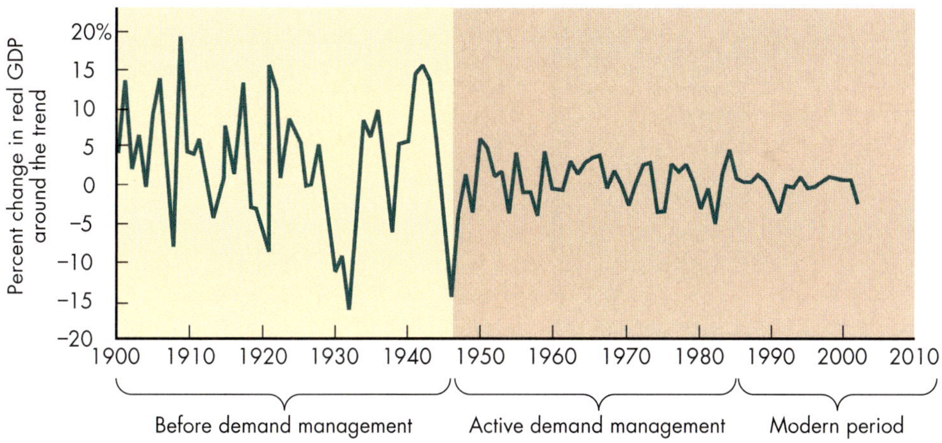

Source: Federal Reserve Historical Charts and Economic Report of the President (www.doc.gov).

Despite these problems, most economists believe that automatic stabilizers have played an important role in reducing fluctuations in our economy. They point to the kind of data we see in Figure 30-3, which they say show a significant decrease in fluctuations in the economy. Other economists aren't so sure; they argue the apparent decrease in fluctuations is an optical illusion. As usual, economic data are sufficiently ambiguous to give both sides strong arguments. The jury is still out.

Conventional Wisdom about Monetary and Fiscal Policy

Now that I've been through the problems with fiscal policy, and how policymakers deal with them, let me summarize the conventional wisdom about the use of both monetary and fiscal policy. They certainly are not tools to fine-tune the economy, but they can be useful in guiding it toward achieving goals of high growth, low inflation, and low unemployment. Of the two, monetary policy is the more important policy for short-run stabilization purposes. Reasons include the political and technical problems of using discretionary fiscal policy. Politics, not the needs of the economy, generally shape fiscal policy. Automatic stabilizers have, however, built in an automatic fiscal response to fluctuations in the economy, and more automatic responses could be built in. Monetary policy has some of the same problems as fiscal policy but is more flexible and less influenced by politics. Expansionary monetary and fiscal policy both have long-run consequences, with the former tending to lead to inflation and the latter raising interest rates and decreasing investment in the long run.

Often, the economy will be in a range where there is some chance that both inflation and unemployment will be problems, which means that these trade-offs must be dealt with. In discussing the trade-offs economists emphasize the limits of what can be achieved with macroeconomic policy. Economists often tell governments that they're asking for too much. These governments are like a patient who asks his doctor for a health program that will enable him to forget about a training program, eat anything he wants, and run a four-minute mile. Some things just can't be done, and it's

Figure 30-4 Conventional Wisdom about Macroeconomic Policy

	Option	Advantages	Disadvantages
Monetary policy	Expansionary	1. Interest rates may fall. 2. Economy may grow. 3. Decreases unemployment.	1. Inflation may worsen. 2. Capital outflow. 3. Trade deficit may increase.
	Contractionary	1. Helps fight inflation. 2. Trade deficit may decrease. 3. Capital inflow.	1. Risks recession. 2. Increases unemployment. 3. Slows growth. 4. May help cause short-run political problems. 5. Interest rates may rise.
Fiscal policy	Expansionary	1. May increase output growth in the short run. 2. May help solve short-run political problems. 3. Decreases unemployment.	1. Budget deficit worsens. 2. Hurts country's ability to borrow in the future. 3. Trade deficit may increase. 4. Upward pressure on interest rate, discouraging growth.
	Contractionary	1. May help fight inflation. 2. May allow a better monetary/fiscal mix. 3. Trade deficit may decrease. 4. Interest rates may fall stimulating investment and growth in the long run.	1. Risks recession. 2. Increases unemployment. 3. Slows output growth in the short run. 4. May help cause short-run political problems.

important for governments to recognize the inevitable limitations and trade-offs, at least with the monetary and fiscal policy tools currently available. Good economics are continually pointing out those limits.

The conventional wisdom about monetary and fiscal policy is summarized in Figure 30-4.

Alternatives and Supplements to Monetary and Fiscal Policy

Since there are serious questions about the effectiveness of both monetary and fiscal policy, attempts to control the economy often include a variety of alternative policies to affect aggregate demand. You can understand these policies by thinking about the various components of aggregate demand: consumption, investment, government spending, and net exports. Both monetary and fiscal policy work because they affect at least one of these four components. For example, an increase in government spending increases government spending directly. Alternatively, a tax cut gives consumers more income to spend and leads to increased consumption. So fiscal policy works by affecting consumption and government spending. Similarly, monetary policy works because it changes interest rates and the availability of credit. (Expansionary monetary policy lowers interest rates and increases credit availability; contractionary monetary policy does the opposite.) Thus, monetary policy works because it changes the interest-sensitive portions of consumption and investment spending.

Monetary and fiscal policies aren't the only policies that affect aggregate demand; any policy that affects any of the four components of autonomous spending *without having offsetting effects on other expenditures* can achieve the same results. The addendum in italics is important because, in reality, no expenditure is totally autonomous. If you push on one type of expenditure, you pull on another, and the net effect is often far more ambiguous than assumed.

We considered government spending policy before when we talked about fiscal policy. Let us briefly consider some of the other policies that could be used to influence income. I discuss investment first, then net exports, and, finally, consumption.

Directed Investment Policies: Policy Affecting Expectations

Early macro economists thought that the Depression was caused by some type of collective psychological fear on the part of investors who, because they predicted that the economy was going into a recession, decided not to invest. If somehow government could have supported investment, it could have avoided the Depression.

A Numerical Example To give you some practice with the model, let's consider a numerical example. Say that income is \$400 less than desired and that the marginal propensity to expend is .5. How much will government policy have to increase autonomous investment in order to achieve the desired level of income? Working backward, we see that the multiplier is 2, so autonomous investment must be increased by \$200.

Rosy Scenario: Talking the Economy into Fiscal Health I'll call the first policy I want to discuss the rosy scenario policy. Listen to government officials on the radio or television. Almost inevitably you will hear rosy scenarios from them: the **rosy scenario policy**—*government policy of making optimistic predictions and never making gloomy predictions*. You almost never hear a policy-level government economist telling the newspapers how bad the economy is going to be. Why? Because a gloomy prediction could affect expectations and decrease investment and consumption spending. If you're a high-level government policy economist and you have a gloomy forecast, you're told to keep quiet or quit.

Q-5 How is it possible to "talk" the economy into a boom?

There are many examples of government's use of this policy. For example, after the September 11, 2001, terrorist attacks, politicians went out of their way to argue that the events would not have a major negative effect on the economy, and the economic forecast for the economy was positive. President Bush went on television to tell people that the best way they could contribute to the war on terrorism was to go about their daily routines as before—to go to the mall and spend, rather than to save. The economy would be all right if Americans did the patriotic thing and supported businesses by spending.

Financial Guarantees Another way to influence investment directly is to protect the financial system by government guarantees or promises of guarantees. Nothing can decrease business confidence quite like a large number of bank and financial institution failures.

Let's consider how such policies work in practice. Say the economy is in a slight recession and, because of that, banks are in financial trouble. The government recognizes that if the public decides that banks are in trouble, they will try to get their money out of the banks, in which case banks will have to close. As banks close, loans will dry up, investment will decrease, and the economy will fall into a deep recession. To prevent that, the government comes along and tells everyone that it will bail out the banks so that people's money is safe. If the government is believed, everything stays fine and the recession doesn't happen (and, hopefully, the banks get themselves out of their financial trouble).

Japan used such a "save the financial institutions" policy in the 1990s. When the Japanese stock and real estate markets collapsed in the early 1990s, the Japanese government loosened bank accounting rules in order to prevent banks from failing. In the late 1990s, the U.S. central bank, the Fed, arranged a $3.6 billion bailout of a private U.S. investment firm, Long-Term Capital Management (LTCM), which had lost billions of dollars when the Russian ruble (Russia's currency) collapsed. Guaranteeing LTCM's solvency worked. The Asian crisis that had spread to Russia did not pull the U.S. economy into a recession.

Autonomous Consumption Policy

Q-6 By how much do autonomous expenditures need to change to decrease income by $60 if the *mpe* is 2/3?

Increasing the availability of consumer credit to individuals can also expand aggregate demand by making the institutional environment conducive to credit, thereby expanding aggregate demand. For example, the growth of the U.S. economy from the 1950s through the 1980s was marked by significant institutional changes that made credit available to a larger and larger group of people. This increase in consumer credit allowed significant expansion in income of the U.S. economy. In the early 1990s, some consumers cut back as they tried to consolidate their financial obligations, and that cutback played a major role in the slow growth of the U.S. economy at that time. Similarly, the resolution of those problems played a major role in the rise in growth in the early 2000s. Thus, economists keep a close eye on indexes of consumer credit and consumer confidence, since they know that any significant change in consumer confidence is likely to signal a major change in the state of the economy.

Trade Policy and Export-Led Growth

Any policy that increases autonomous exports or decreases autonomous imports (and thereby increases autonomous expenditures) will also increase aggregate demand. Examples of such policies abound. The U.S. Commerce Department has entire subdepartments that help firms develop their export markets. Similarly, U.S. trade delegations visit other nations, pushing to get the other nations' trade restrictions on U.S. goods lowered. Those policies are called **export-led growth policies**—*policies designed to stimulate U.S. exports and increase aggregate expenditures on U.S. goods, and hence to have a multiplied effect on U.S. income.*

Export-led growth policies are policies designed to stimulate exports and hence have a multiplied effect on U.S. income.

Notice that it is the trade balance (exports minus imports) that affects aggregate expenditures, so any policy that will reduce imports, such as tariffs, will have the same expansionary effect on income. That's why you hear so much about trade restrictions from Washington. They're a way of protecting U.S. jobs and of stimulating the U.S. economy in the short run. (In the long run most economists believe that tariff policies have serious problems.)

Interdependencies in the Global Economy I'll discuss these trade policies in much more detail in later chapters, but for now let me remind you that one country's exports are another country's imports, so every time the United States is out pushing its exports in an attempt to follow an export-led growth policy, it is the equivalent to getting another country to follow an *import-led decline* for its economy. Similarly, every trade restriction on foreign goods has an offsetting effect on another country's economy, an effect that will often lead to retaliation. So a policy of trying to restrict imports can often end up simultaneously restricting exports as other countries retaliate. Expectations of such retaliation is one of the reasons many economists support free trade agreements, such as the North American Free Trade Agreement (NAFTA), in which member countries agree not to engage in restrictive trade policies on imports.

Exchange Rate Policies A final way in which the trade balance can be affected is through **exchange rate policy**—*a policy of deliberately affecting a country's exchange rate in order to affect its trade balance*. You were introduced to this policy when I presented the shift factors of aggregate demand. A low value of a country's currency relative to currencies of other countries encourages exports and discourages imports; a high value of a country's currency relative to other countries' currency discourages exports and encourages imports.

Q-7 In the early 2000s, the value of the U.S. dollar fell. What effect would that have had on income in the United States?

The effect of such exchange rates can be seen in the automobile industry. In the 1970s and 1980s, Japanese exports of cars were increasing enormously. An important reason for that was the relative value of the Japanese yen (somewhere around 300 to the dollar). In the 1990s, the value of the dollar fell relative to the yen so that it was about one-third the value (around 100 to the dollar) of what it was in the 1970s. With this change, cars produced in Japan no longer seemed the good buy that they had been, and the U.S. automobile industry made a comeback as U.S. production facilities became more attractive. Again, we'll discuss such policies in more detail in Chapters 33 and 34.

A Final Comment

Aggregate demand policy is more than monetary and fiscal policy. You can see the use of these additional policies in the comments policymakers make and in the trade and exchange rate policies that a country follows. This isn't surprising. For policymakers, keeping unemployment low and the growth rate high is generally a prime objective of policy, and any policy that can help achieve that end will likely be tried, assuming it doesn't interfere with another policy objective.

Credibility in Aggregate Demand Policy

A theme that dominates modern discussions of macro policy is the importance of expectations, and economists have devoted a great deal of thought to expectations and their role in the economy. Changes in expectations can shift the *AD* curve; expectations of inflation can cause inflation. For this reason expectations are central to all policy discussions, and what people believe policy will be significantly influences the effectiveness of the policy.

Effective policy must be credible policy.

Expectations complicate models and policymaking enormously; they change the focus from discussions about a mechanical policy—a response that can be captured by simple models—to much more complicated discussions in which any policy is seen as part of a broader policy regime.

Rational Expectations

People's expectations are generally rational, in the sense that they are forward looking. People aren't stupid; they will use available evidence to form their expectations about the future. Thus, it is reasonable to assume that rational expectations are based on the best current information available. That said, there is enormous debate about what rational expectations will be. The term *rational expectations* is interpreted by some economists to mean expectations consistent with economic models, but that definition is a technical one, and is not the one policymakers use. What's important for policymakers is the forward-looking aspect of rational expectations, and in this chapter I use the term in this broader sense. Thus, a reasonable way to think of **rational expectations** is as *forward-looking expectations that use available information*.

The influence of economists' work on rational expectations is woven into much of the discussion of modern policy. It is why, for example, when I discussed monetary policy, I talked about the Fed posturing—*seeming* to be absolutely resolute about fighting inflation—in addition to *being* resolute. If the Fed convinces the public that its sole goal is to fight inflation, people will react differently than if they do not believe that. One Fed economist nicely summarized the distinction between making people believe the Fed's goal and the policy of actually pursuing that goal when he differentiated "bark policy" from "bite policy." If the Fed barks loudly and convincingly enough, it doesn't have to bite.

Q-8 Why does bark policy sometimes work better than bite policy?

Uncertainty about the Effects of Policy

The central role of expectations means that there is a great deal of uncertainty in the economy. Put simply: What people believe plays a central role in how they react to policy. Expectations can change the effect of a policy.

Most discussion of policy today assumes that people are forward looking, that they think strategically, and that they base their actions on expected policy actions. Thus, in some way their expectations are rational. But modern policy discussion is also built on the belief that the economy is complicated and that many possible expectations are rational. This includes adaptive and extrapolative expectations, and combinations of expectations strategies. The multiplicity of expectational strategies and the speed with which they can shift undermine our ability to develop deterministic models of the economy, and give the economy an unpredictability that precludes fine tuning. It was those assumptions that led me to talk about interpretative models rather than mechanistic models, and to constantly remind you that the models are not directly applicable but are simply for guidance of your thought process.

As people build expectations of policy into their actions, the effects of policy change.

What the above assumptions mean in terms of policy is that depending on the beliefs that individuals hold, monetary and fiscal policy will work in different ways. People aren't stupid, and they aren't superintelligent; they are people. If the government uses an activist monetary and fiscal policy in a predictable way, people will eventually come to build that expectation into their behavior. If the government bases its prediction of the effect of policy on past experience, that prediction will likely be wrong. But government never knows when expectations will change.

Let's consider an example. Say that everyone expects government to run expansionary fiscal policy if the economy is in a recession. In the absence of any expected policy response by government, people will lower their prices when they see a recession coming. Expecting government expansionary policy, however, they won't lower their prices. Thus, the expectation of policy can create its own problems. Such expectational problems can partially be avoided by establishing a set of rules that limits government's policy responses, but they cannot be totally avoided because people may or may not believe that the rules will be followed.

Policy Regimes and Expectations

Q-9 How does a policy regime differ from a policy?

A **policy regime** is a rule; it is *a predetermined statement of the policy that will be followed in various circumstances*. In contrast, a **policy** is *a one-time reaction to a problem;* it is chosen without a predetermined framework. As I stated above, these policy regimes can help generate the expectations that make the government's tools work.

A good way to see how these ideas about expectations have affected macroeconomic policy, or at least the thinking about that policy, is to look at the *Economic Report of the President* in various years. In the 1990 *Economic Report of the President*, there's little or no mention of fiscal policy and sizes of multipliers. Instead, the central theme is: "Fiscal policy should move toward *credible, systematic* policies that would promote strong non-inflationary growth" (p. 77). By *credible, systematic policies*, the report means policies that people believe will be implemented regardless of the consequences.

The report's discussion of monetary policy is similar. A key statement of principle for monetary policy is:

> Monetary policy needs to maintain credibility, because credibility helps ensure that the goals of policy will be attained during a period of dynamic economic and financial developments. Policy credibility is enhanced by building a record of achievement of the stated goals of policy and by consistently following stated policy principles.

I suspect the redundancy in those descriptions is by design. The economists who wrote the report wanted to emphasize that we cannot think of macroeconomic policy without thinking about what effect expectations of macroeconomic policy will have. The policy must be credible, systematic, and consistent. The statements emphasize that we cannot think that policy choices in one time period will not affect individuals' behavior in another time period.

An analogy to raising a child might make the point clear. Say that your child is crying in a restaurant. Do you hand out a piece of candy to stop the crying, or do you maintain your "no candy" rule? Looking only at the one situation, it might make sense to give the candy. But giving the child candy, even once, will undermine your credibility and consistency, and therefore has an additional cost. This emphasis on credibility is the primary effect modern theoretical work has had on macroeconomic policy. In conducting macro policy, we must consider the effect that expectations of that policy will have on the economy generally, and not only in a particular case.

The quotations from the 1990 *Economic Report of the President* reflect the Republican view of traditional macro policy. The same focus on credibility shows up in the 1996 *Economic Report of the President*, which reflects the Democratic view of traditional macro policy. In a section entitled "The Importance of Forward-Looking Expectations" we find:

> Deficit reduction that is viewed as credible and likely to be accompanied by future monetary accommodation leads investors to expect a future decline in short-term rates.

Rules versus Discretion and Credibility

The focus on credibility has led to a call for policy rules that guide the use of policy rather than giving policymakers wide discretion about what policy to implement. In fiscal policy this has meant changing how budgets are created and modified, such as the pay-as-you-go budget system adopted in the early 1990s, which required that all new expenditures be offset by matching spending cuts or tax increases and proposals requiring the federal government to follow a balanced-budget rule. In monetary policy, it has meant pushing for feedback rules, like the Taylor rule or an inflation target, that specify what the policy response will be to an event that has not yet occurred.

Q-10 What are the costs and benefits of adopting a policy rule?

Such guidance is much the same as the advice found in parenting manuals telling parents that, to maintain their credibility, they must never threaten any punishment unless they are prepared to carry it out. But as all, or at least most, parents know, some situations allow for exceptions. Not all contingencies can be planned for in advance. So parents and policymakers will consistently emphasize their credibility and explain how, once the rules are set, they will follow them. And just as consistently, the rule that says "rules were meant to be broken" will intervene, and policymakers and parents will trade off some credibility for some short-term gain, either in the belief that the initial rule did not take into account that particular eventuality or because political forces require it.

Conclusion

One of my favorite economists, G. L. S. Shackle, once said, "The first task of the University teacher of any liberal art is surely to persuade his students that the most important things he will put before them are questions and not answers. He is going to put up for them a scaffolding, and leave them to build within it. He has to persuade them that they have not come to the University to learn as it were by heart things which are already hard-and-fast and cut-and-dried, but to watch and perhaps help in a process, the driving of a causeway which will be made gradually firmer by the traffic of many minds" (Shackle, 1953). Aggregate demand policy fits what Shackle is talking about to a T. Yes, it has models underlying it, but those models are not mechanistic; they are interpretive. They give a sense of the policies to be followed, but in the end the policymaker has to rely on his or her intuition.

But while economic policy is not a cut-and-dried topic; neither is it a totally subjective one. As Keynes once said, economics is a method rather than a doctrine, an apparatus of the mind, a technique of thinking that helps the possessor to draw correct conclusions. The operative word there is *method*, not *doctrine*.

In economics you don't learn correct economic policy; what you learn is a method for thinking about economic policy that others have found useful. That method is to learn some models and then to judiciously apply them to a variety of situations. Past applications of these models have found that expectations and the policy process are often more important than the particular policy, which has led economists to talk about credibility and policy regimes when discussing policy. In such an uncertain world, tools, not rules, are what's needed for guiding policy.

Summary

- Fiscal policy is affected by the following problems, among others:
  1. Interest rate crowding out.
  2. The government knows what the situation is.
  3. The government knows the economy's potential income.
  4. Government's inability to respond quickly enough.
  5. The size of government debt doesn't matter.
  6. Conflicting goals.
- Activist fiscal policy is now built into U.S. economic institutions through automatic stabilizers.
- Economists take a trade-off view of macro policy. Their challenge is to find the appropriate mix of policy to see that unemployment is as low as possible, growth is as high as possible, and inflation is as low as possible.
- Three alternatives to monetary and fiscal policy are directed investment policies, autonomous consumption policy, and trade policy.
- Policy is a process, not a one-time event, and policy regimes are often more important than any particular policy.
- Credibility can be built by establishing policy rules, but the trade-off is that policymakers will be unable to respond to an unforeseen event.

Key Terms

automatic stabilizer *(713)*
crowding out *(709)*
exchange rate policy *(719)*
export-led growth policies *(718)*
policy *(720)*
policy regime *(720)*
procyclical fiscal policy *(714)*
rational expectations *(720)*
rosy scenario policy *(717)*

Questions for Thought and Review

1. Explain how Franklin D. Roosevelt's statement "We have nothing to fear but fear itself" pertains to macroeconomic policy.
2. What two trade policies would you recommend if an economy has a recessionary gap?
3. If government cuts taxes and wants a neutral fiscal policy, what should it do with its trade policy?
4. How does the budget process make fiscal policy difficult to implement?
5. How are state balanced-budget requirements procyclical?
6. How do automatic stabilizers work? How can they slow an economic recovery?
7. Name three alternatives to monetary and fiscal policy.
8. If interest rates have no effect on investment, how much crowding out will occur?
9. Use the *AS/AD* model to explain why most presidents increase government spending programs when running for reelection.
10. Use the *AS/AD* model to explain the maxim in politics that if you are going to increase taxes, the time to do it is right after your election, when reelection is far off.
11. Which is considered the more effective tool: monetary or fiscal policy? Why?
12. Why is policymaking better seen as a process than as a one-time event?
13. How does a policy regime differ from a policy?

Problems and Exercises

1. Congratulations! You've just been appointed chairman of the Council of Economic Advisers in Textland. The *mpe* is .8. There is a recessionary gap of $400.
   a. The government wants to eliminate the gap by changing expenditures. What policy would you suggest?
   b. Your research assistant comes running in and tells you that instead of changing expenditures, the government wants to achieve the same result by decreasing taxes. What policy would you recommend now? (Requires reading and using the math in Appendix A of Chapter 26.)
   c. Your research assistant has a worried look on her face. "What's the problem?" you ask. "I goofed," she confesses. "I thought taxes were exogenous when actually there's a marginal tax rate of .2." Before she can utter another word, you say, "No problem, I'll simply recalculate my answers to parts *a* and *b* and change them before I send them in." What are your corrected answers? (Requires reading Appendix A of Chapter 26.)
   d. She still has a pained expression, "What's wrong?" you ask. "You didn't let me finish," she says. "Not only was there a marginal tax rate of .2; there's also a marginal propensity to import of .1." Again you interrupt to make sure she doesn't feel guilty. Again you say, "No problem," and recalculate your answers to parts *a* and *b* to account for the new information. What are your new answers? (Requires reading Appendix A of Chapter 26.)
   e. That pained look is still there, but this time you don't interrupt. You let her finish. She says, "And they want to see the answers graphically." You do the right thing.
2. A tax cut has just been announced. Congressman Growth states that its effect will be on the supply side. Congressman Stable states that its effect will be on the demand side.
   a. Demonstrate graphically the effect of the tax cut on the price level and output in the standard *AS/AD* model. Which of the two congressmen's views better fit the model?
   b. Demonstrate the effect graphically of the tax cut on the price level and output if the other congressman is correct.
   c. In the short run which of the two congressmen is most likely correct?
   d. How might the existence of significant crowding out change your answer?
3. The government has just increased taxes.
   a. Demonstrate the effect on the price level and output in the standard model.
   b. How would your answer to *a* differ if there were partial crowding out?
   c. How would your answer to *a* differ if there were complete crowding out?
4. When Professor Robert Gordon lowered his estimate of the target unemployment rate from 6 percent to

5.5 percent in early 1995, he quipped, "I've just created 600,000 jobs."
a. What events in the 1990s most likely motivated his revision of the target unemployment rate?
b. Show the effect this revision would have on the *AS/AD* model.
c. The unemployment rate at the time of the revision was 5.5 percent. Income was $7.3 trillion. Within 18 months the unemployment rate had fallen to 5 percent without signs of accelerating inflation. How much higher would the level of potential income have been in 1995 if the target unemployment rate were 5 percent rather than 5.5 percent?

5. President Bill Clinton's policy in 1993 was designed to reduce the deficit but increase employment.
   a. Why would such a policy not fit well in the multiplier model?
   b. Explain in words how such a policy might achieve the desired effect.
   c. Graphically demonstrate your answer in *b*.
   d. What data would you look at to see if your explanation in *b* and *c* is appropriate?

WEB QUESTIONS

1. The Virtual Economy Home Page provides a model of the British economy in which you can play the role of Chancellor, the person who helps determine levels of taxation and spending in Britain. Go to its home page at http://ve.ifs.org.uk and answer the following questions:
   a. Visit the Chancellor's office on the ground floor. What are the four key economic targets?
   b. What are the main policy tools at the Chancellor's disposal? Provide a brief description of each.
   c. Find the economic model on the fourth floor. Use the model to predict what will happen to each of the policy targets within the first three to four years if income taxes are raised 9 percentage points. Report your results.
   d. What does the model predict will happen within the first three to four years if government spending is increased 10 percent?
2. One of the problems with fiscal policy is the delay between the time government recognizes that the economy is in a recessionary gap (or inflationary gap) and the time it takes to change spending or taxes. Go to the home page of the White House's Office of Management and Budget at www.whitehouse.gov/omb to read about the budgetary process. This information is in *A Citizen's Guide to the Budgetary Process*, found by clicking on Citizen's Guide under the President's Budget. Answer the following questions:
   a. What are the major steps in the budget process?
   b. How much time elapses between the time the President formulates his budget and the time that data are available to indicate what were the actual expenditures made and actual revenue collected?
   c. What percentage of total spending *must* the president and Congress act upon each year? What accounts for the remaining expenditures?

ANSWERS TO MARGIN QUESTIONS

1. If interest rates did not affect investment or consumption expenditures, there would be no crowding out. *(709)*
2. If government spending stimulated private spending, the phenomenon of what might be called *crowding in* might occur. The increase in government spending would shift the *AD* from AD_0 to AD_1 as in the diagram at the right. The resulting shift in income would cause a further shift up in investment, shifting the aggregate expenditure curve out further to AD_2. Income would increase from Y_0 to Y_2—by more than what the simple AS/AD model would predict. *(710)*

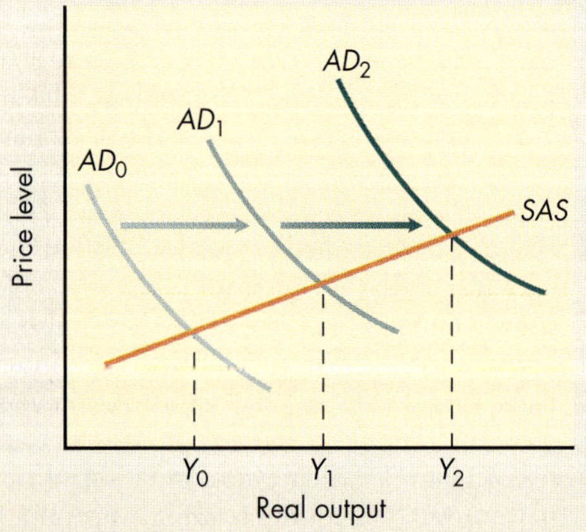

3. Potential income is not a measurable number. It is a conceptual number that must be estimated based on observable information about such phenomena as inflation, productivity, and unemployment. Estimating potential income is a challenge. *(711)*
4. Automatic stabilizers tend to decrease the size of the multiplier, decreasing the fluctuations in the economy. *(714)*
5. Expectations play a central role in both spending and production decisions. If positive talk about the economy can influence expectations, it may be possible to "talk" an economy into a boom by increasing expenditures, or productivity, or both. *(717)*
6. Since the *mpe* is 2/3, the multiplier is 3. Autonomous expenditures need to fall by 20. *(718)*
7. According to the multiplier model, a fall in the value of the dollar should increase exports, which would have had a multiplied positive effect on income. *(719)*
8. A bark policy sometimes works better than a bite policy because it is designed to convince people of the Fed's resolve to fight inflation and thus changes expectations of inflation. Changing the expectations of inflation is an important element to keeping inflation low. *(720)*
9. A policy regime is a predetermined statement of policy rule that will be followed in various circumstances. A policy is a one-time action taken by government; it may or may not follow a policy rule. *(720)*
10. The benefit of adopting a policy rule is that if the rule is followed consistently, policymakers can gain credibility more easily. This is especially helpful with policies to reduce inflation. The costs of adopting a rule is that no rule can account for all contingencies. Adopting a rule most likely means that the rule will be broken. Once policymakers break the rule, they may find it difficult to regain credibility. *(721)*

31 Politics, Deficits, and Debt

After reading this chapter, you should be able to:

- Define the terms *deficit, surplus,* and *debt.*
- Distinguish between a passive deficit and a structural deficit.
- Differentiate between real and nominal deficits and surpluses.
- Explain why the debt needs to be judged relative to assets.
- Describe the historical record for the U.S. deficit, surplus, and debt.
- Summarize the current debate about the budget and Social Security system.

Any government, like any family, can for a year spend a little more than it earns. But you and I know that a continuance of that habit means the poorhouse.

—Franklin D. Roosevelt

After having run budget deficits for many decades, in 1998 the U.S. government started to run budget surpluses. In 2000 economists predicted that the total surpluses would exceed $5.9 trillion over the next 15 years. That was quite a change from the trillion-dollar deficit predictions of the mid-1990s. By 2002 much of that predicted $5.9 trillion in surplus had disappeared. The government's budget returned to deficit, and the government was predicting deficits into the near future. How can the budget picture change so fast? And what do such changes mean for the economy? This chapter considers these and other questions from an economist's perspective in order to give you some deeper insight into policy debates that you will likely hear about in the newspapers.

Let's begin by considering what economic theory has to say about deficits and surpluses. In the long-run framework, surpluses are good because they provide additional saving for an economy and deficits are bad because they reduce saving, growth, and income. In the short-run framework, the view of deficits and surpluses depends on the state of the economy relative to its potential. If the economy is operating below its potential output, deficits are good and surpluses are bad because deficits increase expenditures, moving output closer to potential.

Combining the two frameworks gives us the following policy directive: Whenever possible, run surpluses, or at least a balanced budget, to help stimulate long-run growth. That recommendation is made even stronger when the economy is booming—that is, when it is above its level of potential income. Should the economy fall into a recession, however, policymakers must choose between the different policies suggested by the long-run and short-run frameworks.

At the beginning of 2000, the U.S. economy was booming, unemployment was at historic lows, and there was general agreement that the economy was at its potential output. If ever there was a time to let government build up a surplus and cut debt, it was then; that was the policy both the short- and long-run economic frameworks recommended. What policy did the government follow? It increased spending and cut taxes—precisely the opposite of what economic theory suggested was needed.

In 2001, the situation changed and the economy fell into a mild recession. When the World Trade Center and the Pentagon were attacked on September 11, many feared that the mild recession, which had begun March 2001, would become a severe recession and possibly a depression because consumers would lose confidence in the economy. Suddenly, that earlier tax cut didn't look so bad in economists' short-run framework, and the tax cut played a role in making the recession of 2002 the shortest on record.

Q-1 How can deficits be both good and bad for an economy?

So what's going on here? The answer is complicated. To explain it we need some background on accounting issues that pertain to deficits, some specifics about the demography and institutions of the United States, and some knowledge of politics as it relates to surpluses, deficits, and debt. This chapter is intended to provide you with that background.

Defining Deficits and Surpluses

The definitions of *deficit, surplus,* and *debt* are simple, but this simplicity hides important aspects that will help you understand current debates about deficits and debt. Thus, it's necessary to look carefully at some ambiguities in the definitions.

A **deficit** is *a shortfall of revenues under payments;* both are flow concepts. A **surplus** is *an excess of revenues over payments.* If your income (revenue) is $20,000 per year and your expenditures (payments) are $30,000 per year, you are running a deficit. This definition tells us that a government budget deficit occurs when government expenditures exceed government revenues. Table 31-1 shows federal government total expenditures, total revenue, and the difference between the two for various years since 1980. The federal government ran deficits through the 1980s and most of the 1990s. It began to run surpluses in 1998, and returned to running deficits in 2002.

A *deficit* is a shortfall of incoming revenues under payments. A *surplus* is an excess of revenues over payments.

Financing the Deficit

Just like private individuals, the government must pay for the goods and services it buys. This means that whenever the government runs a deficit, it has to finance that deficit. It does so by selling *bonds*—promises to pay back the money in the future—to private individuals and to the central bank. There's a whole division of the U.S. Treasury devoted to managing the government's borrowing needs.

The government finances its deficits by selling bonds to private individuals and to the central bank.

The United States is fortunate to have people who want to buy its bonds. Some countries, such as Russia, have few people who want to buy their bonds (lend them money) and therefore have trouble financing their deficits. However, countries have an option that individuals don't have. Their central banks can loan them the money (buy their bonds). Since the central bank's IOUs are money, the loans can be made simply by printing money; in principle, therefore, the central bank has a potentially unlimited source of funds. But, as we saw in earlier chapters, printing too much money can lead to serious inflation problems, which have negative effects on the economy. So, whenever possible, governments try not to use the "print money" option to finance their deficits.

Table 31-1 Revenue, Expenditures, and Budget Balance (in billions of dollars)

	1980	1990	2000	2001	2002
Revenues	517.1	1,032.0	2,025.2	1,991.0	1,853
Expenditures	590.9	1,253.2	1,788.8	1,863.9	2,011
(−) Deficit/(+) surplus	−73.8	−221.2	236.4	127.1	−158

Source: Congressional Budget Office, *The Economic and Budget Outlook,* January 2003 (www.cbo.gov).

ARBITRARINESS OF DEFINING DEFICITS AND SURPLUSES

Whether or not you have a deficit or surplus depends on what you count as a revenue and what you count as an expenditure. These decisions can make an enormous difference in whether you have a surplus or deficit. For example, consider the problem of a firm with annual revenues of $8,000 but no expenses except a $10,000 machine expected to last five years. Should the firm charge the $10,000 to this year's expenditures? Should it split the $10,000 evenly among the five years? Or should it use some other approach? Which method the firm chooses makes a big difference in whether its current budget will be in surplus or deficit.

Accounting is central to the debate about whether we should be concerned about a deficit. Say, for example, that the government promises to pay an individual $1,000 ten years from now. How should government treat that promise? Since the obligation is incurred now, should government count as a current expense an amount that, if saved, would allow it to pay that $1,000 later? Or should government not count the amount as an expenditure until it actually pays out the money? The **Social Security system**—*a social insurance program that provides financial benefits to the elderly and disabled and to their eligible dependents and/or survivors*—is based on promises to pay, and thus the accounting procedures used for Social Security play an important role in how big the government's budget deficit actually is.

MANY RIGHT DEFINITIONS

There are many ways to measure expenditures and receipts, so there are many ways to measure deficits and surpluses.

Many accounting questions must be answered before we can determine the size of a budget deficit. Some have no right or wrong answer. For others there are right or wrong answers that vary according to the wording of the question being asked. For still others, an economist's "right way" is an accountant's "wrong way." In short, there are many ways to measure expenditures and receipts, so there are many ways to measure surpluses and deficits.

To say that there are many ways to measure deficits is not to say that all ways are correct. Pretending to have income that you don't have is wrong by all standards. Similarly, inconsistent accounting practices—such as measuring an income flow sometimes one way and sometimes another—are wrong. Standard accounting practices rule out a number of "creative" but improper approaches to measuring deficits. But even eliminating these, there remain numerous reasonable ways of defining deficits, which account for some of the debate.

DEFICITS AND SURPLUSES AS SUMMARY MEASURES

Deficit and surplus figures are simply summary measures of the financial health of the economy. To understand the summary, you must understand the methods that were used to calculate it.

The point of the previous discussion is that a deficit is simply a summary measure of a budget. As a summary, a surplus or deficit figure reduces a complicated set of accounting relationships to one figure. To understand what that summary measure is telling us, you've got to understand the accounting procedures used to calculate it. Only then can you make an informed judgment about whether a deficit is something to worry about. What's important is not whether a budget is in surplus or deficit but whether the economy is healthy.

STRUCTURAL AND PASSIVE DEFICITS AND SURPLUSES

An important distinction to be made when discussing deficits and surpluses is between a structural deficit and a passive deficit. The discussion of fiscal policy in earlier chapters emphasized the effect of the deficit on total income. But in thinking about such policies, it is important to remember that many government revenues and expenditures

ACCOUNTING, ENRON, WORLDCOM, AND XEROX (AND MANY OTHER COMPANIES)

Applying the Tools

It is not only government budgets that have some arbitrariness to them. So, too, do company income and cost accounts. In the early 2000s a number of companies came under fire for using incorrect accounting—calling current costs capital or long-run costs, and calling future revenues current revenues. For example, WorldCom listed payments to local telephone companies as a capital expense (for which only part of the payments shows up this year as a cost) rather than a current expense (where all of the payments shows up as a current cost). This was clearly a violation of standard accounting rules, and the company was prosecuted for it. Other companies, such as Enron, got in trouble for supercreative accounting that went beyond standard accounting principles. (Enron's auditing firm, Arthur Andersen, was found guilty for failing to detect that fraud.) Others, such as Xerox, had problems because of more ambiguous issues involving how to book lease payments.

How can such things happen? The reason is that accounting, at every level, is an art, and when firms are under intense pressure to increase profits (or when governments are under intense pressure to eliminate a deficit), the art allows for some different interpretation. All budget figures—whether of governments, firms, or even colleges—should be interpreted cautiously.

depend on the level of income in the economy. For example, say that the multiplier is 2 and the government is running expansionary policy. Say that that policy increases government spending by $100 (increasing the budget deficit by $100), which causes income to rise by $200. If the tax rate is 20 percent, tax revenues will increase by $40 and the net effect of the policy will be to increase the budget deficit by $60, not $100.

To differentiate between a budget deficit being used as a policy instrument to affect the economy and a budget deficit that is the result of income deviating from its potential, economists ask the question "Would the economy have a budget deficit or surplus if it were at its potential level of income?" If it would, that portion of the budget deficit or surplus is said to be a **structural deficit or surplus**—*the part of a budget deficit or surplus that would exist even if the economy were at its potential level of income*. In contrast, if an economy is operating below its potential, the actual deficit will be larger than the structural deficit. In such an economy, that part of the total budget deficit or surplus is a **passive deficit or surplus**—*the part of the deficit or surplus that exists because the economy is operating below or above its potential level of output*. The passive deficit is also known as the cyclical deficit. When an economy is operating above its potential, it has a passive surplus. Economists believe that an economy can eliminate a passive budget deficit through growth in income, whereas it can't grow out of a structural deficit. Because the economy can't grow out of them, structural budget deficits are of more concern to policymakers than are passive budget deficits.

The structural deficit is the deficit that remains when the cyclical elements of the deficit have been removed.

Let me give an example, say potential income is $11 trillion and actual income is $10.8 trillion, a shortfall of $200 billion. The actual budget deficit is $250 billion and the marginal tax rate is 25 percent. If the economy were at its potential income, tax revenue would be $50 billion higher and the deficit would be $200 billion. That $200 billion is the structural deficit. The $50 billion (25 percent multiplied by the $200 million shortfall) is the passive portion of the deficit. Table 31-2 shows the actual, structural, and passive budget deficits and surpluses for selected years. In 1980 and 1990, the economy was operating below potential and the passive deficit contributed to a greater deficit. In 2000 and 2001 passive surpluses contributed to greater surpluses, but in 2002 the economy was below potential, creating a passive deficit.

Q-2 An economy's actual income is $1 trillion; its potential income is also $1 trillion. Its actual deficit is $100 billion. What is its passive deficit?

In reality there is significant debate about what an economy's potential income level is, and hence there is disagreement about what percentage of a deficit is structural and

Table 31-2 Budget Deficits and Surpluses: Actual, Passive, and Structural

	1980	1990	2000	2001	2002
Passive (−)deficit/(+)surplus	−61	−100	+137	+47	−5
Plus structural (−)deficit/(+)surplus	−13	−121	+99	+80	−153
Equals actual (−)deficit/(+)surplus	−74	−221	+236	+127	−158

Source: *The Economic and Budget Outlook*, Congressional Budget Office, January 2003 (www.cbo.gov).

what percentage is passive. Nonetheless, the distinction is often used and is important to remember. For example, the passive/structural distinction plays a key role in explaining the sudden movement from predictions of surpluses to predictions of deficits that I discussed in the opening part of this chapter. The recession of 2001–2002 decreased the passive surplus, because, as income fell, tax revenues fell. The terrorist attacks in late 2001 also caused economists to lower their growth predictions, which lowered the estimate of the structural surplus. These changes alone reduced trillions of dollars in the predicted surplus. Take these changes, combine them with the tax cut that had previously been passed by Congress, and with the expected increases in government expenditures associated with the war on terror, and—*poof*—the expected $5.9 trillion surplus almost disappeared.

Nominal and Real Deficits and Surpluses

Another distinction that economists make when discussing the budget deficit and surplus picture is the real/nominal distinction. A **nominal deficit** is *the deficit determined by looking at the difference between expenditures and receipts*.[1] It's what most people think of when they think of the budget deficit; it's the value that is generally reported. The **real deficit** is *the nominal deficit adjusted for inflation*. To understand this distinction it is important to recognize that inflation wipes out debt (accumulated deficits less accumulated surpluses). How much does it wipe out? Consider an example: If a country has a $2 trillion debt and inflation is 4 percent per year, the real value of all assets denominated in dollars is declining by 4 percent each year. If you had $100 and there's 4 percent inflation in a year, that $100 will be worth 4 percent less at the end of the year—the equivalent of $96 without inflation. By the same reasoning, when there's 4 percent inflation, the value of the debt is declining 4 percent each year. Four percent of $2 trillion is $80 billion, so with an outstanding debt of $2 trillion, 4 percent inflation will eliminate $80 billion of the debt each year.

Q-3 Explain how inflation can wipe out debt.

Inflation reduces the value of the debt. That reduction is taken into account when the real deficit is calculated.

The larger the debt and the larger the inflation, the more debt will be eliminated by inflation. For example, with 10 percent inflation and a $2 trillion debt, $200 billion of the debt will be eliminated by inflation each year. With 10 percent inflation and a $4 trillion debt, $400 billion of the debt would be eliminated.

If inflation is wiping out debt, and the deficit is equal to the increases in debt from one year to the next, inflation also affects the deficit. Economists take this into account by differentiating nominal deficits from real deficits.

We can calculate the real deficit by subtracting the decrease in the value of the government's total outstanding debts due to inflation. Specifically:[2]

[1]In this section I will discuss deficits only. Since a surplus is a negative deficit, the discussion can be easily translated into a discussion of surpluses.

[2]This is an approximation for low rates of inflation. When inflation becomes large, total debt is multiplied by 1/(1 + Inflation).

Table 31-3 Real and Nominal Deficits (in billions of dollars)

	1980	1990	2000	2002
Nominal (−)deficit/(+)surplus	−74	−221	+236	−158
Plus Inflation × Total debt	86	142	129	68
Government debt	930	3,233	5,629	6,137
GDP inflation	9.3	4.4	2.3	1.1
Equals Real (−)deficit/(+)surplus	+12	−79	+365	−90

Source: *The Economic and Budget Outlook*, Congressional Budget Office, January 2003 (www.cbo.gov); and *The Economic Report of the President*, 2000.

$$\text{Real deficit} = \text{Nominal deficit} - (\text{Inflation} \times \text{Total debt}).$$

Real deficit = Nominal deficit − (Inflation × Total debt)

Let's consider an example. Say that the nominal deficit is \$80 billion, inflation is 6 percent; and total debt is \$3 trillion. Substituting into the formula gives us a real surplus of \$100 billion [\$80 billion − (0.06 × \$3 trillion) = \$80 billion − \$180 billion = −\$100 billion]. (This follows because a surplus is a negative deficit and hence is written here as a negative number.)

This insight into debt is directly relevant to the budget situation in the United States. For example, back in 1990 the nominal U.S. deficit was about \$221 billion, while the real deficit was about one-third of that—\$79 billion; in 2002 the U.S. government deficit was about \$158 billion; there was 1.1 percent inflation and a total debt of about \$6.1 trillion. That means the real deficit was \$90 billion.[3] Table 31-3 shows the U.S. nominal and real deficits and surpluses for selected years. Because the United States has had both debt and inflation for the years shown, the real deficits are smaller than the nominal deficits and the real surpluses are greater than the nominal surpluses.

Q-4 The nominal deficit is \$40 billion, inflation is 2 percent, and the total debt is \$4 trillion. What is the real deficit?

The lowering of the real deficit by inflation is not costless to the government. Persistent inflation becomes built into expectations and causes higher interest rates. When inflationary expectations were low, as they were in the 1950s, the U.S. government paid 3 or 4 percent on its bonds. In 1990, when inflationary expectations were high, the government paid 8 or 9 percent interest, which is about 5 percentage points more than it paid in the 1950s. With its \$3.2 trillion debt, this meant that the United States was paying about \$160 billion more in interest than it would have had to pay if no inflation had been expected and the nominal interest rate had been 3 rather than 8 percent. That reduced the amount it could spend on current services by \$160 billion. In other words, \$160 billion of the 1990 nominal U.S. deficit existed because of the rise in interest payments necessary to compensate bondholders for the expected inflation. As inflationary expectations and nominal interest rates fell through the 1990s and early 2000s, the difference between the real and nominal deficit (surplus) decreased, but the fear that inflation would reignite left bondholders requiring a small inflation premium, meaning that interest rates paid by government were higher than they otherwise would have been.

THE DEFINITION OF DEBT AND ASSETS

Debt is *accumulated deficits minus accumulated surpluses*. Whereas deficits and surpluses are flow measures (they are defined for a period of time), debt is a stock measure (it is defined at a point in time). For example, say you've spent \$30,000 a year for 10 years

Debt is accumulated deficits minus accumulated surpluses. Whereas *deficit* is a flow concept, *debt* is a stock concept.

[3]Because a surplus is the opposite of deficit, you must add inflation times total debt to the nominal surplus to arrive at the real surplus.

and have had annual income of $20,000 for 10 years. So you've had a deficit of $10,000 per year—a flow. At the end of 10 years, you will have accumulated a debt of $100,000 (10 × $10,000 = $100,000)—a stock. (Spending more than you have in income means that you need to borrow the extra $10,000 per year from someone, so in later years much of your expenditure will be for interest on your previous debt.) If a country has been running more surpluses than deficits, the accumulated surpluses minus accumulated deficits are counted as part of its assets.

Q-5 Distinguish between *deficit* and *debt.*

DEBT MANAGEMENT

The U.S. government, through its Treasury Department, must continually refinance the bonds that are coming due by selling new bonds, as well as sell new bonds when running a deficit. This makes for a very active market in U.S. government bonds, and the interest rate paid on government bonds is a closely watched statistic in the economy. If the government runs a surplus, it can either retire some of its previously issued bonds by buying them back or simply not replace the previously issued bonds when they come due.

To judge a country's debt, we must view its debt in relation to its assets.

The Need to Judge Debt Relative to Assets Debt is also a summary measure of a country's financial situation. As a summary measure, debt has even more problems than deficit. Unlike a deficit, which is the difference between outflows and inflows, and hence provides both sides of the ledger, debt by itself is only half of a picture. The other half of the picture is assets. For a country, assets include its skilled workforce, its natural resources, its factories, its housing stock, and its holdings of foreign assets. For a government, assets include not only the buildings and land it owns but also, and more important, a portion of the assets of the people in the country, since government gets a portion of all earnings of those assets in tax revenue.

Q-6 Why is debt only half the picture of a country's financial situation?

To get an idea of why the addition of assets is necessary to complete the debt picture, consider two governments: one has debt of $3 trillion and assets of $50 trillion; the other has only $1 trillion in debt but only $1 trillion in assets. Which is in a better position? The government with the $3 trillion debt is, because its debt is significantly exceeded by its assets. The point is simple: To judge a country's debt, we must view its debt in relation to all its assets.

This need to judge debt relative to assets adds an important caveat to the long-run position that government budget deficits are bad. When the government runs a deficit, it might be spending on projects that increase its assets. If the assets are valued at more than their costs, then the deficit is making the society better off. Government investment can be as productive as private investment or even more productive.

To distinguish between expenditures that are building up assets and those that are not, many businesses have separate capital and expenditures budgets. When they run deficits in their capital account, we do not say that they are spending recklessly; we say that they are investing in the future, and generally we applaud that investment. We say they are running a deficit only in reference to their expenditures budget. While the U.S. government budget separates out investment from noninvestment expenditures, it does not have a separate capital account; it reports a consolidated budget, so it does not take into account the asset accumulation or the depreciation of its assets in determining its deficit.

Web Note 31.1 Treasury Securities

Why aren't government finances generally discussed in relation to separate current and capital budgets? Because with government expenditures it is extraordinarily difficult to determine what an investment is. Business's investments will earn income that allows the business to pay off those investments. Most government goods earn no income; they are supplied free to individuals and are paid for by taxes. Impossible-to-

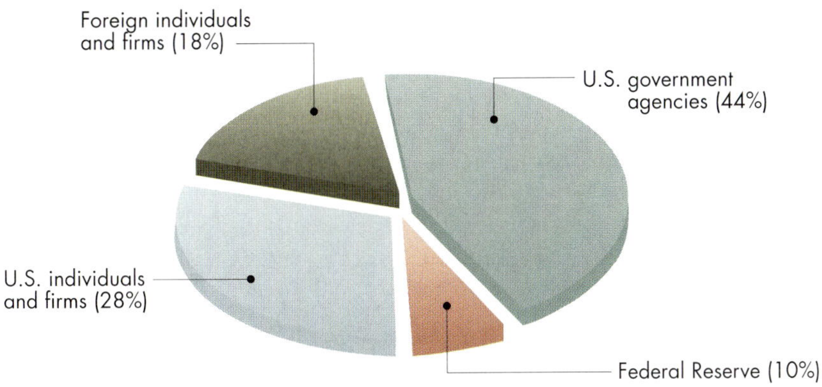

Figure 31-1 Ownership of the Debt This pie chart shows that the debt is held by U.S. citizens, foreign citizens, financial institutions, and other government entities including state and local governments.

Source: *Treasury Bulletin*, U.S. Department of the Treasury, December 2002 (www.fms.treas.gov).

answer questions arise such as: Are expenditures on new teachers an investment in better knowledge? Or: Are expenditures on a poverty program an investment in a better social environment? There are no unambiguous answers to these and similar questions; government accountants believe it is best to avoid such questions altogether.

Arbitrariness in Defining Debt and Assets Like income and revenues, assets and debt are subject to varying definitions. Say, for example, that an 18-year-old is due to inherit $1 million at age 21. Should that expected future asset be counted as an asset now? Or say that the government buys an aircraft for $1 billion and discovers that it doesn't fly. What value should the government place on that aircraft? Or say that a country owes $1 billion, due to be paid 10 years from now, but inflation is ongoing at 20 percent per year. The inflation will reduce the value of the debt when it comes due by so much that its current real value will be $162 million—the approximate present value of $1 billion in 10 years with 20 percent inflation. It will be like paying about $162 million today. Should the country list the debt as a $1 billion debt or a $162 million debt?

As was the case with income, revenues, and deficits, there's no single answer to how assets and debts should be valued. So even after you take assets into account, you still have to be careful when deciding whether or not to be concerned about debt.

The government holds about 44 percent of its own debt, mostly in the Social Security trust fund.

The arbitrariness of the debt figure can be seen by considering the holdings of U.S. debt more carefully. In 2003, the U.S. government had a total of $6.5 trillion in debt, but the actual amount held by people and organizations outside the federal government is much less than that, as shown in Figure 31-1. There you can see that 54 percent of the debt is internal to the government (including the Fed's holdings)—one branch of the federal government owes another branch of the government the debt. It is an asset of one part of government and a debt of another part. When we net out these offsetting debts and assets, the total federal debt decreases from about $6.5 trillion to $2.8 trillion. Of that $2.8 trillion, about 62 percent is held by U.S. individuals and firms, and 38 percent is held by foreign individuals and firms.

Many of the bonds to finance the current deficit are being bought by the Social Security trust fund, a fund managed by the Social Security Administration in order to meet its future obligations. By law, the Social Security trust fund must be held in the form of nonmarketable government bonds. This means that one agency of government (the Social Security Administration) is buying the bonds of another agency (the Treasury Department). Until about 2030, when the Social Security system's outlays will exceed its revenues, the percentage of debt held by government agencies will continue to increase. In 2003, the Social Security trust fund owned 22 percent of the debt. By 2012,

GENERATIONAL ACCOUNTING

Beyond the Tools

As I have emphasized in the text, there are many different accounting procedures that shed light on slightly different issues. Each provides a different perspective of the financial situation, and the combination of them provides you with a full understanding of the issues. One accounting procedure that some economists use is generational accounting. Generational accounting shows government deficits in terms of each generation's net lifetime tax payments and benefits received. Economists such as Larry Kotlikoff and Alan Auerbach have shown that our current system of taxation and transfers results in an intergenerational transfer of resources from younger to older generations. With the older generation becoming larger as the baby boomers age, these transfers are likely to put a severe strain on the tax system and the political foundations of our tax and transfer policies over the next couple of decades.

---

the fund is expected to own 50 percent of the debt. (The Social Security system will be discussed in more detail later in this chapter.)

DIFFERENCE BETWEEN INDIVIDUAL AND GOVERNMENT DEBT

The final point I want to make concerns the quotation from the beginning of the chapter, by Franklin D. Roosevelt, about deficit spending leading to the poorhouse. Roosevelt may have been a great president, but based on that comment, he probably would have failed his economics course. All debt is not the same. In particular, government debt is different from an individual's debt. There are three reasons for this.

Three reasons government debt is different from individual debt are:

1. The government lives forever; people don't.
2. The government can print money to pay its debt; people can't.
3. Government owes much of its debt to itself—to its own citizens.

First, government is ongoing. Government never has to pay back its debt. An individual's life span is limited; when a person dies, there's inevitably an accounting of assets and debt to determine whether anything is left to go to heirs. Before any part of a person's estate is passed on, all debts must be paid. The government, however, doesn't ever have to settle its accounts.

Second, government has an option that individuals don't have for paying off a debt. Specifically, it can pay off a debt by creating money. As long as people will accept a country's currency, a country can always exchange money (non-interest-bearing debt) for bonds (interest-bearing debt).

Third, 82 percent of government debt is **internal debt** *(government debt owed to other governmental agencies or to its own citizens)*. Paying interest on the internal debt involves a redistribution among citizens of the country, but it does not involve a net reduction in income of the average citizen. For example, say that a country has $3 trillion in internal debt. Say also that the government pays $150 billion in interest on its debt each year. That means the government must collect $150 billion in taxes, so people are $150 billion poorer; but it pays out $150 billion in interest to them, so on average, people in the country are neither richer nor poorer because of the debt. **External debt** *(government debt owed to individuals in foreign countries)* is more like an individual's debt. Paying interest on external debt involves a net reduction in domestic income. U.S. taxpayers will be poorer; foreign holders of U.S. bonds will be richer.

Web Note 31.2
External Debts

U.S. GOVERNMENT DEFICITS AND DEBT: THE HISTORICAL RECORD

Now that we have been through the basics of deficits and debt, let's look at the historical record. From World War II until recently, the U.S. government ran almost continual

Figure 31-2 (a and b) U.S. Budget Deficits and Debt Relative to GDP
The size of the deficits and the size of the debt look somewhat different when considered relative to the GDP. Notice specifically how the total debt-to-GDP ratio declined substantially from the 1950s to the 1980s and how it increased in the 1980s and early 1990s. It declined in the late 1990s and early 2000s.

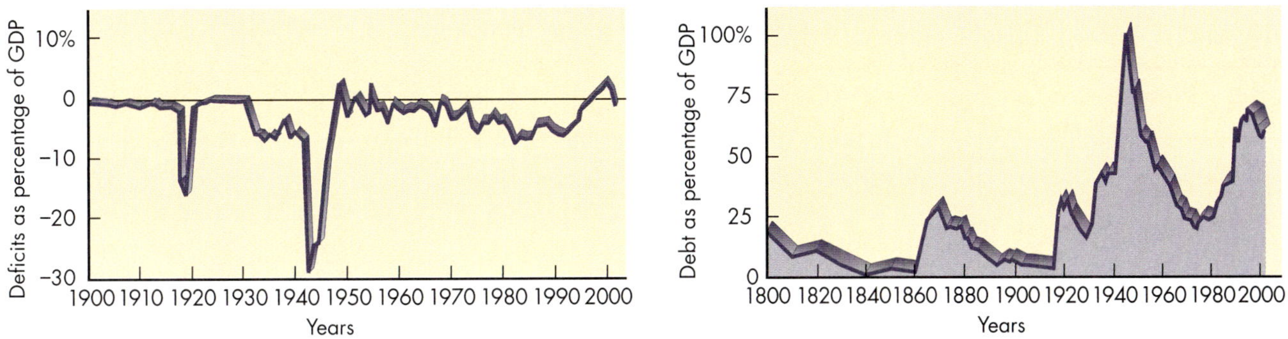

(a) Budget deficits as percentage of GDP **(b) Debt as percentage of GDP**

Source: *The Economic and Budget Outlook*, Congressional Budget Office, 2002 (www.cbo.gov); and U.S. Bureau of the Census, *Historical Statistics*.

deficits. From the 1950s to the early 1970s, the government budget balance fluctuated between small $3 billion surpluses to $25 billion deficits. Beginning in the mid-1970s, deficits grew considerably, from $53 billion in 1975 to $290 billion in 1992, before declining in the mid-1990s, disappearing in 1998, but then reappearing in 2002. Over most of that time total debt has increased. It doubled in the 30 years from 1946 to 1975 and grew more quickly beginning in the mid-1970s, rising by a multiple of 13 to $6.5 trillion in 2003. Most economists, however, are much more concerned with deficits and debt relative to GDP than with the absolute figures.

Figure 31-2 graphs the budget deficit and debt as a percentage of GDP. From this perspective, as you can see in Figure 31-2(a), deficits as a percentage of GDP did not rise significantly in the 1970s and the 1980s, as they did when we considered them in absolute terms. And it's the same with debt. As you can see in Figure 31-2(b) debt, relative to GDP, has not been continually increasing. Instead, from the end of World War II to the 1970s, and from 1988 to 1990, the debt/GDP ratio actually decreased. In the mid-1990s it stabilized at somewhat under 70 percent of GDP, and in the late 1990s and early 2000s it fell to about 60 percent. Then, in 2002 it started rising again.

Economists prefer the "relative to GDP" measurement because it better measures the government's ability to handle the deficit; a nation's ability to pay off a debt depends on its productive capacity (the asset side of the picture). GDP serves the same function for government as income does for an individual. It provides a measure of how much debt, and how large a deficit, government can handle. So when GDP grows, so does the debt the government can reasonably carry.

Deficits and debt relative to GDP provide a measure of a country's ability to pay off a deficit and service its debt.

THE DEBT BURDEN

Most of the decrease in the debt-to-GDP ratio in U.S. history occurred through growth in GDP. There are two ways in which growth in GDP can occur—through inflation (a rise in nominal but not real GDP) or through real growth. Both ways reduce the problem of the debt. As I discussed above, inflation wipes out the value of existing debt; when there is inflation, there can be large nominal budget deficits but a small real deficit.

Figure 31-3 U.S. Debt Compared to Foreign Countries' Debt
The U.S. debt does not appear so large when compared to the debts of other countries in the early 2000s.

Source: *World Economic Outlook*, International Monetary Fund (www.imf.org) and individual country web pages.

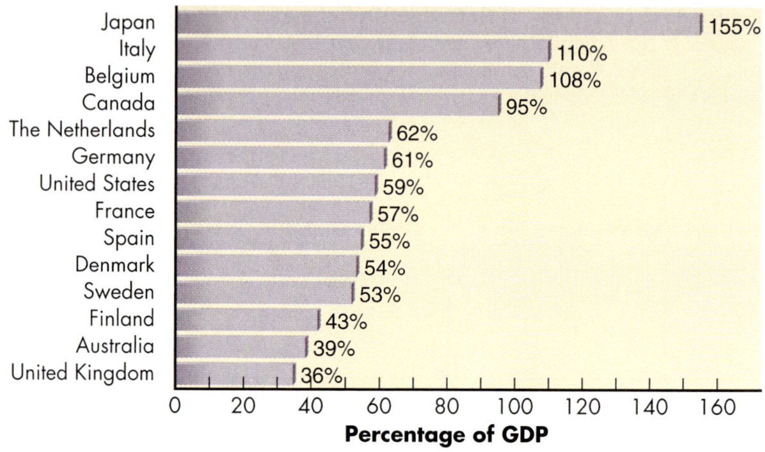

Q-7 What annual deficit could a $5 billion economy growing at a real annual rate of 5 percent have without changing its debt burden?

When an economy experiences real growth, the ability of the government to incur debt is increased; the economy becomes richer and, being richer, can handle more debt. As noted in an earlier chapter, real growth in the United States has averaged about 2.5 to 3.5 percent per year, which means that U.S. debt can grow at a rate of 2.5 to 3.5 percent without increasing the debt/GDP ratio. But for debt to grow, government must run a deficit; so a constant debt/GDP ratio in a growing economy is consistent with a continual deficit.

How much of a deficit are we talking about? U.S. federal government debt in 2003 was about $6.5 trillion and GDP was about $11 trillion, so the government debt/GDP ratio was about 60 percent. A real growth rate of 2.5 percent means that real GDP is growing at about $275 billion per year. That means that government can run a deficit of $163 billion a year without increasing the debt/GDP ratio. Of course, for those who believe that the total U.S. government debt is already too large relative to GDP, this argument (that the debt/GDP ratio is remaining constant) is unsatisfying. They'd prefer the debt/GDP ratio to fall.

U.S. Debt Relative to Other Countries

When judged relative to other countries, the United States does not have an especially large debt burden, as can be seen in Figure 31-3. Notice that the U.S. debt is only 59 percent of GDP. If it were 110 percent, as it is in Italy, the U.S. debt would be approximately $5 trillion higher than it is. This international comparison, combined with the fact that much of the U.S. debt is held by other government agencies, suggests that the U.S. government can have trillions of dollars more in debt before there is significant need for concern.

Interest Rates and Debt Burden

Considering debt relative to GDP is still not quite sufficient to give an accurate picture of the debt burden. How much of a burden a given amount of debt imposes depends on the interest rate that must be paid on that debt. The annual **debt service** is *the interest rate on debt times the total debt.*

In 2002, the U.S. government paid out approximately $170 billion in interest. A larger debt would require even higher interest payments. The interest payment is government revenue that can't be spent on defense or welfare; it's a payment for past

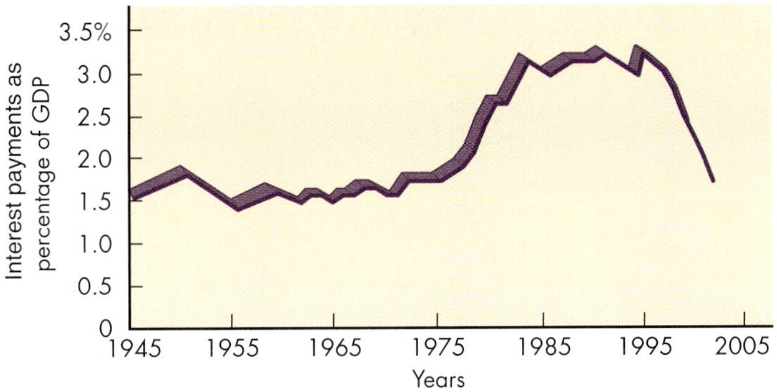

Figure 31-4 Federal Interest Payments Relative to GDP

Interest payments as a percentage of GDP remained relatively constant until the 1970s, after which they rose significantly due to high interest rates and large increases in debt. In the late 1990s they fell as interest rates fell and surpluses reduced the total debt.

Source: *The Economic and Budget Outlook*, Congressional Budget Office, 2002 (www.cbo.gov).

expenditures. Ultimately, the interest payments are the burden of the debt. That's what people mean when they say a deficit is burdening future generations.

Over the past 50 years, the interest rate has fluctuated considerably; when it has risen, the debt service has increased; when it has fallen, debt service has decreased. Figure 31-4 shows the federal interest payments relative to GDP. This ratio increased substantially in World War II and then again in the 1970s and early 1980s. In the early 1990s it rose, but in the late-1990s it fell to under 3 percent of GDP and continued to fall in the early 2000s. As long as the government has a debt, it will make interest payments. In the late 1990s, many predicted the debt would be repaid within 20 years, but the return of budget deficits in 2002 changed their predictions.

The United States can afford its current debt in the sense that it can afford to pay the interest on that debt. In fact, as I discussed above, it could afford a much higher debt/GDP ratio, since U.S. government bonds are still considered one of the safest assets in the world. No one is worried about the U.S. government's defaulting; that's why we stated above that the U.S. debt can be increased by trillions of dollars without problems.

The Current Budget Debate

Now that we've discussed deficits, surpluses, and debt in detail, let me return to the sudden disappearance of the budget surplus that I mentioned in the beginning of the chapter. Let's start with a consideration of why the surplus came about.

Why Did the Surplus Come About?

Until the 1940s, economists and laypeople shared the same view of deficits—they are bad. Then Keynesian economics made clear that that view was too simplistic and that, when the economy was significantly below its potential output, deficits could serve a positive function. The view that all government debt should be paid off as quickly as possible did not follow from economic theory. The more enlightened view of deficits lessened the pressure to eliminate them and contributed to the almost continual deficits that the U.S. government ran after World War II.

The adoption of Keynesian policy—using deficits to stimulate the economy in the 1940s has led to nearly continual budget deficits ever since the end of World War II.

That Keynesian view of deficits was never fully accepted by politicians, or by the public. Both had a deep-seated fear of deficits. They, like Roosevelt in the opening quotation, equated government deficits with individual deficits, when in fact the two are quite different. So, even when the government was running large deficits, most politicians were saying that the deficits should be eliminated. However, they did not act on their statements. Democrats generally came in and enacted new spending programs;

Four Important Points about Deficits and Debt

Knowing the Tools

1. Deficits are summary measures of the state of the economy. They are dependent on the accounting procedures used.
2. It is the health of the economy, not the deficit, with which we should be concerned.
3. Deficits and debt should be viewed relative to GDP to determine their importance.
4. Real deficit = Nominal deficit − (Inflation × Debt).

Republicans tried to stop those new spending programs and increased taxes to maintain fiscal responsibility.

In the 1980s the political landscape changed. Republicans, who opposed large government spending programs, developed a political strategy that focused on cutting taxes. They saw most government spending as unproductive, but saw political forces driving toward higher and higher spending. Their solution was to cut taxes, and to allow the deficits to expand. Some justified this by arguing that the tax cuts would increase incentives to work and expand the economy so much that no deficits would result. The majority of economists, while they agreed that the incentives could play a positive role in the long run, felt that they were too small to play a significant role in expanding the economy in the short run. Whatever the reasoning, the 1980s created a situation where both political parties were pushing the economy toward deficits—Democrats by spending, Republicans by cutting taxes.

Public and political concerns about the size of the deficit led to the passage of the Budget Enforcement Act of 1990, which established spending caps and a pay-as-you-go test on new spending or tax cuts.

This push toward large deficits provoked a reaction in the political center, and in the public, that led to changes in government rules on spending. Specifically it led to the passage of the Budget Enforcement Act of 1990, a law that put caps on certain aspects of federal spending and established a "pay-as-you-go" test for new spending or tax cuts so that, through 1996, any new legislation, except for emergencies, had to be accompanied by offsetting tax increases or spending cuts. In 1997, the act was extended through 2002. There were a number of holes in the act, but it did work in slowing the deficit even though, on its own, it is not what brought about the surplus in the late 1990s.

Q-8 What accounted for the budget surplus of the late 1990s?

Also contributing to the growth in the surplus in the late 1990s was the unexpected growth of the U.S. economy, and the lack of inflation accompanying that growth. As estimates of the level of potential output increased, the predicted future tax revenue increased; and, as it did, the deficit projections moved in the opposite direction. Because inflation remained low, interest rates remained low, holding down government interest payments. Simultaneously, the stock market boomed, which brought in large capital gains revenue for governments. It was that combination of economic growth, low inflation, and the stock market boom that was primarily responsible for turning the budget deficit predictions into the budget surplus predictions.

The emergence of a surplus allowed politics again to enter into budget decisions. The Economic Growth and Tax Relief Reconciliation Act of 2001 cut taxes and increased spending. Then came the September 11 terrorist attacks and the war on terrorism, which opened up the spending gates on defense and homeland security. And with the focus on the war, political considerations led to an increase in still other areas such as agricultural subsidies. With the war on terrorism, the political pressure against deficits melted and the Budget Enforcement Act was not extended. Together, these factors increased the likelihood that deficits will return as the status quo. In 2002, federal government spending grew by 7.5 percent, the largest annual increase since 1990, and the budget fell into deficit and was predicted to remain in deficit for at least the next few years.

Social Security and Lockboxes

One of the debates about how concerned we should be about the deficits involves the Social Security system. To understand this debate about Social Security and deficits, it is important to recognize that the United States uses a **cash flow accounting system**—*an accounting system entering expenses and revenues only when cash is received or paid out.* When it spends or collects money, these outflows or inflows show up on the budget. When the government doesn't have a cash inflow or outflow, nothing shows up on the budget. Thus, if government were to create a drug benefit for future retirees, if no cash is paid out currently, that obligation doesn't show up as part of the deficit.

Because the government uses a cash flow accounting system, a number of obligations incurred by the government do not show up as part of expenditures.

Currently the Social Security system is running a large surplus in its portion of the budget. In the future, however, Social Security will be legally required to pay out significant benefits to retirees that far exceed its revenue. Some politicians have argued that to safeguard the current revenue needed to pay these future obligations, we should create a "lockbox" in which current Social Security revenue would be locked up for future retirees. (In reality there would be no physical lockbox; the word is a metaphor for an accounting rule that would require the government to use the surpluses in the Social Security portion of budget to pay down the debt held by the public.)

While this proposal has certain attractive attributes, they are not those most people identify with the lockbox concept. The proposal would only indirectly help future Social Security recipients. To see how, let's consider the Social Security system more carefully.

The Social Security system began with the passage of the Federal Insurance Contribution Act (FICA) in 1935; FICA requires employees and firms to pay taxes and, in return, gives them a pension after they retire.

A Pay-as-You-Go System

The Social Security system was set up as a **pay-as-you-go system** where *the payments to current beneficiaries are funded through current payroll taxes*. This means that the Social Security system is a partially unfunded pension system. A *funded pension system* is a system where the contributions paid by workers plus interest are used to fund those workers' pensions. An *unfunded pension system*, however, is not necessarily unsound. In an ongoing system, there will always be revenue coming in and payments going out. There are always current workers to support a system that pays the aged. The benefit of the unfunded system is that it allows initial payments to individuals to exceed what they paid in. As long as the population's age distribution, the annual death rate, and the number of people working do not change much, an unfunded system runs smoothly.

The Social Security system is partially unfunded pension system: payments to current beneficiaries are funded through current payroll taxes.

The Effect of the Baby Boom

An unfunded system does, however, present a potential problem if the amount paid in differs from the amount paid out. To see this, say we have only three groups of people: workers, the retired elderly, and the very young (who aren't yet working). Now suddenly we start a pension program. We use the money that we collect from the workers to pay pensions to the elderly retired people, who have paid nothing in because they retired before the system started up. In short, this group gets benefits without having paid anything into the system. In the next generation, the elderly die, the workers become elderly, and the young become workers. The new group of elderly gets paid by the new workers. As long as the three groups remain at

This lithograph, titled "Legislative assault (on the budget)," appeared in a French newspaper in 1835. Bleichroeder Print Collection, Baker Library, Harvard Business School.

equivalent relative sizes, the process works neatly—each generation will get paid when its time comes.

But what happens when there's a "baby boom"—when one group suddenly has a large number of children in a short period of time? In this case, the sizes of the generations are no longer equal. Initially things work out wonderfully. The baby boomers become workers, and there are lots of them relative to the elderly. There's plenty of money coming in and comparatively little going out. This allows for an increase in payments to the elderly, a decrease in the taxes paid by the working group, or both.

Q-9 How can a baby boom cause problems for an unfunded pension system?

In the next generation, the baby-boom workers become elderly. Then, assuming the baby boomers have fewer children than their own parents had, the number of people collecting benefits becomes larger but the number of workers contributing to the system becomes smaller. In this case, payments per beneficiary must decrease, real contributions per worker coming in must increase, or some combination of the two must occur. None of these alternatives is particularly pleasant.

This example doesn't come out of nowhere. It represents the current situation in the U.S. Social Security system. From 1946 through the late 1960s there was a baby boom, and these baby boomers are currently in the labor force. They'll start retiring in large numbers in the early 2020s and, when they do, the number of workers per retiree will decrease dramatically, so that around 2020 there will be about 2.5 workers per retiree instead of more than 15 workers per retiree as in the 1950s and 1960s. Figure 31-5 shows these unpleasant projections.

The Social Security Trust Fund In the 1970s and 1980s, economists pointed out that this problem would be occurring. In response, in 1983 the government passed an amendment to the Social Security Act of 1935. The age of eligibility was raised slightly, Social Security tax rates (FICA) were raised, and Social Security payments became subject to taxation for some beneficiaries. These measures were designed to create surpluses in the coming years.

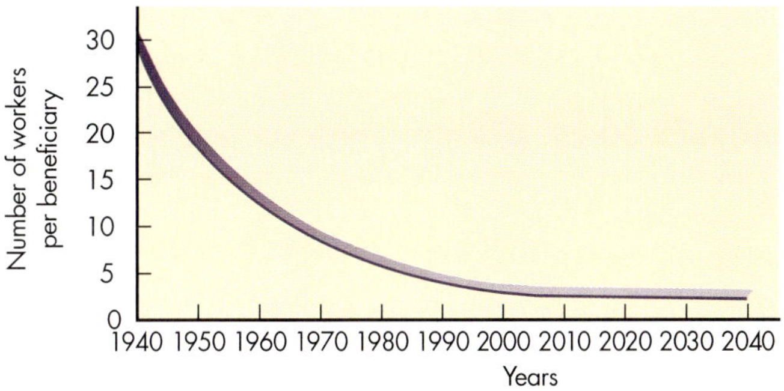

Figure 31-5 Projection of Workers Compared with Social Security Retirees
The number of workers per retiree declined considerably from 1950 to 2000, and it will continue to decline in future decades.

Note: Working-age persons are aged 20–64, and retirement-age persons are aged 65 and over.

Source: Social Security Administration.

Currently, were it not for surpluses in the Social Security system, the budget deficit would be much larger. For example, in 2002 the Social Security system had a $160 billion surplus and the government budget would have had a $318 billion deficit rather than a $158 billion deficit if the government had separated out the Social Security system's surplus from the standard budget.

Most of the current budget surpluses originate from a surplus generated from the Social Security system.

That portion of the surplus is not available for spending; it is earmarked for the Social Security trust fund, which holds special bonds issued by government that cannot be bought and sold on the bond market. The 1983 act was designed to produce surpluses that could be placed into a trust fund to make the payments coming due in the 2020 to 2040 period without requiring huge tax increases or massive borrowing then. The lockbox proposals are designed to ensure that those surpluses held in the trust fund would be available. In the early 2000s, the Social Security Administration estimated that surpluses would continue until about 2020. At that time outlays will begin to exceed revenue, and by about 2040, the Social Security trust fund will be used up and the system will either have to begin borrowing or increase revenue.

The Social Security system is not the only government spending program that will experience significant funding problems in the future. The Medicare program will also face similar problems; since the elderly use significantly more medical services than younger individuals, these expenses will be substantial. It has been estimated that in 2030, 60 percent of the government budget will be spent on Social Security and Medicare, compared to the current 35 percent.

The bottom line is that the United States budget, considered separately from the Social Security budget, is having to borrow much more than the amount of its current deficit. It is also borrowing from the trust fund designed to pay future Social Security claims.

The Real Problem and the Real Solution

While economic theory advocates running a surplus when the economy is booming, it does not suggest that the trust fund will provide the complete answer to the Social Security funding problem. Even if we had a fully funded trust fund, it would not solve the Social Security problem. The reason is that the trust fund is simply a financial solution; the actual solution must be a "real" solution—a solution that deals with the supply and demand of real resources, not with nominal amounts.

Q-10 Why won't a fully funded Social Security trust fund solve the real problem the U.S. economy will face as more and more baby boomers retire?

To understand why this is the case, it is helpful to think of the problem in relation to the *AS/AD* model, which tells us that, in equilibrium, real aggregate demand must equal real aggregate supply—the amount of real goods available to consume must equal the amount of real goods for sale. Herein lies the problem. When baby boomers, like me, retire in 2020 we will stop producing real goods, *but we will continue consuming* real

The real problem that is created by the baby boom is that as baby boomers retire, they will cease to contribute to production but will continue to consume. Workers will have to produce enough both for themselves and for the large number of retirees.

goods. And given our medical needs, we will likely consume quite heavily—medicine, travel, and all that good stuff. Real goods must be provided to us. Our Social Security payments, our other pensions, and our savings will give us significant nominal income to spend. If that nominal income is not matched by significant real production, the quantity of aggregate demand will exceed the quantity of aggregate supply and the result will be inflation. The problem is that someone has to produce the goods that we're spending on. That's where you and your fellow workers come in. Put bluntly, starting in 2020 you must produce not only enough real goods for yourself and your family but also enough for the retired baby boomers.

Put another way, *the real output per worker must increase, but the real consumption of workers must not increase* if the retired baby boomers are to have real goods to consume. This matching of real production with real expenditures could be accomplished if you and your fellow workers save a large portion of your income rather than consuming it; if the government taxes you heavily starting in 2020, so you don't have income to spend; if Social Security recipients choose to save rather than spend their income; or if foreign saving comes in. But some combination of these must occur so that real aggregate demand will not exceed real aggregate supply, which would cause strong inflationary pressures and strong pressure on government to decrease aggregate demand through contractionary fiscal policy.

The Trust Fund Illusion If this real problem—the need to match aggregate supply and aggregate demand—exists whether or not the Social Security trust fund exists, what does the trust fund do? The answer is "not much" directly, but it does have a positive indirect effect. The trust fund, like the lockbox policy meant to protect the trust fund, is an accounting illusion. When the United States created the Social Security system, it created obligations to individuals. What the trust fund does is to back that obligation with government bonds—an obligation of the government to pay a certain amount in the future. It backs one government obligation with another.

As I emphasized in the beginning of this chapter, the concepts of *deficit* and *surplus* are creatures of the accounting system used. The Social Security trust fund essentially changes the accounting system—it changes an unbooked obligation into a booked obligation. Given the political fear of deficits, this change leads government to spend less now, and to keep taxes higher now, than it otherwise would. To the degree the government does this, the trust fund decreases the debt in private hands, making the interest burden of the debt less than it otherwise would have been. The holders of debt will not have the interest payments to spend on real goods in the future, making more real goods available for consumption in the future. So, the trust fund does help, even if it does not completely solve the problem.

Politics and Economic Policy[4] Politics generally mixes illusions with reality, and both Republicans and Democrats have avoided discussing real solutions—solutions that match real production with real expenditures. They both want to assume that the Social Security trust fund will solve the problem. The real solution requires them to deal with the "real" problem that there is no free lunch.

Most of the political proposals being put forward would make matters worse. Consider the proposal to help elderly with their drug expenses. While the desire is laudable, the economics of it are dubious. The increased expenditure will be small now but will

[4]This section reflects my particular view, so treat it as a stimulant for thought, not as the correct view. Your teacher, who grades your exam, will tell you the "correct" view.

The Stock Market Crash of 2014?

Beyond the Tools

Another aspect of the demographic changes brought about by the baby boom relates to stock market prices. Stock prices were soaring in the late 1990s as the baby boomers moved into their peak earning periods and, through pension systems, saved for the future—by buying stock. Even with the fall in stock prices in the early 2000s, stock prices were still high relative to their long-term trend because of this demographic fact.

In 2014, when the boomers start anticipating retiring and selling stock, the effect of the baby boom on the stock market will be in the opposite direction. Many elderly will be redeeming their stocks as they retire, hoping to live off the proceeds of their savings. (These forces are the reverse of those that were pushing the stock market prices up at the turn of the century.) As the expectations of that happening develop, stock prices will likely fall precipitously, and remain low relative to their long-run trend, and there will be much less there than people thought.

---

increase future obligations of the Medicare system enormously, and do it at precisely the time the real problem is at its worst. If that proposal is passed, in the 2020s the elderly will be consuming even more goods, making it necessary to cut future workers' consumption even more.

Another policy being proposed is to invest the trust fund in the stock market. That policy also does not deal with the real problem. If my prediction about the stock market is right (see the box "The Stock Market Crash of 2014?"), and it falls as soon as the market starts expecting baby boomers to decrease their demand for stock as they prepare to spend their savings, then the value of the investments in the trust fund will not be anywhere near as much as people expect.

Politically Unpopular Policies So what does provide a real solution? Any policy that brings the real forces of aggregate demand and aggregate supply into equilibrium. The real amount I and my fellow baby boomers spend when we retire must be reduced if the real amount you and your fellow workers will have to contribute at that time is to be reduced. There are a number of ways this can be accomplished, none of them politically attractive, which is why they are not much talked about. If not accomplished through policy, the spending reduction will be accomplished through inflation.

One policy is to increase taxes on workers starting in 2020. The other is to cut benefits once baby boomers start retiring. One way to cut benefits is to make Social Security "means tested," so that high-income individuals do not receive as much as they were promised. Another way to cut benefits is to increase the retirement age to 72. (It's now 65 to 68.)[5] This increase could be justified by the fact that the elderly live longer and are in better health now than in the past. Since many of us baby boomers will die off between 65 and 72, the savings would be considerable. Moreover, with the delayed Social Security benefits many of us would work longer, increasing the number of people working and decreasing the number of people consuming without producing.

Policies that would help to match real production to real expenditures in 2020 are:

1. Increase taxes on workers to reduce their consumption.
2. Reduce Social Security payments to reduce consumption by retirees.
3. Increase the retirement age to 72 to increase real production.

Neither of these benefit-cutting policies would affect the current budget picture, but both would significantly improve the U.S. economic picture because future real commitments would be decreased. I doubt that either of these policies will be considered,

[5]Government pension systems were started by the 19th-century German leader Otto von Bismarck. He reportedly chose 65 as the retirement age because his advisers told him that vital statistics for the country showed most people died before age 65.

but they are the type of policies that will deal with the "real" macro problem facing the United States in the future.

Conclusion

This has been a relatively short chapter, but the points in it are important. Deficits, debts, and surpluses are all accounting measures. Whether a budget is in surplus or deficit is not especially important. What is important is the health of the economy. The economic framework tells us that if the economy is in a recession, you shouldn't worry much about deficits—they can actually be good for the economy. If you are in an expansion, surpluses make much more sense. It is the state of the economy that we need to consider when making decisions about whether deficits or surpluses are good.

Economics also tells us that there are limits to how much real output one can transfer with financial assets over time. In each time period the real aggregate demand must equal the real aggregate supply; otherwise inflation or deflation will result. When demographic changes cause real supply and demand to differ substantially, as they will begin to do in the 2020s, there will be a real problem that financial transfers cannot solve. The *AS/AD* model tells us that that "real" problem must have a "real" solution. Politically we are unlikely to hear much discussion of such solutions, which is why the future economic health of the United States can be precarious even if the U.S. budget is in surplus.

Summary

- A deficit is a shortfall of revenues over payments. A surplus is the excess of revenues over payments. Debt is accumulated deficits minus accumulated surpluses.
- Budget deficits and surpluses should be judged in light of economic and political conditions.
- Deficits and surpluses are summary measures of a budget. Whether a budget is a problem depends on the budgeting procedures that measure it.
- A structural deficit or surplus is that part of a budget deficit or surplus that would exist even if the economy were at its potential level of income. A passive deficit or surplus is that part of the deficit or surplus that exists because the economy is below or above potential:

  Structural deficit = Actual deficit − Passive deficit
- A real deficit is a nominal deficit adjusted for the effect of inflation:

  Real deficit = Nominal deficit − (Inflation × Debt)
- A country's debt must be judged in relation to its assets. What is counted as a debt and as an asset can be arbitrary. About 44 percent of the government's debt is held by other government agencies.
- Government debt and individual debt differ in three major ways: (1) government is ongoing and never needs to repay its debt, (2) government can pay off its debt by printing money, and (3) most of government debt is internal—owed to its own citizens.
- Deficits, surpluses, and debt should be viewed relative to GDP because this ratio better measures the government's ability to handle the deficit and pay off the debt. Compared to many countries, the United States has a low debt-to-GDP ratio.
- The Budget Enforcement Act of 1990 and the growth in the U.S. economy both contributed to budget surpluses in the late 1990s and early 2000s. The Economic Growth and Tax Relief Reconciliation Act of 2001 and an economic slowdown contributed to a return to budget deficits in 2002.
- The Social Security system makes the surplus look bigger than it is. Beginning in 2020, the Social Security system will run deficits.
- The real problem is not the solvency of the Social Security system but the future mismatch between real production and real expenditures.

Key Terms

cash flow accounting system *(739)*
debt *(731)*
debt service *(736)*
deficit *(727)*
external debt *(734)*
internal debt *(734)*
nominal deficit *(730)*
passive deficit or surplus *(729)*
pay-as-you-go system *(739)*
real deficit *(730)*
Social Security system *(728)*
structural deficit or surplus *(729)*
surplus *(727)*

Questions for Thought and Review

1. "Budget deficits should be avoided, even if the economy is below potential, because they reduce saving and lead to lower growth." Does this policy directive follow from the short-run or the long-run framework? Explain your answer.
2. What are the two ways government can finance a budget deficit?
3. Your income is $40,000 per year; your expenditures are $45,000. You spend $10,000 of that $45,000 for tuition. Is your budget in deficit or surplus? Why?
4. "The deficit should be of concern." What additional information do you need to undertake a reasonable discussion of this statement?
5. If the actual budget deficit is $100 billion, the economy is operating $250 billion above its potential, and the marginal tax rate is 20 percent, what is the structural deficit and the passive deficit?
6. Two economists are debating whether the target rate of unemployment is 4 percent or 6 percent. Mr. A believes it's 4 percent; Ms. B. believes it's 6 percent. One says the structural deficit is $40 billion; the other says it's $20 billion. Which one says which? Why?
7. Inflation is 20 percent. Debt is $2 trillion. The nominal deficit is $300 billion. What is the real deficit?
8. How would your answer to question 5 differ if you knew that expected inflation was 15 percent?
9. "The debt should be of concern." What additional information do you need to undertake a reasonable discussion of this statement?
10. List three ways in which individual debt differs from government debt.
11. If all of the government's debt were internal, would financing that debt make the nation poorer?
12. How can a government that isn't running a deficit still get itself into financial trouble?
13. Why is debt service an important measure of whether debt is a problem?
14. How did the Budget Enforcement Act of 1990 contribute to the budget surpluses of the late 1990s?
15. How did the Economic Growth and Tax Relief Reconciliation Act of 2001 contribute to the return of deficits?
16. How did the Social Security system contribute to the surpluses of the late 1990s?
17. What are two solutions to the "real" problem posed by the growing number of retiring baby boomers beginning in 2020?
18. Economist Paul W. McCracken stated, "A decision to go with budgets that involve deficits is a decision to have a future economy delivering lower incomes." Do you agree or disagree? Why?

Problems and Exercises

1. Canada's debt was $574 billion at the end of 1996. Using the information below (in billions of Canadian dollars), fill in the blanks for Canada's budget balance and debt for the following years:

	Revenues	Expenditures	Debt
1997	$141	$150	$___
1998	153	___	580
1999	156	153	___
2000	___	153	565
2001	179	162	___

2. Say the marginal tax rate is 30 percent and that government expenditures do not change with output. Say also that the economy is at potential output and that the deficit is $200 billion.
   a. What is size of the passive deficit?
   b. What is the size of the structural deficit?
   c. How would your answers to *a* and *b* change if the deficit were still $200 billion but the output were $200 billion dollars below potential?
   d. How would your answer to *a* and *b* change if the deficit were still $200 billion but output were $100 billion dollars above potential?
   e. Which is likely of more concern to policy makers: a passive or a structural deficit?

3. Calculate the real deficit or surplus in the following cases:
   a. Inflation is 10 percent. Debt is $3 trillion. Nominal deficit is $220 billion.
   b. Inflation is 2 percent. Debt is $1 trillion. Nominal deficit is $50 billion.
   c. Inflation is −4 percent. (Price levels are falling.) Debt is $500 billion. Nominal deficit is $30 billion.
   d. Inflation is 3 percent. Debt is $2 trillion. Nominal surplus is $100 billion.
4. Assume a country's nominal GDP is $600 billion, government expenditures less debt service are $145 billion, and revenue is $160 billion. The nominal debt is $360 billion. Inflation is 3 percent and interest rates are 6 percent.
   a. Calculate debt service payments.
   b. Calculate the nominal deficit.
   c. Calculate the real deficit.
5. Assume that a country's real growth is 2 percent per year, while its real deficit is rising 5 percent a year. Can the country continue to afford such deficits indefinitely? What problems might it face in the future?
6. You've been hired by Creative Accountants, economic consultants. Your assignment is to make suggestions about how to structure a government's accounts so that the current deficit looks as small as possible. Specifically, they want to know how to treat the following:
   a. Government pensions.
   b. Sale of land.
   c. Social Security taxes.
   d. Proceeds of a program to allow people to prepay taxes for a 10 percent discount.
   e. Expenditures on F-52 bombers.

Web Questions

1. The Social Security Network is a source of information on the current Social Security debate. Go to its home page (www.socsec.org/facts/Basics) to answer the following questions:
   a. Summarize what's right about Social Security.
   b. Summarize what's wrong about Social Security.
   c. What reforms have been proposed to fix what's wrong?
2. The U.S. Department of Treasury maintains a learning vault at www.publicdebt.treas.gov. Go to this site and click on frequently asked questions (FAQs) about the public debt to answer the following questions:
   a. What percent of the debt is held in each of the following: bills, notes, bonds, inflation-indexed notes, and inflation-indexed bonds?
   b. What are intragovernmental holdings?
   c. When would the debt decline?

Answers to Margin Questions

1. Deficits can be good when an economy is operating below its potential because they increase aggregate demand and total output. Deficits can be bad in the long run if they lead to lower investment, because lower investment will lead to lower growth. *(727)*
2. Since the economy is at its potential income, its passive deficit is zero. All of its budget deficit is a structural deficit. *(729)*
3. Inflation reduces the value of the dollars with which the debt will be repaid and hence, in real terms, wipes out a portion of the debt. *(730)*
4. The real deficit equals the nominal deficit minus inflation times the total debt. Inflation times the total debt in this case equals $80 billion (0.02 × $4 trillion). Since the nominal deficit is $40 billion, the real deficit is actually a surplus of $40 billion. ($40 billion − $80 billion = −$40 billion). *(731)*
5. Deficit is a flow concept, the difference between income and expenditures. Debt—accumulated deficits minus accumulated surpluses—is a stock concept. *(732)*
6. To get a full picture of a country's financial situation, you have to look at assets as well as debt, since a large debt for a country with large assets poses no problem. *(732)*
7. A $5 billion economy growing at a real annual rate of 5 percent could have an annual deficit of $250 million (0.05 × $5 billion) and not increase its debt burden. *(736)*
8. The Budget Enforcement Act of 1990, unexpected growth of the U.S. economy, and the lack of inflation accompanying that growth led to the surpluses of the late 1990s. *(738)*
9. An unfunded pension system is a pay-as-you-go system. It collects taxes from current workers and uses the proceeds

to pay out benefits to current retirees. A baby boom changes the ratio between workers and retirees. Initially, it increases the number of workers to retirees, lowering the tax rate that must be paid to meet given retirement goals per person. However, when the baby boomers retire, it increases the necessary tax rate because there are so many more retirees for whom a retirement goal must be met, and there are fewer working taxpayers from whom the necessary amount of taxes must be collected. *(740)*

10. A fully funded trust fund wouldn't solve the real problem because the trust fund is a financial solution. The solution would make sure that the amount of real goods demanded equals the amount of real goods for sale without significant inflation. *(741)*

32 Macro Policies in Developing Countries

After reading this chapter, you should be able to:

- State some comparative statistics on rich and poor countries.
- Explain why there might be a difference in normative goals between developing and developed countries.
- Explain why economies at different stages in development have different institutional needs.
- Explain what is meant by the term *dual economy.*
- Distinguish between a regime change and a policy change.
- Explain why the statement that inflation is a problem of central bank issuing too much money is not sufficient for developing countries.
- Distinguish between convertibility on the current account and full convertibility.
- List seven obstacles facing developing countries.

Rise up, study the economic forces which oppress you . . .
They have emerged from the hand of man just as the
gods emerged from his brain. You can control them.

—*Paul LaFargue*

Throughout this book I have emphasized that macro policy is an art in which one takes the abstract principles learned in *positive economics*—the abstract analysis and models that tell us how economic forces direct the economy—and examines how those principles work out in a particular institutional structure to achieve goals determined in *normative economics*—the branch of economics that considers what goals we should be aiming for. In this chapter we see another aspect of that art.

Most of this book has emphasized the macroeconomies of Western industrialized economies, the United States in particular. That means I have focused on their goals and their institutions. In this chapter I shift focus and discuss the macroeconomic problems of developing economies.

Developing Countries in Perspective

There are over 6 billion people in the world. Of these, 4.6 billion (about 75 percent) live in developing, rather than developed, countries. Per capita income in developing countries is around $500 per year; in the United States per capita income is about $36,000.

These averages understate the differences between the poorest country and the richest. Consider the African country of Chad—definitely one of the world's poorest. Its per capita income is about $200 per year—less than 1/100 of the per capita income in the United States. Moreover income in Chad goes primarily to the rich, so Chad's poor have per capita income of significantly less than $200.

How does a person live on that $200 per year, as many people in the world do? To begin with, that person can't:

Go out for Big Macs.

Use Joy perfume (or any type of perfume).

Wear designer clothes.

What to Call Developing Countries

Beyond the Tools

In this chapter, following common usage, I call low-income countries *developing countries.* They have not always been called *developing.* In the 1950s they were called *backward,* but it was eventually realized that *backward* implied significant negative value judgments. Then these countries were called *underdeveloped,* but it was eventually realized that *underdeveloped* also implied significant negative value judgments. More recently they have been called *developing,* but eventually everyone will realize that *developing* implies significant negative value judgments. After all, in what sense are these countries "developing" any more than the United States? All countries are evolving or developing countries. Many so-called developing countries have highly refined cultures, which they don't want to lose; they may want to develop economically but not at the cost of cultural change.

What should one call these countries? That remains to be seen, but whatever one calls them, bear in mind that language can conceal value judgments.

And that person must:

Eat grain—usually rice or corn—for all meals, every day.

Mix fat from meat—not meat itself—with the rice on special occasions (maybe).

Live in one room with 9 or 10 other people.

Work hard from childhood to old age (if there is an old age). Those too old to work in the fields stay at home and care for those too young to work in the fields. (But children go out to work in the fields when they're about six years old.)

Go hungry, because no matter how many family members can work in the fields, probably the work and soil don't yield enough to provide the workers with an adequate number of calories per day.

In a poor person's household it's likely that a couple of the older children have gone into the city to find work that pays money wages. If they were lucky and found jobs, they can send money home each month. That money may be the only cash income their family back in the fields has. The family uses the money to buy a few tools and cooking utensils.

The preceding is, of course, only one among billions of different stories. Even Americans and Europeans who are classified as poor find it hard to contemplate what life is really like in a truly poor country.

Don't Judge Society by Its Income Alone

Poor people in developing countries survive and often find pleasure in their hard lives. There are few suicides in the poorest countries. For example, the U.S. suicide rate is approximately 11 per 100,000 people. In Costa Rica it's 6.8; in Mexico it's 2.6; and in Peru it's 0.5. Who has time for suicide? You're too busy surviving. There's little ambiguity and few questions about the meaning of life. Living! That's what life's all about. There's no "Mom, what am I going to do today?" You know what you're going to do: survive if you can. And survival is satisfying.

Often these economically poor societies have elaborate cultural rituals and networks of intense personal relationships that provide individuals with a deep sense of fulfillment and satisfaction.

Often economically poor societies have cultures that provide individuals with a deep sense of fulfillment and satisfaction.

Are people in these societies as happy as Americans are? If your immediate answer is no, be careful to understand the difficulty of making such a judgment. The answer isn't clear-cut. For us to say, "My God! What a failure their system is!" is wrong. It's an inappropriate value judgment about the relative worth of cultures. All too often Americans have gone into another country to try to make people better off, but have ended up making them worse off.

An economy is part and parcel of a culture.

An economy is part and parcel of a culture. You can't judge just an economy; you must judge the entire culture. Some developing countries have cultures that, in many people's view, are preferable to ours. If one increases a country's income but takes away its culture in doing so, one may well have made its people worse off.

That said, if we asked people in developing countries if they believe that they would be better off if they had more income, most would definitely answer yes!

Q-1 In what way is economic development the only choice for developing countries?

Even culturally sensitive people agree that economic growth within the context of a developing country's culture would be a good thing, if only because those countries exist simultaneously with market economies. Given market societies' expansionary tendencies, without economic growth, cultures in economically poor countries would simply be overrun and destroyed by the cultures of market societies. Their land would be taken, their agricultural patterns would be changed, their traditional means of subsistence would be destroyed, and their cultures would be obliterated. So generally the choice isn't between development and preservation of the existing culture (and its accompanying ancient ways to which the poor have adjusted). Rather, the choice is between development (with its attendant wrenching cultural transitions) and continuing poverty and slower, but still painful, cultural transitions.

Some Comparative Statistics on Rich and Poor Nations

The low average income in poor countries has its effects on people's lives. Life expectancy is about 60 years in most very economically poor countries (compared to about 77 years in the United States). In economically poor countries most people drink contaminated water, consume about half the number of calories the World Health Organization has determined is minimal for good health, and do physical labor (often of the kind done by machine in developed countries). Table 32-1 compares developing countries, middle-income countries, and developed countries.

As with all statistics, care must be taken in interpreting the figures in Table 32-1. For example, the income comparisons were all made on the basis of current exchange rates. But relative prices between rich and poor countries often differ substantially; the cost of goods relative to total income tends to be much lower for people in developing countries than for those in developed countries.

Purchasing power parity determines exchange rates by determining what a specified basket of consumer goods will cost in various countries.

To allow for these differences, some economists have looked at the domestic purchasing power of money in various countries and have adjusted the comparisons accordingly. Rather than working with exchange rates, they use **purchasing power parity**—*a method of comparing income by looking at the domestic purchasing power of money in different countries*. They compare what a specified market basket of consumer goods will cost in various countries and use these results to compare currencies' values. Making these adjustments, the World Bank found that income differences among countries are cut by half. In other words, when one uses the World Bank's purchasing power parity method of comparison, it's as if the people in developing countries had twice as much income as they had when the exchange rate method was used.

A similar adjustment can be made with the life expectancy rates. A major reason for the lower life expectancies in developing countries is their high infant mortality rates. Once children survive infancy, however, their life expectancies are much closer to those of children in developed countries. Say a country's overall life expectancy is 50 years and that 10 percent of all infants die within their first year. As a person grows older, at

Table 32-1 Statistics on Selected Developing, Middle-Income, and Developed Countries: 2001

Country	Population per Physician	Daily Calorie Supply	Life Expectancy	Infant Mortality (per 1,000)	Labor Force in Agriculture (%)	Labor Force in Industry (%)	Adult Literacy Rate	People per TV Receiver	GDP per Capita ($)
Developing									
Bangladesh	4,102	2,201	61	68	63%	11%	56%	173	$ 370
Ethiopia	25,000	1,845	44	97	52	11	36	99	100
Haiti	7,180	1,721	50	93	66	9	45	185	480
Middle-Income									
Brazil	1,020	2,797	64	36	23	24	83	4	3,060
Iran	3,140	2,899	70	28	30	25	72	14	1,750
South Korea	817	3,229	75	8	10	22	98	3	9,400
Thailand	4,180	2,365	71	30	54	15	94	4	1,970
Developed									
Japan	530	2,890	81	4	5	30	99	1.5	35,990
Sweden	166	2,914	80	3	2	24	99	1.9	25,400
United States	435	3,609	77	7	2	24	97	1.3	36,000

Sources: *World Development Report, 2002,* The World Bank (www.worldbank.org); *CIA World Factbook, 2002; Encyclopedia Britannica, Book of the Year, 2002.* Because of reporting lags, some data are for earlier years.

each birthday the person's life expectancy is higher. So if a child lives to the age of 3 years, then at that point the child has an actual life expectancy of close to 60 years, rather than 50 years.

Growth versus Development

Economists use the term *developing,* rather than *growing,* to emphasize that the goals of these counties involve more than simply an increase in output; these countries are changing their underlying institutions. Put another way, these economies are changing their production functions; they are not increasing inputs given a production function. Thus, *development* refers to an increase in productive capacity and output brought about by a change in the underlying institutions, and *growth* refers to an increase in output brought about by an increase in inputs.

Growth occurs because of an increase in inputs, given a production function; development occurs through a change in the production function.

The distinction can be overdone. Institutions, and hence production functions, in developed as well as in developing countries are continually changing, and output changes are essentially a combination of both changes in production functions and increases in inputs. For example, in the 1990s the major Western economies have been **restructuring** their economies—*changing the underlying economic institutions*—as they work to compete better in the world economy. As they restructure, they change their methods of production, their laws, and their social support programs. Thus, in some ways, they are doing precisely what developing countries are doing—developing rather than just growing. Despite the ambiguity, the distinction between growth and development can be a useful one if you remember that the two blend into each other.

Q-2 Why does restructuring in developed countries suggest that the distinction between growth and development can be overdone?

The reason economists separate out developing economies is that these economies have (1) different institutional structures and (2) a different weighting of goals than do Western developed economies. These two differences—in institutional structure and in goals—change the way in which the lessons of abstract theory are applied and discussed.

While the lessons of abstract theory do not change when we shift our attention to developing economies, the institutions and goals change enormously.

Differing Goals

When discussing macro policy within Western developed economies, I did not dwell on questions of normative goals of macroeconomics. Instead, I used generally accepted goals in the United States as the goals of macro policy—achieving low inflation, low unemployment, and an acceptable growth rate—with a few caveats. You may have noticed that the discussion focused more on what might be called stability goals—achieving low unemployment and low inflation—than it did on the acceptable growth rate goal. I chose that focus because growth in Western developed countries is desired because it holds unemployment down, and because it avoids difficult distributional questions, as much as it is desired for its own sake. Our economy has sufficient productive capacity to provide its citizens, on average, with a relatively high standard of living. The problem facing Western societies is as much seeing that all members of those societies share in that high standard of living as it is raising the standard.

There are differences in normative goals between developing and developed countries because their wealth differs. Developing countries face true economic needs whereas developed countries' economic needs are considered by most people to be normatively less pressing.

In the developing countries, the weighting of goals is different. Growth and development are primary goals. When people are starving and the economy isn't fulfilling people's **basic needs**—*adequate food, clothing, and shelter*—a main focus of macro policy will be on how to increase the economy's growth rate through development so that the economy can fulfill those basic needs.

Differing Institutions

Developing countries differ from developed countries not only in their goals but also in their macroeconomic institutions. These macroeconomic institutions are qualitatively different from institutions in developed countries. Their governments are different; their financial institutions—the institutions that translate savings into investment—are different; their fiscal institutions—the institutions through which government collects taxes and spends its money—are different; and their social and cultural institutions are different. Because of these differences, the way in which we discuss macroeconomic policy is different.

Economies at different stages of development have different institutional needs because the problems they face are different.

One of the differences concerns very basic market institutions—such as Western-style property rights and contract law. In certain groups of developing countries, most notably sub-Saharan Africa, these basic market institutions don't exist; instead, communal property rights and tradition structure economic relationships. How can one talk about market forces in such economies?[1] On a more mundane level, consider the issue of monetary policy. Talking about monetary policy via open market operations (the buying and selling of bonds by the central bank) is not all that helpful when there are no open market operations, as there are not in many developing countries.

Let's now consider some specific institutional differences more carefully.

In many developing countries, institutional checks and balances on government leaders often do not exist.

Political Differences and Laissez-Faire Views of how activist macroeconomic policy should be are necessarily contingent on the political system an economy has. One of the scarcest commodities in developing countries is socially minded leaders. Not that developed countries have any overabundance of them, but at least in most developed countries there is a tradition of politicians seeming to be fair and open-minded, and a set of institutionalized checks and balances that limits leaders using government for their personal benefit. In many developing countries, those institutionalized checks and balances on governmental leaders often do not exist.

[1]One can, of course, talk about economic forces. But, as discussed in Chapter 1, economic forces become market forces only in a market institutional setting.

Let's consider a few examples. First, let's look at Saudi Arabia, which, while economically rich, maintains many of the institutions of a developing country. It is an absolute monarchy in which the royal family is the ultimate power. Say a member of that family comes to the bank and wants a loan that, on economic grounds, doesn't make sense. What do you think the bank loan officer will do? Grant the loan, if the banker is smart. Thus, despite the wealth of the country, it isn't surprising that many economists believe the Saudi banking system reflects that political structure—and may soon find itself in serious trouble.

A second example is Nigeria, which had enormous possibilities for economic growth in the 1980s because of its oil riches. It didn't develop. Instead, politicians fought over the spoils, and bribes became a major source of their income. Corruption was rampant, and the Nigerian economy went nowhere. I will stop there, but, unfortunately, there are many other examples.

Because of the structure of government in many developing countries, many, economists who, in Western developed economies, favor activist government policies may well favor Classical laissez-faire policies for the same reasons that early Classical economists did—because they have a profound distrust of the governments. That distrust, however, must have limits. As I discussed in Chapter 2, even a laissez-faire policy requires some government role in setting the rules. So there is no escaping the need for socially minded leaders.

The Dual Economy A second institutional difference between developed and developing countries is the dual nature of developing countries' economies. Whereas it often makes sense to talk about a Western economy as a single economy, it does not for most developing countries. A developing country's economy is generally characterized by a **dual economy**—*the existence of two sectors: a traditional sector and an internationally oriented modern market sector.*[2]

The term *dual economy* refers to the existence of the two sectors in most developing countries: a traditional sector and an internationally oriented modern market sector.

Often, the largest percentage of the population participates in the traditional economy. It is a local currency, or no currency, sector in which traditional ways of doing things take precedence. The second sector—the internationally oriented modern market sector—is often indistinguishable from a Western economy. Activities in the modern sector are often conducted in foreign currencies, rather than domestic currencies, and contracts are often governed by international law. This dual economy aspect of developing countries creates a number of policy dilemmas for them and affects the way they think about macroeconomic problems.

Q-3 What is meant by the term *dual economy?*

For example, take the problem of unemployment. Many developing countries have a large subsistence-farming economy. Subsistence farmers aren't technically unemployed, but often there are so many people on the land that, in economic terms, their contribution to output is minimal or even negative, so for policy purposes one can consider the quantity of labor that will be supplied at the going wage unlimited. But to call these people unemployed is problematic. These subsistence farmers are simply outside the market economy. In such cases one would hardly want, or be able, to talk of an unemployment problem in the same way we talk in the United States.

Web Note 32.1
The Modern Sector

Fiscal Structure of Developing and Transitional Economies A third institutional difference concerns developing countries' fiscal systems. To undertake discretionary fiscal policy—running a deficit or surplus to affect the aggregate economy—the

---

[2]I discuss these two economies as if they were separate, but in reality they are interrelated. Portions of the economy devoted to the tourist trade span both sectors, as do some manufacturing industries. Still, there is sufficient independence of the two economies that it is reasonable to treat them as separate.

government must be able to determine expenditures and tax rates, with a particular eye toward the difference between the two. As discussed above, discretionary fiscal policy is difficult for Western developed countries to undertake; it is almost impossible for developing economies.

Often developing countries do not have the institutional structures with which to collect taxes.

In the traditional sector of many developing countries, barter or cash transactions predominate, and such transactions are especially difficult to tax. Often, the governments in these economies don't have the institutional structures with which to collect taxes (or, when they have the institutional structure, it is undermined by fraud and evasion), so their taxing options are limited; that's why they often use tariffs as a primary source of revenue.

Many government expenditures in developing countries are mandated by political considerations.

Similar problems exist with government expenditures. Many expenditures of developing countries are mandated by political considerations—if the government doesn't make them, it will likely be voted out of office. Within such a setting, to talk about activist fiscal policy—choosing a deficit for its macroeconomic implications—even if it might otherwise be relevant, is not much help since the budget deficit is not a choice variable, but instead is a result of other political decisions.

A regime change is a change in the entire atmosphere within which the government and the economy interrelate; a policy change is a change in one aspect of government's actions.

The political constraints facing developing and transitional countries can, of course, be overstated. The reality is that developing countries do institute new fiscal regimes. Take, for example, Mexico. In the early 1980s, Mexico's fiscal problems seemed impossible to solve, but in the late 1980s and early 1990s, Carlos de Salinas, a U.S.-trained economist, introduced a fiscal austerity program and an economic liberalization program that lowered Mexico's deficit and significantly reduced its inflation. But such changes are better called a **regime change**—*a change in the entire atmosphere within which the government and the economy interrelate*—rather than a **policy change**—*a change in one aspect of government's actions, such as monetary policy or fiscal policy*. Regimes can change suddenly. For example, in Mexico soon after President Salinas left office, his brother was implicated in a murder and drug scandal. Foreign investors became worried and pulled money out of Mexico. The peso fell, inflation and interest rates rose, and the Mexican economy fell into a serious recession. In one day the regime of confidence had changed to a regime of uncertainty and confusion, full of questions about what policy actions the Mexican government would take.

Financial Institutions of Developing and Transitional Economies I spent two chapters discussing the complex financial systems of developed countries because you had to understand those financial systems in order to understand macro policy. While some parts of that discussion carry over to developing countries, other parts don't, since financial systems in developing countries are often quite different than those in developed countries.

The primary difference between financial institutions in developing countries and developed countries arises from the dual nature of developing countries' economies.

The primary difference arises from the dual nature of developing countries' economies. In the traditional part of developing economies, the financial sector is embryonic; trades are made by barter, or with direct payment of money; trades requiring more sophisticated financial markets, such as mortgages to finance houses, just don't exist.

In the modern international part of developing economies, that isn't the case. Developing countries' international financial sectors are sometimes as sophisticated as Western financial institutions. A currency trading room in Ecuador or Nigeria looks similar to one in New York, London, or Frankfurt. That modern financial sector is integrated into the international economy (with pay rates that often approach or match those of the West). This dual nature of developing countries' financial sectors imposes constraints on the practice of monetary policy and changes the regulatory and control functions of central banks.

The above is one of many institutional examples of differences that exist and that change the nature of the macro problem. What's important is not so much the specifics of the example but, rather, the general point it brings home. Economies at different stages of development have different institutional, and policy, needs. Institutions with the same names in different countries can have quite different roles. Such institutions can differ in subtle ways, making it important to have specific knowledge of a country's institutions before one can understand its economy and meaningfully talk about policy.

It is important to have specific knowledge of a country's institutions before one can understand its economy and meaningfully talk about policy.

Monetary Policy in Developing Countries

Now that I've discussed some of the ways in which financial institutions differ in developing countries, let's consider some issues of central banking and monetary policy for those economies.

Central Banks Are Less Independent

The first thing to note about central banking in developing countries is that its primary goal is often different than a central bank's primary goal in developed countries. The reason is that, while all central banks have a number of goals, at the top of them all is the goal of keeping the economy running. Western central banks have the luxury of assuming away the problem of keeping the economy running—inertia, institutions, and history hold Western industrial economies together, and keep them running. Central banks in developing countries can't make that assumption.

What this means in practice is that central banks in developing countries generally have far less independence than do central banks in developed countries. With a political and fiscal system that generates large deficits and cannot exist without these deficits, the thought of an independent monetary policy goes out the window.

Central banks in developing countries generally have far less independence than do central banks in developed countries.

A second difference concerns the institutional implementation of monetary policy. In a developing country, a broad-based domestic government bond market often does not exist. So if the government runs a deficit and is financing it domestically, the central bank usually must buy the bonds, which means that it must increase the money supply. As you know, increasing the money supply leads to higher inflation. And developing countries on the whole have experienced high inflation, as Table 32-2 shows. The central banks recognize that increasing the money supply will cause inflation, but often central banks feel as if they have no choice because of the political consequences of issuing too much money.

Q-4 If everyone knows that the cause of inflation in developing countries is the creation of too much money, why don't these countries stop inflation?

As I discussed above, often, in developing countries, the government's sources of tax revenue are limited, and the low level of income in the economy makes the tax base small. A government attempting to collect significantly more taxes might risk being overthrown. Similarly its ability to cut expenditures is limited. If it cuts expenditures, it will almost certainly be overthrown. With new tax sources unavailable and with no ability to cut expenditures, the government uses its only other option to meet its

Central banks recognize that printing too much money causes inflation, but often feel compelled to do so for political reasons.

Table 32-2 Annual Inflation Rates for Selected Areas

	1987–1993	1994–2002
United States	3.8	2.4
European Union	4.4	2.2
Africa	24.3	19.2
Developing Asia	10.3	6.1
Middle East and Turkey	24.3	25.0
Western Hemisphere developing countries	184.3	24.5

Source: World Economic Outlook, 2002; International Monetary Fund.

obligations—it issues debt. And, if the central bank agrees with the conclusion that the government is correct in its assessment that it has no choice, then if the central bank doesn't want the government to be overthrown, it has no choice but to monetize that debt (print money to pay that debt). Sometimes the central bank's choices are even more limited; dictatorships simply tell the central bank to provide the needed money, or be eliminated.

Issuing money to finance budget deficits may be a short-term solution, but it is not a long-term solution. It is an accounting identity that real resources consumed by the economy must equal the real resources produced or imported. If the government deficit doesn't increase output, the real resources the government is getting because the central bank is monetizing its debt must come from somewhere. Where do those real resources come from? From the inflation tax: an implicit tax on the holders of cash and the holders of any obligations specified in nominal terms. Inflation works as a type of tax on these individuals.

Inflation works as a tax on holders of obligations specified in nominal terms.

Faced with the prospect of a collapse of government, the central banks generally choose to keep the governments operating (which isn't surprising, since they are often branches of the government). To do that they increase the money supply enormously, causing hyperinflation in many of these countries. These hyperinflations soon take on a life of their own. The expectation of accelerating inflation creates even more inflationary pressure as individuals try to spend any money they have quickly, before the prices go up. This increases velocity, nominal demand for goods, and inflationary pressures.

Q-5 In an inflation, who else, besides government, gets revenue from an inflation tax?

One problem with the use of an inflation tax is that in an inflation, the government is not the only recipient of revenue; any issuer of fixed-interest-rate debt denominated in domestic currency also gains. And the holder of any fixed-interest-rate debt denominated in domestic currency loses. This income redistribution caused by an inflation can temporarily stimulate real output, but it can also undermine the country's financial institutions.

The point of the above discussion is that the central banks know that issuing large quantities of money will cause inflation. What they don't know, and what the policy discussions are about, is which is worse: the inflation or the unpleasant alternatives. Should the central bank bail out the government? There are legitimate questions about whether countries' budget deficits are absolutely necessary or not. It is those assessments in which the debate about developing countries' inflation exists; the debate is not about whether the inflation is caused by the issuance of too much money.

The fact that inflation is only a temporary solution doesn't stop developing countries' leaders from using it.

Opponents of any type of bailout point out that any "inflation solution" is only a temporary solution that, if used, will require ever-increasing amounts of inflation to remain effective. Proponents of bailouts agree with this argument but argue that inflation buys a bit more time, and the alternative is the breakdown of the government and the economy. Because of the unpleasant alternative, the fact that inflation is only a temporary solution doesn't stop developing and transitional countries' leaders from using it. They don't have time for the luxury of long-run solutions and are often simply looking for policies that will hold their governments together for a month at a time.

Focus on the International Sector and the Exchange Rate Constraint

Another difference between the monetary policies of developed and developing countries concerns the policy options they consider for dealing with foreign exchange markets. Developed countries are generally committed to full exchange rate convertibility. With full exchange rate convertibility, individuals can exchange their currency for any other country's currency without significant government restrictions.

Developing countries often do not have fully convertible currencies. Individuals and firms in these countries face restrictions on their ability to exchange currencies—sometimes general restrictions and sometimes restrictions depending on the purpose for which they wish to use the foreign exchange.

Various Types of Convertibility Since convertibility plays such a central role in developing countries' macro policies, let's review the various types of convertibility. The United States has **full convertibility**—*individuals may change dollars into any currency they want for whatever legal purpose they want*. (There are, however, reporting laws about movements of currency.) Most Western developed countries have full convertibility.

Q-6 Distinguish between convertibility on the current account and full convertibility.

A second type of convertibility is **convertibility on the current account**—*a system that allows people to exchange currencies freely to buy goods and services, but not to buy assets in other countries*. The third type of convertibility is **limited capital account convertibility**—*a system that allows full current account convertibility and partial capital account convertibility*. There are various levels of restrictions on what types of assets one can exchange, so there are many types of limited capital account convertibility.

Almost no developing country has full convertibility.

Almost no developing country allows full convertibility. Why? One reason is that they want to force their residents to keep their savings and to do their investing in their home country, not abroad. Why don't their citizens want to do that? Because when there is a chance of a change in governments—and government seizure of assets as there often is in developing countries—rich individuals generally prefer to have a significant portion of their assets abroad, away from the hands of their government.

These limits on exchange rate convertibility explain a general phenomenon found in most developing countries—the fact that much of the international part of the dual economy in developing countries is "dollarized"—contracts are framed in, and accounting is handled in, dollars, not in the home country's currency. Dollarization exists almost completely in the international sectors of countries that have nonconvertible currencies, and largely in the international sectors of countries where the currency is convertible on the current account but not on the capital account. This dollarization exists because of nonconvertibility, or the fear of nonconvertibility. Thus, ironically, nonconvertibility increases the focus on dollarized contracts in the international sector, and puts that sector beyond effective control by the central bank.

Nonconvertibility does not halt international trade; it merely makes it more difficult.

Nonconvertibility does not halt international trade—it merely complicates it, since it adds another layer of uncertainty and bureaucracy to the trading process. Each firm that is conducting international trade must see that it will have sufficient foreign exchange to carry on its business. Developing governments will often want to encourage this international trade, while preventing outflows of their currencies for other purposes.

When developing countries have partially convertible exchange rates, exchange rate policy—buying and selling foreign currencies in order to help stabilize the exchange rate—often is an important central bank function. This is such an important function because trade in most of these countries' currencies is *thin*—there is not a large number of traders or trades. When trading is thin, large fluctuations in exchange rates are possible in response to a change in a few traders' needs. Even the uncertainties of the weather can affect traders. Say an unexpected oil tanker is kept from landing in port because of bad weather. The financial exchange—paying for that oil—that would have taken place upon landing does not take place, and the supply/demand conditions for a country's currency could change substantially. In response, the value of the country's currency could rise or fall dramatically unless it were stabilized. The central bank often helps provide exchange rate stabilization.

Conditionality and the Balance of Payments Constraint In designing their policies, developing countries often rely on advice from the International Monetary Fund (IMF). One reason is that the IMF has economists who have much experience with these issues. A second reason is that, for these countries, the IMF is a major source of temporary loans that they need to stabilize their currencies.

These loans usually come with conditions that the country meet certain domestic monetary and fiscal stabilization goals. Specifically, these goals are that government deficits be lowered and money supply growth be limited. Because of these requirements, IMF's loan policy is often called **conditionality**—*the making of loans that are subject to specific conditions*. These goals have been criticized by economists such as Joseph Stiglitz, who argues that the contractionary monetary and fiscal policies required by conditionality tend to be procyclical and only worsen the recession. The IMF responds that in a developing country the long-run fiscal and monetary goals must take precedence to establish a basis for development.

The basis for most IMF loans is conditionality.

Even a partially flexible exchange rate regime presents the country with the **balance of payments constraint**—*limitations on expansionary domestic macroeconomic policy due to a shortage of international reserves*. Attempts to expand the domestic economy with expansionary monetary policy continually push the economy to its balance of payments constraint. To meet both its domestic goals and international balance of payments constraints, many developing countries turn to loans from the IMF, not only for the exchange rate stabilization reasons discussed above but also for a more expansionary macro policy than otherwise would be possible. Because of the IMF's control of these loans, macro policy in developing countries is often conducted with one eye toward the IMF, and sometimes with a complete bow.

The balance of payments constraint consists of limitations on expansionary domestic macro policy due to a shortage of international reserves.

The Need for Creativity

The above discussion may have made it seem as if conducting domestic macro policy in developing countries is almost hopelessly dominated by domestic political concerns and international constraints. If by macro policy one means using traditional monetary and fiscal policy tools as they are used in standard ways, that's true. But macro policy, interpreted broadly, is much more than using those tools. It is the development of new institutions that expand the possibilities for growth. It is creating a new production function, not operating within an existing one. Macro policy, writ large to include the development of new institutions, can have enormous effects. To undertake such policies requires an understanding of the role of institutions, the specific nature of the problem in one's country, and creativity.

Obstacles to Economic Development

What stops countries from developing economically? Economists have discovered no magic potion that will make a country develop. We can't say, "Here are steps 1, 2, 3, 4. If you follow them you'll grow, but if you don't follow them you won't grow."

What makes it so hard for developing countries to devise a successful development program is that social, political, and economic problems blend into one another and cannot be considered separately. The institutional structure that we take for granted in the United States often doesn't exist in those countries. For example economists' analysis of production assumes that a stable government exists that can enforce contracts and supply basic services. In most developing countries, that assumption can't be made. Governments are often anything but stable; overnight, a coup d'état can bring a new government into power, with a whole new system of rules under which businesses have to operate. Imagine trying to figure out a reasonable study strategy if every week you had a new teacher who emphasized different things and gave totally different types of tests from last week's teacher. Firms in developing countries face similar problems.

While economists can't say, "Here's what you have to do in order to grow," we have been able to identify some general obstacles that all developing countries seem to face:

1. Political instability.
2. Corruption.
3. Lack of appropriate institutions.
4. Lack of investment.
5. Inappropriate education.
6. Overpopulation.
7. Health and disease.

I consider each in turn.

Seven problems facing developing countries are:

1. Political instability.
2. Corruption.
3. Lack of appropriate institutions.
4. Lack of investment.
5. Inappropriate education.
6. Overpopulation.
7. Health and disease.

Political Instability

A student's parents once asked me why their son was doing poorly in my economics class. My answer was that he could not read and he could hardly write. Until he could master those basics, there was no use talking about how he could better learn economics.

Roughly the same reasoning can be applied to the problem of political instability in developing countries. Unless a country achieves political stability (acceptance within a country of a stable system of government), it's not going to develop economically, no matter what it does.

All successful development strategies require the existence of a stable government. A mercantilist or a socialist development strategy requires an elaborate government presence. A market-based strategy requires a much smaller government role, but even with markets, a stable environment is needed for a market to function and for contracts to be made with confidence.

All successful development strategies require the existence of a stable government.

Many developing countries don't have that stability. Politically they haven't established a tradition of orderly governmental transition. Coups d'état or armed insurrections always remain possible.

One example is Somalia. There, a civil war among competing groups in 1990 led to famine and enormous hardship, which provoked the sympathy of the world. But attempts by the UN and the United States to establish a stable government by sending troops there caused as many, or more, problems than they resolved, and in 1995 the United States withdrew its troops. Today Somalia continues to lack a unified central government.

The problem of political instability exists in most developing countries, but it is strongest in Africa, which in large part accounts for Africa's low rate of economic growth relative to that of the other geographic areas.

Q-7 Why does political instability present an economic problem for developing countries?

Even countries whose governments aren't regularly toppled face threats of overthrow, and those threats are sufficient to prevent individual economic activity. To function, an economy needs some rules—any rules—that will last.

The lack of stability is often exacerbated by social and cultural differences among groups within a country. Political boundaries often reflect arbitrary decisions made by former colonial rulers, not the traditional cultural and tribal boundaries that form the real-life divisions. The result is lack of consensus among the population as a whole as well as intertribal suspicion and even warfare.

For example, Nigeria is a federation established under British colonial rule. It comprises three ethnic regions: the northern, Hausa Fulan, region; the western, Yoruba, region; and the eastern, Ibo, region. These three regions are culturally distinct and so are in continual political and military conflict. Nigeria has experienced an endless cycle of military coups, attempts at civilian rule, and threats of secession by the numerically smaller eastern region. Had each region been allowed to remain separate, economic development might have been possible; but because the British lumped the regions together and called them a country, economic development is next to impossible.

The Influence of Political Instability on Development Do these political considerations affect economic questions? You bet. As I will discuss shortly, any development plan requires financial investment from somewhere—either external or internal. Political instability closes off both sources of investment funds.

Any serious potential investor takes political instability into account. Foreign companies considering investment in a developing country hire political specialists who analyze the degree of risk involved. Where the risk is too great, foreign companies simply don't invest.

Q-8 Income inequality leads to higher levels of savings by the rich and therefore has significant advantages for developing countries. True or false? Explain your answer.

Political instability also limits internal investment. Income distribution in many developing countries is highly skewed. There are a few very rich people and an enormous number of very poor people, while the middle class is often small.

Whatever one's view of the fairness of such income inequality, it has a potential advantage for society. Members of the wealthy elite in developing countries have income to spare, and their savings are a potential source of investment funds. But when there is political instability, that potential isn't realized. Fearing that their wealth may be taken from them, the rich often channel their investment out of their own country so that, should they need to flee a revolution, they'll still be able to live comfortably. Well-off people in developing countries provide major inflows of investment into the United States and other Western countries.

Political Instability and Unequal Distribution of Income The highly skewed distribution of income in most developing countries contributes in another way to political instability. It means that the poor majority has little vested interest in maintaining the current system. A coup? Why not? What have they got to lose? The economic prospects for many people in developing countries are so bleak that they are quite willing to join or at least support a guerrilla insurgency that promises to set up a new, better system. The resulting instability makes development almost impossible.

Corruption

When rights to conduct business are controlled and allocated by the government, economic development can be hindered.

Bribery, graft, and corruption are ways of life in most developing countries. In Egypt it's called *baksheesh* (meaning "gift of money"); in Mexico it's called *la mordida* ("the bite"). If you want to park in a parking spot in Mexico City, you'd better pay the policeman, or your car will get a ticket. If you want to take a photograph of the monument to Rameses II in front of the Cairo railroad station, you'd better slip the traffic officer a few bucks, or else you may get run over.

Without a well-developed institutional setting and a public morality that condemns corruption, economic forces function in a variety of areas that people in developed countries would consider inappropriate. In any country the government has the right to allow imports, to allow development, to determine where you can park your car, to say whether you can take photographs of public buildings, to decide who wins a lawsuit, and so forth. In developing countries, however, those rights can be, and often are, sold. The litigant who pays the judge the most wins. How about the right to import? Want to import a new machine? That will be 20 percent of the cost, please.

Such graft and corruption quickly become institutionalized to the degree that all parties involved feel they have little choice but to take part. Government officials say that graft and bribery are built into their pay structure, so unless they take bribes, they won't have enough income to live on. Businesspeople say that if they want to stay in business they have to pay bribes. Similarly, workers must bribe business in order to get a job, and labor leaders must be bribed not to cause trouble for business.

I'm not claiming that such payments are wrong. Societies decide what is right and wrong; economists don't. The term *bribery* in English has a pejorative connotation. In many other languages the terms people use for this type of activity don't have such negative connotations.

Societies decide what is right and wrong; economists don't.

Q-9 In what way do bribes limit development?

But I am claiming that such payments—with the implied threat that failure to pay will have adverse consequences—make it more difficult for a society's economy to grow. Knowing that those payments must be made prevents many people from undertaking actions that might lead to growth. For example, a friend of mine wanted to build a group of apartments in the Bahamas, but when he discovered the payoffs he'd have to make to various people, he abandoned the whole idea.

Limiting an activity makes the right to undertake that limited activity valuable to the person doing the limiting. When bribery is an acceptable practice, it creates strong incentives to limit an ever-increasing number of activities—including many activities that could make a country grow.

Lack of Appropriate Institutions

Almost all economists agree that, to develop, a country should establish markets. Markets require the establishment of property rights. In a recent book, *The Mysteries of Capital*, Hernando DeSoto argued that developing countries' main problem is that their assets, such as houses, do not have the legal standing to be used as collateral or to be bought and sold easily, so markets cannot work. Unfortunately, establishing property rights is a difficult political process. That is the problem of a number of African countries: how to establish property rights with an undeveloped political process.

Markets do not just exist; they are created, and their existence is meshed with the cultural and social fabric of the society.

Creating markets is not enough. The markets must be meshed with the cultural and social fabric of the society. Thus, questions of economic development inevitably involve much more than supply and demand. They involve broader questions about the cultural and social institutions in a society.

Let me give an example of cultural characteristics not conducive to development. Anyone who has traveled in developing countries knows that many of these countries operate on what they call "_______ time," where the "_______" is the name of the particular country one is in. What is meant by "_______ time" is that in that country, things get done when they get done, and it is socially inappropriate to push for things to get done at specific times. Deadlines are demeaning (many students operate on "_______ time").

As a self-actualizing mentality, "_______ time" may be high-level mental development, but in an interdependent economic setting, "_______ time" doesn't fit. Economic development requires qualities such as extreme punctuality and a strong sense of individual responsibility. People who believe their being two minutes late will make the world come to an end fit far better with a high-production country than do people who are more laid back. The need to take such cultural issues into account explains why development economics tends to be far less theoretical and far more country- and region-specific than other branches of economics.

As a self-actualizing mentality, "_______ time" may be a high-level mental development, but in an interdependent economic setting, "_______ time" doesn't fit.

Lack of Investment

Even if a country can overcome the political, social, and institutional constraints on development, there are also economic constraints. If a country is to grow it must somehow invest, and funds for investment must come from savings. These savings can be either brought in from abroad (as private investment or foreign government aid) or generated internally (as domestic savings). Each source of investment capital has its problems.

With per capita incomes of as low as $300 per year, poor people in developing countries don't have a lot left over to put into savings.

Investment Funded by Domestic Savings In order to save, a person must first have enough to live on. With per capita incomes of $300 per year, poor people in developing countries don't have a whole lot left over to put into savings. Instead you rely on your kids, if they live, to take care of you in your old age. As for the rich, the threat of political instability often makes them put their money into savings abroad, as I discussed before. For the developing country, it's as if the rich didn't save. In fact, it's even worse because when they save abroad, the rich don't even spend the money at home as do poor people, so the rich generate less in the way of short-run income multiplier effects in their home country than do the poor.

Web Note 32.2
Development Economists

That leaves the middle class (small as it is) as the one hope these countries have for domestic savings. For them, the problem is: Where can they put their savings? Often these countries have an underdeveloped financial sector; there's no neighborhood bank, no venture capital fund, no government-secured savings vehicle. The only savings vehicle available may be the government savings bond. But savings bonds finance the government deficit, which supports the government bureaucracy, which is limiting activities that could lead to growth. Few middle-class people invest in those government bonds. After all, what will a government bond be worth after the next revolution? Nothing!

Some governments have taxed individuals (a type of forced savings) and channeled that money back into investment. But again, politics and corruption are likely to interfere. Instead of going into legitimate productive investment, the savings—in the form of "consulting fees," outright payoffs, or "sweetheart contracts"—go to friends of those in power. Before you get up on your high horse and say, "How do the people allow that to happen?" think of the United States, where it's much easier to prevent such activities but where scandals in government spending are still uncovered with depressing regularity.

Investment Funded from Abroad The other way to generate funds for investment is from external savings, either foreign aid or foreign investment.

Foreign Aid The easiest way to finance development is with **foreign aid** *(funds that developed countries lend or give to developing countries)*. The problem is that foreign aid generally comes with strings attached; funds are earmarked for specific purposes. For example, most foreign aid is military aid; helping a country prepare to fight a war isn't a good way to help it develop.

Total foreign aid from all countries comes to about $11 per person in developing countries.

As you can see in Table 32-3, the United States gives about $11 billion (about $38 per U.S. citizen) per year in foreign aid. For the 4.6 billion people in developing countries, total foreign aid from all countries comes to about $11 per person. That isn't going to finance a lot of economic development, especially when much of the money is earmarked for military purposes.

Foreign Investment If a global or multinational company believes that a country has a motivated, cheap workforce, a stable government supportive of business, and sufficient

Table 32-3 Foreign Aid Given by Major Countries, 2001

Country	Development Aid 2001 (millions of U.S. dollars)	Percent of GDP
United States	$10,884	.11%
France	4,293	.34
United Kingdom	4,659	.32
Japan	9,678	.23
Germany	4,879	.27
Italy	1,493	.14
Austria	457	.25
Sweden	1,576	.76
Canada	1,572	.23

Source: *OECD DAC Chairman's Report* (www.oecd.org).

infrastructure investment—*investment in the underlying structure of the economy*, such as transportation or power facilities—it has a strong incentive to invest in the country. That's a lot of ifs, and generally the poorest countries don't measure up. What they have to offer instead are raw materials that the global corporation can develop.

Countries at the upper end of the group of developing countries (such as Mexico and Brazil) may meet all these requirements, but large amounts of foreign investment often result in political problems as citizens of these countries complain about imperialist exploitation, outside control, and significant outflows of profits. Developing countries have tried to meet such complaints by insisting that foreign investment come in the form of joint development projects under local control, but that cuts down the amount that foreign firms are willing to invest.

When the infrastructure doesn't exist, as is the case in the poorest developing countries, few firms will invest in that country, no matter how cheap the labor or how stable the government. Firms require infrastructure investment such as transportation facilities, energy availability, and housing and amenities for their employees before they will consider investing in a country. And they don't want to pay to establish this infrastructure themselves.

Competition for Investment among Developing Countries The world is made up of about 20 highly industrial countries and about 170 other countries at various stages of development. Global companies have a choice of where to locate, and often developing countries compete to get the development located in their country. In their efforts to get the development, they may offer tax rebates, free land, guarantees of labor peace, or loose regulatory environments within which firms can operate.

This competition can be keen, and can result in many of the benefits of development being transferred from the developing country to the global company and ultimately to the Western consumer, since competition from other firms will force the global company to pass on the benefits in the form of lower prices.

Competition for global company investment often leads to the benefits of that investment being passed on to the Western consumer.

An example of the results of such competition can be seen in the production of chemicals. Say a company is planning to build a new plant to produce chemicals. Where does it locate? Considering the wide-ranging environmental restrictions in the United States and Western Europe, a chemical company will likely look toward a developing country that will give it loose regulation. If one country will not come through, the chemical firm will point out that it can locate elsewhere. Concern about

The Odd Couple

Applying the Tools

In 2002 U.S. Treasury secretary Paul O'Neill and U-2 Irish rock star Bono traveled to Africa together to highlight the importance of development and foreign aid. They were an odd couple, but the combination kept the press interested (MTV followed it thoroughly) and generated a lot of publicity about the need for foreign aid. Seeing the plight of millions of Africans firsthand also brought tears to the eyes of the old-line Republican and the then Treasury secretary. (The press reported the tears as genuine.)

Bono went on the trip because he has made helping Africa a personal goal. As the founder of Debt, AIDS and Trade for Africa (DATA), he was instrumental in getting President George W. Bush's administration to take an increased interest in development and to increase the amount it proposed to spend on foreign aid. When Bono visited the White House, President Bush released a plan for "a new compact for global development." Under this plan, called the Millennium Challenge Account Proposal, the United States pledged to increase foreign aid by $10 billion in return for accountability, economic reforms, and a commitment to human rights for "projects in nations that govern justly, invest in their people and encourage economic freedom."

The Bono–O'Neill Africa trip was designed to highlight projects that would meet these criteria. The problem is that almost all previous foreign aid has had precisely those same lofty goals but the actual results have often been quite different—aid efforts have led to corruption, failed projects, and white elephants. Critics wonder whether this new project will be any different, and they point out that at the same time the United States was offering increased foreign aid, it was maintaining quotas, tariffs, and subsidies for U.S. farm production that limited African countries' ability to sell their goods in the United States.

Paul O'Neill and Bono on their trip to Africa in 2002.
Saurabh Das/AP Wide World Photos.

Still, the focus on development and the need for foreign aid that Bono's interest highlights is generally welcomed by advocates of developing countries, although many point out that even with the addition of the Millennium Fund, U.S. foreign aid would still be less than the percentage of GDP given by other developed countries.

Mexico's relatively loose environmental regulatory environment was one of the sticking points of U.S. approval of NAFTA.

Focal Points and Takeoff The scope of competition among developing countries can be overstated. Most companies do not consider all developing countries as potential production and investment sites. To decide to produce in a developing country requires a knowledge of that country—its legal structure, its political structure, and its infrastructure. Gaining this information involves a substantial initial investment, so most companies tend to focus on a few developing countries about which they have specific knowledge, or which they know other companies have chosen as development sites. (If company X chose it, it must meet the appropriate criteria.)

Because of this informational requirement, developing countries that have been successful in attracting investment often get further investment. Eventually they reach a stage called **economic takeoff**—*a stage when the development process becomes self-sustaining.* Other developing countries fall by the wayside. This means that economic development is not evenly spread over developing countries, but rather is concentrated in a few.

Inappropriate Education

The right education is a necessary component of any successful development strategy. The wrong education is an enormous burden. Developing countries tend to have too much of the wrong education and too little of the right education.

The right education is a necessary component of any successful development strategy. The wrong education is an enormous burden.

Often educational systems in developing countries resemble Western educational systems. The reason is partly the colonial heritage of developing countries and partly what might be described as an emulation factor. The West defines what an educated person is, and developing countries want their citizens to be seen as educated. An educated person should be able to discuss the ideas of Vladimir Nabokov, the poetry of Lord Byron, the intricacies of chaos theory, the latest developments in fusion technology, the nuances of the modern Keynesian/Classical debate, and the dissociative properties of Andy Warhol's paintings. So saith Western scholars; so be it.

But, put bluntly, that type of education is almost irrelevant to economic growth and may be a serious detriment to growth. Basic skills—reading, writing, and arithmetic, taught widely—are likely to be more conducive to growth than is high-level education. When education doesn't match the needs of the society, the degrees—the credentials—become more important than the knowledge learned. The best jobs go to those with the highest degrees, not because the individuals holding the degrees are better able to do the job, but simply because they hold the credentials. **Credentialism,** in which *the degrees, or credentials, become more important than the knowledge learned,* serves to preserve the monopoly position of these who manage to get the degree.

If access to education is competitive, credentialism has its advantages. Even irrelevant education, as long as it is difficult, serves a "screening" or "selection" role. Those individuals who work hardest at getting an education advance and get the good jobs. Since selecting hardworking individuals is difficult, even irrelevant education serves this selection role.

But developing countries' current educational practices may be worse than irrelevant. Their educational systems often reflect Western culture, not their own cultures. The best students qualify for scholarships abroad, and their education in a different tradition makes it difficult for them to return home.

In my studies in Europe and the United States, I've come to know a large number of the best and the brightest students from developing countries. They're superb students and they do well in school. But as they near graduation, most of them face an enormously difficult choice. They can return to their home country—to material shortages, to enormous challenges for which they have little training, and to an illiterate society whose traditional values are sometimes hostile to the values these new graduates have learned. Or they can stay in the West, find jobs relevant to their training, enjoy an abundance of material goods, and associate with people to whom they've now learned to relate. Which would you choose?

The choice many of them make results in a **brain drain** *(the outflow of the best and brightest students from developing countries to developed countries)*. Many of these good students don't return to the developing country. Those that do go home take jobs as government officials, expecting high salaries and material comforts far beyond what their society can afford. Instead of becoming the dynamic entrepreneurs of growth, they become impediments to growth.

Many good students from developing countries who study abroad don't return to the developing country.

Q-10 How could too much education cause problems for development?

There are, of course, many counterexamples to the arguments presented here. Many developing countries try to design their education system to fit their culture. And many of the dynamic, selfless leaders who make it possible for the country to develop do return home. As with most issues, there are both positive and negative attributes to the way something is done. I emphasize the problems with educational systems in developing economies because the positive attributes of education are generally accepted. Without education, development is impossible. The question is simply how that education should be structured.

Overpopulation

Two ways a country can increase per capita income are:

1. Decrease the number of people in the country (without decreasing the total income in the country).
2. Increase the income (without increasing the population).

In each case the qualifier is important, for income and population are related in complicated ways: People earn income; without people there would be no income. But often the more people there are, the less income per person there is, because the resources of the country become strained.

A country's population can never be higher than the natural resources that it has, or can import, can support. But that doesn't mean that overpopulation can't be an obstacle to development. Nature has its own ways of reducing populations that are too large: Starvation and disease are the direct opposite to development. That control system works in nature, and it would work with human societies. The problem is that we don't like it.

Thomas Carlyle gave economics the name *the dismal science* as he was verbally sparring with economists of the period about a number of issues. The name stuck with economics in large part because of the writings of Thomas Malthus, who in the early 1800s said that society's prospects are dismal because population tends to outrun the means of subsistence. (Population grows geometrically—that is, at an increasing rate; the means of subsistence grow arithmetically—that is, at a constant rate.) The view was cemented into economic thinking in the law of diminishing marginal productivity: As more and more people are added to a fixed amount of land, the output per worker gets smaller and smaller.

Many developing economies have not avoided the Malthusian fate because diminishing marginal productivity has exceeded technological change.

Through technological progress, most Western economies have avoided the fate predicted by Malthus because growth in output has exceeded growth in population. In contrast, many developing economies have not avoided the Malthusian fate because diminishing marginal productivity has exceeded technological change, and limited economic growth isn't enough to offset the increase in population. The result is a constant or falling output per person.

That doesn't mean that developing countries haven't grown economically. They have. But population growth makes per capita output growth small or negative.

Population grows for a number of reasons, including:

1. As public health measures are improved, infant mortality rates and death rates for the population as a whole both decline.
2. As people earn more income, they believe they can afford to have more kids.
3. In rural areas, children are useful in working the fields.

What to do? Should the government reduce the population growth rate? If it should, how can it do so? Various measures have been tried: advertising campaigns, free condoms, forced sterilization, and economic incentives. For example, in China the government has tried imposing severe economic penalties on couples who have more than one child, while providing material incentives such as a free television set to couples who agreed not to have more than one child.

Even successful population control programs have their problems.

China's vigorous population control campaign has had a number of effects. First, it created so much anger at the government that in rural areas the campaign was dropped.

Second, it led to the killing of many female babies because, if couples were to have only one baby, strong cultural and economic pressures existed to ensure that the baby was a male. Third, it led to an enormous loss of privacy. Dates of women's menstrual periods were posted in factories and officials would remind them at appropriate times that they should take precautions against getting pregnant. Only a very strong government could impose such a plan.

Even successful population control programs have their problems. In Singapore a population control campaign was so successful among educated women that the government became concerned that its "population quality" was suffering. It began a selective campaign to encourage college-educated women to have children. They issued "love tips" to men (since some college-educated women complained that their male companions were nerds and had no idea how to be romantic) and offered special monetary bonuses to college-educated women who gave birth to children. As you might imagine, the campaign provoked a backlash, and it was eventually dropped by the government.

Individuals differ substantially in their assessment of the morality of these programs, but even if one believes that population control is an appropriate government concern, it does not seem that such programs will be successful, by themselves, in limiting population growth.

Health and Disease

Web Note 32.3
Fighting Disease

Before a country can hope to develop, it must have a reasonably healthy population. If you are sick, it's hard to think, to work, or even to do standard daily tasks like growing food. In many developing countries, large portions of the population are undernourished or sick. Disease hits young children particularly hard. Millions of children die from pneumonia, diarrhea, malaria, and measles, all of which, because of the children's general malnutrition, are often aggravated by intestinal worms. Older individuals suffer from HIV/AIDS, tuberculosis, and malaria. For example, more than 26 million people now have AIDS in Africa, and about one-third of today's 15-year-olds in Africa will likely die of AIDS.

These diseases make it difficult for people to work, or even to take care of their kids, and create a vicious cycle. You're sick, you can't work, and so you and your family become malnutritioned. You get even more prone to disease, and less able to work and contribute to development. Thus, maintaining public health is more than a humanitarian issue; it is a key development issue.

What to do? Most of these diseases can be alleviated with drugs, but developing the infrastructure to provide these drugs is often difficult or impossible, even when the money for the drugs becomes available. Thus, one must not only get the drugs but also create the cultural and physical environment in which those drugs can be effective. Drug companies have little incentive to work on developing low-cost medicines to treat diseases in developing countries because the people there don't have much money to pay for them, so the return would be low. Instead, pharmaceutical companies focus their research on providing high-priced drugs to be sold in rich countries. Drug companies created anti-AIDS drugs, but their focus was on markets in wealthy developed countries. Only later, and under significant social and political pressure, did they start offering treatment for AIDS at low cost to developing countries.

Mission Impossible

Economic development is a complicated problem because it is entwined with cultural and social issues.

At this point in my course, I inevitably throw my hands up and admit that I don't know what makes it possible for a country to develop. Nor, judging from what I have read, do the development experts. The good ones (that is, the ones I agree with) admit that they don't know; others (that is, the ones I don't agree with) simply don't know that they don't know.

My gut feeling is that there are no definitive general answers that apply to all developing countries. The appropriate answer varies with each country and each situation. Each proposed solution to the development problem has a right time and a right place. Only by having a complete sense of a country, its history, and its cultural, social, and political norms can one decide whether it's the right time and place for this or that policy.

Summary

- While policies in developed countries focus on stability, developing countries struggle to provide basic needs.
- Development refers to an increase in productive capacity and output brought about by a change in underlying institutions while growth refers to an increase in output brought about by an increase in inputs.
- Many developing economies have serious political problems that make it impossible for government to take an active, positive role in the economy.
- Many developing countries have dual economies—one a traditional, nonmarket economy, and the other an internationalized market economy.
- Many developing countries need a change in the entire atmosphere within which the government and economy relate. They need regime changes rather than policy changes.
- Although developing countries know that printing too much money leads to inflation, their choices are limited. Some central banks lack independence and for others the only alternative is the collapse of government.
- Most monetary policies in developing countries focus on the international sector and are continually dealing with the balance of payments constraint.
- Most developing countries have some type of limited convertibility to limit the outflow of saving.
- Macro policies in developing countries are more concerned with institutional policies and regime changes than are macro policies in developed countries.
- Seven obstacles to economic development are political instability, corruption, lack of appropriate institutions, lack of investment, inappropriate education, overpopulation, and poor health and disease.

Key Terms

balance of payments constraint *(758)*
basic needs *(752)*
brain drain *(765)*
conditionality *(758)*
convertibility on the current account *(757)*
credentialism *(765)*
dual economy *(753)*
economic takeoff *(764)*
foreign aid *(762)*
full convertibility *(757)*
infrastructure investment *(763)*
limited capital account convertibility *(757)*
policy change *(754)*
purchasing power parity *(750)*
regime change *(754)*
restructuring *(751)*

Questions for Thought and Review

1. If you suddenly found yourself living as a poor person in a developing country, what are some things that you now do that you would no longer be able to do? What new things would you have to do?

2. What is wrong with saying that people in developing countries are worse off than people in the United States?
3. Does the fact that suicide rates are lower in developing countries than in the United States imply that Americans would be better off living in a developing country? Why?
4. How does the exchange rate method of comparing incomes differ from the purchasing power method of comparing incomes?
5. What is the difference between development and growth?
6. What are three ways in which the institutions of developing countries differ from those in developed countries?
7. Why do governments in developing countries often seem more arbitrary and oppressive than governments in developed countries?
8. Why might an economist favor activist policies in developed countries and laissez-faire policies in developing countries?
9. What is meant by "the dual economy"?
10. How does a regime change differ from a policy change?
11. What is the inflation tax?
12. Why doesn't the fact that the "inflation solution" is only a temporary solution stop many developing countries from using it?
13. What is conditionality, and how does it relate to the balance of payments constraint?
14. Why are investment and savings so low in developing countries?
15. If developing countries are so unstable and offer such a risky environment for investment, why do foreigners invest any money in them at all?
16. If you were a foreign investor thinking of making an investment in a developing country, what are some things that you would be concerned about?
17. Should developing countries send their students abroad for an education?
18. How does corruption limit investment and economic growth?
19. Should a country control the size and makeup of its population? Why?
20. A 1995 United Nations study reported that more than 300 million low-income women owned businesses in developing countries, but only 5 million had access to credit other than from money lenders. How might the UN alleviate this obstacle to growth? What other obstacles might exist for women entrepreneurs in developing nations?

Problems and Exercises

1. Interview a foreign student in your class or school. Ask about each of the seven obstacles to economic development and how his or her country is trying to overcome them.
2. Spend one day living like someone in a developing country. Eat almost nothing and work lifting stones for 10 hours. Then, that same evening, study this chapter and contemplate the bootstrap strategy of development.
3. In 1991 Germany passed a law requiring businesses to take back and recycle all forms of packaging. A large group of businesses formed a company to collect and recycle these packages. Its costs are 4.5 cents per pound for glass, 9.5 cents per pound for paper, and 74 cents per pound for plastic. This accounts for a recycling cost of about $100 per ton for glass and $2,000 per ton for plastic, and the average recycling cost is $500 per ton. A developing country has offered to create a giant landfill and accept Germany's waste at a host of $400 per ton, which includes $50 per ton sorting and transport costs and a $350-per-ton fee to be paid to the developing country.
   a. Should Germany accept this proposal?
   b. Will the proposal benefit the developing country?
   c. What alternative or modification to the proposal might you suggest?
4. Say that you have been hired to design an education system for a developing country.
   a. What skills would you want it to emphasize?
   b. How might it differ from an ideal educational system here in the United States?
   c. How much of the U.S. educational system involves credentialism, and how much involves the learning of relevant skills?
5. Choose any developing country and answer the following questions about it:
   a. What is its level of per capita income?
   b. What is its growth potential?
   c. What is the exchange rate of its currency in relation to the U.S. dollar?
   d. What policy suggestions might you make to the country?
6. It has been argued that development economics has no general theory; it is instead the application of common sense to real-world problems.
   a. Do you agree or disagree with that statement? Why?
   b. Why do you think this argument about the lack of generality of theories is made for developing countries more than it is made for developed countries?

Web Questions

1. Go to the World Bank's student challenge, Build It!, at www.worldbank.org/challenge to answer the following questions.
   a. What three social challenges face developing countries?
   b. What three economic challenges face developing countries?
   c. What three environmental challenges face developing countries?
   d. What additional challenges to promote sustainable development could have been listed?
2. The Bretton Woods Project is an IMF and World Bank watchdog. Go to its home page at www.brettonwoodsproject.org to answer the following questions:
   a. Select "Background & glossary" to read about criticisms of the IMF World Bank. Provide a brief summary of those criticisms.
   b. Select "Advocacy & action." List two recent criticisms of the IMF or World Bank.

Answers to Margin Questions

1. Given market societies' expansionary tendencies, the cultures in economically poor countries that do not grow would simply be overrun and destroyed by cultures of market societies. This means that the choice is not between development and preservation of existing culture; rather, the choice is between economic development with its attendant wrenching cultural transitions, and continued poverty with exploitation by developed countries and its attendant wrenching cultural transitions. *(750)*
2. Restructuring in developed countries suggests that the distinction between growth and development can be overdone since it is an example of developed countries' growth occurring through changing institutions—development—rather than through increasing inputs—growth. *(751)*
3. *Dual economy* refers to a developing country's tendency to have two economies that have little interaction—one a traditional nonmarket economy, and one an internationally oriented modern market economy. *(753)*
4. While everyone agrees that inflation in developing countries is caused by the central bank issuing too much money, the real policy question concerns what the political consequences of not issuing too much money may be. Sometimes the cure for inflation can be worse than the problem. *(755)*
5. In an inflation, any issuers of fixed-interest-rate debt denominated in the domestic currency gain from the holders of these debts. *(756)*
6. Full convertibility includes convertibility on the capital account as well as on the current account. It means that people are allowed to buy foreign financial assets—to save abroad. Convertibility on the current account means that people are allowed to buy foreign currencies in order to buy foreign goods, but not necessarily in order to buy foreign financial assets. *(757)*
7. In order for a market to operate, a set of rules—any rules—is needed. Lack of stability undermines the existence of any rules and leads to a failure of cooperation among people. *(759)*
8. It depends, but the answer is probably false. Often the wealthy elite in a developing country fear that if they invest in their country their money will be taken away, so they often invest out of their country—meaning that the benefits of their savings go to other countries, not to the investor's own developing country. *(760)*
9. The more it costs to undertake economic activities, the fewer economic activities individuals undertake. *(761)*
10. Education is absolutely necessary for development, but it is most helpful if it is the right type of education—focusing on basic skills such as reading, writing, and arithmetic. When education focuses on abstract issues, determined by different cultures and having little relevance to the country's problems, "too much" education can lead to a brain drain and a diversion of people's talent away from the central development issues. *(765)*

INTERNATIONAL FINANCIAL POLICY

33

A foreign exchange dealer's office during a busy spell is the nearest thing to Bedlam I have struck.

—*Harold Wincott*

After reading this chapter, you should be able to:

- Describe the balance of payments and the trade balance, and relate them to the supply and demand for currencies.
- List four important fundamental determinants of exchange rates.
- Explain how a country fixes an exchange rate.
- Define purchasing power parity and explain its relevance to the debate about whether to have a fixed or flexible exchange rate.
- Differentiate fixed, flexible, and partially flexible exchange rates, and discuss the advantages and disadvantages of each.
- Discuss the advantages and disadvantages of a common currency.
- Explain why Argentina dissolved its currency board and eliminated its fixed exchange rate in 2001.

International currency markets were much in the news in the early 2000s. Argentina went through five presidents in two weeks as it struggled to adjust from a fixed to a flexible exchange rate. At about the same time, 12 European countries gave up their currencies and adopted a common currency, the euro, which they hoped would help expand their economies and challenge the dollar as the international reserve currency.

To understand these issues, you must understand the determination of exchange rates and the balance of payments, so the chapter starts with an in-depth consideration of the balance of payments, showing how it relates to the trade balance and exchange rates. That discussion is then tied to a consideration of the supply of and demand for currencies. Next I discuss exchange rate policy in some depth and present the arguments for and against various exchange rate regimes. I conclude the chapter with a case study—a close look at the Argentinean currency crisis in the early 2000s.

THE BALANCE OF PAYMENTS

The best door into an in-depth discussion of exchange rates and international financial considerations is a discussion of **balance of payments** *(a country's record of all transactions between its residents and the residents of all foreign nations)*.[1] These include a country's buying and selling of goods and services (imports and exports) and interest and profit payments from previous investments, together with all the capital inflows and outflows. Table 33-1 presents the 1987 and 2001 balance of payments accounts for the United States. These accounts record all payments made by foreigners to U.S. citizens and all payments made by U.S. citizens to foreigners in those years.

Goods the United States exports must be paid for in dollars; they involve a flow of payments into the United States, so in the balance of payments accounts

[1]Balance of payments records are not very good. Because of measurement difficulties, many transactions go unrecorded and many numbers must be estimated, leaving a potential for large errors.

Table 33-1 The Balance of Payments Account, 1987 and 2001

	1987 (billions of dollars)		2001 (billions of dollars)	
1. **Current account**				
2. Merchandise				
3. Exports	+250		+ 719	
4. Imports	−410		−1,146	
5. Balance of trade		−160		−427
6. Services				
7. Exports	+ 99		+ 279	
8. Imports	− 99		− 210	
9. Balance on services		+ 8		+ 69
10. Balance on goods and services		−152		−358
11. Net investment income	+ 14		+ 14	
12. Net transfers	− 23		− 49	
13. Invest. trans. balance		− 9		− 35
14. **Balance on current account**		**−161**		**−393**
15. **Capital account**				
16. Capital inflows	+249		+753	
17. Capital outflows	− 87		−370	
18. **Balance on capital account**		**+162**		**+383**
19. Statistical discrepancy		− 9		+ 11
20. **Current and capital account balance**		**− 8**		**+ 1**
21. **Official transactions account**		**+ 8**		**− 1**
22. **Totals**		**0**		**0**

Source: *Survey of Current Business*, 2002 (www.bea.doc.gov).

The balance of payments is a country's record of all transactions between its residents and the residents of all foreign countries.

they have a plus sign. Similarly, U.S. imports must be paid for in foreign currency; they involve a flow of dollars out of the United States, and thus they have a minus sign. Notice that the bottom line of the balance of payments is $0. By definition, the bottom line (which includes all supplies and demands for currencies, including those of the government) must add up to zero.

As you can see in Table 33-1, the balance of payments account is broken down into the current account, the capital account, and the official transactions account. The **current account** (lines 1–14) is *the part of the balance of payments account in which all short-term flows of payments are listed*. It includes exports and imports, which are what we normally mean when we talk about the trade balance. The **capital account** (lines 15–18) is *the part of the balance of payments account in which all long-term flows of payments are listed*. If a U.S. citizen buys a German stock, or if a Japanese company buys a U.S. company, the transaction shows up on the capital account.

The current account is the part of the balance of payments account that lists all short-term flows of payments.

The capital account is the part of the balance of payments account that lists all long-term flows of payments.

The government can influence the exchange rate (the rate at which one currency trades for another) by buying and selling **official reserves**—*government holdings of foreign currencies*—or by buying and selling other international reserves, such as gold. Such buying and selling is recorded in the **official transactions account** (line 21)—*the part of the balance of payments account that records the amount of its own currency or foreign currencies that a nation buys or sells*.

To get a better idea of what's included in the three accounts, let's consider each of them more carefully.

The Current Account

At the top of Table 33-1, the current account is composed of the merchandise (or goods) account (lines 2–5), the services account (lines 6–9), the net investment income account (line 11), and the net transfers account (line 12).

Starting with the merchandise account, notice that in 1987 the United States imported $410 billion worth of goods and exported $250 billion worth of goods. *The difference between the value of goods exported and the value of goods imported* is called the **balance of merchandise trade.** Looking at line 5, you can see that the United States had a balance of merchandise trade deficit of $160 billion in 1987 and $427 billion in 2001.

The merchandise trade balance is often discussed in the press as a summary of how the United States is doing in the international markets. It's not a good summary. Trade in services is just as important as trade in merchandise, so economists pay more attention to the combined balance of goods and services.

Thus, the **balance of trade**—*the difference between the value of goods and services exported and imported*—(line 10) becomes a key statistic for economists. Notice that in both 1987 and 2001 most of the U.S. trade deficit resulted from an imbalance in the merchandise account. The service account worked in the opposite direction. It was slightly positive in 1987; in 2001 the services account reduced the trade deficit by $69 billion. Such services include tourist expenditures and insurance payments by foreigners to U.S. firms. For instance, when you travel in Japan, you spend yen, which you must buy with dollars; this is an outflow of payments, which is a negative contribution to the services account.

The balance on goods and services is the difference between the value of goods and services exported and imported.

Q-1 If you, a U.S. citizen, are traveling abroad, where will your expenditures show up in the balance of payments accounts?

There is no reason that the goods and services sent into a country must equal the goods and services sent out in a particular year, even if the current account is in equilibrium, because the current account also includes payments from past investments and net transfers. When you invest, you expect to make a return on that investment. The payments to foreign owners of U.S. capital assets are a negative contribution to the U.S. balance of payments. The payment to U.S. owners of foreign capital assets is a positive contribution to the U.S. balance of payments. These payments on investment income are a type of holdover from past trade and services imbalances. So even though they relate to investments, they show up on the current account.

The final component on the current account is net transfers, which include foreign aid, gifts, and other payments to individuals not exchanged for goods or services. If you send $1,000 bond to your aunt in Mexico, it shows up with a minus sign here.

Adding up the pluses and minuses on the current account, we arrive at line 14, the current account balance. Notice that in 1987 the United States ran a $161 billion deficit on the current account, and in 2001 the United States had a deficit of $393 billion (line 14). That means that, in the current account, the supply of dollars greatly exceeded the demand for dollars. If the current account represented the total supply of and demand for dollars, the value of the dollar would have fallen. But it doesn't represent the total. There are also the capital account, statistical discrepancies, and the official transactions account.

The Capital Account

The capital account measures the flow of payments between countries for assets such as stocks, bonds, and real estate. As you can see in Table 33-1, in both years there was a significant inflow of capital into the United States in excess of outflows of capital from the United States. In 1987, capital inflows (payments by foreigners for U.S. real and financial assets) were $162 billion more than capital outflows (payments by U.S. citizens for foreign assets). In 2001, there was an inflow of $753 billion (line 16), but there was also an outflow of $370 billion, so the net balance on the capital account was $383 billion as compared to $162 billion in 1987.

To buy these U.S. assets foreigners needed dollars, so these net capital inflows represent a demand for dollars. In 1987 the demand for dollars to buy real and financial assets more than offset the excess supply of dollars on the current account. In 2001 it went a long way toward balancing it. Because of the importance of capital flows, when you think about what's likely to happen to a currency's value, it's important to remember both the demand for dollars to buy goods and services and the demand for dollars to buy assets.

In thinking about what determines a currency's value, it's important to remember both the demand for dollars to buy goods and services and the demand for dollars to buy assets.

Based on the current and capital account balances, it would seem that the government would have had to sell dollars in 1987 and buy dollars in 2001. That wasn't the case, however. The reason is statistical discrepancies, as we see in line 19. In 1987 there was a small −$9 billion discrepancy, and in 2001 there was a +$11 billion discrepancy. These discrepancies arise because many international transactions, especially on the capital account, go unrecorded and hence must be estimated. With these discrepancies taken into account, in the absence of government policy there would have been slight downward pressure on the value of the dollar in 1987 and slight upward pressure in 2001.

While the current and capital accounts offset each other, there is a difference between the long-run effects of the demand for dollars to buy currently produced goods and services and the demand for dollars to buy assets. Assets earn profits or interest, so when foreigners buy U.S. assets, they earn income from those assets just for owning them. The net investment income from foreigners' previous asset purchases shows up on line 11 of the current account. It's the difference between the income U.S. citizens receive from their foreign assets and the income foreigners receive from their U.S. assets. If assets earned equal returns, we would expect that when foreigners own more U.S. capital assets than U.S. citizens own foreign capital assets, net investment income should be negative. And when U.S. citizens own more foreign capital assets than foreigners own U.S. capital assets, net investment income should be positive. Why is this? Because net investment income is simply the difference between the returns on U.S. citizens' assets held abroad and foreign citizens' assets held in the United States.

Since the 1980s, the inflow of capital into the United States has greatly exceeded the outflow of capital from the United States. As a result, the United States has become a net debtor nation; the amount foreigners own in the United States now exceeds the amount U.S. citizens own abroad by well over $1 trillion. So we would expect that U.S. investment income would be highly negative. But looking at line 11 of Table 33-1 we see that was not the case. The reason? Foreigners' returns have been low, and much of the U.S. investment abroad is undervalued. For example, the Japanese bought a lot of U.S. real estate at very high prices and have been losing money on those investments. While this trend has continued much longer than expected, we cannot expect it to continue forever.

Q-2 How can net investment income be positive if a country is a net debtor nation?

The Official Transactions Account

The current account and the capital account measure the private and nongovernment supply of and demand for dollars. The net amount of these two accounts is called the *balance of payments surplus* (if quantity demanded of a currency exceeds quantity supplied) or *deficit* (if quantity supplied of a currency exceeds quantity demanded). In 1987 the private quantity of dollars supplied exceeded the private quantity demanded (taking statistical discrepancies into account), which means that the United States had a small balance of payments deficit in that year (line 20). In 2001 it had a small balance of payments surplus.

A balance of payments deficit will put downward pressure on the value of a country's currency.

A balance of payments deficit will put downward pressure on the value of a country's currency. If a country wants to prevent that from happening, it can buy its own currency. The third component of the balance of payments account, the official transactions account, records the amount of dollars that the United States bought. As you can see on line 21 of Table 33-1 in 1987 the government entered into the foreign exchange market and bought 8 billion U.S. dollars, using $8 billion of the foreign reserves it had. When a government buys its own currency to hold up the currency's price, we say that the government has supported its currency. It's holding the exchange rate higher than it otherwise would have been. If the government sells its currency, it's attempting to depress the value of the currency.[2] In 2001, the government sold a small amount of U.S. dollars.

Now let's return to the point made at the beginning of the chapter: By definition the three accounts (current, capital, and official transactions) must sum to zero. Why is this? Because they are an accounting identity. The identity becomes something more than an identity if the currencies are freely exchangeable. In that case whenever anybody wants, they can take their currency and trade it for another. The quantity of currency supplied, including government's, must equal the quantity demanded, including government's.

The concepts *balance of payments* and *surplus* or *deficit* refer to the balance of payments not counting a country's official reserve transactions. Thus, any deficit in the balance of payments must be offset by an equal surplus in the official reserve transactions, and any surplus must be offset by an equal deficit. This means that the quantity of dollars supplied and the quantity of dollars demanded must be equal by definition.

Exchange Rates

Q-3 Show graphically the effect of an increase in demand for euros on the exchange rate for euros.

Supply and demand are two central forces of economics, so it shouldn't be surprising that our initial discussion of the determination of exchange rates uses supply and demand curves. As I stated above, an exchange rate is the rate at which one country's currency can be traded for another country's currency.

The exchange rate will tell you the price of a foreign currency. Below is an exchange rate table from January 17, 2003. It tells you how much a dollar was worth in terms of other currencies on that day.

Exchange Rates, January 17, 2003

Country	U.S. $ Equivalent	Currency per U.S. $
Argentina (peso)	0.3125	3.20
Britain (pound)	1.6137	0.620
Canada (dollar)	0.6513	1.535
China (renminbi)	0.1208	8.278
Denmark (krone)	0.1435	6.989
Israel (shekel)	0.2061	4.852
Japan (yen)	0.008495	117.72
Pakistan (rupee)	0.01722	58.072
Philippines (peso)	0.01867	53.562
Russia (ruble)	0.03143	31.817
Saudi Arabia (riyal)	0.2666	3.751
Euro	1.0669	0.9373

[2]Support for the dollar can also come from foreign central banks. In 1987, foreign central banks bought $45 billion worth of dollar-denominated assets, thereby playing a big role in holding the value of the dollar higher than it otherwise would have been.

The second column reports the U.S. dollar equivalent. It tells you the price of foreign currencies in terms of dollars. For example, one Argentinean peso costs about 31 cents. You can also look at exchange rates from the viewpoint of the foreign currency. For example, how many pesos are needed to buy one U.S. dollar? The third column tells you that one U.S. dollar costs 3.20 pesos.

As you learned in Chapter 5, people exchange currencies to buy goods or assets in other countries. For example, an American who wants to buy stock of a company that trades on the EU stock exchange first needs to buy euros with dollars. If the stock costs 150 euros, he will need to buy 150 euros. With an exchange rate of $1.07 for 1 euro, he will need to pay $160.50 to buy 150 euros ($1.07 × 150). Only then can he buy the stock.

Let's now turn to the graphs. At first glance, the graphical analysis of foreign exchange rates seems simple: You have an upward-sloping supply curve and a downward-sloping demand curve. But what goes on the axes? Obviously price and quantity, but what price? And what quantity? Because you are talking about the prices of currencies relative to each other you have to specify which currencies you are using.

In Figure 33-1, I present the supply of and demand for euros in terms of dollars. Notice that the quantity of euros goes on the horizontal axis and the dollar price of euros goes on the vertical axis. When you are comparing currencies of only two countries the supply of one currency equals the demand for the other currency. To demand one currency you must supply another. In this figure I am assuming that there are only two trading partners: the United States and the European Union. This means that the supply of euros is equivalent to the demand for dollars. The Europeans who want to buy U.S. goods or assets supply euros to buy dollars. Let's consider an example. Say a European wants to buy an IBM computer made in the United States. She has euros, but IBM wants dollars. So, in order to buy the computer, she or IBM must somehow exchange euros for dollars. She is *supplying* euros in order to *demand* dollars.

To demand one currency you must supply another.

The supply curve of euros is upward-sloping because the more dollars European citizens get for their euros, the cheaper U.S. goods and assets are for them and the greater the quantity of euros they want to supply for those goods. Say, for example, that the dollar price of one euro rises from 75 cents to 80 cents. That means that the price of a dollar to a European has fallen from 1.33 euros to 1.25 euros. For a European, a good that cost $100 now falls in price from 133 euros to 125 euros. U.S. goods are cheaper, so the Europeans buy more U.S. goods and more dollars, which means they supply more euros.

The demand for euros comes from Americans who want to buy European goods or assets. The demand curve is downward sloping because the lower the dollar price of euros, the more euros U.S. citizens want to buy, using the same reasoning I just described.

Figure 33-1 The Supply of and Demand for Euros
As long as you keep quantities and prices *of what* straight, the standard, or fundamental, analysis of the determination of exchange rates is easy. Exchange rates are determined by the supply of and demand for a country's currency. Just remember that if you're talking about the supply of and demand for euros, the price will be measured in dollars and the quantity will be in euros, as in this figure.

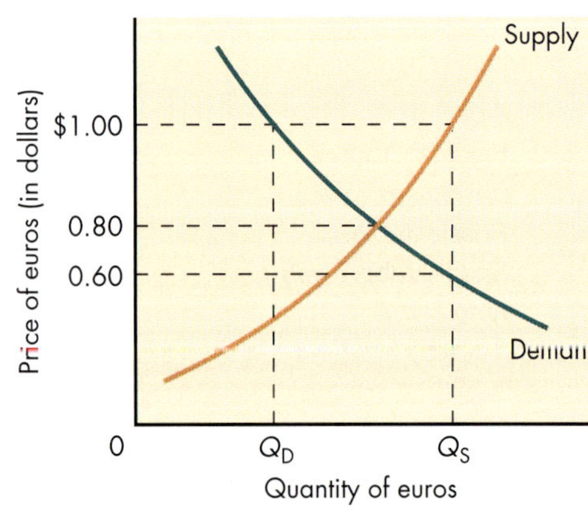

Equilibrium is where the quantity supplied equals the quantity demanded. In my example, equilibrium occurs at a dollar price of 80 cents for one euro. If the price of euros is above or below 80 cents, quantity supplied won't equal the quantity demanded and there will be pressure for the exchange rate to move to equilibrium. Say, for example, that the price is $1.00. The quantity of euros supplied will be greater than the quantity demanded. People who want to sell euros won't be able to sell them. To find buyers, they will offer to sell their euros for less. As they do, the price of euros falls.

Q-4 Show graphically the effect of an increase in the demand for dollars by Europeans on the price of euros.

Exchange Rates and the Balance of Payments

The supply/demand framework directly relates to the balance of payments. When private quantity supplied equals private quantity demanded, the balance of payments is in equilibrium. If the exchange rate is too high, there will be a deficit in the balance of payments; if the exchange rate is too low, there will be a surplus in the balance of payments. Thus, in Figure 33-1, when the price of euros is $1.00, the quantity of euros supplied exceeds the quantity demanded, so Europe is running a balance of payments deficit. When the price of euros is 60 cents, the quantity of euros demanded exceeds the quantity supplied, so Europe is running a balance of payments surplus.

A deficit in the balance of payments means that the private quantity supplied of a currency exceeds the private quantity demanded. A surplus in the balance of payments means the opposite.

Fundamental Forces Determining Exchange Rates

Exchange rate analysis is usually broken down into fundamental analysis and short-run analysis. In this section I discuss fundamental analysis—a consideration of the fundamental forces that determine the supply of and demand for currencies, and hence cause them to shift. These fundamental forces include a country's income, a country's prices, the interest rate in a country, and the country's trade policy. That means that changes in a country's income, changes in a country's prices, changes in interest rates, and changes in trade policy can cause the supply of and demand for a currency to shift. Let's consider how they do so.

Changes in a Country's Income The demand for imports depends on the income in a country. When a country's income falls, demand for imports falls. Hence demand for foreign currency to buy those imports falls, which means that the supply of the country's currency to buy the foreign currency falls. That's why, in my presentation of the *AS/AD* model, I said that imports depend on income.

How important is this relationship? Very important. For example, in 2001 strong economic growth in Brazil relative to its primary trading partners led to increased imports, which increased the supply of Brazilian real. The increase in the supply tended to lower the price of the real relative to foreign currencies.

Q-5 In the early 1980s, the U.S. economy fell into a recession (the government faced the problem of both a high federal deficit and a high trade deficit, called the twin deficits), and the dollar was very strong. Can you provide an explanation for this sequence of events?

Changes in a Country's Prices The United States' demand for imports and foreign countries' demand for U.S. exports depend on prices of U.S. goods compared to prices of foreign competing goods. If the United States has more inflation than other countries, foreign goods will become cheaper, U.S. demand for foreign currencies will tend to increase, and foreign demand for dollars will tend to decrease. This rise in U.S. inflation will shift the dollar supply outward and the dollar demand inward.

Four important fundamental determinants of exchange rates are prices, interest rates, income, and trade policy.

Changes in Interest Rates People like to invest their savings in assets that will yield the highest return. Other things equal, a rise in U.S. interest rates relative to those abroad will increase demand for U.S. assets. As a result, demand for dollars will increase, while simultaneously the supply of dollars will decrease as fewer Americans sell their dollars to buy foreign assets. A fall in the U.S. interest rate or a rise in foreign interest rates will have the opposite effect.

Changes in Trade Policy The demand for imports is affected by a government's trade policy. An increase in trade restrictions, such as the 30 percent tariff President George W. Bush imposed on imported steel in 2002, increases the price of imports, reducing the quantity of imports demanded. Consequently, the demand for foreign currency to buy those imports declines so that the supply of a country's currency falls. In 2002 a number of other countries threatened to impose retaliatory tariffs on American goods. These retaliatory tariffs would reduce U.S. exports and reduce the demand for the U.S. dollar.

Some Examples To make sure that you have the analysis down pat, let's consider some examples. First, the U.S. economy goes into recession with interest rates remaining constant. What will likely happen to exchange rates? Second, the Mexican economy has runaway inflation—what will likely happen to exchange rates? And third, the interest rate on yen-denominated assets increases—what will likely happen to the exchange rate? If you answered: The value of the dollar will rise, the value of the peso will fall, and the value of the yen will rise, you're following the argument. If those weren't your answers, a review is in order.

Why Exchange Rate Determination Is More Complicated than Supply/Demand Analysis Makes It Seem

In day-to-day trading, fundamentals can be overwhelmed by expectations of how a currency will change in value. The supply and demand curves for currencies can shift around rapidly in response to rumors, expectations, and expectations of expectations. As they shift, they bring about large fluctuations in exchange rates that make trading difficult and have significant real effects on economic activity.

Q-6 Why don't most governments leave determination of the exchange rate to the market?

Let me outline just one potential problem. Say you expect the price of the currency to fall one-half of 1 percent tomorrow. What should you do? The correct answer is: Sell that currency quickly. Why? One-half of 1 percent may not sound like much, but, annualized, it is equivalent to a rate of interest per year of 617 percent. Based on that expectation, if you're into making money (and you're really sure about the fall) you will sell all of that currency that you hold, and borrow all you can so you can sell some more. You can make big money if you guess small changes in exchange rates correctly. (Of course if you're wrong you can lose big money.) This means that if the market generally believes the exchange rates will move, those expectations will tend to be self-fulfilling. Self-fulfilling expectations undermine the argument in favor of letting markets determine exchange rates: When expectations rule, the exchange rate may not reflect actual demands and supplies of goods. Instead, the exchange rate can reflect expectations and rumors. The resulting fluctuations serve no real purpose, and cause problems for international trade and the country's economy.

International Trade Problems from Shifting Values of Currencies

Suppose that a firm decides to build a plant in the United States because costs in the United States are low. But suppose also that the value of the dollar then rises significantly; the firm's costs rise significantly too, making it uncompetitive.

In a real-world example, from July to September 1997, the value of the Thai baht fell nearly 40 percent. Goodyear (Thailand), which had been one of the five most profitable companies on the Stock Exchange of Thailand, suddenly faced a 20 percent rise in the costs of raw materials because it paid for those raw materials in dollars. It also faced a decline in tire prices because the demand for tires had fallen 20 to 40 percent when the Thai economy contracted. Within just two months, a highly profitable venture had become unprofitable. Other firms were closing shop because they were unable to pay the interest on loans that were denominated in dollars.

In summary, large fluctuations make real trade difficult and cause serious real consequences. It is these consequences that have led to calls for government to fix or stabilize their exchange rates.

How a Fixed Exchange Rate System Works

The government can fix its exchange rate by *exchange rate intervention*—buying or selling a currency to affect its price. Let's consider an example of exchange rate intervention. Suppose that, given the interaction of private supply and demand forces, the equilibrium value of the euro is 80 cents a euro, but the European Union wants to maintain a value of $1.00 a euro. This is shown in Figure 33-2. At $1.00 a euro, quantity supplied exceeds quantity demanded. The European Union must buy the surplus, $Q_2 - Q_1$, using official reserves (foreign currency holdings). It thus shifts the total demand for euros to D_1, making the equilibrium market exchange rate (including the European government's demand for euros) equal to $1.00. This process, mentioned earlier in this chapter, is called **currency support**—the *buying of a currency by a government to maintain its value at above its long-run equilibrium value*. It is a direct exchange rate policy. If a government has sufficient official reserves, or if it can convince other governments to lend it reserves, it can fix the exchange rate at the rate it wants, no matter what the private level of supply and demand is. In reality governments have no such power to support currencies in the long run, since their reserves are limited. For example, in 2002 the Argentinean government ran out of foreign reserves and was forced to let its currency decline in value.

A country can maintain a fixed exchange rate above its market price only as long as it has the reserves above its market price.

A country fixes the exchange rate by standing ready to buy and sell its currency anytime the exchange rate is not at the fixed exchange rate.

A more viable long-run exchange rate policy is **currency stabilization**—the *buying and selling of a currency by the government to offset temporary fluctuations in supply and demand for currencies*. In currency stabilization, the government is not trying to change the long-run equilibrium; it is simply trying to keep the exchange rate at that long-run equilibrium. The government sometimes buys and sometimes sells currency, so it is far less likely to run out of reserves.

Successful currency stabilization requires the government to choose the correct long-run equilibrium exchange rate. A policy of stabilization can become a policy of

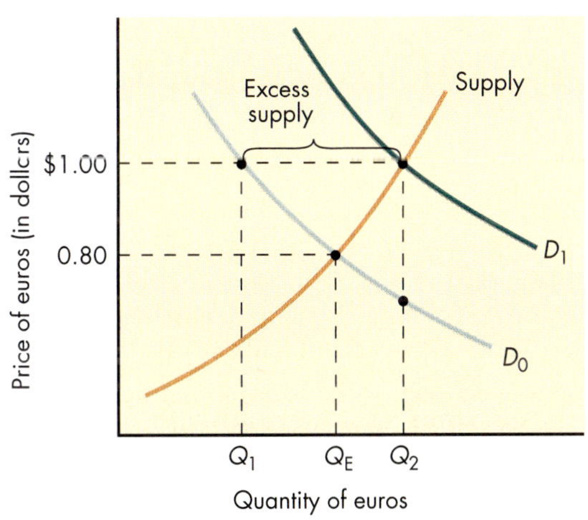

Figure 33-2 A Demonstration of Direct Exchange Policy
If the government chooses to hold the exchange rate at $1.00, when the equilibrium is 80 cents, there is an excess supply given by $Q_2 - Q_1$. The government purchases this excess (using official reserves) and closes the difference, thus maintaining equilibrium.

support if the government chooses too high a long-run equilibrium. Unfortunately, government has no way of knowing for sure what the long-run equilibrium exchange rate is, so how much stabilizing it can do depends on its access to reserves. If it has sufficient reserves, the government buys up sufficient quantities of its currency to make up the difference.

Once the government has dried up the sources of borrowing foreign currencies, if it wants to hold its exchange rate above the private equilibrium exchange rate it must move to indirect methods affecting its economy in order to affect private supplies and demands for its currency. (These indirect measures are discussed in the next chapter.) In short, if a country wants to maintain a fixed exchange rate, it must adjust its economy to the fixed exchange rate.

Q-7 In general, would it be easier for the United States to push the value of the dollar down or up? Why?

The same argument about running out of reserves cannot be made for a country that wants to maintain a below-market exchange rate. Since a government can create all the domestic currency it wants, it's easier for the European Union to push the value of its currency down by selling euros than it is for the government to hold it up by buying euros. By the same token, it's easier for another country (say, Japan) to push the value of the euro up (by pushing the value of the yen down). Thus, if the two governments can decide which way they want their exchange rates to move, they have a large incentive to cooperate. Of course, cooperation requires an agreement on the goals, and often countries' goals conflict. One role of the various international economic organizations is to provide a forum for reaching agreement on exchange rate goals and a vehicle through which cooperation can take place.

Notice that, in principle, any trader could establish a fixed exchange rate by guaranteeing to buy or sell a currency at a given rate. Any "fix," however, is only as good as the guarantee, and to fix an exchange rate would require many more resources than an individual trader has; only governments have sufficient resources to fix an exchange rate, and often even governments run out of resources.

Strategic currency stabilization is the process of buying and selling at strategic moments to affect the expectations of traders, and hence affect their supply and demand.

In reality given the small level of official reserves compared to the enormous level of private trading, significant amounts of stabilization are impossible. Instead governments use *strategic currency stabilization*—buying and selling at strategic moments to affect expectations of traders, and hence to affect their supply and demand. Such issues are discussed in depth in international finance courses.

Stabilizing Fluctuations versus Deviating from Long-Run Equilibrium

The key to whether or not exchange rate intervention is a viable option involves the long-run equilibrium exchange rate. Direct exchange rate policy can succeed if the problem is one of stabilization. If, however, the problem is long run, or if the government estimates the wrong equilibrium, eventually the government will run out of official reserves. Here's the rub: While in theory it is important to make the distinction, in practice it is difficult to do so. The government can only guess at the long-run equilibrium rate, since no definitive empirical measure of this rate exists. The long-run equilibrium must be estimated. If that estimation is wrong, a sustainable stabilization policy becomes an unsustainable deviation from long-run equilibrium policy. Thus, a central issue in exchange rate intervention policy is estimating the long-run equilibrium exchange rate.

Q-8 Ms. Economist always tries to travel to a country where the purchasing power parity exchange rate is lower than the market exchange rate. Why?

Estimating Long-Run Equilibrium Exchange Rates: Purchasing Power Parity Purchasing power parity is one way economists have of estimating the long-run equilibrium rate. **Purchasing power parity (PPP)** is *a method of calculating exchange rates that attempts to value currencies at rates such that each currency will buy an equal basket of goods*. It is based on the idea that the exchange of currencies reflects the exchange

Determining the Causes of Fluctuations in the Dollar's Value

Applying the Tools

As you can see on the graph, the dollar's value has fluctuated considerably since 1973. A good exercise to see if you understand movements in the value of the dollar is to try to choose which factors caused the fluctuation.

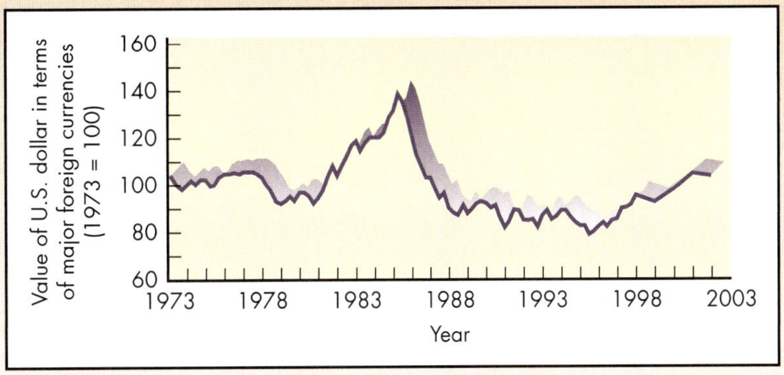

Source: Board of Governors, Federal Reserve System (www.federalreserve.gov).

Let's start with the relatively small fluctuations in 1973 and 1974. These probably reflected expectational bubbles—in which speculators were more concerned with short-run fluctuations than long-run fundamentals—while the dollar's low value in 1979 and 1980 reflected high inflation, relatively low real interest rates, and the booming U.S. economy during this period.

The rise of the dollar in the early 1980s reflected higher real U.S. interest rates and the falling U.S. inflation rate, although the rise was much more than expected and probably reflected speculation, as did the sudden fall in the dollar's value in 1985. Similarly, the fluctuations in the late 1980s and early 1990s reflected both changing interest rates in the United States and changing foreign interest rates, as well as changing relative inflation rates.

In the late 1990s the value of the dollar rose substantially. Part of the explanation for this lies in the weakness of the Japanese economy, which led the Japanese central bank to increase the Japanese money supply, thereby lowering the Japanese interest rate. That weakness also was reflected in the fall in the prices of Japanese stocks. That fall led investors to shift out of Japanese stocks and into U.S. stocks, thereby increasing the demand for the dollar, and pushing up the U.S. effective exchange rate. In the early 2000s the value of the dollar fluctuated as both U.S. and foreign economies slowed.

As you can see, after the fact we economists are pretty good at explaining the movements in the exchange rates. Alas, before the fact we aren't so good because often speculative activities make the timing of the movements unpredictable.

of real goods. If you are able to exchange a basket of goods from country X for an equivalent basket of goods from country Z, you should also be able to exchange the amount of currency from country X that is needed to purchase country X's basket of goods for the amount of currency from country Z that is needed to purchase country Z's basket of goods. For example, say that the yen is valued at 100 yen to \$1. Say also that you can buy the same basket of goods for 1,000 yen that you can buy for \$7. In that case the purchasing power parity exchange rate would be 143 yen to \$1 (1,000/7 = 143), compared to an actual exchange rate of 100 yen to \$1. An economist would say that at 100 to the dollar the yen is overvalued—with 100 yen you could not purchase a basket of goods equivalent to the basket of goods you could purchase with \$1.

Table 33-2 shows various calculations for purchasing power parity for a variety of countries. The second column shows the 2000 actual exchange rates. The third column shows purchasing power parity exchange rates. The fourth column shows the difference between the two, or the 2000 distortion in the exchange rates (if you believe the PPP exchange rates are the correct ones).

Purchasing power parity is a method of calculating exchange rates such that various currencies will each buy an equal basket of goods and services.

Criticisms of the Purchasing Power Parity Method For many economists, estimating exchange rates using PPP has serious problems. If the currency is overvalued

Table 33-2 Actual and Purchasing Power Parity Exchange Rates for 2000

Country	Actual Exchange Rate (currency per dollar)	PPP Exchange Rate (currency per dollar)	Under (−)/ Over (+) valuation
Japan	107.8	153.7	+43%
Switzerland	1.7	2.0	+18
European Union	0.9	0.9	0
United Kingdom	0.7	0.7	0
United States	1	1	0
Brazil	5.1	2.3	−55
Mozambique	15,447.1	3,900.2	−75
China	8.3	1.8	−78
Russia	28.1	5.8	−79
Uganda	1,644.5	347.6	−79
India	44.9	8.7	−81

Source: *World Development Indicators 2002,* World Bank (www.worldbank.org).

Web Note 33.1
The Big Mac Index

and will eventually fall, why don't traders use that information and sell that currency now, making it fall now? After all, they are out after a profit. So if there is open trading in a currency, any expected change in the exchange rate will affect exchange rates now. If traders don't sell now when there are expectations that a currency's overvaluation will eventually make its value fall, they must believe there is some reason that its value won't, in fact, fall.

Purchasing power parity exchange rates may or may not be appropriate long-run exchange rates.

Critics argue that the difficulty with PPP exchange rates is the complex nature of trade and consumption. They point out that the PPP will change as the basket of goods changes. This means that there is no one PPP measure. They also point out that, since all PPP measures leave out asset demand for a currency, the measures are missing an important element of the demand. Critics ask: Is there any reason to assume that in the long run the asset demand for a currency is less important than the goods demand for a currency? Because the asset demand for a currency is important, critics of PPP argue that there is little reason to assume that the short-run actual exchange rate will ever adjust to the PPP exchange rates. And if that rate doesn't adjust, then PPP does not provide a good estimate of the equilibrium rate. These critics further contend that the existing exchange rate is the best estimate of the long-run equilibrium exchange rate.

Advantages and Disadvantages of Alternative Exchange Rate Systems

Three exchange rate regimes are:

1. Fixed exchange rate: The government chooses an exchange rate and offers to buy and sell currencies at that rate.
2. Flexible exchange rate: Determination of exchange rates is left totally up to the market.
3. Partially flexible exchange rate: The government sometimes affects the exchange rate and sometimes leaves it to the market.

The problems of stabilizing exchange rates have led to an ongoing debate about whether a fixed exchange rate, a flexible exchange rate, or a combination of the two is best. This debate nicely captures the macro issues relevant to exchange rate stabilization, so in this section I consider that debate. First, a brief overview of the three alternative regimes:

Fixed exchange rate: *If the government chooses a particular exchange rate and offers to buy and sell currencies at that price*. For example, suppose the U.S. government says it will buy euros at 80 cents per euro and sell dollars at 1.25 euros per dollar. In that case, we say that the United States has a fixed exchange rate of 1.25 euros to the dollar.

Flexible exchange rate: *When the government does not enter into foreign exchange markets at all, but leaves the determination of exchange rates totally up to currency* *traders*. The price of its currency is allowed to rise and fall as market forces dictate.

Partially flexible exchange rate: *When the government sometimes buys or sells currencies to influence the exchange rate, while at other times letting private market forces operate*. A partially flexible exchange rate is sometimes called a dirty float because it isn't purely market-determined or government-determined.

Fixed Exchange Rates

The advantages of a fixed exchange rate system are:

1. Fixed exchange rates provide international monetary stability.
2. Fixed exchange rates force governments to make adjustments to meet their international problems.

The disadvantages of a fixed exchange rate system are:

1. Fixed exchange rates can become unfixed. When they're expected to become unfixed, they create enormous monetary instability.
2. Fixed exchange rates force governments to make adjustments to meet their international problems. (Yes, this is a disadvantage as well as an advantage.)

Let's consider each in turn.

Fixed Exchange Rates and Exchange Rate Stability The advantage of fixed exchange rates is that firms know what exchange rates will be, making trade easier. However, to maintain fixed exchange rates, the government must choose an exchange rate and have sufficient official reserves to support that rate. If the rate it chooses is too high, its exports lag and the country continually loses official reserves. If the rate it chooses is too low, it is paying more for its imports than it needs to and is building up official reserves.

The difficulty is that as soon as the country gets close to its official reserves limit, foreign exchange traders begin to expect a drop in the value of the currency, and they try to get out of that currency because anyone holding that currency when it falls will lose money. For example, in December 1997, when traders found out that South Korea had only $10 billion in reserves instead of the official government announcement of $30 billion, they sold the Korean won and its value dropped. False rumors of an expected depreciation or decrease in a country's fixed exchange rate can become true by causing a "run on a currency," as all traders sell that currency. Thus, at times fixed exchange rates can become highly unstable because expectation of a change in the exchange rate can force the change to occur. As opposed to small movements in currency values, under a fixed rate regime these movements occur in large, sudden jumps.

Fixed exchange rates provide international monetary stability and force governments to make adjustments to meet their international problems. (This is *also* a disadvantage.) If they become unfixed, they create monetary instability.

Fixed Exchange Rates and Policy Independence Maintaining a fixed exchange rate places limitations on a central bank's actions. In a country with fixed exchange rates, the central bank must ensure that the international quantities of its currency supplied and demanded are equal at the existing exchange rate.

Say, for example, that the United States and the Bahamas have fixed exchange rates: $1 B = $1 U.S. The Bahamian central bank decides to run an expansionary monetary policy, lowering the interest rate and stimulating the Bahamian economy. The lower interest rates will cause financial capital to flow out of the country, and the higher income will increase imports. Demand for Bahamian dollars will fall. To prop up its dollar and to maintain the fixed exchange rate, the Bahamian government will have to buy its own currency. They can do so only as long as they have sufficient official reserves of other countries' currencies.

Because most countries' official reserves are limited, a country with fixed exchange rates is limited in its ability to conduct expansionary monetary and fiscal policies. It loses its freedom to stimulate the economy in response to a recession. That's why, when a serious recession hits, many countries are forced to abandon fixed exchange rates. They run out of official reserves, and choose expansionary monetary policy to achieve their domestic goals over contractionary monetary policy to achieve their international goals.

FLEXIBLE EXCHANGE RATES

The advantages and disadvantages of a flexible exchange rate (exchange rates totally determined by private market forces) are the reverse of those of fixed exchange rates. The advantages are:

1. Flexible exchange rates provide for orderly incremental adjustment of exchange rates rather than large, sudden jumps.
2. Flexible exchange rates allow government to be flexible in conducting domestic monetary and fiscal policies.

The disadvantages are:

1. Flexible exchange rates allow speculation to cause large jumps in exchange rates, which do not reflect market fundamentals.
2. Flexible exchange rates allow government to be flexible in conducting domestic monetary and fiscal policies. (This is a disadvantage as well as an advantage.)

Let's consider each in turn.

Flexible Exchange Rates and Exchange Rate Stability Advocates of flexible exchange rates argue as follows: Why not treat currency markets like any other market and let private market forces determine a currency's value? There is no fixed price for TVs; why should there be a fixed price for currencies? The opponents' answer is based on the central role that international financial considerations play in an economy and the strange shapes and large shifts that occur in the short-run supply and demand curves for currencies.

When expectations shift supply and demand curves around all the time, there's no guarantee that the exchange rate will be determined by long-run fundamental forces. The economy will go through real gyrations because of speculators' expectations about other speculators. Thus, the argument against flexible exchange rates is that they allow far too much fluctuation in exchange rates, making trade difficult.

Flexible exchange rate regimes provide for orderly incremental adjustment of exchange rates rather than large sudden jumps, and allow governments to be flexible in conducting domestic monetary and fiscal policies. (This is also a disadvantage.) They are, however, susceptible to private speculation.

Flexible Exchange Rates and Policy Independence The policy independence arguments for and against flexible exchange rates are the reverse of those given for fixed exchange rates. Individuals who believe that national governments should not have flexibility in setting monetary policy argue that flexible exchange rates don't impose the discipline on policy that fixed exchange rates do. Say, for example, that a country's goods are uncompetitive. Under a fixed exchange rate system, the country would have to contract its money supply and deal with the underlying uncompetitiveness of its goods. Under a flexible exchange rate system, the country can maintain an expansionary monetary policy, allowing inflation simply by permitting the value of its currency to fall.

Advocates of policy flexibility argue that it makes no sense for a country to go through a recession when it doesn't have to; flexible exchange rates allow countries more flexibility in dealing with their problems. True, policy flexibility may lead to inflation, but inflation is better than a recession.

Partially Flexible Exchange Rates

Faced with the dilemma of choosing between these two unpleasant policies, most countries have opted for a policy in between: partially flexible exchange rates. With such a policy they try to get the advantages of both fixed and flexible exchange rates.

When policymakers believe there is a fundamental misalignment in a country's exchange rate, they will allow private forces to determine it—they allow the exchange rate to be flexible. When they believe that the currency's value is falling because of speculation, or that too large an adjustment in the currency is taking place, and that that adjustment won't achieve their balance of payments goals, they step in and fix the exchange rate, either supporting or pushing down their currency's value. Countries that follow a currency stabilization policy have partially flexible exchange rates.

If policymakers are correct, this system of partial flexibility works smoothly and has the advantages of both fixed and flexible exchange rates. If policymakers are incorrect, however, a partially flexible system has the disadvantages of both fixed and flexible systems.

Partially flexible exchange rate regimes combine the advantages and disadvantages of fixed and flexible exchange rates.

Which View Is Right?

Q-9 Does government intervention stabilize exchange rates?

Which view is correct is much in debate. Most foreign exchange traders I know tell me that the possibility of government intervention increases the amount of private speculation in the system. In the private investors' view, their own assessments of what exchange rates should be are better than those of policymakers. If private investors knew the government would not enter in, private speculators would focus on fundamentals and would stabilize short-run exchange rates. When private speculators know government might enter into the market, they don't focus on fundamentals; instead they continually try to outguess government policymakers. When that happens, private speculation doesn't stabilize; it destabilizes exchange rates as private traders try to guess what the government thinks.

Many of my economics colleagues who work for the Fed aren't convinced by private investors' arguments. They maintain that some government intervention helps stabilize currency markets. I don't know which group is right—private foreign exchange traders or economists at the Fed. But to decide, it is necessary to go beyond the arguments and consider how the various exchange rate regimes have worked in practice. Appendix A to this chapter gives you an introduction into the history of exchange rate regimes.

The Euro: A Common Currency for Europe

If you think of countries with a fixed exchange rate as being in a marriage, you can think of a common currency as in a marriage for life, from which it is almost impossible to escape. In 2002 the 12 European nations shown in Figure 33-3 with the euro symbol (€) consummated their fixed exchange rate regime established under the EU's plan for monetary union and adopted the euro as their common currency. (Other members of the EU are considering joining in the near future.) They adopted the euro for a number of reasons, some political and some economic; but regardless of why they did it, the euro will have significant effects on international finance over the next decade.

First, let's consider the advantages the EU countries get from adopting a common currency. The first advantage is that, politically, a common currency ties the countries closely together. World Wars I and II started from fights among European countries. An

Web Note 33.2
Multinational Money

Figure 33-3 Map of EU Countries
Members of the European Union as of 2002 included Austria, Belgium, Denmark, Finland, France, Germany, Great Britain, Greece, Ireland, Italy, Luxembourg, The Netherlands, Portugal, Spain, and Sweden. Those countries that also share a common currency are marked with a €, the symbol of the euro.

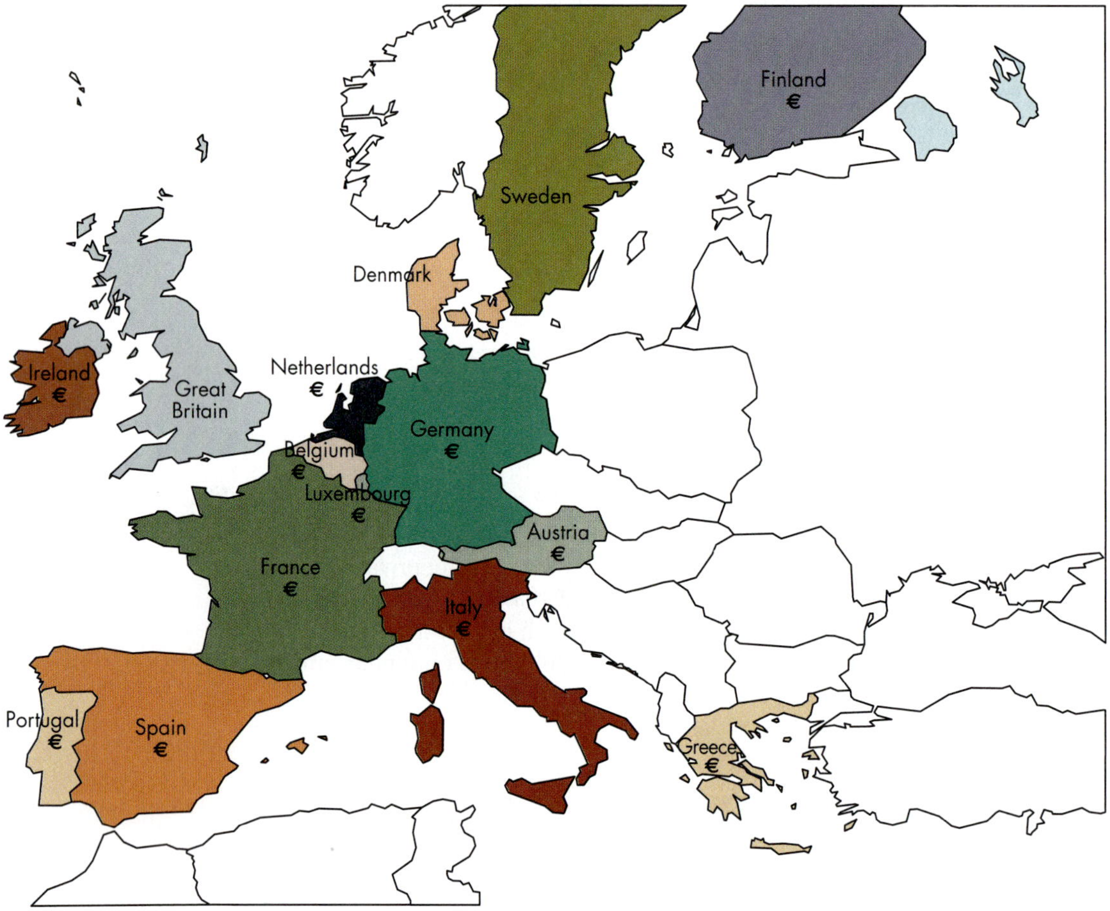

important motive behind the increasing integration of Europe—from initial creation of a common market, to the establishment of the European Union with reduced border controls, to the establishment of the monetary union—has been to prevent large-scale war from ever happening again. Many feel that political reasons drove the countries toward union.

Three economic advantages of a common currency are it (1) eliminates the cost of exchanging currencies, (2) facilitates price comparisons, and (3) creates a larger market.

There are, however, also economic reasons. One is to eliminate the cost of exchanging currencies when trading among members, and hence provide an incentive to increase trade within the EU countries. A second is price transparency. With the adoption of a single currency, consumers and businesses can more easily see price differentials, resulting in greater competition. For example, instead of having to compare a pair of German shoes priced at 60 marks with an Italian pair priced at 48,000 lire, a consumer just needs to compare 30 euros with 25 euros. A third advantage is that the common currency makes it more likely that companies will think of Europe as a single market. Producing for that market would give European consumers more clout and make Europe, as well as the United States, the reference market when new goods are planned. It would also allow European firms to take advantage of economies of scale when producing for the European market. Finally, planners hoped that the importance of the euro would lead individuals throughout the world to hold their assets in euros rather than in dollars. That would mean lower interest rates for Europe relative to what they would have been, and the possibility that the euro will be used as an international reserve currency along with the dollar. An international reserve currency is a currency in which people and firms hold their savings. This means that the EU could create euros and exchange them for other currencies to buy products without increasing the money supply and risking inflation. (For the EU, it would be like getting an interest-free loan.) Because the U.S. dollar has been the world's reserve currency, the United States has been getting those interest free loans, which is one of the reasons it's been able to run continual large trade deficits. If the euro partially replaces the dollar as the world reserve currency, there will likely be a large fall in demand for the dollar and a decrease it its relative value.

One major disadvantage of the common currency area is that members of the EU will no longer have independent monetary policies. So if an external shock hurts one region worse than another, the region hit hard cannot increase the money supply to offset the effect on output. For example, in the early 2000s, Ireland's economy was growing quickly while Germany's economy was contracting, but the two countries shared the same interest rate and monetary policy. A common currency also presents nationalism problems. A country's currency is a symbol to people of their country, and giving it up means losing part of their identity. Loss of nationalism is one reason Britain has been reluctant to adopt the euro.

A major disadvantage of a common currency is the loss of independent monetary policy for member countries.

The initial adoption of the euro has gone relatively smoothly, although realization of the most advantages is still in the future. It will be an experiment that will be followed carefully over the next decade.

A Case Study: The Argentinean Currency Crisis

To understand the difficult policy issues that currency problems raise, it is helpful to consider the ongoing Argentinean currency crisis that I described in the beginning of this chapter. Let's begin the story back in the 1980s, when the Argentinean economy was rocked by hyperinflation. In the late 1980s, Carlos Menem was elected president. In his election platform, he promised to end the hyperinflation that had plagued the Argentinean economy. He planned to do this by (1) limiting money supply growth; (2) liberalizing the Argentinean economy (which meant reducing tariffs and reducing the role of the government in the economy); and (3) ending the continual government budget deficits.

Achieving the Three Goals

This was not an easy set of goals. Limiting money supply growth would most likely cause a major recession and, given the history of broken promises by Argentinean politicians, people were likely not going believe in Menem's resolve. Without credibility, firms would likely continue raising their prices, inflation would remain, and the recession would be worse. One way to gain credibility was to fix the value of the peso to the U.S. dollar. With a fixed exchange rate, money supply growth would be determined by U.S. monetary policy. The value of the peso was legally set to equal one dollar by establishing a currency board that was required to hold one dollar for every peso in circulation. A **currency board** essentially *establishes a fixed exchange rate, along with a fund to defend the price of the currency should it be necessary*. Argentina could increase its money supply only if it increased the number of dollars in reserve. If its dollar reserves fell, it would have to decrease the money supply. The plan worked; inflation dropped enormously (from over 1,000 percent per year in 1990 to almost nothing in 1995) and the Argentinean economy grew at a fast rate. Argentina was hailed as a success story in regard to its inflation policy.

Argentina also progressed toward Menem's second goal of liberalization. The federal government sold a number of its assets, including its oil refineries, and trade restrictions were reduced, substantially increasing trade with its neighbor, Brazil. In 1994 Argentina formed a free-trade zone with Brazil, Uruguay, and Paraguay called Mercosur, which eliminated all tariffs for members while maintaining average tariff rates of about 14 percent for imports from countries outside the free trade zone. Whereas in 1986 nearly half of domestic output was protected by import quotas, today only 2 percent is protected.

Argentina, at first glance, also met its third goal of keeping the federal budget deficits low. The way the Argentine government achieved this goal, however, was problematic. The budget deficit was being reduced by one-time sales of assets, and while the federal government was incurring little new debt, local government debt increased enormously. Because under the Argentinean constitution, the federal government was responsible for paying that debt, the actual federal debt picture was much worse than reported. During 1993–98, when the Argentine economy was expanding, the federal and local debt-to-GDP ratio rose by 12 percentage points. Even so, most observers were satisfied that Argentina was doing well and thought that it would likely weather the slowdown in world growth during the late 1990s.

An External Shock to the Economy

In 1999 the situation changed substantially. Brazil, a significant trading partner to Argentina, suffered a currency crisis. The value of the Brazilian real (pronounced *ree-ahl*) fell 40 percent against the U.S. dollar. Because the American dollar remained high, Argentinean goods were no longer competitive in the world market and could not compete at all in the Brazilian market. The demand for imports remained strong while the demand for exports fell, resulting in a significant trade deficit and a recession. The recession was exacerbated by a slowdown in the world economy and a fall in world agricultural prices, which hit Argentina hard because the country's exports were heavily agricultural.

The recession lowered tax revenues and threw the federal budget even more into deficit. This, combined with the revenue loss from sold industries and the increase in debt from local governments, worsened Argentina's fiscal situation. Argentina tried to cut government spending and raise taxes, but this effort was overwhelmed by the declining revenues caused by the recession. Lenders became more and more concerned about the situation and were unwilling to buy Argentinean bonds except at very high interest rates. The high interest rates, by increasing the interest-payment component of government spending, further worsened the deficit.

Had Argentina not had a currency board, at that point it probably would have done what most developing countries do when faced with such a problem—monetize the debt (let the central bank buy the government debt by increasing the money supply). But because of the currency board, the central bank, by law, could not increase the money supply unless it could increase its holdings of dollars. Initially, Argentina borrowed from the International Monetary Fund (IMF) and outside countries, but that borrowing quickly dried up as people feared a default on the country's debt. The IMF demanded major cuts in federal spending if it was to lend Argentina any more money. Politically, the cuts were almost impossible because it seemed clear that any government that instituted them would be thrown out of office. That was the situation in 2000.

As time progressed, the situation became clearly untenable. More and more people began to expect the value of the peso to fall, and they tried to convert pesos to dollars in whatever way they could. So even more dollars began to flow out of the country. The situation was worsening weekly. As people sold even more pesos (people don't want to hold an asset that is going to fall in value), the number of dollars flowing out of Argentina increased, which required the board to reduce the supply of pesos further. The results were a deepening of the recession in Argentina and a further reduction in tax revenues. With the lack of money, it was almost impossible to get loans even to have enough currency to buy goods. Faced with this major shortage in currency, local governments started paying their debts in IOUs. They encouraged others to accept these IOUs in payment for goods, and governments in parts of Argentina developed a second currency, which traded at a discount to the peso.

Q-10 Demonstrate, using supply and demand analysis, what effect the fear of a falling value of the peso will have on the value of the peso.

In late 2001 there simply weren't enough dollars to support the peso at the set fixed exchange rate, and in early 2002 it was clear that the fixed exchange rate of the peso to the dollar would be impossible to maintain. As it was preparing to eliminate the fix, the Argentinean government limited withdrawals from banks, which created massive riots in the streets and forced the government to resign. A period of political and economic chaos followed. Various presidents were appointed, but they quickly resigned when their proposals were rejected by either the political establishment or the people. The riots continued, and Argentina went through five presidents in two weeks.

In late 2001 Argentina defaulted on its international debt, worth over $150 billion, the largest such default by any country in history, and in early 2002 the currency board and fixed exchange rate were both dropped. As soon as the fix was eliminated, the exchange rate fell from one Argentinean peso to the dollar to under two pesos to the dollar, which meant that all assets denominated in pesos, such as savings accounts, lost about half their value. Argentineans with debt denominated in dollars had to convert more than twice the number of pesos as before to pay their debt. The government instituted a number of plans to partially compensate them, but it was limited by reduced tax revenue. At the same time the government had defaulted on its international debt, leaving its international situation in legal limbo. It turned again to the IMF, but to get any loans it faced the IMF requirement that it had to reduce its budget deficit, which again was politically difficult, if not impossible.

Argentina's crisis continued through 2002, and the level of unemployment rose to 30 percent. With the fall in the value of the peso, import prices rose, which contributed to higher inflation of more than 10 percent per month. This inflation led to a further decline in the value of the peso on the international market and a fear that hyperinflation would return once again to the Argentinean economy.

There are some bright spots on the horizon. Assuming the real value of the peso (the value of the peso adjusted for inflation) falls, eventually the lower value of the peso will increase demand for Argentinean exports, which will help the Argentinean economy come out of the recession. And, as time progressed, the negotiations on the defaulted loans came closer to resolution. But Argentina faces a long and difficult road, loaded with much pain.

Lessons from Argentina's Crisis

Six lessons can be learned from this case study:

1. If a country uses a fixed exchange rate or currency board, it should tie its currency to a set of currencies that closely reflects its major trading partners.
2. Short-run success stories must be put in the perspective of long-run effects.
3. Limiting the money supply may be technically possible but politically impossible.

4. It is the financial health of a country, not the budget deficit figures alone, that needs to be considered when considering fiscal policy.
5. If a country has a fixed exchange rate, it needs an exit strategy (but ideally the fact that it has an exit strategy should not be known).
6. In international finance, chaos can reign; and when problems develop, some institutional method of dealing with defaults and crises is needed.

Most of these lessons have to do with individual countries, but the last one has to do with international agencies. In response to the Argentinean crisis, a number of economists proposed international bankruptcy laws under which a set of rules are established similar to bankruptcy laws for companies and individuals in countries, which would guide the default. The hope is that such rules can ease the pain and reduce the chaos associated with sovereign default of debt such as happened in Argentina. Any change in the rules will not help Argentina, which will likely be bearing the burden of the crisis for years to come. This leads to a final lesson we can learn from this case study. That final lesson is a lesson that we have seen in many other situations: There is no free lunch in the conduct of international monetary affairs.

Conclusion

This chapter began with a quotation suggesting that a foreign exchange dealer's office can be the nearest thing to bedlam that there is. Seeing some order within that bedlam is not easy, but understanding the balance of payments and its relation to the determination of exchange rates is good first step. And it is a necessary step. With international transportation and communication becoming easier and faster and other countries' economies growing, the U.S. economy will become more interdependent with the global economy in the upcoming decades, making understanding these issues more and more necessary to understanding macroeconomics.

Summary

- The balance of payments is made up of the current account, the capital account, and the official transactions account.
- Exchange rates in a perfectly flexible exchange rate system are determined by the supply of and demand for a currency.
- An increase in a country's income increases the demand for foreign currency and leads to a decline in the value of the country's own currency.
- An increase in a country's price level reduces the demand for one's currency and increases the demand for foreign currency and leads to a decline in the value of one's own currency.
- A decrease in a country's interest rates reduces the demand for that country's currency and increases the demand for foreign currency, leading to a decline in the value of one's own currency.
- Increased trade restrictions on imports reduce the demand for foreign currencies, leading to an increase in the value of one's own currency.
- A country can maintain a fixed exchange rate by either directly buying and selling its own currency or adjusting its monetary and fiscal policy to achieve its exchange rate goal.
- It is easier technically for a country to bring the value of its currency down than it is to support its currency.
- It is extraordinarily difficult to correctly estimate the long-run equilibrium exchange rate; one method of doing so is the purchasing power parity approach.

- Fixed exchange rates provide international monetary stability but can create enormous monetary instability if they become unfixed. Fixed exchange rates force governments to make adjustments to meet their international problems.
- Flexible exchange rates allow exchange rates to make incremental changes, but are also subject to large jumps in value as a result of speculation. Flexible exchange rates give governments flexibility in conducting domestic monetary and fiscal policy.
- A common currency creates strong political ties, reduces the cost of trade, facilitates price comparisons, and creates a larger single market. A common currency also makes it impossible to have an independent monetary policy. The 12 countries that share the euro gave up their own national currencies and gave up independent monetary policies.
- The experience of Argentina in the early 2000s demonstrates the difficulties of a fixed exchange rate. Argentina's fixed exchange rate could not hold up against the decline in the value of the currencies of its trading partners or the worldwide recession.

Key Terms

balance of merchandise trade *(773)*
balance of payments *(771)*
balance of trade *(773)*
capital account *(772)*
currency board *(787)*
currency stabilization *(779)*
currency support *(779)*
current account *(772)*
fixed exchange rate *(782)*
flexible exchange rate *(782)*
official reserves *(772)*
official transactions account *(772)*
partially flexible exchange rates *(783)*
purchasing power parity (PPP) *(780)*

Questions for Thought and Review

1. If a country is running a balance of trade deficit, will its current account be in deficit? Why?
2. When someone sends 100 British pounds to a friend in the United States, will this transaction show up on the capital or current account? Why?
3. Support the following statement: "It is best to offset a capital account surplus with a current account deficit."
4. Support the following statement: "It is best to offset a capital account deficit with a current account surplus."
5. In Figure 33-2, a foreign government chooses to maintain an equilibrium market exchange rate of U.S. $1.00 per unit of its own currency. Discuss the implications of the government trying to maintain a higher fixed rate—say at $1.50.
6. If you were the finance minister of Never-Never Land, how would you estimate the long-run exchange rate of your currency, the neverback? Defend your choice as well as discuss its possible failings.
7. Which is preferable: a fixed or a flexible exchange rate? Why?
8. Dr. Dollar Bill believes price stability is the main goal of central bank policy. Is the doctor more likely to prefer fixed or flexible exchange rates? Why?
9. If currency traders expect the government to devalue a currency, what will they likely do? Why?
10. A country eliminates all tariffs. Would you expect that the value of its currency to rise or fall? Explain your answer.
11. Demonstrate, using supply and demand curves, why Argentina had to give up its fixed exchange rate in 2001.
12. Should Canada, the United States, and Mexico adopt a common currency? Why or why not?
13. During the 1995–96 Republican presidential primaries, Patrick Buchanan wrote an editorial in *The Wall Street Journal* beginning, "Since the Nixon era the dollar has fallen 75 percent against the yen, 60 percent against the mark." What trade policies do you suppose he was promoting? He went on to outline a series of tariffs. Agree or disagree with his policies.
14. In an op-ed article, Paul Volcker, former chairman of the Board of Governors of the Federal Reserve, asked the following question: "Is it really worth spending money in the exchange markets, modifying monetary policy, and taking care to balance the budget just to save another percentage or two [of value of exchange rates]?" What's your answer to this question?
15. In mid-1994 the value of the dollar fell sufficiently to warrant coordinated intervention among 17 countries. Still, the dollar went on falling. One economist stated, "[The intervention] was clearly a failure . . . It's a good indication something else has to be done." Why would the United States and foreign countries want to keep up the value of the dollar?

Problems and Exercises

1. Draw the fundamental analysis of the supply and demand for British pound in terms of dollars. Show what will happen to the exchange rate with those curves in response to each of the following events:
   a. The U.K. price level rises.
   b. The U.S. reduces tariffs.
   c. The U.K. economy experiences a boom.
   d. The U.K. interest rates rise.
2. The government of Never-Never Land, after much deliberation, finally decides to switch to a fixed exchange rate policy. It does this because the value of its currency, the neverback, is so high that the trade deficit is enormous. The finance minister fixes the rate at $10 a neverback, which is lower than the equilibrium rate of $20 a neverback.
   a. Discuss the trade or traditional macro policy options that could accomplish this lower exchange rate.
   b. Using the laws of supply and demand, show graphically how possible equilibria are reached.
3. Will the following be suppliers or demanders of U.S. dollars in foreign exchange markets?
   a. A U.S. tourist in Latin America.
   b. A German foreign exchange trader who believes that the dollar exchange rate will fall.
   c. A U.S. foreign exchange trader who believes that the dollar exchange rate will fall.
   d. A Costa Rican tourist in the United States.
   e. A Russian capitalist who wants to protect his wealth from expropriation.
   f. A British investor in the United States.
4. You've been hired as an economic adviser to Yamaichi Foreign Exchange Traders. What buy or sell recommendations for U.S. dollars would you make in response to the following news?
   a. Faster economic growth in the EU.
   b. Expectations of higher interest rates in the United States.
   c. U.S. interest rate rises, but less than expected.
   d. Expected loosening of U.S. monetary policy.
   e. Higher inflationary predictions for the United States.
   f. The government imposes new trade restrictions on imports.
5. State whether the following will show up on the current account or the capital account:
   a. IBM's exports of computers to Japan.
   b. IBM's hiring of a British merchant bank as a consultant.
   c. A foreign national living in the United States repatriates money.
   d. Ford Motor Company's profit in Hungary.
   e. Ford Motor Company uses that Hungarian profit to build a new plant in Hungary.
6. One of the basic laws of economics is the law of one price. It says that given certain assumptions one would expect that if free trade is allowed, the prices of goods in multiple countries should converge. This law underlies purchasing power parity.
   a. Can you list what three of those assumptions likely are?
   b. Should the law of one price hold for labor also? Why or why not?
   c. Should it hold for capital more so or less so than for labor? Why or why not?

Web Questions

1. The Big Mac index is an index of purchasing power parity created by a magazine called *The Economist*. *The Economist* publishes the exchange rate value of various currencies that would make the Big Mac cost the same as in the United States. Go to www.economist.com and search for its Big Mac index. Look up the purchasing power parity of the dollar for five currencies and compare them with the actual exchange rates.
   a. Which currencies were undervalued? Which were overvalued?
   b. What are the shortcomings of the Big Mac index?
   c. If you were to design your own index, what types of goods would you use in your basket of goods? Explain your answer.
   d. How could you check the validity of the Big Mac index?
2. Pick a foreign currency and answer the following questions using www.oanda.com.
   a. What is the name of your country's currency?
   b. In the last year, has the currency risen or fallen in value against the dollar?
   c. Using information from *The Economist* magazine (www.economist.com/countries) about your country, explain why the currency's price rose or fell.
3. Go to the IMF's website at www.imf.org/external/np/exr/center/action/eng/devalue/index.htm to find out how the IMF can help a country facing a shortage of official reserves.
   a. Describe the problem facing the fictitious African economy.
   b. What course of action did you recommend?
   c. What was the outcome of your recommendations?

Answers to Margin Questions

1. The expenditures of a U.S. citizen traveling abroad will show up as a debit on the services account. As tourism or traveling, it is a service. *(773)*
2. Net investment income is the return a country gets on its foreign investment minus the return foreigners get on their investment within a country. A country is a net debtor nation if the value of foreign investment within a country exceeds the value of its investment abroad. A country can be a net debtor nation and still have its net investment income positive if its foreign investment is undervalued at market values (valuation is generally done at book value), or if its foreign investment earns a higher rate of return than foreigners' investment within that country. *(774)*
3. As in the following diagram, an increase in the demand for euros pushes up the exchange rate of euros in terms of dollars. *(775)*

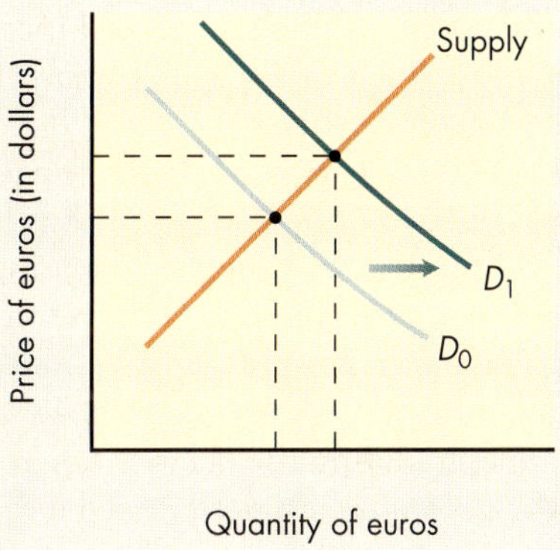

4. An increase in the demand for dollars is the equivalent of an increase in the supply of euros, so an increase in the demand for dollars pushes down the price of euros in terms of dollars, as in the following diagram. *(777)*

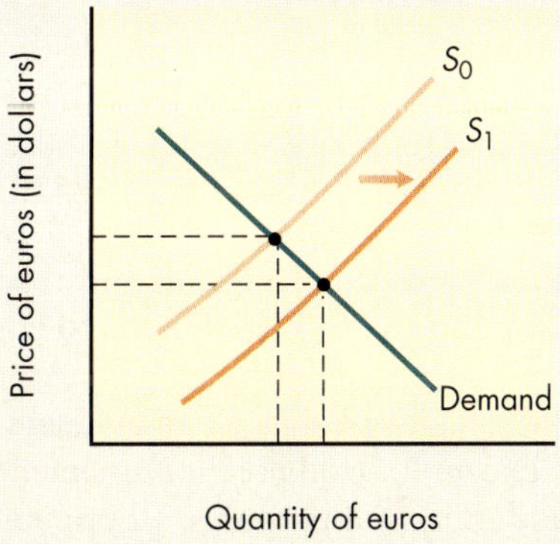

5. In the early 1980s the U.S. government was pursuing tight monetary policy and expansionary fiscal policy. The high interest rate resulted in a strong dollar. Expansionary fiscal policy failed to stimulate domestic demand as export demand fell sharply due to the high dollar. This, accompanied by the high interest rate that had cut investment, drove the economy into a recession with twin deficits, but a strong dollar. *(777)*
6. In the short run, normal market forces have a limited, and possibly even perverse, effect on exchange rates, which is why most governments don't leave determination of exchange rates to the market. *(778)*
7. In general, it would be easier for the United States to push the value of the dollar down because doing so involves the United States buying up foreign currencies, which it can pay for simply by printing more dollars. To push the dollar up requires foreign reserves. *(780)*
8. When a foreign country's purchasing power parity exchange rate is less than the market exchange rate, the price of goods in that country tends to be relatively cheaper than at home. This tends to make traveling there less expensive. *(780)*
9. There is much debate about whether government intervention stabilizes exchange rates—private traders tend to believe it does not; government economists tend to believe that it does. *(785)*
10. People who are holding pesos will try to sell them, increasing the supply of pesos from S_0 to S_1. People who had previously demanded pesos will demand fewer of them, decreasing the demand for pesos from D_0 to D_1. As the figure below shows, the fear of a price decline becomes a self-fulfilling prophecy. *(789)*

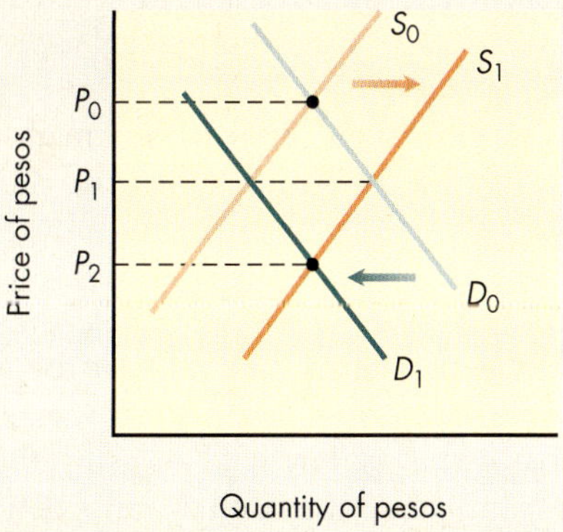

Appendix A

History of Exchange Rate Systems

A good way to give you an idea of how the various exchange rate systems work is to present a brief history of international exchange rate systems.

The Gold Standard: A Fixed Exchange Rate System

Governments played a major role in determining exchange rates until the 1930s. Beginning with the Paris Conference of 1867 and lasting until 1933 (except for the period around World War I), most of the world economies had a system of relatively fixed exchange rates under what was called a **gold standard**—*a system of fixed exchange rates in which the value of currencies was fixed relative to the value of gold and gold was used as the primary reserve asset.*

Under a gold standard, the amount of money a country issued had to be directly tied to gold, either because gold coin served as the currency in a country (as it did in the United States before 1914) or because countries were required by law to have a certain percentage of gold backing their currencies. Gold served as currency or backed all currencies. Each country participating in a gold standard agreed to fix the price of its currency relative to gold. That meant a country would agree to pay a specified amount of gold on demand to anyone who wanted to exchange that country's currency for gold. To do so, each country had to maintain a stockpile of gold. When a country fixed the price of its currency relative to gold, it fixed its currency's price in relation to other currencies as a result of the process of arbitrage.

Under the gold standard, a country made up the difference between the quantity supplied and the quantity demanded of its currency by buying or selling gold to hold the price of its currency fixed in terms of gold. How much a country would need to buy and sell depended on its balance of payments deficit or surplus. If the country ran a surplus in the balance of payments, it was required to sell its currency—that is, buy gold—to stop the value of its currency from rising. If a country ran a deficit, it was required to buy its currency—that is, sell gold—to stop the value of its currency from falling.

The gold standard enabled governments to prevent short-run instability of the exchange rate. If there was a speculative run on its currency, the government would buy its currency with gold, thereby preventing the exchange rate from falling.

But for the gold standard to work, there had to be a method of long-run adjustment; otherwise countries would have run out of gold and would no longer have been able to fulfill their obligations under the gold standard. The **gold specie flow mechanism** was *the long-run adjustment mechanism that maintained the gold standard.* Here's how it worked: Since gold served as official reserves to a country's currency, a balance of payments deficit (and hence a downward pressure on the exchange rate) would result in a flow of gold out of the country and hence a decrease in the country's money supply. That decrease in the money supply would contract the economy, decreasing imports, lowering the country's price level, and increasing the interest rate, all of which would work toward eliminating the balance of payments deficit.

Similarly a country with a balance of payments surplus would experience an inflow of gold. That flow would increase the country's money supply, increasing income (and hence imports), increasing the price level (making imports cheaper and exports more expensive), and lowering the interest rate (increasing capital outflows). These would work toward eliminating the balance of payments surplus.

Thus, the gold standard determined a country's monetary policy and forced it to adjust any international balance of payments disequilibrium. Adjustments to a balance of payments deficit were often politically unpopular; they often led to recessions, which, because the money supply was directly tied to gold, the government couldn't try to offset with expansionary monetary policy.

The gold specie flow mechanism was called into play in the United States in late 1931 when the Federal Reserve, in response to a shrinking U.S. gold supply, decreased the amount of money in the U.S. economy, deepening the depression that had begun in 1929. The government's domestic goals and responsibilities conflicted with its international goals and responsibilities.

That conflict, which was rooted in the aftereffects of World War I and the Depression, led to partial abandonment of the gold standard in 1933. At that time the United States made it illegal for individual U.S. citizens to own gold. Except for gold used for ornamental and certain medical and industrial purposes, all privately owned gold had to be sold to the government. Dollar bills were no longer backed by gold in the sense that U.S. citizens could exchange dollars for a prespecified amount of gold. Instead dollar bills were backed by silver, which meant that any U.S. citizen could change dollars for a prespecified amount of silver. In the late 1960s that changed also. Since that time, for U.S. residents, dollars have been backed only by trust in the soundness of the U.S. economy.

Gold continued to serve, at least partially, as international backing for U.S. currency. That is, other countries could still exchange dollars for gold. However in 1971, in response to another conflict between international and domestic goals, the United States totally cut off the relationship between dollars and gold. After that a dollar could be redeemed only for another dollar, whether it was a U.S. citizen or a foreign government who wanted to redeem the dollar.

The Bretton Woods System: A Fixed Exchange Rate System

As World War II was coming to an end, the United States and its allies met to establish a new international economic order. After much wrangling they agreed upon a system called the **Bretton Woods system,** *an agreement about fixed exchange rates that governed international financial relationships from the period after the end of World War II until 1971*. It was named after the resort in New Hampshire where the meeting that set up the system was held.

The Bretton Woods system established the International Monetary Fund (IMF) to oversee the international economic order. The IMF was empowered to arrange short-term loans between countries. The Bretton Woods system also established the World Bank, which was empowered to make longer-term loans to developing countries. Today the World Bank and IMF continue their central roles in international financial affairs.

The Bretton Woods system was based on mutual agreements about what countries would do when experiencing balance of payments surpluses or deficits. It was essentially a fixed exchange rate system. For example, under the Bretton Woods system, the exchange rate of the dollar for the British pound was set at slightly over $4 to the pound.

The Bretton Woods system was not based on a gold standard. When countries experienced a balance of payments surplus or deficit, they did not necessarily buy or sell gold to stabilize the price of their currency. Instead they bought and sold other currencies. To ensure that participating countries would have sufficient reserves, they established a stabilization fund from which a country could obtain a short-term loan. It was hoped that this stabilization fund would be sufficient to handle all short-run adjustments that did not reflect fundamental imbalances.

In those cases where a misalignment of exchange rate was determined to be fundamental, the countries involved agreed that they would adjust their exchange rates. The IMF was empowered to oversee an orderly adjustment. It could authorize a country to make a one-time adjustment of up to 10 percent without obtaining formal approval from the IMF's board of directors. After a country had used its one-time adjustment, formal approval was necessary for any change greater than 1 percent.

The Bretton Woods system reflected the underlying political and economic realities of the post–World War II period in which it was set up. European economies were devastated; the U.S. economy was strong. To rebuild, Europe was going to have to import U.S. equipment and borrow large amounts from the United States. There was serious concern over how high the value of the dollar would rise and how low the value of European currencies would fall in a free market exchange. The establishment of fixed exchange rates set limits on currencies' relative movements; the exchange rates that were chosen helped provide for the rebuilding of Europe.

In addition, the Bretton Woods system provided mechanisms for long-term loans from the United States to Europe that could help sustain those fixed exchange rates. The loans also eliminated the possibility of competitive depreciation of currencies, in which each country tries to stimulate its exports by lowering the relative value of its currency.

One difficulty with the Bretton Woods system was a shortage of official reserves and international liquidity. To offset that shortage, the IMF was empowered to create *a type of international money* called **special drawing rights (SDRs).** But SDRs never became established as an international currency and the U.S. dollar kept serving as official reserves for individuals and countries. To get the dollars to foreigners, the United States had to run a deficit in its current account. Since countries could exchange the dollar for gold at a fixed price, the use of dollars as a reserve currency meant that, under the Bretton Woods system, the world was on a gold standard once removed.

The number of dollars held by foreigners grew enormously in the 1960s. By the early 1970s, those dollars far exceeded in value the amount of gold the United States had. Most countries accepted this situation; even though they could legally demand gold for their dollars, they did not. But Charles de Gaulle, the nationalistic president of France, wasn't pleased with the U.S. domination of international affairs at that time. He believed Europe deserved a much more prominent position. He demanded gold for the dollars held by the French central bank, knowing that the United States didn't have enough gold to meet his demand. As a result of his and other countries' demands, on August 15, 1971, the United States ended its policy of exchanging gold for dollars at $35 per ounce. With that change, the Bretton Woods system was dead.

The Present U.S. System: A Partially Flexible Exchange Rate System

International monetary affairs were much in the news in the early 1970s as countries groped for a new exchange rate system. The makeshift system finally agreed on involved partially flexible exchange rates. Most Western countries' exchange rates are allowed to fluctuate, although at various times governments buy or sell their own currencies to affect the exchange rate.

Under the present partially flexible exchange rates system, countries must continually decide when a balance of payments surplus or deficit is a temporary phenomenon and when it is a signal of a fundamental imbalance. If they believe the situation is temporary, they enter into the foreign exchange market to hold their exchange rate at what they believe is an appropriate level. If, however, they believe that the balance of payments imbalance is a fundamental one, they let the exchange rate rise or fall.

While most Western countries' exchange rates are partially flexible, certain countries have agreed to fixed exchange rates of their currencies in relation to rates of a group of certain other currencies. For example, a group of European Union countries adopted irreversible fixed exchange rates among their currencies, by electing to have one currency—the euro, which was introduced in 2002. Other currencies are fixed relative to the dollar.

Deciding what is, and what is not, a fundamental imbalance is complicated, and such decisions are considered at numerous international conferences held under the auspices of the IMF or governments. A number of organizations such as the Group of Eight focus much discussion on this issue. Often the various countries meet and agree, formally or informally, on acceptable ranges of exchange rates. Thus, while the present system is one of partially flexible exchange rates, the range of flexibility is limited.

Key Terms

Bretton Woods system *(795)*

gold specie flow mechanism *(794)*

gold standard *(794)*

special drawing rights (SDRs) *(795)*

MONETARY AND FISCAL POLICY IN A GLOBAL SETTING

34

The actual rate of exchange is largely governed by the expected behavior of the country's monetary authority.

—*Dennis Robertson*

After reading this chapter, you should be able to:

- Discuss why there is significant debate about what U.S. international goals should be.
- Explain how a country influences its exchange rate by using monetary or fiscal policy.
- Describe the paths through which monetary policy affects exchange rates and the trade balance.
- Explain the paths through which fiscal policy affects exchange rates and the trade balance.
- Summarize the reasons why governments try to coordinate their monetary and fiscal policies.
- State the potential problem of internationalizing a country's debt.

In the last chapter we learned about the balance of payments and exchange rates. We saw how a country can influence exchange rates directly—by intervening in foreign exchange markets—or indirectly, through trade policy. We also saw how a trade surplus or deficit could exist if the other two international accounts offset that surplus. In this chapter we put that knowledge to work, exploring the policy issues surrounding international goals in reference to the standard macro tools of monetary and fiscal policy.

THE AMBIGUOUS INTERNATIONAL GOALS OF MACROECONOMIC POLICY

Macroeconomic international goals are less straightforward than domestic goals. There is general agreement about the domestic goals of macroeconomic policy: We want low inflation, low unemployment, and high growth. There's far less agreement on what a country's international goals should be.

Most economists agree that the international goal of U.S. macroeconomic policy is to maintain the U.S. position in the world economy. But there's enormous debate about what achieving that goal means. Do we want a high or a low exchange rate? Do we want a balance of trade surplus? Or would it be better to have a balance of trade deficit? Or should we not even pay attention to the balance of trade? Let's consider the exchange rate goal first.

THE EXCHANGE RATE GOAL

Figure 34-1(a) shows the U.S. exchange rate over the last 30 years. You can see how the U.S. exchange rate has fluctuated significantly over that period. There is a debate over whether a country should have a high or a low exchange rate. A high exchange rate for the dollar makes foreign currencies cheaper, lowering the price of imports. Lowering import prices places competitive pressure on U.S. firms and helps to hold down inflation. All of this benefits U.S. residents' living standard. But a high exchange rate encourages imports and discourages exports. In doing so, it can cause a balance of trade deficit that can exert a contractionary effect

Figure 34-1 (a and b) The Value of the Dollar and the Trade Balance
In (**a**) you can see that the value of the U.S. dollar has fluctuated significantly over the last 30 years. Panel (**b**) shows that the United States has had trade deficits nearly every year since 1970.

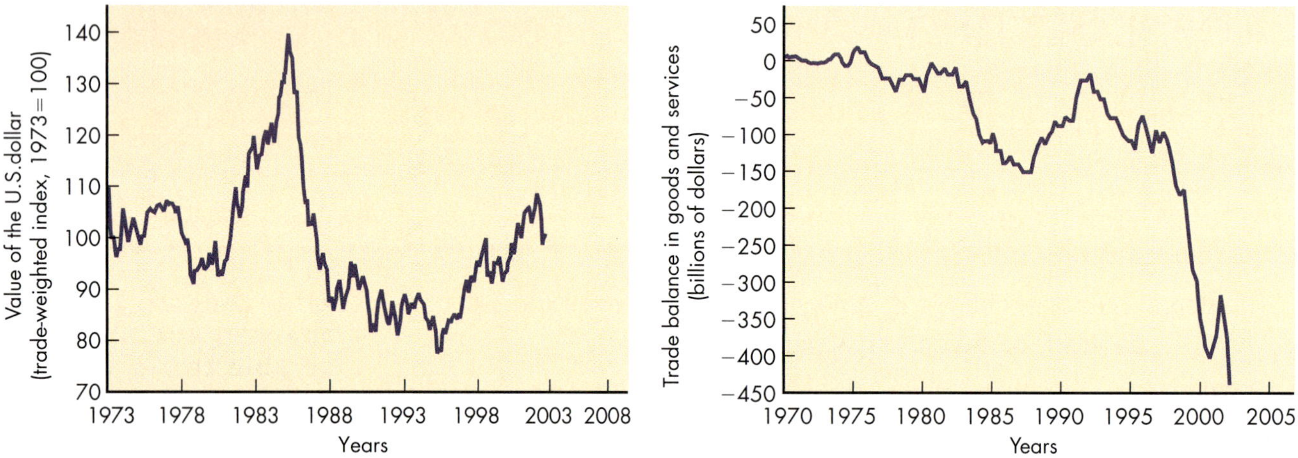

(a) U.S. dollar **(b) U.S. trade balance**

on the economy by decreasing aggregate demand for U.S. output. So a high exchange rate also has a cost to U.S. residents.

Q-1 What effect does a low exchange rate have on a country's exports and imports?

A low exchange rate has the opposite effect. It makes imports more expensive and exports cheaper, and it can contribute to inflationary pressure. But, by encouraging exports and discouraging imports, it can cause a balance of trade surplus and exert an expansionary effect on the economy.

Exchange rates have conflicting effects and, depending on the state of the economy, there are arguments both for high and low exchange rates.

Many economists argue that a country should have no exchange rate policy because exchange rates are market-determined prices that are best left to the market. These economists question whether the government should even worry about the effect of monetary policy and fiscal policy on exchange rates. According to them, government should simply accept whatever exchange rate exists and not consider it in its conduct of monetary and fiscal policies.

The Trade Balance Goal

The trade balance is the difference between a country's exports and imports.

Figure 34-1(b) shows the U.S. trade balance over the past 30 years. You can see that the United States has consistently run a trade deficit over that period, and that that trade deficit has generally increased. A deficit in the trade balance (the difference between imports and exports) means that, as a country, we're consuming more than we're producing. Imports exceed exports, so we're consuming more than we could if we didn't run a deficit. A surplus in the trade balance means that exports exceed imports—we're producing more than we're consuming. Since consuming more than we otherwise could is kind of nice, it might seem that a trade deficit is preferred to a trade surplus.

But wait. A trade deficit isn't without costs, and a trade surplus isn't without benefits. We pay for a trade deficit by selling off U.S. assets to foreigners—by selling U.S. companies, factories, land, and buildings to foreigners, or selling them financial assets such as U.S. dollars, stocks, and bonds. All the future interest and profits on these assets will go to foreigners, not U.S. citizens. That means eventually, sometime in the future, we will have to produce more than we consume so we can pay them *their* profit and

The U.S. Trade Deficit and the Value of the Dollar

Applying the Tools

The continued U.S. trade deficit from the 1970s into the early 2000s has confounded many analysts. Why has it remained so high? Why are other countries willing to give the United States many more real goods and services than they require in return? The answer is that they want to buy U.S. assets. There are a number of reasons why. First, the value of U.S. assets has increased. For example, Japan's stock market and real estate markets were falling while the U.S. stock market was rising, which gave Japanese investors a strong incentive to invest in the United States. Second, the United States is considered a safe haven—a solid economy that is safer than any other. If you want safety, you buy U.S. government bonds. At some point, however, the demand for U.S. assets is expected to end and the U.S. trade deficit is expected to disappear.

Many observers feel that the time for this to happen is soon. There are three reasons: First, the terrorist attacks on the World Trade Center and the Pentagon in 2001 showed that the United States was vulnerable. The United States is not as safe from attacks as it was once believed to be. Second, the fall in the value of the U.S. stock market and the continued slow, or no, growth in stock prices have begun to make foreign markets more attractive to investors. Third, the creation of the euro has given international investors another major currency in which to hold reserves.

If these analysts are correct, we should see a continued fall in the value of the dollar, which will eventually lower the relative price of U.S. exports and increase the cost of imports. Because people don't want to hold assets in currencies whose values are falling, this fall could be much more sudden than policymakers would like, leaving them with serious questions about whether they can do anything to prevent it.

interest on *their* assets. Thus, while in the short run a trade deficit allows more current consumption, in the long run it presents potential problems.

As long as a country can borrow, or sell assets, a country can have a trade deficit. But if a country runs a trade deficit year after year, eventually the long run will arrive and the country will run out of assets to sell and run out of other countries from whom to borrow. When that happens, the trade deficit problem must be faced.

The debate about whether a trade deficit should be of concern to policymakers involves whether these long-run effects should be anticipated and faced before they happen.

Running a trade deficit is good in the short run but presents problems in the long run.

Opinions differ greatly. Some say not to worry—just accept what's happening. These "not-to-worry" economists argue that the trade deficit will end when U.S. citizens don't want to borrow from foreigners anymore and foreigners don't want to buy any more of our assets. They argue that the inflow of financial capital (money coming into the United States to buy our assets) from foreigners is financing new investment that will make the U.S. economy strong enough in the long run to reverse the trade deficit without serious disruption to the U.S. economy. So why deal with the trade deficit now, when it will take care of itself in the future?

Q-2 Why do some people argue that we should not worry about a trade deficit?

Others argue that, yes, the trade deficit will eventually take care of itself, but the accompanying economic distress will be great. By dealing with the problem now, the United States can avoid a highly unpleasant solution in the future.

Both views are reasonable, which is why there's no consensus on what a country's trade balance goal should be.

International versus Domestic Goals

Domestic goals generally dominate international goals.

In the real world, when there's debate about a goal, that goal generally gets far less weight than goals about which there's general agreement. Since there's general agreement about our country's domestic goals (low inflation, low unemployment, and high growth), domestic goals generally dominate the U.S. political agenda.

Even if there weren't uncertainty about a country's international goals, domestic goals would likely dominate the political agenda. The reason is that inflation, unemployment, and growth affect a country's citizens directly. Trade deficits and exchange rates affect them indirectly—and in politics, indirect effects take a back seat.

Web Note 34.1
Putting Exchange Rates First

Often a country responds to an international goal only when the international community forces it to do so. For example, in the 1980s when Brazil couldn't borrow any more money from other countries, it reluctantly made resolving its trade deficit a key goal. Similarly, when other countries threatened to limit Japanese imports, Japan took steps to increase the value of the yen and decrease its trade surplus. When a country is forced to face certain economic facts, international goals can become its primary goals. As countries become more economically integrated, these pressures from other countries become more important.

Monetary Policy and Fiscal Policy with Fixed Exchange Rates

Web Note 34.2
Foreign Exchange Futures

How fast a country must respond to international pressure depends on the exchange rate regime it follows. If an economy sets fixed exchange rates, its monetary and fiscal policies are much more restricted than they are with flexible exchange rates. The reason is that the amount of currency stabilization that can be achieved with direct intervention is generally quite small, since a country's foreign reserves are limited. When this is the case, to keep its currency fixed at the desirable level it must adjust the economy to the exchange rate. Specifically, it must undertake policies that will change either the private supply of its currency or the private demand for its currency. It can do so by traditional macro policy—monetary and fiscal policy—influencing the economy, or by trade policy to affect the level of exports and imports.

Q-3 If a country wants to fix its exchange rate at a rate that is higher than the market rate, what monetary or fiscal policy must it use?

To see the issues involved, consider the case of Europe that we examined in the previous chapter. That case is shown in Figure 34-2. Europe's problem here is that it wants the exchange rate for the euro to be \$1.00, not 80 cents as it currently is. The EU has three options for raising the value of the euro: decrease the private supply of euros (shifting the supply curve in from S_0 to S_1), increase the private demand for euros (shifting the demand curve out from D_0 to D_1), or use some combination of the two. Let's see how it could accomplish its goal with monetary or fiscal policy.

Figure 34-2 Targeting an Exchange Rate with Monetary and Fiscal Policy

To increase the exchange rate value of the euro from 80 cents per euro to \$1.00 per euro, the European Central Bank (ECB) will have to either shift the supply curve for euros from S_0 to S_1 or shift the demand curve for euros from D_0 to D_1. To increase the private demand for euros, the ECB could increase interest rates by running contractionary monetary policy. To decrease the private supply of euros the European Union could induce a recession by running either contractionary monetary or contractionary fiscal policy.

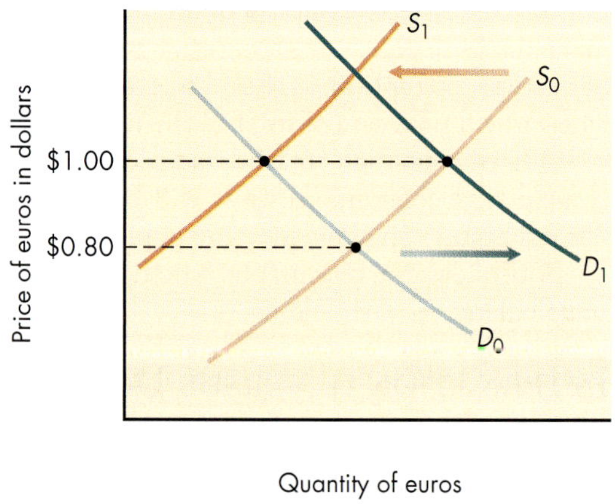

Increase the Private Demand for Euros via Contractionary Monetary Policy

To increase the demand for euros, the EU must create policies that increase the private foreign demand for EU assets, or for EU goods and services. In the short run the European Central Bank (ECB) can increase the interest rate by running contractionary monetary policy. A higher interest rate increases the foreign demand for the EU's interest-bearing assets. The problem with this approach is that to maintain an exchange rate at a certain level, a country must give up any attempt to target its interest rate to achieve domestic goals. To put it another way: A country can achieve an interest rate target or an exchange rate target, but generally it cannot achieve both at the same time.

Decrease the Private Supply of Euros via Contractionary Monetary and Fiscal Policy

To decrease the private supply of euros that comes from imports, the ECB can run contractionary monetary and fiscal policy, slowing down the domestic economy and inducing a recession. This recession decreases the demand for imports and thereby decreases the private supply of euros. Governments are usually loath to use contractionary policy because politically induced recessions are not popular.

Monetary and Fiscal Policy with Flexible or Partially Flexible Exchange Rate Regimes

It is because of the constraints that fixed exchange rates place on domestic monetary and fiscal policy that many countries choose flexible, or at least partially flexible, exchange rate regimes. In this section we shall take an in-depth look at the effect of monetary and fiscal policy on the exchange rate and the trade balance. Those effects often can significantly influence the choice of policies. We begin by considering the effect of monetary policy.

Monetary Policy's Effect on Exchange Rates

Monetary policy affects exchange rates in three primary ways: (1) through its effect on the interest rate, (2) through its effect on income, and (3) through its effect on price levels and inflation.

The Effect on Exchange Rates via Interest Rates Expansionary monetary policy pushes down the U.S. interest rate, which decreases the financial capital inflow into the United States, decreasing the demand for dollars, pushing down the value of the dollar, and decreasing the U.S. exchange rate via the interest rate path. Contractionary monetary policy does the opposite. It raises the U.S. interest rate, which tends to bring in financial capital flows from abroad, increasing the demand for dollars, increasing the value of the dollar, and increasing the U.S. exchange rate. This interest rate effect is the dominant short-run effect, and it often overwhelms the other effects.

Q-4 What effect does the lowering of a country's interest rates have on exchange rates?

The interest rate effect on exchange rates is the dominant short-run effect.

To see why these effects take place, consider a person in Japan in the early 2000s, when the Japanese interest rate was close to 0 percent. He or she reasoned, "Why should I earn 0 percent return in Japan? I'll save (buy some financial assets) in the United States where I'll earn 3 percent." If the U.S. interest rate goes up due to contraction in the money supply, other things equal, the advantage of holding one's financial assets in the United States will become even greater and more people will want to save here. People in Japan hold yen, not dollars, so in order to save in the United States they must buy dollars. Thus, a rise in U.S. interest rates increases demand for dollars and, in terms of yen, pushes up the U.S. exchange rate. This example illustrates that it is relative interest rates that govern the flow of financial capital.

Countries are continually taking into account the effect of monetary policy on exchange rates. For example, in the mid-1990s Taiwan kept its money supply tight, raising its interest rates to keep the new Taiwan dollar high. In 1997 Taiwan cut reserve ratios; interest rates fell and the value of the new Taiwan dollar fell.

The Effect on Exchange Rates via Income Monetary policy also affects income in a country. As money supply rises, income expands; when money supply falls, income contracts.[1] This effect on income provides another way in which the money supply affects the exchange rate. As we saw earlier, when income rises, imports rise while exports are unaffected. To buy foreign products, U.S. citizens need foreign currency, which they must buy with dollars. So when U.S. imports rise, the supply of dollars to the foreign exchange market increases as U.S. citizens sell dollars to buy foreign currencies to pay for those imports. This decreases the dollar exchange rate. This effect through income and imports provides a second path through which monetary policy affects the exchange rate: Expansionary monetary policy causes U.S. income to rise, imports to rise, and the U.S. exchange rate to fall via the income path. Contractionary monetary policy causes U.S. income to fall, imports to fall, and the U.S. exchange rate to rise via the income path.

Q-5 What effect would contractionary monetary policy have on a country's exchange rates via the income and price routes?

The Effect on Exchange Rates via Price Levels A third way in which monetary policy can affect exchange rates is through its effect on prices in a country. Expansionary monetary policy pushes the U.S. price level up. As the U.S. price level rises relative to foreign prices, U.S. exports become more expensive, and goods the United States imports become relatively cheaper, decreasing U.S. competitiveness. This increases demand for foreign currencies and decreases demand for dollars. Thus, via the price path, expansionary monetary policy pushes down the dollar's value for the same reason that an expansion in income pushes it down.

Contractionary monetary policy puts downward pressure on the U.S. price level and slows down any existing inflation. As the U.S. price level falls relative to foreign prices, U.S. exports become more competitive and the goods the United States imports relatively more expensive. Thus, contractionary monetary policy pushes up the value of the dollar via the price path.

The Net Effect of Monetary Policy on Exchange Rates Notice that all these effects of monetary policy on exchange rates are in the same direction. Expansionary monetary policy pushes a country's exchange rate down; contractionary monetary policy pushes a country's exchange rate up. Summarizing these effects, we have the following relationships for expansionary and contractionary monetary policy:

---

[1]When there's inflation, it's the rate of money supply growth relative to the rate of inflation that's important. If inflation is 10 percent and money supply growth is 10 percent, the rate of increase in the real money supply is zero. If money supply growth falls to, say, 5 percent while inflation stays at 10 percent, there will be a contractionary effect on the real economy.

Expansionary monetary policy

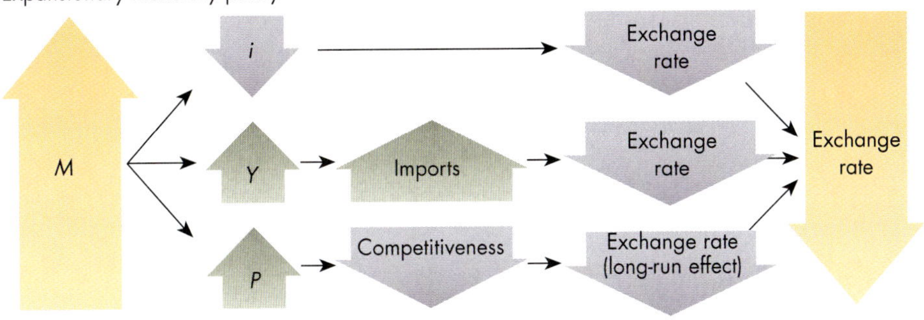

Monetary policy affects exchange rates through the interest rate path, the income path, and the price level path, as shown in the accompanying diagram.

Contractionary monetary policy

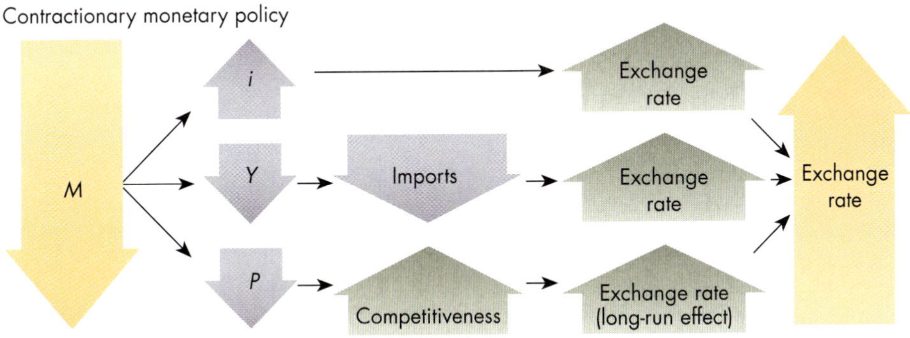

There are, of course, many provisos to the relationship between monetary policy and the exchange rate. For example, as the price of imports goes up, there is some inflationary pressure from that rise in price and hence some pressure for the price level to rise as well as fall. Monetary policy affects exchange rates in subtle ways, but if an economist had to give a quick answer to what effect monetary policy would have on exchange rates it would be:

> Expansionary monetary policy lowers exchange rates. It decreases the relative value of a country's currency.
>
> Contractionary monetary policy increases exchange rates. It increases the relative value of a country's currency.

Expansionary monetary policy lowers exchange rates. It decreases the relative value of a country's currency.

Contractionary monetary policy increases exchange rates. It increases the relative value of a country's currency.

Monetary Policy's Effect on the Trade Balance

When a country's international trade balance is negative (in deficit), the country is importing more than it is exporting. When a country's international trade balance is positive (in surplus), the country is exporting more than it is importing.

Monetary policy affects the trade balance primarily through its effect on income. Specifically, expansionary monetary policy increases income. When income rises, imports rise, while exports are unaffected. As imports rise, the trade balance shifts in the direction of deficit. So expansionary monetary policy shifts the trade balance toward a deficit.

Contractionary policy works in the opposite direction. It decreases income. When income falls, imports fall (while exports are unaffected), so the trade balance shifts in the direction of surplus. Thus, expansionary monetary policy increases the trade deficit; contractionary monetary policy decreases the trade deficit.

Q-6 What effect will contractionary monetary policy have on the trade balance?

Monetary policy will also affect the trade balance in a variety of other ways—for example, through its effect on the price level and the exchange rate. These other effects tend to be more long-run effects and tend to offset one another. So we will not consider them here. So, while many complications can enter the trade balance picture, most economists would summarize monetary policy's short-run effect on the trade balance as follows:

Expansionary monetary policy makes a trade deficit larger.

Contractionary monetary policy makes a trade deficit smaller.

Expansionary monetary policy makes a trade deficit larger.

Contractionary monetary policy makes a trade deficit smaller.

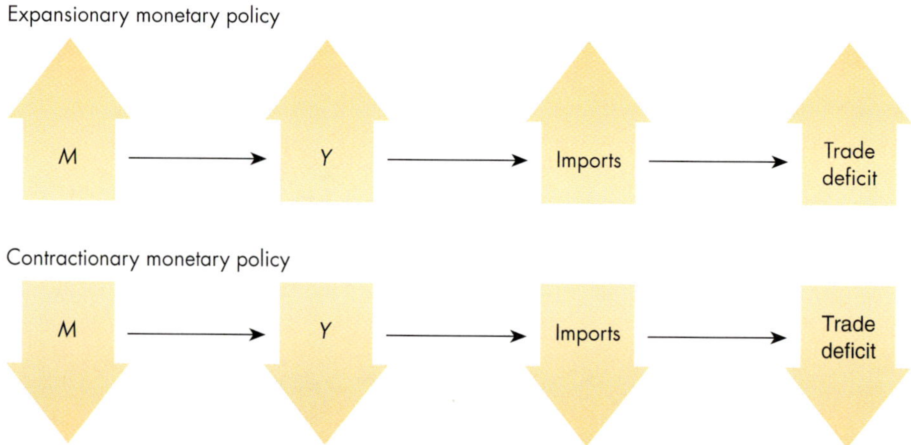

Fiscal Policy's Effect on Exchange Rates

Now we'll consider fiscal policy's effect on exchange rates. Fiscal policy, like monetary policy, affects exchange rates via three paths: income, price, and interest rates. Let's begin with its effect through income.

The Effect on Exchange Rates via Income Expansionary fiscal policy expands income and therefore increases imports, increasing the trade deficit and lowering the exchange rate. Contractionary fiscal policy contracts income, thereby decreasing imports and increasing the exchange rate. These effects of expansionary and contractionary fiscal policies via the income path are similar to the effects of monetary policy, so if it's not intuitively clear to you why the effect is what it is, it may be worthwhile to review the slightly more complete discussion of monetary policy's effect presented previously.

Q-7 What effect does a higher price level have on the exchange rate?

The Effect on Exchange Rates via Price Levels Let's turn to the effect of fiscal policy on exchange rates through prices. Expansionary fiscal policy increases aggregate demand and increases prices of a country's exports; hence it decreases the competitiveness of a country's exports, which pushes down the exchange rate. Contractionary fiscal policy works in the opposite direction. These are the same effects that monetary policy had. And, as was the case with monetary policy, the price path is a long-run effect.

The Effect on Exchange Rates via Interest Rates Fiscal policy's effect on the exchange rate via the interest rate path is different from monetary policy's effect. Let's first consider the effect of expansionary fiscal policy. Whereas expansionary monetary policy lowers the interest rate, expansionary fiscal policy raises interest rates because the government sells bonds to finance that deficit. The higher U.S. interest rate causes foreign capital to flow into the United States, which pushes up the U.S. exchange rate. Therefore expansionary fiscal policy's effect on exchange rates via the interest rate effect is to push up a country's exchange rate.

Contractionary fiscal policy decreases interest rates since it reduces the bond financing of that deficit. Lower U.S. interest rates cause capital to flow out of the United States, which pushes down the U.S. exchange rate. Thus, the U.S. government budget surplus in the late 1990s put downward pressure on the interest rate and downward pressure on the exchange rate value of the dollar.

The Net Effect of Fiscal Policy on Exchange Rates Of these three effects, the interest rate effect and the income effect are both short-run effects. These two work in opposite directions, so the net effect of fiscal policy on the exchange rate is ambiguous. The following diagram summarizes these three effects.

Q-8 What is the net effect of expansionary fiscal policy on the exchange rate?

Fiscal policy affects exchange rates through the income path, the interest rate path, and the price level path, as shown in the accompanying diagram.

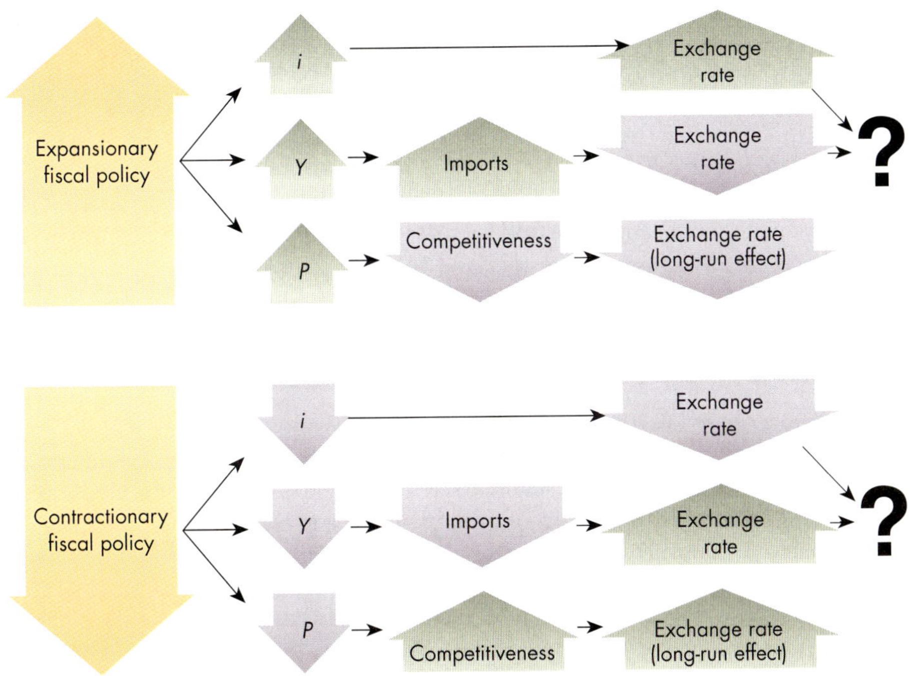

As you can see, it's unclear what the effect of expansionary or contractionary fiscal policy will be on exchange rates.

Fiscal Policy's Effect on the Trade Deficit

Fiscal policy, like monetary policy, works on the trade deficit primarily through its effects on income. (Again, there are other paths by which fiscal policy affects the trade deficit, but this one is the largest.) So if asked for a quick answer, economists would say that contractionary fiscal policy decreases a trade deficit.

Contractionary fiscal policy decreases a trade deficit.

Summarizing the effects of expansionary and contractionary fiscal policy schematically, we have:

Q-9 What is the effect of expansionary fiscal policy on the trade deficit?

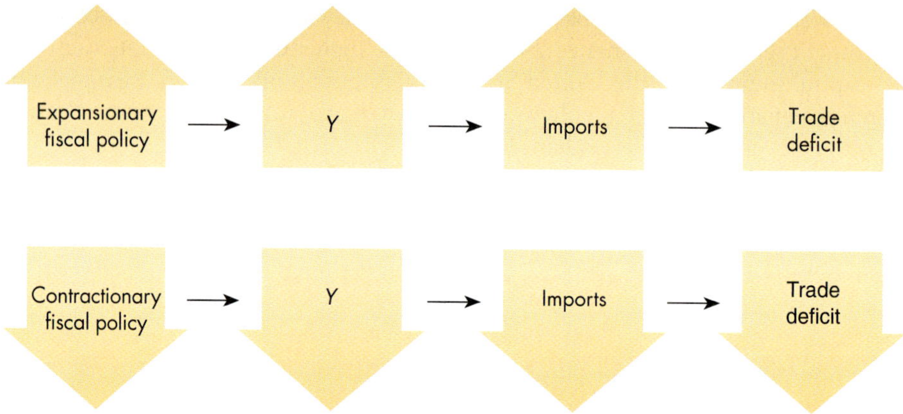

International Phenomena and Domestic Goals

Web Note 34.3 Coordinating Policies

So far, we've focused on the effect of monetary and fiscal policies on international goals. But often the effect is the other way around: International phenomena change and have significant influences on the domestic economy and on the ability to achieve domestic goals.

For example, say that Japan ran contractionary monetary policy. That would increase the Japanese exchange rate and increase Japan's trade surplus, which means it would decrease the U.S. exchange rate and increase the U.S. trade deficit, both of which would affect U.S. domestic goals.

International Monetary and Fiscal Coordination

Governments try to coordinate their monetary and fiscal policies because their economies are interdependent.

Unless forced to do so because of international pressures, most countries don't let international goals guide their macroeconomic policy. But for every effect that monetary and fiscal policies have on a country's exchange rates and trade balance, there's an equal and opposite effect on the combination of other countries' exchange rates and trade balances. When one country's exchange rate goes up, by definition another country's exchange rate must go down. Similarly, when one country's balance of trade is in surplus, another's must be in deficit. This interconnection means that other countries' fiscal and monetary policies affect the United States, while U.S. fiscal and monetary policies affect other countries, so pressure to coordinate policies is considerable.

Coordination Is a Two-Way Street

Q-10 If domestic problems call for expansionary monetary policy and international problems call for contractionary monetary policy, what policy will a country likely adopt?

Coordination, of course, works both ways. If other countries are to take the U.S. economy's needs into account, the United States must take other countries' needs into account in determining its goals. Say, for example, the U.S. economy is going into a recession. This domestic problem calls for expansionary monetary policy. But expansionary monetary policy will increase U.S. income and U.S. imports and lower the value of the dollar. Say that, internationally, the United States has agreed that it must work toward eliminating the U.S. trade deficit in the short run. Does it forsake its domestic goals? Or does it forsake its international commitment?

Each country will likely do what's best for the world economy as long as it's also best for itself.

There's no one right answer to those questions. It depends on political judgments (how long until the next election?), judgments about what foreign countries can do if

Monetary and Fiscal Policy's Effect on International Goals

Knowing the Tools

The effect of expansionary monetary and fiscal policy on international goals in the short run is summarized in the diagram on the right. In the short run, expansionary monetary policy tends to increase a trade deficit and decrease the exchange rate. Expansionary fiscal policy tends to increase the trade deficit. Its effect on the exchange rate is ambiguous. The effects of contractionary policy work in the opposite direction.

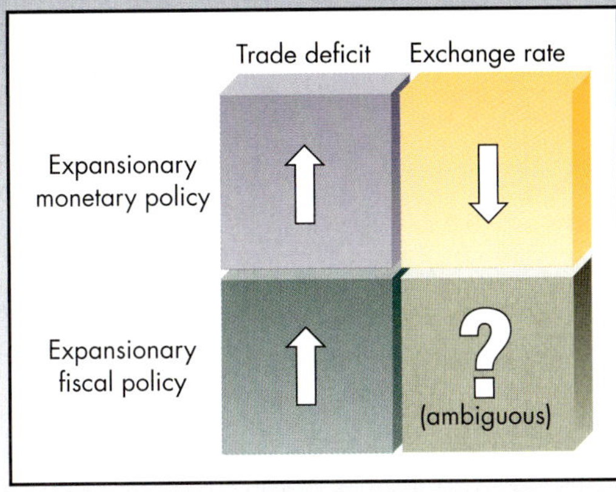

the United States doesn't meet its international commitments, and similar judgments by foreign countries about the United States.

Despite the complications, the above discussion gives you an understanding of many events that may have previously seemed incomprehensible. To show you the relevance of what I have said above about international considerations, let's look at two situations.

The first is an example from the last chapter: Argentina in the early 2000s. In the late 1980s Argentina established a currency board with a promise to maintain parity between the peso and the U.S. dollar forever. Numerous international investors relied on that promise. In the late 1990s, the Argentinean economy went into recession and domestic political pressures called for expansionary aggregate demand policy. Maintaining the fixed exchange rate required contractionary aggregate demand policy. The internal political pressures won, and Argentina abandoned its fixed exchange rate in early 2002.

The second concerns Japan in 1993 and early 1994. Japan was experiencing a recession, in part because its tight monetary policy had pushed up interest rates and hence pushed up the exchange rate for the yen. Other countries, especially the United States and European countries, put enormous pressure on Japan to run expansionary fiscal policy, which would keep the relative value of the yen high but simultaneously increase Japanese income, and hence Japanese demand for imports. In response, the Japanese ran expansionary fiscal policy and this helped to keep the value of the yen higher than it otherwise would have been. Soon thereafter, Japan simultaneously ran expansionary monetary policy, thereby lowering the interest rate and the exchange rate. There are many more examples, but these two should give you a good sense of the relevance of the issues.

Crowding Out and International Considerations

As a final topic in this chapter, let's reconsider the issue of crowding out that we considered in an earlier chapter, only this time we'll take into account international considerations. Say a government is running a budget deficit, and that the central bank has decided it won't increase the money supply to help finance the deficit. (This happened in the 1980s with the Fed and the U.S. government.) What will be the result?

Table 34-1 Selecting Policies to Achieve Goals
This table shows how alternative monetary and fiscal policies can be used to achieve the goal of a lower exchange rate and the goal of a lower trade deficit.

International Goal	Policy Alternatives
Lower exchange rate	Contractionary foreign monetary policy Expansionary domestic monetary policy
Lower trade deficit	Contractionary domestic fiscal policy Expansionary foreign fiscal policy Contractionary domestic monetary policy Expansionary foreign monetary policy

The basic idea of crowding out is that the budget deficit will cause the interest rate to go up. But wait. There's another way to avoid the crowding out that results from financing the deficit: Foreigners could buy the debt at the existing interest rate. This is called *internationalizing the debt,* and is what happened to the U.S. economy in the late 1980s.

In the 1980s, there were massive inflows to the United States of financial capital from abroad. These inflows held down the U.S. interest rate even as the federal government ran large budget deficits. Thus, those large deficits didn't push up interest rates because foreigners, not U.S. citizens, were buying U.S. debt.

While internationalizing a country's debt may help in the short run, in the long run it presents potential problems since foreign ownership of a country's debts means the country must pay interest to those foreign countries and that debt may come due.

But, as we discussed, internationalization of the U.S. debt is not costless. While it helps in the short run, it presents problems in the long run. Today about 40 percent of privately held U.S. government debt is held by foreigners. Foreign ownership of U.S. debt means that the United States must pay foreigners interest each year on that debt. To do so, the United States must export more than it imports, which means that the United States must consume less than it produces at some time in the future to pay for the trade deficits it's running now. As you can see, the issues become complicated quickly.

Conclusion

Let's conclude our discussion by looking at the issues from a different perspective. Throughout this chapter I have organized the discussion around the effects of policies. Another way to organize the discussion would have been around goals, and to show how alternative policies will achieve those international goals. Table 34-1 does this, and will serve as a useful review of the chapter. It shows alternative policies that will achieve specified goals. You can see in the table why coordination of monetary and fiscal policies is much in the news, since a foreign country's policy can eliminate, or reduce the need for, domestic policies to be undertaken.

This brief chapter in no way exhausted the international topics relevant to monetary and fiscal policy. Countries use many policies to effect their international goals. But this chapter has, I hope, made you very aware of the international dimensions of our economic goals, and of how monetary and fiscal policies affect those goals. That awareness is absolutely necessary to discuss real-world macroeconomic policies.

Summary

- The international goals of a country are often in dispute.
- Domestic goals generally dominate international goals, but countries often respond to an international goal when forced to do so by other countries.
- To raise the value of one's currency a country can either increase private demand through contractionary monetary policy or decrease private supply through contractionary monetary and fiscal policy.
- Expansionary monetary policy, through its effect on interest rates, income, and the price level, tends to lower a country's exchange rate and, through its effect on income, increase its trade deficit.
- Contractionary fiscal policy has an ambiguous effect on a country's exchange rate but tends to decrease its trade deficit.
- For every effect that monetary and fiscal policies have on a country's exchange rate and trade balance, there is an equal and opposite effect on the combination of foreign countries' exchange rates and trade balances. Therefore, countries try to coordinate their policies.
- International capital inflows can reduce crowding out.
- Internationalizing a country's debt means that at some time in the future the country must consume less than it produces.

Questions for Thought and Review

1. Look up the current U.S. exchange rate relative to the yen. Would you suggest raising it or lowering it? Why?
2. Look up the current U.S. trade balance. Would you suggest raising it or lowering it? Why?
3. What effect on the U.S. trade deficit and exchange rate would result if Japan ran an expansionary monetary policy?
4. What would be the effect on the U.S. trade deficit and the U.S. exchange rate if Japan ran a contractionary fiscal policy?
5. If expansionary monetary policy immediately increases inflationary expectations and the price level, how might the effect of monetary policy on the exchange rate be different than that presented in this chapter?
6. What effect will a combination of expansionary fiscal policy and contractionary monetary policy have on the exchange rate?
7. Is the United States justified in complaining of Japan's use of an export-led growth policy? Why?
8. In the 1990s, Japan's economic recession was much in the news. What would you suspect was happening to its trade balance during this time? What policies would you guess other countries (such as those in the Group of Eight) were pressuring Japan to implement?
9. How does internationalizing the debt reduce crowding out?
10. What are the costs of internationalizing the debt?

Problems and Exercises

1. Draw the schematics to show the effect of contractionary fiscal policy on exchange rates.
2. Draw the schematics to show the effect of expansionary monetary policy on the trade deficit.
3. You observe that over the past decade a country's competitiveness has been continually eroded and its trade deficit has risen.
   a. What monetary or fiscal policies might have led to such results? Why?
   b. You also observe that interest rates have steadily risen along with a rise in the exchange rate. What policies would lead to this result?
   c. What policy might you suggest to improve the country's competitiveness? Explain how that policy might work.
4. Congratulations! You have been appointed an adviser to the IMF. A country that has run trade deficits for many years now has difficulty servicing its accumulated international debt and wants to borrow from the IMF to meet its obligations. The IMF requires that the country set a target trade surplus.
   a. What monetary and fiscal policies would you suggest the IMF require of that country?
   b. What would be the likely effect of that plan on the country's domestic inflation and growth?

c. How do you think the country's government will respond to your proposals? Why?

5. Congratulations! You've been hired as an economic adviser to a country that has perfectly flexible exchange rates. State what monetary and fiscal policy you might suggest in each of the following situations, and explain why you would suggest those policies.
   a. You want to lower the interest rate, decrease inflationary pressures, and lower the trade deficit.
   b. You want to lower the interest rate, decrease inflationary pressures, and lower a trade surplus.
   c. You want to lower the interest rate, decrease unemployment, and lower the trade deficit.
   d. You want to raise the interest rate, decrease unemployment, and lower the trade deficit.

Web Questions

1. The Census Bureau has an interactive program that reports the top trading partners of the United States. Go to www.census.gov/foreign-trade/top/index.html#top_partners and answer the following questions:
   a. What are the United States' five largest trading partners?
   b. With what five countries does the United States have the largest trade deficits?
   c. What policies could the United States encourage those countries to implement to reduce those deficits?
   d. With what five countries does the United States have the largest trade surpluses?
2. The International Monetary Fund (IMF), which has 183 member countries, was established to promote international monetary cooperation, exchange stability, and orderly exchange arrangements. In the late 1990s it came under increasing criticism. The Hoover Institution launched a public policy inquiry on the IMF in 1999. Go to the official site of this inquiry (www.imfsite.org) to answer the following questions:
   a. What is conditionality?
   b. What are some typical IMF financing preconditions? If implemented, what would be the effect of these preconditions on the country's (a) exchange rate, (b) trade deficit, (c) domestic economy?
   c. Name five countries that have received IMF financing over the past five years.
   d. What is mission creep?

Answers to Margin Questions

1. A low exchange rate of a country's currency will tend to stimulate exports and curtail imports. *(798)*
2. A trade deficit means a country is consuming more than it is producing. Consuming more than you produce is pleasant. It also means that capital is flowing into the country, which can be used for investment. So why worry? *(799)*
3. To increase the value of its currency, a country can increase the private demand for its currency by implementing contractionary monetary policy or it could decrease private supply of its currency by implementing contractionary monetary and fiscal policy. *(800)*
4. A fall in a country's interest rate will push down its exchange rate. *(801)*
5. Contractionary monetary policy pushes up the interest rate, decreases income and hence imports, and has a tendency to decrease inflation. Therefore, through these paths, contractionary monetary policy will tend to increase the exchange rate. *(802)*
6. Contractionary monetary policy will tend to decrease income, decreasing imports and decreasing the trade deficit. *(803)*
7. A higher price level makes exports less competitive and imports more competitive, pushing down the exchange rate. *(804)*
8. The net effect of expansionary fiscal policy on exchange rates is uncertain. Through the interest rate effect it pushes up the exchange rate, but through the income and price level effects it pushes down the exchange rate. *(805)*
9. The effect of expansionary fiscal policy on the trade deficit is to increase the trade deficit. *(806)*
10. Generally, when domestic policies and international policies conflict, a country will choose to deal with its domestic problems. Thus, it will likely use expansionary monetary policy if domestic problems call for that. *(806)*

Answers to Even-Numbered End-of-Chapter Questions

A Note about the Answers

The following answers are meant as guides to answering the end-of-chapter questions, not as definitive answers. The same questions often have many answers; this is especially true of policy-oriented questions. Although we have tried hard to see that mistakes are eliminated, the reality is that, as in any human endeavor, mistakes are inevitable. If you have checked and double-checked your answer and it is substantially different from that found here, assume that our answer is wrong, not yours. If you do come to a different answer, or think an answer misses an important aspect of the question, please check for corrections at my website to see if the answer has changed. If you don't find it there, please e-mail me at Colander@Middlebury.edu with your answer and an explanation of why you think it is better. I will get back to you and if I think you are right, I will post the change on the Web page marked "Corrections," together with your name and a thank-you.

Chapter 1: Economics and Economic Reasoning
Questions for Thought and Review

2. The responses will be varied since this question asks individual students about choices they have made. In these responses students should be encouraged to consider all the costs and benefits, and to be clear about the concept of the marginal costs and marginal benefits.
4. The opportunity cost of buying a $20,000 car is the benefit we would have gained by using that $20,000 for the next-best alternative, which could be spending or saving it.
6. I would spend the $5 million on those projects that provide the highest marginal benefit per dollar spent. The opportunity cost of spending the money on one project is the lost benefit that the college would have received by spending it on some other project. Thus, another way to restate the decision rule is to spend the money on the project that minimizes opportunity cost per dollar.
8. Two examples of social forces are our unwillingness to charge interest to friends, and our unwillingness to "buy" dates with other people. These issues are still subject to economic forces; however, there is no market in "dates" or in loans to friends, and hence the economic force does not become a market force.
10. An economic model is a framework that places the generalized insights of the theory in a more specific contextual setting. Policymakers need to understand the empirical evidence supporting the theory as well as real-world economic institutions to make policy recommendations.
12. Two microeconomic problems are the pricing policies of firms (price fixing in particular) and how wages are determined in labor markets. (Why do athletes and celebrities make so much money anyway?) Two macroeconomic problems are unemployment and inflation.
14. A good economist always tries to be objective. However, no one can ever be completely objective, even some of the time. Sometimes the best we can hope for is to be aware of the cultural norms and value judgments that influence our views and decisions.

Chapter 1: Problems and Exercises

2. a. The opportunity cost of attending college is the sacrifice one must make by attending college. It can be estimated by figuring out the benefit of the next-best alternative. If that alternative is working, one would guess the likely wage that could be earned at a job that does not require a college degree (minimum wage? more?) and then multiply by 40 hours for each week in college.
   b. The opportunity cost of taking this course could also be estimated using the same technique as in *a* if you otherwise would be working for these hours. If you had taken another course instead, the opportunity

cost would be the benefit you would have received from taking that course.

c. The opportunity cost of attending yesterday's lecture again would depend on what you otherwise could have done with the time (sleep? eat lunch with an interesting person?). Although this is no longer a choice to you, past activities do have opportunity costs.

4. Assuming who pays for dates reflects supply and demand considerations, and assuming that the majority of the Chinese are heterosexual, this suggests there will be a shortage of women, and thus men will be paying a higher percentage of the cost of dates in the future.

6. a. In this exercise you are asked to obtain prices on a gallon of milk from a supermarket and a convenience store.

b. Most likely, the price in the convenience store is higher (unless they are being used as a loss-leader). Someone will buy milk at a higher price because it is easier to purchase it at that store or the store may be the only source at a given time.

c. Unlike milk (which is a standardized product), clothes come in different brands, types, and perhaps quality. Saks clothes cost more, but one is also buying the Saks cachet.

8. *The Theory of Moral Sentiments* emphasizes the importance of morality. The invisible hand directs people's selfish desires (tempered by the social and political forces) to the common good but is based on certain presuppositions about the morality of individuals, which constrains individuals' selfish actions. What Smith is suggesting is that the marginal cost and marginal benefit used by individuals must be interpreted within a social context.

Chapter 2: Trade, Trade-Offs, and Government Policy
Questions for Thought and Review

2. If there were decreasing marginal opportunity costs, the production possibility curve would be convex with respect to the origin instead of concave. This means that (in terms of the example on page 24 of the text) we would gain more and more guns for every pound of butter we give up. An example of this is found in a situation in which a practice makes perfect; i.e., smaller and smaller numbers of hours devoted to a task, or sport, will result in bigger and bigger gains in performance.

4. If a society became equally more productive in the production of both widgets and wadgets, the production possibility curve would shift out to the right as shown in the following graph:

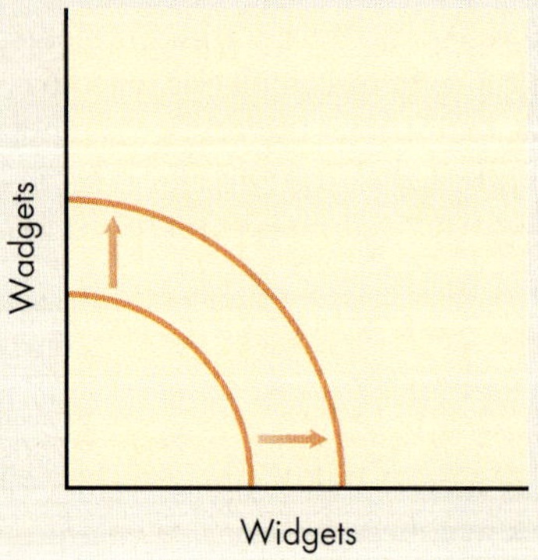

6. This statement is true or false depending on the implicit assumptions made in the analysis. It is true since individuals will eliminate all inefficiencies they see through trading. It might be false if not everyone knows all the benefits and the inefficiencies, but do not have the opportunity to correct the inefficiencies.

8. The combined production possibility curve of two countries that have no comparative advantage in either of two goods will be a straight line with the same slope as the production possibility curve of each of the countries, just shifted out to the right, reflecting the fact that the production levels reflect that of both countries combined. There are no gains to trade.

10. If a particular distribution of income is one of society's goals, a particular production technique that leads to greater output but also an undesirable distribution of income might be considered an inefficient method of production. Remember, efficiency is achieving a goal as cheaply as possible. Maximizing output is not the only goal of a society.

12. The six roles of government in a market economy are (1) providing a stable set of institutions and rules, (2) promoting effective and workable competition, (3) correcting for externalities, (4) ensuring economic stability and growth, (5) providing public goods, and (6) adjusting for undesired market results. Which of the six is the most controversial is open to debate. One possibility is the sixth role, adjusting for undesired market results. The problem is determining what rules should guide government in deciding on the desired result. Intervening in the market might create more problems than it solves.

14. Pollution permits require firms pay the cost of pollution they create. By making these permits tradable, firms that face the lowest cost of reducing pollution will reduce pollution emissions the most. Permits assign rights, thereby correcting for the externality.

Chapter 2: Problems and Exercises

2. a. See the graph below.
   b. The United States has a comparative advantage in the production of wheat because it can produce 200 additional tons of wheat for every 100 fewer bolts of cloth while Japan can produce 50 additional tons for every 100 fewer bolts of cloths. Japan has a comparative advantage in producing cloth.
   c. The joint production possibility curve without specialization or trade is shown in the graph below.
   d. The joint production possibility curve *with* specialization and trade is shown in the graph below. It is the outermost curve.

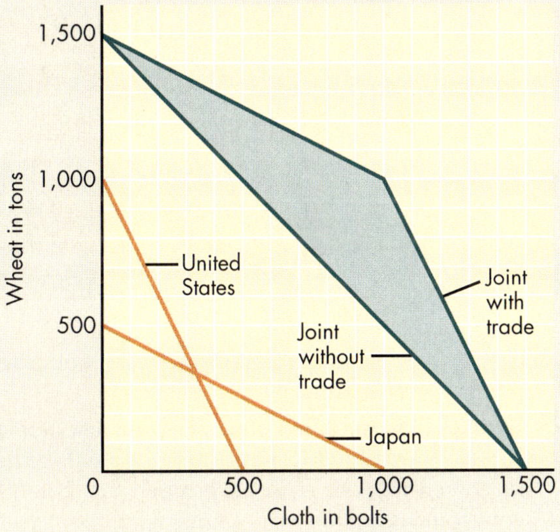

4. The fact that lawns occupy more land in the United States than any single crop does not mean that the United States is operating inefficiently. Although the cost of enjoying lawns is not included in GDP, lawns are nevertheless produced consumption goods and are included in the production possibility curve for the United States. The high proportion of land devoted to lawns implies that the United States has sufficient food that it can devote a fair amount of land to the production of goods for enjoyment such as lawns.

6. This exercise asks students to gather information about the limitations on businesses of different types in their communities. They are then asked to make judgments as to whether the limitations were necessary (are they clear about the goals involved?) and whether the number of limitations is correct. The information is linked to the text's material in part *d*. Part *e* asks students to learn about business taxes in their communities, and part *f* has them gather a sense of business satisfaction.

Chapter 2: Appendix A

2. See the graph at the top of the next page.
   a. The relationship is nonlinear because it is not straight. It is curved.
   b. From 0 to 5, cost declines as quantity rises (inverse). From 5 to 10, cost rises as quantity rises (direct).
   c. From 0 to 5, the slope is negative (slopes down). From 5 to 10, the slope is positive (slopes up).
   d. The slope between 1 and 2 units is the change in cost (30 − 20) divided by the change in quantity (1 − 2), or −10.

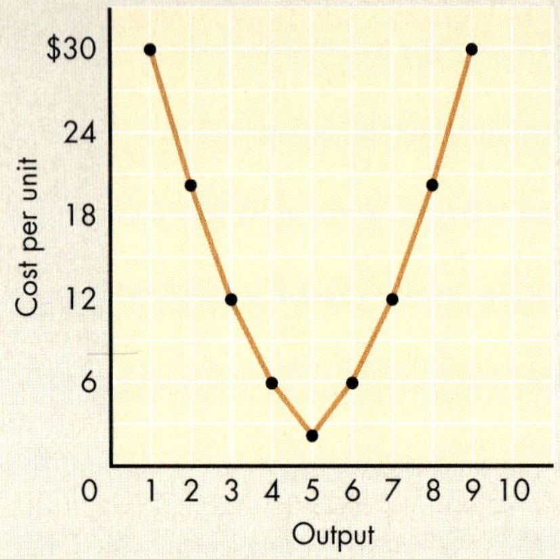

4. a. 1
   b. −3
   c. ⅓
   d. −¾
   e. 0
6. a. See line *a* in the graph in the next column.
   b. See line *b* in the graph in the next column.
   c. See line *c* in the graph in the next column.

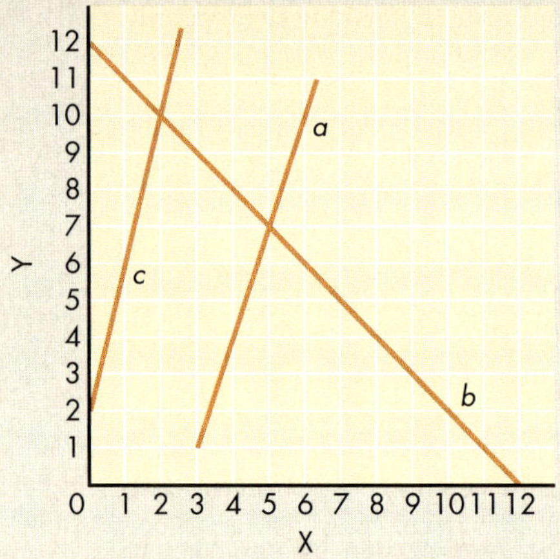

8. a. line graph
   b. bar graph
   c. pie chart
   d. line graph

Chapter 3: The Evolving U.S. Economy in Perspective
Questions for Thought and Review

2. The central coordinating mechanism in Soviet-style socialism is the central planners.
4. Soviet-style socialism solves the three problems by using administrative control. Central planners decide what to produce according to what they believe is socially beneficial. Central planners decide how to produce guided by what they believe is good for the country. Central planners decide distribution based on their perception of individuals' needs.
6. Markets have little role in most families. In most families decisions about who gets what are usually made by benevolent parents. Because families are small and social bonds strong, this benevolence can work. Thus, a socialist organization seems more appropriate to a family and a market-based organization to a large economy where social bonds don't hold the social unit together.
8. An economy depends on coordination, and the mechanisms of coordination depend on people. What is considered a resource depends on technology, and people develop new technologies. It follows that the economy's ultimate strength resides in its people.
10. Business is dynamic; it involves meeting new problems constantly, recognizing needs, and meeting those needs in a timely fashion. These are precisely the skills of entrepreneurship.
12. The two largest categories of federal expenditures are income security and health and education.
14. The Internet has added competition by increasing the amount of information available to consumers and reducing the importance of geographic location to production and sales. Increasing the amount of information to consumers lowers the cost of comparison shopping, which gives consumers more negotiating power with sellers. Because location doesn't matter, the Internet broadens the potential marketplace for both inputs and outputs, increasing competitive pressures in both factor and goods markets.

CHAPTER 3: PROBLEMS AND EXERCISES

2. a. The fact that more money is spent on adults than on children in the family does not imply that the children are deprived or that the distribution is unfair. Children and adults have different needs. Moreover, it is the parents who earn the money, so it is only through their beneficence, and requirements of law, that they provide for their children at all.
   b. Yes, these percentages probably change with income. The lower the income, the larger the percent of total expenditures spent on children. The reason is that most families want to provide a basic level of needs for their children. Many families feel that luxuries should not be given to children until the children have learned how to work for them themselves.
   c. Our suspicion is that the allocation would not be significantly different in Soviet-style socialist countries as compared to capitalist countries. If, however, the average income in socialist countries were lower, the percentage of total expenditure spent on children might be higher, as described in *b*.
4. a. Innovation requires a certain level of freedom of thought and a possibility of profit-making from the innovation. Neither was the case with Soviet-style socialism. Government planners directed production with income based on need, so workers had neither the freedom nor the incentive to innovate.
   b. Both freedom and the possibility of making profits provide the means and incentives for innovation in capitalist countries.
   c. Schumpeter's argument was based on the idea that profit-making by innovators was necessary for innovation to occur. As firms become larger, however, the individual ceases to become the direct beneficiary of his or her innovations.
   d. Since his predictions did not materialize, one must believe either that firms have been able to create incentive structures to foster innovation or that some other venue for innovation has arisen. Firms have large research and development departments designed to promote innovation. In addition, individual innovators have been able to raise enough capital to start their own companies to profit directly from their innovations. In the United States there has been enormous growth in the number of such firms. The U.S. government has been a large motivator of innovation through subsidies to basic research at universities and through support of military innovations, both of which have large spillovers into private industry.

CHAPTER 4: SUPPLY AND DEMAND QUESTIONS FOR THOUGHT AND REVIEW

2. The law of supply states that quantity supplied rises as price increases or, alternatively, that quantity supplied falls as price decreases. Price is directly related to quantity supplied because, as price rises, people and firms rearrange their activities to supply more of that good.
4. A change in the price causes a movement along the demand curve, a movement to a new point on the same curve. A shift in the demand curve means that the quantities will be different at all prices; the entire curve shifts.
6. Shift factors of supply include the price of inputs, technological advances, changes in expectations, and taxes and subsidies. As the price of inputs increase, the supply curve shifts to the left. As technological advances are made that reduce the cost of production, the supply curve shifts to the right. If a supplier expects the price of her good to rise, she may decrease supply now to save and sell later. Other expectional effects are also possible. Taxes paid by suppliers shift the supply curve to the left. Subsidies given to producers shift the supply curve to the right.
8. In the graph in the next column, the demand curve has shifted to the left, causing a decrease in the market price and the market quantity.

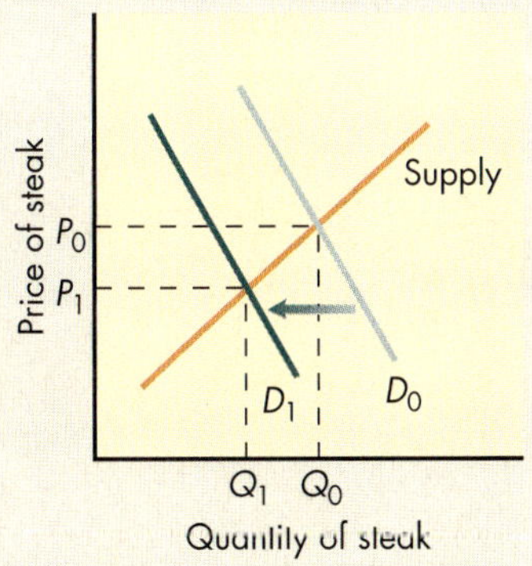

10. Sales volume increases (equilibrium quantity rises) when the government suspends the tax on sales by retailers because the price to demanders falls and hence equilibrium quantity demanded rises. This occurs because the supply curve shifts to the right.
12. Customers will flock to stores demanding that funky "economics professor" look, creating excess demand. This

excess demand will soon catch the attention of suppliers, and prices will be pushed upward.

14. It suggests that the job is being rationed, which means that the wage is above the equilibrium wage.

16. The fallacy of composition is the false assumption that what is true for a part will also be true for the whole. It affects the supply/demand model by drawing our attention to the possibility that supply and demand are interdependent. Feedback effects must be taken into account to made the analysis complete.

18. The greatest feedback effects are likely to occur in the markets that are the largest. This is most likely to be true for housing and manufactured-goods markets.

Chapter 4: Problems and Exercises

2. a. The market demand and market supply curves are shown below.
   b. At a price of \$37, quantity demanded is 32 and quantity supplied is 18. Excess demand is 14. At a price of \$67, quantity demanded is 10 and quantity supplied is 46. Excess supply is 36.
   c. Equilibrium price is \$47. Equilibrium quantity is 24.

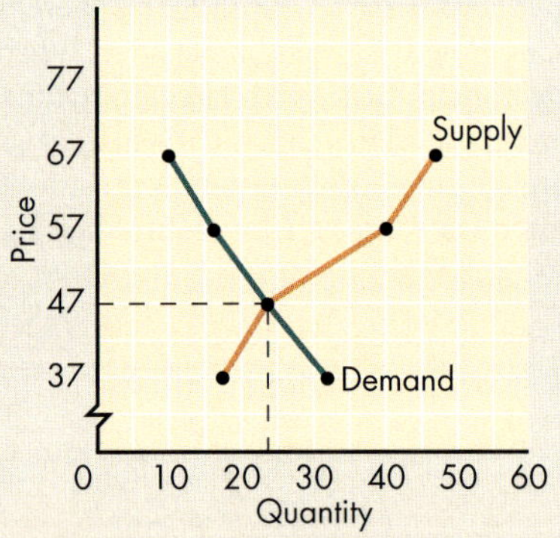

4. a. I would expect wheat prices to decline since the supply of wheat is greater than expected. Wheat commodity markets are very competitive, so the initial 35 percent increase in output was already reflected in the current price of wheat. It is only the additional 9 percent increase that will push down the price of wheat.
   b. This is graphically represented by a shift to the right in the supply of wheat, as shown in the next column.

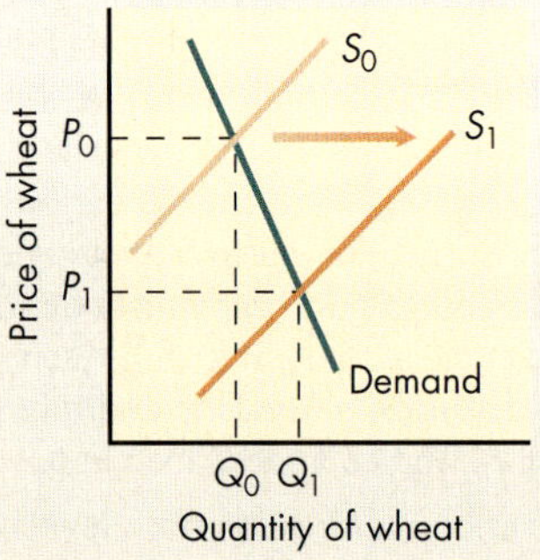

6. a. Because the market for pencils is relatively small, supply/demand analysis would be appropriate without modification.
   b. Because the labor market is very large, supply/demand analysis would not be appropriate without modification. For example, an increase in labor supply will likely lead to greater income and greater demand for goods, which will lead to an increase in quantity of goods produced and therefore an increase in the demand for labor. In this case there are significant feedback effects.
   c. Aggregate markets such as savings and expenditures include feedback effects, so supply/demand analysis would not be appropriate without modification.
   d. The CD market is relatively small. Supply/demand analysis would be appropriate without modification.

Chapter 5: Using Supply and Demand Questions for Thought and Review

2. If price fell and quantity remained constant, a possible cause would be a shift out of the supply curve and a shift of the demand curve in to the left. Another possibility would be a shift of the demand curve in to the left with a vertical supply curve.

4. As you can see in the graph on the next page the rent controls create a situation in which demanders are willing to pay much more than the controlled price and much more than the equilibrium price. These payments are sometimes known as *key money*. In this graph,

landlords are willing to supply Q_S at the current controlled rent, P_C. Consumers are willing to pay up to P_B for the quantity Q_S. Key money can be an amount up to the difference between P_B and P_C.

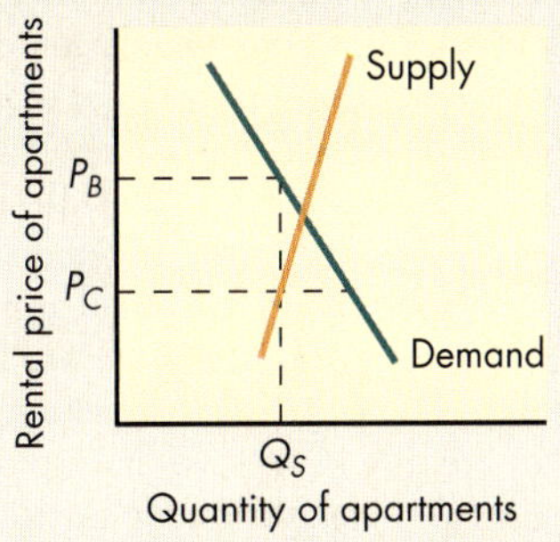

6. A minimum wage, W_{min}, above the equilibrium wage W_E will result in the quantity of laborers looking for work to increase to Q_S and the quantity of employers looking to hire to decrease to Q_D. The difference between the two is a measure of the number of unemployed.

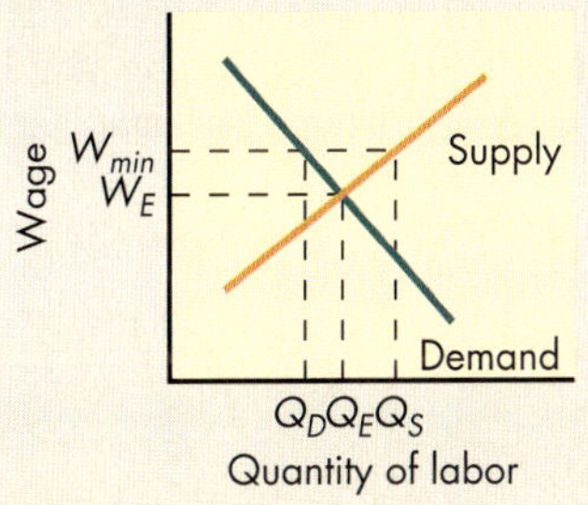

8. Political turmoil in South Africa likely led both foreign and domestic investors to question the economic stability of the country. Foreign investors reduced their demand for South African investments, and therefore their demand for the rand. This shifted the demand for the rand to the left. Domestic investors did likewise, shifting their investments to those outside South Africa, shifting the supply of rand to the right. The combination led to a lower price for the rand in terms of other currencies.
10. Excess supply in U.S. agricultural markets is caused by the government's policy of agricultural price supports, or price floors on agricultural products. The political forces prevent the invisible hand from working.
12. Governments likely support third-party-payer markets for a variety of reasons. It could be that they believe the market does not distribute the good equitably (poorer people have less access to the good); there are positive externalities associated with the good (for example, public education); or that some other market failure exists.

Chapter 5: Problems and Exercises

2. a. A weakly enforced antiscalping law would add an additional cost to those selling scalping tickets and push up the resale cost of tickets to include the expected cost of being caught. In the graph on the right, this shifts the supply curve from S_0 to S_1, raising equilibrium price from P_0 to P_1. (Note: This assumes that only selling, not buying, is illegal.)
   b. A strongly enforced antiscalping law (against suppliers) would push up prices far more. If enforcement were sufficiently strong, a two-tier price system would emerge with a low legal resale price at P_0 and another a very high price, P_2.

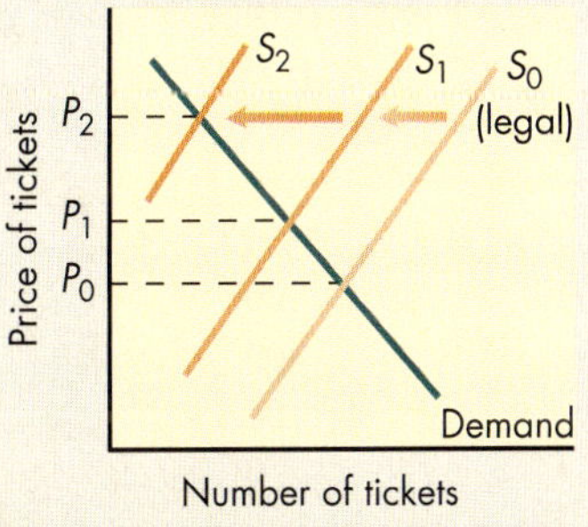

4. a. The government subsidy of mohair provided an enormous incentive for those who were allowed to sell mohair to sell large quantities at lower price than otherwise. The elimination of this subsidy shifted the supply curve to the left (shown below as a shift from S_0 to S_1, increasing the market price for mohair from P_0 to P_1 and decreasing the quantity demanded and supplied from Q_0 to Q_1.
   b. This program was likely kept in existence because not many people knew about it (mohair is a relatively small market), and ranchers had no incentive to broadcast the subsidy.
   c. If a law were passed so that suppliers would receive $3.60 more than the market price, the demand curve would shift to the left to include this tax. The quantity demanded would fall dramatically. Consumers would not support this law because they would have to pay an enormously high price. Suppliers would support this law only if they were guaranteed that they could sell at that high price.

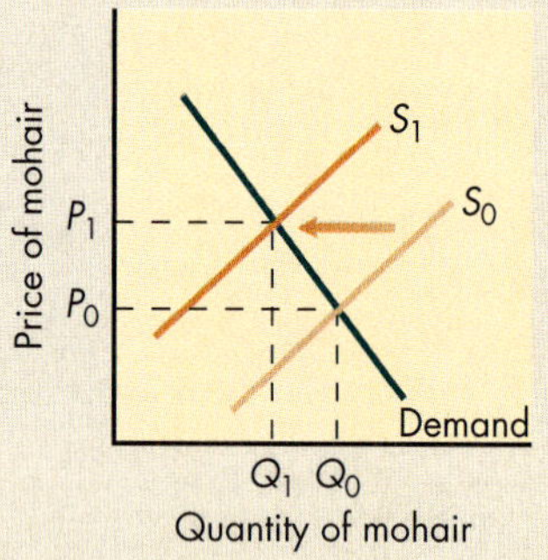

6. a. Boards often exist to benefit the consumer, but also to benefit those who currently produce. Often those who are currently certified attempt to limit the number of new certifications to limit the supply and thus boost the price.
   b. Possible changes include eliminating the board of certification, limiting its regulation to only those skills that it addresses directly, or requiring continual recertification so that skills of those already certified reflect the current demand for skills in that market.
   c. A political difficulty with implementing these changes is that a relatively small group of those currently certified will be hurt and will lobby hard for the status quo. The benefits of the changes are also large, but they are spread out over large groups of consumers, with each consumer benefiting very little. Therefore, it will be easier for the small group, whose benefit per individual is large, to organize.

8. a. Frequent-flyer programs allow companies to lower their effective prices without lowering their reported prices. Companies also use them to get business travelers to choose their airline. Such programs are an example of a third-party-payer system: The business traveler gets the benefit (frequent-flyer miles), while the business pays for the current flight.
   b. Other examples include points that hotels give to travelers and bonus checks based on charges that *Discover* gives those who use its credit card.
   c. Firms likely do not monitor these programs because it would be too costly to do so.

CHAPTER 5: APPENDIX A

2. a. The following are the demand and supply tables after the hormone is introduced:

Price (dollars per gallon)	Quantity Demanded (gallons per year)	Quantity Supplied (gallons per year)
0.00	600	−25
1.00	500	125
2.00	400	275
2.50	350	350
3.00	300	425
4.00	200	575
5.00	100	725
6.00	0	875

   b. The original supply curve is S_0. The growth hormone shifts the supply curve to S_1 (to the right by 125).

Equilibrium price falls to $2.50 a gallon, and equilibrium quantity rises to 350 million gallons (point *B*).

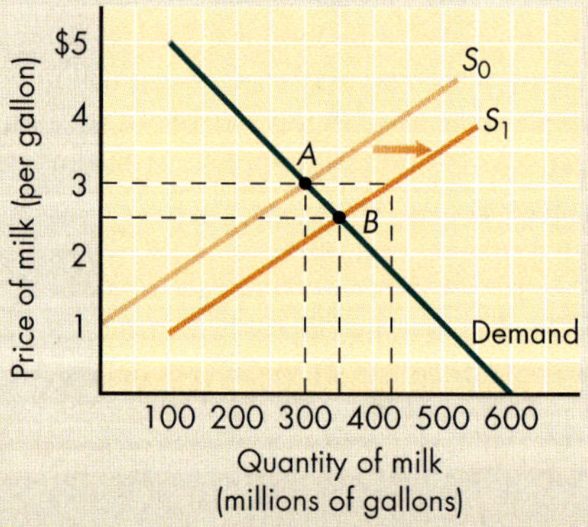

c. The demand curve remains the same at $Q_D = 600 - 100P$. The supply curve becomes $Q_S = -25 + 150P$. To solve the two equations, set them equal to one another: $600 - 100P = -25 + 150P$ and solve for P. Doing so, we get $P = 2.5$. Substituting this value for P into either the demand or supply equation gives us equilibrium quantity of 350.

d. Quantity supplied would be 425 $(-25 + 150 \times 3)$ and quantity demanded would be 300 $(600 - 100 \times 3)$. There would be excess supply of 125. The price floor is shown in the graph above.

4. a. A demand curve follows the formula $Q_D = a - bP$, where a is the price-axis intercept and b is the slope of the curve. A shift in demand is reflected in a change in a. An increase in demand increases a and a decrease in demand reduces a.

b. A supply curve follows the formula, $Q_S = a + bP$, where a is the price-axis intercept and b is the slope of the curve. A shift in supply is reflected in a change in a. An increase in supply reduces a and a decrease in supply increases a.

c. A movement in supply or demand is reflected in the effect of a change in P on either Q_S or Q_D.

6. a. The new supply equation is $Q_S = -150 + 150(P - 1)$ where P is the equilibrium price, or $Q_S = -300 + 150P$.

b. $P = 3.60$; $Q = 240$.

c. Farmers receive $2.60 per gallon.

8. a. The new supply equation is $Q_S = -150 + 150(P + 1)$ where P is the equilibrium price, or $Q_S = 150P$.

b. $P = 2.40$; $Q = 360$.

c. Farmers receive $3.40 per gallon.

Chapter 6: Describing Supply and Demand: Elasticities Questions for Thought and Review

2. I would check to see if other things remained equal, suspecting that they did not. The reason why is that the rise in price did not have the expected effect. If all other things did indeed remain equal, the elasticity would be zero. Percent change in quantity divided by the percentage change in price.

4. Price elasticity of demand is equal to the percentage change in quantity divided by the percentage change in price. Pizzas went from $8 to $2 and quantity from 1 to 100. The price elasticity of demand is (1.96/1.2) = 1.63.

6. They are both the same. Any supply curve that goes through the origin has an elasticity of 1.

8. To the degree that colleges are trying to get as much revenue as possible, they will keep raising tuition until the demand is no longer inelastic. Colleges don't raise their tuition by more than what they currently do because they are not profit maximizers, and because social pressures such as student protests would result if they raised tuition too much.

10. More eager students will agree to go to a school even if they don't get much financial aid. That is, they have less elastic demands and thus will tend to get less financial aid. Whether this practice is justified is a difficult normative issue, with many alternative views.

12. a. Vodka: luxury (except in Russia). Individuals tend to drink more hard liquor as their income rises. (It depends on the type: Absolut vodka is more of a luxury than store brands.)

b. Table salt: necessity. It is a small portion of people's income, and its consumption doesn't increase with income.

c. Furniture: luxury (depends on the type). While we all need some furniture, the wealthy spend large sums on furniture. The rest of us get by with cheap stuff.

d. Perfume: luxury (depends on the type). The rich blow money on perfume; the rest of us get by with toilet water, or we smell a bit.

e. Beer: necessity (depends on the type). Beer tends to be the poor person's drink. However, new micro breweries are trying to change beer's image, and to make certain types of beer be seen as a luxury.

f. Sugar: necessity. It is not used significantly more by rich than by poor.

14. If there were only two (assuming no saving) the goods must be substitutes because if a person doesn't consume one, he or she would have to consume the other.

Chapter 6: Problems and Exercises

2. a. Using standard reasoning, we would answer that firms decreased the size of the coffee cans to hide price increases from consumers. However, in reality people often react differently to changes in the size of packages compared to the equivalent change in price.

b. Examples include candy bars, soap, and canned tuna fish.

4. a. A price rise of 10 percent will reduce fuel consumption anywhere from 4 to 8.5 percent. This translates to 9.15 to 9.6 million gallons demanded.
   b. This suggests that there are other forces besides price at work here; making adjustments to higher prices is much easier than making adjustments to lower prices. This may be due to learning the true cost of substitutes when those substitutes are consumed. One can imagine a scenario in which a price hike significantly changes driving behavior—commuters may switch to ride sharing or public transportation, to which there may be perceived social barriers (costs). Once those barriers are overcome and the perceived costs are lowered after those alternatives are used, a larger decline in the price of gasoline is required to induce those who switched to return to driving their own cars.

6. Point *A*: 3; point *B*: 1/3; point *C*: 3/2; point *D*: 7/6.

8. a. 0.5
   b. 0.60

10. a. The supply shifts in and price rises as in the graph below.
    b. Elasticity of demand is 1.

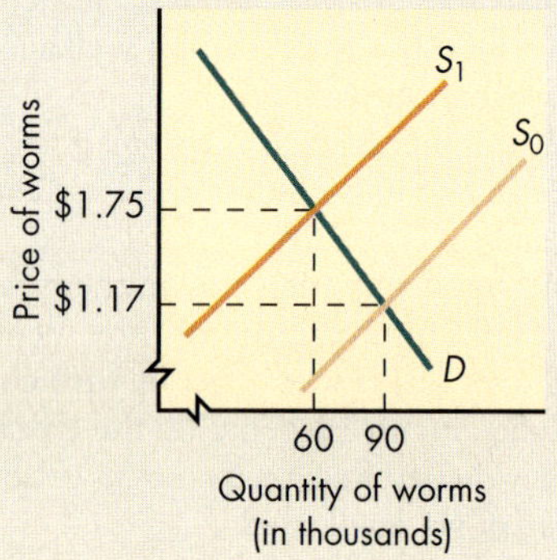

12. a. Peak hour travelers are likely to be commuters who have little choice but to go to work and therefore have lower demand elasticity than those who ride buses during off-peak hours. They could choose to stay at home instead.
    b. Demand tends to be less elastic in the short run because there are fewer substitutes. If fares rose enough, in the long run people could find alternative modes of transportation—purchase a car, find someone to share rides with, etc.
    c. Tolls are likely a much smaller portion of high-income commuter's total income, contributing to a less-elastic demand.

Chapter 7: Taxation and Government Intervention

Questions for Thought and Review

2. Decision making based on costs and benefits means you make purchases if the marginal benefits are greater than the price. The market price yields no benefits for the marginal producer or the marginal good. For all others the consumer gets the surplus.

4. If demand is inelastic, raising a tax increases revenue paid by consumers; similarly with supply. Thus, what happens to total tax revenue depends on the elasticity of both supply and demand.

6. I'd recommend goods with a price elasticity of demand or price elasticity of supply as close to zero as possible. Examples would be cigarettes, salt, required medications, a per capita tax, and land.

8. With a perfectly elastic demand, suppliers will pay the entire cost of the tax regardless of how elastic supply is—unless supply is also perfectly elastic, in which case no goods will be bought or sold after the tax, so no one will bear the burden.

10. If the economist wanted to get as much revenue as possible from as little output reduction as possible, he would suggest taxing inelastic supplies.

12. If the tax were based on street frontage rather than square feet of living space, individuals would have an incentive to build in this style.

14. Rent seeking is the restricting of supply in order to increase price. The firm would have a greater incentive to rent-seek when demand is inelastic.

CHAPTER 7: PROBLEMS AND EXERCISES

2. a. In the graph below, the government requirement has caused an increase in demand, which has raised the price. Consumers used to pay P_0 for Q_0, but now pay P_1 for Q_1. Welfare loss for society is the blue shaded triangle.
   b. If eating beets makes people healthy, their decisions ought to reflect that fact. One could argue that if the government knew better than consumers, this action would be justified if the marginal benefits exceeded the marginal costs. However, if people are choosing not to be healthy, and are rational, then any regulation making them eat beets would make them worse off.

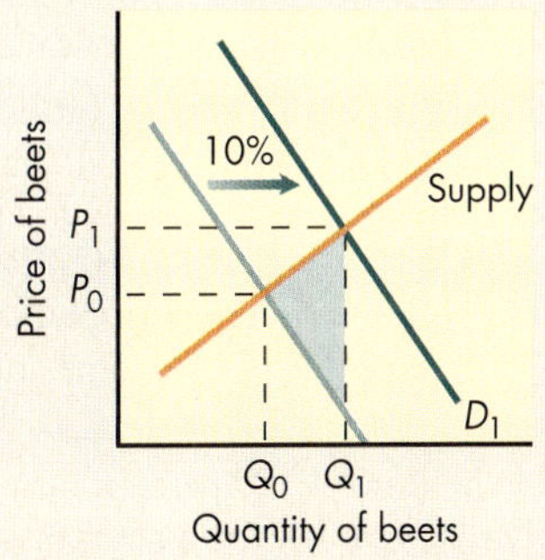

4. a. A poll tax would have no incentive effect, as shown in the graph below. A tax on property, where supply is somewhat elastic, will reduce the quantity of property supplied (negative incentive effect), which may not be desirable.

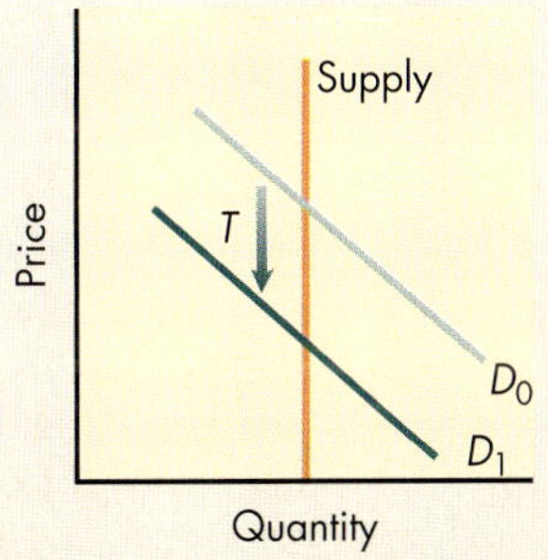

   b. Margaret Thatcher was almost thrown out of office because of this tax, and her successor, John Major, returned to a property tax. Citizens were far more concerned with the distributional consequences associated with a poll tax than they were with the loss of efficiency associated with a property tax.

6. a. With time the job searchers will get discouraged and drop out of the labor force, disguising the unemployment. Another possibility is that firms invest in machinery to replace labor, increasing the productivity of labor and thereby increasing the demand for labor and reducing the shortage of jobs.
   b. It is likely to decrease.

8. a. Before the tax, equilibrium price is \$6 and equilibrium quantity is 200. After the tax, equilibrium price is \$8 and equilibrium quantity is 100.
   b. Producer surplus before the tax is the area above the supply curve and below price. This is a triangle with base 200 and height 4. So, producer surplus is ½ (200)(4) = 400. After the tax, the triangle representing producer surplus has a height of 2 and base of 100. So producer surplus is ½ (100)(2) = 100.
   c. Consumer surplus before the tax is the area below the demand curve and above price. This is a triangle with base 200 and height 4. So consumer surplus is ½ (200)(4) = 400. After the tax, the triangle representing consumer surplus has a height of 2 and base of 100. So consumer surplus is ½ (100)(2) = 100.
   d. Total tax revenue is \$4 times equilibrium quantity, 100, or \$400.

Chapter 8: The Logic of Individual Choice Questions for Thought and Review

2. According to the principle of diminishing marginal utility, marginal utility falls as one consumes more of a good. Marginal utility of the last unit consumed rises as one consumes less of the good.
4. Economists' theory of value depends on the underlying assumptions. Given those assumptions, price and value are related. If those assumptions (such as assumed rationality and freedom of choice) don't hold, the statement is true; if they do hold, the statement is false.
6. There are many psychological explanations for people's actions, but economists use an easy underlying psychological foundation: rational self-interest.
8. The law of demand states that quantity demanded falls as price rises and quantity demanded rises as price falls. If you are already in equilibrium and the price of a good rises, you will no longer be in equilibrium. The marginal utility per dollar of the good whose price has risen is too low. To raise it, you must reduce your consumption of that good. Therefore, as the price of the good rises, you consume less of it—the law of demand.
10. If the supply curve is perfectly inelastic, the supplier has no alternative; thus, the opportunity cost is zero.
12. For Americans, a large part of utility (happiness) is relative to others. As everyone gets more, relative happiness does not increase.
14. Most people buy goods without a lot of thinking. An example of ours is when we buy meat at the store. We have a general idea of what the price should be, and if the price is lower than that (and a sign or sticker says *sale*) we buy it. It follows the principle of rational choice only if that principle takes into account the costs of deciding.

Chapter 8: Problems and Exercises

2. Given the information in the table, the best combination to purchase will be where the (*MU*/*P*) is equal for all three goods. Doing the calculations, we have:

#	(*MU*/*P*) for A	(*MU*/*P*) for B	(*MU*/*P*) for C
1	20	10	8.33
2	18	7	1.67
3	15	6	1.67
4	10	5	1.67
5	5	4	1.67
6	2	4	1.67
7	−7	3	−1.67
8	−20	2	−1.67

(Note that marginal utility should be interpreted between units of consumption.) We start by buying that good with the highest util per dollar. With $20 to spend we would buy 1 of A, for 20 utils per dollar, leaving me with $10 to spend. We would then buy 1 more of A, getting 18 utils to the dollar. This would exhaust our money.

4. You should continue your present pattern of consumption. One more widget will give you 2 more units of utility for $2, and one more wadget will give you 3 more units of utility for $3, and since $(MU_1/P_1) = (MU_2/P_2)$, your present consumption pattern gives you as much total utility, considering your income and prices, as any variation.
6. a. If he or she is not a 100 percent rational economist, it is likely that you will lose your spouse or significant other—or at least lose his or her love or fondness.
   b. The utility gained from a diamond is not just its brilliance or perfection but also the knowledge that it is real (and thus expensive) and that some sacrifice (driven by affection) was made for its purchase. A fake diamond suggests that there was little sacrifice and thus the giver's love was cheap as well.
   c. Who is to say that the utility from the consumption of a product is not just?

Chapter 8: Appendix A

2. With budget constraint in *a*, Zach will be on utility curve II. With budget constraint in *b*, Zach will be on utility curve III. With budget constraint in *c*, Zach will be on a utility curve that is to the right of III.
   a. Zachary prefers the budget constraint that is the furthest to the right, *c*.
   b. The marginal rate of substitution for *a* is −2, for *b* is −1 and for *c* is −1. The marginal rate of substitution equals the slope of the budget constraint at the optimal combination of goods. Even though we do not know the optimal combination with budget constraint *c*, we can still figure out the marginal rate of substitution for that combination.
4. It would be bowed away from the origin if there were increasing marginal utility.

Chapter 9: Production and Cost Analysis I Questions for Thought and Review

2. The terms *long run* and *short run* do not necessarily refer to specific periods of time independent of the production process. The long run, by definition, is a period in which the firm can vary the inputs as much as it wants; in the long run, all inputs are variable. The question is whether a firm ever really gets to this degree of flexibility. It may be true that firms are always constrained in regard to what production decisions they can make, so in reality this statement is probably true.
4. If average productivity is falling, short-run average variable cost is rising; to say that productivity falls is equivalent to saying that cost rises.
6. If average productivity is falling, average costs must be rising; if marginal productivity is falling, marginal cost must be rising. But there is no necessary relationship between average productivity and marginal costs.
8. The shapes of the short-run average cost curve and marginal cost curve would be the same as in the more usual case where machines are the fixed factor. Either way you are still adding more and more of a variable factor to a fixed factor and encountering diminishing marginal productivity as a result. The marginal cost and average cost curves would be U-shaped.
10. Labor does not need to be produced (at least in the time periods that microeconomic analysis usually considers) and hence the choice for individuals is how to divide up that labor among various activities such as work, play, and studying (opportunity costs). Goods that need to be produced ultimately depend on the opportunity costs of the factors producing them, but in the standard economic model, those costs are assumed fixed; thus, the opportunity costs are assumed fixed. This leaves the analysis of production free to focus on technical aspects of production such as diminishing marginal productivity as the determinant of costs, and hence supply.
12. Productivity gains can reduce the percentage of labor costs per vehicle, allowing GM either to lower its price (thereby increasing the quantity of its cars sold) or to increase its profits (making its shareholders happy).

Chapter 9: Problems and Exercises

2. Rent is $4,000; labor is $40,000; utilities are $5,000; total revenue is $100,000; the opportunity cost of the entrepreneur is $50,000; and that of the funds invested is $4,000. By the accounting definition of cost and profit, Economan is making a profit equal to $100,000 − ($4,000 + $40,000 + $5,000) = $51,000. From an economist's point of view, where explicit and implicit costs are considered, Economan now has a loss of $100,000 − ($4,000 + $40,000 + $5,000 + $50,000 + $4,000) = −$3,000.
4. a. Given the price of labor at $15 per hour, and the data in the total product table; the following table represents the average variable costs:

Labor	*TP*	*VC*	*AVC*	*AP*	*MP*	*MC*
1	5	15	3.00	5.0	5	3.00
2	15	30	2.00	7.5	10	1.50
3	30	45	1.50	10.0	15	1.00
4	36	60	1.67	9.0	6	2.50
5	40	75	1.88	8.0	4	3.75

   b. This is done in the next column. The *AVC* curve is shown on the left, and the *AP* curve is shown on the right. You can see that the *AVC* curve and *AP* curve are mirror images of each other.

   c. The *MP* curve is shown below on the right.

   d. As you can see from the graph below, the MC curve and the *MP* curve are approximate mirror images of each other.

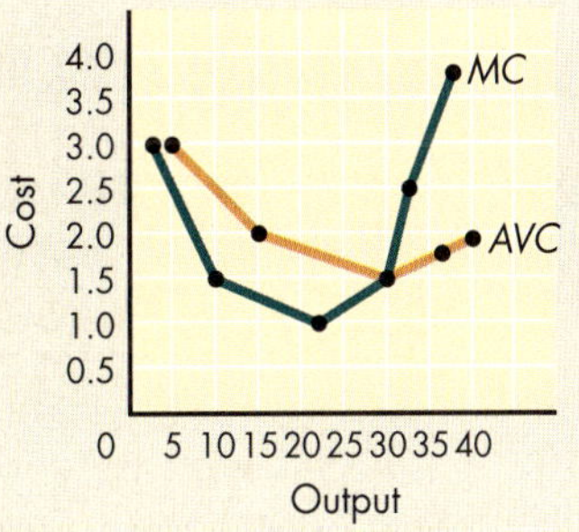

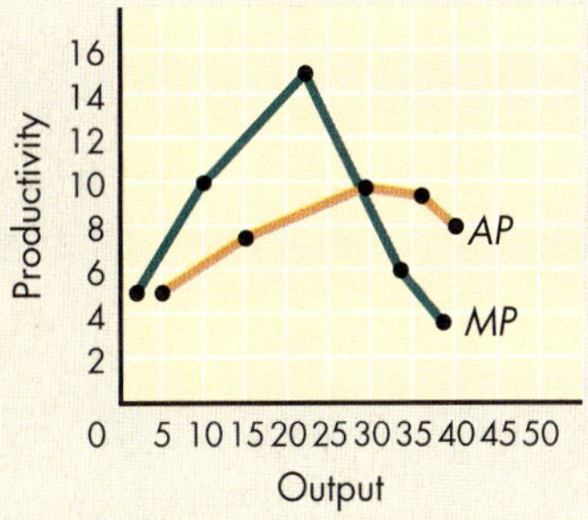

6. a. The *AFC*, *ATC*, *AVC*, and MC curves are shown at the top of the next page on the left.

   b. The *AFC* curve has its normal shape. Because average variable costs do not change, the marginal cost curve is coincident with the average variable cost as shown. The *ATC* curve is always falling since the costs are always above the MC curve. They asymptotically approach $25.

   c The law of diminishing marginal productivity is not operative.

d. The new *AFC*, *ATC*, *AVC*, and MC curves are shown in the second graph on the right. The *AFC* curve remains the same. The MC curve is now upward-sloping, with a slope of 10. The *AVC* curve is also upward-sloping, with a slope of 5. The *ATC* curve now has a more normal shape, with a minimum where it intersects the MC curve.

e. Marginal costs would have to decline at first and then rise for the curves to have their "normal" shapes.

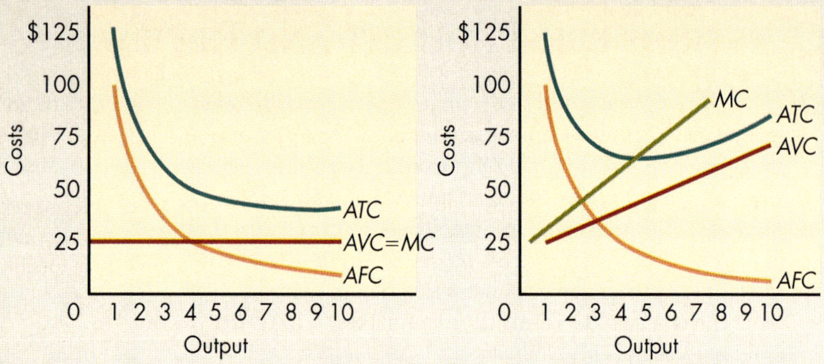

Chapter 10: Production and Cost Analysis II Questions for Thought and Review

2. It is incorrect because in the long run firms can change any input they want. In the long run there would be no fixed cost—all costs would be variable. The shape of the long-run average total cost curve is determined by economies of scale.

4. If production relationships were only technical relationships, diseconomies of scale would never occur because the same technical process could be used over and over again at the same cost. In reality, however, the social dimensions of production relationships introduce the potential for diseconomies of scale because, as the firm size increases, monitoring costs increase and team spirit or morale generally decreases.

6. An entrepreneur is an individual who sees an opportunity to sell an item at a price higher than the average cost of producing it. The entrepreneur then looks at the cost of production to see if a profit can be made. If so, he or she will create supply by organizing production.

8. Cost curves are defined within a period of time. In the short run, technology is assumed constant. In the long run, technological change shifts the cost curves down. It does not explain the downward-sloping portion of cost curves.

10. Producing steel in this fashion involves an enormous fixed cost. These fixed costs must be spread out over sufficient production to lower average total costs and make the average total production costs (which includes fixed costs) less than the price.

Chapter 10: Problems and Exercises

2. a. Variable costs would likely include manufacturing labor and materials and possibly sales costs to the extent that they are for the sale of additional production. Certain other costs have a variable component to them, but they will unlikely vary directly with production.

   b. Fixed costs would likely include factor overhead, operating expenses and profit, R&D, interest, and to some extent advertising. In the real world, the division between fixed and variable costs is not as clear-cut as in the texts.

   c. If output were to rise, average total cost would likely fall because fixed costs seem relatively important. This is the case for many real-world firms.

4. a. The long-run cost curve is shown on the right. Initially it will fall because of economies of scale.

   b. It will later rise due to diseconomies of scale.

   c. The average cost curves in the short run are also U-shaped. Their shape is due initially to increasing marginal productivity and eventually decreasing marginal productivity.

   d. There is no fixed component.

   e. A straight line.

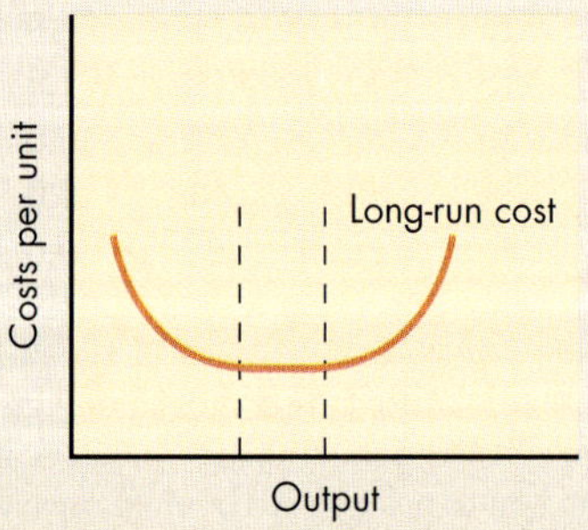

6. a. It is possible that both methods are technically efficient because neither dressmaker is using more of both inputs to produce the same number of garments.
   b. The economically efficient method is the least-cost method. The cost of 800 garments for the first dressmaker is \$46,000 (160 × \$100 + 3,000 × \$10). The cost of the same number of garments for the second dressmaker is \$40,000 (200 × \$100 + 2,000 × \$10). Therefore, the second method is economically efficient. The first method is not.

CHAPTER 10: APPENDIX A

2. See the graph below. The black line is the original isocost curve. Each of the following is shown with respect to the dotted line.
   a. This is line *a* in the graph below.
   b. The isocost curve rotates in along the machinery axis as shown in the graph below to line *b*.
   c. The isocost curve shifts in along both axes as shown below to line *c*.

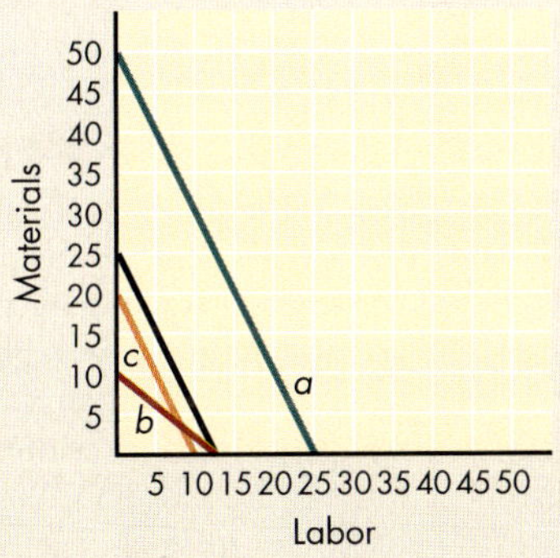

4. Technical efficiency in production means that as few inputs as possible are used to produce a given output. On the graph in the next column, this would be anywhere on the isoquant curve, including points A and B. Economic efficiency means using that method that produces a given level of output at the lowest possible cost. Given the cost of inputs, the efficient point to produce that level of output corresponding to the isoquant curve is point *B*.

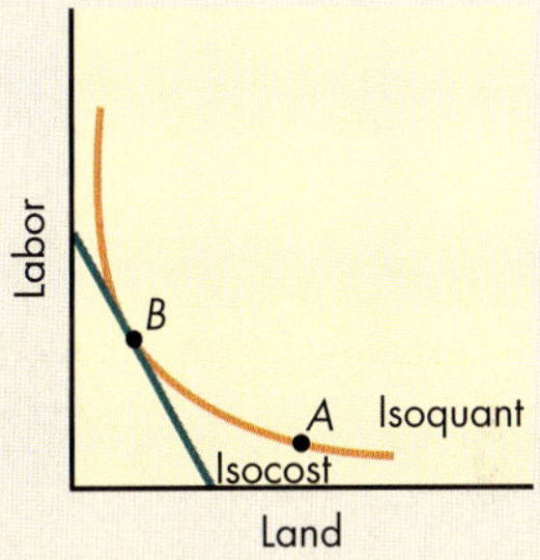

6. If the price of labor falls to \$3, the isocost curve shifts out along the labor axis, intersecting at 20 units of labor. Producing 60 earrings with the new labor costs is now inefficient. The firm can now produce more than 60 earrings, shown by point *D* and the new isoquant curve, I_2, to the right of the one corresponding to 60 earrings, I_1.

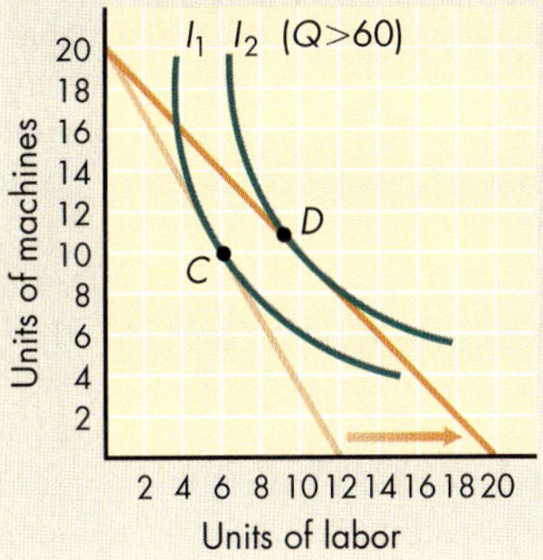

CHAPTER 11: PERFECT COMPETITION QUESTIONS FOR THOUGHT AND REVIEW

2. Typical marginal cost, marginal revenue, and average total cost curves are shown on the next page. The profit-maximizing level of output is Q^*. The total profit is shown by the blue shaded rectangle. As we have drawn it, the firm is not in long-run equilibrium since it is earning a profit.

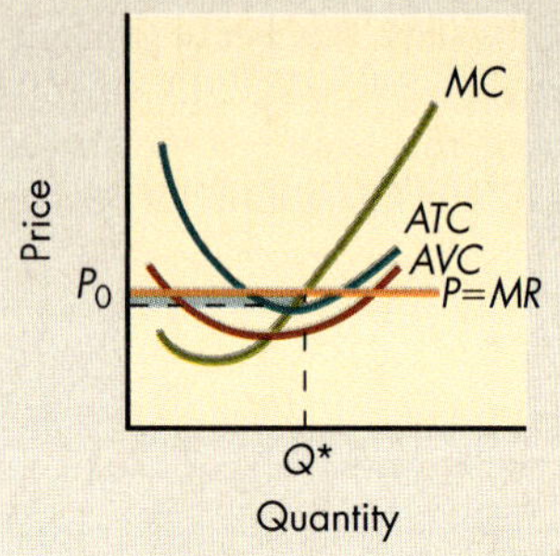

4. The firm's supply curve is that portion of the firm's marginal cost curve that lies above the minimum of the average variable cost curve curve. The sum of all individual firms' marginal cost curves (above the minimum *AVC* curve) is the market supply curve.
6. The shutdown point is the same as the point at which a firm exits a market in the long run when there are no fixed costs. That is, when *AVC* is the same as *ATC*.
8. A technological development that shifts the MC curve down will shift the market supply curve to the right. Market price will fall and output will rise. Profit for each firm will still be zero because the price will decline sufficiently so that each firm earns zero profit.
10. If both firms are producing where *MR* = MC and we could buy either for the same amount, I'd buy the one with the highest total profit. Remember, it is total profit, not profit per unit that is maximized by a firm. If there are perfectly competitive firms, however, eventually both will earn 0 economic profits regardless of which we bought.
12. This question requires students to find current articles in newspapers and apply supply/demand analysis to them.
14. If the older retail stores had higher costs than the new stores, they would be forced to cut prices below their costs. If that happened, they might stay in business in the short run, assuming they were covering their average variable costs, but they wouldn't stay in business in the long run. If the market remains perfectly competitive, equilibrium price will fall.

Chapter 11: Problems and Exercises

2. a. With the information given, the clear answer is to change output in an attempt to lower costs and achieve an economic profit. We are not told whether *MR* = MC at the level of output at which *ATC* = \$4. If it is, then it is maximizing profit, even though at a loss. If the firm is perfectly competitive, in the long run it should close.
   b. If we now know that *AVC* = \$3.50, we know that price is less than the average variable cost but not whether we are at the quantity where *MR* = MC. If *AVC* cannot be reduced, the firm should stop producing since it loses more by producing than it would if it shut down.
4. a. Zapateria will produce 500 pairs of shoes if the market price is \$70 because at 500 pairs, the market price \$70 equals marginal costs of \$70.
   b. The total profit that Zapateria will earn is \$20 times 500 pairs of shoes, or \$10,000.
   c. Since Zapateria is making an economic profit, it should expect other shoe stores to enter the market.
   d. The long-run equilibrium price is \$40 a pair because at \$40 a pair, zero profit is made.
6. a. As demand decreases, price will decrease in the short run. As price declines, some firms will exit the market. As firms exit, marginal costs will decrease. The price at which zero profit is made falls. Market equilibrium price falls in the long run.
   b. The market equilibrium quantity falls.
   c. The number of firms also falls because the decrease in demand decreased economic profits, making firms exit the market.
   d. Profit per firm returns to zero for all firms, and for the industry in the long run.
8. a. Once the new tomato is generally available, it will likely reduce the price of equal-quality tomatoes in the off-season. However, the new, higher-quality tomato may well sell for more than the cardboard-tasting ones normally bought in winter.
   b. Its effects on farmers depends on what the biotechnology firm charges for its seeds. Further, since the demand for tomatoes is fairly inelastic, the increased supply of good tomatoes (reducing their price) in the off-season will reduce revenues of farmers.
   c. Tomatoes will be grown in areas much farther from their point of sale.
   d. To the degree that the price of tomatoes falls, tomatoes in the winter will more likely be moved from the rear to the front of the salad bar.
10. a. Reconstituted milk can be shipped from low-cost production areas to high-cost production areas, threatening local dairy monopolies with competition.
    b. This probably resulted in strong regional lobbies to protect regional markets.
    c. He is most likely incorrect economically, but correct politically. Price supports cause overproduction of milk and its elimination most likely will cut production. He made this statement because he wanted to get reelected and his supporters are dairy farmers who benefit from the price supports.

Chapter 12: Monopoly
Questions for Thought and Review

2. Monopolists may or may not make pure economic profit. In long-run equilibrium perfectly competitive firms tend to break even, which means they make only a normal profit. So profit is not the distinguishing factor. Instead, the distinguishing characteristic is that the monopolist will restrict output to hold up price; a perfect competitor will not.
4. The development of such a machine would probably reduce the demand for college education to the extent that it would be a lower-priced substitute. (But remember, gaining knowledge is not the only aspect of college—what about the social experiences, the sports, etc.?) If one college could monopolize the production of this machine, it could probably charge close to the current price of college and hire professors to do pure research with the proceeds.
6. A monopolist will tend to sell at a point on the demand curve where demand is elastic, but as the fish gets older (and smelly) the monopolist will wish to lower its price. The price will not be likely to be in the inelastic range, but it may if disposing of the fish is costly.
8. The additional costs are the lost profit by Bayer. If drug makers believe that government will ignore patents on future drugs, thereby lowering future profits, they will spend less on developing new drugs. So the cost to society of a policy of disregarding a patent is having fewer drugs to fight disease in the future.
10. The most likely information involves price discrimination. Existing low fares can be used to attract highly price-elastic customers who spend a lot of time searching for the lowest fare. The individuals who happen to see the advertisement for the special fare likely have a less elastic demand, allowing the airlines to price-discriminate against them.
12. A perfectly elastic marginal cost curve is shown below as the horizontal straight line MC_0. Because the opportunity cost of providing additional units does not increase, welfare loss is greatest with constant marginal costs—shown below as the blue shaded triangle. One can see that welfare loss falls with increasing marginal costs by rotating the marginal cost curve up. An example, MC_1, is shown below. Welfare loss is bounded by the MC curve, the demand curve, and the quantity line.

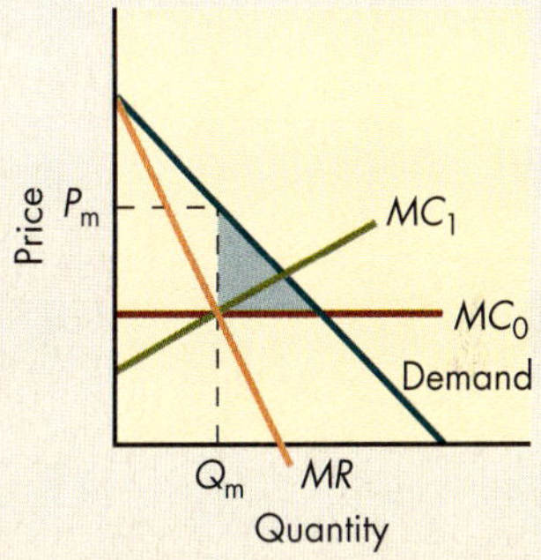

14. The argument for copyrights (and patents) is that without some guarantee of profits from their ideas, people would be unlikely to engage in the effort (and incur the costs) associated with generating new ideas, products, etc. If that is the case, then copyrights may be justified. If people would write good books anyway, then probably society would be better off without copyrights because more books would be sold at a lower price.

Chapter 12: Problems and Exercises

2. This is what is wrong in the graphs shown:
   a. The marginal revenue curve is too steep. It should cut the *x*-axis at *Q*. In addition, quantity should be determined where *MR* = MC.
   b. The curve labeled *ATC* is really the MC curve. Correctly labeled, the profit-maximizing level of output is determined where MC = *MR*.
   c. Quantity should be determined *MR* = MC, not MC = *ATC*. Also, the MC curve should intersect the *ATC* curve at the minimum point of the *ATC* curve.
   d. Quantity should be determined where *MR* = MC.

4.

Q	*P*	*TR*	*MR*	*TC*	*MC*	*ATC*
0	4.20	0.00		3.20		
1	3.80	3.80	3.80	4.20	1.00	4.20
2	3.40	6.80	3.00	5.60	1.40	2.80
3	3.00	9.00	2.20	7.80	2.20	2.60
4	2.60	10.40	1.40	10.40	2.60	2.60
5	2.20	11.00	0.60	13.40	3.00	2.68
6	1.90	11.40	0.40	16.80	3.40	2.80

a. Fixed cost is \$3.20 per month per resident.
b. MC = *MR* at 3 collections per month. The price charged is \$3 per pickup. Profit is 40 cents per pickup per person.
c. *P* = MC at 4 collections per month. The price charged would be \$2.60 per pickup. There would be only normal profits. Economic profit would be zero.
d. The city government should prefer competitive bidding unless there is a natural monopoly. The quality of the pickup would be expected to be greater for the competitive industry because monopolists do not face competitors.

6. a. The limitation of medallions likely increases the price of taxi medallions because it creates a monopoly position for medallion holders. There is no threat of new suppliers to compete away profits. Since the demand for taxis is always shifting to the right as the population grows, the relative monopoly position also grows.
b. Requiring single cab medallion owners to drive their cabs full-time would reduce cab drivers' ability to limit supply and thus would tend to reduce the value of the medallion. However, it would also limit the use of the taxis (since they now rent them out when they are not using them). This effect would be the equivalent to a decrease in the number of medallions and would slightly offset the first effect.
c. The price of medallions would decline as the supply increased. Before the sale, however, the windfall from the sale of new medallions would increase the value of existing medallions mitigating the fall in price from the lower expected revenue from existing medallions.
d. The wealth of existing medallion owners, if one includes the value of the existing medallions, will increase by the windfall but decrease by the reduced value of the medallion from the sale because the expected future stream of profits will have declined. It's unclear what the final result would be.

Chapter 12: Appendix A

2. a. $Q = 2, P = \$39.50$
b. $ATC = \$52$
c. Profit = −\$25

4. a. $Q = 6, P = \$18$
b. $Q = 12, P = 0$

Chapter 13: Monopolistic Competition, Oligopoly, and Strategic Pricing
Questions for Thought and Review

2. Firms differentiate products through advertising. The overriding objective of product differentiation is to maintain or increase market share by creating their own small monopolistic niche.
4. Product differentiation makes us better off to the degree that we prefer having choices of different varieties of the same product. However, in some cases, the differences may be imagined rather than real. Firms reinforce product differentiation with advertising, and so there is a question whether devoting resources to advertising is a benefit (due to increased information) or a waste.
6. The monopolistic competitor does not earn economic profits because of free entry into the market.
8. Strategic pricing is the central characteristic of oligopoly. Monopolistic competitors face too many competitors to price strategically.
10. The contestable market is more interested in the pricing structure and firm behavior arising from free entry into the market. Therefore, the contestable market is more likely to judge by performance.
12. (In answering this question students may be aware of media coverage in the 1990s that suggested colleges colluded in establishing financial aid packages for students and in setting tuition.) Since colleges are not profit maximizers, it is difficult to characterize them as a cartel type of oligopoly. There certainly has been implicit and even explicit collusion; the goals of that collusion are complicated and not simply profit maximization.
14. The breakfast cereal market is definitely oligopolistic; the firms made interdependent decisions.

Chapter 13: Problems and Exercises

2. a. The demand curve is kinked at \$8 and the *MR* curve is discontinuous at \$4. The kink for the demand curve is the opposite to that in the text. There are two places where MC = *MR*, at quantities 4 and 8, as shown.

b. The firm would prefer the equilibrium with the lower output, higher price, and higher profit. This is where output is 4 and price is about $7 a unit.

c. If marginal cost falls, the level of output rises by a lot while the price decline falls by just a little.

d. If marginal cost rises, the level of output falls by a little while the price rises by a lot.

e. This part asks students to survey firms in their area about pricing strategies. The kinked demand model presented in the book is more likely.

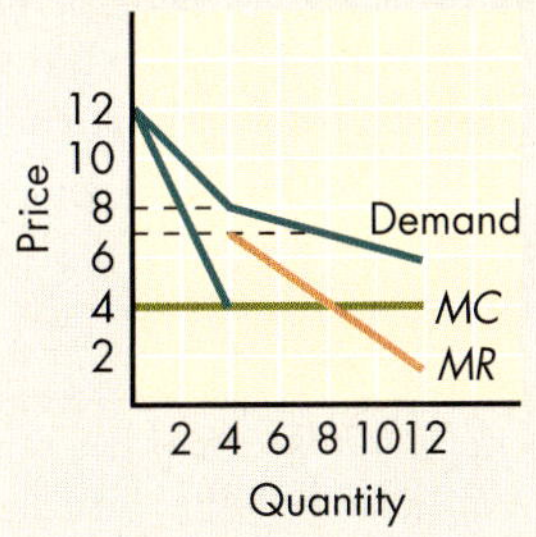

4. a. This market is most likely characterized by oligopoly or possibly monopolistic competition. We say oligopoly because the largest firm will consider the response of its rivals in its decisions. We say monopolistic competition because there are many firms but their products are differentiated. There is some label recognition and loyalty.

b. The Herfindahl index is 428.49 + 289 + 44.9 + 4.84 + 4 + 51.4 = 822.63.

c. The four-firm concentration ratio is 46.6% = 20.7 + 17 + 6.7 + 2.2.

6. a. See the table below.

	A: TweedleDee Does Not Cheat	**A:** TweedleDee Cheats
B: TweedleDum Does Not Cheat	**A:** $2 million **B:** $2 million	**A:** $3 million **B:** $1 million
B: TweedleDum Cheats	**A:** Less than $1 million **B:** $3 million	**A:** Less than $2 million **B:** Less than $2 million

b. If the game is played only once, we would advise that Mr. Notsonice's profit-maximizing strategy is to cheat to maximize expected profit. What his "best" strategy is depends on how much he values being honest.

c. If the game were played over and over, we would advise that his profit-maximizing policy would be to develop some level of trust between the two players and agree not to cheat, avoiding the prisoner's dilemma.

d. The benefit of colluding compared to expected benefit of cheating would have to be greater. It would have to be greater by $2 million.

8. a. The hypothetical payoff matrix is shown below. If neither offers free shipping each earns $1,000 profit. If only Amazon.com offers free shipping its profits are $2,000 while Buy.com loses $300. If both offer free shipping each earns profit of $200.

Buy.com \ **Amazon.com**	No Free Shipping	Free Shipping
No Free Shipping	**A:** $1,000 **B:** $1,000	**A:** $2,000 **B:** −$300
Free Shipping	**A:** −$300 **B:** $2,000	**A:** $200 **B:** $200

b. Amazon.com is best off when it offers free shipping and Buy.com does not. It makes a profit of $2,000.

c. Buy.com is best off when it offers free shipping and Amazon.com does not. It makes a profit of $2,000.

d. Joint profits are maximized when neither offers free shipping. Combined profits are $2,000, instead of $1,700 in the case when one offers free shipping and the other does not.

e. Answers to this question will vary. At the time we answered the question, Amazon.com offered free shipping on purchases of $25 or more and Buy.com offered free shipping with no minimum purchase.

Chapter 14: Real-World Competition and Technology Questions for Thought and Review

2. False. While profits are important to business, because of internal monitoring problems it is not clear that managers maximize profit. They may waste profit potential in high-priced benefits for themselves and in inefficiency generally. The market, however, provides a limit on inefficiency, and firms that exceed the limit and have losses go out of business.
4. X-inefficiency is the result of firms operating far less efficiently than they could technically. The economic forces of a market would knock a firm out of business if it operates less efficiently than the rest of the market. Only a monopolist can produce inefficiently and remain in the game.
6. Even if existing colleges are inefficient, competition from for-profit colleges would not necessarily force them out of business. The political and social forces can keep such colleges from developing. Moreover, some colleges receive state assistance or have endowments that allow them to hold their costs down even if they are inefficient.
8. By the same reasoning used in the answer to question 7, the price could decrease below the competitive equilibrium level. At that below-equilibrium price, some consumers could not get goods, but the consumers who could get goods would be able to hold the prices low nonetheless; it would be in their interest to do so.
10. Natural monopolies, by definition, are the result of a process in which market conditions dictate that monopoly is the most efficient way to produce in that industry. To break up such firms would likely result in higher costs, and thus while there could be more competitors, the benefits associated with more competition (principally, lower prices) would not be achieved.
12. It launched a marketing campaign to retain brand recognition and loyalty to round up before the year 2000. In the year 2000 it also began to lower price to further cement its position in the market and discourage entry.
14. It needs funds to carry on research or new technologies and an ability to earn profits from that research. Oligopoly best meets these criteria.
16. Network externalities lower costs as more people use a product. As network externalities broaden the use of a product, the need for a single standard becomes more important and eventually wins out. The firm with the standard is the big winner and will dominate the market. Even better technology will have a hard time competing with the standard.

Chapter 14: Problems and Exercises

2. If suppliers were able to restrict their output to Q_r, price would rise to P_r. Suppliers kept out of the market lose area E in producer surplus. The consumers, on the other hand, lose both areas D and B. Area B is transferred to suppliers as additional revenue leaving D and E as deadweight loss.

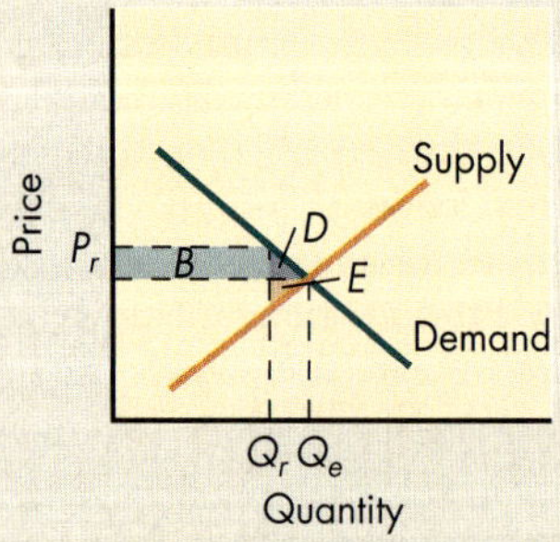

4. See the graph below. The monopolist would be willing to spend any of its profit. This is depicted as the shaded rectangle.

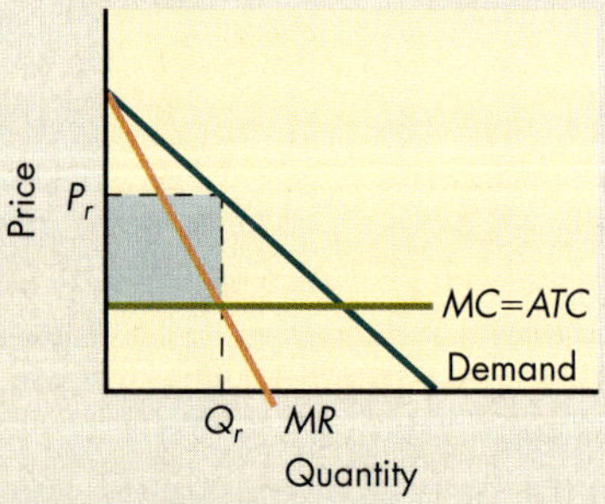

Chapter 15: Antitrust Policy and Regulation Questions for Thought and Review

2. In the Standard Oil case the Court determined that the company was a structural monopoly (it controlled 90 percent of its market), but that alone was not a violation of the Sherman Act. Rather, it was the firm's behavior that brought it into violation. Thus, the firm was found guilty of unfair business practices. In the ALCOA case the key issue was the determination of the firm's market, and hence its share of that market. Determining that ALCOA had 90 percent of the aluminum market, the Court declared it a monopoly, and ALCOA was broken up.
4. The Clayton Antitrust Act gave more guidance and provided for more vigorous enforcement. It is a law that made four specific monopolistic practices illegal when their effect was to lessen competition.
6. Financial aid is often need-based, and so in some sense is an attempt to equalize the price as a proportion of income for students. Again, the test is the impact, and for many students financial aid is the key to access to the college of their choice. It may be more discriminatory in another sense not to have it. Moreover, the fact that something is discriminatory does not necessarily make it bad.
8. As an economist for the firm, I would want the broader definition of the market to make the firm's share a smaller proportion. Thus, I would argue for the three-digit industry as the definition of the market.
10. In some ways the service has improved, but in other ways it has worsened. What would have happened in the absence of the breakup is difficult to say. What this tells us is that making judgments about policy is enormously difficult and requires intricate knowledge of the industry affected.
12. Microsoft was charged with having a monopoly in the personal computer operating systems market. In a dynamic view of the market, technological advances, such as open-source operating systems and the merging of software and hardware, will see the market open to more competition in the future.
14. Conglomerate mergers occur when two relatively unrelated businesses merge. They tend to be approved under our antitrust laws on the assumption that they do not significantly restrict competition. These mergers should be considered like other mergers in terms of their effect, and approved or not on that basis. A blanket policy against such mergers might foreclose some opportunities that would benefit firms and the economy.
16. The two methods government may use to deal with natural monopolies are regulation and government ownership. Price regulation usually takes the form of requiring the firm to charge its average total cost plus a profit margin; this gives the firm no incentive to hold down costs, and cost increases lead directly to price increases. Another problem is that once regulation is established it may extend far beyond the natural monopolies and be introduced into industries where competition could work. Government ownership of natural monopolies is used most often in countries outside the United States, and also has the problem of no incentive to hold costs down or to introduce new technologies. Government-owned firms guarantee jobs and offer high wages, but they pass these higher costs on to the consumers.

Chapter 15: Problems and Exercises

2. In a monopolistic competition model the firms have only a small share of the market and make no profit, so antitrust would have little effect. The graph of monopolistic competition is the relevant graph. In a cartel market, firms get together and allocate market share. Antitrust would prevent that, holding prices down and increasing quantity. The graph of monopoly is the relevant graph. In a contestable market model, potential competition, not market structure, determines equilibrium, so antitrust would have little effect unless it influenced potential competition.
4. a. The likely basis of this suit was predatory pricing to keep price so low that American Airlines' competitors would go out of business and so that the company would enjoy a monopoly position and raise prices.
   b. Knowledge of their financial instability only strengthens the argument. It suggests that American Airlines would not have to hold prices down for too long before its competitors folded.

CHAPTER 16: WORK AND THE LABOR MARKET QUESTIONS FOR THOUGHT AND REVIEW

2. This chapter opens with a quotation from Voltaire: "Work banishes those three great evils: boredom, vice, and poverty." Welfare laws, to the degree that they discourage work, therefore can be said to harm the people they are meant to help. While they help people in the short run, they establish a dependency relationship, which can hurt people in the long run.
4. The elasticity of the labor supply is measured by the percent change in the quantity supplied divided by the percent change in the wage. In this case, 5 divided by 20 is less than 1 (it is 0.25), so the supply is said to be inelastic.
6. Supply/demand analysis is partial equilibrium analysis; immigration policy often affects the general economy and thus requires an analysis of spillover effects and changes that partial equilibrium analysis cannot capture.
8. If the labor market were monopsonistic, so that the pay were less than the competitive wage, the minimum wage could change the effective supply facing the monopsonist and could raise the wage and increase employment simultaneously, as in the graph on the right. In the graph, the monopsonist would hire Q_m workers, paying W_m. With a minimum wage W_e, higher than W_m, the monopsonist would hire Q_e workers, higher than Q_m.

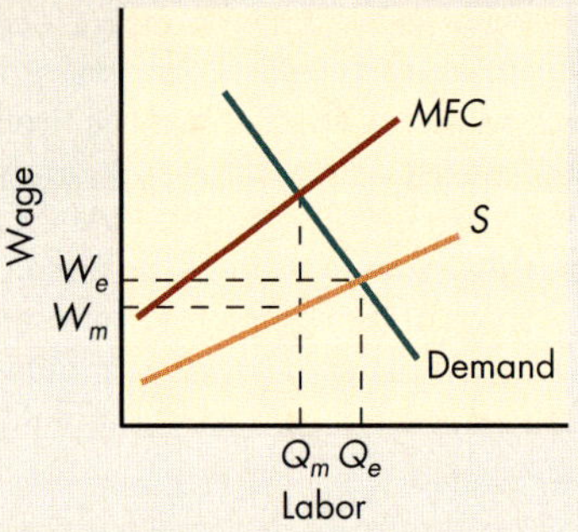

10. The fact that unemployment among blacks is nearly twice as high as it is among whites can be explained by many factors, including discrimination. There are also differences in existing income levels, with the result that many blacks reside in poorer neighborhoods and thus do not have equal access to education and other services that would lead to higher employment. The choices available in terms of opportunities may also lead young people to choose nonmarket activities over participation in the labor force.

CHAPTER 16: PROBLEMS AND EXERCISES

2. a. Based on standard economic theory, one would expect the number of teens employed to rise and the employment of nonteens to decline as the relative wage of teens declines. This assumes that the minimum wage is above the market-clearing wage. Further, one would expect that a large number of employees would lose their jobs at the end of their training period (six months) for "just" reasons, such as not learning the job adequately.
   b. It is likely that the administrative costs of participating in the program were higher than the benefits of hiring teens at the lower training wage. It could also be that market clearing wage in teen labor market was already higher than the subminimum wage. A third possibility is the focal point phenomenon: teens may focus on the mandated minimum wage as their reservation wage and refuse to accept a job at the subminimum training wage.
4. a. Since they will have to pay 20 percent of what they save in added tuition in addition to the 20 percent income tax rate, the implicit marginal tax rate they face on income they save will be 36 percent. The tax on assets is a tax on savings after income taxes have been subtracted, so the tuition tax has to be adjusted to make it a tax on pre-income-tax income. So the relevant tax on tuition as a percent of pretax income is $(1 - t_i) \times t_t = [(1 - 0.2) \times 0.2 = 0.16]$ where t_i is income tax and t_t is the tuition tax. Add this to the 20 percent income tax to get 36 percent.
   b. The second child will raise it to $48.8\% = [(1 - 0.36) \times 0.2 + 0.36] \times 100$. The third child will raise it to $59.04\% = [(1 - 0.488) \times 0.2 + 0.488] \times 100$.
   c. This is a complicated question, but one could argue that divorced parents share in the obligation to pay for college equally and therefore the relative incomes and asset shares of combined incomes and assets should be used to determine contributions. In reality one parent might alone bear the burden of the cost, having to shoulder contributions by both. The second part to this question is for the student to research.
   d. An ability-based scholarship program would attract students of significantly higher caliber if their elasticity of demand is high, but it would most likely compromise the diversity of the student body with respect to income. It would also promote retaliation by other

schools, and the long-run benefit in having brighter students might be very small.

6. a. Firms hire children because children's marginal productivity relative to their wage is higher than it is for alternative workers. Children's marginal product/wage ratio could be higher because the child wage is lower or because the marginal product is higher. Children are often energetic, pliable, and dexterous. For certain jobs these traits could make the children's productivity high. Children may also be more trainable than older employees, and they may work for a lower wage.
   b. Children work for the same reasons that others work—they need money, work is what is expected of them, and so on.
   c. In deciding whether there should be an international ban on child labor, one must look at the effects of that ban. What are the children's opportunity costs of working? If the ban will lead to children starving, the ban does them no good; if it allows them to go to school while the firm hires their parents instead, the ban may help the children. One must also look at the ease with which some firms may get around the ban. If it can be easily avoided in some countries, then the ban will likely hurt children in those countries where it is effective. Also, one should consider whether the work gives children anything useful (such as education) besides pay.

Chapter 16: Appendix A

2. They would likely hire fewer workers since they would take into account the fall in the marginal revenue product that hiring more workers would cause.
4. Yes. Widespread introduction of such programs would likely reduce the demand for teachers and lower their pay.
6. If the firm were a monopolist, the marginal revenue would be less than $3.00, and thus the amount it would be willing to pay would fall.
8. a. The proposal that should be adopted is the one that minimizes costs. Using the cost minimization condition, proposal A is the one that minimizes costs (30/5 = 42/7 = 36/6).
   b. If the price of labor rises to $14, none of the proposals meets the cost minimization condition. There are other combinations that would meet the cost minimization condition.

Chapter 17: Who Gets What? The Distribution of Income Questions for Thought and Review

2. The top 20 percent of individuals in Bangladesh earn 38 percent of the income.
4. Arguments could be made for both approaches. Poverty could be defined relatively since one of our concerns is the distribution of income and the gap between the rich and poor. Poverty could also be defined absolutely since another of our concerns is that people have enough to eat, which is an absolute concept.
6. The observed difference may be due to supply and demand factors. If many people wish to be English teachers and few wish to be garbage collectors, then market factors will result in a higher wage for the garbage collectors—and if one believes in the market mechanism, this is right. That question raises other, more complicated questions about fairness of compensation and the social value of different occupations; it has no right answers.
8. The answer to this question will depend in part on the individual student's circumstances. In general, the incentive effects of a tax may result in a switch from labor to leisure.
10. On the surface the democratic system of one person/one vote would seem to suggest that the politics of redistribution would favor the poor, but it doesn't. One would expect that the poor would use their power to make sure that income was redistributed to them from the rich, but they don't. The reasons for this include the fact that many of the poor don't vote, and so consequently they are not seen as a voting bloc by politicians. Another reason is that when poor people do vote, they vote with other issues in mind. Also, campaigns require financing, which is often supplied by the rich, and so their interests may be more represented than those of the poor.

Chapter 17: Problems and Exercises

2. a. Taking into account in-kind benefits and nonreported income would reduce the number of people seen in poverty. Taking account of the fact that food makes up only a quarter of the family's benefits would suggest

that the inflation adjustment was probably too high in reference to what was defined as poverty in the past, and that the measure of poverty has increased. Taking into account unreported income would reduce the measure of poverty. Taking account of home ownership and cost-of-living differences would involve distributional consequences. It would raise the level of poverty for some and lower it for others.

b. What is fair involves normative judgments. Even if the adjustments were made, one could still argue that the current definition of poverty is too low and that benefits should be increased.

4. Four conditions that you might list before you would favor equality of income are (1) that individuals have essentially the same needs, (2) that they work the same amount, (3) that they have essentially the same health, and (4) that they have put in the same effort up to this point.
   a. Depending on what conditions you listed, it could change your views on welfare in a number of different ways.
   b. Again, it depends on what conditions you chose. If the condition does not include differences in ability, then you would likely favor a progressive income tax.
   c. If the tax were progressive in wage rates, rather than income, hard work would be encouraged and raw ability would be taxed more. If you did not list ability, then you should say that the conditions would be better met.

6. a. This would increase the incentive to work since working longer hours will not push one up into the higher tax bracket.
   b. To the extent that the wage rate measures taxability better than income does, this tax system is fair.
   c. Making the tax system regressive in hours worked would further increase the incentive to work longer hours.
   d. Instituting such a tax system faces enormous difficulties. Wage rates for each individual would have to be measured, and many positions have no explicit wage rate. Some method for calculating wage rates of salaried positions would have to be designed.

Chapter 18: Government Policy and Market Failures

Questions for Thought and Review

2. The marginal social benefit of a good that exhibits positive externalities is greater than the private social benefit because the trade results in a benefit to people outside the trade.

4. An economist might argue about the word *acceptable*. While not many people would argue that any pollution is good, an economist who realizes that eliminating pollution completely is probably an impossible goal would find pollution acceptable if it could be reduced to a cost-efficient level.

6. The tax on oil will affect the pollution coming from oil, but it is possible that users could switch to other fuel sources that actually result in other and greater forms of pollution. Moreover, some types of pollution would be unaffected. Thus, the net impact on the environment is difficult to predict.

8. The public aspect of safety is that if safety provides a safe environment, it is provided for all people and one person enjoying safety does not preclude others from benefiting from that safety. Naming streets allows people to orient themselves in towns and facilitates communication. Once a street is named, it benefits all people. No one can be excluded from referring to that name. In addition, one person using that street name does not preclude others from referring to that street with its name. Before the street is named, however, if a particular name is used to refer to more than one street, the value of that name in providing geographic orientation will be diminished. The public good aspect of the lighthouse and newspaper is that once it is produced it can be consumed over and over again. Though in the case of the newspaper, the owner can keep others from benefiting by keeping it to himself.

10. In a market, when buyers and sellers have different amounts of information about the good for sale, a problem occurs called the adverse selection problem. The problem is that the market for quality products disappears. In commercial dating services, the seller certainly has more information about the negative (and positive) aspects of the product than the buyer. We suspect that the market has fewer "acceptable" dates than the general population.

12. To keep rates to a minimum, insurance companies estimate information about individuals by categorizing them. If everyone paid the same amount, low-cost customers would be paying for high-cost customers and eventually change companies, leaving only high-cost customers. One would expect that, statistically, married drivers are safer drivers.

14. Many answers are possible, beginning with (1) the label on their breakfast cereal, (2) the roads they use to get to school, (3) either the school they go to (if it is public) or the federal funds their school receives (if it is private), (4) the tax they pay on the snack at the snack bar, and (5) the laws that are enforced on the roadways.

16. The advanced degree serves the same purpose as a license. It reduces the supply and increases the wage.

Chapter 18: Problems and Exercises

2. a. Proposal A would force a downward shift in each demand curve, while Proposal B would raise the price at each quantity, also shifting the demand curves down.
   b. The consumers in group 1 have a more elastic demand, so a small increase in price results in a large decrease in quantity; these consumers can more easily adjust their usage and would therefore favor Proposal A. The members of group 2 would be more likely to favor the tax because changing their usage is more difficult. Their inelasticity can be interpreted to mean that they are more willing to pay a higher price than to use less.
4. a. One could explain the Seattle Stomp if there were a per can charge for garbage. To maximize the amount of waste per can (and thus per flat fee), Seattle citizens stomp their garbage.
   b. A fee structure based on weight would eliminate the Seattle Stomp.
6. a. Most likely the price of all cars in California rose, and air quality rose as well.
   b. This law could possibly have increased pollution if consumers held on to their older, less efficient but lower-cost, higher-performance gas cars and delayed purchase of an electric car. This would have increased the average age of cars on the road, increasing pollution. Furthermore, if electric cars (the most likely candidates) were designed to meet the no-pollution requirement, it could be that the process of generating sufficient electricity to run the cars would produce even more pollution, at which point even more regulation might be imposed. (The law was modified and never went fully into effect.)
   c. Economists generally favor market incentive programs over direct regulation. A market incentive program to reduce pollution by a certain percent might be to tax drivers of older, high-pollution cars and use the tax revenue to subsidize those who purchase the new, no-pollution cars. This approach will more likely equate marginal cost with marginal benefit.
8. a Some dairy farmers would probably argue that labeling is unnecessary since the drugs they administer have been certified by the FDA. Dairy farmers who do not use BST would support BST labeling.
   b. If BST were to be listed on milk containers, one could argue that all drugs and antibiotics should be listed. However, such listing (without more information) may cause consumer concern. To support BST labeling and not other labeling, one must argue that BST is different.
   c. One would suspect that dairy farmers who support BST labeling would not support the broader law that might include so many drugs that consumers become outraged at dairy farmers. Only those few farmers who use wholly organic farming would support full labeling.

Chapter 19: Politics and Economics: The Case of Agricultural Markets

Questions for Thought and Review

2. A price support system achieved through acreage restriction is illustrated below. The graph shows that, under this system, the farmers gain rectangle A as income from the government in the form of payments not to grow wheat, and rectangle B from consumers who pay more for the wheat the farmers do grow.

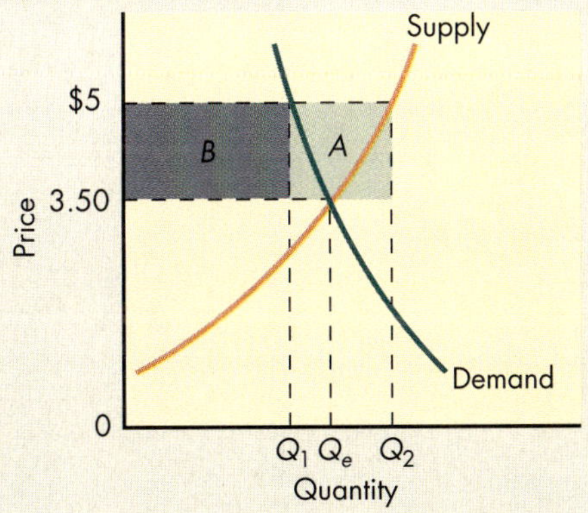

4. As shown below, the method of price support that is most costly to the taxpayer is the subsidies on sales to keep prices down; taxpayers must finance the subsidy payments on all subsidized farm products, represented by areas A, B, and C.

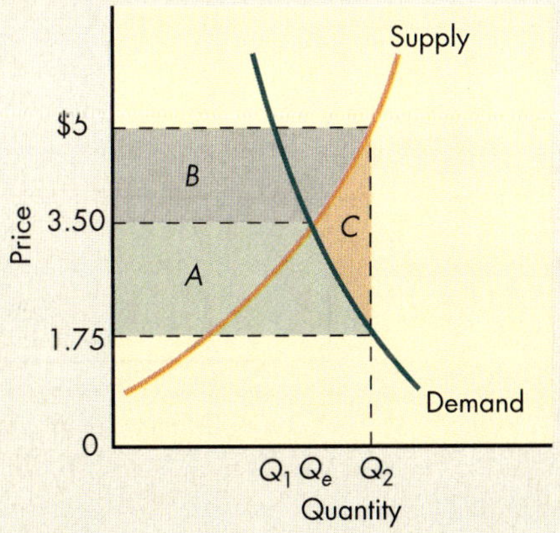

6. Tariffs and quotas generally accompany price support systems in order to prevent lower-priced foreign products from competing in the domestic market.
8. Governments find grandfathering a good option when they institute price supports because it is the easiest way of restricting supply. Existing suppliers retain their level of output, added or new entry is denied or limited, and the policy is easy to enact and easy to enforce.
10. The nonrecourse loan is a price support system in which government buys goods in the form of collateral on defaulting loans. The land bank program is a price support in which the government supports prices by giving farmers economic incentives to reduce supply.

Chapter 19: Problems and Exercises

2. The graph on the right shows an increase in demand sufficient to raise the market price to P_s. The market quantity is also increased to Q_s. The cost to the government is the shaded rectangle. If instead supply is restricted (shown in the far right graph), the government must pay the farmers ($P_s - P_1$) for every unit not grown at price P_s, resulting in a cost equal to the area of the bolded rectangle. Therefore, assuming that you cannot use the corn, the second policy is preferred.

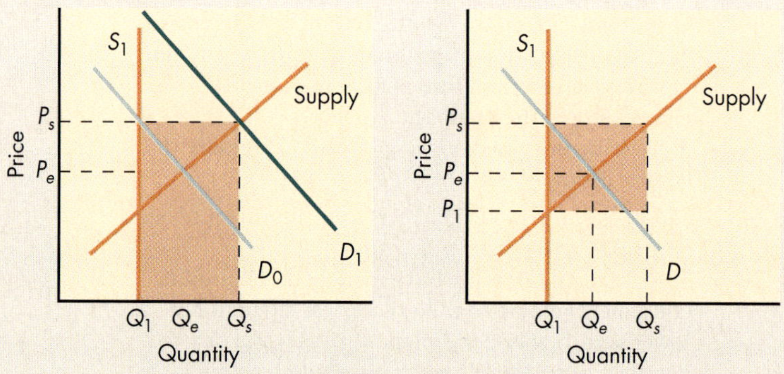

4. a. Consumers of peanuts pay more in higher prices—estimated at between \$190 and \$369 million a year—and suffer from reduced consumption.
   b. See the graph below. Area *B* represents additional costs to consumers, while areas *D* and *E* represent deadweight loss of the program.
   c. The land with peanut quotas is a government license to sell millions of pounds of peanuts and thus is priced higher to include the present value of the future returns to that license.
   d. The government's costs would likely rise enormously in the attempt to keep supply constrained to maintain the 50 percent above competitive equilibrium price.
   e. If the United States limited the guaranteed high price to U.S. producers only, administrative procedures would have to be set up to see that imported peanuts are not passed off as U.S.-produced peanuts.

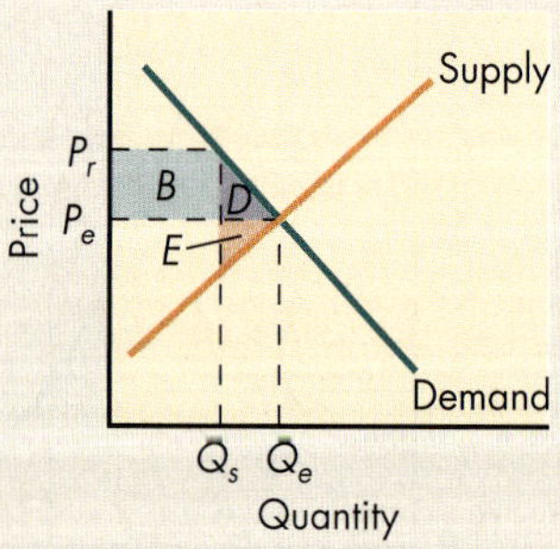

6. a. The reason the difference exists is mostly political. A small group of ranchers benefits greatly from the reduced fee and is a strong lobby for the cause.
   b. The advantage could be that the U.S. government could require more from ranchers in their care of the land.
   c. One would expect excess demand because at the price below equilibrium, the quantity of land owners are willing to supply at \$1.86 is lower than the quantity demanded.

Chapter 20: Microeconomic Policy, Economic Reasoning, and Beyond

Questions for Thought and Review

2. The problem with proposing only Pareto optimal policies would lie in developing them. As the text points out, there are no examples of real-world policies that benefit some people without hurting anyone. If economists seek to propose only Pareto optimal policies, they may end up proposing no policies. Focusing only on Pareto optimality condemns them to irrelevancy in real-world affairs, and to focusing on abstract models rather than on the real world.

4. The usual arguments against the buying and selling of body organs include the concern that people might seek to make such sales for the money involved and exploit the poor, and that those with the ability to pay would get needed organs sooner than those without means, again favoring the well-off over the poor. Some may believe that it is immoral to sell body parts. Arguments for selling body parts include that both parties freely enter the transaction, and that both sellers (since they decided they preferred the money to the body part) and buyers benefit. Economic theory provides no answers to such questions.

6. The textbook suggests a method for valuing one's life. Your answer should consider what you would pay to reduce their chance of dying by a certain amount. The value of life is that amount times the inverse of the reduced probability of dying.

8. An economist might propose a policy that has little chance of adoption because he or she might be removed from the concerns that make policies unadoptable (i.e., political concerns). In so doing, economists put ideas into the real world and may influence the way people think. The goal behind policy proposals is not always to get them implemented.

10. Most politicians say that they are out to do the public good, but in practice they often (in their quest to be reelected) do things that just sound good.

12. Any decision about prisons involves complicated ethical and moral as well as economic considerations. In reference to the economic issues alone, it would seem that it does make sense to build more prisons since, assuming prisons are currently full, the marginal benefits of additional prisons are greater than the marginal costs.

Chapter 20: Problems and Exercises

2. a. A higher percentage of births by C-section are done at for-profit hospitals, most likely because the profit margin for C-sections is higher than that for vaginal births.
   b. The implication that can be drawn is that goodwill cannot be relied on to lead to low-cost health programs. Other mechanisms must be instituted to ensure efficiency.
   c. In the case of fixed payment, the for-profit hospital would probably do more vaginal births, which cost less than C-sections. The C-section rate would most likely rise at nonprofit institutions as necessary C-sections are limited at for-profit hospitals and shift toward nonprofit hospitals.

4. a. Since the supply of teenage baby-sitters shifted to the left just as the demand for them shifted to the right, the equilibrium wage probably rose dramatically, reducing the number of times parents go out without their children.
   b. The price of baby-sitters probably rose as described in *a*.
   c. The average age of baby-sitters probably fell as parents loosened their requirements of baby-sitters in an attempt to find substitutes for the reduced number of 14- to 17-year-olds.

6. a. According to standard economic reasoning, the value of an additional dollar spent in preventing death is (assuming the journal's figures are correct) more valuable in the United States than in Sweden and in Portugal, and thus more money should go to saving lives in the United States. However, there are moral issues that complicate matters and make the answer unclear.
   b. This is a complicated question. First, many Americans fly in Portugal and, second, it would be bad publicity for an airline to value lives of people differently by national origin or to even acknowledge making such a marginal cost/marginal benefit analysis with regard to safety precautions at all. Moreover, there are those sticky moral issues, which lead one to value all life equally.
   c. To the degree that the cost of the standard is the same, the standard economic answer is yes. If noneconomic factors are included, the answer is not so clear-cut.

8. a. The likely effect of that proposal would be a flood of criticism. Certain human rights such as the sanctity of the human body are held in high regard regardless of societal status.

A proposal that, on its face, seems economically sound is not acceptable if it does not include issues of human rights.

b. That was the effect because the economic model did not account for all issues. Morality issues provoke strong political reactions.

CHAPTER 21: INTERNATIONAL TRADE POLICY

QUESTIONS FOR THOUGHT AND REVIEW

2. The opportunity cost of producing 1 widget is 1 wadget in Wadgetland and 4 wadgets in Widgetland. Since the opportunity costs differ, there is a basis for trade. One possibility for trade is for Widgetland to produce 240 widgets, trading 60 widgets for 120 wadgets, and for Wadgetland to produce 720 wadgets, trading 120 wadgets for 60 widgets.
4. Smaller countries tend to get more of the gains from trade because more opportunities are opened up for them. This is true only under the condition that competition among traders prevails. International traders in small countries often have little competition and so keep large shares of the gains from trade for themselves; hence the small country may not get the gains from trade.
6. An equitable method might be to tax those who gain from the trade liberalization and give the proceeds to those who are hurt by it. Assuming the original distribution is equitable and the government is not trying to redistribute income, this method is equitable because the combined policies make everyone better off. The political problems with implementation include: (1) Everyone will try to exaggerate the amount they are hurt and minimize the amount they are helped. Thus actually finding a tax that accomplishes the goal will be difficult. (2) Once the taxes and subsidies are in place, they may not be removed after the adjustment of displaced workers is complete. Losers will be overcompensated and gainers will be taxed too much.
8. When the United States economy fell into a recession in 1991 income and imports fell and the trade balance improved. This is consistent with predictions.
10. Economists support free trade because it forces domestic producers to operate efficiently and it increases consumer welfare.
12. Both increase the price of the import, helping the domestic producers. In the case of the voluntary restraint, increases in price result in increased revenue to foreign firms and increased demand is met entirely by the domestic market.
14. With a price floor, there is a loss of consumer surplus, higher prices, and lower quantities.
16. The WTO is the successor to GATT. Both work toward agreements to reduce trade. WTO includes enforcement mechanisms that GATT did not have.

CHAPTER 21: PROBLEMS AND EXERCISES

2. a. No. Both countries' opportunity cost of producing pickles is 2/1 (they must give up 2 olives to get 1 pickle). Neither has a comparative advantage, so there is no basis for trade.
   b. If there are economies of scale, it definitely pays for both countries to specialize since doing so would lower total costs. Which one should specialize is an open question since neither has a comparative advantage.
4. a. Firms may produce in Germany, because (1) transportation costs in the other countries may be very high, so that if these costs are included, it would not be efficient to produce there; (2) there might be tariffs or quotas for imports into Germany that will prevent producing elsewhere; (3) the productivity of German labor may be so much higher that unit labor costs in Germany are the lowest; and (4) historical circumstances may have led to production in Germany and the cost of moving production may exceed potential gains.
   b. Yes, one would expect some movement from Greece and Italy into Germany, but this is limited by the minimum wage laws in Germany. Also, social restrictions such as language and culture will limit labor mobility. With such high unemployment in Germany already, one would not expect much short-run movement. Movement in the long run, however, may be substantial.
   c. I would need to know how stable the political system is, what the worker productivity rates are, how sound the infrastructure (such as roads) is, and what the tax differences are between the two countries.
6. a. Three assumptions are that the good is tradable, that transportation costs are minimal, and that taxes between the two countries do not differ significantly.

b. To the degree that production facilities and labor can move easily, the law of one price should hold for labor, too. Given the wage differentials that exist among countries with seemingly equivalent productivities, it seems that these conditions do not hold for labor.

c. Since capital is more mobile than labor, the law of one price should have a greater tendency to hold for capital. Financial capital is a great example. Interest rates among countries tend to equate much faster than wages.

CHAPTER 21: APPENDIX A

2. a. The opportunity cost for Greece of making 1 million olives is 1,000 pounds of cheese. The opportunity cost for France of making 1 million olives is 250 pounds of cheese. The opportunity cost for Greece of making 1,000 pounds of cheese is 1 million olives. The opportunity cost for France of making 1,000 pounds of cheese is 4 million olives.
   b. They are worse off since France has a comparative advantage in producing olives and Greece has a comparative advantage in producing cheese. Under the new law France produces 50,000 pounds of cheese and Greece produces 500 million olives—point *A*. They could have had a greater combination: 100,000 pounds of cheese produced by Greece and 600 million olives (200 million by France and 400 million by Greece)—point *B*. Their *combined* possibility curve if they were able to trade is the outermost production possibility curve shown.

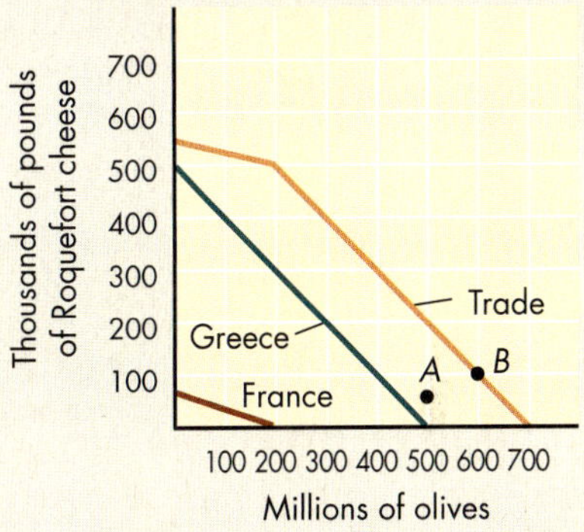

CHAPTER 22: ECONOMIC GROWTH, BUSINESS CYCLES, UNEMPLOYMENT, AND INFLATION

QUESTIONS FOR THOUGHT AND REVIEW

2. The U.S. per capita growth rate of 1.5 to 2.0 percent per year is lower than those of Japan (4.8 percent per year) and China (3.4 percent per year), close to those of Western Europe (2.5 percent per year) and Latin America (1.4 percent per year), and higher than those of Eastern Europe (1.0 percent per year) and Africa (0.8 percent per year).
4. A representative business cycle is shown below. Each of the four phases—peak, downturn, trough, and expansion—is clearly labeled.

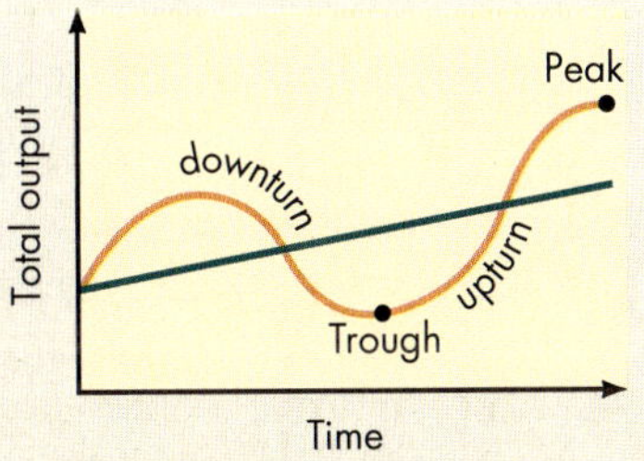

6. Reducing unemployment to 1.2 percent today is not likely for several reasons. One is that a low inflation rate seems to be incompatible with low unemployment. Another is that today's economy differs from that of the World War II period, when there was an enormous ideological commitment to the war effort and an acceptance of strong wage and price controls.
8. Structural unemployment, because it results from changes in the structure of the economy, is best studied in the long-run framework. Cyclical unemployment, which results from fluctuations in economic activity, is best studied in the short-run framework.
10. Okun's rule of thumb states that a 1 percentage point change in the unemployment rate will cause income to change in the opposite direction by 2 percent. Thus, a 2 percentage point rise in unemployment will likely cause income to decrease by 4 percent.
12. While inflation doesn't make the nation any poorer on average, it does have costs. Its costs include capricious distributional effects, the destruction of the informational value of prices, and the breaking down of the institutional structure within which markets work.

Chapter 22: Problems and Exercises

2. a. The index in 2003 is 68/64 × 100 = 106.25.
   b. Real output is Nominal output/Price index × 100 = \$300 billion/115 × 100 = \$260.9 billion.
   c. Percent change in nominal output = Percent change in real output + Percent change in the price level. Thus, change in nominal output = 5 percent + 2 percent = 7 percent.
   d. Percent change in nominal output = Percent change in real output + Percent change in the price level. Thus, inflation = 7 percent − 3 percent = 4 percent.
4. a. Possible explanations include Japanese cultural emphases on tradition, honor, and loyalty. In Japan, firms are less willing to lay off workers in times of excess supply and workers are less likely to change employers in search of higher compensation. Another explanation is the nature of Japanese production. One could suggest that Japanese production does not rely on a changing base of skills so that the skills of workers always match the skills demanded of a particular firm.
   b. It is impossible to say which is better. Each needs to be judged within the broader system of the economy. This requires far more knowledge than is required for this book.
   c. The answer to this question depends on the distribution of layoffs and hires in each of the economies. If layoffs in Japan were unavoidable and occurred among lower-ranking employees, the average tenure of Japanese employees would rise. If instead the elderly were asked to retire, the average tenure would decline. In the United States, assuming that new hires came from those just entering the labor force, the average tenure would most likely decline.

Chapter 23: National Income Accounting Questions for Thought and Review

2. If you add up all transactions, you will include intermediate goods—so the amount will far exceed GDP, which is the measure of final output within a country.
4. The aggregate value added at each stage of production is, by definition, precisely equal to the value of final sales. Thus, the value-added rate should also be 15 percent. (Technical note: This is assuming the value-added tax is an income-based rather than consumption-based.)
6. NDP is actually preferable to GDP as the expression of a country's domestic output because NDP takes depreciation into account. Depreciation is a cost of producing goods. However, measuring true depreciation is difficult because asset values fluctuate, and so GDP rather than NDP is generally used in discussions of economic activity.
8. Transfer payments are not included in national income, so nothing directly would happen to it.
10. The difference between domestic personal income and national personal income is the addition of net foreign factor income to domestic personal income.

Chapter 23: Problems and Exercises

2. a. GDP should fall as nonmarket transactions increase.
   b. GDP would not change.
   c. GDP would rise by the broker's commission.
   d. GDP would not change.
   e. GDP would not change.
   f. GDP would rise.
4. GDP = C + I + G + (X − M) = 500 + 185 + 195 + 4 = 884.
   GNP = GDP + Net foreign factor income = 884 + 2 = 886.
   NNP = GNP − Depreciation = 886 − 59 = 827.
   NDP = GDP − Depreciation = 884 − 59 = 825.
   NI = NNP − Indirect business taxes = 827 − 47 = 780.
   PI = NI + Transfers from government + Nonbusiness interest income − Corporate retained earnings − Social Security taxes = 780 + 72 + 10 − 51 − 35 = 776.
   DPI = PI − Personal taxes = 776 − 91 = 685.
6. a. GDP = C + I + G + (X − M) = 485.
   GNP = GDP + Net foreign factor income = 488.
   NI = Compensation + Rent + Profits + Net interest = 448.

NNP = NI + Indirect business taxes = 475.
NNP = NDP + Net foreign factor income: NDP = 472.

b. Depreciation = GDP − NDP = 13.
c. GDP = C + *I* + G + (X − M) = 480.
GNP = GDP + Net foreign factor income = 483.
NI = Compensation + Rent + Profits + Net interest = 459.
NNP = NI + Indirect business taxes = 486.
NNP = NDP + Net foreign factor income: NDP = 483.
Depreciation = GDP − NDP = −3.

Chapter 24: Growth, Productivity, and the Wealth of Nations

Questions for Thought and Review

2. A person living in 1910 is most likely to work more to buy a dozen eggs than the person living in 1990. The reason is that, since 1910, the United States income has been rising, on average, by more than the growth in the population. This means that the income per person has gone up since 1910. Thus, the person living in 1990 has a higher income than the person living in 1910 and so is likely to work less to buy the dozen eggs.
4. Specialization and division of labor allow a country to take advantage of its comparative advantage. Thus, the individual country can specialize in the production of goods in which it has a comparative advantage and trade them with the goods for which it does not have a comparative advantage. Hence, free trade will, in general, benefit the participating countries.
6. The three types of capital are physical capital, human capital, and social capital. Physical capital includes the buildings and machines that are available for the production process. Human capital includes the workers' skills that are embodied in them through education, experience, and on-the-job training (i.e., through people's knowledge). Social capital includes the habitual way of doing things that guides people in how they approach production in the economy.
8. The two actions governments can take to promote the development of new technologies are (*a*) to create patents and protect property rights, and (*b*) to implement policies to provide funding for research.
10. If individuals suddenly needed more food to subsist, the subsistence line would rotate to the left. Population would decrease and output would fall, as is shown in the graph in the next column.

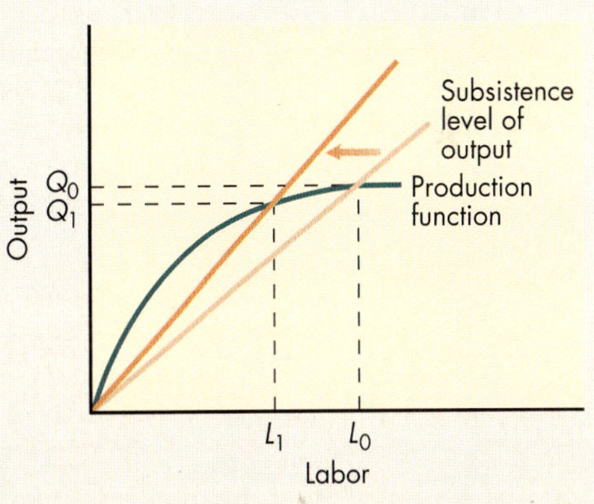

12. The following are three ways in which growth can be undesirable:
    a. Growth may contribute to increased pollution.
    b. Growth changes traditional cultures with beautiful handiwork, music, and dance into cultures of modern gadgets.
    c. Some argue that the number of average working hours has increased because of growth in the economy.
14. To compete with the others, the producer has an incentive to innovate (i.e., to invest in technological advance so that he can increase his efficiency and so take a lead among his competitors). But technological innovation is usually associated with a high cost initially, and the producer who has advanced his production process cannot afford to impose a high price on his product due to competition in the industry and so he cannot sustain his technological improvement.

16. Communities are willing to give tax relief to new-technology firms to help them survive during the initial stages, when the start-up costs are very high. If these companies survive, they will be able to provide employment opportunities to the community members and thereby play a role in increasing the community's total income and standard of living.

Chapter 24: Problems and Exercises

2. Constant returns to scale refers to the relationship between increases in all inputs and output. In this case, only one input rose, so we cannot make any conclusion about returns to scale.
4. a. −4.8%
   b. 4.6%
   c. 4%
   d. 2.0%
6. a. The borrowing circle probably would not work in the United States, because the strong social forces in Bangladesh that eliminate the need for collateral do not exist in the United States. Perhaps there are some minority groups that do not have the necessary collateral to get loans in the traditional way but whose culture could provide the social forces to make repayment of loans more certain.
   b. A possible modification of the program would be to require proof that the "traditional" methods of financing are not open. This would limit the program to those who have few options but do have a good business plan and intention to repay. Another modification would be to require that the business be maintained in the neighborhood where the cosigners live. This would maintain the social forces that ensure repayment.
   c. Minorities often face the same problems because they do not have adequate assets for collateral necessary to gain traditional financing. They also may face discrimination by banks and venture capitalists. Nevertheless, they may have good business plans and an intention to repay.

Chapter 25: Aggregate Demand, Aggregate Supply, and Modern Macroeconomics

Questions for Thought and Review

2. Classicals felt that if the wage was lowered, the Depression would end. They saw unions as preventing the fall in wages, and they saw the government lacking the political will to break up unions.
4. Say there is a rise in the price level. That would make the holders of money poorer (the wealth effect). It would also reduce the real money supply, increasing the interest rate (the interest rate effect). Assuming fixed exchange rates, it would also make goods less internationally competitive (the international effect). All three account for the quantity of aggregate demand decreasing—decreasing spending as the price level rises. These initial increases are then multiplied by the multiplier effect as the initial spending reverberates through the economy.
6. If the economy is in short-run equilibrium below potential output, there will be downward pressures on the price level. The short-run aggregate supply curve will shift down and the price level will fall. This will set the wealth, interest rate, and international effects in motion, increasing the quantity of aggregate demand and thereby bringing the economy into long-run equilibrium at potential output.
8. Yes, they would emphasize the inherent value of the program rather than discussing the program's effect on aggregate demand. This is because programs that increase aggregate demand when the economy is close to potential will ultimately lead to inflation and little increase in real output.
10. To design an appropriate fiscal policy, it is important to know the level of potential income because where the economy is relative to potential income tells you whether you want expansionary or contractionary policy. Conducting fiscal policy without having an estimate of potential income would be like driving without being able to see the road.
12. The simple model abstracts from a number of important issues such as the problem of estimating potential income. Without knowing potential income, we cannot know whether expansionary or contractionary policy is called for.

Chapter 25: Problems and Exercises

2. a. Keynes used models not in a mechanistic way, but in an interpretive way. He was a Marshallian who saw economic models as an engine of analysis, not an end in themselves.
   b. It fits in nicely with the "other things constant" assumption since the policy relevance follows only when one has eliminated that assumption and taken into account all the things held at the back of one's mind.
   c. It definitely was primarily in the art of economics since the above method is the method used in the art of economics.
4. a. An increase in the availability of inputs will shift the *LAS* curve to the right.
   b. A civil war will presumably destroy productive capacity or otherwise halt production and cause a shift in the *LAS* curve to the left.
   c. To the degree that the rise in oil prices results in an overall rise in the price level, this will shift the *SAS* curve up. Otherwise, other relative prices will decline to offset the rise in oil prices and the *SAS* curve will not shift at all.
   d. If wages that were fixed become flexible and aggregate demand increases, the *SAS* curve will shift up as wages rise.
6. a. The slowing of foreign economies will reduce exports, shifting the *AD* curve to the left by a multiple of the initial decline in exports (from AD_0 to AD_1 in the graph below). I would recommend that the government increase expenditures by an amount equal to the initial decline in exports. This will shift the *AD* curve back to its initial position, as shown in the graph.

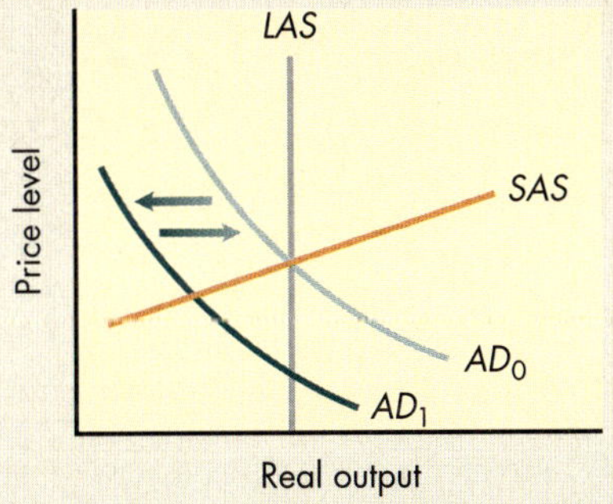

   b. An economy operating above potential is shown by point *A* in the graph below. To keep the inflation from rising (the *SAS* curve from shifting up), the government should reduce expenditures enough (shifting the *AD* curve from AD_0 to AD_1) to bring the economy back to long-run equilibrium at potential output, Y_P, and the price level, P_1, as shown below.

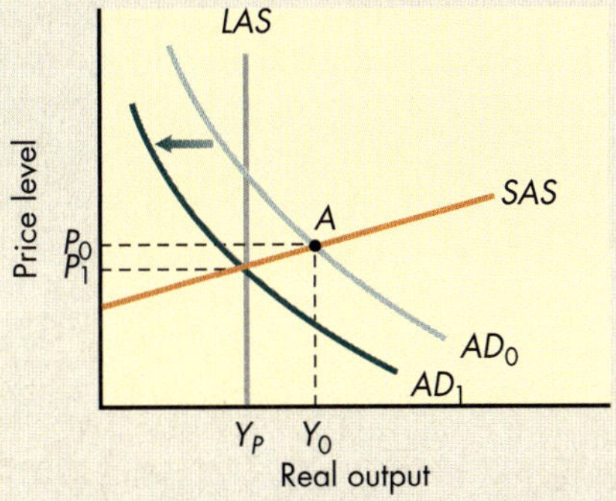

   c. A new technology that increases potential output will shift the *LAS* curve (from LAS_0 to LAS_1), creating excess capacity and downward pressure on factor prices. If left alone, the price level will fall and real output will rise. If the government wants to keep the price level constant, it can increase expenditures enough to increase output to the new potential (shifting the *AD* curve from AD_0 to AD_1).

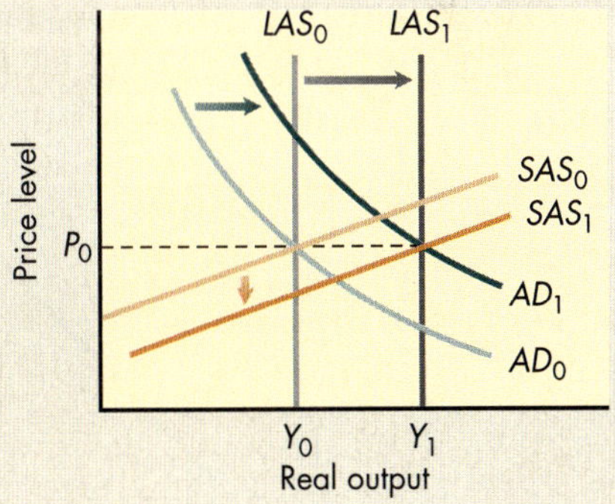

Chapter 26: The Multiplier Model Questions for Thought and Review

2. At levels of output above equilibrium, inventories are building up because planned expenditures are below actual production. People are not buying all that is produced.
4. The *AE* curve becomes steeper when the marginal propensity to expend increases. Equilibrium income rises.
6. Shocks to aggregate expenditures are any sudden changes in factors that affect *C*, *I*, *G*, *X*, or *M*. This includes consumer sentiment, business optimism, foreign income, and government policy. It is possible that people could change their marginal propensities to consume and save, and this could also have an effect on the economy.
8. If the *mpe* is 0.5, the multiplier is 2. Every $1 increase in autonomous expenditures will raise income by $2. To close a recessionary gap of $200 the government needs to generate $100 of additional autonomous spending. It can accomplish this by increasing government expenditures by $100.
10. The effects of this invention on the economy would be manifold and in many ways unpredictable because such major shocks have social, institutional, and political effects, as well as economic effects. The obvious effect is that the demand for the pill would likely be tremendous (after people were sure it was safe), and so production of the pill would gear up to meet the demand. Market structure and pricing decisions will play a big role in determining the new effect of the change. Alternative forms of transportation would suffer decreases in demand (cars, mass transit, airplanes, etc.), and levels of production of those goods and services would adjust, as would employment in those industries and related industries. Measured GDP might actually fall.
12. A mechanistic model states the equilibrium independent of where the economy has been or of what people wanted. A mechanistic model is used as a direct guide for policy prescriptions. An interpretive model is used as a guide that highlights dynamic interdependencies that is suggestive of the direction of the response of aggregate output to various policy initiatives.

Chapter 26: Problems and Exercises

2. a. If the *mpe* is .66, the value of the multiplier is 3. A decrease in autonomous expenditures of $20 will likely result in a decrease in income of $60. This is demonstrated in the graph below.
   b. The analysis in *a* is graphed below.

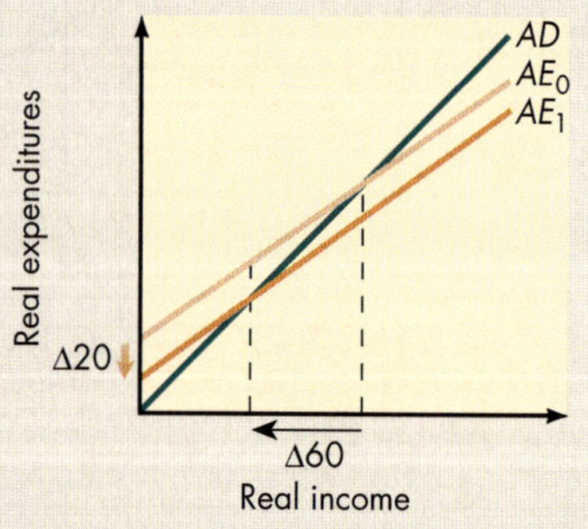

4. Given that the *mpe* is .6, I_0 = 1,000; G_0 = 8,000; C_0 = 10,000; and $(X_0 - M_0)$ = 1,000, then:
   a. $Y = 10{,}000 + .6Y + 1{,}000 + 8{,}000 + 1{,}000$.
   $Y - .6Y = 20{,}000$; $0.4Y = 20{,}000$; $Y = 50{,}000$.
   Thus, the level of income in the country is $50,000. (Note that Examland seems to be on a U.S. dollar currency standard.)
   b. If net exports increase by $2,000, income will increase by $5,000 (the multiplier is 2.5, or 1/.4).
   c. According to Okun's law, a one-percentage-point change in unemployment will cause a 2 percent change in income in the opposite direction. Thus, if income has increased by $5,000, which is a 10 percent increase, then unemployment should drop by 5 percentage points.
   d. If the *mpe* falls from 0.6 to 0.5, the multiplier decreases from 2.5 to 2. The answer to part *a* would now be $40,000; the answer to part *b* would be $4,000; and the answer to part *c* is that unemployment should fall by 5 percentage points.
6. Given that income is $50,000, the *mpe* is .75:
   a. To reduce unemployment by 2 percentage points (again, by Okun's rule of thumb) requires a 4 percent increase in income, which in this case is $2,000. The multiplier is 4.0, calculated as $[1/(1 - mpe)]$. To generate a $2,000 increase in income, increase government spending by $500.
   b. If the *mpe* is .66, the multiplier is 2.94, which means that to generate a $2,000 increase in income, government spending would have to increase by $680.27.
   c. If the *mpe* is .5, then the multiplier is 2.0, which means that to generate a $2,000 increase in income, government spending would have to increase by $1,000.

8. a. If the *mpe* is .5, the multiplier is 2. To eliminate the inflationary gap, the government should undertake a contractionary fiscal policy. Since the economy is $36,000 above potential, we would advise decreasing government spending by $18,000.
   b. Using Okun's rule of thumb, since income falls by 6 percent, we would expect unemployment to rise by 3 percentage points to 8 percent.
   c. The multiplier now becomes 5, so we would advise decreasing spending by $7,200. We would not change our answer to *b*.

Chapter 26: Appendix A

2. We would recommend increasing expenditures by 80.
4. This makes the multiplier 2.08. This means that we would increase expenditures by about 192 or cut taxes by about 213.
6. This would make the multiplier = $1/(1 - c + ct + m - mt)$. It would be a slightly higher multiplier. (The difference between the two assumptions is whether we are assuming government imports.)

Chapter 26: Appendix B

2. a. The *AD* curve will become steeper.
   b. An increase in the size of the multiplier makes the *AD* curve flatter because the effect of changes in the price level on aggregate demand will be augmented even more by the multiplier.
   c. An increase of $20 in autonomous expenditures has no effect on the slope of the *AD* curve; it only affects its position.
   d. A decline in the price level disrupting the financial market will make the *AD* curve steeper because it eliminates the price-level interest rate effect.

Chapter 27: Money, Banking, and the Financial Sector Questions for Thought and Review

2. Money is to the economy as oil is to an engine because money is a financial asset that makes the real economy function smoothly by serving as a medium of exchange, a unit of account, and a store of wealth. Without it, the economy comes to a screeching halt.
4. In order to maintain money's usefulness and to prevent large fluctuations in the price level, the money issuer, which in the United States is the Federal Reserve Bank, must issue neither too much nor too little money. To issue money without restraint would destroy the social convention that gives money its value.
6. The equation for the simple money multiplier is $1/r$; the equation for the approximate real-world multiplier is $1/(r + c)$. Since c is positive, the simple multiplier is larger.
8. If the U.S. government were to raise the reserve requirement to 100 percent, the interest rates banks pay to depositors would decrease and possibly even become negative (you'd have to pay to have the bank handle your money), because significant opportunities for profitable loans would be lost.
10. What brought the S&Ls down were bad loans, particularly in real estate. The reasons that S&Ls made those bad loans are complex. Government deregulation in the 1980s expanded the kinds of loans S&Ls could make and the ways they could compete for deposits. Due to moral hazard and perverse incentives (government, not the bank managers, would have to pay if the S&L went down), S&Ls made risky loans and paid high interest on their deposits. When the real estate market soured, the S&Ls' net worth crumbled and the government had to step in to bail out depositors.
12. To be considered money, the currencies would have to fulfill the functions of money. They only partially fulfill those functions since they have only limited acceptability as a medium of exchange, store of value, and unit of account. Thus, while they are partial moneys, we would not consider them full moneys.

Chapter 27: Problems and Exercises

2. For a deposit of $100 and a reserve ratio of 5 percent,
   a. The bank can lend out $95.
   b. There is now $195 of money.
   c. The multiplier is 20.
   d. John's $100 will ultimately turn into $2,000.
4. a. money
   b. not money
   c. not money
   d. not money
   e. money
   f. not money
   g. not money

Chapter 27: Appendix A

2. It is a financial asset because it has value due to an offsetting liability of the Federal Reserve Bank.
4. No, she is not correct. While a loan is a loan, that loan is a financial asset to the one issuing the loan because it has value just as a bond does.
6. $0.50
8. a. Market rates are above 10 percent because its price is below face value.
   b. Its yield is 12.24 percent.
   c. Its price will rise.
10. Substituting into the present value formula $PV =$ $1,060/1.1, we find that the bond is worth $964 now.
12. Using the present-value table, we see that at a 3 percent interest rate, $1 30 years from now would be worth $0.41; $200 would be worth $82 now.
14. If the interest rate is still 9 percent, the value of a lump sum of $20,000 in 10 years can be calculated using the annuity table in Table A27-1. You should be willing to pay $20,000 × 0.42, or about $8,400 for this offer.
16. An investment bank facilitates borrowing. It does not take in deposits and often does not make loans. A commercial bank takes in deposits and makes loans.
18. The prospects must not be very good, or the interest rate must be extremely high. Generally, stocks sell for a minimum of multiples of 10 or 12 times earnings. This multiple can be roughly determined by dividing the expected earnings (the annuity) by the interest rate. More recently, the average price/earnings ratio has been 30, a historically high figure.
20. Money market assets usually pay lower interest rates than do longer-term capital assets because they offer the buyer more liquidity and less risk of asset value fluctuation.
22. a. Technically, a rise in stock prices does not imply a richer economy. If, however, the rise in stock prices reflects underlying real economic improvement such as finding the cure for cancer or a technological advance, society will be richer not because of the rise in stock prices, but because of the underlying cause of their rise.
   b. We disagree with this statement. If both the real and financial asset are worth $1 million, then they have the same value as long as they are valued at market prices. Just as financial assets bear a risk of no repayment, real assets bear a risk of a fluctuation in prices.
   c. Although financial assets have a corresponding liability, they facilitate trades that could not otherwise have taken place and thus have enormous value to society.
   d. This is false. The value of an asset depends not only on the quantity but also on its price per unit. The price of land per acre in Japan exceeds that in the United States by so much that the total value of land in Japan also exceeds that in the United States.
   e. This is false. The stock market valuation depends on the supply and demand for existing stock. There is, however, a relationship between relative growth in GDP and the rise in stock prices to the extent that growth in stock prices and GDP growth both reflect economic well-being in a country. Also, many of the companies are multinational companies, and where the company is based may not reflect where its value added is generated.

CHAPTER 27: APPENDIX B

2. a.

Assets		Liabilities	
Cash	$ 10,000	Demand deposits	$ 50,000
	−1,000		−1,000
	9,000		49,000
Loans	100,000	Net worth	110,000
Physical assets	50,000		
Total assets	$159,000	Total liabilities and net worth	$159,000

b. The reserve ratio is now 18 percent. This is less than the required 20 percent. The bank must decrease loans by $800 to meet the reserve requirement. But this shows up as $800 less in demand deposits and $800 less in cash. The bank must again reduce loans, but this time by $640. Demand deposits once again decline. This continues until the final position indicated by the following T-account:

Assets		Liabilities	
Cash	$ 9,000	Demand deposits	$ 45,000
Loans	96,000	Net worth	110,000
Physical assets	50,000		
Total assets	$155,000	Total liabilities and net worth	$155,000

c. The money multiplier is 5.
d. Total money supply declined by $5,000.

CHAPTER 28: MONETARY POLICY AND THE DEBATE ABOUT MACRO POLICY QUESTIONS FOR THOUGHT AND REVIEW

2. There are few regional Fed banks in the western part of the United States because in 1913, when the Fed was established, the West and South were less populated and less important economically than the rest of the country. As these regions grew, the original structure remained because no one wanted to go through the political wrangling that restructuring would bring about.
4. Three tools by which the Fed can affect the money supply are: (*a*) changing the reserve requirement, which changes the amount of reserves banks keep and thereby changes the money supply; (*b*) changing the discount rate, which changes the cost of borrowing by banks from the Fed and thereby changes the money supply (actually, it works more as a signal); and (*c*) open market operations, which change reserves as the Fed buys and sells bonds, and thereby changes the money supply.
6. The Fed funds rate is the interest rate that banks charge one another for Fed funds or reserves. As the Fed buys and sells bonds, it changes reserves and thereby directly affects this short-term overnight interest rate. Other, longer-term interest rates, such as the Treasury bill rate, are only indirectly affected.
8. When the Fed takes money out of the economy, banks are in violation of Fed regulations and have no choice but to contract their loans in order to meet their reserve requirements. When the Fed puts money into the economy, banks have excess reserves but there is no regulation that they are violating. Although they may have a financial incentive to make loans, they are not required to do so. Since they are not required to make loans, the saying "You can lead a horse to water, but you can't make it drink" is relevant.
10. The nominal interest rate is equal to the real interest rate plus the expected inflation rate. If the nominal interest rate is 6 percent and the expected inflation rate is 5 percent, the real interest rate is 1 percent.
12. Treasury bills pay interest; cash does not.
14. The Taylor rule suggests that the Fed will target a Fed funds rate of 5.5 percent [2 + 3 + .5(1) + .5(0)].

CHAPTER 28: PROBLEMS AND EXERCISES

2. a. If people hold no cash, the money multiplier is $1/r$. If this is equal to 3, then the current reserve requirement is 33 percent. To increase the money supply by 200, the Fed should lower the reserve requirement to 32 percent.

b. Lowering the discount rate will encourage banks to borrow. This will increase the amount of reserves in the system so that the money supply increases. If the Fed wishes to increase the money supply by 200, and the multiplier is 3, reserves must be increased by

66.67. If banks will borrow an additional 20 for every point the discount rate is lowered, the Fed should lower the rate by 3.33 percentage points.

c. To increase the money supply by using open market operations, the Fed should buy bonds, thus increasing the level of reserves in the banking system. To achieve an increase of 200 (if the multiplier is 3) the Fed should buy 66.67 worth of bonds.

4. a. Increasing the reserve requirement would lower the multiplier, calculated as $[1/(r + c)]$. To calculate exactly how much, we would need to know the current money supply.

b. The money multiplier is $[1/(r + c)] = 2.5$. If the Fed sold $800,000 worth of bonds it would decrease reserves and so decrease the money supply by $2 million.

c. This part of the question requires information from a local bank. Reevaluate *a* and *b* in view of this information.

6. a. This would increase excess reserves enormously.

b. Banks would most likely favor this proposal because they would now earn interest on their assets held at the Fed.

c. Central banks would likely oppose this because it would reduce their superiority and may require that they ask Congress for appropriation to pay the interest, reducing their political independence.

d. This would increase the interest rate paid by banks because the additional interest would increase their profit margin. The initial increased profit margin would shift the demand for depositors out as new banks entered the market and as existing banks competed for more deposits. This would increase the interest paid to depositors until the normal profits are once again earned.

8. a. Since the money multiplier is 2.5, we would issue a directive for the Fed open market window to buy 24 worth of government bonds.

b. We could have also reduced the discount rate and lowered the reserve requirement, although by how much cannot be determined with the information given.

c. Using the quantity theory, we would predict that the price level would rise because of the increase in the money supply.

Chapter 28: Appendix A

2. Let's assume the following initial bank balance sheet:

Initial Bank Balance Sheet

Assets		Liabilities	
Reserves	$100,000,000	Demand deposits	$1,000,000,000
T-bill holdings	0	Net worth	5,000,000
Loans	905,000,000		
Total assets	$1,005,000,000	Total liabilities	$1,005,000,000

First, individuals sell $2 million in T-bills to the Fed, and deposit the $2 million in the bank. The bank now has more reserves than is required:

Assets		Liabilities	
Reserves	$102,000,000	Demand deposits	$1,002,000,000
T-bill holdings	0	Net worth	5,000,000
Loans	905,000,000		
Total assets	$1,007,000,000	Total liabilities	$1,007,000,000

It has excess reserves of $1.8 million, which it lends out. These loans are redeposited at the bank as demand deposits:

Assets		Liabilities	
Reserves	$102,000,000	Demand deposits	$1,002,000,000
Loans given	−1,800,000	New deposits	+1,800,000
New deposits	+1,800,000		
T-bill holdings	0	Net worth	5,000,000
Loans	906,800,000		
Total assets	$1,008,800,000	Total liabilities	$1,008,800,000

It still has excess reserves of 1.62 million, which it lends out. Each round, the amount called in gets smaller and smaller until the bank arrives at its final position with money supply having risen by $20 million.

Assets		Liabilities	
Reserves	$102,000,000	Demand deposits	$1,020,000,000
T-bill holdings	0	Net worth	5,000,000
Loans	923,000,000		
Total assets	$1,025,000,000	Total liabilities	$1,025,000,000

Chapter 29: Inflation and Its Relationship to Unemployment and Growth

Questions for Thought and Review

2. Adaptive or extrapolative expectations.
4. The real interest rate is 5 percent: Real interest rate = Nominal interest rate − Inflation.
6. The three assumptions are that velocity is constant, real income is independent of the money supply, and the direction of causation is from money to prices.
8. Financial institutions have changed enormously and financial markets have become increasingly connected internationally, increasing the flow of money among countries.
10. Governments and central banks sometimes increase money supply even when they know the consequences because sometimes the political ramifications of not increasing the money supply (which can include a collapse of government) are thought to be worse.
12. Quantity theorists are more likely to support rules because they have less trust in government undertaking beneficial actions. Rules limit those actions.
14. The insider/outsider theory of inflation divides workers into insiders and outsiders. It is an example of an institutionalist theory of inflation, which says that social pressures prevent economic pressures from working. In it, insiders push up wages and outsiders find themselves experiencing unemployment. So there is little pressure on insiders not to raise wages. It is an institutionalist theory.
16. Alfred Marshall would say that it is impossible to separate the roles of supply and demand in influencing price and that therefore we cannot distinguish between cost-push and demand-pull inflation.
18. No, as long as expectations of inflation are constant, the economy will stay on the same short-run Phillips curve.
20. Economists see a trade-off between inflation and growth because low inflation reduces price uncertainty and thereby encourages investment, increasing the efficiency of the market system.

Chapter 29: Problems and Exercises

2. a. The economy is at point A on short-run and long-run Phillips curve in the graph below.

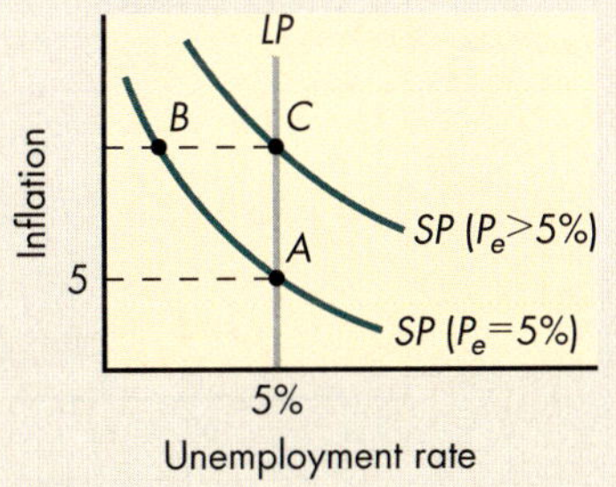

   b. The answer to this question really hinges on what kind of change would be popular. Should you try to cut unemployment further? If so, then we would recommend increasing government expenditures, moving the economy to a point such as *B* in the graph above. Or would a better strategy be cutting inflation? If so, then we would recommend reducing government expenditures, which will increase unemployment while reducing inflation.

   c. We have chosen the "lower unemployment" option. An increase in aggregate expenditures will cause a movement up along the short-run Phillips curve. Unemployment will fall, but inflation will rise. In the long run, as expectations of inflation adjust to actual inflation, the short-run Phillips curve shifts up. Unemployment returns to its target rate of 5 percent, but inflation is higher than before, as shown as point C in the graph.

4. The advantage of indexing grades is that it provides a benchmark with which to measure a student's performance in his or her class. It would distinguish between an A received in a difficult class in which many did not receive A's and an A earned in an easy class in which A's were plenty. The disadvantage is that it would not distinguish between an A earned among A's in a class where A's were given generously without work and an A earned among A's in a class of geniuses. It might result in professors making distinctions among bright students whose abilities are virtually the same just to make a given distribution of grades.

6. a. He would likely be a quantity theorist since quantity theorists see inflation most connected to long-term growth because low inflation means that the informational job of prices is working better and more investment will take place.

   b. Inflation can affect household decisions in a number of ways. It can add uncertainty about the future, leading them to save less. Alternatively, it could lead them to temporarily supply more labor than they would otherwise, causing a temporary spurt in growth and then a fall in growth once they recognize their mistakes.

Chapter 30: Aggregate Demand Policy in Perspective

Questions for Thought and Review

2. If the economy has a recessionary gap, the following trade policies can be adopted:
   a. An export-led growth policy in which the country lobbies to remove other countries' restrictions on its exports.
   b. Allowing its currency to depreciate, which means that the exchange rate of its currency relative to other currencies should fall.
4. The budget process begins a year and a half before the budget is implemented, making it difficult to know what type of fiscal policy will be needed. In addition, many budget decisions are made for political reasons (few politicians would vote for a tax increase in an election year even if such an increase were needed). Finally, nearly two-thirds of the budget is mandated by federal programs and cannot be easily changed.
6. Automatic stabilizers work to reduce taxes and raise expenditures during contractions (and do the opposite during expansions) without additional government action. They therefore act to offset contractions. Likewise, however, during recoveries, automatic stabilizers increase taxes and reduce expenditures, which act to slow the recovery.
8. If interest rates have no effect on investment, there would be no crowding out. Crowding out occurs when the government's sale of bonds to finance expansionary fiscal policy causes interest rates to rise, choking off private investment.
10. Increasing taxes shifts the aggregate demand curve in to the left, decreasing income and making people less likely to vote for them. The maxim holds because people tend to have short memories.
12. Policies followed now affect expectations of future policies, and those expectations can affect how the economy operates. By thinking about policy as a process, not a one-time event, policymakers can take these effects into account.

Chapter 30: Problems and Exercises

2. a. In the standard *AS/AD* model, a tax cut will shift the *AD* curve to the right, leading to an increase in the price level and real output, as shown in the graph below. Congressman Stable's views fit this model well.

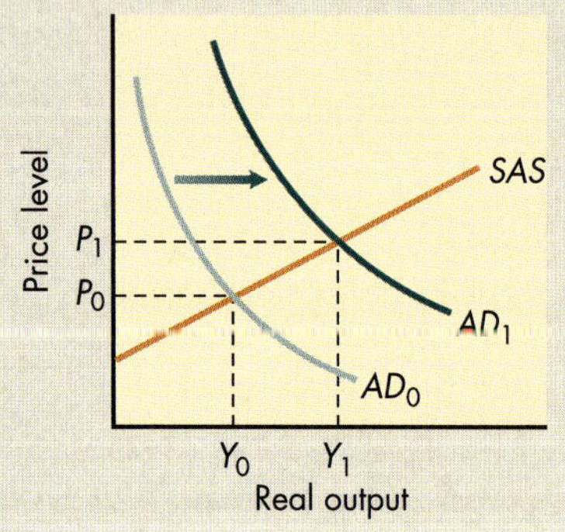

   b. If Congressman Growth is correct, the tax cut will shift the *LAS* curve to the right. If the economy had previously been in long-run equilibrium, the economy will now be below potential and there will be pressures for factor prices to decline. Assuming nothing else happens in the meantime, the *SAS* curve will shift down, leading to a lower price level and higher real output, as shown in the graph in the next column.

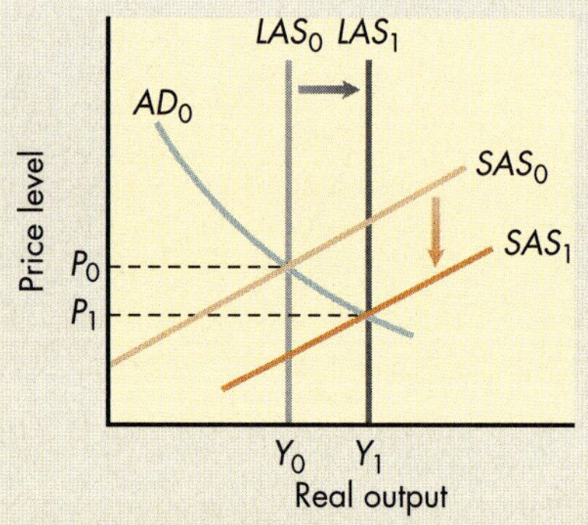

   c. In the short run, Congressman Stable is likely to be correct.
   d. If there is significant crowding out, the tax cut will require government to finance a higher budget deficit. This would lead to higher interest rates and lower investment. If there is perfect crowding out, the decline in investment will completely offset the expansionary effect of the tax cut. In this case, the tax cut will have no effect on either the price level or real output.
4. a. In 1995 the unemployment rate fell below the target rate of 6 percent without generating inflationary pressures. He was probably changing his estimates to reflect that reality.

b. It would shift the *LAS* curve out.
c. Using Okun's rule of thumb—which says that for every 1 percentage point rise in the unemployment rate, income falls by 2 percent—a 0.5 percentage point decline in the target unemployment rate would imply a rise in potential income of 1 percent, or $100 billion.

Chapter 31: Politics, Deficits, and Debt Questions for Thought and Review

2. The government can finance a deficit in either of two ways: by selling bonds or by printing money.
4. There are technical aspects of the deficit that must be understood in order to undertake a meaningful discussion of the problems deficits and debts pose for society. Since a deficit is defined as a shortfall of revenues compared to expenditures, these technical aspects include what you define as revenue and what you define as expenditure.
6. A structural deficit would exist even if the economy were at its potential level of income, which would be at full employment, or at where the unemployment rate is equal to the normal rate of unemployment. If an economist believed that the normal rate of unemployment was 4 percent instead of 6 percent, then the portion of the deficit considered to be structural would be smaller. Thus, it is Mr. A who should also say that the structural deficit is $20 billion.
8. It would not differ; expected inflation does not enter into the determination of the real deficit.
10. Three ways individual debt can be said to differ from government debt are: (*a*) government is ongoing and therefore never needs to pay back the debt; (*b*) government can pay off the debt by creating money; and (*c*) much of the government debt is internal debt.
12. Deficits are only a summary measure of the economy. A government can undertake significant future obligations and therefore get itself into trouble even if it is not running a deficit.
14. The Budget Enforcement Act changed the politics of spending and taxing. It forced Congress to figure out how the government would pay for a program at the same time it instituted the program.
16. Because of the baby boom, there were many people working and relatively few collecting Social Security in the late 1990s. This caused a surplus in the Social Security Trust Fund. Since that Trust Fund is part of the government budget, the Social Security system is a primary reason for the surplus.
18. It depends. Clearly, there is some tendency for the deficit to raise the interest rate, thereby decreasing investment and hence future growth. However, to the degree that the government spending is itself productive, not having the deficit could also decrease future growth. The ultimate effect depends on the relative size of the two effects.

Chapter 31: Problem and Exercises

2. a. The passive deficit must be zero since it is defined as zero at potential output.
   b. The structural deficit is $200 billion.
   c. Now $60 billion of that deficit is passive and $140 is structural since revenue would increase by $60 billion if output rose to potential.
   d. Now there is a passive surplus of $30 billion, and a structural deficit of $230 billion because revenue would decline by $30 billion if output declined to potential.
   e. The structural deficit is likely of more concern to policymakers because normal stabilization policies will not remove it.
4. a. Debt service payments are 0.06 times $360 billion = $21.6 billion.
   b. The nominal deficit is 160 − ($21.6 + 145) = $6.6 billion.
   c. The real deficit equals the nominal deficit ($6.6 billion) less .03 × $360 = $4.2 billion surplus.
6. To make the deficit look as small as possible, we would do the following:
   a. Enter government pensions when they become payable, not on an accrual basis.
   b. Treat the sale of land as current income rather than spreading it out with the sale of an asset.
   c. Include Social Security taxes as a current revenue because at this time revenue from Social Security exceeds payment.
   d. Count prepayment of taxes as current income instead of reserves for future taxes.
   e. Count expenditures on F-52 bombers as capital expenditures and introduce another cost item of depreciation and allow the F-52 to depreciate as little as possible.

Chapter 32: Macro Policies in Developing Countries Questions for Thought and Review

2. You can't just judge an economy; you must judge the entire culture. Some developing countries have cultures that, in some people's view, are preferable to ours.
4. The exchange rate method uses current exchange rates to compare relative incomes while the purchasing power parity method compares incomes by looking at the domestic purchasing power of money in different countries. Because many developing countries' currencies are undervalued, the current exchange rate overstates the income disparity between developed and developing countries.
6. Three ways in which institutions differ in developing countries are that (*a*) basic market institutions with well-defined property rights do not, in many cases, exist; (*b*) there is often a dual nature to the economy; and (*c*) fiscal structures with which to adequately implement fiscal policy often do not exist.
8. An economist might favor activist policies in developed countries and laissez-faire policies in developing countries because the policies one favors depends on the desire and the ability of government to work for and achieve the goals of its policies. Different views of government can lead to different views of policy. Since many economists have a serious concern about the political structure in developing countries, but less concern about it in developed countries, they can favor one set of policies for developing countries and another set for developed countries.
10. A regime change is a change in the entire structure within which the government and economy interact, whereas a policy change is a change in one aspect of government action.
12. The alternative to the inflation tax, possible breakdown of government and the economy, may be worse than the inflation tax, which may buy a bit more time before the difficult decisions must be made.
14. Investment and savings are low in developing countries because income is low, and poor people don't have a whole lot left over to save. The rich often put their savings abroad due to the fear of political instability. As for the middle class, the underdeveloped financial sector leaves them with few opportunities to invest their savings.
16. An investor thinking of making an investment in a developing country should be concerned about the country's political stability and its economic condition (inflation, etc.). The existing amount of debt may also be a matter of concern.
18. Corruption limits investment and growth because knowing that payments of graft must be made prevents many people from undertaking actions that might lead to growth. Tax revenues are often diverted to those in power instead of going into legitimate productive investment, and the same is sometimes true of foreign aid money from abroad. But that does not answer the issue, since one must deal with the political reasons why the government increases the money supply.
20. The UN could encourage the development of microcredit banks, like the Grameen Bank, which provide a low-cost alternative to money lenders. There are also significant social and cultural limitations in many areas that limit women entrepreneurs.

Chapter 32: Problems and Exercises

2. This exercise asks you to spend a day living like someone in a developing country, and then to read this chapter and contemplate the degree to which someone in such a situation can pull himself or herself up by the bootstraps.
4. a. I would want to emphasize those skills which have the highest per-dollar return—those that would lead to development. These would probably be the basic reading, writing, and problem-solving skills that fit the indigenous culture.
   b. This differs from the ideal educational system in the United States because the U.S. culture is different and U.S. economic problems are different. Thus, in the United States the focus would be more abstract analysis, while in developing countries the focus would be agricultural science and basic skills.
   c. This is an open-ended question. The relevant question would be: How much would individuals be willing to pay for courses that do not result in a credential compared to how much they would be willing to pay for a credential without the coursework?
6. a. I agree with this statement because of the differing importance of institutions. A detailed knowledge of a country's institutions and culture is necessary to make prescriptions for development. I disagree with this statement to the degree that the lessons learned from a general theory say that development requires stability of political structures and of economic environment and the need for savings applies across countries. The solutions are specific to the countries but fall within a general framework.
   b. This argument is made for developing countries because culture and traditional institutions play a larger role in the growth in these economies.

Chapter 33: International Financial Policy Questions for Thought and Review

2. When someone sends 100 British pounds to a friend in the United States, the transaction will show up in the component of the current account called net transfers, which include foreign aid, gifts, and other payments to individuals not exchanged for goods or services. It will also appear on the capital account as a receipt of foreign currency just like the purchase of a British stock or bond.
4. A capital account deficit means that capital outflows are more than capital inflows. The excess supply of dollars is balanced by a current account surplus, which means Americans are producing more than they are consuming. In the long run, capital account deficits are nice because you are building up holdings of foreign assets, which will provide a future stream of income.
6. We would use a combination of purchasing power parity, current exchange rates, and estimates of foreign exchange traders to determine the long-run exchange rate of the Neverback. This combination approach can be justified only by the "that's all we have to go on" defense. Since no one really knows what the long-run equilibrium exchange rate is, and since that exchange rate can be significantly influenced by other countries' policies, the result we arrive at could well be wrong.
8. He will more likely prefer fixed exchange rates. They provide an anchor, which restricts government temptations to use expansionary monetary policy.
10. If a country eliminates tariffs, the demand for imports will likely increase. To buy more imports residents of the country will have to supply more of their own currency, depressing their currency's value.
12. A common currency would tie these countries together much more closely, create a larger common market, and make price comparisons among Canada, the United States, and Mexico easier. It would be politically difficult since each country would have to give up its own currency, which is a source of national identity. Since the U.S. dollar would likely predominate, this would be especially problematic for Canada and Mexico. These countries would also have to give up their independent monetary policy. Since the economic conditions in the three countries can differ substantially, doing so would likely be unacceptable for Canada and Mexico.
14. No. It is extremely difficult to affect exchange rates. Since we don't know what the correct exchange rates are, it is probably best not to try to significantly change the exchange rates determined by the market by foreign exchange intervention. If one is going to change exchange rates, one must change one's domestic monetary and fiscal policies.

Chapter 33: Problems and Exercises

2. a. This is an enormous change. In order to bring it about, the Never-Never government would have to run an enormously expansionary monetary policy, reducing the real interest rate possibly to negative amounts and probably generating significant inflation.
   b. Holders of Neverbacks will demand foreign currencies (increase supply of Neverbacks) since the return on Neverback assets has declined. This is shown as a rightward shift in the supply of Neverbacks. Likewise, potential foreign investors will demand fewer Neverbacks for the same reason. This is shown as a leftward shift in the demand for Neverbacks from D_0 to D_1. The effect is to reduce the exchange rate value of the Neverback to $10 per Neverback.
4. a. We would suggest buying U.S. dollars and selling currencies of the EU.
   b. We would suggest buying U.S. dollars since U.S. interest rates are expected to be higher, the quantity of U.S. assets demanded will rise, and thus the demand for dollars will increase.
   c. Since the market will likely already have responded to the higher expected interest rates, the rise will likely have the same effect as a fall in interest rates. Thus, we would suggest selling U.S. dollars.
   d. We suggest selling U.S. dollars by reasoning opposite to that in *b*.
   e. We would suggest selling U.S. dollars in the expectation of a decrease in demand for U.S. dollars as U.S. goods become more expensive. Also U.S.-denominated assets such as bonds will be worth less with greater inflation making foreign assets more attractive to investors.
   f. We would suggest buying because, if the U.S. government imposed new tariffs, the demand for imports would decline, shifting the supply of dollars to the left. This would lead to a higher value of the dollar.
6. a. Three assumptions of the law of one price are that (1) there are zero transportation costs, (2) the goods are tradable, and (3) there are no barriers to trade. (There are many others.)

b. For it to apply directly, labor would have to be completely mobile. Thus, it does not apply directly. However, assuming capital is flexible, there will be significant indirect pressure toward an equalization of wage rates.

c. Since capital is more mobile than labor, we would expect that the law of one price would hold more for capital than for labor.

Chapter 34: Monetary and Fiscal Policy in a Global Setting Questions for Thought and Review

2. At the time that this was written, the U.S. trade deficit had risen to record highs. Still, it is unclear whether we should want to lower the U.S. trade deficit. The trade deficit was in part due to the fact that the economy has been growing for nine consecutive years. As long as the United States can borrow or sell assets, it can have a trade deficit. On the other hand, the more the United States borrows, the more U.S. assets foreigners own. Eventually, the United States will have to run a trade surplus.
4. A contractionary fiscal policy by Japan would have an ambiguous effect on the value of the U.S. dollar because the effect via the interest rate and income paths oppose one another, and the effect through the price level is a long-run effect. Contractionary fiscal policy in Japan will lower income and imports in Japan and therefore lead to a higher U.S. trade deficit.
6. The effect of expansionary fiscal policy on the exchange rate is ambiguous, while contractionary monetary policy has the effect of increasing exchange rates. The net effect will depend on which influence is stronger.
8. If the recession was caused by a fall in domestic expenditures, we would expect that its trade balance was moving toward surplus. If, however, the recession was caused by a fall in exports, we would expect that its trade balance was moving toward deficit. The G-8 countries were trying to get Japan to boost its economy by increasing aggregate expenditures with expansionary monetary policy.
10. The costs of internationalizing the debt are that interest and profits must be paid on the capital owned by foreigners. Future consumption must be reduced to pay that amount.

Chapter 34: Problems and Exercises

2. *money* ↑ → *income* ↑ → *imports* ↑ → *trade deficit* ↑.
4. a. We would suggest that the IMF require a contractionary policy for both monetary and fiscal policy. I would, however, suggest a relatively more contractionary fiscal policy so that the exchange rate would also fall, while inflation falls, boosting exports.

   b. This would tend to slow inflation, after an initial burst due to a fall in the exchange rate. The policy, however, would hinder growth and push the economy into a recession.

   c. We suspect that the country would not be happy about the proposal because its adoption might lead to a deep recession, which is politically unpopular.

Glossary

A

Ability-to-Pay Principle The individuals who are most able to bear the burden of the tax should pay the tax.
Absolute Advantage A country that can produce a good at a lower cost than another country is said to have an absolute advantage in the production of that good. When two countries have absolute advantages in different goods, there are gains of trade to be had.
Acquisition A merger in which a company buys another company and the purchaser has the right of direct control over the resulting operation (but does not always exercise that right).
Adaptive Expectations Expectations based in some way on the past.
Adverse Selection Problem Problem that occurs when buyers and sellers have different amounts of information about the good for sale.
Aggregate Demand (*AD*) Curve A curve that shows how a change in the price level will change aggregate expenditures on all goods and services in an economy.
Aggregate Demand Management Government's attempt to control the aggregate level of spending in the economy.
Aggregate Expenditures The total amount of spending on final goods and services in the economy; consumption (spending by consumers), investment (spending by business), spending by government, and net foreign spending on U.S. goods (the difference between U.S. exports and U.S. imports).
Aggregate Production The total amount of goods and services produced in every industry in an economy.
Annuity Rule The present value of any annuity is the annual income it yields divided by the interest rate.
Antitrust Policy The government's policy toward the competitive process.
Approximate Real-World Money Multiplier One divided by the sum of the percentage of deposits banks hold in reserve (r) and the ratio of money people hold in currency (c) to the money they hold as deposits ($1/(r + c)$).
Art of Economics The application of the knowledge learned in positive economics to the achievement of goals one has determined in normative economics.
Asset Management How a bank handles its loans and other assets.
Austrian Economist Economist who believes in the liberty of all individuals first and social goals second.
Automatic Stabilizer Any government program or policy that will counteract the business cycle without any new government action.
Autonomous Expenditures Expenditures that do not systematically vary with income.
Average Fixed Cost Fixed cost divided by quantity produced.
Average Product Output per worker.
Average Total Cost Total cost divided by the quantity produced.
Average Variable Cost Variable cost divided by quantity produced.

B

Balance of Merchandise Trade The difference between the value of goods exported and the value of goods imported.
Balance of Payments A country's record of all transactions between its residents and the residents of all foreign nations.
Balance of Payments Constraint Limitations on expansionary domestic macroeconomic policy due to a shortage of international reserves.
Balance of Trade The difference between the value of the goods and services a country imports and the value of the goods and services it exports.
Bank A financial institution whose primary function is holding money for, and lending money to, individuals and firms.
Bar Graph Graph where the area under each point is filled in to look like a bar.
Barriers to Entry Social, political, or economic impediments that prevent firms from entering a market.
Basic Needs Adequate food, clothing, and shelter.
Benefit Principle The individuals who receive the benefit of a good or service should pay the tax necessary to supply that good.
Bilateral Monopoly Market with only a single seller and a single buyer.
Bond A promise to pay a certain amount plus interest in the future.
Brain Drain The outflow of the best and brightest students from developing countries to developed countries.
Bretton Woods System An agreement about fixed exchange rates that governed international financial relationships from the period after the end of World War II until 1971.
Budget Constraint A curve that shows us the various combinations of goods an individual can buy with a given income.
Business Private producing unit in our society.
Business Cycle The upward or downward movement of economic activity, or real GDP, that occurs around the growth trend.

C

Capital Account The part of the balance of payments account in which all long-term flows of payments are listed.

Capital Markets Markets in which financial assets having a maturity of more than one year are bought and sold.
Capitalism An economic system based on the market in which the ownership of the means of production resides with a small group of individuals called capitalists.
Cartel A combination of firms that acts as if it were a single firm.
Cartel Model of Oligopoly A model that assumes that oligopolies act as if they were monopolists that have assigned output quotas to individual member firms of the oligopoly so that total output is consistent with joint profit maximization.
Cash Flow Accounting System An accounting system entering expenses and revenues only when cash is received or paid out.
Central Bank A type of bankers' bank.
Certificate of Deposit (CD) A piece of paper certifying that you have a sum of money in a savings account in the bank for a specified period of time.
Classical Growth Model A model of growth that focuses on the role of capital accumulation in the growth process.
Classicals Macroeconomists who generally favor laissez-faire or nonactivist policies.
Clayton Antitrust Act A U.S law that outlawed four specific monopolistic practices: price discrimination, tie-in contracts, interlocking directorships, and buying stock in a competitor's company in order to reduce competition.
Closed Shop Firm where unions control the hiring.
Commercial Paper Short-term promissory note that a certain amount of money plus interest will be paid back on demand.
Comparable Worth Laws Laws mandating comparable pay for comparable work.
Comparative Advantage The ability to be better suited to the production of one good than to the production of another good. As long as the relative opportunity costs of producing goods (what must be given up in one good in order to get another good) differ among countries, then there are potential gains from trade, even if one country has an absolute advantage in everything.
Complements Goods that are used in conjunction with other goods.
Concentration Ratio The percentage of the total industry that the top firms of the industry have.
Conditionality The making of loans that are subject to specific conditions.
Conglomerate Merger The merging of two relatively unrelated businesses.
Conspicuous Consumption The consumption of goods not for one's direct pleasure, but simply to show off to others.
Constant Returns to Scale Situation in which long-run average total costs do not change with an increase in output. Also: Output will rise by the same proportionate increase as all inputs.
Consumer Price Index (CPI) Measure of prices of a fixed basket of consumer goods, weighted according to each component's share of an average consumer's expenditure.
Consumer Sovereignty Principle that the consumer's wishes rule what's produced.
Consumer Surplus The value the consumer gets from buying a product less its price. Also: The difference between what consumers would have been willing to pay and what they actually pay.
Contestable Market Model A model of oligopoly in which barriers to entry and barriers to exit, not the structure of the market, determine a firm's price and output decisions.
Contractionary Monetary Policy Monetary policy that tends to raise interest rates and lower income.
Contractual Intermediary Financial institution that holds and stores individuals' financial assets.
Convertibility on the Current Account A system that allows people to exchange currencies freely to buy goods and services, but not capital.
Coordinate System Two-dimensional space in which one point represents two numbers.
Corporate Takeover An action in which a firm or a group of individuals issues a tender offer for another company (that is, offers to buy up the stock of a company) to gain control and to install its own managers.
Corporation Business that is treated as a person, legally owned by its stockholders. Its stockholders are not liable for the actions of the corporate "person."
Cost Minimization Condition Situation where the ratio of marginal product to the price of an input is equal for all inputs.
Cost/Benefit Approach Assigning costs and benefits, and making decisions on the basis of the relevant costs and benefits.
Cost-Push Inflation Inflation that occurs when the economy is below potential output.
Countercyclical Fiscal Policy Fiscal policy in which the government offsets any change in aggregate expenditures that would create a business cycle.
Credentialism When the degrees, or credentials, become more important than the knowledge learned.
Cross-Price Elasticity of Demand The percentage change in demand divided by the percentage change in the price of a related good.
Crowding Out The offsetting of a change in government expenditures by a change in private expenditures in the opposite direction.
Currency Board Board that establishes a fixed exchange rate, along with a fund to defend the price of the currency, should it be necessary.
Currency Stabilization Buying and selling of a currency by the government to offset temporary fluctuations in supply and demand for currencies.
Currency Support Buying of a currency by a government to maintain its value at above its long-run equilibrium value.
Current Account The part of the balance of payments account in which all short-term flows of payments are listed.
Cyclical Unemployment Unemployment resulting from fluctuations in economic activity.

D

Deadweight Loss The loss of consumer and producer surplus from a tax.
Deacquisition One company's sale of parts of either another company it has bought, or parts of itself.
Debt Accumulated deficits minus accumulated surpluses.
Debt Service The interest rate on debt times the total debt.
Decision Tree A visual description of sequential choices.
Decreasing Returns to Scale Output rises by a smaller proportionate increase than all inputs.
Deficit A shortfall of revenues under payments.
Deflation The opposite of inflation.
Demand A schedule of quantities of a good that will be bought per unit of time at various prices, other things constant.
Demand Curve Graphic representation of the relationship between price and quantity demanded.
Demand-Pull Inflation Inflation that occurs when the economy is at or above potential output.
Demerit Goods or Activities Goods or activities the government deems bad for people even though they choose to use the goods or engage in the activities.
Depository Institution A financial institution whose primary financial liability is deposits in checking or savings accounts.
Depreciation A decrease in the value of a currency or a decrease in an asset's value.
Depression A large recession.
Derived Demand The demand for factors of production by firms, which depends upon consumers' demands.
Derived Demand Curve for Labor Curve that shows the maximum amount of labor, measured in labor hours, that a firm will hire.
Diminishing Marginal Productivity Increasing one input, keeping all others constant, will lead to smaller and smaller gains in output.
Direct Regulation A program in which the amount of a good people are allowed to use is directly limited by the government.
Direct Relationship Relationship in which when one variable goes up, the other goes up too.
Discount Rate The rate of interest the Fed charges for loans it makes to banks.
Diseconomies of Scale Situation when the long-run average total cost increases as output increases.
Disintermediation The process of lending directly and not going through a financial intermediary.
Disposable Personal Income Personal income minus personal income taxes and payroll taxes.
Diversification Spreading the risks by holding many different types of financial assets.
Division of Labor The splitting up of a task to allow for specialization of production.
Downsizing A reduction in the workforce.
Dual Economy The existence of two sectors: a traditional sector and an internationally oriented market sector.
Duopoly An oligopoly with only two firms.
Dynamic Efficiency A market's ability to promote cost-reducing or product-enhancing technological change.

E

E-commerce Buying and selling over the Internet.
Economic Decision Rule If the marginal benefits of doing something exceed the marginal costs, do it. If the marginal costs of doing something exceed the marginal benefits, don't do it.
Economic Efficiency Achieving a goal at the lowest possible cost.
Economic Forces The necessary reactions to scarcity.
Economic Model Framework that places the generalized insights of the theory in a more specific contextual setting.
Economic Policy An action (or inaction) taken by government, to influence economic events.
Economic Principle Commonly held economic insight stated as a law or general assumption.
Economic Profit Explicit and implicit revenue minus explicit and implicit cost.
Economically Efficient Describes a method of production that produces a given level of output at the lowest possible cost.
Economics The study of how human beings coordinate their wants and desires, given the decision-making mechanisms, social customs, and political realities of the society.
Economic Takeoff A stage when the development process becomes self-sustaining.
Economies of Scale Situation when long-run average total costs decrease as output increases. Also: Situation in which costs per unit of output fall as output increases.
Economies of Scope Situation when the costs of producing products are interdependent so that it's less costly for a firm to produce one good when it's already producing another.
Efficiency Achieving a goal as cheaply as possible (using as few inputs as possible).
Efficiency Wages Wages paid above the going-market wage to keep workers happy and productive.
Efficient Achieving a goal at the lowest cost in total resources without consideration as to who pays those costs.
Effluent Fees Charges imposed by government on the level of pollution created.
Elastic The percentage change in quantity is greater than the percentage change in price ($E > 1$).
Embargo A total restriction on the import or export of a good.
Employment Rate Number of people who are working as a percentage of the labor force.
Entrepreneur An individual who sees an opportunity to sell an item at a price higher than the average cost of producing it.
Entrepreneurship The ability to organize and get something done. Also: Labor services that involve high degrees of organizational skills, concern, oversight responsibility, and creativity.
Equation of Exchange An equation stating that the quantity of money times the velocity of money equals the price level times the quantity of goods sold.

Equilibrium A concept in which opposing dynamic forces cancel each other out.
Equilibrium Income The level of income toward which the economy gravitates in the short run because of the cumulative cycles of declining or increasing production.
Equilibrium Price The price toward which the invisible hand drives the market.
Equilibrium Quantity The amount bought and sold at the equilibrium price.
European Union (EU) An economic and political union of European countries that is both an economic free trade area and a loose political organization.
Euro The currency used by 12 members of the European Union.
Excess Demand Quantity demanded is greater than quantity supplied.
Excess Reserves Reserves held by banks in excess of what banks are required to hold.
Excess Supply Quantity supplied is greater than quantity demanded.
Exchange Rate The rate at which one country's currency can be traded for another country's currency.
Exchange Rate Policy Buying and selling foreign currencies in order to help stabilize the exchange rate.
Excise Tax A tax that is levied on a specific good.
Expansion Upturn that lasts for at least two consecutive quarters of a year.
Expansionary Monetary Policy Monetary policy that tends to reduce interest rates and raise income.
Expected Inflation Inflation people expect to occur.
Expenditures Multiplier A number that tells us how much income will change in response to a change in autonomous expenditures.
Export-Led Growth Policies Policies designed to stimulate U.S. exports and increase aggregate expenditures on U.S. goods, and hence to have a multiplied effect on U.S. income.
External Debt Government debt owed to individuals in foreign countries.
Externality An effect of a decision on a third party not taken into account by the decision maker.
Extrapolative Expectations Expectations that a trend will continue.

F

Failure of Market Outcomes A situation in which, even though the market is functioning properly (there are no market failures), it is not achieving society's goals.
Fallacy of Composition The false assumption that what is true for a part will also be true for the whole.
Fed Funds Loans of excess reserves banks make to one another.
Federal Funds Market The market in which banks lend and borrow reserves.
Federal Funds Rate The interest rate banks charge one another for Fed funds.
Federal Open Market Committee (FOMC) The Fed's chief policymaking body.
Federal Reserve Bank (the Fed) The U.S. central bank whose liabilities (Federal Reserve notes) serve as cash in the United States.
Federal Trade Commission Act U.S. law that made it illegal for firms to use "unfair methods of competition" and to engage in "unfair or deceptive acts or practices."
Feudalism Economic system in which traditions rule.
Final Output Goods and services purchased for final use.
Financial Assets Assets such as stocks or bonds, whose benefit to the owner depends on the issuer of the asset meeting certain obligations.
Financial Institution A business whose primary activity is buying, selling, or holding financial assets.
Financial Liabilities Liabilities incurred by the issuer of a financial asset to stand behind the issued asset.
Financial Market Market where financial assets and financial liabilities are bought and sold.
Fine Tuning Fiscal policy designed to keep the economy always at its target or potential level of income.
Firm An economic institution that transforms factors of production into goods and services.
Fiscal Policy The deliberate change in either government spending or taxes to stimulate or slow down the economy.
Fixed Costs Costs that are spent and cannot be changed in the period of time under consideration.
Fixed Exchange Rate The exchange rate is set and government is committed to buying and selling its currency at a fixed rate.
Flexible Exchange Rate The exchange rate is set by market forces (supply and demand for a country's currency).
Foreign Aid Funds that developed countries lend or give to developing countries.
Free Market in Money Policy that would leave people free to use any money they want, and would significantly reduce banking regulation.
Free Rider Person who participates in something for free because others have paid for it.
Free Rider Problem Individuals' unwillingness to share in the cost of a public good.
Free Trade Association Group of countries that have reduced or eliminated trade barriers among themselves.
Frictional Unemployment Unemployment caused by new entrants into the job market and people quitting a job just long enough to look for and find another one.
Full Convertibility Individuals may change dollars into any currency they want for whatever legal purpose they want.
Fundamental Analysis A consideration of the fundamental forces that determine the supply of and demand for currencies.

G

Game Theory An application of economic principles in which players make interdependent choices.

GDP Deflator Index of the price level of aggregate output, or the average price of the components in total output (or GDP) relative to a base year.
General Agreement on Tariffs and Trade (GATT) A regular international conference to reduce trade barriers held from 1947 to 1995. It has been replaced by the World Trade Organization (WTO).
General Rule of Political Economy When small groups are helped by a government action and large groups are hurt by that same action, the small group tends to lobby far more effectively than the large group. Thus, policies tend to reflect the small group's interest, not the interest of the large group.
Global Corporations Corporations with substantial operations on both the production and sales sides in more than one country.
Gold Specie Flow Mechanism The long-run adjustment mechanism that maintained the gold standard.
Gold Standard System of fixed exchange rates in which the value of currencies was fixed relative to the value of gold and gold was used as the primary reserve asset.
Good/Bad Paradox Phenomenon of doing poorly because you're doing well.
Government Failure A situation where the government intervention in the market to improve market failure actually makes the situation worse.
Government Purchases Government payments for goods and services and investment in equipment and structures.
Grandfather To pass a law affecting a specific group but providing that those in the group before the law was passed are exempt from some provisions of the law.
Graph Picture of points in a coordinate system in which points denote relationships between numbers.
Gross Domestic Product (GDP) The total market value of all final goods and services produced in an economy in a one-year period.
Gross National Product (GNP) Aggregate final output of citizens and businesses of an economy in a one-year period.
Gross Private Investment Business spending on equipment, structures, and inventories and household spending on new owner-occupied housing.
Growth An increase in the amount of goods and services an economy produces.

H

Herfindahl Index An index of market concentration calculated by adding the squared value of the individual market shares of all firms in the industry.
Heterodox Economist Economist who doesn't accept the basic underlying model used by a majority of economists as the most useful model for analyzing the economy.
Horizontal Merger The combining of two companies in the same industry.
Hostile Takeover A merger in which the firm being taken over doesn't want to be taken over.
Households Groups of individuals living together and making joint decisions.
Human Capital The skills that are embodied in workers through experience, education, and on-the-job training, or, more simply, people's knowledge.
Hyperinflation Inflation that hits triple digits—100 percent or more per year.

I

Implicit Collusion A type of collusion in which multiple firms make the same pricing decisions even though they have not explicitly consulted with one another.
Incentive Effect How much a person will change his or her hours worked in response to a change in the wage rate.
Incentive-Compatible Contract A contract in which the incentives of each of the two parties to the contract are made to correspond as closely as possible.
Income Payments received plus or minus changes in value in one's assets in a specified time period.
Income Elasticity of Demand The percentage change in demand divided by the percentage change in income.
Incomes Policy A policy that places direct pressure on individuals to hold down their nominal wages and prices.
Increasing Returns to Scale Output rises by a greater proportionate increase than all inputs.
Indicative Planning Macroeconomic policy in which the government sets up an overall plan for various industries and selectively directs credit to certain industries.
Indifference Curve A curve that shows combinations of goods among which an individual is indifferent.
Indivisible Setup Cost The cost of an indivisible input for which a certain minimum amount of production must be undertaken before the input becomes economically feasible to use.
Induced Expenditures Expenditures that change as income changes.
Industrial Policy Formal policy that government takes toward business.
Industrial Revolution A time when technology and machines rapidly modernized industrial production and mass-produced goods replaced handmade goods.
Inefficiency Getting less output from inputs which, if devoted to some other activity, would produce more output.
Inefficient Achieving a goal in a more costly manner than necessary.
Inelastic The percentage change in quantity is less than the percentage change in price ($E < 1$).
Infant Industry Argument With initial protection, an industry will be able to become competitive.
Inferior Goods Goods whose consumption decreases when income increases.
Inflation A continual rise in the price level.
Inflation Tax An implicit tax on the holders of cash and the holders of any obligations specified in nominal terms.
Inflationary Gap A difference between equilibrium income and potential income when equilibrium income exceeds potential income. Also: Aggregate expenditures above potential output that exist at the current price level.

Infrastructure Investment Investment in the underlying structure of the economy.
Input What you put into a production process to achieve an output.
Insider/Outsider Model An institutionalist story of inflation where insiders bid up wages and outsiders are unemployed.
Institutionalist Economist Economist who argues that any economic analysis must involve specific considerations of institutions.
Interest Rate The price paid for use of a financial asset.
Interest Rate Effect The effect that a lower price level has on investment expenditures through the effect that a change in the price level has on interest rates.
Intermediate Products Products used as input in the production of some other product.
Internal Debt Government debt owed to other governmental agencies or to its own citizens.
International Effect As the price level falls (assuming the exchange rate does not change) net exports will rise.
Interpolation Assumption Assumption that the relationship between variables is the same between points as it is at the points.
Inverse Relationship A relationship between two variables in which when one goes up the other goes down.
Invisible Hand The price mechanism; the rise and fall of prices that guides our actions in a market.
Invisible Hand Theory A market economy, through the price mechanism, will allocate resources efficiently.
Isocost Line A line that represents alternative combinations of factors of production that have the same costs.
Isoquant Curve A curve that represents combinations of factors of production that result in equal amounts of output.
Isoquant Map A set of isoquant curves that show technically efficient combinations of inputs that can produce different levels of output.

J

Judgment by Performance To judge the competitiveness of markets by the behavior (performance) of firms in that market.
Judgment by Structure To judge the competitiveness of markets by the structure of the industry.

K

Keynesians Macroeconomists who generally favor activist government policy.

L

L The broadest measure of money.
Labor Force Those people in an economy who are willing and able to work.
Labor Force Participation Rate Measurement of the labor force as a percentage of the total population at least 16 years old.
Labor Market Factor market in which individuals supply labor services for wages to other individuals and to firms that need (demand) labor services.
Labor Productivity The average output per worker.
Laissez-Faire Economic policy of leaving individuals' wants to be controlled by the market.
Land Bank Program Program in which government supports prices by giving farmers economic incentives to reduce supply.
Law of Demand Quantity demanded rises as price falls, other things constant. Also can be stated as: Quantity demanded falls and price rises, other things constant.
Law of Diminishing Marginal Productivity As more and more of a variable input is added to an existing fixed input, eventually the additional output one gets from that additional input is going to fall.
Law of Diminishing Marginal Rate of Substitution As you get more and more of a good, if some of that good is taken away, then the marginal addition of another good you need to keep you on your indifference curve gets less and less.
Law of Supply Quantity supplied rises as price rises, other things constant. Also can be stated as: Quantity supplied falls as price falls, other things constant.
Lazy Monopolist Firm that does not push for efficiency, but merely enjoys the position it is already in.
Learning by Doing As we do something, we learn what works and what doesn't, and over time we become more proficient at it. Also: To improve the methods of production through experience.
Liability Management How a bank attracts deposits and what it pays for them.
Libertarian Economist who believes in liberty of individuals first and in other social goals second.
Limited Capital Account Convertibility A system that allows full current account convertibility and partial capital account convertiblity.
Limited Liability The liability of a stockholder (owner) in a corporation; it is limited to the amount the stockholder has invested in the company.
Line Graph Graph where the data are connected by a continuous line.
Linear Curve A curve that is drawn as a straight line.
Liquidity Ability to turn an asset into cash quickly.
Liquidity Trap Situation in which increasing reserves does not increase the money supply but simply causes excess reserves. Can occur when individuals believe that interest rates are much more likely to rise than fall.
Long-Run Aggregate (*LAS*) Supply Curve A curve that shows the long-run relationship between output and the price level.
Long-Run Decision Decision in which a firm chooses among all possible production techniques.
Long-Run Phillips Curve A vertical curve at the unemployment rate consistent with potential output. (It shows the trade-off [or complete lack thereof] when expectations of inflation equal actual inflation.)

Lorenz Curve A geometric representation of the share distribution of income among families in a given country at a given time.
Luxuries Goods that have an income elasticity greater than 1.

M

M_1 Currency in the hands of the public, checking account balances, and traveler's checks.
M_2 M1 plus savings deposits, small-denomination time deposits, and money market mutual fund shares, along with some esoteric financial instruments.
Macroeconomic Externality Externality that affects the levels of unemployment, inflation, or growth in the economy as a whole.
Macroeconomics The study of the economy as a whole, which includes inflation, unemployment, business cycles, and growth.
Mainstream Economist Economist who accepts the basic underlying model used by a majority of economists as the most useful model for analyzing the economy.
Marginal Benefit Additional benefit above what you've already derived.
Marginal Cost (MC) Additional cost to you over and above the costs you have already incurred. Also: Increase (decrease) in total cost from increasing (or decreasing) the level of output by one unit. Also: The change in total cost associated with a change in quantity.
Marginal Factor Cost The additional cost to a firm of hiring another worker.
Marginal Physical Product (*MPP*) The additional units of output that hiring an additional worker will bring about.
Marginal Product The additional output that will be forthcoming from an additional worker, other inputs constant.
Marginal Propensity to Consume (*mpc*) The ratio of a change in consumption, ΔC, to a change in income, ΔY.
Marginal Propensity to Expend (*mpe*) The ratio of the change in aggregate expenditures to a change in income.
Marginal Propensity to Save (*mps*) The percentage of income flow that is withdrawn from the income/expenditures flow of the economy in each round.
Marginal Rate of Substitution The rate at which one good must be added when the other is taken away to keep the individual indifferent between the two combinations. Also: The rate at which one factor must be added to compensate for the loss of another factor to keep output constant.
Marginal Revenue (*MR*) The change in total revenue associated with a change in quantity.
Marginal Revenue Product (*MRP*) The marginal revenue a firm expects to earn from selling an additional worker's output.
Marginal Social Benefit The marginal private benefit of consuming a good plus the benefits of the positive externalities resulting from consuming that good.
Marginal Social Cost The marginal private costs of production plus the cost of the negative externalities associated with that production.
Marginal Utility The satisfaction one gets from consuming one additional unit of a product above and beyond what one has consumed up to that point.
Market Demand Curve The horizontal sum of all individual demand curves.
Market Economy An economic system based on private property and the market in which, in principle, individuals decide how, what, and for whom to produce.
Market Failure A situation where the market does not lead to a desired result. Also: Situation in which the invisible hand pushes in such a way that individual decisions do not lead to socially desirable outcomes.
Market Force Economic force that is given relatively free rein by society to work through the market.
Market Incentive Plan A plan requiring market participants to certify that they have reduced total consumption—not necessarily their own individual consumption—by a specified amount.
Market Structure The physical characteristics of the market within which firms interact.
Market Supply Curve Horizontal sum of all individual supply curves. Also: Horizontal sum of all the firms' marginal cost curves, taking account of any changes in input prices that might occur.
Marxian (Radical) Model A model that focuses on equitable distribution of power, rights, and income among social classes.
Medicare A multibillion-dollar medical insurance system.
Mercantilism Economic system in which government determines the what, how, and for whom decision by doling out the rights to undertake certain economic activities.
Merger The act of combining two firms.
Merit Good or Activity Good or activity that government believes is good for you, even though you may not choose to consume the good or engage in the activity.
Microeconomics The study of individual choice, and how that choice is influenced by economic forces.
Minimum Efficient Level of Production The amount of production that spreads setup costs out sufficiently for a firm to undertake production profitably.
Minimum Wage Law Law specifying the lowest wage a firm can legally pay an employee.
Monetary Base Vault cash, deposits at the Fed, plus currency in circulation.
Monetary Policy A policy of influencing the economy through changes in the banking system's reserve that influence the money supply and credit available in the economy.
Monetary Regime A predetermined statement of policy that will be followed in various situations.
Money A highly liquid financial asset that's generally accepted in exchange for other goods, is used as a reference in valuing other goods, and can be stored as wealth.
Money Markets Markets in which financial assets having a maturity of less than one year are bought and sold.

Monitoring Costs Costs incurred by the organizer of production in seeing to it that the employees do what they're supposed to do.
Monitoring Problem The need to oversee employees to ensure that their actions are in the best interest of the firm.
Monopolistic Competition A market structure in which there are many firms selling differentiated products; there are few barriers to entry.
Monopoly A market structure in which one firm makes up the entire market.
Monopoly Power The ability of individuals or firms currently in business to prevent other individuals or firms from entering the same kind of business.
Monopsony Market in which a single firm is the only buyer.
Mortgage A special name for a secured loan on real estate.
Most-Favored Nation A country that will be charged as low a tariff on its exports as any other country.
Movement along a Demand Curve The graphic representation of the effect of a change in price on the quantity demanded.
Movement along a Supply Curve The graphic representation of the effect of a change in price on the quantity supplied.
Multiplier Effect The amplification of initial changes in expenditure.
Multiplier Equation An equation that tells us that income equals the multiplier times autonomous expenditures.

N

National Income (NI) The total income earned by citizens and businesses of a country.
National Income Accounting A set of rules and definitions for measuring economic activity in the aggregate economy—that is, in the economy as a whole.
Natural Monopoly An industry in which a single firm can produce at a lower cost than can two or more firms. Also: An industry in which significant economies of scale make the existence of more than one firm inefficient.
Necessity A good that has an income elasticity less than 1.
Negative Externality The effect of a decision that is not taken into account by the decision maker and is detrimental to others.
Net Domestic Product (NDP) The sum of consumption expenditures, government expenditures, net foreign expenditures, and investment less depreciation.
Net Exports Exports minus imports.
Net Foreign Factor Income Income from foreign domestic factor sources minus foreign factor income earned domestically.
Net Private Investment Gross private domestic investment minus depreciation.
Network Externality Phenomenon that the greater use of a product increases the benefit of that product to everyone.
New Growth Theory Theory that emphasizes the role of technology rather than capital in the growth process.
Nominal Deficit The deficit determined by looking at the difference between expenditures and receipts.
Nominal GDP GDP calculated at existing prices.
Nominal Interest Rates The rates you actually see and pay.
Nominal Output Output as measured at current prices.
Nonlinear Curve A curve that is drawn as a curved line.
Nonrecourse Loan Program Program in which government "buys" goods in the form of collateral on defaulting loans.
Normal Goods Goods whose consumption increases with an increase in income.
Normal Profit The amount the owners of business would have received in the next-best alternative.
Normative Economics The study of what the goals of the economy should be.
North American Industry Classification System (NAICS) An industry classification that categorizes firms by type of economic activity and groups firms with like production processes.

O

Official Reserves Government holdings of foreign currencies.
Official Transactions Account The part of the balance of payments account that records the amount of its own currency or foreign currencies that a nation buys or sells.
Okun's Rule of Thumb (sometimes called Okun's Law) A 1 percentage-point change in the unemployment rate will be associated with a 2 percent change in output in the opposite direction.
Oligopoly A market structure in which there are only a few firms; there are often significant barriers to entry.
Open Market Operations The Fed's buying and selling of government securities.
Opportunity Cost The benefit forgone by undertaking a particular activity.
Optimal Policy Policy in which the marginal cost of undertaking the policy equals the marginal benefit of that policy.
Output A result of a productive activity.
Outsourcing A firm shifting production from its own plant to other firms, either in the United States or abroad, where wages are lower.

P

Pareto Optimal Policy Policy that benefits some people and hurts no one.
Partially Flexible Exchange Rate The government sometimes buys and sells currencies to influence the price directly, and at other times the government simply accepts the exchange rate determined by supply and demand forces.
Partnership Business with two or more owners.
Passive Deficit or Surplus The part of the deficit or surplus that exists because the economy is operating below or above its potential level of output.
Patent Legal protection of a technical innovation that gives the person holding it sole right to use that innovation. (Note: A patent is good for only a limited time.)

Pay-as-You-Go System Payments to current beneficiaries are funded through current payroll taxes.
Per Capita Growth Producing more goods and services per person.
Per Capita Real Output Real GDP divided by the total population.
Perfectly Competitive Market A market in which economic forces operate unimpeded.
Perfectly Elastic Quantity responds enormously to changes in price ($E = \infty$).
Perfectly Inelastic Quantity does not respond at all to changes in price ($E = 0$).
Permanent Income Hypothesis Expenditures are determined by permanent or lifetime income.
Personal Consumption Expenditure (PCE) Deflator A measure of prices of goods that consumers buy that allows yearly changes in the basket of goods that reflect consumers' actual purchasing habits.
Personal Consumption Expenditures Payments by households for goods and services.
Personal Income (PI) National income plus net transfer payments from government minus amounts attributed but not received.
Phillips Curve A representation of the relationship between inflation and unemployment. (There is both a short-run and a long-run relationship.)
Pie Chart A circle divided into "pie pieces," where the individual pie represents the total amount and the pie pieces reflect the percentage of the whole pie that the various components make up.
Policy A one-time reaction to a problem.
Policy Change A change in one aspect of government's actions, such as monetary policy or fiscal policy.
Policy Regime A predetermined statement of the policy that will be followed in various circumstances.
Positive Economics The study of what is, and how the economy works.
Positive Externality Positive effect on others not taken into account by the decision maker.
Post-Keynesian Macroeconomist Economist who believes that uncertainty is a central issue in macroeconomics.
Potential Income The level of income that the economy technically is capable of producing without generating accelerating inflation.
Potential Output Output that would materialize at the target rate of unemployment and the target rate of capacity utilization. Also: The highest amount of output an economy can produce from the existing production function and the existing resources.
Poverty Threshold The income below which a family is considered to live in poverty.
Present Value A method of translating a flow of future income or saving into its current worth.
Price Ceiling A government-imposed limit on how high a price can be charged. In other words, a government-set price below the market equilibrium price.
Price-Discriminate To charge different prices to different individuals or groups of individuals.
Price Elasticity of Demand The percentage change in quantity demanded divided by the percentage change in price.
Price Elasticity of Supply The percentage change in quantity divided by the percentage change in price.
Price Floor A government-imposed limit on how low a price can be charged. In other words, a government-set price above equilibrium price.
Price Index A number that summarizes what happens to a weighted composite of goods (often called a market basket of goods) over time.
Price Stabilization Program Program designed to eliminate short-run fluctuations in prices, while allowing prices to follow their long-run trend line.
Price Support Program Program designed to maintain prices at higher levels than the market prices.
Price Taker Firm or individual who takes the market price determined by market supply and demand as given.
Primary Financial Market Market in which newly issued financial assets are sold.
Principle of Diminishing Marginal Utility As you consume more of a good, after some point the marginal utility received from each additional unit of a good decreases with each additional unit consumed, other things equal.
Principle of Increasing Marginal Opportunity Cost In order to get more of something, one must give up ever-increasing quantities of something else.
Principle of Rational Choice Spend your money on those goods that give you the most marginal utility (*MU*) per dollar.
Prisoner's Dilemma Well-known game that demonstrates the difficulty of cooperative behavior in certain circumstances.
Private Good A good that, when consumed by one individual, cannot be consumed by other individuals.
Private Property Rights Control a private individual or firm has over an asset or a right.
Procyclical Fiscal Policy Changes in government spending and taxes that increase the cyclical fluctuations in the economy instead of reducing them.
Producer Price Index (PPI) An index of prices that measures average change in the selling prices received by domestic producers of goods and services over time.
Producer Surplus Price the producer sells a product for less the cost of producing it.
Production The transformation of factors into goods and services.
Production Function The relationship between the inputs (factors of production) and outputs.
Production Possibility Curve A curve measuring the maximum combination of outputs that can be obtained from a given number of inputs.
Production Possibility Table Table that lists a choice's opportunity costs by summarizing what alternative outputs you can achieve with your inputs.
Production Table A table showing the output resulting from various combinations of factors of production or inputs.

Productive Efficiency Achieving as much output as possible from a given amount of inputs or resources.
Productivity Output per unit of input.
Profit A return on entrepreneurial activity and risk taking. Alternatively, what's left over from total revenues after all the appropriate costs have been subtracted. Also: Total revenue minus total cost.
Profit-Maximizing Condition $MR = MC = P$.
Progressive Tax Tax whose rates increase as a person's income increases.
Proportional Tax Tax whose rates are constant at all income levels, no matter what a taxpayer's total annual income is.
Public Assistance Means-tested social programs targeted to the poor and providing financial, nutritional, medical, and housing assistance.
Public Choice (Conservative) Model A model that focuses on economic incentives as applied to politicians.
Public Choice Economists Economists who integrate an economic analysis of politics with their analysis of the economy.
Public Good A good that if supplied to one person must be supplied to all and whose consumption by one individual does not prevent its consumption by another individual.
Purchasing Power Parity (PPP) A method of calculating exchange rates that attempts to value currencies at rates such that each currency will buy an equal basket of goods.

Q

Quantity Demanded A specific amount that will be demanded per unit of time at a specific price, other things constant.
Quantity Supplied A specific amount that will be supplied at a specific price.
Quantity Theory of Money The price level varies in response to changes in the quantity of money.
Quantity-Adjusting Markets Markets in which firms respond to changes in demand primarily by modifying their output instead of changing their prices.
Quota Quantity limits on imports.

R

Radical Economist Economist who believes substantial equality-preferring institutional changes should be implemented to our economic system.
Rational Used to describe behavior individuals undertake in their own best interest.
Rational Expectations Expectations that the economists' model predicts. Also: Forward-looking expectations that use available information.
Rational Expectations Model All decisions are based upon the expected equilibrium in the economy.
Real-Business-Cycle Theory A theory that views fluctuations in the economy as reflecting real phenomena—simultaneous shifts in supply and demand, not simply supply responses to demand shifts.
Real Deficit The nominal deficit adjusted for inflation.
Real Gross Domestic Product (real GDP) The market value of final goods and services produced in an economy, stated in the prices of a given year. Also: Nominal GDP adjusted for inflation.
Real Interest Rates Nominal interest rates adjusted for expected inflation.
Real Output The total amount of goods and services produced, adjusted for price-level changes.
Recession A decline in real output that persists for more than two consecutive quarters of a year.
Recessionary Gap The amount by which equilibrium output is below potential output.
Regime Change A change in the entire atmosphere within which the government and the economy interrelate.
Regressive Tax Tax whose rates decrease as income rises.
Regulatory Trade Restrictions Government-imposed procedural rules that limit imports.
Rent Control A price ceiling on rents, set by government.
Rent-Seeking Activities Activities designed to transfer surplus from one group to another.
Reserve Ratio The ratio of reserves to total deposits.
Reserve Requirement The percentage the Federal Reserve System sets as the minimum amount of reserves a bank must have.
Reserves Currency and deposits a bank keeps on hand or at the Fed or central bank, enough to manage the normal cash inflows and outflows.
Restructuring Changing the underlying economic institutions.
Reverse Engineering The process of a firm buying other firms' products, disassembling them, figuring out what's special about them, and then copying them within the limits of the law.
Rosy Scenario Policy Government policy of making optimistic predictions and never making gloomy predictions.
Rule of 72 The number of years it takes for a certain amount to double in value is equal to 72 divided by its annual rate of increase.

S

Say's Law Supply creates its own demand.
Scarcity The goods available are too few to satisfy individuals' desires.
Secondary Financial Market Market in which previously issued financial assets can be bought and sold.
Share Distribution of Income The relative division of total income among income groups.
Sherman Antitrust Act A U.S. law designed to regulate the competitive process.
Shift in Demand The effect of anything other than price on demand.
Shift in Supply The graphic representation of the effect of a change in other than price on supply.
Short-Run Aggregate Supply (*SAS*) Curve A curve that specifies how a shift in the aggregate demand curve affects the

price level and real output in the short run, other things constant.
Short-Run Decision Decision in which the firm is constrained in regard to what production decisions it can make.
Short-Run Phillips Curve A downward-sloping curve showing the relationship between inflation and unemployment when expectations of inflation are constant.
Shutdown Point Point at which the firm will be better off if it temporarily shuts down than it will if it stays in business.
Simple Money Multiplier The measure of the amount of money ultimately created per dollar deposited in the banking system, when people hold no currency.
Sin Tax A tax that discourages activities society believes are harmful (sinful).
Slope The change in the value on the vertical axis divided by the change in the value on the horizontal axis.
Social Capital The habitual way of doing things that guides people in how they approach production.
Social Security System A social insurance program that provides financial benefits to the elderly and disabled and to their eligible dependents and/or survivors.
Socialism An economic system based on individuals' goodwill toward others, not on their own self-interest, and in which, in principle, society decides what, how, and for whom to produce.
Socioeconomic Distribution of Income The allocation of income among relevant socioeconomic groupings.
Sole Proprietorship Business that has only one owner.
Soviet-Style Socialist Economy Economic system that uses administrative control or central planning to solve the coordination problems: what, how, and for whom.
Special Drawing Rights (SDRs) A type of international money.
Specialization The concentration of individuals in certain aspects of production.
Stagflation Combination of high and accelerating inflation and high unemployment.
Stock Financial asset that conveys ownership rights in a corporation.
Strategic Bargaining Demanding a larger share of the gains from trade than you can reasonably expect.
Strategic Decision Making Taking explicit account of a rival's expected response to a decision you are making.
Strategic Pricing A characteristic of oligopoly in which firms set their price based on the expected reactions of other firms.
Strategic Trade Policies Threatening to implement tariffs to bring about a reduction in tariffs or some other concession from the other country.
Structural Deficit or Surplus The part of a budget deficit or surplus that would exist even if the economy were at its potential level of income.
Structural Unemployment Unemployment caused by the institutional structure of an economy or by economic restructuring making some skills obsolete.
Substitutes Goods that can be used in place of one another.
Sunk Costs Costs that have already been incurred and cannot be recovered.
Supplemental Security Income (SSI) A federal program that pays benefits based on need to the elderly, blind, and disabled.
Supply A schedule of quantities a seller is willing to sell per unit of time at various prices, other things constant. Put another way, a schedule of quantities of goods that will be offered to the market at various prices, other things constant.
Supply Curve Graphical representation of the relationship between price and quantity supplied.
Surplus An excess of revenue over payments.

T

Takeover The purchase of one firm by a shell firm that then takes direct control of all the purchased firm's operations.
Target Rate of Unemployment Lowest sustainable rate of unemployment that policymakers believe is achievable under existing conditions.
Tariff An excise tax on an imported (internationally traded) good.
Tax Incentive Program A program of using a tax to create incentives for individuals to structure their activities in a way that is consistent with the desired ends.
Tax-Based Income Policies Policies in which the government tries to directly affect the nominal wage- and price-setting institutions.
Taylor Rule The rule is: Set the Fed funds rate at 2 percent plus current inflation if the economy is at desired output and desired inflation. If the inflation rate is higher than desired, increase the Fed funds rate by 0.5 times the difference between desired and actual inflation. Similarly, if output is higher than desired, increase the Fed funds rate by 0.5 times the percentage deviation.
Team Spirit The feelings of friendship and being part of a team that bring out people's best efforts.
Technical Efficiency Describes a situation in which as few inputs as possible are used to produce a given output.
Technological Change An increase in the range of production techniques that leads to more efficient ways of producing goods as well as the production of new and better goods.
Technological Development The discovery of new or improved products or methods of production.
Technological Lock-In The use of a technology makes the adoption of subsequent technology difficult.
Technology The way we make goods and supply services.
Third-Party-Payer Market A market in which the person who receives the good differs from the person paying for the good.
Total Cost Explicit payments to the factors of production plus the opportunity cost of the factors provided by the owners of the firm.
Total Revenue The amount a firm receives for selling its product or service plus any increase in the value of the assets owned by the firm.

Total Utility The total satisfaction one gets from consuming a product.
Trade Adjustment Assistance Programs Programs designed to compensate people hurt by the removal of trade restrictions.

U

Unemployment Compensation Short-term financial assistance, regardless of need, to eligible individuals who are temporarily out of work.
Unemployment Rate The percentage of people in the economy who are willing and able to work but who are not working.
Unexpected Inflation Inflation that surprises people.
Union Shop Firm in which all workers must join the union.
Unit Elastic The percentage change in quantity is equal to the percentage change in price ($E = 1$).
Utility The pleasure or satisfaction that one expects to get from consuming a good or service.
Utility-Maximizing Rule Utility is maximized when the ratios of the marginal utility to price of two goods are equal.

V

Value Added The increase in value that a firm contributes to a product or service.
Value of Marginal Product (*VMP*) An additional worker's marginal physical product multiplied by the price at which the firm could sell that additional product.
Variable Costs Costs that change as output changes.
Velocity of Money The number of times per year, on average, a dollar goes around to generate a dollar's worth of income.
Vertical Merger A combination of two companies that are involved in different phases of producing a product.

W

Wealth The value of the things individuals own less the value of what they owe.
Wealth Accounts A balance sheet of an economy's stock of assets and liabilities.
Wealth Effect A fall in the price level will make the holders of money and of other financial assets richer, so they buy more.
Welfare Loss Triangle A geometric representation of the welfare cost in terms of misallocated resources that are caused by a deviation from a supply/demand equilibrium.
World Trade Organization (WTO) An organization whose functions are generally the same as GATT's were—to promote free and fair trade among countries. Also: Organization committed to getting countries to agree not to impose new tariffs or other trade restrictions except under certain limited conditions.

X–Z

X-inefficiency The underperformance of a firm that has a monopoly position.

Colloquial Glossary

A

Ads (noun) Short for "advertisements."
Ain't (verb) An ungrammatical form of "isn't," sometimes used to emphasize a point although the speaker knows that "isn't" is the correct form.
All the Rage (descriptive phrase) Extremely popular, but the popularity is likely to be transitory.
Andy Warhol (proper name) American artist who flourished in the period 1960–1980. He was immensely popular and successful with art critics and the intelligentsia, but, above all, he gained worldwide recognition in the same way and of the same quality as movie stars and sports athletes do. His renown has continued even after his death.
Armada (proper noun) Historic term for the Spanish navy. Now obsolete.
Automatic Pilot (noun) To be on automatic pilot is to be acting without thinking.

B

Baby Boom (noun) Any period when more than the statistically predicted number of babies is born. Originally referred to a specific group: those born in the years 1945–1964.
Baby Boomers (descriptive phrase) Americans born in the years 1945 through 1964. An enormous and influential group of people whose large number is attributed to the "boom" in babies that occurred when military personnel, many of whom had been away from home for four or five years, were discharged from military service after the end of World War II.
Back to the Drawing Board (descriptive phrase) To start all over again after having your plan or project turn out to be useless.
Backfire (verb) To injure a person or entity who intended to inflict injury.
Bailed Out (descriptive phrase) To be rescued. It has other colloquial meanings as well, but they do not appear in this book.
Balloon (verb) To expand enormously and suddenly.
Bear Market (noun) Stock market dominated by people who are not buying (i.e., are hibernating). Opposite of a bull market, where people are charging ahead vigorously to buy.
Bedlam (noun) Chaotic and apparently disorganized activity. Today the word is not capitalized. A few hundred years ago in England the noun meant the Hospital of St. Mary's of Bethlehem, an insane asylum. The hospital was not in Bethlehem; it was in London. "Bedlam" was the way "Bethlehem" was pronounced by the English.
Beluga Caviar (noun) Best, most expensive, caviar.
Benchmark (noun) A point of reference from which measurement of any sort may be made.
Better Mousetrap (noun) Comes from the proverb, "Invent a better mousetrap and the world will beat a path to your door."
Bidding (or Bid) (verb sometimes used as a noun) Has two different meanings. (1) Making an offer, or a series of offers, to compete with others who are making offers. Also the offer itself. (2) Ordering or asking a person to take a specified action.
Big Bucks (noun) Really, really large sum of money.
Big Mac (proper noun) Brand name of a kind of hamburger sold at McDonald's restaurants.
Blow It (verb; past tense: blew it) To do a poor job, to miss an opportunity, to perform unsatisfactorily.
Blowout (noun) Serious release of pent-up emotions or of control over one's actions.
Boost (verb and noun) To give a sudden impetus, or boost, to something or someone.
Botched Up (adjective) Operated badly; spoiled.
Bottleneck (noun) Situation in which no action can be taken because a large number of people or actions is confronted by a very small opening or opportunity.
Brainteaser (noun) Question or puzzle that intrigues the brain, thus "teasing" it to answer the question or solve the puzzle.
Bring Home (verb) To emphasize or convince.
Broke (adjective) (1) To "go broke" or to "be broke" is to become insolvent, to lose all one's money and assets. (2) Usually not as bad as to have gone broke—just to be (hopefully) temporarily out of money or short of funds.
Bucks (noun) American slang for "dollars."
Buffalo (adjective, as used in this book) "Buffalo chicken wings" are a variety of tempting food developed in, and hence associated with, the city of Buffalo. (Not all chicken wings are Buffalo chicken wings.)
Bus Person (noun) Has no relation to transportation. It's a term for the person who clears the tables in a restaurant.

C

Call (verb) In sports refereeing, one meaning of "to call" is for the referee to announce his or her decision on a specific point.
Calvin Coolidge (proper name) President of the United States 1923–1928.
Carriage Maker (noun) Person or firm that makes carriages, a type of horse-drawn conveyance almost never seen any more except in films. Members of the British royal family ride in carriages on important ceremonial occasions, such as weddings.
Caveat (noun) In English, this noun means "caution" or "warning." It come from Latin, where it is a whole little sentence: "Let him beware."

Cellophane (noun) A transparent wrapping material. It differs from plastic wrap in that it is made of cellulose, not plastic.
Center Stage (noun) A dominant position.
Central Park West (proper noun) A fashionable and expensive street in New York City.
CEO (noun) Abbreviation of "chief executive officer."
Charade (noun) A pretense, usually designed to convince someone that you are doing something that you are definitely not doing.
Chit (noun) Type of IOU (which see) or coupon with a designated value that can be turned in toward the purchase or acquisition of some item.
Chump Change (noun) Insignificant amount of money earned by or paid to a person who is not alert enough to realize that more money could rather easily be earned.
Clear-Cut (adjective) Precisely defined.
Clip Coupons (verb) To cut coupons out of newspapers and magazines. The coupons give you a discount on the price of the item when you present the item and the coupon at the cashier's counter in a store. Sometimes you are directed to buy the item and then send the coupon and an identifying code from the item's package to the manufacturer, who will mail you the discount.
Clout (noun) Influence or power.
Coffer (noun) A box or trunk used to hold valuable items; hence, "coffers" has come to mean a vault or other safe storage place to hold money or other valuable items.
Coined (verb) Invented or originated.
Coldhearted (adjective) Without any sympathy; aloof; inhuman.
Come Through (verb) Satisfy someone's demands or expectations.
Come Up Short (descriptive phrase) To be deficient.
Co-opted (adjective) Overwhelmed.
Cornrows (noun) Hair style in which hair is braided in shallow, narrow rows over the entire head.
Corvette (noun) A type of expensive sports car.
Couch (verb) To construct and present an argument.
Crack (noun) A strong form of cocaine.
Cry Over Spilt Milk (verb) To indulge in useless complaint or regret. Note that there is a departure from standard English spelling in this phrase, which uses the spelling "spilt" instead of "spilled." Either is correct, but "spilt" is seldom used. (Another such variation is the rare "spelt" for usual "spelled.")
Cut and Dried (descriptive phrase) Simple, obvious, and settled.

D

Deadbeat (noun) Lazy person who has no ambition, no money, and no prospects.
Deadweight (noun) Literally, the unrelieved weight of any inert mass (think of carrying a sack of bricks); hence, any oppressive burden.
Decent (adjective) One of its specialized meanings is "of high quality."
Doodle (noun and verb) Idle scribbles, usually nonrepresentational and usually made while actively thinking about something else, such as during a phone conversation or sitting in a class.
Down Pat (descriptive phrase) To have something down pat is to know it precisely, accurately, and without needing to think about it.
Drop in the Bucket (noun) Insignificant quantity compared to the total amount available.
Dyed-in-the-Wool (adjective) Irretrievably convinced of the value of a particular course of action or of the truth of an opinion. Literally, wool that is dyed after it is shorn from the sheep but before it is spun into thread.

E

'Em (pronoun) Careless way of pronouncing "them." Written out, it reproduces the sound the speaker is making.
Energizer Bunny (noun) Character in a television commercial for Energizer batteries. Just as the batteries are alleged to do, the Energizer bunny keeps going and going.
Esperanto (noun) An artificial language invented in the 1880s, intended to be "universal." It is based on words from the principal European languages, and the theory was that all speakers of these European languages would effortlessly understand Esperanto. It never had a big following and today is almost unknown.
Establishment (noun and adjective) As a noun, the prevailing theory or practice. As an adjective, something that is used by people whose views prevail over other people's views.

F

Fake (verb) To fake is to pretend or deceive; to try to make people believe that you know what you're doing or talking about when you don't know or aren't sure.
Fire (verb) To discharge an employee permanently. It's different from "laying off" an employee, an action taken when a temporary situation makes the employee superfluous but the employer expects to take the employee back when the temporary situation is over.
Fit to a T (verb) Suit perfectly.
Fix (verb) To prepare, as in "fixing a meal." This is only one of the multiplicity of meanings of this verb.
Fleeting (adverb) This word's usage is elegant and correct, but rare. It means transitory or short-lived.
Flop (noun) A dismal failure.
Follow Suit (verb) To do the same thing you see others do. Comes from card games where if a card of a certain suit is played, the other players must play a card of that suit, if they have one.
Follow the Flag (verb) To be committed to doing business only with firms that produce in your own country or in your "colonies"—that is, territories that belong to your country.
Follow the Leader (noun) Name of a children's game. Metaphorically, it means to do what others are doing, usually without giving it much thought.
Forest for the Trees (descriptive phrase) To be so focused on details that you don't see the overall situation.

Free Lunch (descriptive phrase) Something you get without paying for it in any way. Usually applied negatively: There is no "free lunch."
Funky (adjective) Eccentric in style or manner.

G

G.I. Joe (noun) A toy in the form of a boy (as "Barbie" is a girl). Original meaning was "government issue"—i.e., an item, such as a uniform, issued by the U.S. government to a member of the U.S. armed forces, and, by extension, the person to whom the item was issued.
GM (noun) The General Motors automobile company.
Gadget (noun) Generic term for any small, often novel, mechanical or electronic device or contrivance, usually designed for a specific purpose. For instance, the small wheel with serrated rim and an attached handle used to divide a pizza pie into slices is a gadget.
Gee (expletive) Emphatic expression signaling surprise or enthusiasm.
Get Across (verb) To convince.
Get You Down (descriptive phrase) Make you depressed about something or make you dismiss something altogether. (Do not confuse with "get it down," which means to understand fully.)
Glitch (noun) Trivial difficulty.
Go-Cart (noun) A small engine-powered vehicle that is used for racing and recreation.
Gold Mine (noun) Metaphorically, any activity that results in making you a lot of money.
Goldilocks (fictional character) In a children's story, Goldilocks is a beautiful little girl with blonde curls who emerges unharmed from an encounter with three bears because she is so good and charming.
Good and Ready (descriptive phrase) Really, really ready.
Good Cop/Bad Cop (noun) Alternating mood shifts. It comes from the alleged practice of having two police officers interview a suspect—one officer is kind and coaxing while the other is mean and nasty. This is supposed to make the suspect feel that the nice cop is a safe person to confide in.
Good Offices (descriptive phrase) An expression common in 18th-century England, meaning "services."
Gooey (adjective) Sticky or slimy.
Goofed (verb) Past tense of the verb *goof*, meaning to make a careless mistake.
Got It Made (descriptive phrase) Succeeded.
Grind (noun) Slang for necessary intense effort that may be painful but will likely benefit your understanding.
Groucho Marx (proper name) A famous U.S. comedian (1885–1977).
Gung-ho (adjective) Full of energy and eager to take action.
Guns and Butter (descriptive phrase) Metaphor describing the dilemma whether to devote resources to war or to peace.

H

Haggling (noun) Bargaining, usually in a petty and confrontational manner.
Handout (noun) Unearned offering (as distinct from a gift); charity.
Handy (adjective) Convenient.
Hard Liquor (noun) Alcoholic beverages with a high content of pure alcohol. Beer and wine are not "hard liquor" but most other alcoholic drinks are.
Hard Up (adjective) Seriously worried.
Hassle (noun) Unreasonable obstacle. As a verb, *to hassle* means to place unreasonable obstacles or arguments in the way of someone.
Hawking (adjective) Selling aggressively and widely.
Heat (noun) Anger, blame, outrage, and pressure to change.
Hefty (adjective) Large; substantial.
Hero Sandwich (noun) A type of very large sandwich.
Highfalutin (adjective) American slang term meaning pretentious, self-important, supercilious.
High Horse, Getting on Your (descriptive phrase) Adopting a superior attitude; looking down (from your high horse) on other people's opinions or actions.
Hog Bellies (noun) Commercial term for the part of a pig that becomes bacon and pork chops. (Also called *pork bellies*.)
Holds Its Own (descriptive phrase) Refuses to give up, even in the face of adversity or opposition.
Home Free (descriptive phrase) Safe and successful.
Hot Air (descriptive phrase) An empty promise. Also, bragging.
Hot Dog (noun) A type of sausage.
Hot Potatoes (noun) Slang term for anything that everyone wants to avoid confronting.
How Come (expression) Why? That is, "How has it come about that . . . ?"

I

IOU (noun) A nickname applied to a formal acknowledgment of a debt, such as a U.S. Treasury bond. Also an informal but written acknowledgment of a debt. Pronounce the letters and you will hear "I owe you."
"In" (preposition sometimes used as an adjective) Placed within quotation marks to show it is used with a special meaning. Here it is used as an adjective, to indicate: "fashionable or popular, usually just for a short period." Compare, in this glossary, *all the rage*.
Incidentals (noun) Blanket term covering the world of small items a person uses on a daily basis as the need happens to arise—that is, needed per incident occurring. Examples are aspirin, combs, and picture postcards.
Iron Curtain (noun) Imaginary but daunting line between Western Europe and adjacent communist countries. After the political abandonment of Communism in these countries, the Curtain no longer exists.
It'll (contraction) "It will."

J

Jolt (noun) A sudden blow.

Junk Food (noun) Food that tastes good but has little nutritional value and lots of calories. It is sometimes cheap, sometimes expensive, and it's quick and easy to buy and eat.
Just Say No (admonition) Flatly refuse. This phrase became common in the 1970s after Nancy Reagan, the wife of the then-president of the United States, popularized it in a campaign against the use of addictive drugs.

K

Ketchup (noun) Spicy, thick tomato sauce used on, among other foods, hot dogs.
Kick In (verb) To activate; to start or begin. (Can also mean "to contribute to.")
Kickback (noun) A firm's giving part of the price it has received for its product or service back to the firm or individual who authorized the purchase of that product or service. In effect it is a type of bribe or blackmail demanded or expected by a purchaser's agent.
Klutz (noun) Awkward, incompetent person.
Knockoff (noun) A cheap imitation.

L

Laetrile (noun) Substance derived from peach pits, thought by some people to be a cure for cancer.
Laid Back (adjective) Casual; calm; free from worry and feelings of pressure.
Late Victorian (adjective or noun) Embodying some concept typical of the late period of Queen Victoria. Also, a person from that period or who acts like someone from that period. (Queen Victoria was queen of England from 1837 to 1901.)
Lay Off (verb) To discharge a worker temporarily.
Lead Banker (noun) Primary or principal bank or banker in a joint undertaking.
Leads (noun) Persons or institutions that you think will be interested in whatever you have to sell. Also the information you have that makes you think someone or something is worth pursuing.
Left the Nest (descriptive phrase) To have left one's parental home, usually because one has grown up and become self-sufficient.
Levi's (noun) Popular brand of jeans.
Like Greek to You (descriptive phrase) Incomprehensible (because in the United States, classical Greek is considered to be a language that almost no one learns).
Limbo (noun) To be "in limbo" is to be in a place or situation from which there is no escape.
Lion's Share (noun) By far the best part of a bargain.
Lobby (verb and noun) To lobby is to attempt by organized effort to influence legislation. As a noun, a lobby is an organized group formed to influence legislation. A lobbyist is a member of a lobby.
Lord Tennyson (proper name) Alfred Tennyson, 19th-century English poet who wrote a poem, *Ulysses*, about the nobility of effort ("To strive, to seek, to find and not to yield").
Losing Ground (verb) Regressing.
Lousy (adjective) Incompetent or distasteful.

M

MBA (noun) An academic degree: master of business administration.
Make It (verb) To succeed in doing something; for instance, "make it to the bank" means to get to the bank before it closes.
Mall (noun) Short for "shopping mall." A variety of stores grouped on one piece of land, with ample parking for all the mall's shoppers and often with many amenities such as covered walkways, playgrounds for children, fountains, etc.
MasterCard (proper noun) Brand name of a widely issued credit card.
Mazuma (noun) U.S. slang term for money. It was used in the first half of the 20th century but is now rare, to say the least.
Medicaid (proper noun) Health insurance program for low-income people. It is administered jointly by the U.S. government and the individual states.
Medicare (proper noun) U.S. government health insurance program for people who are disabled or age 65 and over. There is no means test.
Messed Up (adjective) Damaged or badly managed.
Mind Your Own Business (admonition) Don't meddle in other people's affairs; don't ask intrusive questions.
Mind Your Ps and Qs (expression) Pay close attention to distinctions. It comes from the similarity of the small printed letters "p" and "q" where the only visual distinction is the location of the downstroke. Also, the letters are right next to each other in our alphabet.
Mob (noun) Organized criminal activity. Also, the group to which organized criminals belong.
Moot (adjective) Irrelevant because the issue in question has already been decided.
Mousetrap (noun) Producing a better mousetrap is part of the saying, "Make a better mousetrap and the world will beat a path to your door." Metaphorically, producing a better mousetrap stands for doing anything better than it has previously been done.

N

NA (abbreviation) "Not available."
NASDAQ (also sometimes spelled "Nasdaq") (noun) Stock market operated by the National Association of Securities Dealers. The "AQ" stands for "Automated Quotations."
NATO (noun) North American Treaty Organization. Western alliance for joint economic and military cooperation. It includes the United States, Canada, and several European nations.
Nature of the Beast (descriptive phrase) Character of whatever you are describing (need not have anything to do with a "beast").
Nicholas Apert (proper name) Nineteenth-century French experimenter who discovered how to preserve food by canning or bottling it.

Nirvana (noun) This word is adopted from Buddhism. Its religious meaning is complicated, but it is used colloquially to mean salvation, paradise, harmony, perfection.
No Way (exclamation) Emphatic expression denoting refusal, denial, or extreme disapproval.
Not to Worry (admonition; also, when hyphenated, used as an adjective) Don't worry; or, it's nothing to worry about.
Nudge (noun and verb) A little push (noun); to give a little push (verb).

O

Off the Books (descriptive phrase) Not officially recorded (and hence it's an untaxed transaction).
Off-the-Cuff (adjective) A quick, unthinking answer for which the speaker has no valid authority (comes from the alleged practice of writing an abbreviated answer on the cuff of your shirt, to be glanced at during an examination).
Oliver Wendell Holmes (proper name) A justice of the U.S. Supreme Court, famous for his wit, his wisdom, his literary ability, his advocacy of civil rights, and his long life (1841–1935).
On Her (His) Own (descriptive phrase) By herself (himself); without any help.
On Their Toes (descriptive phrase) Alert; ready for any eventuality.
Op-Ed (adjective) Describes an article that appears on the "op-ed" page of a newspaper, which is **OP**posite the **ED**itorial page.

P

Pain, Real (noun) This real pain is not a *real* pain; rather, it is something—anything—that gives you a lot of trouble and that you dislike intensely. For instance, some people think balancing a checkbook is a real pain.
Park Avenue (noun) Expensive and fashionable street in New York City.
Pass the Buck (descriptive phrase) Evade responsibility by forcing someone else to make the relevant decision.
Peanuts (noun) Slang for a small amount, usually money but sometimes anything with a small value.
Pecking Order (noun) Hierarchy.
Peer Pressure (descriptive phrase) Push to do what everyone else in your particular group is doing.
Penny-Pincher (noun) Person who is unusually careful with money, sometimes to the point of being stingy.
Perks (noun) Short for "perquisites."
Philharmonic (adjective) A philharmonic orchestra is an orchestra that specializes in classical music. Sometimes used as a noun, as in "I heard the Philharmonic."
Phoenix from the Ashes (descriptive phrase) Metaphor for coming to life after having been thought to be dead. In ancient Greek mythology, the phoenix was a bird said to (really) rise from the ashes after a fire. (Phoenix, Arizona, was so named because of the hot climate that prevails there.)
Pick Up Steam (verb) As steam pressure increases, the speed of a steam engine increases. When this happens, we say the engine has "picked up steam."
Pickle (noun) Dilemma.
Picky (adjective) Indulging in fine distinctions when making a decision.
Pie (noun) Metaphor for the total amount of a specific item that exists.
Piece of Cake (descriptive phrase) Simple; easy to achieve without much effort or thought.
Pitt, (Sir) William (historical figure) Chief financial officer and prime minister of Britain in the 1780s. He is usually designated "the younger" to distinguish him from his father, who was also a high British government official.
Poorhouse (noun) Public institution where impoverished individuals were housed. These institutions were purposely dreary and unpleasant. They no longer officially exist, but they have a modern manifestation: shelters for the homeless.
Pop-Tart (noun) Brand name of a type of junk food. It's a sweet filling enclosed in pastry that you pop into the toaster and when the pastry is hot, it pops out of the toaster.
Populist (noun and adjective) As a noun, this means a member of a political party that purports to represent the rank and file of the people. As an adjective, it means a political party, a group, or an individual that purports to represent rank and file opinion.
Pound (noun) Unit of British currency.
Practice Makes Perfect (expression) The grammar of this phrase is illogical but the meaning is clear.
Premium Tires All Round (descriptive phrase) Premium tires are tires of superior quality. When all the tires on your vehicle are premium tires, you have them "all round."
Presto! (exclamation) Immediately.
Proxy (noun) A stockholder can give a "proxy" to the firm. It is an authorization that permits the firm's officials to vote for the proposition that the stockholder directs them to vote for. By extension, proxy means a substitute.
Ps and Qs See under *Mind.*
Pub (noun) Short for "public house," a commercial establishment where alcoholic drinks are served, usually with refreshments and occasionally with light meals.

Q

Queen Elizabeth (proper noun) Here the author means Queen Elizabeth the first (reigned in England from 1558 to 1603).
Quote (noun) Seller's statement of what he or she will charge for a good or service.

R

R&D (noun) Research and development.
Rainy Day (noun) Period when you (hopefully) temporarily have an income shortage.
Rainy Day Fund (descriptive phrase) Money set aside when you are doing well financially—i.e., in a financially sunny period—to use in case you have a period when you

are doing less well financially—i.e., when you run into a financially rainy period.

Raise Your Eyebrows (verb) To express surprise, usually by a facial expression rather than vocally.

Red Flag (noun) A red flag warns you to be very alert to a danger or perceived danger. (Ships in port that are loading fuel or ammunition raise a red flag to signal danger.)

Red-Handed (adjective) Indisputably guilty. Comes from being found at a murder or injury scene with the blood of the victim on one's hands.

Red-Lined (adjective) On a motor vehicle's tachometer, a red line that warns at what speed an engine's capacity is being strained.

Right On! (exclamation) Expression of vigorous, often revolutionary, approval and encouragement.

Ring Up (verb) Before the introduction of computer-type machines that record each payment a retail customer makes—say at the supermarket or a restaurant—a "cash register" was used. When you pressed the keys representing the amount offered by the customer, a drawer sprang open and a bell rang.

Ritzy (adjective) Very expensive, fashionable, and ostentatious. Comes from the entrepreneur Caesar Ritz, a Swiss developer of expensive hotels, active in the first quarter of the 20th century.

Robin Hood (proper name) Semifictional English adventurer of the 12th or 13th century. He "stole from the rich and gave to the poor."

Rodeo (noun) Entertainment where a person rides a bull that is wildly trying to throw the rider off. Horses are often exhibited similarly.

Rolodex File (noun) Manual—as opposed to electronic—device for organizing names, addresses, phone numbers, and e-numbers.

Rule of Thumb (descriptive phrase) An estimate that is quick and easy to make and is reliable enough for rough calculations. Comes from using the space from the tip of your thumb to the thumb's first joint to represent an inch.

S

Sacred Cow (noun) An institution or practice that social and/or political forces dictate is absolutely protected from change of any kind.

Saks (proper name) A midsize department store that sells expensive, fashionable items. There are very few stores in the Saks chain, and Saks stores are considered exclusive.

Savvy (adjective) Slang term meaning very knowledgeable. Adaptation of the French verb *savoir*, meaning "to know."

Scab (noun) Person who takes a job, or continues in a job, even though workers at that firm are on strike.

Scraps (noun) Little pieces of leftover food. Also little pieces of anything that is left over: for example, steel that is salvaged from a wrecked car.

Sears Catalog (noun) Sears, Roebuck and Co. is a large chain of stores that sells a wide variety of goods. Before shopping malls, interstate highways, and the Internet, Sears used to have a huge mailing list to which it sent enormous catalogs. A person receiving such a catalog would have information about, and access to, thousands of items, many of which the person might not have known existed before the catalog provided the prospect.

Set Up Shop (verb) To go into business.

Shell Out (verb) To pay money, often somewhat more than you want to pay for the item in question.

Shivering in Their Sandals (descriptive phrase) Adaptation of standard English idiom *shivering in their shoes*, which means being afraid.

Show Up (verb) To put in an appearance, to arrive.

Shorthand (noun) Any of several systems of abbreviated writing or writing that substitutes symbols for words and phrases. Shorthand was widely used in business until the introduction of mechanical and electronic devices for transmitting the human voice gradually made shorthand obsolete. Today it means to summarize very briefly or to substitute a short word or phrase for a long description.

Shy Away (verb) To decisively refrain from something. (Comes from the world of horses, who are said to "shy at" things that startle them.)

Silk Stockings (noun) Silk stockings for women denoted luxury and extravagance, almost like caviar or pearls. With the development of nylon in 1940, silk stockings for anyone, let alone the queens or factory girls mentioned in this book, joined the dinosaurs in oblivion.

Sixpence (noun) A British coin that is no longer in use. It represented six British pennies and its U.S. equivalent in the 2000s would be about a nickel.

Skin of One's Teeth (descriptive phrase) To succeed by the skin of one's teeth means to just barely succeed. A micromeasure less and one would not have succeeded.

Skyrocket (verb and noun) To rise suddenly and rapidly. As a noun, it means the type of fireworks that shoot into the sky and explode suddenly in a shower of brilliant sparks.

Slow as Molasses (descriptive phrase) Very slow. Molasses is a thick, sweet syrup made from sugar cane (known as "treacle" in the United Kingdom) that pours with agonizing slowness from its container.

Small Potatoes (noun) An expression meaning insignificant or trivial.

Smoke Screen (noun) Metaphorically, anything used intentionally to hide one's true intentions.

Smoking Gun (noun) This term has come to stand for any indisputable evidence of guilt or misdeeds.

Snitch (verb) To engage in petty theft. (This verb has another meaning, which is to betray a person by divulging a secret about that person. If you do that, you are not only snitching, you are a snitch.)

Snowball (verb) To increase rapidly, like a ball of wet snow that grows and grows when it is rolled rapidly in more wet snow.

Soft Drink (noun) Nonalcoholic beverage.

Sourpuss (noun) Dour; sulky; humorless. Derives from *sour*, which is self-explanatory, and *puss*, a slang word for "face."

Spending a Penny (descriptive phrase) Spending any money at all. Do not confuse with usage in England, where the phrase means to go to the bathroom.
Squash (verb) To crush or ruin.
Squirrel Away (verb) To hide or conceal in a handy but secret place (as a squirrel stores nuts).
***Star Trek* (title)** Famous U.S. TV series about life in outer space.
Steady (noun) A person to whom you are romantically committed and with whom you spend a lot of time, especially in social activities.
Sticky (adjective) Resistant to change, as if glued on.
Strings Attached (descriptive) phrase A gift that comes with strings attached comes with certain conditions set forth by the donor.
Strongarm (adjective) Repressive and violent.
Super Bowl (noun) Important football game played annually that attracts million of viewers (most of them see the game on TV).
Sucker (noun) A gullible person.

T

Tables Were Turned (descriptive phrase) The advantage of one side over the other reverses so that now the winner is the loser and the loser is the winner.
Tacky (adjective) In very poor taste.
Take the Heat (verb) To accept all criticism of one's action or inaction, whether or not one is actually the person that should be blamed.
Take Title (verb) Legal term meaning to acquire ownership.
Tea Control (noun) A method of resolving differences by informal but powerful social mechanisms, such as inviting your opponents to tea and settling matters while passing teacups and plates of cake around.
Temp (noun) Worker whose job is temporary and who accepts the job with that understanding.
Time-and-a-Half (noun) In labor law, 150 percent of the normal hourly wage.
Tombstone Ad (noun) Newspaper advertisement announcing the completion of a stock or bond offering.
Ton (noun) A ton weighs 2,000 pounds and an English ton (often spelled "tonne") weighs 2,240 pounds. In this book the term is used most frequently to mean simply "a large quantity."
Tough (adjective) Very difficult.
Trendy (adjective) A phenomenon that is slightly ahead of traditional ways and indicates a trend. Something trendy may turn into something traditional, or it may fade away without ever becoming mainstream.
Truck (verb) To exchange one thing for another. This was Adam Smith's definition in 1776 and it is still one of the meanings of the verb.
Turf (noun) Territory, especially the figurative territory of a firm.
Turn of the Century (expression) The few years at the end of an expiring century and the beginning of a new century. For example: 1998–2002.
Turn Up One's Nose (verb) To reject.
Twinkies (noun) Brand name of an inexpensive small cake.

U

Under-the-Counter (adjective) Secret or concealed by an unscrupulous person. Also see *under the table* below.
Under the Table (descriptive phrase) To accept money surreptitiously in order to avoid paying taxes on it or to conceal the income for other reasons. Also, to proffer such money to avoid having it known that you are making a particular deal.
Union Jack (noun) Nickname for the British flag.
Up in Arms (adjective) Furious and loudly protesting. Comes from the use of *arms* to stand for *firearms*.

V

Vanity License Plate (descriptive phrase) One-of-a-kind motor vehicle license plate issued to your individual specification. It might have your name, your profession, or any individual set of letters and numbers you choose that will fit on the plate.
Village Watchman (descriptive phrase) Before modern communication technology, in small communities local news was gathered and reported by an official, the village watchman or town crier, who walked around collecting facts and gossip.

W–X

Wadget (noun) Term used by economists to stand for any manufactured good except goods designated as widgets, which see.
Wal-Mart (proper name) A very large store that sells thousands of inexpensive items. There are hundreds of Wal-Marts in the United States and the company is beginning to expand into foreign markets.
Wampum (noun) String of beads made of polished shells, formerly used by North American Indians as money.
Whatever (noun) Designates an unspecified generic item or action when the speaker wants to let you know that it doesn't matter whether you know the exact item or place.
Wheaties (proper noun) Name of a brand of dry breakfast cereal.
White Elephant (noun) Something large and useless that you can't get rid of.
White Knight (noun) A company that comes to the rescue of another company. The term comes from the game of chess—some chess sets have white pieces and black pieces—and from the children's book, *Alice Through the Looking Glass*, where the story is structured as a game of chess and a chess piece, the white knight, tries to rescue Alice.
Whiz (noun) An expert.
Whopper (proper noun) Brand name of a kind of hamburger sold at Burger King restaurants.
Widget (noun) The opposite of a wadget, which see.
Wild About (descriptive phrase) Extremely enthusiastic about undertaking a particular action or admiring a particular object or person.

Wind Up (descriptive phrase) To discover that you have reached a particular conclusion or destination.
With-It (adjective) Current in one's knowledge.
Wodget (noun) A made-up term for a produced good. Variation of *widget*, which see.
Working Off the Books (descriptive phrase) Being paid wages or fees that are not reported to the tax or other authorities by either the payer or the payee.
Wound Up (past tense of verb *wind up*) To have found oneself in a particular situation after having taken particular actions.
Writing on the Wall (descriptive phrase) To see the writing on the wall is to realize that a situation is inevitably going to end badly. It comes from the Biblical story that Nebuchadnezzar, king of Babylon, saw a fatal prediction written on a wall.

Y–Z

You Bet! (exclamation) Expression meaning "It certainly is!" or "Absolutely!"

Index

A

C

E

F

H

O

P

U

V

W

Hours and Earnings in Private Nonagricultural Industries, 1959–2002[1]

[monthly data seasonally adjusted]

Year	Average Weekly Hours: Total Private	Average Weekly Hours: Manufacturing: Total	Average Weekly Hours: Manufacturing: Overtime	Average Hourly Earnings: Total Private: Current Dollars	Average Hourly Earnings: Total Private: 1982 Dollars[2]	Average Hourly Earnings: Manufacturing (current dollars)	Average Weekly Earnings, Total Private: Level: Current Dollars	Average Weekly Earnings, Total Private: Level: 1982 Dollars[2]	Average Weekly Earnings, Total Private: Percent Change from Year Earlier: Current Dollars	Average Weekly Earnings, Total Private: Percent Change from Year Earlier: 1982 Dollars[2]
1959	39.0	40.3	2.7	$ 2.02	$6.69	$ 2.19	$ 78.78	$260.86	4.9	4.2
1960	38.6	39.7	2.5	2.09	6.79	2.26	80.67	261.92	2.4	.4
1965	38.8	41.2	3.6	2.46	7.52	2.61	95.45	291.90	4.5	2.9
1970	37.1	39.8	3.0	3.23	8.03	3.35	119.83	298.08	4.6	−.9
1975	36.1	39.5	2.6	4.53	8.12	4.83	163.53	293.06	5.7	−3.0
1980	35.3	39.7	2.8	6.66	7.78	7.27	235.10	274.65	6.9	−5.8
1985	34.9	40.5	3.3	8.57	7.77	9.54	299.09	271.16	2.1	−1.3
1990	34.5	40.8	3.6	10.01	7.52	10.83	345.35	259.47	3.3	−1.8
1995	34.5	41.6	4.4	11.43	7.39	12.37	394.34	255.07	2.2	−.6
1996	34.4	41.6	4.5	11.82	7.43	12.77	406.61	255.73	3.1	.3
1997	34.6	42.0	4.8	12.28	7.55	13.17	424.89	261.31	4.5	2.2
1998	34.6	41.7	4.6	12.78	7.75	13.49	442.19	268.32	4.1	2.7
1999	34.5	41.7	4.6	13.24	7.86	13.90	456.78	271.25	3.3	1.1
2000	34.5	41.6	4.6	13.76	7.89	14.37	474.72	271.45	3.9	0
2001	34.2	40.7	3.9	14.31	7.99	14.83	489.4	272.93	3.1	0.5
2002	34.1	40.9	4.1	14.77	8.14	15.30	503.66	277.95	2.9	1.9

[1]For production or nonsupervisory workers; total includes private industry groups.

[2]Current dollars divided by the consumer price index for urban wage earners and clerical workers on a 1982 = 100 base.

Source: Department of Labor, Bureau of Labor Statistics.

Industrial Production and Consumer Prices, Percent Change, 1980–2002

Year	Industrial Production: United States	Industrial Production: Canada	Industrial Production: Japan	Industrial Production: European Union	Consumer Prices: United States	Consumer Prices: Canada	Consumer Prices: Japan	Consumer Prices: European Union
1980	−2.8	−3.1	4.6	0.0	13.5	10.0	7.7	13.4
1985	1.0	5.1	3.7	3.0	3.6	4.1	2.1	6.1
1990	0.8	−2.8	4.3	3.5	5.4	4.8	3.1	5.9
1991	−1.7	−3.5	1.7	0.2	4.2	5.6	3.2	5.2
1992	2.6	1.3	−5.6	−1.3	3.0	1.5	1.7	4.5
1993	3.3	4.9	−3.4	−3.6	3.0	1.8	1.4	3.6
1994	5.3	6.2	1.2	4.9	2.6	0.2	0.6	3.1
1995	4.8	4.6	3.2	3.5	2.8	2.2	−0.1	3.1
1996	4.4	1.3	2.3	0.5	3.0	1.6	0.1	2.5
1997	7.3	5.6	3.5	3.8	2.3	1.6	1.8	2.1
1998	5.6	3.5	−6.5	3.7	1.6	1.0	0.6	1.8
1999	4.3	5.1	0.6	1.9	2.2	1.7	−0.3	1.3
2000	4.7	5.7	5.7	4.7	3.4	2.7	−0.7	2.5
2001	−3.6	−3.5	−7.2	−0.1	2.8	2.5	−0.7	2.5
2002	−0.6				1.6	2.2		

Sources: Bureau of Labor Statistics and Bureau of Economic Analysis.